APPROXIMATION ALGORITHMS FOR NP-HARD PROBLEMS

Edited by DORIT S. HOCHBAUM

University of California — Berkeley

PWS PUBLISHING COMPANY

I(T)P

An International Thomson Publishing Company

BOSTON • ALBANY • BONN • CINCINNATI • DETROIT
LONDON • MADRID • MELBOURNE • MEXICO CITY
NEW YORK • PACIFIC GROVE • PARIS • SAN FRANCISCO
SINGAPORE • TOKYO • TORONTO • WASHINGTON

PWS PUBLISHING COMPANY
20 Park Plaza, Boston, MA 02116-4324

Copyright © 1997 by PWS Publishing Company,
a division of International Thomson Publishing Inc.

I(T)P™
International Thomson Publishing
The trademark ITP is used under license.

Library of Congress Cataloging-in-Publication Data

Approximation algorithms for NP–hard problems / Dorit Hochbaum, editor.
p.   cm.
Includes bibiliographical references and index.
ISBN 0-534-94968-1 (hardcover)
1. Programming (Mathematics)   2. Approximation theory.
3. Algorithms.   I. Hochbaum, Dorit (Dorit S.)
T57.7A68   1995   95-31849
511'.42—dc20   CIP

Sponsoring Editor: *Michael J. Sugarman*
Editorial Assistant: *Susan Garland*
Marketing Manager: *Nathan Wilbur*
Production Coordinator: *Elise S. Kaiser*
Interior/Cover Designer: *Monique A. Calello*
Manufacturing Coordinator: *Wendy Kilborn*

Composition: *SuperScript Typography*
Prepress: *Pure Imaging*
Cover Printer: *John Pow Company*
Text Printer/Binder: *Phoenix Color*
Cover Art: *"Comings and Goings"* © *1993 by Adriana Díaz Used by permission of the artist.*

Printed and bound in the United States of America.
03 — 10 9 8 7 6 5 4

 This book is printed on recycled, acid-free paper.

For more information, contact:
PWS Publishing Company
20 Park Plaza
Boston, MA 02116

International Thomson Publishing Europe
Berkshire House I68-I73
High Holborn
London WC1V 7AA
England

Thomas Nelson Australia
102 Dodds Street
South Melbourne, 3205
Victoria, Australia

Nelson Canada
1120 Birchmont Road
Scarborough, Ontario
Canada M1K 5G4

International Thomson Editores
Campos Eliseos 385, Piso 7
Col. Polanco
11560 Mexico D.F., Mexico

International Thomson Publishing GmbH
Königswinterer Strasse 418
53227 Bonn, Germany

International Thomson Publishing Asia
221 Henderson Road
#05-10 Henderson Building
Singapore 0315

International Thomson Publishing Japan
Hirakawacho Kyowa Building, 31
2-2-1 Hirakawacho
Chiyoda-ku, Tokyo 102
Japan

LIST OF CONTRIBUTORS

Sanjeev Arora
Computer Science Department
Princeton University
35 Olden Street
Princeton, NJ 08544
arora@cs.princeton.edu

Marshall Bern
Xerox PARC
3333 Coyote Hill Road
Palo Alto, CA 94304
bern@parc.xerox.com

Ed G. Coffman
Room 2D-150
AT&T Bell Laboratories
600 Mountain Avenue
Murray Hill, NJ 07974-2070
egc@research.att.com

David Eppstein
Department of Information
    and Computer Science
University of California at Irvine
Irvine, CA 92717-3425
eppstein@ics.uci.edu

Mike R. Garey
Room 2D-150
AT&T Bell Laboratories
600 Mountain Avenue
Murray Hill, NJ 07974-2070
mrg@research.att.com

Michel X. Goemans
Department of Mathematics
Room 2-382
MIT
Cambridge, MA 02139
goemans@math.mit.edu

Leslie Hall
Mathematical Sciences
Maryland Hall
Johns Hopkins University
3400 North Charles Street
Baltimore, MD 21218-2694
leslie@noether.mts.jhu.edu

Dorit S. Hochbaum
Department of Industrial Engineering
    & Operations Research
Etcheverry Hall
University of California
Berkeley, CA 94720-1777
dorit@hochbaum.berkeley.edu

Sandy Irani
Department of Information
    and Computer Science
University of California at Irvine
Irvine, CA 92717-3425
irani@ics.uci.edu

Mark Jerrum
Department of Computer Science
University of Edinburgh
King's Buildings
Mayfield Road
Edinburgh EH9 3JZ
U.K.
mrj@dcs.ed.ac.uk

David S. Johnson
Room 2D-150
AT&T Bell Laboratories
600 Mountain Avenue
Murray Hill, NJ 07974-2070
dsj@research.att.com

Anna R. Karlin
Department of Computer Science
 and Engineering
FR-35
University of Washington
Seattle, WA 98195
karlin@cs.washington.edu

Samir Khuller
Computer Science Department
University of Maryland
College Park, MD 20742
samir@cs.umd.edu

Carsten Lund
AT&T Bell Laboratories
Room 2C-324
600 Mountain Avenue
Murray Hill, NJ 07974
lund@research.att.com

Rajeev Motwani
Department of Computer Science
Stanford University
Stanford, CA 94305-2140
rajeev@cs.stanford.edu

Joseph (Seffi) Naor
Department of Computer Science
Technion—Israel Institute of Technology
Haifa 32000
Israel
naor@cs.Technion.ac.il

Balaji Raghavachari
Computer Science Department
University of Texas at Dallas
Richardson, TX 75083-0688
rbk@utdallas.edu

Prabhakar Raghavan
IBM, Box 218
Yorktown Heights, NY 10598
pragh@watson.ibm.com

David B. Shmoys
204 E&TC Building
School of Operations Research
 and Industrial Engineering
Cornell University
Ithaca, NY 14853-3801
shmoys@cs.cornell.edu

Alistair Sinclair
Computer Science Department
University of California
Berkeley, CA 94720
sinclair@cs.berkeley.edu

David P. Williamson
IBM TJ Watson Research Center
Room 33-219
P.O. Box 218
Yorktown Heights, NY 10598
dpw@watson.ibm.com

CONTENTS

INTRODUCTION

Approximation algorithms have developed in response to the impossibility of solving a great variety of important optimization problems. Too frequently, when attempting to get a solution for a problem, one is confronted with the fact that the problem is NP-hard. This, in the words of Garey and Johnson, means "I can't find an efficient algorithm, but neither can all these famous people" ([GJ79] p. 3). While this is a significant theoretical step, it hardly qualifies as a cheering piece of news.

If the optimal solution is unattainable then it is reasonable to sacrifice optimality and settle for a "good" feasible solution that can be computed efficiently. Of course, we would like to sacrifice as little optimality as possible, while gaining as much as possible in efficiency. Trading-off optimality in favor of tractability is the paradigm of approximation algorithms.

The main themes of this book revolve around the design of such algorithms and the "closeness" to the optimum that is achievable in polynomial time. To evaluate the limits of approximability, it is important to derive lower bounds or inapproximability results. In some cases, approximation algorithms must satisfy additional structural requirements such as being on-line, or working within limited space. This book reviews the design techniques for such algorithms and the developments in this area since its inception about three decades ago.

WHAT CAN APPROXIMATION ALGORITHMS DO FOR YOU: AN ILLUSTRATIVE EXAMPLE

0.1

Consider the following problem that motivates the study of approximation algorithms and also happens to be the first ever treated in the approximation algorithms framework.

Picture yourself at 9 a.m., on the shop floor, facing 8 machines that will be ready for work at 10 a.m., and 147 jobs of various durations waiting to be processed. There is a 9 p.m. basketball game on TV which you would hate to miss, but you have to stay until all the jobs are finished. You would want to assign jobs to machines so that you can get home as early as possible.

However, there is one catch: the problem is an instance of the well-known *minimum makespan* problem which is *NP*-hard. Being *NP*-hard means not only that there is no known efficient algorithm for solving the problem, but also that it is quite unlikely that one exists.

Given that this optimization problem is *NP*-hard, what is the next step? For years *NP*-hard problems were treated with integer programming tools or "heuristics." Integer programming tools are forms of implicit enumeration algorithms that combine efficient derivations of lower and upper bounds with a hopeful search for an optimal solution. The amount of time required to solve even a typical moderate-size optimization problem is exorbitant. Instead, the user interrupts the enumeration process either when the current solution is deemed satisfactory, or when the running time has exceeded reasonable limit. The point is that integer programming algorithms provide no *guarantee*. It is impossible to tell if 5 additional minutes of running time would get you a significantly better solution, or if 5 more days of running time would yield no improvement at all.

Besides the issues of guarantee of quality of solution and reasonable running time, the classic integer programming tool, *Branch-and-Bound*, needs good bounds which are feasible solutions as well as good estimates of the value of the optimum (lower bounds for minimization problems—upper bounds for maximization). Approximation algorithms address both the issue of guarantee and of making good feasible solutions available. The analysis of approximation algorithms always involves deriving estimates on the value of the optimum. As such, approximation algorithms and their analysis are useful in traditional integer programming techniques.

...back on the "floor" the time is a few minutes before 10:00 a.m. and it is too late to start running a branch-and-bound procedure since you may end up worse off compared to a solution that you can quickly guess. Indeed how about using some rules of thumb to guess a reasonable solution? Say, place any job on any machine as soon as the machine becomes available. That sounds sensible, but a quick calculation shows that the machine that finishes last will do so at 10 p.m. It would certainly help to get a clue as to how much better an optimal schedule value can be, even if the schedule itself is unattainable. In essence we would like to know how good is the solution delivered by the above rule compared to the optimum. Indeed, Graham proved in 1966 [Gra66] that this rule gives a solution with relative error no more than 100%. In other words, while the rule delivers a schedule lasting 12 hours, the optimum could be as short as 6 hours, but no less. At this point you are assured that no solution will get you off before 4 p.m.

Heuristics is the nomenclature for rules-of-thumb which in itself is a euphemism for simple and invariably polynomial algorithms. Heuristics work quickly and efficiently. The quality of the solution they deliver is another matter altogether. Prior to the advent of the approximation algorithms' method of analysis, the performance of a heuristic was judged by running it on a benchmark set of problem instances and comparing it with the performance of other heuristics on the same benchmark.

The obvious setbacks to such an approach were already evident in the pre-complexity days. The benchmark set is typically a small sample which is not necessarily a good representative of general problem instances. In addition, improvements in the quality of a solution as measured by the benchmark set are not necessarily a good predictor of possible improvements in general cases. There was clearly a need for well-defined analysis to evaluate the quality of heuristics. When such an analysis emerged it had the added benefit of enhancing our understanding of the problem and providing insight as to what makes a solution "right." This insight made it possible to improve the heuristics and the integer programming algorithms. On the other hand, many heuristics with excellent empirical performance have so far eluded formal analysis.

Garey, Graham, and Ullman [GGU72] and later Johnson [Joh74] formalized the concept of an *approximation algorithm*. An approximation algorithm is necessarily polynomial, and is evaluated by the worst case possible relative error over all possible instances of the problem. An algorithm $\mathcal{A}$ is said to be a δ-approximation algorithm for a minimization problem P if for every instance I of P it delivers a solution that is at most δ times the optimum. Naturally, $\delta > 1$ and the closer it is to 1, the better. Similarly, for maximization problems a δ-approximation algorithm delivers for every instance I a solution that is at least δ times the optimum. In that case $\delta < 1$. δ is referred to as the *approximation ratio*, or *performance guarantee*, or *worst case ratio*, or *worst case error bound*, or *approximation factor*. For the maximization problem it is also common to refer to $1/\delta$ as the approximation factor.

As stated above, the sensible rule described for the minimum makespan problem gives a solution with relative error no more than 100%. As such, it is a 2-approximation algorithm. (Details on the analysis of this approximation algorithm, called List Scheduling algorithm, are given in Chapter 1.) Graham further showed that a different heuristic that assigns the longest remaining job to the first available machine gives a better worst case error ratio of $4/3$. With this slightly modified rule you get a 10-hour schedule that ends at 8 p.m. Furthermore, now you know that the best solution—the optimum schedule—will last 7 and a $1/2$ hours and thus will not end before 5:30 p.m.

For the minimum makespan problem, considerably better approximation algorithms have been devised by Hochbaum and Shmoys [HS87]. They described a family of approximation algorithms for the minimum makespan problem so that algorithm $\mathcal{A}_\epsilon$ is a $(1 + \epsilon)$-approximation algorithm (Section 9.3.2 contains a description of this family of algorithms). This means you can get an error as small as you like, but have to pay significantly in terms of increased running time. The rate of increase in running time is a known function of ϵ, so one can decide on the appropriate trade-off for the situation. For instance, an algorithm that guarantees a ratio no more than $6/5$ works in several hundred steps (more precisely, in $O(n \log n)$ steps for n jobs) and hence can deliver a solution in a fraction of a second with a guarantee of no more than 20% relative error (this specific algorithm is described in [HS87]). Applying that $6/5$-approximation algorithm gives you an assignment of the 147 jobs that is 9 hours long, terminates at 7 p.m. and guarantees that the optimum is no earlier than 5:30 p.m. Considering it satisfactory you can use this schedule, or, if there is still time till 10 a.m., run one of the better approximation algorithms in the family to see if it results in yet a better schedule. Even if not, we at least end up with a higher estimate for the finish time of the optimum, thus reducing "regret."

This trade-off family of algorithms is called an approximation scheme. While such success is not typical for other *NP*-hard problem it demonstrates that the detailed analysis and insight gained lead to the generation of this tool of approximation scheme for the makepsan problem. With the increased interest in the area of approximation algorithms, more and more empirically successful heuristics for other problems are being analyzed and theoretically understood. This results in the ability to derive closer to optimum solutions for these problems than previously done.

Having introduced informally the main concepts, we now proceed to a more systematic introduction of the basic definitions.

FUNDAMENTALS AND CONCEPTS

0.2

Foremost among the concepts is that of a δ-approximation algorithm. An approximation algorithm is always assumed to be "efficient" or more precisely, polynomial. We also assume that the approximation algorithm delivers a feasible solution to some *NP*-hard problem that has a set of instances $\{I\}$.

DEFINITION 0.1   A polynomial algorithm, $\mathcal{A}$, is said to be a δ-approximation algorithm if for every problem instance I with an optimal solution value $OPT(I)$,

$$OPT(I) \leq \delta.$$

As mentioned before, $\delta \geq 1$ for minimization problems and ≤ 1 for maximization problems. The smallest value of δ is the approximation (or performance) ratio $R_\mathcal{A}$ of the algorithm $\mathcal{A}$.

The value of δ is referred to by any of the following terms or their variations

- Worst case bound
- Worst case performance
- Approximation factor
- Approximation ratio
- Performance bound
- Performance ratio
- Error ratio

and several others.

For maximization problems, sometimes $\frac{1}{\delta}$ is considered to be the approxmiation ratio/factor.

Unless otherwise specified, we always mean for δ to be the *absolute performance ratio*. However, in some cases the error involves an additive term. In those cases the notion of asymptotic performance ratio is relevant.

DEFINITION 0.2   The *absolute performance ratio*, $\cdot R_A$, of an approximation algorithm $\mathcal{A}$ is,

$$R_\mathcal{A} = \inf\{r \geq 1 | R_\mathcal{A}(I) \leq r \text{ for all problem instances } I\}.$$

and the *asymptotic performance ratio* $R_\mathcal{A}^\infty$ for $\mathcal{A}$ is,

$$R_\mathcal{A}^\infty = \inf\{r \geq 1 | \exists n \in Z^+, R_\mathcal{A}(I) \leq r \; \forall I \text{ s.t. } I \geq n\}.$$

In Chapter 9 we illustrate examples where the difference between these two ratios is significant. For online algorithms there is an analogous concept of *competitive ratio* (asymptotic). There, however, the input instance is a sequence and the comparison is to the performance of an optimal offline algorithm on the same sequence, rather than to an optimal solution value. Chapter 12 provides details on the motivation and definition of this concept.

The concept of R_A is a *worst case* notion meaning that it suffices to have a single "bad" instance to render the value of δ larger than it is for all other encountered instances. Typically, the observed performance of an approximation algorithm, as reflected in the gap between the optimal solution and the delivered solution, is considerably better than would be indicated by the performance ratio. This has been evident in every experimental study on specific problem instances. Ideally we would like to be able to predict the actual performance of the algorithm.

One way of addressing this concern is through the use of *average case analysis*. In average case analysis we assume knowledge of the distribution of the problem's instances. This knowledge permits a tightening of the assessment of the optimal value as well as allows for tailor-fitting algorithms to the features of the distribution. Average case analysis is illustrated in Chapter 2 of the book, primarily for the bin packing problem.

The efficiency of an approximation algorithm is another important issue. While we assume that every approximation algorithm is polynomial, there is a vast variety of polynomial algorithms some of which are decidedly inefficient and impractical. Within the range of "practical" polynomiality we may want to invest more running time in order to get a better approximation bound. Such a trade-off comes in several versions of *approximation schemes*.

DEFINITION 0.3   A family of approximation algorithms for a problem $\mathcal{P}$, $\{\mathcal{A}_\epsilon\}_\epsilon$, is called a *polynomial approximation scheme* or PAS, if algorithm $\mathcal{A}_\epsilon$ is a $(1+\epsilon)$-approximation algorithm and its running time is polynomial in the size of the input for a fixed ϵ.

DEFINITION 0.4   A family of approximation algorithms for a problem $\mathcal{P}$, $\{\mathcal{A}_\epsilon\}_\epsilon$, is called a *fully polynomial approximation scheme* or FPAS, if algorithm $\mathcal{A}_\epsilon$ is a $(1+\epsilon)$-approximation algorithm and its running time is polynomial in the size of the input **and** $1/\epsilon$.

When a FPAS is a family of *randomized* algorithms it will be called *fully polynomial randomized approximation scheme* or FPRAS. In that case the approximation is guaranteed with probability that is large enough (e.g. 3/4 as in Chapter 12). Chapter 9 discusses examples of PAS and FPAS, and Chapter 12 discusses examples of FPRAS. Chapter 10 reviews the class of Max-$\mathcal{SNP}$-hard problems that cannot have PAS, unless $NP = P$.

Lower bounds on approximability are a major concern as we always want to know whether a better approximation exists which we simply failed to identify, or if better approximations are impossible. For a large number of important problems there have recently been a slew of discouraging results in the sense that their approximability limits are quite bad. Among these problems the maximum clique is prominent. In the maximum clique problem the aim is to find the largest number of vertices in a graph all of which are linked with each other via edges. A trivial solution, and not a very good one, is to take a single vertex as the clique. The inapproximability results demonstrate that unless $NP = P$ we cannot guarantee to do substantially better. This problem, and the recent techniques for proving lower bounds, are the main topics of Chapter 10. More traditional techniques that prove lower bounds on approximability are described in Chapter 9.

In a number of practical situations an algorithm is required to have a specific structure. For instance, when the data instance is not available *a-priori*, then the decision, or the algorithm, has to be executed *on-line* with only partial information. This is, for example, the case with the minimum makespan problem when jobs arrive continually and the machines have to be assigned and running without waiting for the stream of jobs to end. Graham's 2-approximation algorithm previously described offers the extra bonus of also being on-line: a job in the pool is assigned to the first available machine. When we want to assess the performance of an on-line algorithm the notion of worst case ratio is inappropriate as it would be meaningless to compare the solution delivered by such algorithm with optimal value that does not depend on the arrival sequence of the jobs. Instead we compare it with an optimal algorithm that is off-line, meaning that it has the *a-priori* information about the sequence of the arriving jobs. For this purpose the concept of *competitive ratio* and related concepts are introduced (see Chapter 13) for analyzing on-line problems. These concepts measure the effects of partial information.

Other types of approximation algorithms are required to work in *restricted space* or in dynamic fashion. Such algorithms, as well as several other interesting variants, are described in Chapter 2.

Randomized algorithms were found to be extremely useful in general algorithm design (see the recent book by Motwani and Raghavan [MR95]). These algorithms make random choices during execution. In the context of approximation algorithms, the randomized approach had a dramatic affect in introducing novel approaches. Randomization is generally combined with the continuous techniques of linear programming and semidefinite programming. Randomized algorithms are also the only algorithms known that provide any sort of estimate for solutions to *counting* problems. Problems, such as counting the number of perfect matchings in a graph or assessing the volume of a polytope are harder than the corresponding optimization problems. For the few instances when solutions are known (Chapter 12) they are achieved via randomized techniques.

Finally, the continuous optimization problems of *linear programming* and *semidefinite programming* are of prime importance in approximations. Since it is possible to formulate optimization problems as integer programming, linear programming relaxations, (in which the requirement of integrality is omitted), provide a bound (lower bound for a minimization problem, upper bound for maximization). If a semidefinite programming relaxation of the problem is known, then the bound is frequently tighter (closer to the actual optimum) than that obtained by linear programming. It is likely that other, more general, nonlinear relaxations can be tighter still, but for that to be useable, those nonlinear problems need to be solvable in polynomial time. This is promising to be the direction of future developments in approximations.

The reader will need to have some background in linear programming, as pertains to duality theory, and the knowledge that the problem is polynomial. A good introduction to linear programming is given in a recent book by Saigal [S95]. For semidefinite programming the relevant references are mentioned in Chapter 11.

OBJECTIVES AND ORGANIZATION OF THIS BOOK

0.3

This book is aimed at practitioners interested in specific application areas, as well as the computer science and operations research community interested in design tools for algorithms in general and approximation algorithms in particular. Our goal here is to layout the variety of approaches and techniques that are typical and most effective for approximations.

The variety and versatility make it difficult to navigate in this area. One goal of this book is to introduce a framework, review of applications and unifying techniques in the analysis of approximation algorithms. Such unifying features have only emerged recently as the area has matured.

The chapters in this book are written so as to be self-contained to the greatest extent. Each chapter has its own list of references that provide a perspective on the work done in the particular subarea. The reader is assumed to have prior background in the design and complexity of algorithms, as well as in linear programming and stochastic processes. Each chapter gives references to appropriate tutorial material. There are exercises scattered throughout the text that highlight important extensions or ask the reader to verify some of the claims.

The chapters of the book can be read in any order. The reader can identify specific techniques or problems of interest in the index and in the glossary of problems that include pointers to chapters where the problems are discussed. The glossary is arranged in an alphabetical order relating to some particular key words in the problem title. The glossary, however, is not organized by topics and it may be necessary to use the index in order to pinpoint a specific problem definition.

The first three chapters follow the chronological developments in the field. We chose to have the topic of scheduling as the opening chapter since scheduling problems were the first historically to be analyzed for approximations. The area of scheduling has remained very active and novel techniques have been devised and used. Chapter 1, indeed, reviews the early work, but is mostly devoted to the discussion of recent developments. Another problem that was extensively analyzed in the early days of approximation algorithms analysis is the *bin packing* problem. Chapter 2 focuses on this problem and its extensions. It is the only chapter to cover average case analysis, for which bin packing has been a showcase problem. The chapter also reviews on-line algorithms that are space restricted and *dynamic* algorithms and *open* versus *closed* on-line algorithms.

The *set cover* problem has been considered one of the most prominent problems in optimization. The first algorithm to use linear programming and duality was devised for this problem and its special case—the vertex cover problem. Not surprisingly, this algorithm came shortly after the discovery that linear programming is a polynomial problem.While the performance of the first algorithms was not improved since the early 1980s, there has been substantial progress on specially structured set cover problem, as well as for the vertex cover problem and it complement—the independent set problem. Chapter 3 reviews these algorithms and provides an up-to-date summary of best approximations. It includes an analysis that explains the particular usefulness of linear programming relaxation for the vertex cover and independent set and other integer programs with two variables per inequality. The chapter also reviews the important greedy algorithm and its properties.

Chapter 4 presents refinements of the linear programming based technique described in Chapter 3. It describes a number of problems in the context of network design applications, that can be posed as covering problems. It then shows how the technique using primal and dual solutions leads to the design of stronger approximation algorithms than does general covering for a surprisingly vast collection of problems.

Chapter 5 is concerned with problems that involve partitioning of graphs such as separation or cut problems. The techniques here, again, are dominated by the use of linear programming relaxations and their duals. Several randomized algorithms are reviewed as well. The chapter addresses problems that make use of separation, or divide-and-conquer algorithms for problems such as the multicommodity and the linear arrangement.

Chapters 6 is devoted to connectivity problems. While these problems can be thought of as network design problems, the focus here is on graph algorithmic techniques. Chapter 7 uses graph algorithms to solve problems of network design characterized by the objective of minimizing the maximum degree node in the required structure (a recurring scenario in limited capacity setups). One of the most dramatic successes of approximation algorithms is described in this chapter—the derivation of a solution which is within one unit of the optimum for the problem of finding a spanning tree for which the maximum vertex degree is minimized. This problem was previously the target of a variety of heavy duty machinery, none of which approached the quality of the solution and the efficiency of the approximation described in this chapter.

Chapter 8 is devoted to the algorithms and techniques that are most successful when the problems are given in the plane or in a Euclidean space. These problems include the Traveling Salesman problem (TSP), the Steiner tree problem, triangulations, and a variety of clustering problems. Approximation algorithms for these types of problems use different techniques, compared to those used for non-Euclidean problems, that rely on the field of computational geometry. The TSP is not covered comprehensively in this book, as it has been extensively covered in the literature to date. The bottleneck version of TSP is analyzed in the next chapter.

Chapter 9 addresses problems that are not otherwise covered in the book, with emphasis on the "quality" of the approximation bound and on how much it can be improved. It includes samples of constant approximation algorithms: PASs, FPASs; approximation algorithms that are provably best (unless $NP = P$); some lower bound results; illustrations of the differences between absolute and asymptotic worst case ratios and approximation algorithms that are within one unit of the optimum. The chapter discusses problems with a wide scope of applications including location, clustering network communication, covering and packing with certain objects, scheduling, and more.

The recent lower bound techniques based on probabilistically checkable proofs are reviewed in Chapter 10. This chapter is concerned with the limits on approximability of problems rather than with the design of approximation algorithms.

In Chapter 11 there are randomized algorithms analyzed in conjunction with linear programming and semidefinite programming. (It is interesting that these two continuous techniques work so well together with the technique of randomization that has been proven successful for algorithm design in general.) The randomization makes use of the fractional values and interprets them as probabilities for rounding up the given variable.

As was the case for the use of linear programming in approximations, the discovery that semidefinite programming is useful for approximations came shortly after it was established that semidefinite programming is a polynomial problem. The chapter also describes the important topic of *derandomization*—the conversion of a randomized algorithm to a deterministic one.

Chapter 12 is about Markov chain techniques that have proven useful for providing an approximate answer to various counting problems. The idea is to use sampling in an efficient way in order to estimate the magnitude of the answer from a polynomially restricted search.

Chapter 13 describes extensively online (on-line) algorithms and their major applications. It reviews the various design techniques and recent results on lower and upper bounds for the paging, k-server, metrical task system, and other online problems.

ACKNOWLEDGMENTS

0.4

I would like to thank all the contributors for their expertise and enthusiasm for this project. In particular, I benefited from David Shmoys' editorial help, from Marshall Bern's hawk-eye for fonts and design details, and from Samir Khuller and Sanjeev Arora's helpful feedback. Through the arduous months (that extended to years) that it took to complete the book, I enjoyed the help and encouragement of my students, Anu Pathria, Youxun Shen, and Eli Olinick. The numerous conversations I had with Anu formed my views on the orientation of the book and the presentation of the material.

Along the way I had substantial help from my friends and colleagues. I would like to note in particular Ilan Adler, who always helped me put things in perspective, Olivier Goldschmidt, and Seffi Naor. Cliff Stein was most helpful in providing information and pointers on the superstring problem.

The technical production of the book turned out to be a mammoth task for which I needed all the help I could get. I thank Mandy Simondson for her supportive response to emergencies, and to William Baxter, the LaTeX wiz, from whom I learned more than I ever cared to know about LaTeX, LaTeX 2_ε, and their intricacies. I wish to acknowledge the continuing support from ONR of my research on algorithms and approximation algorithms. Finally, to Adriana for her warm friendship and inspiring paintings, to Aharon, Allon, and Daniel whose enthusiasm for seeing the Hochbaum name on a book cover helped compensate for extended work days, and to Belle and Ivan for always being there for us.

Dorit S. Hochbaum

REFERENCES

[GGU72] M. R. Garey, R.L. Graham and J. D. Ullman. Worst case analysis of memory allocation algorithms. in Proc. of the 4th ACM Symp.on Theory of Computing. 143-150, 1972.

[GJ79] M. R. Garey and D. S. Johnson, *Computers and Intractability: A guide to the theory of NP-completeness.* W. H. Freeman, San Francisco, 1979.

[Gra66] R.L. Graham. Bounds for certain multiprocessing anomalies. *Bell System Tech. J. 45,* 1563–1581, 1966.

[HS87] D. S. Hochbaum, D. B. Shmoys. Using dual approximation algorithms for scheduling problems: practical and theoretical results. *Journal of ACM* 34:1, 144–162, 1987.

[Joh74] D. S. Johnson. Approximation algorithms for combinatorial problems. *J. Comput. System Sci.,* 9, 256-278, 1974.

[MR95] R. Motwani and P. Raghavan. *Randomized algorithms.* Cambridge University Press, Cambridge, 1995.

[S95] R. Saigal. *Linear programming: a modern integrated analysis.* Kluwer Academic Publishers, Boston, 1995.

1

APPROXIMATION ALGORITHMS FOR SCHEDULING

Leslie A. Hall

Scheduling problems provide a good starting point for the study of approximation algorithms, and historically they were among the first problems to be analyzed this way. This chapter provides a broad sampling of results that span three decades of research.

INTRODUCTION

1.1

When was the first time that someone presented a worst-case analysis of an approximation algorithm? It was probably 1966, the year that Ron Graham analyzed a simple procedure for one of the most basic scheduling problems: minimizing makespan in an identical parallel machine environment [Gr66]. In this model, we have a set of n jobs, $J_1, \ldots, J_n$, and m identical machines, $M_1, \ldots, M_m$. Each job J_j must be processed without interruption for a time $p_j > 0$ on one of the m machines, each of which can process at most one job at a time.

Graham considered the following algorithm, known as *list scheduling* (LS): we are given a list of the jobs in some arbitrary order. Whenever a machine becomes available, the next job on the list is assigned to begin processing on that machine. Graham used the following simple geometric argument to show that the total *makespan* of this schedule, that is, the time by which all jobs complete their processing, would never be more than $2 - (1/m)$ times the makespan of the optimal schedule. Let us denote the starting time and completion time of job J_j in the heuristic schedule as s_j and C_j, respectively, for $j = 1, \ldots, n$. Graham observed that, if we focus on the last job to complete processing (call it J_k), then no machine can be idle at any time prior to s_k, since otherwise job J_k would have been processed there (see Figure 1.1).

This observation allows us to partition the heuristic schedule into two time intervals as follows. Suppose we use $C_{\max}^{LS}$ to denote the makespan of the heuristic schedule produced by list scheduling and $C_{\max}^*$ to denote the makespan of an optimal schedule. First,

$$C_{\max}^* \geq p_k,$$

since job J_k must be processed on some machine; and second,

$$C_{\max}^* \geq (1/m) \sum_{j=1}^{n} p_j,$$

since this lower bound represents the best possible situation in which all machines complete processing at exactly the same time. The final step of the analysis hinges on observing that we can break up the heuristic schedule's makespan as

$$C_{\max}^{LS} = C_k = s_k + p_k \leq (1/m) \sum_{j \neq k} p_j \; + p_k$$

$$= (1/m) \sum_{j=1}^{n} p_j \; + (1 - 1/m) p_k$$

$$\leq C_{\max}^* + (1 - 1/m) C_{\max}^* = (2 - 1/m) C_{\max}^*.$$

We will have more to say about extensions of this basic result in Section 1.3.1.

In all of the models considered in this chapter, once a job (or an operation in the shop scheduling models) begins processing on a machine it must complete its processing without interruption; this contrasts with *preemptive* scheduling models in which the processing of jobs can be interrupted and later resumed. In most of this chapter, we will consider scheduling problems whose objective functions, like makespan, represent minimizing a maximum over all jobs J_j of a job-dependent, non-decreasing function f_j of the completion time of job J_j. In the case of makespan, the function f_j is just the identity, for all j: we wish to minimize the maximum completion time C_j over all jobs $J_j, j = 1, \ldots, n$. In Section 1.7 we consider scheduling problems with so-called *min-sum* objective criteria. These models include, for example, minimizing the sum of completion times of all jobs.

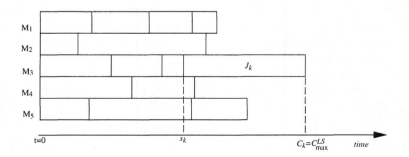

FIGURE 1.1

Analysis of Graham's list scheduling algorithm.

Throughout this chapter we use the following notation[1]. Jobs are denoted as J_j, and n denotes the number of jobs. Machines are denoted M_i, and when there is more than one machine, we use m to denote the number of machines. A *schedule* Σ is an assignment of jobs to machines and associated starting times $s_1(\Sigma), \ldots, s_n(\Sigma)$ of jobs $J_1, \ldots, J_n$, respectively. When the intended schedule is not ambiguous we simply write $s_1, \ldots, s_n$. A feasible schedule will have the property that at any point in time a machine processes at most one job at a time; that is, if two jobs J_j and J_k are assigned to the same machine then either $s_j + p_j \leq s_k$ or $s_k + p_k \leq s_j$. As we already mentioned, we use C_j to denote the time at which job J_j completes processing in a given schedule, i.e., $s_j + p_j = C_j$. A schedule associated with a given algorithm A is denoted $\Sigma(A)$, and we use the shortened notation $C_{\max}^A$ to denote $C_{\max}(\Sigma(A))$ (and similarly with other schedule-dependent parameters).

For describing problems, we will adhere to the conventional terminology, introduced by Graham, Lawler, Lenstra, and Rinnooy Kan [G+79, L+93]. Problems are described by three fields: the first represents the machine environment, the second describes any special conditions or constraints in the model, and the third describes the objective function criterion. Possible machine environments include $1, \mathcal{P}, R$: machine environments consisting of a single machine, identical parallel machines, and unrelated parallel machines, respectively; and for shop models, O, F, J: open, flow, and job shops, respectively (see Section 1.5). The middle field might indicate, for example, that all jobs have unit processing times ("$p_j = 1$"). Thus, for example, "$\mathcal{P}|p_j = 1|C_{\max}$" is the problem of scheduling unit-time jobs on identical parallel machines to minimize the makespan.

The sum of the job processing times of a set of jobs S is denoted

$$P(S) = \sum_{J_j \in S} p_j;$$

and we use P to denote $P(\{J_1, \ldots, J_n\})$, the sum of all processing times.

In some cases we have *precedence constraints* among jobs; that is, there is a partial order $\prec$ on the set of jobs whereby $J_j \prec J_k$ implies that job J_k cannot begin until J_j has completed processing. We say that the jobs are *independent* when there are no precedence constraints in the model.

SEQUENCING WITH RELEASE DATES TO MINIMIZE LATENESS

1.2

In this section we will consider scheduling problems on a single machine. In a given instance, each job J_j has a *due date* d_j associated with it, as well as a *processing time* $p_j > 0$; for a given schedule Σ we define the *lateness* of a job as its completion time minus its due date, $L_j(\Sigma) = C_j(\Sigma) - d_j$; in particular, if the job completes before its due date, its "lateness" can be negative. Our goal is to find a schedule that minimizes the

---

[1]In Section 1.5 on shop scheduling we use slightly different notation.

maximum lateness over all jobs,

$$L_{\max} = \max_{1 \le j \le n} L_j.$$

We denote the minimum value of $L_{\max}$ over all schedules as $L_{\max}^*$.

In such a model approximation algorithms defined by a relative, multiplicative error are meaningless; since, for example, if the optimal maximum lateness is negative, then a ρ-approximation algorithm with $\rho > 1$ would have to deliver a super-optimal schedule! A simple observation allows us to sidestep this problem and to provide a meaningful baseline for approximation algorithms. Consider an instance of scheduling with due dates and an associated schedule. Observe that, if some constant K is subtracted from each of the due dates, then the overall maximum lateness of a schedule increases by exactly K. In fact, one way to ensure that the maximum lateness is always positive in any schedule is to require that all due dates are non-positive, a condition that can be obtained by subtracting a sufficiently large constant from every due date of an instance.

Requiring due dates to be non-positive seems somewhat unnatural; and in fact an equivalent, more intuitive model is that of sequencing with *delivery times*. In this model, each job J_j must be processed on the machine and then spend an additional amount of time $q_j \ge 0$ being delivered. This "delivery" can be interpreted as an additional processing requirement on a non-bottleneck machine (a machine that can process an arbitrary number of jobs at once), or as a physical delivery (travel) time; but the key property is that different jobs' deliveries can overlap in time. Thus the *delivery-completion time* of a job J_j is $s_j + p_j + q_j$. For an instance of the lateness model with non-positive due dates, we can set $q_j = -d_j$ to obtain an equivalent instance in the new model, since for any schedule

$$L_{\max} = \max_{1 \le j \le n} s_j + p_j - d_j = \max_{1 \le j \le n} s_j + p_j + q_j.$$

We will continue to use L_j to represent $C_j + q_j$, even though the new model does not contain a direct reference to "lateness," but we will refer to L_j as the delivery-completion time of job J_j.

On a single machine it is easy to see that an optimal ordering of the jobs to minimize $L_{\max}$ is given by ordering the jobs according to non-increasing delivery time (i.e., non-decreasing due date); this rule is known as the "earliest due date" (EDD) rule in the due-date model. To see why such an ordering is optimal, consider any schedule in which the jobs are not ordered in this fashion. Then there must exist a pair of jobs J_j and J_k with J_k sequenced immediately after J_j, but with $q_j < q_k$. A simple interchange argument shows that interchanging these two jobs in the schedule cannot degrade $L_{\max}$, and after a finite number of such interchanges, we obtain the EDD ordering.

Next, we introduce job *release dates* into the model: each job J_j cannot begin its processing before its release date r_j. We refer to this model as $1|r_j|L_{\max}$. This problem is strongly NP-hard [LRB77]; a reduction from 3-PARTITION is relatively straightforward. In spite of this hardness result, however, $1|r_j|L_{\max}$ remains one of the "easiest" strongly NP-hard scheduling problems both in theory and practice. In the rest of this section, we analyze several simple heuristics, provide a polynomial approximation scheme, and finally describe preprocessing techniques for incorporating job precedence constraints into the model.

There is an interesting symmetry between release dates and delivery times in this model. We can view r_j, p_j, and q_j as the head, body, and tail of job J_j, respectively; and then our task is to find a schedule for the jobs so that the bodies do not overlap and the heads and tails, which are allowed to overlap, "stick out" as little as possible. Indeed, by reversing the roles of delivery times and release dates, we obtain an equivalent scheduling problem in which time runs backward; the value L_{max} associated with an ordering for an instance of the original problem, when reversed, gives an ordering with value L_{max} for the instance with release dates and delivery times interchanged!

In what follows we will repeatedly use the following lower bounds on the optimal length of a schedule for an instance I of the single-machine problem:

$$L_{max}^* \geq P = \sum_{j=1}^{n} p_j; \tag{1.1}$$

$$L_{max}^* \geq r_j + p_j + q_j, \quad j = 1, \ldots, n. \tag{1.2}$$

1.2.1   JACKSON'S RULE

Let us first consider a straightforward generalization of Graham's list scheduling algorithm LS: whenever the machine becomes available, schedule the first *available* job on the list. A job is defined as "available" if it has already been released.

THEOREM 1.1 $L_{max}^{LS} < 2L_{max}^*$, and this bound is tight.

Proof.   Consider an instance I of the scheduling problem and an associated list-processing schedule given by Algorithm LS. Let J_k be the job whose lateness attains that of the schedule, i.e., $L_{max}^{LS} = C_k + q_k$. Since there is no idle time on the machine between time r_k and s_k, we have

$$L_{max}^{LS} = s_k + p_k + q_k < (r_k + P) + p_k + q_k = (r_k + p_k + q_k) + P \leq 2L_{max}^*.$$

A simple two-job example illustrates that the bound is tight. Consider the instance with $r_1 = q_1 = 0$, $r_2 = p_2 = 1$, and $p_1 = q_2 = M$. Both lists $\{1, 2\}$ and $\{2, 1\}$ generate the schedule in which job J_1 is scheduled before J_2, while the optimal schedule puts J_2 before J_1. The ratio of the list schedule's value to the optimal schedule's is $(2M + 1)/(M + 1)$, for M arbitrarily large.   ■

We might consider a more sophisticated version of list scheduling that takes the delivery times into account; that is, we apply list scheduling to a list with jobs ordered by non-increasing delivery times (equivalent to an EDD, or earliest due-date, ordering). This approach is sometimes called *Schrage's heuristic* or *Jackson's rule* [Sc71, Ja55]; we will refer to it as Algorithm J (for "Jackson"). Of course, the two-job instance just given illustrates that the worst-case performance does not improve over arbitrary list scheduling.

COROLLARY 1.1 $L_{max}^{J} < 2L_{max}^*$, and this bound is tight.

It is worthwhile examining this heuristic J in slightly more detail. Consider an instance of $1|r_j|L_{\max}$ and a schedule given by Jackson's rule. Let us define a *critical job* J_c as one whose lateness attains that of the schedule,

$$L_c(J) = L_{\max}^J.$$

Associated with a critical job J_c is a *critical sequence* consisting of those jobs tracing backward from J_c in $\Sigma(J)$ to the first idle time in the schedule (or to the start of the schedule). Let us fix a critical job J_c and denote the first job in its associated critical sequence as J_a, and the set of jobs in the critical sequence as S. Then,

$$L_{\max}^J = L_c(J) = r_a + P(S) + q_c,$$

since the machine is idle just before it begins processing job J_a (or if the sequence begins at time zero, then $r_a = 0$ and the equation still holds).

To begin, we make two simple observations. First, for every job J_j in the critical sequence, $r_a \le r_j$, since either $r_a = 0$ or the machine is idle just before time r_a. Second, for *any* set of jobs S, (and in particular for the set of jobs in the critical sequence),

$$L_{\max}^* \ge \min_{J_j \in S} r_j + P(S) + \min_{J_j \in S} q_j. \tag{1.3}$$

This second observation implies that, if $q_c \le q_j$ for all $J_j \in S$, then the schedule is optimal, since then,

$$L_{\max}^J = r_a + P(S) + q_c = \min_{J_j \in S} r_j + P(S) + \min_{J_j \in S} q_j.$$

Furthermore, it implies the following important inequality:

$$L_{\max}^J \le L_{\max}^* + q_c \tag{1.4}$$

for any critical job J_c.

So how, then, does Jackson's rule go wrong? If the set S associated with the critical sequence contains a job J_b for which $q_b < q_c$, then the sequence might not be optimal; for example, in a two-job example with $r_1 = q_1 = 0$, $p_1 = M$, and $r_2 = p_2 = 1$, $q_2 = M$, Jackson's rule schedules job J_1 before J_2 and produces a schedule almost twice as bad as the optimal schedule, for M large. In this example, the large processing time of job J_1 delays the processing and subsequent large delivery time of job J_2, which should take priority.

Let J_b be chosen as the *last* job in the critical sequence with $q_b < q_c$; we call such a job an *interference job* for the critical sequence. Then we have a second important inequality relating $L_{\max}^J$ to $L_{\max}^*$: for any critical sequence,

$$L_{\max}^J < L_{\max}^* + p_b \tag{1.5}$$

for the interference job J_b associated with that sequence. To see why this relation is true, consider the subset $S' \subset S$ of those jobs processed after job J_b in the critical sequence. By the way that J_b was chosen, clearly $q_j \ge q_c$ for all jobs $J_j \in S'$; that implies that $q_j > q_b$ for all $J_j \in S'$.

Notice, however, that for Jackson's rule to schedule job J_b at time s_b implies that no job $J_j \in S'$ could have been available at time s_b, since otherwise such a job J_j would have taken priority over job J_b. Thus, $r_j > s_b$ for all $J_j \in S'$. Now we can bound the length of an optimal schedule, using (1.3), as

$$L^*_{\max} \geq \min_{J_j \in S'} r_j + P(S') + \min_{J_j \in S'} q_j > s_b + P(S') + q_k,$$

while we also know that

$$L^J_{\max} = s_b + p_b + P(S') + q_k < L^*_{\max} + p_b,$$

i.e., (1.5) holds.

1.2.2   A SIMPLE 3/2-APPROXIMATION ALGORITHM

The first approximation algorithm to beat the list scheduling bound of 2 was a 3/2-approximation algorithm given by Potts [Po80]. It involves iteratively using Jackson's rule, updating certain data between iterations, and its running time is $O(n^2 \log n)$. The more efficient 3/2-approximation algorithm presented here is due to Nowicki and Smutnicki [NS94] and runs in time $O(n \log n)$. We refer to it as Algorithm NS, after the authors' names.

Consider an instance of $1|r_j|L_{\max}$. Let job J_d, if it exists, be the unique job with $p_d > P/2$. Notice by (1.5), if no such job exists then the schedule given by Jackson's rule satisfies $L^J_{\max} < (P/2) + L^*_{\max} \leq (3/2)L^*_{\max}$. We define a partition of jobs other than J_d as follows:

$$A = \{J_j : j \neq d, \; r_j \leq q_j, \; j = 1, \dots, n\}, \quad \text{and}$$
$$B = \{J_j : j \neq d, \; r_j > q_j, \; j = 1, \dots, n\}.$$

In those instances in which P_d exists, clearly $P(A) + P(B) < P/2$.

Algorithm NS

Step 1: Construct the schedule given by Jackson's rule, and determine a critical job J_c and critical sequence for the schedule. If there exists no interference job J_b, then stop and return this schedule.

Step 2: If $\min\{p_b, q_c\} \leq P/2$, then stop and return the schedule of Step 1. Otherwise, order the jobs of A according to nondecreasing release dates and of B according to nonincreasing delivery times. (Note that $J_b = J_d$.) Construct a schedule given by the ordered set A, followed by J_b, followed by the ordered set B. Return the better of this schedule and that constructed in Step 1.

We claim that the schedule generated is guaranteed to have length $L^{NS}_{\max} \leq (3/2)L^*_{\max}$. Let S denote the set of jobs in the critical sequence constructed in Step 1, and let a and c be the first and last sequenced jobs of S, so that the first schedule constructed has length $r_a + P(S) + q_c$. By (1.4) and (1.5), if the algorithm stops after constructing the first schedule using Jackson's rule, then the result clearly holds; moreover, even if the second schedule gets constructed, if $p_b \leq (1/2)L^*_{\max}$ then the first schedule constructed will still attain the bound.

Thus, all we have left to show is that the bound is attained in the case that $p_b > (1/2)L^*_{\max}$. In this case, notice that J_b must be the large job J_d, i.e., $b = d$. Now, if $a = b = c$, then the critical sequence consists of a single job and by (1.2) the schedule must be optimal. Otherwise, if $a \neq c$, we claim that the second schedule constructed, which we denote as Σ_2, satisfies $L_{max}(\Sigma_2) < (3/2)L_{max}^*$. We proceed by considering an arbitrary job J_k and showing that, in every possible case, the delivery completion time of job J_k in Σ_2 satisfies $L_k(\Sigma_2) \leq (3/2)L_{max}^*$. Throughout the proof we refer to a particular optimal schedule Σ^* as a point of comparison.

In each of the cases to follow, we fix a job J_k and define a sequence tracing backward in time from J_k in Σ_2 to the first idle time (or to the beginning of the schedule). We denote the job that begins processing at that point in time by J_h (which is, of course, dependent on the choice of J_k). We use Q to denote the set of jobs beginning with J_h and ending with J_k in Σ_2, so that $L_k = r_h + P(Q) + q_k$. We delineate cases based on the status of the jobs J_h and J_k and proceed to show that in every case $L_k(\Sigma_2) < (3/2)L_{max}^*$.

Case 1: both J_h, $J_k \in A$, or both J_h, $J_k \in B$. Recall that job J_b is scheduled between sets $\overline{A}$ and B. Thus in both of these situations, $J_b \notin Q$, and so $P(Q) \leq P - P_b < L_{max}^*/2$. If J_h and J_k are in A, then $r_h \leq r_k$ since J_h precedes J_k in A, whereas if both are in B, $q_k \leq r_k$ since J_k succeeds J_h in B. Thus, if both are in A then

$$L_k = r_h + P(Q) + q_k \leq r_k + P(A) + q_k < (3/2)L_{max}^*,$$

while if both are in B,

$$L_k = r_h + P(Q) + q_k \leq r_h + P(B) + q_h < (3/2)L_{max}^*,$$

by (1.2).

Case 2: $J_k = J_b$ or $J_h = J_b$. First, notice that if $J_h = J_k = J_b$, then $L_k(\Sigma_2) \leq L_{max}^*$ by (1.2). Next, consider $J_k = J_b$, and $J_h \in A$. Suppose first that all of the jobs of $Q \setminus \{J_b\}$ are processed before job J_b in Σ^*, so that

$$L_{max}^* \geq \min_{J_j \in Q \setminus \{J_b\}} r_j + P(Q) + q_b.$$

Then, since

$$r_h = \min_{J_j \in Q \setminus \{J_b\}} r_j, \tag{1.6}$$

job J_k actually completes delivery by time L_{max}^* in the second schedule, since $L_k = L_b = r_h + P(Q) + q_b$. Now suppose that at least one job of $Q \setminus \{J_b\}$ is processed after job J_b in Σ^*. In that case, since $Q \setminus \{J_b\} \subseteq A$,

$$L_{max}^* \geq P(Q) + \min_{J_j \in Q \setminus \{J_b\}} q_j \geq P(Q) + r_h,$$

by the definition of A and (1.6). But since $p_b > L_{max}^*/2$ we have $q_b < L_{max}^*/2$, and so $L_k = L_b = r_h + P(Q) + q_b < (3/2)L_{max}^*$.

The proof for the case $J_h = J_b$ with $J_k \in B$ is virtually identical to the proof just given, with the roles of k and h, release dates and delivery times, and "before" and "after" interchanged. Suppose first that all of the jobs of $Q \setminus \{J_b\}$ are processed after job J_b in Σ^*, so that

$$L_{max}^* \geq \min_{J_j \in Q \setminus \{J_b\}} q_j + P(Q) + r_b.$$

Then, since

$$q_k = \min_{J_j \in Q \setminus \{J_b\}} q_j, \tag{1.7}$$

job J_k actually completes delivery by time L_{max}^* in the second schedule, since

$L_k = r_b + P(Q) + q_k$. Now suppose that at least one job of $Q \backslash \{J_b\}$ is processed before job J_b in Σ^*. In that case, $Q \backslash \{J_b\} \subseteq B$,

$$L_{max}^* \geq P(Q) + \min_{J_j \in Q \backslash \{J_b\}} r_j \geq P(Q) + q_k,$$

by the definition of B and (1.7). But since $p_b > L_{max}^*/2$ we have $r_b < L_{max}^*/2$, and so $L_k = r_b + P(Q) + q_k < (3/2) L_{max}^*$.

Case 3: $J_h \in A$ and $J_k \in B$. In this case, notice that $r_h \leq q_h$, while $q_k \leq r_k$. These relationships imply that

$$r_h < L_{max}^*/2 \quad \text{and} \quad q_k < L_{max}^*/2. \tag{1.8}$$

Let job J_i be that job of Q that gets processed first in Σ^*, so that $L_{max}^* \geq r_i + P(Q)$. If $J_i \in A$, then $r_h \leq r_i$ and so $L_{max}^* \geq r_h + P(Q)$. If $J_i \in B$, then $r_i \geq q_i \geq q_k$, and so $L_{max}^* \geq q_k + P(Q)$. Finally, if $P_i = P_b$, then since the rest of Q follows job P_b in Σ^*,

$$L_{max}^* \geq P(Q) + \min_{J_j \in Q \backslash \{J_b\}} q_j \geq P(Q) + \min\{q_k, r_h\}, \tag{1.9}$$

and indeed, (1.9) thus holds regardless of what type of job J_i is. Combining (1.9) with (1.8) gives us

$$L_k = r_h + P(Q) + q_k = \max\{r_h, q_k\} + \min\{r_h, q_k\} + P(Q) < L_{max}^*/2 + L_{max}^*.$$

Since all cases have been established, we have shown that $L_{max}(\Sigma_2) \leq (3/2) L_{max}^*$ whenever p_b and q_c are both greater than $L_{max}^*/2$, and so we have established the result.

THEOREM 1.2 Nowicki and Smutnicki [NS94]. Algorithm NS is a (3/2)-approximation algorithm.

The proof presented here was modified from one by Paul Martin (unpublished).

1.2.3 A POLYNOMIAL APPROXIMATION SCHEME

While $1|r_j|L_{max}$ is strongly NP-hard, there do exist polynomial approximation schemes for it, that is, a family of $(1 + 1/k)$-approximation algorithms, for $k = 1, 2, 3, \ldots$. Two such schemes were first given by the author and Shmoys [HS92]; for one of these, the running time of the associated $(1 + 1/k)$-approximation algorithm was $O(n \log n + nk^{O(1)k^2})$. It is worth noting that the running time contains no exponent on n dependent on k. The simpler-to-analyze scheme presented here is due to E. Lawler (unpublished).

To explain the polynomial approximation scheme, we first examine an artificial situation that we shall use as a tool in analyzing the eventual algorithm. Let us focus on a specific instance I and a particular optimal sequence for that instance, Σ^* with value $L_{max}^*(I)$. Let us denote the starting time of job J_j in Σ^* as s_j^*, for $j = 1, \ldots, n$. In addition, we introduce a parameter $\delta > 0$ to be specified later.

Now consider a modified instance $\tilde{I}$ as follows: for all jobs J_j with $p_j < \delta$, $\tilde{r}_j = r_j$ and $\tilde{q}_j = q_j$, while for those jobs J_j with $p_j \geq \delta$, $\tilde{r}_j = s_j^*$ and $\tilde{q}_j = L_{max}^*(I) - p_j - s_j^*$. The processing times of all jobs remain unchanged in $\tilde{I}$. Observe that $\tilde{r}_j \geq r_j$ and $\tilde{q}_j \geq q_j$ for all jobs J_j, so that clearly $L_{max}^*(\tilde{I}) \geq L_{max}^*(I)$; in fact, it is easy to see that Σ^* is an optimal schedule for the modified instance and that $L^*_{max}(\tilde{I}) = L^*_{max}(I)$. Moreover, any schedule that is optimal for $\tilde{I}$ is also optimal for the original instance I. We shall use L^*_{max} to denote this common optimal value.

Let us use A and B to denote, respectively, those jobs J_j whose processing times $p_j < \delta$ and $p_j \geq \delta$. Notice that, for jobs $J_j \in B$,

$$L^*_{max} = \tilde{r}_j + p_j + \tilde{q}_j.$$

Let us analyze the schedule delivered by Jackson's rule on instance $\tilde{I}$. Consider a critical sequence as defined in the last section. If the sequence has no interference job, then this sequence is optimal for $\tilde{I}$ and hence also for I. Now suppose that there is an interference job J_b. We claim that $J_b \notin B$, and thus by (1.5)

$$L^J_{max}(\tilde{I}) < L^*_{max} + \delta;$$

that is, on the modified instance, the value of the heuristic schedule is within δ of the optimal value.

We now prove that J_b cannot be in B. Suppose that $J_b \in B$, and recall that $\tilde{r}_b = s^*_b$. In particular, job J_c begins processing after job J_b in Σ^*, since $\tilde{r}_c > \tilde{r}_b$. But since $\tilde{q}_c > \tilde{q}_b$, we have

$$\Sigma^* \geq \tilde{r}_b + p_b + p_c + \tilde{q}_c > \tilde{r}_b + p_b + \tilde{q}_b + p_c = \Sigma^* + p_c,$$

which is a contradiction.

Let us refer to the heuristic schedule just constructed as Σ. Since we do not in fact know the optimal starting times s^*_j of the jobs of B, we cannot reconstruct Σ; or can we? In fact, in order to reconstruct Σ it is sufficient to know simply the positions that each of the jobs of B have in Σ; we can then run Jackson's rule with the exception that, when a position belonging to a job of B is reached, we place that job next in the ordering. Of course, we also do not know the positions of the jobs of B in Σ, but by trying *every* possible choice for positioning the jobs of B in the sequence and selecting the best schedule generated, we are guaranteed to find a schedule as good as Σ. There are $O(n^{|B|})$ such choices. Now we observe the tradeoff with δ: by choosing $\delta = P/k$, we can guarantee that we produce a schedule of value at most $L^*_{max} + P/k \leq (1 + 1/k)L^*_{max}$. On the other hand, the number of jobs in B is bounded by $P/\delta = k$, and so the number of possible choices for positions that we need to try is $O(n^k)$. For any fixed k we thus have a polynomial-time algorithm with a performance guarantee of $(1 + 1/k)$.

The preceding argument was taken from an unpublished manuscript by Lawler, Lenstra, Rinnooy Kan, and Shmoys.

1.2.4 PRECEDENCE CONSTRAINTS AND PREPROCESSING

In this section we show how the results of subsections 1.2.1 and 1.2.2 can be modified to work for models with precedence constraints among the jobs, $1|r_j, prec|L_{max}$.

Because most of the algorithms in the previous subsections work by implementing essentially "greedy" rules, it turns out that by applying certain preprocessing to the data of the problem we can ensure that these algorithms automatically enforce the precedence relations. Lageweg, Lenstra, and Rinnooy Kan [LLR76] first observed that it is possible to preprocess the data so that Jackson's rule automatically enforces the precedence constraints and, moreover, each feasible schedule remains feasible and retains its original objective value. The release times and delivery times are updated separately. For the former, the jobs are processed in any topologically sorted order (from sources to sinks), and when job J_k is processed, then r_k is set to the maximum of its original value and $r_j + p_j$ for any job J_j such that $J_j \prec J_k$. For the latter, the jobs are processed in the reverse order, and when job J_j is processed, then q_j is set to the maximum of its original value and $q_k + p_k$ for any job J_k such that $J_j \prec J_k$. These changes ensure that, if $J_j \prec J_k$, then $r_j < r_k$ and $q_j > q_k$.

Notice that these relationships are sufficient to ensure that, if $J_j \prec J_k$, then Jackson's rule will always select job J_j to be processed before it selects job J_k: first, job J_k will never become available before J_j; and if both are available, job J_j will receive priority since its delivery time is smaller. Moreover, it is straightforward to verify that a schedule feasible for the original instance remains feasible after preprocessing, and that its objective value does not change.

Next we show that preprocessing can be applied to the 3/2-approximation algorithm, Algorithm NS, as well. Consider the following version of Algorithm NS that incorporates preprocessing.

Algorithm NS-prec

Step 0: Preprocess release dates and delivery times with respect to the precedence relation $\prec$.

Step 1: Identical to Step 1 of Algorithm NS.

Step 2: Identical to Step 2 of Algorithm NS, except that if the newly constructed schedule is infeasible, then return the schedule of Step 1.

First, our previous observations ensure that the Step 1 schedule will always be feasible with respect to the precedence constraints. Thus, all we need to establish is that, if the Step 2 schedule is not feasible with respect to $\prec$, then the Step 1 schedule achieves the 3/2-approximation bound. We begin by considering jobs other than the interference job J_b in the Step 2 schedule.

LEMMA 1.1   Consider two jobs J_i and J_j, $i, j \neq b$, with $J_i \prec J_j$. Then it is never the case that $J_i \in B$ and $J_j \in A$.

Proof.   Suppose that $J_j \in A$, so that $r_j \leq q_j$. Then after preprocessing, $r_i < r_j \leq q_j < q_i$, and so $J_i \in A$, as well. Similarly, suppose that $J_i \in B$, so that $r_i > q_i$. After preprocessing, $r_j > r_i > q_i > q_j$, so that $J_j \in B$, as well.   ∎

Now suppose that there is an interference job J_b with $p_b > P/2$, and that the Step 2 schedule violates the precedence relation. Due to the preceding lemma, the only such violation can occur between job J_b and some other job, since the jobs of A and B will all get scheduled consistently with respect to their precedence constraints; and no job of B precedes any job of A. Suppose first that there is a job $J_j \in A$ with $J_b \prec J_j$, so that the Step 2 schedule violates the precedence constraint between J_j and J_b. After preprocessing, we have $r_j \geq r_b + p_b$; moreover, $J_j \in A$ implies $q_j \geq r_j$. Thus, $L^*_{\max} \geq r_j + q_j \geq 2r_j \geq 2p_b$. Similarly, if some job $J_j \prec J_b$ is in B, then $q_j \geq q_b + p_b$ and $r_j \geq q_j$. Hence, $L^*_{\max} \geq r_j + q_j > 2q_j \geq 2p_b$. In both cases, $p_b \leq L^*_{\max}/2$ and the Step 1 schedule is within a factor of 3/2 of $L^*_{\max}$. Thus, we have established the following result.

THEOREM 1.3   Algorithm NS-prec is a $3/2$-approximation algorithm for the scheduling problem $1|r_j, prec|L_{max}$.

Unfortunately, it is not possible to apply preprocessing to the polynomial approximation scheme outlined in the last section. However, more sophisticated preprocessing applied to a different polynomial approximation scheme results in a polynomial approximation scheme for the precedence-constrained problem [HS90].

As we mentioned earlier, Potts [Po80] constructed the first $3/2$-approximation algorithm for the problem of sequencing with respect to release dates and delivery times; preprocessing can also be used on this algorithm to handle precedence constraints. Moreover, Potts' algorithm can be modified to a $4/3$-approximation algorithm that runs in $O(n^2 \log n)$ time [HS92], essentially by exploiting the symmetry between running time forwards and backwards (and interchanging the symmetric roles of release dates and delivery times).

IDENTICAL PARALLEL MACHINES: BEYOND LIST SCHEDULING

1.3

This section considers scheduling problems in which each job must be processed on one of a set of identical parallel machines. First, we consider list scheduling applied to a more general model, and then discuss improvements to list scheduling for some models. Finally, we recall some related results that are discussed in other sections of the book.

1.3.1 $\mathcal{P}|r_j, prec|L_{max}$: LIST SCHEDULING REVISITED

In the introduction we presented Graham's analysis of a simple heuristic known as list scheduling (LS) for the problem of scheduling jobs on identical parallel machines to minimize makespan. We demonstrated that it is a $(2 - 1/m)$-approximation algorithm. Graham actually gave a stronger result: namely, even if there are precedence constraints among jobs, list scheduling is still a $(2 - 1/m)$-approximation algorithm. Here, we present a generalization of that result that imposes release dates and delivery times on jobs, and the objective is to minimize the maximum delivery-completion time (equivalent to "lateness") of any job; it is due to the author and Shmoys [HS89]. In this model we modify the definition of list scheduling so that whenever the machine becomes available we process the next *available* job on the list, meaning one that has been released and whose predecessors have all completed processing.

THEOREM 1.4   List scheduling is a 2-approximation algorithm for the scheduling problem $\mathcal{P}|r_j, prec|L_{max}$ (delivery-completion-time version).

Proof.   Consider a schedule produced by the algorithm, and let J_{j_1} be a job whose delivery completion time attains that of the schedule,

$$L_{j_1}(LS) = L_{\max}^{LS}.$$

We will partition the total time of the schedule into two sets of intervals such that the total time of the intervals belonging to each of the sets is bounded above by $L_{\max}^*$. Thus, the constructed schedule will have $L_{\max} \le 2L_{\max}^*$.

Consider the latest time t_1 before s_{j_1} that some machine is idle. Since job J_{j_1} was not scheduled in this idle slot, it was not available at time t_1, either because one of its predecessors had not completed processing or because it had not been released. In the former case, consider a job $J_{j_2} \prec J_{j_1}$ that was undergoing processing at time t_1. Now, we repeat this argument with job J_{j_2}: we consider the latest idle time t_2 preceding the start of processing for J_{j_2}, and again we see that either one of its predecessors has not completed processing or it has not been released. Eventually we construct a string of jobs $J_{j_k} \prec \cdots \prec J_{j_2} \prec J_{j_1}$ whereby job J_{j_k} is not available before time t_k because it has not been released by time t_k.

We now partition the schedule into two sets of intervals, as follows. The first set consists of the disjoint intervals $[0, r_k)$, $[C_{j_1}, C_{j_1} + q_{j_1}]$, and

$$\bigcup_{i=1}^{k}[s_{j_i}, C_{j_i});$$

in other words, it consists of all of those times that some job in the constructed chain is undergoing processing, plus the release date of the first job in the chain and the delivery time of the last job in the chain. The sum of these intervals is a lower bound on $L_{\max}^*$, since the jobs involved form a precedence chain; see Figure 1.2.

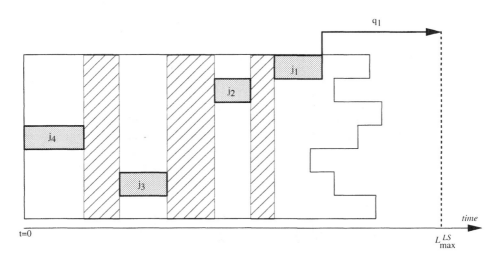

FIGURE 1.2

*The diagonally shaded strips comprise the second set of
intervals; no machine is idle during these intervals.*

The second set of intervals is the remaining time in the schedule. We claim that during these intervals no machine is idle. Indeed, by the choice of the jobs $J_{j_1}, \ldots, J_{j_k}$ this fact is clear. Let us denote an optimal schedule by Σ^*, and let $C_{\max}(\Sigma^*)$ denote the time at which all jobs have completed processing (but have not necessarily been delivered). We can now argue as we did in the introduction that, since the intervals contain no idle time, their total length is bounded above by $P/m \leq C_{\max}(\Sigma^*) \leq L^*_{\max}$. Thus, we have shown that list scheduling is indeed a 2-approximation algorithm for this problem.   ∎

It is not hard to show that both this approximation bound and the Graham's bound of $(2 - 1/m)$ for processing independent jobs to minimize makespan are tight. For Graham's result, consider an instance with $m^2 - m + 1$ jobs, $m^2 - m$ with processing requirement equal to one, and the last with processing requirement m. If the last job is last in the list, the resulting schedule will have makespan $m - 1 + m = 2m - 1$, while the optimal schedule has length m. We have already seen that Jackson's rule for single-machine scheduling can yield a schedule with lateness arbitrarily close to 2 (see Section 1.2), and the same example shows that list scheduling in the presence of release dates and delivery times has the same tight worst-case bound.

1.3.2   THE LPT RULE FOR $\mathcal{P}||C_{\max}$

Graham's seminal work on list scheduling included an analysis of a special case known as the LPT (*longest processing time*) rule for $\mathcal{P}||C_{\max}$. In this case, we apply list scheduling, ordering the job list by non-increasing processing times. Intuitively such a rule should help, since the worst-case example for list scheduling involves scheduling a very long job last.

THEOREM 1.5   [Gr69] For $\mathcal{P}||C_{\max}$, $C^{LPT}_{\max} \leq 4/3 - 1/3m$, and this bound is tight.

Proof.   Let us assume that the jobs are indexed so that $p_1 \geq p_2 \geq \cdots \geq p_n$. We delineate two cases, depending on the length of J_k, the job that completes last. First, suppose that $p_k \leq C^*_{\max}/3$; then the bound follows directly from our analysis of list scheduling (Section 1.1). Now, suppose that $p_k > C^*_{\max}/3$. Without loss of generality, we can assume that job J_k was the last job on the list, since otherwise we can truncate the instance at this point and obtain a new instance on which LPT performs at least as badly relative to the optimal schedule. For such an instance, in the optimal schedule at most two jobs can be processed on any machine. Suppose that the instance has $2m - h$ jobs total. It is not hard to see that the following schedule is optimal in this case: schedule jobs $J_1, \ldots, J_h$ alone on machines, and then pair up jobs J_{h+1} with J_n, J_{h+2} with J_{n-1}, and so on. In fact, this schedule is precisely the one delivered by the LPT rule, up to tie-breakers; so in this case, the LPT rule delivers the optimal schedule.

We leave it to the reader to verify that the following class of instances is tight at the $4/3 - 1/3m$ bound: let $n = 2m + 1$, and let there be two jobs of length $m + 1, \ldots, 2m - 1$, and three jobs of length m.   ∎

1.3.3   THE LPT RULE FOR $\mathcal{P}|r_j|C_{\max}$

We may consider a dynamic version of the LPT rule in the case that jobs have release dates: whenever a machine is idle, schedule a longest *available* (already released) job, if there is one. Chen and Vestjens [CV95] have shown that, in the presence of release dates, LPT is a 3/2-approximation algorithm. The proof given here is theirs.

THEOREM 1.6   [CV95] For $\mathcal{P}|r_j|C_{\max}$, $C_{\max}^{LPT} \leq (3/2)C_{\max}^*$.

Proof.   Assume that we have an instance in which $C_{\max}^{LPT} > (3/2)C_{\max}^*$. By carefully analyzing the structure of this schedule, we will conclude that it cannot exist. First, we observe that without loss of generality we can assume that at no point in the LPT schedule are all machines idle; if that is the case, by considering the set of jobs processed after this idle period we have a smaller instance for which the LPT schedule can only be worse relative to the optimal schedule than was the original instance, and thus we can focus on this smaller instance.

Let J_ℓ be the last job to finish, and let $[t_s, t_f]$ be the last interval of idle time (if there is such an interval) before J_ℓ begins processing. First, we observe that $s_\ell - r_\ell > (1/2)C_{\max}^*$, since

$$(3/2)C_{\max}^* < C_{\max}^{LPT} = s_\ell + p_\ell = s_\ell - r_\ell + (r_\ell + p_\ell) \leq s_\ell - r_\ell + C_{\max}^*.$$

In particular, there are m jobs undergoing processing just before J_ℓ begins. Each of these either begins before or after r_ℓ. Those J_j that begin after must satisfy $p_j \geq p_\ell$, since the LPT rule was used to build the schedule; and for those J_j that begin before r_ℓ, $p_j \geq s_\ell - r_\ell > (1/2)C_{\max}^*$. We conclude from these observations that $p_\ell \leq (1/2)C_{\max}^*$, since otherwise we would have $m + 1$ jobs with processing time strictly larger than $(1/2)C_{\max}^*$, two of which would have to be processed on the same machine. From this fact we further deduce that there is indeed a non-empty interval $[t_s, t_f]$, before r_ℓ, during which some machine is idle; otherwise, all machines would be busy up to time s_ℓ, and we would have $C_{\max}^{LPT} \leq (3/2)C_{\max}^*$. We need, however, a stronger bound on p_ℓ.

LEMMA 1.2   Let t_f be the latest point before r_ℓ that some machine is idle. Then, $p_\ell \leq (1/2)(C_{\max}^* - t_f)$.

Proof.   Consider again the m jobs that are processing just before J_ℓ begins. We divide them into two groups, Type-I and Type-II, according to whether they begin before or after t_f, respectively; note that, from our previous analysis, Type-I jobs have processing times greater than $C_{\max}^*/2$. Let J_ℓ be considered a Type-II job, as well. For the Type-II jobs J_j, clearly $r_j \geq t_f$, since some machine was idle just before t_f. For the Type-I jobs J_j, we claim that $s_j \leq t_s$; otherwise, the job begins processing at its release date, which would imply $C_{\max}^{LPT} \leq r_j + p_j + p_\ell \leq (3/2)C_{\max}^*$.

Let us fix an optimal schedule Σ^*. Now, two of these $m + 1$ Type-I and Type-II jobs must be scheduled on the same machine, in Σ^*. We claim that the first of these must be a Type-II job. Clearly they cannot both be Type-I jobs, since these jobs have processing times greater than $C_{\max}^*/2$. Suppose that the first was a Type-I job J_i, and the second a

Type-II job (whose processing time, recall, is at least p_ℓ). Then,

$$C^*_{\max} \geq r_i + p_i + p_\ell = (r_i - s_i) + s_i + p_i + p_\ell \geq C^{LPT}_{\max} - (s_i - r_i),$$

i.e., $s_i - r_i > C^*_{\max}/2$. There could be no idle machines during this long interval $[r_i, s_i]$; but there is also no idle time in the interval $[r_\ell, s_\ell]$, whose length is also greater than $C^*_{\max}/2$. Because these two intervals $[r_i, s_i]$ and $[r_\ell, s_\ell]$ are disjoint, we have a contradiction. Thus, the first of the two jobs scheduled on the same machine in Σ^* must be a Type-II job; call it J_i. If both jobs are Type-II jobs, then we have $C^*_{\max} \geq r_i + 2p_\ell \geq t_f + 2p_\ell$, while if the second is a Type-I job, then $C^*_{\max} \geq r_i + p_\ell + (s_I - t_s) > t_f + 2p_\ell$. In either case, $p_\ell \leq (1/2)(C^*_{\max} - t_f)$, and we have proved the lemma. ∎

LEMMA 1.3   In the LPT schedule, some job begins at or before t_s and completes at or after t_f.

Proof.   Suppose that such a job did not exist; then consider the set $\mathcal{J}$ of jobs that begin processing after time t_s in the LPT schedule. Each such job begins either at its release date (if it begins on or before t_f) or after t_f, when all machines become busy. Now consider when these jobs get processed in some optimal schedule Σ^*. Let t_i and t_i^* denote the time at which M_i begins processing jobs of $\mathcal{J}$ in the LPT schedule and in Σ^*, respectively, $i = 1, \ldots, m$; further, let us assume that the machines have been numbered in each case so that $t_1 \leq t_2 \leq \ldots \leq t_m$ and $t_1^* \leq t_2^* \leq \ldots \leq t_m^*$. Clearly $t_i \leq t_i^*$, for all i, since in the LPT case no machine has been delayed from starting on a job of $\mathcal{J}$ for any reason. On the other hand, the LPT schedule keeps all machines busy between t_f and s_ℓ, and so

$$C^*_{\max} \geq t_f + (1/m)\left[\sum_{j \in \mathcal{J}} p_j - \sum_{i=1}^{m}(t_i^* - t_f)\right]$$

$$\geq t_f + (1/m)\left[\sum_{j \in \mathcal{J}} p_j - \sum_{i=1}^{m}(t_i - t_f)\right] \geq t_f + (s_\ell - t_f) = s_\ell.$$

But $C^{LPT}_{\max} > (3/2)C^*_{\max}$ precludes this possibility, since $C^{LPT}_{\max} = s_\ell + p_\ell \leq s_\ell + (1/2)C^*_{\max}$. Thus, the second lemma is proved. ∎

Suppose that there are k such jobs ($1 \leq k \leq m - 1$) that begin on or before t_s and complete at or after time t_f, and let $\alpha = max_{1 \leq j \leq k}(s_j - r_j)$. In particular, all machines are busy during a block of α units before t_s, since some job was delayed by that amount. We shall derive two lower bounds on the length of $C^*_{\max}$, and together these will imply a contradiction on the length of the LPT schedule. First, consider the total load across the LPT schedule: we have a busy interval of length α, and a busy interval disjoint from that one of length $s_\ell - t_f$. Additionally, recall that we have assumed that in the LPT schedule at least one machine is always busy; thus, in particular, we obtain an additional load, before the second busy period begins, of $t_f - \alpha$ (α has been subtracted because it was already counted in the first busy interval). Thus, we have a load-based lower bound of

$$C^*_{\max} \geq \alpha + (s_\ell - t_f) + (1/m)(t_f - \alpha).$$

Next, we consider the total machine load that must occur after time t_f. The most we could possibly save over LPT on the k jobs that process across the interval is $k\alpha$. Thus, we have $C^*_{\max} \geq t_f + (s_\ell - t_f) - k\alpha/m$. Averaging these two lower bounds and possibly throwing out an α-term results in the new lower bound

$$C^*_{\max} \geq s_\ell - t_f + t_f/2. \tag{1.10}$$

Finally, by combining (1.10) with the bound in Lemma 1.2 we derive that

$$C^{LPT}_{\max} = s_\ell + p_\ell \leq (s_\ell - t_f + t_f) + (1/2)C^*_{\max} - (1/2)t_f \leq (3/2)C^*_{\max},$$

contradicting our original assumption on $C^{LPT}_{\max}$. Thus, we have shown that no such schedule can exist, and the theorem is proved.

We make one final observation concerning the LPT rule and list scheduling. There is a complementary rule known as the *SPT* rule that list schedules jobs from shortest to longest processing times. Ironically, this rule is optimal when minimizing the average (or sum) of all job completion times! See Section 1.7 for more about this model.

1.3.4 OTHER RESULTS FOR IDENTICAL PARALLEL MACHINES

There are several additional approximation results on identical parallel machines. In particular, Hochbaum and Shmoys constructed a polynomial approximation scheme for $\mathcal{P}||C_{\max}$; for a description of that algorithm, see Chapter 9, Section 9.3.2. Their result was generalized by the author and Shmoys to a polynomial approximation scheme for $\mathcal{P}|r_j|L_{\max}$ [HS89]. There is one noteworthy lower bound on approximation; namely, for $\mathcal{P}|prec, p_j = 1|C_{\max}$ there is no $(4/3 - \epsilon)$-approximation algorithm, for any $\epsilon > 0$, unless $P = NP$. Section 1.6 describes this result. We make one final observation: some of the algorithms discussed in the preceding sections can be interpreted as on-line algorithms, in particular the 2-approximation algorithm for $P|r_j, prec|L_{\max}$ of Section 1.3.1 and the 3/2-approximation algorithm for $P|r_j|C_{\max}$ of Section 1.3.3.

UNRELATED PARALLEL MACHINES

1.4

The packing arguments of the previous section for identical parallel machines seem to break down for the case of unrelated parallel machines. Instead, we use solutions to linear programs to guide heuristics. The basic thrust of these methods is that optimal fractional solutions to these linear programs provide reasonable starting points for analysis: If they can somehow be modified to produce integral solutions, either by clever rounding or by other means, then perhaps some performance guarantee can be attained without paying too large a price in running time. Indeed, as in many areas of combinatorial optimization, linear programming proves to be a powerful tool.

1.4.1   A 2-APPROXIMATION ALGORITHM BASED ON LINEAR PROGRAMMING

To begin, we present a simple approach suggested by Potts [Po85] for $R||C_{max}$; the running time is exponential in the number of machines. Consider the following integer linear program that represents the problem of assigning jobs to machines ($x_{ij} = 1$ means that job J_j has been assigned to machine M_i):

$$\text{Minimize} \quad t$$

$$\text{subject to} \quad \sum_{i=1}^{m} x_{ij} = 1, \qquad j = 1, \dots, n;$$

$$\sum_{j=1}^{n} p_{ij} x_{ij} \leq t, \qquad i = 1, \dots, m;$$

$$x_{ij} \in \{0, 1\}, \quad i = 1, \dots, m, \ j = 1, \dots, n.$$

The first constraints ensure that every job gets assigned, while the second set relates the makespan t to the processing time on each of the machines. Since t is minimized in the objective function, at optimality t will represent the maximum processing time of any machine.

Suppose that we relax the binary constraints and require only that $x_{ij} \geq 0$ for all i, j; this linear program is called the *LP relaxation* of the integer program. A *basic* optimal solution to this linear program has the property that the number of positive variables is at most the number of rows in the constraint matrix, $m + n$. Since t is always positive, at most $m + n - 1$ of the x_{ij} variables are positive; moreover, every job J_j has at least one positive variable associated with it. By simple counting we conclude that at most $m - 1$ jobs have been split onto two or more machines in the assignment. Notice, moreover, that the LP solution value $t(LP)$ is a lower bound on the integral optimal makespan.

Now we construct a schedule in two stages, as follows. For all of those jobs with integral assignments in the linear programming solution, we assign them according to the linear programming solution; this first piece of the schedule is guaranteed to have a length that is at most the value of the linear program, which is clearly at most C_{max}^*. For the remaining set of at most $m - 1$ jobs, by complete enumeration we find an optimal assignment in time at most $O(m^{m-1})$; this optimal schedule on a partial set of jobs is also guaranteed to have makespan at most C_{max}^*, and so by concatenating the two constructed schedules we obtain a schedule of length at most $2C_{max}^*$.

The drawback, of course, is that constructing the second piece of the schedule potentially requires time exponential in the number of machines, and so this algorithm is polynomial-time only if the number of machines is fixed. Moreover, it seems very suggestive that only $m - 1$ of the jobs get split; the "average" number of jobs assigned to a machine in the second piece of the schedule is less than one! If there was a direct way to assign at most one job to each machine, in a manner such that each machine got a job whose processing time was not too large for it, perhaps we could avoid the total enumeration for the fractional jobs.

This intuition is what motivates our modified algorithm, due to Lenstra, Shmoys, and Tardos [LST90]. This algorithm is based on a 2-relaxed decision procedure; that is, given a "target" length of T, the procedure will either correctly deduce that no schedule with length T exists, or it will construct a schedule with makespan at most $2T$ (possibly even if no schedule of length T exists). It is then possible, using binary search on T, to convert such a procedure into a 2-approximation algorithm.

Given the target schedule length T, we construct sets of machine and job indices as follows: for each job J_j,

$$\mathcal{M}(j) := \{i : p_{ij} \leq T\},$$

and for each machine M_i,

$$\mathcal{J}(i) := \{j : p_{ij} \leq T\}.$$

In other words, $\mathcal{M}(j)$ represents all of the machines that J_j could possibly be scheduled on in any schedule of length at most T, and $\mathcal{J}(i)$ represents those jobs that could get processed on M_i, in any schedule of length at most T.

Now we consider the following linear feasibility system:

$$
\begin{aligned}
\sum_{i \in \mathcal{M}(j)} x_{ij} &= 1, & j &= 1, \ldots, n; \\
\sum_{j \in \mathcal{J}(i)} p_{ij} x_{ij} &\leq T, & i &= 1, \ldots, m; \\
x_{ij} &\geq 0, & i &= 1, \ldots, m, \ j = 1, \ldots, n.
\end{aligned}
\tag{1.11}
$$

Notice that, if an (integral) schedule of length T exists, then this linear program is guaranteed to be feasible, since the zero-one solution corresponding to the schedule would be feasible. Moreover, a basic feasible solution to this system has the property that at most $n + m$ variables are positive, as before, and so we can conclude that at most m jobs get split (fractional) assignments. As before, we will construct the approximate schedule in two pieces: First, we assign each unsplit job to its proper machine, and then we focus on assigning the jobs with fractional assignments.

By the construction of the sets $\mathcal{J}(i)$ and $\mathcal{M}(j)$, if $x_{ij} > 0$ then $p_{ij} \leq T$; so if we can construct a matching of the fractional jobs to the machines in such a way that each job gets matched to a machine it is already partially assigned to, then we will have constructed an assignment of the fractional jobs that is guaranteed, as a partial schedule, to have length at most T.

How can we be sure that such a matching exists? Fortunately, the structure of basic feasible solutions can be exploited to prove existence constructively, and to thus provide us with a simple way of producing the desired matching from the linear programming solution. The feasibility system above is an example of a *generalized assignment* problem, whose basic feasible solutions are well known to have a very special form (see, e.g., [AMO93]). Let us construct the underlying graph, whose nodes are the jobs and machines of the instances, and whose edges (i, j) correspond to those variables $x_{ij} > 0$. If the solution x is basic, then the graph constructed will consist of a forest of trees and 1-trees (a tree plus one edge), in which job nodes and machine nodes alternate. Now, if we delete the job nodes with integral assignments from the graph, we will still have such a "forest," all of whose leaves correspond to machine nodes (since the remaining "split" job nodes have at least two incident edges); see Figure 1.3. Our task is to construct a matching in this graph, in which every job node gets matched. The matching will correspond to the desired assignment.

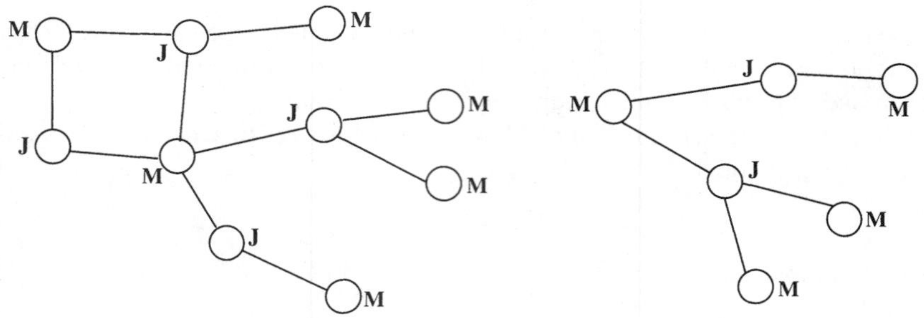

FIGURE 1.3

*Trees and 1-trees after all jobs with integral assignments
have been removed, so that all leaves are machine nodes.
Job nodes and machine nodes are labeled
"J" and "M," respectively.*

We construct the matching as follows. For each of the 1-trees, we first focus on the unique cycle in the 1-tree. This cycle contains an equal number of (alternating) job nodes and machine nodes. We arbitrarily orient the cycle in one direction and assign each job node to the machine node succeeding it on the cycle. In this manner, each machine on the cycle receives exactly one job. We now delete all of the nodes along the cycles. What remains overall is a forest of trees, each containing at most one job leaf node. (Job leaf nodes might be created upon the deletion of the cycles, but there will be at most one such leaf per resulting tree.)

By rooting each tree either at its unique job leaf node or to an arbitrary node (if no job leaf node exists), we can now assign each job node to one of its machine children in the tree. Since each machine node has a unique parent, it is guaranteed to receive at most one job in this assignment. Thus, we have completed constructing the desired assignment. Since each machine is assigned at most one job, and since that job's processing time is guaranteed to be at most T, the schedule corresponding to this part of the assignment is guaranteed to have a length of at most T.

We now paste the two pieces of the schedule together, as before, to obtain a schedule with a length of at most $2T$.

1.4.2   AN APPROXIMATION ALGORITHM FOR MINIMIZING COST AND MAKESPAN

In this section we present an alternative linear programming approach to minimizing makespan on unrelated parallel machines. The advantage of this new approach is that it does not rely on finding *basic* solutions to certain linear programs and expoiting their special structure. Instead, it uses a more sophisticated grouping and an assignment of fractional jobs to obtain a schedule for the "fractionally" assigned jobs. Moreover, this approach is more powerful in that it allows us to construct approximation algorithms that simultaneously approximate two objective functions and also works for more general models, such as *controllable processing times*. The algorithm presented here is due to Shmoys and Tardos [ST93]; it builds on earlier work of Lin and Vitter [LV92] and Trick [Tr90].

We focus on the following bicriterion scheduling problem. In addition to processing times, each job J_j incurs a cost c_{ij} if it is assigned to machine M_i. The *cost* of a schedule is the sum of the costs of each of the assignments. The two objectives to be minimized are the makespan and the cost. Suppose that there exists a schedule with total cost C and makespan T. Then the approximation algorithm will deliver a schedule with makespan at most $2T$, and with total cost at most C.

First, we solve a linear program Minimize $\sum_{i,j} c_{ij} x_{ij}$ subject to the feasibility system (1.11) from the previous section. Notice that the cost of any optimal solution to the linear program is guaranteed to be at most C; for simplicity, we assume from now on that it is exactly C. Given *any* optimal solution to the linear program (not necessarily basic), we will construct an integral assignment with total cost C and total makespan at most $2T$.

Consider an optimal solution x^* to the linear program. We construct a bipartite graph $G(V, W, E)$ as follows. Nodeset W contains a node corresponding to each job; nodeset V contains a *set* of nodes corresponding to each machine. The number of nodes associated with each machine will depend on the construction to follow. The edges of the graph will correspond to job-machine pairs whose associated value in x^* is positive, and each edge (v, w) will have an associated *weight* $\overline{y}(v, w)$.

The bipartite graph $G(V, W, E)$ will have the following useful properties:

(i)   Any matching in $G(V, W, E)$ that matches every job node will represent a schedule with makespan at most $2T$;

(ii) The fractional schedule x^* will have a natural interpretation as a "fractional matching" in $G(V, W, E)$, with cost C (that is, an assignment of fractional weights to the edges so that no node has more than a total of 1 total incident weight);

(iii) There will exist a matching in $G(V, W, E)$ that matches every job node and has cost at most C, the cost of the fractional matching.

We make a couple of easy observations. First, if statements (i) and (iii) are true, then clearly a matching in $G(V, W, E)$ will represent a schedule with the desired properties of cost equal to at most C and makespan at most $2T$. Second, it is not hard to see that (ii) implies (iii): if there is a fractional matching in $G(V, W, E)$ of cost C in which all nodes of W are matched, then that fractional matching can be decomposed into a convex combination of integral matchings, at least one of which has cost at most C. We justify this remark later on.

Now we explain the construction. Let us focus on a particular machine M_i, and temporarily renumber the jobs so that $p_{i1} \geq p_{i2} \geq \cdots \geq p_{in}$. Let $k_i = \left\lceil \sum_{j=1}^n x_{ij}^* \right\rceil$; then the nodes of V corresponding to machine M_i will be $v_{i1}, \ldots, v_{ik_i}$.

For the sake of simplicity, let us assume that $k_i = 3$. The idea for the general construction is easily extrapolated from this case. We construct edges and edge weights

$\overline{y}(v, w)$ as follows. Let q be that job index for which

$$\sum_{j=1}^{q-1} x_{ij}^* < 1 \le \sum_{j=1}^{q} x_{ij}^*. \tag{1.12}$$

We add edges from node v_{i1} to job nodes $1, \ldots, q-1$ with weights $\overline{y}(v_{i1}, j) := x_{ij}^*$, $j = 1, \ldots, q-1$; and we add an edge from node v_{i1} to job node q with weight

$$\overline{y}(v_{i1}, q) := 1 - \sum_{j=1}^{q-1} x_{ij}^*.$$

These are the only edges to node v_{i1}; observe that the sum of the weights of the edges incident to v_{i1} is exactly equal to 1. Moreover, these are the only edges from jobs $1, \ldots, q-1$ to a job node of M_i.

Now we consider v_{i2}. First, if $x_{iq}^* > \overline{y}(v_{i1}, q)$, we construct an edge (v_{i2}, q) with weight $\overline{y}(v_{i2}, q) = x_{iq}^* - \overline{y}(v_{i1}, q)$. Next, we find that index r for which

$$\overline{y}(v_{i2}, q) + \sum_{j=q+1}^{r-1} x_{ij}^* < 1 \le \overline{y}(v_{i2}, q) + \sum_{j=q+1}^{r} x_{ij}^*. \tag{1.13}$$

We add edges from node v_{i2} to job nodes $q+1, \ldots, r-1$ with weights $\overline{y}(v_{i2}, j) = x_{ij}^*$, $j = q+1, \ldots, r-1$; and we add an edge from node v_{i2} to job node r with weight

$$\overline{y}(v_{i2}, r) = 1 - \overline{y}(v_{i2}, q) - \sum_{j=q+1}^{r-1} x_{ij}^*.$$

These are the only edges to node v_{i2}; observe that the sum of the weights of the edges incident to v_{i2} is exactly equal to 1.

Finally, we consider v_{i3}. First, if $x_{ir}^* > \overline{y}(v_{i2}, r)$, we construct an edge (v_{i3}, r) with weight $\overline{y}(v_{i3}, r) = x_{ir}^* - \overline{y}(v_{i2}, r)$. Next, we observe that

$$\overline{y}(v_{i3}, r) + \sum_{j=r+1}^{n} x_{ij}^* \le 1,$$

since $k_i = 3$. We now add edges from node v_{i3} to job nodes $r+1, \ldots, n$ with weight $\overline{y}(v_{i3}, j) = x_{ij}^*$, $j = r+1, \ldots, n$.

Perhaps the easiest way to understand the construction is with a simple example (see Figure 1.4). Let us focus on the assignments only on the first machine. Suppose that the jobs have been renumbered according to non-increasing processing time on M_1, and suppose that $x_{1,1}^* = 2/3, x_{1,3}^* = x_{1,6}^* = x_{1,8}^* = 1/2, x_{1,9}^* = 1$, and for all other jobs $J_j, x_{1j} = 0$. The number of nodes associated with M_1 would be four, since $2/3 + 1 + 3/2 = 3\frac{1}{6}$. The assigned edges would be $(v_{11}, 1)$ with weight $2/3$; $(v_{11}, 3)$ with weight $1/3$; $(v_{12}, 3)$ with weight $1/6$; $(v_{12}, 6)$ with weight $1/2$; $(v_{12}, 8)$ with weight $1/3$; $(v_{13}, 8)$ with weight $1/6$; $(v_{13}, 9)$ with weight $5/6$; and $(v_{14}, 9)$ with weight $1/6$. Notice that the total "weight" of edges matched to each machine node is at most one, and is exactly one for all except the final machine node v_{14}. Also notice that the most processing time that a matching in the graph on v_{11} through v_{14} could allocate to M_1 is $p_{11} + p_{13} + p_{18} + p_{19}$, obtained by matching each v-node to its costliest (in terms of processing time) w-node. In addition, this time is bounded above by p_{11} plus the cost (in terms of processing time) of the partial fractional matching shown.

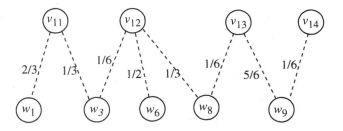

FIGURE 1.4

In general, the step just used to construct the second machine node for M_i would be iterated as long as the total remaining processing time was strictly greater than 1. Notice that in the more general construction, all of the machine nodes associated with M_i except possibly the last one, v_{ik_i}, has the sum of the weights of its incident edges exactly equal to 1. The last node might have a total incident weight strictly less than 1. In addition, once the entire bipartite graph has been constructed, it is easy to verify that the sum of the weights of the edges incident to each job node is exactly 1. Each job node j might have several incident edges but is incident to at most two nodes associated with the same machine M_i; those one or two incident edges have a total weight that is equal to x_{ij}^*, for each job J_j and machine M_i.

We now construct an assignment of jobs to machines, using the constructed bipartite graph $G(V, W, E)$. First, we observe that the variables $\overline{y}(v, w)$ form a feasible, fractional solution to the following linear program:

$$\text{Minimize} \quad \sum_{j=1}^{n}\sum_{i=1}^{m}\sum_{s=1}^{k_i} c_{ij}\, y(v_{is}, w_j)$$

subject to

$$\sum_{i=1}^{m}\sum_{s=1}^{k_i} y(v_{is}, w_j) = 1, \quad j = 1, \ldots, n;$$

$$\sum_{j=1}^{n} y(v_{is}, w_j) \leq 1, \quad s = 1, \ldots, k_i,\ i = 1, \ldots, m;$$

$$y(v, w) \geq 0, \quad \forall\, v, w.$$

It is well known that a feasible linear program of this form has integral extreme-point (or basic) solutions; in particular, the solution $\overline{x}$ is a convex combination of such integral basic solutions (see, e.g., [AMO93]). Any such integral solution represents a matching in $G(V, W, E)$ in which every node of W is matched. Moreover, at least one of the matchings in the convex combination has cost (in the new linear program) at most C, the cost of $\overline{x}$; but this cost is equal to $\sum_{i,j} c_{ij}x_{ij}^*$, the cost of the original assignment, as well.

We claim that this matching, when reinterpreted as an assignment of jobs to machines, has a makespan of at most $2T$; (in fact, every matching in $G(V, W, E)$ does). Let us focus on a particular machine M_i. Notice that in the matching, at most k_i jobs are assigned to machine M_i, since there are k_i machine nodes associated with M_i. We will show that the total processing time assigned to M_i in the matching is no more than T plus the total processing time of the fractional solution on M_i, $\sum_j p_{ij} x_{ij}$.

Let p_{is}^{min} and p_{is}^{max} denote respectively the minimum and maximum processing times of jobs whose nodes in $G(V, W, E)$ are adjacent to machine node v_{is}, for $s = 1, \ldots, k_i$, and observe that, by the construction, $p_{is}^{min} \geq p_{i,s+1}^{max}$. The amount of processing time assigned to M_i by the matching is clearly bounded by

$$
\sum_{s=1}^{k_i} p_{is}^{max} = p_{i1}^{max} + \sum_{s=2}^{k_i} p_{is}^{max} \leq p_{i1}^{max} + \sum_{s=1}^{k_i-1} p_{is}^{min}
$$

$$
\leq p_{i1}^{max} + \sum_{s=1}^{k_i-1} p_{ij} \overline{y}_{ij} \leq p_{i1}^{max} + \sum_{j=1}^{n} p_{ij} x_{ij} \leq 2T,
$$

where the final inequality follows from the facts that p_{i1}^{max} represents a job whose processing time is at most T, and that the fractional load on machine M_i is at most T.

Thus, we have constructed a matching whose overall cost is C and whose makespan is at most $2T$. Notice that in this algorithm and the one of Section 1.4.1, at no time did the analysis depend upon the fact that the right-hand side of the machine capacity constraint was the same for all machines. We could have had machine-dependent righthand sides, e.g., $\sum_{j=1}^{n} p_{ij} x_{ij} \leq T_i$, and we would have been able to construct a schedule such that the makespan on M_i was bounded by $2T_i$, $i = 1, \ldots, m$. This fact will come in handy in Section 1.7.3, where we will utilize the result of this section in a different context.

1.4.3   A RELATED RESULT FROM NETWORK SCHEDULING

A result due to Phillips, Stein, and Wein [PSW94] builds upon the previous work in an elegant manner. In their model, there is a network of processors, or machines, and a set of jobs, each of which is located at some processor node in the network. Each job must be processed by exactly one processor, and so it can either be scheduled on the processor where it is located, or it can move to another processor and get processed there. Job processing times are machine dependent, and the time to move from any processor to any other is given by a shortest path distance in the network. Each processor can process at most one job at a time, and a job must first move to the processor where it will be processed, and then begin processing sometime thereafter. The object is to minimize the makespan of the schedule.

The problem is equivalent to one in which each job has a machine-dependent release date r_{ij}; if we set r_{ij} to the shortest path distance between job J_j's origin machine and machine i, then we obtain an instance equivalent to that for the network representation. (The reduction works in the other direction as well.) We will use this notation in what follows.

Again here, we assume that we have a target T for the length of the schedule; and moreover we assume that a schedule of length T exists. In any schedule of length at most T, an assignment of job J_j to machine M_i is only possible if $r_{ij} + p_{ij} \leq T$. Thus, we will define sets of eligible machines for jobs, and jobs for machines, as

$$
\mathcal{M}(j) := \{i : r_{ij} + p_{ij} \leq T\} \text{ and } \mathcal{J}(i) := \{j : r_{ij} + p_{ij} \leq T\},
$$

for $j = 1, \ldots, n$ and $i = 1, \ldots, m$, respectively.

Now, suppose that we have a feasible solution to the system (1.11), with $\mathcal{M}(j)$ and $\mathcal{J}(i)$ in their new definitions; the system is guaranteed to be feasible, since there exists a schedule of length T. First, we construct an assignment of jobs to machines using the 2-approximation algorithm of Lenstra, Shmoys and Tardos [LST90]. Now we focus on scheduling a particular machine M_i. Recall that in the earlier algorithm, each machine's schedule could be partitioned into two pieces of length at most T, and one of the pieces contained all of the jobs except (possibly) one. Now, we schedule the jobs on M_i as follows: first, we schedule the (possible) extra job J_k at time $T - p_{ik}$; then, we schedule the remaining jobs in any order beginning at time T. Clearly, the machine completes processing by time $2T$; but in addition, we must argue that each job's release date is respected. Because of the definitions of $\mathcal{J}(i)$ and $\mathcal{M}(k)$, the extra job J_k does not violate its release date; and all of the remaining jobs have release dates smaller than T, so their release dates are not violated either. Thus, we have constructed a 2-approximation algorithm.

This algorithm can be generalized to handle the bicriterion targets of cost and makespan by using the algorithm of Shmoys and Tardos [ST93] as a black box, instead of that of Lenstra, Shmoys, and Tardos. The critical property required by the black-box schedule is that on each machine all of the jobs except at most one can be processed within time T.

SHOP SCHEDULING

1.5

In shop scheduling problems, each job consists of a set of *operations* whose processing cannot overlap in time. The set of all operations is denoted $\{O_1, \ldots, O_K\}$; each operation O_k belongs to some job J_j and must be processed on a specific machine M_i. As in earlier sections, we assume that there are n jobs and m machines in total. In an *open shop*, the operations of a job can be processed in any order; in a *job shop*, they must be processed in a specific, job-dependent order. A *flow shop* is a special type of job shop in which each job has exactly m operations, one per machine, and the order in which they must be processed is the same for all jobs. Throughout this section, we use the following notation: p_k denotes the processing time of operation O_k. We use P_j to denote the total processing time of a job, and $P_{\max}$ denotes $\max_j P_j$; Π_i denotes the total processing time that must take place on M_i, and $\Pi_{\max}$ denotes $\max_i \Pi_i$. Throughout the section we consider the problem of minimizing the makespan of the schedule, the time at which all operations complete processing.

All of these problems are strongly NP-hard in their most general forms; moreover, they are notoriously difficult in practice. In the case of the job shop, extremely restricted versions of the problem are already strongly NP-hard; for example, even if each job has at most three operations and there are only two machines, or each job has at most two operations and there are three machines, the problem is weakly NP-hard; and if there are two machines and all operations have processing times equal to one or two time units, the problem is strongly NP-hard [L+93]. For flow shops, if there are three machines the problem is strongly NP-hard, although the two-machine version is polynomially solvable [Jo54]. For open shops, the general version is strongly NP-hard, while the complexity of scheduling an open shop with a fixed number of machines greater than or equal to three is weakly NP-hard, and its status relative to being strongly NP-hard is open. Scheduling a two-machine open shop is polynomially solvable [GS76].

In this section we describe a variety of results. We begin by showing that a simple greedy heuristic, akin to list scheduling, results in a 2-approximation algorithm for the open-shop problem. Beyond this result, little is known about open shops. Next, we consider job shops and flow shops, and present an algorithm with an *additive* error that is the basis for an approximation algorithm when the number of machines is fixed; the result relies on a vector-sum theorem. Finally, we consider two simplified versions of a constant-factor approximation algorithm for job shops with unit-length operations [LMR94, LM95]; the model is related to packet-routing in networks.

Non-trivial lower bounds on approximation are known for all three models; see Section 1.6.

1.5.1   A GREEDY 2-APPROXIMATION ALGORITHM FOR OPEN SHOPS

Consider the following greedy rule for scheduling an open shop: whenever a machine becomes idle, if there is an operation available to be scheduled on that machine, schedule it. By "available" we mean that the operation belongs to a job which is currently not undergoing any processing.

THEOREM 1.7 Rácsmány; see [BF82, SSW94]   The greedy algorithm is a 2-approximation algorithm for $O||C_{\max}$.

Proof.   We will show that the makespan of the greedy schedule is bounded by $\Pi_{\max} + P_{\max}$; since each of these terms is a lower bound on the makespan, the result will follow. Consider the machine M_i that finishes last, and let J_j be the job whose operation O_k completes last on that machine. We claim that, at every point in time during the schedule, either job J_j is undergoing processing on some machine, or machine M_i is busy (or both). If such were not the case, operations O_k would have been scheduled earlier, since if M_i and J_j were both available earlier, clearly O_k would have been processed at that time. Thus the schedule's makespan is less than $\Pi_i + P_j \leq 2C^*_{\max}$.   ∎

A simple example shows that the greedy algorithm does not do better than $2 - 1/m$ in the worst case. In particular, consider an instance with $m + 1$ jobs, each having a unit-length operation on each machine. It is not hard to see that the optimal schedule has length $m + 1$, since the jobs can simply be rotated through the machines. On the other hand, suppose that the m machines spend the first m time units processing only jobs $J_1, \ldots, J_m$. Then the operations of job J_{m+1} must undergo processing sequentially, and the overall schedule produced has length $2m$ (see Figure 1.5). Such a schedule could be generated by the greedy algorithm.

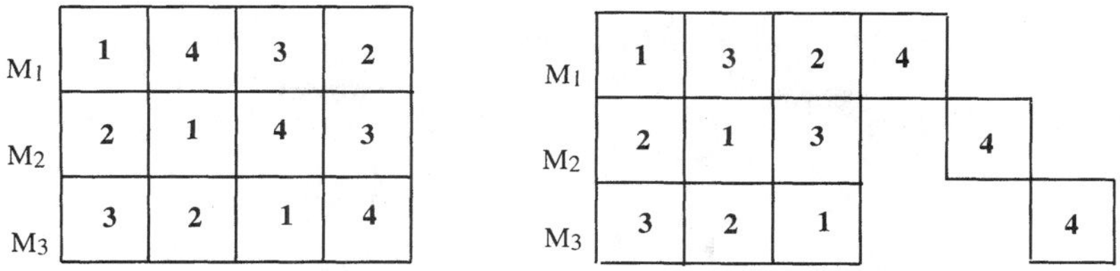

FIGURE 1.5

An optimal schedule versus a possible greedy schedule, for an open shop instance with four jobs and three machines.

1.5.2 AN ALGORITHM WITH AN ABSOLUTE ERROR BOUND

In this section we present an algorithm that delivers a schedule whose makespan is within an additive term of optimal, a term that depends on the maximum length of an operation, p_{max}. We describe an algorithm for flow shops; versions exist for open and job shops as well, although the latter is somewhat more intricate. Then we show how such an algorithm can be used to obtain a $(2 + \epsilon)$-approximation algorithm for flow shops (and job shops) in the case that the number of machines m is fixed (as opposed to part of the input).

In order to prove the result, we first prove a general fact about sums of vectors. Recall that, for $x \in \mathbb{R}^d$, $||x||_\infty = \max_{1 \le i \le d} |x_i|$.

LEMMA 1.4 Consider a set of vectors $v_1, \dots, v_n \in \mathbb{R}^d$ with the property that $\sum_{k=1}^n v_k = 0$. Then it is possible to find, in polynomial time, a permutation π of $1, \dots, n$ such that, for $j = 1, \dots, n$,

$$|| \sum_{k=1}^j v_{\pi(k)} ||_\infty \le d \max_{1 \le k \le n} ||v_k||_\infty.$$

Proof. If $n \le d$ the result is true for any permutation since $|| \sum_{k=1}^j v_{\pi(k)} ||_\infty \le j \max_{1 \le k \le j} ||v_\pi(k)||_\infty \le d \max_{1 \le k \le n} ||v_k||_\infty$. Thus, we assume that $n > d$.

For a given permutation π, we define $V_j = \{v_{\pi(1)}, \dots, v_{\pi(j)}\}$, for $j = 1, \dots, n$. It suffices to show that we can find a permutation π with the following property: for each $j, n \ge j > d$, there exist scalar multipliers $\{\lambda_{jv} : v \in V_j\}$ such that:

$$\sum_{v \in V_j} \lambda_{jv} v = 0; \tag{1.14}$$

$$\sum_{v \in V_j} \lambda_{jv} = j - d; \tag{1.15}$$

$$\lambda_{jv} \le 1, \qquad \forall v \in V_j; \tag{1.16}$$

$$\lambda_{jv} \ge 0, \qquad \forall v \in V_j. \tag{1.17}$$

To see why this condition suffices, notice that then

$$\sum_{k=1}^{j} \mathbf{v}_{\pi(k)} = \sum_{\mathbf{v} \in V_j} \mathbf{v} - \sum_{\mathbf{v} \in V_j} \lambda_{j\mathbf{v}} \mathbf{v} = \sum_{\mathbf{v} \in V_j} (1 - \lambda_{j\mathbf{v}}) \mathbf{v},$$

and hence,

$$|| \sum_{k=1}^{j} \mathbf{v}_{\pi(k)} ||_{\infty} = || \sum_{\mathbf{v} \in V_j} (1 - \lambda_{j\mathbf{v}}) \mathbf{v} ||_{\infty} \leq \sum_{\mathbf{v} \in V_j} (1 - \lambda_{j\mathbf{v}}) \max_{k} ||\mathbf{v}_k||_{\infty}$$
$$= (j - (j - d)) \max_{k} ||\mathbf{v}_k||_{\infty} = d \max_{k} ||\mathbf{v}_k||_{\infty}.$$

We construct $\pi(d+1), \ldots, \pi(n)$ in reverse order by determining the sets $V_n, V_{n-1},$ $\ldots, V_d$. At each stage we also find a set of λ-values for the corresponding set V_j. Let $V_n = \{\mathbf{v}_1, \ldots, \mathbf{v}_n\}$; notice that $\lambda_{n\mathbf{v}} = (n - d)/n$, $\mathbf{v} = \mathbf{v}_1, \ldots, \mathbf{v}_n$, satisfies conditions (1.14)–(1.17). In general, suppose that we have constructed set V_j. We construct V_{j-1} by first finding an extreme point solution λ to the following set of $d + 1$ linear equalities and $2j$ inequalities (upper and lower bounds on the $\lambda_{\mathbf{v}}$):

$$\sum_{\mathbf{v} \in V_j} \lambda_{\mathbf{v}} \mathbf{v} = 0;$$

$$\sum_{\mathbf{v} \in V_j} \lambda_{\mathbf{v}} = j - 1 - d;$$

$$0 \leq \lambda_{\mathbf{v}} \leq 1, \qquad \forall \mathbf{v} \in V_j.$$

First, we observe that this system is feasible since the values $\lambda_{\mathbf{v}} = (j - 1 - d)/(j - d)\lambda_{j\mathbf{v}}$ yield a feasible solution. Second, we claim that an extreme point solution will have at least one variable set to zero. To see why, recall from linear programming theory that an extreme point to a system with j variables must have at least j of its equalities and inequalities satisfied at equality. In this case, that means that at least $j - (d + 1) = j - 1 - d$ of the $2j$ inequalities hold at equality. Now, suppose that none of the j variables were equal to zero; then necessarily, $j - 1 - d$ of them would be equal to 1, while the rest were strictly positive. But in that case, $\sum_{\mathbf{v} \in V_j} \lambda_{\mathbf{v}} > j - 1 - d$, and the solution is not feasible after all. So we have proved the claim.

Suppose we have found such an extreme point solution $\tilde{\lambda}$; we know that $\tilde{\lambda}_{\mathbf{v}^*} = 0$, for some $\mathbf{v}^* \in V_j$. We now set $V_{j-1} := V_j \setminus \{\mathbf{v}^*\}$, and $\lambda_{j-1,\mathbf{v}} = \tilde{\lambda}_{\mathbf{v}}$, for all $\mathbf{v} \in V_{j-1}$. Notice that these values satisfy (1.14)–(1.17) for set V_{j-1}. Thus, we have completed the construction, and we may iterate until we have constructed $\mathbf{v}_{\pi(n)}, \ldots, \mathbf{v}_{\pi(d+1)}$, at which point we have set V_d. We can set the first d elements of the permutation in an arbitrary order to complete the construction. ■

Since finding an extreme point of a system of linear inequalities requires polynomial time, the algorithm just described is clearly polynomial. In fact, these vectors can be found more efficiently using a direct combinatorial method in $O(n^2 d^2)$ time ([Se80]; see Sevast'janov [Se94] for a survey of vector-sum theorems and applications).

Now let us consider flow shop scheduling. In a flow shop there is exactly one operation per machine, and thus we notate the operation of job J_j on M_i as O_{ij}, and its processing time as p_{ij}. A particularly structured type of schedule for a flow shop is a *permutation schedule*, one in which the jobs are processed in the same order on all machines. In fact, if $m \leq 3$ there is always a permutation schedule that is optimal, but such is not the case in general. Consider, for example, a two-job, four-machine instance in which $p_{11} = p_{41} = p_{22} = p_{32} = 1$, while the remaining four operations have very large length M. It is not hard to show that the optimal makespan for this instance is $2M + 4$, while both permutation schedules have makespan $3M + 2$.

We shall use Lemma 1.4 to construct a permutation schedule with length at most $C^*_{\max} + m(m-1)p_{\max}$, where $C^*_{\max}$ of course refers to the optimal length of any schedule, not just any permutation schedule. In order to carry out the construction, we first transform our instance into one in which $\Pi_i = \Pi_{\max}$ for all machines M_i, by iteratively lengthening operations on M_i to $p_{\max}$ until the bound is met. Notice that a schedule for this new instance is feasible for the old instance.

Now consider a permutation schedule with the associated permutation π; for simplicity, assume that the jobs are renumbered so that π is the identity permutation, $\pi(j) = j$. In order to determine the makespan of any schedule, observe that it is sufficient to determine how much idle time occurs on M_m, since in a flow shop, M_m always finishes last, and since the makespan is just the idle time plus $\sum_{j=1}^{n} p_{mj}$. We will construct a schedule whose total idle time is bounded by $m(m-1)p_{\max}$.

Let C_{ij} denote the finishing time of O_{ij} in the given schedule, and let I_{ij} denote the amount of idle time incurred on M_i up to the completion of J_j; that is, $C_{ij} = I_{ij} + \sum_{k=1}^{j} p_{ik}$. Notice that $I_{1j} = 0$ for all j, and that we seek to bound I_{mn} by $m(m-1)p_{\max}$. Let us analyze the relationship among the I_{ij} values: for any i and j, job J_j begins processing on M_i as soon as both its operation on $M_{i-1,j}$ completes and machine M_i completes the processing of J_{j-1}. Thus the completion time of J_j on M_i can be written $C_{ij} = \max\{C_{i-1,j}, C_{i,j-1}\} + p_{ij}$. If $C_{ij} = C_{i,j-1} + p_{ij}$ then $I_{ij} = I_{i,j-1}$. On the other hand, if $C_{ij} = C_{i-1,j} + p_{ij}$, then we have $I_{ij} + \sum_{k=1}^{j} p_{ik} = I_{i-1,j} + \sum_{k=1}^{j} p_{i-1,k} + p_{ij}$, which implies

$$I_{ij} = I_{i-1,j} + p_{ij} + \sum_{k=1}^{j}(p_{i-1,k} - p_{ik}).$$

We claim that, using the vector-sum lemma, we can find a permutation π satisfying

$$\sum_{k=1}^{j}(p_{i-1,\pi(k)} - p_{i\pi(k)}) \leq (m-1)p_{\max}. \tag{1.18}$$

If so, notice that we would then have $I_{i\pi(j)} \leq \max\{I_{i\pi(j-1)}, I_{i-1,\pi(j)} + mp_{\max}\}$, which together with the conditions $I_{1\pi(j)} = 0$ for all j yields $I_{mn} \leq m(m-1)p_{\max}$ as we need.

Thus, all that remains is to find a permutation satisfying (1.18). For each j we define an $(m-1)$-dimensional vector $\mathbf{v}_j = (p_{1j} - p_{2j}, p_{2j} - p_{3j}, \ldots, p_{m-1,j} - p_{mj})$. Notice that, since we ensured that $\Pi_i = \Pi_{\max}$ for all i, we have, for each component ℓ of the vectors $\mathbf{v}_1, \ldots, \mathbf{v}_n$,

$$\sum_{j=1}^{n} \mathbf{v}_j(\ell) = \sum_{j=1}^{n}(p_{\ell j} - p_{\ell+1,j}) = \Pi_\ell - \Pi_{\ell+1} = 0,$$

and hence our vectors sum to zero, the condition needed for Lemma 1.4. Letting $d = m - 1$ in the lemma and noting that $||\mathbf{v}_j||_\infty \leq p_{\max}$ for all j, we see that we can find a permutation π satisfying, for all j, $|| \sum_{k=1}^{j} \mathbf{v}_{\pi(k)} ||_{\infty} \leq (m-1) p_{\max}$, or componentwise, $\sum_{k=1}^{j} (p_{\ell-1,j} - p_{\ell j}) \leq (m-1) p_{\max}$, as required. Thus, we have proved the following theorem.

THEOREM 1.8   [Se80] There is a polynomial time algorithm for finding a permutation schedule for a flow shop with $C_{\max} \leq C_{\max}^* + m(m-1) p_{\max}$, where $p_{\max}$ is the maximum length of any operation, and $C_{\max}^*$ is the optimal makespan over all schedules.

In fact, by implementing the vector sum construction efficiently we obtain a running time of $O(n^2 m^2)$. Moreover, the theorem extends to job shops and open shops.

The results of this section are due to Sevast'janov [Se80, Se94]. The presentation here was adapted from an unpublished manuscript by David Shmoys.

1.5.3   A $(2+\epsilon)$-APPROXIMATION ALGORITHM FOR FIXED JOB AND FLOW SHOPS

The result of the previous section can be used to produce an algorithm with a relative performance guarantee as follows [SSW94]; since the additive performance guarantee holds for job shops as well as flow shops, this algorithm also works for job shops. The algorithm depends exponentially on m, the number of machines, and so it is polynomial only if m is fixed.

A theme throughout this chapter has been to focus on a small set of the very largest operations or jobs, and to deal with them more carefully and directly, while treating the small jobs in a more aggregated fashion; for example, see Sections 1.2.3 and 1.4. The previous result tells us that if $p_{\max}$ is quite small relative to $\Pi_{\max}$, then the schedule delivered is quite good; in particular, if $m(m-1) p_{\max}/\Pi_{\max} \leq \epsilon$, then $C_{\max} \leq (1+\epsilon)\Pi_{\max} \leq (1+\epsilon)C_{\max}^*$.

We construct a $(2+\epsilon)$-approximation algorithm using these two observations. Given $\epsilon > 0$, we partition the jobs into two sets: those containing an operation of size greater than $\epsilon \Pi_{\max}/m(m-1)$, and the remaining jobs, all of whose operations are at most $\epsilon \Pi_{\max}/m(m-1)$. We treat the partition as two separate instances. Notice that, for the instance containing the "small" jobs, we can apply the technique of the previous section to obtain a schedule with makespan at most $(1+\epsilon)\Pi_{\max}$. On the other hand, in the instance with the "large" jobs there can be at most $m(m-1)/\epsilon$ of these large operations on any machine; and thus there are at most $m^2(m-1)/\epsilon$ jobs total, a constant number if m is fixed. By trying every possible job ordering on every machine for these jobs, we can find the optimal schedule in "constant" (perhaps quite a large constant!) time. We now concatenate these two schedules to obtain a schedule with makespan at most $(2+\epsilon)C_{\max}^*$ for the original instance.

In fact, while this is the best result known for job shops, there is a polynomial approximation scheme for flow shop scheduling with a fixed number of machines [Ha95]. This scheme also partitions the jobs into "large" and "small," and it relies on the near-integrality of a certain linear program to show that most of the small jobs can be scheduled feasibly as well.

1.5.4   THE GENERAL JOB SHOP: UNIT-TIME OPERATIONS

One of the most remarkable facts in the shop scheduling literature is that for any instance of a job shop in which all operations have unit-length and each job has at most one operation per machine, there is a schedule whose makespan comes within a constant factor of $\Pi_{\max} + P_{\max}$ (recall that $\Pi_{\max}$ and $P_{\max}$ are the maximum machine- and job-load, respectively, and are lower bounds on the makespan). This surprising result was proved by Leighton, Maggs, and Rao [LMR94], whose primary interest was in packet routing through networks. The result relies on the following probabilistic lemma, known as the Lovász Local Lemma. Consider a set of events $A_1, \ldots, A_m$ and an integer b with the property that for each i, A_i is mutually independent of a set of at least $m - b - 1$ of other events A_j. In that case the set of events $A_1, \ldots, A_m$ is said to have *dependence at most b*.

LEMMA 1.5 Lovász; see, e.g., [AS92]   Consider a set of events $A_1, \ldots, A_m$ with dependence at most b such that $prob(A_i) < q$, for all i, where $4bq < 1$. Then the probability that none of the A_i occurs is strictly positive.

An algorithmic version of the lemma was proved by Beck [Be91]; Leighton and Maggs used it to construct (from their previous existential result with Rao) a constant-factor approximation algorithm for $\mathcal{J}|p_j = 1, \mu = 1|C_{\max}$ [LM95].

In this section, we present two simple results on job-shop scheduling, both of which are weaker versions of the existence result just referred to. First, we give a randomized algorithm that, with high probability, produces a schedule with length $O(\log(mn\mu))(\Pi_{\max} + P_{\max}))$, where μ is the maximum number of operations of a job that belong to the same machine. Second, building on that result and invoking the Lovász Local Lemma, we show that in the case that each job has at most one operation per machine, there exists a schedule whose makespan is $(\Pi_{\max} + P_{\max})2^{O(\log^*(\Pi_{\max} + P_{\max}))}$; although this is obviously not the constant-factor approximation algorithm, this weaker performance guarantee is much simpler to analyze and yet similar in spirit to the stronger result's analysis. For the constant-factor approximation algorithm we refer the reader to Leighton, Maggs, and Rao [LMR94]. Our discussion is mainly based on this paper but also draws upon that of Shmoys, Stein, and Wein [SSW94].

Consider an instance of job-shop scheduling with unit-length operations. Notice that we can now bound $P_{\max}$ and $\Pi_{\max}$, respectively, as $m\mu$ and $n\mu$, since all operations have unit-length. First, for each job consider the "greedy" schedule in which the job begins processing at time zero and continues processing until it is completed. (Of course, the independent greedy schedules for all of the jobs will almost certainly yield an infeasible schedule overall, since the individual jobs' schedules will interfere, and machine capacities will be violated.) Now, suppose we take each job's greedy schedule and delay it by an amount between 0 and Δ time units; we call such a (possibly infeasible) schedule a *greedy pseudo-schedule with $[0, \Delta]$ delays*; observe that the makespan of such a pseudo-schedule is at most $P_{\max} + \Delta$. Intuitively, we see that if these delays are chosen randomly, then the larger Δ is, the smaller the probability that two operations will get scheduled to run simultaneously on the same machine. We wish to quantify this tradeoff more precisely. In particular, we can prove the following lemma.

LEMMA 1.6   With high probability, a pseudo-schedule with random $[0, \Pi_{max}]$ delays has at most $O(\log(mn\mu))$ operations overlapping on any one machine at any time.

Notice that a pseudo-schedule with this structure can be converted to one of length $O(\log(mn\mu))(\Pi_{max} + P_{max}))$ by simply stretching each time interval out to accommodate the congestion; accordingly, with high probability it yields an $O(\log(mn\mu))$-approximate schedule. We now prove the lemma.

Proof.   Consider a particular time t, a machine M_i, and the (at most) Π_{max} operations that are run on M_i over the duration of the schedule. The probability that a particular one of those operations gets scheduled at time t is at most $1/\Pi_{max}$; for a particular subset of k such operations, the probability that they all get scheduled at time t is either zero (if two of the operations belong to the same job) or at most $(1/\Pi_{max})^k$ (since, if the operations come from different machines, their schedules are delayed by independent amounts). Thus, the probability that at least k operations get scheduled at time t is bounded above by

$$\sum_{\ell=k}^{\Pi_{max}} \binom{\Pi_{max}}{\ell} (1/\Pi_{max})^\ell \leq \sum_{\ell=k}^{\Pi_{max}} \binom{\Pi_{max}}{k} (1/\Pi_{max})^k$$

$$\leq (\Pi_{max} - k) \left(\frac{e\Pi_{max}}{k}\right)^k \left(\frac{1}{\Pi_{max}}\right)^k$$

$$= (\Pi_{max} - k) \left(\frac{e}{k}\right)^k,$$

where the second inequality follows from a well-known general inequality that $\binom{a}{b} \leq (ae/b)^b$, for $0 < b < a$. Now, we can bound the probability that more than $O(\log(mn\mu))$ operations get scheduled at *any* time t on *any* machine by the product of the expression above with the number of machines, m, and the total number of time slots, or the length of the pseudo-schedule, $\Pi_{max} + P_{max}$. This yields an upper bound on the overall probability of

$$m(\Pi_{max} + P_{max})(\Pi_{max} - k) \left(\frac{e}{k}\right)^k \leq m\Pi_{max}(\Pi_{max} + P_{max}) \left(\frac{e}{k}\right)^k \tag{1.19}$$

Suppose we wish to bound this probability by $1/(nm\mu)^c$, for some constant $c > 1$. Let $k = \alpha \log(mn\mu)$; since $\Pi_{max} \leq n\mu$ and $P_{max} \leq m\mu$, simple algebra shows that for a sufficiently large, but fixed, constant α, the righthand side of 1.19 is bounded by $1/(nm\mu)^c$. Thus, we have proved the lemma.   ∎

The second result is also built around the idea of scheduling each job in a greedy manner and then assigning a random delay to the start of the schedule. For this result, we require that $\mu = 1$; also, without loss of generality, we assume that $\Pi_{max} \geq P_{max}$. Suppose we have a greedy pseudo-schedule with $[0, \Delta]$ delays. Consider a time interval of length T during the pseudo-schedule's duration, and let C be the largest number of operations that get scheduled on any one machine over the time interval of length T; then we say that the *relative congestion* of that time interval is C/T.

LEMMA 1.7 There exists a greedy pseudo-schedule with $[0, \alpha \Pi_{max}]$ delays, where α is a constant, such that the relative congestion of any time interval of length at least $\log P_{max}$ is at most 1.

Proof. We will analyze a greedy pseudo-schedule with random $[0, \alpha \Pi_{max}]$ delays, as before; and then we will apply the Lovász Local Lemma to the randomized schedule to demonstrate the existence of the desired schedule. The parameter α will be specified later on. Let us focus on a specific machine M_i and consider the probability that in some interval of length $T \geq \log P_{max}$, more than T operations get assigned to M_i; call this event A_i, for $i = 1, \ldots, m$. We would like to show that there is a positive probability that this does not happen on *any* of the m machines, and for that we shall invoke the Lovász Local Lemma. In order to do so, we need to determine two things: first, an upper bound q on the probability that A_i occurs; and second, an upper bound b on the dependence of the events A_i. Then we will show that it is possible to choose a fixed constant α to ensure that $4bq < 1$, so that we can apply the Lemma.

First, we claim that the dependence of the events A_i is at most $\Pi_{max} P_{max}$. Consider a particular machine M_i and the event A_i. Clearly, for any machine M_h that does not process a job in common with M_i, A_h is independent of A_i; but an upper bound on the number of machines that do have a job in common with M_i is the number of jobs that run on M_i multiplied by the number of operations per job. The former is bounded by Π_{max}, while the latter is bounded by P_{max}, and so the claimed dependence follows.

Next, we wish to determine a useful upper bound on the probability q that the event A_i occurs. Now given a particular interval of length T, what is the probability that more than T operations get assigned to that interval? There are at most Π_{max} operations that use M_i, and each of these belongs to a different job, by assumption; thus we can view this probability as a binomial distribution over Π_{max} Bernoulli trials. The probability that a particular job's M_i operation falls into the interval is at most $T/\alpha \Pi_{max}$, and thus an upper bound on the probability that a particular interval is "bad" on M_i is bounded above by

$$\binom{\Pi_{max}}{T} \left(\frac{T}{\alpha \Pi_{max}}\right)^T \leq \left(\frac{\Pi_{max}e}{T}\right)^T \left(\frac{T}{\alpha \Pi_{max}}\right)^T = \left(\frac{e}{\alpha}\right)^T \leq \left(\frac{e}{\alpha}\right)^{\Pi_{max}}.$$

Notice that intervals of length larger than Π_{max} cannot have more operations assigned than their total length, and so the only potentially bad intervals have lengths between $\log P_{max}$ and Π_{max}. For a given T in that range, the total number of intervals of size T over the entire horizon is at most $P_{max} + \alpha \Pi_{max} \leq (1 + \alpha) \Pi_{max}$, and thus we have the following bound on q:

$$q \leq \sum_{T=\log P_{max}}^{\Pi_{max}} (1+\alpha) \Pi_{max} \left(\frac{e}{\alpha}\right)^{\Pi_{max}} \leq (1+\alpha) \Pi_{max}^2 \left(\frac{e}{\alpha}\right)^{\Pi_{max}}.$$

Thus, we have

$$4qb \leq 4 \Pi_{max}^3 P_{max}(1+\alpha) \left(\frac{e}{\alpha}\right)^{\Pi_{max}},$$

and it is not hard to see that for a sufficiently large fixed α, this product can be made strictly smaller than 1, since we have assumed that $\Pi_{max} \geq P_{max}$. ∎

Now we use this lemma to prove the main theorem.

THEOREM 1.9 Under the assumptions given, there exists a schedule with makespan $(\Pi_{max} + P_{max}) \cdot 2^{O(\log^*(\Pi_{max}))}$.

Proof. By the previous Lemma, there exists a pseudo-schedule in which each time interval of length $\log(\Pi_{max})$ contains at most $\log(\Pi_{max})$ operations, on each machine M_i. Now, we can break up this pseudo-schedule, whose overall length is at most $P_{max} + \alpha\Pi_{max} \leq (1+\alpha)\Pi_{max}$, into subintervals, each of length $\log(\Pi_{max})$. The partial schedule that takes place during one of these subintervals can be viewed as a scheduling instance itself with the property that each machine's and job's load is bounded by $\log(\Pi_{max})$. We can now construct pseudo-schedules for these sub-instances that have the property that all intervals of length $\log\log(\Pi_{max})$ contain at most $\log\log(\Pi_{max})$ operations, on any machine. We continue to proceed in this manner for $\log^*(\Pi_{max})$ iterations, at which point we have generated an actual schedule, not just a pseudo-schedule, on each machine at each time unit. All of these partial schedules can now be pieced together into a schedule for the original whose overall length is at most $(\Pi_{max} + P_{max}) \cdot 2^{O(\log^*(\Pi_{max}))}$. ∎

Shmoys, Stein, and Wein [SSW94] extend the previous results to give a randomized $\log^2(m\mu)/\log\log(m\mu)$-approximation algorithm and a deterministic $\log^2(m\mu)$-approximation algorithm for scheduling general job shops; their result was subsequently improved by Schmidt, Siegel, and Srinivasan [SSS93] to a deterministic $\log^2(m\mu)/\log\log(m\mu)$-approximation algorithm.

LOWER BOUNDS ON APPROXIMATION FOR MAKESPAN SCHEDULING

1.6

In this section we present the few known results on lower bounds on approximation for scheduling. All of these rely on the same technique of focusing on very short schedules in which all processing times are integral. We outline the basic technique here.

Suppose we have an instance of a scheduling problem in which all processing times are integer, and suppose we are given a schedule with makespan z and starting times for jobs or operations that are not necessarily integral. In such a situation we can easily convert the schedule into one with makespan $\lfloor z \rfloor$ by simply rounding all starting times down to the nearest integer. Notice that this technique is guaranteed to produce a feasible schedule. Now suppose further that we have, for example, the following type of NP-completeness result: determining whether a schedule of length 3 exists is NP-complete. (Of course, the "3" here is only significant because we have required all of the processing times to be integral.) We claim that such a result implies that there can be no $(4/3 - \epsilon)$-approximation algorithm for the problem, unless $P = NP$. For, suppose that such an algorithm existed; in particular, if we are given an instance to solve whose optimal length is 3, then the schedule generated by the approximation algorithm has length < 4. But as we have already observed, such a schedule can be converted into one with length 3.

In contrast, if the instance has optimal length ≥ 4, then of course the algorithm will generate a schedule of length at least 4; hence, we have a polynomial-time method of distinguishing whether or not an instance has a schedule of length 3, which implies $P = NP$. Of course, if we replace "3" in this discussion with a fixed k, the implication is that no $(1 + 1/k - \epsilon)$-approximation algorithm can exist unless $P = NP$.

We briefly state here the known results of this flavor, and the implications for approximation. For a full discussion of these results we refer the reader to the survey of Lenstra and Shmoys [LS94], or to the references cited.

1.6.1 IDENTICAL PARALLEL MACHINES AND PRECEDENCE CONSTRAINTS

The first result of this type to be proved was for the classical problem of scheduling identical parallel machines to minimize makespan under job precedence constraints. We define the following recognition version of this problem.

3MAKESPAN
Instance: n jobs with unit processing time, m machines, and an arbitrary precedence relation $\prec$ on the jobs.
Question: Does there exist a schedule with makespan at most 3?

EXERCISE 1.1 [LR78] Show that 3MAKESPAN is NP-complete by transforming CLIQUE to 3MAKESPAN (for the solution, see, e.g., the survey by Lawler, Lenstra, Rinnooy Kan, and Shmoys [L+93]).

Notice that by our previous comments we immediately have the following corollary to the exercise.

COROLLARY 1.2 There is no $(4/3 - \epsilon)$-approximation algorithm for $P|prec, p_j = 1|C_{max}$, for any $\epsilon > 0$, unless $P = NP$.

1.6.2 UNRELATED PARALLEL MACHINES

We now consider the problem $R||C_{max}$. Recall that in Sections 1.4.1 and 1.4.2 we showed that 2-approximation algorithms exist for this problem.

THEOREM 1.10 [LST90] Given an instance of $R||C_{max}$ with integral processing times, determining whether a schedule of length 2 exists is NP-complete.

COROLLARY 1.3 There is no $(3/2 - \epsilon)$-approximation algorithm for $R||C_{max}$, for any $\epsilon > 0$, unless $P = NP$.

1.6.3 SHOP SCHEDULING

Finally, we show that for open-, flow-, and job-shop scheduling, there is a lower bound of $5/4$ on approximability.

THEOREM 1.11 [W+96] Determining whether an instance of $O||C_{max}$ with integral processing times (or an instance of $F||C_{max}$) has a schedule of length 4 is NP-complete.

Since flow shops are special cases of job shops, the result holds for general job shops as well. Of course, again we have a corollary on the approximability of these problems.

COROLLARY 1.4 There is no $(5/4 - \epsilon)$-approximation algorithm for $O||C_{max}$ (or for $F||C_{max}$), for any $\epsilon > 0$, unless $P = NP$.

MIN-SUM OBJECTIVES

1.7

In this section we consider the problem of scheduling to minimize the sum of completion times or of weighted completion times. What is particularly striking about these results is that, while the objective function is very different in character from min-max objectives, we can nonetheless use the familiar tools of list scheduling and linear programming to tackle them. Indeed, not only are the algorithms similar but their analyses are as well.

Notice that the sum (or average) of job completion times is an important measure from a practical point of view. If individual jobs are associated with specific deliverables for customers, then in many situations this objective function might better reflect a scheduler's priorities than would the makespan of the schedule. Indeed, scheduling a single machine to minimize total weighted completion time is one of the most exhaustively studied problems in the scheduling literature.

We let w_j denote the *weight* associated with job J_j, so that the problem is to minimize $\sum_{j=1}^{n} w_j C_j$. For the unconstrained single-machine variant, a simple interchange argument proves that ordering the jobs according to non-decreasing p_j/w_j ratio is optimal (Smith [Sm56]); this policy is known as *Smith's Rule*. When $w_j = 1$ for all j so that we are minimizing the sum of (unweighted) completion times, Smith's rule says simply to process the jobs from shortest to longest.

As soon as constraints such as release dates or precedence constraints are introduced into the model, even the single-machine versions of these problems become strongly NP-hard. In the next two sections we focus on approaches for two single-machine problems. First, we present a simple, elegant result of Phillips, Stein, and Wein [PSW95] that constructs a schedule within a factor-of-two of the preemptive schedule's value for minimizing sum of completion times. In the following section, we show how linear programming is a powerful tool in constructing approximation algorithms for precedence-constrained models. Finally, we present an approximation algorithm for minimizing the weighted sum of completion times on unrelated parallel machines.

1.7.1   SEQUENCING WITH RELEASE DATES TO MINIMIZE SUM OF COMPLETION TIMES

First, let us consider the *preemptive* version of the release-date constrained problem; that is, the processing of one job may be interrupted so that another job can be processed, and then the first job can be resumed later on. Consider the following dynamic version of the SPT rule for scheduling jobs.

Algorithm DSPT
At any point in time, schedule an available job with the least amount of remaining processing time.

We leave the proof of the following well-known result to the reader.

LEMMA 1.8   Algorithm DSPT constructs an optimal preemptive schedule with $O(n)$ preemptions.

Now, consider the following heuristic for the non-preemptive problem: schedule the jobs in the order in which they complete in an optimal preemptive schedule. We claim that this algorithm is a 2-approximation algorithm; in fact, we will demonstrate that the sum of completion times is within a factor of two of the preemptive optimum. Consider a particular optimal preemptive schedule, and let $\tilde{C}_j$ denote the completion time of job J_j in that schedule. Let C_j denote the completion time of J_j in the constructed *non-preemptive* schedule.

LEMMA 1.9 $C_j \le 2\tilde{C}_j$, for $j = 1, \ldots, n$.

Proof.   For simplicity assume that the jobs have been scheduled in the order $1, \ldots, n$. Consider a particular job J_k, whose preemptive finishing time is $\tilde{C}_k$. Clearly $\tilde{C}_k \ge \sum_{j=1}^{k} p_j$, since jobs $J_1, \ldots, J_k$ have all completed their processing by time $\tilde{C}_k$. Moreover, $r_j < \tilde{C}_k$ for all $j \le k$. Thus, it is possible to schedule all jobs $J_1, \ldots, J_k$ from time $\tilde{C}_k$ to time $2\tilde{C}_k$. The constructed schedule will perform at least as well as this artificial construction, and thus $C_k \le 2\tilde{C}_k$.   ■

The lemma guarantees that $\sum_{j=1}^{n} C_j \le 2\sum_{j=1}^{n} \tilde{C}_j \le 2\sum_{j=1}^{n} C_j^*$, where C_j^* is the completion time of job J_j in some optimal non-preemptive schedule. This result is due to Phillips, Stein, and Wein [PSW95].

1.7.2   SEQUENCING WITH PRECEDENCE CONSTRAINTS

Notice that the construction in the previous subsection of the non-preemptive schedule from the preemptive one ensured that each job's individual completion time increased by at most a factor of two. If we had a way of generating preemptive schedules for more complex models, such as unequal weights or precedence-constrained problems, then the same analysis would provide 2-approximation algorithms for these models as well.

Unfortunately, no one knows of an algorithm for obtaining an optimal preemptive schedule in the precedence-constrained case. In fact, the analysis cannot even be generalized to the weighted version, for the same reason: $1 \mid r_j, pmtn \mid \sum w_j C_j$ is strongly NP-hard. Thus in order to generate approximation algorithms for these problems, we require a different relaxation (one that is computable in polynomial time) that will provide a lower bound on the optimum and a structural starting point for a non-preemptive schedule.

We will use a linear programming relaxation to guide our construction of schedules. In some sense, a linear programming solution and a preemptive schedule can both be viewed as "fractionalized" versions of non-preemptive schedules. In the linear programming formulations we consider there will also be a natural interpretation of the "completion time" of a job. Our goal is to produce a feasible schedule with the property that each job's completion time is relatively close to its "completion time" in the linear programming solution. We present two different linear programming relaxations. The first one contains a pseudopolynomial number of variables and constraints and so the algorithm derived from it will not be polynomial-time; however, it can be modified to produce a solution in polynomial time by altering the linear program appropriately. The second is based on a different type of linear program which itself contains an exponential number of constraints but which nonetheless is solvable in polynomial time via the ellipsoid algorithm for linear programming ([Qu93]).

Recall that we assume all data are integer, and moreover, we will assume that each job's processing time is at least 1 (although, as in other models, this restriction is easily removed). We can restrict our attention to schedules in which each job begins and completes at an integral point in time. That said, our first integer linear programming formulation uses binary decision variables

$$x_{jt} = \begin{cases} 1, & \text{if job } J_j \text{ completes at time } t; \\ 0, & \text{otherwise}, \end{cases}$$

where for each job J_j we take $t = p_j, \ldots, T$, and T is an upper bound on the makespan of any schedule with unforced idle time; for example, $T = P$ is large enough in this case. If job J_j completes at time t, then it contributes $w_j t$ to the overall sum of weighted completions. Thus, our objective is to

$$\text{Minimize} \sum_{j=1}^{n} \sum_{t=1}^{T} w_j t \, x_{jt}$$

subject to

$$\sum_{t=p_j}^{T} x_{jt} = 1, \qquad j = 1, \ldots, n; \qquad (1.20)$$

$$\sum_{j=1}^{n} \sum_{u=t}^{t+p_j-1} x_{ju} \leq 1, \qquad t = 1, \ldots, T; \qquad (1.21)$$

$$\sum_{u=1}^{t} x_{ju} - \sum_{u=1}^{t+p_k} x_{ku} \geq 0, \qquad \text{if } J_j \prec J_k, t = 1, \ldots, T - p_k; \qquad (1.22)$$

$$x_{jt} \geq 0, \qquad j = 1, \ldots, n; \ t = p_j, \ldots, T.$$

Of course, we have relaxed the integrality restriction on x_{jt} in order to have a linear (instead of integer) program. Constraints (1.20) ensure that each job gets assigned a position in the schedule. Constraint (1.21) ensures that, during time interval $(t - 1, t]$, at most one job is undergoing processing; thus it sums up all of those job-position pairs that overlap the interval $(t - 1, t]$. Finally, constraints (1.22) enforce the precedence constraints by enforcing that if job J_j does not complete by time t then J_k cannot complete by time $t + p_k$, for all t.

Suppose we solve this linear program for a given instance and obtain an optimal solution $\tilde{x}$. Notice first of all that we can define a *fractional completion time* associated with J_j that represents its completion time in the LP objective function:

$$\tilde{C}_j := \sum_{t=p_j}^{T} t \tilde{x}_{jt}.$$

But what is striking about the fractional LP solution is that it has an interpretation as a fractional schedule; in particular, it is possible to view $x_{jt} = \alpha$ as a rectangular piece of processing whose *length* stretches from time $t - p_j$ to time t, and whose *height* is exactly α. In this way, we can view the machine as perhaps processing more than one *fraction* of different jobs at the same time, but never exceeding its capacity of "one" job.

Next, for each job J_j we define the *halfway point* $\tilde{t}_j$ of J_j as the smallest value of t such that

$$\sum_{u=p_j}^{t} \tilde{x}_{jt} \geq 1/2,$$

for all j. For example, if $p_j = 10$ and $\tilde{x}_{j,15} = \tilde{x}_{j,32} = \tilde{x}_{j,36} = 1/3$, then $\tilde{t}_j = 32$ (in particular, $\tilde{t}_j \neq 27$, which is the time at which half of J_j's processing has completed).

We construct a heuristic schedule by ordering the jobs according to non-decreasing halfway point. Notice that the precedence constraints (1.22) ensure that if $J_j \prec J_k$ then $\tilde{t}_j < \tilde{t}_k$, and so the ordering produced is feasible with respect to the precedence constraints. Suppose that $\overline{C}_j$ is the completion time of J_j in the heuristic schedule. We claim that $\overline{C}_j \leq 4\tilde{C}_j$, from which it follows immediately that we have produced a schedule with value within a factor of 4 of the optimal schedule's value.

To prove the claim, we make the following two observations for each j: (i) $\overline{C}_j \leq 2\tilde{t}_j$; and (ii) $\tilde{C}_j \geq (1/2)\tilde{t}_j$. For simplicity, suppose the jobs have been renumbered so that $\tilde{t}_1 \leq \tilde{t}_2 \leq \cdots \leq \tilde{t}_n$. Notice that because of inequality (1.21), by time $\tilde{t}_j$, the machine has completed processing at least half of all jobs $1 \ldots, j$; i.e., $\tilde{t}_j \geq \frac{1}{2}\sum_{k=1}^{j} p_k$. Since $\overline{C}_j = \sum_{k=1}^{j} p_k$, observation (i) follows. The second observation is equally straightforward to prove: by the definition of $\tilde{t}_j$, it follows that

$$\sum_{u=p_j}^{\tilde{t}_j - 1} x_{ju} < 1/2,$$

and thus,

$$\tilde{C}_j = \sum_{t=p_j}^{T} t x_{jt} \geq \sum_{t=\tilde{t}_j}^{T} t x_{jt} \geq \tilde{t}_j \sum_{t=\tilde{t}_j}^{T} x_{jt} > (1/2)\tilde{t}_j,$$

where the final inequality follows from the previous observation and (1.20). Thus we have demonstrated that it is possible to construct a 4-approximate schedule from the solution to this time-indexed linear program. Of course, the algorithm given is not polynomial-time; modifying it to run in polynomial-time requires further work and leads to a $(4+\epsilon)$-approximation algorithm (see [HSW96]). Since we are about to present a result that dominates this one, however, we omit the modification here.

Next, we consider a different LP relaxation of the scheduling problem that is based on considering Smith's Rule for optimally ordering jobs for $1||\sum w_j C_j$. Since Smith's Rule tells us that an optimal schedule is obtained by any ordering in which the ratio p_j/w_j is non-decreasing, it stands to reason that if we were to set $w_j = p_j$ for all jobs, all orderings would have the same objective value. This is indeed the case, and so we have the following valid inequality for the completion times of jobs in any feasible schedule:

$$\sum_{j=1}^{n} p_j C_j \geq \sum_{j=1}^{n} p_j \left(\sum_{i=1}^{j} p_i \right) = \sum_{j=1}^{n} \sum_{i=1}^{j} p_i p_j.$$

In fact, the same inequality is valid when restricted to subsets of jobs (notice that we have reorganized the righthand side):

$$\sum_{j \in A} p_j C_j \geq \frac{1}{2} \sum_{j \in A} p_j^2 + \frac{1}{2} \left(\sum_{j \in A} p_j \right)^2.$$

We use these inequalities to formulate a linear program whose decision variables y_j represent the completion times of J_j, $j = 1, \ldots, n$.

Minimize $\displaystyle\sum_{j=1}^{n} w_j y_j$

subject to $\displaystyle\sum_{j \in A} p_j y_j \;\geq\; \frac{1}{2}\left[\sum_{j \in A} p_j^2 + \left(\sum_{j \in A} p_j \right)^2 \right], \quad \forall A \subseteq \{1, \ldots, n\};$

$\qquad\qquad\qquad y \;\geq\; 0.$

In fact, the extreme point solutions to this linear program actually do represent feasible completion-time vectors. However, that will not be the case once we add constraints to model the precedence constraints among jobs:

$$y_i + p_j \leq y_j, \quad \text{for all } i, j : i \prec j. \tag{1.23}$$

Observe that release dates are also easily modeled, by simply specifying

$$y_j \geq r_j + p_j, \quad j = 1, \ldots, n; \tag{1.24}$$

however, for simplicity we will not consider release dates here.

Now, suppose that we solve this linear program to obtain an optimal solution $\tilde{y}_j$ for all j, which can be interpreted as a completion time of job J_j even though these values do not generally represent a feasible schedule. Still, we can use them to order the jobs and then, based on this ordering, produce a heuristic schedule by scheduling the jobs in this order. Notice that, as in the previous case, such an ordering automatically obeys the precedence constraints because of (1.23). Suppose the jobs have been renumbered so that $\tilde{y}_1 \leq \cdots \leq \tilde{y}_n$. Let $\overline{C}_j = \sum_{k=1}^{j} p_i$ be the completion time of job J_j in the heuristic schedule. Then, by the LP constraints,

$$\tilde{y}_j \sum_{k=1}^{j} p_k \geq \sum_{k=1}^{j} p_k \tilde{y}_k \geq \frac{1}{2} \sum_{k=1}^{j} p_k{}^2 + \frac{1}{2} \left(\sum_{k=1}^{j} p_k \right)^2 \geq \frac{1}{2} \left(\sum_{k=1}^{j} p_k \right)^2,$$

and thus,

$$\tilde{y}_j \geq \frac{1}{2} \sum_{k=1}^{j} p_k = (1/2)\overline{C}_j.$$

This implies that the heuristic schedule is a 2-approximate schedule. Because of our earlier observations that this linear program is solvable in polynomial time [Qu93], we have the following result.

THEOREM 1.12   There is a 2-approximation algorithm for $1|prec|\sum w_j C_j$.

Further extensions of this result lead to 3-approximation algorithms for $1|r_j, prec|\sum w_j C_j$, $\mathcal{P}|r_j, prec, p_j = 1|\sum w_j C_j$, and $\mathcal{P}|r_j, prec, pmtn|\sum w_j C_j$; a 4-approximation algorithm for $\mathcal{P}|r_j|\sum w_j C_j$; and a 7-approximation algorithm for $\mathcal{P}|r_j, prec|\sum w_j C_j$. These results can be generalized to models in which the machines have different speeds, as well (so-called "uniformly related" machines). See [HSW96, Sc95, H+95] for details. An interesting, closely related problem is the *storage-time product* problem (see Chapter 5, Section 5.2). It is interesting to note that so far the techniques used here have failed to provide a constant-factor approximation algorithm for that problem.

   The algorithm's analysis is tight, as the following example indicates: suppose we have n unit-length jobs, and the first $n-1$ jobs must precede J_n but are otherwise independent. Let $w_j = 1$ for $j = 1, \dots, n-1$, and $w_n = M$. If M is sufficiently large, the optimal LP solution will set $\tilde{y}_j = (n+1)/2 - 1/n$ for $j = 1, \dots, n-1$, and $\tilde{y}_n = (n+3)/2 - 1/n$; thus the overall LP objective value is $(M+1)[(n+3)/2 - 1/n] - 1$. On the other hand, the heuristic schedule, (which happens to be the optimal schedule), has value $Mn + n(n-1)/2$. As n gets large, and M gets large relative to n, the ratio between the two values approaches two. No such example is known for the unweighted case, however (i.e., $w_j = 1$ for all j). Finally, we note that the linear program given is valid for $1|prec, pmtn|\sum w_j C_j$ as well, and thus this result implies that the optimal non-preemptive schedule's value is never more than a factor of two greater than the preemptive one.

1.7.3   UNRELATED PARALLEL MACHINES

In this section we consider how to use linear programming techniques to minimize the weighted sum of completion times on unrelated parallel machines: we give an 8-approximation algorithm for $R|r_j|\sum w_j C_j$. In fact, this algorithm and its analysis can be refined to a 16/3-approximation algorithm [HSW96].

   The basic idea is to introduce an *interval-indexed* linear program, akin to the time-indexed linear program of the previous subsection. Let $\tau_0 = 1$, and let $\tau_\ell = 2^{\ell-1}$, $\ell = 1, \dots, L$, where L is large enough that every feasible schedule of interest completes by time 2^{L-1}. (By a slight abuse of notation, we let $(\tau_0, \tau_1] = (1, 1]$ indicate the point interval $[1, 1]$.) Let

$$x_{ij\ell} = \begin{cases} 1, & \text{if } J_j \text{ is assigned to } M_i \text{ to complete in interval } (\tau_{\ell-1}, \tau_\ell], \\ 0, & \text{otherwise}, \end{cases}$$

for $i = 1, \ldots, m$, $j = 1, \ldots, n$, and $\ell = 1, \ldots, L$. Let p_{ij} be the processing time of J_j on M_i, for all i, j. We can then write down the following linear programming formulation whose objective function gives a lower bound on the total weighted completion time:

$$\text{Minimize} \sum_{j=1}^{n} \sum_{i=1}^{m} \sum_{\ell=1}^{L} \tau_{\ell-1} x_{ij\ell}$$

subject to

$$\sum_{i=1}^{m} \sum_{\ell=1}^{L} x_{ij\ell} = 1, \qquad j = 1, \ldots, n \tag{1.25}$$

$$\sum_{j=1}^{n} p_{ij} x_{ij\ell} \le \tau_\ell, \qquad i = 1, \ldots, m, \ \ell = 1, \ldots, L \tag{1.26}$$

$$x_{ij\ell} = 0 \qquad \text{if } r_j + p_{ij} > \tau_\ell, \ \forall i, j, \ell \tag{1.27}$$

$$x_{ij\ell} \ge 0 \qquad \forall i, j, \ell. \tag{1.28}$$

Observe that the machine load constraints (1.26) are sufficiently relaxed to accommodate the possibility that a job could start at time zero and yet contribute to the load of interval $(\tau_{\ell-1}, \tau_\ell]$; thus, any solution vector x corresponding to an integral, feasible schedule is feasible for this LP. Further observe that if job J_j completes in $(\tau_{\ell-1}, \tau_\ell]$, then its contribution to the objective function is $w_j \tau_{\ell-1}$, a lower bound on its contribution to the actual schedule.

We will demonstrate how to construct a schedule whose total weighted completion time is within a factor of 8 of the optimal value to this linear program. First, we solve the linear program to obtain an optimal solution vector $\tilde{x}$. Notice that constraints (1.25) and (1.26) look exactly like the feasibility system (1.11) in Section 1.4.1, with two differences. First, in this case we associate the machine index of (1.11) with machine-interval pairs; and second, the right-hand side of the machine capacity constraints are not identical. However, as we have noted at the end of Section 1.4.2, the algorithms of Sections 1.4.1 and 1.4.2 go through in precisely the same manner even if these capacities differ.

We now show how to obtain the 8-approximation algorithm. First, we apply the technique of Shmoys and Tardos (see Section 1.4.2) to obtain an integral assignment x^* of jobs to machine-interval pairs with the property that the load of any machine-interval pair increases by at most a factor of 2, and the overall cost does not increase. For each job j, if $x_{ij\ell}^* = 1$ we set $\overline{C}_j = \tau_{\ell-1}$; hence, $\sum w_j \overline{C}_j$ is equal to the LP optimal value. Now let us focus on a particular machine M_i. Since originally the fractional load assigned to interval $(\tau_{\ell-1}, \tau_\ell]$ was bounded by τ_ℓ, now the load is at most $\tau_{\ell+1}$. We schedule this piece of the overall schedule for M_i from time $\tau_{\ell+1}$ to $\tau_{\ell+2}$, $\ell = 1, \ldots, L$; clearly, the pieces do not overlap. Moreover, all jobs get scheduled to begin after their release dates; and finally, each job assigned to interval $(\tau_{\ell-1}, \tau_\ell]$ completes by time $\tau_{\ell+2}$ in the constructed schedule. Thus, for each job J_j, its completion time in the constructed schedule is bounded by, for some ℓ, $(\tau_{\ell+2}/\tau_{\ell-1})\overline{C}_j = 8\overline{C}_j$, and so the construction yields an 8-approximation algorithm.

FINAL REMARKS

1.8

The results presented in this chapter are by no means a comprehensive treatment of approximation algorithms for scheduling. We have attempted to focus on what we consider to be the most basic models and have presented what is known about these. Beyond these models is practically an infinite number of variants, including models that incorporate constraints such as machine setup times, special classes of precedence constraints, and other objective functions, to name just a few possibilities. Moreover, there is a massive literature on scheduling outside of what is traditionally called "deterministic" or "combinatorial" scheduling; researchers in manufacturing, in particular, have analyzed a broad range of stochastic models. Good starting points for further reading include the survey by Lawler, Lenstra, Rinnooy Kan, and Shmoys [L+93] and the recent book by Pinedo [Pi95].

Acknowledgments The author would like to thank David Shmoys for his input and helpful comments. This work was supported in part by NSF grant DMI-9496153.

REFERENCES

[AMO93] R. Ahuja, T. Magnanti, and J. Orlin. *Network Flows: Theory, Algorithms, and Applications*. Prentice Hall, 1993.

[AS92] N. Alon and J. H. Spencer. *The Probabilistic Method*. John Wiley and Sons, 1992.

[BF82] I. Bárány and T. Fiala. Többgépes ütemezési problémák közel optimális megoldása. *Szigma-Mat.-Közgazdasági Folyóirat* 15:177–191, 1982.

[Be91] J. Beck. An algorithmic approach to the Lovász Local Lemma I. *Random Structures and Algorithms* 2:343–365, 1991.

[CV95] B. Chen and A. Vestjens. On-line scheduling of identical machines. Unpublished manuscript, 1995.

[GS76] T. Gonzalez and S. Sahni. Open shop scheduling to minimize finish time. *J. Assoc. Comput. Mach.* 23:665–679, 1976.

[Gr66] R. L. Graham. Bounds for Certain Multiprocessing Anomalies. *Bell System Technical Journal* 45:1563–1581, 1966.

[Gr69] R. L. Graham. Bounds on multiprocessing timing anomalies. *SIAM J. Appl. Math.* 17:416–426, 1969.

[G+79] R. L. Graham, E. L. Lawler, J. K. Lenstra, and A. H. G. Rinnooy Kan. Optimization and approximation in deterministic sequencing and scheduling: a survey. *Ann. Discrete Math.* 5:287–326, 1979.

[Ha95]   L. A. Hall. Approximability of flow shop scheduling. In *Proc. IEEE 36th Annual Symp. Foundations of Computer Science*, 1995.

[H+95]   L. A. Hall, A. S. Schulz, D. B. Shmoys, and J. Wein. Scheduling to minimize average completion time: off-line and on-line algorithms. In preparation.

[HS89]   L. A. Hall and D. B. Shmoys. Approximation algorithms for constrained scheduling problems. In *Proc. IEEE 30th Annual Symp. Foundations of Computer Science*, 1989.

[HS90]   L. A. Hall and D. B. Shmoys. Near-optimal sequencing with precedence constraints. In *Proc. Math. Prog. Soc. Conference on Integer Programming and Combinatorial Optimization*, University of Waterloo, 249–260, 1990.

[HS92]   L. A. Hall and D. B. Shmoys. Jackson's rule for single-machine scheduling: making a good heuristic better. *Math. Oper. Res.* 17:22–35, 1992.

[HSW96]   L. A. Hall, D. B. Shmoys, and J. Wein. Scheduling to minimize average completion time: off-line and on-line algorithms. *Proc. of the Sixth ACM-SIAM Symposium on Discrete Algorithms*, January 1996.

[Ja55]   J. R. Jackson. Scheduling a production line to minimize maximum tardiness. Research Report 43, Mgmt. Sci. Research Project, UCLA, 1955.

[Jo54]   S. M. Johnson. Optimal two- and three-stage production schedules with setup times included. *Naval Research Logistics Quarterly* 1:61–68, 1954.

[LLR76]   B. J. Lageweg, J. K. Lenstra, and A. H. G. Rinnooy Kan. Minimizing maximum lateness on one machine: Computational experience and some applications. *Statist. Neerlandica*, 30:25–41, 1976.

[L+93]   E. L. Lawler, J. K. Lenstra, A. H. G. Rinnooy Kan, and D. B. Shmoys. Sequencing and scheduling: algorithms and complexity. In *Handbooks in Operations Research and Management Science, Vol. 4*, North Holland, 445–522, 1993.

[LMR94]   F. T. Leighton, B. Maggs, and S. Rao. Packet routing and job-shop scheduling in O(Congestion + Dilation) steps. *Combinatorica* 14:167–186, 1994.

[LM95]   F. T. Leighton and B. Maggs. Fast algorithms for finding O(Congestion + Dilation) packet routing schedules. *Proc. of the 28th Hawaii International Conference on System Sciences (HICSS)*, 1995.

[LRB77]   J. K. Lenstra, A. H. G. Rinnooy Kan, and P. Brucker. Complexity of machine scheduling problems. *Annals of Discrete Mathematics* 1:343–362, 1977.

[LR78]   J. K. Lenstra and A. H. G. Rinnooy Kan. The complexity of scheduling under precedence constraints. *Operations Research* 26:22–35, 1978.

[LS94]   J. K. Lenstra and D. B. Shmoys. Computing near-optimal schedules. In *Scheduling Theory and its Applications*, edited by P. Chrétienne, E. G. Coffman, Jr., J. K. Lenstra, and Z. Liu. Wiley, 1–14, 1995.

[LST90]   J. K. Lenstra, D. B. Shmoys, and É. Tardos. Approximation algorithms for scheduling unrelated parallel machines. *Mathematical Programming* 46:259–271, 1990.

[LV92]   J.-H. Lin and J. S. Vitter. ϵ-approximations with minimum packing constraint violation. In *Proceedings of the 24th Annual ACM Symposium on the Theory of Computing*, 771–782, 1992.

[NS94]   E. Nowicki and C. Smutnicki. An approximation algorithm for a single-machine scheduling problem with release times and delivery times. *Discrete Appl. Math.* 48:69–79, 1994.

[PSW94]   C. Phillips, C. Stein, and J. Wein. Task scheduling in networks. In *Proceedings of the Fourth Scandinavian Workshop on Algorithm Theory*, 290–301, 1994.

[PSW95]   C. Phillips, C. Stein, and J. Wein. Scheduling jobs that arrive over time. *Proceedings of the Fourth Workshop on Algorithms and Data Structures, Lecture Notes in Computer Science 955*, Springer, Berlin, 86–97, 1995.

[Pi95]   M. Pinedo. *Scheduling: Theory, Algorithms, and Systems.* Prentice-Hall, Englewood Cliffs, NJ, 1995.

[Po80]   C. N. Potts. Analysis of a heuristic for one machine sequencing with release dates and delivery times. *Operations Research* 28:1436–1441, 1980.

[Po85]   C. N. Potts. Analysis of a linear programming heuristic for scheduling unrelated parallel machines. *Discrete Appl. Math.* 10:155–164, 1985.

[Qu93]   M. Queyranne. Structure of a simple scheduling polyhedron. *Math. Prog.* 58:163–185, 1993.

[SSS93]   J. P. Schmidt, A. Siegel, and A. Srinivasan. Chernoff-Hoeffding bounds for applications with limited independence. *Proc. 4th ACM-SIAM Symp. on Discrete Algorithms.* Society for Industrial and Applied Mathematics, Philadelphia, PA. 331–340, 1993.

[Sc71]   L. Schrage. Obtaining optimal solutions to resource constrained network scheduling problems. Unpublished manuscript, 1971.

[Sc95]   A. Schulz. Scheduling to minimize total weighted completion time: performance guarantees of LP-based heuristics and lower bounds. Preprint 474/1995, Dept. of Mathematics, Technical University of Berlin, 1995.

[Se80]   S. V. Sevast'janov. Approximation algorithms for Johnson's and vector summation problems. *Upravlyaemye Systemy* 20:64–73 (in Russian), 1980.

[Se94]   S. V. Sevast'janov. On some geometric methods in scheduling theory: a survey. *Discrete Applied Math.* 55:59–82, 1994.

[SSW94]   D. B. Shmoys, C. Stein, and J. Wein. Improved approximation algorithms for shop scheduling problems. *SIAM J. Comput.* 23:617–632, 1994.

[ST93]   D. B. Shmoys and É. Tardos. An approximation algorithm for the generalized assignment problem. *Mathematical Programming* 62:461–474, 1993.

[Sm56]   W. Smith. Various optimizers for single-stage production. *Naval Res. Logist. Quart.* 3:59–66, 1956.

[Tr90]   M. A. Trick. Scheduling multiple variable-speed machines. In *Proceedings of the 1st Conference on Integer Programming and Combinatorial Optimization*, 485–494, 1990.

[W+96]   D. P. Williamson, L. A. Hall, J. A. Hoogeveen, C. A. J. Hurkens, J. K. Lenstra, S. V. Sevast'janov, and D. B. Shmoys. Short Shop Schedules. *Operations Research*, 1996 (to appear).

2

APPROXIMATION ALGORITHMS
FOR BIN PACKING: A SURVEY

E. G. Coffman, Jr.   M. R. Garey   D. S. Johnson

The classical one-dimensional bin packing problem has long
served as a proving ground for new approaches to the analysis of approximation algorithms. In the early 1970s it was
one of the first combinatorial optimization problems for
which the idea of worst-case performance guarantees was
investigated. It was also in this domain that the idea
of proving lower bounds on the performance of online
algorithms was first developed, and it is here that the probabilistic analysis of approximation algorithms has truly flow-
ered. The chapter surveys the literature on worst-case and
average-case behavior of approximation algorithms for one-
dimensional bin packing, using each type of analysis to put
the other in perspective.

INTRODUCTION

2.1

In the classical one-dimensional bin packing problem, we are given a sequence $L = (a_1, a_2, \ldots, a_n)$ of *items*, each with a *size* $s(a_i) \in (0, 1]$ and are asked to pack them into a minimum number of unit-capacity bins (i.e., partition them into a minimum number m of subsets $B_1, B_2, \ldots, B_m$ such that $\sum_{a_i \in B_j} s(a_i) \leq 1, 1 \leq j \leq m$).

This *NP*-hard problem has many potential real-world applications, from loading trucks subject to weight limitations to packing television commercials into station breaks [Bro71], to *stock-cutting* problems, where the bins correspond to standard lengths of some material, (say cable, lumber, or paper) from which items must be cut.

Bin packing has also been of fundamental theoretical significance, serving as an early proving ground for many of the classical approaches to analyzing the performance of approximation algorithms. These include determining worst-case performance ratios (currently called *competitive ratios*) [Ull71] [JDU74], identifying lower bounds on the best possible online performance [Yao80], and analyzing average-case behavior [Sha77] [Lue82].

In this chapter we survey the literature that has grown from these early papers, and concentrate on results for the basic problem defined above. A subsequent survey [CGJ97] will cover the wide variety of variants that it has spawned, including generalizations to higher dimensions, generalizations to include other constraints beyond bin capacity, and variants with different optimization criteria. The chapter can be viewed as a partial successor to two earlier surveys by the same authors, written in 1981 [GJ81] and 1984 [CGJ84]. As evidence of growth in the field, the number of references doubled between the first and second versions, and although this survey is restricted to the classical one-dimensional case, it has more references than [CGJ84] which covered the basic problem and all its variants.

We divide our coverage into two parts. The first (Section 2.2), covers worst-case results, while the second (Section 2.3), covers the average case. In both sections we consider the distinction between online and offline algorithms, where in the former, items arrive in some given order and must be assigned to bins as they arrive, without knowledge of the items yet to arrive. A brief final section (Section 2.4) offers general conclusions, and sketches the variations of the basic problem that have been studied.

WORST-CASE ANALYSIS

2.2

In the case of bin packing, the standard metric for worst-case performance is the *asymptotic worst-case performance ratio*. For a given list L and algorithm A, let $A(L)$ be the number of bins used when algorithm A is applied to list L; let $\mathrm{OPT}(L)$ denote the optimum number of bins for a packing of L; and let $R_A(L) \equiv A(L)/\mathrm{OPT}(L)$. The *absolute* worst-case performance ratio R_A for algorithm A is defined as

$$R_A \equiv \inf\{r \geq 1 : R_A(L) \leq r \text{ for all lists } L\}$$

The *asymptotic* worst-case performance ratio R_A^∞ is defined as

$$R_A^\infty \equiv \inf\{r \geq 1 : \text{for some } N > 0, R_A(L) \leq r \text{ for all } L \text{ with } \mathrm{OPT}(L) \geq N\}$$

In addition, if one restricts lists to those for which all items have sizes at most α, one can analogously define the *bounded-size* performance ratios, $R_A(\alpha)$ and $R_A^\infty(\alpha)$. Note that $R_A^\infty(1) = R_A^\infty$.

The remainder of this section is organized as follows. Sections 2.2.1 through 2.2.5 are all concerned with various types of online bin packing algorithms. Although for the general bin packing problem we assume that the entire list and its items' sizes are known before the packing begins, in many applications this may not be the case. A common situation is where the items arrive in some order and must be assigned to a bin as soon as they arrive, without knowledge of the remaining items. This models situations in which items are physical objects, and there is no intermediate space to store them in before placing them in bins. A bin packing algorithm that can construct its packings under this regime is called an *online* algorithm.

We begin in Sections 2.2.1 and 2.2.2 by introducing perhaps the two simplest and best known online algorithms, Next Fit and First Fit. Section 2.2.3 then considers generalizations and variations on First Fit, including Best Fit and the Almost Any Fit algorithms, all of which share with First Fit an asymptotic worst-case performance ratio of 1.7. Sections 2.2.4 and 2.2.5 examine the question of what is the best possible worst-case performance under the online constraint.

Section 2.2.4 does this first in the context of a second type of online constraint, that of *bounded space*. Now not only do the items arrive in an online fashion, but only a fixed number of partially-filled bins may be open to further items at any point in the packing process; and once a bin is closed it must remain so. This models situations in which bins are exported once they are packed, and there is limited storage space for partially-filled ones. We present bounded-space online algorithms that perform as well as, and even slightly better than First Fit, but also note that the best possible behavior under this constraint is only marginally better than that obtained by First Fit.

Section 2.2.5 then considers arbitrary online algorithms and whether more substantial improvements over First Fit can be obtained when the bounded-space constraint is removed. There is a limit on how much improvement can be obtained, as it can be shown that any online algorithm A must have $R_A^\infty > \beta$ for a constant $\beta > 1.5$. We discuss the best current upper and lower bounds known on β, and the algorithms on which the upper bounds depend (algorithms whose main motivation is this theoretical question, rather than potential applications in practice, where they are unlikely to perform as well as some of their simpler competitors).

Sections 2.2.6 through 2.2.9 cover offline algorithms. Section 2.2.6 covers what might be called *semi-online* algorithms, where the only relaxation of the online constraint is that each assignment of an item to a bin may be accompanied by a limited amount of rearrangement of the other items in the current packing. Section 2.2.7 then covers what are perhaps the most famous of the offline algorithms, First and Best Fit Decreasing, with asymptotic worst-case ratios of $11/9 = 1.222\ldots$. Section 2.2.8 covers other simple offline algorithms, including both ones that give up a little in worst-case performance for the sake of flexibility, simplicity, or speed, and ones that outperform First Fit Decreasing at a minor cost in increased algorithmic complexity. The best of these "simple" algorithms still has $R_A^\infty > 1.15$, but more complicated approximation schemes exist with asymptotic worst-case performance ratios approaching 1, and indeed there exist impractical but still polynomial-time bin packing algorithms with R_A^∞ (but not R_A) equal to 1.0 exactly. These algorithms are discussed in Section 2.2.9.

Our discussion of worst-case results for the classical one-dimensional bin packing problem concludes in Section 2.2.10 by examining other questions that have been asked about the classic algorithms, (besides the questions about R_A^∞ and $R_A^\infty(\alpha)$ that we concentrate on in Sections 2.2.1 through 2.2.9). Included are results about absolute worst-case performance ratios and bounds on anomalies, such as the situation in which deleting an item from a list causes the algorithm to use more bins.

2.2.1   NEXT FIT

Perhaps the simplest algorithm for the classical one-dimensional bin packing problem is Next Fit (NF), apparently first described under this name in [Joh73]. This is a bounded-space online algorithm in which the only partially-filled bin that is open is the most recent one to be started, i.e., the nonempty bin B_j in the current packing with the largest index j. (In this and subsequent discussions, we assume that bins are indexed $B_1, B_2, \ldots$ in the order in which they are created, i.e., receive their first items.) Let $level(B)$ be the sum of the sizes of the items in bin B. In packing item a_i, Next Fit tests whether $s(a_i) \leq 1 - level(B_j)$. If so, it places a_i in bin B_j, leaving that bin open. Otherwise, it closes bin B_j and places a_i in a new bin B_{j+1}, which now becomes the open bin.

This algorithm can be implemented to run in linear time, and it is not difficult to show that for all lists L, $\mathrm{NF}(L) \leq 2 \cdot \mathrm{OPT}(L) - 1$. Furthermore, there exist lists L with arbitrarily large values of $\mathrm{OPT}(L)$ such that $\mathrm{NF}(L) = 2 \cdot \mathrm{OPT}(L) - 1$, as illustrated in Figure 2.1. Thus, we conclude that $R_{\mathrm{NF}}^{\infty} = 2$.

$$L = \left(\tfrac{1}{2}, \tfrac{1}{2N}, \tfrac{1}{2}, \tfrac{1}{2N}, \cdots, \tfrac{1}{2}, \tfrac{1}{2N} \right)$$

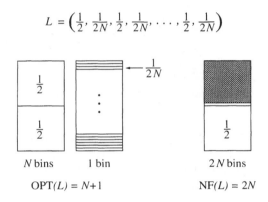

FIGURE 2.1

Worst-case examples for Next Fit.

Note that the lists in the figure contain no items with $s(a) > 1/2$, so we can also conclude that $R_{\mathrm{NF}}^{\infty}(\alpha) = 2$ for all $\alpha \geq 1/2$. As α continues to decrease beyond this point, $R_{\mathrm{NF}}^{\infty}(\alpha)$ decreases in a continuous fashion, with the specific result being $R_{\mathrm{NF}}^{\infty}(\alpha) = 1/(1-\alpha)$ for $\alpha \leq 1/2$ [Joh73].

2.2.2   FIRST FIT

As the worst-case examples of Figure 2.1 illustrate, Next Fit can be made to suffer because of the bounded-space constraint inherent in its definition. In Section 2.2.5, we consider the effect of partially relaxing this constraint to allow more than one but still a bounded number of open bins, as in the Next-K Fit algorithms of [Joh73]. For now, we shall go directly to the historically more important First Fit algorithm, in which the restriction is removed entirely, and we consider *all* partially-filled bins as possible destinations for the item to be packed. The particular rule followed is implicit in the algorithm's name: we place an item in the first (lowest indexed) bin into which it will fit, i.e., if there is any partially-filled bin B_j with $level(B_j) + s(a_i) \leq 1$, we place a_i in the lowest-indexed bin having this property. Otherwise, we start a new bin with a_i as its first item. Note that in removing the bounded-space restriction, we forfeit the benefits of a linear running time enjoyed by Next Fit. We do not have to settle for the naive quadratic-time implementation, however, as it is possible to construct the First Fit packing in time $O(n \log n)$ using an appropriate data structure [Joh73]. (This is the best possible case for a comparison-based implementation, since one can use the First Fit packing rule to sort [Joh73].)

First Fit manages to take good advantage of the wider range of destinations it considers, as the following result shows.

THEOREM 2.1 [GGJ76].   For all lists L, FF$(L) \leq \lceil (17/10) \cdot \text{OPT}(L) \rceil$.

This is a slight tightening of what was essentially the first nontrivial bin packing result, proved by Ullman in 1971 [Ull71] [GGU71] with the slightly larger upper bound of $(17/10) \cdot \text{OPT}(L) + 3$. The bound's additive term was reduced to 2 in the journal version of this paper [JDU74], and to 1 or less by the result of [GGJ76] highlighted above, although these improvements only reflected minor changes in the original proof. That proof has served as a model for many of the results that followed, so let us say a little bit about it.

The key idea is to use a *weighting* function $W : L \rightarrow \Re$, and to relate both $A(L)$ and OPT(L) to $W(L) \equiv \sum_{i=1}^{n} W(a_i)$ in such a way that the desired bound is implied. For Theorem 2.1, a static function suffices, i.e., one under which an item's weight depends only on its size. The version of W used in [GGJ76] is illustrated in Figure 2.2. Given this function one can use case analyses to prove two key lemmas: (i) If A is a set of

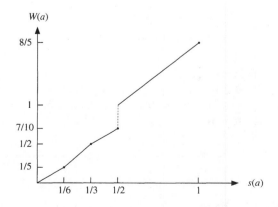

FIGURE 2.2

Weighting function W used in proof of Theorem 2.1.

items with $s(A) \equiv \sum_{a \in A} s(a) \leq 1$, then $w(A) \equiv \sum_{a \in A} W(a) \leq 17/10$, which implies $\text{OPT}(L) \leq (17/10) \cdot W(L)$, and (ii) $W(L) > \text{FF}(L) - 1$. The theorem follows.

The upper bound of Theorem 2.1 is asymptotically tight, in that for arbitrarily large values of N one can construct lists L_N with $\text{FF}(L_N) > (17/10) \cdot \text{OPT}(L_N) - 2$ [JDU74]. These lists are fairly intricate, but simple examples that are almost as bad are readily constructed. Figure 2.3 illustrates a family of lists for which $\text{FF}(L)/\text{OPT}(L) = 5/3 = 1.666\ldots$ when the items are sorted in increasing order by size.

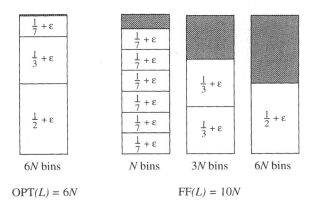

$$\text{OPT}(L) = 6N \qquad\qquad \text{FF}(L) = 10N$$

FIGURE 2.3

Bad lists for First Fit.

Note that still worse examples can be devised using the idea behind those in the figure. For instance, assuming ϵ is small enough, one could include an additional item of size $(1/43) + \epsilon$ in each bin of the optimal packing. Placing these at the beginning of the list will force First Fit to put them in an extra $N/42$ bins (assuming N is divisible by 42). Generalizing this idea, let $t_1 = 2$ and $t_{i+1} = (t_i)(t_i - 1) + 1$, $i > 1$. Then, for any $k < \infty$ we can construct examples in which the optimal bins each contain k items, one each of size $(1/t_i) + \epsilon$, $1 \leq i \leq k$. When First Fit is given these items sorted in order of non-decreasing size, it will require roughly $\sum_{i=1}^{k} 1/(t_i - 1)$ bins. The best we can conclude from this, however, is that

$$R_{\text{FF}}^{\infty} \geq T_{\infty} \equiv \sum_{i=1}^{\infty} \frac{1}{t_i - 1} = 1 + \frac{1}{2} + \frac{1}{6} + \frac{1}{42} + \frac{1}{1805} + \cdots \approx 1.69103\ldots.$$

Although this simple scheme for worst case examples is thus insufficient to characterize the worst-case behavior of First Fit, we shall see below that there are other algorithms for which it and the constant T_{∞} are more relevant. Moreover, the scheme is correct in suggesting that for First Fit to behave at its worst, the instance to which it is applied must contain relatively large items. As with Next Fit, First Fit's worst-case behavior improves dramatically as the size of the largest item declines. Moreover, it maintains its advantage over Next Fit in such situations, although the size of its advantage depends on the precise value of α and shrinks with the size of the largest item.

THEOREM 2.2 [Joh73][JDU74].   Let $m \in \mathbf{Z}$ be such that $\frac{1}{m+1} < \alpha \le \frac{1}{m}$.

A. For $m = 1$, $R_{FF}^{\infty}(\alpha) = 17/10$

B. For $m \ge 2$, $R_{FF}^{\infty}(\alpha) = 1 + 1/m$.

Figure 2.4 plots both $R_{NF}^{\infty}(\alpha)$ and $R_{FF}^{\infty}(\alpha)$ as functions of α. Note that although the value for NF approaches that for FF each time α approaches the reciprocal $1/t$ of an integer from above, it never catches it, as $R_{FF}^{\infty}(\alpha)$ is a step function that changes value at precisely those points.

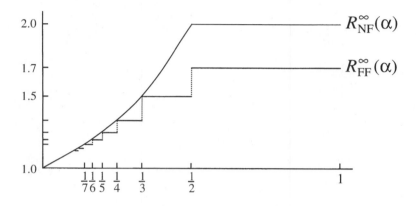

FIGURE 2.4

Comparison of $R_{NF}^{\infty}(\alpha)$ and $R_{FF}^{\infty}(\alpha)$ as functions of α.

2.2.3   BEST FIT, WORST FIT, AND ALMOST ANY FIT ALGORITHMS

How crucial is the packing rule used by First Fit to the improved worst-case behavior outlined in the previous section? It turns out that other packing rules can do essentially as well. The most famous of these rules is the one used by the Best Fit (BF) algorithm. In this packing rule, which like the First Fit packing rule can be implemented to run in time $O(n \log n)$, item a_i is packed in the partially-filled bin B_j with the highest level $level(B_j) \le 1 - s(a_i)$, ties are broken in favor of lower index. Best and First Fit can give strikingly different packings for individual lists. Examples are given in [Joh73] of lists L with arbitrarily large values of $OPT(L)$ both such that $BF(L) = (4/3) \cdot FF(L)$ and such that $FF(L) = (3/2) \cdot BF(L)$. Nevertheless, all the results mentioned in the previous section for $R_{FF}^{\infty}(\alpha)$ hold for $R_{BF}^{\infty}(\alpha)$ as well [Joh73] [Joh74] [JDU74].

There are plausible packing rules for which these results do not hold, however. Consider the algorithm Worst Fit (WF), in which each item a_i is packed in the partially-filled bin with the *lowest* level (ties broken by index), assuming it fits, and otherwise starts a new bin. It is not difficult to see that $R_{WF}^{\infty}(\alpha) = R_{NF}^{\infty}(\alpha)$, $0 < \alpha \le 1$, so that in a worst-case sense, Worst Fit gets no value out of the fact that it never closes a bin.

Surprisingly, it takes only a slight modification to this algorithm to improve it dramatically. Consider the close variant Almost Worst Fit (AWF), in which a_i is placed in the partially-filled bin with the second lowest level (ties broken by index) unless there is only one bin into which it fits, in which case it goes in that bin. If a_i fits in no partially-filled bin, it of course starts a new bin. As shown in [Joh73] [Joh74], the worst-case behavior of Almost Worst Fit is just as good as that for First and Best Fit. Again, however, there can be significant differences on individual lists. Almost Worst Fit can be just as far off from Best Fit (in either direction) as was First Fit, and examples exist such that $\text{AWF}(L) = (5/4) \cdot \text{FF}(L)$ and that $\text{FF}(L) = (9/8) \cdot \text{AWF}(L)$ [Joh73].

More generally, let us say that an online bin packing algorithm is an *Any Fit* (AF) algorithm if it never starts a new bin unless the item to be packed does not fit in any partially-filled bin in the current packing, and additionally it is an *Almost Any Fit* (AAF) algorithm if it never packs an item into a partially-filled bin with the lowest level unless there is more than one such bin—or that bin is the only one that has enough room. Then we have the following result.

THEOREM 2.3 [Joh73][Joh74].   For all α, $0 < \alpha \leq 1$,

A. If A is an AF algorithm, then $R_{\text{FF}}^{\infty}(\alpha) \leq R_A^{\infty}(\alpha) \leq R_{\text{NF}}^{\infty}(\alpha)$, and

B. If A is an AAF algorithm, then $R_A^{\infty}(\alpha) = R_{\text{FF}}^{\infty}(\alpha)$.

Thus, if we want to obtain better worst-case behavior than that of First Fit, we shall either have to abandon the Any Fit constraint or the online restriction itself. In the next two sections we shall discuss what can be done while still obeying the online restriction.

2.2.4   BOUNDED-SPACE ONLINE ALGORITHMS

One disadvantage of the Any Fit constraint beside that implied by Theorem 2.3, is that under it no bin can ever be permanently closed to further items. Consequently, no Any Fit algorithm can be used in situations where the *bounded-space* constraint described at the beginning of Section 2.2 holds, i.e., where at most K bins can remain open at any given time for some fixed K. In this section we consider what can be accomplished when space *is* bounded.

We have already seen one bounded-space online algorithm, Next Fit, and observed that it paid a substantial worst-case performance penalty in comparison to the unbounded-space algorithms First and Best Fit. Such a penalty is unavoidable if the bound K on the number of open bins is 1. When $k > 1$, four natural hybrids between Next Fit and First and Best Fit suggest themselves. Note that in constructing a bounded-space online algorithm we need to specify a *closing* rule in addition to a packing rule. First and Best Fit each suggest one rule of each type.

Assuming some open bin has room for the current item b, the First Fit packing rule places b in the lowest indexed open bin that has room for it, and the Best Fit packing rule places b in the highest-level open bin that has room (ties broken in favor of lowest index). When there are already K open bins and none of them has room for b, one bin must be closed before a new bin can be opened to receive b. The First Fit closing rule closes the lowest indexed open bin, and the Best Fit closing rule closes the fullest open bin (ties broken in favor of lowest index).

The Next-K Fit algorithm (NF_K), introduced in [Joh73], combines the First Fit packing and closing rules. The K-Bounded Best Fit algorithm (BBF_K), introduced in [CJ91] combines the Best Fit packing and closing rules. The two remaining hybrids mix Best and First Fit rules and are denoted by ABF_K and AFB_K in [CJ91]. The first algorithm, ABF_K, uses the Best Fit packing rule and the First Fit closing rule and was analyzed by [Mao93a] under the name *Best-K Fit*. The second, AFB_K, uses the First Fit packing rule and the Best Fit closing rule. All four algorithms reduce to Next Fit when $K = 1$, and all can be implemented to run in linear time for any fixed K, as opposed to the $\Omega(n \log n)$ time needed by our implementations of First and Best Fit. The next theorem summarizes what is known about the asymptotic worst-case ratios for the algorithms when $K \geq 2$.

THEOREM 2.4 [CI89] [Mao93b] [Mao93a] [Zha94] [CJ91].   For $K \geq 2$,

A. $R_{NF_K}^\infty = R_{AFB_K}^\infty = 1.7 + \frac{3}{10(K-1)}$

B. $R_{ABF_K}^\infty = 1.7 + \frac{3}{10K}$

C. $R_{BBF_K}^\infty = 1.7$

The lower bound examples for $R_{NF_K}^\infty$ were discovered by Csirik and Imreh [CI89], and the matching upper bound was proved by Mao [Mao93b], who also proved the result for $R_{ABF_K}^\infty$ [Mao93a]. The result for $R_{AFB_K}^\infty$ was proved by Zhang [Zha94], and that for $R_{BBF_K}^\infty$ was proved by Csirik and Johnson [CJ91]. All the upper bound proofs rely on weighting function arguments similar to those used for FF in Theorem 2.1.

The surprise here is the result for BBF_K, which yields the same performance guarantee as do First and Best Fit as soon as $K \geq 2$, although as might be expected, the penalty for the space bound approaches 0 for the other three algorithms as $K \to \infty$. One could not have expected any of these algorithms to do *better* than First and Best Fit, for although they do not obey the Any Fit constraint, they do obey the bounded-space analog of that constraint. Also, the proof of Theorem 2.3 implies that any such algorithm must have $R_A^\infty \geq 1.7$. If we are to find an algorithm with $R_A^\infty < 1.7$, we will thus have to consider algorithms that start new bins even when the current item fits in one of the currently open bins.

The worst-case examples of Figures 2.1 and 2.3 suggest the following series of bounded-space algorithms, introduced by Lee and Lee in [LL85] as the *Harmonic$_K$* algorithms (H_K). Divide the unit interval into K subintervals I_k, $1 \leq k \leq K$, where $I_k = (1/(k+1), 1/k]$, $1 \leq k < K$, and $I_K = (0, 1/K]$. An item a will be identified as having *type k* if $s(a) \in I_k$. Similarly, bins will be divided into K types, with bins of type k only receiving items of type k, and at most one bin of each type open at any time. Each item a is then packed as follows: Let k be the type of item a. If there is an open bin of type k and that bin has room for a, then place a in that bin. Otherwise, close the open bin of type k if one exists, and place a in a new (open) bin of type k. For K sufficiently large, these algorithms finally break the 1.7 barrier with a limiting value that equals the constant that we encountered in Section 2.2.2.

THEOREM 2.5 [LL85]. $\lim_{K \to \infty} R_{\mathrm{H}_K}^{\infty} = T_{\infty} = 1.69103\ldots.$

Indeed, as soon as $K \geq 7$, we have $R_{\mathrm{H}_K}^{\infty} \leq 1.695$. One can actually get performance guarantees less than 1.7 for K as small as 6, but this requires a variant on the original Harmonic scheme introduced by Woeginger [Woe93]. Woeginger's algorithms, which he calls the *Simplified Harmonic* algorithms (SH$_K$), rely on a more complicated interval structure, derived from the sequence of t_i's defined in Section 2.2.2. Table 2.1 summarizes what is known about the values of R_A^{∞} as a function of K for the various bounded-space algorithms discussed in this section. Tight bounds for H$_K$ are not known for all values of K, so the table gives the best upper and lower bounds currently known. In this table, the upper bounds for all values of K except 4 and 5 are from [LL85]. The upper bounds for $K \in \{4, 5\}$ are due to van Vliet [Vli95] and are tight. The lower bounds for $K \geq 4$ are due independently to [CJ92] and to [Vli95] [Vli96].

K	NF$_K$	ABF$_K$	BBF$_K$	H$_K \geq$	H$_K \leq$	SH$_K$
2	2.00000	1.85000	1.70000	2.00000	2.00000	2.00000
3	1.85000	1.80000	1.70000	1.75000	1.75000	1.75000
4	1.80000	1.77500	1.70000	1.71429	1.71429	1.72222
5	1.77500	1.76000	1.70000	1.70000	1.70000	1.70000
6	1.76000	1.75000	1.70000	1.70000	1.70000	1.69444
7	1.75000	1.74286	1.70000	1.69444	1.69444	1.69388
8	1.74286	1.73750	1.70000	1.69377	1.69388	1.69106
9	1.73750	1.73333	1.70000	1.69326	1.69345	1.69104
10	1.73333	1.73000	1.70000	1.69287	1.69312	1.69104
∞	1.70000	1.70000	1.70000	1.69103	1.69103	1.69103

Table 2.1: Values of R_A^{∞} under fixed space bounds, rounded to five decimal places.

Note that BBF$_K$ provides the best guarantee for $K \in \{2, 3, 4\}$, BBF$_K$, H$_K$, and SH$_K$ are tied for the best when $K = 5$, and thereafter SH$_K$ is the best. Asymptotically, it uses only $O(\log \log K)$ as many open bins to obtain the same performance guarantee as H$_K$, although its margin over H$_K$ for particular values of K is never more than about 0.3%, and rapidly declines to 0 as $K \to \infty$. Asymptotically, both are only about 0.5% better than FF, BF, and BBF$_K$. This is not a major advantage, but it is all that is possible for bounded-space online algorithms in light of the following result of Lee and Lee.

THEOREM 2.6 [LL85]. If A is any bounded-space online bin packing algorithm, then $R_A^{\infty} \geq T_{\infty} = 1.69103\ldots.$

It should be noted that at present no online bounded-space algorithm A is known for which $R_A^{\infty} = T_{\infty}$. The worst-case ratios for the sequences of algorithms H$_K$ and SH$_K$ only approach this value in the limit. If one is willing to consider bounded-space algorithms that are only semi-online, however, there are algorithms whose worst-case ratios match the limiting value, as has recently been shown by Galambos and Woeginger [GW93b] and [Gro94]. The relaxation used by [GW93b] is to allow *repacking* of the current open bins, i.e., to allow us to take all the items out of the current open bins and reassign them before packing the current item. The conclusion of Theorem 2.6 continues to hold even if we allow repacking [GW93b], but Galambos and Woeginger present an "online with repacking" algorithm REP$_3$ that never uses more than three open bins and yet has $R^\infty_{\text{REP}_3} = T_\infty$. Grove [Gro94] independently constructed an algorithm with the same behavior using an alternative notion he calls *lookahead*. In such an algorithm, one is given a fixed *warehouse size* W, and an item a_i need not be packed until one has looked at all items a_i through a_j, for $j > i$ such that $\sum_{h=i}^{j} s(a_h) \leq W$. Allowing lookahead does not allow us to escape from the constraints of Theorem 2.6 either, but if one allows sufficiently large (fixed) values of K and W, Grove's *Warehouse* algorithm can again guarantee an asymptotic worst-case ratio of T_∞.

As remarked above, however, $T_\infty = 1.691\ldots$ is not that great an improvement over 1.7. If an online algorithm is to improve significantly over the worst-case behavior of First Fit, it must exploit something stronger than bounded-space repacking or lookahead, i.e., it must allow for the use of unbounded space. In light of Theorem 2.3, it must also be prepared to disobey the Any Fit constraint and start new bins even when the current item will fit in some already-started bin. We discuss such algorithms in the next section.

2.2.5 ARBITRARY ONLINE ALGORITHMS

The first unbounded-space algorithms to be proposed that did not obey the Any Fit constraint were the Group-X Fit (GXF) algorithms of Johnson [Joh73] [Joh74]. One gets different versions of the algorithm depending on the choice of X, which is an increasing sequence $0 = x_0 < x_1 < \ldots < x_p = 1$ of real numbers. At any given time, a partially-filled bin with gap g is viewed as having a *de facto* gap equal to $\max\{x_i \leq g : 0 \leq i < p\}$. This in effect partitions the bins into p groups. Items are then packed via Best Fit with respect to the de facto gaps. Note that, like our bounded-space algorithms, this algorithm can be implemented to run in linear time for any fixed X. Now, however, the only bins to be effectively closed are those with gaps smaller than x_1, which hence get *de facto* gaps of 0. Unfortunately, the main advantage of GXF seems to be its linear running time, as the algorithm does not avoid the worst-case examples for First Fit and so has $R^\infty_{\text{GXF}} > 1.7$. Johnson did show, however, that for $m = \lfloor 1/\alpha \rfloor \geq 2$, $R^\infty_{\text{GXF}}(\alpha) = R^\infty_{\text{FF}}(\alpha)$ whenever $\{1/(m+1), 1\} \subseteq X$, and conjectured that the same equality held for $m = 1$ whenever $\{1/6, 1/3, 1/2\} \subseteq X$ [Joh73].

The first online algorithm with $R^\infty_A < T_\infty$ (and actually the first one to beat First Fit, since it preceded the Harmonic algorithm of [LL85]), was the Refined First Fit (RFF) algorithm of Yao [Yao80]. This algorithm classified items as to which of the intervals $(0, 1/3]$, $(1/3, 2/5]$, $(2/5, 1/2]$, and $(1/2, 1]$ their sizes fell, and classified bins according to a related scheme. Each item was then packed into a particular class of bins according to the First Fit rule, with the bin class being determined by the item class and, in the case of the items with sizes in $(1/3, 2/5]$, the number of such items previously encountered in the list. For this type of item, one in 6 are treated specially, the idea being to occasionally start a new bin with an item of this size in hopes of subsequently adding an item of size greater than 1/2 to that bin. This will allow the algorithm to defeat the worst-case examples for

First Fit (and the Harmonic algorithms), while not opening the way for an adversary to do too much damage by providing many items with sizes in $(1/3, 2/5]$ but no later items in $(1/2, 1]$ that will pair up with them. Yao showed that $R_{\text{RFF}}^{\infty} = 5/3 = 1.666\ldots$.

This paper set off something of a race, which has led to more and more elaborate variants. The first was the Refined Harmonic (RH_K) algorithms of [LL85], a hybrid of the Harmonic algorithms with Refined First Fit. RH_K uses the partitioning scheme of HK_{20}, with the modification that the two size-intervals $(1/3, 1/2]$ and $(1/2, 1]$ are replaced by the four intervals $(1/3, y]$, $(y, 1/2]$, $(1/2, 1 - y]$, and $(1 - y, 1]$, where $y = 37/96$. Packing proceeds much as in a Harmonic algorithm, except now one attempts to pair items whose sizes are in the first of the new intervals with items whose sizes are in the third new interval, since such pairs can always fit in the same bin. As in Refined First Fit, one must hedge one's bet when doing this, and here only one in 7 of the items with sizes in the first interval get the special treatment. Lee and Lee showed that $R_{\text{RH}_{20}}^{\infty} \leq 373/228 = 1.6359\ldots$, with little to be gained by increasing K further.

Next came Ramanan, Brown, Lee, and Lee [RBL89], with what they called the Modified Harmonic (MH_K) algorithms, which added the possibility of packing still smaller items with items of size in $(1/2, 1/2 + y]$, and a consequently more complicated algorithmic structure (as well as a different value for y, in this case $y = 265/684$). The details are too complex to be gone into here, but Ramanan et al. were able to show that $1.6156146 < R_{\text{MH}_{38}}^{\infty} \leq 1.(615)^* \equiv 1.615615\ldots$. Shortly after drafts of [RBL89] began to circulate, Hu and Kahng [HK88] used somewhat similar principles to construct an (unnamed) variant for which they claimed $R_A^{\infty} \approx 1.6067$. Ramanan et al. themselves sketched further variants which they thought might take the asymptotic worst-case ratio down to as little as 1.59, but proved that the basic approach could never yield $R_A^{\infty} < 1.(583)^*$.

The current champion, Richey's Harmonic+1 algorithm [Ric91], uses somewhat different principles, but essentially attains the limit claimed by Ramanan et al., at least to the first three decimal places. Although it runs in linear time like its predecessors, it is substantially more complicated, with a significantly more complex interval structure involving over 70 intervals and with a packing rule that itself depends on an almost full-page table of constants. Richey shows that for this algorithm, $1.5874 \leq R_A^{\infty} \leq 1.588720$, and that the lower bound will hold for any variant that takes roughly the same approach.

Whether some other approach might do better remains an open question. Given the complicated nature of Harmonic+1 and the fact (as we shall see in Section 2.2.2) that all algorithms that do better than First Fit in the worst case seem to do much worse in the average case, this is perhaps not an open question that needs an answer. We can, however, place bounds on how much improvement might be possible, analogous to the bound on bounded-space online algorithms of Theorem 2.6.

The first such bound was proved by Yao in [Yao80], and actually preceded the abovementioned bounded-space result. Yao showed that no online algorithm could have $R_A^{\infty} < 1.5$, using an adversary argument that required only three item sizes: $1/2 + \epsilon$, $1/3 + \epsilon$, and $1/7 + \epsilon$. Note that these item sizes are simply $1/t_i + \epsilon$ for $1 \leq i \leq 3$ and the t_i used in the definition of T_{∞} given in Section 2.2.2. Shortly thereafter, Brown and Liang independently generalized this approach to use items of size $1/2 + \epsilon$, $1/3 + \epsilon$, $1/7 + \epsilon$, $1/43 + \epsilon$, and $1/1807 + \epsilon$, i.e., $1/t_i + \epsilon$ for $1 \leq i \leq 5$, and proved that no online algorithm could have $R_A^{\infty} < 1.536346\ldots$ [Bro79] [Lia80] . A simplified version of this proof has recently been presented in [GF93]. Because of the rapid growth in the values t_i, attempts to improve this bound by allowing the adversary additional item sizes $1/t_i + \epsilon$ for $i > 5$ do not seem likely to yield much increase in the bound. More careful analysis using just the values for $i \leq 5$ can make a difference however, as shown by van Vliet [Vli95] [Vli96]. Building on an approach first proposed by Galambos [Gal86], van Vliet constructs a linear program whose solution specifies the best possible way of exploiting these item sizes, and derives the currently best lower bound known as shown in Theorem 2.7:

THEOREM 2.7 [Vli95][Vli96].   For any online algorithm A, $R_A^\infty \geq 1.540$.

This sort of lower bound analysis can be extended to questions about $R_A^\infty(\alpha)$, and Table 2.2 summarizes the current best bounds known for $\alpha = 1/m$, $1 \leq m \leq 5$, comparing them with the best values known for $R_A^\infty(\alpha)$ with A online, with the limiting value of $R_{H_K}^\infty(\alpha)$ (as $K \to \infty$), and with $R_{FF}^\infty(\alpha)$. The lower bounds are due again to [Vli95] [Vli96], improving on earlier results of [Gal86]. Note that by the time $\alpha = 1/5$, even First Fit is providing guarantees within 1% of best possible.

m	Lower Bound	Best Known	$R_{H_K}^\infty(1/m)$	$R_{FF}^\infty(1/m)$
1	1.540 ...	1.588 ...	1.691 ...	1.700 ...
2	1.389 ...	1.423 ...	1.423 ...	1.500 ...
3	1.291 ...	1.302 ...	1.302 ...	1.333 ...
4	1.229 ...	1.234 ...	1.234 ...	1.250 ...
5	1.188 ...	1.191 ...	1.191 ...	1.200 ...

Table 2.2: Best possible and actual values of $R_A^\infty(1/m)$ for online algorithms.

The proofs of the above lower bound results all assume that the online algorithm is deterministic. It appears, however that this is not necessarily a required assumption. Chandra [Cha92] has shown that even if we allow an online algorithm to base its assignments on random coin flips, and use the expected length of the resulting packing as our metric, there still exist lists that yield ratios of $E[A(L)]/OPT(L)$ approaching $1.536 \ldots$ (Chandra's proof technique seems general enough to extend as well to the other lower bounds summarized above).

2.2.6   SEMI-ONLINE ALGORITHMS

As we saw at the end of Section 2.2.4 for bounded-space online algorithms, relaxing the online restriction slightly by allowing bounded repacking or lookahead can yield better algorithms. However, whereas in the case of bounded space such relaxations only allowed us to attain rather than beat the online lower bound, the situation is quite different in the general online case, at least for sufficiently powerful notions of bounded repacking.

Note first that if no limit on repacking is imposed, then one can do as well as the best offline algorithm, simply by repacking everything according to that algorithm each time an item arrives. This, however, would multiply the overall running time by a factor of n, and introduce at least linear-time delays each time a new item arrives. (By delaying the repackings appropriately, one can reduce the amortized delay per new item to $T(n) \log n / n$, where $T(n)$ is the offline algorithm's running time, but the worst-case delay would remain $T(n)$ [IL94].) In applications that still retain something of an online flavor, one would presumably need stronger restrictions on how much repacking is allowed; for instance, allowing only constant or $O(\log n)$ time per item in a worst-case sense. Even under such restrictions, however, major improvements can be obtained over the 1.540 lower bound on R_A^∞ for pure online algorithms.

The first authors to observe this were Gambosi et al. [GPT90]. They designed two algorithms that beat the bound. The first yielded $R_A^\infty \leq 1.5$ using only constant time per item. In the worst case, $\Omega(n)$ items might have to be moved while accommodating a single new item, but with the aid of appropriate data structures Gambosi et al. could treat large collections of small items as a group and move them all at once in constant time. In a physical bin packing situation, this might correspond to keeping collections of small items in boxes and moving entire boxes from one bin to another. In this algorithm, which was based on a simple classification of items into four types by size, no more than 3 group or single-item moves are ever required when a new item has to be assigned.

The second algorithm of [GPT90] had six types of items, required $\Theta(\log n)$ time but at most 7 group/item moves per new item, and yielded $R_A^\infty \leq 4/3 = 1.333\ldots$. More recently, Ivković and Lloyd [IL93] have devised an algorithm with $R_A^\infty \leq 5/4 = 1.25$, although for this they need as many as $O(\log n)$ group/item movements as well as $O(\log n)$ time per new item. They also have significantly more complicated packing/repacking rules, although part of this is because their algorithm can also handle the dynamic bin packing problem where items can depart as well as arrive. (It has the same bound on asymptotic worst-case performance in this more generalized situation.)

This is currently the best worst-case behavior currently known for such semi-online algorithms. If we want provably better asymptotic worst-case ratios, we must turn to algorithms that are offline and hence have access to all the items before any of them need to be assigned to bins. The next section covers the most famous of these, ones that were investigated long before many of the above questions about the online case were even considered.

2.2.7 FIRST FIT DECREASING AND BEST FIT DECREASING

Looking at the instances in Figure 2.3 that make First Fit misbehave, it is clear that there are dangers in lists of items sorted by increasing size. Thus, a natural idea for improving on First Fit once the online restriction is removed would be to sort the list in some other way before applying the First Fit packing rule. In the *First Fit Decreasing* (FFD) algorithm, the items are first sorted in order of non-increasing size, and then the First Fit packing rule is applied. The algorithm *Best Fit Decreasing* (BFD) is defined analogously, using the Best Fit packing rule. The improvement over First and Best Fit is dramatic.

THEOREM 2.8 [Joh73]. $R_{\text{FFD}}^{\infty} = R_{\text{BFD}}^{\infty} = 11/9 = 1.222\ldots.$

Examples of instances that provide the lower bound for this result are given in Figure 2.5, and first appeared in [GGU71]. The upper bound in [Joh73] was more precisely $\text{FFD}(L) \le (11/9) \cdot \text{OPT}(L) + 4$ for all lists L. The proof of this was much more complicated than that for Theorem 2.1, with a weighting function that depended not only on item sizes but locations in the packing, and 70 pages of case analysis. Subsequently, Baker devised a somewhat simpler proof and reduced the additive constant from 4 to 3 [Bak83]; and Yue has claimed a much simpler proof and a reduction of the additive constant to 1 [Yue91].

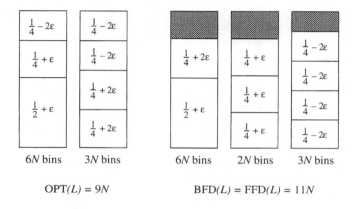

FIGURE 2.5

Worst-case examples for First and Best Fit Decreasing.

The analogous results for Best Fit Decreasing follow from the fact that for all lists L with no item smaller than $1/6$, $\text{BFD}(L) \le \text{FFD}(L)$ [Joh73] [JDU74]. This is enough, since any list in which an item of size less than $1/6$ starts a bin under BFD must have a BFD packing in which all bins except the last have level exceeding $5/6$. Hence, for such lists $\text{BFD}(L) \le (6/5) \cdot \text{OPT}(L) + 1$. BFD can produce worse packings than FFD, however, if smaller items are allowed. Lists L are shown in [Joh73] [JDU74] for which $\text{BFD}(L) = (10/9) \cdot \text{FFD}(L)$. BFD can produce *better* packings than FFD as well, so long as items as small as $1/5 - \epsilon$ are allowed, and lists L of this sort for which $\text{FFD}(L) = (11/10) \cdot \text{BFD}(L)$ are shown in the same reference.

As with the earlier algorithms, the worst-case ratios for First and Best Fit Decreasing improve as the maximum item size α declines, although now the dependence on α is more complicated than it was for the earlier algorithms. The examples in Figure 2.5 imply that $R_{\text{FFD}}^{\infty}(\alpha) = 11/9$ for $1/2 < \alpha \le 1$. In [Joh73], it was shown that

$$R_{\text{FFD}}^{\infty}(\alpha) = \begin{cases} \frac{71}{60}, & \frac{8}{29} < \alpha \le \frac{1}{2} \\ \frac{7}{6}, & \frac{1}{4} < \alpha \le \frac{8}{29} \\ \frac{23}{20}, & \frac{1}{5} < \alpha \le \frac{1}{4} \end{cases}.$$

It was also conjectured that for integers $m \geq 4$,

$$R_{\text{FFD}}^{\infty}(1/m) = F_m \equiv 1 + \frac{1}{m+2} - \frac{2}{m(m+1)(m+2)}.$$

This conjecture turns out to hold only when m is even. When m is odd, Csirik [CS93] subsequently showed that

$$R_{\text{FFD}}^{\infty}(1/m) = G_m \equiv 1 + \frac{1}{m+2} - \frac{1}{m(m+1)(m+2)}.$$

The question of what the situation is for general values of α was answered by Xu in [Xu93], which showed that when m is even, $R_{\text{FFD}}^{\infty}(\alpha)$ equals F_m throughout the interval $(1/(m+1), 1/m]$. But when m is odd, there is a d_m, $1/(m+1) < d_m < 1/m$, such that $R_{\text{FFD}}^{\infty}(\alpha)$ equals G_m only in the interval $(d_m, 1/m]$ while equaling F_m in the interval $(1/(m+1), d_m]$. (The precise value of d_m is $(m+1)^2/(m^3 + 3m^2 + m + 1)$.)

Note that both F_m and G_m represent significant improvements over the results for First Fit cited above, where $R_{\text{FF}}^{\infty}(1/m) = 1 + (1/m)$.

2.2.8   OTHER SIMPLE OFFLINE ALGORITHMS

The choice of a packing rule could make a big difference in the case of online algorithms. One might wonder whether it is so crucial in the context of lists sorted by decreasing size. In the case of the NF versus FF comparison, use of decreasing lists actually amplifies the difference in worst-case behavior. Consider Next Fit Decreasing (NFD), the algorithm that puts the items in decreasing order by size and then applies Next Fit. As proved in [BC81], we have $R_{\text{NFD}}^{\infty} = T_{\infty} = 1.69103\dots$. Note that this limit exceeds $11/9$ by more than $R_{\text{NF}}^{\infty} - R_{\text{FF}}^{\infty} = 3/10$.

More typically, however, the difference between packing rules shrinks when we consider only lists ordered by decreasing item size. For Any Fit packing rules the maximum difference shrinks from the .3 we saw in Section 2.2.3 to .0277..., as a consequence of the following.

THEOREM 2.9 [Joh73][Joh74].   For any algorithm A that sorts the items by decreasing size and then applies an Any Fit packing rule,

A. $\frac{11}{9} \leq R_A^{\infty} \leq \frac{5}{4}$, and

B. $\frac{1}{m+2} - \frac{2}{m(m+1)(m+2)} \leq R_A^{\infty}(\alpha) \leq \frac{1}{m+2}$, where $m = \lfloor 1/\alpha \rfloor$.

The maximum discrepancy so far identified between Any Fit Decreasing algorithms is that between First Fit Decreasing and Worst Fit Decreasing, each of which can for certain classes of lists produce packings that are only 8/9 as long as the packings produced by the other [Joh73]. As might be expected, given the examples in Figure 2.3, the alternative of first sorting the items in *increasing* order by size is counterproductive, and indeed, any algorithm A that applies an Any Fit algorithm after first performing such a sort must have $R_A^{\infty} \geq T_{\infty} = 1.69103\dots$.

One potential drawback of First and Best Fit Decreasing is that they require $\Omega(n \log n)$ time to pack n items, both for the initial sorting phase and for the subsequent packing phase, at least if one assumes simple comparison-based implementations [Joh73]. How well can one do if one restricts attention to algorithms with linear-time implementations?

In the previous section, we have already seen one linear-time offline algorithm that beats the online bound (although there we were viewing it as a semi-online algorithm). This is the first algorithm of [GPT90], which had $R_A^\infty = 1.5$. The same worst-case bound was attained earlier by the more fully offline Group-X Fit Grouped algorithm (GXFG) of [Joh73] [Joh74]. This algorithm applies the Group-X Fit algorithm mentioned in Section 2.2.5 after first classifying the items by size using the set X of breakpoints and then reordering them so that items in each class go together, with the classes themselves being ordered by decreasing size. In [Joh73] [Joh74] it is shown that for all $m \geq 1$ if X contains $1/m$, $1/(m+1)$, and $1/(m+2)$ then for all $\alpha \leq 1$ such that $m = \lfloor 1/\alpha \rfloor$, $R_{GXFG}^\infty(\alpha) = 1 + 1/m$. For the special case of $\alpha = 1$, this yields $R_{GXFG}^\infty = 1.5$ when $X = \{1/2, 1/3, 1/4\}$.

If one reorders items according to this last set of breakpoints and then packs using an Any Fit packing rule, one gets $R_A^\infty = 4/3$ [Joh73], but this will not be a linear-time algorithm. One can, however, obtain an asymptotic worst-case ratio of $4/3$ in linear time if one uses an algorithm due to Martel [Mar85]. This algorithm uses the breakpoint set $X = \{1/4, 1/3, /1/2, 2/3\}$ but does not easily fit into the two-part paradigm in which the list is first reordered according to a simple rule and then an online packing algorithm is applied. For details, see [Mar85].

No algorithm is currently known that does better than this $4/3$ bound and runs in linear time on a sequential computer, although if one is fortunate enough to have an EREW PRAM with $n/\log n$ processors, one can in fact construct a packing in parallel $O(\log n)$ time that obeys the same worst-case bound as FFD (i.e, $11/9$ asymptotically) [AMW89]. The algorithm performs a two-stage process, with the first stage constructing the FFD packing of all items with $s(a) > 1/6$, and the second stage adding the remaining small items to the packing efficiently. It is unlikely that the FFD packing for the full set of items can be precisely constructed in polylogarithmic parallel time, as constructing the FFD packing is a P-hard problem [AMW89].

Having seen what we can do with less than the $\Theta(n \log n)$ time required by FFD, the next question is what can we do if we are allowed more than $\Theta(n \log n)$ time? Can we devise algorithms with $R_A^\infty < 11/9$? This question was first answered in the positive by Yao [Yao80], who showed that there exists an $O(n^{10} \log n)$ time algorithm (called *Refined First Fit Decreasing* by Yao) with $R_A^\infty \leq 11/9 - 10^{-7}$.

This existence proof was later followed by more practical contenders. Garey and Johnson [GJ85] proposed an algorithm they called *Modified First Fit Decreasing* (MFFD) that improves on FFD much more substantially. It differs from First Fit Decreasing only in the way it packs the items with sizes in $(1/6, 1/3)$, but in handling these it also departs from the reordering-plus-online-packing paradigm. In packing these items, one considers the bins currently containing a single item of size exceeding $1/2$ (the "A-bins" in the terminology of [GJ85]) from right to left, i.e., in order of decreasing gaps. To treat the current A-bin, one first checks if the two smallest still-unpacked items with size in $(1/6, 1/3)$ will fit together in the bin. If so, we place the smallest such item in the bin, together with the largest remaining such item that will fit with it. If not, this special phase is over, and all the remaining unpacked items are added to the current packing according to First Fit Decreasing. This algorithm has the same $O(n \log n)$ running time as FFD, and has roughly the same constant of proportionality. Its worst-case behavior is characterized as follows:

THEOREM 2.10 [GJ85]. $R^\infty_{\text{MFFD}} = \frac{71}{60} = 1.18333\ldots.$

An alternative approach to beating FFD was subsequently proposed by Friesen and Langston [FL91]. They modify FFD as follows. First, note that the FFD packing can be constructed bin by bin using the following rule: To pack the next bin, continue adding the largest unpacked item that will fit until no such items remain. The algorithm Best Two Fit (B2F) also proceeds bin by bin, but now does some postprocessing after FFD is used to first fill the bin. If the bin contains more than one item at this point, we check to see if the smallest item in it can be replaced by the two smallest currently unpacked items with size 1/6 or greater. If so, it is replaced by the pair of such items that has the largest total size that will fit, and is added back to the list of unpacked items. This process continues until there are no unpacked items left of size greater than 1/6, at which point we revert to FFD. Friesen and Langston showed that $R^\infty_{\text{B2F}} = 5/4 = 1.25$, which isn't better than what FFD can provide, but they also showed that the worst-case instances for the two algorithms were complementary. Thus, if we denote by CFB the compound algorithm that runs *both* B2F and FFD and outputs the better of the two packings, we do much better than either algorithm separately, in only twice the overall running time. More specifically, we have the following:

THEOREM 2.11 [FL91]. $1.164\ldots = \frac{227}{195} \leq R^\infty_{\text{CFB}} \leq \frac{6}{5} = 1.2.$

MFFD and B2F try to improve the packings of individual bins by considering *pairs* of items as well as individual items in making their packing decisions. One might think that even better results would be possible (at the price of increased running time) if one was allowed to consider larger sets of items as units. With this idea in mind, Johnson [Joh73] proposed a sequence of algorithms called *Most-k Fit* (MF$_K$), $k \geq 1$. As with B2F, these algorithms construct packings bin by bin. To pack the next bin, one starts by placing the largest as-yet-unpacked item in the bin. Then, so long as the smallest unpacked item will fit in the gap, one repeatedly adds the set of k or fewer items that will fit with the least space left over. Once the gap is too small for the smallest unpacked item, we go on to the next bin. The running time for MF$_K$ is $O(n^k \log n)$ and hence not all that practical for k much greater than 2. Johnson observed that MF$_2$ did much better than FFD on its own worst-case examples, and conjectured that $\lim_{k\to\infty} R^\infty_{\text{MF}_k}$ might equal 10/9. Unfortunately, the worst case examples of [FL91] for B2F imply that in fact $R^\infty_{\text{MF}_K} \geq 5/4$ for all $k \geq 2$, so even going from MF$_1 = $ FFD to MF$_2$ causes a degradation in performance.

An even greater degradation occurs if one eliminates the requirement that the largest unpacked item start each bin. Graham [Gra72] has analyzed the algorithm that proceeds by packing each bin in turn so as to contain the set of unpacked items of largest total size no more than 1 (whether that set contains the largest item or not). Not only does this algorithm have to solve an NP-hard problem at each step, its worst-case behavior is much worse than that for FFD. For this algorithm, $R^\infty_A = \sum_{k=1}^{\infty} 1/(2^k - 1) \approx 1.60669\ldots$ [Gra72]. (The examples that imply this bound are described in [Joh73].)

As a final candidate for a simple algorithm that might have better worst-case behavior than MFFD, let us consider an algorithm proposed by Kenyon [Ken96]. This is a variant on Best Fit Decreasing that we might call *Best Fit Randomized* (BFR). Like BFD, this algorithm applies the Best Fit packing rule after first re-ordering the list, but instead of sorting the list, it simply performs a random permutation on it. Unlike our previous algorithms, Best Fit Randomized thus does not produce a unique packing for any given list, but a random distribution of packings. For such an algorithm A, a reasonable measure of its performance on a list of items L would be the *expected* number of bins it uses $E[A(L)]$. For worst-case behavior, one then looks for those lists L that maximize $E[A(L)]/\text{OPT}(L)$, and define R_A^∞ correspondingly. Using these definitions, we have the following:

THEOREM 2.12 [Ken96]. $1.08 = \frac{227}{195} \leq R_{\text{BFR}}^\infty \leq 1.5.$

It is likely that R_{BFR}^∞ is bigger than the stated lower bound. One can generate million-item lists L that, based on a sampling of permutations, appear to have $E[\text{BFR}(L)]/\text{OPT}(L) \approx 1.144$ [JKS95]. Nevertheless, 1.08 represents the largest ratio so far obtained for instances whose value of $E[\text{BFR}(L)]$ can be analytically determined. No examples have been found that empirically yield expected ratios exceeding 1.144, however, so it is possible that in fact $R_{\text{BFR}}^\infty < 1.15$.

This concludes our discussion of "practical" offline bin packing algorithms. If the only running time constraint one worries about is the theoretical one of polynomial time, one can do significantly better, as we shall see in the next section.

2.2.9   SPECIAL-CASE OPTIMALITY, APPROXIMATION SCHEMES, AND ASYMPTOTICALLY OPTIMAL ALGORITHMS

There are basically two approaches to improving on the worst-case ratios highlighted in the previous section. Before we discuss the approach that is the main subject of this section, let us briefly mention the other way to get better worst-case performance ratios. This is to restrict attention to specific types of input lists. For instance, for most of the algorithms we have considered so far, worst-case ratios approach 1 as the maximum item size approaches 0, i.e., $\lim_{\alpha \to 0} R_A^\infty(\alpha) = 1$.

A second class of instances that yield substantially improved worst-case results are those with *divisible item sizes*. As described in [CGJ87], a sequence of item sizes $s_1 > s_2 > \cdots > s_i > s_{i+1} > \cdots$ is a *divisible sequence* if for each $i > 1$, s_i exactly divides s_{i+1}. A list L of items is *weakly divisible* if the sizes of the items when sorted form a divisible sequence. It is *strongly divisible* if it is weakly divisible and the largest item size is of the form $1/k$ for some integer k, i.e., if it exactly divides the bin capacity. A natural example would be a list where all item sizes are of the form $1/2^j$ for various integers j. It is shown in [CGJ87] that, so long as L is weakly divisible, First Fit Decreasing always produces optimal packings; and if L is strongly divisible, then First Fit produces optimal packings as well. (Analogous results hold for many bin packing variants [CGJ87].)

Another class of instances that theoretically can be solved optimally in polynomial time are those in which the number of item sizes is bounded, independent of the number of items. If there are only k item sizes, and the smallest is bigger than $1/j$, then there are $O(k^{j-1})$ possible ways in which a bin can be filled by items of the various sizes, and hence at most $O(n^{k^{j-1}})$ possible packings, (assuming we treat items of the same size as indistinct). This is a polynomial-bounded number of options, and one can in polynomial time check each one to see if it is feasible, given the number of items of each size in the given list. Obviously, the actual list of potential packings can be substantially pruned, but even so, the resulting running time bound will still be far from a "low order polynomial."

From a theoretical point of view, there is a better way to solve this problem than simply trying all possible packings [BE83]. Determining the number of bins needed of each type can be formulated as an integer program (IP) with a variable for each bin type and constraints that insure that the total number of occurrences of items of size s is precisely the number of such items in the instance. This IP will have an A-matrix with k rows (constraints) and $O(k^{j-1})$ columns (variables). Because the number of variables is bounded, it can be solved in time polynomial in the number of constraints using the algorithm of [Len83] (although the time is exponential in the number of variables). Because the number of constraints is also bounded, the total time for constructing and solving the IP is thus just a constant, albeit one that is exponential in k and doubly exponential in j. To this constant must be added linear time for turning the solution of the IP into an explicit bin-by-bin description of the packing. Thus, one can find an optimal packing in linear time. (We assume, as is standard in discussions of running times for bin packing algorithms, that the item sizes are rational numbers whose numerators and denominators are integers with binary representations that will fit in a single register of our computer, and that the registers are also big enough to contain the binary representation of the number n of items in the input.)

If one is willing to settle for asymptotic optimality rather than exact optimality, one can follow Gilmore and Gomory [GG61] [GG63] and simply solve the linear programming (LP) relaxation of the above IP. Using the ellipsoid method or a polynomial-time interior point algorithm along with appropriate post-processing techniques, one can find a basic optimal solution to the LP in time that is polynomial in k and only singly-exponential in j, a major reduction in the amount of "constant time" needed for the original IP. Such a basic solution will have at most k non-zero variables. These variables can then be rounded up to induce a packing of a superset of our original list, which can be converted in linear time to a bin-by-bin description of a packing of L that has at most k more bins than the optimal number.

By giving up a bit more in the worst-case guarantee, one can extend this approach to arbitrary instances, as shown by Fernandez de la Vega and Lueker.

THEOREM 2.13 [FL81].   For any $\epsilon > 0$, there exists a linear time algorithm A_ϵ such that $R_{A_\epsilon}^\infty \leq 1 + \epsilon$.

In standard terminology, the algorithms A_ϵ constitute an *approximation scheme* [GJ79] for one-dimensional bin packing. Or more precisely, an *asymptotic* approximation scheme, since here we deal with asymptotic as opposed to absolute worst-case ratios. Here is a sketch of how algorithm A_ϵ works, adapted from [FL81]. Note that to prove the theorem, we need only show that for all lists L, $A_\epsilon(L) \leq (1+\epsilon) \cdot \text{OPT}(L) + K_\epsilon$ bins for some constant $K_\epsilon \geq 1$ depending only on ϵ. (As we shall see, $K_\epsilon = 4/\epsilon$ will suffice.)

We may assume without loss of generality that $\epsilon \leq 1$. For a suitably chosen $\epsilon' < \epsilon$, we begin by partitioning the given input list L into two parts L' and L_ϵ, where the latter part consists of all items a with $s(a) \leq \epsilon'$ and can be identified in linear time. If we can pack L' into $(1 + \epsilon) \cdot \text{OPT}(L) + K_\epsilon$ bins, we will essentially be done, as the following procedure will suffice to construct an overall packing that satisfies the same bound: Add the elements of L_ϵ to the packing one bin at a time, continuing to add items to a bin until the next one does not fit. This is a linear-time operation. If no new bins are created, our final packing will still obey the desired bound. If a new bin *is* created, all bins except the last must be filled at least to the level $1 - \epsilon'$, which implies that the total number of bins used is at most $\text{OPT}(L)/(1 - \epsilon') + 1$. This will be less than $(1 + \epsilon) \cdot \text{OPT}(L) + 1$ and hence less than $(1 + \epsilon) \cdot \text{OPT}(L) + K_\epsilon$ so long as $\epsilon' \leq \epsilon/(1 + \epsilon)$. (For future reference, note that because of this we may assume that $\epsilon' > \epsilon/2$.)

So let us concentrate on L'. Let $n' = |L'|$, $m = \lceil 4/\epsilon^2 \rceil$, and $h = \lfloor n'/m \rfloor$. Now pretend L' is sorted in nondecreasing order by size as $a_1, a_2, \ldots, a_{n'}$. Let $L_1 = (b_1, b_2, \ldots, b_{(m-1)h})$ be a list consisting of h items of size $s(a_{jh})$, $1 \leq j \leq m - 1$, sorted in nondecreasing order. Note that we must have $s(b_i) \leq s(a_{i+h})$, $1 \leq i \leq (m-1)h$, and so $\text{OPT}(L_1) \leq \text{OPT}(L')$. Moreover, the items of L_1 are restricted to $m - 1 < 4/\epsilon^2$ distinct sizes, all larger than $\epsilon/2$. Thus, by the above argument, one can for fixed ϵ construct in linear time a packing for L_1 that uses at most $\text{OPT}(L_1) + m - 1 \leq \text{OPT}(L') + 4/\epsilon$ bins. Moreover, note that for $1 \leq i \leq (m-1)h$, $s(b_i) \geq s(a_i)$, and so we can in linear time convert our packing of L_1 to a packing of the smallest $(m-1)h$ items in L' that uses just $\text{OPT}(L') + 4/\epsilon$ bins, leaving at most $2h - 1$ items unpacked. If we pack these leftover items one per bin, we obtain an overall packing of L' that uses at most $\text{OPT}(L') + 2h - 1 + 4/\epsilon$ bins. But by definition, $h \leq (n')(\epsilon^2/4)$ and $\text{OPT}(L') \geq (n')(\epsilon') \geq (n')(\epsilon/2)$. Thus, $2h - 1 \leq \epsilon \cdot \text{OPT}(L')$, and we have constructed a packing of L' using at most $(1 + \epsilon) \cdot \text{OPT}(L') + 4/\epsilon$ bins, as desired.

For fixed ϵ, the running time for this algorithm remains linear (assuming a model of computation as described above). This is because we do not actually have to sort L' in order to identify the key $m - 1$ item sizes, which can be found by use of linear-time median-finding techniques. More precisely, the running time is $C_\epsilon + Cn \log(1/\epsilon)$, where C is a fixed constant independent of ϵ and C_ϵ is a constant reflecting the cost of constructing and solving the key linear program. Assuming we use the ellipsoid method or an appropriate polynomial-time interior point algorithm for solving the LP, C_ϵ should be polynomial in $(4/\epsilon)^{(1+\epsilon)/\epsilon}$. This is probably too large to yield feasible computations even for $\epsilon = .18333$, which would yield the same asymptotic worst-case ratio as MFFD.

Since we are being theoretical, however, it is interesting to note what happens when we let ϵ grow slowly with $\text{OPT}(L) \leq n$. (We can determine close bounds on $\text{OPT}(L)$ using FFD, so such growth can easily be arranged.) Suppose for instance that we let $\epsilon \approx (\log \log \text{OPT}(L))/(\log \text{OPT}(L))$. The worst-case guarantee would then be

$$A(L) \leq (1 + \frac{\log \log (\text{OPT}(L))}{\log(\text{OPT}(L))}) \cdot \text{OPT}(L) + \frac{4 \log(\text{OPT}(L))}{\log \log(\text{OPT}(L))}$$

which would imply that $R_A^\infty = 1$. Moreover, for some fixed constant d, the running time would then be bounded by a polynomial in $d^{(\log \log n)(1 + (\log n)/(\log \log n))}$, which is a (possibly high-order) polynomial in n. Thus, we have the following corollary to the result of [FL91], first observed in [Joh82].

THEOREM 2.14.   Polynomial-time bin packing algorithms exist with $R_A^\infty = 1$.

A much better guarantee of this sort was subsequently discovered by Karmarkar and Karp [KK82], who demonstrated a polynomial-time algorithm A that guarantees $A(L) \leq OPT(L) + \log^2(OPT(L))$. They exploit many additional techniques beyond those in [FL81] to obtain this result. One key idea is to avoid actually generating the entire linear program. For this they concentrate on the dual of the LP described above (actually, the dual of an LP that is similar to that of [FL81] but is constructed using somewhat more sophisticated rounding procedures). In the dual, the variables correspond to items and the constraints correspond to the packings. Karmarkar and Karp then apply the ellipsoid method, which only generates constraints as they are needed for separation purposes. Moreover, these separating constraints turn out to be solutions to knapsack problems, as in the column-generation approach that Gilmore and Gomory proposed decades ago for solving the original problem using the simplex method [GG61] [GG63]. The knapsack problems are NP-hard, but fortunately we can settle for near-optimal as opposed to optimal solutions in this context, since we only need to solve the LP to within an additive constant. Thus, existing polynomial-time approximation algorithms for the knapsack problem can be used. Once the LP has been approximately solved, Karmarkar and Karp exploit additional ideas to eliminate unneeded constraints (bin-types) so as to get down to a near-basic solution, from which a final packing can be derived.

Unfortunately, all this cleverness comes at a price, and the best running-time bound proved in [KK82] is worse than $O(n^8)$. Better running times are possible, however, if one is willing to settle for less than asymptotic optimality. Whereas in the [FL81] scheme a guarantee of the form $A_\epsilon(L) \leq (1 + \epsilon) \cdot OPT(L) + K_\epsilon$ required time exponential in $1/\epsilon$, an analogous guarantee based on the [KK82] approach can be obtained in running time bounded by a polynomial in $1/\epsilon$ (although the dependence on n is $\Theta(n \log n)$ rather than linear, as it was in the [FL81] scheme). Thus, we have a fully polynomial (asymptotic) approximation scheme (FPAS) for bin packing. For full details see [KK82]. An alternative sketch of the results of [FL81] and [KK82] is given in Chapter 9.

From the theoretical point of view, the Karmarkar-Karp algorithm leaves little room for further improvement in the level of approximation obtainable by polynomial-time algorithms. We should point out, however, that there are to date no NP-hardness results that rule out the possibility (assuming P $\neq$ NP) of a polynomial-time heuristic A that guarantees $A(L) \leq OPT(L) + d$ for some fixed constant d.

2.2.10   OTHER WORST-CASE QUESTIONS

2.2.10.1   Absolute worst-case ratios

The results we have mentioned so far concentrate on *asymptotic* worst-case ratios R_A^∞, but the question of absolute worst-case ratios $R_A \equiv \inf\{r \geq 1 : R_A(L) \leq r$ for all lists $L\}$ is also of interest, especially when we are considering relatively short lists of items. For these, the current best results are as follows:

THEOREM 2.15   [Sim94].

   A. For $A \in \{FF, BF\}$, $R_A \leq 1.75$.

   B. For $A \in \{FFD, BFD\}$, $R_A = 1.5$.

Note that the former bound is actually quite close to the asymptotic bound of $R_{FF}^\infty = R_{BF}^\infty = 1.7$. The latter is further from the asymptotic bound of $R_{FFD}^\infty = R_{BFD}^\infty = 11/9$, but in comparing the latter conclusion to the specific results underlying the asymptotic conclusion, we see that Theorem 2.15 provides a better bound at least for $OPT(L) \leq 3$. To be specific, if it is true that $FFD(L) \leq (11/9) \cdot OPT(L) + \alpha$ for all L, then the absolute bound is stronger only for $OPT(L) \leq (18/5)\alpha$. Baker shows in [Bak83] that $\alpha = 3$ suffices, implying that the asymptotic result dominates for $OPT(L) > 10$. In [Yue91] a proof is claimed for $\alpha = 1$, which would imply that the asymptotic result dominates the absolute one for $OPT(L) > 3$. More recently, [CSB94] presents a tighter result that dominates both [Yue91] and [Sim94] when $OPT(L) \in \{3, 4, 5\}$. Using techniques that exploit linear programming lower bounds on the optimal packing, the authors prove that both $FFD(L)$ and $BFD(L)$ are no more than $(4/3) \cdot OPT(L) + 1/3$.

2.2.10.2   Bounds on anomalous behavior

One difficulty that often must be confronted in proving worst-case guarantees for bin packing algorithms is the fact that certain natural monotonicity properties can be violated by the better heuristics. Let us say that a list L_2 is *dominated* by a list L_1 if L_2 can be obtained from L_1 by deleting items and/or reducing their size. A bin packing algorithm A is *monotone* if for any two lists L_1 and L_2 where L_1 dominates L_2, $A(L_2) \leq A(L_1)$ [Mur88]. Such a property clearly might be helpful in proving results about algorithm A. Indeed, in Section 2.3 we shall introduce a monotone algorithm *Matching Best Fit* as a key intermediary in proving results about the average-case behavior of the non-monotone Best Fit algorithm. Unfortunately, few of the algorithms we have discussed so far are monotone. In a comprehensive study, Murgolo [Mur88] was able to identify only two: Next Fit and Next-2 Fit. Monotonicity does not hold even for Next-3 Fit or for ABF_2 (the algorithm that replaces the First Fit packing rule in Next-2 Fit by the Best Fit rule). Nor does it hold for such simple algorithms as the Harmonic algorithms H_K, $K \geq 3$ (although it holds trivially for H_1 and H_2).

Given that most of the algorithms worth studying are non-monotonic, the question then arises, just how non-monotonic can they be? For the four most famous bin packing heuristics, FF, BF, FFD, and BFD, the non-monotonicity can be arbitrarily large; that is it can grow with n. This was implicit in examples discovered by Halász [Hal74], but has been studied in most detail by Murgolo, who constructed lists implying the following result. If A is a bin packing algorithm, define the *asymptotic worst-case nonmonotonicity* of A, denoted by N_A^∞ to be the maximum value ϕ such that for all $N > 0$ there exists a pair of lists (L_1, L_2) with $OPT(L_1) \geq N$, L_1 dominating L_2, and $A(L_2)/A(L_1) - 1 \geq \phi$. In other words, the nonmonotonicity is the asymptotic fraction by which the number of bins may increase when items are shrunk or deleted.

THEOREM 2.16 [Mur85][Mur88].   With respect to asymptotic worst-case non-monotonicity,

A. Both N_{WF}^∞ and N_{WFD}^∞ are at least $1/15$,

B. Both N_{FF}^∞ and N_{BF}^∞ are at least $1/42$, and

C. Both N_{FFD}^∞ and N_{BFD}^∞ are at least $1/75$.

In general, no upper bounds on nonmonotonicity besides the trivial that $N_A^\infty \leq R_A^\infty - 1$ are currently known. For more details on nonmonotonicity, see [Mur85] [Mur88].

AVERAGE-CASE ANALYSIS

2.3

One drawback of relying on worst-case analysis is that in many applications the worst case never seems to occur. Indeed, quite intricate and unlikely lists of items were needed to prove many of the lower bounds in the previous section. Thus, there is a strong need for results that tell us more about typical behavior. Proving results about the average-case behavior of heuristics under a variety of item-size distributions is one step in this direction. Objections can be lodged against any single choice of distribution, since real-world applications rarely generate instances that obey the sorts of probability distributions for which tight analysis is currently possible. Objections might also be made to the standard assumption that each item size is chosen independently of all the rest. Nevertheless, if results are obtained for a variety of such distributions, a broader picture may begin to emerge, and at the very least the worst-case results can be put into perspective. In the case of the classical one-dimensional bin packing problem, just such a broad-based average-case approach has begun to emerge, and we survey it in this section. In spite of the difficulty of probabilistic analysis, both the general theory and average-case results for specific algorithms have grown impressively in the past decade.

Let us begin with some terminology. Although a variety of item-size distributions have been studied, the common assumption is that the items in a list have independent, identically distributed sizes. Let F denote the item-size distribution, and denote its mean and variance by μ and σ^2. For purposes of asymptotic analysis, we are typically concerned with a list L_n of n randomly generated items. For simplicity, our notation does not specify what distribution F is under consideration, but the identity of F will always be made clear.

In this context, many of our standard functions of lists become random variables: $s(L_n)$ (the sum of the item sizes), $\text{OPT}(L_n)$, $A(L_n)$ (where A is a bin packing algorithm), and $R_A(L_n) \equiv A(L_n)/\text{OPT}(L_n)$. We are also interested in the derived random variable $W_A(L_n) \equiv A(L_n) - s(L_n)$, which is the amount of wasted space in the bins of the packing of L_n by algorithm A. It is often easier to prove average-case results about $W_A(L_n)$ than about $R_A(L_n)$ directly. Fortunately, the former typically imply the latter, since for most of the distributions that have been studied $\lim_{n\to\infty} E[\text{OPT}(L_n)/s(L_n)] = 1$. Moreover, even for those distributions F and algorithms A where $\lim_{n\to\infty} E[A(L_n)/s(L_n)]$ also equals 1, we typically have $E[W_{\text{OPT}}(L_n)] = o(E[W_A(L_n)])$, so that $E[W_A(L_n)] = \Theta(E[A(L_n) - \text{OPT}(L_n)])$.

In what follows, we use average-case notation that mirrors the worst-case notation of Section 2.2. For a given item-size distribution F and algorithm A, define

$$\bar{R}_A^n(F) \equiv E[R_A(L_n)] = E\left[\frac{A(L_n)}{\text{OPT}(L_n)}\right]$$

and

$$\bar{W}_A^n(F) \equiv E\left[A(L_n) - s(L_n)\right]$$

for lists L_n generated according to F. We then can define the *asymptotic expected ratio* for A under F to be

$$\bar{R}_A^\infty(F) \equiv \lim_{n \to \infty} \bar{R}_A^n(F).$$

(No asymptotic notation is needed for expected wasted space, as this is unbounded for most algorithms and distributions.)

Although there have been some general average-case results that hold for arbitrary distributions F, most of the specific expected values that have been computed concern *continuous uniform* or *discrete uniform* distributions. A distribution of the former type is denoted by $U[a, b]$, where $0 \leq a < b \leq 1$, and item-sizes are chosen uniformly from the (continuous) interval $[a, b]$. Typically $a = 0$, although we shall present some results for $a > 0$ in Section 2.3.5. Distributions of the second type are denoted by $U\{j, k\}$, $1 \leq j \leq k$, where item sizes are chosen uniformly from the finite set $\{1/k, 2/k, \ldots, j/k\}$. Note that as m approaches ∞, the discrete distributions $U\{jm, km\}$ become more and more like the continuous distribution $U[0, j/k]$. As we shall see, however, this does not prevent the two types of distribution from yielding results that are mathematically very different.

Our discussion of the average case parallels our earlier discussion of worst-case results, and we organize the presentation by algorithm rather than by distribution. In Section 2.3.1 we survey average-case results for bounded-space online algorithms. Section 2.3.2 covers results for arbitrary online algorithms, with special emphasis on the much-studied First and Best Fit algorithms. Section 2.3.3 describes results for the offline case. These three sections all concentrate on questions about $\bar{R}_A^\infty(F)$ and $\bar{W}_A^n(F)$. Section 2.3.4 considers two other average-case questions that have received attention: (1) what is the expected optimal number of bins under various distributions, and (2) what can we say about the probability distribution of $A(L_n)$ as a function of n for various algorithms and distributions. The results relating to question (1) help back up the claims made above about the relationship between $E[s(L_n)]$ and $E[\text{OPT}(L_n)]$. The results relating to question (2) allow us to reach conclusions about $\bar{R}_A^\infty(F)$, which measures expected ratios, from results about ratios of expectations. This is something we shall do regularly in Sections 2.3.1 through 2.3.3, and only justify when we get to Section 2.3.4.2. We shall not provide much detail about proof techniques beyond highlighting the different types of approaches taken. Readers interested in more details about these approaches are referred to the corresponding references and to the monograph by Coffman and Lueker [CL91].

2.3.1 BOUNDED-SPACE ONLINE ALGORITHMS

The first probabilistic analysis of bin packing algorithms appears to be that of Shapiro [Sha77], who proposed an approximate analysis of Next Fit based on the exponential distribution. The first precise average-case asymptotics were those of Coffman, So, Hofri, and Yao [CSH80], again for Next Fit. They proved that, if $F = U[0, 1]$, then the distribution of the level of the highest indexed closed bin converges geometrically fast to the stationary distribution $V(x) = x^3, 0 \le x \le 1$ with mean $3/4$. From this we can conclude the following:

THEOREM 2.17 [CSH80]. $\bar{R}^\infty_{\mathrm{NF}}(U[0, 1]) = \frac{4}{3}$.

Karmarkar [Kar82a] subsequently extended the NF results to cover the distributions $U[0, b]$. His analysis came down to the solution of linear systems of differential equations. Closed-form results were obtained for $1/2 \le a \le 1$ and showed that $E[\mathrm{NF}(L_n)] \sim \rho n$ as $n \to \infty$, where

$$\rho = \frac{1}{12b^3}(15b^3 - 9b^2 + 3b - 1) + \sqrt{2}\left(\frac{1-b}{2b}\right)^2 \tanh\left(\frac{1-b}{\sqrt{2}b}\right),$$

which gave numbers confirming the experimental results of Ong, Magazine, and Wee [OMW84]. A numerical calculation using this expression verified that, asymptotically, the packing efficiency $\bar{R}^\infty_{\mathrm{NF}}(U[0, b])$ is not monotone in b as one might expect; it reaches a maximum at $b \approx 0.841$.

The average-case performance of the Harmonic algorithms H_K is relatively easy to obtain for general distributions F. Lee and Lee [LL87] showed that, for all $K \ge 3$, $\bar{R}^\infty_{H_K}(U[0, 1]) < 1.306$, and hence is significantly better than the asymptotic expected ratio of $4/3$ for Next Fit, even for relatively small K. As K goes to ∞ we have

THEOREM 2.18 [LL87][CL91]. $\displaystyle\lim_{K \to \infty} \bar{R}^\infty_{H_K}(U[0, 1]) = \pi^2/3 - 2 \approx 1.2899$.

Note, however, that even the limiting difference of $4/3 - 1.2899$ is far smaller than the 2.0 versus 1.691 ... worst-case gap between the two algorithms. For a pictorial comparison of the results for Next Fit and the Harmonic algorithms, see Figure 2.6, which originally appeared in [CJ91] and covers results for $F = U[0, b], 0 < b \le 1$. The curve labeled H_∞ in the figure represents $\lim_{K \to \infty} \bar{R}^\infty_{H_K}(U[0, b])$. Note that the expected values for H_∞ are not uniformly better than those for Next Fit. Indeed, they oscillate as a function of b. The local minima occur whenever b is of the form $1/m$ for m an integer. Values for Next Fit when $b < 1/2$ are experimentally determined, as are the curves included for some of the other algorithms of Section 2.2.6.

The figure also includes the curve for an interesting modification of Next Fit devised and analyzed by Ramanan [Ram89], called *Smart Next Fit* (SNF). This algorithm works as follows: The next item p to be packed is put by SNF into the current bin B if it fits, as in NF. But if p does not fit in B, then SNF puts p into a new bin B' and retains as the new current bin whichever of B and B' has the most space remaining. (Note that this algorithm lies somewhere between Next Fit and the 2-Bounded Best Fit algorithm of Section 2.2.6.) Ramanan applied Karmarkar's techniques and showed that improvements are possible under SNF when $F = U[0, b]$ with $1/2 < b \le 1$. For $b = 1$, $\bar{R}^\infty_{\mathrm{SNF}}(U[0, b])$ is roughly 1.227 versus 1.333 for Next Fit, although the difference declines to 0 as $b \to 1/2$.

The curves in the figure for versions of Next-K Fit (NF_K) and K-Bounded Best Fit (BBF_K) raise interesting issues. Presumably as K goes to ∞ these curves should converge to those for First and Best Fit respectively, and one wonders just what those

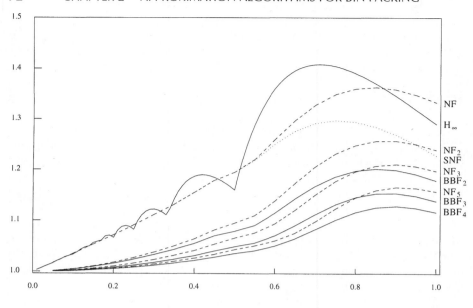

FIGURE 2.6

$\bar{R}_A^\infty(U[0, b])$ *as a function of b.*

limiting curves will look like, given the rapid improvement (and flattening) of the curves depicted here. We will return to this question in the next section.

In the meantime we should note that, just as there are lower bounds on how well bounded-space online algorithms can perform in the worst-case, there are also nontrivial bounds on what they can do on average. In particular, no bounded-space online algorithm A can have $\bar{R}_A^\infty(U[0, 1]) = 1$. Coffman and Shor [CS93] proved that such algorithms inevitably waste a constant fraction of the allocated space on average. More specifically, they show the following:

THEOREM 2.19 [CS93].   If A is an online algorithm limited to K active bins, then

$$\bar{W}_A^n(U[0, 1]) \geq \frac{n}{16(K + 1)}.$$

Analogous results (with different constants of proportionality) also hold for the distributions $U[0, b]$, $0 < b < 1$. The lower bound of Theorem 2.19 can probably be improved substantially by tighter analysis, and it remains to be seen whether a tight lower bound can be obtained.

As to other sorts of distributions, results for discrete uniform distributions $U\{j, k\}$ should roughly track those for the corresponding continuous uniform distributions. There has been work on the average-case behavior of Next Fit under further sorts of distributions, for example the abovementioned study by Shapiro [Sha77] along with that of Halfin [Hal89], which were based on the exponential distribution, but these dealt with different questions and did not yield results that are directly comparable to the ones reported here.

2.3.2 ARBITRARY ONLINE ALGORITHMS

2.3.2.1 Results for $U[0, 1]$

As pointed out in Section 2.2.5, relaxing the bounded-space requirement allows one to design algorithms with substantially better worst-case behavior than any bounded-space online algorithm. One of the improved algorithms covered in that section, the Modified Harmonic algorithm MH_{38} of Ramanan, Brown, Lee, and Lee [RBL89], has been analyzed from an average-case point of view. In [RT89f], Ramanan and Tsuga show that this algorithm improves on the basic Harmonic algorithms on average as well as in the worst case, at least when $F = U[0, 1]$. In particular, they show that $\bar{R}^{\infty}_{MH_{38}}(U[0, 1])$ lies between 1.27684 and 1.27688. This is significantly less than the $1.333 \ldots$ ratio for Next Fit and the $1.2899 \ldots$ limiting value for the Harmonic algorithms, although not as good as the ratio of 1.227 for Smart Next Fit. However, Ramanan and Tsuga then describe a sequence of variants on the Modified Harmonic algorithms (obtained simply by altering certain parameters but not the boundaries of the item-size classes) which have $\bar{R}^{\infty}_{MH_K}(U[0, 1]) < 1.2$ as soon as $K \geq 5$, and $\lim_{K \to \infty} \bar{R}^{\infty}_{MH_K}(U[0, 1]) \approx 1.189$.

This last-mentioned sequence of algorithms obtains its improved average-case performance at the cost of degraded worst-case performance with respect to MH_{38}. At a further cost in worst-case behavior, one can improve average-case performance still more. Indeed, as first observed by Hoffman [Hof82], there exist $\Theta(n \log n)$ time online algorithms whose expected behavior when $F = U[0, 1]$ is in a sense asymptotically optimal. We illustrate Hoffman's approach using a variant studied by Coffman and Lueker [CL91, pp. 148–150]. The approach actually involves yet another indexed sequence of algorithms, which we shall call the *Online Match* algorithms (OM_K for $K \geq 3$) and which are closely related to the Interval First Fit algorithms of Csirik and Galambos [CG86]. Call p and p' *companions* for algorithm OM_K if $1 - 1/K \leq s(p) + s(p') \leq 1$. Algorithm OM_K maintains two initially empty packings; one is *partial match* packing, and the other is a NF packing that contains only items $\leq 1/2$. The algorithm packs the next item p according to the following two-part rule: If $s(p) \geq 1/2$, pack p into an empty bin and add the bin to the partial match packing. If $s(p) < 1/2$ and there exists a bin B in the partial match packing that contains only a companion of p, pack p in B along with its companion. If $s(p) < 1/2$ and no such bin exists, pack p into the NF packing. It is easily verified that the asymptotic worst-case ratio $R^{\infty}_{OM_K} = 2$. The average case result is as follows:

THEOREM 2.20 [CL91]. For some universal constant c,

$$\bar{R}^{\infty}_{OM_K}(U[0, 1]) = 1 + c\sqrt{\frac{K}{n}} + O\left(\frac{1}{K}\right).$$

Thus, $\lim_{K \to \infty} \bar{R}^{\infty}_{OM_K}(U[0, 1]) = 1$, although of course for each particular value of K we still have $\bar{R}^{\infty}_{OM_K}(U[0, 1]) > 1$. Note that we could presumably get a single algorithm with $\bar{R}^{\infty}_A(U[0, 1]) = 1$ by letting K grow with N, say by setting $K = \log n$. Strictly speaking, however, this would be a violation of the online restriction, since it would require us to know n in advance. Let us call an algorithm that is online, (except for the fact that it knows n in advance) a *closed* online algorithm. Thus, it appears that there exist closed online algorithms A with $\bar{R}^{\infty}_A(U[0, 1]) = 1$.

The question thus becomes whether there exist *open* online algorithms, i.e., ones that do not know n in advance, with this same optimality property. The answer is yes. One could devise such an algorithm from the Online Match approach above by adaptively increasing K as more items arrive, but fortunately something much simpler will suffice. In 1984, Bentley, Johnson, Leighton, McGeoch, and McGeoch [BJL84] proved the following surprising result:

THEOREM 2.21 [BJL84]. $\bar{R}_{FF}^{\infty}(U[0, 1]) = 1$.

This result was viewed as surprising because of earlier conjectures based on simulation results. Johnson in [Joh73] had conjectured based on samples lists with $n = 200$ that $\bar{R}_{FF}^{\infty}(U[0, 1]) \approx 1.07$. Ong, Magazine, and Wee [OMW84], (based on sample lists with n ranging from 40 to 1000) updated this conjecture to $\bar{R}_{FF}^{\infty}(U[0, 1]) \approx 1.056$; still quite far from 1. It turned out, however, that much larger values of n were needed to get a true picture of asymptotic behavior. For instance, based on much more extensive experiments [BJL83] we now know that $\bar{R}_{FF}^{n}(U[0, 1])$ still exceeds 1.01 for n as large as 250,000. The question thus becomes how fast does $\bar{R}_{FF}^{n}(U[0, 1])$ approach 1.

This question can be addressed by turning our attention to expected waste, in particular the function $\bar{W}_{FF}^{n}(U[0, 1])$. It was shown by a complicated argument in [BJL84] that this function was $O(n^{0.8})$. Much simpler arguments have since been derived and we now know the precise order of the function.

THEOREM 2.22 [Sho86][CJS95]. $\bar{W}_{FF}^{n}(U[0, 1]) = \Theta(n^{2/3})$.

The algorithm Best Fit turns out to be even better:

THEOREM 2.23 [Sho86][LS89]. $\bar{W}_{BF}^{n}(U[0, 1]) = \Theta(\sqrt{n} \log^{3/4} n)$.

The proofs of these results embody fascinating connections to the theory of stochastic planar matching, a theory that has had a surprising variety of applications. The foundation for the modern theory of stochastic planar matching is the work of Ajtai, Komlós, and Tusnády [AKT84]. Chapter 3 in [CL91] gives a broad coverage of the area, but the definitive treatment can be found in the more recent work of Talagrand [Tal94].

There are many variants on the original planar matching problem of [AKT84], several of which come up in bin packing contexts. As a primary example, let us consider the *up-right matching* problem. An instance of this problem is a set of n points chosen independently and uniformly at random in the unit square. The points are colored red and blue, with each point having equal probability of receiving either color, and the choices for all points being independent. We ask for a maximum matching of blue points to red points such that in each matched pair, the blue point is above and to the right of the red point, i.e., in both coordinates, the blue point is at least as far from the origin as the red point. This problem originated in an analysis of a two-dimensional bin packing problem by Karp, Luby, and Marchetti-Spaccamela [KLM84b], who were the first to apply stochastic planar matching problems to bin packing.

The connection is to Best Fit and comes about as follows. Consider a random list L_n generated according to $F = U[0, 1]$. An item a_i is identified with a blue point at location

$(s(a_i), i/n)$ if $s(a_i) \leq 1/2$ and with a red point at location $(1 - s(a_i), i/n)$ if $s(a_i) > 1/2$. An edge in an up-right matching thus corresponds to a pair of items such that the first-arriving has size exceeding $1/2$ and the total size of the two items does not exceed 1, i.e., the pair can fit in a bin together. Thus, the following simplified variant on Best Fit, called *Matching Best Fit* (MBF), will construct an up-right matching. Proceed as in Best Fit, except that bins are closed as soon as they receive an item a with $s(a) \leq 1/2$. It is easy to see that the number of unmatched points that result will be roughly proportional to the amount of wasted space in the MBF packing of L_n. Shor proves three additional key facts about Matching Best Fit in [Sho86]:

- MBF constructs an *optimal* up-right matching.
- MBF$(L) \geq$ BF(L) for all lists L.
- $\bar{W}_{BF}^n(U[0, 1]) = \Omega(\bar{W}_{MBF}^n(U[0, 1]))$ so long as the latter is $\Omega(\sqrt{n \log n})$.

Thus, assuming that $\bar{W}_{MBF}^n(U[0, 1])$ grows quickly enough, we will have $\bar{W}_{BF}^n(U[0, 1]) = \Theta(\bar{W}_{MBF}^n(U[0, 1])) = \Theta(E[U_n])$, where U_n is defined to be the number of unmatched points in an optimal up-right matching on $2n$ random points. The initial results in [KLM84b] gave an $\Omega(\sqrt{n \log n})$ lower bound and a $O(\sqrt{n} \log n)$ upper bound on $E[U_n]$. A lower bound of $\Omega(\sqrt{n} \log^{3/4} n)$ was proved by Shor in [Sho86] and the tight upper bound $E[U_n] = O(\sqrt{n} \log^{3/4} n)$ was proved by Leighton and Shor in [LS89], thus completing the proof of Theorem 2.23. Rhee and Talagrand [RT88a] independently proved the same bounds on $E[U_n]$. Simpler proofs were discovered later by Coffman and Shor [CS91], and then, in a more general setting, by Talagrand [Tal94].

The proof of Theorem 2.22 for First Fit is derived in a similar fashion, based on an appropriately defined variant on up-right matching and using an analogously defined *Matching First Fit* algorithm as an intermediary. The $\Omega(n^{2/3})$ lower bound for $\bar{W}_{FF}^n(U[0, 1]$ was proved by Shor in [Sho86]; Shor's original $O(n^{2/3} \log n)$ upper bound was subsequently tightened to $O(n^{2/3})$ by Coffman, Johnson, Shor, and Weber in [CJS95].

Stochastic planar matching results can also be used to obtain lower bounds on the best possible average case performance for an online algorithm when $F = U[0, 1]$. Here the relevant variant is the *rightward matching* problem. Instances are as in up-right matching, but now a point P can be matched either to a point of the other color, in which case the blue point must be to the right of the red point, or to a point directly beneath P on the lower boundary of the square. The objective is a matching with a minimum total vertical distance between matched points, i.e., a matching such that the sum of the vertical components of straight-line segments connecting matched points is minimized. Let us call this quantity the *vertical discrepancy* of the matching. Shor showed in [Sho86] that any open online algorithm operating a list L_n generated according to $F = U[0, 1]$ will generate a rightward matching whose vertical discrepancy roughly equals the average wasted space during the course of the packing. Thus, if we let V_n denote the vertical discrepancy of an optimal rightward matching for a random point set, we have $\bar{W}_A^n(U[0, 1]) = \Omega(E[V_n])$ for all open online algorithms A. In [Sho86] he proved that $E[V_n] = \Omega(\sqrt{n \log n})$. In [Sho91] he exhibited an $O(n \log n)$-time open online algorithm that achieved this bound on wasted space. Thus, we have the following:

THEOREM 2.24 [Sho86][Sho91].   For any open online algorithm A,

$$\bar{W}_A^n(U[0, 1]) = \Omega(\sqrt{n}\log n)$$

and this is the best possible such lower bound.

The above bound does not hold for closed online algorithms (ones that know n in advance). For these the only lower bound is the trivial one of $\bar{W}_A^n(U[0, 1]) = \Omega(\sqrt{n})$ (trivial because $\bar{W}_{OPT}^n(U[0, 1]) = \Omega(\sqrt{n})$, as is easily seen). Moreover, as is shown in [Sho86], this bound is achieved by the simple algorithm that begins by packing the first $\lfloor n/2 \rfloor$ items one per bin, and then packs the remaining items using Best Fit. Note however, that there are drawbacks to algorithms that optimize their behavior for a particular distribution like $U[0, 1]$. Both this algorithm and the one in Theorem 2.24 have unbounded worst-case behavior and indeed can have arbitrarily bad average-case behavior under natural distributions. For example, each has $\lim_{b\to 0} \bar{R}_A^\infty(U[0, b]) = \infty$.

2.3.2.2   Results for $U[0, b]$, $0 < b < 1$

Although the distribution $F = U[0, 1]$ gives rise to interesting behavior and appealing mathematical connections, the very fact that simple matching algorithms suffice to yield good average-case behavior makes this distribution somewhat suspect. In real-world applications, one often has to put more than two items in a bin to get good packings. As a first step to obtaining a more realistic picture of real-world behavior, let us see what has been learned about average-case behavior under the distributions $F = [0, b], 0 < b < 1$.

For such distributions $\bar{W}_{OPT}^n(F) = O(1)$, as we shall see in the next section, but a lower bound of $\Omega(n^{1/2})$ on $\bar{W}_A^n(F)$ holds for all open online algorithms A [CCG91]. No algorithm achieving this bound has yet been found, although one can come close. Rhee and Talagrand [RT93b, RT93c] have shown that, with only a slight weakening, results similar to those for Best Fit can be derived for any distribution F. They exhibit an online algorithm in [RT93c] that packs L_n into at most $OPT(L_n) + K\sqrt{n}\log^{3/4} n$ bins with a probability at least $1 - n^{-\alpha\sqrt{\log n}}$, where K and α are universal constants, and where, as one might suspect, the $\sqrt{n}\log^{3/4} n$ term comes from the algorithm's connection with Best Fit. The algorithm works for all F, dynamically changing its packing strategy as it "learns" more about F from items already packed. For the case of $F = U[0, b], b < 1$, the above bound implies that $\bar{W}_A^n(F) = \Theta(\sqrt{n}\log^{3/4} n)$. Unfortunately, even if one is able to specialize the algorithm in advance to the distribution in question, it is still likely to be complex; it will only come into its own for huge values of n, and it will behave poorly in a worst-case sense.

More natural and robust alternatives have yet to be found. First and Best Fit in particular do not appear to be good candidates. Based on extensive simulations [BJL83] [Joh96], it appears that for all b, $0 < b < 1$ both Best and First Fit have linear expected waste, i.e., $\bar{W}_A^n(U[0, b]) = \Theta(n)$ and hence, $\bar{R}_A^\infty(U[0, b]) > 1$. See Figure 2.7, which illustrates the case for First Fit and $.70 \le b \le 1$. The figure presents experimentally-derived curves for $\bar{R}_{FF}^\infty(U[0, b])$ with b increasing in increments of $.01$ from $.70$ to 1.00, and with n increasing by factors of 2 from $16,000$ to $8,192,000$. Note that the curves are consistent with the above conclusion about $\bar{R}_{FF}^n(U[0, b])$, but also suggest (as one would hope given Theorem 2.21) that $\lim_{b\to 1} \bar{R}_{FF}^\infty(U[0, b]) = 1$. As was the case for Next Fit,

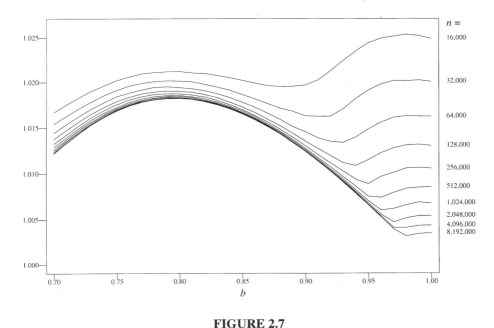

FIGURE 2.7

$\bar{R}^n_{FF}(U[0,b])$ *as a function of b for increasing values of n.*

the value of $\bar{R}^\infty_{FF}(U[0,b])$ takes on its maximum for b roughly equal to .81, although now the maximum value is quite small, i.e, less than 1.02. In general the values are so small that for small n they are overwhelmed by the $\Theta(n^{2/3})$ expected waste term, with $\bar{R}^n_{FF}(U[0,b])$ actually increasing as $b \to 1$.

The cases for Best Fit and for $0 < b < .70$ are similar, except that $\bar{R}^\infty_{BF}(U[0,b])$ appears always to be a bit less than $\bar{R}^\infty_{FF}(U[0,b])$ for any fixed $b < 1$, and both approach 1 in the limit as b approaches 0. Unfortunately, although the evidence of the experiments reported in Figure 2.7 seems incontrovertible, no one so far has been able to rigorously prove that either $\bar{R}^\infty_{FF}(U[0,b])$ or $\bar{R}^\infty_{BF}(U[0,b])$ exceeds 1 for any b, $0 < b < 1$. To find proofs of such behavior we must turn to the analogous discrete uniform distributions $U\{j,k\}$ defined at the beginning of Section 2.3. As was the case for the bounded-space online algorithms of Section 2.3.1, the behavior of First and Best Fit on such distributions roughly mimics that for the corresponding continuous cases, although now there are a few interesting differences.

2.3.2.3   Results for discrete distributions

The major difference between results for discrete and continuous uniform distributions is that for certain combinations of j and k, we have $\bar{W}^n_{BF}(U\{j,k\}) = O(1)$. That is, the expected waste is bounded independent of n, something that is impossible in the continuous uniform case. Before discussing such cases, however, let us first see what happens for the discrete uniform analogues of the continuous uniform distribution $U[0,1]$.

THEOREM 2.25 [CCG91][CJS95].   For $k > 1$,

   A. $\bar{W}^n_{\mathrm{FF}}(U\{k,k\}) = \Theta(\sqrt{nk})$.

   B. $\bar{W}^n_{\mathrm{BF}}(U\{k,k\}) = O(\sqrt{n}\log k)$.

   C. For any open online algorithm A, $\bar{W}^n_A(U\{k,k\}) = \Omega(\sqrt{n\log k})$.

Note that this means that for fixed k, both Best and First Fit have $\Theta(\sqrt{n})$ expected waste, something that is impossible for any open online algorithm under $U[0,1]$. However, if one allows k to grow with n, say as $n^{1/3}$, one obtains the bounds reported above for the $U[0,1]$ case, except for a small discrepancy in case (B). Indeed, the upper bound on $\bar{W}^n_{\mathrm{FF}}(U[0,1])$ in Theorem 2.22 was obtained from the proof of claim (A) in the above theorem by taking $k = \lceil n^{1/3} \rceil$. We conjecture that the bound in (B) can be replaced by $\Theta(\sqrt{n}\log^{3/4} k)$, thus eliminating the one discrepancy. We also conjecture that there exists an open online algorithm meeting the lower bound of (C), operating along much the same principles as the algorithm in the corresponding continuous result.

    For $j = k - 1$, the results of Theorem 2.25 continue to hold, since the only significant difference between $U\{k,k\}$ and $U\{k-1,k\}$ is the presence of items of size $k/k = 1$. Such an item fills a single bin with no waste and no impact on the remainder of the packing. Reducing j just one step further, however, gives rise to bounded expected waste results of the type mentioned above.

THEOREM 2.26 [CJS93][KRS96].   For all $k > 2$, $\bar{W}^n_{\mathrm{BF}}(U\{k-2,k\}) = O(1)$.

This was proved for $k \leq 10$ by Coffman, Johnson, Shor, and Weber in [CJS93]. They modeled the packing process as a multi-dimensional Markov chain and used linear programming to derive for each individual distribution a potential function that could be used to show that the Markov chain was stable. Kenyon, Rabani, and Sinclair generalized this to arbitrary k in [KRS96] by deriving a simple potential function that works for all k (but needs significantly more sophisticated arguments to show that it works).

    The Best Fit algorithm is well suited for a Markov chain approach, since the ordering of the bins in the packing is irrelevant as far as wasted space is concerned. Thus, a packing can be represented by the numbers N_i of bins with gaps of size i/k, $0 \leq i < k$. This not only facilitates Markov chain proofs, but also allows for much faster simulations of the algorithm. No similar advantage holds for First Fit, which helps explain why much less is known about First Fit. Moreover, limited experiments suggest that the analog of Theorem 2.26 does not hold for First Fit, and indeed that $\bar{W}^n_{\mathrm{FF}}(U\{k-2,k\})$ may still be $\Omega(n^{1/2})$ for large enough fixed k.

    When we consider distributions $U\{j,k\}$ with $j \leq k - 3$, behavior can become much worse, even for Best Fit, and begins to mimic that for the continuous case, where $\bar{W}^n_{\mathrm{BF}}(U[0,b])$ is apparently linear for all $b \in (0,1)$. We conjecture that for any such b there exists an integer K_b such that $\bar{W}^n_{\mathrm{BF}}(U\{j,k\})$ is linear whenever $k > K_b$ and $|b - j/k| < \min\{(b/2, (1-b)/2\}$. Simulations reported in [CJS93] support this conjecture, with the conclusions summarized in Table 2.3. Most of the empirical conclusions in the table have now been rigorously proved, the exceptions being those entries marked by a "*". The results along the diagonal follow from Theorem 2.26, while the remaining bounded-waste results can be proved using individually-derived potential functions. (The linear-programming-based technique for generating these potential

j	k	5	6	7	8	9	10	11	12	13	14
3		B	B	B	B	B	B	B	B	B	B
4			B	B	B	B	B	B	B	B	B
5				B	B	B	B	B	B	B	B
6					B	B	B	B	B	B	B
7						B	B	B	B	B	B
8							B	L	B*	B*	B
9								B	L	L*	B*
10									B	L*	L*
11										B	L*
12											B

Table 2.3: Simulation results for $\bar{W}_{\mathrm{BF}}^{n}(U\{j,k\})$ when $j < k - 1$.

B = Bounded Waste; L = Linear Waste; * = Unproved

functions seems to run out of gas once $k \geq 15$ [CJS93].) The proofs that $\bar{W}_{\mathrm{BF}}^{n}(U\{8, 11\})$ and $\bar{W}_{\mathrm{BF}}^{n}(U\{9, 12\})$ are both linear rely on much more complicated Markov chain arguments that involve lengthy computer-aided numerical computations. To date no general approach has been found to prove such linear-waste conjectures.

To complete the picture for discrete uniform distributions, we note that for sufficiently small values of j, one can get bounded-waste results much more easily, and even extend them to First Fit. For instance, it is easy to see that under both First and Best Fit, the expected waste is bounded for all $U\{j, k\}$ with $j \in \{1, 2\}$. More generally, we have the following:

THEOREM 2.27 [CCG91].

A. $\bar{W}_{\mathrm{BF}}^{n}(U\{j, k\}) = O(1)$ whenever $k \geq j(j+3)/2$.

B. $\bar{W}_{\mathrm{FF}}^{n}(U\{j, k\}) = O(1)$ whenever $k \geq j^2$.

This completes our discussion of what is known about the performance of standard online algorithms like First and Best Fit under the discrete uniform distributions. The normal question to ask next is what is the *best* performance one can hope for from an online algorithm on such distributions. Given the lower bounds we saw in the continuous case, the answer is surprising.

THEOREM 2.28 [CCG91]. For any distribution $F = U\{j, k\}$ with $1 \leq j < k - 1$, there exists an open online algorithm A_F such that $\bar{W}_{A_F}^{n}(F) = O(1)$.

This theorem is an application of an earlier result of Courcoubetis and Weber [CW86a] [CW86b] which applies to all discrete distributions, and provides an explicit test by which the expected waste under any such distribution can be determined up to a constant factor. In general, performing the test is an NP-hard problem, but it can be done efficiently in several important special cases (such as that of the distributions $U\{j, k\}$). In these situations, the Courcoubetis-Weber result can yield much tighter bounds than does the general result of Rhee and Talagrand [RT93b] [RT93c] mentioned in Section 2.3.2.2 that holds for all distributions, both continuous and discrete. Moreover, most real-world bin packing applications involve discrete rather than continuous distributions. Here is a sketch of what is involved in the Courcoubetis-Weber test.

A *discrete distribution* $F = (s_F, P_F)$ is specified by a finite set of item sizes $s_F = \{s_F(1), \ldots, s_F(j)\}, 0 < s_F(i) \leq 1$ for $1 \leq i \leq j$, together with a list of probabilities $P_F = (P_F(1), \ldots, P_F(j))$ where $\sum_{i=1}^{j} P_F(i) = 1$. Let us call an integer vector $(c_1, \ldots, c_q)$ a *packing configuration* for F if c_i items of size $s_F(i), i = 1, \ldots, j$, can all be packed into a bin, i.e., if $\sum_{i=1}^{j} c_i s_F(i) \leq 1$. If this sum is equal to 1 (there is no wasted space), then $(c_1, \ldots, c_j)$ is a *perfect* packing configuration. Let Λ_F be the convex cone in $\mathbf{R}^q$ spanned by all non-negative linear combinations of perfect packing configurations for F. The Courcoubetis-Weber test asks whether P_F, considered as a vector, lies in the convex cone Λ_F. The answer to the test not only determines the best possible expected waste for an online algorithm, but also characterizes the expected waste in an optimal packing, which turns out to be the same to within a constant factor.

THEOREM 2.29 [CW86a][CW86b].   For any discrete distribution F, there exists an open online algorithm A_F with $\bar{W}_{A_F}^n(F) = \Theta(\bar{W}_{\mathrm{OPT}}^n(F))$. Moreover,

A. $\bar{W}_{\mathrm{OPT}}^n(F) = O(1)$ if P_F is in the interior of Λ_F.

B. $\bar{W}_{\mathrm{OPT}}^n(F) = \Theta(n^{1/2})$ if P_F is on the surface of Λ_F.

C. $\bar{W}_{\mathrm{OPT}}^n(F) = \Theta(n)$ if P_F is outside Λ_F.

For specific classes of distributions one can avoid the NP-hardness inherent in the general Courcoubetis-Weber result by proving combinatorial theorems about perfect packings that imply that one of the three cases always holds. This is what is done in [CCG91] to prove Theorem 2.28. The specific perfect packing theorem proved in [CCG91] is stronger than what is needed, and much harder to prove, but it is easier to state: *For positive integers k, j, and r, with $k \geq j$, the list L of rj items, r each of sizes 1 through j, can be packed perfectly into bins of size k if and only if the sum of the rj item sizes is a multiple of k.*

The specific online algorithms embodied in Theorem 2.29 are randomized, but can be efficiently derandomized when F is a discrete uniform distribution. In their randomized form, they maintain a separate pool of bins for each of the possible perfect packing configurations, and assign each new item randomly to an appropriate pool, using probabilities determined by a linear program over the current numbers of partially-packed bins of each type. As described, a separate algorithm is needed for each distribution, although in the case of the discrete uniform distribution, a single algorithm can be constructed that has $O(1)$ expected waste for all such distributions [CCG91]. As with the more general but less-effective algorithm of Rhee and Talagrand [RT93b] [RT93c], this algorithm works by learning the distribution as it goes along. Also, as with the Rhee and Talagrand algorithm, it is only of theoretical interest, a statement that holds for the specific algorithms A_F as well. For more practical results, let us now turn to the offline case.

2.3.3 OFFLINE ALGORITHMS

Given the impressive average-case performance of online algorithms, it is not clear whether offline algorithms have much of an advantage as far as expected performance is concerned. However, at least for continuous uniform distributions, First and Best Fit Decreasing still outperform First and Best Fit in important ways. A first result (both in our presentation and historically) is the following:

THEOREM 2.30 [Kno81][Lue82]. For $A \in \{\text{FFD}, \text{BFD}\}$,

$$\bar{W}_A^n(U[0, 1]) = \Theta(\sqrt{n}).$$

Note that this is better than can be obtained by the best possible open online algorithm by a factor of $\sqrt{\log n}$.

The determination of the growth rate for $\bar{W}_{\text{FFD}}^n(U[0, 1])$ was the first significant average-case result proved for bin packing. Frederickson in [Fre80] showed that it was $O(n^{2/3})$. Knödel [Kno81] and Lueker [Lue82] then independently improved this to the correct bound. Once again a simple algorithm was needed as an intermediary to make the analysis go through, and the main advantage that Knödel and Lueker had over Frederickson was a better choice of an intermediary. Perhaps the simplest choice for the intermediary is the algorithm *Match* (MA) given by Karp in [Kar82b]. This algorithm is the same as FFD except that as soon as a bin receives its second item it is closed. It is easy to show that $\text{MA}(L) \geq \max\{\text{FFD}(L), \text{BFD}(L)\}$ for all lists L. The analysis of Match when $F = U[0, 1]$ easily reduces to computing the expected maximum excursion of a symmetric random walk above its original position and yields $\bar{W}_{\text{MA}}^n(U[0, 1]) = \Theta(n^{1/2})$ thus implying the desired upper bound for both FFD and BFD. The corresponding lower bound follows from the fact that $\bar{W}_{\text{OPT}}^n(U[0, 1]) = \Theta(n^{1/2})$, which itself is proved via an analysis of the expected value of the lower bound $\text{OPT}(L) \geq \max\{s(L), |\{a \in L : s(a) > 1/2\}|\}$ (see also [CL91, p. 122]).

It should be noted, as observed in [Kno81], that the above results hold for any distribution F that is symmetric about $1/2$, where a random variable X and its distribution function F are *symmetric about a* if $X - a$ and $a - X$ have the same distribution [CL91, p. 103].

For the distributions $U[0, b], 0 < b < 1$, the average-case advantage of Best and First Fit Decreasing over their online counterparts increases substantially, although to date this has only been proved for FFD, as shown by Bentley, Johnson, Leighton, McGeoch, and McGeoch [BJL84].

THEOREM 2.31 [BJL84].

$$\bar{W}_{\text{FFD}}^n(U[0, b]) = \begin{cases} \Theta(1) & \text{if } b \leq 1/2 \\ \Theta(n^{1/3}) & \text{if } 1/2 < b < 1. \end{cases}$$

These results should be compared to our earlier result that any open online algorithm must have expected waste at least $\Omega(\sqrt{n})$ for $0 < b < 1$, and our observation that both First and Best Fit appear to have linear expected waste for all such b.

When $b \leq 1/2$, the constant bound appears to be no more than 0.7 based on simulations reported in [BJL83], meaning that FFD is typically optimal or at most one bin off. The proof in [BJL84] unfortunately only provided a bound of something like 10^{10}. A later analysis of the case $0 < b \leq 1/2$ by Floyd and Karp [FK91] reduced the bound on the constant hidden in the $\Theta(1)$ notation to 11.3, albeit at a slight change in the probabilistic model. Their technique was to take the number of items in L to be Poisson distributed with mean n, and then to reduce the problem to the analysis of a queueing system; the discontinuity from bounded to unbounded expected wasted space when $b = 1/2$ was then explained by its correspondence with the stability point of the queueing system.

As to the situation when $b > 1/2$, it is claimed in [BJL84] that one can do substantially better than FFD by modifying the algorithm slightly.

THEOREM 2.32 [BJL84].   There exists an $O(n \log n)$-time offline algorithm A such that for $1/2 < b < 1$, $\bar{W}_A^n(U[0, b]) = O(1)$.

It should be noted that the proofs of Theorem 2.32 and the second half of Theorem 2.31 currently still exist only in the form of handwritten notes, and so we may have been generous in calling these results "theorems" at this point.

When we turn to discrete uniform distributions, the advantages of FFD and BFD are no longer so clear in light of Theorem 2.29, which says for any discrete distribution there is an online algorithm with the same expected waste as an optimal packing to within a constant factor. Moreover, although as one might expect these two algorithms can outperform First and Best Fit, they do not do so consistently. For instance, for $F = U\{8, 11\}$ we have $\bar{W}_{\text{BFD}}^n(F) = O(1)$ and $\bar{W}_{\text{BF}}^n(F) = \Theta(n)$, while for $F = U\{6, 13\}$ we have $\bar{W}_{\text{BFD}}^n(F) = \Theta(n)$ and $\bar{W}_{\text{BF}}^n(F) = O(1)$. These results for BFD are based on a *fluid packing* theorem mentioned in [CCG91] and proved in [CJM96].

In the fluid packing of a discrete distribution $F = (s_F, P_f)$ by First or Best Fit Decreasing, one views the distribution as made up of continuous quantities of each item-size, with an amount $P_F(i)$ of item-size $s_F(i)$. One then performs a version of the algorithm that treats each item-size in turn (in decreasing order), building up a packing that contains fractional amounts of the resulting bin-types. For example, when $F = U\{6, 13\}$, FFD begins by using up the given amount $1/6$ of item-size $6/13$ to create an amount $1/12$ of the bin-type that consists of two items of size $6/13$. When it comes time to pack item-size $1/13$, half of the amount of this item-size will fill the gaps in these "bins." The final packing resulting from this fluid packing process is called *perfect* if all the bin types occurring in the final packing in nonzero quantities contain no wasted space. Coffman, Johnson, McGeoch, Shor, and Weber [CJM96] prove the following general result.

THEOREM 2.33 [CJM96].   Let $F = (s_F, P_f)$ be a discrete distribution with j item sizes and let $A \in \{\text{FFD}, \text{BFD}\}$. Then,

A. If the fluid packing of A for F is not perfect, then $\bar{W}_A^n(F) = \Theta(n)$.

B. If the fluid packing of A for F is perfect, then $\bar{W}_A^n(F)$ is either $O(1)$ or $\Theta(\sqrt{n})$. The first option occurs if and only if there exists a $\delta > 0$ such that for all probability distributions Q on S_F with $\max\{|Q(i) - P_F(i)| : 1 \leq i \leq j\} < \delta$, the fluid packing of A for $F' = (s_F, Q)$ is perfect.

The theorem actually holds for a more general class of offline algorithms called *bin type priority algorithms* in [CJM96]. The condition stated in (B) can be tested by solving a finite number of linear programs, but in general is NP-hard even for BFD and FFD [CJM96]. In the case of the discrete uniform distribution $U\{j, k\}$, however, it can be tested in time $O(j \log j)$.

The above results are similar in form to those we saw in Theorem 2.29 for the best possible online algorithms when F is discrete. The consequences are not nearly so simple, however. For $j \in \{k - 1, k\}$ and $k > 3$ the expected waste is always $\Theta(\sqrt{n})$, although now the constant of proportionality need not depend on k, as can be proved using arguments like those used in the continuous case for $U[0, 1]$. Using the fluid packing test, the nature of $\bar{W}_F^n(F)$ when $j < k - 1$ has been determined for both BFD and FFD for all $U\{j, k\}$ with $k \leq 1,000$ [CCG91] (and in the case of FFD for all $k \leq 2,500$ [CJM96]). All cases examined so far yield expected waste $O(1)$ or $\Theta(n)$ with the same answer for both BFD and FFD, but the patterns of pairs (j, k) for which these two options occur is not at all straightforward. For a given k, the values of j for which linear waste occurs are often broken up into multiple intervals separated by j's for which the expected waste is $O(1)$; and k's exist with as many as 10 such intervals. See [CCG91] for more details.

Certain global observations are possible, however. When $\bar{W}_A^\infty(U\{j, k\}) = \Theta(n)$ for $A \in \{\text{FFD}, \text{BFD}\}$, the fluid packing process can be used to determine the precise value of $\bar{R}_A^\infty(U\{j, k\})$, and based on the computations for $k \leq 2,500$ and additional arguments, one can show the following:

THEOREM 2.34 [CCG91][CJM96]. For $A \in \{\text{FFD}, \text{BFD}\}$ and all pairs (j, k) with $j < k - 1$,

    A. $\bar{R}_A^\infty(U\{j, k\}) \leq \bar{R}_A^\infty(U\{6/13\}) \approx 1.00596$.

    B. $\bar{R}_A^\infty(U\{j, k\}) = O(\log k / k)$.

Thus, the asymptotic expected ratios are bounded and go to 0 as $K \to \infty$. The proof uses a simplified version of FFD as an intermediary that shares the name *Modified First Fit Decreasing* (and abbreviation MFFD) with the quite different algorithm of [GJ85] discussed in Section 2.2.8. In this version of MFFD, a bin is closed as soon as it receives its first *fallback item*—an item that is added to a bin after a subsequent bin has been started. (This version of MFFD is also used by Floyd and Karp [FK91] in their analysis of FFD for $U[0, b]$ when $b \leq 1/2$.)

This concludes our coverage of First and Best Fit Decreasing. The only other offline algorithm whose average case behavior has received serious attention is Next Fit Decreasing (NFD), with the attention probably due more to the ease with which it can be analyzed than to any likely applications for the algorithm. The average-case analysis of NFD began with Hofri and Kamhi [HK86] (see also Hofri [Hof87]) and continued soon after with Csirik et al. [CFF86]. These papers contain several results including the fact that $\bar{R}_{\text{NFD}}^\infty(U[0, 1]) = \pi^2/3 - 2 \approx 1.2899$ (the same value we saw in Theorem 2.18 for $\lim_{K \to \infty} \bar{R}_{H_K}^\infty(U[0, 1])$, for much the same reason). This result is easily generalized to arbitrary distributions F [Rhe87]. With F general, let α_k be the probability that an item size falls in $(1/(k + 1), 1/k]$, and define $\sigma_F = \sum_{k \geq 1} \alpha_k / k$. Rhee shows that $\bar{R}_{\text{NFD}}^\infty(F) = \sigma_F$

2.3.4   OTHER AVERAGE-CASE QUESTIONS

In this section we consider two additional questions about average-case behavior that bear on the results presented above. The first concerns the quality of optimal packings.

2.3.4.1   When is the expected optimal packing "perfect"?

A distribution F is said to *allow perfect packings* if $\bar{W}_{\text{OPT}}^n(F) = o(n)$. Note that this implies that $\lim_{n\to\infty} E[\text{OPT}(L_n)/s(L_n)] = 1$ under F, since $E[s(L_n)] = \mu n$, where μ is the mean of F. The question of which distributions allow perfect packings, originally posed by Karp as reported in [Kar82a], has been a subject of much study. It is germane to our concerns about the performance of heuristics, since for those F that allow perfect packing, we can simplify our estimates of $\bar{R}_A^\infty(F)$ by simply comparing values of $E[A(L_n)]$ to μn.

Fortunately for our analysis, all the discrete and continuous uniform distributions that we have been examining do allow perfect packings, as is implied by the results already presented. On the other hand, perhaps our understanding of algorithmic performance would be more thorough if it contained some knowledge about average-case results for distributions that do not allow perfect packings. Be that as it may, the distributions on which we have concentrated in fact allow even more "perfect" packings than the definition requires. For all the continuous uniform distributions $F = U[0, b], 0 < b < 1$, and all the discrete uniform distributions $F = U\{j, k\}, k > 1$ and $j \leq k - 2$, we have $\bar{W}_{\text{OPT}}^n(F) = O(1)$ as a consequence of Theorems 2.28, 2.31, and 2.32. For the remaining cases, $F = U[0, 1]$ and $F \in \{U\{k-1, k\}, U\{k, k\} : k \geq 3\}$, we have $\bar{W}_{\text{OPT}}^n(F) = \Theta(\sqrt{n})$.

For the case of $U[0, 1]$, even more detailed information is known, as various authors have attempted to estimate the multiplicative constant of the $\sqrt{n}$ term. The current best estimate, due to Csirik, Frenk, Galambos, and Rinnooy Kan [CFG91], is that

$$\bar{W}_{\text{OPT}}^n(U[0, 1]) = \sqrt{\frac{n}{32\pi}} + o(\sqrt{n}).$$

In contrast, most searches for distributions that allow perfect packings have been willing to settle for simply showing that the expected waste is $o(n)$, which is all that the definition requires, or $O(\sqrt{n})$, which is typically the case. Although the original proof that $U[0, 1]$ allows perfect packings was implicit in the 1980 analysis of FFD by Frederickson [Fre80], the first explicit study of the question appears to be that of Karmarkar [Kar82a]. Implicit in Frederickson's result was the fact that any symmetric distribution (as defined in the previous section) allows perfect packings. Karmarkar extended this to show that the same held for any *decreasing* distribution, i.e., one whose density function is non-increasing. The proof is based on the fact that any such distribution can be decomposed into the union of a sequence of distributions that are symmetric around powers of $1/2$, an observation also made by Loulou [Lou84a] and partially attributable to Knödel [Kno81].

When Karp originally asked the question about perfect packings, he was concerned with the class of continuous uniform distributions $U[a, b]$ with $0 < a < b \leq 1$. For this class there exist examples of distributions that trivially do not allow perfect packings. For instance, all those with $a > 1/2$ or $a \leq 1/2$ and $b > 1 - a$, as well as others with more subtle reasons for being bad. Lueker in [Lue83] identified all of these using a proof technique motivated by linear programming duality. He also showed that $U[a, b]$ allows perfect packings whenever $(a + b)/2$ is the reciprocal of an integer $m \geq 3$, although he was unable to show that all the distributions outside of his bad class allowed perfect packings.

Rhee [Rhe88, Rhe90] and Rhee and Talagrand [RT88b, RT89d, RT89e] continued this research, addressing the general problem of characterizing *all* distributions on [0, 1] that allow perfect packing. Incorporating results in topology and functional analysis, they developed a comprehensive and deep theory. We present here a few of the major results, starting with a fundamental characterization of the set $\mathcal{B}$ of measures allowing perfect packing. Let $R_k, k \geq 1$, be the set of k-tuples $(x_1, \ldots, x_k)$ such that $0 \leq x_i \leq k$ and $\sum_{i=1}^{k} x_i = 1$. Let M_k denote the set of all probability measures on R_k, and let $\mathcal{B}_k$ denote the set of all probability measures $\hat{\nu}$ on [0, 1] induced by the measure $\nu \in M_k$ as follows: Sample R_k according to ν, then choose a single component of the sample, with all k components equally likely. Rhee [Rhe88] proved that $\mathcal{B}$ is the class of all probability measures obtainable as (countable) positive linear combinations of measures chosen from the sets $\mathcal{B}_k$. Following up on this work, Rhee and Talagrand [RT88b] derived more explicit sufficient conditions for F to allow perfect packings, and as a corollary resolved the questions left open by Lueker's earlier work on the uniform distributions. Thus, they completed the solution to Karp's perfect packing problem.

In general, the proofs that various classes of distributions allow perfect packing have not been constructive, i.e., optimal packing algorithms have not been given. Exceptions are the cases mentioned above of decreasing distributions and distributions $U[a, b]$ with $(a + b)/2 = 1/m$, as well the case of any triangular density whose expectation is $1/m$ with $m \geq 3$ an integer, for which Krause, Larmore, and Volper [KLV87] gave a constructive proof that perfect packings are allowed.

2.3.4.2   What can we say about the probability distribution of $A(L_n)$?

It is one thing to know the expected number of bins $A(L_n)$ that an algorithm A will produce given a list L_n generated under distribution F. In many applications, however, it is useful to know more about the distribution of $A(L_n)$, such as the nature of its tails. This might have practical significance in the computation of safety margins, but it also has theoretical significance for our analysis. Although we have defined $\bar{R}_A^n(F)$ in terms of the expected ratio $E[A(L_n)/\text{OPT}(L_n)]$, it is often much easier to prove results about $E[A(L_n)]/E[\text{OPT}(L_n)]$, the ratio of expectations. Fortunately, for any distribution F the tails of the distribution of $\text{OPT}(L_n)$ decline sufficiently rapidly with n that these ratios must converge to the same limit as $n \to \infty$; and this is all we are interested in when we talk about $\bar{R}_A^\infty(F)$.

To be specific, consider the following result of Rhee and Talagrand [RT87]. Recall from Section 2.2.10.2 that we call an algorithm A *monotone* if an increase in the sizes or numbers of items in L never causes $A(L)$ to decrease for any list L. Say an algorithm is *k-conservative* if inserting a new item in L never increases $A(L)$ by more than k. Next Fit is one the few of our standard heuristics that meet both these constraints (the latter with $k = 2$). However, OPT, viewed as an algorithm, also meets these criteria, in this case with $k = 1$. Using martingale techniques, Rhee and Talagrand proved the following result:

THEOREM 2.35 [RT87].   For any monotone, k-conservative algorithm A, and any distribution F,

$$P(|A(L_n)) - E[A(L_n)]| \geq t) \leq 2e^{-\alpha t^2/n}$$

where $\alpha > 0$ is a constant depending on the value of k but not on F.

For OPT we have $\alpha = 1/2$ and for NF we have $\alpha = 1/8$. Thus, if we take $t = \sqrt{4n \ln n}$, we get that the probability that $OPT(L_n)$ exceeds its mean by more than t is no more than $2/n^2$. Given that no algorithm A can have a worst-case ratio $R_A^n(F) > n$, it is then an easy exercise to show that $E[A(L_n)/OPT(L_n)]$ and $E[A(L_n)]/E[OPT(L_n)]$ go to the same limit as $n \to \infty$.

In addition to Theorem 2.35, there have been many other results giving similar exponential type bounds on tail probabilities. These include ones that tighten up Theorem 2.35 for particular distributions F [Rhe89] [Rhe93a] [Rhe94], as well as weaker results covering algorithms not captured by Theorem 2.35, such as MFFD (the version discussed in Section 2.3.3) [Rhe91], BFD and FFD [RT89b] [RT89c], and stronger results for algorithms like Next Fit Decreasing that were captured by the theorem [Rhe87]. See also [Rhe85] [Rhe89] [Rhe93b] [RT89a] [CL91].

CONCLUSION

2.4

In this chapter we have tried to give a relatively complete picture of the state of the art with respect to the classical one-dimensional bin packing problem, both from the worst-case point of view that is the common outlook of this book and from an average-case point of view that helps to put those worst-case results into perspective. The field of bin packing is much wider than the single classical problem studied here, however, and many of the same questions have been studied in great detail for a wide range of variants. Among these are generalizations to higher dimensions [CR89], variants in which additional constraints are present, such as precedence relations [WM82] or bounds on the maximum number of items allowed in a bin [KSS75]; variants in which bins of different sizes are allowed [FL86a]; variants in which items have lifetimes and may leave the packing before subsequent items arrive [CGJ83]; variants in which each non-empty bin must contain items of total size of *at least* a given amount and we wish to maximize the number of bins used [AJK84]; and variants in which the number of bins is fixed and some other objective function is considered, such as minimizing the maximum bin contents (the multiprocessor scheduling problem [Gra69]).

The literature on such generalizations is vast, and the references given above should only be viewed as existence proofs for work on the problems in question. The current authors' earlier survey [CGJ84] elaborates on the variety of problems and covers the literature through 1984. There are many important references that have appeared since it was written, however, especially in the multidimensional cases, and an expanded version of this chapter is planned that will bring the entire picture up to date [CGJ97].

REFERENCES

[AJK84] S. B. Assman, D. S. Johnson, D. J. Kleitman, and J. Y-T. Leung. On a dual version of the one-dimensional bin packing problem. *J. Algorithms*, 5:502–525, 1984.

[AKT84] M. Ajtai, J. Komlós, and G. Tusnády. On optimal matchings. *Combinatorica*, 4:259–264, 1984.

[AMW89] R. J. Anderson, E. W. Mayr, and M. K. Warmuth. Parallel approximation algorithms for bin packing. *Inf. and Comput.*, 82:262–277, 1989.

[Bak83] B. S. Baker. A new proof for the first-fit decreasing bin-packing algorithm. *J. Algorithms*, 6:49–70, 1985.

[BC81] B. S. Baker and E. G. Coffman, Jr. A tight asymptotic bound for next-fit-decreasing bin-packing. *SIAM J. Alg. Disc. Meth.*, 2:147–152, 1981.

[BE83] J. Blazewicz and K. Ecker. A linear time algorithm for restricted bin packing and scheduling problems. *Oper. Res. Lett.*, 2:80–83, 1983.

[BJL83] J. L. Bentley, D. S. Johnson, F. T. Leighton, and C. C. McGeoch. An experimental study of bin packing. In *Proceedings of the 21st Annual Allerton Conference on Communication, Control, and Computing*, pages 51–60, Urbana, 1983. University of Illinois.

[BJL84] J. L. Bentley, D. S. Johnson, F. T. Leighton, C. C. McGeoch, and L. A. McGeoch. Some unexpected expected behavior results for bin packing. In *Proceedings of the Sixteenth Annual ACM Symposium on Theory of Computing*, pages 279–288, 1984.

[Bro71] A. R. Brown. *Optimum Packing and Depletion*. American Elsevier, New York, 1971.

[Bro79] D. J. Brown. A lower bound for on-line one-dimensional bin packing algorithms. Technical Report R-864, Coordinated Science Laboratory, University of Illinois, Urbana, IL, 1979.

[CCG91] E. G. Coffman, Jr., C. A. Courcoubetis, M. R. Garey, D. S. Johnson, L. A. McGeogh, P. W. Shor, R. R. Weber, and M. Yannakakis. Fundamental discrepancies between average-case analyses under discrete and continuous distributions: A bin packing case study. In *Proceedings of the 23rd Annual ACM Symposium on Theory of Computing*, pages 230–240. ACM Press, 1991.

[CFF86] J. Csirik, J. B. G. Frenk, A. Frieze, G. Galambos, and A. H. G. Rinnooy Kan. A probabilistic analysis of the next fit decreasing bin packing heuristic. *Oper. Res. Lett.*, 5:233–236, 1986.

[CFG91] J. Csirik, J. B. G. Frenk, G. Galambos, and A. H. G. Rinnooy Kan. Probabilistic analysis of algorithms for dual bin packing problems. *J. Algorithms*, 12:189–203, 1991.

[CG86] J. Csirik and G. Galambos. An $O(n)$ bin-packing algorithm for uniformly distributed data. *Computing*, 36:313–319, 1986.

[CGJ83] E. G. Coffman, Jr., M. R. Garey, and D. S. Johnson. Dynamic bin packing. *SIAM J. Comput.*, 12:227–258, 1983.

[CGJ84] E. G. Coffman, Jr., M. R. Garey, and D. S. Johnson. Approximation algorithms for bin-packing: An updated survey. In G. Ausiello, M. Lucertini, and P. Serafini, editors, *Algorithm Design for Computer System Design*, pages 49–106. Springer-Verlag, Wien, 1984. CISM Courses and Lectures Number 284.

[CGJ87] E. G. Coffman, Jr., M. R. Garey, and D. S. Johnson. Bin packing with divisible item sizes. *J. Complexity*, 3:405–428, 1987.

[CGJ97] E. G. Coffman, Jr., M. R. Garey, and D. S. Johnson. To appear.

[Cha92] B. Chandra. Does randomization help in on-line bin packing? *Information Proc. Lett.*, 43:15–19, 1992.

[CI89] J. Csirik and B. Imreh. On the worst-case performance of the NkF bin-packing heuristic. *Acta Cybernetica*, 9:89–105, 1989.

[CJ91] J. Csirik and D. S. Johnson. Bounded space on-line bin packing: Best is better than first. In *Proceedings, Second Annual ACM-SIAM Symposium on Discrete Algorithms*, pages 309–319, Philadelphia, 1991. Society for Industrial and Applied Mathematics.

[CJ92] J. Csirik and D. S. Johnson. Bounded space on-line bin packing: Best is better than first. *Algorithmica*, submitted.

[CJM96] E. G. Coffman, Jr., D. S. Johnson, L. A. McGeoch, P. W. Shor, and R. R. Weber. Bin packing with discrete item sizes, part III: Average-case behavior of FFD and BFD, 1996. In preparation.

[CJS93] E. G. Coffman, Jr., D. S. Johnson, P. W. Shor, and R. R. Weber. Markov chains, computer proofs, and best fit bin packing. In *Proceedings of the 25th ACM Symposium on the Theory of Computing*, pages 412–421, New York, 1993. ACM Press.

[CJS95] E. G. Coffman, Jr., D. S. Johnson, P. W. Shor, and R. R. Weber. Bin packing with discrete item sizes, part II: Average-case behavior of first fit, 1995. manuscript.

[CL91] E. G. Coffman, Jr. and G. S. Lueker. *Probabilistic Analysis of Packing and Partitioning Algorithms*. Wiley, New York, 1991.

[CR89] D. Coppersmith and P. Raghavan. Multidimensional on-line bin packing: Algorithms and worst-case analysis. *Oper. Res. Lett.*, 8:17–20, 1989.

[CS91] E. G. Coffman, Jr. and P. W. Shor. A simple proof of the $O(\sqrt{n}\log^{3/4} n)$ up-right matching bound. *SIAM J. Disc. Math.*, 4:48–57, 1991.

[CS93] E. G. Coffman, Jr. and P. W. Shor. Packing in two dimensions: Asymptotic average-case analysis of algorithms. *Algorithmica*, 9:253–277, 1993.

[CSB94] L. M. A. Chan, D. Simchi-Levi, and J. Bramel. Worst-case analyses, linear programming, and the bin-packing problem, 1994. Manuscript.

[CSH80] E. G. Coffman, Jr., K. So, M. Hofri, and A. C. Yao. A stochastic model of bin-packing. *Inf. and Cont.*, 44:105–115, 1980.

[CW86a] C. Courcoubetis and R. R. Weber. A bin-packing system for objects with sizes from a finite set: Necessary and sufficient conditions for stability and some applications. In *Proceedings of the 25th IEEE Conference on Decision and Control*, pages 1686–1691, Athens, Greece, 1986.

[CW86b] C. Courcoubetis and R. R. Weber. Necessary and sufficient conditions for stability of a bin packing system. *J. Appl. Prob.*, 23:989–999, 1986.

[FK91] S. Floyd and R. M. Karp. FFD bin packing for item sizes with distributions on $[0, 1/2]$. *Algorithmica*, 6:222–240, 1991.

[FL81] W. Fernandez de la Vega and G. S. Lueker. Bin packing can be solved within $1 + \epsilon$ in linear time. *Combinatorica*, 1:349–355, 1981.

[FL86a] D. K. Friesen and M. A. Langston. Variable sized bin packing. *SIAM J. Comput.*, 15:222–230, 1986.

[FL91]   D. K. Friesen and M. A. Langston. Analysis of a compound bin-packing algorithm. *SIAM J. Disc. Math*, 4:61–79, 1991.

[Fre80]   G. N. Frederickson. Probabilistic analysis for simple one- and two-dimensional bin packing algorithms. *Inf. Proc. Lett.*, 11:156–161, 1980.

[Gal86]   G. Galambos. Parametric lower bound for on-line bin-packing. *SIAM J. Alg. Disc. Meth.*, 7:362–367, 1986.

[GF93]   G. Galambos and J. B. G. Frenk. A simple proof of Liang's lower bound for on-line bin packing and the extension to the parametric case. *Disc. Appl. Math.*, 41:173–178, 1993.

[GG61]   P. C. Gilmore and R. E. Gomory. A linear programming approach to the cutting stock problem. *Oper. Res.*, 9:948–859, 1961.

[GG63]   P. C. Gilmore and R. E. Gomory. A linear programming approach to the cutting stock program — Part II. *Oper. Res.*, 11:863–888, 1963.

[GGJ76]   M. R. Garey, R. L. Graham, D. S. Johnson, and A. C. Yao. Resource constrained scheduling as generalized bin packing. *J. Comb. Th. Ser. A*, 21:257–298, 1976.

[GGU71]   M. R. Garey, R. L. Graham, and J. D. Ullman. Worst-case analysis of memory allocation algorithms. In *Proceedings, 4th Annual Symposium on Theory of Computing*, pages 143–150, New York, 1972. ACM.

[GJ79]   M. R. Garey and D. S. Johnson. *Computers and Intractability: A Guide to the Theory of NP-Completeness*. W. H. Freeman and Co., San Francisco, 1979.

[GJ81]   M. R. Garey and D. S. Johnson. Approximation algorithms for bin-packing problems: A survey. In G. Ausiello and M. Lucertini, editors, *Analysis and Design of Algorithms in Combinatorial Optimization*, pages 147–172. Springer-Verlag, New York, 1981.

[GJ85]   M. R. Garey and D. S. Johnson. A 71/60 theorem for bin packing. *J. of Complexity*, 1:65–106, 1985.

[GPT90]   G. Gambosi, A. Postiglione, and M. Talamo. New algorithms for on-line bin packing. In R. Petreschi, G. Ausiello, D. P. Bovet, editor, *Algorithms and Complexity, Proceedings of the First Italian Conference*, pages 44–59, Singapore, 1990. World Scientific.

[Gra69]   R. L. Graham. Bounds on multiprocessing timing anomalies. *SIAM J. Appl. Math.*, 17:263–269, 1969.

[Gra72]   R. L. Graham. Bounds on multiprocessing anomalies and related packing algorithms. In *Proc. 1972 Spring Joint Computer Conference*, pages 205–217, Montvale, NJ, 1972. AFIPS Press.

[Gro94]   E. F. Grove. Online bin packing with lookahead. Unpublished manuscript, July 1994.

[GW93b]   G. Galambos and G. J. Woeginger. Repacking helps in bounded space on-line bin-packing. *Computing*, 49:329–338, 1993.

[Hal74]   S. Halász. Private communication, 1974.

[Hal89]   S. Halfin. Next-fit bin packing with random piece sizes. *J. Appl. Prob.*, 26:503–511, 1989.

[HK86]   M. Hofri and S. Kamhi. A stochastic analysis of the NFD bin-packing algorithm. *J. Algorithms*, 7:489–509, 1986.

[HK88]   T. C. Hu and A. B. Kahng. Anatomy of on-line bin packing. Technical Report CSE-137, Department of Computer Science and Engineering, University of California at San Diego, La Jolla, CA, 1988.

[Hof82]   U. Hoffman. A class of simple stochastic online bin packing algorithms. *Computing*, 29:227–239, 1982.

[Hof87]   M. Hofri. *Probabilistic Analysis of Algorithms*. Springer-Verlag, New York, 1987.

[IL93]   Z. Ivković and E. Lloyd. Fully dynamic algorithms for bin packing: Being myopic helps. In *Proceedings of the First European Symposium on Algorithms*, No. 726 in Lecture Notes in Computer Science, pages 224–235, New York, 1993. Springer-Verlag. Journal version to appear in *SIAM J. Comput.*

[IL94]   Z. Ivković and E. Lloyd. Partially dynamic bin packing can be solved within $1 + \epsilon$ in (amortized) polylogarithmic time. Technical report, Department of Computer and Information Sciences, University of Delaware, Newark, DE 19716, 1994.

[JDU74]   D. S. Johnson, A. Demers, J. D. Ullman, M. R. Garey, and R. L. Graham. Worst-case performance bounds for simple one-dimensional packing algorithms. *SIAM J. Comput.*, 3:299–325, 1974.

[JKS95]   D. S. Johnson, C. Kenyon, P. W. Shor, and N. Young, 1995. Private communication.

[Joh73]   D. S. Johnson. *Near-Optimal Bin Packing Algorithms*. PhD thesis, Massachusetts Institute of Technology, Department of Mathematics, Cambridge, 1973.

[Joh74]   D. S. Johnson. Fast algorithms for bin packing. *Journal of Computer and System Sciences*, 8:272–314, 1974.

[Joh82]   D. S. Johnson. The NP-completeness column: An ongoing guide. *J. Algorithms*, 3:288–300, 1982.

[Joh96]   D. S. Johnson, 1996. Unpublished results.

[Kar82a]   N. Karmarkar. Probabilistic analysis of some bin-packing algorithms. In *Proceedings of the 23rd Annual Symposium on Foundations of Computer Science*, pages 107–111, 1982.

[Kar82b]   R. M. Karp. Lecture notes. Computer Science Division, University of California, Berkeley, 1982.

[Ken96]   C. Kenyon. Best-fit bin-packing with random order. In *Proceedings, The Seventh Annual ACM-SIAM Symposium on Discrete Algorithms*, pages 359–364, Philadelphia, 1996. Society for Industrial and Applied Mathematics.

[KK82]   N. Karmarkar and R. M. Karp. An efficient approximation scheme for the one-dimensional bin packing problem. In *Proc. 23rd Ann. Symp. on Foundations of Computer Science*, pages 312–320, 1982. IEEE Computer Soc.

[KLM84b]   R. M. Karp, M. Luby, and A. Marchetti-Spaccamela. A probabilistic analysis of multidimensional bin packing problems. In *Proceedings of the Sixteenth Annual ACM Symposium on Theory of Computing*, pages 289–298, 1984.

[KLV87]   K. Krause, L. Larmore, and D. Volper. Packing items from a triangular distribution. *Inf. Proc. Lett.*, 25:351–361, 1987.

[Kno81]   W. Knödel. A bin packing algorithm with complexity $O(n \log n)$ and performance 1 in the stochastic limit. In J. Gruska and M. Chytil, editors, *Proceedings 10th Symp. on Mathematical Foundations of Computer Science*, Lecture Notes in Computer Science, 118, pages 369–378, Berlin, 1981. Springer-Verlag.

[KRS96] C. Kenyon, Y. Rabani, and A. Sinclair. Biased random walks, Lyapunov functions, and stochastic analysis of best fit bin packing. In *Proc. Seventh Annual ACM-SIAM Symposium on Discrete Algorithms*, pages 351–358, Philadelphia, 1996. Society for Industrial and Applied Mathematics.

[KSS75] K. L. Krause, Y. Y. Shen, and H. D. Schwetman. Analysis of several task-scheduling algorithms for a model of multiprogramming computer systems. *J. Assoc. Comput. Mach.*, 22:522–550, 1975.

[Len83] H. W. Lenstra, Jr. Integer programming with a fixed number of variables. *Math. Oper. Res.*, 8:538–548, 1983.

[Lia80] F. M. Liang. A lower bound for on-line bin packing. *Inf. Proc. Lett.*, 10:76–79, 1980.

[LL85] C. C. Lee and D. T. Lee. A simple on-line packing algorithm. *J. ACM*, 32:562–572, 1985.

[LL87] C. C. Lee and D. T. Lee. Robust on-line bin packing algorithms. Technical report, Department of Electrical Engineering and Computer Science, Northwestern University, Evanston, IL, 1987.

[Lou84a] R. Loulou. Probabilistic behavior of optimal bin-packing solutions. *Oper. Res. Lett.*, 3:129–135, 1984.

[LS89] F. T. Leighton and P. Shor. Tight bounds for minimax grid matching with applications to the average case analysis of algorithms. *Combinatorica*, 9:161–187, 1989.

[Lue82] G. S. Lueker. An average-case analysis of bin packing with uniformly distributed item sizes. Technical Report 181, University of California at Irvine, Department of Information and Computer Science, 1982.

[Lue83] G. S. Lueker. Bin packing with items uniformly distributed over intervals $[a, b]$. In *Proceedings of the 24th Annual Symposium on Foundations of Computer Science*, pages 289–297, 1983.

[Mao93a] W. Mao. Best-k-fit bin packing. *Computing*, 50:265–270, 1993.

[Mao93b] W. Mao. Tight worst-case performance bounds for next-k-fit bin packing. *SIAM J. Comput.*, 22:46–56, 1993.

[Mar85] C. U. Martel. A linear time bin-packing algorithm. *Oper. Res. Lett.*, 4:189–192, 1985.

[Mur85] F. D. Murgolo. *Approximation Algorithms for Combinatorial Optimization Problems*. PhD thesis, Univesity of California at Irvine, 1985.

[Mur88] F. D. Murgolo. Anomalous behavior in bin packing algorithms. *Disc. Appl. Math.*, 21:229–243, 1988.

[OMW84] H. L. Ong, M. J. Magazine, and T. S. Wee. Probabilistic analysis of bin packing heuristics. *Oper. Res.*, 32:993–998, 1984.

[Ram89] P. Ramanan. Average-case analysis of the smart next fit algorithm. *Inf. Proc. Lett.*, 31:221–225, June 12 1989.

[RBL89] P. Ramanan, D. J. Brown, C. C. Lee, and D. T. Lee. On-line bin packing in linear time. *J. Algorithms*, 10:305–326, 1989.

[Rhe85] W. T. Rhee. Convergence of optimal stochastic bin packing. *Oper. Res. Lett.*, 4:121–123, 1985.

[Rhe87] W. T. Rhee. Probabilistic analysis of the next fit decreasing algorithm for bin packing. *Oper. Res. Lett.*, 6:189–191, 1987. Correction: *Oper. Res. Lett.*, 7:211, 1988.

[Rhe88]   W. T. Rhee. Optimal bin packing with items of random sizes. *Math. Oper. Res.*, 13:140–151, 1988.

[Rhe89]   W. T. Rhee. Some inequalities for bin packing. *Optimization*, 20:299–304, 1989.

[Rhe90]   W. T. Rhee. A note on optimal bin packing and optimal bin covering with items of random size. *SIAM J. Comput.*, 19:705–710, 1990.

[Rhe91]   W. T. Rhee. Stochastic analysis of a modified first fit decreasing packing. *Math. Oper. Res.*, 16:162–175, 1991.

[Rhe93a]   W. T. Rhee. Optimal bin packing of items of sizes uniformly distributed over [0, 1]. *Math. Oper. Res.*, 18:694–704, 1993.

[Rhe93b]   W. T. Rhee. Inequalities for Bin Packing – II. *Math. Oper. Res.*, 18:685–693, 1993.

[Rhe94]   W. T. Rhee. Inequalities for Bin Packing – III. *Optimization*, 29:381–385, 1994.

[Ric91]   M. B. Richey. Improved bounds for harmonic-based bin packing algorithms. *Disc. Appl. Math.*, 34:203–227, 1991.

[RT87]   W. T. Rhee and M. Talagrand. Martingale inequalities and NP-complete problems. *Math. Oper. Res.*, 12:177–181, 1987.

[RT88a]   W. T. Rhee and M. Talagrand. Exact bounds for the stochastic upward matching problem. *Trans. Amer. Math. Soc.*, 307:109–125, 1988.

[RT88b]   W. T. Rhee and M. Talagrand. Some distributions that allow perfect packing. *Assoc. Comp. Mach.*, 35:564–578, 1988.

[RT89a]   W. T. Rhee and M. Talagrand. The complete convergence of best fit decreasing. *SIAM J. Comput.*, 18:909–918, 1989.

[RT89b]   W. T. Rhee and M. Talagrand. The complete convergence of first fit decreasing. *SIAM J. Comput.*, 18:919–938, 1989.

[RT89c]   W. T. Rhee and M. Talagrand. Optimal bin covering with items of random size. *SIAM J. Comput.*, 18:487–498, 1989.

[RT89d]   W. T. Rhee and M. Talagrand. Optimal bin packing with items of random sizes—II. *SIAM J. Comput.*, 18:139–151, 1989.

[RT89e]   W. T. Rhee and M. Talagrand. Optimal bin packing with items of random sizes – III. *SIAM J. Comput.*, 18:473–486, 1989.

[RT89f]   P. Ramanan and K. Tsuga. Average-case analysis of the modified harmonic algorithm. *Algorithmica*, 4:519–533, 1989.

[RT93b]   W. T. Rhee and M. Talagrand. On-line bin packing with items of random size. *Math. Oper. Res.*, 18:438–445, 1993.

[RT93c]   W. T. Rhee and M. Talagrand. On-line bin packing with items of random sizes – II. *SIAM J. Comput.*, 22:1251–1256, 1993.

[Sha77]   S. D. Shapiro. Performance of heuristic bin packing algorithms with segments of random length. *Inf. and Cont.*, 35:146–148, 1977.

[Sho86]   P. W. Shor. The average-case analysis of some on-line algorithms for bin packing. *Combinatorica*, 6(2):179–200, 1986.

[Sho91]   P. W. Shor. How to pack better than best-fit: Tight bounds for average-case on-line bin packing. In *Proceedings, 32nd Annual Symposium on Foundations of Computer Science*, pages 752–759, New York, 1991. IEEE Computer Society Press.

[Sim94]   D. Simchi-Levi. New worst-case results for the bin packing problem. *Nav. Res. Log.*, 41:579–585, 1994.

[Tal94]   M. Talagrand. Matching theorems and empirical discrepancy computations using majorizing measures. *J. Amer. Math. Soc.*, 7:455–537, 1994.

[Ull71]   J. D. Ullman. The performance of a memory allocation algorithm. Technical Report 100, Princeton University, Princeton, NJ, October 1971.

[Vli95]   A. van Vliet. *Lower and Upper Bounds for On-Line Bin Packing and Scheduling Heuristic*. PhD thesis, Erasmus University, Rotterdam, Netherlands, 1995.

[Vli96]   A. van Vliet. On the asymptotic worst case behavior of harmonic fit. *J. Algorithms*, 20:113–136, 1996.

[WM82]   T. S. Wee and M. J. Magazine. Assembly line balancing as generalized bin-packing. *Oper. Res. Lett.*, 1:56–58, 1982.

[Woe93]   G. Woeginger. Improved space for bounded-space, on-line bin-packing. *SIAM J. Disc. Math.*, 6:575–581, 1993.

[Xu93]   K. Xu. *A Bin-Packing Problem with Item Sizes in the Interval $(0, \alpha]$ for $\alpha \leq \frac{1}{2}$*. PhD thesis, Chinese Academy of Sciences, Institute of Applied Mathematics, Beijing, China, 1993.

[Yao80]   A. C. Yao. New algorithms for bin packing. *J. Assoc. Comput. Mach.*, 27:207–227, 1980.

[Yue91]   M. Yue. A simple proof of the inequality $\mathrm{FFD}(L) \leq \frac{11}{9}\mathrm{OPT}(L) + 1 \ \forall L$, for the FFD bin-packing algorithm. *Acta Math. App. Sinica*, 7:321–331, 1991.

[Zha94]   G. Zhang. Tight worst-case performance bound for AFB_k. Technical Report 015, Institute of Applied Mathematics, Academia Sinica, Beijing, China, May 1994.

3

APPROXIMATING COVERING AND PACKING PROBLEMS: SET COVER, VERTEX COVER, INDEPENDENT SET, AND RELATED PROBLEMS

Dorit S. Hochbaum

This chapter presents the developments that lead to the use of linear programming formulation as an essential approximation tool. These tools were initially developed for the set cover—the most important and general covering problem—and the vertex cover problem. We describe here the use of linear programs' optimal solution and feasible dual solution for effective approximations for the set cover problem and several closely related problem of covering and packing type. The problems analyzed here in detail include (in addition to the set cover and vertex cover problems), the independent set problem, the multicover problem, the set packing problem, the maximum coverage problem, and the problem of integer programming that extends the vertex cover and independent set problems. We also analyze the properties of the greedy algorithm for covering problems.

INTRODUCTION

3.1

One of the most important tools to have emerged in the design of approximation algorithms is the use of linear programming relaxation of the problem and its dual. We trace the history and development of this approach as it evolved for the set cover, set packing, and related problems.

The problems discussed in this chapter include the vertex cover problem and the independent set problem, the set cover problem, the multicover problem, and the set packing problem. In addition, we address the problem of maximum covering of elements with minimum number of sets and the problem of integer programs with two variables per inequality. The latter problem is neither a covering nor a packing problem; yet it engulfs in its structure the very properties of the vertex cover problem and the independent set problem that are instrumental in making improved approximation algorithms possible. The analysis of integer programs with two variables per inequality deepens our insights for the reasons that make vertex cover and related problems approximable within a factor of 2 or better.

Other forms of covering and packing problems that are more structured can have improved approximations exploiting the special structure. Some Euclidean covering and packing approximations are described in Chapter 8 and Section 9.3.3. Some network design problems and connectivity problems are possible to present as covering problems, and then techniques that extend those in this chapter are applicable (see Chapter 4 and Section 9.2.1). Also, the vertex cover and independent set problems defined on special classes of graphs have better approximations than the general cases. These special cases are described in detail in Section 3.7.

The linear programming (LP) relaxation plays an important role for all these problems. All known approximation algorithms for the set cover problem [Chv79] [Hoc82] use the (weak) duality theorem of linear programming and the superoptimality of the linear programming relaxation. For the vertex cover, the best known approximation algorithms are provided by independent set and integer programs with two variables per inequality; i.e., the preprocessing technique based on the properties of the linear programming solutions [Hoc83] [HMNT93]. We start by defining the problems discussed in this chapter and how they are related.

3.1.1 DEFINITIONS, FORMULATIONS, AND APPLICATIONS

A *vertex cover* in an undirected graph $G = (V, E)$ is a set of vertices C such that each edge of G has at least one endpoint in C. The *vertex cover problem* is the problem of finding a cover of the smallest weight in a graph whose vertices carry positive weights. This problem is known to be *NP*-complete even when the input is restricted to planar cubic graphs with unit weights [GJS76]. An *independent set* in a graph is a set of pairwise nonadjacent vertices (also referred to as *vertex packing*). The largest weight independent set is the complement of the smallest weight vertex cover.

A natural integer programming formulation of the vertex cover problem with node weights w_j for $j \in V$, $|V| = n$, is,

$$
\begin{array}{lll}
\text{Min} & \sum_{j=1}^{n} w_j x_j & \\
\text{(VC)} \quad \text{subject to} & x_i + x_j \geq 1 & \text{(for every edge } (i, j) \text{ in the graph)} \\
& 0 \leq x_j \leq 1 & (j = 1, \ldots, n) \\
& x_j \text{ integer} & (j = 1, \ldots, n).
\end{array}
$$

The formulation of the independent set problem (IS) is similar, with "Max" replacing "Min" and with the direction of the first set of inequalities reversed. The independent set problem is also known as the "vertex packing" problem or as the "stable set" problem. To illustrate the problems, consider the graph in Figure 3.1 with all weights equal to 1. The minimum vertex cover is the set of nodes $\{1, 3, 4, 6\}$ and the maximum independent set is the set of nodes $\{2, 5\}$. The linear programming relaxation of (VC) is obtained by removing the integrality constraints on the x_j's.

Among the multiple applications of the vertex cover and the independent set problems are finding nonconflicting schedules. Then assigning the smallest number of watch guards located at vertices so that all links (edges) have at least one guard surveying them.

A general packing problem is the *set packing problem*. Here the goal is to find the maximum weight collection of sets so that no two overlap:

maximize $\{\mathbf{wx}|\ A \cdot \mathbf{x} \le \mathbf{e}\}$ for $\mathbf{x}$ binary, $\mathbf{e}$ a column vector of ones and A a zero-one matrix.

This problem can be represented as the independent set problem by constructing a graph (called the derived graph) whose vertices are columns of A, and two such vertices being adjacent if the two columns have a nonzero dot product. The independent set problem is also a special case of the set packing problem, and hence the two problems are polynomially equivalent. As such, any result for the independent set problem is also applicable to the set packing problem. Therefore the set packing problem will not be discussed here separately.

The vertex cover problem is a special case of the set cover problem. Given a set I of m elements to be covered and a collection of sets $S_j \in I$, $j \in J = \{1, \ldots, n\}$. Each set has weight w_j associated with it. The characteristic vector of set S_j is the $0-1$ vector $\{a_{ij}\}_{i=1}^m$. The *set cover problem* is to identify the smallest weight collection of sets so that all elements of I are included in their union (or "covered"): minimize $\{\mathbf{wx}|\ A \cdot \mathbf{x} \ge \mathbf{e}\}$ for $\mathbf{x}$ binary. A vertex cover problem is a set cover problem where each element can be covered by exactly two sets. These two sets correspond to the endpoints of an edge in the graph. Unlike the set packing problem which is equivalent to the vertex packing problem, the set cover problem is a strict generalization of the vertex cover problem, and the two problems are distinguished by the quality of approximation algorithms that can be devised for them.

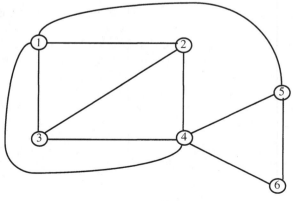

FIGURE 3.1

The set cover problem has applications in diverse contexts such as efficient testing, statistical design of experiments, [FNT74], and crew scheduling for airlines [MMK79]. It also arises as a subproblem of many integer programming problems. For surveys on the set cover problems see Garfinkel and Nemhauser [GN72], Christofides and Korman [CK75], Balas and Padberg [BP76], Padberg [Pad79], and an annotated bibliography by Trotter [Tro85].

Some applications of the set cover problem require an extension where each element is to be covered a specified number of times. This extension is called the *multicover* problem. The multicover problem has applications where reliability of coverage requires extra redundancy. Among the applications of the problem are the location of emergency service facilities, communication systems, military applications marketing applications, crew scheduling, and security checking (Van Slyke 81 [VS81]). In the formulation of the multicover problem, each element i is to be covered at least b_i times.

$$
\begin{aligned}
\text{(MC)} \qquad \text{Min} \qquad & \sum_{j=1}^{n} w_j x_j \\
\text{subject to} \qquad & \sum_{j=1}^{n} a_{ij} x_j \geq b_i \quad (\text{for } i = 1, \ldots, m) \\
& 0 \leq x_j \leq 1 \quad (j = 1, \ldots, n) \\
& x_j \text{ integer} \quad (j = 1, \ldots, n).
\end{aligned}
$$

When the amount of required coverage $b_i = 1$ for all i, the multicover problem reduces to the set cover problem (SC).

The maximum coverage problem generalizes the set cover problem and the multicover problem. Here, instead of seeking the smallest number of sets that cover all elements, we seek the largest number of elements (accounting for their multiplicities) that can be covered by a prespecified number of sets, k. When this largest number is m—the total number of elements to be covered—the solution is also a set cover. The maximum coverage problem is also defined in a weighted context: find the largest number of elements that can be covered by sets of total weight not exceeding W—the budget limit.

Both formulations of the vertex cover and independent set problems have two variables per inequality. Another problem that is formulated as integer programming optimization with two variables per inequality is the problem of minimizing the weight of true variables in a 2-satisfiability truth assignment. In the 2-SAT problem we are given a collection of clauses in conjunctive normal form (CNF) of length 2 each, where each variable has a certain weight associated with setting it to True. The vertex cover problem could be viewed as 2-SAT with no negation of variables. As such, integer programming with two variables per inequality, IP2, captures in its structure a number of other problems. Indeed, as we shall see, much of the insight about these three problems can be derived from the analysis of IP2. The formulation of IP2 is,

$$
\begin{aligned}
\text{(IP2)} \qquad \text{Min} \qquad & \sum_{j=1}^{n} w_j x_j \\
\text{subject to} \qquad & a_i x_{j_i} + b_i x_{k_i} \geq c_i \quad (\text{for } i = 1, \ldots, m) \\
& 0 \leq x_j \leq u_j \quad (j = 1, \ldots, n) \\
& x_j \text{ integer} \quad (j = 1, \ldots, n),
\end{aligned}
$$

where $1 \leq j_i, k_i \leq n$, $w_i \geq 0$ $(i = 1, \ldots, n)$, and all the coefficients are integer. We denote the largest upper bound by $U = \max_{j=1,\ldots,n} u_j$.

IP2 with $a_i = b_i = c_i = u_i = 1$ is the vertex cover problem. With $u_i = 1$ and $a_i, b_i, c_i \in \{-1, 0, 1\}$ IP2 is the 2-SAT problem.

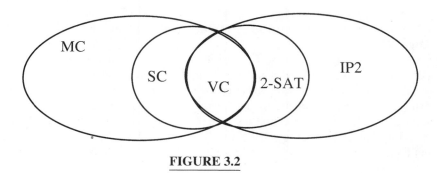

FIGURE 3.2

Figure 3.2 depicts schematically the relationship between vertex cover and the other minimization problems.

3.1.2   LOWER BOUNDS ON APPROXIMATIONS

All problems discussed here are Max-$\mathcal{SNP}$-complete, which means that there are no polynomial approximation schemes, PASs, for these problems unless $NP = P$. Stronger lower bounds have been derived for these problems (and are getting improved continuously). The strongest lower bounds at the time of this writing are:

- For vertex cover problem there is no δ-approximation for $\delta < 16/15$ unless $NP = P$, [BGS95].

- The independent set problem is equivalent to the maximum clique problem on the complement graph. The maximum clique problem has been studied extensively for lower bounds, and there are extremely large (and thus discouraging) lower bounds that apply also to the independent set problem. The current champion lower bound is $\sqrt{n}$ [Håstad, private communication] meaning that we cannot guarantee an approximation factor $n^{\frac{1}{2}-\delta}$ for any positive δ unless $NP = P$.

- There have been some constant lower bounds proved for approximating set cover that hold unless $NP = P$. Stronger bounds were proved under the assumption that $NP \neq DTIME(n^{O(\log\log n)})$. In other words, if NP problems are not solvable in time that is quasi-polynomial, or exponential in $\log\log n$, then the lower bound holds. A lower bound proved recently by Feige [F95] is $(1 - \epsilon)\ln n$ provided that $NP \neq DTIME(n^{O(\log\log n)})$.

A lower bound for multicover follows from that of set cover, and a lower bound to IP2 follows from the bound for vertex cover.

When considering these lower bounds one has to keep in mind that these are worst case lower bounds. Indeed, there are approximation algorithms for set cover instances that have small set sizes or have small coverage duplicity (the number of sets covering a given element), that have performance better than the lower bound. For instance, the approximation factor for an independent set on bounded degree graphs is substantially better than the lower bound of $\sqrt{n}$ implies, and similarly for many other special classes of problems demonstrated in this chapter. Table 3.1 summarizes such results.

3.1.3   OVERVIEW OF CHAPTER

The chapter is arranged in chronological order of developments—with some minor exceptions. We begin with a discussion of the set cover problem and the greedy algorithm which was the first approximation algorithm devised for it. The analysis of the greedy was the first use of linear programming duality in approximations. We then present the Linear Programming (LP) approximation algorithm that mades use of the dual optimal solution; then the dual-feasible algorithm making use of a dual solution that is only feasible rather than optimal, and finally using other relaxations of the set cover problem that lead to a variety of dual-feasible algorithms. These are applicable to the set cover problem, and some are only applicable to its special case—the vertex cover problem. We then extend the analysis of the linear programming algorithm and the dual-feasible algorithm to the multicover problem.

Next, we demonstrate the value of the *optimal* dual solution in a preprocessing approach that yields improved approximation bounds to the vertex cover or the independent set problems. In this section we describe a large number of special classes of these problems along with the improved approximation bounds. All known approximation algorithms to date for these problems are then summarized in Table 3.1.

Section 3.8 investigates the nature of the factor of 2 approximation for the vertex cover problem (which we also conjecture to be best possible), and describes how the ideas of preprocessing and the use of the optimal linear programming solution apply also in the more general set up of integer programming with two variables per inequality.

Finally, we discuss the performance of the greedy algorithm for the maximum coverage problem, which is an extension of the set cover problem (as a decision problem). This problem is of particular interest because of the analysis of the generic type of greedy algorithm involved.

The notation used in this chapter includes bold fonts for vectors; $\mathbf{e}$ denotes the vector of all 1's, and $\mathbf{e}_i$ denotes the vector of all 0's except for a 1 in the ith position.

THE GREEDY ALGORITHM FOR THE SET COVER PROBLEM

3.2

A greedy algorithm is the most natural heuristic for set cover. It works by selecting one set at a time that covers the most elements among the uncovered ones. Johnson and

Lovász ([Joh74], [Lov75]) were the first to demonstrate that the greedy algorithm is a $\mathcal{H}(d)$- approximation algorithm for the unweighted set cover problem, where $\mathcal{H}(d) = \sum_{i=1}^{d} \frac{1}{i}$ and d is the size of the largest set. $\mathcal{H}(d)$ is bounded by $1 + \log d$.

Chvátal [Chv79] extended the applicability of the greedy to the weighted set cover. This version of greedy selects a set with the minimum ratio of weight to remaining coverage. Chvátal proved that this greedy algorithm is still a $\mathcal{H}(d)$-approximation algorithm. Although the algorithm is easily stated, its analysis is far from trivial. That analysis is particularly instructive as it introduces the use of linear programming duality in approximations, which we will present next. The formal statement of the greedy is,

THE GREEDY ALGORITHM [CHVÁTAL]

Step 0: Set $C^G = \emptyset$; $S_j^1 = S_j$, $j \in J$; $I = \{1, \dots, m\}$; $k = 0$.

Step 1: $k \leftarrow k + 1$. Select a set S_{j_k}, such that $\frac{w_{j_k}}{|S_{j_k}^k|} = \min_{j \in J} \frac{w_j}{|S_j^k|}$.

Step 2: Set $C^G \leftarrow C^G \cup \{j_k\}$ and $S_j^{k+1} = S_j^k \setminus S_{j_k}^k$, $j \in J$, $I \leftarrow I \setminus S_{j_k}^k$.

Step 3: If $I = \emptyset$, stop and output cover C^G. Else, go to Step 1.

Consider the linear programming relaxation of (SC), with the upper bound $x_j \leq 1$ constraints omitted (an optimal solution will satisfy those constraints automatically). The dual problem is

$$
\begin{aligned}
&\text{Max} && \sum_{i=1}^{m} y_i \\
\text{(SC-dual)} \quad &\text{subject to} && \sum_{i=1}^{m} a_{ij} y_i \leq w_j \quad \text{(for } j = 1, \dots, n\text{)} \\
& && y_i \geq 0 \quad (i = 1, \dots, m).
\end{aligned}
$$

The analysis of greedy relies on allocating the weights of the set selected by the greedy heuristic to the elements covered, and interpreting those as a form of dual, not quite feasible, solution.

THEOREM 3.1   The greedy heuristic is a $\mathcal{H}(d)$-approximation algorithm.

Proof.   To prove the desired result, it suffices to show that for *any* cover C, indicated by the characteristic vector $\{x_j\}$, and a cover delivered by the greedy C^G,

$$
\sum_{j \in C} \mathcal{H}(d) w_j = \sum_{j=1}^{n} \mathcal{H}(d) w_j x_j \geq \sum_{j \in C^G} w_j . \tag{3.1}
$$

Applying this inequality to C^*, the optimal cover, yields that the value of the solution delivered by the greedy is at most $\mathcal{H}(d)$ times the value of the optimal solution. To prove (3.1), it is sufficient to find an "almost feasible" dual solution $\mathbf{y}$ such that,

$$
\sum_{i=1}^{m} a_{ij} y_i \leq \mathcal{H}(|S_j|) w_j \quad j = 1, \dots, n \tag{3.2}
$$

and so that the weight of the sets selected is accounted for by **y**,

$$\sum_{i=1}^{m} y_i = \sum_{j \in C^G} w_j. \tag{3.3}$$

Such **y** satisfying these inequalities is feasible within a factor of $\mathcal{H}(d)$, and it satisfies (3.1) since,

$$\sum_{j=1}^{n} \mathcal{H}(d) w_j x_j \overset{(3.2)}{\geq} \sum_{j=1}^{n} (\sum_{i=1}^{m} a_{ij} y_i) x_j = \sum_{i=1}^{m} (\sum_{j=1}^{n} a_{ij} x_j) y_i \geq \sum_{i=1}^{m} y_i \overset{(3.3)}{=} \sum_{j \in C^G} w_j. \tag{3.4}$$

Let S_j^k be the set S_j with the remaining elements at the beginning of iteration k, and its size, $|S_j^k| = s_j^k$. The dual vector **y** that will satisfy (3.2) and (3.3) has for y_i the average price paid by the greedy to cover an element i. Whenever a set is selected, its weight is divided evenly among the elements it has newly covered, $y_i = \frac{w_k}{s_k^k}$.

Let the sets greedy selects in the first k iterations be $\{1, 2, \dots, k\}$. Since k is the index for which the ratio is minimum

$$\frac{w_k}{s_k^k} \leq \frac{w_j}{s_j^k} \qquad \forall j. \tag{3.5}$$

Assume that there are t iterations altogether. Then, $\sum_{j \in C^G} w_j = \sum_{j=1}^{t} w_j$. Each element $i \in I$ belongs to one set $S_k^k, k = 1, \dots, t$, so for $i \in S_k^k$, $y_i = \frac{w_k}{s_k^k}$. (3.3) now follows as,

$$\sum_{i=1}^{m} y_i = \sum_{k=1}^{t} \sum_{i \in S_k^k} y_i = \sum_{k=1}^{t} s_k^k (\frac{w_k}{s_k^k}) = \sum_{k=1}^{t} w_k .$$

To prove (3.2) observe that, $S_j \cap S_k^k = S_j^k \setminus S_j^{k+1}$ and $I = \bigcup_{k=1}^{t} S_k^k$. Hence,

$$\sum_{i=1}^{m} a_{ij} y_i = \sum_{k=1}^{t} \sum_{i \in S_j \cap S_k^k} y_i = \sum_{k=1}^{t} \sum_{i \in S_j^k \setminus S_j^{k+1}} y_i = \sum_{k=1}^{t} \left(s_j^k - s_j^{k+1} \right) \frac{w_k}{s_k^k} .$$

For a given set S_j, let p be the largest index such that $s_j^p > 0$, then

$$\sum_{i=1}^{m} a_{ij} y_i = \sum_{k=1}^{p} (s_j^k - s_j^{k+1}) \frac{w_k}{s_k^k} \overset{(3.5)}{\leq} w_j \sum_{k=1}^{p} \frac{s_j^k - s_j^{k+1}}{s_j^k} .$$

We now use the inequality $\frac{s_j^k - s_j^{k+1}}{s_j^k} \leq \mathcal{H}(s_j^k) - \mathcal{H}(s_j^{k+1})$ to establish,

$$\sum_{i=1}^{m} a_{ij} y_i \leq w_j \sum_{k=1}^{p} \left(\mathcal{H}(s_j^k) - \mathcal{H}(s_j^{k+1}) \right) \leq w_j \mathcal{H}(s_j^1) .$$

∎

The greedy algorithm is thus an $O(\log n)$-approximation algorithm for any set cover. This matches the recently proved lower bound for approximating the set cover [F95]. Still considerably better results are possible for special cases. Consider for instance the performance of the greedy on *high coverage* instances of unweighted set cover.

EXERCISE 3.1 [KZ95]:   Let an unweighted set cover instance be of α-coverage if every element of I belongs to at least $\alpha|J|$ sets. Then the greedy delivers a solution of size $\log_{\frac{1}{1-\alpha}} n$ for instances of α-coverage.

As a corollary an enumeration algorithm solves the α-coverage instance in $O(m^{O(\log n)})$ steps. The high coverage problem—where α is close to 1—is thus unlikely to be *NP*-hard.

THE LP-ALGORITHM FOR SET COVER

3.3

A different approximation algorithm—which is duality based—was devised for the set cover problem by Hochbaum [Hoc82]. This was motivated by an approximation to the *unweighted* vertex cover problem by Gavril (reported as private communication in [GJ79]). Gavril's algorithm is based on the idea of solving for a maximal (not necessarily maximum) matching, and taking both endpoints of the edges in the matching. The number of edges in the maximal matching $|M|$ is a lower bound on the optimum $|VC^*|$. This is because a single vertex cannot cover two edges in M. On the other hand, if we pick both endpoints of each matched edge we get a feasible cover, VC^M, as otherwise there would be an edge with both endpoints unmatched. Therefore this edge could be added to the matching M—contradicting its maximality. These two statements lead to the inequalities,

$$|VC^M| = 2|M| \leq 2|VC^*|. \tag{3.6}$$

Hence, this cover is at most twice the optimal cover.

The extension of this idea to the weighted case and to the set cover problem was inspired by an alternative way of viewing the maximal matching algorithm as a feasible dual solution. To see that, consider the dual of the linear programming relaxation of the unweighted vertex cover problem.

$$
\begin{array}{lll}
& \text{Max} & \sum_{(i,j)\in E} y_{ij} \\
\text{(VC-dual)} & \text{subject to} & \sum_{(i,j)\in E} y_{ij} \leq 1 \quad \text{for } j = 1,\ldots,n \\
& & y_{ij} \geq 0, \quad \forall\, (i,j) \in E.
\end{array}
$$

An integer feasible solution to (VC-dual) is a matching in the graph. Consider a feasible solution to the dual, $\bar{\mathbf{y}}$, and let $\bar{x}_j = 1$ whenever the dual constraint is binding, $\sum_{(i,j)\in E} \bar{y}_{ij} = 1$. We show that the solution $\bar{\mathbf{x}}$ is a feasible vertex cover. To that end, we introduce the concept of maximality: a feasible solution to (VC-dual), $\bar{\mathbf{y}}$, is said to be *maximal* if there is no feasible solution $\mathbf{y}$ such that $y_{ij} \geq \bar{y}_{ij}$ and $\sum_{(i,j)\in E} y_{ij} > \sum_{(i,j)\in E} \bar{y}_{ij}$.

LEMMA 3.1   Let $\bar{\mathbf{y}}$ be a maximal feasible solution to (VC-dual). Then the set $VC = \{i \mid \sum_{(i,j) \in E} \bar{y}_{ij} = 1\}$ is a feasible solution to (VC).

Proof.   Suppose that VC is not a feasible cover. Then there is an edge (u, v) which is uncovered, i.e., $\sum_{(u,j) \in E} y_{uj} < 1$ and, $\sum_{(v,j) \in E} y_{vj} < 1$.

Let $\delta = \text{Min} \{1 - \sum_{(u,j) \in E} y_{uj}, 1 - \sum_{(v,j) \in E} y_{vj}\}$. Then the vector, $\mathbf{y} = \bar{\mathbf{y}} + \delta \cdot \mathbf{e}_{uv}$ (for $\mathbf{e}_{uv}$ denoting the vector of all zeros except for a 1 in the uv entry), is a feasible solution satisfying $y_{ij} \geq \bar{y}_{ij}$ and $\sum_{(i,j) \in E} y_{ij} > \sum_{(i,j) \in E} \bar{y}_{ij}$. This contradicts the maximality of $\bar{\mathbf{y}}$. Hence, every edge must be covered by VC and VC is therefore a feasible cover.   ∎

Consider now the generalization of this approach for the set cover problem.

DEFINITION 3.1   A feasible solution to (SC-dual) $\bar{\mathbf{y}}$ is said to be *maximal* if there is no feasible solution $\mathbf{y}$ such that $y_i \geq \bar{y}_i$ and $\sum_{i=1}^n y_i > \sum_{i=1}^n \bar{y}_i$.

THE LP-ALGORITHM [HOCHBAUM]

> *Step 1:*   Find a maximal dual feasible solution for (SC), $\bar{\mathbf{y}}$.
> *Step 2:*   Output the cover $C^H = \{j \mid \sum_{i=1}^n a_{ij} \bar{y}_i = w_j\}$.

LEMMA 3.2 C^H is a feasible solution to (SC).

Proof.   The proof is an obvious extension of Lemma 3.1: Consider an element q that is not covered. Let $\delta = \text{Min}_{j \mid q \in S_j} \{w_j - \sum_{j=1}^n a_{ij} \bar{y}_i\} > 0$. Then the vector, $\mathbf{y} = \bar{\mathbf{y}} + \delta \cdot \mathbf{e}_q$, is a feasible solution contradicting the maximality of $\bar{\mathbf{y}}$.   ∎

Let C^* be the optimal cover. Define for any set cover C, $w(C) = \sum_{j \in C} w_j$. The following lemma shows that the the LP- algorithm is a $\max_i\{\sum_j a_{ij}\}$- approximation algorithm due to the dual constraint being binding for every $j \in C^H$.

LEMMA 3.3 $w(C^H) \leq \max_i\{\sum_j a_{ij}\} w(C^*)$.

Proof.   First, $w(C^H) = \sum_{j \in C^H} w_j = \sum_{j \in C^H} (\sum_{i=1}^m a_{ij} y_i)$. Using the weak duality theorem we get that for any solution to the linear programming relaxation, and in particular for the optimal solution $\mathbf{x}^*$,

$$\sum_{j \in C^H} (\sum_{i=1}^m a_{ij} y_i) \quad \leq \max_i\{\sum_{j \in C^H} a_{ij}\} \sum_{i=1}^m y_i \leq \max_i\{\sum_{j \in C^H} a_{ij}\} \sum_{j=1}^n w_j x_j^*$$
$$\leq \max_i\{\sum_{j \in C^H} a_{ij}\} w(C^*).$$

Now the value of the optimal solution to the linear programming relaxation is a lower bound to the optimal integer solution. It follows that,
$w(C^H) \leq \max_i\{\sum_{j \in C^H} a_{ij}\} w(C^*)$.   ∎

This proves a slightly stronger approximation factor as we can consider the row sums restricted only to those sets in the cover (alternatively the row sums are calculated in the submatrix of the columns in the cover). For instance, if the cover C^H has only one set covering each element, then it is optimal. Let the maximum number of sets covering an element, $\max_i\{\sum_j a_{ij}\}$ be denoted by p.

An immediate corollary of the p-approximation is that the LP-algorithm is a 2-approximation algorithm for the (weighted) vertex cover problem.

COROLLARY 3.1   The LP-algorithm is a 2-approximation algorithm for the vertex cover problem.

Proof.   (VC) is a special case of (SC) with each element—an edge—belonging to precisely two "sets" representing its endpoints. Hence, $\sum_j a_{ej} = 2$ for all edges $e \in E$.   ∎

The implementation of the LP-algorithm proposed in [Hoc82] used the optimal dual solution as a maximal feasible solution. Still, the role of the dual solution is only to aid the analysis of the algorithm. It need not be generated explicitly by the algorithm:

THE ROUNDING ALGORITHM [HOCHBAUM]

Step 1:   Solve optimally the linear programming relaxation of (SC). Let an optimal solution be $\{x_j^*\}$

Step 2:   Output the cover $C^H = \{j \,|\, x_j^* > 0\}$. Equivalently, set $x_j^H = \left\lceil x_j^* \right\rceil$.

The rounding algorithm is indeed a special case of the LP-algorithm as $x_j^* > 0$ implies that the corresponding dual constraint is binding by complementary slackness optimality conditions, $\sum_{i=1}^m a_{ij} y_i = w_j$.

A minor variation of the rounding algorithm is still a p-approximation algorithm. We replace Step 2 by:

Step 2':   Output the cover $C^H = \{j \,|\, x_j^* \geq \frac{1}{p}\}$.

The feasibility of this cover is obvious, as in any fractional solution **x** corresponding to a cover C, $\sum_{j=1}^n x_j \geq 1$, and there are at most p positive entries per such inequality. So at least one must be at least as large as the average $\frac{1}{p}$. This rounding algorithm (rounding II) will always produce a cover no larger than the rounding algorithm; although it does not offer any advantage in terms of worst case analysis. Moreover, for any cover produced by an approximation algorithm, it is easy to prune it of unnecessary extra sets, and leave a "prime" cover, which is a *minimal* cover. Although a prime cover can only be a better solution, this approach has not provided *guaranteed* tighter approximation factors.

In the next section we see that it is not necessary to compute an *optimal* solution to the linear programming problem. Rather, there are more efficient ways of finding a maximal dual solution, two of which are described in the next section. On the other hand, as discussed in the section on the preprocessing algorithm, 3.7, the linear programming solution carries some extra valuable information for the vertex cover and independent set problems. In addition, for the vertex cover problem it is possible to solve the linear programming relaxation by applying a max-flow min-cut algorithm which is more efficient than solving the respective linear program.

It is also shown that the LP-algorithm can also be used in the presence of covering matrices with coefficients other than 0 or 1. In Section 3.5 it is demonstrated for a different formulation of the set cover problem. Chapter 4 is devoted entirely to applications of the algorithm of finding maximal dual solutions to a large variety of covering-type problems.

THE FEASIBLE DUAL APPROACH

3.4

Solving the linear programming relaxation of set cover can be done in polynomial time. Yet, much more efficient algorithms are possible that find a feasible and maximal dual solution. The advantage of such algorithms is in the improved complexity. The approximation ratios derived are the same as for the dual optimal solution.

Bar-Yehuda and Even [BYE81] devised an efficient algorithm for identifying a maximal feasible dual solution to be used in the LP-algorithm. The idea is to identify a feasible primal constraint and then to increase its dual variable till at least one of the dual constraints becomes binding.

As before, the derivation of the dual solution is implicit and exists only in order to analyze the approximation factor. This dual information is placed in square brackets in the description of the algorithm to stress that it is not an integral part of the procedure.

THE DUAL-FEASIBLE I ALGORITHM [BAR-YEHUDA AND EVEN]

Step 0: Set $C = \emptyset$; $I = \{1, \ldots, m\}$; $[\mathbf{y} = 0]$.

Step 1: Let $i \in I$. Let $w_{j(i)} = \min_{a_{ij}=1} w_j$. $[y_i = w_{j(i)}]$; $C \leftarrow C \cup \{j(i)\}$.

Step 2: {update} For all j such that $a_{ij} = 1$, $w_j \leftarrow w_j - w_{j(i)}$, $I \leftarrow I \setminus S_j(i)$.

Step 3: If $I = \emptyset$, stop and output cover C. Else, go to Step 1.

Throughout this procedure the updated w_js remain nonnegative. The weights w_j are in fact the reduced costs corresponding to the solution $\mathbf{y}$, and at each iteration they quantify the amount of slack in the dual constraint. In this sense, the algorithm is dual-feasible—throughout the procedure it maintains the feasibility of the dual vector $\mathbf{y}$. For any set added to the cover, the updated value of the reduced cost is 0, i.e. the corresponding dual constraint is binding. The resulting dual vector is maximal since each element belongs to some set in the cover, and therefore to some set with a binding dual constraint. Hence, there is no vector that is larger or equal to $\mathbf{y}$ in all its components which is feasible, unless it is equal to $\mathbf{y}$.

Lemma 3.3 applies to the cover delivered by the dual-feasible I algorithm, namely, dual-feasible I is a p-approximation algorithm to the set cover problem. The complexity of the dual-feasible algorithm is $O(mn)$, which is linear in the size of the input matrix, and hence a considerable improvement to the complexity of the respective linear program.

As in Corollary 3.1, this algorithm is a 2-approximation to the vertex cover problem. However, as discussed in the next section, there is additional information in the optimal linear programming solution to the vertex cover problem that is lost in the dual-feasible algorithm.

Another variation on the theme of dual feasible solutions was proposed by Clarkson [Clar83] for the vertex cover problem. This algorithm is superficially similar to the greedy algorithm: instead of choosing a vertex based on its minimum weight per edge covered, it is choosing a vertex based on minimum *reduced* weight. Clarkson did not use the concept of duality, and his proof for the bound of 2 is consequently more involved. We adapt this idea for the set cover problem:

THE DUAL-FEASIBLE ALGORITHM II [AFTER CLARKSON]

Step 0: Set $C = \emptyset$; $S_j^1 = S_j$, $j \in J$; $I = \{1, \ldots, m\}$; $k = 0$; $[\mathbf{y} = 0]$.

Step 1: $k = k + 1$. Select a set S_{j_k}, such that $\frac{w_{j_k}}{|S_{j_k}^k|} = \min_{j \in J} \frac{w_j}{|S_j^k|}$.

Step 2: {update} Set $C \leftarrow C \cup \{j_k\}$ and $S_j^{k+1} = S_j^k \setminus S_{j_k}^k$, $\forall j \in J$, $I \leftarrow I \setminus S_{j_k}^k$.
$w_j \leftarrow w_j - \frac{w_{j_k}}{|S_{j_k}^k|} \cdot |S_j^k \cap S_{j_k}^k|$. $[y_i = \frac{w_{j_k}}{|S_{j_k}^k|} \forall i \in S_{j_k}^k.]$

Step 3: If $I = \emptyset$, stop and output cover C. Else, go to Step 1.

Dual-feasible II has several interesting aspects. Whenever a set is selected, its corresponding dual constraint becomes binding as each of the elements covered by it is assigned an equal share of the set's (reduced) weight. This symmetry among the elements in the allocation of the dual weights makes the algorithm particularly amenable to parallel and distributed implementations. Indeed Khuller, Vishkin, and Young, [KVY94], devised a parallel algorithm that runs in time $O(\log^2 m \log \frac{1}{\epsilon})$, and produces a solution that is at most $\frac{p}{(1-\epsilon)}$ times the optimum.

In the next section we demonstrate how Dual-feasible II could have been conceived from a different formulation of the set cover problem. This underlies the connection between formulations and algorithms.

USING OTHER RELAXATIONS TO DERIVE DUAL FEASIBLE SOLUTIONS

3.5

Imagine an alternative formulation of the set cover problem that has many additional constraints compared to the standard formulation. Let $\bar{C}$ be any feasible set cover and any $S \subseteq I = \{1, \ldots, m\}$. Then, obviously $\sum_{j \in \bar{C}} |S_j \cap S| \geq |S|$. This leads to a new formulation with the following LP relaxation of the set cover problem:

$$\text{Min} \quad \sum_{j=1}^{n} w_j x_j$$
$$\text{subject to} \quad \sum_{j=1}^{n} |S_j \cap S| x_j \geq |S| \quad \forall S \subseteq I$$
$$x_j \geq 0, \quad j \in J.$$

Observe that this formulation contains all the constraints of (SC) for $S = i$, $i \in I$. All the additional constraints are redundant. The coefficients in the constraint matrix are no longer 0 and 1 as before. The dual to this relaxation is

$$\text{Max} \quad \sum_S |S| y_S$$
$$\text{subject to} \quad \sum_S |S_j \cap S| y_S \leq w_j, \quad j \in J$$
$$y_S \geq 0 \quad S \subseteq I.$$

Consider now the dual feasible algorithm applied to this formulation. For every violated primal constraint (uncovered element), we increase the corresponding y_S proportionally to its coefficient in all dual constraints until at least one becomes binding. This means setting

$$y_S = \min_{j|S_j \cap S \neq \emptyset} \frac{w_j}{|S_j \cap S|}.$$

In particular, we may choose $S = I$ and add the set S_k for which the minimum is attained to the cover; update $I \leftarrow I \setminus S_k$ and repeat.

Notice that this algorithm is precisely Dual-feasible II. To see that the same p-approximation follows notice that for every pair of feasible covers C and $\bar{C}$,

$$\sum_{j \in C} |S_j \cap S| \leq p|S| \leq p \sum_{j \in \bar{C}} |S_j \cap S|.$$

Let the optimal integer solution be $|SC^*|$. We now have similar inequalities as before,

$$\sum_{j \in C} w_j = \sum_{j \in C} \sum_S |S_j \cap S| y_S = \sum_S \sum_{j \in C} |S_j \cap S| y_S \leq p \sum_S |S| y_S \leq p|SC^*|.$$

This type of approach that uses alternative formulations has lead to considerably better approximations for specific types of covering problems and network design problems as described in Chapter 4. For an alternative 2-approximation for the vertex cover problem, see Section 9.2.1.

APPROXIMATING THE MULTICOVER PROBLEM

3.6

In this section we present variations of the LP-algorithm, the rounding algorithm, and the dual-feasible algorithm that also work for the multicover problem (MC). The description of the dual-feasible algorithm and its analysis are from [HH86]. Consider the linear programming relaxation of the multicover problem and its dual:

$$MC^* = \text{Min} \quad \sum_{j=1}^{n} w_j x_j$$

(MCR)   subject to $\sum_{j=1}^{n} a_{ij} x_j \geq b_i$ (for $i = 1, \ldots, m$)

$$0 \leq x_j \leq 1 \quad (j = 1, \ldots, n)$$

MC^* obviously bounds from below the optimal value to the multicover problem. The dual to the linear programming relaxation above reads:

$$\text{Max} \quad \sum_{i=1}^{m} b_i y_i - \sum_{j=1}^{n} v_j$$

(MC-dual)   subject to $\sum_{i=1}^{m} a_{ij} y_i - v_j \leq w_j$ (for $j = 1, \ldots, n$)

$$y_i, v_j \geq 0 \quad (i = 1, 2, \ldots, m, j = 1, \ldots, n)$$

Here a feasible dual solution $(\bar{y}, \bar{v})$ is called *maximal* if it satisfies:

(i)   There is no other feasible solution (y, v) such that $y_i \geq \bar{y}_i$, $v_i \geq \bar{v}_i$ and $\sum_{i=1}^{m} b_i y_i - \sum_{j=1}^{n} v_j > \sum_{i=1}^{m} b_i \bar{y}_i - \sum_{j=1}^{n} \bar{v}_j$.

(ii) $\bar{v}_j = 0$ whenever $\sum_{i=1}^{m} a_{ij} y_i < w_j$.

(iii) $\sum_{i=1}^{m} \bar{y}_i \leq \sum_{i=1}^{m} b_i \bar{y}_i - \sum_{j=1}^{n} \bar{v}_j$

With this definition of maximality, the following LP-algorithm works as a p-approximation algorithm, where $p = \max_i \{\sum_j a_{ij}\}$.

THE LP-ALGORITHM FOR MULTICOVER

Step 1: Find a maximal dual feasible solution for (MC), $\bar{y}, \bar{v}$.

Step 2: Output the cover $C^H = \{j \mid \sum_{i=1}^{n} a_{ij} \bar{y}_i - \bar{v}_j = w_j\}$.

LEMMA 3.4   The LP-algorithm is a p-approximation algorithm for (MC).

Proof.   First, we establish that C^H is a feasible multicover. Consider an uncovered element (row) q. Notice that for the problem to be feasible, every row i needs at least b_i sets covering it. Let $\delta = \text{Min}_{j \mid q \in S_j} \{\delta_j = w_j - \sum_{j=1}^{n} a_{ij} \bar{y}_i$ and $\delta_j > 0\}$. Since there must be at least b_q sets that q belongs to, and at most $b_q - 1$ of them are in C^H, it follows that δ is well defined. Now set, $\mathbf{y} = \bar{y} + \delta \cdot e_q$ and $\mathbf{v} = \bar{v} + \sum_{j \in C^H \mid q \in S_j} \delta e_j$.

It is easy to verify that the vector $(\mathbf{y}, \mathbf{v})$ is a feasible solution, thus contradicting property (i) of the maximality of $(\bar{y}, \bar{v})$. This is because the first term has at least increased by $b_q \delta$ whereas the second term has at most increased by $(b_q - 1)\delta$, thus contributing to a net increase of the objective function by at least δ.

Now $(\bar{y}, \bar{v})$ is a feasible dual solution, hence the weak duality theorem applies:

$$\sum_{i \in I} b_i \bar{y}_i \leq \min \left(\sum_{j \in J} w_j x_j \right) + \sum_{j \in J} \bar{v}_j \leq MC^* + \sum_{j \in J} \bar{v}_j.$$

From that and property (iii),

$$\sum_{i \in I} y_i \leq MC^*. \tag{3.7}$$

Using the construction of C^H:

$$\sum_{j \in C^H} w_j + \sum_{j \in C^H} v_j = \sum_{j \in C^H} \sum_{i \in I} a_{ij} \bar{y}_i = \sum_{i \in I} \left(\sum_{j \in C^H} a_{ij} \right) \bar{y}_i$$

$$\leq \left(\max_{i \in I} \sum_{j \in C^H} a_{ij} \right) \cdot \sum_{i \in I} \bar{y}_i \leq p \cdot MC.$$

The last inequality follows from 3.7 and the definition of p. Recalling that the $\bar{v}_j$'s are nonnegative and that $MC^* \leq w(C^*)$ where $w(C^*)$ is the value of the optimal integer solution, we derive the stated result. ∎

A rounding algorithm is also a p-approximation algorithm. It offers the advantage of a smaller weight multicover.

THE ROUNDING ALGORITHM [HALL AND HOCHBAUM]

Step 1: Solve the linear programming relaxation of (MC) optimally. Let an optimal solution be $\{x_j^*\}$

Step 2: Output the cover $C^H = \{j \,|\, x_j^* \geq \frac{1}{p}\}$.

The feasibility of this cover is obvious, as in any fractional solution **x** corresponding to a cover C, $\sum_{j=1}^n a_{ij} x_j \geq b_i$. So at least b_i entries must be at least as large as the average $\frac{1}{p}$.

Next we present a dual-feasible algorithm that delivers a p-approximate solution to the multicovering problem. This algorithm has a better complexity than the one required to solve the relaxation optimally.

The input to the algorithm is the matrix A and the vectors **b** and **w**. The output is COVER – the indices of the sets selected and a vector $(y_i, i = 1, \ldots, m; v_j, j = 1, \ldots, n)$ that will later be proved to constitute a feasible dual solution.

THE DUAL-FEASIBLE MC ALGORITHM

Step 0: (initialize) $v_j = 0, j \in J$. $y_j = 0, i \in J$. COVER $= \emptyset$.

Step 1: Let $i \in I$. Let $w_k = \min\{w_j \,|\, j \in J\text{-COVER and } a_{ij} = 1\}$. ($k$ is the minimum cost column covering row i.) If no such minimum exists, stop - the problem is infeasible.

Step 2: Set $y_i \leftarrow y_i + w_k$. COVER $\leftarrow$ COVER $\cup \{k\}$. For all $j \in J$ such that $a_{ij} = 1$ set $w_j \leftarrow w_j - w_k$. If $w_j < 0$ then $v_j \leftarrow v_j - w_j$ and $w_j \leftarrow 0$.

Step 3: Set $b_i \leftarrow b_i - 1, i = 1, \ldots, m$. For all i' such that $b_{i'} = 0, I \leftarrow I - \{i'\}$. If $I = \emptyset$ stop. Else, go to Step 1.

The algorithm repeats Step 1 at most n times, since if following n iterations the set I is not yet empty, then there is no feasible solution. This could occur for instance if the amount of required coverage exceeds the number of covering sets, n. At each iteration there are at most $(\max\{n, m\})$ operations resulting in a total complexity of $O(\max\{n, m\} \cdot n)$.

The output of the algorithm is the set COVER of indices of the selected sets that multicover all elements, or a statement that the problem is infeasible. We shall now prove that dual vector derived is maximal and satisfies the three properties.

In the proofs of the facts that follow we shall use the notation $S_j = \{i \,|\, a_{ij} = 1\}$, i.e., S_j denotes the jth set.

Fact 1. For each $j \in$ COVER, $w_j = \sum_{i \in S_j} y_i - v_j$.

Proof.   By construction $w_j + v_j = \sum_{i \in S_j} y_i$.   ∎

Fact 2. $\sum_{i \in S_j} y_i \leq w_j + v_j \quad \forall j \in J$.

Proof.   This follows from Fact 1 and from Step 1 since the minimum cost column is always selected.   ∎

Fact 3. The output of the algorithm $(\mathbf{y}, \mathbf{v}) = \left(\{y_i\}_{i=1}^m, \{v_j\}_{j=1}^n \right)$ is a feasible solution to the dual problem.

Proof.   First, y_i, v_j are always nonnegative. This follows since y_i is equal to a cost w_j during one of the iterations and the $w_j's$ are always maintained as nonnegative numbers. Each v_j is a sum of positive numbers, and hence, nonnegative as well. Finally, Fact 2 establishes the feasibility with respect to the constraints.   ∎

Fact 4. $v_j = 0$ for all $j \in J$-COVER. This fact follows from the selection made at Step 1 of the algorithm.

The following lemma is useful in the proof of property (iii).

LEMMA 3.5 $\sum_{j \in \text{COVER}} v_j \leq \sum_{i \in I} (b_i - 1) y_i$ (note that $b_i \geq 1, i \in I$).

Proof.   The values of the left-hand side and the right hand side of the inequality vary during the algorithm's iteration.

We let the value of v_j and y_i after iteration t be denoted by $v_j^{(t)}$ and $y_i^{(t)}$ respectively. Let T be the number of iterations. We shall prove by induction on t that

$$\sum_{j \in \text{COVER}} v_j^{(t)} \leq \sum_{i \in I} (b_i - 1) y_i^{(t)}, \quad i = 1, \ldots, T.$$

For $t = 1$, the left-hand side is zero and the right-hand side nonnegative. We shall assume by induction that the inequality holds for $t = 1, \ldots, l - 1$ and prove for l.

Let $M = w_k$ be the minimum column cost selected at iteration l; then the right-hand side increases by $(b_i - 1) \cdot M$ with y_i increasing by M. Each $v_j^{(l)}$ might be increased by at most M compared to the previous iteration but for no more than $(b_i - 1)$ columns. This is the case since a cost of a column could become negative (thus triggering the increase in $v_j^{(l)}$), only if it is already b_i columns or more covering row i in COVER. Then this row would have been removed from the set I, and thus could not be considered at iteration l. Therefore, the inequality is preserved at each iteration, and hence, the desired result. ∎

From the proof of the theorem it follows that the heuristic solution value does not in fact exceed $(\max_{\substack{i \in I \\ i \in \text{COVER}}} \sum a_{ij})$ times the value of the optimum. This quantity could be much smaller than p.

The derivation of the dual vector as a by-product of the heuristic also provides a certificate of optimality for the selected set COVER (or any other solution) satisfying $\sum_{i \in \text{COVER}} w_j = \sum_{i=1}^{n} b_i y_i - \sum_{j=1}^{n} v_j$.

THE OPTIMAL DUAL APPROACH FOR THE VERTEX COVER AND INDEPENDENT SET PROBLEMS: PREPROCESSING

3.7

As we saw earlier, finding the optimal dual solution rather than a feasible one does not offer improved approximation bounds in general but requires more running time. Still, for the vertex cover and independent set (and the more general integer programs with two variables per inequality), the optimal dual solution provides important information about the problem, and allows it to improve the approximation bounds. For vertex cover, the use of the optimal dual solution guarantees that any heuristic used along with that information as preprocessing, yields an approximation ratio strictly better than 2.

Many intuitively reasonable heuristics for the vertex cover problem, (with the exception of the LP-algorithm), may fare quite badly compared to the optimal solution to the problem. For instance, a natural heuristic to consider is to take the largest degree vertex in the graph for the unweighted problem. This is the greedy algorithm, and, as shown by Johnson [Joh74], this heuristic applied to a graph of maximum degree k may deliver a cover whose weight exceeds the weight of an optimal cover by a factor of $\mathcal{H}(k)$ even if all weights are unit.

Another heuristic is available when the set of vertices of the graph V is split into independent sets $\{V_1, \ldots, V_k\}$. (Methods of obtaining such a split will be described later.) Each set $V \setminus V_i$ is a cover. In particular, $V \setminus V_i$ of the smallest weight may seem to be a good candidate for a cover C. Still, the ratio $\frac{w(C)}{w(C^*)}$ may be arbitrarily large even when G is fixed. Indeed, consider the path with vertices $\{1, 2, 3, 4\}$ and weights $w_1 = w_4 = M$, $w_2 = w_3 = 1$ for some large M. When V is partitioned into two independent sets, the strategy proposed here yields a cover C with $w(C) = M + 1$ and yet the optimal cover C^* has $w(C^*) = 2$. Some more illustrations of such undesirable behavior of other heuristics are quite common. Still, it seems that the LP-heuristic alone employs relatively little information about the underlying structure of the graph, and one should be able to fare better with additional graph information taken into account.

This idea has motivated the use of the preprocessing procedure of [Hoc83] that makes use of the linear programming information *and* additional information about the graph. Indeed, the quality of the solution delivered by any heuristic can be improved if we first partition the graph into two subgraphs with the property that in one subgraph an optimal selection of a cover is known and in the other the weight of the optimal cover is at least half of the total weight of all vertices. The existence of such a partition, implied by the fractional solution to the problem, has been established by Nemhauser and Trotter [NT75].

More precisely, Nemhauser and Trotter [NT75], Balinski and Spielberg [BS69], and Lorentzen [Lor66] have shown that there exists an optimal solution to the linear programming relaxation of (VC), $\mathbf{x}^*$, such that $x_j^* \in \{0, 1, \frac{1}{2}\}$. We call this property the *half integrality property*. Nemhauser and Trotter have further proved that there exists an optimal integer solution that is equal to $\mathbf{x}^*$ in its integer components. We refer to this property as the *"fixing variables" property*. Both the half integrality property and the "fixing variables" property were proved to hold also for IP2 (see [HMNT93] or 3.8).

One possible algorithmic use of fixing variables is that an optimal integer solution may be obtained by rounding the components of $\mathbf{x}^*$ that are equal to $\frac{1}{2}$. The rounding could be up or down to 1 or 0 respectively. Since there are 2^n possible rounding schemes (some of which may not lead to a feasible solution), this fact in itself does not aid in speeding up the search for an optimal solution. It does, however, provide us with a head-start in the search towards a solution: consider an optimal solution $\mathbf{x}^*$ to (VCR), and the implied partition:

$$j \in P \text{ if } x_j = 1$$

$$j \in Q \text{ if } x_j = \frac{1}{2}$$

$$j \in R \text{ if } x_j = 0.$$

Then, using the fixing variables property we conclude,

(i) at least one optimal cover in C contains P,

(ii) each vertex in R has all its neighbors in P,

(iii) each cover in G has weight at least $w(P) + \frac{1}{2}w(Q)$.

From (i) and (ii), it follows instantly that at least one optimal cover in G consists of the set P and of an optimal cover in the subgraph H induced by Q. Thus, it suffices to find an optimal cover in H; working with H rather than with G is what we mean by "fixing variables."

Fixing variables is a trick which can be applied not only in the context of finding optimal covers but also in the context of heuristics for finding near-optimal covers. In this context, the trick has a nice corollary: If C is any cover in H, then (by (ii)) $P \cup C$ is a cover in G, and (by (iii)) its weight is at most twice the weight of an optimal cover. Thus any heuristic for finding near-optimal covers can be made to deliver a cover whose weight is at most twice the weight of an optimal cover: it suffices to preprocess G by finding P, Q, R, and then to apply the heuristic to H rather than directly to G. Formally, let C^H be the cover delivered by the heuristic on the subgraph H. Then,

$$\frac{w(C^H \cup P)}{w(C^*)} \leq \frac{w(C^H) + w(P)}{\frac{1}{2}w(Q) + w(P)} \leq 2\frac{w(C^H)}{w(Q)}.$$

The consequence of using the preprocessing technique is that *any* heuristic for the vertex cover problem delivers a solution that is less than twice times the optimum. C^H is a subset of Q, and one can always remove just one vertex from Q that is of maximum weight and consider the rest as the heuristic cover.

The preprocessing technique has become the basis of most "good" heuristics for the vertex cover problem, and it can be used to improve by a factor of two the approximation ratio for the independent set problems. Unlike the vertex cover, we cannot guarantee an approximation ratio better than half (or factor of two off the optimum) for the independent set problem. To see why, consider a heuristic applied to the subgraph H delivering an independent set IS^H. The ratio of the weight of the resulting independent set to the optimal independent set IS^* is,

$$\frac{w(IS^H \cup R)}{w(IS^*)} \geq \frac{w(IS^H) + w(R)}{\frac{1}{2}w(Q) + w(R)} \geq 2\frac{w(IS^H)}{w(Q)}.$$

Now IS^H could be arbitrarily small, so the ratio may be arbitrarily close to 0. If on the other hand the heuristic procedure guarantees a certain positive ratio, the use of the preprocessing technique may double this ratio. Whether or not the ratio is doubled depends on whether the graph property is hereditary and maintained for the subgraph. When applying the procedure to a graph with a small largest claw number, for instance, there is no improvement with preprocessing (as this property is not hereditary), and the bound on the optimum relies on the bounded claw number of the graph. This algorithm will be demonstrated in a later section.

Pulleyblank [Pul79] observed the following with regard to the size of the subsets P and Q. He proved that almost all graphs (randomly generated) have an LP-relaxation for which the solution is a vector of $\frac{1}{2}$s and no integer entries. In that sense, the use of the preprocessing is more to guarantee that the graph has no integer nodes, rather than to attempt to find many integer values.

3.7.1 THE COMPLEXITY OF THE LP-RELAXATION OF VERTEX COVER AND INDEPENDENT SET

In order to apply the preprocessing solution, the optimal LP solution must be available. Although in principle it is possible to solve linear programs in polynomial time (using Ellipsoid method or interior-point methods), such procedures are less efficient than many combinatorial algorithms. In particular, the LP-relaxation of the vertex cover is solvable by the max-flow min-cut algorithm.

The LP-relaxation of the vertex cover problem can be solved by finding an optimal cover in a bipartite graph with two vertices for each vertex in the original graph, and two edges for each edge in the original graph (see Figure 3.3). In the bipartite graph a vertex cover may be identified from the solution of a corresponding minimum cut problem. Specifically, as suggested by Edmonds and Pulleyblank and noted in [NT75], the LP-relaxation can be solved by finding an optimal cover C in the bipartite graph with two vertices a_j, b_j of weight w_j for each vertex j of G, and two edges $(a_i, b_j), (a_j, b_i)$ for each edge (i, j) of G: then it suffices to set

$$x_j = 1 \text{ if } a_j, b_j \in C,$$

$$x_j = \frac{1}{2} \text{ if } a_j \in C, b_j \notin C, \text{ or } a_j \notin C, b_j \in C,$$

$$x_j = 0 \text{ if } a_j \notin C, b_j \notin C.$$

In turn, the problem of finding C can be reduced into a minimum cut problem: the bipartite graph can be converted into a network by making each edge (a_i, b_j) into a directed arc (a_i, b_j) of an infinite capacity, adding a source s with an arc (s, a_i) of capacity w_i for each i, and adding a sink t with an arc (b_j, t) of capacity w_j for each j. Now a minimum cut (S, T) with $s \in S$ and $t \in T$ points out the desired C: it suffices to set $a_i \in C$ iff $a_i \in T$ and $b_j \in C$ iff $b_j \in S$. A description of the resulting graph is given in Figure 3.3.

The minimum cut can be found by efficient algorithms for maximum flow on (bipartite) graphs. For instance, if one uses Goldberg and Tarjan's algorithm, [GT88], it takes only $O(mn \log \frac{n^2}{m})$ steps to preprocess G with n vertices and m edges by partitioning the set of vertices into P, Q and R. This algorithm is a special case of the algorithm used to find the half integer solution for IP2 where min cut is also used for preprocessing (see Section 3.8).

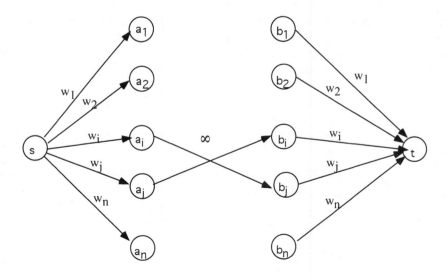

FIGURE 3.3

We now present an alternative method of reducing the LP-relaxation to a flow problem that is illuminating as to why min cut solves this problem. Consider the LP-relaxation of the vertex cover problem (VCR),

$$\text{Min} \qquad \sum_{j=1}^{n} w_j x_j$$
(VCR)   subject to $x_i + x_j \geq 1$ (for every edge (i, j) in the graph)
$$0 \leq x_j \leq 1 \quad (j = 1, \ldots, n).$$

Replace each variable x_j by two variables, x_j^+ and x_j^-, and each inequality by two inequalities:

$$x_i^+ - x_j^- \geq 1$$
$$-x_i^- + x_j^+ \geq 1 .$$

The two inequalities have one 1 and one -1 in each, and thus correspond to a dual of a network flow problem. The upper and lower bounds constraints are transformed to

$$0 \leq x_j^+ \leq 1$$
$$-1 \leq x_j^- \leq 0 .$$

In the objective function, the variable x_j is substituted by $\frac{1}{2}(x_j^+ - x_j^-)$.

The resulting constraint matrix of the new problem is totally unimodular. Hence, the linear programming (optimal basic) solution is integer, and in particular can be obtained using a minimum cut algorithm. When the original variables are recovered, they are integer multiples of $\frac{1}{2}$.

We will see in Section 3.8 that this transformation is applicable to all integer programs with two variables per inequality. That, in addition to the "fixing variables" property that applies, guarantees that *any* heuristic will give a bound of 2 or better.

Remark: When the problem is *unweighted*, the network flow that solves the LP relaxation is defined on *simple* networks. These are networks with all arcs of capacity 1, and every node has either one incoming arc or one outgoing arc. In this case, the arcs in the bipartition of the type (a_i, b_j) can be assigned capacity 1 instead of ∞. For simple networks, Dinic's algorithm for maximum flow works in $O(\sqrt{n}m)$ time—a significant improvement in running time.

3.7.2   EASILY COLORABLE GRAPHS

It is now demonstrated how to exploit certain graph properties with the preprocessing technique so as to obtain approximation factors better than 2 for the vertex cover problem, and improved approximations for the independent set problem. For many classes of graphs it is easy to split the nodes into independent sets. Assigning each independent set a color results in a valid coloring with adjacent vertices having distinct colors.

THEOREM 3.2   Let G be a weighted graph with n vertices and m edges; let k be an integer greater than one. If it takes only s steps to color the vertices of G in k colors, then it takes only $s + O(nm \log \frac{n^2}{m})$ steps to find an independent set whose weight is at least $2/k$ times the weight of an optimal independent set and to find a cover whose weight is at most $2 - 2/k$ times the weight of an optimal cover.

Proof.   It takes only $s + O(nm \log \frac{n^2}{m})$ steps to color G in k colors and to find the set P, Q, R of the preceding section. (Note that it suffices to color only the vertices of Q.) The coloring of G splits Q into k color classes; if S denotes the heaviest of them then $W(S) \geq W(Q)/k$. The set $R \cup S$ is independent since

$$w(R \cup S) \geq w(R) + \frac{1}{k}w(Q) \geq \frac{2}{k}\left((w(R) + \frac{1}{2}w(Q)\right),$$

its weight is at least $2/k$ times the weight of an optimal independent set. The complement C of $R \cup S$ is a cover since

$$w(C) \leq w(P) + \frac{k-1}{k}w(Q) \leq \frac{2(k-1)}{k}\left(w(P) + \frac{1}{2}w(Q)\right),$$

its weight is at most $2 - 2/k$ times the weight of an optimal cover.   ■

The remainder of this section consists of various corollaries of Theorem 3.2. To begin with, let $D(G)$ denote the largest d such that G contains a subgraph in which each vertex has degree at least d. As proved by Szekeres and Wilf [SW68], every graph G can be colored in $D(G) + 1$ colors. For the sake of completeness, we shall describe a way of finding such a coloring and evaluating $D(G)$ in only $O(n+m)$ steps. To evaluate $D(G)$, it suffices to dismantle G by successive removals of vertices of minimum degree.

MAXIMUM MINIMUM DEGREE SUBGRAPH

Step 0:   Set $d = 0$.

Step 1:   If G has no vertices left, then stop; otherwise choose a vertex v of the smallest degree.

Step 2:   Replace d by the maximum of d and the degree of v. Then remove v (and all the edges incident with v) from G and return to Step 1.

If v_i denotes the vertex removed from G in the ith iteration, then each v_i has at most d neighbors among the vertices $v_{i+1}, v_{i+2}, \ldots, v_n$. To color G in no more than $d + 1$ colors, it suffices to scan the sequence of $v_i's$ from v_n to v_l, assigning to each v_i the smallest positive integer not yet assigned to any of its neighbors.

COROLLARY 3.2   It takes only $O(nm \log \frac{n^2}{m})$ steps to find, in any weighted graph G with n vertices and m edges such that $m > 0$, an independent set whose weight is at least $2/(D(G)+1)$ times the weight of an optimal independent set and a cover whose weight is at most $2 - 2/(D(G)+1)$ times the weight of an optimal cover.

The celebrated theorem of Brooks [Bro41] asserts the following: if G is a connected graph of a maximum degree Δ such that $\Delta > 3$ and if G is not the complete graph with $\Delta + 1$ vertices, then G is Δ-colorable. An elegant and constructive proof of this theorem, due to Lovász [Lov75a], provides an algorithm which finds the coloring in only $O(\Delta n)$ steps. (The algorithm requires finding cutpoints and endblocks in a graph. This can be done in $O(m)$ steps by depth-first search as described, for instance, in [Baa78]).

COROLLARY 3.3 It takes only $O(\Delta n^2 \log \frac{n^2}{m})$ steps to find, in any weighted graph with n vertices and a maximum degree Δ such that $\Delta \geq 2$, an independent set whose weight is at least $2/\Delta$ times the weight of an optimal independent set and a cover whose weight is at most $2 - 2/\Delta$ times the weight of an optimal cover.

Proof. We may assume that $\Delta \geq 3$; otherwise each component is a cycle or a path and a straightforward dynamic programming algorithm finds an optimal independent set and an optimal cover in only $O(n)$ steps. Furthermore, we may assume that the graph is connected; otherwise each component may be treated separately. Finally, we may assume that the graph is not complete: otherwise an optimal independent set and an optimal cover may be found trivially in $O(n)$ steps. But then the desired conclusion follows directly from Brooks' theorem and Theorem 3.2. ∎

We will show in the next subsection that the $\frac{2}{\Delta}$ guarantee for independent set can be improved by using a better partition.

The coloration heuristics are not counterexamples to our conjecture that vertex cover is impossible to approximate within a ratio strictly less than 2. To show that, we let a graph G be defined as follows. Consider Δ Δ-cliques and Δ $(\Delta - 1)$-independent sets. Each clique has one edge connecting it to one of the vertices of an independent set. $\Delta - 1$ of the independent sets are one set of vertices in a complete bipartite graph with the Δth independent set as the second set of vertices. For such family of graphs, one can easily verify that G is Δ chromatic and $G = H$. One feasible[1] Δ-coloration consists of each one of the independent sets colored by one of the Δ-colors. The heuristic then delivers a cover C of size $(2\Delta - 1)(\Delta - 1)$. The optimum cover C^* is of size $\Delta(\Delta - 1) + (\Delta - 1)$ and the ratio

$$w(C)/w(C^*) = 2 - \frac{2 - 3/\Delta}{\Delta - 1/\Delta}$$

which could be arbitrarily close to 2.

The standard proof due to Heawood that every planar graph is five-colorable (see, for instance, [Har69]) has been converted into linear time algorithms [CNS81] [MST80].

COROLLARY 3.4 It takes only $O(n^2 \log \frac{n^2}{m})$ steps to find, in any weighted planar graph with n vertices, an independent set whose weight is at least 0.4 times the weight of an optimal independent set and a cover whose weight is at most 1.6 times the weight of an optimal cover.

Furthermore, the proof that every planar graph is four-colorable [AH77] [AHK77] is convertible into an algorithm which actually finds the coloring in a polynomial number of steps.

COROLLARY 3.5 It takes a polynomial number of steps to find, in any weighted planar graph, an independent set whose weight is at least 0.5 times the weight of an

---

[1]In order to make this coloration unique we add a few edges to the graph: The vertices in the cliques that connect each clique to each independent set are linked together to make a complete subgraph. The ith independent set is connected to all these vertices except for the ith vertex.

optimal independent set and a cover whose weight is at most 1.5 times the weight of an optimal cover.

3.7.3   A GREEDY ALGORITHM FOR INDEPENDENT SET
IN UNWEIGHTED GRAPHS

Sparse graphs have large independent sets. More precisely, the celebrated Theorem of Turán [Tur41] asserts that every graph with n vertices and an average degree δ (this quantity is not necessarily an integer) contains a independent set of size at least $\frac{n}{\delta+1}$. An elegant proof of Turán's theorem, due to Erdös [Erd70], is easily converted into the following algorithm for finding a independent set S in at most $O(m)$ steps.

GREEDY ALGORITHM [ERDÖS]

Step 0: Set $S = 0$.

Step 1: If G has no vertices then stop; otherwise choose a vertex v with the smallest degree d in the current graph.

Step 2: Add v to S, delete v and all its neighbors (along with all the edges incident with at least one of these vertices) from G, and return to Step 1.

To show that the size of the independent set S delivered upon termination is at least $\frac{n}{\delta+1}$, we observe that whenever a vertex v_i of degree d_i (this is the degree of v_i in the reduced graph from which v_i is selected and subsequently removed) is chosen and deleted, we eliminate a total of $d_i + 1$ vertices from the graph and the sum of the degrees of the vertices deleted is at least $d_i(d_i + 1)$. If $q = |S|$ is the number of vertex selections performed in the greedy algorithm, then

$$\sum_{i=1}^{q} d_i(d_i + 1) \leq n\delta \quad \text{and} \quad \sum_{i=1}^{q}(d_i + 1) = n . \tag{3.8}$$

By adding these two equations together and then applying the Cauchy-Schwarz inequality, we get that

$$n(\delta + 1) \geq \sum_{i=1}^{q}(d_i + 1)^2 \geq \frac{n^2}{q} ,$$

from which it follows that $q \geq \frac{n}{\delta+1}$.

By using the greedy algorithm in conjunction with preprocessing, we get the following result.

THEOREM 3.3 [Hoc83]   In any graph G with n vertices and average degree δ it takes $O(\delta n^{\frac{3}{2}})$ steps to find an independent set of size at least $\frac{2}{\delta+1}$ times the size of maximum independent set.

Proof. Preprocessing an unweighted graph can be executed in only $O(m\sqrt{n})$ steps [HK73]. Once the partition P, Q, R is obtained we apply the algorithm above to the subgraph H. The total number of steps does not exceed $O(\delta n^{\frac{3}{2}})$. The size of the independent set delivered by the algorithm is at least $|R| + \frac{|Q|}{\delta_H + 1}$, where δ_H is the average degree in H. (Incidentally, note that $\delta_H \geq 2$ as there is always a solution with no vertices of degree one in the subgraph H.) Now we note that:

Fact 1. G is a connected graph, hence,

$$\delta \geq \frac{|Q|\delta_H + |R| + |P|}{|Q| + |R| + |P|}$$

(note that $n = |Q| + |R| + |P|$).

Fact 2. $|R| \geq |P|$, otherwise setting $G = H$ (i.e., all vertices are assigned the value $\frac{1}{2}$) implies an "LP relaxation" solution of value larger than $|R| + \frac{1}{2}|Q|$, contradiction.

To complete the proof it suffices to show (using Fact 1) that

$$\frac{|R| + \frac{|Q|}{\delta_H + 1}}{|R| + \frac{1}{2}|Q|} \geq 2\left(\frac{|Q|\delta_H + |R| + |P|}{|Q| + |R| + |P|}\right)^{-1}.$$

Rearranging this inequality we reduce it to

$$|Q|\,(|R|\delta_H(\delta_H - 1) - |P|(\delta_H - 1) - |P|(\delta_H - 1)) \geq 0.$$

The validity of this inequality follows easily from Fact 2. ∎

Halldórsson and Radhakrishnan ([HR94]) have recently tightened this analysis to achieve an improved bound on q. Consider an optimal independent set, and let k_i be the number of nodes from this independent set deleted at stage i of the greedy algorithm. Then, because an edge can have only one of its endpoints in the maximum independent set, the equations (3.8) can be tightened:

$$\sum_{i=1}^{q} d_i(d_i + 1) + k_i(k_i - 1) \leq n\delta \quad \text{and} \quad \sum_{i=1}^{q}(d_i + 1) = n .$$

Adding these two equations along with $\sum_{i=1}^{q} k_i = IS^*$, and applying the Cauchy-Schwarz inequality yields,

$$(\delta + 1)n + \alpha \geq \sum_{i=1}^{q}(d_i + 1)^2 + k_i^2 \geq \frac{n^2 + (IS^*)^2}{q} ,$$

which implies that $q \geq \frac{n^2 + (IS^*)^2}{n(\delta+1) + IS^*}$. Because this quantity is maximized at $IS^* = n$, the following improved bound for the quality of the greedy solution is found:

$$q \geq \frac{2}{\delta + 2} .$$

When used in conjunction with the preprocessing technique, as in Theorem 3.3, a better performance bound of $\frac{5}{2\delta+3}$ is achieved.

[HR94] also provides an analysis that yields a performance guarantee in terms of the maximum degree Δ in an unweighted graph of $q \geq \frac{3}{\Delta+2}$ for the greedy algorithm. This is better than the bound in Corollary 3.3 when the graph is unweighted and $\Delta \geq 5$.

As we discuss in the next subsection, the idea of *subgraph removal* can be incorporated to further improve the performance guarantee given for the greedy algorithm.

3.7.4   A LOCAL-RATIO THEOREM AND SUBGRAPH REMOVAL

In some cases, the absence of a particular family of subgraphs $\mathcal{H}$ (for example, odd cycles) from a graph G can imply an improved approximation guarantee for finding an optimal structure in G. Bar-Yehuda and Even [BE85] have developed a local-ratio theorem that, by removing problematic subgraphs, yields several new approximation algorithms which improve upon previously known results for the weighted vertex cover problem. Their main result is a $(2 - \frac{\log\log n}{2\log n})$-approximation algorithm that relies on eliminating "small" odd cycles. This subsection describes their approach and its extension to other approximation problems.

Let $\mathcal{H}$ be a set of graphs. Let $A_{\mathcal{H}}$ be an approximation algorithm for the weighted vertex cover problem. Consider the following algorithm to find a vertex cover in the graph $G = (V, E)$, with weight function w.

SUBGRAPH REMOVAL ALGORITHM [BAR-YEHUDA AND EVEN]

Step 0: Set $w_0 \leftarrow w$.

Step 1: While there exists a subgraph H of G that is isomorphic to some member of $\mathcal{H}$ and whose vertices have positive weight, do: $\forall v \in V(H)$ set $w_0(v) \leftarrow w_0(v) - \delta$, where $\delta \leftarrow \min\{w_0(v) | v \in V(H)\}$.

Step 2: Set: $VC_0 \leftarrow \{v \in G | w_0(v) = 0\}$; $V_1 \leftarrow V - VC_0$.

Step 3: Let VC_1 be returned by applying $A_{\mathcal{H}}$ on $G(V_1)$, with the weight function w_0. Return $VC \leftarrow VC_0 \cup VC_1$.

For each entry in $H \in \mathcal{H}$, let $r_H = \frac{n_H}{c_H}$, where n_H is the number of vertices in H and c_H is the cardinality of a minimum unweighted vertex cover in H. r_H is called the *local-ratio* of the graph H. The quality of solution returned by the above algorithm is given by the following theorem from [BE85]:

THEOREM 3.4 Local-Ratio Theorem   Let $r_{\mathcal{H}} = \max_{H \in \mathcal{H}}\{r_H\}$ and $r_{A_{\mathcal{H}}}$ be the approximation factor guaranteed by the algorithm $A_{\mathcal{H}}$ on input $G(V_1)$. Then, the vertex cover VC returned by the Subgraph Removal Algorithm has weight at most $r = \max\{r_{\mathcal{H}}, r_{A_{\mathcal{H}}}\}$ times that of the optimal vertex cover.

In order to establish Theorem 3.4, we need a preliminary lemma.

LEMMA 3.6   Let $G = (V, E)$ be a graph, and w, w_1, and w_2 be weight functions on the vertices V, with optimal vertex covers VC^*, VC_1^* and VC_2^*, respectively. Suppose that $w(v) \geq w_1(v) + w_2(v)$, for every $v \in V$. Then,

$$w(VC^*) \geq w_1(VC_1^*) + w_2(VC_2^*) .$$

Proof.

$$w(VC^*) = \sum_{v \in VC^*} w(v) \geq \sum_{v \in VC^*} (w_1(v) + w_2(v))$$
$$= w_1(VC^*) + w_2(VC^*) \geq w_1(VC_1^*) + w_2(VC_2^*) \ .$$

∎

Proof. (**Local-Ratio Theorem**) The proof is by induction on k, the number of times that the *do-while* loop in Step 1 of the Subgraph Removal Algorithm is iterated through. For $k = 0$ the theorem is obviously true.

Now consider the case $k = 1$. Let VC^* and VC_0^* be the optimal solutions with respect to w and w_0, and let VC be the vertex cover returned by the algorithm. Then,

$$w(VC) \leq w_0(VC) + \delta n_H \leq r_{A_{\mathcal{H}}} w_0(VC^*) + r_H \delta c_H$$
$$\leq r \left(w_0(VC^*) + \delta c_H \right) \leq r \, w(VC^*) \ .$$

For $k > 1$, imagine running Step 1 through one iteration. Then, by considering the remainder of the algorithm as "$A_{\mathcal{H}}$" with performance guarantee r (from the induction hypothesis), we are in the $k = 1$ case, from which the result follows.   ∎

By selecting $\mathcal{H}$ appropriately and designing the approximation algorithm $A_{\mathcal{H}}$ to take advantage of the absence of such subgraphs, the *Subgraph Removal Algorithm* achieves approximation procedures with improved efficiency and/or approximation guarantee over previously known algorithms. The following is a summary of the results presented in [BE85].

1. $\mathcal{H}$ *is an edge:* An edge has a local-ratio of 2. By removing edges during Step 1 of the *Subgraph Removal Algorithm*, we are left with an empty graph at Step 2 (for which $r_{\mathcal{H}}$ vacuously equals 1). Thus, the algorithm gives a 2-approximation.

2. $\mathcal{H}$ *is a triangle:* By removing triangles during Step 1, which have a local-ratio of 1.5, we are left with a triangle-free graph at Step 2. Then, by using the $2 - \frac{2}{k}$ approximation algorithm from [Hoc83] as $A_{\mathcal{H}}$, where k is the number of colors needed to color the remaining graph, two results follow:

   a. Wigderson has shown [Wig83] that triangle free graphs can be colored with $k = 2\sqrt{n}$ colors in linear time. This yields a $\min\{1.5, 2 - \frac{1}{\sqrt{n}}\} = 2 - \frac{1}{\sqrt{n}}$ (for $n \geq 4$) approximation guarantee for general graphs. (Halldórsson [H94] has noted the existence of a nice algorithm [She83] that colors triangle free graphs with $k = 2\sqrt{\frac{n}{\log n}}$ colors, yielding a $2 - \sqrt{\frac{\log n}{n}}$ approximation guarantee.)

   b. Triangle-free planar graphs can be colored with $k = 4$ colors in linear time (see [Har69]), yielding an algorithm that matches the known 1.5 approximation guarantee of [Hoc83] for planar graphs. The advantage is that the complexity of the general 4-coloring algorithms for planar graphs is avoided.

3. $\mathcal{H}$ *is the set of "small" odd cycles:* Odd cycles up to length $2k - 1$, where $(2k - 1)^k \geq n$ (so, $k \leq \frac{2 \log n}{\log \log n}$), are removed. This set of cycles has local ratio $r_{\mathcal{H}} = \frac{2k-1}{k} = 2 - \frac{1}{k}$. For $A_{\mathcal{H}}$ we use an algorithm, with the same performance ratio, developed in [BE85] for graphs in which all odd cycles have length at

least $2k + 3$. This yields an approximation ratio guarantee of $2 - \frac{1}{k} \leq 2 - \frac{\log\log n}{2\log n}$. (Monien and Speckenmeyer [MS85] have used a similar approach to achieve improved results for the unweighted vertex cover problem.)

Halldórsson and Radhakrishnan [HR94] have used the strategy of triangle removal, in conjunction with preprocessing, to achieve several additional results for finding vertex covers in unweighted graphs:

1. Removing triangles and applying the coloring algorithm of [She83] yields a $2 - \frac{\log\Delta + O(1)}{\Delta}$ approximation guarantee, where Δ is the maximum degree of a vertex in the graph.

2. Consider a graph that is p-claw free. After removing triangles, the size of the largest claw is equal to the maximum degree of the remaining graph. Thus, the preceding result holds with Δ replaced by $p - 1$.

Halldórsson and Radhakrishnan [HR94] also employ a strategy of subgraph removal to achieve improved approximation algorithms for finding large (unweighted) independent sets. Their general schema, which entails removing all cliques of a given size from the graph and then running any particular independent set algorithm on the resulting graph, is used to achieve improved performance bounds for the particular independent set algorithm. Used in conjunction with the greedy algorithm, for instance, they achieve an asymptotic performance ratio of $\frac{3.76}{\Delta}$ by removing 8-cliques. Better performance bounds may be achievable if it is used in conjunction with other heuristics.

3.7.5   ADDITIONAL ALGORITHMS WITHOUT PREPROCESSING

3.7.5.1   Independent Set in Weighted Graphs

By applying a graph theoretic result of Lóvasz [Lov66], it is possible to improve the approximation guarantee for the weighted independent set problem in bounded degree graphs from $\frac{2}{\Delta}$ to $\frac{1}{\lceil \frac{\Delta+1}{3} \rceil}$, where Δ is the maximum degree of a vertex in the graph.

The idea is to consider a partition of a graph into k subgraphs, for some integer k; that is, partition the vertices into k subsets and consider the k subgraphs induced by each of the k subsets. Being able to find an optimal independent set in each subgraph implies being able to find an independent set with weight within a factor of $\frac{1}{k}$ of the optimal in the original graph. This fact is established in the next theorem.

THEOREM 3.5   Consider a weighted graph $G = (V, E)$, and let $V_1, \ldots, V_k$ be a partition of the vertices V into k subsets. If IS_i^* is an optimal independent set in G_i (where G_i is the subgraph of G induced by the vertices V_i) for $i = 1, \ldots, k$, and IS^* an optimal independent set in G, then

$$\max_{i=1,\ldots,k} \{w(IS_i^*)\} \geq \frac{1}{k} w(IS^*) .$$

Proof.   Because IS^* is an independent set in G, $IS^* \cup V_i$ is an independent set in G_i. So,

$$\sum_{i=1}^{k} w(IS_i^*) \geq \sum_{i=1}^{k} (w(IS^*) \cap V_i) = w(IS^*) \,.$$

Now, the result follows by the pigeonhole principle.   ■

Thus, being able to partition a graph into k subgraphs in which optimal independent sets can be found in polynomial time leads to a $\frac{1}{k}$-approximation algorithm for weighted independent set. Of the optimal independent sets in the subgraphs, select the one with maximum weight. More generally, being able to solve the independent set problem for each subgraph within a factor β of the optimal implies a $\frac{\beta}{k}$-approximation algorithm. Halldórson has noted the existence of a partitioning that can be used in this manner by applying the following theorem due to Lovász:

THEOREM 3.6 Lovász   Let $G(V, E)$ be a graph with maximum degree Δ. Let k be any integer such that $1 \leq k \leq \Delta$, and let $\Delta_1, \ldots, \Delta_k$ be nonnegative integers such that,

$$\Delta_1 + \Delta_2 + \ldots + \Delta_k = \Delta - k + 1 \,.$$

Then, V can be partitioned into k subsets $V_1, \ldots, V_k$, such that Δ_i is the maximum degree of a vertex in the subgraph of G induced by V_i, for $i = 1, \ldots, k$.

Moreover, a crude analysis of the algorithm implied by the proof of the above theorem shows that the partitioning of the graph can be carried out in $O(mk)$ time. The previous two theorems lead to the following corollary:

COROLLARY 3.6   Let G be a weighted graph with maximum degree Δ. An independent set with weight within a factor of $\frac{1}{\lceil \frac{\Delta+1}{3} \rceil}$ of the optimal can be found in $O(m\Delta)$ time.

Proof.   Applying Theorem 3.6, a graph can be partitioned into $k = \lceil \frac{\Delta+1}{3} \rceil$ subgraphs, each with maximum degree 2, in $O(m\Delta)$ time. Now, an optimal independent set in such graphs can be found in linear time. Thus, by Theorem 3.5, we can find an independent set with weight within $\frac{1}{\lceil \frac{\Delta+1}{3} \rceil}$ of the optimal.   ■

3.7.5.2   Vertex cover in unweighted large min-degree graphs

Karpinski and Zelikovsky [KZ95] recently proposed an algorithm for which the approximation is improved for graphs with large minimum degree. Let a graph be called $\underline{\delta}$-dense if each vertex is adjacent to at least $\underline{\delta}n$ vertices. Let $N(v)$ be the set of neighbors of v in $G = (V, E)$. The following is a $\frac{2}{1+\underline{\delta}}$- approximation algorithm:

procedure $\frac{2}{1+\underline{\delta}}$- approximation
for all $v \in V$ do
  $V(v) \leftarrow V \setminus \{N(v) \cup v\}$
  apply **dual-feasible I algorithm** to find a feasible vertex cover
  $VC(v)$ in the graph induced on $V(v)$.
  $VC(v) \leftarrow VC(v) \cup \{N(v)\}$
Return $VC(u)$ where $|VC(u)| = \min_{v \in V}|VC(v)|$.

The algorithm makes n calls to dual-feasible I, hence its complexity is $O(mn)$. The proof that the bound is valid is derived by assessing the ratios for the cases when the optimum cover OPT satisfies $|OPT| \le (1 - \underline{\delta})n$ and $|OPT| \ge (1 - \underline{\delta})n$.

3.7.6   SUMMARY OF APPROXIMATIONS FOR VERTEX COVER AND INDEPENDENT SET

We present here two tables along with a notation legend with the best known approximation results to date for vertex cover and independent set. The following legend explains the meanings of the symbols used in Table 3.1:

Symbol	Meaning
n	number of vertices in the graph
m	number of edges in the graph
α	value of optimal independent set
χ	chromatic number
Δ	maximum vertex degree
δ	average vertex degree
$D(G)$	$\max_{H \subseteq G}\{\min_{v \in H}\{degree(v)\}\}$
p-claw	a subset of $(p + 1)$ vertices that induces a p-star
$T(n,m)$	complexity of finding a minimum cut in a network with n nodes, m arcs
S	complexity of applying Shearer's coloring algorithm
$\underline{\delta}$	minimum vertex degree

References and comments: (1) [Hoc83]; (2) [Hoc83], Δ-coloring via Brooks' theorem; (3) [HR94]; (4) [HR94]; (5) [Hoc83],(δ_H is ave degree in subgraph H.); (6) [Hoc83]; (7) [Hoc83]; this running time is from [BE85]; (8) [Bak83], approximation scheme; (9) [BE85], via coloring algorithm in [Wig83]; (10) [BE85]; (11) [Hoc83] c is a fixed constant; (12) [MS85]; (13) [Hoc83]; (14) [YG92]; (15) [HR94]; (16) [KZ95]; (17) [Hoc83]; (18) [H94], using graph decomposition of [Lov66]; (19) [HR94], analysis of greedy algorithm; (20) [Hoc83]; (21) [HR94]; (22) [HR94], analysis of greedy algorithm; (23) [Hoc83]; (24) [Hoc83]; (25) [Bak83], approximation scheme; (26) [Hoc83]; (27) [YG92].

Table 3.1: Approximation Results for Vertex Cover and Independent Set

Vertex Cover Problem					
Graph Parameter	Approximation Guarantee	Complexity	Unweighted Only	No Pre-processing	Ref
χ	$2 - \frac{2}{\chi}$				1
Δ	$2 - \frac{2}{\Delta}$	$O(\Delta n^2 \log n)$			2
	$2 - \frac{3}{\Delta+2}$	$T(n,m)$	★		3
	$2 - \frac{\log \Delta + O(1)}{\Delta}$	$T(n,m)+S$	★		4
δ	$2 - \frac{2}{\delta_H+1}$	$O(\delta_H n^{\frac{3}{2}})$	★		5
$D(G)$	$2 - \frac{2}{D(G)+1}$	$T(n,m)$			6
Planar	$\frac{3}{2}$	$T(n,m)$			7
	$1+\epsilon$	$O(\frac{1}{\epsilon} 8^{\frac{1}{\epsilon}} n)$	★	★	8
n	$2 - \frac{1}{\sqrt{n}}$	$T(n,m)$			9
	$2 - \frac{2\log n}{\log\log n}$	$T(n,m)$			10
	$2 - \frac{2c}{n}$				11
	$2 - \frac{2\log n}{\log\log n}$	$O(nm)$	★		12
p-claw free	$2 - \frac{1}{p-1}$	$T(n,m)$			13
	$(2 - \frac{2}{p})$	$O(nm\log n + n^3)$	★		14
	$2 - \frac{\log p + O(1)}{p}$	$T(n,m)+S$	★		15
$\underline{\delta}$	$\frac{2}{1+\underline{\delta}}$	$O(mn)$	★	★	16

Independent Set Problem					
Graph Parameter	Approximation Guarantee	Complexity	Unweighted Only	No Pre-processing	Ref
χ	$\frac{2}{\chi}$				17
Δ	$\frac{1}{\lceil \frac{\Delta+1}{3} \rceil}$	$O(\Delta)$		★	18
	$\frac{3}{\Delta+2}$	$O(m)$	★	★	19
δ	$\frac{2}{\delta+1}$	$O(\delta n^{\frac{3}{2}})$	★		20
	$\frac{5}{2\delta+3}$	$O(\delta n^{\frac{3}{2}})$	★		21
	$\frac{2}{\delta+2}$	$O(m)$	★	★	22
$D(G)$	$\frac{2}{D(G)+1}$	$T(n,m)$			23
Planar	$\frac{1}{2}$	4-coloring			24
	$1-\epsilon$	$O(\frac{1}{\epsilon} 8^{\frac{1}{\epsilon}} n)$	★	★	25
p-claw free	$\frac{1}{p-1}$	$O(n\log n + m)$			26
	$\max\{\frac{2}{p}, \frac{k}{2}\alpha - \frac{n}{\alpha}(\frac{k}{2} - 1)\}$	$O(n^3)$	★	★	27

Table 3.1: *continued*

INTEGER PROGRAMMING WITH TWO VARIABLES PER INEQUALITY

3.8

The analysis of integer programming with two variables per inequality (IP2 for short) provides insight as to why approximations to vertex cover, independent set, and the 2SAT problems work. Moreover, any minimization IP2 is at least as hard to approximate as the vertex cover problem (Section 3.8.3). That means that such problems are Max-$\mathcal{SNP}$-hard and approximating them with a factor better than 2 will imply similar factor approximation for the vertex cover problem.

As this book goes to print we have discovered another problem that is a special case of IP2, the minimum satisfiability problem, where one seeks a minimum weight collection of clauses that are satisfied. We also found an extension of IP2, [Hoc96], that implies a 2-approximation for the feasible cut problem, and gives, in polynomial time, super optimal half integral solution for several other problems, including the sparsest cut (see Chapter 5 for a discussion of this problem).

3.8.1   THE HALF INTEGRALITY AND THE LINEAR PROGRAMMING RELAXATION

Many linear programming relaxations have solutions that are integer multiples of $\frac{1}{2}$. These include the vertex cover, independent set, and the dual of matching. Here we show that the reason for this property lies with the formulation's structure of two variables per constraint.

As discussed later, many IP2 problems have LP relaxations whose solutions are *not* integer multiples of $\frac{1}{2}$. One way of deriving half integral solutions is to convert the system of constraint inequalities into a system of *monotone* inequalities where the conversion may map integer solution to half integers. A polynomial time algorithm (Hochbaum and Naor [HN94]) is then used for optimizing over a system of *monotone* inequalities in bounded integer variables. An inequality in two variables is called *monotone* if it is of the form

$$ax_{j_i} - bx_{k_i} \geq c$$

where a and b are both nonnegative. Although, as proved by Lagarias [Lag85], even the problem of finding a feasible solution of a system of monotone inequalities in integers is *NP*-complete, the algorithm of Hochbaum and Naor [HN94] finds an optimal solution in time $O(mnU^2 \log(Un^2/m))$ where U is the largest upper bound, i.e. in pseudo-polynomial time. For IP2s that include nonmonotone inequalities, we use a transformation of nonmonotone inequalities to monotone inequalities proposed by Edelsbrunner, Rote, and Welzl [ERW89]. The transformation does not preserve integrality, yet each solution to the transformed problem corresponds to a feasible solution of the original problem; and in addition it consists of integer multiples of $\frac{1}{2}$.

Consider a generic nonmonotone inequality of the form $ax + by \geq c$ where a and b are positive. (Any nonmonotone inequality can be written in this form, perhaps with a reversed inequality.) Replace each variable x by two variables, x^+ and x^-, and each inequality by two inequalities:

$$ax^+ - by^- \geq c$$
$$-ax^- + by^+ \geq c .$$

The two resulting inequalities are monotone. Note that upper and lower bounds constraints $\ell_j \leq x_j \leq u_j$ are transformed to

$$\ell_j \leq x_j^+ \leq u_j$$
$$-u_j \leq x_j^- \leq -\ell_j .$$

In the objective function, the variable x is substituted by $\frac{1}{2}(x^+ - x^-)$.

Monotone inequalities remain so by replacing the variables x and y in one inequality by x^+ and y^+, and in the second, by x^- and y^-, respectively. Note that the alternative formulation of the vertex cover problem that yields a minimum cut problem on a bipartite graph (presented in Section 3.7.1), is a special case of this transformation of nonmonotone to monotone inequalities.

Let $\mathcal{A}$ be the matrix of the constraints in the original system and let $\mathcal{A}^{(2)}$ be the matrix of the monotone system resulting from the above transformation. The matrix $\mathcal{A}^{(2)}$ consists of $2m$ inequalities with two variables per inequality, and $2n$ upper and lower bound constraints. The order of this matrix is therefore $(2m + 4n) \times 2n$.

We now sketch the algorithm of [HN94] which finds an optimal solution for an integer programming problem over monotone inequalities in time

$$O(mnU^2 \log(Un^2 / m)).$$

Consider the optimization problem over a monotone system (IPM),

$$\text{Min} \quad \sum_{j=1}^{n} w_j x_j$$

(IPM) subject to $a_i x_{j_i} - b_i x_{k_i} \geq c_i \quad (i = 1, \dots, m)$

$$\ell_j \leq x_j \leq u_j , \; x_j \text{ integer} \quad (j = 1, \dots, n),$$

where a_i, b_i, c_i $(i = 1, \dots, m)$, and w_j $(j = 1, \dots, n)$ are rational, and ℓ_j and u_j $(j = 1, \dots, n)$ are integers. The coefficients a_i and b_i $(i = 1, \dots, m)$ are nonnegative but the objective function coefficients w_j $(j = 1, \dots, n)$ may be negative. Note that we allow nonzero lower bounds on the variables that can be made nonnegative by translation.

A directed graph G is created where for each variable x_j in the interval $[\ell_j, u_j]$, there are $u_j - \ell_j + 1$ nodes representing it, one for each integer value in the range. A set of nodes is said to be *closed* if it contains all the nodes that can be reached via a directed path from any node in the set. It is shown that a maximum weight closed set in this graph corresponds to an optimal solution of (IPM). A section of the graph created is depicted in Figure 3.4

For each integer p in the range, there is an arc $(p, p-1)$ from the node representing the value p to the node representing the value $p - 1$. The node representing ℓ_j has an arc directed to it from the source node s. Thus, if the source node is in a closed set then so are all ℓ_j nodes. The monotone inequalities are represented by arcs. For each potential value p of variable x_{p_i}, all inequalities in which x_{p_i} appears with a negative coefficient

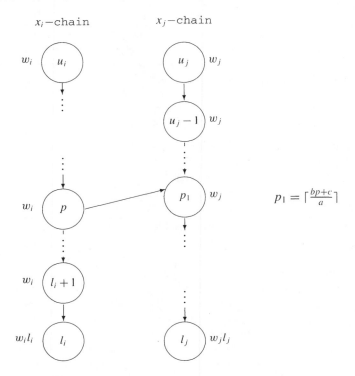

FIGURE 3.4

*Representing the inequality $ax_i - bx_j \geq c$ between the
chains for x_i and x_j.*

impose a minimum value on the variable x_{j_i} that appears in the same inequality with a positive coefficient,

$$x_{j_i} \geq \left\lceil \frac{b_i p + c_i}{a_i} \right\rceil = p_1 .$$

This is represented by an arc going from node p of x_{p_i} to node p_1 of x_{j_i}. If $p_1 > u_{j_i}$, then the value p of the variable x_{p_i} is infeasible, and the upper bound of x_{p_i} is reset to $p - 1$. A closed set containing s corresponds to a feasible solution to (IPM) where the variable x_j assumes the value of the largest node representing it in the closed set.

The nodes are now assigned weights as follows: node ℓ_j of variable x_j is assigned the value $-w_j \ell_j$, and all other nodes representing variable x_j are assigned the value $-w_j$. A maximum weight closed set corresponds then to an optimal solution to the minimization problem (IPM). The maximum closure in a graph is derived from solving a minimum cut problem in the graph after adding a source and a sink, placing arcs from the source to all nodes of positive weight with capacity equal to that weight, and placing arcs from all nodes with negative weight to the sink with capacity equal to the absolute value of that weight. All other arcs are assigned infinite capacity. The source set of a minimum cut in this graph corresponds to a maximum weight closed set with the weights as specified. The justification for the algorithm of maximum closure is given by Picard [Pic7]. For the case of vertex cover, the algorithm reduces to the minimum cut in the bipartite network described in Figure 3.3 on page 114.

Whereas, for (VC) an optimal solution to the LP-relaxation of (VC) consists of integer multiples of $\frac{1}{2}$, such is not necessarily the case for IP2 where the use of the above transformation is necessary. IP2 problems may have LP relaxation solutions that are not integer multiple of $\frac{1}{2}$, and in fact it is even *NP*-hard to get an optimal solution among all those that are an integer multiple of $\frac{1}{2}$ as we demonstrate next.

Given a system of inequalities with two variables per inequality, let the set of feasible solutions for this system be

$$S = \{\mathbf{x} \in \mathbf{R}^n \mid \mathcal{A}\mathbf{x} \leq \mathbf{c}\},$$

and the feasible solutions to the monotone system resulting from the transformation above,

$$S^{(2)} = \{(\mathbf{x}^+, \mathbf{x}^-) \mid \mathcal{A}^{(2)}(\mathbf{x}^+, \mathbf{x}^-) \leq \mathbf{c}^{(2)}, \ \mathbf{x}^+, \mathbf{x}^- \in \mathbf{R}^n\}.$$

If $\mathbf{x} \in S$, $\mathbf{x}^+ = \mathbf{x}$, and $\mathbf{x}^- = -\mathbf{x}$, then $(\mathbf{x}^+, \mathbf{x}^-) \in S^{(2)}$. So, for every feasible solution in S, there exists a feasible solution in $S^{(2)}$. Conversely, if $(\mathbf{x}^+, \mathbf{x}^-) \in S^{(2)}$, then $\mathbf{x}^{(2)} = \frac{1}{2}(\mathbf{x}^+ - \mathbf{x}^-) \in S$. Hence, for every feasible solution in $S^{(2)}$, there is a feasible solution in S.

Let $S_I = \{\mathbf{x} \in S \mid \mathbf{x} \text{ integer}\}$, and let

$$S_I^{(2)} = \left\{\frac{1}{2}(\mathbf{x}^+ - \mathbf{x}^-) \mid (\mathbf{x}^+, \mathbf{x}^-) \in S^{(2)} \text{ and } \mathbf{x}^+, \mathbf{x}^- \text{ integer}\right\}.$$

If $\mathbf{x} \in S_I$, then $\mathbf{x} \in S_I^{(2)}$. Thus, $S_I \subseteq S_I^{(2)} \subseteq S$.

In fact, the set of solutions $S_I^{(2)}$ is even smaller than the set of feasible solutions that are integer multiples of $\frac{1}{2}$. To see that, let

$$S^{(\frac{1}{2})} = \{\mathbf{x} \mid \mathcal{A}\mathbf{x} \leq \mathbf{c} \text{ and } \mathbf{x} \in \frac{1}{2}Z^n\}.$$

The claim is that $S_I^{(2)} \subset S^{(\frac{1}{2})}$, and $S^{(\frac{1}{2})}$ may contain points not in $S_I^{(2)}$. The following example illustrates such a case:

$$5x + 2y \leq 6$$
$$0 \leq x, y \leq 1.$$

Obviously, $(x = 1, \ y = \frac{1}{2})$ is a feasible solution in $S^{(\frac{1}{2})}$. But there is no corresponding integer solution in $S_I^{(2)}$ as $x^+ = -x^- = 1$ implies that $y^+ = y^- = 0$. It follows that the bound derived from optimizing over $S_I^{(2)}$ is tighter than a bound derived from optimizing over $S^{(\frac{1}{2})}$. Not only is this latter optimization weaker, but it is also in general *NP*-hard as stated in the following Lemma (proved in [HMNT93]).

LEMMA 3.7 Minimizing over a system of inequalities with two variables per inequality for $\mathbf{x} \in \frac{1}{2} \cdot Z^n$, is *NP*-hard.

3.8.2   COMPUTING AN APPROXIMATE SOLUTION

Here we show how to obtain a 2-approximation for the optimum of a bounded integer program with two variables per inequality in $O(mnU^2 \log(Un^2/m))$ time. Assume that the given integer program has a feasible integer solution denoted by $z_1, \ldots, z_n$. (This can be tested in polynomial time as proved in Lemma 3.9.)

We first transform the integer program into a monotone integer system and compute an optimal solution for the monotone system as in the previous section. For every variable x_i $(i = 1, \ldots, n)$, let m_i^+ and m_i^- denote the respective values of x_i^+ and x_i^- in the optimal solution of the monotone system. For $i = 1, \ldots, n$, let $m_i^* = \frac{1}{2}(m_i^+ - m_i^-)$. We define the following solution vector, denoted by $\ell = (\ell_1, \ldots, \ell_n)$, where for $i = 1, \ldots, n$:

$$
\ell_i = \begin{cases}
\min\{m_i^+, -m_i^-\} & \text{if } z_i \leq \min\{m_i^+, -m_i^-\}, \\
z_i & \text{if } \min\{m_i^+, -m_i^-\} \leq z_i \leq \max\{m_i^+, -m_i^-\}, \\
\max\{m_i^+, -m_i^-\} & \text{if } z_i \geq \max\{m_i^+, -m_i^-\}.
\end{cases}
\tag{3.9}
$$

LEMMA 3.8   The vector ℓ is a feasible solution of the given integer program.

Proof.   Let $ax_i + bx_j \geq c$ be an inequality where a and b are nonnegative. We check all possible cases. If ℓ_i is equal to z_i or $\min\{m_i^+, -m_i^-\}$, and ℓ_j is equal to z_j or $\min\{m_j^+, -m_j^-\}$, then clearly, $a\ell_i + b\ell_j \geq az_i + bz_j \geq c$. Suppose $\ell_i \geq z_i$ and $\ell_j = \max\{m_j^+, -m_j^-\}$. By construction, we know that

$$
am_i^+ - bm_j^- \geq c \quad \text{and} \quad -am_i^- + bm_j^+ \geq c.
$$

If $\ell_i \geq -m_i^-$, then, $a\ell_i + b\ell_j \geq -am_i^- + bm_j^+ \geq c$. Otherwise, $a\ell_i + b\ell_j \geq am_i^+ - bm_j^- \geq c$. The last case is when $\ell_i = \max\{m_i^+, -m_i^-\}$, and $\ell_j = \max\{m_j^+, -m_j^-\}$. In this case,

$$
a\ell_i + b\ell_j \geq am_i^+ - bm_j^- \geq c.
$$

The other types of inequalities are handled similarly.   ∎

We showed that vector ℓ is a feasible solution. We now argue that it also approximates the optimum.

THEOREM 3.7

1. The vector ℓ is a 2-approximate solution of the bounded integer program.
2. The value of the objective function at the vector $\mathbf{m}^*$ is at least a half of the value of the objective function of the best integer solution.

Proof.   By construction, $\ell \leq 2\mathbf{m}^*$. From the previous subsection we know that the vector $\mathbf{m}^*$ provides a lower bound on the value of the objective function for any integral solution. Hence, the theorem follows.   ∎

The complexity of the algorithm is dominated by the complexity of the procedure in [HN94] for optimizing over a monotone system. The running time is $O(mnU^2 \log(Un^2/m))$.

3.8.3 THE EQUIVALENCE OF IP2 TO 2-SAT AND 2-SAT TO VERTEX COVER

The integer programming problem in two variables per inequality is in fact *equivalent* to a 2-SAT problem. Hence, 2-SAT already captures all the interesting properties of IP2. This has also algorithmic consequences—implying a fast algorithm for finding a feasible solution to IP2. We also demonstrate a reduction of 2-SAT to (VC). That implies the "fixing variables" property for 2-SAT and therefore for IP2.

The equivalence to 2-SAT is shown using an idea of T. Feder: Recall that for each variable x_i we have $0 \leq x_i \leq u_i < \infty$ $(i = 1, \ldots, n)$. We replace each variable x_i by u_i binary variables $x_{i\ell}$ $(\ell = 1, \ldots, u_i)$, with the constraints $x_{i\ell} \geq x_{i,\ell+1}$ $(\ell = 1, \ldots, u_i - 1)$. Subject to these constraints, the correspondence between x_i and the u_i-tuple $(x_{i1}, \ldots, x_{iu_i})$ is one-to-one and is characterized by $x_{i\ell} = 1$ if and only if $x_i \geq \ell$ $(\ell = 1, \ldots, u_i)$, or, equivalently, $x_i = \sum_{\ell=1}^{u_i} x_{i\ell}$.

We now explain how to transform the constraints of the given system into constraints in terms of the $x_{i\ell}$'s. Suppose

$$a_{ki} x_i + a_{kj} x_j \geq b_k$$

is one of the given constraints. There are several cases to be distinguished. Without loss of generality, assume both a_{ki} and a_{kj} are nonzeros. Consider the case where both are positive, and assume without loss of generality that $0 < b_k < a_{ki} u_i + a_{kj} u_j$. For every ℓ $(\ell = 0, \ldots, u_i)$, let

$$\alpha_{k\ell} = \left\lceil \frac{b_k - \ell a_{ki}}{a_{kj}} \right\rceil - 1 .$$

It is easy to see that for an integer solution $\mathbf{x}$, $a_{ki} x_i + a_{kj} x_j \geq b_k$ if and only if for every ℓ $(\ell = 0, \ldots, u_i)$,

$$\text{either } x_i > \ell \text{ or } x_j > \alpha_{k\ell}$$

or, equivalently,

$$\text{either } x_i \geq \ell+1 \text{ or } x_j \geq \alpha_{k\ell}+1 .$$

Under the above transformation between the x_i's and the $x_{i\ell}$'s, this is equivalent to:

1. For every ℓ $(\ell = 0, 1, \ldots, u_i - 1)$, if $0 \leq \alpha_{k\ell} < u_j$, then either $x_{i,\ell+1} = 1$ or $x_{j,\alpha_{k\ell}+1} = 1$, and if $\alpha_{k\ell} \geq u_j$, then $x_{i,\ell+1} = 1$.

2. For $\ell = u_i$, if $\alpha_{ku_i} \geq 0$, then $x_{j,\alpha_{ku_i}+1} = 1$ (since we have $\alpha_{ku_i} < u_j$).

The disjunction in (i) can be written as

$$x_{i,\ell+1} + x_{j,\alpha_{k\ell}+1} \geq 1 .$$

Thus, altogether we have replaced one original constraint on x_i and x_j by at most $u_i + 1$ constraints on the variables $x_{i\ell}$ and $x_{j\ell}$. The other cases, corresponding to different sign combinations of a_{ki}, a_{kj}, and b_k, can be handled in a similar way.

If the above transformation is applied to a monotone system of inequalities, then the resulting 2-SAT integer program is also monotone.

To summarize, we replace the n original variables and m original constraints by $\bar{u} = \sum_{j=1}^{n} u_j$ new variables and at most $mU + \bar{u}$ new constraints, where $U = \max_i u_i$.

The time bounds for finding a feasible solution are as follows.

LEMMA 3.9 A feasible solution to a bounded integer program with two variables per inequality can be computed in $O(m + n + \bar{u} + mU)$ time.

Proof. A feasible solution to a 2-SAT integer program can be found in linear time using the algorithm of [EIS76]. Encoding a bounded integer program as a 2-SAT integer program generates $\bar{u}$ variables and at most $mU + \bar{u}$ constraints. Hence, the time bound follows. ∎

We now show that any 2-SAT is *equivalent* to a vertex cover problem, i.e. to a nonmonotone form of 2-SAT. This has been observed by Seffi Naor. Given a 2-CNF formula F. We compute the transitive closure of F, $T(F)$. This is done by repeating the following step until no more new clauses are generated: For every pair of clauses of the form $x \vee y$ and $\bar{x} \vee z$, add the clause $y \vee z$.

In an alternative approach for computing $T(F)$, one can create a directed graph. For each variable we have two nodes in the graph, one corresponding to the variable x, and the other to $\bar{x}$. Given a clause $x \vee y$, we replace it by two directed arcs, $\bar{y} \to x$ and $\bar{x} \to y$. We now consider the set of directed edges in the transitive closure of the graph. This transitive closure is symmetric and corresponds to the transitive closure of the set of clauses, F, by replacing every pair of symmetric directed arcs (of the form $\bar{y} \to x$ and $\bar{x} \to y$) by a clause.

Now generate a new undirected graph $G = (V, E)$ from the transitive closure of the clauses. For each variable we have two nodes in the graph, one corresponding to the variable x being true, and the other $\bar{x}$ corresponding to the variable x being false. Given a clause $x \vee y$ we place an edge $(x, y) \in E$. Finally, add the edges $(x, \bar{x})$ to the set E.

The claim is that a vertex cover in G corresponds to a satisfying assignment and vice versa. Obviously at least one of the endpoints of the edges of the form $(x, \bar{x})$ must be in the cover. We need to show that both x and $\bar{x}$ cannot be selected simultaneously in some optimal cover. Let $N(x)$ be the set of neighbors of x. Then the set of edges induced by $N(x)$ and $N(\bar{x})$ contains a complete bipartite graph, due to the transitive closure property. Any feasible vertex cover in a complete bipartite graph must contain at least one set of the bipartition. Therefore, either x or $\bar{x}$ are redundant in the cover and exactly one of the two is in the vertex cover. So, with the reduction above we showed that any 2-SAT problem on n variables and m clauses is equivalent to a vertex cover problem on $O(n)$ variables and $O(m^2)$ edges.

Since we have established that IP2 is equivalent to 2-SAT, which in turn is equivalent to vertex cover (VC), it follows in particular that IP2 is equivalent to vertex cover. The 2-approximation to IP2 could hence be also deduced from this equivalence.

The solution to the relaxation of the vertex cover problem (VCR) has the "fixing variables" property that there exists an optimal solution that coincides with the relaxed solution in all integer components. The following lemma demonstrates that precisely the same idea applies to any integer programming problem IP2, after it is transformed to a 2-SAT.

With the reduction of 2-SAT to vertex cover, the direct proof to this lemma may be substituted by the corresponding lemma of Nemhauser and Trotter [NT75].

LEMMA 3.10 [HMNT93]   Let $\mathbf{x}^{(2)}$ be an optimal solution of 2-SAT in the set $S_I^{(2)}$. Let

$$\text{INT} = \{j \mid x_j^{(2)} = 0 \ \text{or} \ x_j^{(2)} = 1\} \, .$$

Then there is an optimal integer solution $\mathbf{z}$ of 2-SAT such that $z_j = x_j^{(2)}$ for $j \in \text{INT}$.

For the integer problem IP2 the fixing of variables imply that there exists an optimal solution $\mathbf{z}^*$ such that,

$$\min\{m_i^+, -m_i^-\} \le z_i^* \le \max\{m_i^+, -m_i^-\}.$$

If the upper and lower bounds are equal, then z_i may be fixed at that value. The interval gets smaller as more of the 2-SAT binary variables are fixed.

3.8.4   PROPERTIES OF BINARY INTEGER PROGRAMS

In this section we further investigate the properties of 2-SAT integer programs (or binary IP2s). We first consider the linear relaxation of a 2-SAT integer programming problem. It turns out that solutions of this relaxation always have denominators not greater than 2. Consequently, the basic solutions are integer multiples of $\frac{1}{2}$. This follows from the statement in the next lemma about the determinants of 2-SAT's *nonseparable* submatrices. A matrix is *nonseparable* if there is no partition of the columns and rows to two subsets (or more) C_1, C_2 and R_1, R_2 such that all nonzero entries in every row and column appear only in the submatrices defined by the sets $C_1 \times R_1$ and $C_2 \times R_2$. The following lemma applies only to nonseparable matrices, since one can construct a separable 2-SAT or (VC) matrix with an arbitrary number, K, of nonseparable ones on its diagonal, each of determinant 2. Thus, we achieve a matrix with a determinant that is 2^K.

LEMMA 3.11   The determinants of all nonseparable submatrices of a 2-SAT linear programming problem have absolute value at most 2.

Proof.   Let $\mathbf{A}$ denote the constraint matrix of a 2-SAT integer program. Thus, $\mathbf{A}$ has at most two non-zero entries in every row. We show that the absolute value of the determinant of any nonseparable square submatrix of $\mathbf{A}$ can be either 0, 1, or 2. The proof of this claim is by induction on the size of the submatrix. Since the entries of $\mathbf{A}$ are from $\{-1, 0, 1\}$, the claim holds for 1×1 submatrices. Assume it holds for any $(m-1) \times (m-1)$ submatrix and we show that the claim holds for any $m \times m$ submatrix. We may assume that each row and column in $\mathbf{A}$ has exactly two non-zero entries. Otherwise, there must be a row or a column where all entries, possibly with the exception of one, are zero. In either case, we can apply the inductive assumption directly and prove the claim. Let $\mathbf{A}_{ij}$ denote the submatrix obtained by deleting the i'th row and the j'th column from $\mathbf{A}$.

Without loss of generality, we may assume that the two non-zero elements in row i of $\mathbf{A}$ are in columns i and $i+1$ (modulo m). (Due to the nonseparability of the submatrix, this can be achieved by appropriate row and column interchanges.) Hence,

$$\det(\mathbf{A}) = A[1,1] \cdot \det(\mathbf{A}_{11}) - (-1)^m A[m,1] \cdot \det(\mathbf{A}_{m1}) \, .$$

The absolute values of the determinants of $\mathbf{A}_{11}$ and $\mathbf{A}_{m1}$ are equal to 1, since both are triangular matrices with nonzero diagonal elements. Therefore, the absolute value of the determinant of $\mathbf{A}$ is at most 2. ∎

An immediate corollary of Lemma 3.11 is the fact that the value of every variable in a basic solution of the 2-SAT linear program is in the set $\{0, \frac{1}{2}, 1\}$. Although for binary integer problems the subdeterminants can be of value greater than 2, and hence the solutions would not be in this set, we get rid of these "unnecessary" solutions by reducing the problem first to 2-SAT. In a 2-SAT system the variables are assumed to be binary. Lemma 3.11, however, applies to any linear programming problem with a constraint matrix with coefficients $0, 1, -1$, and at most two nonzero elements in each row. We call such a system *generalized* 2-SAT. Note that we do not assume the existence of finite upper bounds on the variables. We will show that a 2-approximation can be achieved even for such systems.

LEMMA 3.12   A generalized 2-SAT has the property that $S_I^{(2)} = S^{(\frac{1}{2})}$.

Proof.   It suffices to prove that $S^{(\frac{1}{2})}$ is contained in $S_I^{(2)}$. Let $\mathbf{x} \in S^{(\frac{1}{2})}$. Define a solution $(\mathbf{x}^+, \mathbf{x}^-)$ as follows. For $j = 1, \dots, n$,

1. If x_j is an integer, set $x_j^+ = -x_j^- = x_j$.
2. If x_j is a noninteger, then set $x_j^+ = x_j + \frac{1}{2}$ and $x_j^- = -x_j + \frac{1}{2}$.

It is easy to show that $(\mathbf{x}^+, \mathbf{x}^-)$ satisfies the (three) generic types of constraints defining $S_I^{(2)}$. For example, consider a constraint of the form $x_j^+ - x_k^- \geq c$. Since $\mathbf{x}$ is feasible, we have $x_j + x_k \geq c$. If either both x_j and x_k are integer or both are noninteger, then we have $x_j^+ - x_k^- = x_j + x_k \geq c$. Assuming that $x_j + x_k$ is noninteger, if $x_j + x_k \geq c$ then $x_j + x_k - \frac{1}{2} \geq c$. Using the fact that $x_j^+ \geq x_j$ and $-x_k^- \geq x_k - \frac{1}{2}$, it follows that $x_j^+ - x_k^- \geq x_j + x_k - \frac{1}{2} \geq c$. The other cases follow from similar considerations. ∎

One corollary of Lemmas 3.11 and 3.12 is that the linear programming relaxation of a 2-SAT and a generalized 2-SAT can be solved by optimizing over the respective monotone system. Both problems are then solvable in strongly polynomial time: the 2-SAT as a maximum flow (or rather minimum cut) problem, and the generalized 2-SAT as a dual of a linear flow problem. Note that one could also solve these linear programs in strongly polynomial time without using the transformation to a monotone system by directly applying the algorithm of [Tar86]. The latter, however, is not as efficient as the best-known algorithms for solving maximum flow problems or linear flow problems.

We next show how to obtain a 2-approximation for a generalized 2-SAT integer program. First, we note that the procedure described above for IP2 is not applicable here since the variables might not have finite upper bounds. Since we already know how to solve the monotone system, the difficulty lies in finding a feasible integer solution or verifying that none exists. We perform this latter task as follows.

Let $(\mathbf{x}^+, \mathbf{x}^-)$ be an optimal solution of the monotone system, *i.e.*, $\mathbf{x} = \frac{1}{2}(\mathbf{x}^+ - \mathbf{x}^-)$ solves the linear programming relaxation. Using, if necessary, the transformation in the proof of Lemma 3.12, we may assume that $x_j^+ = -x_j^-$ or $x_j^+ = -x_j^- + 1$ ($j = 1, \dots, n$). Next, we apply Lemma 3.8 to conclude that the given generalized 2-SAT integer program is feasible if and only if there exists a feasible rounding of **x**. The latter can be tested by the linear time algorithm in [EIS76]. Moreover, Theorem 3.8 ensures that if such a rounding exists, then it is a 2-approximation.

3.8.5   DUAL FEASIBLE SOLUTIONS FOR IP2

The approach described for devising a 2-approximation algorithm for IP2 is analogous to the preprocessing or dual optimal approach for the vertex cover. Exploring this analogy more carefully raises the question whether an analogue of the dual feasible approach could apply as well. The advantage would be to do away with the need to solve the minimum cut problem on a graph optimally (or solving the respective linear program).

This turns out to be possible by reducing IP2 to an equivalent vertex cover problem and then applying any dual-feasible algorithm. For instance, if we choose the algorithm of Bar-Yehuda and Even (dual-feasible I), its running time is linear in the number of edges in the resulting graph which is $O(m^2 U^2)$. This represents a minor improvement (if at all) compared to the running time of the min-cut-based procedure, $O(mnU^2 \log(Un^2 / m))$.

THE MAXIMUM COVERAGE PROBLEM AND THE GREEDY

3.9

Consider the *maximum coverage* problem. Given a set system S and a parameter k, the *maximum coverage* problem is to find k sets such that the total weight of elements covered is maximized. This problem is clearly *NP*-hard, as *set cover* is reducible to it.

For the maximum coverage problem we are interested in describing the performance of a simple greedy algorithm. Consider the performance of a greedy algorithm, as depicted in Figure 3.5, that selects k sets by iteratively picking the set that covers the maximum weight group of currently uncovered elements. The performance of the greedy heuristic when optimizing a submodular function has been studied by Nemhauser and Wolsey [NW72] and Conforti and Cornuejols [CC84]; Vohra and Hall [VH93] have

```
GREEDY ← ∅
for                 l = 1 … k do
                    select Gₗ ∈ S that maximizes wt(GREEDY ∪ Gₗ)
                    GREEDY ← GREEDY ∪ Gₗ
end
output GREEDY
```

FIGURE 3.5

Greedy heuristic for the maximum coverage problem

explicitly noted that *maximum coverage* falls into this context. Applications of the *maximum coverage* problem can be found in Section 3.9.2; the method discussed next for dealing with this problem is from [HP94].

3.9.1   THE GREEDY APPROACH

We establish the following theorem regarding the quality of solution returned by the greedy heuristic, where wt(GREEDY) and wt(OPT) are the total weight of elements covered by the greedy solution and the optimal solution, respectively. G_l refers to the l'th set selected by the greedy algorithm.

THEOREM 3.8 $\text{wt(GREEDY)} \geq \left[1 - \left(1 - \frac{1}{k}\right)^k\right]\text{wt(OPT)} > (1 - \frac{1}{e})\text{wt(OPT)}.$

Thus, the greedy heuristic is a $(1 - \frac{1}{e})$-approximation algorithm for the *maximum coverage* problem.

In fact, there is an example given in [HP94], taken from [DJS93], that shows this bound to be tight.

In order to prove the bound, we need to establish two lemmas.

LEMMA 3.13 $\text{wt}(\cup_{i=1}^{l} G_i) - \text{wt}(\cup_{i=1}^{l-1} G_i) \geq \frac{\text{wt}(OPT) - \text{wt}(\cup_{i=1}^{l-1} G_i)}{k}$, for $l = 1, 2, \ldots, k$.

Proof.   At least $\text{wt(OPT)} - \text{wt}(\cup_{i=1}^{l-1} G_i)$ worth of elements not covered by the first $(l-1)$ sets selected by the greedy heuristic are covered by the k sets of OPT. Hence, by the pigeonhole principle, one of the k sets in the optimal solution must cover at least $\frac{\text{wt(OPT)} - \text{wt}(\cup_{i=1}^{l-1} G_i)}{k}$ worth of these elements. Since G_l is a set that achieves maximum additional coverage, it must also. (Note that $\text{wt}(\cup_{i=1}^{l} G_i) - \text{wt}(\cup_{i=1}^{l-1} G_i)$ represents the additional coverage achieved by G_l.) ∎

LEMMA 3.14 $\text{wt}(\cup_{i=1}^{l} G_i) \geq \left[(1 - (1 - \frac{1}{k})^l)\right]\text{wt(OPT)}$, for $l = 1, 2, \ldots, k$.

Proof.   We proceed by induction on l. For $l = 1$, the result holds: $\text{wt}(G_1) \geq \frac{\text{wt}(OPT)}{k}$, from Lemma 3.13. Now,

$$\text{wt}(\cup_{i=1}^{l+1} G_i) = \text{wt}(\cup_{i=1}^{l} G_i) + (\text{wt}(\cup_{i=1}^{l+1} G_i) - \text{wt}(\cup_{i=1}^{l} G_i))$$

$$\geq \text{wt}(\cup_{i=1}^{l} G_i) + \frac{\text{wt(OPT)} - \text{wt}(\cup_{i=1}^{l} G_i)}{k}$$

$$= (1 - \frac{1}{k})\text{wt}(\cup_{i=1}^{l} G_i) + \frac{\text{wt(OPT)}}{k}$$

$$\geq (1 - \frac{1}{k})(1 - (1 - \frac{1}{k})^l)\,\text{wt(OPT)} + \frac{\text{wt(OPT)}}{k}$$

$$= (1 - (1 - \frac{1}{k})^{l+1})\,\text{wt(OPT)},$$

where the first inequality comes from Lemma 3.13, and the second inequality is from the induction hypothesis. ∎

Theorem 3.8 follows directly from Lemma 3.14 by letting $l = k$, and noting that because $\lim_{k \to \infty} 1 - \left(1 - \frac{1}{k}\right)^k = 1 - \frac{1}{e}$ and $1 - \left(1 - \frac{1}{k}\right)^k$ is decreasing, it follows that $1 - \left(1 - \frac{1}{k}\right)^k > 1 - \frac{1}{e} > .632$.

The quality of the greedy heuristic for the *maximum coverage* problem was also studied in [VH93] in the context of a "maximal covering location problem." By interpreting the problem as one of maximizing a submodular function, they were able to apply results from [CC84] and [NW72] to achieve the performance guarantee of Theorem 3.8 for their location problem. As discussed in [HP94], however, in some applications of the *maximum coverage* problem the sets in S may be implicitly defined rather than explicitly given. For instance, consider the problem of covering a maximum weight set of edges of a graph with k cutsets; this problem arises in an application involving the testing of printed circuit boards for short-circuits [Lou92]. The greedy heuristic entails selecting a maximum cut in a graph at each step, which is itself *NP*-hard!

Thus, in some cases finding the optimal set at a given stage may itself be *NP*-hard. Suppose, however, that a solution within a factor of β of the optimal is selected at each step of the greedy heuristic; what can we then say about the quality of solution returned by this greedy-like algorithm? By modifying the analysis used to prove Theorem 3.8, the following theorem from [HP94] can be obtained:

THEOREM 3.9   Suppose that a modified version of the algorithm of Figure 3.5 is run so that G_l, is a set that causes an increase in coverage that is within a factor β of the maximum increase possible rather than being the set that causes the maximum increase in overall coverage at iteration l. Then, the solution returned by the algorithm achieves coverage with weight within a factor of

$$(1 - \frac{\beta}{k})^k > 1 - \frac{1}{e^\beta}$$

of the optimal.

Proof.   First of all, Lemma 3.13 can be easily generalized to establish that, for $l = 1, 2, \ldots, k$,

$$\text{wt}(\cup_{i=1}^l G_i) - \text{wt}(\cup_{i=1}^{l-1} G_i) \geq \beta \frac{\text{wt}(OPT) - \text{wt}(\cup_{i=1}^{l-1} G_i)}{k} .$$

Secondly, Lemma 3.14 can be easily generalized to establish that, for $l = 1, 2, \ldots, k$,

$$\text{wt}(\cup_{i=1}^l G_i) \geq \left[(1 - (1 - \frac{\beta}{k})^l) \right] \text{wt}(OPT) .$$

Then, the theorem follows by setting $l = k$ in the above result, and noting that $1 - (1 - \frac{\beta}{k})^k$, which is decreasing in k, has limit $1 - \frac{1}{e^\beta}$ as k approaches ∞.   ∎

For the maximum cut problem, there exists a polynomial algorithm with $\beta = .878\ldots$ (see [GW94]), yielding a polynomial time algorithm with an approximation ratio guarantee of $(1 - \frac{1}{e^\beta}) > .584$ for the circuit-testing application.[2]

---

[2]It has been pointed out by M. Goemans that for this problem of covering edges with k cut sets, employing an algorithm based on the method of conditional expectations provides a performance guarantee of $1 - \frac{1}{2^k}$. See Chapter 11 for more on the method of conditional expectation.

We next briefly describe some additional problems that are instances of the *maximum coverage* problem.

3.9.2   APPLICATIONS OF THE MAXIMUM COVERAGE PROBLEM

Problems, are considered from a variety of applications regarding covering graphs with subgraphs, packing, and fixed parameter combinatorial optimization.

- *Covering Graphs by Subgraphs:* As already mentioned, the problem of covering edges by cut-sets arises in testing printed circuit boards for short-circuits. At each stage of the greedy algorithm, we are to find a maximum cut in the graph consisting of those edges not already covered. Now, although MAX CUT is itself *NP*-hard (see [GJ79]), there is a simple greedy MAX CUT algorithm with $\beta = \frac{1}{2}$, and a more involved one with $\beta = \min_{0 \le \theta \le \pi} \frac{2}{\pi} \frac{\theta}{1 - \cos \theta} = .878 \ldots$ (see [GW94] and Chapter 11).

    Problems of covering the edges of a graph by subgraphs satisfying some particular structure arise in other contexts as well. For example, we may wish to cover the maximum weight set of edges in a graph G using k subgraphs from a class $\mathcal{R}$; $\mathcal{R}$ may consist of triangles or other small cliques (see [GHY94]), or spanning trees, etc. At each stage, an optimal structure from the class $\mathcal{R}$ is selected in the graph that is identical to G except that previously covered edges have weight 0.

    Consider a k-stage forestry problem in which a set of cells are to be harvested at each stage, under the restriction that no two adjacent cells can be harvested during a given stage; that is, at each stage an *Independent Set* set must be selected in a corresponding graph (see [BWE92]). At each stage, a maximum weight independent set is to be found. While the independent set problem is *NP*-hard for general graphs (indeed, guaranteeing a β-approximate solution for any fixed $\beta > 0$ is *NP*-hard), for certain classes of graphs (as we have seen) approximation algorithms of varying quality are available.

- *Packing and Layout Problems:* Now consider packing problems with a given set U of objects to pack. The common nature of these applications is that the objective is to pack the maximum weight set of objects into k identical *bins*. Our greedy approach is to pack, as best possible, a single bin at a time using objects of U not already packed. Some examples:

    1. Circuit Layout and Design: Recent advances in multilayer IC technology have led to design problems in which an optimal assignment of objects to layers is to be made. For example, it has been shown that the topological planar routing problem, in which a maximum weight set of nets is to be assigned to k given layers such that all nets assigned to a given layer can be routed without any two nets crossing each other, is *NP*-hard (see [CL90]). On the other hand, finding a maximum weighted subset of nets to assign to a *single* layer can be solved in polynomial time (see [Sup87]), yielding a $(1 - \left(1 - \frac{1}{k}\right)^k)$-approximation algorithm to the topological planar routing problem using the greedy heuristic.

2. *Scheduling:* Suppose we are given a set of jobs to assign to k identical machines, where each machine has a set of restrictions as to which jobs can be grouped together The goal is is to schedule the largest weight set of jobs to the k machines. How well a single machine can be packed in a stage of our greedy approach will depend on the restrictions as to what can be scheduled together on a machine, and depend, on the set of jobs to be scheduled.

3. *Logistics:* Consider a logistics problem in which k identical vehicles are to be packed with a maximum weight set of items for delivery to a common destination. Given a set of items to be delivered, each having a specified benefit, we attempt to pack the vehicles, one at a time, with items of maximum total benefit.

- *Fixed Parameter Combinatorial Optimization:* In some standard optimization problems, the goal is to cover all the elements in a set using the smallest number of subsets. We will look at the versions of these problems in which, given a fixed parameter k that limits the number of subsets that we can select, we wish to cover the maximum weight set of elements.

  For instance, consider *Vertex Cover* in which we need to cover the maximum weight set of edges in a graph G using k vertices. At each stage, we select a vertex that covers the maximum weight set of edges not previously covered.

  Other such $(1 - \left(1 - \frac{1}{k}\right)^k)$-approximation algorithms can be derived for fixed parameter versions of well-known combinatorial optimization problems such as *Dominating Set, Minimum Test Set, Hitting Set,* and *Minimum Test Collection.* Refer to the glossary and [GJ79] for complete specifications of these problems.

  We note that several location problems, in which the goal is to locate k facilities so that as many customers as possible can each be served within a prespecified cost, can be modeled as a fixed-parameter version of the *Dominating Set* problem. For example, a problem in which the goal is to locate k new facilities so as to maximize market share (see [MZH83]), can be modeled as such; while the results in [MZH83] give special cases of the problem that can be solved in polynomial time, our greedy approach provides an α_k-approximation algorithm for general instances of the problem considered. We also note that a similar problem concerning the optimal location of bank accounts was given in [CFN77]; indeed, they provide a greedy algorithm that is shown to have a α_k-approximation guarantee via a different, and more complicated, analysis than the one presented here.

References

[AH77]   K. Appel and W. Haken. Every planar map is four colorable. Part I: Discharging. *Illinois J. Math.* 21:429–490, 1977.

[AHK77] K. Appel, W. Haken, and J. Koch. Every planar map is four colorable. Part II: Reducibility," *Illinois J. Math.* 21:491–567, 1977.

[Baa78] S. Baase. *Computer Algorithms: Introduction to Design and Analysis,* Addison-Wesley, Reading, MA, 1978.

[BP76]   E. Balas and M. Padberg. Set partitioning: A survey. *SIAM Review* 18: 710–760, 1976.

[BS69]   M. Balinski and K. Spielberg. Methods for integer programming: algebraic, combinatorial and enumeration. *J. Aronofsky, editor, Progress in Operations Research, III* 295–292, 1969.

[Bak83]   B. S. Baker. Approximation algorithms for *NP*-complete problems on planar graphs. In *Proceedings of the 24th Annual Symposium on Foundations of Computer Science*, IEEE, 265–273, 1983.

[BWE92]   F. Barahona, A. Weintraub, and R. Epstein. Habitat dispersion in forest planning and the stable set problem. *Operations Research*, 40:14–21, 1992.

[BYE81]   R. Bar-Yehuda and S. Even. A linear time approximation algorithm for the weighted vertex cover problem. *J. of Algorithms* 2:198–203, 1981.

[BE85]   R. Bar-Yehuda and S. Even. A local-ratio theorem for approximating the weighted vertex cover problem. *Annals of Discrete Mathematics* 25:27–45, 1985.

[BGS95]   M. Bellare, O. Goldreich, and M. Sudan. Free bits and nonapproximability. *Proceedings of the 36th Annual IEEE Symposium on Foundations of Computer Science (FOCS95).* 422–431, 1995.

[Bro41]   R. L. Brooks. On coloring the nodes of a network. *Proc. Cambridge Philos. Soc.* 37:194–197, 1941.

[CC84]   M. Conforti and G. Cornuejols. Submodular functions, matroids and the greedy algorithm: tight worst-case bounds and some generalizations of the Rado-Edmonds theorem. *Discrete Applied Mathematics* 7:257–275, 1984.

[CFN77]   G. Cornuejols, M. L. Fisher, and G. L. Nemhauser. Location of bank accounts to optimize float: an analytic study of exact and approximate alogrithms. *Management Science*, 23(8):789–810, 1977.

[CL90]   J. Cong and C. L. Liu. On the *k*-layer Planar Subset and Via Minimization Problems. In *Proceedings of the European Design Automation Conference*, pages 459–463, 1990.

[CNS81]   N. Chiba, T. Nishizeki and N. Saito. A linear 5-coloring algorithm of planar graphs. *J. of Algorithms* 2:317–327, 1981.

[CM91]   E. Cohen and N. Megiddo. Improved algorithms for linear inequalities with two variables per inequality. In *Proceedings of the Twenty Third Symposium on Theory of Computing,* New Orleans, 145–155, 1991.

[CK75]   N. Christofides and S. Korman. A computational survey of methods for the set covering problem. *Management Science* 21:591–599, 1975.

[Chv79]   V. Chvátal. A Greedy Heuristic for the Set-Covering Problem *Math. of Oper. Res.* Vol. 4, 3, 233–235, 1979.

[Clar83] K. L. Clarkson. A modification of the Greedy algorithm for the vertex cover. *Info. Proc. Lett.* 16:23–25, 1983.

[DJS93]   B. Dasgupta, R. Janardan, and N. Sherwani. On the greedy algorithm for a covering problem. Unpublished manuscript, February 1993.

[ERW89]   H. Edelsbrunner, G. Rote, and E. Welzl. Testing the necklace condition for shortest tours and optimal factors in the plane. *Theoretical Computer Science* 66:157–180, 1989.

[Erd70]   P. Erdös. On the Graph-Theorem of Turán. *Math. Lapok*, 21:249–251, 1970.

[EIS76]   S. Even, A. Itai, and A. Shamir. On the complexity of timetable and multicommodity flow problems. *SIAM Journal on Computing* 5:691–703, 1976.

[F95]   U. Feige. A threshold of ln n for approximating set cover. Manuscript, 1995.

[FNT74]   D. R. Fulkerson, G. L. Nemhauser, and L. E. Trotter, Jr. Two computationally difficult set covering problems that arise in computing the 1-width incidence matrices of steiner triple systems. *Mathematical Programming Study* 2:72–81, 1974.

[GHY94]   O. Goldschmidt, D. S. Hochbaum, and G. Yu. Approximation Algorithms for the k-clique covering problem. To appear *SIAM J. of Discrete Math*, 1994.

[GJ79]   M. R. Garey and D. S. Johnson. *Computers and Intractability*, W. H. Freeman, San Francisco, 1979.

[GJS76]   M. R. Garey, D. S. Johnson, and L. Stockmeyer. Some simplified *NP*-complete graph problems. *Theoret. Comput. Sci.* I 237–267, 1976.

[GN72]   R. S. Garfinkel and G. L. Nemhauser. Optimal set covering: A survey. In *Perspectives on optimization: A collection of expository articles*, A. M. Geoffrion, ed., 164–183, 1972.

[GP92]   D. Gusfield and L. Pitt. A bounded approximation for the minimum cost 2-SAT problem. *Algorithmica* 8:103–117, 1992.

[GT88]   A. V. Goldberg and R. E. Tarjan. A new approach for the maximum flow problem. *J.of ACM* 35:921–940, 1983.

[GW94]   M. X. Goemans and D. P. Williamson. Improved approximation algorithms for maximum cut and satisfiability problems using semidefinite programming. Submitted to *Journal of the ACM*, 1994.

[H94]   M. M. Halldórsson. Private communication, 1994.

[HR94]   M. M. Halldórsson and J. Radhakrishnan. Greed is good: approximating independent sets in sparse and bounded-degree graphs. *Proceedings of 26th ACM Symposium on Theory of Computing*, 439–448, 1994.

[HH86]   N. G. Hall and D. S. Hochbaum. A fast approximation algorithm for the multicovering problem. *Discrete Applied Mathematics* 15:35–40, 1986.

[Har69]   F. Harary. *Graph Theory*, Addison-Wesley, Reading, MA, 1969.

[Hoc82]   D. S. Hochbaum. Approximation algorithms for the set covering and vertex cover problems. *SIAM J. Comput.* 11(3) 1982, an extended version: W.P. #64-79-80, GSIA, Carnegie-Mellon University, April 1980.

[Hoc83]   D. S. Hochbaum. Efficient bounds for the stable set, vertex cover and set packing problems. *Discrete Applied Mathematics* 6:243–254, 1983.

[Hoc96]   D. S. Hochbaum. A framework for half integrality and 2-approximations with applications to feasible cut and minimum satisfiability. Manuspcript, 1996.

[HN94]   D. S. Hochbaum and J. Naor. Simple and fast algorithms for linear and integer programs with two variables per inequality. *SIAM Journal on Computing*, 23(6) 1179–1192, 1994.

[HMNT93] D. S. Hochbaum, N. Megiddo, J. Naor and A. Tamir. Tight bounds and 2-approximation algorithms for integer programs with two variables per inequality. *Mathematical Programming* 62:69–83, 1993.

[HK73]   J.E. Hopcroft and R.M. Karp. A $n^{\frac{5}{2}}$ algorithm for maximum matchings in bipartite graphs. *SIAM J. Comput.* 2:225–231, 1973.

[HP94]   D. S. Hochbaum and A. Pathria. Analysis of the greedy approach in covering problems. Unpublished manuscript, 1994.

[HSVW90] J. M. Ho, M. Sarrafzadeh, G. Vijayan, and C. K. Wong. Layer Assignment for Multichip Modules. *IEEE Transactions on Computer-Aided Design*, 9:1272–12 77, 1990.

[Joh74] D. S. Johnson. Approximation Algorithms for Combinatorial Problems. *J. Comput. System Sci.*, 9:256–278, 1974.

[KZ95] M. Karpinski and A. Zelikovsky. Approximating dense cases of covering problems (preliminary draft). Manuscript, Sept. 1995.

[KVY94] S. Khuller, U. Vishkin, and N. Young. A primal-dual parallel approximation technique applied to weighted set and vertex cover. *J. of Algorithms*, 17(2):280–289, 1994.

[Lag85] J. C. Lagarias. The computational complexity of simultaneous diophantine approximation problems. *SIAM Journal on Computing* 14:196–209, 1985.

[Lor66] L. C. Lorentzen. Notes on covering of arcs by nodes in an undirected graph. *Technical Report ORC 66.16, University of California, Berkeley*, 1966.

[Lou92] R. Loulou. Minimal Cut Cover of a Graph with an Application to the Testing of Electronic Boards. *Operations Research Letters*, 12(5):301–306, 1992.

[Lov66] L. Lovász. On Decomposition of Graphs. *Studia Scientiarum Mathematicarum Hungarica* 1:237–238, 1966.

[Lov75a] L. Lovász. Three short proofs in graph theory. *J. Combin. Theory (B)* 19:269–271, 1975.

[Lov75] L. Lovász. On the Ratio of Optimal Integral and Fractional Covers. *Discrete Math.* 13 383–390, 1975.

[MMK79] R. E. Marsten, M. R. Muller, and C. L. Killion. Crew Planning at Flying Tiger: A successful application of integer programming. *Management Science* 25:1175–1183, 1979.

[MST80] D. Matula, Y. Shiloach, and R. Tarjan. Two linear-time algorithms for 5-coloring a planar graph. Stanford Department of Computer Science, Report No. STAN-CS-80-830, 1980.

[MS85] B. Monien and E. Speckenmeyer. Ramsey Numbers and an approximation algorithm for the vertex cover problem. *Acta Informatica* 22:115–123, 1985.

[MZH83] N. Megiddo, E. Zemel, and S. L. Hakimi. The maximum coverage location problem. *SIAM Journal of Algebraic and Discrete Methods*, 4(2):253–261, 1983.

[Meg83] N. Megiddo. Towards a genuinely polynomial algorithm for linear programming. *SIAM Journal on Computing* 12:347–353, 1983.

[NT75] G. L. Nemhauser and L. E. Trotter, Jr. Vertex packings: Structural properties and algorithms. *Mathematical Programming* 8:232–248, 1975.

[NW72] G. L. Nemhauser and L. Wolsey. Maximizing submodular set functions: formulations and analysis of algorithms. In *Studies of Graphs and Discrete Programming* North-Holland, Amsterdam, 279–301, 1972.

[Pad79] M. W. Padberg. Covering and packing and knapsack problems. *Annals of Discrete Mathematics* 4:265–287, 1979.

[Pic7] J. C. Picard. Maximal closure of a graph and applications to combinatorial problems. *Management Science* 22:1268–1272, 1976.

[Pul79] W. R. Pulleyblank. Minimum node covers and 2-bicritical graphs. *Mathematical Programming* 17:91–103, 1979.

[She83] J. B. Shearer. A note on the independence number of triangle-free graphs. *Discrete Mathematics* 46:(1983) 83–87.

[Sup87] K. Supowit. Finding a Maximum Planar Subset of a Set of Nets in a Channel. *IEEE Transactions on Computer-Aided Design*, 6:93–94, 1987.

[SW68] G. Szekeres and W. S. Wilf. An inequality for the chromatic number of a graph. *Combin. Theory* 4:1–3, 1968.

[Tar86] É. Tardos. A strongly polynomial algorithm to solve combinatorial linear programs. *Operations Research* 34:250–256, 1986.

[Tro85] L. E. Trotter. Discrete packing and covering. in, O'hEigeartaigh et al. 21–31, 1985.

[Tur41] P. Turán. An External Problem in Graph Theory. *Mat. Fiz. Lapok*, 48:436–452, 1941.

[VH93] R. V. Vohra and N. G. Hall. A probabilistic analysis of the maximal covering location problem. *Discrete Applied Mathematics* 43:175–183, 1993.

[VS81] R. van Slyke. Covering problems in CCCI systems. Report to the Air Force Office of Scientific Research, 1981.

[Wig83] A. Wigderson. Improving the performance guarantee for approximate graph coloring. *Journal of the ACM* 30:729–735, 1983.

[YG92] G. Yu and O. Goldschmidt. On locally optimal independent sets and vertex covers. *Technical Report ORP92-01: Graduate School in Operations Research The University of Texas at Austin*, 1992.

4

THE PRIMAL-DUAL METHOD FOR APPROXIMATION ALGORITHMS AND ITS APPLICATION TO NETWORK DESIGN PROBLEMS

Michel X. Goemans   **David P. Williamson**

Dedicated to the memory of Albert W. Tucker

The primal-dual method is a standard tool in the design of algorithms for combinatorial optimization problems. This chapter shows how the primal-dual method can be modified to provide good approximation algorithms for a wide variety of *NP*-hard problems. We concentrate on results from recent research applying the primal-dual method to problems in network design.

INTRODUCTION

4.1

In the last four decades, combinatorial optimization has been strongly influenced by linear programming. With the mathematical and algorithmic understanding of linear programs came a whole host of ideas and tools that were then applied to combinatorial optimization. Many of these ideas and tools are still in use today, and form the bedrock of our understanding of combinatorial optimization.

One of these tools is the *primal-dual method*. It was proposed by Dantzig, Ford, and Fulkerson [DFF56] as another means of solving linear programs. Ironically, their inspiration came from combinatorial optimization. In the early 1930s, Egerváry [Ege31] proved a min-max relation for the assignment problem (or the minimum-cost bipartite perfect matching problem) by reducing it to a known min-max result for maximum cardinality matchings. This lead Kuhn to propose his primal-dual "Hungarian Method" for solving the assignment problem [Kuh55], which then inspired Dantzig, Ford, and Fulkerson. Although the primal-dual method in its original form has not survived as an algorithm for linear programming, it has found widespread use as a means of devising algorithms for problems in combinatorial optimization. The main feature of the primal-dual method is that it allows a weighted optimization problem to be reduced to a purely combinatorial, unweighted problem. Most of the fundamental algorithms in combinatorial optimization either use this method or can be understood in terms of it, including Dijkstra's shortest path algorithm [Dij59], Ford and Fulkerson's network flow algorithm [FF56], Edmonds' non-bipartite matching algorithm [Edm65] and, of course, Kuhn's assignment algorithm.

The primal-dual method as described above has been used to solve problems that can be modelled as linear programs; the method simply leads to efficient polynomial-time algorithms for solving these problems. Since NP-hard problems cannot be modelled as polynomially-sized linear programs unless $P = NP$, the primal-dual method does not generalize straightforwardly to generate algorithms for the NP-hard optimization problems that are the interest of this book. Nevertheless, with modifications the primal-dual method leads to approximation algorithms for a wide variety of NP-hard problems. In this chapter we will explain the current state of knowledge about how the primal-dual method can be used to devise approximation algorithms.

One of the benefits of the primal-dual method is that it leads to a very general methodology for the design of approximation algorithms for NP-hard problems. Until quite recently, whenever one wanted to design an approximation algorithm, one usually had to tailor-make an algorithm using the particular structure of the problem at hand. However, in the past few years several general methods for designing approximation algorithms have arisen. The primal-dual method is one of these, and we will see in this chapter that it leads to approximation algorithms for a large number of problems.

Linear programming has long been used to design and analyze approximation algorithms for NP-hard problems, particularly for problems which can be naturally formulated as integer programs. Several approximation algorithms from the seventies use linear programming (LP) in their analysis (see [Chv79, Lov75, CFN77], for example). A 1980 paper by Wolsey [Wol80] highlighted the use of linear programming, and showed that several previously known approximation algorithms could be analyzed using linear programming, including Christofides' algorithm for the TSP [Chr76] and Johnson et al.'s bin packing algorithms [JDU+74]. In the eighties, several papers appeared which used the optimum solution of a linear program to derive an integer solution; the most common technique given rounds fractional solutions to integer solutions. The reader can find examples of deterministic rounding and other techniques (as in [Hoc82]) in Chapter 3 of this book, while randomized rounding [RT87] is presented in Chapter 11. In the primal-dual method for approximation algorithms, an approximate solution to the problem and a feasible solution to the dual of an LP relaxation are constructed simultaneously; the performance guarantee is proved by comparing the values of both solutions. Many of the approximation algorithms with an LP-based analysis can be viewed as primal-dual, but the first truly primal-dual approximation algorithm in which the integer primal and the dual solutions are constructed at the same time is the algorithm of Bar-Yehuda and Even [BYE81] for the vertex cover problem. In the past few years, the power of the primal-dual method has become apparent through a sequence of papers developing this technique for *network design problems* [AKR95, GW95a, SVY92, KR93, WGMV95, GGW93, AG94, GGP⁺94, RW95]. This line of research started with a paper by Agrawal, Klein, and Ravi [AKR95], who introduced a powerful modification of the basic method. Our survey will focus mostly on these problems and results.

In basic versions of network design problems we are given a graph $G = (V, E)$ (undirected or directed) and a cost c_e for each edge $e \in E$ (or for each arc in the directed case), and we would like to find a minimum-cost subset E' of the edges E that meets some design criteria. For example, we may wish to find the minimum-cost set of arcs in a directed graph such that every vertex can reach every other vertex; that is, we wish to find the minimum-cost strongly connected subgraph. Network design problems arise from many sources, including the design of various transportation systems (such as highways and mass-transit systems), as well as telephone and computer networks. We direct the reader to the book edited by Ball et al. [BMMN94] for a broad overview of network design problems, models, and algorithms. For the most part, our survey will concentrate on network design problems on undirected graphs $G = (V, E)$ with nonnegative edge costs c_e.

We will present the primal-dual method as developed for network design problems in a somewhat different fashion than in the original references. We isolate the essential ideas or *design rules* present in all these approximation results and develop generic primal-dual algorithms together with generic proofs of their performance guarantees. Once this is in place, it becomes quite simple to apply these algorithms and proofs to a variety of problems, such as the vertex cover problem [BYE81], the edge covering problem, the minimum-weight perfect matching problem [GW95a], the survivable network design problem [AKR95, WGMV95], the prize-collecting traveling salesman problem [GW95a], and the minimum multicut problem in trees [GVY96]. We show that each of these design rules is implicit in several long-known primal-dual algorithms that solve network design problems exactly, namely Dijkstra's shortest *s-t* path algorithm [Dij59], Edmonds' minimum-cost branching algorithm [Edm67], and Kruskal's minimum spanning tree algorithm [Kru56]. The generic algorithms reduce to these exact algorithms for these problems.

The survey is structured as follows. In the next section, we review the classical primal-dual method for solving linear programs and optimization problems that can be modelled as linear programs. In Section 4.3 we gradually develop a primal-dual method for the design of approximation algorithm by modifying the classical method and introducing a sequence of design rules. This yields our generic primal-dual algorithm and generic theorems for proving good performance guarantees of the algorithm. We then apply the algorithm and theorems to a number of network design problems in the following sections. The general model of network design problems that we consider is given in Section 4.4. We introduce a number of network design problems in Sections 4.5 through 4.7, and show that the generic algorithm yields near optimal results. In Section 4.8 we show that the primal-dual method can even be applied to other problems that do not fit in our model, and we conclude in Section 4.9.

THE CLASSICAL PRIMAL-DUAL METHOD

4.2

Before we begin to outline the primal-dual method for approximation algorithms, we first review the classical primal-dual method as applied to linear programs and polynomial-time solvable optimization problems. We refer the reader unfamiliar with the basic theorems and terminology of linear programming to introductions in Chvátal [Chv83] or Strang [Str88, Ch. 8]. For a more detailed description of the primal-dual method for polynomial-time combinatorial optimization problems, see Papadimitriou and Steiglitz [PS82].

Consider the linear program

$$\text{Min} \quad c^T x$$

subject to:

$$Ax \geq b$$
$$x \geq 0$$

and its dual

$$\text{Max} \quad b^T y$$

subject to:

$$A^T y \leq c$$
$$y \geq 0,$$

where $A \in \mathbf{Q}^{m \times n}$, $c, x \in \mathbf{Q}^n$, $b, y \in \mathbf{Q}^m$, and ^{T} denotes the transpose. For ease of presentation we assume that $c \geq 0$. In the primal-dual method of Dantzig, Ford, and Fulkerson, we assume that we have a feasible solution y to the dual; initially we can set $y = 0$. In the primal-dual method, either we will be able to find a primal solution x that obeys the complementary slackness conditions with respect to y, thus proving that both x and y are optimal, or we will be able to find a new feasible dual solution with a greater objective function value.

First consider what it means for x to be complementary slack to y. Let A_i denote the ith row of A and A^j the jth column of A (written as a row vector to avoid the use of transpose). For the linear program and dual given above, there are two types of complementary slackness conditions. First, there are *primal complementary slackness conditions*, corresponding to the primal variables, namely

$$x_j > 0 \Rightarrow A^j y = c_j.$$

Let $J = \{j \mid A^j y = c_j\}$. Second, there are *dual complementary slackness conditions*, corresponding to the dual variables, namely

$$y_i > 0 \Rightarrow A_i x = b_i.$$

Let $I = \{i \mid y_i = 0\}$.

Given a feasible dual solution y we can state the problem of finding a primal feasible x that obeys the complementary slackness conditions as another optimization problem:

find a solution x which minimizes the "violation" of the primal constraints and of the complementary slackness conditions. The notion of violation can be formalized in several ways leading to different *restricted primal* problems. For example, the following restricted linear program performs the required role:

$$z_{INF} \quad = \quad \text{Min} \quad \sum_{i \notin I} s_i + \sum_{j \notin J} x_j$$

subject to:

$$A_i x \geq b_i \qquad\qquad i \in I$$
$$A_i x - s_i = b_i \qquad\qquad i \notin I$$
$$x \geq 0$$
$$s \geq 0.$$

(To ensure feasibility of the restricted primal, we are implicitly assuming the existence of an $x \geq 0$ satisfying $Ax \geq b$.) If this linear program has a solution (x, s) such that the objective function value z_{INF} is 0, then we will have found a primal solution x that obeys the complementary slackness conditions for our dual solution y. Thus x and y are optimal primal and dual solutions, respectively. However, suppose that the optimal solution to the restricted primal has $z_{INF} > 0$. Consider now the dual of the restricted primal:

$$\text{Max} \quad b^T y'$$

subject to:

$$A^j y' \leq 0 \qquad\qquad j \in J$$
$$A^j y' \leq 1 \qquad\qquad j \notin J$$
$$y'_i \geq -1 \qquad\qquad i \notin I$$
$$y'_i \geq 0 \qquad\qquad i \in I.$$

Since the optimal solution to its primal has value greater than 0, we know that this program has a solution y' such that $b^T y' > 0$. We will now show that we can find an $\epsilon > 0$ such that $y'' = y + \epsilon y'$ is a feasible dual solution. Thus, if we cannot find an x that obeys the complementary slackness conditions, we can find a feasible y'' such that $b^T y'' = b^T y + \epsilon b^T y' > b^T y$; that is, we can find a new dual solution with greater objective function value. Observe that, by definition of I, $y'' \geq 0$ provided that $\epsilon \leq \min_{i \notin I : y'_i < 0} (-y_i / y'_i)$ while, by definition of J, $A^T y'' \leq c$ provided that $\epsilon \leq \min_{j \notin J : A^j y' > 0} \frac{c_j - A^j y}{A^j y'}$. Choosing the smaller upper bound on ϵ, we obtain a new dual feasible solution of greater value, and we can reapply the procedure. Whenever no primal feasible solution obeys the complementary slackness conditions with y, the above restricted primal outputs the least infeasible solution, and this can be used to trace the progress of the algorithm towards finding a primal feasible solution.

Since the method outlined above reduces the solution of a linear program to the solution of a series of linear programs, it does not seem that we have made much progress. Notice, however, that the vector c has disappeared in the restricted primal and its dual. In network design problems, this vector corresponds to the edge-costs. The classical primal-dual method thus reduces weighted problems to their unweighted counterparts, which are often much easier to solve. Furthermore, for combinatorial optimization problems (such as network design problems), these unweighted problems can usually be solved combinatorially, rather than with linear programming. That is, we can use combinatorial algorithms to find an x that obeys the complementary slackness conditions, or failing that, to find a new feasible dual with greater dual objective value. In this way, the method leads to efficient algorithms for these optimization problems.

As an example, we quickly sketch the primal-dual method as it is applies to the assignment problem, also known as the minimum-weight perfect matching problem in bipartite graphs. Suppose we have a bipartite graph $G = (A, B, E)$, with $|A| = |B| = n$, and each edge $e = (a, b)$ has $a \in A$, $b \in B$. We assume that a perfect matching exists in E. Let $c_e \geq 0$ denote the cost of edge e; throughout this section we will use c_e and c_{ab} interchangeably for an edge $e = (a, b)$. We would like to find the minimum-cost set of edges such that each vertex is adjacent to exactly one edge. This problem can be formulated as the following integer program:

$$\text{Min} \quad \sum_{e \in E} c_e x_e$$

subject to:

$$\sum_{b:(a,b)\in E} x_{ab} = 1 \qquad\qquad a \in A$$

$$\sum_{a:(a,b)\in E} x_{ab} = 1 \qquad\qquad b \in B$$

$$x_e \in \{0, 1\} \qquad\qquad e \in E.$$

It is well-known that the LP relaxation of this integer program has integer solutions as extreme points (Birkhoff [Bir46], von Neumann [vN53]), so we can drop the integrality constraints and replace them with $x_e \geq 0$. The dual of this LP relaxation is

$$\text{Max} \quad \sum_{a \in A} u_a + \sum_{b \in B} v_b$$

subject to:

$$u_a + v_b \leq c_{ab} \qquad\qquad (a, b) \in E.$$

The primal-dual method specifies that we start with a dual feasible solution, in this case $u = v = 0$. Given our current feasible dual solution, we look for a primal feasible solution that obeys the complementary slackness conditions. In this case, we only have primal complementary slackness conditions. Let $J = \{(a, b) \in E : u_a + v_b = c_{ab}\}$. Then the restricted primal is

$$\text{Min} \quad \sum_{a \in A} s_a + \sum_{b \in B} s_b$$

subject to:

$$\sum_{b:(a,b)\in E} x_{ab} + s_a = 1 \qquad\qquad a \in A$$

$$\sum_{a:(a,b)\in E} x_{ab} + s_b = 1 \qquad\qquad b \in B$$

$$x_e = 0 \qquad\qquad e \in (E - J)$$

$$x_e \geq 0 \qquad\qquad e \in J$$

$$s \geq 0.$$

As with the original primal, every basic feasible solution to the restricted primal has every component equal to 0 or 1. This implies that solving the restricted primal reduces to the problem of finding the largest cardinality matching in the bipartite graph $G' = (A, B, J)$. Efficient algorithms are known for finding maximum matchings in bipartite graphs. If we find a perfect matching in G', then we have found an x that obeys the complementary slackness conditions with respect to (u, v), and x and (u, v) must be optimal solutions. Initially, J is likely to be empty and, as a result, our initial primal infeasible solution is $x = 0$. One can show that the infeasibility of x gradually decreases during the course of the algorithm.

The dual of the restricted primal is

$$\text{Max} \quad \sum_{a \in A} u'_a + \sum_{b \in B} v'_b$$

subject to:

$$
\begin{aligned}
u'_a + v'_b &\leq 0 & (a, b) &\in J \\
u'_a &\leq 1 & a &\in A \\
v'_b &\leq 1 & b &\in B.
\end{aligned}
$$

It can easily be seen that every basic solution (u', v') has all its components equal to ± 1. Given the maximum matching, there is a straightforward combinatorial algorithm to find an optimum solution to this dual. If the optimum value of the restricted primal is not zero then an improved dual solution can be obtained by considering $u'' = u + \epsilon u'$ and $v'' = v + \epsilon v'$, for $\epsilon = \min_{(a,b) \in E-J} (c_{ab} - u_a - v_b)$. It is not hard to see that this choice of ϵ maintains dual feasibility, and it can be shown that only $O(n^2)$ dual updates are necessary before a perfect matching is found in G'. At this point we will have found a feasible x that obeys the complementary slackness conditions with a feasible dual u, v, and thus these solutions must be optimal.

EXERCISE 4.1   Show how to formulate a restricted primal by using only one new variable. Make sure that your restricted primal is always feasible.

THE PRIMAL-DUAL METHOD FOR APPROXIMATION ALGORITHMS

4.3

Most combinatorial optimization problems have natural integer programming formulations. However, unlike the case of the assignment problem, the LP relaxations typically have extreme points which do not correspond to solutions of the combinatorial optimization problem. Therefore, we cannot use the classical primal-dual method to find an optimum integer solution. In this section, however, we will show that a suitable modification of the method is very useful for finding approximate integer solutions. In addition, we will show a sequence of design rules that leads to good approximation algorithms for network design problems.

The central modification made to the primal-dual method is to relax the complementary slackness conditions. In the classical setting described in the previous section, we imposed both primal and dual complementary slackness conditions, and we used the dual of the restricted primal problem to find a direction to improve the dual solution if the complementary conditions were not satisfied. For the design of approximation algorithms, we will impose the primal complementary slackness conditions, but relax the dual complementary slackness conditions. Furthermore, given these conditions, if the current primal solution is not feasible, we will be able to increase the value of the dual.

To illustrate this modification of the method, we will examine a specific combinatorial optimization problem, the *hitting set problem*. The hitting set problem is defined as follows: Given subsets $T_1, \ldots, T_p$ of a ground set E and given a nonnegative cost c_e for every element $e \in E$, find a minimum-cost subset $A \subseteq E$ such that $A \cap T_i \neq \emptyset$ for every $i = 1, \ldots, p$ (i.e. A "hits" every T_i). The problem is equivalent to the more well-known set cover problem in which the goal is to cover the entire ground set with the minimum-cost collection of sets (see Chapter 3).

As we proceed to construct piece by piece a powerful version of the primal-dual method for approximation algorithms, along the way we will "rediscover" many classical (exact or approximation) algorithms for problems that are special cases of the hitting set problem. From these classical algorithms, we will infer design rules for approximation algorithms which we will later show lead to good approximation algorithms for other problems. The particular special cases of the hitting set problem we study are as follows. The *undirected $s - t$ shortest path problem* with nonnegative lengths can be formulated as a hitting set problem by noticing that any $s - t$ path must intersect every $s - t$ cut $\delta(S)$, where $\delta(S) = \{e = (i, j) \in E : i \in S, j \notin S\}$ and $s \in S$ and $t \notin S$. Thus, we can let E be the edge set of the undirected graph $G = (V, E)$; c_e be the length of the edge e; and $T_1, \ldots, T_p$ be the collection of all $s - t$ cuts, i.e. $T_i = \delta(S_i)$ where S_i runs over all sets containing s but not t. Observe that the feasible solutions consist of subgraphs in which s and t are connected; only *minimal* solutions (i.e. solutions for which no edge can be removed without destroying feasibility) will correspond to $s - t$ paths. The directed $s - t$ path problem can be similarly formulated. The *minimum spanning tree problem* is also a special case of the hitting set problem; here we would like to cover all cuts $\delta(S)$ with no restriction on S. The *vertex cover problem* (see Chapter 3) is the problem of finding a minimum (cardinality or cost) set of vertices in an undirected graph such that every edge has at least one endpoint in the set. The vertex cover is a hitting set problem in which the ground set E is now the set of vertices and T_i corresponds to the endpoints of edge i. In the *minimum-cost arborescence problem*, we are given a directed graph $G = (V, E)$ with nonnegative arc costs and a special root vertex r, and we would like to find a spanning tree directed out of r of minimum cost. Here the sets to hit are all r-directed cuts, i.e. sets of arcs of the form $\delta^-(S) = \{(i, j) \in E : i \notin S, j \in S\}$ where $S \subseteq V - \{r\}$. All these special cases, except for the vertex cover problem, are known to be polynomially solvable. Dijkstra's algorithm [Dij59] solves the shortest path problem, Edmonds' algorithm [Edm67] solves the minimum-cost arborescence problem, while Kruskal's greedy algorithm [Kru56] solves the minimum spanning tree problem. For many special cases (again excluding the vertex cover problem), the number of sets to hit is exponential in the size of the instance. We will see shortly that this does not lead to any difficulties.

The hitting set problem can be formulated as an integer program as follows:

$$\text{Min} \quad \sum_{e \in E} c_e x_e$$

subject to:

$$\sum_{e \in T_i} x_e \geq 1 \qquad\qquad i = 1, \dots, p$$

$$x_e \in \{0, 1\} \qquad\qquad e \in E,$$

where x represents the incidence (or characteristic) vector of the selected set A, i.e. $x_e = 1$ if $e \in A$ and 0 otherwise. Its LP relaxation and the corresponding dual are the following:

$$\text{Min} \quad \sum_{e \in E} c_e x_e$$

subject to:

$$\sum_{e \in T_i} x_e \geq 1 \qquad\qquad i = 1, \dots, p$$

$$x_e \geq 0 \qquad\qquad e \in E,$$

and

$$\text{Max} \quad \sum_{i=1}^{p} y_i$$

subject to:

$$\sum_{i : e \in T_i} y_i \leq c_e \qquad\qquad e \in E$$

$$y_i \geq 0 \qquad\qquad i = 1, \dots, p.$$

For the incidence vector x of a set A and a dual feasible solution y, the primal complementary slackness conditions are

$$e \in A \Rightarrow \sum_{i : e \in T_i} y_i = c_e \tag{4.1}$$

while the dual complementary slackness conditions are

$$y_i > 0 \Rightarrow |A \cap T_i| = 1. \tag{4.2}$$

As we said earlier, the central modification made to the primal-dual method is to enforce the primal complementary slackness conditions and relax the dual conditions. Given a dual feasible solution y, consider the set $A = \{e : \sum_{i : e \in T_i} y_i = c_e\}$. Clearly, if A is infeasible then no feasible set can satisfy the primal complementary slackness conditions (4.1) corresponding to the dual solution y. As in the classical primal-dual method, if we cannot find a feasible primal solution given the complementary slackness conditions, then there is a way to increase the dual solution. Here, the infeasibility of A means that there exists k such that $A \cap T_k = \emptyset$. The set T_k is said to be *violated*. By increasing y_k, the value of the dual solution will improve; the maximum value y_k can take without violating dual feasibility is

$$y_k = \min_{e \in T_k} \left\{ c_e - \sum_{i \neq k : e \in T_i} y_i \right\}. \tag{4.3}$$

Observe that $y_k > 0$ since no element e in T_k is also in A. For this value of y_k, at least one element e (the argmin in (4.3)) will be added to A since now $\sum_{i:e\in T_i} y_i = c_e$. We can repeat the procedure until A is a feasible primal solution.

This basic version of the primal-dual method is formalized in Figure 4.1. In the description of the algorithm in the figure, we are adding only one element e at a time to A, although other elements f could satisfy $\sum_{i:f\in T_i} y_i = c_f$. This means that in a later stage such an element f could be added while the corresponding increase of y_l for some $T_l \ni f$ would be 0. This does not affect the algorithm.

The primal-dual method as described is also referred to as a *dual-ascent algorithm*. See for example the work of Erlenkotter [Erl78] for the facility location problem, Wong [Won84] for the Steiner tree problem, Balakrishnan, Magnanti, and Wong [BMW89] for the fixed-charge network design problem, or the recent Ph.D. thesis of Raghavan [Rag94].

The main question now is whether the simple primal-dual algorithm described in Figure 4.1 produces a solution of small cost. The cost of the solution is $c(A) = \sum_{e\in A} c_e$ and since e was added to A only if the corresponding dual constraint was tight, we can rewrite the cost as $\sum_{e\in A} \sum_{i:e\in T_i} y_i$. By exchanging the two summations, we get

$$c(A) = \sum_{i=1}^{p} |A \cap T_i| y_i.$$

Since y is a dual feasible solution, its value $\sum_{i=1}^{p} y_i$ is a lower bound on the optimum value z_{OPT} of the hitting set problem. If we can guarantee that

$$|A \cap T_i| \le \alpha \text{ whenever } y_i > 0 \tag{4.4}$$

then this would immediately imply that $c(A) \le \alpha z_{OPT}$, i.e. the algorithm is an α-approximation algorithm. In particular, if α can be guaranteed to be 1, then the solution given by the algorithm must certainly be optimal, and equation (4.4) together with primal feasibility imply the dual complementary slackness conditions (4.2). Conditions (4.4) certainly hold if we choose α to be the largest cardinality of any set T_i: $\alpha = \max_{i=1}^{p} |T_i|$. This α-approximation algorithm for the general hitting set problem was discovered by Bar-Yehuda and Even [BYE81]; the analysis appeared previously in a paper of Hochbaum [Hoc82], who gave an α-approximation algorithm using an optimal dual solution. In the special case of the vertex cover problem, every T_i has cardinality two, and therefore, the algorithm is a 2-approximation algorithm. We refer the reader to the Chapter 3 for the history of these results, as well as additional results on the vertex

1	$y \leftarrow 0$
2	$A \leftarrow \emptyset$
3	While $\exists k : A \cap T_k = \emptyset$
4	Increase y_k until $\exists e \in T_k : \sum_{i:e\in T_i} y_i = c_e$
5	$A \leftarrow A \cup \{e\}$
6	Output A (and y)

FIGURE 4.1

The basic primal-dual algorithm.

cover problem and the general set cover problem. The algorithm above is functionally equivalent to the "dual feasible" algorithm of Chapter 3.

Before refining the basic algorithm, we discuss some implementation and efficiency issues. First, since A has at most $|E|$ elements, the algorithm performs at most $|E|$ iterations and outputs a dual feasible solution y with at most $|E|$ nonzero values. This observation is particularly important when there are exponentially many sets T_i (and these sets are given implicitly) as in the case of the $s - t$ shortest path problem or the minimum-cost arborescence problem. In such cases, the algorithm does not keep track of every y_i but only of the nonzero components of y. Also, the algorithm must be able to find a set T_k not intersecting A. If there are many sets to hit, we must have a *violation oracle*: given A the oracle must be able to decide if $A \cap T_i \neq \emptyset$ for all i and, if not, must output a set T_k for which $A \cap T_k = \emptyset$.

For the shortest path problem, the minimum-cost arborescence problem, or the network design problems we will be considering, the sets T_i to be hit are naturally associated to vertex sets S_i ($T_i = \delta(S_i)$, or for the minimum-cost arborescence problem, $T_i = \delta^-(S_i)$). For simplicity, we shall often refer to these vertex sets instead of the corresponding cuts; for example, we will say that the set S_i is violated, rather than $T_i = \delta(S_i)$ is violated. Also, we shall denote the dual variable corresponding to the cut induced by S as y_S.

We obtain our first design rule by considering a violation oracle for the $s - t$ shortest path problem. For this problem, the oracle simply computes the connected components of (V, A) and check if s and t belong to the same component; if not, the component containing s (or the one containing t, or the union of components containing s or t) is a violated set. This comment raises the issue of which violated set to select in the basic primal-dual algorithm when there are several sets which are not hit by A. For network design problems in which the T_i's naturally correspond to vertex sets, a good selection rule is to take among all violated edge sets T one for which the corresponding vertex set S is (inclusion-wise) minimal, i.e. there is no violated S' with $S' \subset S$. We refer to this rule as the *minimal violated set rule*. In the case of the undirected shortest path problem, this rule consists of selecting the connected component containing s, provided that this component does not contain t. Here there is a *unique* minimal violated set, although this is not always the case.

Let us consider the resulting primal-dual algorithm for the shortest path problem in greater detail. Initially, all y_S are 0, $A = \emptyset$, and the minimal violated set is simply $S = \{s\}$. As y_S is increased, the shortest edge (s, i) out of s is selected and added to A. In a later stage, if S denotes the current minimal violated set, an edge (i, j) with $i \in S$ and $j \notin S$ is added to A and the minimal violated set becomes $S \cup \{j\}$ (unless $j = t$ in which case there are no more violated sets). Thus, A is a forest consisting of a single non-trivial component containing s. To see which edges get added to A, it is useful to keep track of a notion of *time*. Initially, time is 0 and is incremented by ϵ whenever a dual variable is increased by ϵ. For every edge e, let $a(e)$ denote the time at which e would be added to A *if* the minimal violated sets were not to change. We refer to $a(e)$ as the *addition time* of edge e. Similarly, let $l(j)$ be the time at which a vertex j would be added to S. Clearly, $l(j)$ is simply the smallest $a(e)$ over all edges e incident to j. The next vertex to be added to S is thus the vertex attaining the minimum in $\min_{j \notin S} l(j)$. As j is added to S, we need to update the $a(.)$ and $l(.)$ values. Only the $a(.)$ values of the edges incident to j will be affected; this makes their update easy. Also, for $k \notin S$, $l(k)$

simply becomes $\min\{l(k), l(j) + c_{jk}\}$. By now, the reader must have realized that the $l(.)$ values are simply the labels in Dijkstra's algorithm [Dij59] for the shortest path problem. Keeping track of the $a(.)$ values is thus not necessary in this case, but will be useful in more sophisticated uses of the primal-dual method.

The primal-dual algorithm with minimal violated set rule thus reduces to Dijkstra's algorithm in the case of the shortest path. Or not quite, since the set A output by the algorithm is not simply an $s - t$ path but is a shortest path forest out of s. The cost of this forest is likely to be higher than the cost of the shortest $s - t$ path. In fact, if we try to evaluate the parameter α as defined in (4.4), we observe that α could be as high as $|V| - 1$, if all edges incident to s have been selected. We should therefore eliminate all the unnecessary edges from the solution. More precisely, we add a *delete step* at the end of the primal-dual algorithm which discards as many elements as possible from A without losing feasibility. Observe that, in general, different sets could be output depending on the order in which edges are deleted; in this case, we simply keep only the path from s to t in the shortest path forest. It is not difficult to show (this follows trivially from the forthcoming Theorem 4.1) that the resulting $s - t$ path P satisfies $|P \cap \delta(S)| = 1$ whenever $y_S > 0$, implying that the algorithm finds an optimal solution to the problem.

In some cases, however, the order of deletion of elements is crucial to the proof of a good performance guarantee; this leads to our next design rule. We adopt a *reverse delete step* in which elements are considered for removal in the *reverse* order they were added to A. This version of the primal-dual algorithm with the reverse delete step is formalized in Figure 4.2. We first analyze the performance guarantee of this algorithm in general, then show that it leads to Edmonds' algorithm for the minimum-cost arborescence problem.

To evaluate the performance guarantee of the algorithm, we need to compute an upper bound on α as given in (4.4). To avoid any confusion, let A_f be the set output by the algorithm of Figure 4.2. Fix an index i such that $y_i > 0$, and let e_j be the edge added when y_i was increased. Because of the reverse delete step, we know that when e_j is considered for removal, no element e_p with $p < j$ was removed already. Let B denote the set of elements right after e_j is considered in the reverse delete step. This means that $B = A_f \cup \{e_1, \ldots, e_{j-1}\}$, and that B is a *minimal augmentation* of $\{e_1, \ldots, e_{j-1}\}$, i.e. B is feasible, $B \supseteq \{e_1, \ldots, e_{j-1}\}$ and for all $e \in B - \{e_1, \ldots e_{j-1}\}$ we have that $B - \{e\}$ is

```
1     y ← 0
2     A ← ∅
3     l ← 0
4     While ∃k : A ∩ T_k = ∅
5         l ← l + 1
6         Increase y_k until ∃e_l ∈ T_k : ∑_{i:e_l∈T_i} y_i = c_{e_l}
7         A ← A ∪ {e_l}
8     For j ← l downto 1
9         if A − {e_j} is feasible then A ← A − {e_j}
10    Output A (and y)
```

FIGURE 4.2

Primal-dual algorithm with reverse delete step.

not feasible. Moreover, $|A_f \cap T_i| \leq |B \cap T_i|$ and this continues to hold if we maximize over *all* minimal augmentations B of $\{e_1, \ldots, e_{j-1}\}$. Thus, as an upper bound on α, we can choose

$$\beta = \max_{\left\{\begin{array}{c} \text{infeasible} \\ A \subset E \end{array}\right\}} \max_{\left\{\begin{array}{c} \text{minimal} \\ \text{augmentations } B \text{ of } A \end{array}\right\}} |B \cap T(A)|, \qquad (4.5)$$

where $T(A)$ is the violated set selected by the primal-dual algorithm when confronted with the set A. We have therefore proved the following theorem:

THEOREM 4.1   The primal-dual algorithm described in Figure 4.2 delivers a feasible solution of cost at most $\beta \sum_{i=1}^{p} y_i \leq \beta z_{OPT}$, where β is given in (4.5).

The reverse delete step has thus allowed us to give a bound on the performance of the algorithm without looking at the entire run of the algorithm, but simply by considering any *minimal augmentation* of a set. As an exercise, the reader is invited to derive the optimality of the primal-dual algorithm for the shortest path problem from Theorem 4.1.

Consider now the minimum-cost arborescence problem. For any subset A of arcs, the violation oracle with minimal violated set rule can be implemented by first computing the strongly connected components and then checking if any such component not containing the root, say S, has no arc incoming to it (i.e. $\delta^-(S) \cap A = \emptyset$). If no such component exists then one can easily derive that A contains an arborescence. Otherwise, the algorithm would increase the dual variable corresponding to such a strongly connected component (observe that we have the choice of which component to select if there are several of them). Any minimal augmentation of A must have only *one* arc incoming to a strongly connected component S, since one such arc is sufficient to reach all vertices in S. Thus, the parameter β is equal to 1, and the primal-dual algorithm delivers an optimum solution. This elegant algorithm is due to Edmonds [Edm67]. We should point out that in the case of the arborescence problem, deleting the edges *in reverse* is crucial (while this was not the case for the shortest path problem). The use of the reverse delete step will also be crucial in the design of approximation algorithms for network design problems described in the following sections; in this context, this idea was first used by Klein and Ravi [KR93] and Saran, Vazirani, and Young [SVY92].

Several variants of the primal-dual algorithm described in Figure 4.2 can be designed, without affecting the proof technique for the performance guarantee. One useful variant is to allow the algorithm to increase the dual variable of a set which does not need to be hit. More precisely, suppose we also add to the linear programming relaxation the constraints

$$\sum_{e \in T_i} x_e \geq 1$$

$i = p+1, \ldots, q$, for a collection $\{T_{p+1}, \ldots, T_q\}$ of sets. This clearly may affect the value of the relaxation. Assume we now use the primal-dual algorithm by increasing the dual variable corresponding to any set T_i, where i now runs from 1 to q. Thus, in step 4 of Figure 4.2, a solution A is considered feasible if it hits every set T_i for $i = 1, \ldots, q$. However, in the reverse delete step 9, A only needs to hit every T_i for $i = 1, \ldots, p$. Although the addition of sets T_i's has made the relaxation invalid, we can still use the dual solution we have constructed. Indeed, $\sum_{i=1}^{p} y_i$ is still a lower bound on the optimum value, and, as before, it can be compared to the cost $\sum_{i=1}^{q} |A \cap T_i| y_i$ of the output solution A. The proof technique we have developed for Theorem 4.1 still applies, provided we can guarantee that $A \cap T_i = \emptyset$ for $i = p+1, \ldots, q$. In this case, the performance guarantee will again be β as given by (4.5). As an application, assume that in the minimum-cost arborescence problem, we also include the constraints corresponding to sets S containing the root (this would constitute a formulation for the strongly connected subgraph problem). Then, as long as A does not induce a strongly connected graph, we increase the dual variable corresponding to any strongly connected component with no arc incoming to it (whether or not it contains r). This step is thus independent of the root. It is only in the reverse delete step that we use knowledge of the root. This algorithm still outputs the optimum arborescence (for any specific root r) since it is easy to see that any arc incoming to a strongly connected component containing r and selected by the algorithm will be deleted in the reverse delete step. The algorithm therefore constructs a *single* dual solution proving optimality for *any* root. This observation was made by Edmonds [Edm67]. Another application of this variant of the primal-dual algorithm will be discussed in Section 4.5.

Our final design rule comes from considering the minimum spanning tree problem and the associated greedy algorithm due to Kruskal [Kru56]. In the case of the minimum spanning tree problem, the violation oracle with minimal violated set rule can be implemented by first computing the connected components of (V, A) and, if there are k components where $k > 1$, by selecting any such component, say S. It is easy to see that any minimal augmentation of A must induce a spanning tree if we separately shrink every connected component of (V, A) to a supervertex. The resulting algorithm has a bad performance guarantee since a minimal augmentation of A could therefore have as many as $k - 1$ edges incident to S. Recall that Kruskal's greedy algorithm repeatedly chooses the minimum-cost edge spanning two distinct connected components. This choice of edge is equivalent to *simultaneously* increasing the dual variables corresponding to *all* connected components of (V, A), until the dual constraint for an edge becomes tight.

To see this, consider the notion of *time* as introduced for the shortest path problem. As in that context, we let the addition time $a(e)$ of an edge e to be the time at which this edge would be added to A if the collection of minimal violated sets were not to change. Initially, the addition time of e is $c_e/2$ (since the duals are increased on both endpoints of e), and it will remain so as long as both ends are in different connected components of (V, A). The next edge to be added to A is the one with smallest addition time and is thus the minimum-cost edge between two components of (V, A). Thus, the algorithm mimics Kruskal's algorithm.

This suggests that we should revise our primal-dual algorithm and increase *simultaneously and at the same speed* the dual variables corresponding to several violated sets. We refer to this rule as the *uniform increase* rule. This is formalized in Figure 4.3, in which the oracle VIOLATION returns a collection of violated sets whose dual variables will be increased. In the case of network design problems, the study of the minimum spanning tree problem further suggests that the oracle VIOLATION should return *all* minimal violated sets. In the context of approximation algorithms for network design problems, this uniform increase rule on minimal violated sets was first used by Agrawal, Klein, and Ravi [AKR95] without reference to linear programming; its use was broadened and the linear programming made explicit in a paper of the authors [GW95a]. The

1	$y \leftarrow 0$
2	$A \leftarrow \emptyset$
3	$l \leftarrow 0$
4	While A is not feasible
5	$\quad l \leftarrow l + 1$
6	$\quad \mathcal{V} \leftarrow \text{VIOLATION}(A)$
7	$\quad$ Increase y_k uniformly for all $T_k \in \mathcal{V}$ until $\exists e_l \notin A : \sum_{i:e_l \in T_i} y_i = c_{e_l}$
8	$\quad A \leftarrow A \cup \{e_l\}$
9	For $j \leftarrow l$ downto 1
10	$\quad$ if $A - \{e_j\}$ is feasible then $A \leftarrow A - \{e_j\}$
11	Output A (and y)

FIGURE 4.3

Primal-dual algorithm with uniform increase rule
and reverse delete step.

algorithm of Agrawal et al. can be considered the first highly sophisticated use of the primal-dual method in the design of approximation algorithms.

The analysis of the performance guarantee can be done in a similar way as for the primal-dual algorithm of Figure 4.2. Remember we compared the cost of the solution output A_f, which can be written as $\sum_{i=1}^{p} |A_f \cap T_i| y_i$, to the value $\sum_{i=1}^{p} y_i$ of the dual solution. However, instead of comparing the two summations term by term, we may take advantage of the fact that several dual variables are being increased at the same time. Let $\mathcal{V}_j$ denote the collection of violated sets returned by the oracle VIOLATION in the jth iteration of our primal-dual algorithm of Figure 4.3 and let ϵ_j denote the increase of the dual variables corresponding to $\mathcal{V}_j$ in iteration j. Thus, $y_i = \sum_{j:T_i \in \mathcal{V}_j} \epsilon_j$. We can rewrite the value of the dual solution as

$$\sum_{i=1}^{p} y_i = \sum_{j=1}^{l} |\mathcal{V}_j| \epsilon_j,$$

and the cost of A_f as:

$$\sum_{i=1}^{p} |A_f \cap T_i| y_i = \sum_{i=1}^{p} |A_f \cap T_i| \sum_{j:T_i \in \mathcal{V}_j} \epsilon_j = \sum_{j=1}^{l} \left(\sum_{T_i \in \mathcal{V}_j} |A_f \cap T_i| \right) \epsilon_j.$$

From these expressions (comparing them term by term), it is clear that the cost of A_f is at most the value of the dual solution times γ if, for all $j = 1, \ldots, l$,

$$\sum_{T_i \in \mathcal{V}_j} |A_f \cap T_i| \leq \gamma |\mathcal{V}_j|.$$

Again using the reverse delete step, we can replace A_f, (which depends on the entire algorithm in an intricate fashion) by any minimal augmentation B of the infeasible solution at the start of iteration j. We have thus proved the following theorem.

THEOREM 4.2 The primal-dual algorithm described in Figure 4.3 delivers a feasible solution of cost at most $\gamma \sum_{i=1}^{p} y_i \leq \gamma z_{OPT}$, if γ satisfies that for any infeasible set A

and any minimal augmentation B of A

$$\sum_{T_i \in \mathcal{V}(A)} |B \cap T_i| \leq \gamma |\mathcal{V}(A)|,$$

where $\mathcal{V}(A)$ denotes the collection of violated sets output by VIOLATION on input A.

Let us consider again the minimum spanning tree problem. For any set A, $\mathcal{V}(A)$ denotes the set of connected components of A, and we know that any minimal augmentation B of A must induce a spanning tree when shrinking all connected components. Therefore, $\sum_{T_i \in \mathcal{V}(A)} |B \cap T_i|$ corresponds to the sum of the degrees of a spanning tree on a graph with $k = |\mathcal{V}(A)|$ supervertices, and is thus equal to $2k - 2$, independent of the spanning tree. The upper bound γ on the performance guarantee can thus be set to 2. Theorem 4.2 will be used repeatedly in the next sections to prove the performance guarantee of approximation algorithms for many network design problems.

The reader may be surprised that we did not prove optimality of the spanning tree produced since the algorithm reduces to Kruskal's greedy algorithm. The reason is simply that our linear programming formulation of the minimum spanning tree problem is not strong enough to prove optimality. Instead of increasing the dual variables corresponding to all sets $S \in \mathcal{V}$, we could also view the algorithm as increasing a single dual variable corresponding to the aggregation of the inequalities for every $S \in \mathcal{V}$. The resulting inequality $\sum_{S \in \mathcal{V}} \sum_{e \in \delta(S)} x_e \geq |\mathcal{V}|$ can in fact be strengthened to

$$\sum_{S \in \mathcal{V}} \sum_{e \in \delta(S)} x_e \geq 2|\mathcal{V}| - 2$$

since any connected graph on k vertices has at least $k - 1$ edges. The value of the dual solution constructed this way is therefore greater, and with this stronger formulation, it is easy to see that the proof technique developed earlier will prove the optimality of the tree produced. The use of valid inequalities in this primal-dual framework is also considered in Bertsimas and Teo [BT95].

We would like to point out that the bound given in Theorem 4.2 is tight in the following sense. If there exists a set A and a minimal augmentation B of A for which

$$\sum_{T_i \in \mathcal{V}(A)} |B \cap T_i| = \gamma |\mathcal{V}(A)|,$$

then the algorithm can return solutions of value equal to γ times the value $\sum_{i=1}^{p} y_i$ of the dual solution constructed by the algorithm. For this, one simply needs to set the cost of all elements of A to 0 and to set appropriately the cost of the elements in $B - A$ so that they would all be added to A at the same time during the execution of the algorithm.

As a final remark, we could also allow the oracle VIOLATION to return sets which do not need to be hit, as we did in the case of the minimum-cost arborescence problem. The performance guarantee is given in the following theorem. Its proof is similar to the proof of Theorem 4.2 and is therefore omitted.

THEOREM 4.3 If the oracle VIOLATION may return sets which do not need to be hit then the performance guarantee of the primal-dual algorithm described in Figure 4.3 is

γ, provided that for any infeasible set A and any minimal augmentation B of A

$$\sum_{T_i \in \mathcal{V}(A)} |B \cap T_i| \leq \gamma c,$$

where $\mathcal{V}(A)$ denotes the collection of sets output by VIOLATION, and c denotes the number of sets in $\mathcal{V}(A)$ which need to be hit.

EXERCISE 4.2   Prove the correctness of Dijkstra's algorithm by using Theorem 4.1.

EXERCISE 4.3   Find an instance of the minimum-cost arborescence problem where the use of a non-reverse delete step leads to a non-optimal solution.

EXERCISE 4.4   Consider the minimum spanning tree problem on a complete graph with all edge costs equal to 1. Given a set A of edges, write a restricted primal in the spirit of Section 4.2. Show that the unique optimum solution to its dual is to set the dual variables corresponding to all connected components of (V, A) to 0.5 and all other dual variables to 0.

EXERCISE 4.5   Prove Theorem 4.3.

A MODEL OF NETWORK DESIGN PROBLEMS

4.4

With a primal-dual method for approximation algorithms in place, we show how to apply it to various other network design problems. In this and following sections, we will discuss various problems and prove that the design principles listed above lead to good approximation algorithms for these problems.

Most of the network design problems we discuss have as input an undirected graph $G = (V, E)$ with nonnegative edge costs c_e, and can be modelled by the following integer program:

$$\text{Min} \quad \sum_{e \in E} c_e x_e$$

subject to:

$$(IP) \qquad \sum_{e \in \delta(S)} x_e \geq f(S) \qquad \emptyset \neq S \subset V$$

$$x_e \in \{0, 1\} \qquad e \in E.$$

This integer program is a variation on some of the hitting set problems discussed above, parametrized by the function $f : 2^V \to \mathbf{N}$: here, our ground set is the set of edges E and a feasible solution must contain at least $f(S)$ edges of any cut $\delta(S)$. Sometimes we consider further variations of the problem in which the constraint $x_e \in \{0, 1\}$ is replaced by $x_e \in \mathbf{N}$; that is, we are allowed to take any number of copies of an edge e in order to satisfy the constraints. If the function f has range $\{0, 1\}$, then the integer program

(IP) is a special case of the hitting set problem in which we must hit the sets $\delta(S)$ for which $f(S) = 1$.

We have already seen that (IP) can be used to model two classical network design problems. If we have two vertices s and t, and set $f(S) = 1$ when S contains s but not t, then edge-minimal solutions to (IP) model the undirected $s - t$ shortest path problem. If $f(S) = 1$ for all $\emptyset \neq S \subset V$, then (IP) models the minimum spanning tree problem.

The integer program (IP) can also be used to model many other problems, which we will discuss in subsequent sections. As an example, (IP) can be used to model the *survivable network design problem*, sometimes also called the *generalized Steiner problem*. In this problem we are given nonnegative integers r_{ij} for each pair of vertices i and j, and must find a minimum-cost subset of edges $E' \subset E$ such that there are at least r_{ij} edge-disjoint paths for each i, j pair in the graph (V, E'). This problem can be modelled by (IP) with the function $f(S) = \max_{i \in S, j \notin S} r_{ij}$; a min-cut/max-flow argument shows that it is necessary and sufficient to select $f(S)$ edges from $\delta(S)$ in order for the subgraph to have at least r_{ij} paths between i and j. The survivable network design problem is used to model a problem in the design of fiber-optic telephone networks [GMS94, Sto92]. It finds the minimum-cost network such that nodes i and j will still be connected even if $r_{ij} - 1$ edges of the network fail.

The reader may notice that the two network design problems mentioned above are special cases of the survivable network design problem: the undirected $s - t$ shortest path problem corresponds to the case in which $r_{st} = 1$ and $r_{ij} = 0$ for all other i, j, while the minimum spanning tree problem corresponds to the case $r_{ij} = 1$ for all pairs i, j. Other well-known problems are also special cases. In the *Steiner tree problem*, we are given a set of terminals $T \subseteq V$ and must find a minimum-cost set of edges such that all terminals are connected. This problem corresponds to the case in which $r_{ij} = 1$ if $i, j \in T$ and $r_{ij} = 0$ otherwise. In the *generalized Steiner tree problem*, we are given p sets of terminals $T_1, \ldots, T_p$, where $T_i \subseteq V$. We must find a minimum-cost set of edges such that for each i, all the vertices in T_i are connected. This problem corresponds to the survivable network design problem in which $r_{ij} = 1$ if there exists some k such that $i, j \in T_k$, and $r_{ij} = 0$ otherwise. We will show how the primal-dual method can be applied to these two special cases (and many others) in Section 4.6, and show how the method can be applied to the survivable network design problem in general in Section 4.7.

It is not known how to derive good approximation algorithms for (IP) for any given function f. Nevertheless, the primal-dual method can be used to derive good approximation algorithms for particular classes of functions that model interesting network design problems, such as those given above. In the following sections we consider various classes of functions f, and prove that the primal-dual method (with the design rules of the previous section) gives good performance guarantees.

4.4.1   0-1 FUNCTIONS

First we focus our attention on the case in which the function f has range $\{0, 1\}$. We often refer to such functions as 0-1 functions. The shortest path, minimum spanning tree, and (generalized) Steiner tree problems all fit in this case, as well as many other problems to be discussed in the coming sections. For functions with range $\{0, 1\}$, the integer program

(IP) reduces to

$$\text{Min} \sum_{e \in E} c_e x_e$$

subject to:

(IP)

$$\sum_{e \in \delta(S)} x_e \geq 1 \qquad\qquad S : f(S) = 1$$

$$x_e \in \{0, 1\} \qquad\qquad e \in E,$$

and the dual of its LP relaxation is:

$$\text{Max} \sum_{S : f(S) = 1} y_S$$

subject to:

$$\sum_{S : e \in \delta(S)} y_S \leq c_e \qquad\qquad e \in E$$

$$y_S \geq 0 \qquad\qquad S : f(S) = 1.$$

Observe that the edge-minimal solutions of (IP) are forests since one can remove arbitrarily any edge from a cycle without destroying feasibility. In Figure 4.4, we have specialized the algorithm of Figure 4.3 to this case, assuming the oracle VIOLATION returns the minimal violated sets. As already mentioned in the previous section, we will often stretch our terminology to say that a vertex set S is violated, instead of saying that the associated cut $T = \delta(S)$ is violated. Let $\delta_A(S) = \delta(S) \cap A$. Then a set $S \subset V$ is violated when $\delta_A(S) = \emptyset$ and $f(S) = 1$. We can restate Theorem 4.2 as follows.

THEOREM 4.4   The primal-dual algorithm described in Figure 4.4 delivers a feasible solution of cost at most $\gamma \sum_{S : f(S) = 1} y_S \leq \gamma z_{OPT}$, if γ satisfies that for any infeasible set A and any minimal augmentation B of A

$$\sum_{S \in \mathcal{V}(A)} |\delta_B(S)| \leq \gamma |\mathcal{V}(A)|,$$

where $\mathcal{V}(A)$ denotes the collection of minimal violated sets.

1	$y \leftarrow 0$
2	$A \leftarrow \emptyset$
3	$l \leftarrow 0$
4	While A is not feasible
5	$\quad l \leftarrow l + 1$
6	$\quad \mathcal{V} \leftarrow \{\text{minimal violated sets } S\}$
7	$\quad$ Increase y_S uniformly for all $S \in \mathcal{V}$ until $\exists e_l \in \delta(T), T \in \mathcal{V} : \sum_{S : e_l \in \delta(S)} y_S = c_{e_l}$
8	$\quad A \leftarrow A \cup \{e_l\}$
9	For $j \leftarrow l$ downto 1
10	$\quad$ if $A - \{e_j\}$ is feasible then $A \leftarrow A - \{e_j\}$
11	Output A (and y)

FIGURE 4.4

Primal-dual algorithm for (IP) with uniform increase rule on minimal violated sets and reverse delete step.

For general functions f with range $\{0, 1\}$, there could be exponentially many sets S for which $f(S) = 1$. As a result, we assume that f is implicitly given through an oracle taking a set S as input and outputting its value $f(S)$. But, for arbitrary 0-1 functions, it might not be easy to check whether an edge set A is feasible, i.e. whether it hits all cuts $\delta(S)$ for which $f(S) = 1$. Also, the minimal violated sets might not have any nice structure as they do for the shortest path or minimum spanning tree problems. However, consider the class of functions satisfying the *maximality* property:

- [Maximality] If A and B are disjoint, then $f(A \cup B) \leq \max(f(A), f(B))$.

For functions with range $\{0, 1\}$, this can also be expressed as:

- [Maximality] If A and B are disjoint, then $f(A) = f(B) = 0$ implies $f(A \cup B) = 0$.

This is equivalent to requiring that if $f(S) = 1$ then for any partition of S at least one member of the partition has an $f(.)$ value equal to 1. For this class of functions, the following lemma shows how to check whether an edge set is feasible and, if it is not, how to find the minimal violated sets.

LEMMA 4.1 Let f be a function with range $\{0, 1\}$ satisfying the maximality property. Let A be any edge set. Then,

1. A is feasible for f if and only if every connected component C of (V, A) satisfies $f(C) = 0$,

2. the minimal violated sets of A are the connected components C of (V, A) for which $f(C) = 1$.

Proof. Consider a violated set S, i.e. a set S for which $f(S) = 1$ but $\delta_A(S) = \emptyset$. Clearly, S must consist of the union of connected components of (V, A). But, by maximality, one of these components, say C, must satisfy $f(C) = 1$, and is thus a violated set. Thus, only connected components can correspond to minimal violated sets, and A is feasible only if no such component has $f(C) = 1$. ∎

In the case of functions satisfying the maximality property, the collection $\mathcal{V}(A)$ of minimal violated sets can thus easily be updated by maintaining the collection $\mathcal{C}(A)$ of connected components of (V, A). This is exploited in Figure 4.5, where we present a more detailed implementation of the primal-dual algorithm of Figure 4.4 in the case of functions satisfying maximality. When implementing the algorithm, there is no need to keep track of the dual variables y_S. Instead, in order to be able to decide which edge to select next, we compute for every vertex $i \in V$ the quantity $d(i)$ defined by $\sum_{S : i \in S} y_S$. Initially, $d(i)$ is 0 (lines 5-6) and it increases by ϵ whenever the dual variable corresponding to the connected component containing i increases by ϵ (line 12). As long as i and j are in different connected components C_p and C_q (respectively), the quantity $(c_e - d(i) - d(j))/(f(C_p) + f(C_q))$ being minimized in line 10 represents the difference between the addition time of edge $e = (i, j)$ and the current time. This explains why the edge with the smallest such value is being added to A. When an edge is added to A, the collection $\mathcal{C}$ of connected components of (V, A) is updated in line 15. We are also maintaining and outputting the value LB of the dual solution, since this allows us to

1	$A \leftarrow \emptyset$
2	*Comment: Implicitly set* $y_S \leftarrow 0$ *for all* $S \subset V$
3	$LB \leftarrow 0$
4	$\mathcal{C} \leftarrow \{\{v\} : v \in V\}$
5	For each $i \in V$
6	$\quad d(i) \leftarrow 0$
7	$l \leftarrow 0$
8	While $\exists C \in \mathcal{C} : f(C) = 1$
9	$\quad l \leftarrow l + 1$
10	$\quad$ Find edge $e_l = (i, j)$ with $i \in C_p \in \mathcal{C}$, $j \in C_q \in \mathcal{C}$, $C_p \neq C_q$ that minimizes $\epsilon = \frac{c_{e_l} - d(i) - d(j)}{f(C_p) + f(C_q)}$
11	$\quad A \leftarrow A \cup \{e_l\}$
12	$\quad$ For all $k \in C_r \in \mathcal{C}$ do $d(k) \leftarrow d(k) + \epsilon \cdot f(C_r)$
13	$\quad$ *Comment: Implicitly set* $y_C \leftarrow y_C + \epsilon \cdot f(C)$ *for all* $C \in \mathcal{C}$.
14	$\quad LB \leftarrow LB + \epsilon \sum_{C \in \mathcal{C}} f(C)$
15	$\quad \mathcal{C} \leftarrow \mathcal{C} \cup \{C_p \cup C_q\} - \{C_p\} - \{C_q\}$
16	For $j \leftarrow l$ downto 1
17	$\quad$ If all components C of $A - \{e_j\}$ satisfy $f(C) = 0$ then $A \leftarrow A - \{e_j\}$
18	Output A and LB

FIGURE 4.5

Primal-dual algorithm for (IP) *for functions satisfying*
the maximality property.

estimate the quality of the solution on any instance. The algorithm can be implemented quite easily. The connected components can be maintained as a union-find structure of vertices. Then all mergings take at most $O(n\alpha(n, n))$ time overall, where α is the inverse Ackermann function and n is the number of vertices [Tar75]. To determine which edge to add to A, we can maintain a priority queue of edges, where the key of an edge is its addition time $a(e)$. If two components C_p and C_q merge, we only need to update the keys of the edges incident to $C_p \cup C_q$. Keeping only the smallest edge between two components, one derives a running time of $O(n^2 \log n)$ for all queue operations and this is the overall running time of the algorithm. This is the original implementation as proposed by the authors in [GW95a]. Faster implementations have been proposed by Klein [Kle94] and Gabow, Goemans, and Williamson [GGW93].

Even for 0-1 functions obeying maximality, the parameter γ of Theorem 4.4 can be arbitrarily large. For example, consider the problem of finding a tree of minimum cost containing a given vertex s and having at least k vertices. This problem corresponds to the function $f(S) = 1$ if $s \in S$ and $|S| < k$, which satisfies maximality. However, selecting $A = \emptyset$ and B a star rooted at s with k vertices, we observe that $\gamma \geq k - 1$. As a result, for this problem, the primal-dual algorithm can output a solution of cost at least $k - 1$ times the value of the dual solution produced.

In the following two sections, we apply the primal-dual algorithm to some subclasses of 0-1 functions satisfying maximality. We show that, for these subclasses, the primal-dual algorithm of Figures 4.4 and 4.5 is a 2-approximation algorithm by proving that γ can be set to 2. Before defining these subclasses of functions, we reformulate γ in terms of the average degree of a forest. This explains why a performance guarantee of 2 naturally arises. To prove that $\gamma = 2$, we need to show that, for any infeasible set A and any minimal augmentation B of A, we have $\sum_{S \in \mathcal{V}(A)} |\delta_B(S)| \leq 2|\mathcal{V}(A)|$. For functions satisfying the maximality property, the collection $\mathcal{V}(A)$ of minimal violated sets consists of the connected components of (V, A) whose $f(.)$ value is 1 (Lemma 4.1). Now, construct a graph H formed by taking the graph (V, B) and shrinking the connected components of (V, A) to vertices. For simplicity, we refer to both the graph and its vertex set as H. Because B is an edge-minimal augmentation, there will be a one-to-one correspondence between the edges of $B - A$ and the edges in H, and H is a forest. Each vertex v of H corresponds to a connected component $S_v \subset V$ of (V, A); let d_v denote the degree of v in H, so that $d_v = |\delta_B(S_v)|$. Let W be the set of vertices of H such that for $w \in W$, $f(S_w) = 1$. Then, each of these vertices corresponds to a minimal violated set; that is, $\mathcal{V}(A) = \{S_w \mid w \in W\}$. Thus, in order to prove the inequality $\sum_{S \in \mathcal{V}(A)} |\delta_B(S)| \leq 2|\mathcal{V}(A)|$, we simply need to show that

$$\sum_{v \in W} d_v \leq 2|W|. \tag{4.6}$$

In other words, the average degree of the vertices in H corresponding to the violated sets is at most 2. In the next two sections, we show that equation (4.6) holds for two subclasses of functions satisfying the maximality property.

EXERCISE 4.6 Show that the function f corresponding to the generalized Steiner tree problem satisfies the maximality property.

DOWNWARDS MONOTONE FUNCTIONS

4.5

In this section, we consider the network design problems that can be modelled by the integer program (IP) with functions f that are *downwards monotone*. We say that a function is downwards monotone if $f(S) \leq f(T)$ for all $S \supseteq T \neq \emptyset$. Notice that any downwards monotone function satisfies maximality and, as a result, the discussion of the previous section applies. Later in the section, we will prove the following theorem.

THEOREM 4.5 The primal-dual algorithm described in Figure 4.5 gives a 2-approximation algorithm for the integer program (IP) with any downwards monotone function $f : 2^V \to \{0, 1\}$.

In fact, we will also show that applying the reverse delete procedure to the edges of a minimum spanning tree is also a 2-approximation algorithm for the problem; see Figure 4.6 for the algorithm. The advantage of the algorithm in Figure 4.6 is that its running time is that of computing the minimum spanning tree and sorting its edges, rather than $O(n^2 \log n)$ time. Thus, the algorithm takes $O(m + n \log n)$ time in general graphs, and $O(n \log n)$ time in Euclidean graphs.

1	$A \leftarrow$ MINIMUM-SPANNING-TREE
2	Sort edges of $A = \{e_1, \dots, e_{n-1}\}$ so that $c_{e_1} \leq \cdots \leq c_{e_{n-1}}$
3	For $j \leftarrow n - 1$ downto 1
4	If $A - \{e_j\}$ is feasible then $A \leftarrow A - \{e_j\}$.

FIGURE 4.6

Another 2-approximation algorithm for downwards monotone functions f.

THEOREM 4.6   The primal-dual algorithm described in Figure 4.6 gives a 2-approximation algorithm for the integer program (IP) with any downwards monotone function $f : 2^V \rightarrow \{0, 1\}$.

Before we get to the proofs of these theorems, we consider the kinds of network design problems that can be modelled by (IP) with a downwards monotone function $f : 2^V \rightarrow \{0, 1\}$.

4.5.1   THE EDGE-COVERING PROBLEM

The edge-covering problem is that of selecting a minimum-cost set of edges such that each vertex is adjacent to at least one edge. The problem can be solved in polynomial time via a reduction to the minimum-weight perfect matching problem (see Grötschel, Lovász, and Schrijver [GLS88, p. 259]). The problem can be modelled by the downwards monotone function $f(S) = 1$ iff $|S| = 1$. Thus, the primal-dual algorithm yields a 2-approximation algorithm for this problem. It is interesting to observe that another primal-dual algorithm for the hitting set problem (or the set cover problem) due to Chvátal [Chv79] (see Chapter 3) gives a performance guarantee of $\frac{3}{2}$ for the edge-covering problem.

4.5.2   LOWER-CAPACITATED PARTITIONING PROBLEMS

In the *lower-capacitated partitioning problems* we wish to find a minimum-cost set of edges that partitions the vertices into trees, paths, or cycles such that each tree, path, or cycle has at least k vertices for some parameter k. When $k = 3$, the lower-capacitated cycle partitioning problem is also known as the binary two-matching problem; when $k = 4$, it is also known as the triangle-free binary two-matching problem. The lower-capacitated cycle partitioning problem is *NP*-complete for $k \geq 5$ (Papadimitriou in Cornuéjols and Pulleyblank [CP80] for $k \geq 6$ and Vornberger [Vor79] for $k = 5$), polynomially solvable for $k = 2$ or 3 (Edmonds and Johnson [EJ70]), while its complexity for $k = 4$ is open. Imielińska, Kalantari, and Khachiyan [IKK93] have shown that the lower-capacitated tree partitioning problem is *NP*-complete for $k \geq 4$, even if the edge costs obey the triangle inequality.

The lower-capacitated tree partitioning problem can be modelled by (IP) with the downwards monotone function $f(S) = 1$ if $0 < |S| < k$ and 0 otherwise. If the edge costs obey the triangle inequality, we can also obtain an approximation algorithm for the lower-capacitated path partitioning problem. Obviously the cost of the optimal tree partition is a lower bound on the cost of the optimal lower-capacitated path partition. Given the tree partition produced by our algorithm, we duplicate each edge and find a tour of each component by shortcutting the resulting Eulerian graph on each component; this gives a cycle partition of no more than twice the cost of the original solution. Removing an edge from each cycle gives a path partition; thus we have a 4-approximation algorithm for the lower-capacitated path partitioning problem.

If the edge costs obey the triangle inequality, then we can obtain a 2-approximation algorithm for the lower-capacitated cycle problem. The algorithm constructs a cycle partition as above. To show that the cost of solution is no more than twice optimal, notice that the following linear program is a relaxation of the lower-capacitated cycle problem:

$$\text{Min} \quad \sum_{e \in E} c_e x_e$$

subject to:

$$\sum_{e \in \delta(S)} x_e \geq 2f(S) \qquad \emptyset \neq S \subset V$$

$$x_e \geq 0.$$

The dual of this relaxation is

$$\text{Max} \quad 2 \sum_{S \subset V} f(S) y_S$$

subject to:

$$\sum_{S:e \in \delta(S)} y_S \leq c_e \qquad \forall e \in E$$

$$y_S \geq 0.$$

The dual solution generated by the primal-dual algorithm for the lower-capacitated tree problem is feasible for this dual, but has twice the objective function value. Let y denote the dual solution given by the primal-dual algorithm, let T denote the set of tree edges produced by the algorithm for the lower-capacitated tree problem, let C denote the set of cycle edges produced by doubling and shortcutting the tree edges, and let Z_C^* denote the cost of the optimal cycle partition. We know $c(T) \leq 2 \sum_S f(S) y_S$ and $c(C) \leq 2c(T)$, so that $c(C) \leq 2(2 \sum_S f(S) y_S) \leq 2Z_C^*$, proving that the algorithm is a 2-approximation algorithm for the cycle partitioning problem. This illustrates one of the benefits of the primal-dual method: the dual lower bound can be used to prove stronger results.

A paper of the authors [GW95a] provided the first 2-approximation algorithms for these problems. Imielińska, Kalantari, and Khachiyan [IKK93] showed how to select a subset of the edges of a minimum spanning tree to get a 2-approximation algorithm for the tree partitioning problem and a 4-approximation algorithm for the cycle partitioning problem. A subsequent paper of the authors [GW94] showed how spanning tree edges could be used for any downwards monotone function.

4.5.3   LOCATION-DESIGN AND LOCATION-ROUTING PROBLEMS

The primal-dual method can be used to solve a problem in network design and vehicle routing. Many problems of this type require two levels of decisions. In the first level the location of special vertices, such as concentrators or switches in the design of communication networks, or depots in the routing of vehicles, needs to be decided. There is typically a set of possible locations and a fixed cost is associated with each of them. Once the locations of the depots are decided, the second level deals with the design or routing per se. These problems are called location-design or location-routing problems (Laporte [Lap88]).

The algorithm can be applied to one of the simplest location-routing problems. In this problem (Laporte et al. [LNP83, Lap88]), we need to select depots among a subset D of vertices of a graph $G = (V, E)$ and cover all vertices in V with a set of cycles, each containing a selected depot. The goal is to minimize the sum of the fixed costs of opening our depots and the sum of the costs of the edges of our cycles. In order to approximate this NP-complete problem we consider an augmented graph $G' = (V \cup D', E')$, which we obtain from G by adding a new copy u' of every vertex $u \in D$ and adding edges of the form (u, u') for all $u \in D$. Edge (u, u') has a cost equal to half the value of the fixed cost of opening a depot at u. Consider the downwards monotone function $f(S) = 1$ if $\emptyset \neq S \subseteq V$ and 0 otherwise. We apply the 2-approximation algorithm for this function f. As in the case of the lower-capacitated cycle partitioning problem, doubling the edges and shortcutting the solution obtained can be shown to result in a 2-approximation algorithm for the original location-design problem.

4.5.4   PROOF OF THEOREMS 4.5 AND 4.6

We now turn to the proof of Theorems 4.5 and 4.6.

Proof of Theorem 4.5.   Using the arguments developed in Section 4.4.1, we simply need to show that, for downwards monotone functions, equation (4.6) holds.

Recall that we construct a graph H by taking the graph (V, B) and shrinking the connected components of (V, A) to vertices. Each vertex v of H corresponds to a connected component S_v of (V, A), and has degree d_v. The set W is the set of vertices $\{v \in H : f(S_v) = 1\}$. We first claim that each connected component of H has at most one vertex v such that $f(S_v) = 0$. Suppose this is false, and some connected component of H has two vertices, v and w, such that $f(S_v) = f(S_w) = 0$. Let e be an edge of B corresponding to an edge on the path between v and w in H. By minimality of B, $B - \{e\}$ is not feasible. Thus, there is a set $S \subset V$ such that $e \in \delta(S)$ and $f(S) = 1$, but $(B - \{e\}) \cap \delta(S) = \emptyset$. The removal of e must split a connected component of H. In order that $e \in \delta(S)$ and $(B - \{e\}) \cap \delta(S) = \emptyset$, it must be the case that S contains the vertices of one of the two parts of this component. Thus, either $S_v \subseteq S$ or $S_w \subseteq S$. By the downwards monotonicity of f, $f(S) = 0$, a contradiction.

Let c be the number of components of H. Then

$$\sum_{v \in W} d_v \leq \sum_{v \in H} d_v = 2(|H| - c) \leq 2|W|,$$

as desired, since H is a forest, and $|H - W| \leq c$ by the claim above.   ∎

Proof of Theorem 4.6.   If we increase the dual variables on all connected components $\mathcal{C}(A)$ of (V, A), rather than the minimal violated sets $\mathcal{V}(A)$, then, as was argued in Section 4.3, the first part of the algorithm reduces to Kruskal's algorithm for the minimum spanning tree. We can therefore use Theorem 4.3 to prove a performance guarantee of 2 for the algorithm of Figure 4.6 if we can show that

$$\sum_{S \in \mathcal{C}(A)} |\delta_B(S)| \leq 2|\{S \in \mathcal{V}(A)\}|,$$

where B is any minimal augmentation of A, $\mathcal{C}(A)$ is the set of connected components of (V, A), and $\mathcal{V}(A) = \{C \in \mathcal{C}(A) : f(C) = 1\}$ is the set of minimal violated sets. Using the notation developed in the previous section, this reduces to $\sum_{v \in H} d_v \leq 2|W|$, which was proved above. This proves that the algorithm of Figure 4.6 is also a 2-approximation algorithm.   ∎

Further variations on the algorithm also yield 2-approximation algorithms. Imielińska et al. [IKK93] give a 2-approximation algorithm for the lower capacitated tree problem that selects appropriate edges of a minimum spanning tree in order of increasing cost, rather than deleting edges in order of decreasing cost. The authors have generalized this algorithm to a 2-approximation algorithm for downwards monotone functions $f : 2^V \to \mathbf{N}$ for the integer program (IP) with the constraint $x_e \in \mathbf{N}$ [GW94].

EXERCISE 4.7   Show that the performance guarantee in the statement of Theorem 4.5 can be improved to $2 - 1/l$ where $l = |\{v : f(\{v\}) = 1\}|$.

EXERCISE 4.8   Give a very simple proof of the fact that the algorithm of Figure 4.6 is a 2-approximation algorithm for the edge covering problem.

0-1 PROPER FUNCTIONS

4.6

In this section we consider the network design problems which can be modelled by the integer program (IP) with a proper function f with range $\{0, 1\}$. A function $f : 2^V \to \mathbf{N}$ is proper if

- $f(V) = 0$,
- f satisfies the maximality property, and
- f is symmetric, i.e. $f(S) = f(V - S)$ for all $S \subseteq V$.

Under symmetry it can be shown that, for 0-1 functions, the maximality property is equivalent to requiring that if $f(S) = f(A) = 0$ for $A \subseteq S$ then $f(S - A) = 0$. We will refer to this property as *complementarity*. The class of 0-1 proper functions is incomparable to the class of downwards monotone functions; neither class is contained in the other.

The class of network design problems which can be formulated by proper functions is particularly rich. It encompasses very diverse problems such as the shortest path problem, the minimum-weight T-join problem, the generalized Steiner tree problem, or the point-to-point connection problem. Later in this section we elaborate on some of these applications. The work described in this section appeared in [GW95a], the first paper of the authors on the use of the primal-dual method for network design problems.

As with downwards monotone functions, the primal-dual algorithm described in Figure 4.5 is a 2-approximation algorithm.

THEOREM 4.7   The primal-dual algorithm described in Figure 4.5 gives a 2-approximation algorithm for the integer program (IP) with any 0-1 proper function $f : 2^V \to \{0, 1\}$.

The proof of this theorem is given below. With regard to the (reverse) delete step, proper functions behave very much as in the case of the shortest path problem. No matter how the delete step is implemented, the same subgraph is output, since, as is shown in the next lemma, there is a unique minimally feasible subset of any feasible solution.

LEMMA 4.2   Let f be any 0-1 proper function and let A be any feasible solution. Let $R = \{e : A - \{e\}$ is feasible$\}$. Then $A - R$ is feasible.

Notice that R represents the set of all edges that can possibly be removed without losing feasibility. The lemma shows that *all* these edges can be simultaneously removed without losing feasibility. For 0-1 proper functions, we can thus replace the reverse delete step (lines 16-17) in Figure 4.5 by the following command:

16      $A \leftarrow \{e \in A :$ For some connected component N of $(V, A - \{e\})$, $f(N) = 1\}$.

Proof of Lemma 4.2.   Let N be any connected component of $(V, A - R)$. We first claim that $f(N) = 0$. Clearly, $N \subseteq C$ for some connected component C of (V, A). Now let $e_1, \ldots, e_k$ be the edges of A such that $e_i \in \delta(N)$ (possibly $k = 0$). Let N_i and $C - N_i$ be the two components created by removing e_i from the edges of component C, with $N \subseteq C - N_i$ (see Figure 4.7). Since $e_i \in R$, it must be the case that $f(N_i) = 0$. Note also that the sets $N, N_1, \ldots, N_k$ form a partition of C. Therefore, by maximality, $f(C - N) = f(\cup_{i=1}^{k} N_i) = 0$. Since $f(C) = 0$, complementarity now implies that $f(N) = 0$. Since every connected component of $(V, A - R)$ has $f(.)$ value equal to 0, Lemma 4.1 implies that $A - R$ is feasible. ∎

Proof of Theorem 4.7.   As discussed at the end of Section 4.4.1, the proof of the theorem can be reduced to the proof of inequality (4.6), as was the case for downwards monotone functions.

In order to prove (4.6) for 0-1 proper functions, we first claim that no leaf v of H satisfies $f(S_v) = 0$. Suppose otherwise. Let e be the edge incident to v and let C be the connected component of (V, B) that contains S_v. By feasibility of B, $f(C) = 0$. The assumption that $f(S_v) = 0$ together with complementarity now implies that $f(C - S_v) = 0$. But by minimality of B, $B - \{e\}$ is not feasible, which implies that either S_v or $C - S_v$ has an $f(.)$ value equal to 1, which is a contradiction. Thus, every leaf v of H belongs to W.

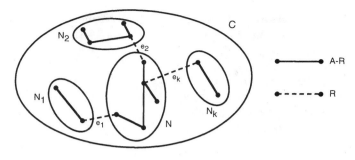

FIGURE 4.7

Illustration for the proof of Lemma 4.2.

Showing that the average degree over the vertices in W is at most 2 is now easy. First discard all isolated vertices from H (they do not contribute in any way). Now,

$$\sum_{v \in W} d_v = \sum_{v \in H} d_v - \sum_{v \notin W} d_v \le (2|H| - 2) - 2(|H| - |W|) = 2|W| - 2,$$

since H is a forest of at most $|H| - 1$ edges, and since all vertices not in W have degree at least two. This proves inequality (4.6), and completes the proof of the theorem. ∎

Since the inequality proved is a bit stronger than what was claimed, the proof can be refined to show that the performance guarantee is in fact equal to $2 - \frac{2}{l}$, where $l = |\{v : f(\{v\}) = 1\}|$. Also, observe the similarities and differences between the proofs of the performance guarantee for downwards monotone functions and proper functions. In both cases, the argument hinges on the fact that the average degree of a forest remains at most 2 if we discard certain vertices. In the former we discard at most one vertex per component, and in the latter we discard only inner vertices (i.e. non-leaves). The result would still hold if we discard any number of inner vertices, but at most one leaf (or even two leaves) per component. By using the same arguments as in the proofs of Theorems 4.5 and 4.7, this for example shows that the algorithm of Figure 4.5 is still a 2-approximation algorithm for the class of functions satisfying maximality and the following condition: there do not exist a set S and two disjoint subsets A, B of S such that $f(S) = f(A) = f(B) = 0$ and $f(S - A) = f(S - B) = 1$. This class of functions contains both the downwards monotone functions and the proper functions, but we are not aware of any interesting application of this generalization not covered by the previous two classes.

We now discuss network design problems that can be modelled as integer programs (IP) with a proper function f.

4.6.1   THE GENERALIZED STEINER TREE PROBLEM

The generalized Steiner tree problem is the problem of finding a minimum-cost forest that connects all vertices in T_i for $i = 1, \ldots, p$. The generalized Steiner tree problem corresponds to the proper function f with $f(S) = 1$ if there exists $i \in \{1, \ldots, p\}$ with

$\emptyset \neq S \cap T_i \neq T_i$ and 0 otherwise. In this case, the primal-dual algorithm we have presented simulates an algorithm of Agrawal, Klein, and Ravi [AKR95]. Their algorithm was the first approximation algorithm for this problem and has motivated much of the authors' research in this area.

When $p = 1$, the problem reduces to the classical Steiner tree problem. For a long time, the best approximation algorithm for this problem had a performance guarantee of $(2 - \frac{2}{k})$ (for a survey, see Winter [Win87]) but, recently, Zelikovsky [Zel93] obtained an $\frac{11}{6}$–approximation algorithm. Further improvements have been obtained; we refer the reader to Chapter 8.

4.6.2   THE T-JOIN PROBLEM

Given an even subset T of vertices, the T-join problem consists of finding a minimum-cost set of edges that has an odd degree at vertices in T and an even degree at vertices not in T. Edmonds and Johnson [EJ73] have shown that the T-join problem can be solved in polynomial time. The problem corresponds to the proper function f with $f(S) = 1$ if $|S \cap T|$ is odd and 0 otherwise. When $|T| = 2$, the T-join problem reduces to the shortest path problem. The primal-dual algorithm for 0-1 proper functions in this case reduces to a variant of Dijkstra's algorithm that uses bidirectional search (Nicholson [Nic66]).

4.6.3   THE MINIMUM-WEIGHT PERFECT MATCHING PROBLEM

The minimum-weight perfect matching problem is the problem of finding a minimum-cost set of non-adjacent edges that cover all vertices. This problem can be solved in polynomial time by a primal-dual algorithm discovered by Edmonds [Edm65]. The fastest strongly polynomial time implementation of Edmonds' algorithm is due to Gabow [Gab90]. Its running time is $O(n(m + n \log n))$. For integral costs bounded by C, the best weakly polynomial algorithm runs in $O(m \sqrt{n \alpha(m, n)} \log n \, \log nC)$ time and is due to Gabow and Tarjan [GT91].

These algorithms are fairly complicated and, in fact, time-consuming for large instances that arise in practice. This motivated the search for faster approximation algorithms. Reingold and Tarjan [RT81] have shown that the greedy procedure has a tight performance guarantee of $\frac{4}{3} n^{0.585}$ for general nonnegative cost functions. Supowit, Plaisted and Reingold [SPR80] and Plaisted [Pla84] have proposed an $O(\min(n^2 \log n, m \log^2 n))$ time approximation algorithm for instances that obey the triangle inequality. Their algorithm has a tight performance guarantee of $2 \log_3(1.5n)$.

As shown by Gabow and Tarjan [GT91], an exact scaling algorithm for the maximum-weight matching problem can be used to obtain an $(1 + 1/n^a)$-approximation algorithm ($a \geq 0$) for the minimum-weight perfect matching problem. Moreover, if the original exact algorithm runs in $O(f(m, n) \log C)$ time, the resulting approximation algorithm runs in $O(m \sqrt{n \log n} + (1 + a) f(m, n) \log n)$. Vaidya [Vai91] obtains a $(3 + 2\epsilon)$-approximation algorithm for minimum-weight perfect matching instances satisfying the triangle inequality. His algorithm runs in $O(n^2 \log^{2.5} n \log(1/\epsilon))$ time.

The primal-dual algorithm for problems modelled with a proper function can be used to approximate the minimum-weight perfect matching problem when the edge costs obey the triangle inequality. We use the algorithm with the proper function $f(S)$ being the parity of $|S|$, i.e. $f(S) = 1$ if $|S|$ is odd, and 0 if $|S|$ is even. This function is the same as the one used for the V-join problem. The algorithm returns a forest whose components have even size. More precisely, the forest is a V-join, and each vertex has odd degree: if a vertex has even degree, then, by a parity argument, some edge adjacent to the vertex could have been deleted so that the resulting components have even size. Thus, this edge would have been deleted in the delete step of the algorithm. The forest can be transformed into a perfect matching with no increase of cost by repeatedly taking two edges (u, v) and (v, w) from a vertex v of degree three or more and replacing these edges with the edge (u, w). This procedure maintains the property that the vertices have odd degree. This algorithm has a performance guarantee of $2 - \frac{2}{n}$.

Often the vertices of matching instances are given as points in the plane; the cost of an edge is then the Euclidean distance between its endpoints. Jünger and Pulleyblank [JP91] have observed that the dual variables of matching problems in this case correspond nicely to "moats" around sets of points. That is, a dual variable y_S corresponds to a region of the plane of width y_S surrounding the vertices of S. The dual program for these instances attempts to find a packing of non-overlapping moats that maximizes the sum of the width of the moats around odd-sized sets of vertices. The algorithm of Figure 4.5 applied to Euclidean matching instances can thus be interpreted as growing odd moats at the same speed until two moats collide, therefore adding the corresponding edge, and repeating the process until all components have even size. The reverse delete step then removes unnecessary edges. See Figure 4.8 for an example.

The notion of moats is not particular to matching problems: one can also consider moat packings for Euclidean instances of other problems modelled by (IP). The moats for a feasible dual solution y can be drawn in the plane whenever the non-zero dual variables y_S form a laminar family (any two sets in the family are either disjoint or one is contained in the other). One can show that whenever f is a 0-1 proper function, there exists an optimal dual solution y such that $\{S : y_S > 0\}$ is laminar (this even holds when f is an uncrossable function; see Section 4.7 for a definition). This is also clearly true for the dual solutions constructed by our primal-dual algorithms.

4.6.4   POINT-TO-POINT CONNECTION PROBLEMS

In the point-to-point connection problem we are given a set $C = \{c_1, \ldots, c_p\}$ of sources and a set $D = \{d_1, \ldots, d_p\}$ of destinations in a graph $G = (V, E)$, and we need to find a minimum-cost set F of edges such that each source-destination pair is connected in F [LMSL92]. This problem arises in the context of circuit switching and VLSI design. The fixed destination case in which c_i is required to be connected to d_i is a special case of the generalized Steiner tree problem where $T_i = \{c_i, d_i\}$. In the non-fixed destination case, each component of the forest F is only required to contain the same number of sources and destinations. This problem is NP-complete [LMSL92]. The non-fixed case can be modelled by the proper function f with $f(S) = 1$ if $|S \cap C| \neq |S \cap D|$ and 0 otherwise.

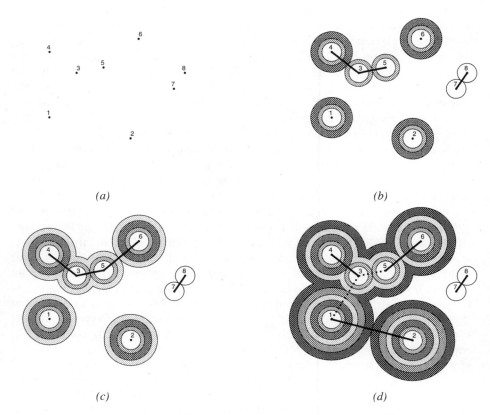

FIGURE 4.8

(a) A Euclidean matching instance. (b) An intermediate stage of the primal-dual algorithm of Figure 4.5 with a partial moat packing. The odd connected components are {1}, {2}, {3, 4, 5} and {6}. (c) When growing odd moats uniformly, the edge (5, 6) becomes tight and is added to A. (d) The final solution. The edges removed in the reverse delete step are dashed, the others belong to the matching (or the V-join) output by the algorithm. Observe that every moat is intersected by exactly one edge of the matching, implying that the matching and the dual solution (or moat packing) are both optimal.

4.6.5   EXACT PARTITIONING PROBLEMS

In the exact tree (cycle, path) partitioning problem, for a given k we must find a minimum-cost collection of vertex-disjoint trees (cycles, paths) of size k that cover all vertices. These problems generalize the minimum-weight perfect matching problem (in which each component must have size exactly 2), the traveling salesman problem, the Hamiltonian path problem, and the minimum-cost spanning tree problem.

We can approximate the exact tree, cycle, and path partitioning problems for instances that satisfy the triangle inequality. For this purpose, we consider the proper function $f(S) = 1$ if $S \not\equiv 0 \pmod{k}$ and 0 otherwise. Our algorithm finds a forest in which each component has a number of vertices that are multiples of k, and such that the cost of the forest is within $2 - \frac{2}{n}$ of the optimal such forest. Obviously, the cost of the optimal such forest is a lower bound on the optimal exact tree and path partitions. Given the forest, we duplicate each edge and find a tour of each component by shortcutting the resulting Eulerian graph on each component. If we remove every kth edge of the tour, starting at some edge, the tour is partitioned into paths of k nodes each. Some choice of edges to be removed (i.e., some choice of starting edge) accounts for at least $\frac{1}{k}$ of the cost of the tour, and so we remove these edges. Thus, this algorithm is a $\left(4(1 - \frac{1}{k})(1 - \frac{1}{n})\right)$-approximation algorithm for the exact tree and path partitioning problems.

To produce a solution for the exact cycle partitioning problem, we add the edge joining the endpoints of each path; given the triangle inequality, this at most doubles the cost of the solution produced. However, the resulting algorithm is still a $\left(4(1 - \frac{1}{k})(1 - \frac{1}{n})\right)$-approximation algorithm for the cycle problem by the same argument as was used in Section 4.5.2.

The proper functions corresponding to the non-fixed point-to-point connection problem, the T-join problem and the exact partitioning problems, are all of the form $f(S) = 1$ if $\sum_{i \in S} a_i \not\equiv 0 \pmod{p}$ and 0 otherwise, for some integers $a_i, i \in V$, and some integer p.

EXERCISE 4.9 Prove that, for symmetric functions f, the maximality property is equivalent to complementarity.

EXERCISE 4.10 Consider a (non necessarily symmetric) function f satisfying maximality and complementarity. Consider the symmetrization of f defined by $f_{sym}(S) = \max(f(S), f(V - S))$. Observe that the integer programs corresponding to f and f_{sym} are equivalent. Show that f_{sym} is a proper function.

EXERCISE 4.11 Prove that the performance guarantee of Theorem 4.7 is in fact $2 - 2/l$, where $l = |\{v : f(\{v\}) = 1\}|$. What is the resulting performance guarantee for the shortest path problem (i.e. for $f(S) = 1$ iff $|S \cap \{s, t\}| = 1$)?

EXERCISE 4.12 Prove that the algorithm of Figure 4.5 is a 2-approximation algorithm for the class of functions f satisfying maximality and the property that there do not exist a set S and two disjoint subsets A, B of S such that $f(S) = f(A) = f(B) = 0$ and $f(S - A) = f(S - B) = 1$.

GENERAL PROPER FUNCTIONS

4.7

We now turn from 0-1 proper functions to the case of general proper functions in which the function f can range over the nonnegative integers. In the previous two sections we discussed special cases of the hitting set problem in which we considered the integer program (IP) with a 0-1 function f. Now consider the case in which we must hit a set $\delta(S)$ at least $f(S)$ times. We will give a $2\mathcal{H}(f_{max})$-approximation algorithm for any proper function f, where $f_{max} = \max_S f(S)$ and $\mathcal{H}(k) = 1 + \frac{1}{2} + \cdots + \frac{1}{k} \approx \ln k$. The results presented in this section were initially given in [WGMV95, GGW93, GGP+94].

The main application of an algorithm for general proper functions is the survivable network design problem, as discussed in Section 4.4. As we previously observed, this problem can be modelled by (IP) with the function $f(S) = \max_{i \in S, j \notin S} r_{ij}$. It is not hard to show that this function is proper: first, it is obviously symmetric. To see that it obeys maximality, let A and B be disjoint sets, and pick $i \in A \cup B$, $j \notin A \cup B$ that attain the maximum $\max_{i \in A \cup B, j \notin A \cup B} r_{ij} = f(A \cup B)$. If $i \in A$, then $f(A) \geq f(A \cup B)$, else $f(B) \geq f(A \cup B)$, ensuring that $f(A \cup B) \leq \max(f(A), f(B))$.

In order to apply the primal-dual method to this class of problems, we reduce the overall problem to a sequence of hitting set problems, and apply the primal-dual approximation algorithm to each subproblem. Thus, we build a solution to the original problem in a series of *phases*. We start with an empty set of edges $F_0 = \emptyset$. In each phase p, we consider a hitting set problem with the ground set of elements $E_p = E - F_{p-1}$. Let $\Delta_p(S) = f(S) - |\delta_{F_{p-1}}(S)|$ be the *deficiency* of the set S; that is, the number of edges we must still choose from $\delta(S)$ since a feasible solution to the overall problem must contain $f(S)$ edges, but our current solution F_{p-1} contains only $|\delta_{F_{p-1}}(S)|$ edges. Let $\Delta_{p,max}$ denote the maximum deficiency, $\Delta_{p,max} = \max_S \Delta_p(S)$. In the hitting set problem for phase p, the sets to be hit are defined as the sets $\delta(S)$ for which $\Delta_p(S) = \Delta_{p,max}$. If A is a feasible solution to this problem, then the maximum deficiency of $A \cup F_{p-1}$ can be no greater than $\Delta_{p,max} - 1$. Thus, we apply the algorithm of Figure 4.4 to this hitting set problem; given the resulting set of edges A, we set F_p to $A \cup F_{p-1}$ and we proceed to phase $p + 1$. Since the maximum deficiency in the first phase is f_{max}, where $f_{max} = \max_S f(S)$, at most f_{max} phases are necessary before we have a feasible solution to the overall problem. It is possible to show that given this scheme all f_{max} phases are necessary, and the maximum deficiency in phase p is exactly $f_{max} - p + 1$. The algorithm for general proper functions is formalized in Figure 4.9 on page 177. The idea of augmenting a graph in phases has been previously used in many graph algorithms; in terms of primal-dual approximation algorithms it was first used by Klein and Ravi [KR93] and Saran et al. [SVY92].

The central difficulties of obtaining an algorithm for general proper functions become applying the algorithm of Figure 4.4 to the hitting set problems generated by the algorithm above, and showing that a good performance guarantee for the solution of each hitting set problem leads to the performance guarantee of $2\mathcal{H}(f_{max})$ for the overall problem. We postpone the second difficulty for a moment in order to deal with the first. Given a hitting set problem from phase p, let $h_p(S) = 1$ if we must hit $\delta(S)$ and $h_p(S) = 0$ otherwise. Unfortunately, it is easy to come up with examples such that h_p does not obey maximality, and so we cannot straightforwardly apply the discussion of the previous two sections. Fortunately, the functions h_p arising from the hitting set problems of the phases have a particularly nice structure. We will prove below that the functions belong to the class of *uncrossable* functions. A function $h : 2^V \to \{0, 1\}$ is uncrossable if

- $h(V) = 0$; and
- if $h(A) = h(B) = 1$ for any sets of vertices A, B, then either $h(A \cup B) = h(A \cap B) = 1$ or $h(A - B) = h(B - A) = 1$.

1	$F_0 \leftarrow \emptyset$
2	**for** $p \leftarrow 1$ **to** f_{max}
3	*Comment: Phase p.*
4	$\Delta_p(S) \leftarrow f(S) - |\delta_{F_{p-1}}(S)|$ for all $S \subset V$
5	$h_p(S) \leftarrow \begin{cases} 1 & \text{if } \Delta_p(S) = \max_S \Delta_p(S) = f_{max} - p + 1 \\ 0 & \text{otherwise} \end{cases}$
6	$E_p \leftarrow E - F_{p-1}$
7	Let A be the edge set returned by the algorithm of Figure 4.4 applied to the hitting set problem associated with the the graph (V, E_p) and the function h_p
8	$F_p \leftarrow F_{p-1} \cup A$
9	Output $F_{f_{max}}$

FIGURE 4.9

Primal-dual algorithm for proper functions f.

The class of uncrossable functions contains all functions satisfying the maximality property. We will show below that the minimal violated sets of uncrossable functions are disjoint.

LEMMA 4.3   Let f be a proper function, $F \subseteq E$, $\Delta(S) = f(S) - |\delta_F(S)|$, and $\Delta_{max} = \max_S \Delta(S)$. Then the function $h(S) = 1$ if $\Delta(S) = \Delta_{max}$ and $h(S) = 0$ otherwise is uncrossable.

Proof.   Since $f(V) = |\delta_F(V)| = 0$, we have $h(V) = 0$. By the maximality of f, we have the following four inequalities for any two sets X and Y:

- $\max\{f(X - Y), f(X \cap Y)\} \geq f(X)$.
- $\max\{f(Y - X), f(X \cup Y)\} \geq f(X)$.
- $\max\{f(Y - X), f(X \cap Y)\} \geq f(Y)$.
- $\max\{f(X - Y), f(X \cup Y)\} \geq f(Y)$.

Summing the two inequalities involving the minimum of $f(X - Y)$, $f(Y - X)$, $f(X \cup Y)$, and $f(X \cap Y)$ shows that $f(X) + f(Y) \leq \max\{f(X - Y) + f(Y - X), f(X \cap Y) + f(X \cup Y)\}$. To prove the lemma, we use the well-known fact that $\delta_F(S)$ is submodular; that is, for any sets of vertices X and Y

$$|\delta_F(X)| + |\delta_F(Y)| \geq |\delta_F(X \cap Y)| + |\delta_F(X \cup Y)|,$$

and

$$|\delta_F(X)| + |\delta_F(Y)| \geq |\delta_F(X - Y)| + |\delta_F(Y - X)|.$$

Then we can see that $\Delta(X) + \Delta(Y) \leq \max\{\Delta(X - Y) + \Delta(Y - X), \Delta(X \cap Y) + \Delta(X \cup Y)\}$. From this inequality it is easy to see that h is uncrossable. ∎

LEMMA 4.4   Let h be any uncrossable function. Then the minimal violated sets of any subset A are disjoint.

Proof.   Note that a set S is violated if $h(S) = 1$ and $\delta_A(S) = \emptyset$. Suppose there exist two minimal violated sets X and Y that are not disjoint. Then we know that $h(X) = h(Y) = 1$ and $\delta_A(X) = \delta_A(Y) = \emptyset$. Since the sets are minimal, $Y - X \neq \emptyset$ and $X - Y \neq \emptyset$; since they are not disjoint, $X \cap Y \neq \emptyset$. By the definition of uncrossable functions, either $h(X - Y) = h(Y - X) = 1$ or $h(X \cap Y) = h(X \cup Y) = 1$. Suppose the latter is true. Then by submodularity, $\delta_A(X \cup Y) = \delta_A(X \cap Y) = \emptyset$, implying that $X \cup Y$ and $X \cap Y$ are also violated, and contradicting the minimality of X and Y. The other case is similar. ∎

Despite Lemma 4.4, it is still difficult to find the minimal violated sets (or even just check feasibility, see Exercise 4.17) for an arbitrary uncrossable function if the function is given only as an oracle. Consider a function taking the value 1 for only one arbitrary set S; this function is uncrossable but the oracle would not allow us to find S without testing all sets in the worst case. Nevertheless, for the uncrossable functions generated by our algorithm, it is possible to find these minimal violated sets in polynomial time by using minimum cut computations. See Williamson et al. [WGMV95], Gabow et al. [GGW93], Williamson [Wil93], and Exercise 4.19 for details.

Williamson et al. [WGMV95] have shown that the algorithm of Figure 4.4 is a 2-approximation algorithm for any uncrossable function; it runs in polynomial time given a polynomial-time algorithm to compute h and the minimal violated sets.

THEOREM 4.8   The primal-dual algorithm of Figure 4.4 is a 2-approximation algorithm for any uncrossable function f.

This theorem can again be proved using the proof technique developed in Section 4.3 (see Theorem 4.4). However, the proof that γ can be set to 2 is more complicated than in the previous cases, and is therefore omitted.

We must now tackle the second difficulty and show that the performance guarantee of 2 for the uncrossable functions arising in each phase leads to a performance guarantee of $2\mathcal{H}(f_{max})$ for the overall algorithm of Figure 4.9.

THEOREM 4.9   The primal-dual algorithm described in Figure 4.9 gives a $2\mathcal{H}(f_{max})$-approximation algorithm for the integer program (IP) with any proper function f, where $\mathcal{H}(k) = 1 + \frac{1}{2} + \frac{1}{3} + \ldots + \frac{1}{k}$.

In order to prove Theorem 4.9 from Theorem 4.8, we first show that the dual solution y constructed in phase p by the algorithm can be mapped to a feasible solution to the dual of the LP relaxation of (IP). This dual is:

$$\text{Max} \quad \sum_{S \subset V} f(S) y_S - \sum_{e \in E} z_e$$

subject to:

(D)

$$\sum_{S: e \in \delta(S)} y_S \leq c_e + z_e \qquad\qquad e \in E,$$

$$y_S \geq 0 \qquad\qquad \emptyset \neq S \subset V,$$

$$z_e \geq 0 \qquad\qquad e \in E.$$

Given the dual variables y constructed by the algorithm in phase p, define $z_e = \sum_{S:e\in\delta(S)} y_S$ for all $e \in F_{p-1}$, and $z_e = 0$ otherwise. It is easy to verify that (y, z) is a feasible solution for (D). We now provide a proof of Theorem 4.9.

Proof.   Observe that

$$\sum_{e\in E} z_e = \sum_{e\in F_{p-1}} \sum_{S:e\in\delta(S)} y_S = \sum_S |\delta_{F_{p-1}}(S)| y_S.$$

Comparing the value of the dual solution produced by the algorithm in phase p to the optimum value Z_D^* of the dual (D), we deduce

$$Z_D^* \geq \sum_S f(S) y_S - \sum_{e\in E} z_e$$
$$= \sum_S (f(S) - |\delta_{F_{p-1}}(S)|) y_S$$
$$= (f_{max} - p + 1) \sum_S y_S,$$

where we have used the fact that in phase p the dual variable $y_S > 0$ only if the deficiency of S $(f(S) - |\delta_{F_{p-1}}(S)|)$ is $f_{max} - p + 1$. Using the proof of the performance guarantee for uncrossable functions and summing over all phases, we obtain that

$$\sum_{e\in F_{f_{max}}} c_e \leq 2 \sum_{p=1}^{f_{max}} \frac{1}{f_{max} - p + 1} Z_D^* = 2\mathcal{H}(f_{max}) Z_D^*,$$

proving the desired result.   ∎

Notice that the algorithm for uncrossable functions constructs a dual feasible solution is crucial for the proof of the above theorem. An improved approximation algorithm for uncrossable functions would be useless for proving any performance guarantee for proper functions if it only compared the solution produced to the optimum value rather than to a dual feasible solution.

It is an interesting open question whether the primal-dual method can be used to design approximation algorithms for general proper functions or the survivable network design problem with a performance guarantee *independent* of f_{max}.

EXERCISE 4.13   Prove that, for a proper function f, $f_{max} = \max\{f(\{v\}) : v \in V\}$.

EXERCISE 4.14   Show that any 0-1 function satisfying the maximality property is uncrossable.

EXERCISE 4.15   Dijkstra's algorithm corresponds to the algorithm of Figure 4.4 with $f(S) = 1$ if $s \in S$ and $t \notin S$, and $f(S) = 0$ otherwise. Show that this function does not satisfy the maximality property but is uncrossable.

EXERCISE 4.16   Show that Lemma 4.3 also holds for the more general class of *skew supermodular* functions. A function f is skew supermodular if $f(V) = 0$ and $f(A) + f(B) \leq \max(f(A - B) + f(B - A), f(A \cup B) + f(A \cap B))$ for all sets A and B.

EXERCISE 4.17 Let h be an uncrossable function and assume we have an oracle for deciding the feasibility of a set A of edges. First prove that if $S \subset V$ is a *maximal* set such that $A \cup \{(i, j) : i, j \in S\}$ is not feasible, then $V - S$ is a minimal violated set for A. Then deduce that the set of minimal violated sets can be obtained by less than $|V|^2$ calls to the feasibility oracle. Given a general proper function f, consider the problem of checking the feasibility of a set F of edges. Prove that F is feasible if and only if the $|V| - 1$ cuts induced by the Gomory-Hu cut equivalent tree [GH61] of F have the required number of edges [GGW93].

EXERCISE 4.18 Consider the uncrossable function h_p defined in phase p of the algorithm of Figure 4.9. Show that A is feasible for h_p if and only if $A \cup F_{p-1}$ is feasible for the function $g_p(S) = \max(f(S) - f_{max} + p, 0)$. Moreover, show that this function g_p is proper.

EXERCISE 4.19 Using Exercises 4.17–4.18, show how to find the minimal violated sets for the uncrossable function h_p of the algorithm of Figure 4.9 in polynomial time. More efficient solutions to this exercise can be found in [WGMV95, GGW93, Wil93].

EXERCISE 4.20 Prove Theorem 4.8. Can you improve the performance guarantee to $2 - 2/l$ where l denotes the maximum number of disjoint sets $C_1, \ldots, C_l$ such that $f(C_i) = 1$ for all i?

EXTENSIONS

4.8

Up to this point, we have concentrated on showing how the primal-dual method can be applied to various network design problems that can be modelled by the integer program (IP) with different classes of functions f. In this section, we show that the method can be applied to other problems as well.

4.8.1 MINIMUM MULTICUT IN TREES

The primal-dual method can be applied to problems that are not network design problems. For example, Garg, Vazirani, and Yannakakis [GVY93a] have given a primal-dual 2-approximation algorithm for the problem of finding a *minimum multicut* in a tree. In the general minimum multicut problem, we are given an undirected graph $G = (V, E)$ with nonnegative capacities u_e on the edges, and pairs $s_i, t_i \in V$, for $i = 1, \ldots, k$. We must remove a minimum-capacity subset of edges E' so that no s_i, t_i pair is in the same connected component of $(V, E - E')$. In the minimum multicut problem in trees, the set of edges E is a tree on V. In this case, we can formulate the problem as a hitting set problem: E is the ground set of elements, the cost of each element is u_e, and for each i we must hit a set T_i, where T_i contains the edges on the unique path from s_i to t_i in the tree.

The minimum multicut problem in trees generalizes the vertex cover problem. Indeed, consider a star graph G with center vertex r, with leaves $v_1, \cdots, v_n$, and with terminal pairs (s_i, t_i) for $i = 1, \cdots, k$. Construct a graph H with vertex set $\{v_1, \cdots, v_n\}$, edge set $\{(s_i, t_i) : i = 1, \cdots, k\}$ and assign a weight of u_{rv} to any vertex v. Then $\{(r, v_i) : i \in C\}$ is a multicut of G of capacity U *if and only if* $\{v_i : i \in C\}$ is a vertex cover of H of weight U.

We can get a 2-approximation algorithm for this problem by applying the algorithm in Figure 4.2. In order to do this, we must specify how to select a violated set. At the beginning of the algorithm, we root the tree at an arbitrary vertex r. Define the *depth* of a vertex v to be the number of edges in the path from v to r, and define the *least common ancestor* of vertices u and v to be the vertex x of smallest depth that lies on the path from u to v. For each i, we compute the depth d_i of the least common ancestor of s_i and t_i. Then, among the violated sets T_i, we choose a set that maximizes d_i. The resulting algorithm is the algorithm proposed by Garg et al. [GVY93a].

THEOREM 4.10 The algorithm given in Figure 4.2 is a 2-approximation algorithm for the minimum multicut problem in trees.

Proof. We will apply Theorem 4.1. For this purpose, let A be any infeasible solution, let T be the violated set selected by the algorithm (i.e., the one that maximizes the depth of the least common ancestor), and let B be any minimal augmentation of A. We only need to prove that $|T \cap B| \leq 2$. Recall that T corresponds to a path from s_i to t_i in the tree, and let a_i be the least common ancestor of s_i and t_i. Let T_1 denote the path from s_i to a_i and T_2 denote the path from a_i to t_i. Then the theorem will follow by showing that $|B \cap T_1| \leq 1$ (the proof that $|B \cap T_2| \leq 1$ is identical). Suppose that $|B \cap T_1| \geq 2$. We claim that removing all edges in $B \cap T_1$ from B except the edge closest to a_i is still a feasible solution, contradicting the minimality of B. To see this, notice that by the choice of T, for any other violated sets T_j such that $T_1 \cap T_j \neq \emptyset$, the set $T_1 \cap T_j$ is a path from some vertex in T_1 to a_i; if not, T_j would have a least common ancestor of depth $d_j > d_i$, a contradiction. Therefore, if T_j contains any edge in $B \cap T_1$, it contains the edge in $B \cap T_1$ closest to a_i. ∎

The algorithm of Figure 4.2 not only constructs an approximate primal solution but also constructs an approximate dual solution. Moreover, if the capacities are integral, so is the dual solution constructed. In the case of the multicut problem, the (integral) dual is referred to as the *maximum (integral) multicommodity flow problem*: one needs to pack a maximum number of paths between terminal pairs without using any edge e more than u_e times. By Theorem 4.1, the algorithm of Figure 4.2 constructs a multicut and an integral multicommodity flow whose values are within a factor of 2 of each other.

4.8.2 THE PRIZE-COLLECTING PROBLEMS

We next show how to derive 2-approximation algorithms for extensions of the traveling salesman problem and the Steiner tree problem. These extensions are known as the *prize-collecting traveling salesman problem* and the *prize-collecting Steiner tree problem*.

In the prize-collecting traveling salesman problem, the input is an undirected graph $G = (V, E)$, nonnegative edge costs c_e, and nonnegative penalties on the vertices π_i. The goal is to find a tour on a subset of the vertices that minimizes the sum of the cost of the edges in the tour and the penalties on the vertices not in the tour. We will consider a variant in which a prespecified root vertex r must be in the tour; this is without loss of generality, since we can repeat the algorithm $n = |V|$ times, setting each vertex to be the root. The version of the prize-collecting TSP is a special case of a more general problem introduced by Balas [Bal89]. The prize-collecting Steiner tree problem is defined analogously; one needs to find a tree containing the root r which minimizes the sum of the cost of the edges of the tree plus the penalties of the vertices not spanned. The first approximation algorithms for these problems were given by Bienstock, Goemans, Simchi-Levi, and Williamson [BGSLW93]: they gave a 5/2-approximation algorithm for the TSP version (assuming the triangle inequality) and a 3-approximation algorithm for the Steiner tree version. The 2-approximation algorithms that we describe here are due to the authors [GW95a].

We first concentrate on deriving a 2-approximation algorithm for the prize-collecting Steiner tree problem; we will then show how a 2-approximation algorithm for the prize-collecting TSP can be derived from it. The 2-approximation algorithm is simply going to be the algorithm of Figure 4.3 for an appropriate formulation of the hitting set problem. Given the input graph (V, E) and root vertex r, the set of ground elements for the hitting set problem is the set of all edges E together with the set of all subsets of V not containing r; that is, the set of ground elements is $E \cup \{S : S \subseteq V - \{r\}\}$. The cost of a ground element $e \in E$ is c_e, while the cost of a ground element $S \subset V$ is $\sum_{v \in S} \pi_v$. The sets that must be hit are the sets $T_i = \delta(S_i) \cup \{S : S \supseteq S_i\}$ ranging over all $\emptyset \neq S_i \subseteq V - \{r\}$. Throughout the section, we assume that A denotes a subset of the ground set, so A contains vertex sets as well as edges; we will denote the collection of edges of A by A_e and the collection of vertex sets by A_s.

We now argue that this hitting set problem exactly models the prize-collecting Steiner tree problem. First, any feasible solution A to this hitting set problem is a feasible solution of no greater cost to the prize-collecting Steiner tree problem. Let S be the set of vertices not connected to the root r by the edges in A_e. The set $T = \delta(S) \cup \{S' \supseteq S\}$ must be hit, so some $S' \supseteq S$ must be in A. Thus, the cost of A includes the penalty $\sum_{v \in S} \pi_v$. Furthermore, given any feasible solution to the prize-collecting Steiner tree problem, we get a feasible solution to the hitting set problem of no greater cost by taking the set of all edges in the Steiner tree plus the set S of the vertices not connected to the root.

Since the ground set contains two types of elements, the dual of the LP relaxation will contain two types of constraints; the one corresponding to an edge e is as usual

$$\sum_{S : e \in \delta(S)} y_S \leq c_e,$$

while the one corresponding to a set C is

$$\sum_{S : S \subseteq C} y_S \leq \sum_{v \in C} \pi_v.$$

If a dual feasible solution y satisfies the dual constraints for C_1 and C_2 at equality then it can easily be seen that it also satisfies the dual constraint for $C_1 \cup C_2$ at equality. This means that, given a solution A and a dual feasible solution y satisfying the primal complementary slackness conditions, the solution obtained by replacing the sets in A_s by their union still satisfies the primal complementary slackness conditions with y. Although it will be important to keep track of the different sets in A_s, we will always assume that the union of the sets in A_s is implicitly taken before checking feasibility of A. Thus, we will regard A as feasible if the set of vertices not connected to the root r by edges in A_e can be covered by subsets of A_s.

Since the sets to be hit naturally correspond to vertex sets, we will again refer to the vertex sets S_i instead of referring to the associated subsets T_i of the ground set. In particular, we can use the algorithm of Figure 4.4 on page 162 rather than the one of Figure 4.3. But, for this, we first need to understand what sets are violated and which ones are minimal. Given the definition of T_i, a violated set for the current solution A will be a union of connected components of (V, A_e) provided the union (i) does not contain the root and (ii) cannot be covered by sets of A_s. Thus, the *minimal* violated sets $\mathcal{V}$ are the connected components $\mathcal{C}$ of (V, A_e) which do not contain the root and which cannot be covered by sets in A_s. We give the specialization of the algorithm of Figure 4.4 to the prize-collecting Steiner tree problem in Figure 4.10. In the figure, $\mathcal{C}$ denotes the connected components of (V, A_e) and $\mathcal{V}$ denotes the collection of minimal violated sets. Also, for simplicity, we have allowed a set $S \notin A_s$ to be violated even though it can be covered by sets of A_s. The algorithm would then simply add S to A_s without increasing any dual variable.

THEOREM 4.11 The primal-dual algorithm described in Figure 4.10 gives a 2-approximation algorithm for the prize-collecting Steiner tree problem.

1	$y \leftarrow 0$
2	$A \leftarrow \emptyset$
3	$\mathcal{C} \leftarrow \{\{v\} : v \in V\}$
4	$l \leftarrow 0$
5	While A is not feasible
6	$\quad l \leftarrow l + 1$
7	$\quad \mathcal{V} \leftarrow \{S \in \mathcal{C} : r \notin S \text{ and } S \notin A_s\}$
8	$\quad$ Increase y_S uniformly for all $S \in \mathcal{V}$ until
9	$\quad\quad$ either (i) $\exists e_l \in \delta(T), T \in \mathcal{V}$ such that $\sum_{S:e_l \in \delta(S)} y_S = c_{e_l}$
10	$\quad\quad$ or (ii) $\exists S_l \in \mathcal{V}$ such that $\sum_{S:S \subseteq S_l} y_S = \sum_{v \in S_l} \pi_v$
11	$\quad$ If (i) then
12	$\quad\quad a_l \leftarrow e_l$
13	$\quad\quad$ merge the two components of $\mathcal{C}$ spanned by e_l
14	$\quad$ else $a_l \leftarrow S_l$
15	$\quad A \leftarrow A \cup \{a_l\}$
16	For $j \leftarrow l$ downto 1
17	$\quad$ if $A - \{a_j\}$ is feasible then $A \leftarrow A - \{a_j\}$
18	Output A_e (and the union of the sets in A_s and y)

FIGURE 4.10

Primal-dual algorithm for the prize-collecting Steiner tree problem.

Before we present the proof of this theorem, it is useful to understand what the reverse delete step really achieves in this case. First, observe that at any point during the execution of the algorithm the sets in A_s form a laminar family; i.e., any two sets in A_s are either disjoint or one is contained in the other. Moreover, if $S_1 \subset S_2$ are two sets of A_s, then S_2 was added after S_1 and will be considered for removal before S_1. Because of the reverse delete step, in any solution B output by the algorithm, the sets in B_s will be disjoint. Furthermore, a set S in A_s will be considered for removal after all the edges in $\delta(S)$, but before all the edges with both endpoints within S. This implies that S must be kept in the reverse delete step only if all the edges in $\delta(S)$ have been removed.

Proof. Since the algorithm is equivalent to the algorithm of Figure 4.3, we can use Theorem 4.2. We must therefore show that for any infeasible solution A and any minimal augmentation B of A,

$$\sum_{i:S_i \in \mathcal{V}(A)} |B \cap T_i| \le 2|\mathcal{V}(A)|,$$

where $\mathcal{V}(A)$ is the the collection of violated sets. In fact, looking back at the proof of Theorem 4.2, we don't need to show the inequality for *any* minimal augmentation B, but only for those which could be produced by the algorithm. Given the above discussion, we can thus assume that the sets in B_s are disjoint, that they all consist of unions of connected components of (V, A_e), and that no edge $e \in B_e$ belongs to $\delta(S)$ for some set $S \in B_s$.

Consider now the graph H formed by shrinking the connected components of (V, A_e). Let W denote the vertices of H corresponding to the sets in $\mathcal{V}(A)$, and let $W' \subseteq W$ denote the subset of these vertices corresponding to the union of the sets in B_s. Then, $\sum_{i:S_i \in \mathcal{V}(A)} |B \cap T_i| = \sum_{S_i \in \mathcal{V}(A)} (|B_e \cap \delta(S_i)| + |B_s \cap \{S : S \supseteq S_i\}|) = \sum_{v \in W} d_v + |W'|$, and we must show that this quantity is no more than $2|W|$. By the observations about B_s above, if $v \in W'$, then $d_v = 0$, so that we must prove that $\sum_{v \in W - W'} d_v + |W'| \le 2|W|$. The fact that the reverse delete step produces a minimal solution implies that any leaf of H must be a vertex of W; if a leaf of H is not in W, we could delete the corresponding edge of B_e without affecting the feasibility of B. Then, as before, we derive that $\sum_{v \in W - W'} d_v \le 2|W - W'|$ since we are only discarding vertices of degree at least 2. Thus,

$$\sum_{v \in W - W'} d_v + |W'| \le 2|W - W'| + |W'| = 2|W| - |W'| \le 2|W|,$$

which is the desired inequality.   ■

Given that edge costs obey the triangle inequality, a 2-approximation algorithm for the prize-collecting TSP can be obtained as follows: given the input graph G, edge costs c_e, penalties π_i, and root vertex r, we apply the above algorithm for the prize-collecting Steiner tree to the graph G, edge costs c_e, penalties $\pi_i' = \pi_i/2$, and root vertex r. The resulting tree is converted to a tour by the usual technique of doubling the edges and shortcutting the resultant Eulerian tour. The proof that this algorithm is a 2-approximation algorithm for the prize-collecting TSP is similar to the proof used in Section 4.5.2 for the lower capacitated cycle problem, and we leave it as an exercise for the reader. This 2-approximation algorithm has been used for deriving approximation algorithms for more complex problems; see [BCC+94, GK96, AABV95, BRV95].

4.8.3 VERTEX CONNECTIVITY PROBLEMS

So far all network design problems discussed have involved finding minimum-cost sub-graphs with certain edge-connectivity properties. However, the primal-dual method can also be applied to some vertex-connectivity problems. Ravi and Williamson [RW95] have shown that the primal-dual method gives a $2\mathcal{H}(k)$-approximation algorithm for the minimum-cost k-vertex-connected subgraph problem, in which one must find a minimum-cost set of edges such that there are at least k vertex-disjoint paths between any pair of vertices. They also present a 3-approximation algorithm for the survivable network design problem when there must be r_{ij} vertex-disjoint paths between i and j, and $r_{ij} \in \{0, 1, 2\}$ for all i, j. No approximation algorithms were previously known for either of these problems.

We briefly sketch how the primal-dual algorithm is used in the case of the minimum-cost k-vertex-connected subgraph problem. As in the case of general proper functions (Section 4.6), the solution is constructed in a sequence of k phases. In phase p, the current solution is augmented to a p-vertex-connected graph. By Menger's Theorem, a graph is p-vertex-connected if there does not exist any set of $p - 1$ or fewer vertices such that removing the set divides the graph into two non-empty pieces. Let (V, E) be the input graph, and let F_{p-1} denote the set of edges selected at the end of phase $p - 1$. To augment a $(p - 1)$-vertex-connected graph (V, F_{p-1}) to a p-vertex-connected graph, we apply the algorithm of Figure 4.4 to the hitting set problem in which the ground elements are the edges of $E - F_{p-1}$. For any set of $p - 1$ vertices whose removal separates (V, F_{p-1}) into two pieces S_i and S_i', we must hit the set $T_i = \delta(S_i : S_i') \cap (E - F_{p-1})$, where $\delta(S : S')$ denotes the set of edges with one endpoint in S and one in S'. If A is any feasible solution to this hitting set problem, then $A \cup F_{p-1}$ is a p-vertex-connected graph by Menger's Theorem. We correspond the smaller of S_i and S_i' to each violated set T_i; one can then show for this problem that the minimal violated sets S are disjoint. The algorithm of Figure 4.4 can then be applied in a straightforward way to find a low-cost augmentation A of F_{p-1}; we set F_p to $A \cup F_{p-1}$. As with Theorem 4.8, it is possible to show that the algorithm yields a 2-approximation algorithm for this hitting set problem, and using a proof similar to that of Theorem 4.9, it can be proven that the overall algorithm gives a $2\mathcal{H}(k)$-approximation algorithm for the k-vertex-connected subgraph problem.

Other results known for vertex-connectivity problems can be found in Chapter 6.

EXERCISE 4.21 Show that for star graphs and unit capacities, finding the maximum integral multicommodity flow is equivalent to a maximum matching problem.

EXERCISE 4.22 Prove that the primal-dual algorithm for the prize-collecting TSP is a 2-approximation algorithm.

EXERCISE 4.23 Show that the algorithm of Figure 4.10 returns a tree such that the sum of the cost of the edges plus *twice* the sum of the penalties of the vertices not visited is at most twice the cost of the optimum solution. For an application, see [GK96, BRV95].

EXERCISE 4.24 Does the fact that the elements are deleted *in reverse* matter for the algorithm of Figure 4.10?

CONCLUSIONS

4.9

Up to this point, we have concentrated mainly on showing how the primal-dual method allows the proof of good performance guarantees, and have mostly set aside the issues of running time and performance in practice. A common criticism of approximation algorithms is that they might not generate "nearly-optimal" solutions in practice. A practitioner will seldom be satisfied with a solution guaranteed to be of cost less than twice the optimum cost, as guaranteed by most of the algorithms of this chapter, and would prefer an algorithm that finds solutions within a few percent of optimal. The good news is that the studies of the primal-dual method performed thus far show that it seems to perform very well in practice, at least on some problems. The authors [WG94] report computational results with the 2-approximation algorithm for the minimum-weight perfect matching problem under the triangle inequality. They consider both random and real-world instances having between 1,000 and 131,072 vertices. The results indicate that the algorithm generates a matching within 2% of optimal in most cases. In over 1,400 experiments, the algorithm was never more than 4% from optimal. Hu and Wein [Wei94] implemented the algorithm for the generalized Steiner tree problem, and found that the algorithm was usually within 5% of optimal. Because of the difficulty of finding the optimal solution in this case, their instances had at most 64 vertices. Finally, Mihail and Shallcross implemented a modification of the algorithm given for the survivable network design problem for inclusion in a network design software package. Although they did no rigorous testing, they report that the algorithm does well in practice, coming within a few percent of the expected optimal solution [MSDM96].

In this chapter, we have shown the power of the primal-dual method for designing approximation algorithms for a wide variety of problems. Most of the problems considered in this chapter were network design problems, but the method is so general that it is likely to have interesting applications for many kinds of problems. Indeed, primal-dual techniques have also been applied to derive approximation algorithms for other problems, such as the feedback vertex set problem (see Chapter 9) or some of its variants in planar graphs [GW95b]. For network design problems, the moral of the chapter is that two design rules are very important. First, one should grow uniformly the dual variables corresponding to the minimal violated sets. Secondly, one should delete unnecessary edges in a reverse order before the solution is output. These rules should lead to approximation algorithms for many more problems.

Acknowledgments The first author was supported by NSF grant 9302476-CCR. The second author was supported by an NSF Postdoctoral Fellowship, and by the IBM Corporation.

REFERENCES

[AABV95] B. Awerbuch, Y. Azar, A. Blum, and S. Vempala. Improved approximation guarantees for minimum-weight k-trees and prize-collecting salesmen. In *Proceedings of the 27th Annual ACM Symposium on Theory of Computing*, pages 277–283, 1995.

[AG94] M. Aggarwal and N. Garg. A scaling technique for better network design. In *Proceedings of the 5th Annual ACM-SIAM Symposium on Discrete Algorithms*, pages 233–240, 1994.

[AKR95] A. Agrawal, P. Klein, and R. Ravi. When trees collide: An approximation algorithm for the generalized Steiner problem on networks. *SIAM Journal on Computing*, 24:440–456, 1995.

[Bal89] E. Balas. The prize collecting traveling salesman problem. *Networks*, 19:621–636, 1989.

[BCC+94] A. Blum, P. Chalasani, D. Coppersmith, W. Pulleyblank, P. Raghavan, and M. Sudan. The minimum latency problem. In *Proceedings of the 26th ACM Symposium on Theory of Computing*, pages 163–171, 1994.

[BGSLW93] D. Bienstock, M. X. Goemans, D. Simchi-Levi, and D. Williamson. A note on the prize collecting traveling salesman problem. *Mathematical Programming*, 59:413–420, 1993.

[Bir46] G. Birkhoff. Tres observaciones sobre el algebra lineal. *Revista Facultad de Ciencias Exactas, Puras y Aplicadas Universidad Nacional de Tucuman, Serie A*, 5:147–151, 1946.

[BMMN94] M. Ball, T. L. Magnanti, C. L. Monma, and G. L. Nemhauser. *Network Models*. Handbooks in Operations Research and Management Science. North-Holland, 1994.

[BMW89] A. Balakrishnan, T. L. Magnanti, and R. Wong. A dual-ascent procedure for large-scale uncapacitated network design. *Operations Research*, 37:716–740, 1989.

[BRV95] A. Blum, R. Ravi, and S. Vempala. A constant-factor approximation algorithm for the k-MST problem. Manuscript, 1995.

[BT95] D. Bertsimas and C.-P. Teo. From valid inequalities to heuristics: A unified view of primal-dual approximation algorithms in covering problems. In *Proceedings of the 6th Annual ACM-SIAM Symposium on Discrete Algorithms*, pages 102–111, 1995.

[BYE81] R. Bar-Yehuda and S. Even. A linear time approximation algorithm for the weighted vertex cover problem. *Journal of Algorithms*, 2:198–203, 1981.

[CFN77] G. Cornuéjols, M. L. Fisher, and G. L. Nemhauser. Location of bank accounts to optimize float: An analytical study of exact and approximate algorithms. *Management Science*, 23:789–810, 1977.

[Chr76] N. Christofides. Worst case analysis of a new heuristic for the traveling salesman problem. Report 388, Graduate School of Industrial Administration, Carnegie-Mellon University, Pittsburgh, PA, 1976.

[Chv79] V. Chvátal. A greedy heuristic for the set-covering problem. *Mathematics of Operations Research*, 4:233–235, 1979.

[Chv83] V. Chvátal. *Linear Programming*. W.H. Freeman and Company, New York, NY, 1983.

[CP80] G. Cornuéjols and W. Pulleyblank. A matching problem with side constraints. *Discrete Mathematics*, 29:135–159, 1980.

[DFF56]   G. B. Dantzig, L. R. Ford, and D. R. Fulkerson. A primal-dual algorithm for linear programs. In H. W. Kuhn and A. W. Tucker, editors, *Linear Inequalities and Related Systems*, pages 171–181. Princeton University Press, Princeton, NJ, 1956.

[Dij59]   E. W. Dijkstra. A note on two problems in connexion with graphs. *Numerische Mathematik*, 1:269–271, 1959.

[Edm65]   J. Edmonds. Maximum matching and a polyhedron with 0,1-vertices. *Journal of Research of the National Bureau of Standards B*, 69B:125–130, 1965.

[Edm67]   J. Edmonds. Optimum branchings. *Journal of Research of the National Bureau of Standards B*, 71B:233–240, 1967.

[Ege31]   E. Egerváry. Matrixok kombinatorius tujajdonságairól. *Matematikai és Fizikai Lapok*, 38:16–28, 1931.

[EJ70]   J. Edmonds and E. Johnson. Matching: A well-solved class of integer linear programs. In R. Guy, H. Hanani, N. Sauer, and J. Schonheim, editors, *Proceedings of the Calgary International Conference on Combinatorial Structures and Their Applications*, pages 82–92. Gordon and Breach, 1970.

[EJ73]   J. Edmonds and E. L. Johnson. Matching, Euler tours and the Chinese postman. *Mathematical Programming*, 5:88–124, 1973.

[Erl78]   D. Erlenkotter. A dual-based procedure fo uncapacitated facility location. *Operations Research*, 26:992–1009, 1978.

[FF56]   L. R. Ford and D. R. Fulkerson. Maximal flow through a network. *Canadian Journal of Mathematics*, 8:399–404, 1956.

[Gab90]   H. N. Gabow. Data structures for weighted matching and nearest common ancestors with linking. In *Proceedings of the 1st Annual ACM-SIAM Symposium on Discrete Algorithms*, pages 434–443, 1990.

[GGP+94] M. Goemans, A. Goldberg, S. Plotkin, D. Shmoys, E. Tardos, and D. Williamson. Improved approximation algorithms for network design problems. In *Proceedings of the 5th Annual ACM-SIAM Symposium on Discrete Algorithms*, pages 223–232, 1994.

[GGW93]   H. N. Gabow, M. X. Goemans, and D. P. Williamson. An efficient approximation algorithm for the survivable network design problem. In *Proceedings of the Third MPS Conference on Integer Programming and Combinatorial Optimization*, pages 57–74, 1993.

[GH61]   R. Gomory and T. Hu. Multi-terminal network flows. *SIAM Journal of Applied Mathematics*, 9:551–570, 1961.

[GK96]   M. X. Goemans and J. M. Kleinberg. Improved approximation algorithms for the minimum latency problem. To appear in the *Proceedings of the Seventh Annual Symposium on Discrete Algorithms*, 1996.

[GLS88]   M. Grötschel, L. Lovász, and A. Schrijver. *Geometric Algorithms and Combinatorial Optimization*. Springer-Verlag, Berlin, 1988.

[GMS94]   M. Grötschel, C. L. Monma, and M. Stoer. Design of survivable networks. In *Handbook in Operations Research and Management Science*. North-Holland, 1994.

[GT91]   H. N. Gabow and R. E. Tarjan. Faster scaling algorithms for general graph-matching problems. *Journal of the ACM*, 38:815–853, 1991.

[GVY93a] N. Garg, V. Vazirani, and M. Yannakakis. Primal-dual approximation algorithms for integral flow and multicut in trees, with applications to matching and set cover.

In *Proceedings of the 20th International Colloquium on Automata, Languages and Programming*, 1993. To appear in *Algorithmica* under the title "Primal-dual approximation algorithms for integral flow and multicut in trees".

[GVY93b] N. Garg, V. V. Vazirani, and M. Yannakakis. Approximate max-flow min-(multi)cut theorems and their applications. In *Proceedings of the 25th Annual ACM Symposium on Theory of Computing*, pages 698–707, 1993.

[GW94] M. X. Goemans and D. P. Williamson. Approximating minimum-cost graph problems with spanning tree edges. *Operations Research Letters*, 16:183–189, 1994.

[GW95a] M. X. Goemans and D. P. Williamson. A general approximation technique for constrained forest problems. *SIAM Journal on Computing*, 24:296–317, 1995.

[GW95b] M. X. Goemans and D. P. Williamson. Primal-dual approximation algorithms for feedback problems in planar graphs. Manuscript, 1995.

[Hoc82] D. S. Hochbaum. Approximation algorithms for the set covering and vertex cover problems. *SIAM Journal on Computing*, 11:555–556, 1982.

[IKK93] C. Imielińska, B. Kalantari, and L. Khachiyan. A greedy heuristic for a minimum-weight forest problem. *Operations Research Letters*, 14:65–71, 1993.

[JDU+74] D. Johnson, A. Demers, J. Ullman, M. Garey, and R. Graham. Worst-case performance bounds for simple one-dimensional packing problems. *SIAM Journal on Computing*, 3:299–325, 1974.

[JP91] M. Jünger and W. Pulleyblank. New primal and dual matching heuristics. Research Report 91.105, Universität zu Köln, 1991.

[Kle94] P. N. Klein. A data structure for bicategories, with application to speeding up an approximation algorithm. *Information Processing Letters*, 52:303–307, 1994.

[KR93] P. Klein and R. Ravi. When cycles collapse: A general approximation technique for constrained two-connectivity problems. In *Proceedings of the Third MPS Conference on Integer Programming and Combinatorial Optimization*, pages 39–55, 1993. Also appears as Brown University Technical Report CS-92-30.

[Kru56] J. Kruskal. On the shortest spanning subtree of a graph and the traveling salesman problem. *Proceedings of the American Mathematical Society*, 7:48–50, 1956.

[Kuh55] H. W. Kuhn. The Hungarian method for the assignment problem. *Naval Research Logistics Quarterly*, 2:83–97, 1955.

[Lap88] G. Laporte. Location-routing problems. In B. L. Golden and A. A. Assad, editors, *Vehicle routing: Methods and studies*, pages 163–197. North-Holland, Amsterdam, 1988.

[LMSL92] C.-L. Li, S. T. McCormick, and D. Simchi-Levi. The point-to-point delivery and connection problems: Complexity and algorithms. *Discrete Applied Mathematics*, 36:267–292, 1992.

[LNP83] G. Laporte, Y. Nobert, and P. Pelletier. Hamiltonian location problems. *European Journal of Operations Research*, 12:82–89, 1983.

[Lov75] L. Lovász. On the ratio of optimal integral and fractional covers. *Discrete Mathematics*, 13:383–390, 1975.

[MSDM96] M. Mihail, D. Shallcross, N. Dean, and M. Mostrel. A commercial application of survivable network design: ITP/INPLANS CCS network topology analyzer. To appear in the *Proceedings of the Seventh Annual Symposium on Discrete Algorithms*, 1996.

[Nic66]   T. Nicholson. Finding the shortest route between two points in a network. *Computer Journal*, 9:275–280, 1966.

[Pla84]   D. A. Plaisted. Heuristic matching for graphs satisfying the triangle inequality. *Journal of Algorithms*, 5:163–179, 1984.

[PS82]   C. H. Papadimitriou and K. Steiglitz. *Combinatorial Optimization: Algorithms and Complexity*. Prentice-Hall, Englewood Cliffs, NJ, 1982.

[Rag94]   S. Raghavan. *Formulations and algorithms for network design problems with connectivity requirements*. PhD thesis, MIT, 1994.

[RT81]   E. M. Reingold and R. E. Tarjan. On a greedy heuristic for complete matching. *SIAM Journal on Computing*, 10:676–681, 1981.

[RT87]   P. Raghavan and C. Thompson. Randomized rounding: a technique for provably good algorithms and algorithmic proofs. *Combinatorica*, 7:365–374, 1987.

[RW95]   R. Ravi and D. Williamson. An approximation algorithm for minimum-cost vertex-connectivity problems. In *Proceedings of the 6th Annual ACM-SIAM Symposium on Discrete Algorithms*, pages 332–341, 1995. To appear in *Algorithmica*.

[SPR80]   K. J. Supowit, D. A. Plaisted, and E. M. Reingold. Heuristics for weighted perfect matching. In *Proceedings of the 12th Annual ACM Symposium on Theory of Computing*, pages 398–419, 1980.

[Sto92]   M. Stoer. *Design of Survivable Networks*, volume 1531 of *Lecture Notes in Mathematics*. Springer-Verlag, 1992.

[Str88]   G. Strang. *Linear Algebra and its Applications*. Harcourt Brace Jovanovich, San Diego, CA, Third edition, 1988.

[SVY92]   H. Saran, V. Vazirani, and N. Young. A primal-dual approach to approximation algorithms for network Steiner problems. In *Proceedings of Indo-US Workshop on Cooperative Research in Computer Science*, pages 166–168, 1992.

[Tar75]   R. E. Tarjan. Efficiency of a good but not linear set union algorithm. *Journal of the ACM*, 22:215–225, 1975.

[Vai91]   P. Vaidya. Personal communication, 1991.

[vN53]   J. von Neumann. A certain zero-sum two-person game equivalent to the optimal assignment problem. In H. W. Kuhn and A. W. Tucker, editors, *Contributions to the Theory of Games, II*, pages 5–12. Princeton University Press, Princeton, NJ, 1953.

[Vor79]   O. Vornberger. *Complexity of path problems in graphs*. PhD thesis, Universität-GH-Paderborn, 1979.

[Wei94]   J. Wein. Personal communcation, 1994.

[WG94]   D. P. Williamson and M. X. Goemans. Computational experience with an approximation algorithm on large-scale Euclidean matching instances. In *Proceedings of the 5th Annual ACM-SIAM Symposium on Discrete Algorithms*, pages 355–364, 1994. To appear in *ORSA Journal on Computing*.

[WGMV95] D. P. Williamson, M. X. Goemans, M. Mihail, and V. V. Vazirani. An approximation algorithm for general graph connectivity problems. *Combinatorica*, 15:435–454, 1995.

[Wil93]   D. P. Williamson. *On the design of approximation algorithms for a class of graph problems*. PhD thesis, MIT, Cambridge, MA, September 1993. Also appears as Tech Report MIT/LCS/TR-584.

[Win87]   P. Winter. Steiner problem in networks: a survey. *Networks*, 17:129–167, 1987.

[Wol80]   L. A. Wolsey. Heuristic analysis, linear programming and branch and bound. *Mathematical Programming Study*, 13:121–134, 1980.

[Won84]   R. Wong. A dual ascent approach for Steiner tree problems on a directed graph. *Mathematical Programming*, 28:271–287, 1984.

[Zel93]   A. Zelikovsky. An 11/6-approximation algorithm for the network Steiner problem. *Algorithmica*, 9:463–470, 1993.

5

CUT PROBLEMS AND THEIR APPLICATION TO DIVIDE-AND-CONQUER

David B. Shmoys

Divide-and-conquer is one of the most basic techniques in the design and analysis of algorithms, and yet, until recently, there have been essentially no performance guarantees known for approximation algorithms based on this approach. This chapter will present approximation algorithms for several *NP*-hard graph-theoretic cut problems and their subsequent application as a tool for the "divide" part of divide-and-conquer approximation algorithms for a wide variety of problems.

INTRODUCTION

5.1

One of the most important paradigms in the design and analysis of algorithms is the notion of a divide-and-conquer algorithm. Every undergraduate course on algorithms teaches this method as one of its staples: to solve a problem quickly, one carefully splits the problem into two subproblems, each substantially smaller than the original, then one recursively solves each of these, and then pieces together the solution to each part into the overall solution desired.

This approach has also been used in the design of heuristics for *NP*-hard optimization problems, but until recently, the heuristics designed in this way were either too complicated to analyze or had extremely poor performance guarantees. In one of the most important breakthroughs in the design and analysis of approximation algorithms in the past decade, Leighton and Rao [LR88, LR94] devised an elegant approach for using divide-and-conquer in a way that produced superior performance guarantees for a wide range of problems. The key ingredient to their approach is the design of approximation algorithms for certain cut problems. These algorithms, which are of independent interest, provide approximate max-flow min-cut theorems for multicommodity flow problems that are analogous to the famous max-flow min-cut theorem for (single-commodity) network flow of Ford and Fulkerson [FF56]. In this chapter, we will survey the techniques that were introduced by Leighton and Rao, as well as a number of advances that have been obtained subsequently in the area.

Although the methods that we will describe are much more general, we shall first illustrate this approach on a concrete example, the *minimum cut linear arrangement problem*. Suppose that we are given an undirected graph $G = (V, E)$ with n vertices, and we wish to lay out the graph on integer points of the real line; that is, for $i = 1, \ldots, n$, we assign one vertex to i, in such a way that each vertex is assigned to a value in this range; let $\sigma(i)$ denote the vertex assigned to i, for each $i = 1, \ldots, n$. We can evaluate this layout in the following way: for each $i = 1, \ldots, n$, let S_i denote the set of edges in E of the form $(\sigma(j), \sigma(k))$, where $j \leq i$ and $k > i$; we wish to choose a layout so that $\max_{i=1,\ldots,n} |S_i|$ is minimized. More generally, in the weighted version of this problem, each edge $e \in E$ has a non-negative cost $c(e)$ associated with it, and we wish to lay out the graph on the line so as to minimize

$$\max_{i=1,\ldots,n} \sum_{e \in S_i} c(e). \tag{5.1}$$

Let $OPT_{LA}(G)$ denote the optimal value. Figure 5.1 gives an instance of this problem, and feasible solution σ.

The results of Leighton and Rao are based on an algorithm for the *graph bisection problem*, which serves as the engine for the divide-and-conquer approach. In words, this is the problem of finding a minimum-cost subset of edges whose deletion separates the graph into two components of essentially equal size. More formally, we are given an undirected graph $G = (V, E)$ where each edge $e \in E$ has a given non-negative cost $c(e)$; once again, and throughout this chapter, we shall let n denote the number of vertices in the given graph. We wish to partition the vertex set into V_1 and V_2 such that $|V_1| = \lfloor n/2 \rfloor$ (and hence $|V_2| = \lceil n/2 \rceil$) so as to minimize $\sum_{e \in \delta(V_1)} c(e)$, where for any $S \subseteq V$, $\delta(S)$ denotes the set of edges $\{(u, v) = e \in E : u \in S, v \notin S\}$.

Suppose that we have a ρ-approximation algorithm for the graph bisection problem: that is, the cost of the bisection found, $\mathcal{B}(G)$, is no more than ρ times the cost of the optimal bisection. This can be used to derive the following divide-and-conquer algorithm for the minimum cut linear arrangement problem. Apply the bisection algorithm to your input G to obtain V_1 and V_2; we shall lay out V_1 on the set $\{1, 2, \ldots, \lfloor n/2 \rfloor\}$ and lay out V_2 on the set $\{\lfloor n/2 \rfloor + 1, \ldots, n\}$. Thus, we have divided the problem into two problems of half the size, and we recursively compute good layouts for the graphs induced by V_1 and V_2, which we call G_1 and G_2, respectively. Of course, when there is only one vertex to be laid out, there is no need for further recursion.

How good is this divide-and-conquer algorithm for the minimum cut linear arrangement problem? Let $\mathcal{A}(G)$ denote the objective function value of the solution produced by this algorithm on input G. We will show that $\mathcal{A}(G) = O(\rho \log n) \cdot OPT_{LA}(G)$ for any graph G; that is, it is a $O(\rho \log n)$-approximation for the minimum cut linear

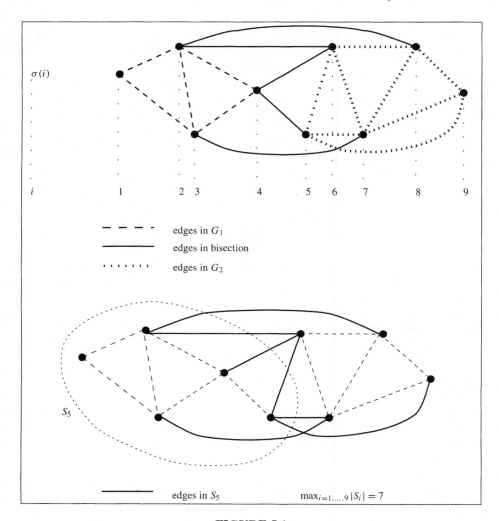

FIGURE 5.1

*An instance of the minimum cut linear
arrangement problem.*

arrangement problem. Consider the top level of the recursion: the edges of the graph G
can be partitioned into three sets: the edges of G_1, the edges of G_2, and the edges in
$\delta(V_1)$. The graphs G_1 and G_2 are independent problems in the sense that in evaluating
the objective function value (5.1) of a layout, for $i = 1, \ldots, \lfloor n/2 \rfloor$, none of the edges in
G_2 are relevant, and for $i = \lfloor n/2 + 1 \rfloor, \ldots, n$, none of the edges in G_1 are relevant (see
Figure 5.1). More precisely, each subset of edges $S_i, i = 1, \ldots, \lfloor n/2 \rfloor$, can be partitioned
into two subsets: those in G_1 and those in $\delta(V_1)$, and hence, the total cost of those edges
can be bounded by $\mathcal{A}(G_1) + \mathcal{B}(G)$. For each subset $S_i, i = \lfloor n/2 + 1 \rfloor, \ldots, n$, the total
cost of these edges can be similarly bounded by $\mathcal{A}(G_2) + \mathcal{B}(G)$. Hence,

$$\mathcal{A}(G) \le \max\{\mathcal{A}(G_1), \mathcal{A}(G_2)\} + \mathcal{B}(G).$$

Observe that we can construct a bisection from any linear arrangement σ: let V_1 and V_2 be, respectively, those vertices mapped by σ to values no more than $\lfloor n/2 \rfloor$ and those mapped to values greater than $\lfloor n/2 \rfloor$. The cost of the linear arrangement σ is, by definition, at least the cost of this bisection. Consequently, the cost of the optimal bisection is at most $OPT_{LA}(G)$, and hence the bisection used in the algorithm has cost $\mathcal{B}(G) \leq \rho OPT_{LA}(G)$. But this implies that

$$\mathcal{A}(G) \leq \max\{\mathcal{A}(G_1), \mathcal{A}(G_2)\} + \rho OPT_{LA}(G). \tag{5.2}$$

It is easy to see that this implies the claimed performance guarantee. With each level of recursion, the size of the relevant graphs is reduced by a factor of 2. Hence, there are $\lceil \log n \rceil$ levels of recursion (unless explicitly noted, any logarithm in this chapter has base equal to 2). With each level of recursion, we incur a cost of $\rho OPT_{LA}(\bar{G})$ for some subgraph $\bar{G}$ of G; clearly, $OPT_{LA}(\bar{G}) \leq OPT_{LA}(G)$. Hence, $\mathcal{A}(G) = O(\rho \log n) \cdot OPT_{LA}(G)$. A straightforward inductive argument can be used to write out a more formal proof.

In fact, this analysis did not require that we find a near-optimal bisection. It would have been sufficient to produce a partition in which, say, both V_1 and V_2 have at most $2n/3$ vertices. So if we can produce such a *balanced cut* for which the cost $\sum_{e \in \delta(V_1)} c(e)$ is within a factor of ρ of the optimal bisection cost, then we could still apply the same analysis. This is precisely what Leighton and Rao did: they gave an algorithm that produced a balanced cut of cost within a factor of $O(\log n)$ of the optimal bisection cost. Consequently, they obtained an $O(\log^2 n)$-approximation algorithm for the minimum cut linear arrangement problem. In Section 5.5 we will discuss a variety of balanced cut theorems and their application to several different optimization problems. It is important to note that this framework for obtaining approximation algorithms by divide-and-conquer was proposed by Bhatt and Leighton [BL84], who focused attention on designing an approximation algorithms for the graph bisection problem.

We shall next try to motivate the mathematical ideas underlying Leighton and Rao's algorithm to find a good balanced cut. The balanced cut problem seems superficially related to the *minimum (s,t)-cut problem*, where one is given a graph and two specified nodes $s, t \in V$, and wishes to find a minimum-cost subset of edges whose deletion disconnects the nodes s and t. One of the most fundamental results in combinatorial optimization is the max-flow min-cut theorem of Ford and Fulkerson [FF56], which states that the total cost of the minimum cut is exactly equal to the *maximum flow* value in the graph between s and t. In the latter problem, flow may be shipped along any path between s and t, and the aim is to maximize the total flow shipped, subject to the constraint that for each edge $e \in E$, the total flow shipped on paths that contain e is at most $c(e)$. It is easy to see that for any flow and any cut, the value of the flow can be no more than the total cost of the cut. Ford and Fulkerson gave an algorithm that simultaneously constructed a flow and a cut of equal value, and hence each is an optimal solution to its respective optimization problem.

The balanced cut problem is more closely related to a so-called multicommodity generalization of the maximum flow problem. In multicommodity network flow problems, there are k pairs of terminals (s_i, t_i), $i = 1, \ldots, k$, and the edge capacity $c(e)$ limits the total flow, over all commodities, that can be shipped through edge e, for each $e \in E$. There are two variants of this problem that we will consider. In the *maximum multicommodity flow*, we simply want to maximize the total amount that is shipped between pairs of terminals. In the *maximum concurrent flow problem*, there is a specified demand $d(i)$, for each commodity $i = 1, \ldots, k$. One might ask: can we find a feasible solution in which the total flow between s_i and t_i is at least $d(i)$, for each $i = 1, \ldots, k$? In the maximum concurrent flow problem, we wish to maximize λ such that the demands $\lambda d(i)$, $i = 1, \ldots, k$, can be met.

It is common to view the single-commodity max-flow min-cut theorem as having two parts: the weak duality theorem, which states that for any instance, the maximum flow value is at most the minimum cut capacity; and the strong duality theorem, which states that for any instance, there exists a feasible flow and a feasible cut for which their objective function values are equal. It is easy to obtain generalizations of the weak duality theorem in these multicommodity settings: for any instance, the maximum multicommodity flow value is at most the optimal value of the *minimum multicut problem*, and the maximum concurrent flow value is at most the optimal value of the *sparsest cut problem*. Unfortunately, the strong duality theorem does not generalize to either of these pairs of problems. Furthermore, whereas both multicommodity generalizations of the flow problem can be solved (via linear programming algorithms) in polynomial time, the minimum multicut and sparsest cut problems are *NP*-hard. (In contrast, the variants of these multicommodity flow problems in which we restrict attention to integer-valued flows are *NP*-hard.) Leighton and Rao [LR88] gave an approximate multicommodity max-flow min-cut theorem, by giving an algorithm that finds a feasible concurrent flow and a corresponding sparse cut for which the objective function values are within a logarithmic factor of each other. Consequently, this algorithm is an approximation algorithm for the sparsest cut problem with a logarithmic performance guarantee. This algorithm can be adapted to yield the approximation algorithm for the balanced cut problem that was claimed above, in the discussion of the minimum cut linear arrangement problem.

The work of Leighton and Rao provided an exciting starting point for research on approximation algorithms for cut problems and their application to divide-and-conquer algorithms for other types of problems. Furthermore, their techniques for cut problems have subsequently been applied *directly* to other problems, such as the feedback arc set problem in directed graphs; a divide-and-conquer approach is still employed, but the "divide" part of the algorithm exploits the structure of the problem at hand to obtain a superior performance guarantee. In this chapter, we shall try to highlight some of the algorithmic techniques that have been developed in this area, and give an overview of the results that have been obtained.

MINIMUM MULTICUTS AND MAXIMUM MULTICOMMODITY FLOW

5.2

In this section, we will consider the *minimum multicut problem* and the *maximum multicommodity flow problem* for undirected graphs. We shall see that these problems are closely related, and we shall exploit this relationship to derive an approximation algorithm for the cut problem.

5.2.1   MULTICUTS, MAXIMUM MULTICOMMODITY FLOW, AND A WEAK DUALITY THEOREM

Given an undirected graph $G = (V, E)$ and k pairs of vertices $(s_1, t_1), \ldots, (s_k, t_k)$, a *multicut* is a subset of edges $F \subseteq E$, such that if all edges in F are deleted, none of the pairs (s_i, t_i), $i = 1, \ldots, k$, are in the same connected component in the remaining graph $\bar{G} = (V, E - F)$. In the minimum multicut problem, we are also given a positive cost $c(e)$ for each edge $e \in E$, and we wish to find the multicut of minimum total cost. We shall let m denote the number of edges, $|E|$.

Let $\mathcal{P}_i$ denote the set of all paths between s_i and t_i, $i = 1, \ldots, k$. The minimum multicut problem can be stated as the following integer linear programming problem:

$$\text{minimize} \quad \sum_{e \in E} c(e)x(e) \tag{5.3}$$

subject to

$$\sum_{e \in P} x(e) \geq 1, \qquad \text{for each } P \in \mathcal{P}_i, i = 1, \ldots, k, \tag{5.4}$$

$$x(e) \in \{0, 1\}, \qquad \text{for each } e \in E. \tag{5.5}$$

It is easy to see that if $k = 1$, then this problem reduces to the traditional minimum (s, t)-cut problem in undirected graphs. Unfortunately, the more general problem is NP-hard [DJP$^+$94], and hence, we shall consider approximation algorithms for it. Just as the optimization algorithm for the minimum (s, t)-cut is based on solving a maximum (single-commodity) flow problem, we shall derive an approximation algorithm for the multicut problem that is based on solving a maximum multicommodity flow problem, which is dual to it.

The *maximum multicommodity flow problem* is as follows: given an undirected graph $G = (V, E)$, where each edge $e \in E$ has an associated positive capacity $c(e)$, and k pairs of terminal vertices, (s_i, t_i), $i = 1, \ldots, k$, assign a flow value $f(P)$ to each path $P \in \mathcal{P}_i$, $i = 1, \ldots, k$, so that, for each edge $e \in E$, the total flow value assigned to paths that contain this edge is at most $c(e)$. The aim is to maximize the total flow between all of the given pairs of vertices. Let $\mathcal{P}_i(e)$ denote the set of all paths between s_i and t_i that contain edge e; that is, $\mathcal{P}_i(e) = \{P : e \in P, P \in \mathcal{P}_i\}$, $i = 1, \ldots, k$. This problem can be formulated as the following linear programming problem:

$$\text{maximize} \quad \sum_{i=1}^{k} \sum_{P \in \mathcal{P}_i} f(P) \tag{5.6}$$

subject to

$$\sum_{i=1}^{k} \sum_{e \in \mathcal{P}_i(e)} f(P) \leq c(e), \qquad \text{for each } e \in E, \tag{5.7}$$

$$f(P) \geq 0, \qquad \text{for each } P \in \mathcal{P}_i, i = 1, \ldots, k. \tag{5.8}$$

Note that in this case, we do not require that the variables be restricted to integer values, i.e., it is a linear programming problem, not an integer linear programming problem.

The reader should note that the same input is required for both the maximum multi-commodity flow problem and the minimum multicut problem. We shall argue next that, for any such input, if we consider any multicut and any feasible multicommodity flow, then the total flow value is at most the cost of the multicut; that is, the weak duality theorem for single-commodity case generalizes to this setting. Consider any unit of flow that uses the path P between s_i and t_i. The multicut must contain at least one of edges in this path P. As in the single-commodity case, we can view the total cost of a cut as the capacity of this cut. Thus, each unit of flow of the total multicommodity flow "uses up" at least one unit of the total capacity of the multicut, which implies the claim. Hence, we have obtained the following weak duality theorem.

LEMMA 5.1   For any input to the maximum multicommodity flow and the minimum multicut problems, the total flow value of any feasible flow is at most the cost of any multicut.

5.2.2   FRACTIONAL MULTICUTS, PIPE SYSTEMS, AND A STRONG DUALITY THEOREM

Garg, Vazirani, and Yannakakis [GVY96] give an approximation algorithm for the minimum multicut problem that first solves the linear relaxation of (5.3)-(5.5), in which the constraints (5.5) are replaced by

$$x(e) \geq 0, \qquad \text{for each } e \in E, \tag{5.9}$$

and then uses this optimal *fractional multicut* to guide the search for a good (integer) multicut. Consequently, it is useful to have a good understanding of this linear relaxation.

Feasible solutions to the linear relaxation (5.4) and (5.9) have a natural physical interpretation. For each edge $e \in E$, one can view its decision variable $x(e)$ as specifying the length of edge e. From this perspective, the constraints (5.4) can be described as requiring that the edge lengths have the following property: for each path P between s_i and t_i, the total length of P is at least 1. Equivalently, we could require that the length of the shortest path between s_i and t_i is at least 1. What physical interpretation does this imply for the objective function? The contribution of each edge $e \in E$ to the objective function is $c(e)$ times its length. Suppose that we view the graph as a system of pipes, where the edges correspond to the pipes themselves, and the vertices correspond to junction points at which the pipes meet. In this case, if we interpret $c(e)$ as the cross-section area of the pipe corresponding to the edge e, then $c(e)$ times its length is exactly equal to the volume of this pipe, and the overall objective function is the total volume of the pipe system. So the linear relaxation is to find the minimum-volume pipe system for the input in which s_i and t_i are at least 1 unit apart from each other, for each $i = 1, \ldots, k$.

The linear program for the maximum multicommodity flow problem, (5.6)-(5.8), is the dual linear program of minimum fractional multicut problem, (5.3), (5.4), and (5.9). To reinforce our intuition about these linear programs, we shall argue directly that any feasible length function for the pipe system gives an upper bound on the total value of any feasible multicommodity flow. Consider any unit of flow that uses the path P between s_i and t_i. This unit of flow "uses up" $\sum_{e \in P} x(e)$ units of volume. However, we have constrained this sum to be at least 1; that is, each unit of flow sent between an (s_i, t_i) pair consumes at least one unit of volume. Hence, the total flow value is at most the total volume of the pipe system. Of course, the strong duality theorem of linear programming states that the optimal value of the primal is equal to the optimal value of the dual, provided that an optimal solution exists (see, for example, Chvátal [Chv83]); hence, the minimum feasible pipe-system volume is equal to the total value of the maximum multicommodity flow.

5.2.3   SOLVING THE LINEAR PROGRAMS

We have already indicated that the approximation algorithm of Garg, Vazirani, and Yannakakis will first find an optimal fractional multicut. As presently stated, this might appear to be a daunting task, since the size of this linear program is exponential. However, we shall argue that one can still find an optimal solution in polynomial time, and that there are a number of approaches to doing so.

Perhaps the simplest approach is to observe that both the minimum fractional multicut problem and the maximum multicommodity flow problems have equivalent formulations that are of polynomial size. We first consider the maximum multicommodity flow problem. We define a flow variable $f_i(e)$ for each commodity $i = 1, \dots, k$, and each edge $e \in E$. For each vertex $v \in V - \{s_i, t_i\}$, we require that the total flow of commodity i into v is equal to the total flow of commodity i out of vertex v. For each edge $e \in E$, we require that the total flow (in both directions) on e over all commodities is at most $c(e)$. The total flow of commodity i is computed by considering the net flow of commodity i out of vertex s_i, and the objective function is, as before, the sum of these totals over all commodities.

It is not hard to show that this more compact linear program is equivalent to (5.6)-(5.8). The more compact version has $O(km)$ variables and $O(m + kn)$ constraints, and hence, can be solved in polynomial time using any polynomial-time linear programming algorithm (e.g., that of Khachiyan [Kha79] or Karmarkar [Kar84]). Furthermore, this optimal solution can be converted, in polynomial time, to an optimal solution to the linear program (5.6)-(5.8) by standard "flow decomposition" methods (see, e.g., Ahuja, Magnanti, and Orlin [AMO93]). Hence, we can find an optimal solution to the maximum multicommodity flow problem in polynomial time.

If we consider the dual linear program of this more compact formulation of the maximum multicommodity flow, then we obtain a linear program equivalent to (5.3), (5.4), and (5.9). In fact, we can easily compute an optimal pipe system from the optimal primal and dual solutions to the compact formulation: set $x(e)$, the length of edge e, to be the optimal value to the dual variable corresponding to the primal constraint so that the total flow on edge e is at most $c(e)$.

Another option is to rely on the nature of the first polynomial-time algorithm for linear programming, the ellipsoid algorithm. One of the most important features of this algorithm is that in order to obtain a polynomial-time algorithm for a linear program with an exponential number of constraints, we need only provide a polynomial-time subroutine that, given a solution x, either proves that x is feasible, or else finds a violated constraint (see, for example, Grötschel, Lovász, and Schrijver [GLS88]). This subroutine is said to solve the *separation problem* for this linear program. For the minimum fractional multicut problem, given by (5.3), (5.4), and (5.9), the subroutine required is just a shortest-path procedure: we need to verify that the length (with respect to x) of the shortest path between s_i and t_i is at least 1, for each $i = 1, \ldots, k$. Either we have identified an (s_i, t_i) pair for which the length of the shortest path is less than 1, in which case this shortest path corresponds to a violated constraint, or else we have shown that the current length function is feasible. Hence, the ellipsoid algorithm can be used to solve our (exponential-sized) linear program in polynomial time.

Finally, we will see that a nearly-optimal length function would work essentially as well in finding a good multicut. There has been a sequence of results obtained in designing fully polynomial approximation schemes for the maximum concurrent flow problem and other related problems. The goal of this line of research is to design algorithms that take advantage of the combinatorial structure of these problems (as opposed to a general purpose LP algorithm) in order to obtain more efficient algorithms, albeit with the disadvantage of finding solutions of objective function value within a factor of $(1 + \epsilon)$ of optimal. It is important to note that these approximation schemes are for problems that are solvable in polynomial time. Since we are losing a logarithmic factor in finding a multicut from the LP solution, it makes sense to relax our aim to finding a near-optimal LP solution, especially since this appears to be an easier computational problem.

Shahrokhi and Matula [SM90] have proposed a combinatorial algorithm for a rather special case of the maximum concurrent flow problem that delivers a flow of objective function value within a factor of $(1 + \epsilon)$ of optimal in time bounded by a polynomial in the size of the graph and $1/\epsilon$. The key to analyzing the running time of this algorithm is an exponential potential function, which has been the basis for several subsequent papers as well. Klein, Plotkin, Stein, and Tardos [KPST94] and Leighton, Makedon, Plotkin, Stein, Tardos, and Tragoudas [LMP+95] subsequently improved and extended this result to derive an algorithm for the maximum concurrent flow problem for which the running time for a k-commodity problem is competitive with the running time for k single-commodity maximum flow computations. This was generalized by Plotkin, Shmoys, and Tardos [PST95] to yield a fully polynomial approximation scheme for a wide range of combinatorially defined linear programming problems, called *fractional packing and covering problems*. Results similar to those in [PST95] were independently obtained by Grigoriadis and Khachiyan [GK94].

We will explain the main ideas behind the framework proposed in [PST95] and show how it can be applied to the problem of computing a maximum multicommodity flow. A *fractional packing problem* is a linear programming problem of the following form: for a given matrix $A \in \Re^{m \times n}$ and vector $b \in \Re^m$, we wish to minimize λ subject to $Az \le \lambda b$, $z \in Q$, where Q is a polytope such that $Az \ge 0$ for each $z \in Q$. The idea of the algorithm is that Q is supposed to represent "easy" constraints, and that $Az \le \lambda b$ are supposed to represent "complicating" constraints. The sense in which Q is "easy" is that the algorithm assumes that there is a fast subroutine that, given a positive row vector $y \in \Re^m$, computes $z^* = \mathrm{argmin}\{cz : z \in Q\}$, where $c = yA$.

Before explaining the ideas underlying this algorithm, we will first show how to cast the maximum multicommodity flow problem in this setting. We will perform a bisection search for the maximum value f such that there is feasible flow of total value f. We will work from the exponential linear programming formulation (5.6)-(5.8). The objective function (5.6) has been transformed into a constraint that the total flow value is exactly equal to f. The polytope Q is the set of solutions satisfying this total flow constraint as well as the non-negativity constraints (5.8); note that this is just a rescaled simplex. The constraints $Az \leq \lambda b$ correspond to the capacity constraints (5.7), where λ reflects the amount by which the capacities need to be multiplied so as to ensure that z is a feasible flow. Thus, for a candidate flow value f, we must decide if the optimum λ^* is at most 1. If we can approximate λ within a factor of $(1 + \epsilon)$, then we can also approximate the optimal flow value within a factor of $(1 + \epsilon)$.

Finally, we need to provide the subroutine to optimize over Q. There always exists an optimal solution at one of its extreme points; each extreme point of Q has exactly one coordinate set equal to f, and the rest set equal to 0. Hence, an optimal solution can be found by determining the smallest objective coefficient and setting the corresponding co-ordinate to f. In this setting, each coordinate of y corresponds to the capacity constraint of one edge $e \in E$. The vector yA specifies the objective function coefficients, and the coordinate of yA corresponding to the flow variable $f(P)$ has value equal to $\sum_{e \in P} y(e)$. Hence, we wish to find the coordinate, or equivalently the path between some (s_i, t_i) pair, for which the total edge length (with respect to the lengths y) is smallest. This can be done, for example, by Dijkstra's algorithm, starting at each source node $s_i, i = 1, \ldots, k$, and then choosing the minimum-length path found over all k computations. Hence, the maximum multicommodity flow problem can be cast into the framework of [PST95].

The main idea of the algorithm of [PST95] is as follows: iteratively maintain a solution z (or in our case, a flow of value f). This solution is feasible for some choice of λ, and we wish to change z so that the corresponding minimal choice of λ decreases over the execution of the algorithm. In our application, λ can be viewed as the minimum value so that the current flow is feasible with respect to the *adjusted capacities* $\lambda c(e)$. For the current solution (z, λ), we wish to focus on the constraints $Az \leq \lambda b$ that are most important in determining λ; in the flow setting, these correspond to the edges e that are saturated, or nearly saturated, to their adjusted capacity. For each of these constraints, we wish to perturb the current z so as to reduce the value of the left-hand side; in our example, the total flow on each nearly saturated edge should be reduced. In our particular case, one way to do this would be to find a $s_i - t_i$ path for which none of the edges is nearly saturated, increase the flow on that path, and decrease the flow on all other paths (uniformly) so that once again the total flow value is f. Instead, the algorithm selects a path as follows: for each edge e, we set $y(e) = (1/c(e)) \cdot \exp(\alpha f(e)/c(e))$, where $f(e)$ denotes the total flow on e in the current solution and α is a parameter that is proportional to $1/\lambda$; then compute a shortest $s_i - t_i$ path with respect to these lengths $y(e)$. Observe that this approach can be viewed as a continuous version of the path selection rule described above: short edge lengths correspond to undersaturated edges. In general, we compute $y_i = (1/b_i) \cdot \exp(\alpha a_i z/b_i)$, where a_i is the ith row of A, compute $z^* = \text{argmin}\{yAz : z \in Q\}$, and set $z = (1 - \sigma)z + \sigma z^*$, where $0 < \sigma < 1$ is a parameter set by the algorithm.

The analysis of the running time of the algorithm is based on showing that each iteration decreases the exponential potential function $\Phi = \sum_i \exp(\alpha a_i z/b_i)$. The overall running time depends on the *width* ρ of the formulation, which is the minimum λ such that *every* $z \in Q$ is feasible: $\rho = \max_{z \in Q} \max_i a_i z/b_i$. Plotkin, Shmoys, and Tardos show that $O(\rho \epsilon^{-2} \log(m\epsilon^{-1}))$ iterations suffice to find a solution within a factor of $(1 + \epsilon)$ of optimal, where m denotes the number of rows in A.

The width of the formulation proposed above for the maximum multicommodity flow is at most $\max_e f/c(e)$; if there are small capacity edges, then this quantity can be quite large. However, if we delete all edges of capacity at most $\epsilon f/m$, then the resulting width is at most m/ϵ. Furthermore, by modifying the instance in this way we can change the optimum by at most a further $(1+\epsilon)$ factor. The subroutine required for each iteration is nothing more than k shortest path computations, and so if we ignore log factors and set ϵ to a constant, we get an overall running time of $\tilde{O}(km^2)$. Significantly, by rescaling y, we can also show that the algorithm produces a near-optimal solution x for the linear program (5.3), (5.4), and (5.9), or in other words, a near-optimal fractional multicut. Finally, we should note that there exist more sophisticated approaches to formulate the maximum multicommodity flow problem as fractional packing problem, which lead to improved running times, but we shall instead discuss these ideas in the context of the maximum concurrent flow in Section 5.3.

5.2.4   FINDING A GOOD MULTICUT

Garg, Vazirani, and Yannakakis [GVY96] gave an algorithm that takes as input a pipe system of volume ϕ, and computes a multicut of cost $O(\log k)\phi$. If we start with the optimal pipe system of volume ϕ^*, since ϕ^* is a lower bound on the minimum-cost multicut, the resulting algorithm is an $O(\log k)$-approximation algorithm.

Next we describe the algorithm Pipe-Cut of Garg, Vazirani, and Yannakakis, which is summarized in Figure 5.2.

The algorithm iteratively produces the desired multicut. At the start of iteration l, the Pipe-Cut has already produced a sequence of disjoint sets of vertices $V_1, \ldots, V_{l-1}$, with the property that, for each $j = 1, \ldots, l-1$, the set V_j contains at most one of s_i and t_i, for each $i = 1, \ldots, k$; furthermore, for each set V_j we have specified one commodity $i(j)$, such that the set V_j contains exactly one of the terminals $s_{i(j)}$ and $t_{i(j)}$. Let $\bar{V} = V - (V_1 \cup \cdots \cup V_{l-1})$, and consider the graph induced by $\bar{V}$ and its corresponding pipe system. If there does not exist a commodity i such that both s_i and t_i are in $\bar{V}$, then we have found a multicut: $\{e \in E : e = (u, v), u \in V_j, v \in V_{j'}, j \neq j'\}$, where $V_l = \bar{V}$, and this is the desired output. Otherwise, select any commodity i such that both s_i and

---

> **procedure** Pipe-Cut(G, x)
> { we shall assume that $x(e)$ is given as a fraction with denominator at most Δ }
> $\bar{V} \leftarrow V(G); \quad l \leftarrow 0; \quad \epsilon \leftarrow 1/(2\Delta^2);$
> **repeat**
>   fix i such that $\{s_i, t_i\} \subseteq \bar{V}$;
> $r^* = \operatorname{argmin}\{C_x(s_i, r)/V_x(s_i, r) : r = dist_x(s_i, v) - \epsilon, v \in \bar{V}\};$
> $l \leftarrow l+1; V_l \leftarrow B_x(s_i, r^*); \bar{V} \leftarrow \bar{V} - V_l;$
> **until** $|\{s_i, t_i\} \cap \bar{V}| \leq 1$, for each $i = 1, \ldots, k$;
> **output** $(V_1, V_2, \ldots, V_l, \bar{V})$.

FIGURE 5.2

The algorithm Pipe-Cut.

t_i are in $\bar{V}$. In this iteration we find a particular subset $V_l \subset \bar{V}$ such that exactly one of s_i and t_i are in V_l, and hence, we can set $i(l) = i$.

Before describing the details of the remainder of this iteration, we first introduce some notation. Let $B_x(s_i, r)$ denote the set of vertices that are contained within a ball of radius r centered at vertex s_i in the pipe system, where the distances are given with respect to the length function x. Figure 5.3 gives an example of a portion of a pipe system and ball centered at one of its vertices. More formally, let $dist_x(u, v)$ denote length of the shortest path between vertices u and v with respect to the length function x, and, for each $v \in V$, set

$$B_x(v, r) = \{u \in V : dist_x(u, v) \le r\}. \tag{5.10}$$

We shall define the part of the pipe system that is within radius r of s_i in the following way: first, we include each pipe that corresponds to an edge with both of its endpoints in $B_x(s_i, r)$; second, for each edge with exactly one endpoint in $B_x(s_i, r)$, we include the fraction of the corresponding pipe that is still within a distance r of s_i; finally, we will add a "point volume" at s_i of volume ϕ / k. More formally, the volume of the pipe system within radius r of vertex s_i is defined to be

$$V_x(s_i, r) = \phi / k + \sum_{u, v \in B_x(v, r)} c(u, v)x(u, v) + \sum_{(u, v) \in \bar{\delta}(B_x(s_i, r))} c(u, v)(r - dist_x(v, u)), \tag{5.11}$$

where $\bar{\delta} = \{(u, v) \in E : u \in B_x(s_i, r) \text{ and } v \in \bar{V} - B_x(s_i, r)\}$.

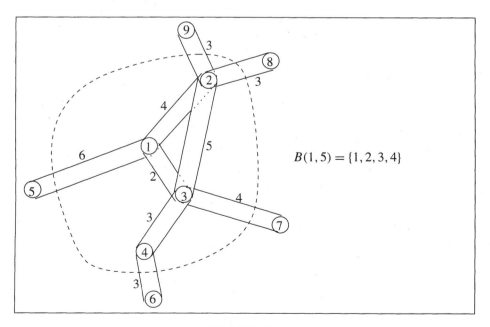

$$B(1, 5) = \{1, 2, 3, 4\}$$

FIGURE 5.3

A pipe system and a ball of radius 5 centered at vertex 1.

We shall set $V_l = B_x(s_i, r)$ for a judicious choice of radius r. Let the cost

$$C_x(s_i, r) = \sum_{(u,v) \in \delta(B_x(s_i, r))} c(u, v). \qquad (5.12)$$

We shall choose the radius r to be a value less than $1/2$ such that $C_x(s_i, r)/V_x(s_i, r)$ is sufficiently small. More precisely, to guarantee the claimed performance, we need only choose a radius $r = \rho_l$ for which this ratio is at most $2 \ln 2k$; in fact, it is possible to choose the radius essentially minimizing this ratio, and the minimum will be guaranteed to be this small.

We shall see that it is easy to find a good choice for ρ_l, but first we will prove a few useful facts about the function $V_x(s_i, r)$ (as a function of r). If there does not exist a vertex v such that $dist_x(s_i, v) = r$, then this function is differentiable at r, and its derivative is equal to the total cost of the cut defined by the current radius r, $C_x(s_i, r)$. The function might not even be continuous at these breakpoints corresponding to vertices in $\bar{V}$, but it is an increasing function of r nonetheless. Furthermore, the cost $C_x(s_i, r)$ changes only at these breakpoints. Hence, if we want to minimize the cost per volume ratio, this minimum is achieved as the radius approaches one of these breakpoints. Since the algorithm depends on the radius only in selecting $V_l = B_x(s_i, \rho_l)$, we need only set ρ_l to a value sufficiently close to the limiting point.

There are two main points in analyzing the performance of the algorithm Pipe-Cut. The first step is to show that the algorithm does produce a feasible multicut. This is quite simple, since we must only prove that the set V_l contains at most one terminal for each commodity. To prove this, we observe that the feasibility of the length function implies that, for each commodity i, its two terminals s_i and t_i are at least distance 1 apart from each other. However, we set V_l to be a ball of radius less than $1/2$, and the distance between any two points within it must be less than 1. The second main point is to show that $C_x(s_i, \rho_l)/V_x(s_i, \rho_l) \leq 2 \ln 2k$, and then show that this implies the claimed performance for the algorithm.

For notational simplicity, let $f(r) = V_x(s_i, r)$. Recall that

$$C_x(s_i, r) = \frac{\partial V_x(s_i, r)}{\partial r} = \frac{df}{dr},$$

whenever the derivative is well-defined. Suppose that for each radius r within the interval $(0, 1/2)$, the ratio $C_x(s_i, r)/V_x(s_i, r) > 2 \ln 2k$. If we consider any interval (r_1, r_2) throughout which $f(r)$ is differentiable, we have that $f'(r)/f(r) > 2 \ln 2k$, or equivalently, that

$$\frac{d}{dr}(\ln f(r)) > 2 \ln 2k.$$

If we integrate both sides, we see that this implies that

$$\ln f(r_2) - \ln f(r_1) > (r_2 - r_1)(2 \ln 2k). \qquad (5.13)$$

If f were differentiable throughout the interval $(0, 1/2)$, (5.13) would imply that

$$\ln(f(1/2)/f(0)) > \ln 2k;$$

that is, $f(1/2) > 2kf(0) = 2\phi$. But this is impossible, since the total volume in the pipe system, including the additional point volume, is at most $(1 + 1/k)\phi$, and hence, $f(1/2)$ cannot exceed this value. Of course, f might not be differentiable throughout the interval $(0, 1/2)$. We can apply the same trick to each interval throughout which f is differentiable. By combining the results of these integrals, along with the fact that f does not decrease at any of the breakpoints, we can still conclude that $\ln f(1/2) - \ln f(0) > \ln 2k$, which is not possible. Hence, we have shown the following lemma:

LEMMA 5.2   There exists a radius $r < 1/2$, such that $C_x(s_i, r)/V_x(s_i, r) \leq 2\ln 2k$.

Finally, we must bound the total cost of the multicut found by the algorithm Pipe-Cut. Consider some edge (u, v) for which $u \in V_j$, $v \in V_{j'}$, $j \leq j'$. The cost of this edge, $c(u, v)$, is included in the sum $C_x(s_{i(j)}, \rho_j)$. Thus, we can upper bound the cost of the multicut found by the algorithm by $\sum_j C_x(s_{i(j)}, \rho_j)$. By Lemma 5.2, for each iteration j we have that $C_x(s_{i(j)}, \rho_j) \leq 2\ln(2k) V_x(s_{i(j)}, \rho_j)$. If we consider the balls $B_x(s_{i(j)}, \rho_j)$ found in each iteration, they each have an associated volume that corresponds to disjoint portions of the original pipe system. The total volume in the original pipe system is at most 2ϕ: there were ϕ units of volume originally, and at most k point volumes, each of volume ϕ/k, that are added throughout the course of the algorithm. Hence, the cost of the multicut is no more than

$$\sum_j 2\ln(2k) V_x(s_{i(j)}, \rho_j) \leq 4\ln(2k)\phi,$$

and we have obtained the result of Garg, Vazirani, and Yannakakis [GVY96].

THEOREM 5.1   The algorithm Pipe-Cut, when applied to an optimal fractional multicut x^*, is a $4\ln(2k)$-approximation algorithm for the minimum multicut problem.

Since we have shown that there always exists a multicut of cost at most $4\ln(2k)$ times the cost of the optimal fraction multicut, we have also proved the following approximate max-flow min-cut theorem for multicommodity flow.

COROLLARY 5.1   For any instance with k terminal pairs, the cost of the minimum multicut is always at least the maximum multicommodity flow value, and is always at most $O(\log k)$ times as much.

SPARSEST CUTS AND MAXIMUM CONCURRENT FLOW

5.3

In this section we will present approximation algorithms for the sparsest cut problem for undirected graphs; these algorithms will also play a central role in the design of approximation algorithms for the balanced cut problem.

5.3.1   THE SPARSEST CUT PROBLEM

In the *sparsest cut problem*, we are given an undirected graph $G = (V, E)$, where there is a positive cost $c(e)$ associated with each edge $e \in E$, and k pairs of vertices (s_i, t_i), $i = 1, \ldots, k$, where there is a positive demand $d(i)$ for the commodity corresponding to (s_i, t_i). For each subset of nodes $S \subseteq V$, let $I(S)$ indicate those terminal pairs that are disconnected by deleting the edges in $\delta(S) = \{(u, v) \in E : u \in S, \ v \notin S\}$; more formally, $I(S) = \{i : |S \cap \{s_i, t_i\}| = 1\}$. The *sparsity ratio* of the set S, $\rho(S)$, is the ratio of the total cost of the edges connecting S with $V - S$ to the total demand separated by this cut:

$$\rho(S) = \frac{\sum_{e \in \delta(S)} c(e)}{\sum_{i \in I(S)} d(i)}.$$

We wish to find the set S for which $\rho(S)$ is minimum. Observe that the definition of the sparsity ratio of a cut captures the fact that in some settings we might be most interested in "getting our money's worth" (in that we are willing to pay more for a cut if it succeeds in disconnecting a greater amount of the demand). Figure 5.4 illustrates these notions for a particular instance.

Although we have defined the sparsity ratio of a cut in terms of a subset of vertices, we can instead view a cut as a subset of edges whose deletion disconnects the graph. We can extend the notion of sparsity ratio to apply to a subset of edges F whose deletion leaves a graph with more than two connected components. Let $\mathcal{S} = \{S_1, S_2, \ldots, S_c\}$ be

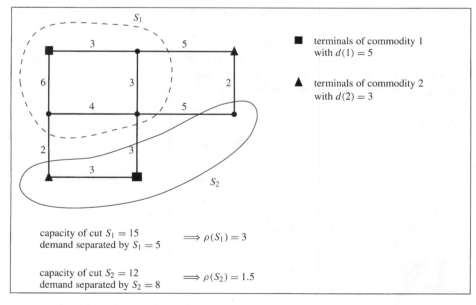

FIGURE 5.4

Illustrating the sparsity ratio of a cut.

a partition of V such that each S_j denotes the vertex set of a connected component in $\bar{G} = (V, E - F)$. Let $I(S)$ denote the set of terminal pairs that are disconnected by S: $\{i : s_i \in S_j, \ t_i \in S_k, \ j \neq k\}$. The sparsity ratio of S is then

$$\rho(S) = \frac{\sum_{e \in F} c(e)}{\sum_{i \in I(S)} d(i)}.$$

The following proposition merely asserts that an average cannot be less than the minimum of its components.

PROPOSITION 5.1 For any non-negative integers, $a_1, \ldots, a_n$, and positive integers, $b_1, \ldots, b_n$, $\min_{i=1,\ldots,n} a_i/b_i \leq (\sum_{i=1}^n a_i)/(\sum_{i=1}^n b_i)$.

Applying this to our setting, we obtain the following lemma:

LEMMA 5.3 Let $S = \{S_1, S_2, \ldots, S_c\}$ be a partition of V such that each S_j, $j = 1, \ldots, c$, denotes the vertex set of a connected component in $\bar{G} = (V, E - F)$. Then,

$$\min_{j=1,\ldots,c} \rho(S_j) \leq \rho(S).$$

This lemma implies that we can find a good set of edges to delete without concern for the number of connected components in the remaining graph (provided that it is at least two). Furthermore, it implies that we can obtain a simple (non-linear) integer programming formulation of the sparsest cut problem. We let $x(e), e \in E$ be a 0-1 variable that indicates whether edge e is cut, and let $y(i), i = 1, \ldots, k$, be a 0-1 variable that indicates whether commodity i is disconnected by this cut. As in the previous section, let $\mathcal{P}_i$ denote the set of paths between s_i and t_i, $i = 1, \ldots, k$.

minimize
$$\frac{\sum_{e \in E} c(e)x(e)}{\sum_{i=1}^k d(i)y(i)} \tag{5.14}$$

subject to

$$\sum_{e \in P} x(e) \geq y(i), \qquad \text{for each } P \in \mathcal{P}_i, \ i = 1, \ldots, k, \tag{5.15}$$

$$y(i) \in \{0, 1\}, \qquad \text{for each } i = 1, \ldots, k, \tag{5.16}$$

$$x(e) \in \{0, 1\}, \qquad \text{for each } e \in E. \tag{5.17}$$

Consider the relaxation of this formulation in which constraints (5.16) and (5.17) are replaced by $y(i) \geq 0$, $i = 1, \ldots, k$, and $x(e) \geq 0$, $e \in E$, respectively. First, observe that if (x, y) is a feasible fractional solution, then for any constant $\alpha > 0$, the solution $(\alpha x, \alpha y)$ is also feasible, and the two solutions have equal objective function value. Consequently, it is without loss of generality that we have not constrained each variable to be at most 1. Furthermore, we can choose a normalization of the variables by requiring that $\sum_{i=1}^k d(i)y(i) = 1$, and by doing this, we have obtained the following linear programming relaxation of the sparsest cut problem:

minimize $\quad \displaystyle\sum_{e \in E} c(e)x(e)$

$\qquad\qquad\qquad\qquad\qquad\qquad\qquad\qquad\qquad\qquad\qquad\qquad$ (5.18)

subject to

$$\sum_{i=1}^{k} d(i)y(i) = 1, \qquad\qquad\qquad\qquad\qquad\qquad\qquad (5.19)$$

$$\sum_{e \in P} x(e) \geq y(i), \qquad\quad \text{for each } P \in \mathcal{P}_i, \ i = 1, \ldots, k, \qquad (5.20)$$

$$y(i) \geq 0, \qquad\quad \text{for each } i = 1, \ldots, k, \qquad\qquad (5.21)$$

$$x(e) \geq 0, \qquad\quad \text{for each } e \in E. \qquad\qquad\qquad (5.22)$$

This linear program can be solved in polynomial time; we defer further discussion of this until Section 5.3.5

Rao [Rao87] focused attention on the sparsest cut problem, and showed its importance in computing a balanced cut (albeit only in the context of planar graphs). Leighton and Rao [LR88] considered arbitrary graphs, but restricted attention to the case in which there is a commodity for each pair of vertices, and each demand $d(i) = 1$. For this case, they showed how to construct a cut of sparsity ratio within a $O(\log n)$ factor of the optimal value of the linear relaxation. Klein, Rao, Agrawal and Ravi [KRAR95] considered the general case, and gave an $O(\log C \log D)$-approximation algorithm, where C denotes the sum of the edge costs in the graph and D denotes the total demand; Tragoudas [Tra91] subsequently improved this performance guarantee to $O(\log n \log D)$. Kahale [Kah93] showed how to obtain a bound of $O(\log k \log D)$ by showing, in effect, how to reduce the sparsest cut problem to the minimum multicut problem. Plotkin and Tardos [PT95] gave a sophisticated rounding technique that yields an improved performance guarantee of $O(\log^2 k)$. Finally, work of London, Linial, and Rabinovich [LLR95] and Aumann and Rabani[AR95] led to a much simpler $O(\log k)$-approximation algorithm for the general case, thereby matching the performance of Leighton and Rao for the all-pairs unit-demand problem.

5.3.2   REDUCING THE SPARSEST CUT PROBLEM TO THE MINIMUM MULTICUT PROBLEM

We will show how to use the information given by an optimal fractional solution to (5.18)-(5.22) to construct a sparse cut. We shall actually give two algorithms to do this. In this subsection, we will present the result of Kahale [Kah93], which relies on Theorem 5.1 to produce a cut of sparsity ratio within a factor of $O(\log D \log k)$ of the fractional optimum, where D denotes the total demand $\sum_{i=1}^{k} d(i)$.

The main idea of this algorithm is quite simple. We use the optimal fractional solution (x, y) to identify a particular subset S of the commodities and apply the approximation algorithm of Section 5.2 to find a multicut that separates each commodity in S.

The choice of S will ensure that the multicut found is sparse, and hence, by Lemma 5.3, we find a sparse cut. Let $\bar{D} = \sum_{i \in S} d(i)$ and $y_{\min} = \min_{i \in S} y(i)$. We will choose S such that

$$y_{\min} \geq \frac{1}{\bar{D} \cdot \mathcal{H}(\bar{D})}, \tag{5.23}$$

where $\mathcal{H}(k) = 1 + 1/2 + 1/3 + \cdots + 1/k$ is the kth Harmonic number; it is straightforward to show that $\mathcal{H}(k) \leq \log_e k + 1$. Suppose that we apply the multicut approximation algorithm given in Section 5.2 to the modified instance in which S specifies the terminal pairs that must be separated (and there are no specified demands). Given any feasible fractional solution (x, y) for the sparsest cut relaxation, (5.18)-(5.22), we can construct a solution $\bar{x}(e) = x(e)/y_{\min}$, for each $e \in E$. We shall argue that $\bar{x}$ is a feasible fractional multicut for the modified instance. To see this, observe that the constraints (5.20) imply that

$$\sum_{e \in P} \bar{x}(e) \geq 1, \qquad \text{for each } P \in \mathcal{P}_i,\ i \in S.$$

By (5.23), $\sum_e c(e)\bar{x}(e) \leq \bar{D} \cdot \mathcal{H}(\bar{D}) \cdot (\sum_e c(e)x(e))$; since $\bar{x}$ is a feasible fractional multicut, the cost of the optimal fractional multicut is clearly at most this much. The multicut approximation algorithm of Garg, Vazirani, and Yannakakis produces a multicut S of cost within an $O(\log|S|)$ factor of the optimal fractional solution, and hence, the cost of S is $O(\log k \cdot \bar{D} \cdot \mathcal{H}(\bar{D}) \cdot (\sum_e c(e)x(e)))$. Since S is a multicut that disconnects each terminal pair in S, $\sum_{i \in I(S)} d(i) \geq \sum_{i \in S} d(i) = \bar{D}$; hence, $\rho(S)$ is $O(\log k \cdot \mathcal{H}(\bar{D})) \cdot \sum_e c(e)x(e)$. Since (x, y) is an optimal solution to the linear relaxation (5.18)-(5.22), we see that $\rho(S)$ is within $O(\log k \cdot \mathcal{H}(\bar{D}))$ factor of optimal.

We must still show how to construct the required set S that satisfies (5.23). Assume, without loss of generality, that the commodities are indexed such that $y(1) \geq y(2) \geq \cdots \geq y(k)$. Let $D(j) = \sum_{i=1}^{j} d(i)$. We shall show that there exists j^* such that $y(j^*) \geq 1/(D(j^*) \cdot \mathcal{H}(D))$ and hence, $S = \{1, 2, \ldots, j^*\}$ satisfies (5.23). Suppose, for a contradiction, that

$$y(i) < \frac{1}{D(i)\mathcal{H}(D)}, \qquad \text{for each } i = 1, \ldots, k.$$

This would imply that

$$\sum_{i=1}^{k} d(i)y(i) < \sum_{i=1}^{k} \frac{d(i)}{\mathcal{H}(D) \cdot D(i)}$$

$$= \frac{1}{\mathcal{H}(D)} \sum_{i=1}^{k} \frac{D(i) - D(i-1)}{D(i)}$$

$$\leq \frac{1}{\mathcal{H}(D)} \sum_{i=1}^{k} \sum_{s=D(i-1)+1}^{D(i)} \frac{1}{s}$$

$$= 1,$$

which contradicts (5.19).

5.3.3   EMBEDDINGS AND THE SPARSEST CUT PROBLEM

In this section, we give an improved rounding method due to Linial, London, and Rabinovich [LLR95] and Aumann and Rabani [AR95]; this yields an $O(\log k)$-approximation algorithm for the sparsest cut problem. In Section 5.2, we viewed the fractional multicut x as specifying a length function on the edges. We can similarly interpret the variables x in the linear programming relaxation of the sparsest cut problem; the variable $y(i)$ correspondingly represents the distance between s_i and $t_i, i = 1, \ldots, k$. Suppose that this length function were derived from an embedding of the input graph $G = (V, E)$ in some low-dimensional space with L_1 norm: that is, there is a function $f : V \to \Re^d$ such that $x(e) = \|f(u) - f(v)\|_1$, for each edge $e = (u, v) \in E$, and $y(i) = \|f(s_i) - f(t_i)\|_1$ for each $i = 1, \ldots, k$. We first shall show if such an embedding were achievable, then we could find a cut of sparsity ratio at most $\sum_e c(e)x(e)$; that is, if the optimal fractional solution (x, y) has the property that it can be derived from such an embedding, then, given the embedding, we can find an optimal sparsest cut.

It is, of course, too much to hope for that the optimal length function admits such an embedding. The crux of the approximation algorithm for the sparsest cut problem is an algorithm to find an embedding that roughly corresponds to the distances. The embedding algorithm that we shall give is due to Linial, London, and Rabinovich [LLR95], which is based on a result of Bourgain [Bou85], which gives an exponential algorithm to find an embedding. The application of this embedding algorithm to the sparsest cut problem was discovered by Aumann and Rabani [AR95], based on a preliminary version of [LLR95], and an essentially identical result was independently discovered by Linial, London, and Rabinovich [LLR95], and published together with their embedding algorithm.

LEMMA 5.4   Let (x, y) be a feasible solution to the linear program (5.18)-(5.22) of objective function value α such that there exists a function $f : V \to \Re^d$ with the property that

$$x(e) = \|f(u) - f(v)\|_1, \quad \text{for each } e = (u, v) \in E, \tag{5.24}$$

and

$$y(i) = \|f(s_i) - f(t_i)\|_1, \quad \text{for each } i = 1, \ldots, k. \tag{5.25}$$

Then, given f, one can find a cut S of sparsity ratio $\rho(S)$ at most α in polynomial time.

Proof.   We first try to understand some simple consequences of the existence of the embedding f. This embedding defines a metric μ on the set of vertices V: that is, for each pair of vertices $u, v \in V$, we have a value $\mu(u, v) = \|f(u) - f(v)\|_1$, and these values satisfy the triangle inequality: for each $u, v, w \in V, \mu(u, v) + \mu(v, w) \geq \mu(u, w)$. (If $e = (u, v) \in E$, then we shall also use $\mu(e)$ to denote $\mu(u, v)$.) We can also derive a metric corresponding to each subset $S \subseteq V$: let $\mu_S(u, v)$ be 1 if $|\{u, v\} \cup S| = 1$, and 0 otherwise. To see that this defines a metric, observe that for any $u, v, w \in V$, if (u, w) crosses the cut defined by S, then exactly one of (u, v) and (v, w) must also cross this cut.

The crucial property of μ that we shall use is that it is in the cone defined by the cut metrics μ_S: that is, there exists $\lambda_S \geq 0$ such that

$$\mu(u, v) = \sum_{S \subseteq V} \lambda_S \cdot \mu_S(u, v), \quad \text{for each } u, v \in V. \tag{5.26}$$

To show this, we start by considering just the contribution of the first coordinate of our d-dimensional space to μ, $|f_1(u) - f_1(v)|$. Suppose that the vertices of V are indexed $v_1, \ldots, v_n$ such that

$$f_1(v_1) \leq f_1(v_2) \leq \cdots \leq f_1(v_n).$$

Then, for each pair of vertices $v_j, v_{j'}, j > j'$, we can rewrite the contribution of the first coordinate to $\mu(v_j, v_{j'})$ as

$$f_1(v_j) - f_1(v_{j'}) = \sum_{\ell=j'}^{j-1} f_1(v_{\ell+1}) - f_1(v_\ell).$$

Let $S(\ell) = \{v_1, \ldots, v_\ell\}, \ell = 1, \ldots, n$. Note that the term $f_1(v_{\ell+1}) - f_1(v_\ell)$ is included in this sum precisely when the distance, with respect to the metric $\mu_{S(\ell)}$, between v_j and $v_{j'}$ is 1. In other words,

$$f_1(v_j) - f_1(v_{j'}) = \sum_{\ell=1}^{n} (f_1(v_{\ell+1}) - f_1(v_\ell)) \cdot \mu_{S(\ell)}(v_j, v_{j'}).$$

Observe that if $j < j'$, then the right-hand side of this equation still gives $|f_1(v_j) - f_1(v_{j'})|$. Hence, we have shown that the contribution of the first coordinate to μ can be expressed in the claimed form. By repeating this construction for each coordinate and adding them together, we have produced a decomposition of μ satisfying (5.26).

Note that although there are 2^n sets $S \subseteq V$, we have produced a decomposition that uses at most nd sets. Second, we have given an efficient algorithm to produce this decomposition. Finally, it is not hard to show that (5.26) precisely characterizes those metrics that correspond to an embedding in L_1; they are precisely those metrics that lie in the cone defined by the cut metrics, or more simply, the *cut cone*. For much more information on the cut cone, and its relationship to embeddings and multicommodity flows, the reader is referred to the expository paper of Avis and Deza [AvisD91].

However, we shall now see that (5.26) easily implies the lemma. Let $\mu = \sum_{S \in \mathcal{S}} \lambda_S \mu_S$, as in (5.26), where $\lambda_S > 0$ for each $S \in \mathcal{S}$. But then, by substituting $\mu(e)$ for $x(e)$, $\mu(s_i, t_i)$ for $y(i)$, and recalling that (x, y) is feasible, we see that

$$\alpha = \sum_{e \in E} c(e)x(e) = \frac{\sum_{e \in E} c(e) \sum_{S \in \mathcal{S}} \lambda_S \cdot \mu_S(e)}{\sum_{i=1}^{k} d(i) \sum_{S \in \mathcal{S}} \lambda_S \cdot \mu_S(s_i, t_i)} = \frac{\sum_{S \in \mathcal{S}} \lambda_S \sum_{e \in E} c(e)\mu_S(e)}{\sum_{S \in \mathcal{S}} \lambda_S \sum_{i=1}^{k} d(i)\mu_S(s_i, t_i)}.$$

Using the fact that $\mu(S)(u, v) = 1$ exactly when (u, v) crosses the cut defined by S, we see that

$$\alpha = \frac{\sum_{S \in \mathcal{S}} \lambda_S \sum_{e \in \delta(S)} c(e)}{\sum_{S \in \mathcal{S}} \lambda_S \sum_{i \in I(S)} d(i)} \geq \min_{S \in \mathcal{S}} \frac{\sum_{e \in \delta(S)} c(e)}{\sum_{i \in I(S)} d(i)} = \min_{S \in \mathcal{S}} \rho(S),$$

where the inequality follows from Proposition 5.1. Hence, we have shown that one of the cuts $S \in \mathcal{S}$ has sparsity ratio at most α.

The algorithm Embed-Cut, given in Figure 5.5, summarizes this quite trivial procedure to find a good cut, given an embedding.   ∎

---

procedure Embed-Cut(G, f)
{ Each vertex $v \in V(G)$ is embedded at $(f_1(v), \ldots, f_d(v))$ }
$(j^*, \xi^*) \leftarrow \operatorname{argmin}\{\rho(S(j, \xi)) : \xi = f_j(v), v \in V(G), j = 1, \ldots, d\}$;
output $S(j^*, \xi^*) = \{v : f_{j^*}(v) \leq \xi^*\}$.

FIGURE 5.5

The algorithm Embed-Cut.

Finally, it is not hard to show that if there are only two commodities, then there exists an optimal length function (x^*, y^*) for which a suitable embedding f is easy to construct; by applying Lemma 5.4, one obtains the min-max theorem of Hu [Hu63].

5.3.4   FINDING A GOOD EMBEDDING

We can view equations (5.24) and (5.25) as taking an embedding f, and from that embedding, constructing a fractional solution (x, y). This solution is not necessarily feasible, since although (x, y) satisfies constraints (5.20), it need not satisfy (5.19). However, this is not significant, since this is just a question of normalization: if $\sum_i d(i) y(i) = \beta$, then $(x/\beta, y/\beta)$ is a feasible fractional solution; we shall refer to this solution as the one *induced by the embedding* f.

The $O(\log k)$-approximation algorithm for the sparsest cut problem is an immediate corollary of the following result: given any feasible solution (x, y) to (5.19)-(5.22), we can construct an embedding f which induces a feasible fractional solution $(\bar{x}, \bar{y})$ such that $\sum_{e \in E} c(e) \bar{x}(e)$ is $O(\log k) \sum_{e \in E} c(e) x(e)$. The embedding is constructed by a randomized algorithm: that is, for any input, the solution induced by the embedding is sufficiently good with high probability, where the probability depends only on the random choices made by the algorithm, and not on any (probabilistic) assumption about the input. Randomized approximation algorithms are discussed in much greater detail in Chapter 11, and we shall rely on basic tools of analysis that are developed in that chapter. Alternatively, the reader can consult the recent book of Motwani and Raghavan [MR95] for an even more thorough investigation of this area.

Let T denote the set of terminal vertices $\{s_i, t_i : i = 1, \ldots, k\}$; for simplicity of notation, we shall assume that $|T|$ is a power of 2, i.e., $|T| = 2^\tau$. We shall use the notation $dist_x(u, v)$ to denote the length of the shortest path between vertices u and v with respect to the length function x. Furthermore, for any set of vertices $A \subseteq V$, let $dist_x(u, A) = \min_{v \in A} dist_x(u, v)$.

Given a feasible fractional solution (x, y), our embedding will be quite easy to compute. We shall let $L = q \log k$ where q is a constant that will be determined later. The dimension of the embedding is $d = \tau L = O(\log^2 k)$. For $\ell = 1, \ldots, L$, $t = 1, \ldots, \tau$, construct the set $A_{t\ell}$ by choosing $2^{\tau-t} = k/2^t$ points from T uniformly at random with replacement (that is, a given element of T may be selected more than once). The embedding function f is then defined to be

$$f_{t\ell}(v) = dist_x(v, A_{t\ell}), \quad \text{for each } v \in V. \tag{5.27}$$

We first state the two key lemmas, show how they imply that the embedding is good, and then give their proofs.

LEMMA 5.5   For each edge $e = (u, v)$, $\|f(u) - f(v)\|_1 \leq d \cdot x(e)$.

LEMMA 5.6   With probability at least $1/2$,

$$\|f(s_i) - f(t_i)\|_1 \geq L \cdot y(i)/88, \quad \text{for each } i = 1, \ldots, k. \tag{5.28}$$

Since it is easy to check if a particular embedding f satisfies (5.28), we can arbitrarily increase the probability of success by repeatedly constructing independent embeddings. Furthermore, by iterating until an embedding satisfying (5.28) is found, we can obtain a Las Vegas-style algorithm, where the performance is guaranteed, and the expected running time is polynomial.

We can combine Lemmas 5.5 and 5.6 in the obvious way. We focus on the case in which f satisfies the property (5.28). In this case,

$$\sum_{i=1}^{k} d(i)\|f(s_i) - f(t_i)\|_1 = \Omega\left(\log k \sum_{i=1}^{k} d(i)y(i)\right) = \Omega(\log k). \tag{5.29}$$

On the other hand, Lemma 5.5 implies that

$$\sum_{(u,v)=e\in E} c(e)\|f(u) - f(v)\|_1 = O(\log^2 k) \sum_{e\in E} c(e)x(e). \tag{5.30}$$

Combining these two equations, we get the following theorem:

THEOREM 5.2   With probability at least $1/2$, the embedding f induces a feasible fractional solution $(\bar{x}, \bar{y})$ of objective function value

$$\sum_{e\in E} c(e)\bar{x}(e) = O(\log k) \sum_{e\in E} c(e)x(e).$$

By applying this theorem starting with an optimal solution (x, y) to the linear program (5.18)-(5.22), we obtain the following corollary.

COROLLARY 5.2   There is a randomized polynomial-time algorithm that, with probability at least $1/2$, computes a cut of sparsity ratio within an $O(\log k)$ factor of optimal.

As we observed above, it is possible to verify efficiently if the embedding found is sufficiently good, and hence, we can obtain an improved algorithm for which the performance guarantee holds with high probability; furthermore, by running the embedding algorithm until a good one is found, we obtain a randomized algorithm that runs in polynomial expected time, and is guaranteed to produce a cut of sparsity ratio within an $O(\log k)$ factor of optimal.

Linial, London, and Rabinovich and, independently, Garg [Gar95] have subsequently shown that, like many other randomized algorithms whose analysis is based on Chernoff-type calculations, this algorithm can be derandomized. However, this deterministic version does not simply follow from an application of standard derandomization techniques to this algorithm; we shall omit the details.

THEOREM 5.3   There is a deterministic polynomial-time $O(\log k)$-approximation algorithm for the sparsest cut problem.

We now return to the proofs of Lemmas 5.5 and 5.6.

Proof of Lemma 5.5.   This is quite straightforward to show. For any set $A \subseteq V$ and edge $(u, v) = e \in E$,

$$dist_x(u, A) \le x(e) + dist_x(v, A).$$

Equivalently, we have that

$$dist_x(u, A) - dist_x(v, A) \le x(e).$$

By the same argument, we see that

$$dist_x(v, A) - dist_x(u, A) \le x(e).$$

By definition,

$$\|f(u) - f(v)\|_1 = \sum_{t,\ell} |f_{t\ell}(u) - f_{t\ell}(v)| = \sum_{t,\ell} |dist_x(u, A_{t\ell}) - dist_x(v, A_{t\ell})|.$$

Combining this with the inequalities above, we see that

$$\|f(u) - f(v)\|_1 \le \tau L x(e) = d \cdot x(e).$$

∎

Proof of Lemma 5.6.   This is the crucial observation that drives the embedding-based proof of Bourgain [Bou85] and Linial, London, and Rabinovich [LLR95], and its proof is rather involved.

We first focus on one particular commodity i, and prove that with probability at least $1 - (1/2k)$, $\|f(s_i) - f(t_i)\|_1 = \Omega(L \cdot y(i))$. Before proving this, observe that this claim implies the lemma: the probability that property (5.28) fails to hold is at most k times the probability that it fails for one particular commodity.

For $v \in \{s_i, t_i\}$, let

$$B_x(v, r) = \{w \in T : dist_x(v, w) \le r\},$$

and let

$$B_x^\circ(v, r) = \{w \in T : dist_x(v, w) < r\}.$$

Let $r_0 = 0$, and let r_t be the smallest value of r such that $|B_x(v, r)| \ge 2^t$, for both $v \in \{s_i, t_i\}$. Furthermore, we let $\hat{t}$ denote the smallest value of t for which $r_{\hat{t}} \ge y(i)/4$, and reset $r_{\hat{t}} = y(i)/4$. Observe that since $y(i) \leq dist_x(s_i, t_i)$ (by constraints (5.20)), we have ensured that $B(s_i, r_{\hat{t}})$ and $B(t_i, r_{\hat{t}})$ are disjoint.

To give some intuition of the proof, we wish to show that f embeds s_i and t_i so that they are reasonably far apart as compared to $y(i)$. Since we are computing distances in the L_1 norm, we can prove this by showing that, with sufficiently high probability, each coordinate of f contributes a certain distance to the total distance between s_i and t_i. More precisely, we will show that each of the coordinates $f_{t\ell}$ is likely to contribute a distance $r_t - r_{t-1}$. By summing this over the L choices for ℓ, we get that those coordinates are likely to contribute $\Omega(L(r_t - r_{t-1}))$. By summing this bound for $t = 1, \ldots, \hat{t}$, we get that this sum is $\Omega(Lr_{\hat{t}}) = \Omega(Ly(i))$, which is what we wish to prove.

Observe that $A \cap B_x^{\circ}(s_i, r_t) = \emptyset$ if and only if $dist_x(s_i, A) \geq r_t$; alternatively, we have that $A \cap B_x(t_i, r_{t-1}) \neq \emptyset$ if and only if $dist_x(t_i, A) \leq r_{t-1}$. Thus, if we let $E_{t\ell}, t = 1, \ldots, \hat{t}$, $\ell = 1, \ldots, L$, denote the event that

$$A_{t\ell} \cap B_x^{\circ}(s_i, r_t) = \emptyset \quad \text{and} \quad A_{t\ell} \cap B_x(t_i, r_{t-1}) \neq \emptyset,$$

then $E_{t\ell}$ implies that

$$|f_{t\ell}(s_i) - f_{t\ell}(t_i)| = |dist_x(s_i, A_{t\ell}) - dist_x(t_i, A_{t\ell})| \geq r_t - r_{t-1}.$$

Hence, we are interested in showing that $E_{t\ell}$ is likely to occur. In order to bound this probability, we shall first do some preliminary calculations. Suppose that we are given a ground set X in which there is a specified good subset G and disjoint bad subset B; finally, A is formed by selecting p elements of X independently and uniformly at random from X (with replacement). Then,

$$Pr[A \cap G \neq \emptyset \text{ and } A \cap B = \emptyset] = Pr[A \cap G \neq \emptyset \mid A \cap B = \emptyset] \cdot Pr[A \cap B = \emptyset]$$
$$\geq Pr[A \cap G \neq \emptyset] \cdot Pr[A \cap B = \emptyset],$$

where the last inequality follows from the observation that knowing that the elements of A are not selected from B can only increase the likelihood that they are selected from G. For any subset $Y \subseteq X$, the probability that $A \cap Y = \emptyset$ is $(1 - \frac{|Y|}{|X|})^p$. If $p = |X|/|Y|$, then this bound approaches $1/e$ as p tends to infinity, and is always within the interval $[1/4, 1/e]$ (provided $|X|/|Y| > 1$). More generally, if $p = \beta(|X|/|Y|)$, then the probability that $A \cap Y = \emptyset$ is within the interval $[(1/4)^{\beta}, (1/e)^{\beta}]$.

Now consider the event $E_{t\ell}, t = 1, \ldots, \hat{t}, \ell = 1, \ldots, L$. We can assume without loss of generality that it was the ball around s_i that determined the radius r_t (since otherwise we could interchange s_i and t_i). We can apply the previous probability calculations by setting $A = A_{t\ell}$, $X = T$, $B = B_x^{\circ}(s_i, r_t)$ and $G = B_x(t_i, r_{t-1})$. We have that $p = 2^{\tau-t}$, $|X| = 2^{\tau}$, $|B| < 2^t$ and $|G| \geq 2^{t-1}$; hence, $p < |X|/|B|$ and $p \geq (1/2)|X|/|G|$. This implies that $Pr[A \cap B = \emptyset] \geq 1/4$ and $Pr[A \cap G \neq \emptyset] \geq (1 - (1/e)^{1/2})$. Hence, $Pr[E_{t\ell}] \geq (1 - (1/e)^{1/2})/4 \geq 1/11, t = 1, \ldots, \hat{t}, \ell = 1, \ldots, L$. (It is important to note that the above calculation applies verbatim to the seemingly exceptional case when $t = \hat{t}$.)

If we fix a particular $t = 1, \ldots, \hat{t}$, and define $X_\ell, \ell = 1, \ldots, L$, to be the 0-1 variable that indicates whether (or not) event $E_{t\ell}$ occurs, then we can apply the Chernoff bound to show that $\sum_{\ell=1}^{L} X_\ell$ does not deviate too much from its expectation, which is at least $L/11$. We shall apply this bound in a very crude way, and will pay no attention to optimizing the constants involved. In particular, we shall use the following statement of the

Chernoff bound: if $E[\sum_\ell X_\ell] = \mu$, then

$$Pr[\sum_\ell X_\ell < \mu/2] \leq \exp(-\mu/8).$$

(This follows, for example, from Theorem 4.2 of [MR95].) Since $\mu \geq L/11 = q \log k/11$, we see that if we set q to be, say, 200, then this probability is less than $\frac{1}{(2k)\log(2k)}$. Most importantly, if $\sum_\ell X_\ell \geq L/22$, then we know that for $L/22$ of the components $f_{t\ell}$, $\ell = 1, \ldots, L$, the event $E_{t\ell}$ occurs, and so

$$\sum_{\ell=1}^{L} |f_{t\ell}(s_i) - f_{t\ell}(t_i)| \geq (r_t - r_{t-1})L/22. \tag{5.31}$$

We have shown that for any fixed value of $t = 1, \ldots, \hat{\imath}$, (5.31) fails to hold with probability at most $1/(2k \log(2k))$. Since $\hat{\imath} \leq \log(2k)$, it follows that (5.31) holds for *every* $t = 1, \ldots, \hat{\imath}$, with probability at least $1 - (1/2k)$. But this implies that, with probability at least $1 - (1/2k)$,

$$\sum_{t=1}^{\hat{\imath}} \sum_{\ell=1}^{L} |f_{t\ell}(s_i) - f_{t\ell}(t_i)| \geq \sum_{t=1}^{\hat{\imath}} (r_t - r_{t-1})L/22 = r_{\hat{\imath}} L/22 = y(i)L/88. \tag{5.32}$$

This completes the proof of Lemma 5.6. ∎

5.3.5   THE MAXIMUM CONCURRENT FLOW PROBLEM

We have just seen that one can compute a cut S of sparsity ratio $\rho(S)$ within a factor of $O(\log k)$ of the optimal fractional solution to (5.18)-(5.22). By considering the linear programming dual to this, we can obtain an elegant approximate max-flow-min-cut theorem for multicommodity flow.

The dual of (5.18)-(5.22) is as follows:

maximize α

$$\tag{5.33}$$

subject to

$$\sum_{P \in \mathcal{P}_i} f(P) \geq \alpha d(i), \qquad \text{for each } i = 1, \ldots, k, \tag{5.34}$$

$$\sum_{i=1}^{k} \sum_{P \in \mathcal{P}_i(e)} f(P) \leq c(e), \qquad \text{for each } e \in E, \tag{5.35}$$

$$f(P) \geq 0, \qquad \text{for each } P \in \mathcal{P}_i, i = 1, \ldots, k. \tag{5.36}$$

This problem is called the *maximum concurrent flow*; it is the version of the multicommodity flow problem in which there is a given demand $d(i)$ for each commodity $i = 1, \ldots, k$, and one wishes to maximize the fraction α such that a α fraction of each commodity's demand is met, subject to the joint capacity constraints of the network.

It is straightforward to see that the maximum concurrent flow value, α^* is at most $\rho(S)$, for any cut S, and hence at most the minimum sparsity ratio. If the total cost (or equivalently, capacity) of S is $\bar{C}$, and it disconnects terminal pairs of total demand $\bar{D}$, then if one just focuses on these commodities, the maximum fraction of the demand that can be met is at most $\bar{C}/\bar{D} = \rho(S)$. Since LP duality implies that the maximum concurrent flow value is exactly equal to the optimal value of the linear relaxation (5.18)-(5.22), we can reinterpret Theorem 5.2 as the following approximate max-flow-min-cut theorem.

THEOREM 5.4   For any instance with k terminal pairs, the minimum sparsity ratio is always at least the maximum concurrent flow value, and is always at most $O(\log k)$ times as much.

Throughout this section, we have ignored the question of computing an optimal solution to the linear relaxation (5.18)-(5.22) and its dual, the maximum concurrent flow problem, (5.33)-(5.36). As for the maximum multicommodity flow problem, there are three distinct options. First, one can give polynomial-sized LP reformulations. Second, one can apply the ellipsoid algorithm. And finally, we will see that the maximum concurrent flow problem can be easily formulated as a fractional packing problem.

To give a fractional packing formulation of this problem, we first make a simple change of variables, where maximizing α is replaced by minimizing a variable λ, which corresponds to $1/\alpha$. This results in the following equivalent linear program.

minimize λ

$$(5.37)$$

subject to

$$\sum_{P \in \mathcal{P}_i} f(P) = d(i), \qquad \text{for each } i = 1, \dots, k, \qquad (5.38)$$

$$\sum_{i=1}^{k} \sum_{P \in \mathcal{P}_i(e)} f(P) \leq \lambda c(e), \qquad \text{for each } e \in E, \qquad (5.39)$$

$$f(P) \geq 0, \qquad \text{for each } P \in \mathcal{P}_i,\ i = 1, \dots, k. \qquad (5.40)$$

The most natural way to formulate this as a fractional packing problem is to let Q denote the set of flows f satisfying the demand constraints (5.38) and the non-negativity constraints (5.40), and to let the packing constraints $Az \leq \lambda b$ correspond to the capacity constraints (5.39). However, one obtains a more efficient algorithm by also adding to Q the constraints that each commodity alone must not violate the given capacity constraint.

$$\sum_{P \in \mathcal{P}_i(e)} f(P) \leq c(e), \quad \text{for each } e \in E,\ i = 1, \dots, k. \qquad (5.41)$$

It is easy to see that, even with these additional constraints, the two linear programs (5.33)-(5.36) and (5.37)-(5.41) are equivalent. However, by strengthening Q in this way, the width of the formulation can now be bounded by k, since for each $f \in Q$, the total flow on each edge e can be at most $kc(e)$. Furthermore, the required subroutine to optimize over Q is still relatively easy: it requires k (single-commodity) maximum flow computations. By incorporating randomization as first proposed by Klein, Plotkin, Stein, and Tardos [KPST94], the effort for this step can be reduced to, in effect, a single max flow computation. This algorithm for the maximum concurrent flow problem is due to Leighton, Makedon, Plotkin, Stein, Tardos, and Tragoudas [LMP+95]. Finally, the dual variables maintained by this algorithm can be easily adapted to yield the required near-optimal solution for (5.18)-(5.22).

MINIMUM FEEDBACK ARC SETS AND RELATED PROBLEMS

5.4

The techniques described in the previous two sections were limited to undirected graphs. Leighton and Rao [LR88] also considered a rather special case in which the graphs are directed: they were able to extend Theorem 5.4, which bounds the ratio between the optimal values to the maximum concurrent flow and the sparsest cut problems, to the case in which there is a unit-demand commodity between each (ordered) pair of vertices. One of the primary applications of this generalization is an $O(\log^2 n)$-approximation algorithm for the minimum-cost feedback arc set in directed graphs. This was improved by Seymour [Sey95], who gave an $O(\log n \log \log n)$-approximation algorithm. His algorithm is quite similar in spirit to the techniques that we have described in the previous two sections, and hence we shall give his result, even though it does not explicitly rely on any connection to multicommodity flow problems. We shall present a more intuitive description of Seymour's result that is due to [ENRS95]. Even, Naor, Rao, and Schieber [ENRS95] have also extended this approach to yield similarly improved performance guarantees for a number of other problems.

5.4.1   AN LP-BASED APPROXIMATION ALGORITHM

A *feedback arc set* in a directed graph $G = (V, A)$ is a subset of arcs $F \subseteq A$, such that if all arcs in F are deleted, the remaining graph $(V, A - F)$ is acyclic. Equivalently, we can require that for each cycle C in G, at least one arc of C is contained in F. In the minimum-cost feedback arc set problem, we are given a directed graph $G = (V, E)$, a cost $c(a)$ for each arc $a \in A$, and we wish to find a feedback arc set F of minimum total cost $\sum_{a \in F} c(a)$.

It is straightforward to show that the minimum-cost feedback arc set problem in directed graphs is equivalent to the minimum-cost feedback vertex set problem in directed graphs (where the aim is to delete a cheap set of vertices so that no cycle remains), in that any performance guarantee obtained for one problem would translate into the same guarantee for the other. Hence, we see that there is a dramatic difference between our current knowledge for the minimum-cost feedback vertex set problem in undirected and directed graphs (see Chapter 9).

We are given a directed graph $G = (V, A)$, and a cost $c(a)$ for each arc $a \in A$. We shall assume, without loss of generality, that each cost $c(a)$ is a positive integer. Let $\mathcal{C}$ denote the set of all cycles in G. We can formulate the minimum-cost feedback arc set problem as the following integer programming problem:

minimize $$\sum_{a \in A} c(a)x(a)$$

$$(5.42)$$

subject to

$$\sum_{a \in C} x(a) \geq 1, \qquad \text{for each } C \in \mathcal{C}, \tag{5.43}$$

$$x(a) \in \{0, 1\}, \qquad \text{for each } a \in A. \tag{5.44}$$

In its linear relaxation, we replace (5.44) with

$$x(a) \geq 0, \qquad \text{for each } a \in A. \tag{5.45}$$

Seymour's algorithm, which we call Feedback, has the following outline: solve the linear relaxation (5.42), (5.43), and (5.45) and then interpret the optimal fractional solution x^* as a length function for the arcs; use the length function to compute a partition of the nodes (V_1, V_2) (in a way to be specified later), delete all arcs from V_1 to V_2 or vice versa (whichever is cheaper), and recurse on the graphs induced by V_1 and V_2. Of course, in order to initiate this approach, one must observe that the linear program can be solved in polynomial time by the ellipsoid algorithm, since the separation problem required is essentially an all-pairs shortest path computation [GLS88]. Alternatively, one can obtain a more efficient algorithm by formulating the problem as a fractional covering problem, and then applying the algorithm of Plotkin, Shmoys, and Tardos [PST95].

From this outline, it is clear that the key to the performance bound is the way in which the graph is partitioned. Let ϕ denote the value of the optimal fractional solution x^*. Furthermore, for a subset of vertices S, let $G[S]$ denote the subgraph of G induced by S; that is, the graph with vertex set S and arc set $A[S] = \{(u, v) : (u, v) \in A, \ u, v \in S\}$. Finally, let $\delta^+(S) = \{(u, v) : (u, v) \in A, \ u \in S, \ v \in \bar{S}\}$, and analogously, let $\delta^-(S) = \{(v, u) : (v, u) \in A, \ u \in S, \ v \in \bar{S}\}$.

LEMMA 5.7   For a given strongly connected directed graph $G = (V, A)$, suppose that there exists a feasible solution x to (5.43) and (5.45) of objective function value ϕ. There exists a partition $(S, \bar{S})$ of V such that, for some $\epsilon, 0 < \epsilon < 1$, the following three conditions hold:

$$\sum_{a \in A[S]} c(a)x(a) \leq \epsilon\phi; \tag{5.46}$$

$$\sum_{a \in A[\bar{S}]} c(a)x(a) \leq (1 - \epsilon)\phi; \tag{5.47}$$

and either

$$\sum_{a \in \delta^+(S)} c(a) \leq 20\epsilon\phi \log(1/\epsilon) \log\log\phi \tag{5.48}$$

or

$$\sum_{a \in \delta^-(S)} c(a) \leq 20\epsilon\phi \log(1/\epsilon) \log\log\phi. \tag{5.49}$$

Furthermore, this partition can be found in polynomial time.

We will first show that Lemma 5.7 suffices to show that Feedback has the claimed performance guarantee, and then give its proof. We should note that there is some slack in the constant given in Lemma 5.7 (that is, 20), and that we are not attempting to give the best constant that is obtainable via this line of proof.

5.4.2   ANALYZING THE ALGORITHM FEEDBACK

We next show that Feedback is an $O(\log n \log \log n)$-approximation algorithm for the minimum-cost feedback arc set in directed graphs (see Figure 5.6). In computing a feedback arc set, a natural first step is to partition the graph into its strongly connected components. Since each cycle is contained in some strongly connected component, we can solve each component separately, and obtain a solution for the original graph by taking the union of the solutions found for the components. Of course, one need only consider the non-trivial strongly connected components; for example, if a graph is acyclic, each strongly connected component consists of a single vertex, and the empty set is a feedback arc set.

---

function Feedback(G, x)
    if G is acyclic **then return** $\emptyset$;
    else
        find strongly connected components $\mathcal{C}$ of G;
        for each non-trivial strongly connected component $C \in \mathcal{C}$
          $S \leftarrow$ Feedback-Cut(C, x)
          if $\sum_{e \in \delta^+(S)} c(e) \leq \sum_{e \in \delta^-(S)} c(e)$
            then $F \leftarrow \delta^+(S)$
            else $F \leftarrow \delta^-(S)$;
          let G_1 and G_2 be the graphs induced by S and $V(G) - S$;
          return $F \cup$ Feedback(G_1, x)$\cup$Feedback(G_2, x)

FIGURE 5.6

The algorithm Feedback.

We can view the input to the algorithm Feedback as the graph G, the cost function c, and a feasible solution x to the linear relaxation (5.43) and (5.45). First, we compute the strongly connected components of G. For each non-trivial component, we apply Lemma 5.7 to partition its vertex set into S and $\bar{S}$. Either the arcs from S to $\bar{S}$ are added to the feedback arc set, or those from $\bar{S}$ to S, whichever is cheaper. We apply the algorithm recursively to each of $G[S]$ and $G[\bar{S}]$; it is useful to note that, for any subgraph of G, the restriction of x to its arcs is a feasible solution to its linear relaxation. The recursion stops when the input is acyclic. It is clear that the algorithm finds a feasible feedback arc set.

As observed above, we can assume without loss of generality that the input is strongly connected. Let $F(\phi)$ denote the maximum value of the cost of a solution produced by the algorithm when given a graph and a feasible fractional solution of cost at most ϕ. By Lemma 5.7, we see that the function F obeys the following recurrence relation:

$$F(\phi) \leq \max_{0 < \epsilon < 1} \{F(\epsilon\phi) + F((1 - \epsilon)\phi) + 20\epsilon\phi \log(1/\epsilon)\log\log\phi\};$$
$$F(\phi) = 0 \text{ if } \phi < 1.$$

We shall prove by induction on ϕ that this implies that

$$F(\phi) \leq 20\phi \log\phi \log\log\phi. \tag{5.50}$$

The claim is clearly true for $\phi = 0$, since the existence of a feasible fractional solution of cost 0 implies that the graph is acyclic. Let $\bar{\epsilon} = 1 - \epsilon$. Since $\epsilon\phi$ and $\bar{\epsilon}\phi$ are both less than ϕ, we apply the inductive hypothesis to the recurrence relation to get that

$$
\begin{aligned}
F(\phi) &\leq \max_{0 < \epsilon < 1} \{20\epsilon\phi \log(\epsilon\phi)\log\log(\epsilon\phi) + \\
&\qquad 20\bar{\epsilon}\phi \log(\bar{\epsilon}\phi)\log\log(\bar{\epsilon}\phi) + 20\epsilon\phi \log(1/\epsilon)\log\log\phi\} \\
&\leq \max_{0 < \epsilon < 1} \{20\epsilon\phi(\log\phi - \log(1/\epsilon))\log\log\phi + \\
&\qquad 20\bar{\epsilon}\phi \log\phi \log\log\phi + 20\epsilon\phi \log(1/\epsilon)\log\log\phi\} \\
&= 20\phi \log\phi \log\log\phi
\end{aligned}
$$

If we apply the algorithm with an optimal fractional solution x^*, its objective function value ϕ^* is a lower bound on the integer optimum; hence, we have shown that the algorithm is a $20 \log\phi^* \log\log\phi^*$-approximation algorithm.

As was observed in [ENSS95], the following standard ideas allow this to be converted to an $O(\log n \log\log n)$-approximation algorithm. The main idea is that we use an optimal fractional solution x^* to round and rescale the weights for an equivalent input so that the new fractional optimal value is upper bounded by a polynomial in n. First observe that the ratio between the optimal integer value and the optimal fractional value is at most n. To see this, take the optimal fractional solution x^*, and for each $a \in A$, set $\bar{x}(a) = 1$ if $x^*(a) \geq 1/n$, and set $\bar{x}(a) = 0$ otherwise. This is a feasible integer solution, since for any cycle $C \in \mathcal{C}$, there must exist some arc $a \in C$ such that $x^*(a) \geq 1/n$. Hence, each arc such that $c(a) > n\phi^*$ is not in any optimal feedback arc set. This implies that we can contract each such edge and obtain an equivalent instance.

Furthermore, if we include each arc a such that $c(a) < \phi^*/m$ in our feedback arc set, then the total cost of these arcs is at most ϕ^*. If we delete these arcs and apply a ρ-approximation algorithm to the resulting graph, the sum of the total costs of the deleted arcs and of the solution found is at most $\rho + 1$ times the optimum. Furthermore, we can now round down each cost $c(a)$ to its nearest integral multiple of ϕ^*/m, and then rescale by dividing ϕ^*/m to obtain a new input, in which each cost is an integer between 0 and nm. The rescaling changes only the units in which the costs are expressed, and the rounding down can introduce an error of at most ϕ^*. Hence, if we apply a ρ-approximation algorithm to our modified data, we obtain a solution of cost within a factor of $\rho + 2$ of optimal. Hence, we have achieved our goal of reducing the problem to instances in which ϕ^* can be bounded by a polynomial in n.

THEOREM 5.5 Given an optimal fractional solution x^* of value ϕ^*, Feedback is an $O(\log\phi^* \log\log\phi^*)$-approximation algorithm; and by preprocessing the input, yields an $O(\log n \log \log n)$-approximation algorithm for the minimum-cost feedback arc set problem in directed graphs.

One corollary of Theorem 5.5 is that the ratio between the optimal value of the integer program (5.42)–(5.44), and its linear relaxation is $O(\log \phi^* \log \log \phi^*)$. Alon and Seymour [Sey95] have shown that there are instances for which this ratio is $\Omega(\log \phi^*)$. Consequently, in order to improve this algorithm by more than a $\log \log \phi^*$ factor, it will be necessary to rely on a stronger lower bound.

5.4.3   FINDING A GOOD PARTITION

We return now to the proof of Lemma 5.7. The algorithm to find the claimed cut is quite similar to the one used in the proof of Theorem 5.1. As in the proof of that theorem, we can think of the graph G, the length function x, and the cost function c as defining a system of pipes: for each $(u, v) \in A$, there is a (one-way) pipe from u to v of length $x(u, v)$ and cross-section area $c(u, v)$. Hence, the objective function value ϕ corresponds to the total volume in the system.

Let $dist_x(u, v)$ denote the length of the shortest path from u to v in G with respect to the arc-length function x. For a given vertex $\hat{v} \in V$, we can compute the set of vertices reachable from $\hat{v}$ within a given radius r:

$$B_x^+(\hat{v}, r) = \{u \in V : dist_x(\hat{v}, u) \le r\}. \tag{5.51}$$

Analogously, let $B_x^-(\hat{v}, r) = \{u \in V : dist_x(u, \hat{v}) \le r\}$. Furthermore, we can compute the total volume of the pipe system that is contained within a radius r of vertex $\hat{v}$:

$$V^+(\hat{v}, r) = \sum_{u, v \in B_x^+(\hat{v}, r)} c(u, v)x(u, v) + \sum_{(u, v) \in \delta^+(B_x^+(\hat{v}, r))} c(u, v)(r - dist_x(\hat{v}, u)) \tag{5.52}$$

and

$$V^-(\hat{v}, r) = \sum_{u, v \in B_x^-(\hat{v}, r)} c(u, v)x(u, v) + \sum_{(u, v) \in \delta^-(B_x^-(\hat{v}, r))} c(u, v)(r - dist_x(v, \hat{v})). \tag{5.53}$$

Throughout the remainder of this section, we will omit the explicit reference to the particular length function x in our notation, with the understanding that it should be understood unambiguously.

Given the graph G, its cost function c, and a length function x of objective function value ϕ, we select a vertex $\hat{v}$ and then consider a sequence of radii from $\hat{v}$. For each radius r, we can consider the cuts defined by setting S to $B^+(\hat{v}, r)$ or to $B^-(\hat{v}, r)$; in the former case, we aim to bound the cost of $\delta^+(S)$, whereas in the latter we aim to bound the cost of $\delta^-(S)$.

For the purpose of the proof, we shall consider radii defined in the following way. We let the initial radius $r = 1/8$. While $V^+(\hat{v}, r) \le \phi/2$, we define an increment

$$d(r) = \frac{1}{10 \log(\phi/V^+(\hat{v}, r)) \log \log \phi};$$

If $V^+(\hat{v}, r + d(r)) < 2V^+(\hat{v}, r)$, then we claim that we can identify a good cut of the form $S = B^+(\hat{v}, \rho)$, where $r \le \rho \le r + d(r)$. If the volume repeatedly doubles until the volume captured exceeds $\phi/2$, then we enter a second phase in which the analogous steps are taken with respect to $V^-(\hat{v}, r)$ and $B^-(\hat{v}, r)$.

To complete the proof of the lemma, we need to establish three claims:

1. if the volume does not double, then we can identify a good cut;

2. the volume cannot expand beyond $\phi/2$ in both phases;

3. the good cut is of a form that is easy to compute.

To prove the first claim, it is useful to recall some facts about the behavior of the function $V^+(\hat{v}, r)$ for a fixed vertex $\hat{v}$. If there does not exist a vertex u such that $dist_x(\hat{v}, u) = r$, then this function is differentiable at r, and its derivative is equal to the total cost of the cut defined by the current radius r:

$$\sum_{(u,v) \in \delta^+(B^+(\hat{v},r))} c(u, v).$$

So the function consists of fewer than n linear pieces. There might be discontinuities at the breakpoints, each of which corresponds to a vertex at the prescribed distance from $\hat{v}$. However, it is a non-decreasing function of r. Hence, if we have identified an interval $[r, r + d]$ over which the volume increases by at most v, there must exist a point within that interval at which the derivative is at most v/d, and hence there is a cut of a total cost at most v/d.

Suppose that we have found a radius $\bar{r}$ for which $V^+(\hat{v}, \bar{r} + d(\bar{r})) < 2V^+(\hat{v}, \bar{r})$. Hence, the increase in volume over this range is less than $V^+(\hat{v}, \bar{r})$, and so the overall rate of increase is less than

$$\frac{V^+(\hat{v}, \bar{r})}{d(\bar{r})} = 10V^+(\hat{v}, \bar{r}) \log \frac{\phi}{V^+(\hat{v}, \bar{r})} \log\log\phi.$$

Let ρ, $\bar{r} \le \rho \le \bar{r} + d(\bar{r})$, denote a value of r for which

$$\frac{\partial V^+(\hat{v}, r)}{\partial r} < 10V^+(\hat{v}, \bar{r}) \log \frac{\phi}{V^+(\hat{v}, \bar{r})} \log\log\phi,$$

and let $S = B^+(\hat{v}, \rho)$.

We shall show S satisfies the properties required by the lemma. Let $\epsilon = V^+(\hat{v}, \rho)/\phi$. Since

$$V^+(\hat{v}, \bar{r}) \le V^+(\hat{v}, \rho) = \epsilon\phi \le 2V^+(\hat{v}, \bar{r}),$$

we have that

$$\sum_{a \in \delta^+(S)} c(a) \le 10\epsilon\phi \log(2/\epsilon) \log\log\phi;$$

applying the crudest of estimates, we see that the cost of the cut defined by S attains the claimed bound. Furthermore, the objective function value of x restricted to the arcs $A[S]$ is at most the volume $V^+(\hat{v}, \rho)$; hence, this is at most $\epsilon\phi$. On the other hand, the objective function value of x restricted to the arcs $A[\bar{S}]$ is at most the volume $\phi - V^+(\hat{v}, \rho)$; hence, this is at most $\bar{\epsilon}\phi$. Repeating the analogous argument with respect to V^-, we see that a cut S found in either phase satisfies the conditions of the lemma.

We next turn to the proof of the second claim: that at some point in the two phases, we find some interval $[r, r + d(r)]$ for which the volume does not double. We shall assume, for a contradiction, that this is not the case, and then show that this assumption implies that there exists a directed cycle C of length $\sum_{a \in C} x(a)$ is less than 1; this contradicts the fact that x is a feasible solution to the linear relaxation. In fact, we will show that there exists some vertex $\hat{u}$ such that $dist_x(\hat{u}, \hat{v}) < 1/2$ and $dist_x(\hat{v}, \hat{u}) < 1/2$.

First, we compute an upper bound on the final radius computed in the first phase; that is, the radius $\hat{r}$ such that $V^+(\hat{v}, \hat{r}) > \phi/2$ that causes the phase to end. To give an upper bound on $\hat{r}$, we upper bound the increments $d(r)$ computed along the way. For each increment $d(r)$ computed, there is a corresponding volume $V^+(\hat{v}, r)$, where $1/8 \le V^+(\hat{v}, r) \le \phi/2$. Since the volume doubles with each iteration, at most one of these values lies in the interval $(\phi/2^{\ell+1}, \phi/2^\ell]$, for each $\ell = 1, \ldots, \lfloor \log \phi \rfloor + 4$. If there is an increment that corresponds to the interval $(\phi/4, \phi/2]$, then it is at most

$$\frac{1}{(10 \log(\phi/(\phi/2))) \log \log \phi} = \frac{1}{(10 \log \log \phi)};$$

the increment corresponding to the interval $(\phi/2^{\ell+1}, \phi/2^\ell]$ is at most $1/(10\ell \log \log \phi)$. Hence, we see that

$$\hat{r} \le \frac{1}{8} + \sum_{\ell=1}^{\lfloor \log \phi \rfloor + 4} \frac{1}{10\ell \log \log \phi} = \frac{1}{8} + \frac{1}{10 \log \log \phi} \mathcal{H}(\lfloor \log \phi \rfloor + 4). \tag{5.54}$$

Using even the crudest estimates, it is easy to verify that this implies that $\hat{r} < 1/2$.

The identical calculation also shows that if the second phase does not end until the current radius yields a volume greater than $\phi/2$, then the final radius for the second phase is less than 1/2. However, between the two phases, more than ϕ units of volume have been captured. Since there are only ϕ units of volume overall, some part of the pipe system must be captured in both phases. But then, there must exist some vertex $\hat{u}$ such that $dist_x(\hat{v}, \hat{u}) < 1/2$ and $dist_x(\hat{u}, \hat{v}) < 1/2$. This contradicts the fact that x is a feasible solution to the linear relaxation. Hence, in one of the two phases, we must indentify a good cut.

Finally, we must argue that we can find a good cut. For any cut S, it is straightforward to check if there exists some ϵ for which conditions (5.46)-(5.48) hold. We have already shown that there exists a good cut of the form $B^-(\hat{v}, \rho)$ or $B^+(\hat{v}, \rho)$. However, for any given $\hat{v}$, there are at most n distinct cuts of the form $B^+(\hat{v}, \rho)$: one need only consider $\rho = dist(\hat{v}, v)$ for some $v \in V$. Of course, the same is true for $B^-(\hat{v}, \rho)$. Hence, the algorithm Feedback-Cut, used in the algorithm Feedback, need only enumerate these cuts until it finds a good one (see Figure 5.7).

---

function Feedback-Cut(G, x)
    fix $\hat{v} \in V$;
    for each $v \in V - \{\hat{v}\}$
        $S \leftarrow \{u \in V : dist_x(\hat{v}, u) \le dist_x(\hat{v}, v)\}$;
        if S satisfies (5.46)-(5.48) **then return** S;
        $T \leftarrow \{u \in V : dist_x(u, \hat{v}) \le dist_x(v, \hat{v})\}$;
        if T satisfies (5.46),(5.47), and (5.48) **then return** T.

FIGURE 5.7

The algorithm Feedback-Cut.

Note that we can give a much better implementation of Feedback-Cut by considering the vertices v in order of their distance from $\hat{v}$; this implies that the algorithm is just a slight modification to Dijkstra's algorithm for the single-source shortest path problem (see, for example, the textbook of Cormen, Leiserson, and Rivest [CLR90]). Dijkstra's algorithm repeatedly identifies the next closest vertex to a given vertex $\hat{v}$, and hence continually maintains a cut S of the appropriate form; after finding the next closest vertex to $\hat{v}$, we need only check if the current S satisfies the conditions of Lemma 5.7.

FINDING BALANCED CUTS AND OTHER APPLICATIONS

5.5

While the sparsest cut problem is of interest in its own right, it is just the starting point for a host of applications. In particular, we will show how a subroutine that produces sparse cuts can be used to compute near-optimal balanced cuts; the approximation algorithm for the balanced cut problem can then be used in a variety of settings to derive divide-and-conquer approximation algorithms.

5.5.1   FINDING BALANCED CUTS

In the α-*balanced cut problem* we are given an undirected graph $G = (V, E)$, where each edge $e \in E$ has a positive cost $c(e)$; an α-balanced cut is a subset of vertices $S \subseteq V$ such that $\alpha n \leq |S| \leq (1 - \alpha)n$, where $n = |V|$, and the objective is to find such a cut for which its total cost, $\sum_{e \in \delta(S)} c(e)$, is minimized. Let C_α denote the total cost of the optimal α-balanced cut. The special case in which $\alpha = 1/2$ is sometimes referred to as the *graph bisection problem*. We have already discussed in Section 5.1 that an approximation algorithm for this problem can be quite useful in designing divide-and-conquer approximation algorithms. We shall next show that the algorithm of Section 5.3 for the sparsest cut problem can be used in this setting.

Given an instance of the α-balanced cut problem, we can construct an instance of the sparsest cut problem by letting there be $\binom{n}{2}$ terminal pairs, one for each pair of vertices $u, v \in V$, and setting the demand of each commodity to be 1. We shall call this the *all-pairs unit-demand problem*. For any cut $S \subseteq V$, its sparsity ratio $\rho(S)$ is equal to the ratio of its total cost $\sum_{e \in \delta(S)} c(e)$ to $|S||V - S|$, since the latter quantity is the total demand of terminal pairs that are disconnected by deleting the edges in $\delta(S)$. This denominator is made large by keeping S and $V - S$ of roughly the same size; that is, the cut is balanced. In fact, if S is α-balanced, then the denominator is at least $n^2\alpha(1 - \alpha)$, and hence the sparsity ratio is at most $C_\alpha/[n^2\alpha(1 - \alpha)]$. Of course, the sparsity ratio need not be minimized by finding the cheapest balanced cut: there might be very imbalanced cuts for which the total cost is sufficiently small so as to offset the fact that the denominator is smaller.

The greedy set covering algorithm computes a cover by repeatedly choosing a set which is the cheapest per element covered (see Chapter 3 for an analysis of this algorithm). The following algorithm Greedy-Ratio for the α-balanced cut problem is analogous: we repeatedly choose additional vertices to add to a cut $\bar{S}$ by choosing additional vertices for which the cost of the new edges cut per vertex selected is small. We initialize $V_1 = V$; in general, V_i will denote the set of vertices remaining at the start of the ith iteration of the algorithm. In iteration i, we apply our sparsest cut approximation algorithm to the all-pairs unit-demand problem for the graph induced by V_i; the cut found by this algorithm is a partition of the vertices into two sets S_i and $V_i - S_i$, where we shall assume that S_i is the smaller of the two. If $\bar{S} = \cup_{\ell=1}^{i} S_\ell$ is such that $|\bar{S}| > \alpha|V|$, then the algorithm terminates. Otherwise, we set $V_{i+1} = V_i - S_i$, and the algorithm continues.

LEMMA 5.8   For any $\alpha \leq 1/3$, the algorithm Greedy-Ratio finds an α-balanced cut.

Proof.   The algorithm must clearly halt at some point; let ℓ denote the iteration in which it halts. Let $k = |\cup_{i=1}^{\ell-1} S_i|$. The set $\bar{S}$ found by the algorithm has size

$$k + |S_\ell| \leq k + (n-k)/2 \leq n/2 + k/2 < (1+\alpha)n/2 \leq (1-\alpha)n.$$

∎

We next turn to showing that the cut found by Greedy-Ratio is near-optimal. We will not show that it is an approximation algorithm in the traditional sense, since we will not compare the cost of the cut found to the optimal α-balanced cut, C_α. Instead, we will compare the cost of the α-balanced cut found to the cost of the optimal β-balanced cut, C_β, where $\beta > \alpha$. Since it is more restrictive to require a cut to be β-balanced than to be α-balanced, it is possible that C_β is much greater than C_α.

Before completing the analysis of the performance of this algorithm, we first introduce some notation. The input graph evolves over the course of the execution of the algorithm, as more and more of its vertices are deleted. Thus, a notation such as $\delta(S)$ is ambiguous, since it is not clear to which graph we are referring. For any set of vertices $S \subseteq V_i$, we shall let

$$c_i(S) = \sum_{e \in \delta_i(S)} c(e),$$

where $\delta_i(S)$ denote the set of edges (u, v) such that $u \in S$ and $v \in V_i - S$. Since $V = V_1$, we will define $c(S) = c_1(S)$ for any $S \subseteq V$. If ℓ denotes the number of iterations that the algorithm makes, we shall set $n_i = |V_i|$ and $s_i = |S_i|$, for each $i = 1, \ldots, \ell$.

THEOREM 5.6   If the Greedy-Ratio algorithm uses a ρ-approximation algorithm to find a sparse cut in each iteration, then, for any $\beta > \alpha$, where $\alpha \leq 1/3$, the algorithm finds an α-balanced cut of cost at most $\frac{3\rho}{\beta-\alpha} C_\beta$.

Proof.   Let R denote an optimal β-balanced cut in the input $G = (V, E)$. Consider the cut S_i found in iteration i, $i = 1, \ldots, \ell$. We know that $R_i = R - \cup_{j=1}^{i-1} S_j$ contains more than $(\beta - \alpha)n$ vertices; in fact, we also know that $V_i - R_i$ also has this many vertices, and since one of these two sets has size greater than $(1-\alpha)n/2 \geq n/3$, we know that the product of their sizes is greater than $(\beta - \alpha)n^2/3$. Hence, for the graph considered in iteration i, the sparsest cut value is at most $\frac{c_i(R_i)}{(\beta-\alpha)n^2/3}$. This implies that

$$\frac{c_i(S_i)}{s_i(n_i - s_i)} \leq \rho \cdot \frac{c_i(R_i)}{(\beta - \alpha)n^2/3} \leq \rho \cdot \frac{c(R)}{(\beta - \alpha)n^2/3},$$

and hence,

$$c_i(S_i) \leq \frac{\rho C_\beta}{(\beta - \alpha)n/3} \cdot s_i.$$

Summing this inequality for $i = 1, \ldots, \ell$, we see that

$$c(\bar{S}) \leq \sum_{i=1}^{\ell} c_i(S_i) \leq \sum_{i=1}^{\ell} \frac{\rho C_\beta}{(\beta - \alpha)n/3} \cdot s_i \leq \frac{3\rho C_\beta}{(\beta - \alpha)}.$$

∎

The relationship between the sparsest cut problem and obtaining a balanced cut was independently discovered by Leighton and Rao [LR88] and Plaisted [Pla90]. By combining Theorem 5.6 with the $O(\log k)$-approximation algorithm for the sparsest cut problem that was given in Section 5.3, we obtain the following corollary:

COROLLARY 5.3 For any fixed ϵ, $0 \leq \epsilon \leq 1/6$, there is a polynomial-time algorithm that finds a $1/3$-balanced cut of cost within an $O(\log n)$ factor of the cost of the optimal $1/3 + \epsilon$-balanced cut.

5.5.2 APPLICATIONS OF BALANCED CUT THEOREMS

In Section 5.1 we showed that an algorithm to find near-optimal balanced cuts could be used to derive an approximation algorithm for the minimum cut linear arrangement problem, via a divide-and-conquer approach. In this section we will consider two other applications of this philosophy. Each of these applications will rely on a good balanced cut algorithm, but in each case we will need a different sort of balanced cut. However, the techniques discussed in this chapter can be extended to yield the required subroutines.

We first consider a problem related to the solution of a linear system of equations $Ax = b$, where A is a positive-definite symmetric matrix, and we wish to compute x for a given input (A, b). A well-known method for solving such a system of equations is to apply Gaussian elimination. Since we are applying this method to a symmetric positive-definite matrix, we may restrict attention to the variant of Gaussian elimination in which we use only diagonal pivot entries. Furthermore, in each iteration of the algorithm, we maintain a symmetric matrix as we gradually transform the system of equations into an equivalent system (A', b') in which A' is the identity matrix. In most applications, the matrix A is extremely sparse; that is, most of its entries are zeroes. The processing of A can be made much more efficient if its sparsity can be maintained as it is transformed to A'. One very stringent requirement of this type is to require that each 0 in the matrix A should remain a 0 throughout the matrix's transformation. For example, in the following sequence we perform Gaussian elimination without introducing any non-zeroes, where the starred element is the pivot element in the current iteration:

$$\begin{bmatrix} 4 & 1 & 1 \\ 1 & 1 & 0 \\ 1 & 0 & 1^* \end{bmatrix} \rightarrow \begin{bmatrix} 3 & 1 & 0 \\ 1 & 1^* & 0 \\ 0 & 0 & 1 \end{bmatrix} \rightarrow \begin{bmatrix} 2^* & 0 & 0 \\ 0 & 1 & 0 \\ 0 & 0 & 1 \end{bmatrix} \rightarrow \begin{bmatrix} 1^* & 0 & 0 \\ 0 & 1 & 0 \\ 0 & 0 & 1 \end{bmatrix}$$

This is a consequence of the order in which we chose the pivot elements. Had we started by pivoting on the 4, we would have obtained the matrix

$$\begin{bmatrix} 1 & 0 & 0 \\ 0 & 3 & -1 \\ 0 & -1 & 3 \end{bmatrix}$$

If we pivot on the diagonal element a_{tt}, then the i, jth entry of the new matrix is $a_{ij} - a_{it}a_{tj}/a_{tt}$, $i, j \neq t$. Hence, we are assured that no new non-zero is created if we select an index t such that

$$a_{ij} = 0 \text{ implies that } a_{it} = 0 \text{ or } a_{tj} = 0, \text{ for each } i, j \neq t. \tag{5.55}$$

For simplicity, we shall assume that any non-zero remains a non-zero throughout the computation; in other words, if Gaussian elimination computes an element of the form $c - c$, where $c \neq 0$, then we shall still treat this new element as a non-zero.

We shall first focus on the following question: for which symmetric positive-definite matrices A does there exist a sequence of pivots so that no new non-zeroes are created throughout Gaussian elimination? This question has a rather elegant answer. Symmetric matrices can be easily modeled by graphs. For each index $1, \ldots, n$ create a vertex. For each non-zero entry a_{ij}, create the edge (i, j). Note that the fact that the matrix A is symmetric implies that this construction yields an undirected graph. If we consider the contrapositive of condition (5.55) and translate this into this graph setting, we see that a pivot can be performed on a_{tt} without creating a non-zero if there is an edge connecting i and j whenever there are edges (t, i) and (t, j); in other words, the neighbors of vertex t induce a clique in the graph. Hence, a matrix can be reduced to the identity without introducing non-zeroes whenever the corresponding graph has the following property: the vertices can be ordered $v_1, \ldots, v_n$, such that, for each $j = 1, \ldots, n - 1$, the neighbors of v_j in $\{v_{j+1}, \ldots, v_n\}$ induce a clique in the original graph. Such an ordering of the vertices is a called a *perfect elimination ordering*. Hence, we are interested in those graphs which admit a perfect elimination ordering. These graphs can be nicely characterized. They are precisely the class of *chordal graphs*: those graph for which any cycle of length at least 4 has an edge connecting some pair of vertices that are not consecutive in the cycle (a so-called *chord* of the cycle). These graphs are also commonly called *triangulated graphs*. It is beyond the scope of this chapter to prove this characterization of chordal graphs, and the reader is referred to the textbook of Golumbic [Gol80].

However, not all graphs are chordal, and hence in some cases, non-zeroes must be introduced in the process of performing Gaussian elimination. We shall be interested in finding an ordering of pivot elements so that the resulting number of non-zeroes is minimized. We shall call this the *minimum fill-in problem* for symmetric positive-definite matrices. By the previous discussion, this problem is equivalent to the following graph theoretic question: given a graph $G = (V, E)$, find a superset of edges $F \supseteq E$ such that the graph (V, F) is a chordal graph, so that the size of F is as small as possible. We shall call this the *minimum chordal extension problem*. Yannakakis [Yan81] showed that this problem is *NP*-complete.

Agrawal, Klein, and Ravi [AKR93] focus on the case in which the maximum degree in the given graph is a constant Δ, or equivalently, there are a constant number of non-zeroes in each row of the given matrix. They gave the first approximation algorithm with a non-trivial performance guarantee for this problem, and we shall present the main ideas of this result. This result relies on several sophisticated results on the structure of chordal graphs, and it is beyond the scope of this chapter to prove the correctness and performance of this algorithm. For these results, and for a concise history of research on this problem, the reader is referred to [AKR93].

For a given ordering of the vertices $v_1, \ldots, v_n$, we compute a sequence of graphs G_i, $i = 0, \ldots, n$. The graph G_0 is the input graph G. The graph G_i is computed from G_{i-1} by adding each edge (v_j, v_k), $i < j < k$, such that v_j and v_k are non-adjacent neighbors of v_i in G_{i-1}. The graph G_n is a chordal graph; it can be viewed as the unique chordal graph corresponding to this *elimination ordering* of the vertices of G.

Suppose that we can find a small subset of nodes S in G whose deletion separates G into two substantially smaller connected components with vertex sets V_1 and V_2. Consider any elimination ordering of G in which we first order V_1, then V_2, and then S. Consider the sequence of graphs G_i, $i = 0, \ldots, n$, for this ordering. At any step i in which $v_i \in V_1$, we introduce only edges induced by $V_1 \cup S$; in any step in which $v_i \in V_2$, we introduce only edges induced by $V_2 \cup S$; finally, in any step in which $v_i \in S$, we introduce only edges induced by S. Hence, we never introduce edges between V_1 and V_2, and hence we have decomposed the original problem into two substantially smaller problems. This approach has long been applied in this context; this divide-and-conquer philosophy has been referred to as *nested dissection*. The key to the performance of any nested dissection algorithm is the manner in which the set S is computed.

Agrawal, Klein, and Ravi proposed a nested dissection algorithm in which the separator is a near-optimal balanced node separator. Such a separator was known to be computable (Leighton and Rao [LR94] and Tragoudas [Tra91]). A subset of nodes S is an α-*balanced node separator* of an n-vertex graph $G = (V, E)$ if each connected component of $V - X$ has at most $(1 - \alpha)n$ vertices. Let C_α denote the minimum size of an α-balanced node separator.

THEOREM 5.7   There exists a polynomial-time algorithm to find a 1/3-balanced node separator of a graph of size $O(\log n C_{1/2})$.

While the algorithm of Agrawal, Klein, and Ravi [AKR93] is a quite natural one, its analysis relies on a number of structural characterizations of chordal graphs that are beyond the scope of this chapter. For example, one key ingredient for the performance guarantee of this approximation algorithm is a result of Gilbert, Rose, and Edenbrandt [GRE84] that states that for each m-edge chordal graph, $C_{1/2} \leq \sqrt{2m}$. Agrawal, Klein, and Ravi show that for graphs in which the maximum degree is bounded by a constant, the resulting nested dissection algorithm has a polylogarithmic performance guarantee.

THEOREM 5.8   For any graph G of maximum degree Δ, the nested dissection algorithm based on near-optimal node-separators computes a chordal extension of G in which the number of edges is within an $O(\sqrt{\Delta} \log^4 n)$ factor of optimal.

We shall consider one final application of this divide-and-conquer approach. In the *storage-time product problem*, the input consists of a directed acyclic graph, which corresponds to the dependency graph of a computation; that is, each node v corresponds to an intermediate result that is computed, and if there are arcs entering v from $u_1, \ldots, u_k$, this means that the result computed for each of the predecessors is needed to compute the result for v. Each node v requires a specified processing time $p(v)$, and for each edge $(u, v) = e$, there is a cost $c(e)$ which corresponds to the amount of storage needed for the intermediate result computed at node u for node v. One can interpret the input graph as defining a precedence relation $\prec$ on the nodes (where $u \prec v$ if there is a path from u to v), and then a feasible solution for this problem is a total ordering $v_1, v_2, \ldots, v_n$ of the nodes that is consistent with $\prec$ (that is, $v_i \prec v_j$ implies that $i < j$). Then the cost associated with this solution is

$$\sum_{e=(v_i, v_j) \in E} c(e) \left(\sum_{k=i}^{j-1} p(v_k) \right), \tag{5.56}$$

that is, the total storage-time product needed to maintain intermediate results. That is, the storage-time product problem is to compute the ordering of V consistent with $\prec$ for which the cost (5.56) is minimized.

Ravi, Agrawal, and Klein [RAK91] have given an $O(\log n \log P)$-approximation algorithm for this problem, where P denotes the total processing time. For ease of exposition, we will present their algorithm for the special case in which each processing time $p(v) = 1$. By focusing on this case, we reduce the problem to one quite similar to the minimum cut linear arrangement problem discussed in Section 5.1. As in that case, let $\sigma(i)$ denote the vertex assigned to be processed in the ith position, for each $i = 1 \ldots, n$. Furthermore, let S_i denote the set of edges in E of the form $(\sigma(j), \sigma(k))$, where $j \leq i$ and $k > i$. Then the problem can be rephrased as follows: find σ consistent with $\prec$ such that $\sum_{i=1}^{n-1} \sum_{e \in S_i} c(e)$ is minimized. In effect, the minimum cut linear arrangement problem is the bottleneck (or min-max) version of this min-sum problem (but we are also constrained here to permutations σ that are consistent with $\prec$).

The idea underlying the approximation algorithm of Ravi, Agrawal, and Klein is exactly as for the minimum cut linear arrangement problem. That is, we need to compute a balanced partition of the nodes, and recursively solve the two subproblems. Of course, for the partition to make sense, we need to find a partition of V into S and $V - S$ such that there does not exist an edge (v, u) in G where $u \in S$ and $v \in V - S$; that is, $\delta^-(S) = \emptyset$. Thus, we shall focus on such $\prec$-*consistent cuts* S and their corresponding edge sets $\delta^+(S)$. Once again, we will say that such a cut is α-balanced if $\alpha n \leq |S| \leq (1 - \alpha)n$. The cost of such a cut S is $\sum_{e \in \delta^+(S)} c(e)$. Ravi, Agrawal, and Klein have observed that the approach of Leighton and Rao can be extended to yield the following theorem:

THEOREM 5.9 There is a polynomial-time algorithm to find a 1/4-balanced $\prec$-consistent cut in a directed acyclic graph of cost within an $O(\log n)$ factor of the minimum cost of a 1/3-balanced $\prec$-consistent cut.

The algorithm for the storage-time product minimization problem is quite natural: we apply the algorithm of Theorem 5.9 to the graph to partition the problem into two subproblems. Let $\mathcal{A}(G)$ denote the cost of the solution found by the algorithm on input

G, and let $\mathcal{B}(G)$ denote the cost of the cut S found by the algorithm of Theorem 5.9. Furthermore, let G_1 denote the graph induced by S, and let G_2 denote the graph induced by $V - S$. Since each edge in G is either in G_1, in G_2, or in the cut $\delta^+(S)$, we can derive the following recurrence relation:

$$\mathcal{A}(G) \le \mathcal{A}(G_1) + \mathcal{A}(G_2) + (n - 1)\mathcal{B}(G),$$

where the last term is a consequence of the fact that each edge in $\delta^+(S)$ might occur in each of the $n - 1$ sets $S_i, i = 1, \dots, n - 1$.

The crux of the analysis of the performance guarantee of this algorithm lies in devising a good lower bound on the optimum. Consider an optimal solution σ^*. If we consider any set $S_i, i = \lceil n/3 \rceil, \dots, \lfloor 2n/3 \rfloor$, then we see that it defines a 1/3-balanced $\prec$-consistent cut. Hence, the cost of each of these is at least B^*, where B^* is the minimum cost of a 1/3-balanced $\prec$-consistent cut. Hence $nB^*/3$ is a lower bound on the optimal value, $OPT_{S \times T}(G)$, and hence we have the recurrence:

$$\mathcal{A}(G) \le \mathcal{A}(G_1) + \mathcal{A}(G_2) + O(\log n) \cdot OPT_{S \times T}(G).$$

By relying on the fact that each G_i has at most $(3/4)n$ vertices, it is easy to show by induction that $\mathcal{A}(G) = O(\log^2 n)OPT_{S \times T}(G)$. It is not hard to extend this argument to give the bound claimed for the general case in which there are arbitrary processing times. This somewhat more general approach to using a balanced cut as a lower bound was first introduced in a different context by Hansen [Han89].

Although we have only given a few examples, there are quite a number of applications for which this approach has led to the first approximation algorithm with polylogarithmic performance guarantee. Leighton and Rao considered several applications from the domain of VLSI design: among these are results for the crossing number of a graph (i.e., embedding a graph in the plane so as to minimize the number of pairs of edges that cross each other in this embedding); and for the problem of laying out a graph in the plane so as to minimize the area required for the layout. Many of these applications were first proposed by Bhatt and Leighton [BL84] who focused attention on obtaining approximation algorithms for the graph bisection problem.

CONCLUSIONS

5.6

In this chapter, we have tried to present the highlights of an approach to the design of approximation algorithms that seeks to capitalize on good algorithms for cut problems in order to design and analyze divide-and-conquer algorithms. We have not attempted to catalog all of the work done in this area, and therefore, have not discussed a number of closely related results. However, we will briefly mention two of the most prominent areas that we have omitted.

The first success in applying divide-and-conquer based on finding good cuts was for the restricted case of planar graphs; as one of the initial applications of their planar separator theorem, Lipton and Tarjan [LT80] observed that one could derive polynomial approximation schemes for a wide variety of combinatorial problems. However, in the subsequent years, Baker [Bak94] has given a better approach for exploiting planarity, and her work is discussed in Chapter 9. Furthermore, we have also omitted discussion of work on better performance guarantees of approximation algorithms for these cut problems when restricted to planar graphs, which includes results of Rao [Rao87], Garg, Saran, and Vazirani [GSV94], Tardos and Vazirani [TV93], and Klein, Plotkin, and Rao [KPR91].

Randomized rounding has also been applied in the context of multicut approximation algorithms; Bertsimas, Teo, and Vohra [BV94, BTV95] have given other mathematical programming formulations which are more amenable to this approach. However, the bounds obtained from this approach do not dominate the ones presented here, and in some sense, build on the earlier work. Randomized rounding is extensively discussed in Chapter 11.

This area of research is still extremely active, and there is still much work to be done. For example, very little is known about multicommodity max-flow min-cut bounds when the input graph is directed. Even more importantly, for each of the problems discussed, there is no complexity-theoretic evidence that a significantly better performance guarantee cannot be obtained; in fact, there may well be approximation algorithms with constant performance guarantees. In fact, Chung and Yau [CY94] gave an algorithm for which they claimed such a performance guarantee for the balanced cut problem, but the proof contained in [CY94] is not correct, and a correct proof of this claim has not been published. Finally, it is ironic that the pivotal result in this chapter, Corollary 5.3, which finds a good balanced cut, is *not* an approximation algorithm in the traditional sense. While this deficiency is unimportant for any of the applications, it would, nonetheless, be an important advance to find a good approximation algorithm for this problem.

Acknowledgments First and foremost, I would to thank Éva Tardos, from whom I first learned most of the results in this chapter. I would also like to thank Satish Rao for explaining his insights into Seymour's algorithm at a time they were still evolving as part of his own research. This chapter benefited greatly from the perceptive comments of Yuval Rabani, David Williamson, Yuri Rabinovich, and this volume's editor, Dorit Hochbaum. This work was partially supported by NSF grant CCR-9307391.

References

[AKR93] A. Agrawal, P. Klein, and R. Ravi. Cutting down on fill using nested dissection: provably good elimination orderings. In: J.A. George, J.R. Gilbert, and J. Liu, editors. *Sparse Matrix Computations: Graph Theory Issues and Algorithms, IMA Volumes in Mathematics and Its Applications*, Springer-Verlag, New York, 1993, pages 31–55.

[AMO93] R.K. Ahuja, T. L. Magnanti, and J. B. Orlin. *Network flows: theory, algorithms, and applications*. Prentice Hall, Englewood Cliffs, NJ, 1993.

[AR95] Y. Aumann and Y. Rabani. An $O(\log k)$ approximate min-cut max-flow theorem and approximation algorithm. *SIAM J. Comput.*, to appear.

[AvisD91] D. Avis and M. Deza. The cut cone, L^1 embeddability, complexity, and multicommodity flows. *Networks*, 21:595–617, 1991.

[Bak94] B. S. Baker. Approximation algorithms for *NP*-complete problems on planar graphs. *J. Assoc. Comput. Mach.*, 41:153–180, 1994.

[BTV95] D. Bertsimas, C. Teo, and R. Vohra. Nonlinear formulations and improved randomized approximation algorithms for multicut problems. In E. Balas and J. Clausen, editors, *Integer Programming and Combinatorial Optimization, Lecture Notes in Computer Science 920*, pages 29–40. Springer-Verlag, New York, 1995.

[BV94] D. Bertsimas and R. Vohra. Linear programming relaxations, approximation algorithms, and randomized rounding: a unified approach to covering problems. Working paper #-3654-94 MSA, Sloan School of Management, MIT, Cambridge, MA, 1993.

[BL84] S.N. Bhatt and F.T. Leighton. A framework for solving VLSI graph layout problems. *J. Comput. Sys. Sciences*, 28:300–343, 1984.

[Bou85] J. Bourgain. On Lipschitz embedding of finite metric spaces in Hilbert space. *Israel J. Math.*, pages 46–52, 1985.

[CY94] F.R.K. Chung and S.T. Yau. A near optimal algorithm for edge separators. In *Proceedings of the 26th Annual ACM Symposium on Theory of Computing*, pages 1–8, 1994.

[Chv83] V. Chvátal. *Linear programming*. W.H. Freeman, New York, 1983.

[CLR90] T. H. Cormen, C. E. Leiserson, and R. L. Rivest. *Introduction to Algorithms*. MIT Press and McGraw Hill, Cambridge, MA and New York, 1990.

[DJP$^+$94] E. Dahlhaus, D. S. Johnson, C. H. Papadimitriou, P. D. Seymour, and M. Yannakakis. The complexity of multiway cuts. *SIAM J. Comput.*, 23:864–894, 1994.

[ENRS95] G. Even, J. Naor, S. Rao, and B. Schieber. Divide-and-conquer approximation algorithms via spreading metrics. In *Proceedings of the 36th Annual IEEE Symposium on Foundations of Computer Science*, pages 62–71, 1995.

[ENSS95] G. Even, J. Naor, B. Schieber, and M. Sudan. Approximating minimum feedback sets and multi-cuts in directed graphs. In E. Balas and J. Clausen, editors, *Integer Programming and Combinatorial Optimization, Lecture Notes in Computer Science 920*, pages 14–28. Springer-Verlag, New York, 1995.

[FF56] L. R. Ford, Jr. and D. R. Fulkerson. Maximal flow through a network. *Canadian J. Math*, 8:399–404, 1956.

[Gar95] N. Garg. A deterministic $O(\log k)$-approximation algorithm for the sparsest cut problem. Preprint, 1995.

[GSV94] N. Garg, H. Saran, and V.V. Vazirani. Finding separator cuts in planar graphs within twice the optimal. In *Proceedings of the 35th Annual IEEE Symposium on Foundations of Computer Science*, pages 14–23, 1994.

[GK94] M. D. Grigoriadis and L. G. Khachiyan. Fast approximation schemes for convex programs with many blocks and coupling constraints. *SIAM J. Optimization*, 4:86–107, 1994.

[GLS88] M. Grötschel, L. Lovász, and A. Schrijver. *Geometric algorithms and combinatorial optimization*. Springer-Verlag, Berlin, 1988.

[Gol80] M.C. Golumbic. *Algorithmic Graph Theory and Perfect Graphs*. Academic Press, New York, 1980.

[GRE84] J.R. Gilbert, D.J. Rose, and A. Edenbrandt. A separator theorem for chordal graphs. *SIAM J. Alg. Discrete Methods*, 5:306–313, 1984.

[GVY96] N. Garg, V. V. Vazirani, and M. Yannakakis. Approximate max-flow min-(multi)cut theorems and their applications. *SIAM J. Comput.*, 25:235–251, 1994.

[Han89] M. Hansen. Approximation algorithms for geometric embeddings in the plane with applications to parallel processing problems. In *Proceedings of the 30th Annual IEEE Symposium on Foundations of Computer Science*, pages 604–609, 1989.

[Hu63] T.C. Hu. Multicommodity network flows. *Operations Res.*, 11:344–360, 1963.

[Kah93] N. Kahale. On reducing the cut ratio to the multicut problem. Technical Report 93–78, DIMACS, 1993.

[Kar84] N. Karmarkar. A new polynomial-time algorithm for linear programming. *Combinatorica*, 4:373–395, 1984.

[Kha79] L.G. Khachiyan. A polynomial algorithm in linear programming (in Russian). *Doklady Akademiia Nauk SSSR*, 244:1093–1096, 1979. English translation: *Soviet Mathematics Doklady* 20:191–194.

[KPR91] P. Klein, S. Plotkin, and S. Rao. Planar graphs, multicommodity flow, and network decomposition. In *Proceedings of the 23rd Annual ACM Symposium on Theory of Computing*, pages 682–690, 1991.

[KPST94] P. Klein, S. Plotkin, C. Stein, and É. Tardos. Faster approximation algorithms for the unit capacity concurrent flow problem with applications to routing and finding sparse cuts. *SIAM J. Comput.*, 23:466–487, 1994.

[KRAR95] P. Klein, S. Rao, A. Agrawal, and R. Ravi. An approximate max-flow min-cut relation for undirected multicommodity flow, with applications. *Combinatorica*, 15:187–202, 1995.

[LLR95] N. Linial, E. London, and Y. Rabinovich. The geometry of graphs and some of its algorithmic applications. *Combinatorica*, 15:215–246, 1995.

[LMP+95] T. Leighton, F. Makedon, S. Plotkin, C. Stein, É. Tardos, and S. Tragoudas. Fast approximation algorithms for multicommodity flow problems. *J. Comput. Sys. Sciences*, 50:228–243, 1995.

[LR88] T. Leighton and S. Rao. An approximate max-flow min-cut theorem for uniform multicommodity flow problems with applications to approximation algorithms. In *Proceedings of the 29th Annual IEEE Symposium on Foundations of Computer Science*, pages 422–431, 1988.

[LR94] T. Leighton and S. Rao. An approximation max-flow min-cut theorem for uniform multicommodity flow problems with applications to approximation algorithms. Unpublished manuscript, 1994.

[LT80] R.J. Lipton and R.E. Tarjan. Applications of a planar separator theorem. *SIAM J. Comput.*, 9:615–627, 1980.

[MR95] R. Motwani and P. Raghavan. *Randomized algorithms*. Cambridge University Press, Cambridge, 1995.

[Pla90] D. Plaisted. A heuristic algorithm for small separators in planar graphs. *SIAM J. Comput.*, 19:267–280, 1990.

[PST95] S. A. Plotkin, D. B. Shmoys, and É. Tardos. Fast approximation algorithms for fractional packing and covering problems. *Math. Oper. Res.*, 20:257–301, 1995.

[PT95] S. Plotkin and É. Tardos. Improved bounds on the max-flow min-cut ratio for multicommodity flows. *Combinatorica*, 15:425–434, 1995.

[RAK91] R. Ravi, A. Agrawal, and P. Klein. Ordering problems approximated: single-processor scheduling and interval graph completion. In *Proceedings of the 18th International Colloquium on Automata, Languages, and Processing, Lecture Notes in Computer Science 510*, pages 751–762, 1991.

[Rao87] S. Rao. Finding near optimal separators in planar graphs. In *Proceedings of the 28th Annual IEEE Symposium on Foundations of Computer Science*, pages 225–237, 1987.

[Sey95] P.D. Seymour. Packing directed circuits fractionally. *Combinatorica*, 15:281–288, 1995.

[SM90] F. Shahrokhi and D.W. Matula. The maximum concurrent flow problem. *J. Assoc. Comput. Mach.*, 37:318–334, 1990.

[Tra91] S. Tragoudas. *VLSI partitioning approximation algorithms based on multicommodity flow and other techniques*. PhD thesis, University of Texas, Dallas, 1991.

[TV93] É. Tardos and V. V. Vazirani. Improved bounds for the max-flow min-multicut ratio for planar and $K_{r,r}$-free graphs. *Inform. Proc. Lett.*, 47:77–80, 1993.

[Yan81] M. Yannakakis. Computing the minimum fill-in is *NP*-complete. *SIAM J. Alg. Discrete Methods*, 2:77–79, 1981.

6

APPROXIMATION ALGORITHMS FOR FINDING HIGHLY CONNECTED SUBGRAPHS

Samir Khuller

In honor of Richard Karp's 60th birthday

This chapter discusses approximation algorithms for the problem of finding minimum weight spanning subgraphs of desired connectivity. Algorithms addressing both edge and vertex connectivities are discussed for weighted and unweighted graphs. We also address the case of directed graphs.

INTRODUCTION

6.1

Let a graph $G = (V, E)$ denote the feasible links of a (proposed) communications network. An edge $e = (a, b)$ denotes the feasibility of adding a link between sites a and b. The weight of this edge, $w(e)$, represents the cost of constructing link e. A *connected* graph is one that contains a path between each pair of vertices. A minimum spanning tree is the minimum weight connected subgraph that includes all the vertices in G, i.e., the cheapest network that will allow all the sites to communicate. Such a network is highly susceptible to failures, since it cannot even survive a single link or site failure. A *spanning* subgraph refers to a subgraph that has the same vertex set as the original graph G.

For more reliable communication, one desires spanning subgraphs of higher connectivity. A network of edge-connectivity λ continues to allow communication between functioning sites even after as many as $\lambda - 1$ links have failed. A graph is said to be λ edge-connected if the deletion of any $(\lambda - 1)$ edges leaves it connected. These definitions extend in a straightforward way to λ vertex-connectivity. The only requirement is that the graph should have at least $\lambda + 1$ vertices, and the deletion of any $(\lambda - 1)$ vertices should leave it connected. Given a graph G with non-negative edge weights, and an integer λ, we consider the problem of finding a minimum-weight λ-connected spanning subgraph. We address the cases of edge and vertex connectivity. For most connectivity versions, the associated problems are NP-hard. In this case we would like to obtain suboptimal solutions in polynomial time. From now on we will refer to sites as vertices and links as edges.

A directed graph is called *strongly connected* if there is a directed path between each ordered pair of vertices u and v. We address the following elementary question for directed graphs: given a directed graph, how does one find a minimum weight strongly connected spanning subgraph? We show that this problem has intimate connections with the Minimum Equivalent Graph (MEG) problem as well.

In this chapter, we address only *uniform* connectivity problems. For results on non-uniform connectivity requirements, see Chapter 4 by Goemans and Williamson. The non-uniform connectivity problems are solved using the "primal-dual" method of linear programming; this usually results in approximation factors that are not as good as the ones obtained here.

Edge connectivity augmentation problems were first studied by Eswaran and Tarjan [ET76]. They studied the problem of making a given graph 2-connected (both vertex and edge connectivities were considered) and strongly connected with the addition of the least number of edges. They showed that when all potential edges are feasible and have weight 1, the problem can be solved optimally in polynomial time, and when the edges have arbitrary weights, the problem is NP-hard.

Subsequently, a lot of work was done on the problem of "increasing" the connectivity of a given graph to any desired value λ; most of these papers deal with the unweighted case where an edge may be added between *any* pair of vertices. This problem can be solved *optimally* in polynomial time, at least for the edge-connectivity case. We will not survey this body of research here since we are primarily interested in approximation techniques for NP-hard problems. For more information on such problems, see recent papers by Frank [F92], and Naor, Gusfield and Martel [NGM90]. For the vertex-connectivity case, the problem appears to be significantly harder, and no polynomial time algorithm is known for finding the optimal solution. Hsu and Ramachandran[HR91] and Hsu [H93] give algorithms for vertex connectivity for small connectivity values. These algorithms are quite complex. The problem of constructing a graph with n vertices, and connectivity λ with the least number of edges was first addressed by Harary [H62].

The first paper to address the issue of obtaining approximate solutions for the case when edges have weights is by Frederickson and JáJá [FJ81]. They provide approximation algorithms for the cases of 2-connectivity (edge and vertex) as well as strong connectivity problems. Subsequently, their algorithm was simplified by Khuller and Thurimella [KT92, KT93]. When the edge weights satisfy the triangle inequality, Frederickson and JáJá [FJ82] provided a 1.5 approximation for the minimum weight biconnected subgraph problem. In particular, they showed that Christofides heuristic for the traveling salesman problem [GJ79] gives a 1.5 approximation for this problem as well. This involves proving that the matching found by the heuristic is no more than half the weight of an optimal solution (this step is easy to argue for the traveling salesman problem). For 2-connectivity, the unweighted case was explored by Khuller and Vishkin [KV94], and Garg, Santosh and Singla [GSS93]. Recently, Chong and Lam [CL95, CL96] have given parallel approximation algorithms that achieve factors better than 2. These use algorithms to find approximate maximum matchings in parallel [FGHP93].

For any λ, fast algorithms for finding sparse certificates were given by Nagamochi and Ibaraki [NI92] and Cheriyan, Kao and Thurimella [CKT93]. The strong connectivity case is addressed by Khuller, Raghavachari and Young [KRY95, KRY94]. When parallel edges are allowed, Goemans and Bertsimas provide an approximation algorithm [GB93].

6.1.1   OUTLINE OF CHAPTER AND TECHNIQUES

The problems we deal with are divided broadly into four categories: edge connectivity, vertex connectivity, strong connectivity, and connectivity augmentation. In each case, we study both the weighted and unweighted problems.

In Section 6.2 we discuss the edge-connectivity results. This section surveys known results for both the weighted case as well as the $\{1/\infty\}$ case (where each edge has weight either 1 or ∞). In other words, the feasibility network is treated as an undirected graph, and each possible link is either feasible or infeasible. In this case we are interested in minimizing the total number of edges in our solution. Section 6.3 discusses the results on vertex connectivity. In Section 6.4 we discuss the problem of finding strongly connected spanning subgraphs in directed graphs. In Section 6.5 we study the problem of increasing the edge-connectivity of a given graph having an arbitrary connectivity, to being λ edge-connected.

The main techniques use the idea of "sparse-certificates" for unweighted graphs. For the general problem, when edges have weights, we use minimum weight branchings, as well as finding a collection of minimum weight disjoint branchings. Both these problems can be solved in polynomial time.

EDGE-CONNECTIVITY PROBLEMS

6.2

We begin this section by describing the algorithm for obtaining an approximation factor of 2 when the edges have weights. In Subsection 6.2.2 we consider the special case when the weights are either 1 or ∞; for this special case we can achieve approximation ratios less than 2.

6.2.1   WEIGHTED EDGE-CONNECTIVITY

Given a graph $G = (V, E)$ with weights on the edges and an integer λ, consider the problem of finding a *minimum* weight spanning subgraph $H = (V, E_H)$ that is λ edge-connected.

The algorithm given by Frederickson and JáJá [FJ81] achieves an approximation factor of 3 for $\lambda = 2$. First, find a minimum spanning tree. Now consider the problem of finding the least weight set of edges to add to the tree to obtain a 2 edge-connected subgraph. Not surprisingly, this is *NP*-hard as well [FJ81]. They give an algorithm with an approximation factor of 2 for the problem of augmenting connectivity, yielding an approximation factor of 3 for the least weight 2 edge-connected spanning subgraph. (In Section 6.5 we describe a simplification of their algorithm due to Khuller and Thurimella [KT92].)

We now briefly review the method given by Khuller and Vishkin [KV94] that yields an approximation algorithm for undirected graphs. Take the undirected graph G, and replace each undirected edge $e = (u, v)$ by two directed edges (u, v) and (v, u) with each edge having weight $w(e)$. Call this graph G^D. Now consider the following problem for directed graphs: given a directed graph G^D with weights on the edges, and a fixed root r, how does one find the *minimum weight* directed subgraph H^D that has at least λ edge-disjoint paths from a fixed root r to each vertex v? Gabow [G91] gives the fastest implementation of a weighted matroid intersection algorithm due to Edmonds [E79] to solve this problem optimally in $O(\lambda n(m + n \log n) \log n)$ time. Run Gabow's algorithm on the graph G^D, with an arbitrary vertex r chosen as the root. If at least one of the directed edges (u, v) or (v, u) is picked in H^D, then we add (u, v) to E_H.

LEMMA 6.1 The graph $H = (V, E_H)$ is a λ edge-connected spanning subgraph of G.

Proof. Suppose (for contradiction) that there is a $\lambda - 1$ edge cut in H that separates H into pieces C_1 and C_2. Let r be in C_1; now consider a vertex v in C_2. It is clear that r cannot have λ edge-disjoint directed paths to v. Thus, there is no cut set of size $\lambda - 1$. ∎

THEOREM 6.1 The total weight of E_H is at most twice the weight of the optimal solution.

Proof. Consider an optimal solution $\mathcal{OPT}(G)$ for the minimum weight λ edge-connected subgraph problem. Consider all the anti-parallel edges corresponding to edges in $\mathcal{OPT}(G)$. We get a directed subgraph in G^D of weight $2w(\mathcal{OPT}(G))$ (where $w(\mathcal{OPT}(G))$ is the total weight of the edges in $\mathcal{OPT}(G)$). From r there are λ edge-disjoint undirected paths to any vertex v; these also yield λ directed paths from r to v that are edge-disjoint. Thus, this subgraph has the property of having λ directed edge-disjoint paths from r to any vertex v. The optimum solution found by Gabow's algorithm has lower weight. ∎

6.2.2 UNWEIGHTED EDGE-CONNECTIVITY

Given an undirected graph G with n vertices and m edges, we would like to find a subgraph H that is λ edge-connected and has as few edges as possible. For the general case, Nagamochi and Ibaraki [NI92] showed how to find a spanning subgraph with at most λn edges (see also Thurimella's doctoral thesis [T89]) that has edge-connectivity

λ if and only if the original graph G has edge connectivity λ. Since each vertex is required to have degree at least λ, we get $\frac{\lambda n}{2}$ as a lower bound on any λ edge-connected spanning subgraph. Thus, this yields an approximation algorithm with a performance ratio of 2. In this section we describe a simple algorithm that finds a 2 edge-connected spanning subgraph by using Depth First Search (DFS). Moreover, it is shown that this algorithm achieves an approximation ratio of 1.5. Combining this with the ideas of [NI92, NP94, T89] yields an approximation ratio of $2 - \frac{1}{\lambda}$ for the problem of finding a λ edge-connected spanning subgraph.

6.2.2.1   2 edge-connectivity

In this section we present a linear time algorithm given by Khuller and Vishkin [KV94] to obtain a 2 edge-connected spanning subgraph from a given graph G. This algorithm obtains a solution that is at most $\frac{3}{2}$ times the optimal solution.

High-level Description of the Algorithm
We traverse G using DFS. A DFS-rooted tree T is computed; T has at most $n - 1$ edges, and all the non-tree edges are *back* edges (i.e., one of the endpoints of the edge is an ancestor of the other in T). All edges of T are picked for E_H. During the depth-first search the algorithm also picks a set of non-tree edges that will increase the edge connectivity by "covering" all the edges in T (since each edge in T is a potential bridge). A back edge may be chosen just before *withdrawing from a vertex for the last time*. Before withdrawing from a vertex v, we check whether the edge $(v, p(v))$, joining v to its parent, is currently a bridge or not. If $(v, p(v))$ is still a bridge, we cover it by adding to E_H a back edge from a descendant of v to low[v], where **low**[v] is the vertex with the smallest dfs-number that can be reached by following zero or more downgoing tree edges from v, and a single back edge.

   To implement the algorithm in linear time we need some simple data structures; the details of the algorithm may be found in [KV94].

Data Structures:
dfs[v]: A serial number given to a vertex the first time it is visited during DFS. For simplicity, we will assume that vertices are numbered by their dfs-number (i.e., $v = $ dfs[v]).
state of a vertex: Each vertex is initially "*unvisited*." After the DFS traversal visits it for the first time, it becomes "*discovered*." When we finally exit from the vertex it becomes "*finished*."
low[v]: defined earlier.
low$_H$[v]: This is defined to be the smallest numbered vertex that can be reached by following zero or more downgoing tree edges from v, and a *single* back edge that belongs to E_H.
savior[v]: This is defined to be the descendant end vertex of the back edge that goes to low[v].

The Approximation Analysis
Our analysis finds a partition of the vertices, called a *tree-carving* (see Figure 6.1), which is used to prove a lower bound on $\mathcal{OPT}(G)$, the number of edges in the optimal solution.

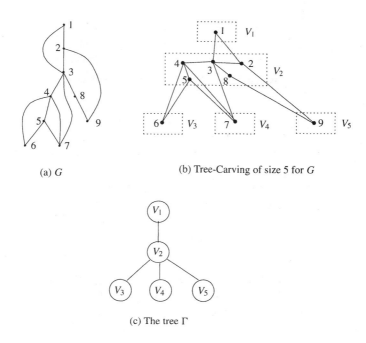

(a) *G*

(b) Tree-Carving of size 5 for *G*

(c) The tree Γ

FIGURE 6.1

*Example to show 2 edge-connectivity algorithm
and a tree-carving.*

The upper bound of $\frac{3}{2}$ on the approximation factor is established using this lower bound. After presenting the concept of a tree-carving, we apply it to the approximation analysis.

DEFINITION 6.1 A **tree-carving** of a graph is a partition of the vertex set V into subsets $V_1, V_2, \ldots, V_k$ with the following properties. Each subset constitutes a node of a tree Γ. For every vertex $v \in V_j$, all the neighbors of v in G belong either to V_j itself, or to V_i where V_i is adjacent to V_j in the tree Γ. The **size** of the tree-carving is k.

We will refer to the vertices of Γ as *nodes*, and the edges of Γ as *arcs*.

THEOREM 6.2 (Tree-Carving Theorem)
If graph $G = (V, E)$ has a tree-carving of size k, then a lower bound on the number of edges of any 2 edge-connected spanning subgraph in G is $2(k - 1)$.

It is interesting to note that the same proof implies that the smallest λ-connected subgraph of G must have at least $\lambda(k - 1)$ edges.

Proof. There are $k - 1$ arcs in the tree Γ. Each such arc $e = (V_i, V_j)$ partitions the vertices in G into two sets S_e and $V - S_e$. (Deletion of arc e breaks Γ into two trees Γ_1 and Γ_2, where V_i belongs to Γ_1. S_e is defined to be the union of the sets V_y that belong to Γ_1.) In any 2 edge-connected spanning subgraph we have: (1) at least two edges going from S_e to $V - S_e$, and (2) both these edges must have one endpoint in V_i and another in V_j; from the disjointness of V_i's it follows that for each arc e, there are two distinct edges in the subgraph. Since Γ has $k - 1$ arcs, we get a lower bound of $2(k - 1)$.   ■

Given T, the DFS-spanning tree, we will be interested in the following partition of the vertices of G, called the *DFS-tree partition*. Some recursive calls end by adding the back edge (savior[v], low[v]) to E_H, and some do not add any edge. For each call where a back edge is added to E_H, "remove" the tree edge from T; the resulting connected components of T (with some tree edges removed) provide the DFS-partition. Furthermore, T induces a *rooted tree structure* Γ on the sets in the DFS-tree partition. In fact, it is easy to modify the approximation algorithm to find the tree-carving as well; however this is not essential since it is only used for the analysis of the algorithm.

THEOREM 6.3   The DFS-tree partition yields a tree-carving of G.

Proof.   Let (v_1, v_2) be any non-tree edge in G. Suppose that v_1 is in set V_1 of the DFS-tree partition and v_2 is in set V_2. Let us assume that v_1 is an ancestor of v_2. Clearly, low[v_2] $\leq v_1$. Thus, by the algorithm there can be at most one deleted tree edge between them. Hence, either $V_1 = V_2$, or set V_1 is the parent set of set V_2 (in the rooted tree structure Γ).   ■

COROLLARY 6.1   Since the number of arcs in the tree-carving is exactly the same as the number of back edges that are added to E_H, we conclude that $\mathcal{OPT}(G) \geq 2(k - 1)$, where $k - 1$ is the number of added back edges.

THEOREM 6.4   The algorithm outputs a solution of size no more than $\frac{3}{2} \mathcal{OPT}(G)$.

Proof.   The number of edges added by the algorithm to H is: (i) $(n - 1)$, for the tree edges, plus (ii) $k - 1$ back edges, where k is also the size of the tree-carving. Hence, the number of edges in E_H is $n - 1 + k - 1$. Let $\mathcal{OPT}(G)$ be the number of edges in an optimal solution. A lower bound on $\mathcal{OPT}(G)$ is $\max(n, 2(k - 1))$, since n is the minimum number of edges in a 2 edge-connected graph with n vertices (each vertex should have degree at least 2), and $2(k - 1)$ follows from Corollary 6.1. Hence, the ratio of the algorithm's solution to $\mathcal{OPT}(G)$ is

$$\leq \frac{n - 1 + k - 1}{\max(n, 2(k - 1))}.$$

If $n \geq 2(k - 1)$, then clearly the ratio is $< 3/2$. If $n \leq 2(k - 1)$, it is again easy to see that the ratio is $< 3/2$.   ■

6.2.2.2 λ edge-connectivity

We now describe a linear time algorithm given by Nagamochi and Ibaraki [NI92] that finds a λ edge-connected spanning subgraph of a given graph G that has edge-connectivity at least λ. The algorithm finds a subgraph with at most $\lambda(n - 1)$ edges; since every vertex has degree at least λ, we get a lower bound of $\frac{\lambda n}{2}$ for $\mathcal{OPT}(G)$. Hence, this is a factor 2 approximation. We then use the previous DFS-based algorithm for 2 edge-connectivity to improve this ratio by $\frac{1}{\lambda}$.

The main idea behind their algorithm is to repeatedly find *maximal* spanning forests in the graph, and to delete them. After λ iterations of this method, we obtain λ forests, which form a λ edge-connected spanning subgraph assuming that the input graph was λ edge-connected. More formally, we state the following lemma (also due to [T89, NP94]).

LEMMA 6.2   For a graph $G = (V, E)$ that has edge connectivity λ, let $F_i = (V, E_i)$ be a maximal spanning forest in $G - E_1 \cup \ldots \cup E_{i-1}$, for $i = 1 \ldots \lambda$; then $G_\lambda = (V, E_1 \cup \ldots \cup E_\lambda)$ has edge connectivity λ.

Proof.   Assume (for contradiction) that G_λ contains a cut C of size $k < \lambda$ whose removal disconnects the graph G_λ into G'_λ and G''_λ. Clearly, at least one forest, say F_j, does not have any edges in C. Since the original graph G was λ edge-connected, it must be the case that there is at least one edge in G between the two components G'_λ and G''_λ that is not in C. Hence, in iteration j when we were picking F_j, we would pick at least one edge connecting G'_λ and G''_λ.   ∎

It is easy to find the set of forests by repeatedly scanning the graph λ times [T89, NP94]. The amazing fact about Nagamochi and Ibaraki's algorithm is that they can find all the forests in a *single* scan of the graph. During the search, for each edge e we compute the integer i satisfying $e \in E_i$. In fact, the algorithm assigns each edge to the forest it would have been assigned to, if we repeatedly removed spanning forests until the graph was completely exhausted.

For each vertex v, we maintain the rank $r(v)$, and $r(v) = i$ if v has been reached by an edge of the forest F_i.

We now argue that the algorithm in Figure 6.2 implements the algorithm that repeatedly finds forests and deletes them. Formally, what is shown is that each $F_i = (V, E_i)$ is a maximal spanning forest in $G - E_1 \cup \ldots \cup E_{i-1}$.

```
λ EDGE-CONNECTIVITY —
1    Label all nodes and edges as "unscanned"
2    r(v) = 0 for all v ∈ V
3    E_i = ∅
4    while there exist "unscanned" nodes do
5        Choose an "unscanned" node x with the largest r
6        for each "unscanned" edge e = (x, y) do
7            if r(x) = r(y) then r(x) = r(x) + 1
8            r(y) = r(y) + 1
9            E_r(y) = E_r(y) ∪ e
10           Mark e scanned
11       Mark x scanned
```

FIGURE 6.2

Nagamochi and Ibaraki's algorithm to find a λ edge-connected subgraph.

In Figure 6.3 we illustrate the execution of the algorithm via a small example.

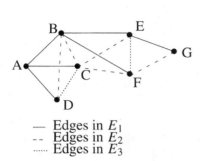

— Edges in E_1
-- Edges in E_2
······ Edges in E_3

Table to show r(v) values

	A	B	C	D	E	F	G
Initial	0	0	0	0	0	0	0
Scan A	1	1	1	1	0	0	0
Scan B	1	2	2	2	1	1	0
Scan C	1	2	3	3	2	2	0
Scan D	1	2	3	3	2	2	0
Scan E	1	2	3	3	3	3	1
Scan F	1	2	3	3	3	3	2
Scan G	1	2	3	3	3	3	2

FIGURE 6.3

Example to show the running of λ Edge Connectivity
algorithm.

PROPOSITION 6.1   For a vertex v let $E(v)$ denote the edges incident to v. At the start of each iteration of scanning an unscanned edge

$$E(v) \cap E_i \neq \emptyset \text{ for } i = 1, \dots, r(v)$$

$$E(v) \cap E_i = \emptyset \text{ for } i = r(v) + 1, \dots, \lambda.$$

Proposition 6.1 immediately implies that each subgraph F_i is acyclic, since we add edge $e = (x, y)$ to E_i only when $r(y)$ first becomes i, so there is no edge in E_i incident on y when e is added.

Before we prove that each forest F_i is maximal in $G - E_1 \cup \dots \cup E_{i-1}$, we give some definitions. If an edge $e = (u, v)$, with $E(u) \cap E_i = \emptyset$ and $E(v) \cap E_i = \emptyset$ is added to E_i, then the edge e is called the root edge of E_i. The vertex u is called the root vertex of E_i if it is scanned before v. (The reader should convince themselves that this edge is unique for each tree in E_i.) The key intuition is that once we create a tree T in E_i, *before* starting a new tree T' in E_i, we will have scanned all the nodes in T. This would guarantee that we do not process an edge between T and T' at some later point of time.

LEMMA 6.3   When we add an edge $e = (u, v)$ to E_i, there exists a path $P_{i-1} \subseteq E_{i-1}$ connecting u and v.

Proof.   Suppose there is no path connecting u and v in E_{i-1}. Then there must be two trees T_u and T_v that contain u and v respectively (observe that the labels of u and v are at least $i - 1$). Let u_0 and v_0 be the roots of these trees. Let the path from u_0 to u be $P = [u_0, u_1, \dots, u_k = u]$. Without loss of generality, u_0 was scanned before v_0. When

u_0 was scanned, $r(u_0) = i - 2$ and $r(v_0) \leq i - 2$. After scanning (u_0, u_1), $r(u_1) = i - 1$ and is scanned before v_0. In a similar manner we can argue that all the nodes on P are scanned before v_0 including v (after we scan the node u). This is a contradiction to the assumption that v_0 is the root of T_v. ∎

LEMMA 6.4 If there is a path $P_j \subseteq E_j$ connecting u and v, then there are paths $P_i \subseteq E_i$ connecting u and v, for all $i < j$.

Proof. For each edge in P_j, (by Lemma 6.3) we know that there is a path in E_{j-1} connecting the endpoints of that edge. Taking the union of all the paths for each edge gives us a path P_{j-1} from u to v in E_{j-1}. Similarly, we can prove this for $i = j - 2, \ldots, 1$ etc. ∎

THEOREM 6.5 Each graph $F_i = (V, E_i)$ is a maximal spanning forest in $G - E_1 \cup \ldots \cup E_{i-1}$.

Proof. We argued earlier that F_i is acyclic. If it is not maximal in $G - E_1 \cup \ldots \cup E_{i-1}$ then there is an edge $e \in E_j$ (with $j > i$) such that $(V, E_i \cup e)$ is a forest. By Lemma 6.3 we know that E_i must contain a path P_i from u to v. This would give a contradiction to the fact that $(V, E_i \cup e)$ is a forest. ∎

We now show how to find a subgraph of edge connectivity λ that is at most $2 - \frac{1}{\lambda}$ times the optimal. Find a 2 edge-connected graph by using the DFS-based algorithm described earlier. Let this graph be called H_2. Now add $\lambda - 2$ forests to H_2, by repeatedly removing the edges on each forest (see Figure 6.4).

A simple proof that this yields a λ edge-connected graph can be obtained in a manner similar to the proof of Lemma 6.2. The proof is left as an exercise for the reader.

Now let us bound the total number of edges added by this procedure. The number of edges in H_2 is (i) $n - 1$ tree edges plus (ii) $k - 1$ back edges, where k is the size of the tree-carving. In Step 4, we add at most $(\lambda - 2)(n - 1)$ edges to make the graph λ connected.

An obvious lower bound on the optimal solution is $\frac{\lambda n}{2}$ (by a degree argument); and $\lambda(k - 1)$ using the tree-carving lower bound. Putting this together we get

$$\frac{(n - 1) + (k - 1) + (\lambda - 2)(n - 1)}{\max\{\lambda(k - 1), \frac{\lambda n}{2}\}}.$$

Simplifying, we get the upper bound of $(2 - \frac{1}{\lambda})$.

λ EDGE-CONNECTIVITY —
1 Find H_2 a 2-edge connected subgraph using the DFS-based algorithm.
2 **for** $i = 3, \ldots, \lambda$
3   Let T_i be a spanning forest in $G - H_{i-1}$.
4   Let $H_i = H_{i-1} \cup T_i$.

FIGURE 6.4

Algorithm to find a λ edge-connected graph.

Remark: Recently, Khuller and Raghavachari [KR95] were able to obtain an algorithm with a performance ratio of at most 1.85 for *any* λ. The key idea is to augment the connectivity by two in each stage. The proof requires a subtle argument, and also uses the notion of tree-carvings.

OPEN PROBLEM 6.1   It seems likely that one should be able to obtain algorithms for which the performance ratio improves as λ increases, at least for the unweighted case. However, we have not been able to do this as yet. An increased understanding of higher connectivity seems essential before this can be done.

VERTEX-CONNECTIVITY PROBLEMS

6.3

We begin this section by describing the algorithm for obtaining an approximation factor approaching 2 when the edges have weights for biconnectivity. When the edge weights satisfy the triangle inequality, then a factor approaching 2 is possible for any λ [KR95]. In Subsection 6.3.2 we consider the special case when the weights are either 1 or ∞; for this special case we can achieve approximation ratios less than 2.

6.3.1   WEIGHTED VERTEX-CONNECTIVITY

For the general problem no constant factor approximation algorithms are known. The best known algorithm to find a λ vertex-connected subgraph for the weighted case is the algorithm due to Ravi and Williamson [RW95] that achieves a factor of $2H(\lambda)$, where $H(\lambda) = 1 + \frac{1}{2} \ldots + \frac{1}{\lambda}$. For the case of finding a 2 vertex-connected graph, an approximation algorithm achieving a factor of 3 was given by Frederickson and JáJá [FJ81], through solving the more general graph augmentation problem. It is possible to obtain an approximation factor of $2 + \frac{1}{n}$ by using a technique similar to the one used in Subsection 6.2.1.

Frank and Tardos [FT89] extended Edmonds method [E79] to show that the following problem can be solved in polynomial time: Given a directed graph G^D with weights on the edges and a fixed root r find the *minimum weight* directed subgraph H^D that has λ *internally vertex-disjoint* paths from a fixed root r to each vertex v.

Using this algorithm as a subroutine it is possible to obtain a factor 2 approximation for the weighted case, when $\lambda = 2$.

The idea is as follows: Create a new graph G^D as follows: for each undirected edge $e = (u, v)$ in G create bi-directional edges (u, v) and (v, u) in G^D, each of weight $w(e)$. Let $e' = (x, y)$ be the lowest weight edge in G.

We create a new vertex r as the root and add directed edges (r, x) and (r, y) of weight 0. We now run Frank and Tardos's algorithm to find the minimum weight subgraph H^D with $\lambda = 2$. This will provide two directed vertex-disjoint paths from r to each vertex v. Let E_H be the subset of edges in G such that at least one of its copies was chosen in H^D. We claim that the graph $H = (V, E_H \cup \{e'\})$ is 2-vertex connected (observe that r is not in H).

PROPOSITION 6.2   For any vertex v in G, there are paths $P(x, v)$ and $P(y, v)$ in H that are internally vertex disjoint.

LEMMA 6.5   The graph $H = (V, E_H \cup \{e'\})$ is 2 vertex-connected.

Proof.   Suppose H contains a cut vertex a. Let the deletion of a from $H \cup \{e'\}$ break the graph into components $C_1, \ldots, C_k$. Since x and y are adjacent they will be in $a \cup C_i$ (for some i). Without loss of generality assume that x and y belong to $a \cup C_1$. Consider a vertex $v \in C_2$. Clearly, there cannot be two vertex disjoint paths from x and y to v. ∎

THEOREM 6.6   The total weight of $E_H \cup \{e'\}$ is at most $(2 + \frac{1}{n})$ times the optimal solution.

Proof.   Since every 2 vertex-connected graph contains at least n edges, the minimum weight edge in G is at most $\frac{1}{n} w(\mathcal{OPT}(G))$, where $w(\mathcal{OPT}(G))$ is the weight of a minimum weight 2 vertex-connected spanning subgraph.

Now consider an optimal solution $\mathcal{OPT}(G)$ for the problem. Consider all the anti-parallel edges corresponding to edges in $\mathcal{OPT}(G)$. We get a directed subgraph in G^D of weight $2w(\mathcal{OPT}(G))$. From x and y there are 2 vertex-disjoint paths to any vertex v; these also yield 2 directed paths from r to v that are also internally vertex-disjoint. Thus, this subgraph has the property of having 2 directed vertex-disjoint paths from r to any vertex v. The optimum solution found by Frank and Tardos's algorithm has lower weight. ∎

Remark: Recently, Penn and Shasha-Krupnik [PS95] showed that the factor of $\frac{1}{n}$ can be removed by trying every possible edge, rather than simply picking the minimum weight edge.

Remark: For the case when the edge weights satisfy triangle inequality, Khuller and Raghavachari [KR95] present algorithms using similar techniques that achieve a performance ratio of $2 + 2\frac{(\lambda-1)}{n}$.

6.3.2   UNWEIGHTED VERTEX-CONNECTIVITY

Given an undirected graph G with n vertices and m edges, we would like to find a subgraph H that is λ vertex-connected and has as few edges as possible. Even though we proved the correctness of the Nagamochi and Ibaraki algorithm for edge-connectivity, what is surprising is that it finds a spanning subgraph with at most λn edges that has vertex-connectivity λ if and only if the original graph G has vertex connectivity λ. Since each vertex is required to have degree at least λ, we get that $\frac{\lambda n}{2}$ is a lower bound on any λ edge-connected spanning subgraph. This yields an approximation algorithm with a ratio of 2.

We now describe the algorithm due to Cheriyan and Thurimella [CT91]. The idea is to "peel" away maximal spanning forests from G, and to repeat this procedure λ times as was done for the edge connectivity case. To obtain a λ vertex-connected subgraph, one cannot use arbitrary maximal forests. Cheriyan and Thurimella suggest the use of the forest obtained by running Breadth First Search from an arbitrary vertex in each connected component. Taking the union of these forests yields a λ vertex-connected subgraph. The proof of the fact that this yields a λ vertex-connected subgraph is a little complicated. The reader is referred to the paper [CT91, CKT93].

6.3.2.1   2 vertex-connectivity

In this section we describe an algorithm that finds a 2 vertex-connected spanning subgraph by using depth first search [KV94]. Combined with the edge discarding technique of Garg, Santosh, and Singla [GSS93] one obtains an approximation ratio of 1.5. Garg, Santosh, and Singla [GSS93] improved the performance ratio of the algorithm due to Khuller and Vishkin [KV94] from $\frac{5}{3}$ to $\frac{3}{2}$. The algorithm has two phases. The first phase is similar to the algorithm for the 2 edge-connectivity case described earlier. The second phase achieves two goals: (i) an attempt is made to expunge tree edges and (ii) an attempt is made to modify the choice of back edges so that it will help in expunging tree edges.

High-level Description of the Algorithm
The *first* phase is as follows: In the graph G, do a depth first search to compute a DFS spanning tree T. We now pick a set of back edges that will increase the vertex connectivity of the tree to two by "detouring" around each vertex of the tree T. During the Depth First Search all the tree edges are added to E_H, as well as some subset of back edges. The back edges are chosen when the DFS traversal is visiting a vertex for the last time. When DFS *retreats out of a vertex v for the last time*, we check if the vertex u (parent of v) is potentially a cut vertex or not. If so, we can cover it by adding to E_H the *highest* going back edge from a descendant of v. (This will at least prevent the separation of v from $p(u)$ under the deletion of u.)

Before discussing the second phase, we define the notion of *carving* of a graph. The key difference between the carving and tree-carving is that in the latter, edges are only allowed to go to the parent node. In a carving, edges are allowed to go to a single vertex in the grandparent node as well.

DEFINITION 6.2   A **carving** of a graph is a partitioning of the vertex set V into a collection of subsets $V_1, V_2, \ldots, V_k$ with the following properties. Each subset constitutes a node of a rooted tree Γ. Each non-leaf node V_j of Γ has a special vertex denoted by $g(V_j)$ that belongs to $p(V_j)$. For every vertex $v \in V_i$, all the neighbors of v that are in ancestor sets of V_i belong to either

> *I.* V_i, or
>
> *II.* V_j, where V_j is the parent of V_i in the tree Γ, or
>
> *III.* V_ℓ, where V_ℓ is the grandparent in the tree Γ. In this case however, the neighbour of v can only be $g(p(V_i))$.

We will refer to the vertices of Γ as *nodes*, and the edges of Γ as *arcs*. The root vertex belongs to a special set called the root-set.

Given T, the DFS spanning tree, we will be interested in the partition of the vertices of G called the *DFS-tree partition*. Some recursive calls end by adding the back edge (savior[v], low[v]) to E_H. For each such call "remove" the corresponding tree edge from T; the resulting connected components of T (with some tree edges removed) provide the DFS-partition. Furthermore, T induces a *rooted tree structure* on the sets in the DFS-tree partition.

The proof of the following theorem is given in [KV94].

THEOREM 6.7   The DFS-tree partition yields a carving of G.

In the *second* phase the carving is processed "top-down" (starting with the root-set). At each step a modification is made to the choice of the back edge (going upwards) from a carving set. This method is able to delete some of the tree edges as it proceeds (a similar trick was used in [KV94] but was not powerful enough to give an approximation factor of $\frac{3}{2}$). The deletion of tree edges is justified by the following lemma.

LEMMA 6.6   Let G' be a 2 vertex-connected graph; C is a simple cycle in G', and $e = (u, v)$ is a chord in C. Then $G' - \{e\}$ is also 2 vertex-connected.

The *parent* vertex of a *carving-set* S is the special vertex of S. Each carving-set (except for the root-set) has a unique parent vertex.

During the "top-down" phase, each time we process a carving-set we either discard a tree edge, or find a new vertex to add to an independent set. Suppose $k - 1$ back edges were added in the first phase (k is the number of sets in the carving). In the second phase, for each added back edge, we either discard a tree edge (so the back edge does not cost us anything) or we add a new vertex to the independent set. On termination, if we have p back edges remaining, we are able to find an independent set of size p. Clearly, $2p$ is a lower bound on the optimal solution since an independent set trivially yields a carving of size $p + 1$ (by making each vertex of the independent set into a carving set, and all the other vertices into a single carving set).

We shall now jump into the guts of the second phase. When processing a carving-set, we decide which back edges to add out of its child blocks. Consider a set S with the back edge out of S being (v, u) with $v \in S$. Consider the path in T from v to $q = g(S)$, the parent vertex (or special vertex) of set S. Let w be the first vertex (excluding v) along this path that has no tree edge (other than the edges on the $v - q$ path) incident on it. If there is no such vertex then w is q.

If there is a back edge (x, w) with $x \in S'$, a child block of S in Γ. Instead of picking the highest going back edge from S' we pick the back edge (x, w). For all other child blocks we do not modify the choice of back edges. Picking this back edge allows the deletion of the edge connecting w to its child in T. There are two cases:

Case 1 $w = p(v)$: observe that the edge (v, w) is a chord on the cycle $u - v - - x - w - -q - - u$ and can be deleted (see Figure 6.5(a)).

Case 2 $w \neq p(v)$: let (r', r) and (r, w) be the last two edges on the path in the DFS tree from v to w. We now have two cases: the first case is when x is a descendant

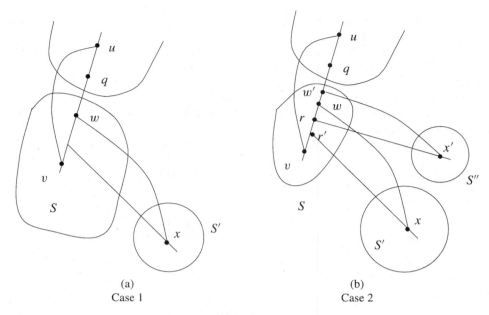

(a)
Case 1

(b)
Case 2

FIGURE 6.5

of r'. By our assumption on w, there must be a tree edge incident on vertex r other than the ones going to r' and w. Assume that this tree edge goes to a child S'' of S in Γ. There must be a back edge (x', w') where $x' \in S''$ and w' is on the path from w to q in the DFS tree. The edge (r, w) is a chord on the cycle $r - -x - w - -w' - x' - -r$ and can be deleted (see Figure 6.5(b)). The second case is when x is not a descendant of r'. In this case the edge (r, w) is a chord on the cycle $w - -q - -u - v - -r - -x - w$ and can be deleted.

We can use this tree edge to account for the back edge emanating from the set S, and this back edge is thus paid for. We label the set S as "free."

If w has no back edges from any child block, we *mark* w and label the set S as "marked." The root-set has no back edge emanating from it, and is marked "free." In addition, each leaf of the DFS tree forms a singleton set that is *marked*, and the set is labeled "marked." To argue that the set of marked vertices form an independent set, observe that no two marked vertices belong to the same set in the carving. Further, a marked vertex has no edge from any descendant set of the set that contains it. Thus, no two marked vertices can have an edge between them.

Upon termination, if we have p "marked" sets, we have $n - 1 + p$ edges in our solution, and the lower bound on the optimal solution is $\max(n, 2p)$. It is easy to see that this is at most $\frac{3}{2}$.

OPEN PROBLEM 6.2 The main open problem is to obtain a constant factor approximation when the edge weights do not satisfy the triangle inequality. Unlike the edge-connectivity case, we do not know how to obtain factors *less* than 2, even for the unweighted case.

STRONG-CONNECTIVITY PROBLEMS

6.4

Most of the network design literature addresses the problem of finding subgraphs having certain connectivities, only for undirected graphs. We now turn our attention to perhaps the most elementary corresponding problem in directed graphs. Given a strongly connected directed graph, find a minimum strongly connected spanning subgraph (SCSS). Not surprisingly, this problem is *NP*-hard by a simple reduction from Hamilton Cycle in directed graphs. This problem was first studied by Frederickson and JáJá [FJ81] for the weighted case, and an algorithm achieving an approximation factor of 2 was obtained. (This is obtained by taking the union of a minimum weight in-branching and a minimum weight out-branching, rooted at an arbitrary vertex.) For the unweighted case, Khuller, Raghavachari, and Young [KRY95] obtained an approximation algorithm with a performance ratio of about 1.64, which was subsequently improved to 1.61 [KRY94]. The algorithms have a relatively high running time, albeit polynomial. An almost linear time algorithm that achieves a ratio of 1.75 is also described.

The MEG (minimum equivalent graph) problem is the following: Given a directed graph, find a smallest subset of the edges that maintains all reachability relations between nodes. This problem is *NP*-hard; in fact, the heart of the MEG problem is the minimum SCSS (strongly connected spanning subgraph) problem — the MEG problem restricted to strongly connected digraphs. The MEG problem reduces in linear time [CLR89] to a single acyclic problem given by the so-called "strong component graph," together with one minimum SCSS problem for each strong component (given by the subgraph induced by that component). Furthermore, the reduction preserves approximation, in the sense that *c*-approximate solutions to the subproblems yield a *c*-approximate solution to the original problem. Hence, an approximation algorithm for the SCSS problem implies an approximation algorithm for the MEG problem. Moyles and Thompson [MT69] observe this decomposition and give exponential-time algorithms for the restricted problems. Hsu [H75] gives a polynomial-time algorithm for the acyclic MEG problem.

First we describe the basic algorithm that achieves a factor of 1.64 in polynomial time. The algorithm and its analysis are based on the simple idea of contracting long cycles. After that we will describe the nearly linear-time algorithm that achieves a ratio of 1.75. To learn about the improvement to 1.61 the reader is referred to [KRY94].

6.4.1   POLYNOMIAL TIME APPROXIMATION ALGORITHMS

Given a strongly connected graph, the basic algorithm finds as long a cycle as it can, contracts the cycle, and recurses. The contracted graph remains strongly connected. When the graph finally collapses into a single vertex, the algorithm returns the set of edges contracted during the course of the algorithm as the desired SCSS. The algorithm achieves a performance guarantee of any constant *greater* than $\pi^2/6 \approx 1.645$ in polynomial time.

Before describing the algorithm we discuss some basic notation used in the rest of the section. To *contract* a pair of vertices u, v of a digraph is to replace u and v

(and each occurrence of u or v in any edge) by a single new vertex, and to delete any subsequent self-loops and multi-edges. Each edge in the resulting graph is identified with the corresponding edge in the original graph or, in the case of multi-edges, the single remaining edge is identified with any one of the corresponding edges in the original graph. To contract an edge (u, v) is to contract the pair of vertices u and v. To contract a set S of pairs of vertices in a graph G is to contract the pairs in S in arbitrary order. The contracted graph is denoted by G/S. Contracting an edge is also analogously extended to contracting a set of edges.

Let $\mathcal{OPT}(G)$ be the minimum size of any subset of the edges that strongly connects G. In general, the term "cycle" refers only to simple cycles.

We begin by showing that if a graph has no long cycles, then the size of any SCSS is large.

LEMMA 6.7 Cycle Lemma   For any directed graph G with n vertices, if a longest cycle of G has length $\mathcal{C}$, then

$$\mathcal{OPT}(G) \geq \frac{\mathcal{C}}{\mathcal{C}-1}(n-1).$$

Proof.   Starting with a minimum-size subset that strongly connects the graph, repeatedly contract cycles in the subset until no cycles are left. Observe that the maximum cycle length does not increase under contractions. Consequently, for each cycle contracted the ratio of the number of edges contracted to the decrease in the number of vertices is at least $\frac{\mathcal{C}}{\mathcal{C}-1}$. Since the total decrease in the number of vertices is $n - 1$, at least $\frac{\mathcal{C}}{\mathcal{C}-1}(n-1)$ edges are contracted.   ■

Note that the above lemma gives a lower bound which is existentially tight. For all values of $\mathcal{C}$, there exist graphs for which the bound given by the lemma is equal to $\mathcal{OPT}(G)$. Also note that $\mathcal{C}$ has a trivial upper bound of n and, using this, we get a lower bound of n for $\mathcal{OPT}(G)$, which is the known trivial lower bound.

LEMMA 6.8 Contraction Lemma   For any directed graph G and set of edges S,

$$\mathcal{OPT}(G) \geq \mathcal{OPT}(G/S).$$

Proof.   Any SCSS of G, contracted around S (treating the edges of S as pairs), is an SCSS of G/S.   ■

The algorithm is the following. Fix k to be any positive integer.

CONTRACT-CYCLES$_k(G)$ —
1   **for** $i = k, k - 1, k - 2, ..., 2$
2   **while** the graph contains a cycle with at least i edges
3   Contract the edges on such a cycle.
4   **return** the contracted edges

We will show that the algorithm runs in polynomial time for any fixed value of k. (Note that it runs in polynomial time for any value of k, if we can find a cycle of length at least k, if one exists.) It is clear that the edge set returned by the algorithm strongly connects the graph. The following theorem establishes an upper bound on the number of edges returned by the algorithm.

THEOREM 6.8   CONTRACT-CYCLES$_k(G)$ returns at most $c_k \cdot \mathcal{OPT}(G)$ edges, where

$$\frac{\pi^2}{6} \leq c_k \leq \frac{\pi^2}{6} + \frac{1}{(k-1)k}.$$

Proof.   Initially, let the graph have n vertices. Let n_i vertices remain in the contracted graph after contracting cycles with i or more edges ($i = k, k-1, ..., 2$).

How many edges are returned? In contracting cycles with at least k edges, at most $\frac{k}{k-1}(n - n_k)$ edges are contributed to the solution. For $i < k$, in contracting cycles with i edges, $\frac{i}{i-1}(n_{i+1} - n_i)$ edges are contributed. The number of edges returned is thus at most

$$\frac{k}{k-1}(n - n_k) + \sum_{i=2}^{k-1} \frac{i}{i-1}(n_{i+1} - n_i) \leq \left(1 + \frac{1}{k-1}\right)n - 2n_2 + \sum_{i=3}^{k} \frac{n_i}{(i-1)(i-2)}$$

$$= \left(1 + \frac{1}{k-1}\right)n - 2 + \sum_{i=3}^{k} \frac{n_i}{(i-1)(i-2)} \leq \left(1 + \frac{1}{k-1}\right)n + \sum_{i=3}^{k} \frac{n_i - 1}{(i-1)(i-2)}.$$

(To prove the last inequality, we use the fact that $\sum_{i=3}^{k} \frac{1}{(i-1)(i-2)} \leq 1$.)

Clearly $\mathcal{OPT}(G) \geq n$. For $2 \leq i \leq k$, when n_i vertices remain, no cycle has more than $i-1$ edges. By Lemmas 6.7 and 6.8, $\mathcal{OPT}(G) \geq \frac{i-1}{i-2}(n_i - 1)$. Thus, the number of edges returned, divided by $\mathcal{OPT}(G)$, is at most

$$\frac{\left(1 + \frac{1}{k-1}\right)n}{\mathcal{OPT}(G)} + \sum_{i=3}^{k} \frac{\frac{n_i - 1}{(i-1)(i-2)}}{\mathcal{OPT}(G)} \leq \frac{\left(1 + \frac{1}{k-1}\right)n}{n} + \sum_{i=3}^{k} \frac{\frac{n_i - 1}{(i-1)(i-2)}}{\frac{i-1}{i-2}(n_i - 1)} = \frac{1}{k-1} + \sum_{i=1}^{k-1} \frac{1}{i^2} = c_k.$$

Using the identity (from [K73, p.75]) $\sum_{i=1}^{\infty} \frac{1}{i^2} = \frac{\pi^2}{6}$, we get

$$\frac{\pi^2}{6} \leq c_k = \frac{\pi^2}{6} + \frac{1}{k-1} - \sum_{i=k}^{\infty} \frac{1}{i^2}$$

$$\leq \frac{\pi^2}{6} + \frac{1}{k-1} - \sum_{i=k}^{\infty} \frac{1}{i(i+1)}$$

$$= \frac{\pi^2}{6} + \frac{1}{k-1} - \frac{1}{k}$$

$$= \frac{\pi^2}{6} + \frac{1}{(k-1)k}.$$

∎

If desired, standard techniques can yield more accurate estimates of c_k, e.g., $c_k = \frac{\pi^2}{6} + \frac{1}{2k^2} + O\left(\frac{1}{k^3}\right)$. If the graph initially has no cycle longer than ℓ ($\ell \geq k$), then the analysis can be generalized to show a performance guarantee of $\frac{k^{-1} - \ell^{-1}}{1 - k^{-1}} + \sum_{i=1}^{k-1} 1/i^2$. For instance, in a graph with no cycle longer than 5, the analysis bounds the performance guarantee (when $k = 5$) by 1.424.

Table 6.1 gives lower and upper bounds on the performance guarantee of the algorithm for small values of k and in the limit as $k \to \infty$. The lower bounds on the performance of our algorithm are shown in [KRY95].

k	Upper Bound	Lower Bound
3	1.750	1.750
4	1.694	1.666
5	1.674	1.625
∞	1.645	1.500

Table 6.1: Bounds on the performance guarantee.

For any fixed k, CONTRACT-CYCLES$_k$ can be implemented in polynomial time using exhaustive search to find long cycles. For instance, if a cycle of size at least k exists, one can be found in polynomial time as follows. For each simple path P of $k - 1$ edges, check whether a path from the head of P to the tail exists after P's internal vertices are removed from the graph. If k is even, there are at most $m^{k/2}$ such paths; if k is odd, the number is at most $n \, m^{(k-1)/2}$. It takes $O(m)$ time to decide if there is a path from the head of P to the tail of P. For the first iteration of the for loop, we may have $O(n)$ iterations of the while loop. Since the first iteration is the most time consuming, the algorithm can be implemented in $O(n \, m^{1+k/2})$ time for even k and $O(n^2 \, m^{(k+1)/2})$ time for odd k.

6.4.2 NEARLY LINEAR-TIME IMPLEMENTATION

We now describe a practical, near linear-time implementation of CONTRACT-CYCLES$_3$. The performance guarantee achieved is $c_3 = 1.75$. CONTRACT-CYCLES$_3$ consists of two phases: (1) repeatedly finding and contracting cycles of three or more edges (called *long* cycles), until no such cycles exist, and then (2) contracting the remaining 2-cycles.

High-level description of the algorithm
To perform Phase (1), the algorithm does a DFS of the graph from an arbitrary root. During the search, the algorithm identifies edges for contraction by adding them to a set S. At any point in the search, G' denotes the subgraph of edges and vertices traversed so far. The rule for adding edges to S is as follows: when an edge is traversed, if the new edge creates a long cycle in G'/S, the algorithm adds the edges of the cycle to S. The algorithm thus maintains that G'/S has no long cycles. When the DFS finishes, G'/S has only 2-cycles. The edges on these 2-cycles, together with S, are the desired SCSS.

Because G'/S has no long cycles and the fact that the original graph is strongly connected, G'/S maintains a simple structure:

LEMMA 6.9 After the addition of any edge to G' and the possible contraction of a cycle by adding it to S: (i) The graph G'/S consists of an outward branching and some of its reverse edges. (ii) The only reverse edges that might not be present are those on the "active" path: from the super-vertex containing the root to the super-vertex in G'/S containing the current vertex of the DFS.

Proof.   Clearly the invariant is initially true. We show that each given step of the algorithm maintains the invariant. In each case, if u and w denote vertices in the graph, then let U and W denote the vertices in G'/S containing u and w, respectively.

When the DFS traverses an edge (u, w) to visit a new vertex w:

Vertex w and edge (u, w) are added to G'. Vertex w becomes the current vertex. In G'/S, the outward branching is extended to the new vertex W by the addition of edge (U, W). No other edge is added, and no cycle is created. Thus, part (i) of the invariant is maintained. The super-vertex containing the current vertex is now W, and the new "active path" contains the old "active path". Thus, part (ii) of the invariant is also maintained.

When the DFS traverses an edge (u, w) and w is already visited:

If $U = W$ or the edge (U, W) already exists in G'/S, then no cycle is created, G'/S is unchanged, and the invariant is clearly maintained. Otherwise, the edge (u, w) is added to G' and a cycle with the simple structure illustrated in Figure 6.6 is created in G'/S. The cycle consists of the edge (U, W), followed by the (possibly empty) path of reverse edges from W to the lowest-common-ancestor (lca) of U and W, followed by the (possibly empty) path of branching edges from lca(U, W) to U. Addition of (U, W) to G'/S and contraction of this cycle (in case it is a long cycle) maintains part (i) of the invariant. If the "active path" is changed, it is only because part of it is contracted, so part (ii) of the invariant is maintained.

When the DFS finishes visiting a vertex w:

No edge is added and no cycle is contracted, so part (i) is clearly maintained. Let u be the new current vertex, i.e., w's parent in the DFS tree. If $U = W$, then part (ii) is clearly maintained. Otherwise, consider the set D of descendants of w in the DFS tree.

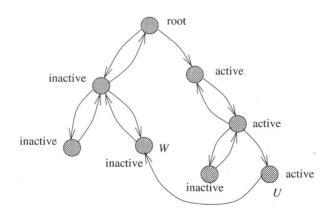

FIGURE 6.6

*Contracted graph G'/S while examining
an edge from U to W.*

Since the original graph is strongly connected, some edge (x, y) in the original graph goes from the set D to its complement $V - D$. All vertices in D have been visited, so (x, y) is in G'. By part (i) of the invariant, the vertex in G'/S containing x must be W, while the vertex in G'/S containing y must be U. Otherwise, the edge corresponding to (x, y) in G'/S would create a long cycle.   ∎

The algorithm maintains the contracted graph G'/S using a union-find data structure [T83] to represent the vertices in the standard way. When a cycle arises in G'/S, it must be of the form described in the proof of Lemma 6.9 and illustrated in Figure 6.6. Using these data structures, the algorithm discovers it and, if it is long, contracts it in a number of union-find operations proportional to the length of the cycle. This yields an $O(m\alpha(m, n))$-time algorithm.

THEOREM 6.9   There is an $O(m\alpha(m, n))$-time approximation algorithm for the minimum SCSS problem achieving a performance guarantee of 1.75 on an m-edge, n-vertex graph.

Here $\alpha(m, n)$ is the inverse-Ackermann function associated with the union-find data structure [T83].

Remark: A natural improvement to the cycle-contraction algorithm is to modify the algorithm to solve the problem *optimally* once the contracted graph has no cycles longer than a given length c. We use SCSS_c to denote the minimum SCSS problem restricted to digraphs with no cycle longer than c. The minimum SCSS_2 problem is trivial. For instance, for $c = 3$, this modification improves the performance guarantee to $\pi^2/6 - 1/36 \approx 1.617$. The minimum SCSS_3 problem can be solved in polynomial time, as shown by Khuller, Raghavachari and Young [KRY94]. However, further improvement in this direction is limited: we show that the minimum SCSS_5 problem is *NP*-hard.

OPEN PROBLEM 6.3   Is a performance ratio better than 2 possible for the weighted strong connectivity problem?

CONNECTIVITY AUGMENTATION

6.5

Let $G = (V, E)$ be a graph with a non-negative weight function w on the edges. Let $G_0 = (V, E_0)$ be a subgraph of G. The goal is to add a minimum weight set of edges, *Aug*, to G_0, such that the resulting graph is λ-connected for a given λ. The edges in $E - E_0$ are also referred to as the *Feasible* edges. We are permitted to only add edges from the graph G. For $\lambda > 1$, the problem is *NP*-hard. For $\lambda = 2$, an approximation algorithm that achieved a factor of 2 was given by Frederickson and JàJà [FJ81] when G_0 is a connected graph. (If G_0 is not connected initially, we may add a minimum spanning tree to connect its connected components.) Here we present a simplification of the algorithm developed by Khuller and Thurimella [KT93]. We describe algorithms for both the edge and vertex connectivity problems. We also show that an approximation factor of 2 can be achieved in polynomial time for any λ. This is done by an extension of the algorithm described in Subsection 6.2.1.

We first describe some notation used in this section. The 2 vertex-connected components of a graph are also referred to as *blocks*. For a vertex v in a rooted tree Γ, let the components formed by the deletion of v be called $C_1(v), C_2(v), \ldots, C_{d(v)}(v)$, where $d(v)$ is the degree of v in Γ. If v is not the root, we will assume that $C_1(v)$ is the component that contains the root, and the other components correspond to subtrees rooted at the children of vertex v. In a rooted tree, for a vertex u we denote its parent by $p(u)$.

We refer to an undirected edge between two vertices x and y as (x, y). On the other hand, a directed edge from x to y is denoted by $x \to y$.

6.5.1 INCREASING EDGE CONNECTIVITY FROM 1 TO 2

Notice that we only need to show how to increase the edge connectivity of a tree due to the following observation. If we are given G_0 with nontrivial 2 edge-connected components, then we can shrink the vertex sets of these components into single vertices, resulting in a tree whose edges are the bridges of G_0. The edges to be retained from *Feasible* are the minimum weight edges that connect vertices in different 2 edge-connected components of G_0. (Observe that the edges of *Feasible* that connect vertices of the same 2 edge-connected component are of no use in augmenting G_0. Similarly, among the edges that connect two distinct 2 edge-connected components, only the minimum weight edge is of interest.)

From G_0, we will construct a directed graph G^D and find a minimum weight out-branching from a vertex r. (If there is no branching that spans all the vertices, we can show that there is no way to increase the connectivity of the network.) Using a minimum weight branching of G^D, we can find a set of edges of $G - G_0$ whose addition will increase the connectivity of G_0. We can also show that the total weight of the edges added by this technique is no more than twice the weight of an optimal augmentation.

The algorithm is as follows:

1. (*Construct $G^D = (V, E_D)$*)

   a. Pick an arbitrary node r and root the tree G_0 at r by directing all the edges towards the root. Denote the resulting tree by Γ.

   b. Add to E_D the directed tree edges of Γ and set their weight to zero.

   c. Consider the edges that belong to $G = (V, E)$ but do not belong to G_0 (edges in $E - E_0$). For each such edge (u, v), we add directed edges to E^D. (We will refer to these directed edges as *images* of (u, v), and we say these directed edges are *generated* by (u, v).)
   Suppose that the edge e with weight $w(e)$, joins vertices u and v belonging to the tree Γ. There are two cases depending on the relative locations of u and v in the tree Γ (see Fig 6.7).

      i. If u is an ancestor of v (the converse is symmetric): then add an edge $u \to v$ in G^D with weight $w(e)$.

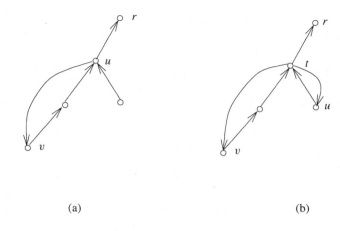

(a)   (b)

FIGURE 6.7

Construction of G^D.

> ***ii.*** If neither u nor v is an ancestor of the other: let $t = l.c.a(u, v)$ (least common ancestor in the rooted tree Γ). Add edges $t \to u$ and $t \to v$ in G^D, each with weight $w(e)$.

> **2.** Find a minimum weight branching in G^D rooted at r. For each directed edge e that is picked as part of the branching, and that does not belong to the directed tree Γ, add the corresponding edge in $E - E_0$ that generated e. The set of edges added is *Aug*.

Observe that all edges of $G^D - \Gamma$ are such that they connect a vertex to one of its descendants in Γ.

LEMMA 6.10   If G is 2 edge-connected, then the directed graph G^D is strongly connected.

Proof.   Clearly, all the vertices of G^D can reach the root r using edges from the tree Γ. Further, let us assume that G^D is not strongly connected. Of all the vertices that cannot be reached from the root, let u be the vertex that is closest to the root in Γ. Clearly, the entire subtree rooted at u must consist of unreachable vertices. Since the edge $(u, p(u))$ in G is not a bridge in G, there must be another edge (v, s) in G going from a vertex v (that is in the subtree rooted at u), to vertex s that is not in this subtree.

Such an edge would have generated a directed edge from a vertex w to v in G^D where w is an ancestor of v (specifically the least common ancestor of v and s). Since w is a proper ancestor of u, it is reachable from r in G^D. Therefore v is reachable from r, and hence, u as well. Thus, we obtain a contradiction. ∎

LEMMA 6.11   If G is 2 edge-connected, then the edge connectivity of the graph G_0 together with the edges in *Aug* is at least 2.

Proof. Assume G is 2 edge-connected. Then by the previous lemma, we can find a minimum weight branching in G^D. Next, assume that despite the addition of the edges in Aug to G_0, the resulting graph has bridges. All such bridges are the tree edges in Γ. Let $(u, p(u))$ be one such edge of Γ that is closest to the root (it does not have to be unique). Since vertices in the subtree rooted at u are reached from r in the branching it must be the case that there is a directed edge $w \rightarrow v$ from a vertex w (proper ancestor of u) to v (descendant of u) in the minimum weight branching. Such an edge would have been generated by an edge connecting v to a vertex not in the subtree rooted at u. This edge would belong to Aug, and hence, the edge $(u, p(u))$ is not a bridge. ∎

LEMMA 6.12 The weight of Aug is less than twice the optimal augmentation.

Proof. We prove the lemma by exhibiting a branching whose weight is at most twice the weight of the optimal augmentation. Consider the minimum weight set of edges $\mathcal{OPT}(G)$ that would increase the connectivity from 1 to 2. Consider all the directed edges that are "generated" by edges that belong to $\mathcal{OPT}(G)$. These directed edges together with the tree edges yield a strongly connected graph with total weight on the edges at most $2w(\mathcal{OPT}(G))$ (each edge of weight w generated at most two directed edges, each of weight w). Hence, the branching that we find has total weight of at most $2w(\mathcal{OPT}(G))$. ∎

THEOREM 6.10 There is an approximation algorithm to find an augmentation to increase the edge connectivity of a connected graph to 2 with weight less than twice the optimal augmentation that runs in $O(m + n \log n)$ time.

Proof. The correctness of the algorithm follows from Lemma 6.11 and Lemma 6.12. The bridge-connected components can be found in $O(m + n)$ time [AHU74] and a minimum weight branching can be found in $O(m + n \log n)$ time [GGST86]. Least common ancestors for the m pairs can be found in $O(m + n)$ time by using the algorithm of Harel and Tarjan [HT84]. ∎

6.5.2 INCREASING VERTEX CONNECTIVITY FROM 1 TO 2

We can assume without loss of generality that G_0 is a connected graph just as in the case of edge connectivity. Our overall strategy is similar to the one used in the previous section. That is, we first obtain a tree structure Γ of the blocks of G_0, construct a weighted, directed graph G^D using Γ and G. We then find a minimum weight branching in G^D which will indicate the edges of $E - E_0$ that are to be added to increase the connectivity of G_0. We remark that Γ, in the case of vertex connectivity, is quite different from that of the previous section.

We first describe an algorithm to construct the "block cut tree" (see Figure 6.8).

1. be the cut vertices and blocks of $G_0 = (V, E_0)$, respectively. The vertex set $V(\Gamma)$ is a union of V_a and V_b where $V_a = \{a_1, a_2, ...\}$ and $V_b = \{b_i \mid B_i \text{ is a block of } G_0\}$. Associated with each vertex in $V(\Gamma)$ is a set. For $a_i \in V_a$, $X_i = \{a_i\}$. For $b_i \in V_b$, $Y_i = \{v_j \mid v_j \in B_i$, and v_j is not a cut vertex in $G_0\}$.

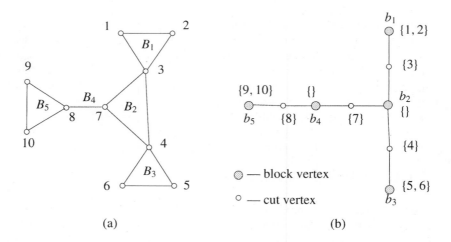

FIGURE 6.8

Construction of block cut vertex tree Γ.

2. The edge set $E(\Gamma)$ consists of edges (a_i, b_j) where a_i is a cut vertex that belongs to block B_j.

In the block cut tree Γ, each edge is between a vertex in V_a and a vertex in V_b.

For a vertex u of V, the vertex of Γ that *corresponds* to u is u if u is a cut vertex, and b_i otherwise, where B_i is the unique block containing u. In the following, by *superimposing* an edge $(x, y) \in G$ on Γ, we mean adding an edge between $a_i, b_j \in V(\Gamma)$ where the associated sets X_i and Y_j contain x and y respectively.

The algorithm is as follows:

1. Superimpose all the edges of $E - E_0$ on Γ. Discard all the self-loops. Among the multiple edges retain the cheapest edge, discarding the rest.

2. a. Pick an arbitrary leaf of Γ to be the root r, and direct all the edges of Γ towards r. Continue to denote the resulting tree by Γ.

b. Add to E_D the directed tree edges of Γ and set their weight to zero.

c. Consider the superimposed edges of $E - E_0$ on Γ. Let (u, v) be one such superimposed edge. For each such edge we add directed edges to E^D. (We will refer to these directed edges as *images* of (u, v), and we say these directed edges are *generated* by (u, v).)

Suppose that the edge e with weight $w(e)$, joins vertices u and v belonging to the tree Γ. There are two cases depending on the relative locations of u and v in the tree Γ (see Figure 6.9 on page 261).

i. symmetric): then add an edge $u \to v$ in G^D with weight $w(e)$.

ii. let $t = l.c.a(u, v)$ (least common ancestor in the rooted tree Γ). Add edges $t \to u$ and $t \to v$ in G^D, each with weight $w(e)$. Also add edges $u \to v$ and $v \to u$, each with weight $w(e)$.

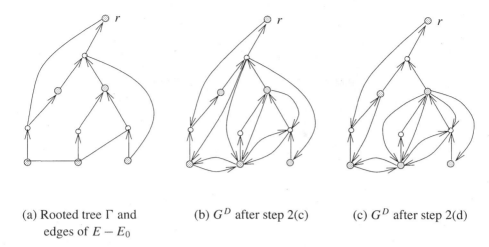

(a) Rooted tree Γ and edges of $E - E_0$

(b) G^D after step 2(c)

(c) G^D after step 2(d)

FIGURE 6.9

Construction of G^D in the case of vertex connectivity.

    d. Modify E_D as follows. For every $u \in V_a$, if there is an outgoing edge from u to a descendant v, then replace that edge with $u_v \to v$ where u_v is the child of u on the tree path from u to v.

  3. Find a minimum weight branching in G^D rooted at r. For each directed edge e that is picked as part of the branching, and does not belong to the directed tree Γ, add the corresponding edge in $E - E_0$ that generated e. The set of edges added is *Aug*.

In the directed graph G^D there are no outgoing edges from a cut vertex to any of its descendants in Γ.

Observation: Consider the components formed on the deletion of a vertex $u \in V_a$ from Γ. The edges of G when superimposed on $\Gamma - u$ connect all these components.

The proof of the following lemma is somewhat technical, and is omitted.

LEMMA 6.13 If G is 2 vertex-connected, then the directed graph G^D is strongly connected.

LEMMA 6.14 If G is 2 vertex-connected, then the vertex connectivity of the graph G_0, together with the edges in *Aug*, is at least 2.

Proof. Assume that despite the addition of the edges in *Aug* to G_0, the resulting graph has a cut vertex u. We will now show that u is destroyed as a cut vertex in the tree Γ, and hence, in G_0. Consider the components $C_1(u), \ldots, C_{d(u)}(u)$ in Γ. Partition the components into two groups as follows. The first group contains all the components that get connected to $C_1(u)$ (by an edge or a path) when the edges of Aug are superimposed on Γ. The second group contains the rest. Notice that both the groups are non-empty. Since G^D is strongly connected all the vertices are reachable from the root in the minimum weight branching. Since there are no outgoing edges from u to its descendants by the previous observation, there must be an edge $s \to v$ in the branching that satisfies the following. This edge has the property that $s \in C_i(u)$ and $v \in C_j(u)$, where $C_i(u)$ and $C_j(u)$ belong to the first and second groups respectively. The edge that generated $s \to v$ in Aug would connect $C_i(u)$ to $C_j(u)$ in $G_0 + Aug$, yielding a contradiction. ∎

LEMMA 6.15   The weight of Aug is less than twice the optimal augmentation.

Proof.   We prove the lemma by exhibiting a branching whose weight is at most twice the weight of the optimal augmentation. Consider the minimum weight set of edges $\mathcal{OPT}(G)$ that would increase the connectivity from 1 to 2. Consider all the directed edges that are "generated" by edges that belong to $\mathcal{OPT}(G)$.

These directed edges together with the tree edges yield a strongly connected graph with total weight on the edges at most $4w(\mathcal{OPT}(G))$ (each edge of weight w generated at most four directed edges, each of weight w). Now pick a minimum weight branching in this graph. Notice that for each cross edge (u, v) (when neither u nor v is an ancestor of the other) even though we generate four directed edges in G^D, no minimum weight branching will use more than two of these four edges. (Otherwise, it will not be a valid branching.) Hence, the branching that we find has total weight at most $2w(\mathcal{OPT}(G))$. ∎

THEOREM 6.11   There is an approximation algorithm to find an augmentation to increase the vertex connectivity of a connected graph to 2 with weight less than twice the optimal augmentation that runs in $O(m + n \log n)$ time.

Proof.   The correctness of the algorithm follows from Lemma 6.14 and Lemma 6.15. The biconnected components can be found in $O(m + n)$ time [AHU74] and a minimum weight branching can be found in $O(m + n \log n)$ time [GGST86]. The least common ancestors for the m pairs can be found in $O(m + n)$ time by using the algorithm of Harel and Tarjan [HT84]. ∎

6.5.3   INCREASING EDGE-CONNECTIVITY TO λ

We argue that it is possible to obtain an approximation factor of 2 for increasing the edge connectivity of a graph to any λ. The algorithm takes as input an undirected graph $G_0(V, E_0)$ on n vertices and a set *Feasible* of m weighted edges on V, and finds a subset *Aug* of edges which when added to G_0 make it λ edge-connected. The weight of *Aug* is no more than twice the weight of the least weight subset of edges of *Feasible* that increases the connectivity. We also observe that the problem is *NP*-hard (for any λ) by extending the proof that was given by [FJ81] for incrementing one connected graphs to 2-connected optimally.

Consider a directed graph G with weights on the edges, and a fixed root r. How does one find the *minimum weight* directed subgraph H^D that has λ-edge disjoint paths from a fixed root r to each vertex v? Gabow [G91] gives the fastest implementation of a weighted matroid intersection algorithm to solve this problem in $O(\lambda n (m + n \log n) \log n)$ time.

To solve our problem (approximation algorithm), in the undirected graph G_0 replace each undirected edge (u, v) by two directed edges $u \rightarrow v$ and $v \rightarrow u$ with each edge having weight 0. For each edge (u, v) in the set *Feasible*, we replace it by two directed edges $u \rightarrow v$ and $v \rightarrow u$ with each having weight $w(u, v)$ (the weight of the undirected edge). Call this graph G^D. Now run Gabow's algorithm on the graph G^D, asking for λ-edge disjoint paths from each vertex to the root. If the directed edge $u \rightarrow v$ is picked in H^D and $w(u, v) > 0$ (we can assume all edges of set *Feasible* have non-negative weight, else we can always include it in *Aug*) we add (u, v) to *Feasible*. (This is a generalization of the scheme for the case when E_0 is empty.)

OPEN PROBLEM 6.4 The main open problem is to obtain factors better than 2 for the unweighted augmentation problem. Even simple greedy algorithms appear to have a worst case performance ratio of 1.5.

Acknowledgments I am grateful to Dorit Hochbaum, Balaji Raghavachari and Yoram Sussmann for useful comments. Support by NSF grant CCR-9307462 is gratefully acknowledged. This chapter is dedicated to Prof. Richard Karp whose Turing Award Lecture "Combinatorics, Complexity and Randomness" (*Communications of the ACM*, Feb 1986) inspired me to start working in the field of algorithms.

REFERENCES

[AHU74] A. V. Aho, J. E. Hopcroft and J. D. Ullman. *The design and analysis of computer algorithms*, Addison-Wesley, 1974.

[CKT93] J. Cheriyan, M. Y. Kao, and R. Thurimella. Algorithms for parallel k-vertex connectivity and sparse certificates. *SIAM Journal on Computing*, 22(1):157-174, 1993.

[CL95] K. W. Chong and T. W. Lam. Approximating biconnectivity in parallel. *Proc. of 7th Annual ACM Symp. on Parallel Algorithms and Architectures*, 224-233, 1995.

[CL96] K. W. Chong and T. W. Lam. Improving biconnectivity approximation via optimization. *Proc. 7th Annual ACM-SIAM Symposium on Discrete Algorithms,* 26-35, 1996.

[CT91] J. Cheriyan and R. Thurimella. Algorithms for parallel k-vertex connectivity and sparse certificates. *Proc. 23rd Annual Symposium on Theory of Computing*, 391-401, 1991.

[CLR89] T. H. Cormen, C. E. Leiserson, and R. L. Rivest. *Introduction to algorithms*, The MIT Press, 1989.

[E79] J. Edmonds. Matroid intersection. *Annals of Discrete Mathematics,* 4:185-204, 1979.

[ET76] K. P. Eswaran and R. E. Tarjan. Augmentation problems. *SIAM Journal on Computing,* 5(4):653-665, 1976.

[F92] A. Frank. Augmenting graphs to meet edge-connectivity requirements. *SIAM Journal on Discrete Mathematics,* 5(1):25-53, 1992.

[FGHP93] T. Fischer, A. V. Goldberg, D. J. Haglin, and S. Plotkin. Approximating matchings in parallel. *Information Processing Letters* 46:115-118, 1993.

[FJ81] G. N. Frederickson and J. JáJá. Approximation algorithms for several graph augmentation problems. *SIAM Journal on Computing,* 10(2):270-283, 1981.

[FJ82] G. N. Frederickson and J. JáJá. On the relationship between the biconnectivity augmentation and traveling salesman problems. *Theoretical Computer Science*, 19(2):189-201, 1982.

[FT89] A. Frank and E. Tardos. An application of submodular flows. *Linear Algebra and its Applications,* 114/115:320-348, 1989.

[G91] H. N. Gabow. A matroid approach to finding edge connectivity and packing arborescences. *Proc. 23rd Annual Symposium on Theory of Computing,*112-122, 1991.

[GGST86] H. N. Gabow, Z. Galil, T. Spencer, and R. E. Tarjan. Efficient algorithms for finding minimum spanning trees in undirected and directed graphs. *Combinatorica,* 6(2):109-122, 1986.

[GJ79] M. R. Garey and D. S. Johnson. *Computers and intractability: A guide to the theory of NP-completeness*, Freeman, San Francisco, 1979.

[GSS93] N. Garg, V. Santosh, and A. Singla. Improved approximation algorithms for biconnected subgraphs via better lower bounding techniques. *Proc. 4th Annual ACM-SIAM Symposium on Discrete Algorithms,* 103-111, 1993.

[GB93] M. Goemans and D. Bertsimas. Survivable Networks, Linear Programming Relaxations and the Parsimonious Property. *Mathematical Programming,* 60:145-166, 1993.

[GW92] M. Goemans and D. Williamson. A general approximation technique for constrained forest problems. *Proc. 3rd Annual ACM-SIAM Symp. on Discrete Algorithms,* 307-316, 1992.

[H62] F. Harary. The maximum connectivity of a graph. *Proc. Nat. Acad. Sci.*, 48:1142-1146, 1962.

[H75] H. T. Hsu. An algorithm for finding a minimal equivalent graph of a digraph. *Journal of the ACM,* 22(1):11-16, 1975.

[H93] T. S. Hsu. Graph Augmentation and Related Problems: Theory and Practice. Ph. D thesis, Dept. of Computer Science, University of Texas, Austin, Texas, 1993.

[HR91] T. S. Hsu and V. Ramachandran. A linear time algorithm for triconnectivity augmentation. *Proc. 32nd Annual Symposium on Foundations of Computer Science*, 548-559, 1991.

[HT84] D. Harel and R. E. Tarjan. Fast algorithms for finding nearest common ancestors. *SIAM Journal on Computing,* 13(2):338-355, 1984.

[KR95] S. Khuller and B. Raghavachari. Improved Approximation Algorithms for Uniform Connectivity Problems. *Proc. 27th ACM Symposium on Theory of Computing,*1-10, 1995. To appear in *Journal of Algorithms,* 1996.

[KRY95] S. Khuller, B. Raghavachari, and N. Young. Approximating the minimum equivalent digraph. *SIAM Journal on Computing,* 24(4):859-872, 1995.

[KRY94] S. Khuller, B. Raghavachari and N. Young. On strongly connected digraphs with bounded cycle length. UMIACS-TR-94-10/CS-TR-3212, 1994. To appear in *Discrete Applied Mathematics*.

[KT92]   S. Khuller and R. Thurimella. Approximation algorithms for graph augmentation. *Proc. 19th International Colloquium on Automata, Languages and Programming Conference*, 330-341, 1992.

[KT93]   S. Khuller and R. Thurimella. Approximation algorithms for graph augmentation. *Journal of Algorithms,* 14(2):214-225, 1993.

[KV94]   S. Khuller and U. Vishkin. Biconnectivity approximations and graph carvings. *Journal of the ACM,* 41(2):214-235, 1994.

[K73]   D. E. Knuth. *Fundamental Algorithms,* Addison-Wesley, Menlo Park, CA, 1973.

[MT69]   D. M. Moyles and G. L. Thompson. An algorithm for finding the minimum equivalent graph of a digraph. *Journal of the ACM,* 16(3):455-460, 1969.

[NGM90] D. Naor, D. Gusfield, and C. Martel. A fast algorithm for optimally increasing the edge-connectivity. *Proc. 31st IEEE Symposium on Foundations of Computer Science,* 698-707, 1990.

[NI92]   H. Nagamochi and T. Ibaraki. Linear time algorithms for finding sparse k-connected spanning subgraph of a k-connected graph. *Algorithmica,* 7 (5/6):583-596, 1992.

[NP94]   T. Nishizeki and S. Poljak. Highly connected factors with a small number of edges. *Discrete Applied Mathematics,* 55(3):295-297, 1994.

[PS95]   M. Penn and H. Shasha-Krupnik. Improved Approximation Algorithms for Weighted 2 & 3 Vertex Connectivity Augmentation Problems. Technical Report TR-95-IEM/OR-1, Industrial Engineering and Management, Technion, Haifa, Israel, May 1995.

[RW95]   R. Ravi and D. Williamson. An approximation algorithm for minimum-cost vertex-connectivity problems. *Proc. 6th Annual ACM-SIAM Symposium on Discrete Algorithms,* 332-341, 1995.

[T83]   R. E. Tarjan. *Data structures and network algorithms*, Society for Industrial and Applied Mathematics, 1983.

[T89]   R. Thurimella. Techniques for the design of parallel graph algorithms. Ph. D thesis, Dept. of Computer Science, University of Texas, Austin, Texas, 1989.

7

ALGORITHMS FOR FINDING
LOW DEGREE STRUCTURES

Balaji Raghavachari

Finding subgraphs of low degree is an important problem for reliable communication. Most of the associated problems are *NP*-complete. In this chapter we discuss various approximation techniques for obtaining solutions that are "close" to the optimal. The minimum-degree problems discussed include spanning trees, f-joins, and two-connected subgraphs.

INTRODUCTION

7.1

The problem of computing low degree subgraphs satisfying given connectivity properties of a given graph arises naturally in the design of communication networks. The criterion of minimizing the maximum degree reflects decentralization of the communication network. Keeping the maximum degree small is also essential in designing switching networks where the same switch is installed at each node, and this implies that the switches must be designed to handle as many connections as the maximum degree of any node in the network in which it is to be used. In telecommunication applications, switches have a limited capacity, as do hubs in service networks, and the optimization problems that arise in the design of these networks include constraints on the degree of the network. Minimum-degree networks are also useful in building networks for broadcast where we wish to minimize the amount of work done at each site.

The simplest of these problems is the *Minimum-Degree Spanning Tree* (MDST) problem. Here the input is an arbitrary graph $G = (V, E)$ and the problem is to compute a spanning tree of G whose maximal degree is the smallest among all spanning trees of G. Let $\Delta^*(G)$ denote the degree of a MDST of G. The MDST problem is a generalization of the Hamiltonian Path problem and is NP-hard. In fact, for any $k \geq 2$, the problem of deciding if a given graph has a spanning tree whose degree is at most k, is NP-complete [GJ79]. The first result on approximating a minimum-degree spanning tree was that of Fürer and Raghavachari [FR90]. They gave a polynomial time approximation algorithm with an approximation ratio of $O(\log n)$. Their algorithm further generalizes to find rooted spanning trees (also known as branchings) in directed graphs of approximately minimum indegree. Ravi, Marathe, Ravi, Rosenkrantz, and Hunt [RMR$^+$93] used a similar strategy to approximate the problem of computing low-weight bounded-degree subgraphs satisfying given connectivity properties. Given a graph with nonnegative weights on the edges, and a degree bound b, their algorithm computes a spanning tree of G whose degree is at most $O(b \log \frac{n}{b})$, and whose cost is at most $O(\log n)$ times the cost of a minimum-weight tree of G with degree at most b. Their techniques extend to the Steiner tree and generalized Steiner tree problems, with the same ratio. They also studied similar problems in the special case when the edge weights satisfy the triangle inequality and presented efficient algorithms for computing subgraphs which have low weight and small bottleneck cost. In subsequent work Fürer and Raghavachari [FR92] improved their previous results and provided another polynomial time algorithm to approximate the minimum-degree spanning tree to within one of optimal. Clearly no better approximation algorithms are possible for this problem.

The MDST problem can be extended to its "Steiner" version (*minimum-degree Steiner tree problem*) as follows: the input is a graph $G = (V, E)$ and a distinguished subset of the vertices $D \subseteq V$. We seek a Steiner tree (spanning at least the set D) whose maximum degree is minimum. The first polynomial-time approximation algorithm was provided by Agrawal, Klein and Ravi [AKR91]. The approximation ratio is a factor of $O(\log k)$, where k is the cardinality of D. Fürer and Raghavachari [FR92] gave an improved polynomial-time approximation algorithm for the problem with an approximation ratio of a constant along with an additive $O(\log n)$ term, and they [FR94] later demonstrated a polynomial-time algorithm that finds a tree whose degree is within one from optimal.

A further generalization of the MDST problem is the minimum-degree f-join problem, defined as follows. The input is a graph $G = (V, E)$ and a *proper* cut-function f that specifies which cuts of the graph are active (see Chapter 4 for the definition of proper functions). A forest which crosses all active cuts is called an f-*join*. The problem is to compute a minimum-degree f-join. Note that the minimum-degree Steiner tree problem is a special case of the minimum-degree f-join problem in which a cut is made active if it separates any two vertices of D. Ravi, Raghavachari, and Klein [RRK92] gave a quasi-polynomial time approximation algorithm for the f-join problem with an approximation ratio of a constant with an additive $O(\log n)$ term.

In related work, Lawler [Law76] showed that matroid methods are sufficient to solve the following variant of the minimum-degree spanning tree problem in polynomial time: given a graph G and an independent set I of nodes of G, find a spanning tree that minimizes the maximum degree of any node in I. Gavish [Gav82] formulated the MDST problem as a mixed integer program and provided an exact solution using the method of Lagrangian multipliers. Ravi [Rav94] gave an approximation algorithm with an approximation ratio of $O(\log n / \log \log n)$ for the problem of finding the "poise" of a graph, defined as follows. The poise of a tree is the sum of its diameter and its maximum degree; the poise of a graph is the minimum poise achieved by any spanning tree of that graph. He used the algorithm that approximates poise to design an approximation algorithm for the minimum broadcast time problem in graphs.

The organization of the chapter is as follows. In Section 7.2 the notion of the *toughness* of a graph is introduced and its relation to the MDST problem is explored. In Section 7.3 the use of the matching problem in approximating the MDST problem is discussed. *Witness sets* are defined in Section 7.4, and these sets are crucial in obtaining good lower bounds on the degree of a MDST. An algorithm that computes a spanning tree of a graph whose degree is within one of the degree of a MDST is also provided. In Section 7.5 a simple local search scheme for approximating several minimum degree problems is introduced. The analysis of the local-search algorithm is shown for three problems: the MDST problem, the minimum degree f-join problem, and the minimum degree two-connected spanning subgraph problem. Then the problem of computing minimum-weight bounded degree spanning trees in graphs which have weights on the edges is considered in Section 7.6. The special case of Euclidean graphs—graphs defined by points on the plane, where the weight of an edge is the Euclidean distance between the endpoints—is considered. An algorithm for approximating a minimum-weight degree-3 spanning trees for an arbitrary set of points in the plane is analyzed. Finally, a few open problems are discussed in Section 7.7.

TOUGHNESS AND DEGREE

7.2

Chvátal [Chv73] defined the following notion of toughness of a graph G. Let $X \subset V$ be an arbitrary subset of vertices. Let $c(X)$ denote the number of connected components in the graph induced by $V - X$.

DEFINITION 7.1   The *toughness* of a graph G, denoted by $\tau(G)$, is the minimum ratio $|X|/c(X)$ over all subsets X of V with $c(X) > 1$.

The toughness of a graph is the minimum ratio generated by a subset X^* that gives the largest number of components per vertex removed. The notion can be extended to *Steiner-toughness* and f-*toughness* in the Steiner and f-join versions of the problem, by counting in $c(X)$ only those components which contain a vertex of D in the Steiner problem, and active components in the f-join problem.

Toughness of a graph, as defined above, is closely related to the degree of a MDST of the graph. Recall that $\Delta^*(G)$ denotes the degree of a MDST of G. The following proposition follows directly from the definition of toughness:

PROPOSITION 7.1   Let G be an arbitrary, connected graph. The inverse of the toughness of G is a lower bound on the degree of a MDST of G, i.e.,

$$\Delta^*(G) \geq \frac{1}{\tau(G)}.$$

The proposition can be extended to the Steiner and f-join versions of the minimum degree problem.

DEFINITION 7.2   A k-*tree* is a spanning tree in which the degree of each vertex in the tree is at most k.

Win [Win89] showed that the relationship between the two quantities $\tau(G)$ and $\Delta^*(G)$ is almost tight by proving the following theorem:

THEOREM 7.1   For $k \geq 2$, G has a k-tree if for any $S \subset V$,

$$c(S) \leq (k-2) \cdot |S| + 2.$$

The above theorem will be proved later. It has the following interesting corollary:

COROLLARY 7.1   If $\tau(G) \geq \frac{1}{k-2}$, with $k \geq 3$, then $\Delta^*(G) \leq k$.

Theorem 7.1 is proved as follows. Let G be a graph that satisfies the conditions of the theorem. For any subset S of vertices, $c(S)$, the number of connected components in $G - S$, is at most $(k-2)|S| + 2$. Suppose for a contradiction G does not contain a k-tree. Let H be a k-tree of a subset of the vertices, with the property that H is of maximal size. In other words, of all the subsets of V that have a k-tree within them, $V(H)$ is one that has the most vertices, where $V(H)$ denotes the vertices that are spanned by the tree H. The crux of the proof of the theorem is in showing that there exists a subset W of degree-k vertices in H such that the following properties are true:

1. The connected components of $H - W$ and $G - W$ are identical, i. e., if the vertices of W are deleted from H, breaking H into a forest F, then there are no edges of G between two different trees of F.

2. There are no edges in G that connect a vertex in $V - V(H)$ to a vertex in $V(H) - W$.

Once these conditions are established, a simple counting argument shows that $c(W)$ is at least $(k-2)|W| + 3$, which establishes the necessary contradiction, thus proving that G has a k-tree.

Theorem 7.1 has another important consequence. It shows that if a graph G does not have a k-tree, then there is a subset W of vertices, whose removal splits the graph into at least $(k-2)|W| + 3$ connected components. Therefore, W establishes an upper bound on the toughness of G, and hence, by Proposition 7.1 a lower bound (which in this case is $k-1$) on $\Delta^*(G)$. Therefore, if a graph G does not have a k-tree, then it has a "witness set" W that establishes $k-1$ to be a lower bound on $\Delta^*(G)$. One can therefore "search" (approximately) for the right value of $\Delta^*(G)$ using the techniques described in Win's paper — either construct a k-tree of G or find a witness set that shows that $\Delta^*(G) \geq k-1$, and keep increasing k until a k-tree of G is found. Such an algorithm would output a spanning tree whose degree is within two of optimal, but unfortunately, it is not clear if it would run in polynomial time.

We now prove Theorem 7.1. The proof is non-constructive. The following technical lemma shows that H can be chosen to satisfy additional structural properties:

LEMMA 7.1   There is a k-tree T of $V(H)$, and subsets B and R of vertices with B nonempty, that satisfy the following properties:

> *I.* The degree of each vertex of $B \cup R$ in T is k.
>
> *II.* Every edge of G that connects two different components of $T - B$ is incident to some vertex of R.
>
> *III.* For any tree $A \in T - B$, if there exists a k-tree that spans the vertices of $V(A) \cup B$ in which the vertices of B are all leaves, then the vertices of R in that tree all have degree k.
>
> *IV.* Any edge of G that connects a vertex in $V(H)$ to a vertex in $V - V(H)$ is incident to $B \cup R$.

Proof.   Consider a vertex t of $V(H)$ that is adjacent in G to a vertex in $V - V(H)$. In any k-tree of $V(H)$, the degree of t must be k; otherwise it contradicts the assumption that $V(H)$ is the largest induced subgraph of G that allows a k-tree. Let (u, v) be an edge in G that connects two different trees T_u and T_v in $H - \{t\}$. Then, for at least one of $i \in \{u, v\}$, the following condition is satisfied:

> *The degree of i is k in any k-tree spanning $T_i \cup \{t\}$ that has t as a leaf.*

Otherwise, we can replace the trees T_u and T_v with trees in which t is a leaf vertex in both trees and the degree of u and v being less than k. Then, add (u, v) and delete an edge incident to t and obtain a k-tree of $V(H)$ in which the degree of t is less than k. This is impossible, since t is connected by an edge to a vertex outside $V(H)$, and the addition of this edge generates a k-tree with more vertices than H.

We call vertices that satisfy the above condition *blocking* vertices. Let $B = \{t\}$ and let R be the set of blocking vertices satisfying the above condition. It can be verified that all four conditions of the lemma are satisfied by H, B, and R, due to the manner in which B and R were chosen.   ■

LEMMA 7.2   Let H, B, and R satisfy the conditions of Lemma 7.1 such that $|B \cup R|$ is maximized. There is no edge of G joining components of $H - \{B \cup R\}$.

Proof.   We give a proof by contradiction. Suppose there exists an edge (u, v) in G that connects different trees of $H - \{B \cup R\}$. Observe that by Condition 2 of Lemma 7.1, u and v must be in the same tree S of $H - B$, as otherwise either u or v must be in R, which is clearly not true. Let $w \in R$ be a vertex in the cycle generated in H by the addition of (u, v). Let T_u and T_v be the trees containing u and v respectively in $H - \{w\}$. As in the proof of the previous lemma, at least one of $i \in \{u, v\}$ must satisfy the following condition:

> *The degree of i is k in any k-tree spanning $T_i \cup \{w\}$ that has w as a leaf.*

Let R_w be the vertices of $H - \{w\}$ that satisfy the above condition. R_w is not empty, since at least one of $\{u, v\}$ is in it. Let $B' = B \cup \{w\}$ and $R' = R_w \cup R - \{w\}$. The sets B' and R' also satisfy the conditions of Lemma 7.1, but $|B' \cup R'| > |B \cup R|$, which is a contradiction since B and R were chosen such that $|B \cup R|$ is maximal.   ■

Proof of Theorem 7.1. Let H, B, and R be chosen as in Lemma 7.2. Since H is an induced proper subgraph of G, Condition 4 of Lemma 7.1 implies that the components of $G - \{B \cup R\}$ are the components of $V(H) - \{B \cup R\}$ together with the components of $G - V(H)$ of which there is at least one. But Lemma 7.2 shows that there are as many components of $V(H) - \{B \cup R\}$ as there are of $H - \{B \cup R\}$. Accounting for the maximum possible edges within $B \cup R$ in H, we get a lower bound on the number of these components as

$$k|B \cup R| - 2(|B \cup R| - 1) = (k - 2)|B \cup R| + 2.$$

Combined with the components of $G - V(H)$, the number of components in $G - \{B \cup R\}$ is at least $(k - 2)|B \cup R| + 3$, which is a contradiction since it violates the condition of the theorem. ∎

MATCHINGS AND MDST

7.3

Fürer and Raghavachari [FR90] observed the following relationship between matchings and the MDST problem:

DEFINITION 7.3 A *complete spanning forest* (CSF) of a graph G is a spanning forest of G in which the degree of every vertex is at least one. In other words, a CSF is a forest that has no isolated vertices.

The following theorem can be inferred from [FR90] (see also [LP86, RMR+93]) and it forms the basis of an approximation algorithm for the MDST problem.

THEOREM 7.2 The problem of computing a minimum-degree complete spanning forest of a graph can be reduced in polynomial time to the perfect matching problem.

The intuition behind the above theorem is as follows. A minimal CSF is one that does not contain another CSF as a proper subgraph. Each tree of a minimal CSF has a star-like structure—a central vertex connected by edges to a number of leaves. There is no loss of generality in assuming that a minimum-degree CSF is minimal. First observe that if G has a perfect matching M, then M is a minimum-degree CSF of G. If a maximum matching M is not perfect, then the matched vertices of M have to be "replicated" before the unmatched vertices of M can be matched. The degree of a resulting CSF is the fewest number of times that the matched vertices of M have to be replicated for the resulting graph to have a perfect matching. The above discussion is meant to be informal, and some of the details have been skipped. See one of the above references for further details.

Theorem 7.2 yields a polynomial-time approximation algorithm for the MDST problem which outputs a tree whose degree is within a factor of $O(\log n)$ of optimal. The algorithm finds a minimum degree CSF, shrinks each connected component into a single vertex, and recurses. Since the number of vertices reduces by at least a half in each stage, there are at most $\log n$ stages. In each stage, the graph is always guaranteed to have a CSF whose degree is at most $\Delta^*(G)$. Hence, the degree of a vertex increases by at most $\Delta^*(G)$ in each stage. Therefore, the degree of the tree output by the algorithm is $O(\Delta^*(G) \log n)$.

The above algorithm can also be adapted to find rooted spanning trees (branchings) in directed graphs with the same approximation ratio. The algorithm also generalizes to the weighted case of the MDST problem, where we want to find a minimum-weight spanning tree whose degree is restricted to be at most a given Δ. Ravi, Marathe, Ravi, Rosenkrantz, and Hunt [RMR+93] observed that Theorem 7.2 has a natural extension to the weighted case. This can be used to obtain an approximation algorithm which outputs a tree of degree $O(\Delta \log n)$, whose cost is at most $O(\log n)$ of a minimum-weight Δ-tree of G.

MDST WITHIN ONE OF OPTIMAL

7.4

We now provide a polynomial-time algorithm for the MDST problem that finds a spanning tree whose degree is within $\Delta^*(G) + 1$ for any given graph G. The algorithm also outputs a vertex set W of G that establishes a lower bound on $\Delta^*(G)$.

7.4.1   WITNESS SETS

For minimization problems, the most challenging task is usually establishing a lower bound on an optimal solution. For the MDST problem, how does one show that the degree of every spanning tree must be more than some value? *Witness sets*, introduced in [FR92], help in establishing a lower bound on $\Delta^*(G)$.

DEFINITION 7.4   A *witness set* W is a proper subset of the vertex set V. Let $|W| = w$, and suppose the removal of W from G disconnects G into t components. Then W is a *witness* to the fact that $\Delta^*(G)$ is at least $\frac{w+t-1}{w}$ as shown in the following lemma:

LEMMA 7.3   Let W be a witness set of size w whose removal splits G into t components. Then $\Delta^*(G) \geq \lceil \frac{w+t-1}{w} \rceil$.

Proof.   Consider the following partition of the vertices of G:

> **I.** t subsets corresponding to the connected components in $G - W$.

> **II.** w singleton subsets, one for each element of W.

These $w + t$ subsets form a partition of V. In any spanning tree of G, there are at least $w + t - 1$ edges between these subsets. By the condition of the lemma, every edge of G which connects two vertices in different subsets is incident to W. Hence, in any spanning tree, there are at least $w + t - 1$ edges incident to W. Therefore, the average degree of the vertices in W in any spanning tree is at least $d = \lceil \frac{w+t-1}{w} \rceil$, and there is at least one vertex in W whose degree is at least d.   ∎

We call the set W as a witness set since it acts as a witness to the fact that $\Delta^*(G) \geq \lceil (w + t - 1)/w \rceil$. The following theorem captures the kind of witness sets that the algorithms obtain:

THEOREM 7.3   Let $G = (V, E)$ be a given graph and let T be a tree of maximal degree k. Let S be the set of vertices of degree k in T. Let B be an arbitrary subset of vertices of degree $k - 1$ in T. Let $S \cup B$ be removed from the graph, breaking the tree T into a forest F. Suppose G satisfies the condition that there are no edges between different trees in F. Then $k \leq \Delta^*(G) + 1$.

Proof.   There are no edges of G between components in $T - (S \cup B)$, and hence, the connected components of $T - (S \cup B)$ and $G - (S \cup B)$ are the same. Hence, if we count the number of components in $T - (S \cup B)$, we can use Lemma 7.3 to obtain a lower bound on $\Delta^*(G)$.

The sum of degrees in T of vertices of $S \cup B$ is $|S|k + |B|(k - 1)$. Since T is acyclic, there are at most $|S \cup B| - 1$ edges in T having both endpoints in $S \cup B$. Hence, the number of edges incident to vertices of $S \cup B$ is at least $|S|k + |B|(k - 1) - (|S \cup B| - 1)$. The forest F obtained from T by removing these edges has at least $|S|k + |B|(k - 1) - (|S \cup B| - 1) + 1$ components. Not counting the vertices of $S \cup B$, therefore, we obtain $|S|(k - 2) + |B|(k - 3) + 2$ components. An application of Lemma 7.3 yields the theorem.   ∎

7.4.2   THE $\Delta^* + 1$ ALGORITHM

The algorithm starts with an arbitrary spanning tree T of G and tries to reduce its degree. The maximal degree of T is always denoted by k. Let $\rho(u)$ denote the degree of vertex u in T. Let S_i denote the vertices of T whose degree is at least i. The following operation forms the building block of the algorithm:

DEFINITION 7.5   Let (u, v) be an edge of G which is not in T. Let C be the cycle generated when (u, v) is added to T. Suppose there is a vertex w of degree k in C, and the degrees of vertices u and v are at most $k - 2$. An *improvement* to T is the modification of T by adding the edge (u, v) to T and deleting one of the edges in C incident to w. In such an improvement, we say that w *benefits* from (u, v).

Improvements can be used to reduce the number of maximal degree vertices repeatedly. Progress is impeded only when either u or v or both have degree $k - 1$.

DEFINITION 7.6   Let T be a spanning tree of degree k. Let $\rho(u)$ denote the degree of a vertex $u \in T$. Let $(u, v) \notin T$ be an edge in G. Suppose w is a vertex of degree k in the cycle generated by adding (u, v) to T. If $\rho(u) \geq k - 1$, we say that u *blocks* w from (u, v).

For example, in Figure 7.1, in the current spanning tree, vertex u has degree 4 and vertex w has degree 5. Adding the nontree edge (u, v) to the tree creates a cycle that includes w. Vertex u blocks w from the edge (u, v). Trying to reduce the degree of w to 4 by exchanging an edge incident to w on this cycle with the edge (u, v) increases the degree of u to 5.

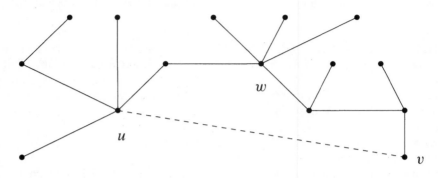

FIGURE 7.1

Example of blocking.

The algorithm is implemented in a bottom-up fashion as follows. At the beginning of each phase of the algorithm, all vertices in S_{k-1} (vertices of degree k and degree $k - 1$ in T) are removed from T and marked as *bad*. All other vertices are marked as *good*. We call the components formed by tree edges between good vertices as good components. If there are no edges of G between good components, the algorithm stops. In this case, Theorem 7.3 shows that the set of bad vertices remaining is a witness set to the fact that $k \leq \Delta^*(G) + 1$. Otherwise, let (u, v) be an edge between two good components F_u and F_v. Consider the cycle generated in T by the addition of (u, v). If there is a vertex of degree k in this cycle, a set of improvements which propagate to this vertex has been identified. Making these changes reduces the size of S_k by one. Otherwise, there is at least one bad vertex of degree $k - 1$ on the cycle. Mark all bad vertices on this cycle as good and form the union of all components on this cycle along with all of its vertices of degree $k - 1$. We then go back to look for other edges between good components. In all cases, the algorithm either finds a way to reduce the degree of some vertex in S_k or finds a blocking set with which Theorem 7.3 may be applied. Algorithm MDST:Opt+1 implements the above ideas and outputs a spanning tree whose maximal degree is at most one more than the optimal degree.

Algorithm MDST:Opt+1

Input: A graph G.
Output: A spanning tree of G which approximates a MDST.

Step 1: Find a spanning tree T of G. Let k be its degree.
Step 2: Mark vertices of degree k and $k - 1$ as bad. Remove these vertices from T generating a forest. Mark all other vertices as good. Let F be the set of connected components in the forest.

Step 3: While there is an edge (u, v) connecting two different components of F, and all vertices of degree k are marked bad, do

  (a) Find the bad vertices in the cycle C generated by T together with (u, v) and mark them as good.

  (b) Update F by combining the components along the cycle C and these newly marked vertices into a single component. Note that more than two components of F may be combined into one in this step.

Step 4: If there is a vertex w of degree k marked as good, find a sequence of improvements which propagate to w and update T (and if necessary k) and go back to Step 2.

Step 5: Output the final tree T, its degree k, and the witness set W consisting of the vertices still marked bad.

7.4.3   PERFORMANCE ANALYSIS

The algorithm proceeds in iterations. In each iteration, some vertices are designated good. We therefore speak of a vertex being marked good at iteration i. A vertex whose degree in T is less than $k - 1$ is said to be good at iteration 0. Let F_i be the subgraph of T generated by the nodes marked good at iteration i or less. Note that $F_i \subset F_{i+1}$ for all i, so each connected component of F_i is contained entirely within some component of F_{i+1}. The following lemmas establish the approximation quality and the running time of the algorithm.

LEMMA 7.4   Suppose that a vertex w is marked good in iteration i when edge (u, v) is added in Step 3(a) of algorithm MDST:Opt+1. Then, w can be made nonblocking by applying improvements to the components of F_i containing u and v.

Proof.   The proof proceeds by induction on i. If w was marked good at iteration 0, it has degree less than $k - 1$ in T, and is therefore nonblocking by definition. Otherwise, w belongs to the cycle C found in Step 3(a) in the ith iteration. The cycle C is the simple cycle in $T \cup \{(u, v)\}$, where (u, v) is an edge between two good components X_u and X_v of F_{i-1}. Since u was marked good at an iteration $j \leq i - 1$, by the inductive hypothesis u can be made nonblocking by applying improvements to the component of F_j containing u, a component itself contained in X_u. Similarly, v can be made nonblocking by applying improvements to X_v. Since X_u and X_v are disjoint, there is no interference between them. A final improvement involving the edge (u, v) suffices to reduce the degree of w, rendering it nonblocking. ∎

LEMMA 7.5   When the algorithm stops, $k \leq \Delta^*(G) + 1$.

Proof.   Let S be S_k and B be the bad vertices of degree $k - 1$. Note that the algorithm only stops when there are no edges between the good components. Hence, the tree T along with these sets S and B satisfies the conditions of Theorem 7.3, and we get the desired result. ∎

LEMMA 7.6   Algorithm MDST:Opt+1 runs in polynomial time.

Proof.   The sum of the degrees of the vertices of a tree is exactly $2n - 2$. Hence, the number of vertices of degree k in a tree on n vertices is $O(n/k)$. Since the size of S_k decreases by one in each phase (except the last one), there are $O(n/k)$ phases when the maximal degree is k. Summing up the harmonic series corresponding to different values of k, we conclude that there are $O(n \log n)$ phases. In each phase we try to find improvements which propagate to vertices of S_k. Lemma 7.4 assures that whenever we find a vertex w of degree k which is marked as good, we can indeed find a sequence of improvements which propagates to w. Lemma 7.5 shows that when the algorithm stops, the degree of the resulting tree is within one from the optimal degree. Each phase of the algorithm can be implemented in nearly linear time using Tarjan's fast disjoint set union-find algorithm for maintaining connected components (e.g., see [CLR89]). Therefore, the entire algorithm runs in $O(m n \alpha(m, n) \log n)$, where m is the number of edges and α is the inverse of Ackermann's function that is associated with the union-find problem.   ∎

Fürer and Raghavachari [FR94] showed that the above algorithm can be generalized to obtain a polynomial-time algorithm for the Steiner case that finds a tree whose degree is within one from optimal. The definition of an improvement has to be generalized to include the possibility of adding a path that may go through vertices that are not currently in the tree instead of just a single edge, and the proofs have to be rewritten correspondingly. The reader is referred to the paper for further details.

LOCAL SEARCH TECHNIQUES

7.5

The notion of improvements introduced in Subsection 7.4.2 can be used directly to yield a local search algorithm for the MDST problem as follows.

Start with an arbitrary spanning tree of G. Search for improvements to the tree using nontree edges, and perform them. Stop when no more improvements are possible. Such a tree is called a locally optimal tree.

DEFINITION 7.7   A spanning tree T of a graph G is a *locally optimal tree* for the MDST problem, if every edge (u, v) in G but not in T satisfies the following condition: for any vertex w in the u–v path of T, $\rho(w)$, the degree of w in T is at most $\max(\rho(u), \rho(v)) + 1$.

Fürer and Raghavachari [FR92] showed that the degree of a locally optimal tree is at most $O(c \Delta^*(G) + \log_c n)$ for any constant $c > 1$. Though the approximation ratio of this algorithm is worse than the algorithm in Section 7.4, it has the advantage of being useful for approximating a larger class of minimum degree problems.

Fischer [Fis93] extended the results of [FR92] to weighted graphs. He showed how to find minimum spanning trees whose degree is within a constant multiplicative factor plus an additive $O(\log n)$ of the optimal degree. The degree bound is improved further in the case when the number of different edge weights is bounded by a constant. Ravi, Raghavachari, and Klein [RRK92] used local optimization techniques to obtain approximation algorithms for the unweighted minimum-degree f-join and the minimum-degree 2-connected spanning subgraph problems.

7.5.1 MDST PROBLEM

Let δ be the maximal degree of a locally optimal tree T. Let S_i be the set of vertices whose degree, at least i in T. The following proposition follows from a simple counting argument.

PROPOSITION 7.2 There is some $i \in [\delta - \lceil \log_c n \rceil, \delta]$ with $|S_{i-1}| \leq c|S_i|$. More generally, for a positive integer a, there is some $i \in [\delta - a \lceil \log_c n \rceil, \delta]$ with $|S_{i-a}| \leq c|S_i|$.

The proof of the above proposition is left as an exercise.

THEOREM 7.4 For any $c > 1$, the maximal degree δ of a locally optimal tree T is at most $c\Delta^*(G) + \lceil \log_c n \rceil$. Therefore, $\delta = O(\Delta^*(G) + \log n)$.

Proof. Let i be an index as in Proposition 7.2. Let the removal of S_i split T into a forest F with t trees. Each vertex in S_i has degree at least i, and hence we count at least $i|S_i|$ edges incident to these vertices. Since T is a tree, at most $|S_i| - 1$ of these edges are within S_i itself, and thus, counted twice. Therefore, we have $t \geq i|S_i| - 2(|S_i| - 1)$.

By the local optimality condition, every edge between trees in F is incident to a vertex of degree $i - 1$. Hence, the removal of S_{i-1} generates at least t components in G. Therefore, by Lemma 7.3,

$$\Delta^*(G) \geq \frac{t + |S_i| - 1}{|S_{i-1}|} \geq \frac{(i-1)|S_i| + 1}{c|S_i|} > \frac{i-1}{c}.$$

Combining this with the condition on the range of i, we get $\delta \leq c\Delta^*(G) + \lceil \log_c n \rceil$. ∎

This can now be converted into a polynomial time algorithm with the desired performance as follows. Note that in the above theorem we used the local optimality condition only on "high" degree vertices. Therefore, the same result holds for any tree satisfying the local optimality condition for the vertices in S_i with $i = \delta - \lceil \log_c n \rceil + 1$. As before, start with an arbitrary spanning tree T of G. Let k be its maximal degree. The algorithm tries to reduce the degree of some vertex whose degree is between k and $k - \lceil \log_c n \rceil$, using local improvement steps. The algorithm stops when no vertex of high degree (in the above range) has a local improvement. Algorithm MDST:Local-Opt gives a description of the algorithm. A potential function is used to show that the algorithm terminates in a polynomial number of steps.

Algorithm MDST:Local-Opt

Input: A graph G, and a constant $c > 1$.
Output: A spanning tree of G which approximates a MDST.

    Step 1: Find a spanning tree T of G. Let k be its degree.

    Step 2: While there is an improvement that benefits a vertex in $S_{k-\lceil \log_c n \rceil}$, make that improvement to T, and update k if necessary.

    Step 3: Output T.

LEMMA 7.7   Algorithm MDST:Local-Opt runs in polynomial time.

Proof.   Each improvement step can be implemented in polynomial time using standard techniques for searching graphs. We show that the number of such steps is bounded by a polynomial in n. Consider an exponential potential function ϕ on the vertices. If the degree of a vertex u is d in the tree T, its potential $\phi(u)$ is defined to be b^d, for any constant $b > 2$. The total potential $\phi(T)$ of the tree is defined to be the sum of the potentials of all the vertices. If k is the maximal degree of T, $\phi(T) \leq nb^k$. Any improvement step on T reduces the degree of some vertex in S_i for $i = k - \lceil \log n \rceil$. Therefore, the reduction in potential due to any improvement is at least

$$(b^i + 2b^{i-2}) - (3b^{i-1}) = (b-1)(b-2)b^{i-2} \geq \frac{(b-1)(b-2)b^k}{b^3 n} = \Omega\left(\frac{\phi(T)}{n^2}\right).$$

Hence, the potential reduces by at least a polynomial factor. In $O(n^2)$ steps, the potential reduces by a constant factor, and therefore the number of improvement steps is $O(n^3)$. ∎

7.5.2   CONSTRAINED FOREST PROBLEMS

Goemans and Williamson [GW92] formulated a general class of connectivity constraints using a $\{0, 1\}$ function defined on the cuts of a graph. The "active" cuts (those cuts for which the function is 1) satisfy certain well-specified structural properties. The functions were named *proper* functions and were shown to be powerful enough to capture a number of constrained-forest problems under a uniform framework. Some examples of problems that can be formulated in this framework include the generalized Steiner forest problem, the T-join problem, and the point-to-point connection problem. For more details, see Chapter 4. We now consider the problem of computing minimum-degree forests where the connectivity constraints are specified by proper functions.

    For a node-subset S, let $\Gamma(S)$ denote the set of edges each having exactly one endpoint in S. To specify that the cut $\Gamma(S)$ is active, we set $f(S)$ to be 1. Using this formalism, one can formulate an integer program (IP) for a minimum-degree network crossing all active cuts as follows. The objective is to find a $\{0, 1\}$ solution to the variables x_e ($e \in E$) that minimizes the degree bound d subject to the feasibility constraints:

$$\sum_{e \in \Gamma(S)} x_e \geq f(S), \text{ for } \phi \neq S \subset V,$$

and degree constraints:

$$\sum_{e \in \Gamma(\{v\})} x_e \le d.$$

A feasible solution to (IP) is called an f-join. It can be verified that minimal f-joins are forests. Therefore, we also refer to an f-join as a feasible forest. We are interested in solutions to (IP) for the class of proper functions f.

We now describe the algorithm for providing an approximate solution to (IP). The input is an undirected graph $G = (V, E)$, an arbitrary constant $c > 1$ (performance accuracy), and a proper function f defined on the cuts of G. It is assumed without loss of generality that G is connected. The algorithm uses iterative local-improvements as in the previous section and outputs a forest F that is feasible for the covering constraints of (IP).

The algorithm starts with any spanning tree T of the given connected graph as the initial feasible solution to (IP). Since a spanning tree crosses all non-trivial cuts of the graph, T is an f-join. The algorithm then iteratively applies improvement steps aimed at reducing the degree of high-degree vertices. Intuitively, if we find a cycle in the graph that contains a node w of high degree, and if all edges that must be added to the current feasible solution to form this cycle are incident to low degree nodes, then we can improve the current solution by adding in the cycle and deleting an edge incident to w. This reduces the degree of w by one.

As before, denote the set of nodes in the current forest with degree at least i by S_i. An improvement step with target i tries to reduce the degree of a node in S_i. The definition of an improvement step is more complicated: starting from G, we delete all the edges in $E - F$ that are incident to nodes in the forest having degree at least $i - 2$, i.e., edges that are incident to nodes in S_{i-2}. In this graph, we examine if any node in S_i lies on a cycle. If so, we add all the edges in $E - F$ in this cycle to the forest F and delete an edge of F incident to the the node in S_i in this cycle. This gives a new f-join F'. If F' contains cycles, drop the minimal number of edges to make it a forest.

Note that after performing an improvement step with target i, the degree of a node in S_i reduces by one, and the resulting degree of each of the affected vertices increases by at most two and is at most $i - 1$. Since the components of F' are unions of forests of F, F' is also an f-join.

Let n be the number of vertices of G. Let $\Delta^*(G)$ be the degree of a minimum-degree f-join. Let the maximum degree of any node in the current feasible solution be k. The algorithm applies improvement steps with target i for $i \ge k - 2\lceil \log_c n \rceil$ until no such improvements are possible. Between two such steps, the forest is made minimal by deleting those edges whose removal does not affect the feasibility of F. The resulting forest is our *locally optimal* approximate solution.

DEFINITION 7.8   An edge e of a feasible forest F is *critical* if $F - \{e\}$ is not feasible. If e is not critical, then it is *unnecessary*.

Note that since the algorithm keeps dropping unnecessary edges from F, all edges of the solution output by it are critical. Each improvement step is polynomial-time implementable. We now show an upper bound on the number of phases of the algorithm.

LEMMA 7.8   The number of phases of the algorithm is at most $n^{2\log_c n + 4}$.

Proof. Define the potential of a vertex v with degree i in the forest F to be $\phi(v) = n^i$. The potential of F is defined as $\phi(F) = \sum_v \phi(v)$. If the maximal degree of any vertex in F is at most k, then $\phi(F) \leq n^{k+1}$. Each improvement step with target i reduces the potential by at least n^{i-2}, since the degree of a node of degree i is reduced by 1 and the degree of all the other nodes may increase to $i - 1$. Since the algorithm makes sure that whenever it applies an improvement to a vertex of degree i that $i \geq k - 2\lceil \log_c n \rceil$ (k is the maximum degree of the current forest), this reduction in potential is at least a fraction $n^{-2\log_c n - 4}$ of the current potential of the forest $\phi(F)$. It follows that the number of improvement steps is at most $n^{2\log_c n + 4}$. ∎

The approximation ratio of the algorithm is proved by identifying a node separator from the solution subgraph whose f-toughness is close to the f-toughness of the graph. Recall that the f-toughness of a graph is the minimum ratio of $|X|/c(X)$, where X ranges over subsets of vertices with $c(X)$, the number of active components in $G - X$ is greater than one.

LEMMA 7.9 Let F be the locally optimal forest with maximal degree k, and let i be an index as in Proposition 7.2. The number of active components in $G - S_{i-2}$ is at least $(i - 1 - c)|S_i|$.

Proof. Define a tree in F to be *relevant* if it contains a node in S_i. Define an equivalence relation R on the edges of F by the rule: $e_1 R e_2$ if there is a path between an endpoint of e_1 and an endpoint of e_2 in F avoiding S_i. Define an auxiliary forest F_i whose nodes are S_i together with the equivalence classes of R. F_i is bipartite, and there is an edge between a node $v \in S_i$ and an equivalence class C of R if there is an edge in C incident to v. Note that since F is acyclic, there is at most one edge in any equivalence class C incident on any node v in S_i. Thus, if a node $v \in S_i$ has degree j in F, it also has degree j in F_i. Note also that F_i is acyclic and has exactly as many components as the number of relevant trees in F.

Let t be the number of classes of degree one, p be the number of other classes, and r be the number of relevant trees in F. The number of edges in the forest F_i is the number of nodes in the forest minus the number of components in it. This is exactly $t + p + |S_i| - r$. The sum of the degrees of the nodes of F_i is twice the number of edges. That sum is at least $i \cdot |S_i| + 2p + t$. Therefore, the number of equivalence classes C of degree one in F_i is at least $(i - 2)|S_i| + 2r$.

Each class C of degree one defines a set X_C of nodes as follows: a node v is in X_C if C contains all the edges of F that are incident on v. Note that each X_C is a component of $F - S_i$ and thus represents a subset of nodes of a relevant tree. In Figure 7.2, v is a node in S_i and three sets identified using degree-one equivalence classes of R are shown.

Consider an edge e in F incident on a node in S_i. Since F is feasible, the component of F containing e is inactive. Since e is critical, the two distinct components formed in F on removing e and containing its endpoints must both be active. Consider an edge in a degree-one equivalence class C of R that is incident on a node in S_i. One of the connected components formed on its removal from F is X_C, and so this set is active. Hence, each set X_C defined by a class C of degree one in F_i is an active set.

We now derive a lower bound on the number of active components of $G - S_{i-2}$. Most of the node sets representing degree-one classes of F_i are useful in forming these

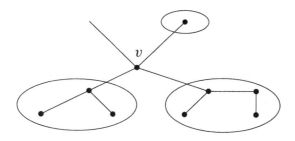

FIGURE 7.2

Identifying active sets using high-degree nodes.

active components. There are two ways in which such a set might fail to be an active component of $G - S_{i-2}$. When nodes of $S_{i-2} - S_i$ are removed, some of these components may break up, but few can break up this way. By choice of i, the number of such components is at most $|S_{i-2}| - |S_i|$, which is at most $(c-1)|S_i|$. We will account for these broken-up components when we count the number of active components. Secondly, when nonforest edges are added, some of the remaining components may merge, possibly resulting in fewer components and inactive components. We show that in fact there remain many active components.

CLAIM 7.1 The total number of such sets X_C's that merge with others on adding edges of $G - S_{i-2}$ is at most $2(r-1)$.

Proof. Suppose for a contradiction that more than $2(r-1)$ such X_C's merge on adding the edges of $G - S_{i-2}$. We show that this identifies a cycle in $F \cup (G - S_{i-2})$ containing a node of S_i, and so F permits an improvement.

Consider the auxiliary graph F_i and augment it with edges representing merging X_C's. For every pair of X_C's that merge, we include an edge between the nodes corresponding to them in F_i. If more than $2(r-1)$ such X_C's merge, then more than $r-1$ edges must be included in the auxiliary graph in addition to F_i. Since F_i has exactly r connected components, and more than $r-1$ edges are added to it, the resulting graph must be cyclic. A cycle in this graph directly corresponds to a cycle in $F \cup (G - S_{i-2})$ containing a node of S_i, and so F permits an improvement. This contradicts the local optimality of F.

The sets X_C's that remain might merge with inactive components of F on adding the nonforest edges of $G - S_{i-2}$. By the properties of a proper function, the resulting component in $G - S_{i-2}$ containing X_C is also active. We already showed that the number of degree-one equivalence classes is at least $(i-2)|S_i| + 2r$, and that each of these defines an active set. We discount at most $(c-1)|S_i|$ of them that may break up on removing nodes in $S_{i-2} - S_i$. The number of such classes that may merge with one another is at most $2(r-1)$ by Claim 7.1. Thus, the number of such active sets that remain is at least $i|S_i| - (1+c)|S_i|$. This completes the proof of Lemma 7.9. ∎

THEOREM 7.5   Let $\Delta^*(G)$ be the degree of a minimum-degree f-join of G. The algorithm outlined earlier returns an f-join whose degree is at most $c\Delta^*(G) + 2\lceil \log_c n \rceil + 1 + c$.

Proof.   Let i be as in Proposition 7.2, with $|S_{i-2}| \leq c|S_i|$. The theorem is proved by estimating the f-toughness of S_{i-2}. By Lemma 7.9 the number of active components in $G - S_{i-2}$ is at least $(i - 1 - c)|S_i|$. Therefore, the average degree of vertices in S_{i-2} in any f-join (which is a lower bound on $\Delta^*(G)$) is at least $\frac{i-1-c}{c}$. The degree of the solution F is at most $i + 2\log_c n$. Combining these with the range of i proves the theorem. ∎

7.5.3   TWO-CONNECTED SUBGRAPHS

In this section we consider minimum-degree networks of a different type. Given as input a 2-edge-connected undirected graph, we consider the problem of finding a 2-edge-connected spanning subgraph of minimum degree. This problem can be shown to be NP-hard by a reduction from the Hamiltonian cycle problem. A local-improvement algorithm similar to the ones described in the earlier sections can be used to obtain an approximate solution for this problem as well. See Chapter 6 for definitions of k-connectivity and k-connected components (in the context of edge connectivity). In this section *connectivity* always refers to edge connectivity (and not vertex connectivity). We refer to a 2-edge-connected component as a 2-component. Let $\Delta^*(G)$ denote the minimum degree of a 2-connected spanning subgraph of G.

DEFINITION 7.9   For a graph H, the *bridge-connected forest (bcf)* of H is obtained by contracting each 2-component of H to a supervertex and deleting self-loops. A *leaf 2-component* of H is a 2-component that has degree one in the *bcf* of H. An *isolated 2-component* of H is one of degree zero in the *bcf* of H.

The following proposition follows from the definition of 2-edge-connectivity:

PROPOSITION 7.3   Let N be any 2-connected spanning subgraph of G, and let X be any subset of vertices. Let C be a 2-component of $G - X$. If C is a leaf 2-component, then there is at least one edge of N between C and X. If C is an isolated 2-component, then there are at least two edges of N between C and X.

The above observation motivates the following definition:

DEFINITION 7.10   Let H be a graph with ℓ leaf 2-components and i isolated 2-components. Then the *deficiency* of H, $def(H)$, is defined to be $\ell + 2i$.

We now derive an easy lower bound on the minimum degree of a 2-connected spanning subgraph.

LEMMA 7.10   Let X be a subset of the nodes of a graph G. Then,

$$\Delta^*(G) \geq \frac{\text{def}(G - X)}{|X|}.$$

Proof.   Consider removing X from G. The remaining graph has deficiency $\text{def}(G - X)$. By Proposition 7.3, in any 2-connected spanning subgraph of G, there must be at least $\text{def}(G - X)$ edges going between $G - X$ and the nodes in X. Thus, the maximum degree of a node in X in any 2-connected spanning subgraph of G is at least $\text{def}(G - X)/|X|$. ∎

    The local-search algorithm proceeds as follows. Let c be an arbitrary constant greater than one. The algorithm starts with an arbitrary 2-connected subgraph, and iteratively applies local improvement steps to reduce the degrees of high-degree vertices. When a local optimum is reached, the algorithm outputs the current subgraph.

    Now we give definitions pertaining to an improvement step. Let N denote a 2-connected subgraph of G. For an edge $e \in N$, we define N_e to be the *bcf* of $N - \{e\}$. Since N is 2-connected, it follows that N_e is a simple path.

DEFINITION 7.11   The *degree-d candidate graph* for an edge e in N is obtained from G as follows: contract each 2-component of $N - \{e\}$, and then delete e and the edges of $G - N$ incident to nodes of degree d or more in N. A vertex w of degree d in N *admits* an improvement if there is an edge e incident to w in N such that the degree-$(d - 3)$ candidate graph for e is 2-connected.

    See Figure 7.3 for an example of a degree-5 candidate graph for an edge $e = \{1, 10\}$. The figure (a) on top, illustrates the network N with thick edges, and the edges in G that are not in N with dashed edges. There are four 2-components in $N - \{e\}$, formed by the vertex sets $\{1, 2, 3\}$, $\{4, 5, 6\}$, $\{7\}$, and $\{8, 9, 10, 11, 12, 13\}$. The figure (b) in the bottom, is the degree-5 candidate graph for the edge e formed by contracting each of the four 2-components of $N - \{e\}$ to single nodes and deleting edges in $G - N$ incident to nodes of degree five or more in N. The vertices in this graph corresponding to the above 2-components are a, b, c, and d respectively. Note that the edge $\{4, 10\}$ in G, but not in N, does not result in an edge between b and d because the degree of vertex 10 is already 5 in N.

    An improvement step consists of replacing e with edges from the candidate graph so that the resulting network remains 2-connected. We require that the degree of no vertex be increased beyond $d - 1$. The following lemma shows that this can be done. We use $deg_H(v)$ to denote the degree of a node v in the subgraph formed by a collection H of edges.

LEMMA 7.11   Let Q be a minimal collection of edges whose addition two-connects N_e. Then, for every node v of N_e, $deg_Q(v) \leq 2$.

Proof.   Suppose that $deg_Q(v) \geq 3$. Since N_e is a path, v splits N_e into two subpaths. Then, at least two of v's three incident edges must be incident on nodes in the same subpath. Let g be the one whose other endpoint is closer to v in the subpath. Then, $Q - \{g\}$ also 2-connects N_e, contradicting the minimality of Q. ∎

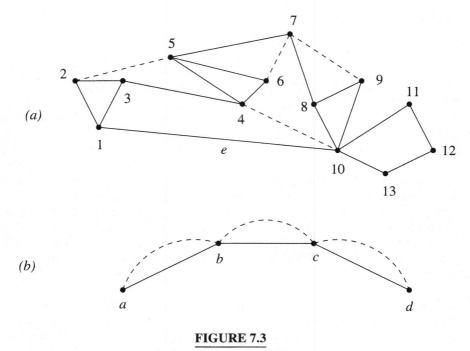

FIGURE 7.3

Candidate graph for local improvement.

Note that an improvement step for a vertex w reduces w's degree by one, and does not increase the degree of any vertex to more than w's new degree.

DEFINITION 7.12 Let N be a 2-connected spanning subgraph of G, and let Δ be the degree of N. Then, N is called *locally optimal* if no vertex of degree at least $\Delta - 2\lceil \log_c n \rceil$ admits an improvement.

A locally optimal solution can be computed by starting from an arbitrary 2-connected spanning subgraph of G, and iteratively applying improvements to high-degree nodes. Using a potential function argument as in Section 7.5.2, it can be shown that the number of improvement steps taken by the algorithm is $O(n^{O(1)+2\log_c n})$. Each improvement step can be executed in polynomial time. We now show that the degree of a locally optimal subgraph is not much more than $\Delta^*(G)$.

THEOREM 7.6 The degree Δ of a locally optimal 2-connected spanning subgraph of a graph G with n nodes is at most $c\Delta^*(G) + 2\lceil \log_c n \rceil + 4c$.

Let S_i denote the set of nodes whose degree in N is at least i. We first show that there is an i in the range $[\Delta - 2\lceil \log_c n \rceil, \Delta]$ for which $G - S_i$ has many leaf and isolated 2-components. We show this in Lemma 7.13. The proof of the above theorem then follows from Lemma 7.10.

LEMMA 7.12 Let G be a 2-connected graph, and let S be a set of vertices of G. Then there is a 2-connected subgraph A of G that contains all vertices of S, such that $\sum_{v \in S} \deg_A(v) \leq 4|S|$.

Proof. We provide an algorithm to compute A. A graph H is defined to be a minor of graph G if one can obtain H from G by repeatedly contracting or deleting edges. For a minor H of G, we say a vertex v of H is *active* if one of the vertices contracted to form v belongs to S. Consider the following algorithm:

- Initialize $H_0 := G$.
- Let $j := 0$ and let A_0 be the empty graph.
- While S is not 2-connected via A_j, do
    - Let C_{j+1} be a shortest cycle in H_j containing at least two active vertices.
    - Let $A_{j+1} := A_j \cup C_{j+1}$.
    - Obtain H_{j+1} from H_j by contracting together all vertices of C_{j+1}.
    - $j := j + 1$.

Let k be the number of iterations. By the termination condition, S is 2-connected in A_k. For each j, let x_j be the number of active vertices in C_j. Since the edges of C_j form a cycle in H_j, the degree due to these edges on active vertices in the cycle is at most twice the number of active vertices in the cycle.

$$\sum_{v \in S} deg_{C_j}(v) \leq 2x_j. \tag{7.1}$$

It follows that

$$\sum_{v \in S} \deg_A(v) = \sum_{j=1}^{k} \sum_{v \in S} \deg_{C_j}(v) \leq \sum_{j=1}^{k} 2x_j. \tag{7.2}$$

Next we bound the right-hand side of (7.2). Since at each iteration j, we contract x_j active vertices of H_j into a single active vertex in H_{j+1}, we have the following claim. Let $Act[H_j]$ denote the number of active vertices in H_j.

CLAIM 7.2 $Act[H_{j+1}] = Act[H_j] - (x_j - 1)$.

Since H_0 contains $|S|$ active vertices and H_k contains 1 active vertex, it follows by Lemma 7.2 that

$$\sum_{j=1}^{k} (x_j - 1) = |S| - 1. \tag{7.3}$$

In each iteration $x_j - 1 \geq 1$, so the number of iterations k is at most $|S| - 1$. Hence, $\sum (x_j - 1) \geq \sum x_j - (|S| - 1)$. Combining this inequality with (7.3) yields $\sum x_j \leq 2(|S| - 1)$. Combining this with (7.2) yields $\sum_{v \in S} \deg_A(v) \leq 4(|S| - 1)$. This completes the proof of Lemma 7.12. ∎

LEMMA 7.13 Let N be a locally optimal 2-connected subgraph with degree Δ. There is an integer i in the range $[\Delta - 2\lceil \log_c n \rceil, \Delta]$ such that the deficiency of $G - S_{i-2}$ is at least $(i - 4c)|S_i|$ and $|S_{i-2}| \leq c|S_i|$.

Proof.   By Proposition 7.2, there is an i in the given range with $|S_{i-2}| \leq c|S_i|$. By Lemma 7.12, there exists a 2-connected subgraph A of N such that S_{i-2} is contained in A and $\sum_{v \in S_{i-2}} \deg_A(v) \leq 4|S_{i-2}|$. By choice of i, the value $4|S_{i-2}|$ is at most $4c|S_i|$. To continue the proof, we show that a large portion of the degree of the nodes in S_{i-2} can be used to infer that $G - S_{i-2}$ has high deficiency.

DEFINITION 7.13   An edge e of a 2-connected graph H is *critical in H* if $H - \{e\}$ is not 2-connected.

By local optimality, for every edge e of N incident on S_i, the degree-$(i-3)$ candidate graph for e is not 2-connected. Note that this also implies that the edge e is critical in N. The following claim is used in the remainder of the proof.

CLAIM 7.3   Let e be an edge of N not in A such that one endpoint of e belongs to S_i. Then the other endpoint of e belongs to a leaf 2-component or isolated 2-component of the *bcf* of $G - S_{i-2}$.

Proof.   We give a proof by contradiction. Let $e = \{u, v\}$, where u belongs to S_i. First, suppose that v belongs to A; this includes the case where v belongs to S_{i-2}. Since A is 2-connected and contains u, it follows that e is noncritical, which is a contradiction. It follows that v belongs to some 2-component C of $G - S_{i-2}$. By the same argument as above, C contains no vertices of A.

Next suppose that C has degree two or more in $bcf(G - S_{i-2})$. Then C is internal to some path in $bcf(G - S_{i-2})$ between leaf 2-components L_1 and L_2 (see Figure 7.4). For $j = 1, 2$, let P_j be the subpath from C to L_j. By Proposition 7.3, there is an edge e_j

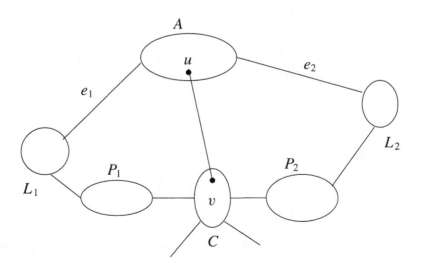

FIGURE 7.4

of N between each L_j and S_{i-2} for $j = 1, 2$. We have constructed edge-disjoint paths $P_1 e_1$ and $P_2 e_2$ from C to A. The edges of these paths are in $N \cup (G - S_{i-2})$. Recall that A is 2-connected and contains only edges in N, and that u is in A. It follows that C is 2-connected to u using edges in $(N \cup (G - S_{i-2}) - \{e\})$. This contradicts the fact that the degree-$(i - 3)$ candidate graph for e is not 2-connected.

To complete the proof of Lemma 7.13, note that the sum of the degrees of all the nodes of S_i in N is at least $i \cdot |S_i|$. By choice of the set A, we have $\sum_{v \in S_{i-2}} \deg_A(v) \leq 4c|S_i|$. Hence, there are at least $(i - 4c)|S_i|$ edges incident on S_i not in A. By Lemma 7.3, each of these edges goes to a leaf 2-component or isolated 2-component of $bcf(G - S_{i-2})$. By the criticality of these edges in N, it also follows that there is at most one such edge to a leaf-component and at most two such edges to a isolated-component in $bcf(G - S_{i-2})$. Hence, each such edge contributes one to the deficiency of $G - S_{i-2}$. This completes the proof of Lemma 7.13.   ■

PROBLEMS WITH EDGE WEIGHTS – POINTS IN EUCLIDEAN SPACES

7.6

Consider the edge-weighted version of the MDST problem. The input is a graph $G = (V, E)$, a nonnegative weight function on the edges and integer k. The output is a spanning tree of minimum weight among those in which each vertex has degree at most k. The problem is known as the minimum-weight degree-k spanning tree problem.

In this section, we consider the minimum-weight degree-k problem for Euclidean graphs, i.e., graphs defined implicitly by a set of points in Euclidean space. Here the weight of an edge between two points is defined to be the Euclidean distance between them. The problem is a generalization of the Hamilton Path problem which is known to be *NP*-hard even for points in the plane [GJ79, IPS82]. When $k = 3$, it was shown to be *NP*-hard by Papadimitriou and Vazirani [PV84], who conjectured that it is *NP*-hard for $K = 4$ as well. Other problems in a geometric setting, such as the traveling salesperson problem (TSP) and the Steiner tree problem, are discussed in Chapter 8.

For $\dim 2$, Papadimitriou and Vazirani [PV84] showed that any minimum spanning tree (MST) whose vertices have integer coordinates has maximum degree at most five. Monma and Suri [MS92] showed that for *every* set of points in the plane, there exists a degree-5 MST.

In any metric space, it is known that there always exists a TSP tour (and hence a spanning tree of degree 2) whose cost is at most twice the cost of an MST. Christofides [Chr75] gave a simple and elegant polynomial time approximation algorithm with an approximation ratio of 1.5 for computing a TSP tour for points satisfying the triangle inequality (points in a metric space). See Chapter 8 for a detailed discussion.

Khuller, Raghavachari, and Young [KRY94] showed that for an arbitrary collection of n points in the plane, there exists a degree-3 spanning tree whose weight is at most 1.5 times the weight of a minimum spanning tree. They also showed that there exists a degree-4 spanning tree whose weight is at most 1.25 times the weight of a minimum spanning tree. Moreover, if a minimum spanning tree is given as part of the input, the trees can be computed in $O(n)$ time. They also generalized the results to points in higher dimensions and showed that for any $d > 2$, an arbitrary collection of points in $\Re^d$ contains a degree-3 spanning tree whose weight is at most 5/3 times the weight of a minimum spanning tree.

In this section we describe the result of computing degree-3 trees for points in the plane.

Let $V = \{v_1, \dots, v_n\}$ be a set of n points in the plane. Let G be the complete graph induced by V, where the weight of an edge is the Euclidean distance between its endpoints. We use the terms points and vertices interchangeably. Let $\overline{uv}$ be the Euclidean distance between vertices u and v. Let $T_{\min}$ be an MST of V. Let $w(T)$ denote the total weight of a spanning tree T. Let T_k denote a spanning tree in which every vertex has degree at most k. Let $\deg_T(v)$ be the degree of a vertex v in the tree T. Let $\triangle ABC$ denote the triangle formed by points A, B, and C. Let $\angle ABC$ denote the angle formed at B between line segments AB and BC. Let $\overline{ABC}$ denote the perimeter of $\triangle ABC$; and more generally, let $\overline{v_1 v_2 \dots v_k}$ denote the perimeter of the polygon formed by the line segments $v_i v_{i+1}$ for $1 \leq i \leq k$, where $v_{k+1} = v_1$.

We first observe some useful properties of minimum spanning trees.

PROPOSITION 7.4 [PV84]   Let AB and BC be two edges incident to a point B in a minimum spanning tree of a set of points in $\Re^d$. Then, $\angle ABC$ is the largest angle in $\triangle ABC$.

COROLLARY 7.2   Let AB and BC be two edges incident to a point B in a minimum spanning tree of a set of points in $\Re^d$. Then,

- $\angle ABC \geq 60°$
- $\angle BAC, \angle BCA \leq 90°$.

We now prove an upper bound on the perimeter of an arbitrary triangle in terms of distances to its vertices from an arbitrary point. This lemma is useful in proving the performance of the algorithm.

LEMMA 7.14   Let X, A, B, and C be points in $\Re^d$ with $\overline{XA} \leq \overline{XB}, \overline{XC}$. Then,

$$\overline{ABC} \leq (3\sqrt{3} - 4)\overline{XA} + 2(\overline{XB} + \overline{XC}). \tag{7.4}$$

Note that $3\sqrt{3} - 4 \approx 1.2$. Recall that $\overline{ABC}$ is the perimeter of the triangle and $\overline{XY}$ is the distance from X to Y.

Proof.   Let B' and C' be points on XB and XC respectively such that $\overline{XA} = \overline{XB'} = \overline{XC'}$ (see Figure 7.5). First we observe that the lemma is true if it is true for the points X, A, B' and C'. This follows because by the triangle inequality,

$$\overline{ABC} \leq \overline{AB'C'} + 2\overline{BB'} + 2\overline{CC'}.$$

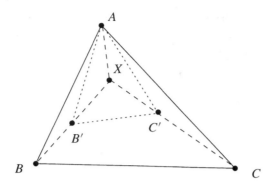

FIGURE 7.5

Shrinking to obtain canonical form.

By our assumption,

$$\overline{AB'C'} \le (3\sqrt{3} - 4)\overline{XA} + 2(\overline{XB'} + \overline{XC'}).$$

Combining the two inequalities yields the desired result. Therefore, in the rest of the proof we show that the lemma is true when the "arms" $\overline{XA}$, $\overline{XB'}$ and $\overline{XC'}$ are equal.

The perimeter of the triangle is maximized when X is in the plane defined by A, B', and C', and thus, X is at the center of a circle passing through A, B', and C'.

By scaling, it suffices to consider the case when the circle has unit radius. In this case, the right-hand side of (7.4) is exactly $3\sqrt{3}$. Thus, it suffices to show that the maximum perimeter achieved by any triangle whose vertices lie on a unit circle is $3\sqrt{3}$. This was proved by Lillington [Lil75]. ∎

Note that in an arbitrary metric space it is possible to have an (equilateral) triangle of perimeter six and a point X at distance one from each vertex.

We now assume that we are given a Euclidean minimum spanning tree T of degree at most five. We show how to convert T into a tree of degree at most three. The weight of the resulting tree is at most 1.5 times the weight of T.

High Level Description: The tree T is rooted at an arbitrary leaf vertex. Since T is a degree-5 tree, once it is rooted at a leaf, each vertex has at most four children. For each vertex v, the shortest path P_v starting at v and visiting every child of v, is computed. The final tree T_3 consists of the union of the paths $\{P_v\}$. In analyzing the algorithm, we think of each vertex v as replacing its edges from its children with the path P_v. The above technique of "shortcutting" the children of a vertex by "stringing" them together is used often, especially in the context of computing degree-3 trees in metric spaces (see [RMR+93, Sal92]).

Algorithm Euclidean:3-Tree
***

Input: A Euclidean graph G, and a MST T of G.
Output: A degree-3 tree of G of approximately minimum weight.

> *Step 1:* Root the MST T at a leaf vertex r.
>
> *Step 2:* **For** each vertex $v \in V$ do
>
>> **(a)** Compute P_v, the shortest path starting at v and visiting all the children of v.
>
> *Step 3:* Return T_3, the tree formed by the union of the paths $\{P_v\}$.

Note: Typically, the initial MST has very few nodes with degree greater than three. In practice, it is worth modifying the algorithm to scan the vertices in preorder, maintaining the partial tree T_3 of edges added so far, and to add paths to T_3 as follows. When considering a vertex v, if the degree of v in the partial T_3 is two, add the path P_v as described in the algorithm. Otherwise, its degree is one and, in this case, relax the requirement that the added path must start at v. That is, add the shortest path that visits v and all of v's children to T_3. This modification will never increase the cost of the resulting tree, but may offer substantially lighter trees in practice.

LEMMA 7.15   Algorithm Euclidean:3-Tree outputs a spanning tree of degree three.

Proof.   A proof by induction shows that the union of the paths forms a tree. Each vertex v is on at most two paths and is in the interior of at most one.   ∎

LEMMA 7.16   Let v be a vertex in a MST T of a set of points in $\Re^2$. Let P_v be a shortest path visiting $\{v\} \cup \text{child}_T(v)$ with v as one of its endpoints.

$$w(P_v) \le 1.5 \times \sum_{v_i \in \text{child}_T(v)} \overline{vv_i}.$$

By the above lemma, each path P_v has weight at most 1.5 times the weight of the edges it replaces. Thus,

THEOREM 7.7   Let T be a minimum spanning tree of a set of points in $\Re^2$. Let T_3 be the spanning tree output by algorithm Euclidean:3-Tree. Then,

$$w(T_3) \le 1.5 \times w(T).$$

Proof of Lemma 7.16.   We consider the various cases that arise depending on the number of children of v. The cases when v has no children or exactly one child are trivial. *Case 1: v has 2 children, v_1, v_2.* There are two possible paths for P_v, namely $P_1 = [v, v_1, v_2]$ and $P_2 = [v, v_2, v_1]$. Clearly,

$$w(P_v) = \min(w(P_1), w(P_2)) \le \frac{w(P_1) + w(P_2)}{2} = \frac{\overline{vv_1}}{2} + \frac{\overline{vv_2}}{2} + \overline{v_1v_2} \le 1.5\,(\overline{vv_1} + \overline{vv_2}).$$

Case 2: v has 3 children, v_1, v_2, v_3. Let v_1 be the child that is nearest to v. Consider the following four paths (see Figure 7.6): $P_1 = [v, v_1, v_2, v_3]$, $P_2 = [v, v_1, v_3, v_2]$, $P_3 = [v, v_2, v_1, v_3]$ and $P_4 = [v, v_3, v_1, v_2]$.

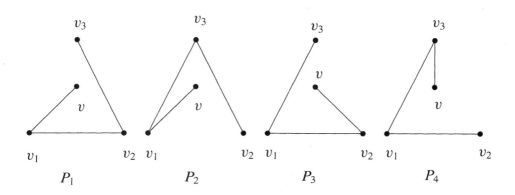

FIGURE 7.6

T_3, three children.

The path P_v is at most as heavy as the lightest of $\{P_1, P_2, P_3, P_4\}$. The weight of the lightest of these paths is at most any convex combination of the weights of the paths. Specifically,

$$w(P_v) \leq \min(w(P_1), w(P_2), w(P_3), w(P_4)) \leq \frac{w(P_1)}{3} + \frac{w(P_2)}{3} + \frac{w(P_3)}{6} + \frac{w(P_4)}{6}.$$

We will now prove that

$$\frac{w(P_1)}{3} + \frac{w(P_2)}{3} + \frac{w(P_3)}{6} + \frac{w(P_4)}{6} \leq 1.5\,(\overline{vv_1} + \overline{vv_2} + \overline{vv_3}).$$

This simplifies to

$$\overline{v_1v_2} + \overline{v_2v_3} + \overline{v_3v_1} \leq 1.25\,\overline{vv_1} + 2(\overline{vv_2} + \overline{vv_3}),$$

which follows from Lemma 7.14.

Case 3: v has 4 children, v_1, v_2, v_3, v_4, ordered clockwise around v. Let v' be the point of intersection of the diagonals $\overline{v_1v_3}$ and $\overline{v_2v_4}$. Note that the diagonals do intersect because the polygon $v_1v_2v_3v_4$ is convex (follows from Corollary 7.2).

Let v_3 be the point that is furthest from v', among $\{v_1, v_2, v_3, v_4\}$. Consider the following two paths (see Figure 7.7): $P_1 = [v, v_4, v_1, v_2, v_3]$, $P_2 = [v, v_2, v_1, v_4, v_3]$.

Clearly,

$$w(P_v) \leq \min(w(P_1), w(P_2)) \leq \frac{w(P_1)}{2} + \frac{w(P_2)}{2}.$$

We will show that

$$\frac{1}{2}(w(P_1) + w(P_2)) \leq 1.5(\overline{vv_1} + \overline{vv_2} + \overline{vv_3} + \overline{vv_4}).$$

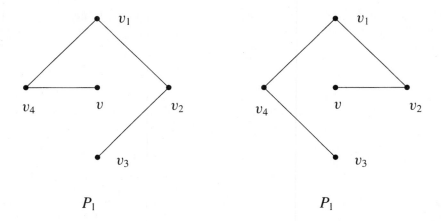

FIGURE 7.7

T_3, *four children.*

This simplifies to

$$\overline{v_1 v_2 v_3 v_4} + (\overline{v_1 v_2} + \overline{v_1 v_4}) \leq 3(\overline{v v_1} + \overline{v v_3}) + 2(\overline{v v_2} + \overline{v v_4}). \tag{7.5}$$

We will first prove that

$$\overline{v_1 v_2 v_3 v_4} + (\overline{v_1 v_2} + \overline{v_1 v_4}) \leq 3(\overline{v' v_1} + \overline{v' v_3}) + 2(\overline{v' v_2} + \overline{v' v_4}). \tag{7.6}$$

Once we prove (7.6), by the triangle inequality we can conclude that (7.5) is true. (Since $\overline{v v_1} + \overline{v v_3} \geq \overline{v_1 v_3} = \overline{v' v_1} + \overline{v' v_3}$ and $\overline{v v_2} + \overline{v v_4} \geq \overline{v_2 v_4} = \overline{v' v_2} + \overline{v' v_4}$.)

We prove (7.6) by contradiction. Suppose there exists a set of points which does not satisfy (7.6). Suppose we shrink $v' v_3$ by δ. The left side of the above inequality decreases by at most 2δ, whereas the right side of the inequality decreases by exactly 3δ. Therefore, as we shrink $v' v_3$, the inequality stays violated. Suppose $v' v_3$ shrinks and becomes equal to another edge $v' v_i$ for some $i \in \{1, 2, 4\}$. We now shrink both $v' v_3$ and $v' v_i$ simultaneously at the same rate. Again, it can be verified that the inequality continues to be violated as $v' v_3$ and $v' v_i$ shrink. Hence, we reach a configuration where three of the edges are equal.

Without loss of generality, the length of the three edges is 1 and the length of the fourth edge is some $\epsilon \leq 1$.

There are two cases to consider. The first is when $v' v_1 = \epsilon$ and the second is when $v' v_2 = \epsilon$. (The case when $v' v_4 = \epsilon$ is the same as the second case due to symmetry.)

Case 3a. $v' v_1 = \epsilon$. We wish to prove that

$$\overline{v_1 v_2 v_3 v_4} + (\overline{v_1 v_2} + \overline{v_1 v_4}) \leq 7 + 3\epsilon.$$

We show that the function $F(\epsilon) = \overline{v_1 v_2 v_3 v_4} + (\overline{v_1 v_2} + \overline{v_1 v_4}) - 7 - 3\epsilon$ is non-positive in the domain $0 \leq \epsilon \leq 1$. Simplifying, we get

$$F(\epsilon) = 2\overline{v_1 v_2} + \overline{v_2 v_3} + \overline{v_3 v_4} + 2\overline{v_1 v_4} - 7 - 3\epsilon.$$

Each of $\overline{v_i v_j}$ in the definition of F is a convex function of ϵ due to the following reason. Let p be the point closest to v_j on the line connecting v_i and v'. Observe that as v_i moves towards v', $\overline{v_i v_j}$ decreases if v_i is moving towards p and increases otherwise. Since F is a sum of convex functions minus a linear function, it is a convex function of ϵ. Therefore, it is maximized at either $\epsilon = 0$ or $\epsilon = 1$.

When $\epsilon = 1$, all four points are at the same distance from v'. If angle $\angle v_4 v' v_1 = \alpha$ then F can be written as a function of a single variable α and it can be verified that F reaches a maximum value of $10\sqrt{0.8} - 10$, which is non-positive.

When $\epsilon = 0$, $\overline{v_1 v_2} = \overline{v_1 v_4} = 1$. Simplifying we get $F = \overline{v_2 v_3} + \overline{v_3 v_4} - 3$, and it reaches a maximum value of $2\sqrt{2} - 3$, which is non-positive (when $\epsilon = 0$, note that v_1 is the midpoint of the line segment $v_2 v_4$).

Case 3b. $v' v_2 = \epsilon$. We wish to prove that

$$\overline{v_1 v_2 v_3 v_4} + (\overline{v_1 v_2} + \overline{v_1 v_4}) \leq 8 + 2\epsilon.$$

We show that the function $F'(\epsilon) = \overline{v_1 v_2 v_3 v_4} + (\overline{v_1 v_2} + \overline{v_1 v_4}) - 8 - 2\epsilon$ is non-positive in the domain $0 \leq \epsilon \leq 1$.

As a function of ϵ, function F' is a sum of convex functions minus a linear function, and thus is convex. Therefore, it is maximized at either $\epsilon = 0$ or $\epsilon = 1$.

The case $\epsilon = 1$ leads to the same configuration as in Case 3a.

When $\epsilon = 0$, $\overline{v_1 v_2} = \overline{v_2 v_3} = 1$. Here $F' = 2\overline{v_1 v_4} + \overline{v_3 v_4} - 5$. If angle $\angle v_4 v' v_1 = \alpha$, then F' can be written as a function of a single variable α and it can be verified that F' reaches a maximum value of $5\sqrt{0.8} - 5$, which is non-positive.

This concludes the proof of Lemma 7.16. ∎

OPEN PROBLEMS

7.7

We conclude the chapter with a few open problems.

OPEN PROBLEM 7.1 [Locally optimal f-joins] Definition 7.7 of a locally optimal tree for the MDST problem can be generalized to locally optimal forests for the minimum-degree f-join problem (see Subsection 7.5.2). Is it possible to compute such forests in polynomial time?

OPEN PROBLEM 7.2 [Minimum degree k-connected subgraphs] No approximation algorithms are known for the minimum-degree k-connected spanning subgraph problem, for $k > 2$. Do local search techniques extend to this problem for general k?

OPEN PROBLEM 7.3 [Weighted MDST problem] For the general MDST problem with arbitrary edge weights, the current best approximation algorithm is that of Ravi et al. [RMR$^+$93] and it generates a tree of degree $O(\Delta \log n)$ whose weight is within $O(\log n)$ of any Δ-tree. It can be shown that no approximation factor is possible (unless $P = NP$) if the output spanning tree is forced to be of degree Δ and it is compared against a minimum-weight Δ-tree. Is it possible to use the techniques of Section 7.4 to find a tree of degree at most $\Delta + 1$, whose weight is not much more than an optimal Δ-tree?

OPEN PROBLEM 7.4 [Euclidean MDST problems]   Improve the current best ratios of 1.25 for degree-4 spanning trees and 1.5 for degree-3 spanning trees for Euclidean graphs induced by points in the plane, and 5/3 for degree-3 trees for points in d-dimensions ($d > 2$). Problems of approximating degree-k trees in higher dimensions and in general metric spaces within factors better than 2 are still open.

Acknowledgments I thank Dorit Hochbaum and Samir Khuller for useful comments. This work was supported in part by the National Science Foundation under grant CCR-9409625.

REFERENCES

[AKR91] A. Agrawal, P. Klein, and R. Ravi. How tough is the minimum-degree steiner tree? a new approximate min-max equality. Technical Report TR CS-91-49, Brown University, August 1991.

[Chr75] N. Christofides. Worst-case analysis of a new heuristic for the traveling salesman problem. Technical Report Report 388, Graduate School of Industrial Administration, Carnegie Mellon University, 1975.

[Chv73] V. Chvátal. Tough graphs and Hamiltonian circuits. *Disc. Math.*, 5:215–228, 1973.

[CLR89] T. H. Cormen, C. E. Leiserson, and R. L. Rivest. *Introduction to Algorithms*. The MIT Press, 1989.

[Fis93] T. Fischer. Optimizing the degree of minimum weight spanning trees. Technical Report TR 93-1338, Dept. of Computer Science, Cornell University, April 1993.

[FR90] M. Fürer and B. Raghavachari. An NC approximation algorithm for the minimum degree spanning tree problem. In *Proc. of the 28th Annual Allerton Conf. on Communication, Control and Computing*, pages 274–281, 1990.

[FR92] M. Fürer and B. Raghavachari. Approximating the minimum degree spanning tree to within one from the optimal degree. In *Proc. of 3rd ACM-SIAM Symp. on Disc. Algorithms*, pages 317–324, 1992.

[FR94] M. Fürer and B. Raghavachari. Approximating the minimum-degree steiner tree to within one of optimal. *J. Algorithms*, 17:409–423, 1994.

[Gav82] B. Gavish. Topological design of centralized computer networks – formulations and algorithms. *Networks*, 12:355–377, 1982.

[GJ79] M. R. Garey and D. S. Johnson. *Computers and intractability: A guide to the theory of NP-completeness*. W. H. Freeman, 1979.

[GW92] M. X. Goemans and D. P. Williamson. A general approximation technique for constrained forest problems. In *Proc. of the 3rd Annual ACM-SIAM Symposium on Discrete Algorithms*, pages 307–316, 1992.

[IPS82]   A. Itai, C. H. Papadimitriou, and J. L. Szwarcfiter. Hamilton paths in grid graphs. *SIAM J. Comput.*, 11(4):676–686, 1982.

[KRY94]   S. Khuller, B. Raghavachari, and N. Young. Low degree spanning trees of small weight. In *Proc. of the 26th Annual ACM Symp. on the Theory of Computing*, pages 412–421, 1994. To appear in *SIAM J. Comput.*

[Law76]   E. L. Lawler. *Combinatorial optimization: networks and matroids*. Holt, Rinehart and Winston, New York, 1976.

[Lil75]   J. N. Lillington. Some extremal properties of convex sets. *Math. Proc. Cambridge Philosophical Society*, 77:515–524, 1975.

[LP86]   L. Lovász and M. D. Plummer. *Matching Theory*. Akadémiai Kiadó, Budapest, 1986.

[MS92]   C. Monma and S. Suri. Transitions in geometric minimum spanning trees. *Discrete & Computational Geometry*, 8(3):265–293, 1992.

[PV84]   C. H. Papadimitriou and U. V. Vazirani. On two geometric problems related to the traveling salesman problem. *J. Algorithms*, 5:231–246, 1984.

[Rav94]   R. Ravi. Rapid rumor ramification: approximating the minimum broadcast time. In *Proc. of 35th Annual IEEE Symposium on Foundations of Computer Science*, pages 202–213, November 1994.

[RMR+93]   R. Ravi, M. V. Marathe, S. S. Ravi, D. J. Rosenkrantz, and H. B. Hunt III. Many birds with one stone: multi-objective approximation algorithms. In *Proc. of 25th Annual ACM Symp. on the Theory of Computing*, pages 438–447, May 1993.

[RRK92]   R. Ravi, B. Raghavachari, and P. Klein. Approximation through local optimality: designing networks with small degree. In *Proc. of 12th Conf. on Foundations of Software Tech. and Theoret. Comp. Sci.*, pages 279–290. Lect. Notes in Comp. Sci. 652, 1992.

[Sal92]   J. S. Salowe. Euclidean spanner graphs with degree four. In *Proc. of 8th Annual ACM Symp. on Computational Geometry*, pages 186–191, June 1992.

[Win89]   S. Win. On a connection between the existence of k-trees and the toughness of a graph. *Graphs and Combinatorics*, 5:201–205, 1989.

8

APPROXIMATION ALGORITHMS FOR GEOMETRIC PROBLEMS

Marshall Bern   **David Eppstein**

This chapter discusses approximation algorithms for hard geometric problems. We cover three well-known shortest network problems—traveling salesman, Steiner tree, and minimum weight triangulation—along with an assortment of problems in areas such as clustering and surface approximation.

INTRODUCTION

8.1

This chapter surveys approximation algorithms for hard geometric problems. The problems we consider typically take inputs that are point sets or polytopes in two- or three-dimensional space, and seek optimal constructions, which may be trees, paths, or polytopes. We limit attention to problems for which no polynomial-time exact algorithms are known, and concentrate on bounds for worst-case approximation ratios, especially bounds that depend intrinsically on geometry.

We illustrate our intentions with two well-known problems. Given a finite set of points S in the plane, the Euclidean traveling salesman problem asks for the shortest tour of S. Christofides' algorithm achieves *approximation ratio* $\frac{3}{2}$ for this problem, meaning that it always computes a tour of length at most three-halves the length of the optimal tour. This bound depends only on the triangle inequality, so Christofides' algorithm works equally well in any metric space, even the finite metric space induced by the shortest-path distance on a network (edge-weighted graph).

The Steiner tree problem asks for the shortest tree that includes S in its vertex set. Approximation ratios for this problem depend quite intimately on geometry. For example, the current best bound for the rectilinear version of the problem is $\frac{19}{15} \approx 1.267$; for the Euclidean version, it is arbitrarily close to $1 + \ln \frac{2}{\sqrt{3}} \approx 1.144$; and for the network version, arbitrarily close to $1 + \ln 2 \approx 1.693$. The proof of a certain geometric conjecture would change the algorithm of choice for the Euclidean case and improve the ratio to 1.114. Because of the more prominent role of geometry, we shall discuss the Steiner tree problem at greater length than the traveling salesman problem.

8.1.1 OVERVIEW OF TOPICS

We have selected five major problems or problem areas as section topics in this chapter: the traveling salesman problem, the Steiner tree problem, minimum-weight triangulation, clustering, and separation. Although we shall not discuss applications, all five of the selected problems arise naturally in a variety of contexts. Four of the five problems— all except minimum-weight triangulation—are known to be *NP*-hard. Our treatments include fairly detailed proof sketches, because proofs are the *sine qua non* of approximation algorithms: that which distinguishes them from mere heuristics.

We have relegated some other work to a sixth, miscellaneous, section. The problems in this section include rectangle packing and covering, embedding graphs onto points, and finding long graphs without edge crossings. We omit all work on approximations of polynomially solvable problems and all results that assume random inputs.

8.1.2 SPECIAL NATURE OF GEOMETRIC PROBLEMS

A geometric input is typically more constrained than its non-geometric counterpart. First, geometric problems can often be reduced to combinatorial optimization problems involving graphs or set systems, only the resulting problem instances are usually quite special. Geometric packing and covering problems can be reduced to independent set or clique cover; the polyhedron separation problem, discussed in Section 8.6.2, can be reduced to a special case of the set cover problem. Secondly, geometric problems sometimes admit decompositions related to planar separator theorems. For example, the Euclidean traveling salesman problem (TSP) can be exactly solved in time $n^{O(\sqrt{n})}$ [Smi88]. Finally, and most significantly, a set of n points in the plane has only $2n$ degrees of freedom, while a network on n vertices may have up to $\binom{n}{2}$ independent distances.

The constrained nature of geometric problems often helps in approximation. In Section 8.7.2 we shall approximate a packing problem better than the bound implied by an approximation to independent set. The geometric origin of the set cover problem in Section 8.6.2 also leads to an improved ratio. Whether planar separators help in approximations to geometric problems is currently unclear. Grigni, Koutsoupias, and Papadimitriou [GEP95] devised a separator-based polynomial time approximation scheme for the traveling salesman problem on planar graphs with unit edge lengths; this result leads them to speculate that the Euclidean TSP has such an approximation scheme as well. Finally, improvements due to constraints on distances appear throughout this chapter. In a recent paper, Barvinok [Bar94] showed that the distance matrix implied by n points and a "polyhedral metric" has low "combinatorial rank," and exploited this fact to approximate the longest Euclidean traveling salesman tour arbitrarily well.

The same constraints that aid in approximation, however, create difficulties for problem reductions. For the purpose of reductions, planar geometric problems resemble problems on planar graphs, and proving a geometric problem *NP*-hard is usually much trickier than proving the same result for its non-geometric counterpart. For example, finding a longest traveling salesman tour is known to be *NP*-hard for general graphs, but is still open for planar graphs and for points in the Euclidean plane.

Even when reductions to geometric or planar-graph problems are known, they typically blow up the size of the instance by polynomial factors, and hence, do not preserve approximability. There are currently very few non-approximability results for these types of inputs. (A *non-approximability result* gives a lower bound on the approximation ratio achievable in polynomial time, assuming that $P \neq NP$.) The recent breakthrough results on non-approximability—see Chapter 10 by Arora and Lund—have had virtually no implications for geometric problems. Hence, we list the following as our foremost open problem. (Note added as this book goes to press: Arora [Aro96] has largely solved this problem; see our conclusion.)

OPEN PROBLEM 8.1   Are the famous geometric problems, such as the Euclidean traveling salesman problem, hard to approximate arbitrarily well?

A final consequence of geometric constraints is perhaps the most curious. Many problems involving Euclidean distance are not even known to be in *NP* due to a certain "technicality" [GGJ77]. For example, the straightforward decision-problem version of the traveling salesman problem asks whether there exists a tour of length at most k. The length of a tour is a sum of n square roots. Comparing this sum to the integer k may require very high precision arithmetic—for example, removing the square roots by repeated squaring gives numbers of about 2^n bits. This difficulty is quite distinct from *NP*-hardness; it arises even for decision-problem versions of easy problems such as the Euclidean minimum spanning tree. Algorithms in computational geometry typically skirt precision issues by assuming exact real arithmetic [Mul94, PS85]. This "real RAM" model of computation, however, is unsuitable for problem reductions.

OPEN PROBLEM 8.2   Is there a polynomial-time algorithm to compare an integer to the sum of n square roots of integers?

TRAVELING SALESMAN PROBLEM
8.2

We start with the most famous hard problem. The *Euclidean traveling salesman problem* is given by a set of points $S = \{s_1, s_2, \ldots, s_n\}$ in the plane with Euclidean metric, and asks for a shortest *tour* that visits all points. In other words, we seek a permutation σ

that minimizes the sum of distances

$$|s_{\sigma(1)}s_{\sigma(2)}| + |s_{\sigma(2)}s_{\sigma(3)}| + \cdots + |s_{\sigma(n-1)}s_{\sigma(n)}| + |s_{\sigma(n)}s_{\sigma(1)}|.$$

The triangle inequality implies that the diagonals of a convex quadrilateral are always longer than either pair of opposite sides; thus a pair of crossing edges in a tour can be replaced by a pair of disjoint edges, decreasing the overall length. Hence, the optimal tour must be a simple polygon.

Euclidean TSP is NP-hard [GJ79]. A network version of the problem is Max-$\mathcal{SNP}$-hard (see Chapter 10), even if edge lengths are restricted to 1 and 2 [PY93]. Hence, the network version cannot be approximated arbitrarily well (no polynomial-time approximation scheme exists) unless $P = NP$.

The best approximation algorithm for the Euclidean TSP is Christofides' algorithm, discovered in 1976. This algorithm achieves an approximation ratio of $\frac{3}{2}$. Remarkably, the algorithm uses no geometry beyond the triangle inequality, so it achieves this same ratio in any metric space. Failure to find a better approximation has led researchers to investigate ancillary questions, such as the approximation ratios of commonly used heuristics. We describe this work below. For more on the traveling salesman problem—mostly non-geometric—see the book edited by Lawler et al. [LLKS85]. For valuable practical information on the geometric case, consult the paper by Bentley [Ben92].

8.2.1 CHRISTOFIDES' ALGORITHM

Let $TSP(S)$ denote an optimal traveling salesman tour and $MST(S)$ denote a minimum spanning tree for points S, with lengths $|TSP(S)|$ and $|MST(S)|$ respectively. Notice that $|MST(S)| \leq |TSP(S)|$. Christofides' algorithm (see [GJ79, JP85]) starts by computing $MST(S)$. The minimum spanning tree alone gives a tour with an approximation ratio 2: simply walk around the "outside" of the tree to obtain a sequence $s_{t(1)}, s_{t(2)}, \ldots, s_{t(2n)}$ that visits each point twice. Eliminating repeats from the sequence $t(1), t(2), \ldots, t(2n)$, say by removing all occurrences of each index after the first, cannot lengthen the solution.

To improve the ratio, Christofides computes a minimum-length matching on the odd-degree vertices of $MST(S)$, as in Figure 8.1. Such a matching has length at most $\frac{1}{2}|TSP(S)|$, since the optimal traveling salesman tour has length at least that of an optimal

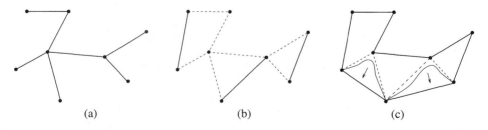

(a) (b) (c)

FIGURE 8.1

(a) The MST. (b) A minimum-length matching on odd-degree vertices. (c) The final tour.

tour on these odd-degree vertices, which can be partitioned into two matchings by taking every other edge. The MST along with the matching edges has only even-degree vertices, so it is Eulerian, and an Euler tour of this graph has length at most $\frac{3}{2}|TSP(S)|$. Eliminating repeats as above can only improve this tour. Figure 8.2 shows that the ratio of $\frac{3}{2}$ is tight. The running time of Christofides' algorithm depends on the time bound for Euclidean matching. Vaidya [Vai88] gave an $O(n^{2.5}\log^4 n)$ matching algorithm.

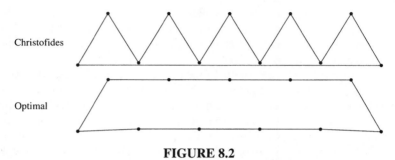

FIGURE 8.2

The tour found by Christofides' algorithm can have length
$\frac{3}{2}$ *times optimal.*

8.2.2   HEURISTICS

An *insertion method* [RSL77] adds the points of S one by one in some order. A newly inserted point s_j is incorporated into the current tour by removing an edge $s_i s_k$, and adding edges $s_i s_j$ and $s_j s_k$. Edge $s_i s_k$ is always chosen to minimize the increase in the cost of the tour, $|s_i s_j| + |s_j s_k| - |s_i s_k|$. However, various rules are used to pick the point to insert. Examples are *nearest insertion*, which inserts the point s_j nearest to a point already in the tour; *farthest insertion*, which inserts the point s_j that is farthest from any point in the tour; and *random insertion*, which chooses s_j uniformly at random. Rosenkrantz, Stearns, and Lewis [RSL77] proved the following upper bound.

THEOREM 8.1   Rosenkrantz et al.   Any insertion order for S gives a tour of length at most $(\lceil \log_2 n \rceil + 1) \cdot |TSP(S)|$.

Proof.   Let $s_1, s_2, \ldots, s_n$ be an arbitrary insertion order, and let $INS(S)$ denote the resulting tour. Let $cost(s_j)$ denote the increase in the length of the tour upon the insertion of s_j. As above, if s_j is inserted between s_i and s_k, then $cost(s_j) = |s_i s_j| + |s_j s_k| - |s_i s_k|$. We define $cost(s_1) = 0$ and $cost(s_2) = 2|s_1 s_2|$, so that $\sum_{j=1}^{n} cost(s_j) = |INS(S)|$.

Now consider vertices s_i and s_j that are consecutive in the optimal tour $TSP(S)$. We assert that

$$2|s_i s_j| \geq \min\{cost(s_i), cost(s_j)\}.$$

Why? If s_i was already in the tour when s_j was inserted, then we could have inserted s_j adjacent to s_i in the tour, and by the triangle inequality, $cost(s_j)$ would have been at most $2|s_i s_j|$. A similar observation applies in the case $j < i$.

We now imagine charging the smaller of $cost(s_i)$ and $cost(s_j)$ to edge $s_i s_j$ in $TSP(S)$. Doing this for consecutive disjoint pairs of vertices from $TSP(S)$, we charge one vertex from each pair—a total of $\lfloor n/2 \rfloor$ vertices—to every other edge in $TSP(S)$. By charging to the shorter set of alternating edges in $TSP(S)$, we see that the total charge is at most $|TSP(S)|$.

We now repeat the argument on the vertices S' not yet paid for. This time insertion costs are assigned to every other edge of a tour on S' that respects the order given by $TSP(S)$. Edges of this tour correspond to disjoint sections of $TSP(S)$, so its length is at most $|TSP(S)|$. After $\lceil \log_2 n \rceil$ stages we get down to a tour on just two vertices, which again has length at most $|TSP(S)|$. ∎

Bafna et al. [BKP94] and Azar [Aza94] (see also [AA93]) independently adapted a construction of Bentley and Saxe [BS80] to show that the bound of Theorem 8.1 is tight up to a factor of $O(\log \log n)$. We use a slightly simpler adaptation [CKT94] below.

THEOREM 8.2 Some insertion orders produce tours of length $\Omega(\log n / \log \log n)$ times optimal.

Proof. The set of points S includes $p + 1$ vertical columns of vertices, numbered 0 to p, an odd integer. Along the top third of column i, there are $p^{2i} + 1$ vertices, evenly spaced along a segment of length p^{2p}. The bottom third of column i is the same as the top third, after a gap of p^{2p}. The horizontal spacing between column i and column $i + 1$ is $p^{2p-1-2i}$, which is $\frac{1}{p}$ times the basic vertical spacing in row i. The total number of vertices is about $3p^{2p}$, so p is $\Omega(\log n / \log \log n)$.

Assume the insertion order is left to right by columns and from the middle outwards, alternating above and below within each column. This order gives the tour on the left in Figure 8.3, which has total length greater than $4p \cdot p^{2p}$. (For clarity, Figure 8.3 does not show all of S; the third column should really have 20 points, and the fourth 164.) The illustration on the far right shows a spanning tree for this same set of points with total length $O(p^{2p})$, proving that $|TSP(S)|$ is also $O(p^{2p})$. ∎

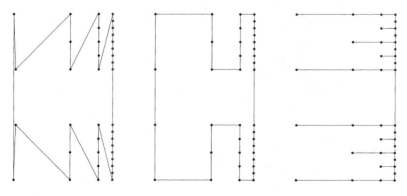

FIGURE 8.3

An insertion tour or a 2-optimized tour can have length
$\Omega(\log n / \log \log n)$ *times the MST.*

We now discuss specific insertion methods. Nearest insertion [RSL77] achieves an approximation ratio of 2, because the jth point never costs more than twice the jth edge chosen by Prim's MST algorithm. This bound is known to be tight. Warburton [War93] considered insertion methods that start with the convex hull instead of a trivial tour, and showed that the bound for nearest insertion then degrades to 3. Somewhat surprisingly, farthest insertion typically outperforms nearest insertion [Ben92], and its exact approximation ratio is currently unknown. However, Hurkens [Hur92] recently showed that this ratio cannot be smaller than 2.43. Azar [Aza94] proved that there are point sets for which random insertion has approximation ratio $\Omega(\log\log n/\log\log\log n)$.

We now move on to another heuristic, that can be used either as an algorithm in its own right, or as a post-processing step to locally optimize a tour. The *2-Opt heuristic* starts from any tour of S, and repeatedly swaps one pair of edges for another pair with the same endpoints and shorter total length. The swapped-out pair may be a crossing pair, but this is not a requirement. The swapped-in pair is determined by the need to form a tour rather than two disjoint cycles, and the new tour is the same as the old only with a contiguous subsequence reversed. The algorithm halts when the tour is *2-optimized*, meaning that there are no 2-Opt swaps that reduce its total length.

There are numerous rules—first found, best first, randomized—that specify which 2-Opt swap to make [Ben92], but in studying the approximation ratio of this heuristic, we shall assume an arbitrary or worst-case order of swaps. Chandra, Karloff, and Tovey [CKT94] showed the following upper bound:

THEOREM 8.3   Any 2-optimized tour has length $O(\log n)$ times optimal.

Proof.   Let $OPT2(S)$ be a 2-optimized tour with edges directed so that each has an "origin" and a "destination." Divide the edges of $OPT2(S)$ into—say—18 equivalence classes, based on directions: an edge belongs to class i, $0 \leq i \leq 17$ if its angle with the horizontal lies in the range $[i \cdot 10°, (i+1) \cdot 10°)$. It is not hard to show that two edges $s_i s_j$ and $s_k s_l$ from the same equivalence class must have origins at least $\frac{1}{2}\min\{|s_i s_j|, |s_k s_l|\}$ apart, for otherwise we could swap them for a shorter pair.

We bound the total length within each equivalence class separately using an argument similar to the proof of Theorem 8.1. Let E_i be the edges of equivalence class i. Sort the edges of E_i by the order of their origins in a walk around $TSP(S)$. Consider consecutive edges $s_i s_j$ and $s_k s_l$ from E_i. By the observation above, $|s_i s_k| \geq \frac{1}{2}\min\{|s_i s_j|, |s_k s_l|\}$. Hence, we can "charge" edge $s_i s_j$ of E_i to edge $s_i s_k$ in $TSP(S)$. Doing this for consecutive disjoint pairs from E_i, we charge all shorter edges—a total of $\lfloor |E_i|/2 \rfloor$ edges—to distinct edges of $TSP(S)$. We now repeat the argument, this time charging to disjoint sections of $TSP(S)$, again halving the number of edges. After $O(\log n)$ stages, all edges are charged. ∎

Theorem 8.3 generalizes in a straightforward way to arbitrary dimension. Chandra et al. proved an almost matching lower bound with the construction of Figure 8.3. A case analysis shows that the tour in the middle illustration is 2-optimized.

THEOREM 8.4   There are 2-optimized tours of length $\Omega(\log n/\log\log n)$ times optimal.

The 2-Opt heuristic can be generalized to the k-Opt heuristic, in which sets of up to k edges are removed and replaced by shorter sets. The upper bound of Theorem 8.3 of course applies to this generalization. Good lower bounds for k-Opt in the geometric case are unknown, although Rosenkrantz et al. [RSL77] proved that even for $k = \frac{n}{4}$, the approximation ratio may be as bad as 2.

OPEN PROBLEM 8.3   Is there a polynomial-time algorithm for the Euclidean TSP with approximation ratio smaller than $\frac{3}{2}$? What is the approximation ratio of the farthest insertion heuristic?

8.2.3   TSP WITH NEIGHBORHOODS

In *TSP with neighborhoods*, we are given a collection of k simple polygons (not necessarily disjoint) with n total vertices, and we seek the shortest tour that passes through each polygon. Obviously, the usual TSP is the special case in which each polygon is simply a point. Arkin and Hassin [AH94b] gave an $O(1)$ approximation algorithm for the case of "round," approximately equal-sized neighborhoods, such as unit disks.

In more recent work, Mata and Mitchell [MM95] provide a general framework that gives an $O(\log k)$ approximation algorithm for this problem. The same framework yields logarithmic approximation ratios for three other problems that generalize the TSP: (1) the *prize-collecting TSP*, in which we seek a shortest tour visiting k out of n points (see Section 8.5.2 for a closely related problem); (2) the *watchman route problem*, in which we seek the shortest tour that can "see" all of a polygon with holes; and (3) the *red-blue separation problem*, in which we are given two point sets—red and blue—and seek the shortest polygon that contains all of the red and none of the blue points. (Using a result on guillotine trees—Lemma 8.6 in Section 8.5.2—Mata and Mitchell have since improved the approximation ratio for problem (3) to $O(1)$.)

The framework's overall strategy has been previously applied to several other geometric approximation problems (Sections 8.5.2 and 8.6.3). The first step is to show that the optimal solution can be approximated within a factor of $O(\log k)$ by a spatial subdivision of a particular form. The second step is to devise a polynomial-time dynamic programming algorithm to compute an optimal subdivision. The last step is to transform the optimal subdivision back into a solution to the original problem with only a constant factor increase in length.

To start the first step, Mata and Mitchell show that the optimal solution for the TSP with neighborhoods can be approximated within a constant factor by an *orthogonal polygon*, meaning one in which each side is either horizontal or vertical. They further show that this orthogonal polygon can be assumed to be a subgraph of the *grid graph* formed by passing a horizontal and a vertical line through each of the n input vertices.

A *binary space partition* (see [PY90, PY92]) is a recursive subdivision of the plane (or of a bounding box) into convex cells, formed by repeatedly cutting cells with line segments that contain portions of input line segments. The following lemma shows that any orthogonal polygon admits a relatively short binary space partition.

LEMMA 8.1   Let P be a k-vertex orthogonal polygon. There is a binary space partition of P (starting from P's bounding box) with total cut length $O(\log k)$ times the perimeter of P.

Proof.   We form a partition by the following method: while some rectangular cell c contains a vertex of P, split c with the line segment that is parallel to the short side of c, and that passes through a vertex of P and lies as close as possible to the center of c. Finally, when all cells contain only edges of P, split the cells along those edges.

Let us add up the total cut length of this partition. The segments in the final stage in which we split along edges of P, add up to at most ℓ, where ℓ is the perimeter of P, so we need only worry about earlier splits. We partition earlier cutting segments into length classes: $[0, \ell/k], [\ell/k, 2\ell/k], [2\ell/k, 4\ell/k]$, and so forth. There are $O(k)$ segments overall, since each one passes through a vertex of P, so the segments in class one have total length at most $O(\ell)$. The length in each remaining class is at most a constant times the length of the minimum spanning tree of the vertices of P, and hence, also $O(\ell)$.   ∎

We now explain the second step: a dynamic programming algorithm that computes a shortest total-length binary space partition that cuts each input polygon at least once. For each rectangle R of the grid graph, in order by size from smallest to largest, we compute the minimum length binary space partition that has R as its root (largest cell). If no input polygons lie entirely interior to R, then the minimum partition is R itself. Otherwise, for each of the $O(n)$ choices for the first cutting segment, we compute the length of the minimum partition of R by combining the lengths of partitions of two smaller rectangles. Since there are $O(n^4)$ rectangles in the grid graph, the overall computation takes $O(n^5)$ time.

Finally, we must translate the optimal partition back to a solution to the original problem. To do this, we compute the points where the optimal partition crosses each input polygon, and then form a tour by doubling the MST of the crossing points.

THEOREM 8.5 Mata and Mitchell   The algorithm above is an $O(\log k)$ approximation algorithm for TSP with neighborhoods.

STEINER TREE PROBLEM

8.3

The *Euclidean Steiner tree problem* is given by a set of points $S = \{s_1, s_2, \ldots, s_n\}$ in the Euclidean plane, and asks for the shortest planar straight-line graph spanning S. The solution takes the form of a tree, called a Steiner minimal tree, that includes all the points of S, called *terminals*, along with zero or more extra vertices, called *Steiner points*. It is well known [GP68] that exactly three edges meet at each Steiner point and form 120° angles. A minimum spanning tree can be considered a suboptimal Steiner tree.

There are several variants of the Steiner problem. The *rectilinear Steiner problem* uses the rectilinear metric, in which the distance between points $s_i = (x_i, y_i)$ and

$s_j = (x_j, y_j)$ is $|x_i - x_j| + |y_i - y_j|$. In the *network Steiner problem*, S is a subset of the vertices in an edge-weighted graph and the desired tree is a subgraph spanning S. Although this version of the problem is not geometric—its most frequent recent use seems to be in the field of phylogeny [HRW92]—approximation algorithms for the geometric versions build on ideas used in the network case. The rectilinear version can be reduced to the network version on the grid graph formed by passing a horizontal and a vertical through each terminal. The books by Hwang, Richards, and Winter [HRW92] and Ivanov and Tuzhilin [IT94] survey the Steiner tree literature.

All three major versions of the Steiner problem are *NP*-hard. Although the network and rectilinear problems are *NP*-complete, the Euclidean problem involves sums of square roots like the traveling salesman and minimum spanning tree problems, and thus is not known to be in *NP* [GJ79]. The network Steiner problem is known to be Max-$\mathcal{SNP}$-hard, even if edge lengths are restricted to 1 and 2 [BP89]. The geometric versions of the problem—like all but a very few geometric problems—are not known to be Max-$\mathcal{SNP}$-hard.

In contrast to the traveling salesman problem, there have been recent breakthroughs in approximating the Steiner tree problem. In 1990, Du and Hwang [DH92a] proved that the Euclidean Steiner ratio—the maximum ratio of the lengths of minimum spanning tree and Steiner minimal tree—is $\frac{2}{\sqrt{3}} \approx 1.1547$, settling a long-open conjecture. In the same year, Zelikovsky [Zel93] gave a polynomial-time algorithm for the network Steiner tree problem with approximation ratio $\frac{11}{6}$, beating the previous bound of 2 given by a minimum spanning tree in which shortest paths between terminals act as tree edges. Zelikovsky's algorithm approximates the optimal Steiner tree by approximating an optimal Steiner tree that has full components of bounded size. (A *full component* is a subtree in which each terminal is a leaf; the tree in Figure 8.4 has three full components, of sizes 5, 3, and 3.) This algorithm has led to improved ratios for the rectilinear and Euclidean cases.

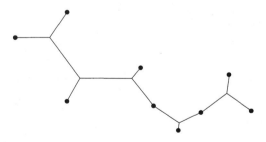

FIGURE 8.4

Terminals are represented by black dots in this Euclidean Steiner minimal tree.

8.3.1 STEINER RATIOS

In this section we view the minimum spanning tree as an approximate Steiner tree and study its worst-case approximation ratio. We define the *Steiner ratio* to be the supremum over all point sets of the length of the minimum spanning tree divided by the length of the Steiner minimal tree.[1] We treat the simpler rectilinear problem first.

8.3.1.1 Rectilinear

The example of four points at the corners of the unit ball—the points $(1, 0)$, $(0, 1)$, $(-1, 0)$, and $(0, -1)$—shows that the rectilinear Steiner ratio may be as large as $\frac{3}{2}$. Hwang [Hwa76] proved that this ratio is never larger.

THEOREM 8.6 Hwang   The rectilinear minimum spanning tree is never longer than three-halves the length of the rectilinear Steiner minimal tree.

Proof Sketch.   We now sketch Hwang's proof. Let S be a set of n terminals in the plane with rectilinear Steiner minimal tree $RST(S)$ and rectilinear minimum spanning tree $RMST(S)$ of lengths $|RST(S)|$ and $|RMST(S)|$. We use induction on n, with basis of the trivial case of $n = 2$.

First assume that some terminal s_i has degree at least two in $RST(S)$. Removing s_i splits $RST(S)$ into two or more components. Let S_1 be the terminals in one of these components along with s_i, and let $S_2 = \{s_i\} \cup S \setminus S_1$. By the inductive hypothesis, Theorem 8.6 holds for S_1 and S_2. Now the minimum spanning tree $RMST(S)$ is no longer than the union of $RMST(S_1)$ and $RMST(S_2)$, and the Steiner tree $RST(S)$ is exactly the union of $RST(S_1)$ and $RST(S_2)$, so Theorem 8.6 must also hold for S.

We may now assume that $RST(S)$ is full, that is, has just one full component. Hwang proves that in this case there always exists a shortest tree that has one of the two canonical forms shown on the left in Figure 8.5: either all Steiner points, or all Steiner points but one, lie along a straight "spine," and straight edges leading to terminals alternate from left to right along this spine. (A Steiner point of degree 4 can be considered the limiting

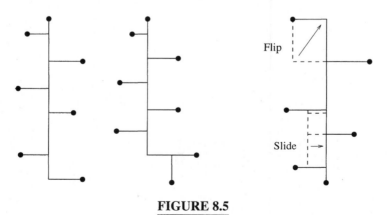

FIGURE 8.5

Canonical forms for full rectilinear Steiner minimal trees.

---

[1]Most authors define the Steiner ratio the other way around: Steiner minimal tree divided by MST. We use the reciprocal so that the Steiner ratio is an approximation ratio.

case of two very closely spaced Steiner points of degree 3.) Any full Steiner minimal tree can be transformed into one of these two forms (or made non-full) by a sequence of *flipping* and *sliding* operations, as shown on the right.

The last step, simplified by Berman et al. [BFK^{+}94, BR94], shows that there must always be a spanning tree of length at most $\frac{3}{2}|RST(S)|$. Assume the full Steiner tree $RST(S)$ has the form shown on the left in Figure 8.6; the other case is similar. On the right are two spanning trees of total length at most three times $|RST(S)|$; the shorter of the two has length at most $\frac{3}{2}|RST(S)|$. The spanning trees (solid lines) charge their excess length to disjoint sets of Steiner tree edges (bold dotted lines). Each of these sets includes alternating segments along the spine, along with longest "ribs" between successive locally minimal ribs. A locally minimal rib is one that is shorter than its two same-side neighbors. ∎

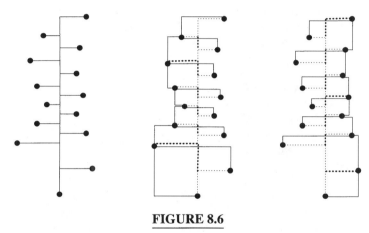

FIGURE 8.6

Two spanning trees (right) have length at most three times the full Steiner tree.

8.3.1.2   Euclidean

Before its recent solution, the Euclidean Steiner ratio was a famous open problem. In 1968 Gilbert and Pollak [GP68] observed that the ratio of $\frac{2}{\sqrt{3}} \approx 1.1547$ holds for the vertices of an equilateral triangle and conjectured that no point set achieves smaller ratio. For years researchers inched towards this conjecture on two fronts: successively establishing that $\frac{2}{\sqrt{3}}$ does indeed hold for 3, 4, 5, and 6 points and that weaker upper bounds (2, 1.75, 1.35, 1.25, and 1.21) hold for arbitrary point sets [DH92b, HRW92]. Finally, in 1990 Du and Hwang [DH92a] announced a proof of the conjecture. Their proof incorporates some ideas of Rubinstein and Thomas [RT91a, RT91b] and Meeks and Yau [MY80].

THEOREM 8.7   Du and Hwang   The Euclidean MST is never longer than $\frac{2}{\sqrt{3}}$ times the length of the Euclidean Steiner minimal tree.

We now give a detailed sketch of Du and Hwang's remarkable proof [DH92a]. Let S denote a set of n points in the Euclidean plane. Let $ST(S)$ and $MST(S)$ denote a Steiner minimal tree and a minimum spanning tree for terminals S of lengths $|ST(S)|$ and $|MST(S)|$. The *topology* of a tree is its pattern of connections (with vertices labeled), which can be specified, among other ways, by an adjacency matrix.

By induction on n, we can, as in the rectilinear problem, limit attention to the case that $ST(S)$ is a full Steiner tree. Du and Hwang simplify matters by fixing a topology T suitable for a full Steiner tree, and bounding the ratio of $|MST(S)|$ to $|ST_T(S)|$, the length of a shortest Steiner tree of topology T. Topology T is arbitrary, so this bound will suffice. Du and Hwang focus attention still further by scaling S so that $|ST_T(S)| = 1$. This step converts the problem of bounding the ratio $|MST(S)|/|ST_T(S)|$ to the problem of bounding $|MST(S)|$. The proof now aims to show that S must be a very special set of points in order to maximize $|MST(S)|$. We preview the approach before diving into the details.

A point set S will be identified—up to rigid motions—with a vector x in $\mathbf{R}^{2n-3}$. For any given MST topology U, the length $|MST_U(S)|$ turns out to be a convex function (like an upwards-opening parabola) in this parametrization of S. The function we are interested in, $|MST(S)|$, is the lower envelope (pointwise minimum) of these convex functions, which implies that its maximum value is attained at a "critical vector," a point set with a maximal set of MST topologies.

We can illustrate the idea with just four points. The set of points shown on the left in Figure 8.7 has two different MSTs, shown solid and dashed. By moving point s_3 slightly, we obtain a point set—the vertices of a 60°–120° rhombus—with the same two MSTs spanning trees along with some others. This new point set in fact supports a maximal set of MST topologies.

In general, a point set with a maximal set of MST topologies must be rather special; for example, many pairs of points determine the same distance. For more than four points, however, such a point set is not so special as to render the Steiner ratio problem easy. An obstacle arises when the union of all MST edges completely encloses a point. To overcome this obstacle, Du and Hwang limit attention to certain spanning tree topologies, called "inner" topologies, that lie inside a polygon induced by $ST_T(S)$. This seemingly small shift clears away a thicket of difficulties. A point set with a maximal set of minimum inner spanning tree topologies is indeed very special: it must be exactly the vertices of a triangulated simple polygon in which each triangle is equilateral, as in the 60°–120° rhombus. The Steiner ratio problem for these very constrained point sets can be solved by elementary arguments, which will complete the proof.

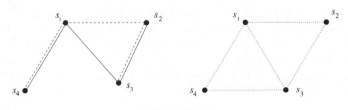

FIGURE 8.7

*Moving s_3 slightly gives a point set with a maximal set of
MST topologies.*

Parametrizing Point Sets. Let T be the topology of a full Euclidean Steiner tree, given by an adjacency matrix with $2n - 2$ rows and columns. In something of a conceptual switch, we can use topology T to parametrize point sets. Point set S $(= S(T, x))$ is specified by the lengths of its edges in a shortest Steiner tree $ST_T(S)$ of topology T. We denote these lengths by a vector $x = (x_1, x_2, \ldots, x_{2n-3})$ and limit attention to vectors x such that $\sum_i x_i = 1$. The $120°$ rule, which holds for any locally minimal Steiner tree such as $ST_T(S)$, fixes the relative directions of edges in $ST_T(S)$, so that any vector x with each $x_i \geq 0$ and $\sum_i x_i = 1$ encodes a single planar point set, modulo equivalence by rigid motions and scaling. Now define

$$\Delta = \left\{ x \in \mathbb{R}^{2n-3} \ \middle| \ \sum_{i=1}^{2n-3} x_i = 1 \text{ and } \forall i, x_i \geq 0 \right\}.$$

So that domain Δ is closed, we must allow zero-length edges in $ST_T(S)$; we regard such a tree as a degenerate version of topology T. Certain x vectors may force edges of $ST_T(S)$ to cross. We can think of such anomalous trees—which cannot be Steiner minimal trees in any case—as embedded in a plane with Riemann sheets attached.

The Lower Envelope of Convex Functions. We now prove that the length of a fixed-topology spanning tree is a convex function of x. Let U be a topology of a spanning tree on n vertices, and let $MST_U(S)$ denote the spanning tree of S of topology U. A function $f : \mathbb{R}^d \mapsto \mathbb{R}$ is *convex* if for each α, $0 < \alpha < 1$, and each x and x' in $\mathbb{R}^d$, $f(\alpha x + (1 - \alpha)x') \leq \alpha f(x) + (1 - \alpha)f(x')$.

LEMMA 8.2 $|MST_U(S)|$ $(= |MST_U(S(T, x))|)$ is a convex function of x.

Proof.   Consider any two terminals s_i and s_j implied by x and T. We first show that edge length $|s_i s_j|$ is a convex function of x. Suppose the path in $ST_T(S)$ connecting s_i and s_j consists of edges with lengths $x_{i_1}, x_{i_2}, \ldots, x_{i_k}$ and directions given by unit vectors $e_1, e_2, \ldots, e_k$. Then, $|s_i s_j|$ is the Euclidean norm of the vector $x_{i_1} e_1 + x_{i_2} e_2 + \cdots + x_{i_k} e_k$. As x varies along a line from x to x', each x_{i_j} varies linearly. The unit vectors $e_1, e_2, \ldots, e_k$ change in concert in order to maintain the $120°$ rule; rotating the coordinate system by the same amount keeps $e_1, e_2, \ldots, e_k$ fixed. The Euclidean norm is itself a convex function, and a convex function of a linear function is convex, so $|s_i s_j|$ is convex. Now $|MST_U(S)|$ is a sum over a fixed subset of $|s_i s_j|$ functions. It is easy to see that a sum of convex functions is convex.   ∎

The length of a minimum spanning tree, or—looking ahead—the length of a minimum inner spanning tree, is the lower envelope of $|MST_U(S)|$ functions. Consider the graph of a function that is the lower envelope of convex functions on the plane. Each of the convex functions forms a bowl-shaped valley. Where two convex functions are both minimum, the lower envelope has a ridge, and where three or more are all minimum, there is a peak. Lemma 8.3 formalizes this observation and generalizes it to arbitrary dimension.

Let f be the lower envelope of a finite set of convex functions $f_1, f_2, \ldots, f_k$, that is, $f(x) = \min_i f_i(x)$. We say that x is a *critical vector* if a maximal set of f_i's have $f_i(x) = f(x)$. In other words, if $I = \{i \mid f_i(x) = f(x)\}$, there is no x' such that $f_i(x') = f(x')$ for each $i \in I$ and $f_j(x') = f(x')$ for some $j \notin I$.

LEMMA 8.3   Let $f : \Delta \mapsto \mathbb{R}$ be the lower envelope of a finite set of convex functions. Then f achieves its maximum either on the boundary of Δ or at a critical vector.

Inner Spanning Trees. We can form a polygon by connecting successive terminals in a walk around the outside of the Steiner tree $ST_T(S)$, as shown in Figure 8.8. We call this polygon the *Steiner tree polygon* and denote it by $P_T(S)$. It is possible for the Steiner tree polygon to self-overlap, but this case is handled with Riemann sheets. A spanning tree $MST_U(S)$ is an *inner spanning tree* if each of its edges lies within the closed region bounded by $P_T(S)$. Let $|MIST(S)|$ denote the length of a *minimum inner spanning tree* for point set S.

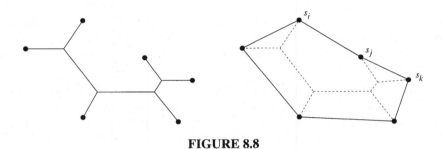

FIGURE 8.8

Full Steiner tree $ST_T(S)$ and the polygon $P_T(S)$ it induces.

The set of inner spanning tree topologies varies with x. For example, in Figure 8.8 a spanning tree with an edge between points s_i and s_k is not an inner spanning tree, but would be one if the edge to s_j were lengthened a little, so that $s_i s_k$ lay below s_j. This variability poses a potential problem. Since each $|MST_U(S)|$ function participates over only part of domain Δ, we cannot apply Lemma 8.3 directly to $|MIST(S)|$. Luckily, a spanning tree $MST_U(S)$ cannot be minimum on the boundary of its "region of innerness". Figure 8.8 shows why: if $MST_U(S)$ is not inner for all small perturbations of S (that is, in a small ball around x), then a terminal s_j must lie in the relative interior of an edge $s_i s_k$. It is not hard to show that Lemma 8.3 still holds for the lower envelope of convex partial functions, so long as the partial functions are never minimal on the boundaries of their domains.

So we now know that $|MIST(S)|$ achieves its maximum either on the boundary of Δ, that is, when some $x_i = 0$, or at a critical vector x. In the former case some edge of $ST_T(S)$ has zero length. If this edge is incident to a terminal, then $ST_T(S)$ is not really a full Steiner tree. On the other hand, if the zero-length edge links two Steiner points, then $ST_T(S)$ violates the degree-3 rule. We have now eliminated the boundary of Δ and can assume that S supports a maximal set of minimum inner spanning trees.

Equilateral Formation. We say that a set of points S is in *equilateral formation* if there exists a simple polygon P with vertex set S that has a triangulation in which each triangle is equilateral (and hence congruent).

LEMMA 8.4   If x is a critical vector, then S is in equilateral formation.

Proof.   Let E be the set of all edges from all minimum inner spanning trees of S. Imagine adding E to Steiner tree polygon $P_T(S)$. It is not hard to show by contradiction that no two edges of E cross. (If two do, remove the longer one and find a shorter path inside $P_T(S)$ reconnecting the connected components.)

Since no two minimum inner spanning tree edges cross, E divides $P_T(S)$ into polygons with vertices from S. Imagine adding extra edges if necessary to triangulate $P_T(S)$. The number of distinct edges in this triangulation—diagonals and boundary—is $2n - 3$. We make two key observations: (1) S is determined (up to rigid motions) by the lengths of these edges, and (2) each of these lengths can be varied independently—for example, lengthening a single edge opens up the opposite angle and spreads out $P_T(S)$ (perhaps causing it to self-overlap). The remainder of the proof repeatedly applies observation (2) to ears (triangles with two boundary sides), in order to establish that each triangle in the triangulation must be equilateral.   ∎

The next lemma completes the proof of Theorem 8.7.

LEMMA 8.5   If S is in equilateral formation, then $\frac{|MST(S)|}{|ST(S)|} \leq \frac{2}{\sqrt{3}}$.

Proof.   To prove this lemma, we introduce another kind of tree, called a *hexagonal Steiner tree*. In such a tree, each edge is parallel to one of three directions: horizontal, $60°$ from horizontal, or $-60°$ from horizontal. Let $HT(S)$ be a shortest hexagonal Steiner tree for S. For any point set, $|HT(S)|/|ST(S)| \leq \frac{2}{\sqrt{3}}$. Why? Any edge of a Steiner minimal tree can be replaced by a dog-leg of two edges of the prescribed directions, expanding its length by at most $\frac{2}{\sqrt{3}}$. The remainder of the proof establishes that for S in equilateral formation, a MST is in fact a shortest hexagonal Steiner tree for some choice of coordinate axes. This is proved by showing that if S consists of points from a hexagonal lattice, flipping and sliding operations reminiscent of the rectilinear Steiner problem can move all Steiner points of $HT(S)$ to lattice points. See Figure 8.9.   ∎

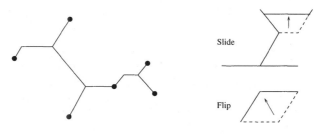

FIGURE 8.9

Hexagonal Steiner tree.

8.3.1.3   Other metrics

We need not limit attention to the rectilinear and Euclidean metrics. Any compact, convex, centrally symmetric shape D can be used to define a *Minkowski metric* on the plane. The distance between points s and s' is measured by translating unit ball D so that its center coincides with s and then shrinking or expanding D until s' lies on its boundary; the factor by which D is dilated is the distance. Basic properties of Steiner minimal trees for such a metric—for example, the degree of Steiner points—depend on whether or not D has a smooth boundary (see [HRW92]). Research on the Steiner ratio question for Minkowski metrics has expanded recently, stimulated by Du and Hwang's solution of the Euclidean problem.

Cieslik [Cie90] and Du, Gao, Graham, Liu, and Wan [DGG+] independently conjectured that for any D the Steiner ratio lies in the range $[\frac{2}{\sqrt{3}}, 1.5] \approx [1.154, 1.5]$, in other words, between the Euclidean and rectilinear cases. Cieslik obtained bounds of 1.106 and 1.634, while Du et al. gave 1.151 and 1.605. Very recently, Gao, Du, and Graham [GDG94] obtained the tight upper bound of 1.5. They showed, moreover, that if a finite point set S has ratio 1.5, then ball D must be a parallelogram and S must have exactly 4 terminals arranged in a parallelogram similar to D. Gao et al. go on to conjecture that for any Minkowski metric some finite point set achieves the Steiner ratio.

We can also imagine generalizing Steiner ratio problems to higher dimensions. Graham and Hwang conjectured that the rectilinear Steiner ratio in $\mathbf{R}^d$ is $\frac{2d-1}{d}$, achieved by the vertices of the unit ball [GH76]. On the basis of some empirical work, Gilbert and Pollak [GP68] speculated that the Euclidean Steiner ratio in $\mathbf{R}^d$ is achieved by the vertices of a regular simplex. Smith [Smi92] disproved this conjecture for $\mathbf{R}^3$ by showing that the ratio for the regular octahedron is greater than that for the regular tetrahedron. (Gilbert and Pollak actually considered the octahedron, but they had the wrong Steiner tree!) The three-dimensional octahedron serves as a counterexample for dimensions up to nine. Du [Du92] gave a counterexample construction—four regular simplices with one vertex in common—that holds for all $d \geq 3$.

OPEN PROBLEM 8.4   Does the Euclidean metric indeed have the smallest Steiner ratio of all Minkowski metrics? What are the Steiner ratios for the rectilinear metric in higher dimensions? For the Euclidean metric?

8.3.2   BETTER APPROXIMATIONS

Does there exist a polynomial-time algorithm with an approximation ratio better than that given by the minimum spanning tree? Heuristics routinely outperform the MST in practice, and a simple, greedy heuristic gives superior results for random points in a square [Ber87, Ber88, HY90]; however, until recently no better worst-case approximation algorithm was known for any *NP*-hard Steiner tree problem, except for the very simple case of a complete graph with all edge lengths either 1 or 2 [BP89]. This situation changed quickly with the circulation of a 1990 manuscript from the former USSR. We now describe Zelikovsky's work [Zel93] and the ensuing extensions to geometric Steiner problems.

8.3.2.1   Greedy k-restricted Steiner trees

We say that a Steiner tree for terminals S is a *k-restricted Steiner tree* if each full component spans at most k terminals. Let $ST_k(S)$ denote the shortest k-restricted Steiner tree and ρ_k be the supremum over all S of $|ST_k(S)| / |ST(S)|$. Notice that ρ_2 is the usual Steiner ratio. For all three versions of the Steiner problem, $ST_k(S)$ for $k > 2$ appears hard to compute; the rectilinear version with $k = 4$ is known to be *NP*-complete, a byproduct of the original reduction [GJ77]. The tree $ST_k(S)$ can, however, be approximated by a simple, greedy algorithm. In this subsection, we shall bound the ratio of the greedy tree to the optimal unrestricted tree $ST(S)$ as a function of ρ_k values. The next subsection then considers the problem of bounding the ρ_k's.

Assume $T_1, T_2, \ldots, T_m$ are full Steiner trees for subsets of S, such that the union of the T_i's does not contain a cycle. Let $MST(S; T_1, \ldots, T_m)$ be a Steiner tree consisting of the trees $T_1, \ldots, T_m$, along with a minimum spanning forest that connects all T_i's and all members of S not in some T_i. In other words, $|MST(S; T_1, \ldots, T_m)|$ is the length of a MST constrained to include all T_i's. Kruskal's algorithm for computing MSTs can also compute $MST(S; T_1, \ldots, T_m)$.

The greedy algorithm starts by choosing a T_1 that minimizes $|MST(S; T)|$ over all choices of T with at most k terminals. At each subsequent step, it continues to choose a full Steiner tree on at most k terminals that offers the most *gain* over the MST. In other words, at step j it chooses a tree T_j that minimizes $|MST(S; T_1, \ldots, T_{j-1}, T_j)|$, or equivalently, maximizes the gain

$$W(T_j \mid T_1, \ldots, T_{j-1}) = |MST(S; T_1, \ldots, T_{j-1})| - |MST(S; T_1, \ldots, T_{j-1}, T_j)|.$$

By allowing full Steiner trees to span only two terminals, the greedy algorithm finishes with a minimum spanning forest when larger full Steiner trees run out. Theorem 8.8 for $k = 3$ is due to Zelikovsky [Zel93]; Du, Zhang, and Feng [DZF91] made the (straightforward) generalization to arbitrary k.

THEOREM 8.8   The greedy algorithm has ratio at most $\frac{k-2}{k-1} \rho_2 + \frac{1}{k-1} \rho_k$.

Proof.   Let $T_1, \ldots, T_\ell$ be the full Steiner trees chosen by the greedy algorithm, including 2-terminal trees (edges). Let $T_1^*, \ldots, T_m^*$ be the full Steiner trees of an optimal k-restricted Steiner tree $ST_k(S)$.

Imagine adding T_1 to the optimal tree $ST_k(S)$. If T_1 spans h terminals, $2 \leq h \leq k$, then $T_1 \cup ST_k(S)$ contains $h - 1$ simple cycles, as shown in Figure 8.10(a). To break these cycles we shall remove $h - 1$ full components, renumbered to be $T_1^*, \ldots, T_{h-1}^*$, from $ST_k(S)$. Now the greedy algorithm chooses T_1 to be the full tree that minimizes $|MST(S; T_1)|$, so $|MST(S; T_1)| \leq \min_{1 \leq j \leq h-1} |MST(S; T_j^*)|$, and no matter how we pick $T_1^*, \ldots, T_{h-1}^*$,

$$|MST(S; T_1)| \leq \frac{(h-2)|MST(S)| + |MST(S; T_1^*, \ldots, T_{h-1}^*)|}{h-1}.$$

Our goal is to pick $T_1^*, \ldots, T_{h-1}^*$ cleverly so that the following statement about "future gains" holds as well:

$$|MST(S; T_1)| - \sum_{j=1}^{\ell} |T_j| \geq \frac{|MST(S; T_1^*, \ldots T_{h-1}^*)| - \sum_{j=1}^{m} |T_j^*|}{h-1}.$$

We can then sum the first inequality with -1 times the second to obtain the result.

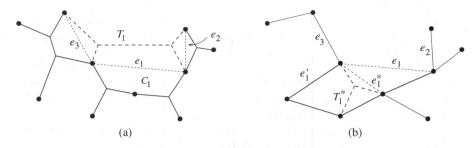

FIGURE 8.10

(a) Adding greedy T_1 to the optimal k-restricted tree $ST_k(S)$. (b) The tree $MST(S; e_2, \ldots, e_{h-1})$ helps locate the full component T_1^* to remove.

Intuitively, we would like T_i^*'s that realize a lot of gain up front, so we look for T_i^*'s that "shortcut" long edges in $MST(S; T_1)$. Let $e_1, e_2, \ldots, e_{h-1}$ be the edges of any spanning tree on the terminals of T_1, as shown in Figure 8.10(a). We use e_1 to pick T_1^*, e_2 to pick T_2^*, and so forth. Let e_1' be the longest edge on the path between the endpoints of e_1 in the tree $MST(S; e_2, \ldots, e_{h-1})$ as shown in Figure 8.10(b). Let C_1 be the cycle formed by adding e_1 to $ST_k(S)$, and imagine connecting successive terminals around C_1. Some edge e_1^* between successive terminals of some full component T_1^* shortcuts e_1', meaning that the path between the endpoints of e_1^* back in $MST(S; e_2, \ldots, e_{h-1})$ includes e_1'. Since edges e_1 and e_1^* remove the same edge (namely e_1') from $|MST(S; e_2, \ldots e_{h-1})|$,

$$|MST(S; e_1, e_2, \ldots, e_{h-1})| - |e_1| = |MST(S; e_1^*, e_2, \ldots, e_{h-1})| - |e_1^*|,$$

which after some algebraic manipulations implies that

$$|MST(S; T_1)| - \sum_{j=1}^{\ell} |T_j| \geq \frac{|MST(S; T_1^*, e_2, \ldots, e_{h-1})| - \sum_{j=1}^{m} |T_j^*|}{h - 1}.$$

Now let e_2' be the longest edge on the path between the endpoints of e_2 in the tree $MST(S; T_1^*, e_3, \ldots, e_{h-1})$. Edge e_2' locates a T_2^* in $ST_k(S) \setminus T_1^*$ that replaces e_2 in the last inequality above. Proceeding in this manner, we choose a set of suitable T_i^*'s. (It is possible that a single T_i^* can span the endpoints of more than one of $e_1, \ldots, e_{h-1}$, in which case we end up with fewer than $h - 1$ T_i^*'s.)   ∎

8.3.2.2   Steiner ratios for k-restricted Steiner trees

Theorem 8.8 implies the existence of approximation algorithms better than the MST whenever $\rho_k < \rho_2$ for some $k = O(1)$, and there exists an algorithm for computing optimal Steiner trees on k vertices. Computing $O(1)$-size optimal Steiner trees is easy for the rectilinear case: reduce the problem to the network problem and use exhaustive search or dynamic programming. The Euclidean case can be solved by a recursive algorithm of Melzak [Mel61] which replaces a pair of terminals adjacent to the same Steiner point by a single new terminal. We now consider the question of bounding ρ_k for various metrics and choices of k. The following bound was proved independently by Zelikovsky [Zel92] and Berman and Ramaiyer [BR94]; combined with Theorem 8.8 it gives an approximation ratio of $\frac{11}{8}$ for the rectilinear Steiner problem.

THEOREM 8.9   For the rectilinear metric, $\rho_3 \leq \frac{5}{4}$.

Proof.   For any full component T of an optimal rectilinear Steiner tree $RST(S)$, we
show how to find four 3-restricted Steiner trees T_1, T_2, T_3, and T_4, that each span the
same terminals as T, with total length five times $|T|$. Thus, the shortest of the four trees
proves the theorem.

Assume T has the canonical form shown on the far left in Figure 8.5 on page 306;
the other case is similar. We create T_1 by first doubling each left-side rib that is longer
than the ribs above and below it. We then replace the spine between two doubled ribs
by a staircase between terminals as shown on the left in Figure 8.11. Tree T_2 is formed
analogously using right-side ribs. Tree T_3 is created by first doubling each left-side rib
not doubled in T_1 as shown on the right in Figure 8.11. This creates components with
three terminals on the left and two on the right. To finish T_3, we add an edge paralleling
the spine on the right and remove one edge of the spine. Tree T_4 is formed analogously
using right-side ribs.   ∎

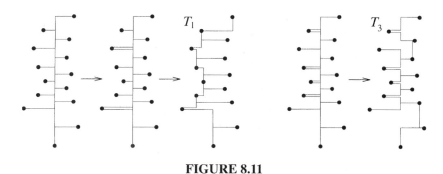

FIGURE 8.11

Transforming a rectilinear full component in canonical
form into a 3-restricted tree.

Berman and Ramaiyer [BR94] generalized the bound to $\rho_k \leq 1 + \frac{1}{2k-2}$ by defining
a collection of $2k - 2$ k-restricted full trees with length at most $2k - 1$ times the length
of any full tree. The bound is tight for $k = 3$, as shown by the corners of the unit ball, but
Berman and Ramaiyer conjectured, and Borchers et al. [BDG95] recently proved, that
the tight bound for $k \geq 4$ is $1 + \frac{1}{2k-1}$.

Du, Zhang, and Feng [DZF91] proved the following theorem for the Euclidean case,
which gives an approximation better than $2/\sqrt{3}$ for the depressingly large value $k = 128$.
They conjecture, however, that $\rho_3 = (\sqrt{2} + \sqrt{6})/(1 + \sqrt{2} + \sqrt{3}) \approx 1.073$, sufficient to
give an improved approximation ratio of 1.114.

THEOREM 8.10   For the Euclidean metric, $\rho_k \leq (\lfloor \log_2 k \rfloor + 1) / \lfloor \log_2 k \rfloor$.

Proof. By induction, we may assume that the optimal Steiner tree $ST(S)$ is full. We root $ST(S)$ in the middle of an edge to turn it into a rooted binary tree. Now from each internal vertex v (a Steiner point) define a path $p(v)$ of length $|p(v)|$ down to a leaf (a terminal), such that each pair of paths is edge-disjoint. (This is easy to do by induction.)

Let U_i be the set of internal vertices of $ST(S)$ with level number (number of edges up to the root) equal to $i \bmod \lfloor \log_2 k \rfloor$. Let the cost of U_i be $\sum_{v \in U_i} |p(v)|$. We remove all vertices of the cheapest U_i, breaking $ST(S)$ into subtrees. The lowest level subtrees have at most k terminals. We attach each leaf v of a higher level subtree to the other endpoint of $p(v)$ using a single edge. The length of the resulting k-restricted Steiner tree is at most $1 + 1/\lfloor \log_2 k \rfloor$ times $|ST(S)|$. ∎

In any metric, Steiner points can be made degree-three by adding zero-length edges, and the proof above will hold, proving that any metric admits a Steiner tree approximation algorithm better than the minimum spanning tree. In fact, $(\lfloor \log_2 k \rfloor + 1) / \lfloor \log_2 k \rfloor$ is the tight bound for ρ_k for some metrics [BD95].

OPEN PROBLEM 8.5 What are the values of ρ_k in the Euclidean metric?

8.3.2.3 A stack-based algorithm

Both ρ_k and the contribution of ρ_k to the approximation ratio decrease with increasing k, so Zelikovsky's algorithm does not give a sequence of better and better algorithms. Berman and Ramaiyer [BR94], however, modified Zelikovsky's algorithm to achieve this result. Their algorithm consists of two phases: evaluation and construction. Both phases keep their work in a tree $M(S)$, a minimum spanning tree for a graph with modified edge weights.

The evaluation phase considers possible full Steiner components, in order of increasing numbers of terminals from 3 to k. At a generic step, if a component T_j offers a gain in the current $M(S)$, it is pushed onto a stack and $M(S)$ is modified to reflect the use of T_j. Specifically, the edges e_i of a spanning tree R_j for the terminals of T_j are added one-by-one to $M(S)$. Edge e_i is given weight equal to the length of the longest edge e'_i in the cycle it forms when first added to $M(S)$, minus the gain $W(T_j \mid T_1, \ldots, T_{j-1})$. Subtracting off $W(T_j \mid T_1, \ldots, T_{j-1})$ prevents overlapping full components with smaller gain from making it onto the stack.

Figure 8.12 gives an example. The upper right figure shows the initial minimum spanning tree $M(S)$, the same as $MST(S)$. When tree T_1 is evaluated and found to offer positive gain, it is pushed onto the stack. Edge e_1 is added to $M(S)$ and e'_1 is removed. The new weight of edge e_1 is $|e'_1| - W(T_1)$. Then edge e_2 is added and e'_2 removed, and e_2 receives weight $|e'_2| - W(T_1)$.

The construction phase pops full components off the stack, transforming $M(S)$ into a Steiner tree as it goes. If, at the time T_j is popped, spanning tree R_j is intact in $M(S)$, then T_j replaces R_j in $M(S)$. Otherwise, whatever edges of R_j remain are replaced by MST edges; that is, edge e_i is replaced by the shortest edge linking the same two pieces of $M(S)$. When the stack is empty, $M(S)$ is the final Steiner tree.

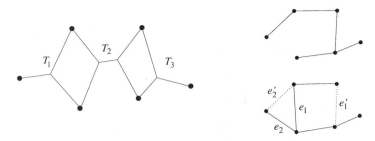

FIGURE 8.12

*Berman and Ramaiyer choose T_1 and T_3 instead of the
inferior, greedy choice of T_2.*

For example, assume that $W(T_1)$ and $W(T_3)$ are both smaller than $W(T_2)$ in Figure 8.12, but their sum is larger. The evaluation phase will push both T_1 and T_3 onto the stack, but by the time it considers 4-terminal subtrees, $W(T_2 \mid T_1, T_3)$ will be negative and T_2 will not offer any gain. Thus, Berman and Ramaiyer's algorithm will choose T_1 and T_3, while Zelikovsky's greedy algorithm will choose only T_2. For the case $k = 3$, however, the two algorithms are identical.

THEOREM 8.11 Berman and Ramaiyer   The stack-based algorithm has approximation ratio

$$\rho_2 - \frac{\rho_2 - \rho_3}{2} - \frac{\rho_3 - \rho_4}{3} - \cdots - \frac{\rho_{k-1} - \rho_k}{k-1}.$$

Proof.   Let us track the cost of tree $M(S)$ during the execution of the algorithm. It is not hard to see that during the evaluation phase, when a full tree T_j spanning i terminals is pushed onto the stack, $|M(S)|$ decreases by $(i-1)W(T_j \mid T_1, \ldots, T_{j-1})$.

We now assert that in the construction phase, each time a full tree T_j spanning i terminals is popped off the stack, $|M(S)|$ increases by at most $(i-2)W(T_j \mid T_1, \ldots, T_{j-1})$. If T_j makes it into $M(S)$, then $|M(S)|$ increases by the length of T_j and decreases by the weight of R_j. We set the edge weights for R_j to guarantee the assertion in this case. (In other words, the net gain is the expected $W(T_j \mid T_1, \ldots, T_{j-1})$.) If T_j does not make it into $M(S)$, then at least one edge of the $i - 1$ edges of R_j has already been removed by the addition of some other full tree to $M(S)$. In this case, each of the $i - 2$ remaining edges of R_j is replaced by a shortest edge crossing a cut. When remaining edge e_l is replaced, $|M(S)|$ increases by at most $W(T_j \mid T_1, \ldots, T_{j-1})$, since e_l has cost $|e_l'| - W(T_j \mid T_1, \ldots, T_{j-1})$, where $|e_l'|$ is the longest edge of a cycle.

Let M_i be $|M(S)|$ after all trees that span i terminals have been pushed onto the stack in the evaluation phase, and set $M_2 = |MST(S)|$. Let N_i be $|M(S)|$ after all trees that span $i + 1$ terminals have been popped off the stack in the construction phase. By the discussion above, the final cost is bounded by

$$N_2 \leq N_k + \sum_{i=3}^{k} (i-2) \sum_j \{ W(T_j \mid T_1, \dots T_{j-1}) \mid T_j \text{ spans } i \text{ terminals} \}$$

$$\leq M_k + \sum_{i=3}^{k} \frac{i-2}{i-1} (M_{i-1} - M_i)$$

$$\leq M_2 - \sum_{i=3}^{k} \frac{(M_{i-1} - M_i)}{i-1}.$$

Using an argument akin to that in the proof of Theorem 8.8, Berman and Ramaiyer show that for each i, $M_i \leq |ST_i(S)|$, which finishes the proof.   ∎

For the rectilinear Steiner problem, Theorem 8.11 coupled with Berman and Ramaiyer's bounds on ρ_k gives a sequence of approximation algorithms with ratios converging to about 1.323. In more recent work, Berman et al. [BFK$^+$94] directly bound linear combinations of the ratios $M_i / |RST(S)|$ (with M_i as in the proof above) rather than using the ρ_k's, thus giving sharper estimates of the approximation ratios for $k = 3$ and $k = 4$. These ratios are now known to be at most $\frac{21}{16} = 1.3125$ (and no better than 1.3) and $\frac{61}{48} \approx 1.271$, respectively. Berman and Ramaiyer's algorithm can be run in $O(n^{3/2})$ time or approximated in $O(n \log^2 n)$ time for k equal to either 3 or 4, and $O(n^{\lfloor k/2 \rfloor + 3/2})$ for general k [BFK$^+$94, BR94]. Most recently, Karpinski and Zelikovsky [KZ94] added a preliminary phase to Berman-Ramaiyer, which—without increasing the running time—further reduces the approximation ratio to $\frac{19}{15} \approx 1.267$ for $k = 4$.

8.3.2.4   The relative greedy algorithm

Very recently, Zelikovsky [Zel94] modified his original greedy algorithm by changing the way full components are chosen. The result is a sequence of algorithms with approximation ratios converging to $1 + \ln \rho_2$. This *relative greedy* algorithm thus gives $1 + \ln 2 \approx 1.693$ for the network Steiner problem, asymptotically beating Berman-Ramaiyer, which converges to about 1.734 [BD95]. It gives $1 + \ln \frac{2}{\sqrt{3}} \approx 1.144$ for the Euclidean problem, winning for now, but losing to Berman-Ramaiyer and even to the original greedy algorithm if ρ_k values are as small as conjectured. The new algorithm already loses in the rectilinear case.

At each step, the relative greedy algorithm chooses the full Steiner tree T_j spanning at most k terminals that minimizes

$$|T_j| \big/ (|MST(S; T_1, \dots, T_{j-1})| - |MST(S; T_1, \dots, T_j)| + |T_j|).$$

The denominator is the decrease, due to the addition of tree T_j, in the length of the minimum spanning forest needed to finish the tree on S. The original greedy criterion minimizes $|T_j|$ minus the denominator.

The approximation ratio bounds are implied by the following theorem:

THEOREM 8.12 Zelikovsky   The relative greedy algorithm finds a tree of length at most $1 + \ln \frac{|MST(S)|}{|ST_k(S)|}$ times $|ST_k(S)|$.

Proof.   Let $T_1, \ldots, T_\ell$ be the full Steiner trees chosen by the relative greedy algorithm, including 2-terminal trees (edges). Let $T_1^*, \ldots, T_m^*$ be the full components of an optimal k-restricted Steiner tree $ST_k(S)$. Let $F_j = |MST(S; T_1, \ldots, T_j)| - \sum_{i=1}^{j} |T_i|$, the length of a minimum spanning forest connecting $T_1, \ldots, T_j$ along with all singleton terminals. Let $F_0 = |MST(S)|$. Because the relative greedy algorithm makes the minimizing choice for T_1,

$$\frac{|T_1|}{|MST(S)| - F_1} \leq \min_{1 \leq j \leq m} \frac{|T_j^*|}{|MST(S)| - |MST(S; T_j^*)| + |T_j^*|} \leq \frac{|ST_k(S)|}{|MST(S)|}.$$

We may apply the same argument after choosing T_1 so that

$$\frac{|T_2|}{F_1 - F_2} \leq \frac{|ST_k(S; T_1)| - |T_1|}{|MST(S; T_1)| - |T_1|} \leq \frac{|ST_k(S)|}{F_1},$$

where $ST_k(S; T_1)$ and $MST(S; T_1)$ denote the optimal k-restricted Steiner tree and the minimum spanning tree constrained to choose T_1. (Imagine contracting T_1 to a point.) Inductively we obtain for each $i \geq 1$, $|T_i|/(F_{i-1} - F_i) \leq |ST_k(S)|/F_{i-1}$, or equivalently $F_i \leq F_{i-1}(1 - |T_i|/|ST_k(S)|)$. Unraveling these inequalities,

$$F_r \leq F_0 \prod_{i=1}^{r} (1 - |T_i|/|ST_k(S)|).$$

Taking the natural logarithm on both sides and using the fact that $\ln(1 + x) \leq x$,

$$\frac{\sum_{i=1}^{r} |T_i|}{|ST_k(S)|} \leq \ln \frac{F_0}{F_r}.$$

Since F_0/F_r grows arbitrarily large, we can choose r such that $F_r > |ST_k(S)| \geq F_{r+1}$. We split $|T_{r+1}|$ proportionately by the position of $|ST_k(S)|$ in the interval $[F_{r+1}, F_r]$. We combine the first portion with F_{r+1} to bring this cost up to exactly $|ST_k(S)|$, and combine the second portion with $|T_r|$. We then split $F_r - F_{r+1}$ into the same proportions, and subtract the second portion from F_r so that the last inequality above still holds when we "pretend" that $|ST_k(S)| = F_{r+1}$. We now finish the proof with the sequence of inequalities

$$\frac{\sum_{i=1}^{\ell} |T_i|}{|ST_k(S)|} \leq \frac{F_{r+1}}{|ST_k(S)|} + \frac{\sum_{i=1}^{r+1} |T_i|}{|ST_k(S)|} \leq 1 + \ln \frac{F_0}{F_{r+1}} = 1 + \ln \frac{|MST(S)|}{|ST_k(S)|}.$$

■

MINIMUM WEIGHT TRIANGULATION

8.4

We now consider approximations to a third geometric network design problem, called *minimum weight triangulation*. The input to this problem is a set of points S in the plane, and the desired output is a *triangulation* that minimizes the total Euclidean edge length. A triangulation of S is a maximal planar straight-line graph with vertex set S, or equivalently a partition of the convex hull of S into triangles that intersect only at common edges and vertices. Unlike the previous two problems, this problem is not known to be

NP-hard, nor is it known to be solvable in polynomial time, and the complexity of minimum weight triangulation is one of the few problems left from Garey and Johnson's original list of open problems [GJ79]. A generalized problem with non-Euclidean distances is *NP*-complete [Llo77].

We consider two versions of minimum weight triangulation. In the more commonly studied version, the vertex set of the triangulation is exactly the set of input points S. In *minimum weight Steiner triangulation*, additional vertices lying anywhere in the plane may be added, and the output is a triangulation of S and the Steiner points.

8.4.1   TRIANGULATION WITHOUT STEINER POINTS

The first approach to minimum weight triangulation considers other standard triangulations as approximations. It was at once believed that the Delaunay triangulation of S actually gives the minimum weight triangulation $MWT(S)$; however, it has since been shown that the Delaunay triangulation can have length as much as $\Omega(n)$ times the optimum [Kir80, MZ79]. Flipping diagonals of quadrilaterals to locally minimize lengths, in analogy with a popular Delaunay triangulation algorithm, does not improve this ratio. See Figure 8.13(a).

Greedy triangulation [Gil79, LL92] is an iterative algorithm, which at each step chooses the shortest edge that does not cross any previous edges. Figure 8.13(b) gives an $\Omega(\sqrt{n})$ lower bound on approximation ratio. The example point set contains an $O(1)$-length slanted line of $\Omega(n)$ vertices and an $\Omega(\sqrt{n})$-length horizontal row of about $\sqrt{n}$ vertices. The greedy triangulation uses a fan of $\Omega(n)$ edges each about $\sqrt{n}$ times longer than the edges in the optimal triangulation's fan. Very recently, Levcopoulos and Krznaric [LK96] established a matching upper bound of $O(\sqrt{n})$. More importantly, they devised a constant-factor approximation algorithm based on greedy triangulation.

The second approach to minimum weight triangulation builds an approximation algorithm from scratch, using minimum weight triangulation of a simple polygon—

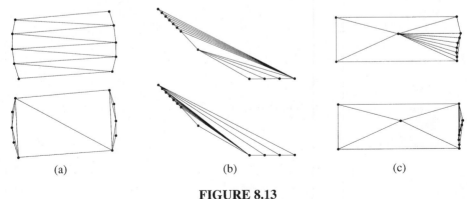

(a)   (b)   (c)

FIGURE 8.13

Bad examples for (a) Delaunay triangulation (and edge flipping), (b) greedy triangulation, (c) Lingas's algorithm. Minimum weight triangulations are below.

solvable in polynomial time by dynamic programming—as a subroutine. The earliest algorithm of this form, due to Lingas [Lin83], adds minimum spanning tree edges until the convex hull of S breaks into simple polygons, and then computes the optimal triangulation within each polygon. In Figure 8.13(c), this algorithm goes wrong by adding the MST edge from the central point to the topmost point of an arc of $\Omega(n)$ points, blocking a much closer point and giving a ratio of $\Omega(n)$. Heath and Pemmaraju [HP94] substitute a subtree of the greedy triangulation for the minimum spanning tree; an example combining features from Figures 8.13(b) and (c) gives an $\Omega(\sqrt{n})$ lower bound for their heuristic. Plaisted and Hong [PH87, Smi89] use a more involved procedure to form the polygons, and achieve an $O(\log n)$ approximation to $MWT(S)$. Finally, there has been recent progress [DM95] on finding large sets of edges guaranteed to be in the minimum weight triangulation. If a connected subgraph of $MWT(S)$ could be found, then the rest could be filled in by dynamic programming, leading to a polynomial-time exact algorithm for the problem.

We now say a little more about the two best approximation algorithms: the polygon-forming method of Plaisted and Hong and the modified greedy algorithm due to Levcopoulos and Krznaric. These two algorithms share a basic idea. Rather than finding a triangulation directly, they try to find a minimum weight partition into convex polygons.

We first sketch Plaisted and Hong's work. Let v be an interior vertex of a planar straight-line graph with convex faces. We can find a *star* of three or four edges forming no reflex angles at v as follows: choose the first star edge arbitrarily, and choose each successive edge to form the maximal non-reflex angle with the previous edge. Conversely, if each interior vertex of a planar straight-line graph has no reflex angles, the graph must have convex faces.

Thus motivated, Plaisted and Hong try to build a convex partition of S by piecing together stars. For each point s_i in the interior of the convex hull of S, they find the minimum weight star of three or four edges. This collection of minimum weight stars, together with the convex hull of S, forms a graph with total edge length less than twice $|MWT(S)|$. Unfortunately, the resulting graph may not be planar. Plaisted and Hong use a complicated case analysis to remove crossings from this graph, ending up with a planar straight-line graph with convex faces having total edge length at most $12|MWT(S)|$.

The convex faces can be triangulated optimally using dynamic programming, but a simple suboptimal algorithm has the advantage that it bounds the overall length as a multiple of the length of the convex partition. The *ring heuristic*, shown in Figure 8.14, connects every other vertex of a convex polygon P to form a polygon P' with $\lfloor n/2 \rfloor$ vertices and a smaller perimeter, and then triangulates P' recursively. Hence, the final Plaisted-Hong triangulation has total length $O(\log n)$ times optimal. Olariu et al. [OTZ88] showed that this bound is tight.

We now sketch Levcopoulos and Krznaric's work. They start by proving that the greedy triangulation achieves approximation ratio $O(\sqrt{n})$. To prove this, they define a convex partition that uses only edges of the greedy triangulation of S. Unlike Plaisted and Hong's collection of stars, the initial result is planar as it is a subgraph of a planar graph. Levcopoulos and Krznaric prove that this convex partition approximates the minimum weight partition into convex polygons within a factor of $O(\sqrt{n})$. Next they prove that any convex partition $CP(S)$ formed by edges of the greedy triangulation can be triangulated by adding diagonals of total length at most $O(1)$ times $|MWT(S)| + |CP(S)|$. The original greedy triangulation includes a greedy triangulation of each cell of $CP(S)$, and

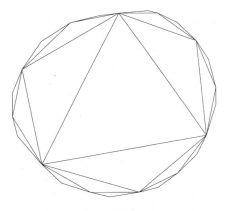

FIGURE 8.14

Ring heuristic triangulation of a convex polygon.

the greedy triangulation approximates the minimum weight triangulation of a convex polygon within a constant factor [LL87], so the greedy triangulation must be an $O(\sqrt{n})$ approximation to $MWT(S)$.

To improve this ratio, Levcopoulos and Krznaric modify the greedy triangulation. The modified algorithm rejects certain greedy edges, replacing them with slightly longer alternative edges, in order to avoid fans of the form shown in Figure 8.13(b). The result is a constant-factor approximation algorithm for the problem of finding a minimum weight convex partition of S, which in turn gives a constant-factor approximation to the minimum weight triangulation. Levcopoulos and Krznaric show that these approximations can be constructed in time $O(n \log n)$, or even $O(n)$ if the Delaunay triangulation is already known.

8.4.2 STEINER TRIANGULATION

We next discuss approximation algorithms for minimum weight Steiner triangulation. For this problem, the complexity of exact algorithms is unclear. It is not even known whether there always exists a minimum weight Steiner triangulation; perhaps there are point sets S for which larger and larger sets of Steiner points give triangulations with smaller and smaller total lengths. In any case, we can define $|MWST(S)|$ as the infimum of the lengths of Steiner triangulations for S, so that the approximation problem remains well defined. It is known that $\Omega(n)$ Steiner points may be needed to achieve a constant-factor approximation to $|MWST(S)|$, and the algorithm described in this section shows that $O(n)$ suffices.

We now explain a quadtree-based approximation algorithm due to Eppstein [Epp94], which gives a constant-factor approximation, improving upon a previous log-factor approximation due to Clarkson [Cla91]. A *quadtree* is a partition of a region of the plane into axis-aligned squares. One square, the *root*, covers the region that is to be partitioned. A square may be recursively divided into four smaller squares.

The basic quadtree triangulation algorithm builds a quadtree covering the set of input points S, by recursively subdividing squares until all points of S lie in different squares and no two adjacent leaf squares differ in size by more than a factor of two. This planar straight-line graph can be triangulated by connecting each input point to the quadtree vertices visible to it, and by adding diagonals to quadtree squares not containing input points. However, due to edges extending outside the convex hull of S, the resulting triangulation may have length $\Omega(\log n)$ times $|MWST(S)|$. To reduce this factor, we clip the triangulation with the convex hull of S, and then retriangulate the cut faces. The steps of the algorithm are depicted in Figure 8.15.

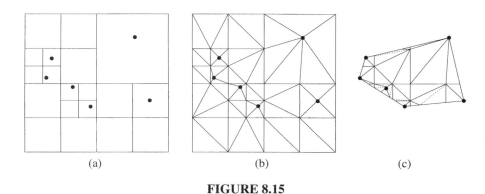

| (a) | (b) | (c) |

FIGURE 8.15

*Steps in quadtree triangulation: (a) construct a "balanced"
quadtree with each input point in a separate square;
(b) add diagonals to form a triangulation; (c) remove edges
outside the convex hull and add diagonals (dotted lines) to
sliced triangles.*

THEOREM 8.13 Eppstein   The quadtree algorithm gives a Steiner triangulation with total length at most $316|MWST(S)|$.

Proof.   We shall not prove the specific constant of 316, but rather just sketch a proof of some constant. Let $QT(S)$ denote the quadtree triangulation and $MWT(S)$ denote the (non-Steiner) minimum weight triangulation of S, with lengths $|QT(S)|$ and $|MWT(S)|$. Below we shall show that $|QT(S)|$ is at most some constant times $|MWT(S)|$. Now imagine adding some Steiner points T to S. Adding T only increases the total length of the (untriangulated) quadtree, so $|QT(S)|$ is at most a constant times $|QT(S \cup T)|$. Since T may be the Steiner points of an optimal or near-optimal Steiner triangulation, we can conclude that $QT(S)$ also approximates $|MWST(S)|$.

We now aim to prove that $|QT(S)|$ has length at most a constant times $|MWT(S)|$. By subdividing squares containing points of S a few extra times, most of the length of $QT(S)$ will be contained in empty squares; that is, squares not containing points of S. We now show how to bound the length in empty squares by charging it to edges of $MWT(S)$.

Let B be an empty quadtree square that lies interior to the convex hull of S. Let R be a concentric square somewhat bigger than 5 times the side length of B. In the quadtree construction, each square has a point of S no farther away than twice its side length, so R cannot be empty. Our aim is to charge the length of $QT(S)$ in B to a "long edge" (length at least a constant times B's side length) of $MWT(S)$ with an endpoint in R.

Some triangle Δ of $MWT(S)$ contains the center c of B. The vertices of Δ lie outside B, and so Δ must have at least two "long" sides. If one of the vertices s_i of Δ is inside R, we charge the length of $QT(S)$ in B to a long edge of Δ incident to s_i. If all three vertices of Δ are far from B, then we choose some other point $s_j \in S$ somewhat interior to R. One of the edges of Δ must cut across R and separate B from s_j. We let Δ' be the triangle on the other side of this edge and apply the same argument to Δ'. By walking from triangle to triangle in this way, as shown in Figure 8.16, we eventually find a long edge e in $MWT(S)$ with an endpoint in region R. This is the edge to which we charge the length of $QT(S)$ inside B.

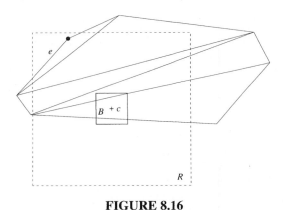

FIGURE 8.16

Walking from triangle to triangle leads to a long edge with
a nearby endpoint.

In this scheme, each edge e in $MWT(S)$ is charged by $O(1)$ quadtree squares of a given size, so that e's total charge adds in a geometric series proportional to its length. Thus, the total quadtree edge length is proportional to $|MWT(S)|$.

The remaining part of the proof deals with those quadtree squares not interior to the convex hull of S. Some such squares have a neighbor entirely contained in the convex hull and can be treated as above. The remaining cases have total length proportional to the convex hull, and hence to $|MWT(S)|$. ∎

The quadtree triangulation can be constructed in time $O(n \log n + k)$, where k denotes the output complexity [BEG94, BET93]. As we have explained the algorithm, however, k need not be bounded by a polynomial in n. Eppstein corrected this flaw by giving an algorithm in which "clusters" of nearby points are triangulated recursively and then treated as a unit in the overall triangulation. This algorithm uses $O(n)$ Steiner points and has $O(n \log n)$ running time. (A straightforward way of achieving the same running time with $O(n \log n)$ output complexity is to stop subdividing quadtree squares when the size reaches $1/n$ times that of the root, and then use any non-Steiner triangulation algorithm within each tiny square.)

We briefly comment on the special case of minimum weight Steiner triangulation for point sets in convex position. For this special case, there are a few results beyond the constant-factor approximation given by the quadtree algorithm. For example, the ring heuristic and the greedy triangulation give approximations with ratios of $\Theta(\log n)$. Eppstein used a similar quadtree triangulation technique as above to show that the minimum weight triangulation, constrained to use Steiner points only on the boundary of the convex hull, has weight $O(1)$ times $|MWST(S)|$.

OPEN PROBLEM 8.6 Does every point set have a Steiner triangulation that achieves the minimum weight? Does every point set in convex position have a minimum weight Steiner triangulation that uses no interior Steiner points?

CLUSTERING

8.5

We now turn away from famous individual problems to a large, loosely defined area. A *clustering problem* is given by a set of points S in the plane or some other metric space, and seeks the "best" partition of S into subsets, or *clusters*. We consider two different styles of problems: *k-clustering*, in which we divide S into k clusters, and *k-point clustering*, in which we seek the single best cluster containing k points.

8.5.1 MINMAX k-CLUSTERING

To measure the quality of a partition of S, some criterion, such as diameter or variance, is applied to each cluster individually. Then individual measures are combined into an overall criterion using a function such as the sum or the maximum.

For the case of fixed k, there are polynomial-time algorithms for minimizing various combinations of cluster diameters [CRW91, HS91b] and for minimizing the sum of variances [BH89, IKI94], but other individual cluster criteria, such as the sum of pairwise distances, give open problems. For example, *Euclidean max cut*, equivalent to asking for the two clusters that minimize the sum of all pairwise intracluster distances, is neither known to be in P nor known to be NP-hard. Letting k vary, however, almost always gives an NP-complete problem, and very few nontrivial approximation results are known. In this section, we describe two k-clustering problems—minmax radius and minmax diameter—that stand out as especially well understood.

Minmax radius clustering, also known as "central clustering" and the "Euclidean k-center problem," seeks a partition $S = S_1 \cup \cdots \cup S_k$ that minimizes $\max_{1 \leq i \leq k} radius(S_i)$, where $radius(S_i)$ is the radius of the smallest disk that covers all points of S_i. The k-center problem is discussed along with other minmax (or bottleneck) problems in

Section 9.4. *Minmax diameter* clustering, also known as "pairwise clustering," seeks to minimize $\max_i diameter(S_i)$, where

$$diameter(S_i) = \max\{|s_j s_l| \mid s_j, s_l \in S_i\}.$$

Gonzalez [Gon85] proposed the following algorithm, called *farthest-point clustering*. Let an arbitrary point s_{i_1} be the representative for the first cluster. Pick the point s_{i_2} farthest from s_{i_1} to represent the second cluster. Pick s_{i_3} to maximize the distance to the nearer of s_{i_1} and s_{i_2}. Continue this process for k steps, at each step picking s_{i_j} to maximize $\min\{|s_{i_1} s_{i_j}|, |s_{i_2} s_{i_j}|, \ldots, |s_{i_{j-1}} s_{i_j}|\}$. After all representatives are chosen, we can define the partition of S: cluster S_j consists of all points closer to s_{i_j} than to any other representative. The following theorem is due to Gonzalez [Gon85]:

THEOREM 8.14   For either radius or diameter clustering, farthest-point clustering computes a partition with maximum cluster size at most twice optimal.

Proof.   Let $s_{i_{k+1}}$ be an input point that maximizes

$$\delta = \min\{|s_{i_1} s_{i_{k+1}}|, \ldots, |s_{i_k} s_{i_{k+1}}|\},$$

in other words, the point that would be chosen if we picked one more representative. All pairwise distances among $s_{i_1}, s_{i_2}, \ldots, s_{i_{k+1}}$ are at least δ. In any k-clustering, two of these points must be in the same cluster, hence δ and $\delta/2$ are respectively lower bounds for the diameter and radius of the worst cluster. Farthest-point clustering places each s_i into a cluster with representative s_{i_j} such that $|s_i s_{i_j}| \leq \delta$. Thus, each cluster has radius at most δ, and by the triangle inequality, diameter at most 2δ.   ∎

This proof uses no geometry beyond the triangle inequality, so Theorem 8.14 holds for any metric space (see Exercise 9.2). The obvious implementation of farthest-point clustering has running time $O(nk)$. Feder and Greene [FG88] give a two-phase algorithm with optimal running time $O(n \log k)$. The first phase of their algorithm clusters points into rectangular boxes using Vaidya's [Vai89] "box decomposition"—a sort of quadtree in which cubes are shrunk to bounding boxes before splitting. The second phase resembles farthest-point clustering on a sparse graph that has a vertex for each box.

The approximation ratio of Theorem 8.14 is, depending upon the metric, optimal or nearly optimal—"best possible" in the terminology of Section 9.4. This non-approximability result, quite rare for a geometric problem, is proved with a problem reduction that creates a "nasty gap," with "no" instances mapped far away from "yes" instances. It is interesting to note that this reduction, for metric spaces, starts from a planar-graph problem that admits a polynomial-time approximation scheme [Bak94]. (Planar graphs [Bak94] and certain geometric intersection graphs [HMR+94] typically admit such approximation schemes for problems in which the solution is simply a set of vertices; see Section 9.3.3.4. Planar graph network-design problems, however, are currently as open as their geometric counterparts.) The specific constructions below are due to Feder and Greene [FG88]; there are also earlier, weaker results [Gon85, MS84].

THEOREM 8.15   It is *NP*-hard to approximate the Euclidean minmax radius k-clustering (or Euclidean k-center) with an approximation ratio smaller than 1.822, or the Euclidean minmax diameter k-clustering with ratio smaller than 1.969.

Proof. Both problem reductions start from vertex cover for 3-regular planar graphs (see [GJ77]). As shown in Figure 8.17(a), any 3-regular planar graph G can be embedded in the plane so that each edge e becomes a path p_e with some odd number of edges, at least 3, which we shall denote by $|p_e|$. The paths meet at 120° angles at vertices, and remain well separated away from vertices. The midpoints S of the unit-length edges form an instance of the k-clustering problem.

It is not hard to see that S has a k-clustering with maximum cluster radius $\frac{1}{2}$ if and only if $k - \sum_e(|p_e| - 2)$ vertices can cover all edges in G. A cluster of radius $\alpha > \frac{1}{2}$ helps reduce this number only if a disk of radius α can cover more than 3 points of S near an original vertex of G. If each original vertex of G has local neighborhood as in the top illustration of Figure 8.17(b), then it takes a disk of diameter $d_1 = \sqrt{13}/2 \approx 1.80$, radius $d_1/2$, to cover 4 points. The bottom illustration shows an improved construction in which a disk must have diameter $d_1' = (1 + \sqrt{7})/2 \approx 1.822$ to cover more than 3 points.

Figure 8.17(c) shows analogous constructions for minmax diameter clustering. In the basic construction (top illustration), a cluster must have diameter $d_2 = (1 + \sqrt{3})/\sqrt{2} \approx 1.93$ to cover more than 3 points. In the improved construction, the critical distance is $d_2' = 2\cos(10°) \approx 1.969$. ∎

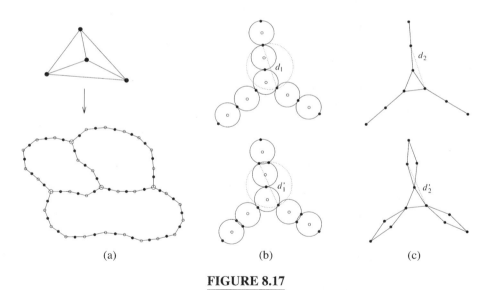

(a) (b) (c)

FIGURE 8.17

(a) Embedding the edges of a 3-regular planar graph as paths. Endpoints of embedded edge are circles; midpoints are dots. (b) Detail of a node for minmax radius clustering. (c) Detail of a node for minmax diameter clustering.

For the rectilinear metric, Feder and Greene give a similar, simpler construction that shows that it is *NP*-hard to approximate either minmax radius or minmax diameter with a ratio smaller than 2.

OPEN PROBLEM 8.7   Is Euclidean max cut solvable in polynomial time? How well can it be approximated? Do other natural k-clustering problems—for example, minimizing the sum of the distances from points to their cluster centers—have good approximation algorithms?

8.5.2 k-MINIMUM SPANNING TREE

We now consider a different sort of clustering problem, in which we seek the best single cluster containing k points of S, rather than the best partition of S into k groups. If the quality measure is radius or diameter (or area or perimeter of convex hull), this problem is polynomially solvable [AIKS91, DLSS93, EE94]. (We note in passing that diameter in $\mathbf{R}^d$ for $d > 2$ is still open.) Another reasonable quality measure, however, leads to an NP-hard problem.

The *Euclidean k-minimum spanning tree* problem measures the cost of interconnecting the cluster: given n points S in the plane, find k points with the shortest minimum spanning tree. Up to constant factors in the approximation ratio, it is equivalent to ask for the shortest cycle (the k-TSP problem) or shortest Steiner tree. Also inessential is the choice of metric. In fact, there has been a flurry of recent work on non-geometric k-MST problems [AABV94, CK94, RSM⁺94, ZL93]. In this section, however, we shall focus on the Euclidean k-MST formulation.

The k-MST problem was introduced by Fischetti et al. [FHJM94] and Zelikovsky and Lozevanu [ZL93], and proved NP-complete by those authors and also by Ravi et al. [RSM⁺94]. Ravi et al. devised an approximation algorithm with ratio $O(k^{1/4})$ for the Euclidean k-MST. The ratio was improved to $O(\log k)$ by Garg and Hochbaum [GH94], $O(\log k / \log \log n)$ by Eppstein [Epp95], $O(1)$ by Blum et al. [BCV95], and $2\sqrt{2}$ by Mitchell [Mit96].

Mitchell builds on the approach of Blum et al., who built on the approach of Hochbaum and Garg. He considers only trees of a special type, and shows that the shortest tree of this type can be found using dynamic programming. A tree falls into the special type if it is rectilinear, meaning that all edges are either horizontal or vertical, and *guillotine*, meaning that there exists a horizontal or vertical cutting line that intersects the tree in a single line segment, and that this property holds recursively within each cut half. It is obvious that an optimal k-MST can be made rectilinear with edge length increasing by at most a factor of $\sqrt{2}$. Lemma 8.6 below shows that the guillotine condition adds at most a factor of 2. Notice that the length of a guillotine tree is the total length of its line segments, not the total length of its cutting lines as in a binary space partition (see Lemma 8.1). The proof of Lemma 8.6 charges segment lengths to parallel, visible edges of R.

LEMMA 8.6 Mitchell   Any connected rectilinear graph R is contained in a guillotine subdivision of total length at most twice R.

A dynamic programming algorithm can now compute an optimal guillotine tree spanning k points of S. We may assume that each line segment of this tree is a segment (union of colinear edges) of a grid graph. The grid graph is formed passing a horizontal and vertical line through each point of S and then adding a horizontal line, say, halfway between each existing horizontal and a vertical line halfway between each vertical. The most straightforward (but not the fastest) dynamic program tries each possible choice of first cutting line and segment, and then recurses within each half. Within the halves, the algorithm considers shortest guillotine trees spanning k_1 and k_2 points of S, for each choice of k_1 and k_2 summing to $k - l$, where l is the number of points of S along the first segment. Each of the smaller guillotine trees is required to connect to the first segment. As we proceed deeper in the recursion, the intersection of the optimal guillotine tree with the bounding box of each subproblem remains connected, so that the number of possible subtrees remains polynomial in n and k. The overall result is the following theorem:

THEOREM 8.16 Mitchell There is a polynomial-time, $2\sqrt{2}$-factor approximation algorithm for the Euclidean k-MST.

SEPARATION PROBLEMS

8.6

We now switch from grouping objects together to cutting them apart. We consider three basic problems: (1) separating k disjoint polygons in the plane by piecewise-linear "fences" with a minimum total number of edges, (2) separating two nested convex polyhedra in $\mathbb{R}^3$ by a polyhedron with a minimum number of facets, and (3) separating two point sets in $\mathbb{R}^3$ by a piecewise-linear function with a minimum number of pieces.

The three problems above depart from the problems of previous sections in two ways. In each case, the input is more complicated than a planar point set, and solutions are evaluated not by a continuous measure such as length, but by minimum combinatorial complexity. Despite these changes, some of the issues important in previous sections carry over to this section. For example, the solution to problem (3) uses dynamic programming methods similar to those for red-blue separation, TSP with neighborhoods, and the k-MST problem. And even though its input consists of two polytopes, problem (2) has a close relationship to a non-geometric problem—the set cover problem. As before, our aim will be to exploit geometry to improve approximation ratios.

8.6.1   POLYGON SEPARATION

The problem of separating two simple polygons by a polygon with a minimum number of sides can be solved in polynomial time [ABO+89]. However, the problem of simultaneously separating a collection of k convex polygons by a minimum-complexity planar straight-line graph is *NP*-complete. Edelsbrunner et al. [ERS90] provided an approximation algorithm for this problem, which Mitchell and Suri [MS92] generalized to separation of arbitrary simple polygons. We describe the generalized algorithm, changing some minor details.

For simplicity, assume that one of the k polygons surrounds the remaining input. The algorithm first forms a triangulation of the space between the polygons, as shown in Figure 8.18(a). The algorithm then uses the triangulation to divide the space into

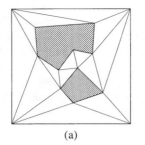
(a)
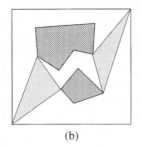
(b)
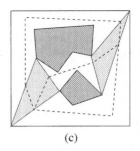
(c)

FIGURE 8.18

(a) Triangulation. (b) Moats (unshaded). (c) Separating graph (dashed).

regions called *moats*. This division is accomplished by forming the graph G that is the planar dual of the triangulation. Degree-one vertices are removed from G, and paths of degree-two vertices are contracted into single curves, resulting in a new planar graph G'. Graph G' is a planar graph with all vertices of degree 3 and with one input polygon per face, so it has $2k - 4$ vertices and $3k - 6$ edges. The moats are the connected components remaining when the triangles corresponding to vertices of G' are removed. See Figure 8.18(b). Each moat is a polygon bounded on two edges by removed triangles, and on the remaining sides by two of the input polygons. Call the two triangle edges of a moat its *terminals*.

Mitchell and Suri connect the two terminals of each moat by a *minimum link path*, a polygonal chain with a minimum number of edges. These paths can be computed in linear time [Sur90]. Within each of the $2k - 4$ removed triangles, three link paths are connected with two more edges, as shown in Figure 8.18(c).

THEOREM 8.17 Mitchell and Suri   The algorithm above gives a separating graph with at most five times as many edges as optimal.

Proof.   Any separating graph must have at least k faces, one for each polygon, and must include a path within each moat in order to separate the polygons bounding the moat. Since the algorithm uses the minimum number of edges within each moat, the only unnecessary vertices are the $6k - 12$ vertices within the $2k - 4$ removed triangles. Thus, if the optimal graph has v vertices and $v + k - 2$ edges, the algorithm above uses at most $v + 6k - 12$ vertices and $v + 7k - 14$ edges. The approximation ratio of this algorithm is $(v + 7k - 14)/(v + k - 2)$, which is at most 5, since any planar graph with k faces has at least $3k/2$ edges.   ∎

8.6.2   POLYHEDRON SEPARATION

Let P and R denote (closed) convex polytopes in $\mathbb{R}^3$ with $P \subseteq R$. We seek a polytope Q, $P \subseteq Q \subseteq R$, with a minimum number of faces. (Since the number of vertices, edges, and faces are linearly related, the precise measure of complexity changes only constant factors; however, the number of faces turns out to be most convenient.) A special case of this *polyhedron separation* problem is *polyhedron approximation*: given a polytope R and a distance ϵ, find a minimum-complexity Q inside R that has a boundary within distance ϵ of the boundary of R. The approximation problem can be reduced to the separation problem by letting P be the polytope formed by moving each face of R inwards by ϵ.

The polyhedron separation problem is due to Silio [Sil79] and Klee [ABO+89]. Das and Joseph [DJ90] proved it *NP*-complete by a reduction from planar 3-SAT. (Whether the special case of polyhedron approximation is *NP*-complete seems to be unknown.) Mitchell and Suri [MS92] gave an $O(\log n)$-approximation algorithm (which works in general dimension). In this section we describe a recent improvement due to Brönnimann and Goodrich [BG94] that achieves a constant-factor approximation in $\mathbb{R}^3$.

Both algorithms reduce the separation problem to the *hitting set* problem [GJ79]: given a collection $\mathcal{S} = \{S_1, S_2, \ldots, S_n\}$ of sets of "points" (elements of a ground set), one seeks a minimum-cardinality set of points S such that each S_i contains at least one point of S. (This problem is equivalent to the *set cover* problem, in which one seeks a minimum-cardinality subset $\mathcal{S}' \subseteq \mathcal{S}$ covering all elements in the union $\bigcup_{1 \le i \le n} S_i$. To transform a hitting set problem to a set cover problem, replace each point x by the set $\{i \mid x \in S_i\}$.) In the polyhedron separation problem, the "points" will be the planes containing faces of the inner polyhedron P.

LEMMA 8.7   There is a separating polyhedron Q with each face coplanar to a face of P that approximates the optimal number of faces within a factor of three.

Proof.   Let polyhedra be represented as intersections of halfspaces, one per face. For each halfspace h of the optimal separating polyhedron Q', we can find three halfspaces of P such that the intersection of the three halfspaces is contained in h (Carathéodory's Theorem). The intersection of all such triples is a polyhedron Q with at most three times as many faces as Q'. Polyhedron Q is contained in the outer polyhedron R since it is contained in Q', and contains the inner polyhedron P.   ∎

We now define the hitting set problem. The points correspond to the planes containing faces of the inner polyhedron P. Let $\mathcal{A}$ denote the arrangement formed by these planes. The sets S_i correspond to the cells of $\mathcal{A}$ that intersect the boundary of the outer polyhedron R. The set for such a cell contains the planes of $\mathcal{A}$ that separate the cell from P. If P has n faces, then the set system $\mathcal{S}$ has n points and $O(n^2)$ sets. Any hitting set for $\mathcal{S}$ induces a separating polyhedron Q of the same complexity. Conversely, Lemma 8.7 shows that the minimum hitting set of $\mathcal{S}$ gives a 3-approximation to the minimum separating polyhedron.

The greedy algorithm for hitting set [Joh74], which repeatedly chooses the point that covers the most uncovered sets, has approximation ratio $1 + \ln n$. To achieve a smaller approximation ratio, we must take advantage of the geometric origin of the set system.

The *Vapnik-Chervonenkis dimension* of a set system is the maximum cardinality of a set of points *shattered* by the system. A set of points A is shattered by the set system if for each of its $2^{|A|}$ subsets A' there is a set S_i in the system with $A' = S_i \cap A$. The fact that our set system $\mathcal{S}$ is defined by an arrangement of planes implies that it has bounded VC-dimension: a set of m cells of $\mathcal{A}$ (points of $\mathcal{S}$) is cut into only $O(m^3)$ subsets by planes of $\mathcal{A}$, which is fewer than 2^m for sufficiently large m.

Now assume that the points of set system S have weights. An ϵ-*net* for S is a set of points N such that for any sufficiently heavy set S_i in S, $N \cap S_i \neq \emptyset$. The parameter ϵ specifies what is meant by "sufficiently heavy": S_i is sufficiently heavy if the total weight of its points is at least ϵ times the total weight of all points of S. Using random sampling, Blumer et al. [BEHW89] proved the following important result: any set system of VC-dimension d has an ϵ-net of cardinality $O(\frac{d}{\epsilon} \log \frac{1}{\epsilon})$. Notice that this bound is independent of n, the number of points in the set system. More recently, Matoušek and others [Mat92, MSW90] have given deterministic algorithms for finding ϵ-nets. These deterministic algorithms find frequent use in computational geometry as replacements for random sampling techniques. Indeed, Brönniman and Goodrich's algorithm can be seen as an application of ϵ-nets to derandomize an algorithm of Clarkson [Cla93], only in this case the derandomized algorithm ends up being better than the randomized one—an $O(1)$- rather than an $O(\log n)$-approximation—due to a better bound on the size of deterministic ϵ-nets for half-spaces in $\mathbb{R}^3$. Any set system defined by a collection of planes in $\mathbb{R}^3$ has an ϵ-net of cardinality $O(\frac{1}{\epsilon})$ that can be computed deterministically in polynomial time [MSW90, MS92].

We now describe how Brönniman and Goodrich use ϵ-nets to approximately solve the hitting set problem defined above. We first assume that the optimal cardinality c of a hitting set is known; we shall soon remove this assumption by binary searching for c. Start each point in the union of S with unit weight. Then find a $\frac{1}{2c}$-net N for S. By the result quoted above, $|N|$ is $O(c)$. If N is a solution to the hitting set problem, we return it as our approximation. Otherwise, we pick any set S_i in S not hit by N, and double the weights of all points in S_i. We then find a $\frac{1}{2c}$-net for the new weights, and repeat this process until it finds a hitting set.

LEMMA 8.8   The process above can continue for at most $4c \log(n/c)$ iterations before a hitting set of cardinality $O(c)$ is found.

Proof.   At each iteration, the unhit set S_i has weight at most $\frac{1}{2c}$ times the total weight of points of S (otherwise N would have to hit it), so doubling the weights of points in S_i increases the total weight by a factor of at most $1 + \frac{1}{2c}$. Now let C be an optimal hitting set. The weight of at least one member of C must double at each iteration. Thus, the total weight of C—and hence the total weight of S—after k iterations is at least $c2^{k/c}$. Finally, $k = 4c \log(n/c)$ is a bound on the maximum k for which $c2^{k/c} \leq n(1 + \frac{1}{2c})^k$.   ∎

We can now assemble the entire algorithm. We start by constructing the weighted set system S. Next we use binary search to find a suitable value of c. At a trial c, we run the weight-doubling algorithm for $4c \log(c/n)$ iterations before changing c. After $O(\log c)$ trials, we find a value of c such that the algorithm's $\frac{1}{2c}$-net is a hitting set but its $\frac{1}{2c-2}$-net is not. By Lemma 8.8, this c is at most the true minimum cardinality of a hitting set. Since the ϵ-net is a hitting set of cardinality $O(c)$ and the optimum hitting set is a 3-approximate solution to the polyhedron separation problem, we have the following result:

THEOREM 8.18 Brönniman and Goodrich   The algorithm above is a constant-factor approximation algorithm for the polyhedron separation problem.

The same technique works equally well if the outer polyhedron R is not convex, but the running time is slower, since there may now be $O(n^3)$ sets in the set system.

8.6.3 POINT SET SEPARATION

Assume we have a set of points in the plane, and each point has a third coordinate called elevation. We turn to the problem of fitting a minimum-complexity, continuous, piecewise-linear function $f(x, y)$ to these "scattered data." In general, we must triangulate the planar point set in order to guarantee an exact fit, meaning an interpolating surface passing through each elevated point, and all triangulations of the input points have the same number of triangles. (Of course, some triangulations may be better than others for considerations quite apart from combinatorial complexity.) If we allow an inexact fit, however, the problem of minimizing the complexity of the surface becomes quite interesting.

To formalize the inexact problem, assume that the input includes an error tolerance $\epsilon > 0$ and the problem asks for a piecewise linear function $f(x, y)$ with a minimum number of faces, such that for each input point (x_i, y_i, z_i), we have $|z_i - f(x_i, y_i)| \leq \epsilon$. This surface fitting problem is a special case of a point set separation problem: separate two given sets of points in $\mathbb{R}^3$ by a terrain with a minimum number of facets. A *terrain* is the graph of a piecewise-linear function, or equivalently a polyhedral surface intersected exactly once by each vertical line.

The two-dimensional version of the surface fitting problem asks for a univariate piecewise-linear function passing through a collection of vertical line segments (error bars); this problem—and more generally, the two-dimensional version of the point set separation problem—can be solved in polynomial time [HS91a]. Notice, however, that a slightly different two-dimensional point set separation problem, which asks for a general separating polygon, is *NP*-hard; this is exactly the red-blue separation problem mentioned in Section 8.2.3.

Agarwal and Suri [AS94] showed that the three-dimensional surface fitting problem is *NP*-hard using a reduction from planar 3-SAT. It is not clear, however, whether the problem is *NP*-complete, as good bounds are not known on the numerical precision needed to represent the optimal function. Agarwal and Suri also devised an algorithm with logarithmic approximation ratio. Their algorithm works for the point-set separation problem as well, so we shall describe it in this more general context.

As in the polyhedron separation problem, the first step is to restrict the output to some canonical form. It is convenient to base the desired piecewise-linear function on trapezoids, rather than triangles. A *canonical trapezoid* T in the xy-plane satisfies the following restrictions: T has two horizontal sides, each passing through (the projection onto the xy-plane of) an input point, and the non-horizontal sides of T must each pass through two input points. If, moreover, some plane in $\mathbb{R}^3$ separates the two sets of points whose projections are covered by T, we call T a *splitting canonical trapezoid*. This last condition can be checked by fixed-dimensional linear programming.

A *canonical function* $f(x, y)$ is a continuous, piecewise-linear function, induced by a collection $\mathcal{C}_f$ of splitting canonical trapezoids with disjoint interiors. The domain of $f(x, y)$ is assumed to be a canonical trapezoid that covers the xy-projections of all input points. The splitting trapezoids in C_f need not cover the entire domain, as $f(x, y)$ can be filled in by triangulating the gaps between the splitting canonical trapezoids. We shall measure the complexity of $f(x, y)$ by $|C_f|$, which is within a constant factor of the number of pieces in the filled-in function. Figure 8.19 shows that any triangle in an optimal (non-canonical) solution can be cut into at most four splitting canonical trapezoids. (Any face of an optimal solution with more than three sides can of course be triangulated, again increasing the total complexity by at most a constant factor.) Hence, restricting attention to canonical functions entails only a constant factor increase in complexity.

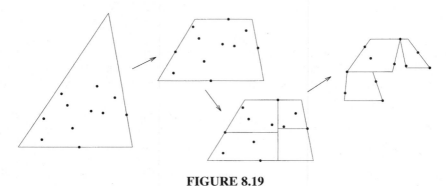

FIGURE 8.19

Any triangle can be shrunk and cut into at most
4 canonical trapezoids.

At this point, we have reduced the problem to covering the (xy-projections of the) n input points by a minimum number of disjoint, splitting canonical trapezoids. We could treat this as a set cover problem; however, this ignores the disjointness requirement. Enforcing disjointness—say by triangulating the planar graph formed by the overlapping trapezoids—blows up the complexity by a quadratic factor, giving $\Omega(k^2)$ pieces when k is optimal.

To improve the approximation ratio, we turn from set covering to dynamic programming. To ensure that the dynamic programming runs in polynomial time, however, we must further restrict the space of piecewise-linear functions. We call a cover of the input by splitting canonical trapezoids *recursively separable* if it can be constructed—starting from a single large canonical trapezoid—by recursively dividing canonical trapezoids in two with cutting lines connecting opposite edges. Agarwal and Suri use an algorithm of Paterson and Yao [PY90], which computes a binary space partition (see Section 8.2.3) for a set of line segments, to show that any disjoint cover by k canonical trapezoids can be transformed into a recursively separable cover with $O(k \log k)$ trapezoids. (There is also a direct proof [Mit93] of this result using horizontal cutting lines determined by a segment tree.)

Now the dynamic programming algorithm computes a globally optimal recursively separable cover. There are $O(n^6)$ different canonical trapezoids—one choice of input point for each horizontal side and two for each of the other sides. The points in any canonical trapezoid T can be partitioned in $O(n^2)$ ways into two smaller canonical trapezoids, and the optimal recursively separable cover for T is the combination of optima for some two smaller trapezoids. The base of this recurrence is the collection of splitting canonical trapezoids. We now have an $O(n^8)$-time dynamic programming algorithm for finding an optimal recursively separable partition.

THEOREM 8.19 Agarwal and Suri Let the optimum piecewise-linear function separating two sets of points in $\mathbb{R}^3$ have k pieces. Then the algorithm sketched above computes a piecewise-linear function with $O(k \log k)$ pieces in polynomial time.

ODDS AND ENDS

8.7

In this section we briefly survey a number of more isolated geometric approximation problems that do not fit into the other sections.

8.7.1 COVERING ORTHOGONAL POLYGONS BY RECTANGLES

An *orthogonal polygon* is a polygonal region in which all sides are either horizontal or vertical. The polygon is *simple* if its boundary has a single connected component, otherwise the polygon has *holes*. Given an orthogonal polygon P, the *rectangle covering* problem asks for a minimum number of (overlapping) rectangles whose union is P. Culberson and Reckhow [CR88] showed that this problem is *NP*-complete, even if P is simple. Berman and DasGupta [BD92] showed that if P has holes, the problem is also Max-$\mathcal{SNP}$-hard. This 1992 result seems to be the first proof of Max-$\mathcal{SNP}$-hardness for a geometric problem.

There are also some approximation results for rectangle covering. The rectangle covering problem can easily be translated into a set cover problem and approximated within a logarithmic factor; however, if the orthogonal polygon is in general position—no two boundary segments collinear—much better approximations are possible. The polygon can be cut into $n/2 + h$ vertical strips, where n is the number of sides and h is the number of holes, by passing a line through each vertical boundary segment. On the other hand, each polygon side requires a separate rectangle side, so any cover has at least $n/4$ rectangles. Thus, the approximation ratio of this method is 3 for polygons with holes and 2 for simple polygons. Berman and DasGupta [BD92] give several similar constant-factor approximations for covering the boundary or vertices of a given orthogonal polygon (not necessarily in general position).

OPEN PROBLEM 8.8 Is there a constant-factor approximation algorithm for covering arbitrary orthogonal polygons by rectangles?

8.7.2   PACKING SQUARES WITH FIXED CORNERS

Formann and Wagner [FW91] (see also [WW95]) define the following packing problem, motivated by the placement of text labels in cartography. The input consists of n points in the plane, along with a not-yet-embedded rectangle for each point. The task is to place all rectangles so that each rectangle is axis-aligned, has its point at one of its corners, and overlaps no other rectangle.

Formann and Wagner prove that this problem is *NP*-complete, even if all rectangles are unit squares. They then define an optimization version of this special case, which seeks the largest value s such that it allows each point to have a square label of side length s, and gives an approximation algorithm. The algorithm starts with s very small and all four candidate squares at each point, and then gradually increases s. At each step, if one of the four candidate squares covers half the distance to a neighboring point, it is removed. A remaining square is called *pending* if it overlaps another remaining square. Formann and Wagner show that a point with only pending squares has at most two remaining squares. This implies that the problem of placing squares for these points can be translated into a 2-SAT instance. If this instance is unsatisfiable, the algorithm halts and returns the last feasible square size found. Overall, this algorithm gives an approximation ratio of 2. Formann and Wagner go on to prove that no better approximation ratio is possible by a careful analysis of the construction used in their *NP*-completeness proof.

8.7.3   LARGEST CONGRUENT SUBSETS

Given a family of finite point sets in $\mathbb{R}^d$, $d \geq 1$, we wish to find a maximum-cardinality set congruent to a subset in each set of the family. Akutsu and Halldórsson [AH94a] define this problem, and show by a reduction from maximum clique, that for some $\epsilon > 0$ no $O(n^\epsilon)$-approximation is possible. This result and Berman and DasGupta's result on rectangle covering currently seem to be the only geometric applications of the new non-approximability results.

Akutsu and Halldórsson also give an $O(n_i / \log n)$-approximation for the same common congruent point set problem, where n_i denotes the size of the smallest input set S_i. In fact, an exhaustive search algorithm works: partition S_i into $O(n_i / \log n)$ pieces of size $O(\log n)$, and test each subset of each piece.

8.7.4   POLYGON BISECTION

Koutsoupias, Papadimitriou, and Sideri [KPS90] consider the following natural problem: given a simple polygon, partition it into two equal-area subsets using curved "fences" of minimum total length. Note that the two subsets need not be connected sets. A construction involving rectangular regions connected by thin "necks" shows the problem to be *NP*-complete; and moreover, that no approximation ratio depending only on n and not also on the geometry, is possible.

To salvage an approximation result, Koutsoupias et al. consider the following relaxation: a partition is an ϵ-bisection if the ratio of the subset sizes is between $1 - \epsilon$ and $1 + \epsilon$. They first show that an optimal bisection consists of circular arcs that meet the polygon either at a vertex or perpendicularly at an edge. Then they pick an area discretization parameter $\delta (= \delta(\epsilon, n))$ and find a collection $\mathcal{A} (= \mathcal{A}(\delta))$ of arcs, such that for any arc of the optimal solution, there is an arc in $\mathcal{A}$ of lesser or equal length that cuts off a similar area with an error of at most δ. Finally, they use dynamic programming to find the shortest subset of $\mathcal{A}$ that cuts off half the discretized area. The result is an algorithm, with time polynomial in n and $1/\epsilon$, that finds an ϵ-bisection at least as short as the optimum true bisection. It remains open whether any similar approximation result can be obtained for non-simple polygons.

8.7.5 GRAPH EMBEDDING

Given an n-vertex graph G and a set S of n points in the plane, the *geometric embedding problem* asks for a mapping of the vertices of G onto the points of S to minimize the total embedded edge length. This problem is *NP*-complete, as it generalizes the Euclidean traveling salesman problem. (Let G be a cycle.) Bern, Karloff, Raghavan, and Schieber [BKRS92] give an $O(\log n)$-approximation for the special case in which G is a bounded-degree tree. Hansen [Han89] considers the embedding problem for highly regular graphs such as d-dimensional grids, hypercubes, and butterfly networks. A ratio of $O(\log n)$ is possible in all these cases, except planar grids, for which the ratio rises to $O(\log^2 n)$. Hansen also considers a different special case, in which G is arbitrary but P is a grid; in this case he achieves an $O(\log^2 n)$ approximation. This last result uses the Leighton-Rao approximation algorithm for graph separators [LR88], so better separator results (claimed in [CY94]) should improve the approximation ratio.

8.7.6 LOW-DEGREE SPANNING TREES

The problem of finding a traveling salesman path can be viewed as a degree-constrained minimum spanning tree problem, in which each vertex has degree at most two. With this in mind, it becomes interesting to consider weaker bounds on the vertex degree of a minimum spanning tree. Khuller, Raghavachari, and Young [KRY94] consider this problem for degree bounds of three and four; they show that one can find constrained spanning trees with length 1.5 and 1.25 times the MST length, respectively. It is no constraint to require the degree to be at most five, as there always exists an MST satisfying this requirement. These results are described in more detail by Raghavachari in Chapter 7.

8.7.7 SHORTEST PATHS IN SPACE

In the Euclidean plane, the shortest path connecting a source and a destination and avoiding a set of polygonal obstacles, is always a subgraph of the *visibility graph*, which connects two vertices u and v if the line segment uv avoids all obstacles. The three-dimensional generalization of this shortest path problem, however, is *NP*-hard [CR87], largely because a shortest path may wrap around a polyhedral obstacle at almost any location on an edge.

Choi et al. [CSY94], building on earlier work of Papadimitriou [Pap85], provide a polynomial-time approximation scheme for this problem, assuming an integer model of computation in which each obstacle vertex has coordinates specified by L-bit integers. The running time is polynomial in n and $1/\epsilon$, and requires computation with numbers of $O(L + \log(n/\epsilon))$ bits. The basic idea is to place a finely-spaced collection of vertices along each obstacle edge, and then compute the shortest path in the visibility graph of these points. Sophisticated techniques are required to keep the number of points polynomially bounded, and to analyze the necessary bit complexity.

8.7.8   LONGEST SUBGRAPH PROBLEMS

We have already mentioned the recent results by Barvinok [Bar94] on the Euclidean longest traveling salesman problem. Alon, Rajagopalan, and Suri [ARS93] consider several other longest-subgraph problems, with the additional constraint that the subgraph may not include any edge crossings. (Shortest subgraphs—matchings, trees, or tours—satisfy this constraint automatically.)

Alon et al. first show how to compute a maximum non-crossing matching with length at least $2/\pi$ times optimal. Choose an angle θ uniformly at random, split the input points in half by a line parallel to θ, and compute any non-crossing matching in which each edge crosses the line. The ratio follows from the observations that a projection of the optimum matching onto a line perpendicular to θ has expected length diminished by only $2/\pi$, and the constructed matching has length at least that of the optimum matching's projection. This algorithm can be derandomized by simply trying all combinatorially distinct bipartitions of the input by lines.

To approximate the maximum non-crossing Hamiltonian path, Alon et al. show that the matching constructed above can be extended to such a path. The result then follows from the fact that the maximum matching contains at least half the weight of the optimal path. Curiously, this method also gives an approximation to the unconstrained maximum Hamiltonian path problem and to the longest traveling salesman tour.

Alon et al. also consider the maximum non-crossing spanning tree, and show that this tree always has a constant-factor approximated by a *star*, a tree in which one vertex is connected to all others. Two similar problems, maximum bounded-degree spanning tree and maximum triangulation, can also be approximated, the first because the tree can be approximated by a matching and the second because the triangulation can be approximated by a spanning tree.

Alon et al. leave open the complexity of exactly solving the problems they treat, although they suspect the problems to be *NP*-complete. Approximating the maximum non-crossing cycle also appears to be open.

CONCLUSIONS

8.8

We now mention a major result of Arora [Aro96], too recent for us to incorporate into the main body of this chapter. Arora has announced a polynomial-time approximation scheme for Euclidean TSP. For any $\epsilon > 0$, a solution of length at most $1 + \epsilon$ times optimal can be found in time $n^{O(1/\epsilon)}$. The result extends to many other geometric problems, including Euclidean Steiner tree, and generalizes to $\mathbb{R}^d$ but with quasi-polynomial running time $n^{O(\log^{d-2} n)/\epsilon^{d-1}}$. The approach is reminiscent of the approach to TSP with neighborhoods and k-MST described in this chapter: there is a near-optimal solution of a special form defined by a recursively constructed tree, and an optimal solution of this form can be found by dynamic programming. Arora's result implies that Euclidean TSP and other famous geometric problems cannot be Max-$\mathcal{SNP}$-hard, unless $P = NP$.

The original conclusion to this chapter, written in December 1994, stressed the immaturity of the geometric area relative to other areas such as graph problems. We observed that each hard geometric problem called for its own approximation method, whereas graph problems admitted unified approaches such as the primal-dual method discussed in Chapter 4. This situation has changed in less than a year and a half. A powerful unified approach has emerged: dynamic programming over a recursively defined subset of solutions. Finally, Arora's new result has clarified the Max-$\mathcal{SNP}$ status of many geometric problems. We look forward to further rapid developments.

Acknowledgments We thank Sanjeev Arora, Ding-Zhu Du, Naveen Garg, Dorit Hochbaum, Joe Mitchell, Günter Rote, Subhash Suri, and Alexander Zelikovsky for valuable suggestions. We remember Gene Lawler, whose clear writing style we have tried to emulate.

REFERENCES

[AA93]   N. Alon and Y. Azar. On-line Steiner trees in the Euclidean plane. *Disc. and Comp. Geometry*, 10:113–121, 1993.

[AABV94] B. Awerbuch, Y. Azar, A. Blum, and S. Vempala. Improved approximation guarantees for minimum-weight k-trees and prize-collecting salesmen. Technical Report CMU-CS-94-173, School of Computer Science, Carnegie Mellon Univ., Pittsburgh, 1994.

[ABO+89] A. Aggarwal, H. Booth, J. O'Rourke, S. Suri, and C.K. Yap. Finding convex minimal nested polygons. *Information and Control*, 83:98–110, 1989.

[AH94a]   T. Akutsu and M.M. Halldórsson. On the approximation of largest common subtrees and largest common point sets. In *Proc. 5th Int. Symp. Algorithms and Computation*, pages 405–413. Springer-Verlag, LNCS 834, 1994.

[AH94b]   E.M. Arkin and R. Hassin. Approximation algorithms for the geometric covering salesman problem. *Disc. Appl. Math.*, 55:197–218, 1994.

[AIKS91] A. Aggarwal, H. Imai, N. Katoh, and S. Suri. Finding k-points with minimum diameter and related problems. *J. Algorithms*, 12:38–56, 1991.

[Aro96]   S. Arora. A polynomial time approximation scheme for Euclidean TSP and other geometric problems. Manuscript, 1996.

[ARS93]   N. Alon, S. Rajagopalan, and S. Suri. Long non-crossing configurations in the plane. In *Proc. 9th ACM Symp. Computational Geometry*, pages 257–263, 1993.

[AS94]   P.K. Agarwal and S. Suri. Surface approximation and geometric partitions. In *Proc. 5th ACM/SIAM Symp. Discrete Algorithms*, pages 24–33, 1994.

[Aza94]   Y. Azar. Lower bounds for insertion methods for TSP. *Combinatorics, Probability, and Computing*, 3:285–292, 1994.

[Bak94]   B.S. Baker. Approximation algorithms for *NP*-complete problems on planar graphs. *J. ACM*, 41:153–180, 1994.

[Bar94]   A.I. Barvinok. Two algorithmic results for the traveling salesman problem. Manuscript, 1994.

[BCV95]   A. Blum, P. Chalasani, and S. Vempala. A constant-factor approximation for the *k*-MST problem in the plane. In *Proc. 27th ACM Symp. Theory of Computing*, 1995.

[BD92]   P. Berman and B. DasGupta. Approximating the rectilinear polygon cover problems. In *Proc. 4th Canad. Conf. Comput. Geom.*, pages 229–235, 1992.

[BD95]   A. Borchers and D-.Z. Du. The *k*-Steiner ratio in graphs. In *Proc. 27th ACM Symp. Theory of Computing*, 1995.

[BDG95]   A. Borchers, D-.Z. Du, and B. Gao. The *k*-Steiner ratio in the rectilinear plane. Technical Report TR 95-028, Dept. of Computer Science, Univ. of Minnesota, 1995.

[BEG94]   M. Bern, D. Eppstein, and J.R. Gilbert. Provably good mesh generation. *J. Comp. System Science*, 48:384–409, 1994.

[BEHW89]   A. Blumer, A. Ehrenfeucht, D. Haussler, and M. Warmuth. Classifying learnable geometric concepts with the Vapnik-Chervonenkis dimension. *J. Assoc. Comput. Mach.*, 36:929–965, 1989.

[Ben92]   J.L. Bentley. Fast algorithms for geometric traveling salesman problems. *ORSA J. Computing*, 4:387–411, 1992.

[Ber87]   M. Bern. *Network Design Problems: Steiner trees and minimum spanning k-trees*. PhD thesis, Computer Science Division, University of California at Berkeley, 1987.

[Ber88]   M. Bern. Two probabilistic results on rectilinear Steiner trees. *Algorithmica*, 3:191–204, 1988.

[BET93]   M. Bern, D. Eppstein, and S.-H. Teng. Parallel construction of quadtrees and quality triangulations. In *Proc. 3rd Workshop on Algorithms and Data Structures*, pages 188–199. Springer-Verlag, LNCS 709, 1993.

[BFK+94]   P. Berman, U. Fößmeier, M. Karpinski, M. Kaufmann, and A. Zelikovsky. Approaching the 5/4-approximation for rectilinear Steiner trees. In *Proc. 2nd Eur. Symp. Algorithms*, pages 60–71. Springer-Verlag, LNCS 855, 1994.

[BG94]   H. Brönnimann and M.T. Goodrich. Almost optimal set covers in finite VC-dimension. In *Proc. 10th ACM Symp. Computational Geometry*, pages 293–302, 1994.

[BH89]   E. Boros and P. Hammer. On clustering problems with connected optima in Euclidean spaces. *Disc. Math.*, 75:81–88, 1989.

[BKP94]   V. Bafna, B. Kalyanasundaram, and K. Pruhs. Not all insertion methods yield constant approximate tours in the Euclidean plane. *Theoretical Computer Science*, 125:345–353, 1994.

[BKRS92] M. Bern, H. Karloff, P. Raghavan, and B. Schieber. Fast geometric approximation techniques and geometric embedding problems. *Theoretical Comp. Sci.*, 106:265–281, 1992.

[BP89] M. Bern and P. Plassmann. The Steiner problem with edge lengths 1 and 2. *Inform. Proc. Lett.*, 32:171–176, 1989.

[BR94] P. Berman and V. Ramaiyer. Improved approximation algorithms for the Steiner tree problem. *J. Algorithms*, 17:381–408, 1994.

[BS80] J.L. Bentley and J.B. Saxe. An analysis of two heuristics for the Euclidean travelling salesman problem. In *Proc. 18th Annual Allerton Conference on Communication, Control, and Computing*, pages 41–49, 1980.

[Cie90] D. Cieslik. The Steiner ratio of Banach-Minkowski planes. In R. Bodendiek, editor, *Contemporary Methods in Graph Theory*, pages 231–248. BI-Wissenschaftverlag, Mannheim, 1990.

[CK94] S.Y. Cheung and A. Kumar. Efficient quorumcast routing algorithms. In *Proc. IEEE INFOCOM '94 Conference on Computer Communications*, volume 2, pages 840–847, 1994.

[CKT94] B. Chandra, H. Karloff, and C. Tovey. New results on the old k-opt algorithm for the TSP. In *Proc. 5th ACM-SIAM Symp. Disc. Algorithms*, pages 150–159, 1994.

[Cla91] K. Clarkson. Approximation algorithms for planar traveling salesman tours and minimum-length triangulations. In *Proc. 2nd ACM-SIAM Symp. Disc. Algorithms*, pages 17–23, 1991.

[Cla93] K.L. Clarkson. Algorithms for polytope covering and approximation. In *Proc. 3rd Worksh. Algorithms and Data Structures*, pages 246–252. Springer-Verlag Lecture Notes in Computer Science 709, 1993.

[CR87] J. Canny and J. Reif. New lower bound techniques for robot motion planning problems. In *Proc. 28th IEEE Symp. Found. Comp. Sci.*, pages 49–60, 1987.

[CR88] J.C. Culberson and R.C. Reckhow. Covering polygons is hard. In *Proc. 29th IEEE Symp. Found. Comp. Sci.*, pages 601–611, 1988.

[CRW91] V. Capoyleas, G. Rote, and G. Woeginger. Geometric clusterings. *J. Algorithms*, 12:341–356, 1991.

[CSY94] J. Choi, J. Sellen, and C.-K. Yap. Approximate Euclidean shortest path in 3-space. In *Proc. 10th ACM Symp. Comp. Geometry*, pages 41–48, 1994.

[CY94] F.R.K. Chung and S.-T. Yau. A near optimal algorithm for edge separators. In *Proc. 26th ACM Symp. Theory of Computing*, pages 1–8, 1994.

[DGG+] D.-Z. Du, B. Gao, R.L. Graham, Z.-C. Liu, and P.-J. Wan. Minimum Steiner trees in normed planes. To appear in *Disc. and Comp. Geometry*.

[DH92a] D.-Z. Du and F.K. Hwang. A proof of Gilbert-Pollak's conjecture on the Steiner ratio. *Algorithmica*, 7:121–135, 1992.

[DH92b] D.-Z. Du and F.K. Hwang. The state of art in Steiner ratio problems. In D.-Z. Du and F.K. Hwang, editors, *Computing in Euclidean Geometry*, pages 163–192. World Scientific, Singapore, 1992.

[DJ90] G. Das and D. Joseph. The complexity of minimum convex nested polyhedra. In *Proc. 2nd Canad. Conf. Computational Geometry*, pages 296–301, 1990.

[DLSS93]   A. Datta, H.-P. Lenhof, C. Schwarz, and M. Smid. Static and dynamic algorithms for k-point clustering problems. In *Proc. 3rd Workshop on Algorithms and Data Structures*, pages 265–276. LNCS 709, Springer-Verlag, 1993.

[DM95]   M. Dickerson and M. Montague. A (usually) connected subgraph of the minimum weight triangulation. In *5th MSI Worksh. Computational Geometry*, 1995.

[Du92]   D.-Z. Du. Disproving Gilbert-Pollak conjecture in high dimensional spaces. Technical Report TR 92-56, Dept. of Computer Science, Univ. of Minnesota, 1992.

[DZF91]   D.-Z. Du, Y. Zhang, and Q. Feng. On better heuristic for Euclidean Steiner minimum trees. In *Proc. 32nd IEEE Symp. Found. Comp. Sci.*, pages 431–439, 1991.

[EE94]   D. Eppstein and J. Erickson. Iterated nearest neighbors and finding minimal polytopes. *Disc. and Comp. Geometry*, 11:321–350, 1994.

[Epp94]   D. Eppstein. Approximating the minimum weight triangulation. *Disc. and Comp. Geometry*, 11:163–191, 1994.

[Epp95]   D. Eppstein. Faster geometric k-point MST approximation. Technical Report 95-13, Dept. of Information and Computer Science, UC-Irvine, 1995.

[ERS90]   H. Edelsbrunner, A.D. Robinson, and X. Shen. Covering convex sets with non-overlapping polygons. *Discrete Math.*, 81:153–164, 1990.

[FG88]   T. Feder and D.H. Greene. Optimal algorithms for approximate clustering. In *Proc. 20th ACM Symp. Theory of Computing*, pages 434–444, 1988.

[FHJM94] M. Fischetti, H.W. Hamacher, K. Jørnsten, and F. Maffioli. Weighted k-cardinality trees: complexity and polyhedral structure. *Networks*, 24:11–21, 1994.

[FW91]   M. Formann and F. Wagner. A packing problem with applications to lettering of maps. In *Proc. 7th ACM Symp. Comp. Geometry*, pages 281–288, 1991.

[GDG94]   B. Gao, D.-Z. Du, and R.L. Graham. The tight lower bound for the Steiner ratio in Minkowski planes. In *Proc. 10th ACM Symp. Computational Geometry*, pages 183–191, 1994.

[GEP95]   M. Grigni, E. Koutsoupias, and C. Papadimitriou. An approximation scheme for the planar graph TSP. In *Proc. 36th IEEE Symp. Found. Comp. Sci.*, pages 640–645, 1995.

[GGJ77]   M.R. Garey, R.L. Graham, and D.S. Johnson. The complexity of computing Steiner minimal trees. *SIAM J. Appl. Math.*, 32:835–859, 1977.

[GH76]   R.L. Graham and F.K. Hwang. Remarks on Steiner minimum trees. *Bull. Inst. Math. Acad. Sinica*, 4:177–182, 1976.

[GH94]   N. Garg and D.S. Hochbaum. An $O(\log k)$ approximation for the k-minimum spanning tree problem in the plane. In *Proc. 26th ACM Symp. Theory of Computing*, pages 432–438, 1994.

[Gil79]   P.D. Gilbert. New results in planar triangulations. Technical Report R–850, Univ. Illinois Coordinated Science Lab, 1979.

[GJ77]   M.R. Garey and D.S. Johnson. The rectilinear Steiner tree problem is *NP*-complete. *SIAM J. Appl. Math.*, 32:826–834, 1977.

[GJ79]   M.R. Garey and D.S. Johnson. *Computers and Intractability: A Guide to the Theory of NP-Completeness*. W. H. Freeman, 1979.

[Gon85]   T. Gonzalez. Clustering to minimize the maximum intercluster distance. *Theoretical Computer Science*, 38:293–306, 1985.

[GP68] E.N. Gilbert and H.O. Pollak. Steiner minimal trees. *SIAM J. Appl. Math.*, 16:1–29, 1968.

[Han89] M.D. Hansen. Approximation algorithms for minimum cost embeddings of graphs in the plane. In *Proc. 30th IEEE Symp. Found. Comp. Sci.*, pages 604–609, 1989.

[HMR⁺94] H.B. Hunt III, M.V. Marathe, V. Radhakrishnan, S.S. Ravi, D.J. Rosenkrantz, and R.E. Stearns. A unified approach to approximation schemes for *NP*- and PSPACE-hard problems for geometric graphs. In *Proc. 2nd Eur. Symp. Algorithms*, pages 424–435. Springer-Verlag, LNCS 855, 1994.

[HP94] L.S. Heath and S.V. Pemmaraju. New results for the minimum weight triangulation problem. *Algorithmica*, 12:533–552, 1994.

[HRW92] F.K. Hwang, D.S. Richards, and P. Winter. *The Steiner Tree Problem*. North-Holland, 1992.

[HS91a] S.L. Hakimi and E.F. Schmeichel. Fitting polygonal functions to a set of points in the plane. *CVGIP: Graphical Models and Image Processing*, 53:132–136, 1991.

[HS91b] J. Hershberger and S. Suri. Finding tailored partitions. *J. Algorithms*, 12:431–463, 1991.

[Hur92] C. Hurkens. Nasty TSP instances for farthest insertion. In *Proc. 2nd Conf. on Integer Programming and Combinatorial Optimization*, pages 346–352. Mathematical Programming Society, 1992.

[Hwa76] F.K. Hwang. On Steiner minimal trees with rectilinear distance. *SIAM J. Appl. Math.*, 30:104–114, 1976.

[HY90] F.K. Hwang and Y.C. Yao. Comments on Bern's probabilistic results on rectilinear Steiner trees. *Algorithmica*, 5:591–598, 1990.

[IKI94] M. Inaba, N. Katoh, and H. Imai. Applications of weighted Voronoi diagrams and randomization of variance-based k-clustering. In *Proc. 10th ACM Symp. Computational Geometry*, pages 332–339, 1994.

[IT94] A.O. Ivanov and A.A. Tuzhilin. *Minimal Networks: The Steiner Problem and its Generalizations*. CRC Press, Inc., 1994.

[Joh74] D.S. Johnson. Approximation algorithms for combinatorial problems. *J. Comput. Syst. Science*, 9:256–278, 1974.

[JP85] D.S. Johnson and C.H. Papadimitriou. Performance guarantees for heuristics. In E.L. Lawler, J.K. Lenstra, A.H.G. Rinnooy Kan, and D.B. Shmoys, editors, *The Traveling Salesman Problem*. John Wiley, 1985.

[Kir80] D.G. Kirkpatrick. A note on Delaunay and optimal triangulations. *Inform. Proc. Lett.*, 10:127–128, 1980.

[KPS90] E. Koutsoupias, C.H. Papadimitriou, and M. Sideri. On the optimal bisection of a polygon. In *Proc. 6th ACM Symp. Computational Geometry*, pages 198–202, 1990.

[KRY94] S. Khuller, B. Raghavachari, and N. Young. Low-degree spanning trees of small weight. In *Proc. 26th ACM Symp. Theory of Computing*, pages 412–421, 1994.

[KZ94] M. Karpinski and A.Z. Zelikovsky. 1.757 and 1.267-approximation algorithms for the network and rectilinear Steiner tree problems. 1994.

[Lin83] A. Lingas. *Advances in minimum weight triangulation*. Ph.D. thesis, Linköping Univ., 1983.

[LK96] C. Levcopoulos and D. Krznaric. Quasi-greedy triangulation approximating the min-imum weight triangulation. In *Proc. 7th ACM-SIAM Symp. Discrete Algorithms*, 1996.

[LL87] C. Levcopoulos and A. Lingas. On approximation behavior of the greedy triangula-tion for convex polygons. *Algorithmica*, 2:175–193, 1987.

[LL92] C. Levcopoulos and A. Lingas. Fast algorithms for greedy triangulation. *BIT*, 32:280–296, 1992. Also in *Proc. 2nd Scand. Worksh. Algorithm Theory*, Springer-Verlag, LNCS 447, 1990, pp. 238–250.

[LLKS85] E.L. Lawler, J.K. Lenstra, A.H.G. Rinnooy Kan, and D.B. Shmoys. *The Traveling Salesman Problem*. John Wiley, 1985.

[Llo77] E.L. Lloyd. On triangulations of a set of points in the plane. In *Proc. 18th IEEE Symp. Found. Comp. Sci.*, pages 228–240, 1977.

[LR88] F.T. Leighton and S. Rao. An approximate max-flow min-cut theorem for uniform multicommodity flow problems with applications to approximation algorithms. In *Proc. 29th IEEE Symp. Found. Comp. Sci.*, pages 422–431, 1988.

[Mat92] J. Matoušek. Reporting points in halfspaces. *Computational Geom. Theory & Appl.*, 2:169–186, 1992.

[Mel61] Z.A. Melzak. On the problem of Steiner. *Canad. Math. Bull.*, 4:143–148, 1961.

[Mit93] J.S.B. Mitchell. Approximation algorithms for geometric separation problems. Manu-script, 1993.

[Mit96] J.S.B. Mitchell. Guillotine subdivisions approximate polygonal subdivisions: a sim-ple new method for the geometric k-MST problem. In *Proc. 7th ACM-SIAM Symp. Discrete Algorithms*, 1996.

[MM95] C.S. Mata and J.S.B. Mitchell. Approximation algorithms for geometric tour and network design problems. In *Proc. 11th ACM Symp. Computational Geometry*, pages 360–369, 1995.

[MS84] N. Megiddo and K.J. Supowit. On the complexity of some common geometric loca-tion problems. *SIAM J. Comput.*, 13:182–196, 1984.

[MS92] J.S.B. Mitchell and S. Suri. Separation and approximation of polyhedral objects. In *Proc. 3rd ACM/SIAM Symp. Discrete Algorithms*, pages 296–306, 1992.

[MSW90] J. Matoušek, R. Seidel, and E. Welzl. How to net a lot with little: small ϵ-nets for disks and halfspaces. In *Proc. 6th ACM Symp. Computational Geom.*, pages 16–22, 1990.

[Mul94] K. Mulmuley. *Computational Geometry: An Introduction through Randomized Al-gorithms*. Prentice-Hall, Englewood Cliffs, 1994.

[MY80] W. Meeks and S.T. Yau. Topology of three-dimensional manifolds and the embed-ding problem in minimal surface theory. *Ann. Math.*, 112:441–485, 1980.

[MZ79] G.K. Manacher and A.L. Zobrist. Neither the greedy nor the Delaunay triangulation approximates the optimum. *Inform. Proc. Lett.*, 9:31–34, 1979.

[OTZ88] S. Olariu, S. Toida, and M. Zubair. On a conjecture by Plaisted and Hong. *J. Algo-rithms*, 9:597–598, 1988.

[Pap85] C. Papadimitriou. An algorithm for shortest-path motion in three dimensions. *In-form. Proc. Lett.*, 20:259–263, 1985.

[PH87] D.A. Plaisted and J. Hong. A heuristic triangulation algorithm. *J. Algorithms*, 8:405–437, 1987.

[PS85]   F.P.Preparata and M.I.Shamos. *Computational Geometry: An Introduction*. Springer-Verlag, 1985.

[PY90]   M.S. Paterson and F.F. Yao. Efficient binary space partitions for hidden-surface removal and solid modeling. *Disc. and Comp. Geometry*, 5:485–503, 1990.

[PY92]   M.S. Paterson and F.F. Yao. Optimal binary space partitions for orthogonal objects. *J. Algorithms*, 13:99–113, 1992.

[PY93]   C. Papadimitriou and M. Yannakakis. The traveling salesman problem with distances one and two. *Math. Oper. Research*, 18:1–11, 1993.

[RSL77]   D.J. Rosenkrantz, R.E. Stearns, and P.M. Lewis. An analysis of several heuristics for the traveling salesman problem. *SIAM J. Comput.*, 6:563–581, 1977.

[RSM+94] R. Ravi, R. Sundaram, M.V. Marathe, D.J. Rosenkrantz, and S.S. Ravi. Spanning trees short and small. In *Proc. 5th ACM-SIAM Symp. Discrete Algorithms*, pages 546–555, 1994.

[RT91a]   J.H. Rubinstein and D.A. Thomas. The Steiner ratio conjecture for six points. *J. of Combinatorial Theory, Ser. A*, 58:54–77, 1991.

[RT91b]   J.H. Rubinstein and D.A. Thomas. A variational approach to the Steiner network problem. In J. MacGregor Smith and P. Winter, editors, *Topological Network Design, Annals of Operations Research 33*, pages 481–500. J.C. Baltzer AG, Basel, 1991.

[Sil79]   C.B. Silio. An efficient simplex coverability algorithm in E^2 with application to stochastic sequential machines. *IEEE Transactions on Computers*, C-28:109–120, 1979.

[Smi88]   W.D. Smith. Finding the optimum N-city traveling salesman tour in the Euclidean plane in subexponential time and polynomial space. Manuscript, 1988.

[Smi89]   W.D. Smith. Implementing the Plaisted-Hong min-length plane triangulation heuristic. Manuscript cited by [Cla91], 1989.

[Smi92]   W.D. Smith. How to find Steiner minimal trees in Euclidean d-space. *Algorithmica*, 7:137–179, 1992.

[Sur90]   S. Suri. On some link distance problems in a simple polygon. *IEEE Trans. Robotics and Automation*, 6:108–113, 1990.

[Vai88]   P. Vaidya. Geometry helps in matching. In *Proc. 20th ACM Symp. Theory of Computing*, pages 422–425, 1988.

[Vai89]   P. Vaidya. An $O(n \log n)$ algorithm for the all-nearest-neighbors problem. *Disc. and Comp. Geometry*, 4:101–115, 1989.

[War93]   A.R. Warburton. Worst-case analysis of some convex hull heuristics for the Euclidean traveling salesman problem. *Oper. Res. Lett.*, 13:37–42, 1993.

[WW95]   F. Wagner and A. Wolff. Map labeling heuristics: provably good and practically useful. In *Proc. 11th ACM Symp. Comp. Geometry*, pages 109–118, 1995.

[Zel92]   A.Z. Zelikovsky. An 11/8-approximation algorithm for the Steiner problem in networks with rectilinear distance. *Coll. Math. Soc. J. Bolyai*, 60:733–745, 1992.

[Zel93]   A.Z. Zelikovsky. An 11/6-approximation algorithm for the network Steiner problem. *Algorithmica*, 9:463–470, 1993.

[Zel94]   A.Z. Zelikovsky. Better approximation bounds for the network and Euclidean Steiner tree problems. Manuscript, 1994.

[ZL93]   A.Z. Zelikovsky and D.D. Lozovanu. Minimal and bounded trees. In *Tezele Congresului XVIII al Academiei Romano-Americane*, pages 25–26. Kishinev, 1993.

9

VARIOUS NOTIONS OF APPROXIMATIONS: GOOD, BETTER, BEST, AND MORE

Dorit S. Hochbaum

How good is an approximation algorithm? We investigate some criteria for evaluating the quality of approximation algorithms. The quality will be measured primarily in terms of the worst-case error ratio, but also in terms of running time. This chapter explores the nature of various approximation criteria with the goal of determining the approximability of *NP*-hard optimization problems.

INTRODUCTION

9.1

A natural question to consider when presented with several approximation algorithms for a problem, is to what extent could these be improved in terms of their error bounds and running times. In other words, what is the true *approximability* of the problem—the best performance ratio achievable in polynomial time? Here we review approximation algorithms with the answer to this question in mind.

The technique of holographic proofs (discussed in Chapter 10) has succeeded in demonstrating that approximation schemes are unlikely for Max-$\mathcal{SNP}$-hard problems. In that, the technique provides lower bounds to the approximability of some problems. There have been additional stronger lower bound results for several other problems such as clique and coloring. Here we consider different approaches for addressing this same question and cases in which the actual approximability of problems has been established.

The purpose of this chapter is to explore the limits of polynomial approximation algorithms for NP-hard problems.

Approximation algorithms for various problems differ quite substantially in terms of the quality of the ratio or worst case error bound. It is tempting to assess the difficulty of a hard problem as proportional to the possible approximation. Consider for instance the Knapsack problem that is viewed as "easy" among NP-hard problems. The Knapsack problem is to maximize the utility of a collection of items that fit in a knapsack of volume $B : \max\{\sum p_j x_j \mid \sum a_j x_j \leq B, \ x \in \{0, 1\}^n\}$. For the Knapsack problem there is a family of algorithms $\{\mathcal{A}_\epsilon\}$ such that $\mathcal{A}_\epsilon$ runs in time polynomial in the length of the input and in $\frac{1}{\epsilon}$, and produces a $(1 - \epsilon)$-approximate solution, i.e. a solution that is at least $(1 - \epsilon)$ times the maximum. We call such a family of algorithms a *fully polynomial approximation scheme* or FPAS. (The corresponding definition for a minimization problem has $(1 + \epsilon)$-approximation algorithms in the family.) In fact, FPASs are quite rare and are known mostly for problems that structurally resemble the Knapsack problem. One such exception is the the problem of minimizing the variance of completion times of jobs on a single machine. A FPAS was described by De Ghosh and Wells [DGW92], and the problem was proved NP-complete by Kubiak [K93] (and earlier by Cai). Another interesting exception is the recent discovery by Barvinok [Bar94] of a FPAS for the Euclidean maximum-tour length traveling salesman problem MAX TSP in a Euclidean space of bounded dimension. This problem is not known to be NP-hard in Euclidean spaces, and one may take the existence of a FPAS as a clue to the polynomiality of the problem in a Euclidean space. If NP-hard, this problem will form a notable and surprising exception compared to other problems that have FPASs.

Another good approximation is a *polynomial approximation scheme*, PAS, where like FPAS there is a family of algorithms $\{\mathcal{A}_\epsilon\}$ such that $\mathcal{A}_\epsilon$ produces a $(1 + \epsilon)$-approximate solution. Unlike FPAS, a PAS runs in time that is polynomial in the length of the input for fixed ϵ. That is, the running time may be exponential in $\frac{1}{\epsilon}$.

The next "level" in the quality of approximations are constant ratio approximations. Here it is reasonable to compare approximation algorithms by how close their worst-case ratio is to 1, and this is for algorithms with "tight" worst case performance bound—namely, where there are instances for which this performance ratio is actually achieved. There is some empirical evidence to suggest that the quality of a solution delivered by an approximation algorithm is correlated to its worst-case ratio.

For constant factor approximations the concept of best possible approximations can be defined. It is the smallest ratio (for minimization problems) that can be achieved in polynomial time, unless $NP = P$. For PAS and FPAS any approximation factor is possible. Yet the running time as a function of $\frac{1}{\epsilon}$ can differ, and quite substantially. In the section on "better" algorithms we show a FPAS for Knapsack with running time $C_1(\epsilon)n + C_2(\epsilon)$ and a PAS for the minimum makespan problems with running time $n + C_3(\epsilon)$ where $C_i(\epsilon)$ are all constants when ϵ is constant. So for fixed ϵ the minimum makespan is presumably more efficiently solvable than the Knapsack in spite of the fact that it is strongly NP-complete, whereas the Knapsack is weakly NP-complete. We elaborate further on these issues in Section 9.3.

Variations in the manner in which the problem is presented or the error ratio is defined can dramatically influence the approximation result. We demonstrate how the formulation of a problem as a maximization problem rather than a minimization problem can affect the outcome. In the section on "better than best" we discuss error criteria that allow for additive error, and hence, deliver results that are seemingly inconsistent with the $NP \neq P$ qualification.

This chapter is an excursion through approximation results sorted according to the "good," "better," "best," "better than best," and "wonderful" categories. We warn the naive reader against interpreting these labels literally.

9.1.1   OVERVIEW OF CHAPTER

Section 9.2 discusses recent developments for the vertex feedback problem in undirected graphs and the implications for the vertex cover problem. Another problem analyzed is the shortest superstring and how it relates to approximating the MAX TSP problem. The algorithms are all "good" in that they guarantee constant ratio approximations. In the context of relating the formulation of the problem as maximization versus minimization, we discuss the k-cluster, k-median, the directed vertex feedback, and the shortest superstring problems.

Section 9.3 includes details of polynomial and fully polynomial approximation schemes (PAS and FPAS, respectively). For the Knapsack problem the PAS described is used to demonstrate the technique of scaling and the separation of "small" and "large" items. A PAS is given for the minimum makespan problem where the technique of dual approximation, "grouping," and the dual relationship between minimum makespan and bin packing is highlighted. Again, we make use of a small/large separation. A new implementation of the dual approximation scheme provides a PAS that runs in linear time for fixed ϵ.

The section describes PAS for geometric problems of the covering and packing type. Examples of such problems include covering points in a Euclidean space with minimum number of spheres or boxes or other geometric objects. In planar graphs the problems that have a similar structure are the independent set, the vertex cover, and the matching problem. The unifying technique that makes these PASs possible is the shifting strategy.

In Section 9.4 we have best possible approximation ratio results that cannot be improved unless $NP = P$. One such problem is the k-center problem where the described 2-approximation algorithm is best possible since a $(2 - \delta)$-approximation for the k-center problem with triangle inequality is NP-complete for any $\delta > 0$. A collection of other problems for which best possible results are obtained is described with the unifying technique of powers of graphs. All these problems for which best possible results were obtained are of "bottleneck type."

In the section on "better than best" algorithms we demonstrate how the introduction of additive errors and different performance criteria leads to results that seemingly provide better approximations than was proved possible. These include a FPAS for the bin-packing problem which is strongly NP-complete and approximation algorithms for edge coloring in multigraphs. The technique of grouping is used for bin-packing, whereas for edge coloring we show how the approximation ratio limits the size of the subgraphs where the recoloring procedure needs to take place.

As for truly astounding approximation algorithms we present in Section 9.6 "Wonderful" several algorithms that deliver a solution within one additive unit of the optimum.

These are the problems of edge coloring in simple graphs, coloring of planar graphs, and minimizing the maximum degree in a spanning tree—a problem elaborated on in Chapter 7.

GOOD: FIXED CONSTANT APPROXIMATIONS

9.2

We consider an approximation algorithm to be *good* if it has a δ-approximation for some constant δ. One difficulty is to determine whether an approximation result obtained could be further improved, and if so—to what extent. This is the main theme of this chapter. To illustrate these difficulties we present some examples of the evolution of approximation results for several *NP*-hard problems.

The vertex cover problem is one such example. Initially, a logarithmic approximation bound was known that later was improved to a factor of 2, with better results known for special classes (see Table 3.1). Hochbaum [Hoc83] conjectured that no approximation better than 2 is possible. Indeed, no such approximation has been discovered to date. On the other hand, Bellare, Goldreich, and Sudan [BGS95] were able to show that approximating vertex cover to within $\frac{16}{15}$ is *NP*-hard. That still leaves the gap between 2 and $\frac{16}{15}$ open. It is open in the sense that we cannot tell if better approximation algorithms do not exist, or that we simply failed to find them so far. Details on various algorithms to approximate the vertex cover problem and its special cases are given in Chapter 3.

Another example is the MAX CUT problem and the related MAX 2SAT. For the MAX 2SAT, approximation ratios progressed from $\frac{1}{2}$ to 0.75 ([Yan92], [GW94a]) to 0.87856 [GW94b], and then to 0.931 (Feige-Goemans in the 1995 Israeli Symposium). For MAXCUT, the progression was from $\frac{1}{2}$ to 0.87856 [GW94b]. For MAX SAT, the progression was from $\frac{1}{2}$ to 0.75 ([Yan92], [GW94a]) to 0.7584 [GW94b]. Again, it is not known to what extent these approximation could be further improved, if at all. Details about some of these algorithms along with the remarkable tools of derandomization and semidefinite programming employed for them are given in Chapter 11.

In this section we focus on two problems that raised a great deal of interest recently. This interest was accompanied by a sequence of approximation algorithms with progressively improved bounds. One problem is the weighted vertex feedback set problem in undirected graphs. The other is finding for a collection of strings the shortest superstring containing each string in the collection. We also talk about the directed version of the vertex feedback set problem and on the affect on the approximation ratio of formulating a problem as a maximization versus a minimization problem.

9.2.1   THE WEIGHTED UNDIRECTED VERTEX FEEDBACK SET PROBLEM

In an undirected graph $G = (V, E)$, a set F of vertices is a *vertex feedback set* (VFS) if it contains at least one vertex from every cycle in G. For each vertex $v \in V$, let $w(v)$ be a nonnegative weight. A vertex feedback set F^* has minimum weight if

$w(F^*) = \sum_{v \in F^*} w(v)$ is minimum among all VFSs. This problem is known to be NP-hard [GJ79] as well as Max-$\mathcal{SNP}$-hard (see Chapter 10) implying that it has no PAS unless $NP = P$.

The *arc feedback set* in an undirected graph is a complement of a spanning tree. As such, the minimum arc feedback set for both minimization and maximization objective in an undirected graph is polynomially solvable.

Both arc and vertex feedback set problems are defined also for directed graphs. Here the objective is to remove a minimum weight collection of arcs (vertices) so that the remaining graph has no directed cycles. For directed graphs the vertex feedback and the arc feedback problems are equivalent using a well-known reduction: replace each vertex i by a pair i', i'' with the arc (i', i''). All incoming arcs to i are then directed into i' and all outgoing arcs leave vertex i''. For the opposite direction, introduce for each arc (i, j) a new vertex v_{ij} and replace the arc by the two arcs (i, v_{ij}) and (v_{ij}, i).

The directed arc feedback problem is closely related to the problem of directed multi-cuts and the multicommodity flow problem. For more on the multicommodity problem and this relationship see Chapter 5. So far the techniques used for the directed problem have been dramatically different from those used for the undirected problem. If there is a way of unifying the approaches to the directed and undirected versions of the problem, this has not been evident to date. We will say more about the directed problem in the context of comparing minimization and maximization objectives in terms of approximations in Section 9.2.3.

Many of the applications of the undirected vertex feedback set problem (VFS problem) use the fact that solving problems on acyclic graphs is substantially easier than on graphs containing cycles. For instance, the testing of circuits with feedback cycles introduces substantial difficulty. To facilitate the process the aim is to find a similar circuit without cycles. Depending on whether vertices or edges are removed from the original circuit, the measure of dissimilarity is increased.

The unweighted version of the problem where all $w(v) = 1$ has been investigated by Erdös and Pósa who proved a $2 \log n$ approximation ratio, [EP62]. This was later improved by Monien and Schultz to a ratio of $\sqrt{\log n}$, [MS81]. In 1994, Bar-Yehuda, Geiger, Naor, and Roth [BGNR94] showed that the problem can be approximated within a constant ratio of 4 in the unweighted case. For the weighted case they described an approximation algorithm with a performance ratio of $\min\{4 \log n, 2\Delta^2\}$ where Δ is the maximum degree in G. They also demonstrated an approximation preserving reduction from the vertex cover problem to the vertex feedback problem (see Subsection 9.2.1.1).

Recently, the approximation ratio for VFS was proved to match that of vertex cover. Becker and Geiger [BG94] and independently Bafna, Berman, and Fujito [BBF94] demonstrated algorithms approximating both the weighted and unweighted cases within a factor of 2. As we shall see, the VFS problem is a specific type of the set cover problem. We will highlight the differences and similarities in approaches between those problems. We then show that approximating the VFS problem is an extension of approximating the vertex cover problem, and the algorithms described here also form new 2-approximations algorithms for the vertex cover problem.

The VFS problem is a covering problem, as the objective is to cover all cycles with smallest cost collection of vertices. As is frequently the case with covering-type problems, a linear programming formulation along with a dual approach (the LP-algorithm in Chapter 3) provides some insight. Given a vertex feedback set F for a graph G with a set of weights $\mathbf{w} = [w(v)]_{v \in V}$, $(G, \mathbf{w})$. Let $\mathbf{x} = [x_v]_{v \in V(G)}$ be the indicator vector of F, namely, $x_v = 1$ if $v \in F$ and $x_v = 0$ otherwise. We denote by $\mathcal{C}$ the set of cycles in G. The problem of finding a minimum-weight vertex feedback set of (G, w) can be formulated as an integer programming problem:

$$\begin{aligned} \text{Min} \quad & \sum_{v \in V(G)} w(v) \cdot x_v \\ \text{subject to} \quad & \sum_{v \in V(\Gamma)} x_v \geq 1 \quad \text{for every} \quad \Gamma \in \mathcal{C} \\ & 1 \geq x_v \geq 0 \text{ integer} \quad (v \in V). \end{aligned}$$

Let $\mathcal{C}_v$ denote the set of cycles passing through vertex v in G, and consider the dual of the linear programming relaxation of the above problem which is a *packing* problem:

$$\begin{aligned} \text{Max} \quad & \sum_{\Gamma \in \mathcal{C}} y_\Gamma \\ \text{subject to} \quad & \sum_{\Gamma \in \mathcal{C}_v} y_\Gamma \leq w(v) \quad \text{for every} \quad v \in V \\ & y_\Gamma \geq 0 \quad \text{for every} \quad \Gamma \in \mathcal{C}. \end{aligned}$$

The goal is now to find a dual-feasible solution that is maximal so that the binding dual constraints correspond to a selection of vertices that is a feasible VFS. The above formulation does not address the question on which quantities to assign as dual costs and to what subgraphs.

Recall from Chapter 3 that there are several approaches for finding a maximal dual feasible solution: An optimal dual solution; a feasible dual solution generated by increasing a dual variable for one violated constraint—uncovered element—at a time (the feasible dual algorithm—see Chapter 3); use of the local ratio lemma that permits an increase of dual costs for an entire subgraph at a time; proportional increase of a dual variable in an alternative formulation that allows constraint matrix coefficients other than 0 or 1.

Bar-Yehuda, Geiger, Naor, and Roth [BGNR94] used a dual feasible algorithm with an assignment of dual costs that gave a solution with a logarithmic performance ratio. Becker and Geiger used in essence the second approach combined with an inequality about the degrees of a VFS. Bafna, Berman, and Fujito used the third approach also combined with an inequality about the degrees of a VFS. We will show that both algorithms are essentially the same and add yet another algorithm using different LP formulations.

A critical factor in deriving a good approximate solution for VFS is that the approximate solution will be minimal (for the set cover problem, whether or not it is minimal has no effect on the performance ratio of any known approximation algorithm). Given a feasible VFS, F, generated in the order $\{v_1, \ldots, v_q\}$, it is easy to achieve a minimal one: remove the vertices of F one at a time in reverse order $\{v_q, \ldots, v_1\}$. With each removal record the set of vertices $\{V_{v_q}, \ldots, V_{v_1}\}$ that got recursively removed as their degree is ≤ 1. All these are placed in a stack. The sets removed by each vertex are now added to the empty graph one at a time $V_{v_q}, \ldots, V_{v_1}$ and with each we add the respective vertex v_i. If v_i creates a cycle in the graph induced by those vertices, it is placed in the minimal VFS, or else it is discarded. When we refer to the step of "removing redundant vertices from F," these are the algorithmic steps that need to be applied.

A key to the analysis of the approximation algorithms is discovering that the degree of a node is a good estimator to the number of cycles it covers. The 2-approximation result relies additionally on a result relating the sum of degrees of a *minimal* vertex feedback set F to that of any other vertex feedback set, $\bar{F}$. In particular, $\bar{F}$ could be chosen to be the minimum VFS. We denote the degree of a vertex v by $d(v)$.

LEMMA 9.1   Let F be a minimal VFS and $\bar{F}$ be any feasible VFS. Let the graph $G = (V, E)$ have all vertices of degree 2 or more. Let k be a lower bound on the cardinality of a minimum VFS, then

$$\sum_{v \in F} d(v) \le 2(|E| - |V| + k) < 2(|E| - |V| + |\bar{F}| + 1) \overset{(a)}{\le} 2 \sum_{v \in \bar{F}} d(v). \qquad (9.1)$$

For graphs G without disjoint cycles and almost disjoint cycles (graphs that are 2-vertex connected),

$$\sum_{v \in F} [d(v) - 1] \le 2(|E| - |V|) < 2(|E| - |V| + 1) \overset{(b)}{\le} 2 \sum_{v \in \bar{F}} [d(v) - 1]. \qquad (9.2)$$

Proof.   The removal of $\bar{F}$ leaves a forest, hence, the subgraph induced on $V \setminus \bar{F}$ can have at most $|V| - |\bar{F}| - 1$ edges. Therefore, $|E| \le |V| - |\bar{F}| - 1 + \sum_{v \in \bar{F}} d(v)$ and,

$$\sum_{v \in \bar{F}} [d(v) - 1] \ge |E| - |V| + 1.$$

This establishes the rightmost inequalities (a) and (b) in (9.1) and (9.2).

Consider now the leftmost inequality in (9.2) restated as

$$\sum_{v \in F} [d(v) - 1] \le \sum_{v \in V} [d(v) - 2].$$

Rewriting this inequality as $|F| + \sum_{v \in F} [d(v) - 2] \le \sum_{v \in V} [d(v) - 2]$ yields that it is equivalent to

$$|F| \le \sum_{v \in V \setminus F} [d(v) - 2]. \qquad (9.3)$$

This inequality is applicable only to graphs without disjoint cycles and almost disjoint cycles.

For a minimal VFS, F, each vertex v of F is contained in a cycle, called an _associated cycle_ of v, in which all the other vertices come from $V \setminus F$. Let vertices x and y be the first vertices of degree ≥ 3 encountered when progressing from v along both directions in the associated cycle. Both x and y belong to $V \setminus F$ (these two vertices may be a single vertex). We call the vertices of degree ≥ 3 encountered, _witness_ vertices for v. Each $v \in F$ has one or two witness vertices. For a given witness vertex w, let $F_2 \subset F$ be the set of vertices of F for which w is the unique witness vertex, and let $F_1 \subset F$ be the set of vertices of F for which w is one of two witness vertices. When following its associated cycle, each vertex of F_2 reaches w along two edges adjacent to w, whereas each vertex of F_1 reaches w along a single edge adjacent to it.

The vertices of F_1 must each lie on its own associated cycle and have no witness vertex between it and w. As a result each pair of vertices of F_1 lie on two adjacent cycles that share a path of edges adjacent to w and contribute a total of 3 units to the degree of w. The set F_1 accounts therefore for a total of $\frac{3}{2}|F_1|$ edges that are adjacent to w, and F_2 accounts for another $2|F_2|$ edges adjacent to w. Therefore,

$$d(w) \ge 2|F_2| + \frac{3}{2}|F_1|.$$

If $F_1 \ne \emptyset$ then $|F_1| \ge 2$ and $d(w) \ge 2|F_2| + |F_1| + 1$. The average "contribution" of each witness vertex from the right hand side of (9.3) to a vertex of F_1 is at least,

$$\frac{d(w)-2}{2|F_2|+|F_1|} \geq \frac{d(w)-2}{d(w)-1} \geq \frac{1}{2}.$$

Since the contribution to a vertex of F_1 comes from two witness vertices, and the contribution to a vertex of F_2 is double, we allocate for each vertex of F a total of 1 unit to the left-hand side of the inequality (9.3) from the right-hand side of (9.3).

In order to prove the leftmost inequality in (9.1), we first restate it as, $2|F| + \sum_{v \in F}[d(v) - 2] \leq \sum_{v \in V}[d(v) - 2] + 2k$. This is equivalent to $2(|F| - k) \leq \sum_{v \in V \setminus F}[d(v) - 2]$.

Let the associated cycles of F be indexed so that a maximum collection of vertex disjoint cycles are indexed $C_1, \ldots, C_k$ followed by $C_{k+1} \ldots, C_{|F|}$. k is obviously a lower bound to a minimum cardinality VFS.

Consider adding recursively one cycle at a time C_{i+1} to the subgraph on $\{C_1, \ldots, C_i\}$ for $i \geq k$. Let v be the vertex of F on C_{i+1} and x and y its witness vertices (as before, x and y may be a single vertex). In the new subgraph there are two edges added adjacent to x and y, hence the right-hand side is increased by 2 for each addition of 2 units to the left-hand side. ∎

We are now ready to state the algorithm of Bafna et al. It implies a decomposition of the graph (indicated in $\{\ \}$ as part of the algorithm's description) which is used solely for the purpose of the analysis. The graphs G_i form the decomposition with $w_i(v)$ being the increase in the dual cost of v during the ith recurrence.

BBF APPROXIMATION ALGORITHM FOR MINIMUM VERTEX FEEDBACK SET

Step 0: $F = \emptyset$. While the graph contains vertices of degree ≤ 1, remove such vertices and adjacent edges recursively. $\{i \leftarrow 1\}$.

Step 1: While there exists a disjoint cycle or an almost disjoint cycle, Γ, let $\delta \leftarrow \min\{w(v) | v \in \Gamma\}$. Set $w(v) \leftarrow w(v) - \delta$ for every $v \in \Gamma$
$\{G_i = \Gamma$ and $w_i(v) = \delta$ for every $v \in \Gamma$. $i \leftarrow i + 1\}$.

Step 2: Set $\delta \leftarrow \min\{\frac{w(v)}{d(v)-1} | v \in V\}$
Set $w(v) \leftarrow w(v) - \delta(d(v) - 1)$ for every $v \in V$
$\{G_i = G$ and $w_i(v) = \delta(d(v) - 1)$ for every $v \in V$, which is the dual cost assigned to the vertex $i \leftarrow i + 1.\}$
$\{update\}$ Remove recursively all vertices of degree ≤ 1.

Step 3: If $V = \emptyset$, set $F = \{v | w(v) = 0\}$. Remove redundant vertices from F. Stop and output cycle cover F. Else go to Step 1.

The algorithm of [BG94] is virtually identical, except that Step 1 is applicable only for disjoint cycles and $d(v) - 1$ is replaced by $d(v)$. It is also possible in that algorithm to do away with Step 1 and not distinguish the case of disjoint cycles. This is because in a disjoint cycle all vertices are of degree 2, and hence, a vertex that minimizes the ratio of weight to the degree also minimizes the weight. Consequently, $G_i = G$ for each iteration i, and the algorithm is somewhat cleaner.

There are two concepts that make algorithm BBF work. One is the inequality on the sum of degrees, (9.2). The other is the concept of decomposition related to the local ratio lemma previously applied to the vertex cover problem (see Chapter 3). A collection of $(G_i, w_i)'s$ $i = 1, \ldots, k$ is said to be a *convex decomposition* of (G, w) if $G = \cup G_i$ and $\Sigma_{1 \leq i \leq k} w_i(v) \leq w(v)$ for each $v \in V$, where $w_i(v) = 0$ if $v \notin V_i$. The algorithm identifies a feasible minimal VFS, F such that $\Sigma_{1 \leq i \leq k} w_i(v) = w(v)$ for each $v \in F$, and such that $\frac{w_i(F \cap V_i)}{w_i(F^* \cap V_i)} \leq 2$ as shown in the next lemma.

LEMMA 9.2   Algorithm BBF is a 2-approximation algorithm for the VFS problem.

Proof.   The set F produced by the algorithm is a minimal VFS, as at termination there are no uncovered cycles in G. Consider the convex decomposition (G, w) implied by the algorithm. For G_i generated in Step 1, it is a cycle—disjoint or almost disjoint. In either case, $\frac{w_i(F \cap V_i)}{w_i(F^* \cap V_i)} = 1$ for cycles. As for the other subgraphs in the convex decomposition, the ratio of 2 will be proved for each G_i by supplying minimal VFS satisfying (9.2). Let $d^{(i)}(v)$ be the degree on node v in G_i. For the convex decomposition produced by the algorithm one has,

$$w(F^*) \geq \sum_i \sum_{v \in F^* \cap V_i} w_i(v) = \sum_i \delta_i \sum_{v \in F^* \cap V_i} (d^{(i)}(v) - 1)$$

$$\overset{(9.2)}{\geq} \frac{1}{2} \sum_i \sum_{v \in F_i} \delta_i [d^{(i)}(v) - 1] = \frac{1}{2} w(F).$$

∎

Alternative relaxations: Goemans and Williamson proposed an interesting approach using an innovative form of relaxation for the problem. Observe that inequalities (a) and (b) in Lemma 9.1 apply to any VFS. Given a graph $G = (V, E)$ and a subset S of vertices, let $G[S]$ denote the subgraph $(S, E[S])$ induced by S. Let $d_S(v)$ denote the degree of vertex v in $G[S]$. Let $b(S) = |E[S]| - |S| + 1$.

Since inequality (b) is valid for any feasible VFS, the following linear program is a relaxation of the VFS problem:

$$\begin{array}{lll} \text{Min} & \sum_{v \in V} w(v) x_v & \\ \text{subject to} & \sum_{v \in S} (d_S(v) - 1) x_v \geq b(S) & S \subseteq V \\ & x_v \geq 0 & v \in V. \end{array}$$

The dual of this relaxation is:

$$\begin{array}{lll} \text{Max} & \sum_S b(S) y_S & \\ \text{subject to} & \sum_{S : v \in S} (d_S(v) - 1) y_S \leq w(v) & v \in V \\ & y_S \geq 0 & S \subseteq V. \end{array}$$

The algorithm now builds a feasible dual solution using proportional increase of the dual costs as described in Chapter 4: Start with $F = \emptyset$ and $\mathbf{y} = 0$. Given a set F, if it is not a feasible VFS there must exist a cycle in $G[V - F]$. Now choose some violated set S in $G[V - F]$ that will be a single 2 vertex-connected component. Increase y_S as much as possible until some dual inequality becomes binding, say for vertex v. Add v to F and repeat. When F is a FVS, remove redundant vertices so as to render it minimal.

LEMMA 9.3   The feasible dual algorithm is a 2-approximation algorithm for the VFS problem.

Proof.   If $y_S > 0$ then from Lemma 9.1 $\sum_{v \in S \cap F}(d_S(v) - 1) \leq 2b(S)$. Now,

$$\sum_{v \in F} w(v) = \sum_{v \in F'} \sum_{S:v \in S}(d_S(v) - 1)y_S = \sum_S [\sum_{v \in S \cap F'}(d_S(v) - 1)]y_S \leq 2\sum_S b(S)y_S.$$

Since y_S is a dual feasible solution, then $\sum_S b(S)y_S$ bounds from below the optimal linear program value, and hence, the optimal integer value—the weight of the minimum weight VFS.

Note that this actually proves that the algorithm guarantees a ratio of $(2 - 1/(|E| - 1))$.   ∎

An almost identical algorithm follows using inequality (a): Let $\tau(S)$ be the *cardinality* of the smallest VFS in $G[S]$. Consider now the relaxation,

$$
\begin{array}{ll}
\text{Min} & \sum_{v \in V} w(v)x_v \\
\text{subject to} & \sum_{v \in S} d_S(v)x_v \geq b'(S) \qquad S \subseteq V \\
& x_v \geq 0 \qquad v \in V
\end{array}
$$

where $b'(S) = |E[S]| + \tau(S) - |S| + 1$. Again consider the dual,

$$
\begin{array}{ll}
\text{Max} & \sum_S b'(S)y_S \\
\text{subject to} & \sum_{S:v \in S} d_S(v)y_S \leq w(v) \qquad v \in V \\
& y_S \geq 0 \qquad S \subseteq V.
\end{array}
$$

A proportional increase algorithm combined with inequality (9.1) is proved analogously to be a 2-approximation algorithm.

9.2.1.1   Approximation preserving reduction between VFS and vertex cover

A vertex cover of an undirected graph is a subset of the vertex set that is incident with every edge in the graph. The vertex cover problem is to find a minimum weight vertex cover. The approximation preserving polynomial reduction from the vertex cover problem to the vertex feedback set problem is as follows: Given a graph G, we extend G to a graph H by adding a vertex v_e for each edge $e \in E(G)$, and connecting v_e with the vertices in G with which e is incident in G. It is easy to verify that there always exists a minimum vertex feedback set in H whose vertices are all in $V(G)$ and this vertex feedback set is also a minimum vertex cover of G. In essence, this reduction replaces each edge in G with a cycle in H, thus transforming any vertex cover of G to a vertex feedback set of H.

The implication of this reduction is that if there is a better than 2-approximation for the vertex feedback problem, then there is such an approximation for the vertex cover problems as well. As described in Chapter 3, there have been many attempts to achieve an approximation ratio smaller than 2 for the vertex cover problem, and so far these attempts were unsuccessful. This does not bode well for efforts to improve the approximation factor of 2 for the VFS problem.

On the positive side, one can use the approximations for VFS in order to derive new approximation algorithms for vertex cover.

9.2.1.2   New vertex cover approximation algorithms

Interestingly, the algorithms presented for the VFS problem translate to new 2-approximation algorithms for the vertex cover problem. We first observe that the two inequalities on the degrees, (9.1) (9.2), apply to the vertex cover problem, with a slight adjustment.

LEMMA 9.4   Let $\bar{C}$ be a feasible vertex cover and C be any set of vertices, then,

$$\sum_{v \in C} d(v) \leq 2|E| \leq 2 \sum_{v \in \bar{C}} d(v). \tag{9.4}$$

Let $\bar{C}$ be a feasible vertex cover and C be a minimal vertex cover in a graph with all nodes not in C of degree at least 2,

$$\sum_{v \in C} [2d(v) - 1] \leq 2(2|E| - |V|) \leq 2 \sum_{v \in \bar{C}} [2d(v) - 1]. \tag{9.5}$$

Proof.   Inequality (9.4) is obvious: a feasible vertex cover set has all edges adjacent to it, hence $|E| \leq \sum_{v \in \bar{C}} d(v)$. For any set of nodes $C \subseteq V$, $\sum_{v \in C} d(v) \leq 2|E|$.

For inequality (9.5), since $\bar{C}$ is a feasible vertex cover,

$$\sum_{v \in \bar{C}} [2d(v) - 1] \geq 2|E| - |\bar{C}| \geq 2|E| - |V| = \sum_{v \in V} [d(v) - 1].$$

It remains to show that $\frac{1}{2}|C| \leq \sum_{v \in V} [d(v) - 1]$. For $v \in C$ let n_v be its associated neighbor (the one corresponding to the edge covered only by v). n_v may be associated with up to $d(n_v)$ other vertices of C. Its contribution to the right-hand side per the vertex of C it is associated with, is at least

$$\frac{d(n_v) - 1}{d(n_v)} \geq \frac{1}{2}.$$

Hence, the left-hand side is accounted for fully as well.   ∎

The four analogous 2-approximation algorithms for vertex cover are based on

- Identifying a vertex with smallest ratio $\frac{w(v)}{d(v)}$.

- Identifying a vertex with smallest ratio $\frac{w(v)}{d(v)-1}$, after recursively removing degree 1 vertices and for each edge thus removed, place the cheaper endpoint in the VFS. When done, redundant vertices must be removed.

- Linear programming relaxation and its dual based on inequality (9.4).

- Linear programming relaxation and its dual based on inequality (9.5). Again, the relaxation can be applied after recursively removing degree 1 vertices and for each edge thus removed, place the cheaper endpoint in the VFS. When done, redundant vertices must be removed.

The algorithms are immediate and are not stated here. It is interesting to note that the algorithm implied by inequality (9.1) is already known for vertex cover (see dual-feasible II algorithm in Chapter 3).

EXERCISE 9.1   Describe and prove the validity of the two vertex cover 2-approximation algorithms resulting from the analogous relaxations of VFS.

9.2.2   THE SHORTEST SUPERSTRING PROBLEM

Given a finite set of strings, the shortest superstring problem is to find a string s such that every string in the set is a substring of s, and such that s is as short as possible. The shortest superstring problem is another example of a problem for which a sequence of results has been produced, and yet little is known about the ultimate approximability of this problem.

Consider two strings s_i and s_j. Let u, v, w be substrings so that $s_i = uv$ and $s_j = vw$. The superstring s_i, s_j is uvw. The length of v, $|v|$ is the *overlap* denoted by $ov(s_i, s_j)$. u is the *prefix* of s_i in s_i, s_j. It is assumed w.l.o.g. that no string in the set given is a substring of another. Such substrings can be discarded at the outset.

The shortest superstring problem has applications in data compression and in the sequencing of DNA. A greedy algorithm that repeatedly merges strings with largest overlap is routinely used to assemble the superstrings. For this reason, it is of particular interest to establish the performance ratio of a solution delivered by the greedy algorithm.

Li established that the greedy algorithm delivers a solution that is at most $\log n$ times the length of the shortest superstring n [Li90]. Blum, Jiang, Li, Tromp, and Yannakakis [BJTY91] achieved a substantial improvement by showing that greedy is a 4-approximation algorithm. They further gave another algorithm that achieves an approximation factor of 3. In addition, Kosaraju, Park and Stein [KPS94] pointed out that the arguments in [BJTY91] imply a relationship between the superstring problem and the longest traveling salesman tour problem (MAX TSP): Given a $(\frac{1}{2} + \epsilon)$-approximation for the directed MAX TSP it is possible to convert into to a $(3 - 2\epsilon)$-approximation for the shortest superstring problem. This relationship has been crucial in the algorithms that further improved the performance bounds. We elaborate in this section on the 4-approximation algorithm and the relationship to MAX TSP.

Any instance of the shortest superstring problem has two types of directed graphs associated with it. The first, the *distance graph*, has a node for each string and for each arc (i, j) the number of characters in the prefix of $s_i s_j$ associated with it as a distance label. After adding a node of distance 0 to and from all other nodes of the graph, the directed traveling salesman problem tour corresponds to a shortest superstring. The second digraph is the *overlap* graph where each arc (i, j) has $ov(s_i, s_j)$ (which is the number of characters in the overlap when the strings $s_i s_j$ are concatenated) associated with it. Again, when such node as above is added, the directed *maximum* traveling salesman problem (MAX TSP) corresponds then to a shortest superstring.

It is interesting to digress at this point about the differences between these two formulations of the shortest superstring problem. Although minimizing the distance or maximizing the overlap will both give the same optimal solution, the two models of the problem differ sharply with regard to approximations. We leave the detailed discussion on the affect of the choice of minimum formulation versus the maximum formulation to the next subsection.

9.2.2.1   A 4-approximation algorithm

To see how the 4-approximation works, consider the following simple algorithm based on finding a minimum weight cycle cover in a graph [BJTY91]. A cycle cover of minimum or maximum weight is determined by setting up the problem as an assignment problem which is solvable in polynomial time. The collection of cycles will minimize the total overlap. When strings overlap, the *prefix* or *label* of a string is the portion of it that is not in an overlap with its successor or predecessor and is always nonempty.

MINIMUM CYCLE COVER

Step 1: Find a minimum weight cycle cover in the distance graph, consisting of cycles c_i.

Step 2: Choose one string from each cycle c_i; call that string r_i.

Step 3: For each cycle, form a string by concatenating the labels on the cycle and r_i; call that string s_i.

Step 4: Concatenate the s_i. Call the length of the resulting string "*total−length*"

When the cycles are opened to form a superstring, the length of each one is only greater than its length as a closed cycle, because the first and last strings no longer overlap. But when one string r_i is removed from a cycle, the length of the cycle when open without r_i is only smaller than its length as a closed cycle. Consequently, if $d(C)$ is the sum of the lengths of all the cycles and $|R|$ is the total length of all strings r_i, the total length of the resulting superstring is, $d(C) + |R|$.

Let *OPT* denote the length of the shortest superstring. The key is to relate R to *OPT*. We do that via the lemma of [BJTY91] that states that for any two strings s, t in different cycles

$$ov(s, t) \leq d(c_s) + d(c_t) \tag{9.6}$$

where c_s (c_t) is the cycle containing s (t).

LEMMA 9.5   Minimum-cycle cover is a 4-approximation algorithm for the shortest superstring problem.

Proof.   Consider an optimal superstring for just the strings r_i. Let $r_1, \ldots, r_k$ be the optimal ordering of these strings, then we know that for $OPT(R)$ denoting the shortest superstring of the strings of R,

$$OPT(R) = |R| - \sum_i ov(r_i, r_i + 1) . \tag{9.7}$$

That is, the optimal length of a superstring for R can be computed by summing the lengths of all strings in R and then subtracting the pairwise overlap. So using (9.7), $total−length = d(C) + |R| = d(C) + OPT(R) + \sum_i ov(r_i, r_i + 1)$.

Applying inequality (9.6) to this sum, notice that since each r_i is in a different cycle, so each cycle gets counted at most twice in the sum above, and we get $\sum_i ov(r_i, r_i + 1) \leq 2d(C)$.

We now replace the bound above, using the fact that $d(C)$ is a lower bound on *OPT*, and the optimal superstring for a subset of the strings is also a lower bound: $total−length \leq d(C) + OPT(R) + 2d(C) \leq 4OPT$.

Hence, minimum cycle cover is a 4-approximation algorithm.   ■

9.2.2.2 Using approximations of MAX TSP to approximate shortest superstring:

To get improved bounds we look more closely at (9.7). For convenience, let Q denote the maximum overlap possible over all orderings of the strings r_i, as this is the same as $\sum_i ov(r_i, r_i + 1)$. Now, if we think about the problem of ordering the strings so as to maximize the overlap, this is just a MAX TSP in the overlap graph corresponding to the strings r_j whose optimal value is Q. So if we have an α-approximation to the MAX TSP problem, we can find a superstring for the strings R_i whose total length is $R - \alpha Q$.

LEMMA 9.6 Given a $(\frac{1}{2} + \epsilon)$-approximation to MAX TSP, there is a $(3 - 2\epsilon)$-approximation for shortest superstring

Proof. We modify the minimum-cycle cover algorithm by replacing Step 4 by one which finds a superstring for the r_i's, and then adding back in the labels of the cycles to form a superstring. We now get a superstring of length $d(C) + |R| - \alpha Q$.

Substituting (9.7) we get, $R = OPT(R) + \sum_i ov(r_i, r_i + 1) = OPT(R) + Q$. That implies that,

$$d(C) + |R| - \alpha Q \leq d(C) + OPT(R) + Q - \alpha Q = d(C) + OPT(R) + (1 - \alpha)Q.$$

We still know by (9.6) that $Q \leq 2d(C)$. Substituting, we get

$$d(C) + OPT(R) + (1 - \alpha)2d(C) = 3d(C) + OPT(R) - 2\alpha d(C).$$

Letting $\alpha = \frac{1}{2} + \epsilon$, we get $3d(C) + OPT(R) - 2(\frac{1}{2} + \epsilon)d(C)$. Since $d(C) \leq OPT$, and $OPT(R) \leq OPT$, we conclude that $d(C) + |R| - \alpha Q \leq (3 - 2\epsilon)OPT$ as required. ∎

The list of subsequent improvements in approximating shortest superstring to date produced the approximation ratios: 3 by Blum, Jiang, Li, Tromp, and Yannakakis [BJTY91], 2.889 by Teng and Yao [TY93], 2.833 by Czumai, Gasieniec, Piotrow, and Rytter [CGPR94], 2.793 by Kosaraju, Park, and Stein [KPS94] and 2.75 by Armen and Stein [AS94]. Most of these improvements rely on improvements in approximating MAX TSP and using Lemma 9.6. Beyond that, the only lower bound known is a proof that the shortest superstring problem is Max-$\mathcal{SNP}$-hard [BJTY91], and hence, cannot be approximated with a PAS.

9.2.3 HOW MAXIMIZATION VERSUS MINIMIZATION AFFECTS APPROXIMATIONS

Some optimization problems could equivalently be posed as either minimization or maximization problems. For instance, finding the maximum-weight independent set is equivalent to the problem of finding the minimum-weight vertex cover in the same graph, as one is the complement of the other. In Chapter 3 it is noted that while there are constant ratio approximation algorithms for the vertex cover problem, none are known for the independent set problem (and none are likely to exist as implied by non-approximability results described in Chapter 10.)

k-cluster problem. Consider the k-cluster problem defined on an edge-weighted graph. The objective is to partition the vertices of the graph to K nonempty components, so that the total weight of edges within components is minimum. When the edge weights represent the dissimilarity (or distance) of the endpoints, this approach yields a partition into clusters, the elements in each cluster bear significant similarity to each other. The problem is known to be *NP*-hard, and a $\frac{1}{K}$-approximation algorithm was described by Sahni and Gonzales [SG76].

Suppose now that the edge weights represent the *similarity* between pairs of objects. In that case we want to find a k-partition so that the sum of edge weights within components is maximum. The complement of this problem is the k-cut problem of finding the minimum weight collection of edges in the cut separating k nonempty components in the graph. This problem is polynomial for fixed k [GH94], and hence, the corresponding maximization version of the k cluster is polynomial as well. Even if k is not fixed, there is a simple $(2 - \frac{2}{k})$-approximation algorithm for the k-cut problem [DJPSY92].

k-median problem. Consider the k-median problem with fixed costs. The objective is to choose up to k locations so as to minimize the total cost of transportation from the customers to the nearest median facility and the fixed costs associated with the locations chosen. The best known approximation for this minimization problem has a ratio of $O(\log n)$ [Hoc82]. For the problem of *maximizing* the sum of transportation costs minus the fixed costs for up to K locations, a greedy type heuristic has worst case of $[\frac{K-1}{K}]^K$ [CFN77]. (A similar approximation algorithm is described in Chapter 3 for maximum coverage problems.) Notice that unlike other examples of complementary problems, the maximization problem of k-median with fixed costs is *not* equivalent to the minimization problem, and one cannot extract a solution to the one problem from the other.

The shortest superstring problem. The shortest superstring problem can be stated as minimizing the distance in the distance graph, or equivalently as maximizing the overlap. The minimum distance model was proved to be Max-$\mathcal{SNP}$-hard [BJTY91], and hence, an approximation scheme is unlikely. There is no such proof for the maximum overlap model of the problem, and therefore an arbitrarily close approximation has not yet been ruled out for the maximum overlap. For instance, it is known that a factor of 2 approximation is possible for the maximum overlap. It follows immediately from solving the maximum weight assignment problem and opening each cycle at the place of smallest overlap. Since each cycle has at least two strings, the amount of overlap lost by opening it is at most $\frac{1}{2}$ of the total overlap (if all cycles consist of at least 3 strings this value goes up to $\frac{2}{3}$). More interestingly, it has been proved also that the greedy algorithm selecting the largest overlap possible at a time and adding it to the existing partial superstring is a $\frac{1}{2}$-approximation algorithm. Yet it is not known for the minimum distance objective that the greedy is a factor of 2 approximation, and such result does not follow. It is indeed conjectured, based on empirical experience (i.e. inability to come up with an example showing otherwise), that the greedy is a 2-approximation for the minimum distance shortest superstring problem.

Here the gap between the two formulations is not that substantial—for overlap maximization we described a 2-approximation algorithm, while for distance minimization the best known approximation to date is 2.75.

Weighted arc feedback set problem. One more example is the directed weighted arc feedback problem which is equivalent to the directed vertex feedback problem. Instead of minimizing the total weight of the arcs in the feedback set, we could consider instead maximizing the weight of the arcs that remain in the acyclic graph. While for the minimization problem the best known approximation algorithm guarantees a bound of $O(\log n \log \log n)$ (the detailed algorithm and analysis are given in Chapter 5), the maximization problem has an easy 2-approximation algorithm. This algorithm was first noted by Grötchel. The input to the problem is a directed graph $G = (V, A)$ with weight w_a associated with each $a \in A$. For a subset of the arcs, $B \subset A$, let $w(B) = \sum_{(i,j) \in B} w_{(i,j)}$.

$\frac{1}{2}$ APPROXIMATION TO THE ARC FEEDBACK SET PROBLEM

Step 1: Assign an arbitrary ordering to the nodes of G.

Step 2: Let $A_1 = \{(i,j) | i < j\}$, and $A_2 = \{(i,j) | i > j\}$. If $w(A_1) \geq w(A_2)$, output A_1; else, output A_2.

Each of the sets of arcs A_1 and A_2 forms an acyclic graph as the indexing is a topological ordering in those graphs. Also these two sets of arcs form a partition of A. Let the larger weight among $w(A_1)$ and $w(A_2)$ be denoted by w_{max} and the weight of the optimal arc feedback set be OPT. Since OPT cannot be more than the weight of all arcs in the graph,

$$w_{max} \geq \frac{1}{2}[w(A_1) + w(A_2)] \geq \frac{1}{2}OPT.$$

This is an illustration of a case where the maximization version of the problem has a ratio 2 approximation that runs in linear time, and the minimization version has a polynomial, but complex, approximation algorithm for delivering a solution that is within a factor of $O(\log n \log \log n)$ of the optimum (Chapter 5).

BETTER: APPROXIMATION SCHEMES

9.3

Approximation schemes are superior to constant ratio approximations in that their performance does not limit the ratio on the error. It can be as close to 1 as desired. The running time of the procedure grows as a function of $\frac{1}{\epsilon}$ where $1 + \epsilon$ is the approximation ratio. In this sense the running time increases to infinity as $\epsilon \to 0$, which establishes, consequently, a threshold on ϵ beyond which complete enumeration algorithm is more efficient than the approximation scheme.

The algorithms in this section are not "best" precisely because of the issue of running time. We focus here on the running time trade-off of polynomial approximation schemes and illustrate the major techniques of scaling, grouping, powers of graphs, and the shifting strategy. We describe a *fully polynomial approximation scheme* FPAS for the Knapsack problem where the running time grows polynomially with the reciprocal of the error bound. We then describe *polynomial approximation schemes* PAS for other problems for which FPAS are not possible unless $NP = P$.

Some problems are known not to have fully polynomial approximation schemes unless $NP = P$. This lower bound applies to *strongly NP-complete* problems. This concept—introduced in [GJ79]—is to relate the cause of the hardness of the problem to its size alone, rather than the occurrence of very large values in the input. One way of defining succinctly strong *NP*-completeness is to give the input in unary encoding. If the problem is still *NP*-complete for unary encoded input (where the number of words is the same as it would have been in binary encoding, but each word is exponentially longer), then the problem is strongly *NP*-complete. With few exceptions, a notable one being the Knapsack problem, most problems studied are strongly *NP*-complete. Garey and Johnson proved the following impossibility result on approximating strongly *NP*-complete problems [GJ78]:

THEOREM 9.1   There is no fully polynomial approximation scheme for a strongly *NP*-complete problem, unless $NP = P$.

The Knapsack problem is weakly *NP*-complete and is known to have FPAS. However, not every weakly *NP*-complete problem is known to have a FPAS. One example where this issue is still unresolved is for integer programs with two variables per inequality and when all constraint inequalities are monotone. This problem, discussed in some detail in Chapter 3, is not known to possess even good approximation algorithms.

We first describe the FPAS for the Knapsack problem. We then give a PAS for the minimum-makespan scheduling problem with an interesting twist. The running time of the PAS is actually *linear* for fixed approximation ratio $1 + \epsilon$. The minimum makespan problem is used to introduce the important technique of dual approximations. The next set of problems are geometric covering and packing problems for which the shifting strategy is extremely useful in deriving PAS. Several problems defined on outerplanar graphs are included in this category and are amenable to the same shifting strategy technique. All the problems described in this section, other than the Knapsack problem, are strongly *NP*-complete. The approximation algorithms PAS and FPAS are hence best in terms of the approximation factors, but the functional dependence of the running time on ϵ can be potentially improved.

The focus of the presentation in this section is on the generality of the techniques employed.

9.3.1   A FULLY POLYNOMIAL APPROXIMATION SCHEME FOR THE KNAPSACK PROBLEM

One of the most significant successes of approximation algorithms has been illustrated for the Knapsack problem. For that problem, there is a polynomial approximation algorithm for any desired approximation with a moderate (polynomial) rate of increase in the running time as the approximation becomes tighter.

We first present the simplest form of the fully polynomial approximation scheme for the 0/1 Knapsack, which is formulated as a singly constrained integer programming problem.

$$P^* = \text{Max} \quad \sum_{j=1}^{N} p_j x_j$$
$$\text{subject to} \quad \sum_{j=1}^{N} a_j x_j \leq B$$
$$x_j \in \{0, 1\}, \quad \text{for } j = 1, \dots, N.$$

The Knapsack problem is solvable by a pseudo-polynomial algorithm which is the essential building block for the FPAS.

9.3.1.1 An $O(NP^*)$-algorithm for solving the 0/1 Knapsack problem

The following Dynamic Programming algorithm solves the problem optimally for integer objective function coefficients:

Let $F_j(i)$ denote the smallest knapsack volume that yields an objective function value of i involving variables in the set $\{1, \ldots, j\}$. The boundary conditions are

$$F_j(0) = 0, \quad j = 1, \ldots, N,$$

and the recursive formula is

$$F_j(i) = \min\{F_{j-1}(i - p_j) + a_j, F_{j-1}(i)\}.$$

Using the boundary conditions, the table of values is evaluated in increasing order of objective function values:

$$F_1(1), F_2(1), \ldots, F_N(1); F_1(2), \ldots, F_N(2); \ldots\ldots$$

The computation terminates once the largest value of i is found so that $F_N(i) \leq B$.

Each function evaluation is done in $O(1)$ steps, and there are a total of $O(NP^*)$ function evaluations, where P^* is the optimal value of the objective function. Hence, the running time of this dynamic programming algorithm is $O(NP^*)$.

9.3.1.2 A "slow" fully polynomial approximation scheme for the 0/1 Knapsack

The idea of the fully polynomial approximation scheme is to exploit the Dynamic Programming algorithm that runs in $O(NP^*)$. The objective function coefficients are scaled, thus reducing the running time of the algorithm to depend on the new scaled value of the optimal solution. On the other hand, for a carefully chosen scaling value, the objective function of the scaled problem is close to that of the original problem.

Consider scaling the objective coefficients by a factor of k. The scaled coefficients are then $p_j(k) = \lfloor \frac{p_j}{k} \rfloor$, and the scaled problem,

$$\begin{aligned} \text{Max} \quad & \sum_{j=1}^{N} p_j(k)x_j \\ \text{subject to} \quad & \sum_{j=1}^{N} a_j x_j \leq B \\ & x_j \in \{0, 1\}, \quad \text{for} \quad j = 1, \ldots, N. \end{aligned}$$

The running time required to solve the scaled problem depends on the value of the optimum. As the value of the optimal solution gets reduced by a factor of k so does the running time. We will be using upper bounds on the optimum that are also reduced by a factor of k for the scaled problem. One such simple upper and lower bound is,

$$P_{\max} \leq P^* \leq N P_{\max}, \tag{9.8}$$

where $P_{\max} = \max_{j=1,\ldots,N}\{p_j\}$. With this upper bound, the running time of the dynamic programming algorithm to solve optimally the scaled problem is $O(N^2 \lfloor \frac{P_{max}}{k} \rfloor)$.

Let S^* be the set of indices of the variables in the optimal solution to the Knapsack problem, and $S(k)$ the set of indices of the variables in the optimal solution to the scaled problem.

$$\sum_{j \in S(k)} p_j \geq \sum_{j \in S(k)} k \lfloor \frac{p_j}{k} \rfloor \geq \sum_{j \in S^*} k \lfloor \frac{p_j}{k} \rfloor \geq \sum_{j \in S^*} (p_j - k) \geq \sum_{j \in S^*} p_j - k |S^*| . \quad (9.9)$$

Hence, the absolute error of the "scaled" solution is at most $k|S^*|$, and the relative error (using the lower bound in 9.8) is

$$\epsilon = \frac{k|S^*|}{P_{\max}} \leq N \frac{k}{P_{\max}} .$$

The running time is $O(N^2 \frac{P_{\max}}{k}) = O(N^3 \frac{1}{\epsilon})$. Hence, this is a fully polynomial approximation scheme. How good is this family of approximation algorithms? Clearly we cannot improve the approximation bound. Yet, it may be possible to get much improved running times, which is indeed the case as we see next.

9.3.1.3   A faster polynomial approximation scheme

Ibarra and Kim introduced several refinements of the algorithm involving other bounds on the optimum and the separation of items to a class of "large" ones versus "small" ones [IK75]. The large items are those with profits larger or equal to a given threshold value T, and the small ones have profits less than T. It was proved that the sum of the errors from the solution of the large items problem and then the small items problem is an upper bound on the total error.

For an improved bound, consider the indices of the variables in the 0/1 Knapsack problem to be arranged in a nonincreasing ratio of $\frac{p_j}{a_j}$. Let $\bar{j}$ be the largest index so that $\sum_{j=1}^{\bar{j}} a_j \leq B$. Let $P_0 = \max\{P_{\max}, \sum_{j=1}^{\bar{j}} p_j\}$, then $P_0 \leq P^* \leq 2P_0$. (The proof for the validity of these bounds is found in [IK75] and [Law79].)

For a chosen value of ϵ, Lawler [Law79] defines large items as those with $p_j \geq T = \frac{1}{2\epsilon P_0}$, and small items are all the others. The scaling factor selected is $k = \frac{1}{4\epsilon^2 P_0}$. The reduced running time is achieved by running the dynamic programming algorithm only for the large items. The small items are then packed in order of nonincreasing $\frac{p_j}{a_j}$ ratio while there is still slack in the packing constraint. The total error resulting from the union of these two sets of selected variables is at most ϵ. To verify that the total error does not exceed ϵ, note that the total error derived from the dynamic programming solution on the large items does not exceed $k\frac{P^*}{T}$ as the number of large items in the optimal solution to the scaled problem is $\frac{P^*}{T}$. For the small items, the error does not exceed the value of T. The sum of the relative errors is hence,

$$\frac{k}{T} + \frac{T}{P^*} \leq \frac{\frac{1}{4\epsilon^2 P_0}}{\frac{1}{2\epsilon P_0}} + \frac{\frac{1}{2\epsilon P_0}}{P_0} = \epsilon .$$

The computational advantage is derived from the relatively small number of large items that need to be considered. The number of different values of $p_j(k)$ is bounded by $\frac{P^*}{k}$. Using that $P^* \leq 2P_0$ and with k defined as above, the number of different values is bounded by $\frac{8}{\epsilon^2}$. As for each value of $p_j(k)$, there could be at most $n_j = \lfloor \frac{P^*/k}{p_j(k)} \rfloor$ items of size $p_j(k)$ in an optimal solution, and among all those of the same scaled profit, those with the smallest weights would be selected. Other large items need not be considered as they are dominated. With this type of argument, Lawler proved that the number of large items to be considered is $\frac{6}{\epsilon^2} \log_2 \frac{4}{\epsilon}$. Consequently, the running time required to solve the dynamic programming algorithm that runs on large items is $O(\frac{NP_0}{k}) = O(\frac{1}{\epsilon^4} \log_2 \frac{1}{\epsilon})$. Lawler further showed that there is a tighter, $O(\frac{1}{\epsilon^2})$, bound on the number of large items resulting in $O(\frac{1}{\epsilon^4})$ running time.

To summarize, the steps of the approximation algorithm A_ϵ for the 0/1 linear Knapsack problem are as follows:

1. Find the value and the set of elements corresponding to P_0.

2. Find the "large" items that are candidates for inclusion in the optimal solution.

3. Solve for the "large" items in the scaled problem, using dynamic programming.

4. Find the largest ratio "small" items that can be packed in the remaining volume of the knapsack.

Steps 1 and 2 can be executed in linear time, Step 4 in $O(n \log_2 \frac{1}{\epsilon})$, and Step 3 in $O(\frac{1}{\epsilon^4})$. Hence, the total running time is $O(n \log_2 \frac{1}{\epsilon} + \frac{1}{\epsilon^4})$.

In the next section we investigate a PAS for a strongly NP-complete problem—the minimum makespan. Although the running time is exponential in $\frac{1}{\epsilon}$, it is of the form $n + C(\epsilon)$ where $C(\epsilon)$ is a function of ϵ only. Hence, for fixed ϵ that approximation scheme is linear, and in that it is a constant factor, more efficient than the FPAS for the Knapsack problem.

9.3.2   THE MINIMUM MAKESPAN AND THE TECHNIQUE OF DUAL APPROXIMATIONS

The scheduling problem of minimizing makespan has probably been studied for approximation algorithms more than any other optimization problem. The first approximation algorithm for the problem was devised by Graham [Gra66]. A variety of of scheduling problems and their approximations are reviewed in Chapter 1. The PAS discussed here is by Hochbaum and Shmoys [HS87].

For the problem of minimizing the makespan of the schedule for a set of jobs, we are given a set of n jobs with designated integral processing times p_j to be scheduled on m identical machines. A schedule of jobs is an assignment of the jobs to the machines, so that each machine is scheduled for certain total time, and the maximum time that any machine is scheduled for is called the *makespan* of the schedule. In the minimum makespan problem, the objective is to find a schedule that minimizes the makespan; this optimum value will be denoted $\text{OPT}_{MM}(I, m)$ where I denotes the set of processing times, and m is the specified number of machines.

During the couple of decades that followed the approximation result of Graham [Gra66], the best known performance guarantee of approximation algorithms for the minimum makespan problem has slowly improved from $2\text{OPT}_{MM}(I, m)$ to $1.20\text{OPT}(I, m)$ in a succession of papers [Gra66], [Gr2], [CGJ78], [Fr84], where the intricacy of the arguments needed to prove these bounds has greatly increased with time as well. Polynomial approximation schemes were known for any *fixed* value of m, but these have running times that are exponential in m [Gr2], [S76].

A problem that is closely related to the minimum makespan problem is the bin-packing problem (which is thoroughly investigated in Chapter 2). In this problem, the input consists of n pieces of size p_j, where each size is in the interval $[0,1]$. The objective is to pack the pieces into bins in such a way that the minimum number of bins are used, and where the sum of the sizes of the pieces packed in any bin cannot exceed 1. This minimum shall be denoted $OPT_{BP}(I)$.

Hochbaum and Shmoys introduced the notion of *dual approximation algorithm* that involves approximating the *feasibility* of a problem, rather than its optimality: Traditional approximation algorithms seek feasible solutions that are suboptimal, where the performance of the algorithm is measured by the degree of suboptimality allowed. In a dual approximation algorithm, the aim is to find an infeasible solution that is *superoptimal*, where the performance of the algorithm is measured by the degree of infeasibility allowed. In addition to employing dual approximation algorithms for the bin-packing problem, we show a general relationship between traditional (or primal) approximation algorithms and dual approximation algorithms.

For the bin-packing problem, an ϵ-dual approximation algorithm is a polynomial-time algorithm that constructs a bin-packing such that at most $OPT_{BP}(I)$ bins are used, and each bin is filled with at most $1 + \epsilon$. There are practical applications where the bin capacity is either not known precisely, or simply not rigid, so that such "overflow" is a natural model of this flexibility.

Let $dual_\epsilon(I)$ denote an ϵ-dual approximation algorithm for the bin-packing problem. Furthermore, let $DUAL_\epsilon(I)$ denote the number of bins actually used by this algorithm. If I denotes a bin-packing instance with piece sizes $\{p_j\}$ it will be convenient to let $\frac{I}{d}$ denote the instance with corresponding piece sizes scaled by d, $\{\frac{p_j}{d}\}$.

It is not hard to see that the optima of the bin-packing and minimum makespan problems are related in that $OPT_{BP}(\frac{I}{d}) \leq m$ if and only if $OPT_{MM}(I, m) \leq d$. In other words, the minimum makespan problem can be viewed as finding the minimum deadline d^* so that $OPT_{BP}(\frac{I}{d^*}) \leq m$. Thus, if we had a procedure for optimally solving the bin-packing problem, we could use it within a binary search procedure to obtain an optimal solution for the minimum makespan problem. A natural extension of this would be to obtain a (traditional) approximation algorithm for the minimum makespan problem by using a (traditional) approximation algorithm for the bin-packing problem within the binary search. It is, however, unlikely that such an approach can succeed as the effect of scaling is dramatically different for bin packing compared to the minimum makespan problem. Instead, we show that the dual approximation algorithm for the bin-packing problem is precisely the tool required.

A useful measure of the size of an instance is $SIZE(I, m) = \max\{\sum_{j=1}^{n} \frac{p_j}{m}, \max_j p_j\}$. It is easy to see that $OPT_{MM}(I, m) \geq SIZE(I, m)$. By another straightforward argument, it can be shown that the makespan of any list processing schedule is at most $2SIZE(I, m)$. (See, for example Chapter 1 or [HS87].) These bounds serve to initialize the binary search bisection algorithm.

```
procedure ε-makespan
   begin
      upper ← 2SIZE(I, m)
      lower ← SIZE(I, m)
      repeat
         begin
            d ← ½(upper + lower)
            call dualₑ(I/d)
            if Dualₑ(I/d) > m then lower ← d else upper ← d
         end
      d* ← upper
      output d*
      call dual(I/d*)
   end
```

This procedure is given with an infinite loop and later we shall remove this simplifying assumption. Since $\text{DUAL}_\epsilon(I)$ is at most $\text{OPT}_{BP}(I)$, and since any list processing schedule has a makespan of at most $2\text{SIZE}(I, m)$, it follows that $\text{DUAL}_\epsilon(\frac{I}{upper}) \leq m$ initially. Furthermore, by the way *upper* is updated, this remains true throughout the execution of the procedure.

Next we show that $\text{OPT}_{MM}(I, m) \geq lower$ throughout the execution of the program. Since $lower \leftarrow \text{SIZE}(I, m)$ initially, this is certainly true before the beginning of the **repeat** loop. Furthermore, any time that *lower* is updated to d, it follows that $\text{OPT}_{BP}(\frac{I}{d}) \geq \text{DUAL}_{BP}(\frac{I}{d}) > m$ and therefore $\text{OPT}_{MM}(I, m) > d$. The makespan of the schedule produced is at most $(1 + \epsilon)d^*$. In this infinite version, $upper = lower$ at "termination," and therefore, the makespan is at most $(1 + \epsilon)lower \leq (1 + \epsilon)\text{OPT}_{MM}(I, m)$. In words, the algorithm is an ϵ-approximation algorithm for the minimum makespan problem, which is what we claimed.

By the fact that all of the processing times are integer we know that $\lceil lower \rceil$ is also a valid lower bound for $\text{OPT}_{MM}(I)$. As a result, when $upper - lower < 1$, the binary search can be terminated. (The procedure *dual* should be called once more with the pieces rescaled by $\lceil lower \rceil$. If this succeeds in using at most m bins, the schedule produced should be output. Otherwise, $\lceil lower \rceil + 1$ is a lower bound on the optimum makespan, so that the schedule produced by $d = upper$, which is less than this bound, can be used instead.) This implies that the algorithm is polynomial in the binary encoding of the input. However, a straightforward computation gives a more practical version of this result is obtained by considering the number of iterations of the binary search that were executed.

THEOREM 9.2 If **procedure** $\epsilon - makespan(I, m)$ is executed with k iterations of the binary search, the resulting solution has makespan at most $(1 + \epsilon)(1 + 2^{-k})\text{OPT}_{MM}(I, m)$.

Notice that since the end goal of this approach is an ϵ-approximation scheme, we could equally well create an ϵ-approximation algorithm for the minimum makespan problem by using an $\epsilon/2$-dual approximation algorithm for the bin-packing problem, and then only $O(\log(1/\epsilon))$ iterations are required to get a total relative error of ϵ. Thus, the algorithm is a strongly polynomial one, in that we do not need to consider the lengths of the binary encoding of the given processing times.

The dual approximation techniques used above are general and can be applied to problems other than minimum makespan problem. For any recognition version of an optimization problem where there are two critical parameters, p_1 and p_2, there are two optimization problems that can be derived from the decision problem, first by fixing one of the two parameters, and then, subject to this constraint, optimizing the other. We shall call one problem the *dual* of the other. The primal problem shall be the one where p_1 is given as part of the input and p_2 is, say, minimized—an instance, is specified by an ordered pair $(I, \bar{p}_1)$. Similarly, an instance of the dual problem consists of a pair $(I, \bar{p}_2)$, and the first parameter is minimized.

Let $\text{OPT}_P(I, \bar{p}_1)$ and $\text{OPT}_D(I, \bar{p}_2)$ denote the optimal values of the specified primal and dual problems, respectively. An ϵ-(primal) approximation algorithm for the primal problem is an algorithm that delivers a solution where the value of the first parameter is at most $\bar{p}_1$ and the value of the second parameter, as derived by the algorithm and denoted $PRIMAL_{P,\epsilon}(I, \bar{p}_1)$, is at most $(1 + \epsilon)\text{OPT}_P(I, \bar{p}_1)$. An ϵ-dual approximation algorithm $dual_{D,\epsilon}(I, \bar{p}_2)$ for the dual problem is an algorithm that delivers a solution where the value of the first parameter, as derived by the algorithm and denoted $\text{DUAL}_{D,\epsilon}(I, \bar{p}_2)$, is at most $\text{OPT}_D(I, \bar{p}_2)$ and the value of the second parameter is at most $(1 + \epsilon)\bar{p}_2$. Finding the ϵ-(primal) approximation algorithm can be reduced to finding an ϵ-dual approximation algorithm by using a binary search algorithm nearly identical to the one discussed above.

It remains to present a polynomial ϵ-dual approximation scheme for the bin-packing problem. By Theorem 9.2, this yields a polynomial ϵ-approximation scheme for the minimum makespan problem. The spirit of this scheme is based on a generalization of the "grouping" ideas used in [HS86a] and is similar to the one given in [FVL81] for a (primal) ϵ-approximation scheme for the bin-packing problem. More on the use of grouping for the bin-packing problem is covered in Section 9.5.1.

9.3.2.1   Polynomial ϵ-dual approximation scheme

The result is presented in two parts: first we argue that the problem of finding an ϵ-dual approximation algorithm can be reduced to finding an ϵ-dual approximation algorithm for the restricted class of instances where all piece sizes are greater than ϵ, and then we give a polynomial scheme for this restricted class of instances.

Suppose that we had a ϵ-dual approximation algorithm for the bin-packing problem which worked only on instances where all piece sizes are greater than ϵ. Such an algorithm could be applied to an arbitrary instance I in the following way:

Step 1: Use the assumed algorithm to pack all of the pieces with size $> \epsilon$ in $m(\epsilon)$ bins.

Step 2: For each remaining piece of size $\leq \epsilon$, pack it in any bin that currently contains ≤ 1. If no such bin exists, start a new bin.

Since the algorithm used in Step 1 is a dual approximation algorithm and since the minimum number of bins for a subset of I is at most $\mathrm{OPT}_{BP}(I)$, it follows that the number of bins used in Step 1, $m(\epsilon)$, is at most $\mathrm{OPT}_{BP}(I)$. Thus, if no new bins are used in Step 2, the algorithm presented is clearly an ϵ-dual approximation algorithm. Suppose now that a new bin was used in Step 2. This implies that the last piece packed could not fit in any started bin. Since the size of the piece is $\leq \epsilon$ and the extended capacity of the bin is $1 + \epsilon$, it follows that every bin is filled to its intended capacity! In other words, in this case it follows that the number of bins used is at most $\lceil \sum p_j \rceil$, and it is clear that $\lceil \sum p_j \rceil \leq \mathrm{OPT}_{BP}(I)$. Furthermore, it is easy to see that no bin is ever packed with more than $1 + \epsilon$. This leads to a complexity improvement in Step 2. If we are only concerned with whether or not the number of bins exceed m and not in the actual assignment, then it suffices to output at Step 2 $\min\{m(\epsilon), \lceil \sum p_j \rceil\}$.

By the reduction given above, we need only produce an ϵ-dual approximation algorithm for instances where all pieces are greater than ϵ. This is done by reducing the problem to a bin packing problem on a fixed number of sizes of items: Partition the interval of allowed piece sizes $(\epsilon, 1]$ into $s = \lceil \frac{\log \frac{1}{\epsilon}}{\epsilon} \rceil$ subintervals $(\epsilon = l_1, l_2], (l_2, l_3], \dots,$ $(l_s, l_{s+1} = 1]$, where $l_j = l_{j-1}(1 + \epsilon)$. For a given instance I, let n_i denote the number pieces with size in the interval $(l_i, l_{i+1}]$. Effectively we consider the size of each piece to be the lower endpoint of the interval in which its size falls.

Consider any feasibly packed bin. Since each piece is of size greater than ϵ, there are at most $\lfloor 1/\epsilon \rfloor$ pieces in this bin. Let x_i denote the number of pieces with size in the interval $(l_i, l_i + 1]$. A *configuration* of the bin can be given by an s-tuple $(x_1, x_2, \dots, x_s)$. A configuration is said to be *feasible* if $\sum_{i=1}^{s} x_i l_i \leq 1$. It is easy to see that any bin that is packed feasibly (with total capacity used at most one) has a corresponding configuration that is feasible. A simple calculation shows that $\mathcal{C}$, the number of feasible configurations, is at most $\mathcal{C} = \lceil \frac{1}{\epsilon} \rceil^s$, which is a (rather large) constant for fixed ϵ.

Consider any bin B that is packed according to some feasible configuration $(x_1, \dots, x_s)$. Let a_i be the fraction of the bin filled by size l_i pieces. Obviously, $x_i \leq \frac{a_i}{l_i}$, hence

$$\sum_{j \in B} p_j \leq \sum_{i=1}^{s} x_i l_{i+1} = \sum_{i=1}^{s} x_i l_i + \sum_{i=1}^{s} x_i (l_{i+1} - l_i)$$

$$\leq 1 + \sum_{i=1}^{s} \frac{a_i}{l_i}(l_{i+1} - l_i) = 1 + \sum_{i=1}^{s} a_i \epsilon = 1 + \epsilon \,. \tag{9.10}$$

In other words, if the pieces are packed according to a feasible configuration, then the overflow in any bin is at most ϵ. Therefore, if we find a partition of the pieces into feasible configurations that has the minimum number of parts, this would yield an ϵ-approximation algorithm. From a slightly different angle, this is nothing more than the bin-packing problem, where the piece sizes are restricted to be one of the s lower bounds l_i. Fortunately, this restricted bin-packing problem can be solved in polynomial time. One approach is to use dynamic programming, based on the recurrence,

$$\mathrm{BINS}(b_1, \dots, b_s) = 1 + \min_{\substack{\text{feasible} \\ \text{configurations} \\ (x_1, \dots, x_s)}} \mathrm{BINS}(b_1 - x_1, \dots, b_s - x_s) \,,$$

where $\mathrm{BINS}(b_1, \dots, b_s)$ denotes the minimum number of bins needed when there are n_i pieces of size l_i. The running time of this approach is $O((\frac{n}{\epsilon})^{\lceil (\log 1/\epsilon)/\epsilon \rceil})$.

Does this polynomial approximation scheme settle entirely the question of approximability of the minimum makespan problem? The running time must be an exponential function of $\frac{1}{\epsilon}$ as otherwise $NP = P$. Yet, the running time can be substantially improved, and in fact can be constant for every fixed ϵ if the input is read and preprocessed first (otherwise an additive linear running time is required to process the input).

9.3.2.2   A linear time approximation scheme

To achieve an improvement to linear time we use the "cutting stock" formulation of the ϵ-dual approximation algorithm and then apply Lenstra's algorithm [Len85] to the resulting integer program. David Shmoys suggested the use of this formulation.

Let y_i be integer variables denoting the number of bins containing feasible configuration i, for $i = 1, ..., C$. Let configuration i be represented by the vector $(a_{i1}, a_{i2}, ..., a_{is})$ where a_{ij} is the number of pieces of length ℓ_j in configuration i. Since $\ell_j > \epsilon$, $a_{ij} < \lceil 1/\epsilon \rceil$. Let n_j be the number of pieces available of size ℓ_j. The ϵ-dual approximation problem is solved with the integer programming formulation:

$$
\begin{array}{ll}
\text{Min} & \sum_{j=1}^{C} y_i \\
\text{subject to} & \sum_{j=1}^{C} a_{ij} y_i \geq n_j \\
& y_i \geq 0 \;\; \text{integer} \quad (i = 1, \dots, C).
\end{array}
$$

We now invoke the result of Lenstra for integer programming feasibility on a fixed number of variables (or constraints) [Len85]. First we observe that in Step 1 we do not need to find an ϵ-dual packing within the smallest number of bins. It suffices to determine whether there exists a packing using no more than m bins. The objective function can therefore be replaced with the constraint:

$$
\sum_{j=1}^{C} y_i \geq m.
$$

So we have an integer programming feasibility problem on C variables and s constraints, which is solvable in time that depends (exponentially) on C. Therefore, the running time which is $O(C^{O(C)})$ is constant for a fixed ϵ. Note that the algorithm also calls for the ellipsoid method, the running time of which depends on the coefficients of the constraints, but can be implemented without depending on the right-hand sides n_j. Consequently, we solve Step 1 of the approximation algorithm in time that is constant for fixed ϵ.

To have the approximation scheme running in constant time for fixed ϵ we need to introduce a preprocessing step, as otherwise determining the large items and the number of items in each subinterval requires at least $O(n)$ steps per each call of the binary search bisection procedure. To achieve that, partition the interval containing all possible large job sizes $[\epsilon \text{SIZE}(I, m), 2\text{SIZE}(I, m)]$, into subintervals,

$$(\epsilon \text{SIZE}(I, m) = l_1, l_2], (l_2, l_3], \dots, (l_\beta, l_{\beta+1} = 2\text{SIZE}(I, m)],$$

where $l_j = l_{j-1}(1 + \epsilon)$. Note that like s, $\beta = O(\frac{\log \frac{1}{\epsilon}}{\epsilon})$. It is possible now to proceed in two different manners. One is to guess values of d on the discrete grid of points of the form l_i in the interval $[\text{SIZE}(I, m), 2\text{SIZE}(I, m)]$. With this choice of d, the partition of the job sizes into the required intervals is already available. The integer programming procedure will provide a solution that is at most $(1 + \epsilon)d$ and at termination, the binary search procedure will guarantee a solution within $(1 + \epsilon)^2 d$. Since $(1 + \epsilon)^2 \leq 1 + 3\epsilon$ for $\epsilon < 1$, it suffices to start the procedure with $\epsilon/3$. The number of calls with this approach to the dual approximation algorithm is $log\beta$.

Another alternative is to use the binary search procedure as before, except that when ϵ falls inside an interval, we let the large piece size be larger than the lower end of that interval. As a result, the smallest large piece is of size a least $\frac{\epsilon}{1+\epsilon}$, and we added at most one subinterval.

This preprocessing requires linear time, so the total running time of the algorithm is $n + \mathbf{C}(\epsilon)$ where $C(\epsilon)$ is a constant for fixed ϵ.

Although this algorithm is theoretically very efficient, the specific algorithms provided by [HS86] for $\frac{1}{5}$ approximation and $\frac{1}{6}$-approximation for the problem are considerably more efficient for any reasonable value of n.

The techniques used for devising PAS to the minimum makespan problem have been extended to apply also to the minimum makespan problem on uniform machines—where each machine has a different processing speed [HS88].

9.3.3 GEOMETRIC PACKING AND COVERING—THE SHIFTING TECHNIQUE

Polynomial approximation schemes are described in this subsection for several strongly *NP*-complete problems that have important applications in the areas of robot motion planning, VLSI design, image processing, and location. These problems appear in the contexts of covering and packing with convex objects. One of them is the *square packing* problem, which comes up in the attempt to increase yield in VLSI chip manufacture. For example, 64K RAM chips, some of which may be defective, are available on a rectilinear grid placed on a silicon wafer. 2 x 2 arrays of such nondefective chips could be wired together to produce 2S6K RAM chips. In order to maximize yield, we want to pack a maximal number of such 2 x 2 arrays into the array of working chips on a wafer. (See the result of Berman et al. [BLS82], reviewed by Johnson [Joh82], and the *NP*-completeness result of Fowler et al. [FPT81].)

Another problem is *covering with disks*; that is, given points in the plane, identifying a minimally-sized set of disks (of prescribed radius) covering all points. One of its applications is in the area of locating emergency facilities such that all potential customers will be within a reasonably small radius around the facility. (The complexity results for this problem are reviewed in [Joh82].)

A third problem considered is *covering with squares* or (rectangles), which has an important application to image processing, discussed in Tanimoto and Fowler [TF80]. Here one wants to store information in square "patches" such that all points with information ("pixels") are contained in at least one of the patches. The general problem can be described as: Given points in a Euclidean space (in this application, on a grid), find a minimally-sized set of squares of prescribed size covering all those points.

None of the above problems was reported to have a bounded error ratio approximation algorithm until the discovery of the approximation schemes in [HM85]. The presentation here follows the unified methodology presented in [HM85]. A similar technique was independently discovered by Baker [B94] and was applied to several problems on planar graphs. The illustration of the scheme for the vertex cover and the independent set problems on planar graphs will be given as well. We call this fundamental technique the *shifting strategy* and outline the necessary conditions for its applicability.

9.3.3.1   The shifting strategy

The shifting strategy allows us to bound the error of the simple divide-and-conquer approach by applying it repetitively and selecting the single most favorable resulting solution. This approach was successfully used for problems of covering with nonconvex objects as well [HM83]. Here we only illustrate the application of the shifting strategy for covering with planar balls (disks).

We use Z^A to denote the value of the solution delivered by algorithm A. An optimal solution set is denoted by OPT and its size by $|\text{OPT}|$. Let the set N of the n given points in the plane be enclosed in an area I. The goal is to cover these points with a minimal number of disks of diameter D. Let the shifting parameter be l. In the first phase the area I is subdivided into vertical strips of width D, where each strip is left closed and right open. Groups of l consecutive strips, resulting in strips of width lD each, are considered. For any fixed subdivision of I into strips of width D, there are l different ways of partitioning I into strips of width lD. These partitions can be ordered such that each can be derived from the previous one by shifting it to the right over distance D. Repeating the shift l times we end up with the same partition we started from. We denote the l distinct shift partitions that result by $S_1, S_2, \ldots, S_l$.

Let A be any algorithm that delivers a solution in any strip of width lD (or less). For a given partition S_i, let $A(S_i)$ be the algorithm that applies algorithm A to each strip in the partition S_i and outputs the union of all disks used. Such a set of disks is clearly a feasible solution to the global problem defined on I. This process of finding a global solution is repeated for each partition $S_i, i = 1, 2, \ldots, l$. The shift algorithm S_A defined for a given local algorithm A, delivers the set of disks of minimum cardinality among the l sets delivered by $A(S_1), \ldots, A(S_l)$.

Let the performance ratio of an algorithm B be denoted by r_B; that is, r_B is defined as the supremum of $Z^B/|\text{OPT}|$ over all problem instances.

LEMMA 9.7   The Shifting Lemma

$$r_{S_A} \leq r_A \left(1 + \frac{1}{l}\right),$$ (9.11)

where A is a local algorithm and I is the shifting parameter.

Proof.   We produce an upper bound on the sum of errors caused by all algorithms $A(S_i)$ for $i = 1, 2, \ldots, l$. By the definition of r_A, we have

$$Z^{A(S_i)} \leq r_A \sum_{j \in S_i} |\text{OPT}_j|,$$ (9.12)

where J runs over all strips in partition S_i and $|\text{OPT}_j|$ is the number of disks in an optimal cover of the points in strip J.

Let OPT be the set of disks in an optimal solution and $\text{OPT}^{(1)}, \ldots, \text{OPT}^{(i)}$ the set of disks in OPT covering points in two adjacent lD strips in the $1, 2, \ldots, l$ shifts, respectively. It can easily be seen that

$$\sum_{j \in S_i} |\text{OPT}_j| \leq |\text{OPT}| + |\text{OPT}^{(i)}| \, . \tag{9.13}$$

There can be no disk in the set OPT that covers points in two adjacent strips in more than one shift partition. Therefore, the sets $\text{OPT}^{(1)}, \ldots, \text{OPT}^{(i)}$ are disjoint and can add up to OPT at most. It follows that

$$\sum_{i=1}^{l} (|\text{OPT}| + |\text{OPT}^{(i)}|) \leq (l+1)|\text{OPT}| \, . \tag{9.14}$$

Expressions (9.13) and (9.14) imply

$$\min_{i=1,\ldots,l} \sum_{j \in S_i} |\text{OPT}_j|^{\cdot} \leq \frac{1}{l} \sum_{i=1}^{l} \left(\sum_{j \in S_i} |\text{OPT}_j| \right) \leq \left(1 + \frac{1}{l} \right) |\text{OPT}| \, . \tag{9.15}$$

Combining inequality (9.15) with (9.12), we obtain

$$z^{S_A} = \min_{i=1,\ldots,l} Z^{A(S_i)} \leq r_A \left(1 + \frac{1}{l} \right) |\text{OPT}| \, , \tag{9.16}$$

which establishes (9.11).   ∎

The local algorithm A may itself be derived from an application of the shifting strategy in lower dimensional space. Repetitive applications of this type yield an approximation scheme as described subsequently.

9.3.3.2   Nested applications of the shifting strategy

THEOREM 9.3   Let $d \geq 1$ be some finite dimension. Then there is a polynomial time approximation scheme H^d such that for every given natural number $l \geq 1$, the algorithm H_l^d delivers a cover of n given points in a d-dimensional Euclidean space by d-dimensional balls of given diameter D in $O(l^d (l\sqrt{d})^d (2n)^{d(l\sqrt{d})^d+1})$ steps with performance ratio $\leq (1 + \frac{1}{l})^d$.

Proof.   The considered problem is *NP*-complete only for $d > 1$. For $d = 1$, one can actually compute an optimal solution in linear time with the following algorithm: We always place the next interval (i.e., 1-dimensional ball) with its left end at the leftmost point that is not yet covered.

For $d = 2$ and fixed $l \geq 1$ we use two nested applications of the shifting strategy from Section 2. We first cut the plane into vertical strips of width lD. Then, in order to cover the points in such a strip, we apply the shifting strategy to the other dimension. Thus, we cut the considered strip into squares of side length lD. We find optimal coverings of points in such a square by exhaustive search. With $(l\sqrt{2})^2 = 2l^2$ disks of diameter D we can cover an $lD \times lD$ square compactly, thus we never need to consider more disks for one square. Further, we can assume that any disk that covers at least two of the given points has two of these points on its border. (For disks that cover only one point, the following estimate holds trivially.) Since there are only two ways to draw a circle of given diameter through two given points, we only have to consider $2\binom{n}{2}$ possible disk positions, where $\tilde{n}$ is the number of given points in the considered square. Thus, we have to check at most $O(\tilde{n}^{2(l\sqrt{2})^2})$ arrangements of disks. We specify the position of each disk by its center. In order to check whether an arrangement of disks is a feasible cover of the n points in the square. we need to determine for each point whether it is within a distance of at most $D/2$ from one of the centers. Such a check will require $O(l^2\tilde{n})$ steps, with the assumption that we can determine in one step the distance between two points on the plane or the center of a disk with the necessary precision. (Note that it is possible to speed up that process by sorting the disk centers in $O(l^2)$ prespecified subsquares of the region and then determining in which of the subsquares there could be the potential covering disk by binary search in time $O(\log l)$.) The two nested applications of the shifting strategy add another factor l^2 to our global time bound.

For $d > 2$ one proceeds analogously with d nested applications of the shifting strategy.   ■

We considered in Theorem 9.3 the problem of covering given points with a minimal number of balls of given size. The method of Theorem 9.3 can easily be generalized to yield approximation schemes for problems in which one covers with objects other than balls. For a fixed type of object (of arbitrary fixed shape) we define D as the maximum diameter of such an object. In a manner similar to Theorem 9.3, we cut the considered d-dimensional space in a number of different ways ("shifting") into d-dimensional cubes with sides of length lD. One can always find a local algorithm that proceeds by enumeration in the same way as the algorithm for balls in Theorem 9.3. But now the number of objects of the considered type that are needed to cover a d-dimensional cube with sides of length lD will depend on the ratio between D and the maximal $\tilde{D}$, such that a d-dimensional cube with sides of length $\tilde{D}$ is contained in a covering object of the considered type. The running time of the resulting approximation algorithm H_l^d will depend exponentially on this ratio $D/\tilde{D}$. For instance, for objects with known orientation the expression $(l\sqrt{d})^d$ in the exponent will be replaced by $(lD/\tilde{D})^d$. This ratio $D/\tilde{D}$ is usually of interest also in other contexts. Note that, e.g., for rectangles of size $a \times b$ in two dimensions this ratio is closely related to the "aspect ratio" $\max\{a/b, b/a\}$. We have shown in another paper [HM83] that in at least one important case, one can eliminate the ratio $D/\tilde{D}$ from the exponent of the running time by replacing the local enumeration algorithm by another approximation scheme.

In certain applications the covering problem is defined in terms of objects with fixed orientation. This is the case, for instance, with the covering with squares problem in the context of image processing [TF80]. This additional constraint simplifies the problem in that the trick illustrated in the following corollary often suffices to eliminate $D/\tilde{D}$ from the exponent of the running time.

COROLLARY 9.1   Consider the problem of covering n given points in d-space with a minimal number of rectilinear blocks (the sides of which have given lengths $D_1, \dots, D_d$) oriented with sides parallel to the axes. There is a polynomial-time approximation scheme H^d such that for every given integer $l \geq 1$, the algorithm H_l^d delivers a cover in $O(l^d n^{2l^d+1})$ steps with performance ratio $\leq (1 + 1/l)^d$.

This corollary is proved in the same way as Theorem 9.3, except that the cuts orthogonal to the ith axis are introduced at a distance $l D_i$ from each other.

9.3.3.3 Applications of the shifting technique to packing problems

In a packing problem one wants to place, without overlap, a maximal number of objects of given shape with a given area. Since the error analysis of the shifting strategy remains true for such problems, we can use algorithms similar to those in Section 9.3. We consider as an example the problem of packing with squares discussed in the introduction. The squares in this case have to be placed so that their sides will also be generalized to packing problems without such a restriction.

THEOREM 9.4   There is a polynomial-time approximation scheme for the problem of packing a maximal number of $k \times k$ squares (for a natural number k) into an area that is given by n squares of unit size on a rectilinear grid. The approximation algorithm with parameter l has an error ratio $\leq (1 + 1/l)^2$ and runs in time $O(k^2 l^2 n^{l^2})$.

Proof.   One reduces the problem via two nested applications of the shifting strategy to a local packing problem in an $lk \times lk$ square. The local packing problem can be solved by enumeration in $O(\tilde{n}^{l^2})$ steps, where n is the number of given unit squares that fall into the considered $lk \times lk$ square. We assume here that a list of all possible placements of $k \times k$ squares that lie totally inside the area of the n given unit squares has been generated as part of the input.

The shifting strategy that has been described in Section 9.2 for the covering problem can be translated to packing problems with the help of the following observation. The absolute error that results from solving the packing problem separately in each strip for a given shift can be bounded by the number of $k \times k$ squares in an optimal global solution of the packing problems that include unit squares in two different strips. ∎

For fixed l one has the option of speeding up the corresponding approximation algorithm by using some faster algorithm for optimal packings in $lk \times lk$ squares (see, e.g., the analogous approach in Section 5 of [HM83]). Note that we also get polynomial approximation schemes for many packing problems in higher dimensions, with arbitrary orientations and with objects other than squares in a manner analogous to the covering in these case.

9.3.3.4 The shifting strategy for planar graphs—Baker's algorithm

There are a number of approximation schemes for the unweighted vertex cover on planar graphs. Lipton and Tarjan [LT80], Chiba et al. [CNS81] and Bar-Yehuda and Even [BE82], all devised approximation schemes based on the linear separator theorem in planar graphs [LT79].

The most efficient approximation scheme for unweighted vertex cover problem, as well as several other graph problems including the maximum independent set and the minimum dominating set problems on planar graphs, is by Baker [B94]. Baker's algorithm does not make use of the separator theorem. Instead, it decomposes the graph to components of bounded outer-planarity. The running time of an ϵ-approximation algorithm in this scheme is $O(8^{1/\epsilon} \frac{1}{\epsilon} n)$. The algorithm relies on a routine that solves the vertex cover problem optimally in k-outerplanar graphs. Since the routine can be easily adapted to the weighted problem, and since the shifting strategy applicability extends to the weighted case, the algorithm is also an approximation scheme for the *weighted* vertex cover and independent set problems.

Intuitively, the idea is that every planar graph is decomposable to "levels" where the outermost is considered level 1, and the level index is increasing as the node is further from the exterior face. All nodes are only adjacent to nodes in the same level or in adjacent levels. When the number of levels is fixed, a dynamic programming procedure solves the problem in linear time.

Given a value of ϵ, we set $k = \lceil \frac{1}{\epsilon} \rceil$. Baker's algorithm for the independent set problem in a planar graph works as follows. The nodes are scanned and assigned to levels. For every value of $i = 1, \dots, k$ the nodes whose levels are congruent to $i \pmod{k}$ are deleted from the graph. Consequently, the remaining components are all $(k-1)$-outerplanar. The dynamic programming is then used to devise a maximum independent set in each component. The union of these independent sets is an independent set in the entire graph. Such an independent set is identified by the algorithm for each value of i, call it ALG_i. The maximum cardinality set among ALG_i, $ALG_{\max}$, is the solution derived by the following approximation algorithm:

LEMMA 9.8 The size of ALG_{max} is at least $1 - \epsilon$ times the optimum.

Proof. Let the optimal independent set be partitioned to its subsets of nodes in the levels i ("*mod*" k), OPT_i. Since $OPT = \cup_i OPT_i$, it follows that there exists an index r such that, $OPT_r \leq \frac{|OPT|}{k}$. Therefore, $OPT - OPT_r$ is an independent set on the graph with the levels $r \pmod{k}$ removed. Hence,

$$|ALG_{\max}| \geq |ALG_r| \geq |OPT| - |OPT_r| \geq \left(1 - \frac{1}{k}\right)|OPT|.$$

∎

The maximum independent set is the complement of a minimum vertex cover. It is therefore tempting to assume that the complement of a good approximate solution of one will be a good approximate solution to the other. However such is not the case. The complement of the approximate independent set delivered by the algorithm above is arbitrarily far from the optimum vertex cover. This is because it would choose the entire set of nodes in the levels i while the optimal vertex cover may consist of arbitrarily small portions of each set of levels. The following is the adaptation of the idea to the minimum vertex cover.

For each value of $i = 1, \dots, k$ decompose the graph into subsets of nodes in $k + 1$ consecutive levels $i \pmod{k}, i \pmod{k} + 1, \dots, i \pmod{k} + k$. So for each value of i, the sets in the decomposition overlap in the $i \pmod{k}$ levels. The minimum vertex cover is found in each subset using the dynamic programming algorithm for $(k + 1)$-outerplanar graphs. The union of these covers for a given value of i, ALG_i, is a feasible vertex cover in the graph. As before, we claim that the set of minimum size among ALG_i is a $(1 + \epsilon)$-approximate solution to the minimum vertex cover problem.

LEMMA 9.9   The size of ALG_{min} is at most $1 + \epsilon$ times the optimum.

Proof.   Let the optimal vertex cover *OPT* be partitioned to its subsets of nodes in the levels $i \pmod k$, OPT_i. Since $OPT = \cup_i OPT_i$, it follows that $OPT = \sum_{i=1}^{k} OPT_i$. Now,

$$|ALG_i| \le |OPT| + |OPT_i| .$$

Therefore,

$$\sum_{i=1}^{k} |ALG_i| \le k|OPT| + \sum_{i=1}^{k} |OPT_i| = (k+1)|OPT|.$$

Hence, $\min_i |ALG_i| \le \frac{k+1}{k}|OPT| \le (1+\epsilon)|OPT|$.   ∎

Hence, the shifting strategy is the building block of PAS for vertex cover and independent set in outerplanar graphs.

BEST: UNLESS $NP = P$

9.4

In the previous section the ultimate limit on approximability was 1. That limit could be approached at an increasing cost of running time. The problems discussed here are harder as there exists a positive ratio error bound that cannot be improved upon unless $NP = P$. A polynomial c-approximation algorithm is called best possible if the problem of approximation within $c - \delta$ is *NP*-complete for any $\delta > 0$. On the other hand, that limit can be reached in polynomial time. To date, all such best possible results were achieved only for bottleneck problems. Another best possible 2-approximation algorithm is discussed in Chapter 8 for the problem of packing squares with fixed corners. Note that this problem is also a bottleneck problem—maximize size of squares so they do not overlap.

In some weaker sense, we will demonstrate a best possible result for a parallel algorithm.

We call the technique that is used to get the best possible results in this section powers of graphs. This technique is widely applicable as is manifested by the list of problems for which best possible algorithms have been devised using that technique. For some of these problems, best possible algorithms were obtained using other techniques (see Exercises 1 and 2.) Yet none has proved to be as uniformly applicable as the powers of graphs.

Examples of bottleneck problems discussed in this section include the k-center problem: Given n cities and the shortest path distances between all pairs of cities, the aim is to choose k cities as centers so that the city farthest from its closest center is as close as possible. A second example is the bottleneck wandering salesperson problem [WSMM]: The salespserson starts in some city u and must wind his or her way to city v, visiting each city exactly once; the salesperson travels to a new city each day, and wishes to choose a route that minimizes the travel time on the longest day of traveling. A third example is the bottleneck k-clustering problem [k-CMM]. Here the goal is to partition

n objects into k clusters so that the longest distance (representing dissimilarity) between two objects in the same cluster is minimized.

For each of these problems, we wish to find a subgraph of the complete graph satisfying certain constraints such that the length of the longest edge included in the subgraph is minimized. We call such problems *bottleneck problems*.

9.4.1   THE k-CENTER PROBLEM

The k-center problem is defined on the complete graph of shortest path distances between each pair of nodes $G = (V, E)$. Let the shortest path distance between i and j be denoted C_{ij}. The problem is to find a subset of the nodes S, with $|S| = k$, so that the longest distance of a node from the nearest node in S is minimized. Formally, the objective is to identify $S \subseteq V$, $|S| = k$ that minimizes the quantity $cost(S) = max_{i \in S} min_j C_{ij}$.

Kariv and Hakimi [KH79] proved that the k-center problem is *NP*-hard. Furthermore, we have the following theorem:

LEMMA 9.10   The problem of approximating the k-center problem with triangle inequality satisfied within a factor of $(2 - \epsilon)$, is *NP*-complete for any $\epsilon > 0$.

Proof.   The proof is by reduction from the dominating set problem. The dominating set problem is to determine whether in a given graph $G = (V, E)$ there is a set of vertices DS of size not exceeding k that dominates all vertices, i.e. such that all vertices are either in DS or are adjacent to a vertex in DS. We construct a complete graph with the following weights, satisfying the triangle inequality:

$$w(e) = \begin{cases} 1 & \text{if } e \in E \\ 2 & \text{if } e \notin E \end{cases}$$

In this complete graph, the existence of k centers of cost less than 2 is equivalent to the existence of a dominating set of size not exceeding k. Moreover, if there are k centers of cost < 2 then the optimal cost is equal to 1.   ∎

Note that this proof can be easily extended to the k-center problem without the triangle inequality. This is done by replacing the constant 2 of the weight function by any positive constant M. In that case the extended proof implies that finding any fixed approximation to the k-center problem is an *NP*-complete problem.

Hochbaum and Shmoys ([HS85]) presented a best possible 2-approximation algorithm for the k-center problem. The main idea of the proof lies in the use of a technique called powers of graphs. Consider for instance the square of a graph $G = (V, E)$, $G^2 = (V, E^2)$. E^2 is the set of edges between vertices that have a path of length 1 or 2 between them. The tth power of a graph is similarly defined as the set of edges between nodes that have a path of length at most t between them. The idea of powers of graphs is particularly useful for bottleneck problems.

We now sketch the 2-approximation algorithm for the k-center problem. In the next section it will be described in full detail and generality. In bottleneck problems the value of the solution is determined by the weight of one of the edges in the graph. The procedure then consists of adding one smallest cost edge at a time, and examining the resulting graph for the required structure. For the k-center problem we examine each such graph for the existence of a dominating set of size $\leq k$. If such dominating set exists then there is a k-center solution the value of which does not exceed the largest edge cost in the graph. Since identifying whether a given graph has a dominating set of size k is an NP-complete problem, we consider instead the square of the graph. If there is a dominating set in the square of the graph, then taking this set as a feasible k-center solution will give an objective value at most twice the optimum. This follows since if there is a solution in the graph itself (and it is the first graph in which there is a dominating set of size $\leq k$), then there must be a dominating set of size $\leq k$ in the square of that graph. Because of the triangle inequality the largest edge in the square of the graph is at most twice the size of the largest edge in the graph, hence establishing the factor of 2. The only snag about this particular procedure is that finding a dominating set in a square of a graph is itself an NP-complete problem, i.e., just as difficult as finding a dominating set in the original graph. We resolve this difficulty by finding instead a *maximal* (not maximum which is NP-hard to find) independent set in the square of the graph. That maximal independent set has the same two required properties as the dominating set in the square of the graph. First, if the graph G has a dominating set of size k, then in G^2 every maximal independent set is also of size k or less. Moreover, a maximal independent set is also a dominating set, and hence, consists of a feasible k-center using only the edges of G^2.

The worst case bound of value 2 now follows easily. At each phase of the algorithm one additional edge of smallest cost among the remaining edges is added to the graph. A maximal independent set is then found in the square of that graph. If it is greater than k, then there is no dominating set in the graph of size k or less, and hence, the value of the optimal k-center solution is greater than the cost of the edge added to the graph. The algorithm then continues to the next phase. When a maximal independent set in the square of the graph is $\leq k$, then we consider it a k-center feasible solution. Since it only uses in the assignment of nodes to centers the edges of the square of the graph, and the value of the optimum is at least the value of the largest edge in the graph, it follows that this feasible k-center uses edge of cost at most twice the optimum.

EXERCISE 9.2   Consider the following 2-approximation algorithm for the k-center problem with triangle inequality:

> Step 0: Select a vertex $v \in V$ arbitrarily. Let $S = \{\}$.
>
> Step 1: Set $S \leftarrow S \cup \{v\}$, $V \leftarrow V - \{v\}$
> if $|S| = K$ stop, output S. Else, continue.
>
> Step 2: Let $max_{v_j \in V} \ min_{v_i \in S} \ d_{ij} = d_{iv}$. Go to Step 1.

Prove that this algorithm is indeed a 2-approximation as claimed.

EXERCISE 9.3   Consider a variation of the k-center problem, known as the k-supplier problem. In the k-supplier problem, one is given a complete weighted graph $G = (V, E)$, and a partition of V into two sets: a set of *suppliers* S, and a set of *customers* C. The objective is to find a subset of k suppliers that minimizes the maximum distance of any customer vertex from the selected subset. As in the k-center problem, the distance of a vertex from a subset of vertices is taken to be the distance between that vertex and its closest neighbor in the subset.

We assume that the edge weights satisfy the triangle inequality.

(a) Prove that finding a $(3 - \epsilon)$-approximation algorithm for any constant $\epsilon > 0$ for the k-supplier problem is *NP*-hard. (Hint: Use a reduction from the Dominating Set problem)

(b) Consider the following algorithm for the k-supplier problem:

> select any $c \in C$
> select $s \in S$ closest to c
> $A_C \leftarrow \{c\}$
> $A_S \leftarrow \{s\}$
> for $\ell = 2, \ldots, k$ do
>> select $c \in C$ farthest from A_S
>> select $s \in S$ closest to c
>> $A_C \leftarrow A_C \cup \{c\}$
>> $A_S \leftarrow A_S \cup \{s\}$
>
> end
> output A_S

Prove that this is a *3*-approximation algorithm.

9.4.2   A POWERFUL APPROXIMATION TECHNIQUE FOR BOTTLENECK PROBLEMS

In this section we present a general technique for designing approximation algorithms for bottleneck problems with strong worst-case performance properties. The material in this section is a summary of the work of Hochbaum and Shmoys [HS86].

The approximation results discussed are tabulated in Table 9.1. For all but one of the problems mentioned, these are the first algorithms that insure *any* constant guarantee; for the clustering problem k-cluster minmax [k-CMM], Gonzalez has reported an identical bound using a different approach [G82].

The main result reported here is that the use of the technique described in this section implies the derivation of approximation algorithms for several bottleneck problems that are *best possible* (and these are indicated in Table 9.1 by an asterisk). That is, if any of these algorithms can be improved to yield a smaller error guarantee (while maintaining polynomial running time) then this improved algorithm could also be used to solve all *NP*-complete problems in polynomial time. (In fact, using only $\log |E|$ "calls" of such a routine would be needed to solve the k-center problem to optimality.)

For each of the problems considered, an instance is specified by an edge-weighted complete undirected graph, where the weights satisfy the triangle inequality; that is, for every triple of nodes, i, j, k, $c_{ij} + c_{jk} \geq c_{ik}$, where c_{ij} denotes the weight of the edge between i and j. The bottleneck problems dealt with in this section are all of the following type: we wish to find a subgraph of the complete graph satisfying certain constraints such that the length of the longest edge included in the subgraph is minimized. The remainder of the specification of each problem is given by the constraints that the feasible subgraphs must satisfy. In some cases these constraints will be purely combinatorial restrictions on

Communication Network Problems	δ
$(k, \mathcal{F})$-partition with diameter d	$2d$
k-cluster minmax *	2
k-center *	2

Weighted Center Problems	δ
(singly) weighted k-center	3
weighted k-center with at most l centers	3
k-supplier *	3

Vehicle Routing Problems	δ
k-path vehicle routing *	2
wandering salesperson *	2
repeated city TSP *	2
single depot k-vehicle routing *	2

(Note that δ denotes an upper bound on $\frac{\text{heuristic solution value}}{\text{optimal solution value}}$.)

Table 9.1: Quality of Approximations using Bottleneck Algorithm

the structure of permissible subgraphs; in others, additional costs will be introduced to limit the range of feasible solutions. This framework is an extremely general one, and yet it permits the following observation.

Observation. For any bottleneck problem, the value of the optimal solution is always one of the edge weights in the original specification of the instance of the problem.

It is convenient to label the edges of the complete graph so that $c_{e_1} \leq c_{e_2} \leq \cdots \leq c_{e_m}$ where $m = \binom{n}{2}$. The following notation will also be used extensively. If $H = (V, F)$ is an arbitrary subgraph of G, let

$$max(H) = \max_{(i,j) \in F} c_{ij} .$$

Example. Returning to the k-center problem, let $K_{m,n}$ denote the complete bipartite graph with the two parts containing m and n vertices. Then $K_{1,i}$, or a *star* graph on $i + 1$ vertices, captures the idea of one vertex dominating i other vertices. Bearing this in mind, we see that the k-center problem falls within the general framework given above, where the class of permissible subgraphs are those graphs that are the union of k-star graphs. By the observation made above, the optimal value must be one of the c_{ij}. This leads us to the following algorithm:

```
i ← 0; S ← ∅
until |S| ≤ k do
    begin
    i ← i + 1
    G_i ← BOTTLENECKG(c_{e_i}) { Recall e_i is the ith shortest edge }
    S ← minimum dominating set of G_i { This is NP-hard }
    end
output S
```

This procedure could be mimicked for all bottleneck problems; the only difference would be that at each iteration of the until loop, a test is made to determine if G_i contains the appropriate feasible subgraph. However, for all of the problems we consider, this decision problem is *NP*-complete.

The key notion used for all of the approximation algorithms given here is that of the power of a graph. If $H = (V, F)$ is an arbitrary subgraph of G and t is a positive integer, let the tth power of H be $H' = (V, F')$ where there is an edge in H' wherever there was a path of length at most t edges in H; more formally, let

$$F' = \{(i_0, i_l) \mid \exists i_1, i_2, \ldots, i_{l-1} \text{ s.t. } (i_{m-1}, i_m) \in F, m = 1, \ldots, l, l \leq t\} .$$

These graphs are useful because of the following simple lemma, which is a consequence of the fact that the edge weights satisfy the triangle inequality.

LEMMA 9.11 $max(H') \leq t \cdot max(H)$.

For a particular instance of some bottleneck problem, let $\mathcal{H}$ denote the set of feasible subgraphs of G. Thus, we wish to minimize $max(H)$ such that $H \in \mathcal{H}$. In the algorithm presented above, at iteration i we want to check if $\mathcal{H}$ contains a graph H that is a subgraph of $G_i = \text{BOTTLENECKG}(c_{e_i})$. Suppose that instead of this, we run a procedure $TEST(\mathcal{H}, G_i, t)$ that has two termination conditions; either $TEST$ produces a "certificate of failure" or it produces a graph $H \in \mathcal{H}$ that is a subgraph of $(G_i)'$. A "certificate of failure" is some proof that there is no subgraph of G_i that is contained in $\mathcal{H}$. This suggests the following algorithm:

> **procedure** *bottleneck*$(\mathcal{H}, G, t)$
> $i \leftarrow 0$
> until *out.test* is not a "certificate of failure" do
>   begin
> $i \leftarrow i + 1$
> $G_i \leftarrow \text{BOTTLENECKG}(c_{e_i})$
>   *out.test* $\leftarrow TEST(\mathcal{H}, G_i, t)$
>   end
> output *out.test*.

The justification for this approach is given by the following theorem:

THEOREM 9.5   Let $\mathcal{H}$ denote the feasible subgraphs for an instance G of a bottleneck problem. Let H^* be the optimal subgraph in $\mathcal{H}$, and let H_A be the graph output by the procedure *bottleneck*$(\mathcal{H}, G, t)$. Then, the value of the approximate solution produced,

$$max(H_A) \leq t\,max(H^*) ,$$

where $max(H^*)$ is the value of the optimal solution.

Proof.   Suppose that the algorithm halts at some iteration i. Since for all previous iterations $TEST$ produces a certificate of failure, it follows that $max(H^*) \geq c_{e_i}$. However, the graph output by the procedure is a subgraph of $(G_i)'$, and thus, by the lemma,

$$max(H_A) \leq max((G_i)') \leq t\,max(G_i) = t c_{e_i}.$$

Combining these inequalities, we get the desired result.   ∎

Thus, for any bottleneck problem the construction of a polynomial-time procedure $TEST(\mathcal{H}, G, t)$ immediately yields a polynomial-time t-approximation algorithm for this problem. The remainder of this section is devoted to exhibiting a wide variety of problems for which this is possible.

9.4.2.1   Communication network design problems

Suppose that we wish to assign each of n locations to one of k communication networks, where the structure of each network is set in some specific way. Furthermore, we wish to do this in such a way so that the length of the longest link used for communication is minimized. More formally, suppose that $\mathcal{F}$ is a family of graphs $\{F_i\}_{i=1,2,\ldots}$ where F_i has i vertices. These are the allowed network structures. Let $part(\mathcal{F}, H)$ denote the minimum number of parts into which the vertices of H can be partitioned such that if a given part has i vertices, the subgraph induced by those vertices contains F_i as a subgraph. Given the complete edge-weighted graph G, we wish to find the minimum value c, such that for $H = \text{BOTTLENECKG}(c), part(\mathcal{F}, H) \leq k$; we call this the $(k, \mathcal{F})$-*partition* problem.

For example, if $\mathcal{F} = \{K_{1,i}\}_{i=0,1,\ldots}$, then $part(\mathcal{F}, H)$ is the domination number $dom(H)$, the size of the smallest dominating set. The corresponding optimization problem is the k-center problem.

Another common example is the family $\mathcal{F} = \{K_i\}_{i=1,2,\ldots}$ where K_i denotes the complete graph on i vertices. In this case, $part(\mathcal{F}, H)$ is the *clique partition number*, $\kappa(H)$, the minimum number of parts into which the vertex set can be partitioned such that the graph induced on each part is a clique. The corresponding optimization problem is the *k-cluster minmax* problem; we wish to partition the nodes such that any two nodes in the same part are as close as possible to each other.

If H is an arbitrary graph, let $diam(H)$ denote the number of edges in the shortest path between the pair of vertices of H that are farthest apart. An alternate, equivalent definition of $diam(H)$ is the minimum value t such that H^t is a complete graph.

In the two examples above, for $F_i = K_{1,i}$, $diam(K_{1,i}) = 2$, and for $F_i = K_i$, $diam(K_i) = 1$. Suppose that $\mathcal{F}$ satisfies the constraint that for all i, $diam(F_i) \leq d$. In this case, we construct a polynomial-time $2d$-approximation algorithm to find a feasible $(k, \mathcal{F})$-partition. As discussed before, if $\mathcal{F}$ denotes the class of feasible subgraphs of G given by $(k, \mathcal{F})$-partitions, we need only construct the procedure $TEST(\mathcal{F}, H, 2d)$.

> **procedure** $TEST(\mathcal{F}, H, 2d)$
> $S \leftarrow$ maximal independent set in H^d
> if $|S| > k$
>> then output "certificate of failure" produced
>> else do
>>> begin
>>> { Note that S is a dominating set of H^d }
>>> if $|S| < k$ then add nodes arbitrarily to make $|S| = k$
>>> { Suppose that $S = \{v_1, v_2, \ldots, v_k\}$ }
>>> partition all of the nodes into $V_1, V_2, \ldots, V_k$ where v_i
>>>> dominates all of the nodes in V_i.
>>> { Note that V_i induces a clique in H^{2d} }

> Form the $(k, \mathcal{F})$-partition by replacing V_i
> by F_j where $j = |V_i|$
> { Note that this $(k, \mathcal{F})$-partition is a subgraph of H^{2d} }
> end

This procedure makes use of a few fundamental facts.

FACT 9.1   If H contains a $(k, \mathcal{F})$-partition, then $\kappa(H^d) \leq k$.

FACT 9.2   If $\kappa(H) \leq k$, then *every* independent set in H has size at most k.

FACT 9.3   If S is a maximal independent set of H, then it is a dominating set of H.

FACT 9.4 $(K_{1,i})^2 = K_{i+1}$.

FACT 9.5 K_i contains all graphs on i vertices as a subgraph.

By combining these facts, it is straightforward to verify that the procedure correctly produces a certificate of failure or a feasible $(k, \mathcal{F})$-partition in H^{2d}. Thus, we have shown the following:

THEOREM 9.6   Let $\mathcal{F}$ be a family of graphs satisfying $diam(F_i) \leq d$ for $i = 1, 2, \ldots$; then the procedure *bottleneck* yields a $2d$-approximation algorithm for the $(k, \mathcal{F})$-partition problem.

COROLLARY 9.2   For the minmax clustering problem, the procedure *bottleneck* produces a clustering of cost at most twice the cost of the optimal clustering.

Consider now the k-center problem; an immediate corollary of the theorem would be a 4-approximation algorithm for this problem. However, it is quite easy to improve this result. In the procedure *TEST* given above, if a certificate of failure is not generated, the set S produced is a dominating set in H^2. This is precisely what is required; therefore, we do not need to resort to H^4.

COROLLARY 9.3   For the k-center problem, the procedure *bottleneck* produces a center of cost at most twice the cost of the optimal.

It is not hard to prove for the clustering problem that unless $P = NP$, there does not exist a polynomial-time algorithm that has a better performance guarantee (for a proof similar to that of the k-center problem, see Lemma 9.10).

For the problems discussed above, the set of feasible subgraphs for each bottleneck problem was constrained by purely combinatorial restrictions. Using generalizations of the k-center problem as examples, we show now how to use this technique for problems where the feasible subgraphs $\mathcal{F}$ are further constrained by additional cost functions.

An instance of the (singly) weighted k-center problem is specified by a complete edge-weighted graph $G = (V, E)$ with edge weights c_{ij} that satisfy the triangle inequality, and node weights w_i. A feasible center is a set S of nodes such that $\sum_{i \in S} w_i \leq k$.

Thus, a certificate of failure for the routine *TEST* must prove that $G_i =$ BOTTLE-NECKG(c_{e_i}) does not contain a dominating set of total weight at most k. Furthermore, if *TEST* does not produce a certificate of failure, then it must find a set of nodes of total weight at most k such that it is a dominating set for G_t for some t. The routine that we provide below yields a dominating set in G_3. It will be useful to define $N_H(v)$ as the neighborhood of v in H; that is, the set of vertices adjacent to v in H as well as v itself.

> **procedure** *TEST*$(G_i, 3)$ { Weighted k-center }
> $S \leftarrow$ maximal independent set in $(G_i)^2$
> for all $j \in S$ do
>   begin
> $w \leftarrow \min_{l \in N_{G_i}(j)}\{w_l\}$
>   let $l(j)$ be a node in $N_{G_i}(j)$ with $w_{l(j)} = w$
>   end
> $S' \leftarrow \cup_{j \in S} l(j)$
> if $\sum_{j \in S'} w_j > k$
>   then output "certificate of failure" produced
>   else output S'

By the observations made above, it is easy to see that that S' must be a dominating set in $(G_i)^3$; S is a dominating set in $(G_i)^2$, and for every vertex v in S there is some vertex in S' that is adjacent to v. We need only show that the certificate of failure is produced correctly. To do this, we show that the total weight of S' is at most the weight of the minimum weight dominating set of G_i. This follows from the greedy way in which we perturb the vertices of S so that we get the following theorem:

THEOREM 9.7   The procedure *bottleneck* yields a 3-approximation algorithm for the weighted k-center problem.

This result can be extended very simply to the weighted k-center problem where we further constrain feasible solutions to have at most l centers without any degradation in the performance guarantee.

9.4.2.2   Routing problems

In the *wandering salesperson problem*, we seek a route for the salesperson from a fixed starting point to a fixed destination that passes through all of the remaining cities. Under the bottleneck cost criterion, we wish to find such a route where the single longest inter-city distance is as small as possible. Another interesting generalization of the traveling salesperson problem is the *vehicle routing problem* [VRMM], where there are some k vehicles that may be used to traverse all of the cities. We consider the following variant: designate some subset of the cities as potential endpoints of routes of the vehicles; this subset may contain no more than $2k$ points. In this model the initial and final endpoints of each route must be distinct. We wish to use at most k vehicles so that all of the cities, both the potential endpoints and the remaining ones as well, are visited exactly once. We will refer to this problem as the *k-path vehicle routing problem*. Note that if $k = 1$ and the subset contains two cities, then this problem reduces to the wandering salesperson problem mentioned above. We will present a 2-approximation algorithm for the k-path vehicle routing problem (and thus for the wandering salesman problem as well). It is possible to show that even in the special case of the wandering salesman problem, improving this guarantee would prove that $P = NP$.

Most of the following algorithms will make use of the following theorem:

THEOREM 9.8   (**Fleischner [F74]**) If G is a biconnected graph with more than 2 vertices, then G^2 contains a Hamiltonian cycle.

Lau [L80] and independently Parker and Rardin [PR85] found a polynomial-time algorithm that constructs a Hamiltonian cycle in the square of a biconnected graph. As Parker and Rardin showed, this immediately leads to a 2-approximation algorithm for the bottleneck traveling salesperson problem, since if $G_i = \text{BOTTLENECKG}(c_{e_i})$ is not biconnected, this is a certificate of failure. Furthermore, biconnectivity can be tested in polynomial time.

As was done above for the k-path vehicle routing problem, we construct a procedure *TEST* that either produces a certificate of failure in G_i or produces a feasible routing in $(G_i)^2$. If X is the set of potential endpoints, G_i has a feasible routing if there exist $l \leq k$ paths with endpoints only in X that cover the vertices of G_i. The following lemma provides us with a suitable certificate of failure:

LEMMA 9.12   If there exists a vertex v such that a component of $G_i - v$ does not contain a vertex of X, then G_i cannot contain a feasible path covering.

To complete the description of the procedure, we must explain how to find a path cover in $(G_i)^2$ in the event that no certificate of failure is found. The routing is found by constructing a biconnected graph H such that any Hamiltonian cycle found in H^2 gives a feasible routing in $(G_i)^2$. Using a slight modification of a result by Chartrand, Hobbs, Jung, Kapoor, and Nash-Williams [CHJKN74], we construct the new graph H by taking five distinct copies of G_i and then adding two additional vertices. Make the two additional vertices adjacent to all of the vertices in the five copies that correspond to vertices in X. It is not hard to prove that any Hamiltonian cycle in H yields a path covering in each of the five copies. Therefore, we have the following result:

THEOREM 9.9   For the bottleneck k-path vehicle routing problem, procedure *bottleneck* yields a 2-approximation algorithm.

In another common routing problem we have one depot and k vehicle that must service all of the cities. (This is aptly referred to as the *single depot k-vehicle routing problem*.) It is not hard to construct a suitable routine *TEST* to prove the following result:

THEOREM 9.10   For the bottleneck single depot k-vehicle routing problem, the procedure *bottleneck* yields a 2-approximation algorithm.

In a well-known relaxation of the bottleneck traveling salesperson problem, cities may be visited more than once, but edges may be used at most once. Thus, for this problem we wish to find the smallest value of c such that $H = \text{BOTTLENECKG}(c)$ contains a Hamiltonian walk. Once again it possible to prove the following result:

THEOREM 9.11 For the bottleneck traveling salesperson problem with multiple visits allowed, the procedure *bottleneck* gives a 2-approximation algorithm.

It is significant to note that *all* of these routing problems have the property that if there existed approximation algorithms for them with a better performance guarantee, then there would exist polynomial-time algorithms to solve them to optimality. For proofs see [PR85] or [HS86].

9.4.3 BEST POSSIBLE PARALLEL APPROXIMATION ALGORITHMS

One of the foremost open questions in the complexity of parallel algorithms is whether $P = NC$. NC problems are polynomial problems for which there exists a parallel algorithm running on a polynomial number of parallel processors in time polynomial in $\log n$, where n indicates the size of the input. Such running time is called *polylog* time.

Among the problems in P, the polynomial problems, the "hardest" are the P-complete problems. If any of the P-complete problems has a polylog algorithm then all problems in P have a polylog algorithm solving them. In that case, $P = NC$.

Another class of polynomial problems containing NC is RNC. These problems possess a *randomized* polylog algorithm. It is not known whether RNC properly contains NC, or whether $P = RNC$ (a weaker form of the $P = NC$ question). There are no known P-complete problems that have an NC or RNC algorithm, so the question $P = RNC$ is still open.

A δ-approximation algorithm for a P-complete problem is called best possible if the existence of a $(\delta - \epsilon)$-approximation algorithm for any fixed $\delta > 0$ would imply that $P = NC$ (or $P = RNC$ as a weaker form of best possibility).

The only example studied for a best possible RNC, (or NC) approximation algorithm is for the maximum minimum degree problem: Given a graph G the problem is to find the maximum value of the minimum degree among all subgraphs of G. This problem is polynomial and there is a linear sequential algorithm solving it described in Section 3.7.2. The maximum minimum degree problem was proved P-complete by Anderson and Mayr [AM85]. Furthermore, Anderson and Mayr also prove that any $(2 - \epsilon)$-approximation to the maximum minimum degree problem is itself P-complete. It follows that an NC 2-approximation algorithm for this problem is best possible and an RNC 2-approximation is best possible in the weaker sense. In [AM85] an NC $(2 + \epsilon)$-approximation algorithm is described for any $\epsilon > 0$. Hochbaum and Shmoys present in [HS87a] a best possible RNC 2-approximation algorithm, i.e., it is a randomized polylog algorithm that finds the value of a degree which is at most a factor of 2 off the maximum minimum degree. An improvement to the performance of this algorithm in terms of the ratio will imply that $P = RNC$. Thus, the algorithm is best possible unless $P = RNC$.

The question whether there exists an NC 2-approximation algorithm for the maximum minimum degree problem is still open.

BETTER THAN BEST

In some cases approximation algorithms have been derived that appear to violate some impossibility results (with the "unless $NP = P$" qualification). Here we describe two such results and explain the apparent contradictions.

When considering the approximation ratio delivered by an algorithm, it is important to distinguish between the absolute and asymptotic ratios. We define the *absolute performance ratio*, R_A, of an approximation algorithm A,

$$R_A = \inf\{r \geq 1 | R_A(I) \leq r \text{ for all problem instances } I\},$$

and the *asymptotic performance ratio* R_A^∞ for A to be

$$R_A^\infty = \inf\{r \geq 1 | \exists n \in Z^+, R_A(I) \leq r \ \forall I \text{ s.t. } I \geq n\}.$$

Unless we are careful as to which type of performance ratio is delivered by an algorithm, we can come across contrasting complexity results. We discuss here two examples. One is the bin-packing problem which is strongly NP-complete and as such would not have a FPAS unless $NP = P$ (see Theorem 9.1). Yet Karp and Karmarkar [KK82] present a scheme that runs in time bounded by a polynomial in the number of items n and in $\frac{1}{\epsilon}$ and delivers a solution for an instance I that is at most $(1+\epsilon)OPT(I) + O((\frac{1}{\epsilon})^6)$. Such a scheme is a polynomial approximation scheme, but the error ratio bound of ϵ is asymptotic and not absolute, which makes this result possible. We will refer to such result as an asymptotic FPAS.

Another example of this phenomenon relates to the edge coloring in multigraphs (or chromatic index). This problem is simply stated: color the edges of a given multigraph $G = (V, E)$ using as few colors as possible, so that no two adjacent edges receive the same color. We denote the minimum number of colors needed by $\chi'(G)$. Holyer [Ho80] proved that the problem is NP-hard. Furthermore, he showed that deciding whether a simple graph (with only a single copy of each edge) has chromatic index of 3 or less is NP-complete. This implies that unless $P = NP$, there does not exist an approximation algorithm that finds an edge coloring for multigraphs that uses at most $(\frac{4}{3} - \epsilon)$ times the chromatic index of the graph for any $\epsilon > 0$.

In contrast to this negative result, there are a number of surprisingly positive results. Let Δ be the the maximum degree of a vertex in the graph G. Hochbaum, Nishizeki, and Shmoys [HNS86] presented an $O(|E|(|V| + \Delta))$-time algorithm to find an edge coloring of G that uses no more than $(\frac{4}{3})\chi'$ colors; more surprisingly, it uses at most $\lfloor \frac{(9\chi'+6)}{8} \rfloor$ colors. This result improved on an algorithm of Nishizeki and Sato which achieved the $(\frac{4}{3})\chi'$ bound as well, but used as many as $\lfloor \frac{(5\chi'+2)}{4} \rfloor$ colors; and an algorithm of Hochbaum and Shmoys which used at most $\lfloor \frac{(7\chi'+4)}{6} \rfloor$ colors. Moreover, this sequence of algorithms can be viewed as part of a family of approximation algorithms, where the ultimate algorithm in this family colors a multigraph using at most $\chi' + 1$ colors. This performance is certainly an improvement over the $\frac{4}{3}$ limit.

These contrasting complexity results have many interesting implications. The hardness results about approximation algorithms that use the absolute performance ratio should be viewed with slight skepticism since a result with superior asymptotic performance might still be obtained. Indeed, as a challenging research topic we propose to get better *asymptotic* bounds for problems that are notoriously hard to approximate, such as the maximum clique problem. By the same reasoning, results that exclude the possibility of approximation algorithms with certain asymptotic performance ratios (assuming that $P \neq NP$), like those for the vertex coloring and independent set problems, are especially desirable.

9.5.1   A FPAS FOR BIN PACKING

Recall that in the bin-packing problem the input instance I consists of n pieces of size p_j, where each size is a rational in the interval $[0,1]$. The objective is to pack the pieces into bins where the sum of the sizes of the pieces packed in any bin cannot exceed 1, in such a way that the minimum number of bins are used. This minimum is denoted here by $OPT(I)$.

The asymptotic FPAS of Karp and Karmarkar was preceded by the important work of Fernandez de la Vega and Lueker [FVL81]. They devised an asymptotic approximation scheme that runs in time polynomial in n but (worse than) exponential in $\frac{1}{\epsilon}$. Fernandez de la Vega and Lueker introduced the ideas of grouping, elimination of small pieces, and most importantly—the role of linear programming relaxation in approximating binpacking.

For a given ϵ and a problem instance I, let $A_\epsilon(I))$ denote the number of bins produced by the algorithm A_ϵ. The running time of the algorithm is polynomial in n and in $\frac{1}{\epsilon}$ and it delivers a solution satisfying $A_\epsilon(I) \leq (1+\epsilon)OPT(I) + O((\frac{1}{\epsilon})^6)$.

The strategy of Karp and Karmarkar used concepts introduced by [FVL81].

1. Elimination of Small Pieces. Let I be an instance of the bin-packing problem and let the parameter ϵ be given. Let instance J be obtained by deleting from I all "small" pieces of size less than or equal to $\frac{\epsilon}{1+\epsilon}$. Suppose a packing for instance J is found using $(1+\epsilon)OPT(J) + B$ bins, then this packing can be extended to one for instance I by inserting the small pieces using a new bin only when necessary. The number of bins required to pack all pieces is then at most $(1+\epsilon)OPT(J) + \max\{1, B\}$.

2. Grouping. Let I be an instance of the bin packing problem with n items. Let the items be divided into m groups of interval sizes such that each interval except the last contains exactly $\lceil \frac{n}{m} \rceil$ items. Let J be the instance obtained by rounding up the size of each item in an interval to the upper end of the interval (the maximum size of an item in the same group.) Instance J will have n items, but they will have only m distinct sizes. It is easy to show that $OPT(I) \leq OPT(J) \leq OPT(I) + \lceil \frac{n}{m} \rceil$.

3. The Linear programming relaxation of bin packing. The following linear programming relaxation of the bin packing problem can be traced back to work done by Gilmore and Gomory in the early 1960s. Consider an instance I of the bin-packing problem in which there are n items of m distinct sizes $s_1, \ldots, s_m$. Let there be n_i items of type i. Define a configuration as a subset of pieces that can be packed within a bin. Let a_{ij} denote the number of items of type i in configuration j and let x_j be the variable indicating the number of occurrences (or bins) of configuration j in a solution.

Then the linear program is:

$$\text{Min} \quad \sum_j x_j$$
$$\text{subject to} \quad \sum_j a_{ij} x_j \geq n_i \qquad i = 1, \ldots, m$$
$$x_j \geq 0 \quad \forall j.$$

The fractional optimal solution can be converted to a feasible integer solution by using configuration j $\lceil x_j \rceil$ times. Then, by deleting excess items as necessary we obtain a packing. The key is that for a linear program with m inequality constraints (not counting the nonnegativity constraints) there is an optimal basic feasible solution in which at most m variables are positive. The process of rounding each variable x_j up to $\lceil x_j \rceil$ will increase the number of configurations, and hence, the number of bins by at most m. Denote by $LIN(I)$ the optimal value of the linear program defining the fractional bin-packing problem on instance I, then $LIN(I) \leq OPT(I) \leq LIN(I) + m$.

EXERCISE 9.4 Let J be the instance derived from I by eliminating small pieces, and let a packing of j use at most $\alpha OPT(J) + B$ bins; then there is an extension of this packing that does not involve moving large pieces from their respective bins that uses at most $\alpha OPT(J) + \max\{1, B\}$ bins.

EXERCISE 9.5 Consider a grouping of an instance I that has $k_1, k_2, \ldots, k_m$ pieces in each of the m intervals. Rounding the size of pieces to the upper endpoint of the interval we obtain an instance J. Prove that $OPT(J) \leq OPT(I) + k_1$.

$\mathcal{A}_\epsilon$ FOR BIN PACKING [KARP AND KARMARKAR]

Step 1: Remove small pieces. Call the resulting instance I.

Step 2: Group big pieces into m groups with $m = \sqrt{n}$ with sizes rounded up. Call the resulting instance J.

Step 3: Solve the linear programming relaxation, round up the solution and remove excess pieces. Output the solution with $c(I)$ bins.

LEMMA 9.13 For $n > \frac{16(1+\epsilon)^2}{\epsilon^3}$, algorithm $\mathcal{A}_\epsilon$ is a $(1+\epsilon)$-approximation algorithm for bin packing.

Proof. Since $c(I)$ is obtained by rounding up the linear programming solution of value $LIN(J)$, then $c(I) \leq LIN(J) + m$, and

$$LIN(J) \leq OPT(J) \leq OPT(I) + \frac{n}{m} + 1.$$

By setting $m = \sqrt{n}$, we obtain $c(I) \leq OPT(I) + 2\sqrt{n} + 1$. The optimum is bounded from below by the sum of piece sizes, which are all big, $OPT(I) \geq n \cdot \frac{\epsilon}{1+\epsilon}$. Hence,

$$c(I) \leq \left(1 + \frac{(2\sqrt{n} + 1)(1+\epsilon)}{n\epsilon}\right) OPT(I).$$

The error term diminishes as $n \to \infty$. In particular, for $n > \frac{16(1+\epsilon)^2}{\epsilon^3}$, the relative error is $< \epsilon$. When the small pieces are added back, the relative error can only decrease. ∎

So this strategy will yield an asymptotic approximation scheme. The running time of this scheme depends on the algorithm used to solve the linear programming relaxation. As stated, the number of variables is the number of potential configurations which is $O(\frac{1}{\epsilon^m})$, which is severely exponential.

The idea of Karp and Karmarkar was to offer an innovative implementation of the Ellipsoid method that would solve the *dual* problem within an additive constant. The dual problem has a very large number of constraints. The solution to the dual is used as an oracle for evaluating a feasible solution to the bin-packing problem within an additive constant and in polynomial time. The key here is that the Ellipsoid method can handle a huge number of constraints if only there is a separation oracle available, and in this case the separation oracle is a simple Knapsack problem. We omit the remaining details of this fascinating implementation of this linear programming algorithm.

9.5.2 A 9/8-APPROXIMATION ALGORITHM FOR EDGE COLORING
OF MULTIGRAPHS AND BEYOND

Here we will only outline the algorithm in brief while stressing the aspects that make it possible to tighten the asymptotic performance bound.

The most naive approach to edge coloring a graph might be described as follows: choose an arbitrary edge of the graph and, if possible, color it with one of the colors used already; otherwise use a new color to color the edge. The most obvious improvement is to use an interchange approach: for each edge, check if some "simple" recoloring of the colored edges would eliminate the need for an additional color. This simple approach is the basis for most of the results about the chromatic index, dating back to Shannon, and is the approach used here. The other common approach is dual to this one—give a coloring that is not feasible (a color is present more than once at a vertex) and improve towards feasibility.

In order to prove better bounds, the "simple" recolorings become more complicated. A description of the algorithm is given in the figure below; the "simple" recolorings are hidden in the subroutine *recolor*.

procedure *color(G)*:
begin { $G = (V, E)$ }
   if $\Delta(G) \leq 2$ then color G with $\chi'(G)$ colors by a trivial method (DFS)
   else { $\Delta \geq 3$ }
     begin
       $q := \lfloor (9\Delta + 6)/8 \rfloor$; { q colors are currently available }
       $G' := (V, \emptyset)$;
       for each $e \in E$ do
         begin
           $G' := G' + e$; { add an uncolored edge $e = (x, y)$ }
           let a and b be any missing colors of x and y, respectively;
           recolor(x, y, a, b) { update coloring }
         end
     end
end

Before proceeding with more details on the subroutine *recolor*, we first introduce a few preliminary definitions. Assume that $G = (V, E)$ is edge colored with a set of q colors. A color c is said to be *missing* at vertex v if color c is not assigned to any of the edges incident to v. The set of all colors missing at v is called the *missing color set of v*, and is denoted by $M(v)$. The set of colors assigned to the multiple edges joining vertices u and v is denoted by $C(u, v)$. An edge colored c is called a *c-edge*. For two colors a and b, the edge subgraph of G induced by all of the edges colored a or b is called an *ab-subgraph,* and is denoted by $G[a, b]$. Each connected component of $G[a, b]$ is either a path or a cycle, in which the edges are alternately colored a and b. Such a path (or cycle) is called an *ab-alternating path (cycle)*. A vertex x is an endpoint of such a path if and only if exactly one of a and b is missing at x. Note that interchanging the colors a and b of the edges in an ab-alternating path or cycle yields another q-coloring of G. If $a \in M(x)$ for a vertex x, then $Apath(x, a, b)$ denotes the ab-alternating path starting from x. As in the procedure above, G' will always denote the graph induced by all of the colored edges and a single uncolored edge (x, y). If, in G', $a \in M(x)$ and $b \in M(y)$, then the ab-alternating path between x and y, if any, is called an *ab-critical path*. Note that every critical path contains an odd number of vertices. If H is a subgraph of G, then let $V(H)$ and $E(H)$ denote, respectively, the vertex and edge sets of H. Finally, define a *k-cycle* to be a cycle containing k vertices.

Let us now consider some easy lower bounds on χ'.

FACT 9.6 $\chi'(G) \geq \Delta(G)$.

FACT 9.7   Let $\mu_k(G)$ be the maximum number of edges in any subgraph induced on $2k + 1$ vertices. Then, $\chi'(G) \geq \lceil \mu_k(G)/k \rceil$.

This follows directly from the fact that each color can be used to color at most k edges of the subgraph. For our purposes it will be convenient to define $\tau(G) = max_{k=1,2,3} \lceil \mu_k(G)/k \rceil$. The following fact is an immediate corollary (and special case) of Fact 9.7.

FACT 9.8 $\chi'(G) \geq \tau(G)$.

LEMMA 9.14   Suppose that the routine *recolor* has the following property: if a new color is added to the color set, a subgraph induced on 3, 5, or 7 vertices has been identified that shows that the number of colors previously used is strictly less than $\tau(G)$. Then the procedure *color* uses at most $min\{\lfloor (9\chi' + 6)/8 \rfloor, (4/3)\chi'\}$ colors.

Proof.   Consider again the procedure *color*. We assume that if the number of colors is ever increased by the routine *recolor* then the number of colors previously used was strictly less than $\tau(G)$. Given this, the algorithm has the very strong property that if an additional color is introduced (beyond the initial $\lfloor (9\Delta + 6)/8 \rfloor$), then the coloring produced is *optimal* (by Fact 9.8). Thus, the only other case is that exactly $\lfloor (9\Delta + 6)/8 \rfloor$ colors are used; but by Fact 9.6, this implies that at most $\lfloor (9\chi' + 6)/8 \rfloor$ colors are ever used. Furthermore, if $\Delta \leq 2$ we color optimally, and if $\Delta \geq 3$, $\lfloor (9\Delta + 6)/8 \rfloor \leq 4\Delta/3 \leq 4\chi'/3$. ∎

Therefore, to prove the claimed performance guarantees we need only show that *recolor* satisfies the property mentioned in Lemma 9.14.

There are five basic cases handled by *recolor*:

Case 1: either x and y have a common missing color, or G' has no ab-critical path.

Case 2: the ab-critical path Q contains two vertices u and v that have a common missing color.

Case 3: the ab-critical path Q contains seven vertices.

Case 4: the ab-critical path Q contains five vertices.

Case 5: the ab-critical path Q contains three vertices.

We first show that these five cases are indeed sufficient. Note that if *recolor* is called, then $\Delta \geq 3$, and therefore $\lfloor (9\Delta + 6)/8 \rfloor \geq \Delta + 1$. Thus, every vertex of G' has at least one missing color, whereas the endpoints of the uncolored edge of G', (x, y), have at least two missing colors. Using a straightforward counting argument, we obtain the following lemma:

LEMMA 9.15 Suppose that $\Delta(G) \geq 3$, and that all of the edges of G' except $e = (x, y)$ are colored with at least $\lfloor (9\Delta + 6)/8 \rfloor$ colors. Let S be any subset of V such that no two vertices have a common missing color.

(a) If $x, y \in S$, then $|S| \leq 8$.

(b) If $x \in S$, then $|S| \leq 16$.

Proof. (a) Assume that q colors are used, where $q \geq \lfloor (9\Delta + 6)/8 \rfloor$. Clearly, $|M(x)|$ and $|M(y)|$ are each at least $q - \Delta + 1$, and $|M(v)| \geq q - \Delta$ for every vertex v other than x and y. Since $\sum_{v \in S} |M(v)| \leq q$, we have that

$$2(q - \Delta + 1) + (|S| - 2)(q - \Delta) \leq q,$$

and using straightforward manipulations we obtain

$$|S| \leq \frac{q - 2}{q - \Delta}.$$

Noting that $\Delta \geq 3$ and $q > (9\Delta + 6)/8 - 1$, we get that $|S| < 9$.

(b) This proof is almost identical to (a). ∎

Lemma 9.15 is the key to the polynomiality of the procedure. It implies that if the ab-critical path Q contains nine or more vertices, then Q contains two vertices that have a common missing color among the first 17 vertices, and hence, Case 2 must occur. Thus, if Cases 1 and 2 do not occur, then Q contains either seven, five, or three vertices (Cases 3, 4, and 5, respectively). These cases are treated with conceptually simple procedures (interchange) that are complex and involved in implementation. For details the reader is referred to [HNS86].

How would we go about improving the asymptotic performance of this algorithm? The algorithm described and its predecessors share the following structure. If a critical path is of length $\geq \ell$ then there exists an "easy" coloring as two vertices on the path are missing the same color. For critical paths of length $< \ell$ specific procedures are devised. With the increasing length of ℓ we can also get better colorings using $\frac{p+1}{p}$ colors for p even and increasingly larger. At this point, however, we lack the tools for compact uniform description of such family of algorithms. Not only the complexity of the algorithm is increasing with the improved coloring, but also the complexity of the description of the algorithm increases exponentially. We do conjecture, however, that ultimately it will be possible to devise a $\chi' + 1$-approximation algorithm for edge coloring in multigraphs.

WONDERFUL: WITHIN ONE UNIT OF OPTIMUM

9.6

Here we review briefly three ultimate approximation algorithms. They each deliver a solution that is at most 1 unit off the optimum.

Edge coloring in simple graphs. The first and oldest is Vizing's algorithm derived from his proof about edge coloring in simple graphs [V64]. Given a simple graph (without multiple edges) $G = (V, E)$ with maximum vertex degree Δ. No coloring can use less than Δ colors. Vizing proved that it is possible to color the edge of a simple graph using no more than $\Delta + 1$ colors. Hence, this is indeed within 1 off the optimum. On the other hand, Holyer [Ho80] proved that identifying the chromatic index of a graph is NP-complete. Vizing's proof has been translated to an $O(mn)$ algorithm. Hence this is a polynomial-time approximation algorithm.

Coloring of planar graphs. The four-color polynomial algorithm [AH77], [AHK77] has received a great deal of attention. In addition to the general interest in the four color theorem, this polynomial algorithm is also an approximation algorithm for the NP-complete planar graph coloring problem. Garey, Johnson, and Stockmeyer [GJS76] proved that it is NP-complete to decide if a planar graph is 3- or 4-colorable. It is trivial to decide whether or not a graph is 2-colorable. This happens if and only if the graph is bipartite, a property that can be verified in linear time. The four-color algorithm is hence a polynomial approximation algorithm within 1 unit off the optimum.

Min max degree spanning tree. The most recent and exciting discovery is the approximation of the NP-complete problem by finding a spanning tree so that the maximum vertex degree in the spanning tree is minimized. This problem, and its relative—the minimum-maximum degree Steiner tree are discussed in detail in Chapter 7. Fürer and Raghavacheri devised polynomial algorithms for these problems that approximate them within one unit off the optimum, [FR92], [FR94]. These algorithms were preceded by a substantial body of literature addressing the problems with tools of branch and bound, heuristics, and approximations. Why this particular problem turned out to be so relatively easy and how we can recognize other problems for which wonderful approximations exist is not known.

One significant use of the min-max degree spanning tree is as a tool for identifying whether a graph is Hamiltonian. When a graph is Hamiltonian it contain a min-max spanning tree with a maximum degree of 2. If the approximation algorithm delivers a solution of value 4 or more, then the graph is not Hamiltonian. It the solution is 2, then the graph is Hamiltonian. The only answer of the algorithm that leaves the existence of Hamiltonian circuit uncertain is when the solution delivered is of value 3. We can now hope that for most non-Hamiltonian graphs the answer is 4 or more. But with the pessimism built into complexity theorists frame of thinking, one should not be surprised if it turns out to be 3 almost every time.

REFERENCES

[AH77] K. Appel and W. Haken. Every planar map is four colorable. Part I: Discharging. *Illinois J. Math.* 21:429–490, 1977.

[AHK77] K. Appel, W. Haken, and J. Koch. Every planar map is four colorable. Part II: Reducibility," *Illinois J. Math.* 21:491–567, 1977.

[AM85] R. Anderson and E. W. Mayr. A *P*-complete problem and approximations to it, Stanford Technical report, 1985.

[AS94] C. Armen and C. Stein. A $2\frac{3}{4}$-approximation algorithm for the shortest superstring problem. Manuscript, 1994.

[B94] B. S. Baker. Approximation algorithms for *NP*-complete problems on planar graphs. *J. of ACM*, 153–180, 1994.

[Bar94] A. I. Barvinok. Two algorithmic results for the traveling salesman problem. Manuscript, 1994, to appear *Mathematics of Operations Research*.

[BE82] R. Bar-Yehuda and S. Even. On approximating a vertex cover for planar graphs. *Proceedings of 14th ACM Symposium on Theory of Computing*, 303–309, 1982.

[BGNR94] R. Bar-Yehuda, D. Geiger, J. Naor, and R. M. Roth. Approximation algorithms for the cycle-cover problem with applications to constraint satisfaction and Bayesian inference. Manuscript, 1994.

[BG94] A. Becker and D. Geiger. Approximation algorithms for the loop cutset problem. *Proc. of the 10th conference on Uncertainty in Artificial Intelligence*, Morgan Kaufman, 60–68, 1994.

[BGS95] M. Bellare, O. Goldreich, and M. Sudan. Free bits and Nonapproximability. *Proceedings of the 36th Annual IEEE Symposium on Foundations of Computer Science (FOCS95)*. 422–431, 1995.

[BLS82] F. D. Berman, F. T. Leighton, and L. Snyder. Optimal tile salvage. Unpublished manuscript, 1982.

[BBF94] V. Bafna, P. Berman, and T. Fujito. Constant ratio approximations of the weighted feedback vertex set problem for undirected graphs. Manuscript, 1994.

[BJTY91] A. Blum, T. Jiang, M. Li, J. Tromp, and M. Yannakakis. Linear approximations of shortest superstrings. In *Proceedings of the 23rd annual ACM symposium on theory of computing*, 328–336, 1991.

[CHJKN74] G. Chartrand, A.M. Hobbs, H.A. Jung, S.F. Kapoor, and C.St.J.A. Nash-Williams. The square of a block is Hamiltonian connected. *J. Comb. Theory Ser. B* 16:290–292, 1974.

[CNS81] N. Chiba, T. Nishizeki, and N. Saito. Applications of the Lipton and Tarjan's planar separator theorem. *J. Information Processing* 4(4):203–207, 1981.

[CGJ78] E.G. Coffman, Jr., M.R. Garey, and D.S. Johnson. An application of bin-packing to multiprocessor scheduling, *SIAM J. Computing* 7:1–17, 1978.

[CFN77] G. Cornuejols, M. L. Fisher, and G. L. Nemhauser. Location of bank accounts to optimize float: An analytic study of exact and approximate algorithms. *Management Science* 23(8):789–810, 1977.

[CGPR94] A. Czumai, L. Gasieniec, M. Piotrow, and W. Rytter. Parallel and sequential approximation of shortest superstrings. In *Proceedings of the 4th Scandinavian workshop on algorithm theory*, 95–106, 1994.

[DJPSY92] E. Dalhaus, D.S. Johnson, C.H. Papadimitriou, P. Seymour, and M. Yannakakis. The complexity of the multiway cuts. Extended Abstract. *Proceedings of the 1992 ACM Symposium on Theory of Computing*, 241–251, 1992.

[DGW92] P. De, J.B. Ghosh, and C.E. Wells. On the minimization of completion time variance with a bicriteria extension. *Operations Research*, 40:1148–1155, 1992.

[EP62] P. Erdös and L. Pósa. On the maximal number of disjoint circuits of a graph. *Publ. Math. Debrechen*, 9:3–12, 1962.

[FVL81] W. Fernandez de la Vega, G. S. Lueker. Bin packing can be solved within $1 + \epsilon$ in linear time. *Combinatorica 1*, 349–355, 1981.

[F74] H. Fleischner. The square of every two-connected graph is Hamiltonian. *J. Comb. Theory Ser. B*, 16:29–34, 1974.

[FPT81] R. J. Fowler, M. S. Peterson, and S. L. Tanimoto. Optimal packing and covering in the plane are *NP*-complete. *Inf. Proc. Lett. 12*, 3:133–137, 1981.

[Fr84] D.K. Friesen. Tighter bounds for the multifit processor scheduling algorithm. *SIAM J. Comput. 13*, 170–181, 1984.

[FR92] M. Fürer and B. Raghavacheri. Approximating the minimum degree spanning tree to within one from the optimal degree. *Proc. of the 3rd ACD-SIAM Symp. on Discrete Algorithms*, 317–324, 1992.

[FR94] M. Fürer and B. Raghavacheri. Approximating the minimum-degree Steiner tree to within one of optimal. *J. Algorithms*, 17:409–423, 1994.

[GJ78] M.R. Garey, and D.S. Johnson. Strong *NP*-completeness results: motivation, examples, and implications, *Journal of ACM*, 25:499–508, 1978.

[GJ79] M. R. Garey and D. S. Johnson. *Computers and Intractability: A guide to the theory of NP-completeness*. W. H. Freeman, San Francisco, 1979.

[GJS76] M. R. Garey, D. S. Johnson and L. Stockmeyer. Some simplified *NP*-complete graph problems. *Theoret. Comput. Sci.* 1:237–267, 1976.

[GH94] O. Goldschmidt and D. S. Hochbaum A polynomial algorithm for the k-cut problem. *Math of Operations Research*, 19(1):24–37, 1994.

[G82] T.F. Gonzales. Clustering to minimize the maximum inter-city distance. Technical report 117, Computer Science Department, U. Texas, Dallas, 1982.

[Gra66] R.L. Graham. Bounds for certain multiprocessing anomalies, *Bell System Tech. J.* 45:1563–1581, 1966.

[GW93] M. X. Goemans and D. P. Williamson. New 3/4-approximation algorithms for MAX-SAT. To appear in *SIAM J. Disc. Math.*, 1993.

[GW94] M.X. Goemans and D.P. Williamson. 0.878-approximation algorithms for MAX-CUT and MAX-2SAT. In *Proceedings of the 26th Annual ACM Symposium on Theory of Computing*, pages 422–431, 1994.

[Gr2] R. L. Graham. Bounds on multiprocessing timing anomalies, *SIAM J. Applied Math.* 17:263–269, 1969.

[Hoc82] D. S. Hochbaum. Heuristics for the fixed cost median problem. *Mathematical Programming*, 222:148–162, 1982.

[Hoc83] D. S. Hochbaum. Efficient bounds for the stable set, vertex cover, and set packing problems, *Discrete Applied Mathematics*, 6:243–254, 1983.

[HM83] D. S. Hochbaum, and W. Maass. Fast approximation schemes for geometric covering and packing problems in robotics and VLSI. Unpublished manuscript, University of California, Berkeley, Calif., 1983.

[HM85] D. S. Hochbaum and W. Maass. Approximation schemes for covering and packing problems in image processing and VLSI. *Journal of ACM*, 32(1):130–136, 1985.

[HNS86] D. S. Hochbaum, T. Nishizeki, and D. B. Shmoys. Better than "Best Possible" algorithm to edge color multigraphs. *Journal of Algorithms*, 7(1):79–104, 1986.

[HS85] D. S. Hochbaum and D. B. Shmoys. A best possible heuristic for the k-center problem. *Mathematics of Operations Research*, 10(2):180–184, 1985.

[HS86] D. S. Hochbaum and D. B. Shmoys. A unified approach to approximation algorithms for bottleneck problems, *Journal of ACM* 33(3):533–550, (July 1986).

[HS86a] D. S. Hochbaum and D. B. Shmoys. A bin packing problem you can almost solve by sitting on your suitcase, *SIAM J. Alg. Disc. Methods*, 7(2):247–257, 1986.

[HS87] D. S. Hochbaum and D. B. Shmoys. Using dual approximation algorithms for scheduling problems: practical and theoretical results. *Journal of ACM* 34(1):144–162, 1987.

[HS87a] D. S. Hochbaum and D. B. Shmoys. A best possible parallel approximation algorithm to a graph theoretic problem. *Operational Research*, 933–938, 1987.

[HS88] D. S. Hochbaum and D. B. Shmoys. A polynomial approximation scheme for machine scheduling on uniform processors: using the dual approximation approach. *SIAM J. on Computing* 17(3):539–551, 1988.

[Ho80] I. J. Holyer. The NP-completeness of edge colorings. *SIAM J. Computing*, 10:718–720, 1980.

[IK75] O.H. Ibarra and C.E. Kim. Fast approximation algorithms for the Knapsack and sum of subset problems. *J. Assoc. Comput. Mach.*, 22, 463–468, 1975.

[Joh82] D. S. Johnson. The NP-completeness column: An ongoing guide. *J. Algorithms 3*,2, 182–195, 1982.

[KH79] O. Kariv and S.L. Hakimi. An algorithmic approach to network location problems, part I: the p-centers. *SIAM J. Appl. Math.* 37:513–538, 1979.

[KK82] R. M. Karp and N. Karmarkar. An efficient approximation scheme for the one-dimensional bin-packing problem. *23rd Symposium on Foundations of Computer Science.* 312–320, 1982.

[KPS94] S. R. Kosaraju, J. K. Park, and C. Stein. Long tours and short superstrings. In *35st IEEE symp. on Foundations of Computer Science*, 166–177, 1994.

[K93] W. Kubiak. Completion time variance minimization on a single machine is difficult. *Operations Research Letters*, 14:49-60, 1993.

[L80] H.T. Lau. Finding a Hamiltonian cycle in the square of a block. Ph.D. Thesis, McGill University, Montreal. 1980.

[Law79] E. Lawler. Fast approximation algorithms for knapsack problems. *Mathematics of Operations Research*, 4:339–356, 1979.

[Len85] H.W. Lenstra Jr. Integer programming with a fixed number of variables. *Mathematics of Operations Research*, 8(4):538–548, 1983.

[Li90] M. Li. Towards a DNA sequencing theory. In *31st IEEE symp. on Foundations of Computer Science*, 125–134, 1990.

[LT79]   R.J. Lipton and R.E. Tarjan. A separator theorem for planar graphs. *SIAM J. Appl. Math.* 36(2):177–189, 1979.

[LT80]   R.J. Lipton and R.E. Tarjan. Applications of a planar separator theorem. *SIAM J. Computing* 9(3):615–627, 1980.

[LY93]   C. Lund and M. Yannakakis. On the hardness of approximating minimization problems. *Journal of the ACM*, 41(5):960–981, 1994.

[MS81]   B. Monien and R. Schultz. Four approximation algorithms for the feedback vertex set problem. In *Proceedings of the 7th conference on graph theoretic concepts of computer science*, 315–390, 1981.

[PR85]   R.G. Parker and R.L. Rardin. Guaranteed performance heuristic for the bottleneck traveling salesman problem. *Oper. Res. Letters*, 6:269–272, 1985.

[S76]   S. Sahni. Algorithms for scheduling independent tasks. *J. Assoc. Comput. Mach.* 23:116–127, 1976.

[SG76]   S. Sahni and T. Gonzales. *P*-complete approximation problems. *J. Assoc. Comput. Mach.* 23:555–565, 1976.

[TF80]   S. L. Tanimoto and R. J. Fowler. Covering image subsets with patches. *Proceedings of the 51st International Conference on Pattern Recognition*, 835–839, 1980.

[TY93]   S.-H Teng and F. Yao. Approximating shortest superstrings. In *Proceedings of the 34th annual IEEE symposium on Foundations of computer science*, 158–165, 1993.

[V64]   V. G.. Vizing. On the estimate of the chromatic class of a *p*-graph (Russian). *Diskret. Analiz*, 3:25–30, 1964.

[Y92]   M. Yannakakis. On the approximation of maximum satisfiability. In *Proceedings of the 3rd ACM-SIAM Symposium on Discrete Algorithms*, 1–9, 1992.

10

HARDNESS OF APPROXIMATIONS

Sanjeev Arora   **Carsten Lund**

This chapter is a self-contained survey of recent results about the hardness of approximating *NP*-hard optimization problems. It reviews techniques for deriving lower bounds on approximations, and surveys inapproximability results for several classes of problems, and their representative "canonical" problems.

INTRODUCTION

10.1

This chapter surveys recent results on the hardness of approximating *NP*-hard optimization problems. According to these results, computing good approximate solutions to many problems is *NP*-hard — and hence no easier than computing exact solutions.

In general, proving the *NP*-hardness of an optimization problem involves a *reduction* from SAT (or any other *NP*-complete problem) to the problem. To prove the hardness of approximation, this reduction must produce a *gap* in the value of the optimum. For instance, proving the *NP*-hardness of approximating the *maximum clique problem* within a factor g requires coming up with a reduction from SAT to CLIQUE that maps satisfiable formulae to graphs with clique number at least K (for some K), and unsatisfiable formulae to graphs with clique number at most K/g.

For a long time it was unclear how to construct such *gap producing* reductions for clique and many other important optimization problems. The Cook-Karp-Levin [Coo71, Kar72, Lev73] techniques for doing reductions seemed more suited for proving the hardness of decision problems (for example, non-optimization problems such as SAT or TILING) than of approximation problems.

Recent work has yielded a fairly general technique for constructing gap-producing reductions. This new technique, which originated in the work of [FGL+91], relies upon new probabilistic characterizations of the *NP* class. The most well-known characterization is the so-called PCP Theorem, written as $NP = PCP(\log n, 1)$ [AS92, ALMSS92]. Section 10.8 provides an introduction to the PCP Theorem.

The proof of the PCP Theorem involves complicated algebraic techniques from complexity theory, and will not be given here. Luckily, understanding the proof is not a prerequisite for using the theorem in inapproximability results. In particular, this survey describes all major inapproximability results, while requiring from the reader only some familiarity with the basic notions of *NP*-completeness. The first few chapters of the well-known book by Garey and Johnson [GJ79] provide all necessary background.

As described in earlier chapters of this book, the chief parameter of interest when studying the approximability of a problem is the *approximation ratio* that can be achieved by a polynomial-time approximation algorithm. An algorithm *achieves an approximation ratio* α for a maximization problem if, for every instance, it produces a solution of value at least OPT/α, where OPT is the value of the optimal solution. (For a minimization problem, achieving a ratio α involves finding a solution of cost at most $\alpha\,OPT$.) Note that the approximation ratio is ≥ 1 by definition. (Other chapters of this book use a slightly different convention, according to which approximation ratios for maximization problems are ≤ 1.)

Recent inapproximability results divide problems into four broad classes, based on the approximation ratio that is provably hard to achieve. These approximation ratios are, respectively, $1 + \epsilon$ for some fixed $\epsilon > 0$, $\Omega(\log n)$, $2^{\log^{1-\gamma} n}$ for every fixed $\gamma > 0$, and n^{δ} for some fixed $\delta > 0$ (throughout, n denotes the input size). The corresponding classes of problems are called Classes I, II, III, and IV respectively. Inapproximability results for problems within a class (sometimes also across classes) share common ideas. We devote a section (from 10.3 to 10.6) to each class. It should be noted that our classification reflects only (the limits of) our current understanding of the area; future work may reveal other natural classes, or collapse two classes, or move problems from one class to another. To give an example, all problems in Class III are believed to also lie in Class IV, although a proof of this eludes us.

This survey also proposes six "canonical" inapproximable problems, which can be used to derive all known inapproximability results in a fairly simple way. (Our framework of canonical problems is derived from the one in [Aro94].) Thus, our six problems play a role in inapproximability results similar to that played by the six canonical problems of [GJ79] in proving the *NP*-completeness of exact optimization. Furthermore, just as 3SAT is the most basic canonical problem in [GJ79], its optimization version, MAX-3SAT, is the most basic canonical problem in this chapter. As we will show, (see Figure 10.1 on page 404) reductions from MAX-3SAT can prove the hardness of all the canonical problems.

We emphasize that the framework presented in this chapter is not a way to prove the best possible results for every problem. Rather, it is meant to be a way to prove results that are "in the same ballpark" as the best results known. To give an example, the best existing result for the clique problem shows the hardness of achieving an approximation ratio roughly $\sqrt[3]{N}$, where N is the number of vertices of the graph. Since the proof of that result is complicated and involves delving deep into the proof of the PCP Theorem, we instead present the weaker result — provable in our framework — that achieving a ratio N^{ϵ} is *NP*-hard for some fixed $\epsilon > 0$.

Class	Factor of Approximation that is hard	Representative Problems
I	$1 + \epsilon$	MAX-3SAT
II	$O(\log n)$	SETCOVER
III	$2^{\log^{1-\gamma} n}$	LABELCOVER
IV	n^ϵ	CLIQUE

Table 10.1: The four classes and their representative problems.

The rest of the survey is organized as follows. Section 10.2 sets up the notational framework as well as the general philosophy of inapproximability results. It also defines the six canonical problems. Sections 10.3 to 10.6 prove inapproximability results for representative problems in Classes I to IV. Section 10.7 is a succinct (by no means exhaustive) overview of other inapproximabilty results and where they are proved. Section 10.8 is an introduction to the PCP Theorem and how it is used in proving inapproximability results. Section 10.9 lists important research problems. Finally, Section 10.10 briefly describes how the results of this chapter were discovered. That section also provides references to further reading.

REMARK 10.1   Notation   We describe, using MAX-3SAT as an example, the notation we will use for describing optimization problems. Such problems involve optimizing some *objective function* on a set of *feasible solutions.* In the MAX-3SAT problem, the input is a 3CNF formula, and the goal is to find an assignment that maximizes the number of satisfied clauses. Thus the feasible solutions are truth assignments, and the value of the objective function on a truth assignment is the *fraction* of clauses that it satisfies. We let MAX-3SAT(I) denote the maximum value of this objective function for a 3CNF formula I. Note that MAX-3SAT(I) ≤ 1. We will likewise express the objective function for many other problems as a ratio (i.e., a pure number).

REMARK 10.2   *Quasi-NP*-hardness   Many inapproximability results in this chapter show that achieving a certain approximation ratio is *NP-hard*. This implies that if some polynomial-time algorithm achieves that approximation ratio, then $NP = P$. Other results in this chapter are slightly weaker; they show only that the approximation is *Quasi-NP-hard*. A problem is *Quasi-NP*-hard if any polynomial-time algorithm for it can be used to solve all *NP*-problems in quasi-polynomial (i.e., $2^{\text{poly}(\log n)}$) time. Since *NP*-complete problems are conjectured to have no sub-exponential algorithms (deterministic or randomized) a proof of *Quasi-NP*-hardness is good evidence that the problem has no polynomial-time algorithm (deterministic or randomized).

HOW TO PROVE INAPPROXIMABILITY RESULTS

10.2

Throughout, we will use the same method to prove the inapproximability of a given problem: We start with a known inapproximable problem, and then perform a *gap-*

preserving reduction from that problem to the given problem. Section 10.2.1 describes six canonical problems that often serve as the "known inapproximable problem" in such situations. Section 10.2.2 describes, without proof, the inapproximability results for the canonical problems; the proofs of these results appear later in the chapter. The concept of a gap-preserving reduction is defined in Section 10.2.3, and illustrated with some examples.

10.2.1 THE CANONICAL PROBLEMS

We describe six canonical problems. The most basic one is MAX-3SAT, an optimization version of the decision problem 3SAT. Reductions from MAX-3SAT will be used to prove all inapproximability results in this chapter. Thus, MAX-3SAT plays a role in the theory of inapproximability analogous to the one played by 3SAT in the classical theory of *NP*-completeness. The next result, which proves that approximating MAX-3SAT is *NP*-hard, can therefore be viewed as the analogue of the Cook-Levin Theorem[1]. Section 10.10 gives a brief history of this and related results.

THEOREM 10.1 [ALMSS92] There is a fixed $\epsilon > 0$ and a polynomial-time reduction τ from SAT to MAX-3SAT such that for every boolean formula I:

$$I \in \text{SAT} \Longrightarrow \text{MAX-3SAT}(\tau(I)) = 1,$$
$$I \notin \text{SAT} \Longrightarrow \text{MAX-3SAT}(\tau(I)) < \frac{1}{1+\epsilon}.$$

In other words, achieving an approximation ratio $1 + \epsilon$ for MAX-3SAT is *NP*-hard.

Theorem 10.1 is proved in Section 10.8.2
Now we describe the other five canonical problems.

Other Canonical Problems:

MAX-3SAT(5): This is the subcase of MAX-3SAT in which every variable appears in at most 5 clauses. We will assume that each variable appears in exactly 5 clauses.

R-CLIQUE: The clique number of the graph, denoted ω, is the size of the largest clique (i.e., a set of vertices all adjacent to each other) in it. In the R-CLIQUE problem the input consists of a positive integer r, and an r-partite[2] graph G along with its r-partition. The goal is to find the largest clique in G. We define R-CLIQUE(G) to be k/r, where k is the size of the largest clique in G. Since a clique can have at most one vertex in common with an independent set, no clique in an r-partite graph has size more than r. Thus, R-CLIQUE(G) ≤ 1.

LABELCOVER: This problem comes in a maximization and a minimization version, both of which are defined below (Definition 10.1).

---

[1]The analogy between Cook's Theorem and Theorem 10.1 is not entirely correct. Cook's Theorem is important also because it motivated other researchers to study *NP*-completeness. The analogous result in the recent work on inapproximability is the paper of Feige et al. [FGL+91] on CLIQUE.

[2]An r-partite graph is one whose vertices can be partitioned into r disjoint independent sets.

SETCOVER: Given a ground set U and a collection of its subsets $S_1, S_2, \ldots, S_m$ satisfying $\bigcup_{i=1}^{m} S_i = U$, find the size of the minimum subcollection that covers U, i.e., the minimum sized $I \subset \{1, 2, \ldots, m\}$ such that $\bigcup_{i \in I} S_i = U$. The objective function is $|I|$, the number of sets in the subcollection.

COLORING: Given a graph G, assign a color (namely, an integer) to each vertex such that no two adjacent vertices have the same color. Minimize the total number of colors used. The objective function is the number of colors in a proper coloring. (The minimum of the objective function is called the *chromatic number* of the graph, denoted $\chi(G)$.)

The only problem unfamiliar from the traditional theory of *NP*-completeness is LABELCOVER, which we describe now.

DEFINITION 10.1 LABELCOVER

Input: (i) A regular[3] bipartite graph $G = (V_1, V_2, E)$ (ii) An integer N. This defines the set of *labels*, which are integers in $\{1, 2, \ldots, N\}$. (iii) For each edge $e \in E$ a partial function $\Pi_e : \{1, 2, \ldots, N\} \to \{1, 2, \ldots, N\}$.

A *labelling* has to associate a non-empty set of labels with every vertex in $V_1 \cup V_2$. It is said to *cover* an edge $e = (u, v)$ (where $u \in V_1$, $v \in V_2$) if, for every label a_2 assigned to v, there is some label a_1 assigned to u such that $\Pi_e(a_1) = a_2$. The collection of all such partial functions is denoted as Π.

LABELCOVER$_{max}$: The output is a labelling that assigns one label per vertex, and maximizes the fraction of covered edges. For a label cover instance $\mathcal{L} = ((V_1, V_2, E), N, \Pi)$, we let LABELCOVER$_{max}(\mathcal{L})$ denote this fraction.

LABELCOVER$_{min}$: The output is a labelling that covers *all* the edges, using more than one label per vertex if necessary. Furthermore, the labelling has minimum *cost,* which is

$$\sum_{v \in V_1} (\text{number of labels assigned to } v)$$

(that is, the total number of labels, counting multiplicities, assigned to vertices in V_1). The objective function is $\text{cost}/|V_1|$, that is, the average number of labels used per vertex.

Note that there is no reason thus far why LABELCOVER$_{min}$ is a well-defined problem, since there may be no feasible solution (i.e., a labelling that covers all edges) at all. So we impose the following condition on the input: (iv) For each edge e, the label 1 has a pre-image under Π_e, that is to say, a $b \in \{1, 2, \ldots, N\}$ for which $\Pi_e(b) = 1$. Thus, we have guaranteed the existence of a feasible solution of cost $\leq N$: the labelling that assigns 1 to each vertex in V_2 and the set $\{1, 2, \ldots, N\}$ to each vertex in V_1. This labelling clearly covers all the edges. (In particular, condition (iv) thus ensures that LABELCOVER$_{min}(\mathcal{L}) \leq N$ for every instance $\mathcal{L}$.)

The reader may wish to read Example 10.1 in Section 10.2.3 to properly understand the definition of LABELCOVER.

---

[3]For our purposes a bipartite graph is *regular* if for some integers d_1, d_2, every vertex on the left (resp., right) has degree d_1 (resp., d_2).

10.2.2   INAPPROXIMABILITY RESULTS FOR THE CANONICAL PROBLEMS

Recall that an inapproximability result involves a reduction from SAT (or any other *NP*-complete decision problem) to instances of the given problem, such that there is a gap in the optimum value of the objective function depending on whether or not the boolean formula is satisfiable. This section describes such results for our canonical problems. (Figure 10.1 gives an overview of the logical dependence between these results.)

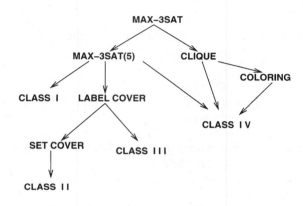

FIGURE 10.1

Diagram of the sequence of transformations used to prove the inapproximability of the six canonical problems. The six problems in turn lead to inapproximability results for problems in Classes I, II, III, and IV.

To do further reductions from the canonical problem, it helps to know the exact nature of the gap produced. As an illustration of this point, consider two hypothetical polynomial-time reductions τ_1 and τ_2 from SAT to MAX-3SAT. For some fixed $\epsilon, c > 0$, reduction τ_1 satisfies

$$I \in \text{SAT} \implies \text{MAX-3SAT}(\tau_1(I)) = 1,$$

$$I \notin \text{SAT} \implies \text{MAX-3SAT}(\tau_1(I)) < \frac{1}{1+\epsilon}$$

and reduction τ_2 satisfies

$$I \in \text{SAT} \implies \text{MAX-3SAT}(\tau_2(I)) = 1 - c,$$

$$I \notin \text{SAT} \implies \text{MAX-3SAT}(\tau_2(I)) < \frac{1-c}{1+\epsilon}.$$

As inapproximability results for MAX-3SAT, the reductions are equally useful: both prove the *NP*-hardness of achieving an approximation ratio of $(1 + \epsilon)$. But as an ingredient of further inapproximability results (which involve further reductions from MAX-3SAT) the first reduction appears to be far more useful. For example, we will later prove the hardness of Set-Cover and Nearest Lattice Vector problems using τ_1, whereas we do not know how to prove these results using τ_2. Luckily for us, Theorem 10.1 shows that reduction τ_1 exists.

Such peculiarities make it essential to know the precise statement of the inapproximability result for our canonical problems. The next theorem gives these statements.

THEOREM 10.2 The following reductions exist.

1. A polynomial-time reduction τ_1 from SAT to MAX-3SAT(5) that, for some fixed $\epsilon > 0$ and for all boolean formulae I, ensures:

$$I \in \text{SAT} \Longrightarrow \text{MAX-3SAT}(\tau_1(I)) = 1,$$
$$I \notin \text{SAT} \Longrightarrow \text{MAX-3SAT}(\tau_1(I)) < \frac{1}{1+\epsilon}.$$

2. A polynomial-time reduction τ_2 from SAT to R-CLIQUE that, for some fixed $\delta > 0$ and for all I, ensures:

$$I \in \text{SAT} \Longrightarrow \omega(\tau_2(I)) = 1,$$
$$I \notin \text{SAT} \Longrightarrow \omega(\tau_2(I)) \leq \frac{1}{n^\delta},$$

where n is the number of vertices in $\tau_2(I)$.

3. A quasi-polynomial-time reduction τ_3 from SAT to $\text{LABELCOVER}_{\max}$ that, for all I, ensures:

$$I \in \text{SAT} \Longrightarrow \text{LABELCOVER}_{\max}(\tau_3(I)) = 1,$$
$$I \notin \text{SAT} \Longrightarrow \text{LABELCOVER}_{\max}(\tau_3(I)) < \frac{1}{2^{\log^{1-\gamma} n}},$$

where γ is an arbitrarily small positive constant and n is the size of $\tau_3(I)$. (Note: Since the reduction runs in quasi-polynomial-time, n is at most $2^{\text{poly}(\log |I|)}$.) There is a similar reduction for $\text{LABELCOVER}_{\min}$ that produces instances with optimum value either 1 or $> 2^{\log^{1-\gamma} n}$.

4. A quasi-polynomial-time reduction τ_4 from SAT to SETCOVER that, for all I, ensures:

$$I \in \text{SAT} \Longrightarrow \text{SETCOVER}(\tau_4(I)) = K(|I|),$$
$$I \notin \text{SAT} \Longrightarrow \text{SETCOVER}(\tau_4(I)) > K(|I|) \cdot \frac{\log n}{48},$$

where $K(|I|)$ is a polynomial-time (in $|I|$) computable function and n is the size of the ground set of the setcover instance $\tau_4(I)$. (The constant 48 can be improved somewhat.)

5. A polynomial-time reduction τ_5 from SAT to COLORING that, for some fixed $\delta > 0$ and for all I, ensures:

$$I \in \text{SAT} \Longrightarrow \chi(\tau_5(I)) = K(|I|),$$
$$I \notin \text{SAT} \Longrightarrow \chi(\tau_5(I)) > K(|I|) n^\delta,$$

where $K(|I|)$ is a polynomial-time (in $|I|$) computable function and n is the number of vertices of $\tau_5(I)$.

Proof.   The proofs appear in the following sections.

- (1). 10.2.3.
- (2). 10.6.1
- (3). 10.5.1 and 10.5.2.
- (4). 10.4.1.
- (5). 10.6.2.   ∎

Notice that the following corollary follows immediately from the statement of Theorem 10.2.

COROLLARY 10.1   There exist fixed $\epsilon, \delta, \delta' > 0$ such that

1. Approximating MAX-3SAT and MAX-3SAT(5) within a factor $(1 + \epsilon)$ is *NP*-hard.
2. Approximating R-CLIQUE and thus CLIQUE within a factor n^δ is *NP*-hard.
3. Approximating LABELCOVER within a factor $2^{\log^{1-\gamma} n}$ is *Quasi-NP*-hard, for any $\gamma > 0$.
4. Approximating SETCOVER within a factor $(\log n)/48$ is *Quasi-NP*-hard.
5. Approximating COLORING within a factor $n^{\delta'}$ is *NP*-hard.

10.2.3   GAP PRESERVING REDUCTIONS

Now we define gap-preserving reductions. We will prove inapproximability results by composing one of the reductions in Theorem 10.2 with a gap-preserving reduction. This technique is explained further in the note following the definition.

DEFINITION 10.2   Let Π and Π' be two maximization problems. A *gap-preserving reduction from* Π *to* Π' *with parameters* $(c, \rho), (c', \rho')$ is a polynomial-time algorithm f. For each instance I of Π, algorithm f produces an instance $I' = f(I)$ of Π'. The optima of I and I', say $OPT(I)$ and $OPT(I')$ respectively, satisfy the following property:

$$OPT(I) \geq c \Longrightarrow OPT(I') \geq c',$$
$$OPT(I) < \frac{c}{\rho} \Longrightarrow OPT(I') < \frac{c'}{\rho'}. \tag{10.1}$$

Here c and ρ are functions of $|I|$, the size of instance I, and c', ρ' are functions of $|I'|$. Also, $\rho(I), \rho'(I') \geq 1$.

Comments on Definition 10.2:

1. Suppose we wish to prove the inapproximability of problem Π'. Suppose further that we have a polynomial time reduction τ from SAT to Π that ensures, for every boolean formula φ:

$$\varphi \in \text{SAT} \implies OPT(\tau(\varphi)) \geq c$$
$$\varphi \notin \text{SAT} \implies OPT(\tau(\varphi)) < \frac{c}{\rho}.$$

Then composing this reduction with the reduction of Definition 10.2 gives a reduction $f \circ \tau$ from SAT to Π' that ensures:

$$\varphi \in \text{SAT} \implies OPT'(f(\tau(\varphi))) \geq c'$$
$$\varphi \notin \text{SAT} \implies OPT'(f(\tau(\varphi))) < \frac{c'}{\rho'}.$$

In other words, $f \circ \tau$ shows that achieving an approximation ratio ρ' for Π' is *NP*-hard. This idea of composing reductions underlies our inapproximability results.

2. Like most known reductions, ours will also map solutions to solutions in an obvious way. For instance, given a solution to I' of value at least c', a solution to I of value at least c can be produced in polynomial time. But we keep this aspect out of the definition for simplicity.

3. The above definition can be modified in an obvious way when one (or both) of the optimization problems involve minimization.

4. The gap-preserving reduction could behave arbitrarily on an instance I for which $c/\rho \leq OPT(I) < c$. Thus, its "niceness" (namely, Equation 10.1) holds only on a partial domain. In this sense the gap-preserving reduction is a weaker notion than the *L-reduction* introduced in [PY91], whose "niceness" has to be maintained on *all* instances of Π. An L-reduction, coupled with an approximation algorithm for Π', yields an approximation algorithm for Π. This statement is false for a gap-preserving reduction. On the other hand, for exhibiting merely the hardness of approximation, it suffices (and is usually easier) to find gap-preserving reductions. For instance, we will prove the inapproximability of SETCOVER and the Nearest Lattice Vector problem using gap-preserving reductions, whereas no corresponding L-reductions are known.

5. The name "gap-preserving" is a bit inaccurate, since the new gap ρ' could be much bigger or much smaller than the old gap ρ.

To illustrate the concept of gap-preserving reductions, we give a reduction from MAX-3SAT to MAX-3SAT(5) that also proves Theorem 10.2, part 1.

Proof of Theorem 10.2, part 1. First we describe a reduction from MAX-3SAT to MAX-3SAT(29) (i.e., each variable appears in at most 29 clauses). Modifying instances of MAX-3SAT(29) to instances of MAX-3SAT(5) (preserving inapproximability) is easy, as we will show.

We describe a reduction τ from MAX-3SAT to MAX-3SAT(29) that is gap-preserving with parameters $(1, (1 - \delta)^{-1}), (1, (1 - \frac{\delta}{43})^{-1})$ for every $\delta > 0$. In other words, it ensures for every fixed $\delta > 0$ and for every 3CNF formula I, that

$$\text{MAX-3SAT}(I) = 1 \implies \text{MAX-3SAT}(\tau(I)) = 1,$$
$$\text{MAX-3SAT}(I) < 1 - \delta \implies \text{MAX-3SAT}(\tau(I)) < 1 - \frac{\delta}{43}.$$

Recall that Theorem 10.1 describes a reduction τ_1 from SAT to MAX-3SAT such that for some fixed $\epsilon > 0$ and for every SAT instance I:

$$I \in \text{SAT} \implies \text{MAX-3SAT}(\tau_1(I)) = 1,$$

$$I \notin \text{SAT} \implies \text{MAX-3SAT}(\tau_1(I)) < \frac{1}{1+\epsilon}.$$

Thus, the composed reduction (that is, τ_1 followed by τ) is a reduction from SAT to MAX-3SAT(29) such that the fraction of satisfied clauses is either 1 or $1 - \epsilon/(43(1+\epsilon))$ depending upon whether or not the SAT instance was satisfiable.

The description of reduction τ uses special types of *expander* graphs. The relevant property of these graphs is that for every subset S of the vertices, the number of edges between S and its complement $\overline{S}$ is at least $\min\{|S|, |\overline{S}|\}$. As shown in [LPS88], such graphs are constructible. There is an algorithm A and a fixed integer n_0 such that given any integer $k > n_0$, algorithm A constructs in poly(k) time a 14-regular graph G_k on k vertices that is an expander.

Let I, the instance of MAX-3SAT, have n variables $y_1, y_2, \ldots, y_n$, and m clauses. Let m_i denote the number of clauses in which variable y_i appears. Let N denote the sum $\sum_i m_i$. Since a clause contains at most 3 variables, $N \le 3m$. Furthermore, since replicating each clause n_0 times does not change the fraction of satisfiable clauses, we can assume without loss of generality that each m_i is greater than n_0, the integer mentioned in the statement about expanders.

To create an instance of MAX-3SAT(29) do the following for each variable y_i. Replace y_i with m_i new variables $y_i^1, y_i^2, \ldots, y_i^{m_i}$. Use the jth new variable, y_i^j, in place of the jth occurrence of y_i. Next, to ensure that the optimum assignment assigns the same value to $y_i^1, y_i^2, \ldots, y_i^{m_i}$, add the following $14m_i$ new clauses. For each $j, l \le m_i$ such that (j, l) is an edge of the expander G_{m_i}, add a pair of new clauses $(y_i^l \vee \neg y_i^j)$ and $(\neg y_i^l \vee y_i^j)$. Together, this pair just says $(y_i^l \equiv y_i^j)$: an assignment satisfies the pair iff it assigns the same value to y_i^l and y_i^j.

Hence, the new formula contains $14N$ new clauses and m old clauses. Each variable occurs in exactly 28 new clauses and 1 old clause. We claim that an optimum assignment, namely, one that satisfies the maximum number of clauses, satisfies all new clauses. For, suppose it does not satisfy a new clause corresponding to y_i. Then it does not assign the same value to all of $y_i^1, y_i^2, \ldots, y_i^{m_i}$. Divide these m_i variables into two sets S and $\overline{S}$ according to the value they were assigned. One of these sets has size at most $m_i/2$; say it is S. In the expander G_{m_i}, consider the set of $|S|$ vertices corresponding to vertices in S. Expansion implies there are at least $|S| + 1$ edges leaving this set. Each such edge yields an unsatisfied new clause. Hence, by flipping the value of the variables in S, we can satisfy at least $1 + |S|$ clauses that were not satisfied before, and possibly stop satisfying the (at most $|S|$) old clauses that contain these variables. The net gain is still at least 1. This contradicts the assumption that we started with an optimum assignment.

We have shown that the optimum assignment satisfies all new clauses, and thus assigns identical values to the different copies $y_i^1, y_i^2, \ldots, y_i^{m_i}$ of y_i for all $i \in \{1, 2, \ldots, n\}$. Thus, the optimum assignment corresponds to an assignment to the old formula. Suppose the original instance of MAX-3SAT was satisfiable. Then so is the instance of MAX-3SAT(29) we created. Now suppose no assignment could satisfy more than $(1 - \delta)m$ clauses in the original formula. Then, in the new formula no assignment can satisfy more than $14N + (1 - \delta)m$ clauses. Since $N \le 3m$, we see that the fraction of unsatisfied clauses is at least $\frac{\delta m}{42m+m} = \frac{\delta}{43}$. Hence, the correctness of the reduction has been proved.

Finally, changing an instance of MAX-3SAT(29) into an instance of MAX-3SAT(5) is similar to the above transformation, but easier. Specifically, replace the expander in the above construction with a simpler graph: the cycle. Thus, if a variable appears l times, replace it by l new variables, and add new clauses corresponding to edges in a cycle on l vertices. The reader can easily check that each variable in the new formula appears in exactly 5 clauses. Further, if only $1 - \gamma$ fraction of clauses could be satisfied in the old formula, then in the new formula the fraction of satisfiable clauses is at most $1 - \frac{\gamma}{29}$.

Note: The fact about expanders that we quoted above is only approximately correct. The construction in [LPS88] may be unable to construct expanders of size n for some integers n. However, it is able to construct an expander of size $\leq n(1 + o(1))$ for every n. The reader can easily check that this does not affect the correctness of our construction. ∎

Next, we give another example of a gap-preserving reduction, which will be useful later.

Example 10.1 We describe a reduction τ from MAX-3SAT(5) to LABELCOVER$_{max}$ that is gap-preserving with $c = c' = 1$, and $\rho = (1 - \epsilon)^{-1}$, $\rho' = (1 - \epsilon/9)^{-1}$. In other words, for every input φ to MAX-3SAT(5) it ensures

$$\text{MAX-3SAT}(\varphi) = 1 \Longrightarrow \text{LABELCOVER}_{max}(\tau(\varphi)) = 1$$

$$\text{MAX-3SAT}(\varphi) < 1 - \epsilon \Longrightarrow \text{LABELCOVER}_{max}(\tau(\varphi)) < 1 - \frac{\epsilon}{9}. \quad (10.2)$$

Given an instance of MAX-3SAT(5), produce an instance of LABELCOVER as follows. Let V_1 have one vertex for each clause and V_2 have a vertex for every variable. Let adjacency correspond to the variable appearing in the clause, whether negated or unnegated. The number of labels, N, is 8. For a vertex in V_1, if the corresponding clause involves variables x_i, x_j, x_k, the reader should think of a label as a 3-bit binary vector (b_1, b_2, b_3), corresponding to the assignment $x_i = b_1, x_j = b_2, x_k = b_3$. For a vertex in V_2, say one corresponding to variable x_i, the labels will be either 0 or 1, corresponding respectively to a truth assignment to x_i (the remaining 6 labels will be dummy labels and not useful to cover any edges).

The edge function Π_e is described as follows. Suppose e is the edge (u, v) where $u \in V_1$ corresponds to clause C, and $v \in V_2$ corresponds to variable x_i. Thus, we know that x_i appears in C and let j be the place where x_i appears. Let $\Pi_e(b_1, b_2, b_3)$ be defined and equal to b_j if and only if the assignment b_1, b_2, b_3 satisfies C.

Since each vertex is allowed only 1 label in the maximization version of LABEL-COVER, the labels on the right-hand side vertices constitute a boolean assignment to $x_1, x_2, \ldots, x_n$. The label on a left-hand vertex also constitutes an assignment to the variables in the corresponding clause. The edge joining a clause-vertex and a variable-vertex is covered iff that variable is assigned the same value by both assignments and the assignment satisfies the clause.

Clearly, if all edges are covered then the assignment is a satisfying assignment. Conversely, if no assignment satisfies more than $1 - \epsilon$ of the clauses, then every labelling must fail to cover an edge incident to at least ϵ fraction of the clause-vertices, in other words a fraction at least $\frac{\epsilon}{3}$ of all edges.

This completes the proof except for the fact that the graph (V_1, V_2, E) is not regular. It can be proven that we can extend the reduction by adding at most $2|E|$ dummy edges such that the new graph is regular and such that all the dummy edges are easily coverable. This will only decrease the gap by a factor of 3. The details are left to the reader. Thus, this completes the proof of the property claimed in (10.2).

INAPPROXIMABILITY RESULTS FOR PROBLEMS IN CLASS I

10.3

Class I contains problems for which achieving an approximation ratio $1 + \epsilon$ is *NP*-hard for some fixed $\epsilon > 0$. To prove that a problem is in Class I, we will give simple gap-preserving reductions from MAX-3SAT.

Papadimitriou and Yannakakis had identified Class I a few years before the discovery of the PCP Theorem. They called it the class of Max-$\mathcal{SNP}$-hard problems. The next section describes their work.

10.3.1   Max-$\mathcal{SNP}$

NP-hard optimization problems exhibit a vast range of behaviors when it comes to approximation. Papadimitriou and Yannakakis [PY91] identified a large sub-class of them that exhibit the same behavior. The authors defined a class of optimization problems, Max-$\mathcal{SNP}$, as well as a notion of completeness for this class. Roughly speaking, a Max-$\mathcal{SNP}$-complete problem is one that behaves just like MAX-3SAT in terms of approximability: MAX-3SAT is hard to approximate up to some constant factor iff so is every Max-$\mathcal{SNP}$-complete problem. (This made MAX-3SAT a plausible candidate problem to prove hard to approximate, and in particular motivated the discovery of the PCP theorem.)

Max-$\mathcal{SNP}$ contains constraint-satisfaction problems, where the constraints are local. The goal is to satisfy as many constraints as possible. The concept of "local" constraints is formalized using logic: constraints are local iff they are definable using a quantifier-free propositional formula.

DEFINITION 10.3   A maximization problem is in Max-$\mathcal{SNP}$ if there is a sequence of relation symbols $G_1, \ldots, G_m$, a relation symbol S, and a quantifier-free formula $\phi(G_1, \ldots, G_m, S, x_1, \ldots, x_k)$ (where each x_i is a variable) such that the following are true (i) there is a polynomial-time algorithm that, given any instance I of the problem produces a set $\mathcal{U}$ and a sequence of relations $G_1^{\mathcal{U}}, \ldots, G_m^{\mathcal{U}}$ on $\mathcal{U}$, where each $G_i^{\mathcal{U}}$ has the same arity ("arity" refers to the number of arguments) as the relation symbol G_i. (ii) The value of the optimum solution on instance I, denoted $OPT(I)$, satisfies

$$OPT(I) = \max_{S^{\mathcal{U}}} | \{(x_1, \ldots, x_k) \in \mathcal{U}^k : \phi(G_1^{\mathcal{U}}, \ldots, G_m^{\mathcal{U}}, S^{\mathcal{U}}, x_1, \ldots, x_k) = \text{TRUE}\} |,$$

where $S^{\mathcal{U}}$ is a relation on $\mathcal{U}$ with the same arity as S, and $\mathcal{U}^k$ is the set of k-tuples of $\mathcal{U}$.

Note: The above definition is inspired by Fagin's model-theoretic characterization of NP [Fag74], and an explanation is in order for those unfamiliar with model theory. The sequence of relation symbols $G_1, \ldots, G_m, S$, as well as their arities, are fixed for the problem. Thus, when the universe $\mathcal{U}$ has size n, the sequence of relations $G_1^{\mathcal{U}}, \ldots, G_m^{\mathcal{U}}$ implicitly defines an "input" of size $O(n^c)$ where c is the largest arity of a relation in G. Solving the optimization problem involves finding a relation $S^{\mathcal{U}} \subseteq \mathcal{U}^k$ that maximizes the number of k-tuples satisfying ϕ. Since $\mathcal{U}^k = n^k$, this relation $S^{\mathcal{U}}$ can be viewed as a "feasible solution" which can be specified using n^k bits.

Example 10.2 Let MAX-CUT be the problem of partitioning the vertex set of an undirected graph into two parts such that the number of edges crossing the partition is maximized. (See glossary for detailed definition.) To see that it is in Max-$\mathcal{SNP}$, let the universe $\mathcal{U}$ be the vertex set of the graph, and let G consist of E, a binary relation whose interpretation is "adjacency." Let S be a unary relation (interpreted as one side of the cut), and $\phi(E, S, (u, v)) = (u < v) \wedge E(u, v) \wedge (S(u) \neq S(v))$. Clearly, the optimum value of MAX-CUT on the graph is $\max_{S \subseteq \mathcal{U}} | \{(u, v) \in \mathcal{U}^2 : \phi(E, S, (u, v)) = \text{TRUE}\} |$.

The reader should check that MAX-3SAT and MAX-3SAT(5) are also in Max-$\mathcal{SNP}$. The paper [PY91] identified many other Max-$\mathcal{SNP}$ problems. It also showed that for every Max-$\mathcal{SNP}$ problem, there is some constant $c \geq 1$ such that some polynomial-time algorithm can achieve an approximation ratio c for the problem (see the exercises and [PY91]). The smallest value of c for which this is true remains an object of research. For example, an algorithm to approximate MAX-CUT within a factor 1.13 appeared recently in [GW94]. (Details on this algorithm are given in Chapter 11.3.1.)

There is a notion of *completeness* in the class Max-$\mathcal{SNP}$. According to the original definition, a Max-$\mathcal{SNP}$ problem is complete for the class if every Max-$\mathcal{SNP}$ problem can be reduced to it using a (so-called) L-reduction. For purposes of proving inapproximability results, it suffices to concentrate on a notion somewhat weaker than an L-reduction, as described in in the following definition:

DEFINITION 10.4 A maximization problem Π is *Max-$\mathcal{SNP}$-hard* if for every Max-$\mathcal{SNP}$ problem Γ and every two constants $c \leq 1, \rho > 1$, there are two constants $c' < 1, \rho' > 1$ such that there is a gap-preserving reduction from Γ to Π with parameters (c, ρ, c', ρ').

(Notes: (i) For notational ease, we are assuming, just as in the case of MAX-3SAT, that the value of the optimum is a fraction. Hence, $c, c' \leq 1$. (ii) The definition implies that if there is a Max-$\mathcal{SNP}$ problem Γ which is hard to approximate within any fixed factor $\rho > 1$, then there is some $\rho' > 1$ such that approximating Π within a factor ρ' is hard.)

Examples of Max-$\mathcal{SNP}$-hard problems include MAX-CUT, MAX-3SAT(5), and many others (see Section 10.7 for a partial list). Note that to prove the hardness of approximating *all* Max-$\mathcal{SNP}$-hard problems, it suffices to exhibit just *one* problem $\Gamma \in$ Max-$\mathcal{SNP}$ and *some* $\epsilon > 0$, such that achieving an approximation ratio $(1 + \epsilon)$ for Γ is *NP*-hard. But we already exhibited such a problem in Max-$\mathcal{SNP}$, namely MAX-3SAT! Thus, the following corollary to Theorem 10.1 is immediate.

COROLLARY 10.2   For every Max-$\mathcal{SNP}$-hard problem, there exists some $c > 1$ such that achieving an approximation ratio c for it is *NP*-hard.

We end this section with another example of a Max-$\mathcal{SNP}$-hard problem: CLIQUE. This proof of Max-$\mathcal{SNP}$-hardness will be used later to show a stronger inapproximability result for CLIQUE.

LEMMA 10.1   For every $\epsilon > 0$, there is a gap-preserving reduction from MAX-3SAT to CLIQUE that has parameters $(c, 1 + \epsilon), (cN/3, 1 + \epsilon)$, where N is the number of vertices in the new graph. In other words, CLIQUE is Max-$\mathcal{SNP}$-hard.

Proof.   A textbook reduction (a modification of the one in [GJ79]) from 3SAT to (the decision version of) CLIQUE works.

Let φ be a 3CNF formula in variables $x_1, x_2 \ldots, x_n$. By replicating literals within clauses we can ensure that each clause has 3 literals (e.g., if the clause is x_i then change it to $x_i \wedge x_i \wedge x_i$). Construct a new graph $\tau(\varphi)$ on $3m$ vertices as follows. Represent each clause with a triple of vertices, one per literal. Put no edges between vertices within the same triple. If u, v are vertices in two different triples, put an edge between them iff the literals they stand for are not the negations of each other.

Notice, a clique in this graph can contain only one vertex per triple. Furthermore, it cannot contain two vertices representing literals that are negations of each other. In other words, by looking at the literals represented in the clique we can write in a natural way a partial assignment that satisfies as many clauses as there are vertices in the clique. Thus,

$$\text{MAX-3SAT}(\varphi) = c \implies \omega(\tau(\varphi)) = cm$$
$$\text{MAX-3SAT}(\varphi) < \frac{c}{1+\epsilon} \implies \omega(\tau(\varphi)) < \frac{cm}{1+\epsilon}.$$

∎

EXERCISE 10.1   Prove the following result from [PY91]: For every Max-$\mathcal{SNP}$ problem, there is some constant $c \geq 1$ such that some polynomial-time algorithm can achieve an approximation ratio c for the problem.

EXERCISE 10.2   Prove that the following optimization problems are in Max-$\mathcal{SNP}$: MAX-3SAT and Minimum Vertex Cover restricted to graphs of degree 5.

INAPPROXIMABILITY RESULTS FOR PROBLEMS IN CLASS II

10.4

In this section we show how to prove the hardness of achieving an approximation ratio $O(\log n)$ for problems in Class II. The canonical problem in Class II is SETCOVER. In Section 10.4.1 we describe the hardness result for SETCOVER, and indicate how to use it to prove the inapproximability of other problems in the class.

10.4.1 SETCOVER

We prove Theorem 10.2, part 4 about the inapproximability of SETCOVER. Specifically, we give a polynomial-time reduction τ from LABELCOVER$_{\text{max}}$ to SETCOVER. Composing it with the inapproximability result for LABELCOVER$_{\text{max}}$ (namely, part 3 of Theorem 10.2, proved Section 10.5.1) gives the desired result.

For every LABELCOVER instance $\mathcal{L} = ((V_1, V_2, E), N, \Pi)$, the reduction in this section produces an instance $\mathcal{S} = \tau(\mathcal{L})$ of SETCOVER such that

$$\text{LABELCOVER}_{\text{max}}(\mathcal{L}) = 1 \implies \text{SETCOVER}(\mathcal{S}) = |V_1| + |V_2|,$$
$$\text{LABELCOVER}_{\text{max}}(\mathcal{L}) \leq \frac{1}{\log^3(|\mathcal{L}|)} \implies \text{SETCOVER}(\mathcal{S}) \geq \frac{\log |\mathcal{S}|}{48} \cdot (|V_1| + |V_2|),$$

where $|\mathcal{L}| = N \cdot |E|$ is the size of $\mathcal{L}$ and $|S|$ is the number of sets in the set-cover instance. (Note: in the instances of SETCOVER produced by the reduction, the number of sets and the size of the ground set are polynomially related. So $|S|$ in the above statement could also stand for the size of the ground set; then we need to change "48" to some other constant.)

The reduction uses the following set system as a basic building block.

DEFINITION 10.5 Let m and l be positive integers, B some finite set, and $C_1, C_2, \ldots,$ C_m a collection of m subsets of B. The subsets form an (m, l) *set-system* if for every set I of at most l indices from $\{1, 2, \ldots, m\}$, $\bigcup_{i \in I} D_i \neq B$, where each D_i is either C_i or complement of C_i.

Lemma 10.3 gives explicit constructions of (m, l) set-system for all m, l, where $|B| = O(2^{2l} m^2)$. Denote the set system as $\mathcal{B}_{m,l}$. We will use $l = O(\log m)$, in which case the size of $\mathcal{B}_{m,l}$ is poly(m).

Now we describe the reduction. First, we assume without loss of generality that $|V_1| = |V_2|$. For, if $|V_1| \neq |V_2|$, then just construct a new bipartite graph (V_1', V_2', E') with $|V_1||V_2|$ vertices on each side (i.e., $|V_2|$ copies of V_1 and $|V_1|$ copies of V_2), and the new set of edges E' consisting of copies of E between each new copy of V_1 and V_2. If the old instance had a labelling that covers all edges (i.e., has value 1), then so does the new one. Conversely, if the old instance had no labelling of value $\geq \rho$ then neither does the new one. Thus, we can assume that $|V_1| = |V_2|$.

Let l be an even integer (to be determined later) and $m = N$. Let $\mathcal{B}_{m,l} = (B; C_1, C_2, \dots, C_m)$ be an (m, l)-system. Since the labels in the LABELCOVER instance are integers from 1 to N, we can talk about the set C_a for any label a. The instance of SET-COVER is as follows. Its ground set U is $E \times B$. The given collection of subsets of $\mathcal{S}$ contains a set $S_{v,a}$ for every vertex v in $G = (V_1, V_2, E)$ and label a. For every $u \in V_1$ and $a_1 \in \{1, 2, \dots, N\}$, let S_{u,a_1} be defined by

$$S_{u,a_1} = \{(e, b) | e = (u, v),\ \Pi_e(a_1) \text{ is defined and } b \notin C_{\Pi_e(a_1)}\}.$$

(That is, S_{u,a_1} is the union of all sets of the type $\{e\} \times (B - C_{a_2})$, where e is an edge containing u and a_2 is the image $\Pi_e(a_1)$ of a_1.)

For every $v \in V_2$ and $a_2 \in \{1, 2, \dots, N\}$, let S_{v,a_2} be defined by

$$S_{v,a_2} = \{(e, b) | e = (u, v) \text{ and } b \in C_{a_2}\}.$$

(That is, $S_{v,a_2} = \cup_{e \ni v} \{e\} \times C_{a_2}$.)

Note that the ground set U can be viewed as $\cup_{e \in E} \{e\} \times B$, that is, as $|E|$ copies of B, one per edge. This observation underlies the next claim.

CLAIM 10.1   If LABELCOVER$_{\max}(\mathcal{L}) = 1$ then SETCOVER$(\mathcal{S}) = |V_1| + |V_2|$.

Proof.   Consider an optimal label cover, which uses one label per vertex to cover all edges. For a vertex $u \in V_1 \cup V_2$, let a_u be the label it assigns to u. We show that the collection of $|V_1| + |V_2|$ sets $\{S_{w,a_w} : w \in V_1 \cup V_2\}$ is a set cover.

Let $e = (u, v)$ be any edge. Since the pair of labels a_u, a_v covers it, a_v must be $\Pi_e(a_u)$. The definition of the set-cover instance ensures that $\{e\} \times C_{a_v}$ is contained in S_{v,a_v} and $\{e\} \times (B - C_{a_v})$ in S_{u,a_u}. Hence, $\{e\} \times B \subseteq S_{u,a_1} \cup S_{v,a_2}$. Since the same is true for every edge e, it follows that $E \times B \subseteq \cup_{w \in V_1 \cup V_2} S_{w,a_w}$. Thus, we have exhibited a set cover of size $|V_1| + |V_2|$.   ∎

The next lemma is more nontrivial. It uses the following restatement of the property of an (m, l)-system $(B; C_1, C_2, \dots, C_m)$: If the union of any collection of l sets out of $\{C_1, C_2, \dots, C_m, \overline{C_1}, \dots, \overline{C_m}\}$ is B, then the collection must contain both C_i and $\overline{C_i}$ for some i.

LEMMA 10.2   Suppose there is a set cover of size less than $\frac{l(|V_1| + |V_2|)}{16}$. Then there is a labelling that uses 1 label per vertex and covers a $\frac{2}{l^2}$ fraction of the edges (in other words, LABELCOVER$_{\max}(\mathcal{L}) \geq \frac{2}{l^2}$).

Proof.   Let I be the collection of sets in the set cover. We say that I *associates a label a with vertex u* if $S_{u,a} \in I$. Since $|V_1| = |V_2|$, and I associates at most $\frac{l}{16}$ labels per vertex on average, at least $\frac{3}{4}$ of the vertices in both V_1 and V_2 have fewer than $\frac{l}{2}$ labels associated with them.

Now define a labelling by picking, for each vertex, a random label from the set of labels associated with it. We show now that the expected fraction of edges covered by this labelling is at least $\frac{2}{l^2}$. Note that this also implies the *existence* of a labelling that covers at least this fraction.

First, we claim that for $\frac{1}{2}$ the edges, the end-points have fewer than $\frac{l}{2}$ labels associated with them. To see this, imagine picking an edge $e = (u, v)$ uniformly at random. Since the bipartite graph is regular, the endpoints u, v of this edge are also distributed uniformly (but not necessarily independently) in V_1, V_2 respectively. With probability at least $1 - 2 \cdot \frac{1}{4} = \frac{1}{2}$, both end points have at most $\frac{l}{2}$ labels. Thus, our claim follows.

Now, let $e = (u, v)$ be an edge such that both u, v have fewer than $\frac{l}{2}$ labels associated with them. We claim that with probability at least $(\frac{2}{l})^2$ the randomly-picked labelling covers this edge. The reason is that C is a set cover, and so

$$\{e\} \times B \subseteq \left(\bigcup_{a_1} S_{u,a_1} \right) \cup \left(\bigcup_{a_2} S_{v,a_2} \right),$$

where the two unions range over the sets of labels associated with u and v respectively. But recall the property of an (m, l)-system: the only way to cover B with fewer than l sets is to use two sets that are complements of one another. In our construction, complementary sets correspond to pairs of labels that can cover the edge. We conclude that there are some labels a_1, a_2 associated with u, v respectively such that $\Pi_e(a_1) = a_2$. Now, let us pick labels randomly for u, v from among all labels associated with them. With probability at least $(\frac{2}{l})^2$ we pick a_1 and a_2, in which case the labelling covers edge e.

To conclude, we have shown that for $\frac{1}{2}$ the edges, the labelling has a probability at least $(\frac{2}{l})^2$ of satisfying that edge. Hence, the expected number of covered edges is at least $\frac{1}{2} \cdot (\frac{4}{l^2}) = \frac{2}{l^2}$. ∎

The following corollary finishes the proof of the correctness of the reduction. The proof also specifies the values of various parameters that were not stated above.

COROLLARY 10.3 Let $\mathcal{L}$ be any instance of LABELCOVER$_{max}$ as described above, and $\mathcal{S}$ be the instance of SETCOVER produced using the above reduction. If LABELCOVER$_{max}(\mathcal{L}) \leq 1/\log^3 |\mathcal{L}|$ then

$$\text{SETCOVER}(\mathcal{S}) > \frac{\log |\mathcal{S}|}{48} (|V_1| + |V_2|),$$

where $|\mathcal{S}| = N(|V_1| + |V_2|)$ is the number of sets in $\mathcal{S}$ and $|\mathcal{L}| = N \cdot |E|$ is the size of $\mathcal{L}$.

Proof. Let $l = 4\lceil \log |\mathcal{L}| \rceil$. Assume that $\mathcal{S}$ has a cover of size less than $\frac{l(|V_1|+|V_2|)}{16}$. Then Lemma 10.2 implies that

$$\text{LABELCOVER}_{max}(\mathcal{L}) \geq 2/l^2 = 1/8\lceil \log |\mathcal{L}| \rceil^2 > 1/\log^3 |\mathcal{L}|$$

for large $|\mathcal{L}|$. This is a contradiction. Hence, SETCOVER$(\mathcal{S}) \geq \frac{l(|V_1|+|V_2|)}{16}$.

Now we express l in terms of $\log |\mathcal{S}|$. Recall that $|B| = O(2^{2l} m^2)$ and $m = N$. Hence, $\log |\mathcal{S}| = \log(N(|V_1| + |V_2|)) \leq \log(m) + 2\log(|\mathcal{L}|) < 3l$. Thus, SETCOVER$(\mathcal{S}) > \frac{\log |\mathcal{S}|}{48} (|V_1| + |V_2|)$. ∎

Note that the previous corollary continues to hold if we define $|\mathcal{S}|$ to be the sum of the number of sets in $\mathcal{S}$ and the size of their ground set.

To finish the description of the reduction, we show how to construct an (m, l)-system.

LEMMA 10.3   There is an explicit algorithm to construct, given integers m, l where $l < m$, an (l, m)-system $(B; C_1, C_2, \dots, C_m)$ with $|B| = O(2^{2l} m^2)$. The algorithm runs in time poly$(|B|)$.

Proof.   We note that to construct the (m, l)-system it suffices to construct a collection X of m-bit vectors with the following property: Given any l distinct coordinates $i_1, i_2, \dots, i_l$ and any l-bit sub-sequence $(y_1, y_2, \dots, y_l)$ there exists a vector $x \in X$ whose components in the indicated coordinates exactly match the bits of y. That is, $x_{i_j} = y_j$ for $j = 1, 2, \dots, l$.

To see that it suffices to construct this collection of vectors, assume we are given a collection X. Define the set-system with $B = X$ and C_i as $\{x \in X \mid x_i = 1\}$, the set of vectors with 1 in the ith coordinate. Suppose $i_1, i_2, \dots, i_l$ is any set of indices in $\{1, 2, \dots, m\}$ and $D_{i_1}, D_{i_2}, \dots, D_{i_l}$ is a collection of subsets of X such that D_{i_j} is equal to either C_{i_j} or the complement of C_{i_j}. We claim that $\cup_{j \le l} D_{i_j}$ cannot be B. For, define an l-bit subsequence y such that $y_j = 0$ if $D_{i_j} = C_{i_j}$ and 1 otherwise. The known property of X implies there exists a vector $x \in X$ such that $x_{i_j} = y_j$ for $j = 1, 2, \dots, l$. By construction, $x \notin D_{i_j}$ for all $j = 1, 2, \dots, l$. Thus, we have shown $\cup_{j \le l} D_{i_j} \ne B$. Since this is true for every sequence $i_1, \dots, i_l$, it follows that $(B, C_1, \dots, C_m)$ is an (m, l)-system.

An explicit construction[4] of the desired collection of vectors follows from a result of Naor and Naor on ϵ-*biased distributions* ([NN93]; for an improved construction, see [AGHP92]).

Given m, l and a rational $\epsilon > 0$ they show how to construct a set X_ϵ of $O(\frac{m^2}{\epsilon^2})$ vectors of m bits each, with the following property. Let $i_1, i_2, \dots, i_l$ be any l distinct coordinates and $(y_1, y_2, \dots, y_l)$ be any l-bit sub-sequence. Consider two experiments: (i) picking a sequence x uniformly at random from X_ϵ, and (ii) picking a sequence z uniformly at random from the set of all 2^m strings of length m. Then, regardless of i_j's and the y_j's, the collection satisfies the inequality $|p_z - p_x| < \epsilon$, where p_z and p_x are the probabilities that z and x respectively matches y in the indicated coordinates. But, $p_z = 2^{-l}$. Hence, $p_x \in [\frac{1}{2^l} - \epsilon, \frac{1}{2^l} + \epsilon]$. By choosing $\epsilon = 2^{-(l+1)}$ we see that the number of vectors is $O(m^2 2^{2l})$. Furthermore, $p_x \ge \frac{1}{2^l} - \frac{1}{2^{l+1}} > 0$, implying there exists a $x \in X_\epsilon$ that matches y. Thus, we have shown how to construct the desired set-system.   ∎

Briefly, we indicate the proof of Theorem 10.2, part 4.

Proof of Theorem 10.2, of part 4.   Part 3 of Theorem 10.2 describes a reduction from SAT to LABELCOVER$_{\max}$. By composing that reduction with the reduction described in this section, part 4 follows.   ∎

REMARK 10.3   The reduction to SETCOVER is easily modified to prove hardness results for HITTING SET, HYPERGRAPH TRANSVERSAL, DOMINATING SET and MINIMUM EXACT COVER (see Table 10.2). Also, the constant $c = \frac{1}{48}$ in the inapproximability result is not optimal. In fact, Feige [Fei95] proved for any $\epsilon > 0$ that approximating SETCOVER within a factor $(1 + \epsilon) \ln |\mathcal{S}|$ is *Quasi-NP-hard*. It is an open

---

[4]A randomized construction is quite trivial; see the exercises.

question whether approximating SETCOVER within a factor $\Omega(\log n)$ is *NP*-hard. A result in [BGLR93] implies that approximating within any constant factor is *NP*-hard. An alternative proof of the [BGLR93] result follows from the reduction of this section, in conjunction with the *product* technique of Section 10.5.1, which implies that approximating LABELCOVER$_{\max}$ within any constant factor is *NP*-hard.

EXERCISE 10.3 (Randomized construction of (m, l) systems) Let l, m be "large enough" positive integers such that $2l < \log m$. Let $X = \{0, 1\}^m$ be the set of sequences of bits of length m. Suppose we pick a set B uniformly at random from among all subsets of X of size $2^{2l} m^2$, and set $C_i = \{x \in B : \text{ the } i\text{th bit of } x \text{ is } 1\}$. Prove that the probability that $(B, C_1, \ldots, C_m)$ is an (m, l) set system is $1 - o(1)$.

EXERCISE 10.4 Use the inapproximability of SETCOVER to prove the inapproximability of HITTING SET, HYPERGRAPH TRANSVERSAL, DOMINATING SET and MINIMUM EXACT COVER. These problems are defined in [GJ79]. (*Hint:* Try to show that SETCOVER is a subcase of these problems.)

INAPPROXIMABILITY RESULTS FOR PROBLEMS IN CLASS III

10.5

In this section we show hardness results for problems in Class III. Achieving a ratio $2^{\log^{1-\gamma} n}$ for these problems is quasi-*NP*-hard, for every fixed $\gamma > 0$. LABELCOVER (in both its minimization and maximization versions) is the canonical problem in this class.

Sections 10.5.1 and 10.5.2 outline the inapproximability result for the max and the min versions of LABELCOVER. A hardness result for the nearest lattice vector problem appears in Section 10.5.3. This result, involving a gap-preserving reduction from LABELCOVER, is illustrative of the hardness results for Class III.

10.5.1 LABELCOVER (MAXIMIZATION VERSION)

We give a quasi-polynomial-time reduction from SAT to LABELCOVER (maximization version) that maps satisfiable formulae to LABELCOVER instances in which some labelling can cover all edges (i.e., the labelling has value 1), and unsatisfiable formulae to instances in which every labelling covers at most $2^{-\log^{1-\gamma} N}$ fraction of edges, where N is the size of the instance. The proof of the correctness of the reduction relies upon a difficult result from [Raz94], which we will not prove.

The starting point is a gap-preserving polynomial-time reduction τ from MAX-3SAT(5) to LABELCOVER$_{\max}$ from Example 10.1. The reduction ensures for all 3CNF formulae I and all $\epsilon > 0$ that:

$$\text{MAX-3SAT}(I) = 1 \implies \text{LABELCOVER}_{\max}(\tau(I)) = 1,$$
$$\text{MAX-3SAT}(I) < (1 - \epsilon) \implies \text{LABELCOVER}_{\max}(\tau(I)) < (1 - \frac{\epsilon}{9}).$$

Note that by composing this reduction with the reduction from SAT to MAX-3SAT(5) in part 1 of Theorem 10.2, we get a polynomial-time reduction τ' from SAT to LABEL-COVER$_{\max}$ which, for some $\delta > 0$, ensures

$$I \in \text{SAT} \implies \text{LABELCOVER}_{\max}(\tau'(I)) = 1,$$
$$I \notin \text{SAT} \implies \text{LABELCOVER}_{\max}(\tau'(I)) < (1 - \delta). \tag{10.3}$$

Thus, the reduction produces a gap: the optimum value in the LABELCOVER$_{\max}$ instance is either 1 or less than $1 - \delta$. We desire a bigger gap: the value should be either 1 or less than $2^{-\log^{1-\gamma} N}$ where N is the size of LABELCoVER instance in question, and γ is any fixed positive rational number. We use the following construction to "boost" the gap.

Given any instance $\mathcal{L} = (V_1, V_2, E, N, \Pi)$ of LABELCOVER$_{\max}$ we define its *kth power*, denoted $\mathcal{L}^k$, as follows. It is another instance of LABELCOVER$_{\max}$ whose underlying bipartite graph is (V_1^k, V_2^k, E^k), where V_i^k is the set of all k-tuples of V_i and E^k, the new set of edges is the set of all k-tuples of old edges. The number of new labels is N^k, and the set of labels are to be viewed as k-tuples of labels of $\mathcal{L}$, i.e., as elements of $\{1, 2, \ldots, N\}^k$. (Thus, a labelling must now assign k-tuples of labels from $\{1, 2, \ldots, N\}$ to vertices in $V_1^k \cup V_2^k$.) The new edge-functions, denoted Π^k, are defined as follows. Let e be a k-tuple of edges $(e_1, e_2, \ldots, e_k)$, where each e_i is an edge in the original graph. Then define

$$\Pi_e^k(a_1^1, a_1^2, \ldots, a_1^k) = (\Pi_{e_1}(a_1^1), \Pi_{e_2}(a_1^2), \ldots, \Pi_{e_k}(a_1^k)).$$

In other words, the pair of k-tuples of labels $((a_1^1, a_1^2, \ldots, a_1^k), (a_2^1, a_2^k, \ldots, a_2^k))$ can be used to cover the new edge $(e_1, \ldots, e_k)$ iff for $i = 1, \ldots, k$ the pair (a_1^i, a_2^i) can be used to cover the edge e_i.

The reduction consists in constructing $\mathcal{L}^k$ for some suitable k. Since $\mathcal{L}^k$ has size $N = n^{O(k)}$, where n is the size of $\mathcal{L}$, the running time of the reduction is poly(N). If LABELCOVER$_{\max}(\mathcal{L}) = 1$ to start with, then LABELCOVER$_{\max}(\mathcal{L}^k) = 1$, as is easily checked. But Lemma 10.4 below shows that if LABELCOVER$_{\max}(\mathcal{L}) < 1 - \delta$ to start with, then LABELCOVER$_{\max}(\mathcal{L}^k) < (1 - \delta)^{ck}$, where $c > 0$ is a fixed constant. (Note that the number of labels, N, is $O(1)$ in instances of LABELCOVER obtained in Example 10.1.) Now, for $k = (\log n)^{O(\frac{1-\gamma}{\gamma})}$ we get that the size of $\mathcal{L}^k$ m is $2^{\text{poly}(\log n)}$ and the gap $1/(1 - \delta)^{ck}$ is at least $2^{\log^{1-\gamma} m}$. This finishes the description of the reduction.

The next lemma, also called Raz's *Parallel Repetition Theorem* [5] shows that if LABELCOVER$_{\max}(\mathcal{L}) < 1$, then LABELCOVER$_{\max}(\mathcal{L}^k)$ decreases exponentially as we increase k.

---

[5]This lemma had been conjectured for many years in the literature on interactive proofs. It can be viewed as saying that parallel repetition of a 2 Prover 1 Round proof system drives down the error probability at an exponential rate.

LEMMA 10.4 Implicit in [Raz94]   There is a fixed constant $c > 0$ such that for any LABELCOVER instance $\mathcal{L}$: $\text{LABELCOVER}_{\max}(\mathcal{L}^k) \leq \text{LABELCOVER}_{\max}(\mathcal{L})^{\frac{ck}{\log N}}$, where N is the number of labels allowed in $\mathcal{L}$.

Raz's result implies that LABELCOVER is in the class of problems with a self-improvement property (see Section 10.6.1). His proof is quite complicated.

10.5.2   LABELCOVER (MIN VERSION)

The hardness result for the min version of LABELCOVER follows from the hardness result for the max version, since the two versions are linked by the following "weak duality."

LEMMA 10.5   For any instance I of LABELCOVER:

$$\text{LABELCOVER}_{\max}(I) \geq \frac{1}{\text{LABELCOVER}_{\min}(I)}.$$

To see why the inapproximability of the min version follows, recall our quasi-polynomial-time reduction τ' from SAT to $\text{LABELCOVER}_{\max}$. It ensures for all I:

$$I \in \text{SAT} \Longrightarrow \text{LABELCOVER}_{\max}(\tau'(I)) = 1,$$
$$I \notin \text{SAT} \Longrightarrow \text{LABELCOVER}_{\max}(\tau'(I)) < \rho,$$

where $\rho = 2^{-\log^{1-\gamma} n}$ for some fixed $\gamma > 0$, and n is the size of the LABELCOVER instance.

But $\text{LABELCOVER}_{\max}(\tau'(I)) = 1$ means there is a way to assign one label per vertex such that all edges are covered, hence, $\text{LABELCOVER}_{\min}(\tau'(I)) = 1$. Further, the weak duality implies that if $\text{LABELCOVER}_{\max}(\tau'(I)) < \rho$, then $\text{LABELCOVER}_{\min}(\tau'(I)) > 1/\rho$.

Thus, τ' can be viewed as a reduction to $\text{LABELCOVER}_{\min}$ as well, with a gap of $2^{\log^{1-\gamma} N}$ in the cost of the minimum label cover depending on whether or not the boolean formula was satisfiable.

Thus, to finish the proof of the inapproximability of $\text{LABELCOVER}_{\min}$ it suffices to prove the weak duality.

Proof of Lemma 10.5.   Let $OPT_{\min}$ and $OPT_{\max}$ be shorthands for $\text{LABELCOVER}_{\min}(I)$ and $\text{LABELCOVER}_{\max}(I)$ respectively. Consider the solution of the minimization version, namely, a labelling using on an average $OPT_{\min}$ labels per vertex in V_1 and covering all the edges. For any vertex $u \in V_1$ let the labelling assign n_u labels to u. Then by definition of cost, $\sum_{u \in V_1} n_u = OPT_{\min} \cdot |V_1|$.

We randomly delete all labels for each vertex in $V_1 \cup V_2$ except one. This gives a labelling that assigns only 1 label per vertex, in other words, a candidate solution for the maximization version. The original labelling covered every edge. In other words, for each edge $e = (u, v)$ and for every label a_2 assigned to v it assigns a label a_1 to u such that $\Pi_e(a_1) = a_2$. The probability that this preimage a_1 survives is $\frac{1}{n_u}$. Therefore, in the new (randomly constructed) labelling the expected number of edges still left covered is at least $\sum_{(u,v)\in E} \frac{1}{n_u}$.

Since each vertex in V_1 has the same degree, say d, the number of edges, $|E|$, is $d|V_1|$, and the above expectation can be rewritten as

$$\sum_{u\in V_1} \frac{d}{n_u} = d\sum_{u\in V_1} \frac{1}{n_u} \geq d\frac{|V_1|^2}{\sum_{u\in V_1} n_u} = d\frac{|V_1|^2}{OPT_{min}|V_1|} = \frac{|E|}{OPT_{min}}.$$

The crucial fact used above is that $\sum_u \frac{1}{n_u}$ is minimized when all n_u are equal.

Thus, we have shown a randomized way to construct a candidate solution to the maximization version, such that the expected fraction of edges covered is at least $\frac{1}{OPT_{min}}$. It follows that there must exist a candidate solution that covers this many edges. Hence, we have proved, $OPT_{max} \geq \frac{1}{OPT_{min}}$. ∎

Remarks: The LABELCOVER problem was implicit in [LY94], and explicitly defined for the first time in [ABSS93]. A weaker version of the "weak duality" described in Lemma 10.5 was implicit in a calculation in [LY94]; the version given here is from [Aro94].

Note that the original proof of the hardness of approximating LABELCOVER$_{max}$ used [FL92] instead of [Raz94].

10.5.3   NEAREST LATTICE VECTOR PROBLEM

Let m, k be integers and $\{b_1, b_2, \ldots, b_m\}$ be a set of independent vectors in $\mathbf{Z}^k$. The *lattice generated by basis* $\{b_1, b_2, \ldots, b_m\}$, denoted $\mathcal{L}(b_1, b_2, \ldots, b_m)$, is the set of all their integer linear combinations, i.e., $\left\{\sum_{i=1}^m \alpha_i b_i : \alpha_i \in \mathbf{Z}\right\}$. Many important optimization problems can be phrased as problems involving lattices (see the survey by Kannan [Kan87]). The following lattice problem is quite basic.

DEFINITION 10.6 *Nearest Lattice Vector Problem (NLVP)*   Given a lattice basis $\{b_1, b_2, \ldots, b_m\}$, and a point $b_0 \in \mathbf{Q}^k$, find the lattice vector nearest (in the Euclidean norm) to b_0.

In conjunction with the inapproximability result for LABELCOVER$_{min}$ (Theorem 10.2, part 3) the next result shows that NLVP is in Class III.

THEOREM 10.3   There is polynomial-time reduction τ from LABELCOVER$_{min}$ to NLVP that ensures for every number $\rho \geq 1$:

$$\text{LABELCOVER}_{min}(I) = 1 \implies \text{NLVP}(\tau(I)) = K(I),$$
$$\text{LABELCOVER}_{min}(I) > \rho \implies \text{NLVP}(\tau(I)) > \sqrt{\rho} \cdot K(I),$$

where $K(I)$ is a polynomial-time computable function.

This is an example (refer to the comments after Definition 10.2) of a gap-preserving reduction for which we do not know an equivalent L-reduction. However, this reduction is still good enough for proving inapproximability in conjunction with the inapproximability result for LABELCOVER stated in Theorem 10.2 part 3, since that result (quite conveniently, it seems) in one of the cases produces instances of LABELCOVER with optimum cost exactly 1.

Proof of Theorem 10.3.   Let (V_1, V_2, E, Π, N) be an instance of LABELCOVER$_{min}$. Remember, a labelling is a function $\mathcal{P}$ from vertices to sets of labels, where $\mathcal{P}(v)$ denotes the set of labels assigned to the vertex $v \in V_1 \cup V_2$. A labelling that covers every edge is called a *total cover*.

The reduction produces a lattice basis containing one vector for every pair (v, a), where v is a vertex and a is a label. For convenience, we index the basis vectors by such pairs, i.e., the basis is denoted by $\{b_{va} | v \in V_1 \cup V_2, a \in \{1, 2, \dots, N\}\}$.

Note, with every lattice vector $x = \sum_{v,a} c_{va} b_{va}$ we may associate a labelling $\mathcal{P}^x$, defined as $\mathcal{P}^x(v) = \{a : c_{va} \neq 0\}$. That is, $\mathcal{P}^x$ assigns a label a to vertex v iff the basis vector b_{va} has a nonzero contribution to x. The reduction will construct a fixed point b_0 in such a way that the cost of the labelling $\mathcal{P}^x$ is related to the distance $||x - b_0||_2$; the distance is small iff $\mathcal{P}^x$ forms a total cover.

The basis vectors (and hence, also the lattice vectors) have $|E|(N+1) + |V_1|N$ coordinates: $N + 1$ coordinates for each edge $e \in E$ and 1 for each pair (v_1, a_1) for $v_1 \in V_1$ and $a_1 \in \{1, 2, \dots, N\}$. Call the coordinates corresponding to e as the *e-projection* of the vector, and the coordinate corresponding to pair (v_1, a_1) as the (v_1, a_1)-projection. The (v_1, a_1)-projection of a basis-vector b_{va} is 1 iff $(v, a) = (v_1, a_1)$. Thus, only the basis vectors corresponding to vertices in V_1 can have a nonzero (v_1, a_1)-projection. As will be clear later, this corresponds to the fact that in the LABELCOVER problem, only labels assigned to vertices in V_1 contribute to the cost of the cover.

Let K be the integer $|E|(N+1)$. For $j = 1, 2, \dots, N$, let U_j be a vector with $N + 1$ coordinates, in which the j'th entry is 1 and all the other entries are 0. Let $\vec{0}$ and $\vec{1}$ denote, respectively, the all-zero vector and all-one vector with $N + 1$ coordinates.

The basis is defined as follows. Let e be any edge and a be a label. For vertex $v_1 \in V_1$,

$$\text{the } e\text{-projection of } b_{v_1 a} = \begin{cases} K \cdot (\vec{1} - U_{\Pi_e(a)}) & \text{if } e \text{ is incident to } v_1 \text{ and } \Pi_e(a) \text{ is defined} \\ \vec{0} & \text{otherwise} \end{cases}$$

For vertex $v_2 \in V_2$, the e-projection of the vector $b_{v_2 a}$ is $K \cdot U_a$ if e is incident to v_2, and $\vec{0}$ otherwise (see Figure 10.2).

The fixed vector b_0 contains, for every edge e, the vector $K \cdot \vec{1}$ in its e-projection. It's (v_1, a_1)-projection is $\vec{0}$ for all pairs (v_1, a_1).

Thus, for every edge e, the e-projections of the basis vectors are either $K \cdot U_a$ for some label a, or $K \cdot (\vec{1} - U_a)$, or $\vec{0}$. Suppose labels a_1, a_2 cover edge $e = (u, v)$. Then $\Pi_e(a_1) = a_2$. Hence, the e-projection of $V_{ua_1} + V_{va_2}$ is

$$K \cdot (\vec{1} - U_{\Pi_e(a_1)}) + K \cdot U_{a_2} = K \cdot \vec{1}.$$

In particular, since the e-projection of b_0 is $K \cdot \vec{1}$, the e-projection of $V_{ua_1} + V_{va_2} - b_0$ is $\vec{0}$.

Now we prove the first property of the reduction. Assume there is a total cover with cost 1, i.e., which uses only one label per vertex. Let $\mathcal{P}(u)$ denote the label it assigns to vertex $u \in V_1 \cup V_2$. Let x be the lattice vector $x = \sum_{v_1 \in V_1} b_{v_1, \mathcal{P}(v_1)} + \sum_{v_2 \in V_2} b_{v_2, \mathcal{P}(v_2)}$. Then the e-projection of $x - b_0$ is $\vec{0}$ for every edge e. Further, exactly $|V_1|$ of the other coordinates in $x - b_0$ are 1. Hence, the distance $||x - b_0||_2$ is exactly $\sqrt{|V_1|}$.

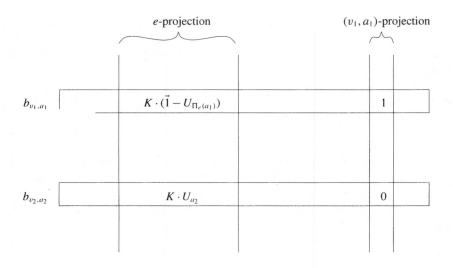

FIGURE 10.2

The e-projections of vectors b_{v_1,a_1} and b_{v_2,a_2} when
$e = (v_1, v_2)$. In the figure we assume that $\Pi_e(a_1)$ is defined;
otherwise the e-projection of b_{v_1,a_1} is $\vec{0}$.

Next, we show the second property of the reduction. The following lemma shows that if the e-projection of any integer combination of basis vectors is $K \cdot \vec{1}$, then the combination contains some vectors b_{u,a_1} and b_{v,a_2} such that a_1, a_2 cover e.

LEMMA 10.6   For some integers $\{d_a : a \in \{1, \dots, N\}\} \cup \{d'_a : a \in \{1, \dots, N\}\}$, if

$$\sum_a (d_a \cdot U_a + d'_a \cdot (\vec{1} - U_a)) = \vec{1},$$

then $d_a = d'_a$ for every a and there exists some a such that d_a and d'_a are nonzero.

Proof.   The vectors $\{U_1, U_2, \dots, U_N\}$ are linearly independent and do not span $\vec{1}$.   ■

Next, we show that if a lattice vector is "near" b_0 then its associated labelling is a total cover.

COROLLARY 10.4   If $||x - b_0||_2 < K$ for a lattice vector x, then $\mathcal{P}^x$ is a total cover.

Proof.   Let $x = \sum_{v,a} c_{va} b_{va}$ and let e be any edge, say (u, v). Every coordinate in the e-projection of $x - b_0$ is an integer multiple of K. If $||x - V_0|| < K$, these coordinates must be all 0. Thus, if $||x - V_0||_2 < K$, the e-projections of the basis vectors form a linear combination as described in the hypothesis of Lemma 10.6, where $\vec{1}$ in the lemma statement comes from the e-projection of b_0. We conclude that $c_{va_2} = \sum_{a_1 : \Pi_e(a_1) = a_2} c_{ua_1}$ for every a_2 and there is at least one a_2 such that $c_{va_2} \neq 0$. Further, if $c_{va_2} \neq 0$, then there exists some a_1 such that $c_{ua_1} \neq 0$ and $\Pi_e(a_1) = a_2$. Hence, $\mathcal{P}^x$ covers e.   ■

The next lemma shows that the distance $||x - b_0||_2$ is related to the cost of labelling $\mathcal{P}^x$. It also proves the second property of the reduction claimed in Theorem 10.3.

LEMMA 10.7   For every lattice vector x,

$$||x - b_0||_2 \geq \sqrt{|V_1| \text{LABELCOVER}_{\min}(\mathcal{L})}.$$

Proof.   The definition of $\text{LABELCOVER}_{\min}$ implies that $\text{LABELCOVER}_{\min}(\mathcal{L}) \leq N$. Since $K = |V_1|(N + 1)$, it follows that $|V_1| \text{LABELCOVER}_{\min}(\mathcal{L}) < K$. Corollary 10.4 implies that if $\mathcal{P}^x$ is not a total cover then $||x - b_0||_2 \geq K$. Thus, the lemma needs to be proven only when $\mathcal{P}^x$ is a total cover. The definitions of $\mathcal{P}^x$ and of the (v_1, a_1)-projections of basis vectors imply that

$$||x - b_0||_2 \geq \sqrt{\text{Number of nonzero coordinates in } x - b_0}$$
$$= \sqrt{|\{(v_1, a_1) : (v_1, a_1)\text{-projection of } x \text{ is} \neq 0\}|}$$
$$\geq \sqrt{\text{cost of } \mathcal{P}^x}$$
$$\geq \sqrt{|V_1| \text{LABELCOVER}_{\min}(\mathcal{L})}$$

Thus, the lemma has been proved.   ■

Remarks: The hardness result for the nearest vector problem is from [ABSS93], which also uses similar constructions to prove the hardness of a variety of problems involving lattices, codes, and linear systems.

EXERCISE 10.5 [ABSS93]   In the NEAREST CODEWORD problem, we are given a matrix M with m rows and n columns ($m < n$) and a vector b_0 with n entries. All entries in M and b_0 are 0 or 1 (interpreted as elements of the field $GF(2)$). The goal is to find a $\frac{0}{1}$ vector $x \in \{0, 1\}^m$ such that $x^T \cdot M$ differs from b_0 in as few positions as possible. Let NEAREST-CODEWORD(M, b_0) denote the number of positions in which $x^T \cdot M$ and b_0 differ. (*Note:* In the language of coding theory, M is the generator matrix of a binary code and b_0 is a received message. We wish to find out the codeword it is nearest to.)

- Show that the NEAREST CODEWORD problem is in Class I.
- Show that the NEAREST CODEWORD problem is in Class III. (*Hint:* Modify our construction for the nearest lattice vector problem.)

EXERCISE 10.6 [ABSS93]   In the MIN-UNSATISFY problem we are given a system of n linear equations in m variables $x_1, \ldots, x_m$. The coefficients of the system are integers and $n > m$ (i.e., there are more equations than variables). The goal is to remove as few equations from the system as possible, such that the remaining system is feasible (i.e., has a solution in which each x_i is a real number). For a system S, let MIN-UNSATISFY(S) denote the minimum number of equations that must be removed to make it feasible.

- Show that the MIN-UNSATISFY problem is in Class I.
- Show that the MIN-UNSATISFY problem is in Class III.
- Consider the version of MIN-UNSATISFY problem in which linear system contains strict inequalities instead of equations. Prove the results in parts 1 and 2 for that problem.

INAPPROXIMABILITY RESULTS FOR
PROBLEMS IN CLASS IV

10.6

In this section we demonstrate problems for which it is *NP*-hard to achieve an approximation ratio of n^ϵ for some $\epsilon > 0$. The canonical problems in this class are CLIQUE (or R-CLIQUE) and COLORING. We describe the inapproximability results for the canonical problems, and indicate how to prove the inapproximability of the other problems.

The inapproximability result for CLIQUE uses the fact that the clique number has a *self-improvement* property [GJ79, BS92]. Problems other than CLIQUE also display this property; see Section 10.7.1 for example. Also, a classical inapproximability result for COLORING[GJ76] uses a similar property.

10.6.1   CLIQUE

The hardness result for clique number relies upon its interesting *self-improvement* behavior when we take graph products. The next example describes this behavior.

DEFINITION 10.7   For a graph $G = (V, E)$ let $\hat{E}$ denote E with all self-loops added; that is, $\hat{E} = E \cup \{\{u, u\} : u \in V\}$. For graphs $G_1 = (V_1, E_1)$ and $G_2 = (V_2, E_2)$, their *product* $G_1 \times G_2$ is the graph whose vertex set is the set $V_1 \times V_2$, and edge set is

$$\left\{((u_1, v_1), (u_2, v_2)) : (u_1, u_2) \in \hat{E}_1 \text{ and } (v_1, v_2) \in \hat{E}_2\right\}.$$

Example 10.3   Let $\omega(G)$ be the size of the largest clique in a graph. It is easily checked that $\omega(G_1 \times G_2) = \omega(G_1)\omega(G_2)$.

Now suppose a reduction exists from SAT to clique, such that the graph G produced by the reduction has clique number either l, or $(1 - \epsilon)l$, depending on whether or not the SAT formula was satisfiable. In other words, achieving an approximation ratio $(1 - \epsilon)^{-1}$ for clique number is *NP*-hard. Then we claim that achieving any constant approximation ratio is *NP*-hard. Consider G^k, the product of G with itself k times. Then $\omega(G^k)$ is either l^k or $(1 - \epsilon)^k l^k$. The gap in clique numbers, $(1 - \epsilon)^{-k}$, can be made arbitrarily large by increasing k enough. This is what we mean by self-improvement.

Note, however, that G^k has size n^k, so k must remain $O(1)$ if the above construction has to work in polynomial time.

The rapid increase in problem size when using self-improvement may seem hard to avoid. Surprisingly, the following combinatorial object (specifically, as constructed in Theorem 10.4) often allows us to do just that.

DEFINITION 10.8   Let n be an integer. A (k, n, α) *booster* is a collection $\mathcal{S}$ of subsets of $\{1, 2, \dots, n\}$, each of size k. For every subset $A \subseteq \{1, 2, \dots, n\}$, the sets in the collection that are subsets of A constitute a fraction between $(\rho - \alpha)^k$ and $(\rho + \alpha)^k$ of all sets in $\mathcal{S}$, where $\rho = \frac{|A|}{n}$. When $\rho < 1.1\alpha$, the quantity $(\rho - \alpha)^k$ should be considered to be 0.

Example 10.4   The set of all subsets of $\{1, 2, \ldots, n\}$ of size k is a booster with $\alpha \approx 0$. This is because for any $A \subseteq \{1, 2, \ldots, n\}$, $|A| = \rho n$, the fraction of sets contained in A is $\binom{\rho n}{k} / \binom{n}{k}$, which is $\approx \rho^k$. The problem with this booster is that its size is $\binom{n}{k} = O(n^k)$, hence k must be $O(1)$ if the booster has to be used in polynomial-time reductions.

The following theorem appears in [AFWZ93]. Its proof uses explicit constructions of expander graphs [GG81].

THEOREM 10.4 [AFWZ93]   For any $k = O(\log n)$ and $\alpha > 0$, an (n, k, α) booster of size poly(n) can be constructed in poly(n) time.

Let G be a graph on n vertices. Using a booster, we can define the *booster product* of a graph, which is similar to the product in [BS92]. This is the graph whose vertices are the sets of the booster $\mathcal{S}$, and there is an edge between sets $S_i, S_j \in \mathcal{S}$ iff $S_i \cup S_j$ is a clique in G.

LEMMA 10.8   For any graph G, and any (k, n, α) booster, the clique number of the booster product of G lies between $(\omega(G)/n - \alpha)^k |\mathcal{S}|$ and $(\omega(G)/n + \alpha)^k |\mathcal{S}|$.

Proof.   Let $A \subseteq \{1, 2, \ldots, n\}$ be a clique of size $\omega(G)$ in graph G. Then the number of sets from $\mathcal{S}$ that are subsets of A is between $(\omega(G)/n - \alpha)^k |\mathcal{S}|$ and $(\omega(G)/n + \alpha)^k |\mathcal{S}|$. Clearly, all such sets form a clique in the booster product.

Conversely, given the largest clique B in the booster product, let A be the union of all sets in the clique. Then A is a clique in G, and hence must have size at most $\omega(G)$. The booster property implies that the size of B is as claimed. ∎

THEOREM 10.5 [ALMSS92]   There is an $\epsilon > 0$ such that approximating CLIQUE within a factor n^ϵ is *NP*-hard, where n is the number of vertices in the input graph.

Proof.   Let G be the graph obtained from the reduction in Lemma 10.1, and suppose it has m vertices. The reduction ensures, for some fixed $\beta > 0$, that $\omega(G)$ is either at least $m/3$ or at most $m(1 - \beta)/3$, and it is *NP*-hard to decide which case holds.

Now construct a $(m, \log m, \alpha)$ booster, $\mathcal{S}$, using Theorem 10.4, by choosing $\alpha = \beta/9$. Construct the booster product of G. The number of vertices in the booster product is $|\mathcal{S}|$, and Lemma 10.8 says the clique number is either at least $((3 - \beta)/9)^{\log m} |\mathcal{S}|$ or at most $((3 - 2\beta)/9)^{\log m} |\mathcal{S}|$. Hence, the gap is now m^γ for some $\gamma > 0$, and further, $|\mathcal{S}| = \text{poly}(m)$, so this gap is $|\mathcal{S}|^\epsilon$ for some $\epsilon > 0$. ∎

The proof in Theorem 10.5 is the easiest known proof of the inapproximability of CLIQUE. Next, we describe the slightly more complicated reduction to R-CLIQUE, which also proves Theorem 10.2, part 2.

Proof of Theorem 10.2, part 2.   For each $\epsilon > 0$ we give a gap-preserving reduction τ from MAX-3SAT to R-CLIQUE that has parameters $((1, 1 + \epsilon), (1, n^{-\delta}))$, where n is the size of the new instance and $\delta > 0$ is some constant depending on ϵ. (Remember that R-CLIQUE(G) of an r-partite graph G is the ratio of $\omega(G)/r$.) In other words, τ ensures, for every 3CNF formula φ,

$$\text{MAX-3SAT}(\varphi) = 1 \Longrightarrow \text{R-CLIQUE}(\tau(\varphi)) = 1$$
$$\text{MAX-3SAT}(\varphi) \leq \frac{1}{1 + \epsilon} \Longrightarrow \text{R-CLIQUE}(\tau(\varphi)) \leq n^{-\delta}.$$

Let $C_1 \vee C_2 \vee \cdots \vee C_m$ be a 3CNF formula in n variables $x_1, x_2, \ldots, x_n$. Construct a $(m, \log m, \alpha)$ booster, $\mathcal{S}$, using Theorem 10.4 and with $\alpha = \epsilon/100$. Let k denote the size of each set in the booster (i.e., $\log m$). Interpret each set $S_i \in \mathcal{S}$ as a set of k clauses. Construct a graph H on $n = |\mathcal{S}|3^k$ vertices as follows. Corresponding to each set $S_i \in \mathcal{S}$ it has 3^k vertices, each labelled by a $k + 1$-tuple of the form $(i, t_1, t_2, \ldots, t_k)$, where each $t_i = 1, 2$, or 3. Notice, the first entry in the tuple indicates the set in $\mathcal{S}$ it corresponds to, and the remaining entries pick out a literal (numbered 1 to 3) from each clause appearing in this set. Put edges in the new graph as follows: vertices $(i, t_1, t_2, \ldots, t_k)$ and $(j, s_1, s_2, \ldots, s_k)$ are adjacent iff $i \neq j$ and if the literals picked out by $t_1, t_2, \ldots, t_k, s_1, \ldots, s_k$, do not contain both a variable and its negation.

Note that the graph is $|\mathcal{S}|$-partite; the vertices corresponding to any set in $\mathcal{S}$ are mutually nonadjacent. Also, in any clique of H, a variable and its negation cannot both appear. Thus, a clique corresponds to a (partial) assignment that satisfies all the clauses appearing in the clique.

Suppose the 3CNF formula has a satisfying assignment. Then there is a corresponding clique in H of size $|\mathcal{S}|$: pick a true literal from each clause, and pick the corresponding k-tuple from each set in $\mathcal{S}$. Since all k-tuples involve true literals, they never involve both a variable and its negation. So all $|\mathcal{S}|$ of them are adjacent to each other, and we have thus identified a clique of size $|\mathcal{S}|$.

Conversely, assume every assignment satisfies less than $1/(1 + \epsilon)$ fraction of the clauses. Let B be a clique in H and let A be the set of clauses appearing in it. Then $|A|/m \leq m/(1 + \epsilon)$. The property of the booster implies that $|B|$ is at most $(|A|/m + \alpha)^k |\mathcal{S}| \leq (1/(1 + \epsilon) + \alpha)^k |\mathcal{S}|$. Thus, $\omega(H)$ is upperbounded by $(1/(1 + \epsilon) + \alpha)^k |\mathcal{S}| \leq m^{-\gamma} |\mathcal{S}|$ for some small $\gamma > 0$. Hence, $\omega(H) < \mathcal{S}/n^{-\delta}$ for some small $\delta > 0$. Thus, the correctness of the reduction has been proved.   ∎

Comments: The first inapproximability result for the clique problem, due to [FGL+91], showed that achieving an approximation ratio of $2^{\log^{1-\delta} n}$ is Quasi-*NP*-hard. Then [AS92] showed that the same approximation is actually *NP*-hard. Soon after, [ALMSS92] showed that achieving a ratio n^ϵ is *NP*-hard. The proof given in this section is due to [AFWZ93]; it is a simplification of the original proof in [ALMSS92].

EXERCISE 10.7   Randomized Construction of Boosters   Let α be any positive fraction and c be any fixed positive integer. Let n be a "large enough" integer, and $k = c \log n$. Suppose we randomly pick $O(n/\alpha^k)$ subsets of size k from $\{1, \ldots, n\}$. Prove that the probability that these subsets form a (k, n, α) booster is at least $1 - o(1)$.

10.6.2 COLORING

Now we prove part 5 of Theorem 10.2, concerning the hardness of approximating the chromatic number of graphs. For ease of exposition, we prove the result for a trivial reformulation of chromatic number, the clique cover number. A *clique cover of size k* in a graph is a partition of the vertices into k sets, each of which is a clique. The *clique cover number* of G, denoted $\overline{\chi}(G)$, is the minimum size of a clique cover of graph G. Note that $\omega(G) \geq n/\overline{\chi}(G)$, where n is the number of vertices in G. The reason is that a partition of $V(G)$ into $\overline{\chi}(G)$ cliques must contain some clique of size $\geq n/\overline{\chi}(G)$

A k-coloring of a graph G is a partition of the vertices into k independent sets. Thus, a k-coloring in G can be viewed as as a clique cover of size k in $\overline{G}$, and vice versa, where $\overline{G}$ is the graph containing exactly those edges that are absent in G. Thus, $\chi(G) = \overline{\chi}(\overline{G})$, which shows that the clique cover number is a trivial reformulation of the chromatic number.

Now we give a gap-preserving reduction τ from R-CLIQUE to the clique cover problem. The following definition will be useful:

DEFINITION 10.9 For positive integers r and k, an $r \times k$ *graph* is a graph on rk vertices, which can be partitioned into r independent sets, each of size exactly k. We will assume that the vertices are labelled from the set $R \times K$, where $R = \{0, 1, \ldots, r-1\}$, $K = \{0, 1, \ldots, k-1\}$, and vertices labelled by $\{j\} \times K$ constitute the jth independent set.

Note that given an r-partite graph — in other words, an instance of R-CLIQUE — we can easily convert it into an $r \times k$ graph (for some suitable k) by adding isolated vertices to equalize the sizes of the r-partitions. Thus, we can trivially rephrase Theorem 10.2, part 2, so that it gives us a reduction τ' which reduces SAT to R-CLIQUE as follows, for some $\epsilon > 0$:

$$\forall I \quad I \in \text{SAT} \implies \text{R-CLIQUE}(\tau'(I)) = 1$$
$$I \notin \text{SAT} \implies \text{R-CLIQUE}(\tau'(I)) < \frac{1}{n^\epsilon}, \tag{10.4}$$

where $\tau'(I)$ is an $r \times k$ graph and $n = rk$ is the size of $\tau'(I)$.

In this section we describe a reduction τ that, given an $r \times k$ graph G, produces an $r \times k'$ graph G' such that, for every constant $\epsilon > 0$:

$$\text{R-CLIQUE}(G) = 1 \implies \overline{\chi}(\tau(I)) = k' \tag{10.5}$$
$$\text{R-CLIQUE}(G) < 1/n^\epsilon \implies \overline{\chi}(\tau(I)) > N^{\epsilon/7} \cdot k', \tag{10.6}$$

where $n = rk$ and $N = rk'$ are the numbers of vertices in G and $\tau(G)$ respectively.

Note that the *NP*-hardness of approximating $\overline{\chi}$ follows, once we compose this reduction with the one in (10.4).

Our reduction τ consists of applying two transformations —defined below— on the graph: first make it 2, 3-*uniquely shiftable*, and then produce the *extension* of the resulting graph.

First, we describe the *extension* of an $r \times k$ graph $G = (R \times K, E)$. For $i = 0, 1, \ldots, k-1$, define the *ith copy* of G as a graph $G_i = (R \times K, E_i)$ containing the same number of vertices and edges as G, but whose edges are *shifted* according to the following rule: $((j, q), (j', q'))$ is an edge in G_i if and only if $((j, (q + i) \bmod k),$ $(j', (q' + i) \bmod k))$ is an edge in G. Since this shifting of edges may be viewed also as a renumbering of the vertices, it follows that graphs G and G_i are isomorphic.

DEFINITION 10.10   Let H be an $r \times k$ graph and $H_0, \ldots, H_{k-1}$ be its copies, as described above. The *extension of* H, denoted $\widetilde{H}$, is an $r \times k$ graph with the same number of vertices as H and whose edges are $\bigcup_{i=0}^{K-1} E(H_i)$.

The next proposition suggests how the reduction could ensure the condition in (10.5).

PROPOSITION 10.1   If H is an $r \times k$ graph, then R-CLIQUE$(H) = 1 \implies \overline{\chi}(\widetilde{H}) = k$.

Proof.   Suppose C is a clique in H of size r. Define for $i = 0, 1, \ldots, k - 1$, the set of vertices $C_i \stackrel{def}{=} \{(j, q) : (j, (q + i) \bmod k) \in C\}$. Each C_i is a clique in $\widetilde{H}$ of size r and furthermore, $C_0, \ldots, C_{K-1}$ are disjoint. It follows that $\overline{\chi}(\widetilde{H}) \leq k$. In addition, $\overline{\chi}(\widetilde{H}) \geq k$, since $\widetilde{H}$ contains an independent set of size k and so a clique partition needs to have k cliques just to cover this independent set. Thus, $\overline{\chi}(\widetilde{H}) = k$.   ■

The next proposition suggests how the reduction could ensure the condition in (10.6).

PROPOSITION 10.2   Let H be an $r \times k$ graph such that $\omega(\widetilde{H}) = \omega(H)$. Then for every $\rho > 1$, R-CLIQUE$(H) < \frac{1}{\rho} \implies \overline{\chi}(\widetilde{H}) > k\rho$.

Proof.   Recall that $kr/\omega(\widetilde{H})$ is a lower bound on $\overline{\chi}(\widetilde{H})$, since $\widetilde{H}$ has kr vertices. Hence, if $\omega(H) = \omega(\widetilde{H})$ then $\omega(H) < r/\rho \implies \omega(\overline{\chi}(\widetilde{H}) > k \cdot \rho$.   ■

Unfortunately, Proposition 10.2 is not enough to ensure the condition in (10.6), since not every $r \times k$ graph G satisfies the property $\omega(G) = \omega(\widetilde{G})$. However, even if G does not satisfy this property, we show how to convert it in polynomial time into an $r \times k'$ graph G' that does. Here k' is roughly $(r K)^5$. Further, this new graph G' has the same clique number as G. Thus, it follows from Propositions 10.1 and 10.2 that

$$\text{R-CLIQUE}(G) = 1 \quad \implies \quad \text{R-CLIQUE}(G') = 1 \quad \implies \quad \overline{\chi}(\widetilde{G'}) = k', \text{and}$$

$$\text{R-CLIQUE}(G) < \frac{1}{\rho} \quad \implies \quad \text{R-CLIQUE}(G') < \frac{1}{\rho} \quad \implies \quad \overline{\chi}(\widetilde{G'}) > k'\rho.$$

As we already indicated, our reduction, when given a graph G, first constructs G' and then outputs its extension $\widetilde{G'}$. Thus, it satisfies both properties desired for it.

To finish up, we describe the transformation from G to G'. For a positive integer l, an $r \times k$ graph G is l *uniquely-shiftable* if it satisfies the following: For every clique C in $\widetilde{G}$ of size l, there is a a unique *shift* $i \in \{0, 1, \ldots, k - 1\}$ such that C is a clique in some copy G_i of G, and C is an independent set in every other copy $G_{i'}$ for $i' \neq i$. Graph G is said to be $2, 3$ *uniquely-shiftable* if it is both 2 uniquely-shiftable and 3 uniquely-shiftable.

Note that if G is $2, 3$ uniquely-shiftable then its extension $\widetilde{G}$ has certain special properties. For instance, 2 uniquely-shiftability implies that every edge e of $\widetilde{G}$ is obtained from exactly one edge of G, by using an appropriate shift i. (That is, for every two distinct edges e', e'' in G, the sth shift of e' does not coincide with the tth shift of e'' for every pair of shifts s, t.) Thus, if G is 2 uniquely-shiftable, we may talk of this shift i as *the* shift of the edge e. If in addition G is 3 uniquely-shiftable, then in every triangle in $\widetilde{G}$, all three edges of the triangle have the same shift.

LEMMA 10.9 If an $r \times k$ graph G is $2, 3$ uniquely-shiftable, then $\omega(G) = \omega(\widetilde{G})$.

Proof. Clearly, $\omega(G) \leq \omega(\widetilde{G})$, since a clique in G is a clique in $\widetilde{G}$. Now let C be any clique in $\widetilde{G}$ of size $\omega(\widetilde{G})$. Since G is 2 uniquely-shiftable, we know that every edge in C has a unique shift associated with it. We show that this shift is the same for all edges in C, whence it follows that C is just the shifted version of some clique in G and the proof is complete. So assume the shifts are not all the same. Then there exist three vertices v_1, v_2, v_3 in C such that the edges (v_1, v_2) and (v_2, v_3) have different shifts. But this contradicts the assumption that G is 3 uniquely-shiftable, since $\{v_1, v_2, v_3\}$ is a triangle in $\widetilde{G}$. Hence, it follows that every edge in C has the same shift. ∎

It only remains to show that every $r \times k$ graphs can be made $2, 3$ uniquely-shiftable without much increase in size. We will need the mapping defined in the following lemma.

LEMMA 10.10 For every positive integer m, we can in poly(m) time construct an injective map $T : \{0, 1, \ldots, m - 1\} \to \{0, 1, \ldots, m' - 1\}$, where $m' > 6m^5$ and for all distinct ordered triples (u_1, u_2, u_3) and (v_1, v_2, v_3) (i.e., $u_1 \leq u_2 \leq u_3$, $v_1 \leq v_2 \leq v_3$, and $(u_1, u_2, u_3) \neq (v_1, v_2, v_3)$),

$$T(v_1) + T(v_2) + T(v_3) \neq T(u_1) + T(u_2) + T(u_3) \bmod m'. \tag{10.7}$$

Proof. Construct T by greedily assigning values, in order, to $T(0), T(1), \ldots,$. Assuming all values up to $T(i)$ have been assigned, we only have to ensure that $T(i + 1)$ does not satisfy any of $6i^5$ equality constraints imposed by the values of $T(0), \ldots, T(i)$. Since $6i^5 < m'$, we can choose a value for $T(i + 1)$ easily, and continue on. ∎

The next lemma shows how to make every $r \times k$ graph $2, 3$ uniquely-shiftable.

LEMMA 10.11 Every $r \times k$ graph G can be changed in polynomial time to an $r \times k'$ graph G' that is $2, 3$ uniquely-shiftable and satisfies $\omega(G) = \omega(G')$. Further, this is possible for $k' \leq 6(rk)^5$.

Proof. Transform G as follows. Choose a map T according to Lemma 10.10 by substituting $m = rk = |R \times K|$. Denote the integer m' obtained from the lemma as k', and let $W = \{0, 1, \ldots, k' - 1\}$. We will think of T as a function from $R \times K$, the vertices of G, to W. The vertex set of the new graph G' is $R \times W$, and its edges are defined according to the following rule: For $j_1, j_2 \in R$ and $w_1, w_2 \in W$, the vertices (j_1, w_1) and (j_2, w_2) are adjacent iff there is an edge $((j_1, q_1), (j_2, q_2))$ in G such that $T(j_1, q_1) = w$ and $T(j_2, q_2) = w_2$. In other words, G' is obtained by mapping every vertex (j, q) in G to the vertex $(j, T(j, q))$ in G', and putting in edges accordingly. Since T is injective, it follows that cliques in G and G' correspond to each other, and so $\omega(G) = \omega(G')$.

To show that G' is 2-uniquely shiftable, we need to show that for every edge in $\widetilde{G'}$, the extension of G', there is a unique shift $i \leq k' - 1$ such that the edge belongs to the ith copy G'_i of G. Assume this is not the case. Then there are distinct edges e_1 and e_2 in G and distinct shifts $s, t \leq k' - 1$ such that the sth shift of e_1 coincides with the tth shift of e_2. Hence, if $e_1 = \{(j_1, q_1), (j_2, q_2)\}$ and $e_2 = \{(j_1, q'_1), (j_2, q'_2)\}$ we have

$$(T(j_1, q_1) + s) = (T(j_1, q'_1) + t)$$
$$(T(j_2, q_2) + s) = (T(j_2, q'_2) + t)$$

This implies that $T(j_1, q_1) - T(j_1, q'_1) = T(j_2, q_2) - T(j_2, q'_2)$ and hence, that $T(j_1, q_1) + T(j_2, q'_2) = T(j_2, q_2) + T(j_1, q'_1) + T(j_2, q'_2)$. The property of T from Equation 10.7 implies that $(j_i, q_i) = (j_i, q'_i)$ for $i = 1, 2$, and thus, e_1 and e_2 are the same edge. This is a contradiction. It follows that G' is 2-uniquely shiftable. Similarly, we can prove that G' is also 3 uniquely-shiftable. ∎

Comments. The above reduction is due to Khanna et. al. [KLS93] and is a simplification of the original reduction in [LY94]. Note that it reduces R-CLIQUE to COLORING and strongly uses the structure of the R-CLIQUE problems. Can a similar reduction be done from CLIQUE to COLORING? This is still open, but partial progress was made in [LY94], which contains a reduction from CLIQUE to COLORING that proves the hardness of approximating COLORING within any constant factor.

The inapproximability of the chromatic number implies inapproximability of many other problems, via gap-preserving reductions: CLIQUE PARTITION, CLIQUE COVER [Sim90], BICLIQUE COVER [Sim90], and FRACTIONAL CHROMATIC NUMBER [Lov75] (see Table 10.2).

EXERCISE 10.8   The *fractional chromatic number* of a graph $G = (V, E)$, denoted $\chi_f(G)$, is the optimum value of the following linear program, which contains a variable x_S for every maximal independent set S in G.

$$\begin{aligned} \text{Min} \quad & \sum_S x_S \\ \text{subject to} \quad & \sum_{\{S : v \in S\}} x_S \geq 1 \quad \forall v \in V. \\ & x_S \geq 0 \quad \forall S \end{aligned}$$

- Prove that $\chi_f(G) \leq \chi(G) \leq \chi_f(G) \cdot 2(1 + \ln |G|)$. (*Hint:* Use the randomized rounding technique of Chapter 11.)
- Conclude that there is an $\epsilon > 0$ such that approximating $\chi_f(G)$ within a factor n^ϵ is *NP*-hard.

INAPPROXIMABILITY RESULTS AT A GLANCE

10.7

As already mentioned, optimization problems fall into four classes, based on the approximation ratio that is hard to achieve for them. In earlier sections we described inapproximability results for some of the problems in each class. Table 10.2 lists references where other inapproximability results can be found.

Class I Referenced papers in second column show the given problem is Max-$\mathcal{SNP}$-hard. Hardness first proved in [ALMSS92]; improvements in factors due to [BS94, BGS95]

Problem	Hard Ratio	Assumption
MAX-SAT ([PY91])	1.027	$NP \neq P$
MAX-3SAT ([PY91])	1.027	$NP \neq P$
MAX-CUT ([PY91])	1.012	$NP \neq P$
VERTEX COVER ([PY91])	1.04	$NP \neq P$
SHORTEST SUPERSTRING ([BJL+91])		$NP \neq P$
3D-MATCHING ([Kan92])	$1 + \epsilon$	$NP \neq P$
MAX-2SAT ([PY91])	1.010	$NP \neq P$
METRIC TSP ([PY93])	$1 + \epsilon$	$NP \neq P$
MULTIWAY CUTS ([DJP+92])	$1 + \epsilon$	$NP \neq P$
STEINER TREE ([BP89])	$1 + \epsilon$	$NP \neq P$
MAX-3-COLORABLE-SUBGRAPH ([PY91])	$1 + \epsilon$	$NP \neq P$
INTEGER-MULTICOMMODITY-FLOW ([GVY93])	$1 + \epsilon$	$NP \neq P$

Class II All results are from [LY94]; Improvements are in [BGLR93, Fei95]

Problem	Hard Ratio	Assumption
SETCOVER	$(1 - \delta) \ln N$	$NP \not\subset \tilde{P}$
HITTING SET	$(1 - \delta) \ln N$	$NP \not\subset \tilde{P}$
DOMINATING SET	$(1 - \delta) \ln N$	$NP \not\subset \tilde{P}$
HYPERGRAPH TRANSVERSAL	$(1 - \delta) \ln N$	$NP \not\subset \tilde{P}$
MINIMUM EXACT COVER	$(1 - \delta) \ln N$	$NP \not\subset \tilde{P}$

Class III Referenced papers give reductions from 2-Prover proof systems. These systems are equivalent to LABELCOVER$_{\max}$.

Problem	Hard Ratio	Assumption
LABELCOVER ([ABSS93])	ρ	$NP \not\subset \tilde{P}$
NEAREST LATTICE VECTOR ([ABSS93])	ρ	$NP \not\subset \tilde{P}$
NEAREST CODEWORD ([ABSS93])	ρ	$NP \not\subset \tilde{P}$
MIN-UNSATISFY ([ABSS93, AK93])	ρ	$NP \not\subset \tilde{P}$
LEARNING HALFSPACES WITH ERROR ([ABSS93])	ρ	$NP \not\subset \tilde{P}$
QUADRATIC PROGRAMMING ([FL92, BR93])	ρ	$NP \not\subset \tilde{P}$
MAX-π-SUBGRAPH ([LY93])	ρ	$NP \not\subset \tilde{P}$
SHORTEST LATTICE VECTOR (ℓ_∞ norm) ([ABSS93])	ρ	$NP \not\subset \tilde{P}$
LONGEST PATH ([KMR93]	ρ	$NP \not\subset \tilde{P}$

Class IV Assuming stronger complexity conjectures, the following factors are hard to achieve: $n^{0.5 - \epsilon}$ for CLIQUE [Has95], $n^{1/3 - \epsilon}$ for CHROMATIC NUMBER [FK95]

Problem	Hard Ratio	Assumption
CLIQUE ([FGL+91, AS92, ALMSS92])	n^ϵ	$NP \neq P$
RCLIQUE ([LY94])	n^ϵ	$NP \neq P$
INDEPENDENT SET ([FGL+91, AS92, ALMSS92])	n^ϵ	$NP \neq P$
CHROMATIC NUMBER ([LY94])	n^ϵ	$NP \neq P$
CLIQUE COVER ([Sim90],[LY94])	n^ϵ	$NP \neq P$
BICLIQUE COVER ([Sim90],[LY94])	n^ϵ	$NP \neq P$
FRACTIONAL CHROMATIC NUMBER ([Lov75],[LY94])	n^ϵ	$NP \neq P$
MAX-PLANAR-SUBGRAPH ([LY93])	n^ϵ	$NP \neq P$
MAX-SET-PACKING ([Zuc93]))	n^ϵ	$NP \neq P$
MAX-SATISFY ([ABSS93, AK93]	n^ϵ	$NP \neq P$

Table 10.2: List of known inapproximability results.

All results in the papers mentioned in Table 10.2 are provable using our canonical problems, except one: the result for the Shortest Lattice Vector problem in ℓ_∞ norm, a problem related to the nearest lattice vector problem described in Section 10.5.3. This problem lies in Class III [ABSS93], but its inapproximability result uses special geometric facts about the construction in [FL92].

In Table 10.2 ϵ denotes some fixed positive constant (that might depend upon the problem in question), δ is any positive constant, ρ denotes $2^{\log^{1-\delta} n}$ for any $\delta > 0$, where n is the input size. $NP \not\subset \tilde{P}$ means NP does not have quasipolynomial-time (i.e., time $n^{\text{poly}(\log n)}$ time) deterministic algorithms. For the results in Class I, we estimate ϵ to be of the order of 10^{-2}; for results in Class IV, ϵ is at least 0.1.

We note that inapproximability results for most problems in Class III were originally proved (see Table 10.2) using reductions from 2-Prover 1-Round proof systems for NP. (Such proof systems first appear in [FL92], and predate the PCP Theorem.) In the (unified) framework we have presented here, all those results can be derived using the LABELCOVER$_{\text{max}}$ problem. The reason is that the LABELCOVER$_{\text{max}}$ problem exactly captures the combinatorial structure of 2-Prover 1-Round proof systems [ABSS93].

As mentioned in the introduction, we have not attempted to optimize the results of this chapter. Such optimization is the subject of many recent papers, however. For example, our hardness result for MAX-3SAT asserts the existence of an $\epsilon > 0$ such that achieving an approximation ratio $1 + \epsilon$ is NP-hard. Optimizing the value of ϵ seems to involve delving into the proof of the PCP Theorem. The best result (in [BGS95], following earlier improvements in [BGLR93, FK94, BS94]) says that $\epsilon \geq \frac{1}{38}$. Optimizing the inapproximability result for clique, on the other hand, has involved looking at the *free bit* parameter of the PCP verifier [FK94, BS94]. A recent result [BGS95] shows that the free bit parameter is intimately connected to inapproximability results for clique. In our terminology, the [BGS95] result can be restated thus: Every reduction to CLIQUE can be modified to produce instances of R-CLIQUE (a seemingly more restrictive problem). That paper also shows that approximating clique within a ratio $n^{1/3-o(1)}$ is hard. This has since been improved to $n^{0.5-\epsilon}$ [Has95]. Similarly, we know that achieving approximation ratio $n^{1/3-\epsilon}$ for Chromatic number is hard [FK95] (see also [Für95]).

Despite such encouraging progress, the provably hard approximation ratio for most problems is much worse than the best ratios that we can achieve for these problems in polynomial time. The best ratio achievable for CLIQUE is $O(n/\log^2 n)$ [BH92], for Chromatic number is $O(n(\log\log n)^2/\log^3 n)$ [Hal93], and for MAX-3SAT is ≈ 1.33 [Yan92, GW94]. Can this gap between inapproximability results and algorithmic results be bridged?[6]

Older inapproximability results. Various inapproximability results were obtained in the 1970s, including those for the traveling salesperson problem (TSP) without the triangle inequality [SG76] and for certain maximum-subgraph problems [Yan79]. Many other results of this type have also been discovered (see eg [CK94]). We did not describe these results, since the techniques involved are closer to those occurring in [GJ79], and seem not to generalize to the problems considered here.

---

[6]Håstad has recently circulated a manuscript that shows the hardness of approximating CLIQUE within a ratio $n^{1-\epsilon}$.

10.7.1 HOW TO PROVE OTHER HARDNESS RESULTS: A CASE STUDY

The first step in proving an inapproximability result for a given problem is to check whether it is already known to be inapproximable. For instance, the problem might be listed in the compendium [CK94].

As a second step, one should try to prove that the problem is in Class I, specifically, to prove that it is Max-SNP-hard. Note that Class I is the richest of the four classes in our classification. Usually one can find a problem in this class, such as MAX-3SAT or MAX-CUT, that reduces in a gap-preserving fashion to the problem at hand. (When stuck in this process, leafing through the many reductions in [PY91] is known to help.)

What if one is unable to show in a reasonable amount of time that the problem is in Class I? According to past experience, proving that the problem is in one of the other classes will then be nearly impossible. (Indeed, we know of only one problem — the Shortest Lattice Vector Problem under the ℓ_∞ norm — which is not known to be Max-$\mathcal{SNP}$-hard, but is known to be in a higher class — namely, Class III.)

But if the problem does turn out to be in Class I, then it is worthwhile trying to place it in a higher class as well. For instance, one might try to think which of the other canonical problems it resembles. Is there a way to reduce SETCOVER to it? Or CLIQUE? Is the problem "self-improvable?"

There is no general recipe to the search we have outlined above. Therefore, we illustrate it with a case study: MAX-SATISFY. This is the problem of finding, in a system of m equations in n variables with rational coefficients, the largest feasible subsystem. (Note that the corresponding decision problem, in which we have to decide whether or not the entire system is feasible, is solvable in polynomial time using Gaussian elimination.) The objective function is the fraction of satisfied equations.

A simple greedy algorithm is known to approximate MAX-SATISFY within a factor $n + 1$, and no substantially better algorithm is known. We will describe a proof from [ABSS93, AK93] that the problem is in Class IV, and hence NP-hard to approximate within a factor n^δ for some $\delta > 0$. But to illustrate our methodology, we will first show that the problem is in Classes I and III.

Let us first attempt to show Max-$\mathcal{SNP}$-hardness. We use the fact that the problem MAX-2SAT is Max-$\mathcal{SNP}$-hard, from which it follows that there exist $d, \epsilon > 0$ such that given an 2CNF φ it is NP-hard to distinguish the cases when MAX-2SAT$(\varphi) \geq d$ and when MAX-2SAT$(\varphi) < d(1 - \epsilon)$. Given a 2CNF formula containing m clauses, construct a system of at most $3m$ equations as follows. First, assume without loss of generality that each clause contains exactly 2 literals (which could be the same literal). Introduce a rational variable x_i for each boolean variable z_i. For a clause $z_i \vee z_j$ write the following system of equations.

$$x_i + x_j = 1, \ x_i = 1, \ x_j = 1.$$

(If the clause involves $\neg z_i$ then use $1 - x_i$ instead of x_i). First, we claim that without loss of generality we may assume that the optimal assignment to the x_i's — that is, the one that satisfies the maximum fraction of equations — assigns 0 or 1 to all the variables. For, given an assignment that is not all $\frac{0}{1}$, we can construct the following assignment: if $x_i \geq \frac{1}{2}$, change x_i to 1 and otherwise change x_i to 0. This does not decrease the number of satisfied equations, as is clear by looking at each group of 3 equations representing a clause.

So assume that the optimal assignment is $\frac{0}{1}$. Thus in each group of 3 equations representing a clause, either 2 equations are satisfied or 0 equations are. View this assignment as a boolean assignment in the obvious way. The boolean assignment satisfies a clause iff exactly 2 equations corresponding to it were satisfied. Thus, the number of satisfied clauses is exactly $\frac{1}{2}$ the number of satisfied equations.

Thus, we have shown that given a MAX-SATISFY instance I, it is *NP*-hard to distinguish whether the fraction of satisfiable equations is either $\geq c$ or $< c(1 - \epsilon)$, where $c = \frac{2d}{3}$.

Self-improvement. Now we show a self-improvement property for MAX-SATISFY, which helps us show that it is in Class III. Suppose we have (as above) N equations, in which the answer to MAX-SATISFY is either c or $c \cdot (1 - \epsilon)$ for some $c, \epsilon > 0$. Let the equations be written as $p_1 = 0, p_2 = 0, \ldots, p_N = 0$. Let k, T be integers (to be specified later). Write down a new set of equations containing, for every k-tuple $(p_{i_1}, p_{i_2}, \ldots, p_{i_k})$ of old equations, a set of T equations $\sum_{j=1}^{k} p_{i_j} y^j = 0$, where $y = 1, 2, \ldots, T$. Note that the number of equations in this new system is $\binom{N}{k} \cdot T$, whereas the number of variables is unchanged.

For each assignment to the variables and each k-tuple of the old equations, let us say the assignment *clears* the tuple if it satisfies all k equations in it. Note that if an assignment clears a tuple, then in the new system of equations it satisfies all T new equations corresponding to this tuple. Now we claim that if it does not clear the tuple, then it satisfies at most k of those T equations. The reason for the claim is that if $(p_{i_1}, p_{i_2}, \ldots, p_{i_k})$ is a k-tuple that is not cleared by the assignment, then the following vector is not zero: $(v_{i_1}, v_{i_2}, \ldots, v_{i_k})$, where v_{i_j} denotes the value of the left-hand side of equation p_{i_j} under this assignment. Thus, the univariate polynomial $\sum_{j=1}^{k} v_{i_j} y^j$ is not identically zero, and therefore has at most k roots.

If some assignment to the variables satisfies a fraction c of the equations in the original system, then it clears $\binom{cN}{k}$ k-tuples, so the number of satisfied equations in the new system is at least $\binom{cN}{k} \cdot T$.

Conversely, suppose every assignment satisfies less than $cN \cdot (1 - \epsilon)$ equations in the old system. Then each assignment clears at most $\binom{cN(1-\epsilon)}{k}$ tuples, each of which contributes T satisfied equations in the new system. The assignment does not clear the other $\binom{N}{k} - \binom{cN(1-\epsilon)}{k}$ tuples, so each of those contributes only k satisfied equations each. Thus, no assignment can satisfy more than $\binom{N}{k} \cdot k + \binom{cN(1-\epsilon)}{k} \cdot (T - k)$ equations in the new system.

By choosing $T = N^{k+1}$, we see that the gap between the optima in the two cases is approximately $(1 - \epsilon)^k$. Thus, we have described a simple construction that allows us to "boost" the gap between the optimum value in the two cases. This shows that MAX-SATISFY is self-improvable.

Using $k = \text{poly}(\log N)$ in the above construction, we get a gap of $2^{\log^{1-\gamma} N'}$, where $N' = 2^{\text{poly}(\log n)}$ is the number of equations in the new system. Thus, we have proved that achieving an approximation ratio $2^{\log^{1-\gamma} N'}$ for MAX-SATISFY is Quasi-*NP*-hard, in other words, that MAX-SATISFY is in Class III.

MAX-SATISFY is in Class IV. Finally, it should be clear that instead of using the trivial booster, namely, the set of all subsets of size k, we can use the booster of Theorem 10.4 in the above self-improvement construction. Write down T equations for every subset of k equations that form a set in the booster. Use $k = \log N$, and $\alpha < \epsilon c / 100$. Thus, the *NP*-hardness of N^δ-approximation follows for some $\delta > 0$.

PROBABILISTICALLY CHECKABLE PROOFS AND INAPPROXIMABILITY

10.8

The introduction mentioned the close connection between inapproximability and new probabilistic definitions of *NP*: This section fleshes out the connection.

10.8.1   THE PCP THEOREM

Let a *verifier* be a polynomial-time probabilistic Turing Machine containing an input tape, a work tape, a tape that contains a random string, and a tape called the *proof string* and denoted as Π. The proof string should be thought of as an array of bits; out of which the verifier will examine a few. The verifier works as follows. First, it reads the input and the random string, and writes down on its work tape some addresses of locations in the proof string Π. Next, it examines the bits in those locations in Π. The process of reading a bit from Π is called a *query*. Finally, the verifier decides to accept or reject, based on what the input, the random string, and the queried bits of Π were.

DEFINITION 10.11   A verifier is $(r(n), q(n))$-*restricted* if on each input of size n it uses at most $O(r(n))$ random bits for its computation, and queries at most $O(q(n))$ bits of the proof.

In other words, an $(r(n), q(n))$-restricted verifier has two associated integers c, k. The random string has length $c\, r(n)$. The verifier operates as follows on an input of size n. It reads the random string R, computes a sequence of $k\, q(n)$ locations $i_1(R), i_2(R), \ldots,$ $i_{kq(n)}(R)$, and queries those locations in Π. Depending on what these bits were, it accepts or rejects.

Define $M^\Pi(x, R)$ to be 1 if M accepts input x, with access to the proof Π, using a string of random bits R, and 0 otherwise.

DEFINITION 10.12   A verifier M *probabilistically checks membership proofs* for language L if

- For every input x in L, there is a proof Π_x that causes M to accept for every random string (i.e., with probability 1).

- For any input x not in L, every proof Π is rejected with probability at least $\frac{1}{2}$, i.e., $\Pr_R[M^\Pi(x, R) = 1] < \frac{1}{2}$.

Note: The choice of probability $\frac{1}{2}$ in the second part is arbitrary. By repeating the verifier's program $O(1)$ times (and rejecting if the verifier rejects even once), the probability of rejection $\frac{1}{2}$ in the second part can be reduced to any arbitrary positive constant. Thus, we could have used any constant less than 1 instead of $\frac{1}{2}$.

DEFINITION 10.13   A language L is in $PCP(r(n), q(n))$ if there is an $(r(n), q(n))$-restricted verifier M that probabilistically checks membership proofs for L.

Note that $NP = PCP(0, \text{poly}(n))$, since $PCP(0, \text{poly}(n))$ is the set of languages for which membership proofs can be checked in deterministic polynomial-time. This set is exactly NP. The next theorem, called the PCP Theorem, gives an alternative characterization of NP in terms of PCP.

THEOREM 10.6 PCP Theorem [AS92, ALMSS92] $NP = PCP(\log n, 1)$.

The proof of the PCP Theorem is complicated. Proving that $PCP(\log n, 1) \subseteq NP$ is easier, however; see Lemma 10.12 for a hint on how to proceed.

10.8.2   CONNECTION TO INAPPROXIMABILITY OF MAX-3SAT

The PCP Theorem, specifically, its nontrivial half $NP \subseteq PCP(\log n, 1)$, is both sufficient and necessary to prove Theorem 10.1 about the inapproximability of MAX-3SAT. That is to say, $NP \subseteq PCP(\log n, 1)$ iff there is a reduction τ from SAT to MAX-3SAT that ensures the following for some fixed $\epsilon > 0$:

$$I \in \text{SAT} \implies \text{MAX-3SAT}(\tau(I)) = 1,$$
$$I \notin \text{SAT} \implies \text{MAX-3SAT}(\tau(I)) < \frac{1}{1+\epsilon}. \tag{10.8}$$

Let's first check that the "if" part holds: if the above reduction exists then $NP \subseteq PCP(\log n, 1)$. Given any NP language L and an input, the verifier reduces it to SAT, and then to MAX-3SAT using the above reduction. It expects the membership proof to contain a satisfying assignment to the MAX-3SAT instance. To check this membership proof probabilistically, it picks a clause uniformly at random, reads the values of the variables in it (notice, this requires reading only 3 bits), and accepts iff these values satisfy the clause. Clearly, if the original input is in L, there is a proof which the verifier accepts with probability 1. Otherwise every proof is rejected with probability at least $1 - 1/(1 + \epsilon)$. Of course, repeating the verification $O(1/\epsilon)$ times makes the rejection probability $\geq 1/2$.

Now we turn to the "only if" part. Suppose $NP \subseteq PCP(\log n, 1)$. As a first step in proving the inapproximability of MAX-3SAT, we prove the inapproximability of the following problem.

DEFINITION 10.14 MAX-k-FUNCTION-SAT   Let k be a fixed integer.
Input: Truth tables for m boolean functions, each a function of a set of k variables out of $y_1, y_2, \ldots, y_n$. $\left\{ f_i(y_{i_1}, y_{i_2}, \ldots, y_{i_k}) : 1 \leq i \leq m \right\}$. *Output*: An assignment to $x_1, x_2, \ldots, x_n$

that maximizes the number of functions that evaluate to 1. The objective function is the fraction of functions that evaluate to 1.

The next lemma is based upon the observation that MAX-k-FUNCTION-SAT is exactly the following problem: given the program of a $(\log n, 1)$-restricted verifier that examines k bits in the proof, determine the maximum (over all possible proof strings) probability with which it accepts any proof string. Thus, the statement $NP \subseteq PCP(\log n, 1)$ implies the inapproximability of MAX-k-FUNCTION-SAT for some constant k.

LEMMA 10.12   If $NP \subseteq PCP(\log n, 1)$, then there is an integer k such that there is a reduction τ' from SAT to MAX-k-FUNCTION-SAT that ensures

$$I \in \text{SAT} \implies \text{MAX-}k\text{-FUNCTION-SAT}(\tau'(I)) = 1,$$
$$I \notin \text{SAT} \implies \text{MAX-}k\text{-FUNCTION-SAT}(\tau'(I)) < \frac{1}{2}. \tag{10.9}$$

Proof.   Since SAT $\in NP$, it has a $(\log n, 1)$-restricted verifier. Suppose the verifier uses $c \log n$ random bits and examines k bits in the proof. Note that it has at most $2^{c \log n} = n^c$ different possible runs, and in each run it reads only k bits in the proof-string. Hence, assume without loss of generality that the number of bits in any provided proof-string is at most kn^c. For concreteness, assume this number is N.

For boolean-valued variables $y_1, y_2, \ldots, y_N$, the set of possible assignments to $y_1, y_2, \ldots, y_N$ is in one-to-one correspondence with the set of possible proof-strings. Assume without loss of generality that the proof-string is an assignment to the variables $y_1, y_2, \ldots, y_N$.

Fixing the verifier's random string to $R \in \{0, 1\}^{c \log n}$, fixes the sequence of locations that it will examine in the proof. Let $i_1(R), i_2(R), \ldots, i_k(R)$ be this sequence. The verifier's decision depends only on the assignments to $y_{i_1(R)}, y_{i_2(R)} \ldots, y_{i_k(R)}$. Define a boolean function on k bits, f_R, as $f_R(b_1, \ldots, b_k) = $ true iff the verifier accepts when the assignment to the sequence of variables $y_{i_1(R)}, \ldots, y_{i_k(R)}$ is $b_1, b_2, \ldots, b_k$. Since the verifier runs in polynomial time, we can compute the truth table of f_R in polynomial time by going through all possible 2^k values of $b_1, b_2, \ldots, b_k$, and computing the verifier's decision on each sequence.

The reduction consists in outputting the set of n^c functions $\{f_R : R \in \{0, 1\}^{c \log n}\}$ defined above. By definition of $PCP(\log n, 1)$, when the input is in the language, there is an assignment to the $y_1, y_2, \ldots, y_N$ that makes all functions in this set evaluate to true. Otherwise, no assignment makes more than $\frac{1}{2}$ of them evaluate to true.   ∎

Now we prove the "only if" part of our earlier assertion.

THEOREM 10.7   If $NP \subseteq PCP(\log n, 1)$ then the reduction described in (10.8) exists.

Proof.   Given a SAT instance, reduce it to MAX-k-FUNCTION-SAT using Lemma 10.12. Let $y_1, y_2, \ldots, y_N$ be the set of boolean variables and $\{f_i : 1 \leq i \leq n^c\}$ the collection of functions in the instance of MAX-k-FUNCTION-SAT. We indicate how to rewrite them using a 3CNF formula.

Consider a function f_i from this collection. Let f_i be a function of variables $y_{i_1}, y_{i_2}, \ldots, y_{i_k}$. Then, f_i can be expressed as a conjunction of at most 2^k clauses in these variables, each of size at most k. Let $C_{i,1}, C_{i,2}, \ldots, C_{i,2^k}$ denote these clauses. (From now on we use the terms k-clause and 3-clause to talk about clauses of size k and 3 respectively.)

Then, the k-CNF formula

$$\bigwedge_{i=1}^{n^c} \bigwedge_{j=1}^{2^k} C_{i,j} \tag{10.10}$$

is satisfiable iff $x \in L$. Also, if $x \notin L$, then every assignment fails to satisfy half the f_i's, each of which yields an unsatisfied k-clause. So if $x \notin L$ the fraction of unsatisfied clauses is at least $\frac{1}{2} \cdot \frac{1}{2^k}$, which is some fixed constant.

To obtain a 3CNF formula rewrite every k-clause as a conjunction of clauses of size 3, as follows. For a k-clause $l_1 \vee l_2 \vee \cdots \vee l_k$ (the l_i's are literals), write the formula

$$(l_1 \vee l_2 \vee z_1) \wedge (l_{k-1} \vee l_k \vee \neg z_{k-2}) \wedge \bigwedge_{t=1}^{k-4} (\neg z_t \vee l_{t+2} \vee z_{t+1}), \tag{10.11}$$

where $z_1, z_2, \ldots, z_{k-2}$ are new variables which are not to be used again for any other k-clause. Clearly, a fixed assignment to $l_1, l_2, \ldots, l_k$ satisfies the original k-clause iff there is a further assignment to $z_1, z_2, \ldots, z_{k-2}$ that satisfies the formula in (10.11).

Thus, the formula of (10.10) has been rewritten as a 3CNF formula that is satisfiable iff $x \in L$. Further, if $x \notin L$, every unsatisfied k-clause in (10.10) yields an unsatisfied 3-clause in the new formula, so the fraction of unsatisfied 3-clauses is at least $\frac{1}{k-2} \cdot \frac{1}{2^{k+1}}$.

Hence, the lemma has been proved for the value of ϵ given by

$$\frac{1}{1+\epsilon} = 1 - \frac{1}{(k-2)2^{k+1}}.$$

∎

EXERCISE 10.9   Note that the MAX-k-FUNCTION-SAT problem exactly represents the decision process of a $(\log n, 1)$-restricted verifier that examines k bits in membership proof. The optimum assignment for the MAX-k-FUNCTION-SAT instance can be viewed as a proof that maximizes the verifier's acceptance probability. The next exercise further clarifies the connection between the PCP Theorem and the inapproximability of MAX-SNP-hard problems.

- Prove that MAX-k-FUNCTION-SAT is in Max-$\mathcal{SNP}$ for every fixed k.
- Prove that for every Max-$\mathcal{SNP}$ problem there is some integer k such that every instance of the problem can be represented as instances of MAX-k-FUNCTION-SAT.

Thus, we have shown that MAX-k-FUNCTION-SAT is Max-$\mathcal{SNP}$-hard.

10.8.3   WHERE THE GAP COMES FROM

The gap of a factor of $1 + \epsilon$ in reduction (10.8) came from two sources: the gap 1 versus $\frac{1}{2}$ in the fraction of satisfiable f_i's in Lemma 10.12, and the fact that each f_i involves $O(1)$

variables. But, remember that each f_i just represents a possible run of the $(\log n, 1)$-restricted verifier for SAT. Thus, the description of each f_i — that is, a description of what function it is and which variables it depends upon — is derived from the program of the verifier. The current construction of this verifier is very involved. It involves defining a complicated algebraic object, which exists iff the input boolean formula is satisfiable. The verifier expects a membership proof to contain a representation of this object. In each of its runs the verifier examines a different part of this provided object. Thus, the function f_i representing that run is a correctness condition for that part of the object.

For details on the algebraic object, we refer the reader to the relevant papers. A detail worth mentioning is that each part of the object — and thus, the definition of each f_i — depends on every input bit (i.e., on every clause of the input boolean formula). This imparts the reduction a global structure. In contrast, classical NP-completeness reductions usually perform local transformations of the input.

OPEN PROBLEMS

10.9

We list some open problems about the hardness of approximation.

OPEN PROBLEM 10.1 As shown in this chapter, all known inapproximability results can be derived from the PCP Theorem and Raz's Parallel Repetition Theorem [Raz94] (note that the latter was used to prove the inapproximability of LABELCOVER). The proofs of both these theorems are currently very difficult. Can they be simplified?

OPEN PROBLEM 10.2 For many problems such as CLIQUE, COLORING, and MAX-3SAT, there is a large gap between the approximation ratio that is provably hard to achieve, and the ratio that we can achieve in polynomial time (see Section 10.7). Can this gap be closed?

OPEN PROBLEM 10.3 Prove inapproximability results for edge deletion problems [Yan81], such as (DIRECTED) FEEDBACK ARC SET, GRAPH BISECTION, GRAPH EXPANSION, etc. Algorithms for many of these problems use similar ideas and achieve approximation ratios close to $O(\log n)$ [LR88].

OPEN PROBLEM 10.4 A look at Table 10.2 shows that many inapproximability results rely on an assumption stronger than $P \neq NP$. Can this assumption be weakened to $P \neq NP$? Currently, the reason for resorting to the stronger assumption is that the reduction to LABELCOVER in Theorem 10.2, part 3, uses a self-improvement property, and needs quasipolynomial time. A more efficient reduction could possibly merge Classes III and IV.

OPEN PROBLEM 10.5   Identify limitations of current techniques for proving inapproximability. For example, identify inapproximability results they inherently cannot prove. (A recent paper [Aro95] takes a first step in this direction.)

OPEN PROBLEM 10.6   Prove inapproximability results for the following problems: SHORTEST LATTICE VECTOR (in Euclidean norm), and coloring a 3-colorable graph with the minimum possible number of colors. For the last problem, Khanna *et al.* [KLS93] have shown that it is *NP*-hard to color a 3-colorable graph using only 4 colors.

OPEN PROBLEM 10.7   The best approximation algorithm for GRAPH BISECTION [LR88] outputs an integer that approximates the *cost* of the minimum bisection, without outputting a bisection of this approximate cost (it outputs a $\frac{1}{3} : \frac{2}{3}$ cut of the graph and not a bisection). Approximation algorithms for some other problems also behave similarly; they output an approximation to the cost of the optimal solution without outputting a near-optimal solution. Prove (for any natural problem) that finding approximate solutions is harder than finding an approximation to the cost of the optimum solution.

OPEN PROBLEM 10.8   Explain why inapproximable problems form the four classes we have described. Are these classes "real," or does the classification reflect a limitation of our proof techniques. (A partial answer — namely, a nice explanation of Class I — seems to lie in the Max-$\mathcal{SNP}$ class of [PY91].)

OPEN PROBLEM 10.9   Prove inapproximability results for some of the counting (or #*P*) problems discussed in Chapter 12. For example, no good approximation algorithm is known for the problem of approximating the number of perfect matchings in a graph.

CHAPTER NOTES
10.10

Approximability. The question of approximability started receiving attention [Joh74, SG76] soon after *NP*-completeness was discovered. (See [GJ79] for a discussion.) Much of the work attempted to discover a classification framework for optimization (and approximation) problems analogous to the framework of *NP*-completeness for decision problems. (See [ADP77, ADP80, AMSP80] for some of these attempts.) The most successful attempt was due to Papadimitriou and Yannakakis, who based their classification around a complexity class they called Max-$\mathcal{SNP}$(see Section 10.3.1). They proved that MAX-3SAT is complete for Max-$\mathcal{SNP}$, in other words, any inapproximability result for MAX-3SAT transfers automatically to a host of other problems. The desire to prove such an inapproximability result motivated the discovery of the PCP theorem.

The idea (in [PY91]) of using logical characterizations of optimization problems to understand their approximability has also been extended in many directions [KT91, PR90].

Interactive Proof Systems. The PCP Theorem is a descendant of a long line of results in interactive proofs systems. These proofs systems were invented in [GMR89, Bab85], and quickly found applications in cryptography and complexity theory [GMW87, BGKW88]. The notion of probabilistically checkable membership proofs first appears in [FRS88]. For a survey of all probabilistic proof systems that have been defined and studied, see [Gol94].

Surprisingly, complexity classes defined in terms of interactive proofs are actually equivalent to conventional complexity classes. For example, IP = PSPACE [LFKN92, Sha92] and MIP = NEXPTIME [BFL91]. Lund's dissertation [Lun92] describes these characterizations.

Connection to inapproximability. Feige et al. [FGL⁺91] showed how to extend some of the ideas in the MIP = NEXPTIME result to the class *NP*. They identified the notion of probabilistically checkable proofs (although under a different name) and proved a surprising result that in hindsight is a clear precursor of the PCP Theorem. Their work was paralleled by that in [BFLS91], who defined *transparent math proofs*, a notion related to probabilistically checkable proofs.

All the above results were very surprising. Even more surprising was the following result, which [FGL⁺91] proved as a corollary of their result about proof-checking: Approximating the clique number within a factor $2^{\log^{1-\delta} n}$ is Quasi-*NP*-hard.

The [FGL⁺91] result focused attention on the notion of probabilistically checkable proofs, and raised two important questions. First, could their techniques prove the inapproximability of any important problem other than clique? Second, could their techniques be sharpened to prove the *NP*-hardness of approximation, instead of *Quasi-NP*-hardness. The first question was partially answered in [Bel93, BR93, Zuc93], which showed the inapproximability of a variety of problems. Then the second question was answered — positively— in [AS92], which showed that approximating clique is *NP*-hard. Proving this result involved a new probabilistic characterization of *NP* in terms of PCP (a definition of the class PCP also makes an appearance in this paper). Then [ALMSS92] gave further evidence of the usefulness of PCPs for proving inapproximability results. They proved the PCP Theorem, and showed that Max-$\mathcal{SNP}$-hard problems do not have polynomial-time approximation schemes. The proof of the PCP Theorem uses many ideas from the then-unpublished [AS92] and papers on program checking [BK89, RS92]. Some observers attribute the PCP Theorem to [AS92, ALMSS92] together.

An interesting development that went largely unnoticed is Condon's inapproximability result for the max-word problem [Con93]. She uses a different probabilistic characterization of *NP*.

The connection between interactive proof systems and inapproximability has provided the impetus for new constructions of various interactive proof systems [LS91, FL92, BGLR93, FK94, Raz94, BS94, BGS95].

Further reading. For a self-contained proof of the PCP Theorem and a detailed survey of related topics, see [Aro94]. The surveys by Babai [Bab94], Johnson [Joh92], and Goldreich [Gol94] provide three different perspectives (mostly without proofs) of the developments mentioned above. Sudan [Sud92] describes program checking for algebraic programs and how it figures in the proof of the PCP Theorem. For a listing of optimization problems according to their approximation properties, consult [CK94].

Acknowledgment Sanjeev Arora is supported by NSF CAREER award CCR-9502747.

REFERENCES

[ABSS93] S. Arora, L. Babai, J. Stern, and Z. Sweedyk. The hardness of approximate optima in lattices, codes and linear equations. To appear in Journ. Comp. Sys. Sci., Preliminary version in *Proc. 34th IEEE Symp. on Foundations of Computer Science*, pages 724–733, 1993.

[ADP77] G. Ausiello, A. D'Atri, and M. Protasi. On the structure of combinatorial problems and structure preserving reductions. In *Proc. 4th Intl. Coll. on Automata, Languages and Programming*, 1977.

[ADP80] G. Ausiello, A. D'Atri, and M. Protasi. Structure preserving reductions among convex optimization problems. *Journal of Computer and System Sciences*, 21:136–153, 1980.

[AFWZ93] N. Alon, U. Feige, A. Wigderson, and D. Zuckerman. Derandomized graph products. Manuscript, 1993.

[AGHP92] N. Alon, O. Goldreich, J. Håstad, and R. Peralta. Simple constructions of almost *k*-wise independent random variables. *Random Structures and Algorithms*, 3, 1992.

[AK93] E. Amaldi and V. Kann. The complexity and approximability of finding maximum feasible subsystems of linear relations. Theor. Computer Sci., 147:187–210, 1995. Preliminary version in Proc. STACS, 1994.

[ALM+92] S. Arora, C. Lund, R. Motwani, M. Sudan, and M. Szegedy. Proof verification and intractability of approximation problems. In *Proc. 33rd IEEE Symp. on Foundations of Computer Science*, pages 13–22, 1992.

[AMSP80] G. Ausiello, A. Marchetti-Spaccamela, and M. Protasi. Toward a unified approach for the classification of NP-complete optimization problems. *Theoretical Computer Science*, 12:83–96, 1980.

[Aro94] S. Arora. *Probabilistic checking of proofs and the hardness of approximation problems*. PhD thesis, U.C. Berkeley, 1994. Available via anonymous ftp as Princeton TR94-476 from ftp://ftp.cs.priceton.edu.

[Aro95] S. Arora. Reductions, codes, PCPs, and inapproximability. In *Proc. 36th IEEE Symp. on Foundations of Computer Science*, pages 404–413, 1995.

[AS92] S. Arora and S. Safra. Probabilistic checking of proofs: A new characterization of *NP*. In *Proc. 33rd IEEE Symp. on Foundations of Computer Science*, pages 2–13, 1992.

[Bab85] L. Babai. Trading group theory for randomness. In *Proc. 17th ACM Symp. on Theory of Computing*, pages 421–429, 1985.

[Bab94] L. Babai. Transparent proofs and limits to approximations. In *Proceedings of the First European Congress of Mathematicians*. Birkhauser, 1995.

[Bel93] M. Bellare. Interactive Proofs and approximation: Reductions from two provers in one round. In *Proceedings of the 2nd Israel Symposium on Theory and Computing Systems*. IEEE Computer Press, 1993. Preliminary version: IBM Research Report RC 17969 (May 1992).

[BFL91] L. Babai, L. Fortnow, and C. Lund. Non-deterministic exponential time has two-prover interactive protocols. *Computational Complexity*, 1:3–40, 1991.

[BFLS91] L. Babai, L. Fortnow, L. Levin, and M. Szegedy. Checking computations in polylogarithmic time. In *Proc. 23rd ACM Symp. on Theory of Computing*, pages 21–31, 1991.

[BGKW88] M. Ben-Or, S. Goldwasser, J. Kilian, and A. Wigderson. Multi prover interactive proofs: How to remove intractability assumptions. In *Proc. 20th ACM Symp. on Theory of Computing*, pages 113–121, 1988.

[BGLR93] M. Bellare, S. Goldwasser, C. Lund, and A. Russell. Efficient multi-prover interactive proofs with applications to approximation problems. In *Proc. 25th ACM Symp. on Theory of Computing*, pages 113–131, 1993.

[BGS95] M. Bellare, O. Goldreich, and M. Sudan. Free bits and non-approximability– towards tight results. In *Proc. 36th IEEE Symp. on Foundations of Computer Science*, pages 422–431, 1995. Full version available from the authors.

[BH92] R. B. Boppana and M. M. Halldórsson. Approximating maximum independent sets by excluding subgraphs. *BIT*, 32(2):180–196, June 1992.

[BJL+91] A. Blum, T. Jiang, M. Li, J. Tromp, and M. Yannakakis. Linear approximation of shortest superstrings. In *Proc. 23rd ACM Symp. on Theory of Computing*, pages 328–336, 1991.

[BK89] M. Blum and S. Kannan. Designing programs that check their work. In *Proc. 21st ACM Symp. on Theory of Computing*, pages 86–97, 1989.

[BP89] M. Bern and P. Plassmann. The Steiner problem with edge lengths 1 and 2. *Information Processing Letters*, 32:171–176, 1989.

[BR93] M. Bellare and P. Rogaway. The complexity of approximating non-linear programs. In P.M. Pardalos, editor, *Complexity of Numerical Optimization*. World Scientific, 1993. Preliminary version: IBM Research Report RC 17831 (March 1992).

[BS92] Piotr Berman and Georg Schnitger. On the complexity of approximating the independent set problem. *Information and Computation*, 96(1):77–94, 1992.

[BS94] M. Bellare and M. Sudan. Improved non-approximability results. In *Proc. 26th ACM Symp. on Theory of Computing*, pages 184–193, 1994.

[CK94] P. Crescenzi and V. Kann. A compendium of NP optimization problems. Manuscript, 1994. Available from ftp://www.nada.kth.se/Theory/Viggo-Kann/compendium.ps.Z.

[Con93] A. Condon. The complexity of the max-word problem and the power of one-way interactive proof systems. *Computational Complexity*, 3:292–305, 1993.

[Coo71] S. Cook. The complexity of theorem-proving procedures. In *Proc. 3rd ACM Symp. on Theory of Computing*, pages 151–158, 1971.

[DJP+92] E. Dahlhaus, D. S. Johnson, C. H. Papadimitriou, P. D. Seymour, and M. Yannakakis. The complexity of multiway cuts. In *Proc. 24th ACM Symp. on Theory of Computing*, pages 241–451, 1992.

[Fag74] R. Fagin. Generalized first-order spectra and polynomial-time recognizable sets. In Richard Karp, editor, *Complexity of Computer Computations*, pages 43–73. AMS, 1974.

[Fei95] U. Feige. A threshold of $\ln n$ for approximating set cover. To appear in Proc. ACM STOC. 1996.

[FGL+91] U. Feige, S. Goldwasser, L. Lovász, S. Safra, and M. Szegedy. Approximating clique is almost *NP*-complete. In *Proc. 32nd IEEE Symp. on Foundations of Computer Science*, pages 2–12, 1991.

[FK94] U. Feige and J. Kilian. Two prover protocols–low error at affordable rates. In *Proc. 26th ACM Symp. on Theory of Computing*, pages 172–183, 1994.

[FK95] U. Feige and J. Kilian. Zero knowledge and the chromatic number. Unpublished manuscript, 1995.

[FL92] U. Feige and L. Lovász. Two-prover one-round proof systems: Their power and their problems. In *Proc. 24th ACM Symp. on Theory of Computing*, pages 733–741, 1992.

[FRS88]   L. Fortnow, J. Rompel, and M. Sipser.   On the power of multi-prover interactive protocols. In *Proceedings of the 3rd Conference on Structure in Complexity Theory*, pages 156–161, 1988.

[Für95]   M. Fürer. Improved hardness results for approximating the chromatic number. In *Proc. 36th IEEE Symp. on Foundations of Computer Science*, pages 414–421, 1995.

[GG81]   O. Gabber and Z. Galil. Explicit constructions of linear sized superconcentrators. *Journal of Computer and System Sciences*, 22:407–425, 1981.

[GJ76]   M. R. Garey and D. S. Johnson. The complexity of near-optimal graph coloring. *Journal of the ACM*, 23:43–49, 1976.

[GJ79]   M. R. Garey and D. S. Johnson. *Computers and Intractability: a guide to the theory of NP-completeness*. W. H. Freeman, 1979.

[GMR89]   S. Goldwasser, S. Micali, and C. Rackoff. The knowledge complexity of interactive proofs. *SIAM J. on Computing*, 18:186–208, 1989. Preliminary version in Proc. STOC 1985.

[GMW87]   O. Goldreich, S. Micali, and A. Wigderson. How to play any mental game or a completeness theorem for protocols with honest majority. In *Proc. 19th ACM Symp. on Theory of Computing*, pages 218–229, 1987.

[Gol94]   O. Goldreich. Probabilistic proof systems. Technical Report RS-94-28, Basic Research in Computer Science, Center of the Danish National Research Foundation, September 1994. (*To appear in the Proceedings of the International Congress of Mathematicians, 1994. Birkhauser Verlag.*).

[GVY93]   N. Garg, V.V. Vazirani, and M. Yannakakis. Approximate max-flow min-(multi)-cut theorems and their applications. In *Proc. 25th ACM Symp. on Theory of Computing*, pages 698 –707, 1993.

[GW94]   M. Goemans and D. Williamson. A 0.878 approximation algorithm for MAX-2SAT and MAX-CUT. In *Proc. 26th ACM Symp. on Theory of Computing*, pages 422–431, 1994.

[Hal93]   M. Halldórsson. A still better performance guarantee for approximate graph coloring. *Information Processing Letters*, 45:19–23, 1993.

[Has95]   J. Håstad. Fast and efficient testing of the long code. To appear in Proc. ACM STOC, 1996.

[Joh74]   D. S. Johnson. Approximation algorithms for combinatorial problems. *Journal of Computer and System Sciences*, 9:256–278, 1974.

[Joh92]   D. S. Johnson. The NP-completeness column: an ongoing guide. *Journal of Algorithms*, 13:502–524, 1992.

[Kan87]   R. Kannan. Minkowski's convex body theorem and integer programming. *Mathematics of Operations Research*, 12(3), 1987.

[Kan92]   V. Kann. *On the approximability of NP-complete optimization problems*. PhD thesis, Royal Institute of Technology, Stockholm, Sweden, 1992.

[Kar72]   R. M. Karp. Reducibility among combinatorial problems. In Miller and Thatcher, editors, *Complexity of Computer Computations*, pages 85–103. Plenum Press, 1972.

[KLS93]   S. Khanna, N. Linial, and S. Safra. On the hardness of approximating the chromatic number. In *Proceedings of the 2nd Israel Symposium on Theory and Computing Systems, ISTCS*, pages 250–260. IEEE Computer Society Press, 1993.

[KMR93] D. Karger, R. Motwani, and G.D.S. Ramkumar. On approximating the longest path in a graph. In *Proceedings of Workshop on Algorithms and Data Structures*, pages 421–430. LNCS (Springer-Verlag), v. 709, 1993.

[KT91] P. G. Kolaitis and M. N. Thakur. Approximation properties of *NP* minimization classes. In *Proc. of the 6th Conference on Structure in Complexity Theory*, pages 353–366, 1991.

[Lev73] L. Levin. Universal'nyĭe perebornyĭe zadachi (universal search problems: in Russian). *Problemy Peredachi Informatsii*, 9(3):265–266, 1973.

[LFKN92] C. Lund, L. Fortnow, H. Karloff, and N. Nisan. Algebraic methods for interactive proof systems. *J. of the ACM*, 39(4):859–868, October 1992.

[Lov75] L. Lovász. On the ratio of optimal integral and fractional covers. *Discrete Mathematics*, 13:383–390, 1975.

[LPS88] A. Lubotzky, R. Phillips, and P. Sarnak. Ramanujam graphs. *Combinatorica*, 8:261–277, 1988.

[LR88] T. Leighton and S. Rao. An approximate max-flow min-cut theorem for uniform multicommodity flow problems with applications to approximation algorithms. In *Proc. 29th IEEE Symp. on Foundations of Computer Science*, pages 422–431, 1988.

[LS91] D. Lapidot and A. Shamir. Fully parallelized multi prover protocols for NEXPTIME. In *Proc. 32nd IEEE Symp. on Foundations of Computer Science*, pages 13–18, 1991.

[Lun92] C. Lund. *The Power of Interaction*. MIT Press, Cambridge, Mass., 1992.

[LY93] C. Lund and M. Yannakakis. The approximation of maximum subgraph problems. In *Proceedings of International Colloquium on Automata, Languages and Programming, ICALP*, pages 40–51, 1993.

[LY94] C. Lund and M. Yannakakis. On the hardness of approximating minimization problems. *Journal of the ACM*, 41(5):960–981, 1994.

[NN93] J. Naor and M. Naor. Small-bias probability spaces: efficient constructions and applications. *SIAM J. on Computing*, 22:838–856, 1993. Prelim. version in ACM STOC'90.

[PR90] A. Panconesi and D. Ranjan. Quantifiers and approximation. In *Proc. of the 22nd ACM Symp. on the Theory of Computing*, pages 446–456, 1990.

[PY91] C. Papadimitriou and M. Yannakakis. Optimization, approximation and complexity classes. *Journal of Computer and System Sciences*, 43:425–440, 1991.

[PY93] C. Papadimitriou and M. Yannakakis. The traveling salesman problem with distances one and two. *Mathematics of Operations Research*, 18(1):1–11, 1993.

[Raz94] R. Raz. A parallel repetition theorem. Proc. 27th ACM STOC pages 447–456, 1995.

[RS92] R. Rubinfeld and M. Sudan. Testing polynomial functions efficiently and over rational domains. In *Proc. 3rd Annual ACM-SIAM Symp. on Discrete Algorithms*, pages 23–32, 1992.

[SG76] S. Sahni and T. Gonzalez. *P*-complete approximation problems. *Journal of the ACM*, 23:555–565, 1976.

[Sha92] A. Shamir. IP = PSPACE. *J. of the ACM*, 39(4):869–877, October 1992.

[Sim90] H. U. Simon. On approximate solutions for combinatorial optimization problems. *SIAM J. Algebraic Discrete Methods*, 3:294–310, 1990.

[Sud92]   M. Sudan. *Efficient checking of polynomials and proofs and the hardness of approximation problems*. PhD thesis, U.C. Berkeley, 1992.

[Yan79]   M. Yannakakis. The effect of a connectivity requirement on the complexity of of maximum subgraph problems. *Journal of the ACM*, 26:618–630, 1979.

[Yan81]   M. Yannakakis. Edge deletion problems. *SIAM Journal of Computing*, 10:77–89, 1981.

[Yan92]   M. Yannakakis. On the approximation of maximum satisfiability. In *Proceedings of 3rd Annual ACM-SIAM Symposium on Discrete Algorithms*, pages 1–9, 1992.

[Zuc93]   D. Zuckerman. *NP*-complete problems have a version that's hard to approximate. In *8th Structure in Complexity Theory Conf.*, pages 305–312, 1993.

RANDOMIZED APPROXIMATION ALGORITHMS IN COMBINATORIAL OPTIMIZATION

Rajeev Motwani   **Joseph (Seffi) Naor**   **Prabhakar Raghavan**

Randomization has proved to be a powerful technique in finding approximate solutions to difficult problems in combinatorial optimization. In this chapter, we restrict ourselves to approximation algorithms that are efficient and provably good. The focus of this chapter is the use of randomized rounding. In this approach, one solves a relaxation of a problem in combinatorial optimization, and then uses randomization to return from the relaxation to the original optimization problem. Two kinds of relaxations of difficult combinatorial problems are considered: linear programming relaxations and semidefinite programming relaxations. A number of concrete applications are given.

INTRODUCTION

11.1

The last few years have witnessed the proliferation of randomization in approximation algorithms for difficult combinatorial problems. Probabilistic search techniques such as simulated annealing [LA87] (see also Section 12.6) have enjoyed considerable success in solving large instances of a variety of combinatorial problems. In this chapter we study approximation algorithms that are *efficient*, in that their running times are (provably) bounded by a polynomial in the size of the input; and *provably good*, in that the solution produced by the algorithm is guaranteed to be close to the optimal solution to within a specified, provable tolerance. Further, we insist that these guarantees hold for every instance of the problem being solved; the only randomness in the performance guarantee stems from the randomization in the algorithm itself, and not due to any probabilistic assumptions on the instance.

Among such provably good and efficient randomized algorithms there have been two major areas of success. The first is that of approximation algorithms for combinatorial problems such as graph coloring, multicommodity flow, and finding large cuts in a graph. Additional algorithms for the multicommodity problem and cuts are described in Chapter 5. This will be the focus of this chapter. The second area, which is covered in the chapter on approximate counting in this book (Chapter 12), is that of approximately counting the number of distinct solutions to an instance of a combinatorial problem.

All the algorithms we will discuss follow a common paradigm. They first formulate the problem as an integer program. Next, some constraints in this integer program are relaxed in order that the relaxation be efficiently solvable. Finally, randomization is used to restore the relaxed constraints.

Throughout this chapter, $E[X]$ will denote the expectation of a random variable X, $P[A]$ will denote the probability of an event A, and $\bar{A}$ will denote the complement of event A. We refer the reader to the book by Motwani and Raghavan [MR95] for an introduction to the area of randomized algorithms.

We will consider optimization problems where we seek to either minimize or maximize the value of an objective function $V(I)$, for a given input instance I. Let $V_A(I)$ be the value of the objective function for the solution delivered by an algorithm A for an input instance I, and let $V_*(I)$ denote the optimal value of the objective function for an instance I. For minimization problems, the performance ratio of an algorithm A is the supremum over all I of the ratio $V_A(I)/V_*(I)$; similarly, for maximization problems, the performance ratio of an algorithm A is the infimum over all I of the ratio $V_A(I)/V_*(I)$. We say that an algorithm A is an α-approximation algorithm if it has performance ratio at most α for minimization problems, and performance ratio at least α for maximization problems. In the case of randomized approximation algorithms, we replace $V_A(I)$ by $E[V_A(I)]$ in the definition of performance ratio, where the expectation is taken over the random choices made by the algorithm. In general, the term *approximation algorithm* will denote a *polynomial-time* algorithm.

In Section 11.2 we study linear programming relaxations using an integer multicommodity flow problem, covering and packing problems, multicut problems, and the maximum satisfiability problem as illustrations. In Section 11.3 we study the application of semidefinite programming relaxations to maximum cuts in a graph and to graph coloring. We give a number of ways in which these results can be extended, and the results of some implementations, in Section 11.4.

ROUNDING LINEAR PROGRAMS

11.2

In this section we discuss approximations obtained using the linear programming relaxation of the integer program formulation of an optimization problem. A convenient

abstraction for beginning this study is the *lattice-approximation problem*. After studying this problem in the abstract, we will point out its connections to linear programming
relaxations and to approximation algorithms in a number of concrete settings. In the lattice approximation problem we are given an $n \times n$ matrix $\mathbf{A}$, all of whose entries are 0
or 1. In addition, we are given a column vector $\mathbf{p}$ with n entries, all of which are in the
interval $[0, 1]$. We wish to find a column vector $\mathbf{q}$ with n entries, all of which are from
the set $\{0, 1\}$, so as to minimize $\| \mathbf{A} \cdot (\mathbf{p} - \mathbf{q}) \|_\infty$. (Please refer to problem [LAP] in the
Glossary). We think of the vector $\mathbf{q}$ as an "integer approximation" to the given real vector
$\mathbf{p}$, in the sense that $\mathbf{A} \cdot \mathbf{q}$ is close to $\mathbf{A} \cdot \mathbf{p}$ in every component. Below, we apply the technique of *randomized rounding* to this problem. Following this, we give two instructive
applications of the technique in detail, and finally, mention a number of other interesting
applications.

One solution to this problem is *thresholding*: for all i, if $p_i \geq 0.5$ set q_i to 1, else set
it to 0. Thresholding may yield a vector $\mathbf{q}$ for which $\| \mathbf{A} \cdot (\mathbf{p} - \mathbf{q}) \|_\infty$ may be as large as
order of $\| \mathbf{A} \cdot \mathbf{q} \|_\infty$. Consider the following randomized rounding scheme for determining
the components of $\mathbf{q}$: for each i, independently set q_i to 1 with probability p_i, and to 0
otherwise. Then, letting $\mathbf{A}_i$ denote the ith row of $\mathbf{A}$, we have $E[\mathbf{A}_i \cdot \mathbf{q}] = E[\mathbf{A}_i \cdot \mathbf{p}]$ by
linearity of expectation (this does not require the entries of $\mathbf{A}$ to be 0-1). We now argue
that for all i, $\mathbf{A}_i \cdot \mathbf{q}$ is likely to remain close to $\mathbf{A}_i \cdot \mathbf{p}$ after randomized rounding. To this
end we invoke the following bounds (commonly known as *Chernoff bounds* [MR95])
on the sum of independent 0-1 (or, *Bernoulli*) random variables.

LEMMA 11.1   Let $X_1, \dots, X_n$ be a sequence of independent Bernoulli trials such that
$P[X_i = 1] = p_i$ and $P[X_i = 0] = 1 - p_i$. Let S be any subset of the integers $1, \dots, n$,
and let $s = |S|$. Define $Y = \sum_{i \in S} X_i$, so that $E[Y] = \sum_{i \in S} p_i$. Then,

$$P\left[|Y - E[Y]| > \sqrt{4s \ln s}\right] \leq \frac{1}{s^2}.$$

The following alternative version of the Chernoff bound [MR95] will also be useful in
the sequel:

LEMMA 11.2   Let $X_1, \dots, X_n$ be a sequence of independent Bernoulli trials such that
$P[X_i = 1] = p_i$ and $P[X_i = 0] = 1 - p_i$. Define $Y = \sum X_i$, so that $E[Y] = \sum p_i$.
Then, for $\beta \in [0, 1]$,

$$P[|Y - E[Y]| > \beta\, E[Y]] \leq 2\exp(-0.38\beta^2\, E[Y]).$$

By Lemma 11.1, we know that

$$P\left[|\mathbf{A}_i \cdot \mathbf{q} - \mathbf{A}_i \cdot \mathbf{p}| > \sqrt{4n \ln n}\right] < \frac{1}{n^2}.$$

Now,

$$P\left[\| \mathbf{A} \cdot (\mathbf{p} - \mathbf{q}) \|_\infty > \sqrt{4n \ln n}\right] = P\left[\cup_{i=1}^{n} |\mathbf{A}_i \cdot \mathbf{q} - \mathbf{A}_i \cdot \mathbf{p}| > \sqrt{4n \ln n}\right]$$

$$\leq \sum_{i=1}^{n} P\left[|\mathbf{A}_i \cdot \mathbf{q} - \mathbf{A}_i \cdot \mathbf{p}| > \sqrt{4n \ln n}\right]$$

$$< \frac{1}{n}.$$

We thus have:

THEOREM 11.1   For every instance $\{\mathbf{A}, \mathbf{p}\}$ of the lattice approximation problem, randomized rounding finds a solution $\mathbf{q}$ such that $\| \mathbf{A} \cdot (\mathbf{p} - \mathbf{q}) \|_{\infty} \leq \sqrt{4n \ln n}$, with probability at least $1 - \frac{1}{n}$.

Using slightly stronger versions of the Chernoff bound than Lemma 11.1 [Rag88, RT87, SSS95], it is possible to get slightly sharper results than that in Theorem 11.1. However, in the worst case, we know of no efficient algorithm that can find a solution $\mathbf{q}$ such that $\| \mathbf{A} \cdot (\mathbf{p} - \mathbf{q}) \|_{\infty}$ is $o(\sqrt{4n \ln n})$ on every instance.

The *set-balancing problem* [Spe85, Spe87] is a special case of the lattice-approximation problem, in which every entry of $\mathbf{p}$ is 0.5. (Please refer to problem [SB] in the Glossary). This problem has a rich history in combinatorics, and additionally has a direct application to a problem in integrated circuit design [DR89]. Gao and Kaufmann [GK87] show that a closely related problem arises in the solution of channel-routing problems in VLSI. Theorem 11.1 implies a solution to the set-balancing problem; directions for improving this solution will be suggested later in Section 11.4.3.

What does the lattice approximation problem have to do with linear programs and approximation algorithms? To answer this question, we define the general framework in which randomized rounding is used. Given a combinatorial optimization problem, we first formulate it as a zero-one integer linear program, if possible. We do not know of good ways of solving large zero-one linear programs in general, so we first relax the integrality constraints, and solve the resulting linear program. The linear program can be solved by any one of several algorithms with proven theoretical and/or practical efficiency. Let $\mathbf{x}$ denote the vector of variables in the integer linear program formulation, and let $\widehat{\mathbf{x}}$ denote the vector of solutions resulting from the linear program. We now apply randomized rounding to restore integrality to the variables: for each i, independently set $\mathbf{x}$ to 1 with probability $\widehat{\mathbf{x}}_i$, and to 0 otherwise. Let $\bar{\mathbf{x}}_i$ denote the resulting 0-1 vector of solutions to the integer program. Let $\mathbf{a}$ denote a row of the coefficient matrix of the linear program formulation. By linearity of expectation, $E[\mathbf{a} \cdot \bar{\mathbf{x}}] = \mathbf{a} \cdot \widehat{\mathbf{x}}$. This suggests that the expected value of the left-hand side of any constraint in the linear program will satisfy the bound prescribed by the right-hand side. We note that in certain instances (e.g., maximum satisfiability), better results can be obtained by rounding a variable $\mathbf{x}$ to 1 with probability $f(\widehat{\mathbf{x}})$, where f is a function that maps $\widehat{\mathbf{x}}$ to a value in [0, 1].

We next illustrate the use of this technique in three settings — integer multicommodity flows, covering problems, and maximum satisfiability. These applications have been chosen because they are especially illustrative; a number of others are listed in Section 11.2.4.

11.2.1   THE INTEGER MULTICOMMODITY FLOW PROBLEM

We are given a directed network (V, E) with a set V of nodes and a set E of arcs. Let m denote $|E|$ and n denote $|V|$. Associated with each each arc $e \in E$ is a *capacity*, denoted $c(e)$. In an instance of the *multicommodity flow problem*, (see also problem [Multicom] in the Glossary), we are given a set of k triplets (s_i, t_i, d_i). In each triplet, s_i and t_i are nodes in the network, while d_i is a positive integer *demand*. A solution is a set of *flows*, denoted $f_i(e)$, where we think of $f_i(e)$ as the amount of commodity i that flows through arc e. The flows are subject to the following restrictions:

> **I.** All the flows $f_i(e)$ should be integral.
>
> **II.** The incoming and outgoing flows of each commodity at each node should obey conservation constraints.
>
> **III.** Capacity constraints: for all e, $\sum_i f_i(e) \leq c(e)$.
>
> **IV.** Demand constraints: we must ship d_i units of commodity i from s_i to t_i. In our notation, we write $\sum_{e \in A_i} f_i(e) \geq d_i$, where A_i is the set of arcs leaving s_i.

As stated above, it is possible for the problem to be infeasible — the capacities available may not suffice to sustain the demands. Consider the following optimization version of the problem, for which we seek approximation algorithms. Given the instance, we seek to maximize the total flow of all commodities, which is clearly $\sum_i \sum_{e \in A_i} f_i(e)$. Thus, some commodities may not have their demands satisfied in the process of this maximization.

We now proceed to discuss the case $d_i = 1$ for all i; the same technique applies to the general case $d_i \geq 1$ with minor modifications. Clearly this maximization problem can be written as a 0-1 linear program. By relaxing the integrality constraint $f_i(e) \in \{0, 1\}$ for all i, e, we obtain the relaxation linear program in which $f_i(e) \in [0, 1]$ for all i, e. This linear program can be solved efficiently; in fact, one can use more efficient and direct combinatorial algorithms [KST90, PST91]; see also Chapter 5 in this book. We solve instead a slightly modified linear program, one in which we set the capacity of every arc e to $(1 - \epsilon)c(e)$ for a positive constant $\epsilon < \frac{\sqrt{5}-1}{2}$. We solve this modified linear program to obtain the fractional solutions $\widehat{f_i}(e)$, together with the total flow $\widehat{F} = \sum_i \sum_{e \in A_i} f_i(e)$. Let F denote the value of the total flow in the optimal *integral* solution. Then, $\widehat{F} \geq F(1 - \epsilon)$, and the fractional total flow in any arc is at most $(1 - \epsilon)$ times its capacity. Randomized rounding is now invoked as follows: for each commodity i, we independently perform a random walk from s_i to t_i that is guided by the fractional solutions $\widehat{f_i}(e)$. The random walk for commodity i is as follows: we begin at s_i by flipping a coin with probability of heads equal to $\sum_{e \in A_i} \widehat{f_i}(e) \leq 1$. If the coin comes up heads, we proceed with the random walk as described below; if not, we assign zero flow to commodity i. We now describe the general step of the random walk: suppose that we are at a node v. Let $A(v)$ denote the set of arcs leaving v. The random walk then chooses to proceed along arc $a \in A(v)$ with probability $\frac{\widehat{f_i}(a)}{\sum_{e \in A(v)} \widehat{f_i}(e)}$. The walk for commodity i terminates on reaching t_i, which it must in at most $n - 1$ steps because the set of arcs with non-zero flow may be assumed (without loss of generality) to form a directed acyclic graph. The following lemma is easy to prove by induction:

LEMMA 11.3 The probability that the random walk for commodity i traverses any arc e is equal to $\widehat{f_i}(e)$.

We are now ready for the main result.

THEOREM 11.2 Suppose that we have an instance of multicommodity flow in which every capacity $c(e)$ is at least $5.2 \ln 4m$. Let ϵ be a positive constant less than $\frac{\sqrt{5}-1}{2}$. Then, with probability $1 - \frac{1}{m}$, the above algorithm yields a integer solution of total flow at least $F(1 - \epsilon)^2$ with probability at least $1 - \frac{1}{m} - 2\exp(-0.38\epsilon^2 F)$, where F is the total flow in the optimal integer solution.

Proof. The algorithm always produces an integer solution, so it can only fail to meet the guarantees of the theorem because of the following types of failure:

    I. The rounded flow violates the capacity constraint on some arc.

    II. The rounded flow is of value less than $F(1 - \epsilon)^2$.

We proceed to bound the probability of the first mode of failure by $\frac{1}{m}$ and the second by $2\exp(-0.38\epsilon^2 F)$. Adding together these probabilities yields the theorem.

    The crucial observation is that the event "the random walk for commodity i traverses arc e" is a Bernoulli trial, for any fixed arc e. Likewise, the event "commodity i has non-zero flow in the solution" is also a Bernoulli trial. Then, after randomized rounding the flow in any arc is the sum of independent Bernoulli trials. Likewise, the total flow is a random variable that is the sum of independent Bernoulli trials. We have already observed that the expectation of the total flow after rounding is at least $F(1 - \epsilon)$. Applying Lemma 11.2 with $\beta = \epsilon$ now yields the probability bound for the second mode of failure. We turn now to the flow through a fixed arc of the network, following randomized rounding. Once again, Lemma 11.2 yields that the probability that the capacity constraint of a fixed arc is violated is at most $\frac{1}{m^2}$; we omit the detailed but routine calculations. Summing this probability over all m arcs, we have the desired bound. ∎

    Note that the failure probability of the algorithm can be diminished by independent repetitions. In most applications, it is the computation of the fractional solutions $\widehat{f_i}(e)$ that is computationally intensive. Randomized rounding is itself quite fast, and can be repeated many times.

11.2.2 COVERING AND PACKING PROBLEMS

Covering and packing integer programs are defined as follows. Let Z_+ denote the non-negative integers. Let $\mathbf{A}$ be an $m \times n$ matrix over Z_+, let $\mathbf{b}$ be a vector over Z_+^m, and let $\mathbf{x}$ and $\mathbf{w}$ be vectors over Z_+^n. The *covering problem* is to minimize $\mathbf{w}^T \cdot \mathbf{x}$ subject to $\mathbf{Ax} \ge \mathbf{b}$. The *packing problem* is to maximize $\mathbf{w}^T \cdot \mathbf{x}$ subject to $\mathbf{Ax} \le \mathbf{b}$. (Please refer to problems [PA] and [CO] in the Glossary). In a linear programming setting, covering and packing are dual problems. Randomized rounding is a very useful technique for approximating both covering and packing problems. We will present this technique in the context of an important special case of covering problems, the *set cover* problem. Please refer to Chapter 3 for an extensive discussion of this problem. In Section 11.2.2.1 we present an application of set cover to the undirected multicut problem.

    Let $V = \{v_1, \ldots, v_n\}$ be a set of elements, and let $\mathcal{S} = \{S_1, \ldots, S_m\}$ be a family of subsets defined over V. There are two common ways of formulating the set cover problem, and the reader can easily verify that they are equivalent. (See also the Glossary, problem [SC]). In the first formulation, a non-negative weight function w is attached to V. The goal is to find a minimum weight set of elements $V' \subseteq V$ that intersects all subsets $S \in \mathcal{S}$. The weight of V' is defined to be the sum of the weights of the elements belonging to V'. In the second formulation, a non-negative weight function w is attached to $\mathcal{S}$, and the goal is to find a minimum weight family of subsets $\mathcal{S}' \subseteq \mathcal{S}$, such that their union is equal to V. We will henceforth use the first formulation (which is also known as the *hitting set*) of the problem.

We first write the set cover problem as an integer program. For $1 \leq i \leq n$, let x_i denote the indicator variable for element v_i.

$$\text{Minimize } \sum_{i=1}^{n} w_i \cdot x_i$$
$$\text{subject to } \sum_{i: \, v_i \in S_j} x_i \geq 1 \quad \forall S_j \in \mathcal{S},$$
$$x_i \in \{0, 1\} \quad 1 \leq i \leq n. \tag{11.1}$$

We relax this integer program and allow each variable x_i to assume values in the interval $[0, 1]$. Let $\widehat{x_i}$ be the value assigned to x_i in an optimal fractional solution of the relaxed program. We now apply randomized rounding and set each variable x_i to 1 with probability $\widehat{x_i}$. Clearly, the expected weight of the elements chosen to the cover is equal to $\sum_{i=1}^{n} w_i \widehat{x_i}$.

What is the probability that a subset S_i is covered? Suppose that S_i contains elements $v_1, \ldots, v_k$; recall that $\sum_{j=1}^{k} \widehat{x_j} \geq 1$. The probability that S_i is covered is:

$$1 - \prod_{j=1}^{k}(1 - \widehat{x_j}) \geq 1 - \left(1 - \frac{1}{k}\right)^k \geq 1 - \frac{1}{e}. \tag{11.2}$$

That is, the probability that subset S_i is covered is at least a constant. To increase the probability of covering the family of subsets $\mathcal{S}$, randomized rounding can be repeatedly applied to the set of variables that were not set to 1. For example, by repeating the randomized rounding procedure $t = O(\log m)$ times, we can guarantee that the probability that a subset S_j is not covered is at most $\frac{1}{2m}$. Thus, the probability that $\mathcal{S}$ is not covered after t repetitions is at most $\frac{1}{2}$. The expected weight of the cover after t repetitions is at most $t \cdot \sum_{i=1}^{k} w_i \widehat{x_i}$, i.e., t times the weight of an optimal fractional cover. In fact, repeating the randomized rounding procedure t times is the same as scaling the original probabilities and rounding each variable x_i as follows:

$$P[x_i = 0] = (1 - \widehat{x_i})^t.$$

We thus have:

THEOREM 11.3 For every instance $\{V, \mathcal{S}\}$ of the set cover problem, randomized rounding finds an $O(\log m)$-approximate cover, with probability at least $\frac{1}{2}$.

The result obtained in Theorem 11.3 is not the best possible. It is well known that the approximation factor obtained by the greedy algorithm can be at most $1 + \ln \Delta$, (please refer to Theorem 3.1 in Chapter 3), where Δ denotes the maximum degree of an element in V, i.e., the maximum number of subsets in $\mathcal{S}$ that can be covered by a single element in V. We will now show that the bound obtained in Theorem 11.3 can be improved. We follow the work of Bertsimas and Vohra [BV94] and Srinivasan [Sri95, Sri96].

Let A_i denote the event that subset S_i is not covered. We claim that events A_i and A_j are positively correlated. To verify this, observe that

$$P[A_i \cap A_j] = \prod_{\ell \in S_i - S_j} P[x_\ell = 0] \cdot \prod_{\ell \in S_j - S_i} P[x_\ell = 0] \cdot \prod_{\ell \in S_i \cap S_j} P[x_\ell = 0]$$
$$\geq P[A_i] \cdot P[A_j],$$

implying also that $P[\bar{A}_i \cap \bar{A}_j] \geq P[\bar{A}_i] \cdot P[\bar{A}_j]$. These inequalities are actually implied by the FKG Inequality [AS92], which also implies the more general inequality for any subset J of indices:

$$P\left[\bigcap_{j \in J} A_j\right] \geq \prod_{j \in J} P[A_j].$$

Suppose that randomized rounding is invoked with some scaling parameter t whose value will be determined later. We are interested in evaluating the expected weight of a solution produced by randomized rounding, given that all subsets are satisfied. Let $F = \cap_{i=1}^m \bar{A}_i$; then,

$$E\left[\sum_{i=1}^n w_i x_i | F\right] = \sum_{i=1}^n w_i \cdot P[x_i = 1 | F]$$
$$= \sum_{i=1}^n w_i \cdot \frac{P[F | x_i = 1]}{P[F]} \cdot P[x_i = 1]. \qquad (11.3)$$

For each element v_i, let $N(i)$ denote the indices of the subsets in which v_i is contained, and let d_i denote the degree of v_i, i.e., $d_i = |N(i)|$. Then,

$$\frac{P[F | x_i = 1]}{P[F]} = \frac{P[\cap_{j \notin N(i)} \bar{A}_j]}{P[\cap_{j=1}^m \bar{A}_j]} \leq \frac{1}{P[\cap_{j \in N(i)} \bar{A}_j]},$$

where the latter inequality follows from the positive correlation of the events $\{\bar{A}_i\}$. We then obtain the following inequality from (11.2) and from the positive correlation of the events $\{\bar{A}_i\}$.

$$P[\cap_{j \in N(i)} \bar{A}_j] \geq \prod_{j \in N(i)} P[\bar{A}_j] \geq (1 - e^{-t})^{d_i}.$$

Recall that $\Delta = \max_{i=1}^m d_i$. Substituting back in (11.3), we obtain:

$$E\left[\sum_{i=1}^n w_i x_i | F\right] \leq \sum_{i=1}^n w_i (1 - e^{-t})^{-d_i} \cdot (1 - (1 - \widehat{x}_i)^t)$$
$$\leq (1 - e^{-t})^{-\Delta} \sum_{i=1}^n w_i (1 - (1 - t\widehat{x}_i))$$
$$= t(1 - e^{-t})^{-\Delta} \sum_{i=1}^n w_i \widehat{x}_i.$$

Choosing $t = O(\log \Delta)$ we get

$$E\left[\sum_{i=1}^{n} w_i x_i \mid F\right] = O\left(\log \Delta \cdot \sum_{i=1}^{n} w_i \widehat{x_i}\right).$$

This proof shows that with positive probability, randomized rounding can yield an $O(\log \Delta)$ approximation factor to the set cover problem. However, the probability of success can still be exponentially small. Thus, from the algorithmic point of view, achieving an $O(\log \Delta)$ approximation factor with a randomized algorithm still remains open. Stronger results for covering and packing problems that use the positive correlation of the events $\{A_i\}_{i=1}^{m}$ were shown by Srinivasan [Sri95, Sri96], who also showed how to de-randomize his existential proof by constructing appropriate pessimistic estimators. He obtains the following bound for covering problems:

$$1 + O\left(\max\left\{\frac{\ln\left(\frac{mB}{y^*}\right)}{B}, \sqrt{\frac{\ln\left(\frac{mB}{y^*}\right)}{B}}\right\}\right),$$

where B is defined to be the minimum entry in the vector b and $y^* = \sum_{i=1}^{n} w_i \widehat{x_i}$. This improves on the bound

$$1 + O\left(\max\left\{\frac{\ln m}{B}, \sqrt{\frac{\ln m}{B}}\right\}\right),$$

which is obtained from the (standard) application of randomized rounding to covering problems, e.g., Theorem 11.3 in the case of set cover.

For the unweighted set cover problem, Srinivasan [Sri95] (see also [Sri96]) obtains the following approximation bound:

$$\ln\left(\frac{m}{y^*}\right) + O\left(\ln\ln\left(\frac{m}{y^*}\right)\right) + O(1),$$

which is at least as good as $O(\log \Delta)$.

11.2.2.1   The undirected multicut problem

The undirected multicut problem is defined as follows. Let $G = (V, E)$ be an undirected graph, $c : E \rightarrow \mathbb{R}^+$ a capacity function, and let (s_i, t_i), $1 \leq i \leq k$, be k source-sink pairs. A multicut is a set of edges that separates each source from its corresponding sink, i.e, the removal of a multicut disconnects the graph into connected components such that no source-sink pair is contained in the same connected component. Finding a minimum capacity multicut is an *NP*-complete problem. Garg, Vazirani, and Yannakakis [GVY93] gave a polynomial-time algorithm that approximates the minimum capacity multicut (in an undirected graph) to within a factor of $O(\log k)$. This algorithm is described in detail in Section 5.2.2. We show a set cover formulation of the multicut problem that yields an $O(\log k)$ approximation factor via randomized rounding. We follow the work of Bertsimas and Vohra [BV94].

We first note that the minimum capacity multicut problem can be formulated as a set cover problem in a natural way. Let the elements in the set cover formulation correspond to the edges in the graph and let each source-sink path define a subset. We are looking for a minimum weight set of edges that intersects each source-sink path. However, the approximation factor obtained from this set cover formulation is quite weak, and can be as bad as $\Omega(|V|)$. We now define a different set cover formulation of the multicut problem.

Let F be the collection of all subsets of V with the property that for any $S \in F$, *at most* one of s_i and t_i belong to S, for all $1 \leq i \leq k$. We denote by $\delta(S)$ the set of edges for which exactly one endpoint is in S. Let $c(A)$ denote the sum of the capacities of the edges in a set A. Let a_{iS} (b_{iS}) be the indicator variable of the event $a_i \in S$ ($t_i \in S$). Let $x(S) = 1$ mean that subset S is picked, $x(S) = 0$ otherwise. We are now ready to define the following integer program:

$$\text{Minimize } \frac{1}{2} \sum_{S \in F} c(\delta(S)) \cdot x(S)$$

$$\text{subject to } \sum_{S \in F} a_{iS} \cdot x(S) \geq 1 \quad \forall s_i, \ 1 \leq i \leq k,$$

$$\sum_{S \in F} b_{iS} \cdot x(S) \geq 1 \quad \forall t_i, \ 1 \leq i \leq k,$$

$$x(S) \in \{0, 1\}, \quad \forall S \in F. \tag{11.4}$$

In words, the goal here is to cover all sources and sinks in the graph by subsets belonging to F. Given any feasible multicut C, it is not hard to see that the connected components generated by removing the edges of C induce a feasible solution to the integer program. Conversely, from any feasible solution to the integer program, a feasible multicut can be computed.

Bertsimas and Vohra [BV94] show that a linear relaxation of this integer program, where each variable $x(S)$ is allowed to assume values in the range $[0, 1]$, can be computed in polynomial time, albeit the number of variables is exponential. This follows by observing that there exists a relaxed optimal solution in which the number of variables that have non-zero variables is bounded by a polynomial. Given an optimal fractional solution, we can now apply the set cover randomized rounding procedure to this solution, and obtain a feasible multicut from it. The approximation factor obtained is $O(\log k)$, since the number of elements that need to be covered is $2k$. We note that a greedy algorithm that finds an approximate multicut, and uses the above set cover formulation of the multicut problem, was given by Cheriyan and Yu [CY95].

11.2.3   THE MAXIMUM SATISFIABILITY PROBLEM

The satisfiability problem (SAT) is defined as follows: given a set of clauses in conjunctive normal form over a collection of boolean variables, we wish to decide whether there is an assignment of the variables that satisfies all the clauses. In the MAX SAT problem, we are given an instance of satisfiability and we seek an assignment that *maximizes* the number of satisfied clauses. Since SAT is known to be *NP*-hard, it immediately follows that MAX SAT is also *NP*-hard. Given an instance I, let $M_*(I)$ be the maximum number of clauses that can be satisfied, and let $M_A(I)$ be the number of clauses satisfied by an algorithm A. Recall that the performance ratio of algorithm A is the infimum (over all instances I) of $\frac{M_A(I)}{M_*(I)}$, and that for a randomized algorithm A, the quantity $M_A(I)$ may be a random variable, in which case we replace $M_A(I)$ by $E[M_A(I)]$ in the definition of the performance ratio. Thus, our definition requires us to satisfy a number of clauses close to the best possible for the instance at hand.

We now give a simple randomized algorithm that achieves a performance ratio of $\frac{3}{4}$. We note that the techniques described here can easily be generalized to yield the same performance ratio for the weighted MAX SAT problem, where a non-negative weight is attached to each clause, and the goal is to find an assignment that maximizes the weight of the satisfied clauses.

Consider setting each variable in the instance independently to 1 with probability $\frac{1}{2}$. Clearly, a clause containing k literals is not satisfied by this process with probability $\frac{1}{2^k}$; thus, such a random assignment would work well for instances in which every clause contains many literals: if every clause were to contain k or more literals, we immediately have an α-approximation algorithm for which $\alpha \geq 1 - 2^{-k}$. This idea is implicit in early work of Johnson [Joh74]. It follows that we have a randomized $\frac{3}{4}$-approximation algorithm for instances of MAX SAT in which every clause has at least two literals. It appears that the bottleneck for achieving a performance ratio of $\frac{3}{4}$ stems from clauses consisting of a single literal. We now give a different algorithm that performs especially well when there are many clauses consisting of single literals. This algorithm is due to Goemans and Williamson [GW94a].[1] We then argue that on any instance, one of these two algorithms will yield a (randomized) $\frac{3}{4}$-approximation. Thus, given an instance, we run both algorithms and take the better of the two solutions. In Section 11.3 we will describe a general technique due to Goemans and Williamson [GW94b] that achieves an improved approximation ratio.

The idea again is to formulate the problem as an integer linear program, solve the linear programming relaxation, and then to round using the randomized rounding. To each clause C_j in the instance, we associate an indicator variable $z_j \in \{0, 1\}$ in the integer linear program that is 1 when C_j is satisfied and 0 otherwise. For each variable x_i, we use an indicator variable y_i that is 1 if the variable x_i is set TRUE, and 0 otherwise. Let S_j^+ be the set of variables that appear in the uncomplemented form in clause S_j, and S_j^- be the set of variables that appear in the complemented form in clause C_j. We may then formulate the MAX SAT problem as follows:

$$\text{Maximize} \sum_j z_j$$
$$\text{subject to} \sum_{S_j^+} y_i + \sum_{S_j^-} (1 - y_i) \geq z_j \quad \forall j,$$
$$y_i, z_j \in \{0, 1\} \quad \forall i, j. \tag{11.5}$$

We solve the linear program in which we relax the integrality constraints (11.5), allowing the y_i and the z_j to assume values in the interval $[0, 1]$. Let $\widehat{y_i}$ be the value assigned to y_i in the optimal solution to this linear program, and let $\widehat{z_j}$ be the value assigned to z_j. Clearly, $\sum_j \widehat{z_j}$ is an upper bound on the number of clauses that can be satisfied. We first show that using randomized rounding, we obtain a solution in which the expected number of clauses satisfied is at least $(1 - \frac{1}{e}) \sum_j \widehat{z_j}$.

---

[1]Prior to the work of Goemans and Williamson, Yannakakis [Yan92] had given a deterministic polynomial-time $\frac{3}{4}$-approximation algorithm for MAX SAT.

Randomized rounding independently sets the variable y_i to 1 (corresponding to x_i being set TRUE) with probability $\widehat{y}_i$. Where k is a positive integer, let β_k denote $1 - (1 - \frac{1}{k})^k$. We first show that for a clause C_j with k literals, the probability that it is satisfied by randomized rounding is at least $\beta_k \widehat{z}_j$. Because $\beta_k \geq (1 - \frac{1}{e})$, the expected number of clauses satisfied by randomized rounding is at least $(1 - \frac{1}{e}) \sum_j \widehat{z}_j$.

LEMMA 11.4   Let C_j be a clause with k literals. The probability that it is satisfied by randomized rounding is at least $\beta_k \widehat{z}_j$.

Proof.   Consider a single clause C_j. We may assume without loss of generality that all the variables contained in it appear in uncomplemented form, and that C_j is of the form $x_1 \vee \cdots \vee x_k$. By constraint (11.5) in the linear program,

$$\widehat{y}_1 + \cdots + \widehat{y}_k \geq \widehat{z}_j.$$

Clause C_j remains unsatisfied by randomized rounding only if every one of the variables y_i is rounded to 0. Since each variable is rounded independently, this occurs with probability $\prod_{i=1}^{k}(1 - \widehat{y}_i)$. To show that

$$1 - \prod_{i=1}^{k}(1 - \widehat{y}_i) \geq \beta_k \widehat{z}_j,$$

we observe that the expression on the left is minimized when $\widehat{y}_i = \frac{\widehat{z}_j}{k}$ for all i. It now suffices to show that $1 - (1 - \frac{z_j}{k})^k \geq \beta_k z_j$ in $[0, 1]$; this follows from elementary calculus. ∎

THEOREM 11.4   Given an instance of MAX SAT, the expected number of clauses satisfied by linear programming and randomized rounding is at least $(1 - \frac{1}{e})$ times the maximum number of clauses that can be satisfied on that instance.

We have studied two randomized algorithms MAX SAT: one that set each variable to 1 with probability $\frac{1}{2}$, and a second that used the solutions to the linear program as a basis for randomized rounding. We will now show by a simple convexity argument that on any instance, one of the algorithms is a $\frac{3}{4}$-approximation algorithm. Namely, given any instance, we run both algorithms and choose the better solution. Let n_1 denote the expected number of clauses that are satisfied when each variable is independently set to 1 with probability $\frac{1}{2}$. Let n_2 denote the expected number of clauses that are satisfied when we use the linear programming followed by randomized rounding (corresponding to Theorem 11.4). The following exercise will be used in the proof below.

EXERCISE 11.1   For $k \geq 1$, $\alpha_k = 1 - \frac{1}{2^k}$ and $\beta_k = 1 - (1 - \frac{1}{k})^k$, show that

$$\alpha_k + \beta_k \geq \frac{3}{2}.$$

THEOREM 11.5 $\max\{n_1, n_2\} \geq \frac{3}{4} \sum_j \widehat{z}_j$.

Proof. We show that

$$\max\{n_1, n_2\} \geq \frac{n_1 + n_2}{2} \geq \frac{3}{4} \sum_j \widehat{z}_j.$$

The first inequality is immediate, we prove the second one. Let α_k denote $1 - \frac{1}{2^k}$, and let C^k denote the set of clauses that contain precisely k literals. Then,

$$n_1 = \sum_{k \geq 1} \sum_{C_j \in C^k} \alpha_k \geq \sum_{k \geq 1} \sum_{C_j \in C^k} \alpha_k \cdot \widehat{z}_j$$

since $0 \leq \widehat{z}_j \leq 1$. By Lemma 11.4,

$$n_2 \geq \sum_{k \geq 1} \sum_{C_j \in C^k} \beta_k \cdot \widehat{z}_j.$$

Hence,

$$\frac{n_1 + n_2}{2} \geq \sum_{k \geq 1} \sum_{C_j \in C^k} \frac{\alpha_k + \beta_k}{2} \cdot \widehat{z}_j.$$

This inequality yields the theorem, since $\alpha_k + \beta_k \geq \frac{3}{2}$ for all $k \geq 1$ as proved in Exercise 11.1. ∎

11.2.4 RELATED WORK

There are many other interesting applications of randomized rounding; we mention a few of them. Naor and Roth [NR95] apply the technique to a file distribution problem in networks. Klein and Sairam [KS92] apply it to the computation of approximate shortest paths in a graph. Lin and Vitter [LV92] consider a family of packing problems. Kortsarz and Peleg [KP93] study the construction of a useful class of graphs known as *spanners*. The paper by Bertsimas and Vohra [BV94] is a comprehensive guide to uses of the technique in a variety of covering problems. One of the interesting ideas in their paper is to devise a function that maps each value in the linear program solution to a probability in [0, 1], a generalization of the technique used by Raghavan and Thompson [RT87], and Goemans and Williamson [GW94a]; note that in the above examples, we have only used the obvious identity function. In some applications, as shown in [BV94], it helps to use other mappings from fractional solutions to probabilities. The interested reader is referred to these papers and the ones cited in them for further applications. Before proceeding to semidefinite programming, it is worth pointing out an alternative view of randomized rounding. Instead of thinking of the process as rounding a fraction $\widehat{x}$ to 1 with probability $\widehat{x}$, we may adopt the following equivalent view: We pick a random number y uniformly in [0, 1]. If $\widehat{x} > y$ we round up to 1. Otherwise, we round down to 0. The effect is the same, but we now think of comparing the fraction $\widehat{x}$ to a randomly chosen threshold. This view will be useful in the following section.

SEMIDEFINITE PROGRAMMING

11.3

The linear programming relaxations of Section 11.2 have the property that the value of the optimum for the relaxation is never far from the value of the optimum for the original integer program. Given this, we were able to obtain good approximations to the original integer program by finding an integer solution whose value is close to the optimum for the linear program. For many problems in combinatorial optimization, the linear program and integer program optima can be quite different. For instance, in the multicommodity flow problem of Section 11.2.1, if all arc capacities are 0 or 1, it is easy to construct instances for which the optimal value for the linear program is $\sqrt{n}$ times the optimal value for the integer program. One approach to coping with this large discrepancy between the optima of the original problem and the relaxation is to consider relaxations tighter than linear programming relaxations. In this direction, the use of *semidefinite programming* relaxations has recently enjoyed striking success. We begin by reviewing some of the main ideas behind semidefinite programming. We then illustrate the use of such relaxations using two examples.

We say that an $n \times n$ matrix $\mathbf{A}$ of reals is *positive semidefinite* if, for any vector $\mathbf{x} \in \mathbf{R}^n$, $\mathbf{x}^T \mathbf{A} \mathbf{x} \geq 0$. Recall that a matrix $\mathbf{A}$ is symmetric positive semidefinite if and only if there exists a matrix $\mathbf{B}$ such that $\mathbf{B}^T \mathbf{B} = \mathbf{A}$. It is known that $\mathbf{B}$ is an $m \times n$ matrix for $m \leq n$, and given $\mathbf{A}$ such a matrix $\mathbf{B}$ of full row-rank can be found in time polynomial in n. When all the diagonal entries of $\mathbf{A}$ are equal to 1, each row of $\mathbf{B}$ is a unit vector in $\mathbf{R}^m$. (Refer to the book by Golub and van Loan [GV83] for further details about the various concepts and algorithms in matrix theory that are used in this section.)

In an instance of a semidefinite programming problem, we wish to optimize a linear function of (the entries of) a symmetric matrix $\mathbf{A}$ subject to linear constraints and the additional constraint that $\mathbf{A}$ be positive semidefinite. There has been considerable work on the theory of semidefinite programming that uses the fact that for any positive real ϵ, a semidefinite program can be solved to within an additive error of ϵ in time polynomial in the size of the input and $\log \frac{1}{\epsilon}$ [Ali95, GLS81, GLS87, NN90, NN94]. We now proceed to our first application of semidefinite programming.

11.3.1   THE MAXIMUM CUT PROBLEM

In the MAX CUT problem, we are given an undirected graph $G = (V, E)$ with vertex set V and edge set E. We wish to partition the vertices into two sets V_- and V_+ so as to maximize the number of edges with one end-point in V_- and one end-point in V_+. We refer to such a partition as a *cut*, and the edges between vertices in V_- and vertices in V_+ as *cut-edges*. The problem is *NP*-hard and has a variety of applications, e.g., in lower bounds for network design [Bar96], and in statistical physics and VLSI design [BGJR88]. Sahni and Gonzalez [SG76] give a $\frac{1}{2}$-approximation algorithm for this problem: an algorithm that, on every instance, finds a cut such that number of cut-edges is at least half the number in the optimal cut. This performance can be achieved by assigning each vertex to either V_- or V_+ with equal probability. The expected number of edges in the cut is at least $\frac{|E|}{2}$. Alternatively, the following *greedy algorithm* also achieves this performance: initially, partition the vertices arbitrarily; thereafter, consider each vertex in turn, moving it to the other partition if this increases the number of edges in the cut. We now present an elegant application of semidefinite programming followed by randomized rounding to this problem, which yields a 0.878-approximation algorithm. This algorithm is due to Goemans and Williamson [GW94b].

Consider first the following quadratic integer programming formulation of MAX CUT. We use a variable x_i to indicate which side of the partition the ith vertex of V goes into. Let a_{ij} be 1 if the edge (i, j) exists, and 0 otherwise.

$$\text{Maximize} \sum_{i<j} a_{ij} \frac{1 - x_i x_j}{2}$$
$$\text{subject to } x_i \in \{-1, +1\} \quad \forall i. \tag{11.6}$$

Clearly, the objective function measures the number of edges in the resulting cut. We now relax this formulation using a semidefinite program. Viewing the allowable values of x_i in (11.6) as unit length vectors in one dimension, the relaxation consists of allowing the x_i to be unit length vectors in dimension $m \leq n$ (i.e., $x_i \cdot x_i = 1$). We interpret the product $x_i x_j$ of the objective function in (11.6) as a dot product when considering vectors in higher dimensions. The resulting relaxation becomes:

$$\text{Maximize} \sum_{i<j} a_{ij} \frac{1 - \mathbf{v}_i \cdot \mathbf{v}_j}{2}$$
$$\text{subject to } \mathbf{v}_i \in S_n \quad \forall i, \tag{11.7}$$

where S_n denotes the set of unit length vectors in n dimensions. Letting y_{ij} denote $\mathbf{v}_i \cdot \mathbf{v}_j$, we can rewrite (11.7) as

$$\text{Maximize} \sum_{i<j} a_{ij} \frac{1 - y_{ij}}{2}$$
$$\text{subject to } \mathbf{Y} = (y_{ij}) \text{ being symmetric positive semidefinite,}$$
$$y_{ii} = 1 \quad \forall i. \tag{11.8}$$

The correspondence between the formulations (11.7) and (11.8) is clear: a solution to (11.7) immediately yields a solution to (11.8); further, given a solution to (11.8), an incomplete Cholesky decomposition [GV83] can be used to reconstruct the vectors $\mathbf{v}_i$, without altering the objective function value. Noting that (11.8) is a semidefinite program, we can solve it in polynomial time (to within any desired precision) using the methods of [Ali95, GLS81, GLS87]. The solution $\mathbf{Y}$ can now be factored into the sets of vectors $\mathbf{v}_i$, and it remains to round these vectors to $\{-1, +1\}$. To this end we use the following randomized rounding procedure: we pick a random unit length vector $\mathbf{r}$ in $\mathbf{R}^n$. For each i, we declare x_i (formulation (11.6)) to be $\text{sgn}(\mathbf{v}_i \cdot \mathbf{r})$, where $\text{sgn}(z)$ is the sign of the real z, and is $+1$ if z is non-negative and -1 otherwise. An equivalent view of this process is that we pick a random hyperplane (whose normal is $\mathbf{r}$) through the origin in $\mathbf{R}^n$, and use it as a threshold: vertices corresponding to the vectors on the same side of it are deemed to be in the same partition of the cut. We turn to the quality of this solution.

THEOREM 11.6   Let C denote the size of the cut found by the above algorithm. Then,

$$E[C] \geq 0.878 \sum_{i<j} a_{ij} \frac{1 - \mathbf{v}_i \cdot \mathbf{v}_j}{2}. \tag{11.9}$$

Remark: Since the right-hand side of (11.9) is the value of the optimum for the relaxation (11.7) (which is in turn an upper bound on the size of the optimal cut), we find a cut whose expected size is at least 0.878 times the optimal cut.

Proof.   We first claim that for any two vectors $\mathbf{v}_i$ and $\mathbf{v}_j$ and for a random unit length vector $\mathbf{r}$, the probability that $\mathrm{sgn}(\mathbf{v_i} \cdot \mathbf{r}) \neq \mathrm{sgn}(\mathbf{v_j} \cdot \mathbf{r})$ is arccos $\frac{\mathbf{v_i} \cdot \mathbf{v}_j}{\pi}$. This follows by noting that the set of vectors $\mathbf{r}$ (equivalently, the set of hyperplanes) that separate $\mathbf{v}_i$ and $\mathbf{v}_j$ lie on two spherical sectors on the unit sphere in $\mathbb{R}^n$, each of measure arccos $\frac{\mathbf{v_i} \cdot \mathbf{v}_j}{2\pi}$.

Now, by linearity of expectation and the fact that the $\mathbf{v}_i$ are solutions to (11.7), we have

$$E[C] = \sum_{i<j} a_{ij} \, P\big[\mathrm{sgn}(\mathbf{v_i} \cdot \mathbf{r}) \neq \mathrm{sgn}(\mathbf{v_j} \cdot \mathbf{r})\big], \tag{11.10}$$

which is clearly $\sum_{i<j} \frac{a_{ij} \cdot \arccos(\mathbf{v_i} \cdot \mathbf{v_j})}{\pi}$. The proof is completed by invoking elementary calculus to argue that for any $z \in \{-1, +1\}$, $2\pi^{-1} \cdot \arccos z \geq 0.878(1 - z)$. Substituting this inequality in (11.10) yields the result.   ∎

It follows from work of Delorme and Poljak [DP93] that this semidefinite programming relaxation cannot yield a substantially better result; the reader is referred to [GW94b] for details. An approach very similar to the above leads to a 0.878-approximation algorithm for the MAX 2SAT problem: this is the same as the MAX SAT problem, with the further restriction that every clause contains at most two literals. (Please see the Glossary for problems' definitions.) This result is also described in [GW94b], as is the resulting 0.758-approximation for MAX SAT. Recently, Feige and Goemans [FG95] have extended these techniques to obtain a 0.931-approximation algorithm for MAX 2SAT. Frieze and Jerrum [FJ95] have applied the techniques to be discussed in the next section to the MAX k-CUT and MAX BISECTION problems in graphs.

11.3.2   THE GRAPH COLORING PROBLEM

Given an undirected graph, a *k-coloring* of G is an assignment of an integer in $[1, k]$ to each vertex of G; we call this integer the *color* of that vertex. Such a k-coloring is said to be *legal* if no two adjacent vertices are assigned the same color. The graph coloring problem seeks a legal k-coloring for as small a value of k as possible; the smallest such k is called the *chromatic number* of G. A graph G is said to be k-colorable if there exists a legal k-coloring of G. It is *NP*-hard to decide whether a graph is 3-colorable. The graph coloring problem arises in many applications, e.g., time-table scheduling, register allocation in compilers, and in resource allocation.

The subject of this section is a randomized approximation algorithm for graph coloring due to Karger, Motwani, and Sudan [KMS94]. Although their algorithm is quite general, for clarity and brevity we only describe their algorithm for 3-colorable graphs.

Their algorithm employs an earlier algorithm due to Wigderson [Wig83] that we will describe first. Wigderson's algorithm colors any 3-colorable graph using $O(\sqrt{n})$ colors; this algorithm is the basis for all subsequent improvements in the performance guarantee. The following observations [BM77], stated as exercises, underlie Wigderson's algorithm.

EXERCISE 11.2   Show that any 2-colorable (bipartite) graph can be 2-colored in polynomial time.

EXERCISE 11.3   Show that any graph of maximum degree Δ can be colored with $\Delta + 1$ colors in polynomial time using a greedy algorithm.

THEOREM 11.7   Any 3-colorable graph can be colored with $O(\sqrt{n})$ colors in polynomial time.

Proof.   By Exercise 11.3, it only remains to deal with graphs in which there is a vertex of degree exceeding $\sqrt{n}$. The key observation is that in a 3-colorable graph, the subgraph induced by the neighbors of any vertex is bipartite, and can be colored in polynomial time using 2 colors. Thus, a vertex of degree exceeding $\sqrt{n}$, together with its neighbors, can be colored using 3 colors. We repeatedly color and remove such vertices (and their neighbors) from the graph, expending 3 colors at each iteration. We either finish with the empty graph in at most $\sqrt{n}$ iterations (using $O(\sqrt{n})$ colors in the process), or with a graph of maximum degree $\sqrt{n}$ (this residual graph can now be colored with at most $\sqrt{n} + 1$ colors as before). In either case, the number of colors used is $O(\sqrt{n})$.   ∎

Blum [Blu94] improved on Wigderson's algorithm by devising an algorithm that uses $\tilde{O}(n^{\frac{3}{8}})$ colors.[2]
     Our main focus here will be the approximation algorithm of Karger, Motwani, and Sudan [KMS94] based on semidefinite programming; given a 3-colorable graph, it uses

$$O(\min\{\Delta^{\frac{1}{3}} \log^{\frac{4}{3}} \Delta, n^{\frac{1}{4}} \log n\})$$

colors, where Δ is the maximum degree of any vertex in the graph. In general, for k-colorable graphs, their algorithm achieves a coloring using $\tilde{O}(\Delta^{1-\frac{2}{x}})$ or $\tilde{O}(n^{1-\frac{3}{x+1}})$ colors.

11.3.2.1   A semidefinite relaxation of graph coloring

The relaxation proposed by Karger, Motwani, and Sudan [KMS94] is the following: consider representing the color of each vertex by a unit length vector in n dimensions. The idea is to constrain the vectors corresponding to colors of adjacent vertices to be "far apart." To this end, a *vector k-coloring* of G is defined, as follows.

---

[2]The notation $\tilde{O}(f(n))$ denotes $O(f(n)\text{polylog}(n))$ and allows us to suppress inconsequential poly-logarithmic factors.

DEFINITION 11.1   A *vector k-coloring* of a graph G is an assignment of unit length vectors in $\mathbb{R}^n$ to the vertices of G such that for any two adjacent vertices i and j, the corresponding vectors $\mathbf{u}_i$ and $\mathbf{u}_j$ satisfy $\mathbf{u}_i \cdot \mathbf{u}_j \le -\frac{1}{k-1}$.

Note that k need not be an integer in this definition. The following fact states that a vector coloring is indeed a relaxation of standard graph coloring.

FACT 11.1   If G is k-colorable, then it has a vector k-coloring.

EXERCISE 11.1   Consider the following k vectors in $\mathbb{R}^n$: the last $n - k$ positions have value 0 in each vector; the ith entry in the ith vector is $-\sqrt{\frac{k-1}{k}}$; and, the remaining $k - 1$ entries in each vector is $\frac{1}{\sqrt{k(k-1)}}$.

- Show that this defines a set of unit length vectors such that the dot product of any two vectors is $-\frac{1}{k-1}$.
- Show that the value $-\frac{1}{k-1}$ is the minimum that can be assumed for the maximum dot product of any k unit length vectors.

Using this construction and its properties, verify Fact 11.1

Note that a graph is vector 2-colorable if and only if it is 2-colorable. The assertion in the exercise is tight in that it provides the best possible value for minimizing the mutual dot-product of k unit length vectors. This can be verified from the following exercises.

EXERCISE 11.2   Let G be vector k-colorable and let i be a vertex in G. Show that the induced subgraph on the vertices $\{ j \mid j$ is a neighbor of i in $G\}$ is vector $(k - 1)$-colorable.

EXERCISE 11.3   Using the preceding exercise, show that any graph containing a $(k + 1)$-clique is not k-vector colorable.

Thus, the "vector chromatic number" lies between the clique and chromatic number; recall that the clique number is a lower bound on the chromatic number. This also shows that $-\frac{1}{k-1}$ is the minimum possible value of the maximum of the dot-products of k vectors.

The vector coloring relaxation is related to the concept of an *orthonormal representation* of a graph [Lov79, GLS81]. The definition of an orthonormal representation requires that the given dot products be equal to zero, a weaker requirement. In fact, the semidefinite program formulation has interesting connections to the work of Lovász on the relationship between the clique and chromatic numbers of a graph [GLS81, Lov79, GLS87], and we will return to this issue a bit later.

For establishing the promised result for graph coloring, there are two main issues that need to be addressed. First, how may we compute this relaxation of graph coloring? And, second, given a vector coloring, how do we "round" it into a "good" coloring of the graph? The first question is easier to answer and this is where we resort to semidefinite programming. We defer the second question to the next section.

The computation of the relaxation is explicated via the following observations whose formal verifications are left as exercises. We begin by defining the notion of a matrix k-coloring that is equivalent to a vector k-coloring.

DEFINITION 11.2 Given a graph $G = (V, E)$ on n vertices, a *matrix k-coloring* of the graph is an $n \times n$ symmetric positive semidefinite matrix M, with $m_{ii} = 1$ for all i, and $m_{ij} \leq -\frac{1}{k-1}$ if $\{i, j\} \in E$.

FACT 11.2 A graph has a vector k-coloring if and only if it has matrix k-coloring.

To verify that a vector k-coloring implies a matrix k-coloring, define the matrix $\mathbf{M} = \{m_{ij}\}$ such that $m_{ij} = \mathbf{u}_i \cdot \mathbf{u}_j$. For the other direction, first recall that for every symmetric positive definite matrix $\mathbf{M}$ there exists a square matrix U such that $\mathbf{U}\mathbf{U}^T = \mathbf{M}$ (where $\mathbf{U}^T$ is the transpose of $\mathbf{U}$). Essentially, a positive semidefinite matrix $\mathbf{M}$ is called a matrix k-coloring of G if we can extract from it a matrix $\mathbf{U}$ such that $\mathbf{U}\mathbf{U}^T = \mathbf{M}$, and the rows of $\mathbf{U}$ form a vector k-coloring.

We observe that to solve the vector coloring relaxation it will suffice to find a matrix coloring. More precisely, a "rough" vector k-coloring can be constructed from a matrix k-coloring in polynomial time.

FACT 11.3 For $\epsilon > 0$, a vector $(k + \epsilon)$-coloring can be constructed from a matrix k-coloring in time polynomial in n and $\log(\frac{1}{\epsilon})$ time.

To verify this fact, observe that a δ-close approximation to the matrix $\mathbf{U}$ can be found in time polynomial in n and $\log(\frac{1}{\delta})$ using an Incomplete Cholesky Decomposition [GV83]. (Here by δ-close we mean a matrix $\mathbf{U}'$ such that $\mathbf{U}'\mathbf{U}'^T - \mathbf{M}$ has L_∞-norm less than δ.)

We now show that it is possible to compute a matrix k-coloring of a k-colorable graph via semidefinite programming.

LEMMA 11.5 For $\epsilon > 0$, if G is k-colorable, a vector k-coloring for it can be found using semidefinite programming in time polynomial in n and $\frac{1}{\epsilon}$, to within an additive error ϵ.

Proof. The proof is based on ideas due to Lovász [Lov79] and Goemans and Williamson [GW94b]. Consider the following semidefinite optimization problem (SDP):

$$\text{Minimize } \alpha$$
$$\text{subject to } \mathbf{M} = \{m_{ij}\} \text{ being positive semidefinite,}$$
$$m_{ij} \leq \alpha \text{ if } (i, j) \in E,$$
$$m_{ij} = m_{ji},$$
$$m_{ii} = 1.$$

Note that the identity matrix is a feasible solution to SDP. Note also that its optimum is $-\frac{1}{k-1}$ where k is the smallest real number such that a matrix k-coloring of G exists. Clearly, the optimum solution provides a matrix k-coloring of G.

A k-colorable graph G has a vector k-coloring (Fact 11.1), and hence a matrix k-coloring (Fact 11.2). For such graphs G, there exists a solution to this SDP with $\alpha = -\frac{1}{k-1}$. Thus, in time polynomial in n and $\log \frac{1}{\delta}$, we can find a feasible solution of value bounded by $-\frac{1}{k-1} + \delta$. This means that for all $\{i, j\} \in E$, m_{ij} is at most $\delta - \frac{1}{k-1}$, which is at most $-\frac{1}{k+\gamma-1}$ for $\gamma = 2\delta(k-1)^2$, provided $\delta \leq \frac{1}{2(k-1)}$. In other words, a matrix $(k+\gamma)$-coloring can be found in time polynomial in k, n, and $\log(\frac{1}{\epsilon})$. By Fact 11.3, we can now find the desired vector coloring in polynomial time for a suitable choice of δ in terms of ϵ.   ∎

11.3.2.2   Semicolorings and a weak rounding scheme

One approach to rounding a vector coloring into a C-coloring for a positive integer C is to directly mimic the technique of Goemans and Williamson for the MAX CUT problem: partition $\mathbb{R}^n$ into C "octants" about the origin using $\log_2 C$ random hyperplanes through the origin. Vertices whose vectors fall into the same octant are deemed to be in the same color class. A problem with this approach is that after the rounding, there is a good chance that two adjacent vertices are assigned the same color class. To circumvent this problem Karger, Motwani, and Sudan [KMS94] propose the notion of a so-called semicoloring.

DEFINITION 11.3   A k-semicoloring of $G = (V, E)$ is an association of k colors with the vertices in V such that at most $\frac{|V|}{4}$ edges in E have both end-points in the same color class.

Thus, given a k-semicoloring of a graph, a constant fraction of its vertices are assigned legal colors and can be put aside. Repeating this process yields the result in the following exercise.

EXERCISE 11.4   Let $f(i)$ be a non-decreasing function on the positive integers. Show that: given an algorithm that yields an $f(i)$-semicoloring on every subgraph of G with i vertices, it can be used to color G using $O(f(n)\log n)$ colors. Extend this result to the case of randomized algorithms.

In fact, the number of colors in Exercise 11.4 can be bounded by $O(f(n))$ provided $f(n) = \Omega(n^\epsilon)$ for a constant $\epsilon > 0$.

We now focus our attention on vector 3-colorable graphs, leaving the extension to general k for later. Consider a 3-colorable graph for which we have found a vector 3-coloring. We show that partitioning $\mathbb{R}^n$ into $O(\Delta^{\log_3 2})$ octants using random hyperplanes through the origin is likely to yield a $O(\Delta^{\log_3 2})$-semicoloring, and from this argue that we can obtain a $O(\Delta^{\log_3 2} \log n)$-coloring of G (recall that Δ is the maximum vertex degree in G).

The vector 3-coloring ensures that the dot product of the vectors assigned to any two adjacent vertices is at most $-\frac{1}{2}$, so that the angle between them is at least $\frac{2\pi}{3}$ radians. As in the proof of Theorem 11.6, the probability that a single random hyperplane separates two adjacent vertices is thus at least $\frac{2}{3}$. The probability that an edge of G is not separated by any of $\lceil 1 + \log_3 \Delta \rceil$ random hyperplanes is thus at most $(\frac{1}{3})^{\lceil 1 + \log_3 \Delta \rceil} \leq \frac{1}{3\Delta}$. Since the number of edges in G is at most $\frac{n\Delta}{2}$, the expected number of edges that are not cut is at most $\frac{n}{6}$. By the Markov inequality [MR95] the probability that we have more than $\frac{n}{3}$ uncut edges is less than $\frac{1}{2}$, so that the expected number of independent iterations before we have a valid $O(\Delta^{\log_3 2})$-semicoloring is at most 2.

Wigderson's algorithm [Wig83] now yields a coloring of G using $O(n^{0.387})$ colors. Let $\delta = n^{0.613}$; if there is a vertex of degree greater than δ, color it and its neighbors using 3 colors (since G is 3-colorable, the neighborhood of any vertex is bipartite and thus, 2-colorable in polynomial time). Repeating this process on the subgraph induced by the remaining vertices, we use $O(\frac{n}{\delta})$ colors until we are left with either the empty graph or a graph with maximum degree less than δ. Once the maximum degree is down to δ, we can color the graph with $O(\delta^{\log_3 2})$ colors by rounding the above semidefinite program for a total of $O(\frac{n}{\delta} + \delta^{\log_3 2}) = O(n^{0.387})$ colors.

This guarantee is slightly weaker than that of Blum [Blu94], whose algorithm finds a $n^{\frac{3}{8}} \log^{O(1)} n$-coloring of a 3-colorable graph. In the next section we show how to improve this result by using a more refined rounding scheme to construct a semicoloring with fewer colors.

11.3.2.3   An improved rounding scheme

Our goal now is to prove the following theorem:

THEOREM 11.8   Given a vector k-coloring of graph G, an $\tilde{O}(\Delta^{1-\frac{2}{k}})$-semicoloring can be constructed with high probability in polynomial time.

As in the previous section, this will immediately imply the desired result for approximate coloring.

We start by describing a new method for assigning colors to vertices which provides a significantly better semicoloring than the hyperplane-partition method. Suppose we have a vector coloring that assigns to each vertex i some unit length vector $\mathbf{u_i}$. The idea is to choose t random vectors, called *spokes*, $\mathbf{s_1}, \ldots, \mathbf{s_t} \in \mathbf{R}^n$ and to use them to define a set of t colors, say $1, \ldots, t$. We color a vertex i according to the spoke "nearest" to its associated vector $\mathbf{u_i}$, i.e., the spoke with the largest projection onto $\mathbf{u_i}$.

DEFINITION 11.4   For any vector $\mathbf{a}$, a spoke $\mathbf{s_j}$ is said to *color* $\mathbf{a}$ if for all $i \neq j$,

$$\mathbf{s_i} \cdot \mathbf{a} < \mathbf{s_j} \cdot \mathbf{a}.$$

Note that this definition allows for vectors not to be colored by any spoke at all, but this happens with a limiting probability equal to 0. Assuming that each vector $\mathbf{u_i}$ is colored by a unique spoke, we can assign the index of that spoke to vertex i as its color. The resulting t-coloring of the vertices of G need not be a legal coloring or even a good semicoloring. However, since the vectors corresponding to the endpoints of an edge are "far apart," it is at least plausible that for a random choice of the spokes it is unlikely that both endpoints are colored by the same spoke. In other words, as in the hyperplane-rounding method, an edge is likely to be "cut" by the coloring. Before we formalize this intuition, we need to specify the distribution from which the spokes are to be sampled.

It is intuitively clear that a good method for picking random spokes is to give each spoke a "direction" chosen uniformly at random in $\mathbf{R}^n$. Clearly, the simplest sampling technique for this purpose is to choose the spokes as random unit length vectors determined by points chosen uniformly at random from the surface of the unit sphere in $\mathbf{R}^n$. Unfortunately, this sampling technique is difficult to analyze, and so instead we choose each spoke s_j independently at random from the n-dimensional normal distribution. Basically, this means that each of the n components of s_j is independently chosen from the standard normal distribution (with expectation 0 and variance 1). Note that the lengths of these vectors are random (they are *not* unit length vectors) and, since they are not of equal length, the nearest spoke to a vector **a** may not be the one of minimum angle displacement from **a**. It turns out that the limiting behavior of the random unit length vector approach is exactly the same as for the one we use, but the multi-dimensional normal distribution is significantly easier to analyze.

Why does this assignment of spokes give a semicoloring? We will show that the color assignment is likely to cut an edge since the two endpoints of an edge are unlikely to be colored by the same spoke. More precisely, consider a graph with an n-dimensional vector k-coloring and the assignment of colors induced by t random spokes. Define $P_k(n, t)$ as the probability that two unit length vectors with a dot product bounded by $-\frac{1}{k-1}$ are colored by the same spoke. We will establish that

$$P_k(n, t) \approx t^{-\frac{k}{k-2}}.$$

Therefore, for t about $\Delta^{1-\frac{2}{k}}$ we will have that $P_k(n, t)$ is about $\frac{1}{\Delta}$. Now, proceeding as in the case of hyperplane-rounding, we can obtain a semicoloring with t colors.

How may we determine the value of $P_k(n, t)$? Clearly, this is t times the probability that both endpoints of an edge are colored by a particular spoke, say s_1. To bound the latter probability, we first note that regardless of the direction of s_1 it cannot be "near" both vectors corresponding to the edge's endpoints, since the vector coloring guarantees that these two vectors are far from each other. For example, in the case of a vector 3-coloring, any spoke must subtend an angle of at least 60° from one of the two vectors; consequently, the spoke's projection onto this vector is small, making it likely that some other spoke will have a larger projection and will prevent s_1 from coloring it.

From the preceding discussion, it should be clear that the analysis reduces to determining the probability that a spoke at a "large" angle from a given vector will color that vector. To obtain such a result, we will first derive some useful properties of the normal distribution. Then, we will show that the properties of the normal distribution allow us to reduce the analysis from the n-dimensional case to the two-dimensional one. (This ability to reduce the dimension is precisely the reason behind the choice of the multi-dimensional normal distribution to sample the spokes.) Finally, we will establish the desired bound on the probability $P_k(n, t)$ in the two-dimensional setting.

11.3.2.4   The multi-dimensional normal distribution

The *standard normal distribution* has the density function

$$\phi(x) = \frac{1}{\sqrt{2\pi}} e^{-\frac{x^2}{2}}$$

and has distribution function $\Phi(x)$, mean 0, and variance 1. A random vector $\mathbf{r} = (r_1, \ldots, r_n)$ is said to have the *n-dimensional standard normal distribution* if each component r_i is independently chosen from the standard normal distribution. Subsequently, the phrase "random d-dimensional vector" will always denote a vector chosen from the d-dimensional standard normal distribution.[3]

EXERCISE 11.5 Show that the n-dimensional standard normal distribution is spherically symmetric, in that the direction specified by the vector $\mathbf{r}$ is uniformly distributed.

Another crucial property of the normal distribution (which motivated its use in this application) is the following theorem adapted from Rényi [Ren70] (see also Section III.4 of Feller [Fel68, vol. II]).

THEOREM 11.9 Theorem IV.16.3 [Ren70] Let $\mathbf{r} = (r_1, \ldots, r_n)$ be a random n-dimensional vector. The projections of $\mathbf{r}$ onto two lines ℓ_1 and ℓ_2 are independent (and normally distributed) if and only if ℓ_1 and ℓ_2 are orthogonal.

Equivalently, we have that under any rotation of the coordinate axes, the projections of r along the axes are independent standard normal variables.[4] We employ the following corollary to the preceding theorem:

COROLLARY 11.1 Let $\mathbf{r} = (r_1, \ldots, r_n)$ be a random vector (of i.i.d. standard normal variables). Suppose we fix two orthogonal unit length vectors $\mathbf{u}_1$ and $\mathbf{u}_2$ in $\mathbf{R}^n$. The projections of $\mathbf{r}$ along these two directions, given by the dot products $\mathbf{u}_1 \cdot \mathbf{r}$ and $\mathbf{u}_2 \cdot \mathbf{r}$, are independent random variables with the standard normal distribution.

EXERCISE 11.6 Show that even if $\mathbf{r}$ is a random n-dimensional *unit* length vector, the above corollary still holds in the limit. That is, as n grows, the projections of $\mathbf{r}$ on orthogonal lines approach (scaled) independent normal distributions.

By this exercise, using random unit length vectors for spokes is equivalent to using random multi-dimensional normal vectors in the limit, but the technical details are much more difficult to handle in that case.

The assertions in the following two exercises are also useful in our analysis. The first states that the square of the length of a random vector in two dimensions has the exponential distribution with parameter $\frac{1}{2}$. The exponential distribution with parameter λ has density function $f(x) = \lambda e^{-\lambda x}$, distribution function $F(x) = 1 - e^{-\lambda x}$, and expectation $\frac{1}{\lambda}$.

---

[3]Refer to Feller [Fel68, vol. II], Knuth [Knu71, vol. 2], and Rényi [Ren70] for further details about the multi-dimensional normal distribution.

[4]As a matter of fact, the n-dimensional standard normal distribution is the *only* possible distribution with this strong spherical symmetry property.

EXERCISE 11.7   Let X and Y be independent standard normal random variables. Show that the random variable $S = X^2 + Y^2$ has the exponential distribution with parameter $\lambda = \frac{1}{2}$.

Suppose we have $r + 1$ random vectors $\mathbf{u}$ and $\mathbf{s}_1, \ldots, \mathbf{s}_r$ in two dimensions, such that each of the vectors $\mathbf{s}_i$ lies along a line obtained by rotating $\mathbf{u}$ by an angle of $\theta \leq \frac{\pi}{2}$ radians. Let $||x||$ denote the length of a vector $\mathbf{x}$. Our goal is to compute the probability that the projection of $\mathbf{u}$ along the line containing the $\mathbf{s}_i$'s is of length larger than that of any of the vectors $\mathbf{s}_i$. Let $X = \mathbf{u} \cdot \mathbf{u} = ||u||^2$, $Y_i = \mathbf{s}_i \cdot \mathbf{s}_i = ||\mathbf{s}_i||^2$, and observe that each of these random variables has the exponential distribution with parameter $\frac{1}{2}$. Since $\theta \leq \frac{\pi}{2}$ and the projection of $\mathbf{u}$ is positive, we can equivalently compute the probability of the event $\mathcal{E} = \{\frac{X}{q} \geq \max_i Y_i\}$, where $q = \frac{1}{\cos^2 \theta}$ is the ratio of the square of $\mathbf{u}$'s length to that of its projection. (For example, for $\theta = \frac{\pi}{3}$, we have $\cos\theta = \frac{1}{2}$ and $q = 4$.) Thus, $\mathcal{E} = \{X \geq q \times \max_i Y_i\}$.

EXERCISE 11.8   Let $Y_1, \ldots, Y_r$, and X independently have the exponential distribution with parameter $\lambda = \frac{1}{2}$. Show that the probability of the event $\mathcal{E}$ that $\{X \geq q \times \max_i Y_i\}$ is

$$\binom{r+q}{r}^{-1},$$

where $\binom{r+q}{r}$ is the generalized binomial coefficient when q is not necessarily an integer. (Refer to Exercise 1.2.6 (48) in Knuth [Knu71, vol. 1] for some useful related results.)

Observe that the probability bound is essentially r^{-q} for large r, where in the coloring application $q = \frac{1}{\cos^2 \omega}$ and ω is half the angle between the endpoints of an edge. For example, in the case of 3-colorings, we have $\omega = \frac{\pi}{3}$, $\cos\omega = \frac{1}{2}$, $q = 4$, and the probability bound is $\frac{1}{r^4}$.

11.3.2.5   Analyzing the improved rounding scheme

We are ready to analyze the quality of the semicoloring obtained by using the projections of the spokes to color the vertices of G. The most important part of the analysis is the bounding of the probability that for some edge $\{i, j\}$ the two endpoints i and j get the same color. Let $\mathbf{u}_i$ and $\mathbf{u}_j$ be the unit length vectors associated with the two vertices by the vector coloring. The angle between these two vectors is at least $\frac{2\pi}{3}$. The "bad" event is that the same random spoke, say $\mathbf{s}_1$, colors both $\mathbf{u}_i$ and $\mathbf{u}_j$. We show that assuming that the number of spokes is sufficiently large, this event is unlikely to occur.

Consider two unit length vectors $\mathbf{a}$ and $\mathbf{b}$ in $\mathbf{R}^n$ that subtend an angle of at least $\frac{2\pi}{3}$ (as do the vectors $\mathbf{u}_i$ and $\mathbf{u}_j$). Clearly, by the spherical symmetry of the normal distribution, our analysis for vectors $\mathbf{a}$ and $\mathbf{b}$ will apply to the vectors associated with the endpoints of any edge in the graph. The most critical part of the analysis is a reduction to a two-dimensional setting, as follows.

LEMMA 11.6   Let θ be such that $\cos\theta = -\frac{1}{k-1}$. Let $P_k(d, t)$ denote the probability of the event that, given any two vectors $\mathbf{a}, \mathbf{b} \in \mathbf{R}^d$ subtending an angle of θ, they are both colored by the same member of a collection of t random spokes in $\mathbf{R}^d$. Then, for all $d \geq 2$ and all $t \geq 1$,

$$P_k(d, t) = P_k(2, t).$$

Proof.   Denote by $H(a, b)$ the hyperplane containing the two vectors $\mathbf{a}$ and $\mathbf{b}$. Consider a rotation of the coordinate axes so that the first two axes lie in this plane, and all other axes are perpendicular to it. By Corollary 11.1, the random vectors have the property that their components along the new axes have the standard normal distribution. Further, the projection of any vector in $\mathbf{R}^d$ onto any line of this plane is determined completely by its components along the two coordinate axes lying in $H(a, b)$. That is, any event that depends only on the projection of the random vectors onto the lines in this plane is independent of the components of the vectors along the remaining $d - 2$ axes. We conclude that $P_k(d, t) = P_k(2, t)$.   ∎

By this lemma, we can now restrict ourselves to the case where all vectors belong to $\mathbf{R}^2$. We concentrate on the situation where the angle between the vectors $\mathbf{a}$ and $\mathbf{b}$ is at least $\frac{2\pi}{3}$ and bound $P_3(n, t)$, but it will be easy to see that the analysis generalizes to higher values of k as well.

THEOREM 11.10   For $0 < \epsilon < \frac{\pi}{3}$, let $p = \frac{\epsilon}{\pi}$, $\theta = \frac{\pi}{3} - \epsilon$, and $q = \frac{1}{\cos^2 \theta}$. Then,

$$P_3(n, t) = P_3(2, t) = O(t p^{q - \lceil q \rceil} (pt)^{-q}).$$

Proof.   We will only bound the probability that the spoke $\mathbf{s}_1$ colors both $\mathbf{a}$ and $\mathbf{b}$; clearly, multiplying this by t will give the desired bound. Note that a spoke must subtend an angle at least $\frac{\pi}{3}$ with respect to one of $\mathbf{a}$ and $\mathbf{b}$. Suppose that $\mathbf{s}_1$ subtends a larger angle with $\mathbf{a}$, and hence, is at least $\frac{\pi}{3}$ radians away from it. Clearly, $\mathbf{s}_1$ colors $\mathbf{a}$ only if none of the remaining $t - 1$ vectors has a larger projection onto $\mathbf{a}$. We will bound the probability of this event from above. A symmetric argument applies in the case where $\mathbf{b}$ is the vector further away from $\mathbf{s}_1$.

Denote by W the wedge-shaped region of the plane within an angle of γ from $\mathbf{a}$. Suppose that r spokes belong to this region. The only way that $\mathbf{s}_1$ will color $\mathbf{a}$ is if its projection onto $\mathbf{a}$ is larger than those of the r spokes in W. (Clearly, the projection of $\mathbf{s}_1$ onto the nearer of the two lines bounding W must be larger than the lengths of all the spokes in W; this is a necessary, but not sufficient, condition for $\mathbf{s}_1$ to color $\mathbf{a}$.) We can model the desired condition by the event $\mathcal{F}$ that the projection of $\mathbf{s}_1$ onto a line at an angle of $\theta = \frac{\pi}{3} - \gamma$ is greater than the lengths of the spokes lying in W. It suffices to bound the probability of the event $\mathcal{F}$.

If r spokes fall into the region W, then by Exercise 11.8 we have that the probability of $\mathcal{F}$ is $\binom{r + q}{r}^{-1}$, where $q = \frac{1}{\cos^2 \theta}$. Given that the random spokes have a spherically symmetric distribution, the number of these lying in W has a binomial distribution

$B(t, p)$ with $p = \frac{\gamma}{\pi}$. Consequently, we can bound the probability of $\mathcal{F}$ as follows:

$$
\begin{aligned}
P[\mathcal{F}] &= \sum_{r=0}^{t} \binom{t}{r} p^r (1-p)^{t-r} \cdot \binom{r+q}{r}^{-1} \\
&= \binom{t+q}{t}^{-1} \sum_{r=0}^{t} \binom{t+q}{t-r} p^r (1-p)^{t-r} \\
&= \binom{t+q}{t}^{-1} \sum_{u=0}^{t} \binom{t+q}{u} p^{t-u} (1-p)^{u} \\
&\leq \binom{t+q}{t}^{-1} \sum_{u=0}^{t} \binom{t+\lceil q \rceil}{u} p^{t-u} (1-p)^{u} \\
&= p^{-\lceil q \rceil} \binom{t+q}{t}^{-1} \sum_{u=0}^{t} \binom{t+\lceil q \rceil}{u} p^{t+\lceil q \rceil - u} (1-p)^{u} \\
&\leq p^{q - \lceil q \rceil} \left(p^q \binom{t+q}{t} \right)^{-1} (p + (1-p))^{t + \lceil q \rceil} \\
&= O(p^{q - \lceil q \rceil} (pt)^{-q}).
\end{aligned}
$$

In the first step of the derivation, we use an identity given in Exercise 1.2.6 (Eq. 20) of Knuth's book [Knu71, vol. 1], which applies to generalized binomial coefficients.[5] Multiplying the resulting expression by t gives the desired bound on $P_k(n, t)$. ∎

The result in this theorem is independent of the choice of γ, which determines the values of p and q. The following exercise shows how γ should be chosen so as to ensure that we get a semicoloring.

EXERCISE 11.9   Setting $\gamma = \frac{1}{\log t}$, show that $P_3(2, t) = O(t^{-3} \log^4 t)$.

Suppose we use $t = \Delta^{\frac{1}{3}} \log^{\frac{4}{3}} \Delta$ random vectors and apply the above corollary. Then, the probability that a given edge is not cut is at most $O(\frac{1}{\Delta})$. Therefore, the expected number of edges not cut is at most $O(n)$, and can be reduced below $\frac{n}{4}$ with an appropriate choice of constants. We obtain the following lemma.

LEMMA 11.7   With high probability, the vector projection method provides an $O(\Delta^{\frac{1}{3}} \log^{\frac{4}{3}} \Delta)$-semicoloring of a 3-colorable graph G with maximum degree Δ.

Applying, as before, the technique of finding an independent set of linear size and recursively coloring the remaining graph, we obtain the following result:

THEOREM 11.11   A vector 3-colorable graph G with n vertices and maximum degree Δ can be colored with $O(\Delta^{\frac{1}{3}} \log^{\frac{4}{3}} \Delta \log n)$ colors by a polynomial time randomized algorithm (with high probability).

---

[5]We need to introduce $\lceil q \rceil$ due to two problems with directly applying the binomial theorem of calculus: first, we are outside the radius of convergence of the infinite sum; and second, the infinite sum has negative terms so we cannot immediately make claims about the first few terms being less than the whole sum.

Once again, we can use Wigderson's technique (with $\Delta = \frac{n^{\frac{3}{4}}}{\log n}$) to obtain a $O(n^{\frac{1}{4}} \log n)$-semicoloring of any vector 3-colorable graph. The next result follows from an application of Exercise 11.4.

THEOREM 11.12 A vector 3-colorable graph G with n vertices can be colored with $O(n^{\frac{1}{4}} \log n)$ colors by a polynomial time randomized algorithm (with high probability).

EXERCISE 11.10 Show that the analysis of the vector projection algorithm given above is tight to within polylogarithmic factors.

It is not very difficult to generalize the above to show that for any constant χ, given a vector χ-coloring, we can color a graph of maximum degree Δ using $\Delta^{1-\frac{2}{\chi}+o(1)}$ colors. A minor modification is in the degree of separation between vectors corresponding to the endpoints of an edge. Suppose a graph is χ-colorable; then, it is vector χ-colorable, implying that we have an assignment of unit length vectors in which the vectors assigned to the endpoints of an edge have dot-product bounded by $-\frac{1}{\chi-1}$. We can apply the approach of using random spokes to round this to a vertex coloring. In the analysis, the only modification required is in determining the probability that with t random spokes, the same spoke will color both endpoints of an edge.

THEOREM 11.13 A vector χ-colorable graph can be colored using $\tilde{O}(\Delta^{1-\frac{2}{\chi}})$ or $\tilde{O}(n^{1-\frac{3}{\chi+1}})$ colors.

EXERCISE 11.11 Establish the preceding theorem using the following suggestions. Use $\theta = \frac{1}{2} \cdot \arccos(-\frac{1}{\chi-1}) - \gamma$ and deduce that the probability that an edge is cut is approximately $t^{-\frac{\chi}{\chi-2}}$, showing thereby that $\Delta^{1-\frac{2}{\chi}+o(1)}$ spokes suffice to give a semicoloring.

11.3.2.6 Relation to the Lovász theta function

The Lovász ϑ-function is the relaxation of a semidefinite programming formulation of the clique number of a graph that led to the first polynomial-time algorithm for finding the clique and chromatic numbers of *perfect* graphs [GLS81, GLS87, Lov79]. We describe a connection between ϑ and a minor variant of vector colorings.

There is a duality relationship between cliques and colorings of a graph – since intuitively it is the presence of large cliques that prevents a graph from being colored with few colors. In the case of perfect graphs, the clique number and the chromatic number are equal, and this is what enables us to compute both in polynomial time. The duality theory of linear programming has been extended to semidefinite programming (see Alizadeh [Ali95]), and it can be shown thereby that the ϑ-function and the vector chromatic number are semidefinite programming duals of one another (and hence equal).

DEFINITION 11.5 Given a graph $G = (V, E)$ on n vertices, a *strict vector k-coloring* of G is an assignment of unit length vectors $\mathbf{u_i}$ from the space $\mathbb{R}^n$ to each vertex $i \in V$, such that for any two adjacent vertices i and j the dot product of their vectors satisfies the equality, $\mathbf{u_i} \cdot \mathbf{u_j} = -\frac{1}{k-1}$. A graph is said to be strictly vector k-colorable if it has a strict vector k-coloring. The *strict vector chromatic number* of a graph is the smallest real number k for which it is strictly vector k-colorable.

It is clear that the strict vector chromatic number of a graph is at least as large as the (non-strict) vector chromatic number. Refer to Karger, Motwani, and Sudan [KMS94] for the proof of the following theorem:

THEOREM 11.14   The strict vector chromatic number of G is equal to $\vartheta(\overline{G})$.

11.3.2.7   The relaxation gap and the sandwich theorem

The performance of the randomized rounding approach is far from optimum. In this section we show that the problem is not in the randomized rounding but in the gap between the original problem and its relaxation. We consider the following question: given a vector k-colorable graph G, how large can its chromatic number be in terms of k and n? It turns out that a graph with chromatic number $n^{\Omega(1)}$ can have bounded vector chromatic number. This implies that the technique of Karger, Motwani, and Sudan [KMS94] is tight in the sense that it is not possible to guarantee a coloring with $n^{o(1)}$ colors for all vector 3-colorable graphs.

DEFINITION 11.6   The Kneser graph $K(m, r, t)$ is defined as follows: the vertices are all possible r-sets from a universe of size m; and, the vertices v_i and v_j are adjacent if and only if the corresponding r-sets satisfy $|S_i \cap S_j| < t$.

The following theorem due to Karger, Motwani, and Sudan [KMS94] establishes that the Kneser graphs have a large gap between their vector chromatic number and chromatic numbers.

THEOREM 11.15   There exists a Kneser graph $K(m, r, t)$ which is 3-vector colorable but has chromatic number exceeding $n^{0.016101}$, where $n = \binom{m}{r}$ denotes the number of vertices in the graph. Further, for large k, there exists a Kneser graph $K(m, r, t)$ which is k-vector colorable but has chromatic number exceeding $n^{0.0717845}$.

Given the equivalence of the (strict) vector chromatic number and the ϑ function, it becomes interesting to study the relationship between the ϑ function and the chromatic number of a graph. The following "sandwich theorem" was proved by Lovász [Lov79] (see also Knuth [Knu94]):

$$\omega(G) \le \vartheta(\overline{G}) \le \chi(G),$$

where $\omega(G)$ denotes the clique number of a graph G. Given that $\vartheta(\overline{G})$ can be computed in polynomial time, it is natural to wonder whether this function gives a reasonably close approximation to either the clique or the chromatic number of a graph. The following conjecture is attributed to Lovász (see Knuth [Knu94]).

There exists a constant c such that for any n-vertex graph G, $\vartheta(\overline{G}) < c\sqrt{n} \times \omega(G)$.

A similar conjecture can be formulated to relate the chromatic number to the ϑ function. It is known that the multiplicative gap between these two quantities must be roughly at least $c\sqrt{n}$ given the following observations: Lovász [Lov94] points out that for a random graph G, $\chi(G) = \frac{n}{\log n}$ while $\vartheta(\overline{G}) = \sqrt{n}$; Koniagin has demonstrated the existence of a graph which has $\chi(G) \geq \frac{n}{2}$ and $\vartheta(\overline{G}) = O(n^{\frac{2}{3}}\log n)$; Alon [Alo94] has explicit constructions matching or slightly improving both these bounds. The Kneser graph construction provides graphs with vector chromatic number at most 3 but with $\chi(G) \geq n^{\epsilon}$. In fact, Karger, Motwani, and Sudan [KMS94] provide a construction of graphs with $\vartheta(\overline{G}) \leq 3$ and $\chi(G) \geq n^{\epsilon}$. Further, Szegedy [Sze94b] has also shown that a similar construction yields graphs with vector chromatic number at most 3 but which are not colorable using $n^{0.05}$ colors. Alon [Alo94] has obtained a slight improvement over Szegedy's bound by using an interesting variant of the Kneser graph construction.

Note that none of these negative results invalidate the above conjecture or the following extended version.

There exist ϵ, $\epsilon' > 0$ such that for any graph G on n vertices,

$$\frac{\vartheta(\overline{G})}{n^{1-\epsilon}} \leq \omega(G) \leq \vartheta(\overline{G}) \leq \chi(G) \leq \vartheta(\overline{G}) \times n^{1-\epsilon'}.$$

Szegedy [Sze94a] studies various aspects of the parameter ϑ and, with respect to the second conjecture, shows that there is such an ϵ bounded away from zero if and only if there is an ϵ' bounded away from zero.

The graph coloring results presented here provide support for this conjecture by giving a (weak) upper bound on the chromatic number of G in terms of $\vartheta(\overline{G})$. Alon and Kahale [AK94] have also been able to use the semidefinite programming technique in conjunction with the techniques described above to obtain algorithms for computing bounds on the clique number of a graph with linear-sized cliques, improving upon some results due to Boppana and Halldórsson [BH92].

A recent result due to Feige [Fei95] has demonstrated that both conjectures are false. In particular, Feige uses the randomized graph product techniques of Berman and Schnitger [BS92] and Blum [Blu94] to demonstrate the existence of a family of graphs that invalidate these conjectures.

CONCLUDING REMARKS
11.4

In this section we discuss a number of issues related to the techniques and problems discussed above.

11.4.1 DERANDOMIZATION AND PARALLELIZATION

Most of the algorithms described in this chapter can be *derandomized* using standard techniques [MR95, Rag88, Spe87] to yield deterministic polynomial-time algorithms that (on every instance and on every execution) yield approximations as good as those given by the randomized algorithms they are derived from. In particular, Mahajan and Ramesh [MR95] have derandomized the semidefinite programming algorithms for MAX CUT and graph coloring. However, the process of derandomization typically takes a relatively simple and clean randomized rounding procedure and turns it into a complex and generally slower deterministic algorithm. In practice, thus, the randomized algorithm is likely to be used. At a slight loss in the approximation ratios achieved, these deterministic algorithms can be turned into parallel algorithms that use a polynomial number of processors and a polylogarithmic number of steps [BR91, MNN94]. The study of such parallel algorithms has led to a rich theory of pseudorandom numbers. It is unclear whether these derandomized sequential or parallel algorithms will have any impact on computational practice.

11.4.2   COMPUTATIONAL EXPERIENCE

The multicommodity flow algorithm of Section 11.2.1 has been applied to the problem of global wiring in gate-arrays [RT87]. Experiments have shown that for relatively small gate-arrays, the method performs well [NRT87]. For large, dense gate-arrays, the cost of solving the linear program becomes prohibitive [PR94], although the rounding remains extremely fast and fairly effective. For this problem as well as the set-balancing problem, the bounds given by Theorem 11.1 are pessimistic in comparison to what is empirically observed [DR89]. Goemans and Williamson [GW94b] report that on random graphs, the MAX CUT algorithm of Section 11.3.1 found cuts that were typically within 4% of the bound given by the semidefinite relaxation. In these experiments, they used the best of 50 roundings of the solution given by the semidefinite program solution.

11.4.3   OPEN PROBLEMS

We conclude with a set of open problems related to the techniques we have discussed. In the following list, we omit the obvious question of improving the results presented in the chapter, as well as open problems explicitly mentioned above.

Set-balancing: Devise a (deterministic or randomized) polynomial-time that will solve the set-balancing problem yielding a solution with discrepancy $o(\sqrt{n \log n})$ on every instance. Spencer [Spe85] shows that there is always a solution with discrepancy at most $6\sqrt{n}$, but his proof does not yield an efficient algorithm.

Edge-disjoint paths: We are given an undirected graph G, together with a set of source-sink pairs (s_i, t_i). We wish to find a path joining each source s_i to its sink t_i, such that the resulting paths are edge-disjoint. In the maximization version of the problem, we seek to maximize the number of source-sink pairs that can be thus connected. It is clear that this is a special case of integer multicommodity flow, but the techniques of Section 11.2 do not seem to apply here. Indeed, it is easy to construct instances on N-vertex graphs in which the ratio of the optima of the LP relaxation and the integer program is $\Omega(\sqrt{N})$.

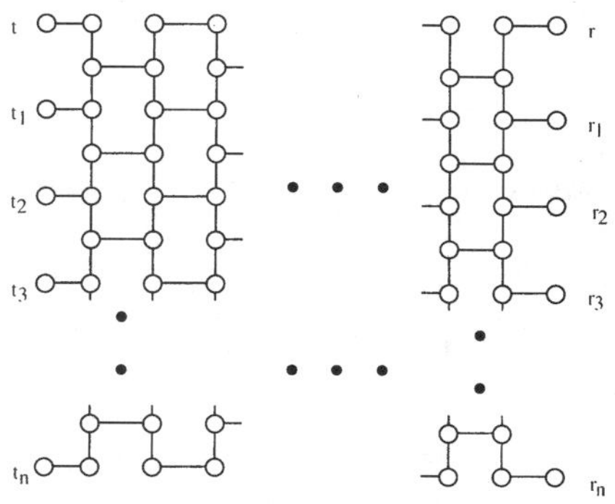

FIGURE 11.1

Example showing large integrality gap for
edge-disjoint paths.

Consider the example in Figure 11.1. Imagine that the graph shown has n layers, so that the total number of vertices $N = \Theta(n^2)$. Consider an instance in which one unit of flow of commodity i is to be shipped from r_i to t_{n-i} for $1 \le i \le n$. Clearly, this is feasible if the flows in all edges were allowed to be from the set $\{0, 0.5, 1\}$. However, by planarity only one commodity can be routed if the flows are restricted to be from the set $\{0, 1\}$.

Independent sets and vertex covers: Given an undirected graph G, a subset of its vertices is said to be *independent* if no two of them are adjacent in G. The independent set problem is to find the largest independent set in G. A *vertex cover* is a subset S of the vertices of G such that every edge is incident to at least one vertex of S. Both these problems are studied in detail in Chapter 3. The vertex cover problem seeks a vertex cover that is as small as possible. Both the independent set problem and the vertex cover problem are *NP*-hard. Given a vertex cover S for a graph G, the vertices of G *not* in S form an independent set (and vice versa). The best approximation algorithm known for the independent set problem achieves an approximation ratio of $O(\frac{n}{\log^2 n})$ [BH92]. For a summary of all known approximation results for this problem see Section 3.1. Szegedy [Sze94a] has recently applied semidefinite programming to this problem. Bellare and Sudan [BS94] give evidence that it is unlikely that the independent set problem can be approximated to within a factor better than $n^{\frac{1}{4}}$. Kleinberg and Goemans [KG95] have considered a natural semidefinite programming relaxation of vertex cover and shown that its value can be twice as bad as the optimum. It remains to be seen whether any improved results can be obtained via such methods.

Acknowledgments We wish to thank David Karger and Madhu Sudan for their help.

Rajeev Motwani was supported by an Alfred P. Sloan Research Fellowship, an IBM Faculty Development Award, NSF Grant CCR-9010517, Mitsubishi Corporation, and NSF Young Investigator Award CCR-9357849, with matching funds from IBM, Schlumberger Foundation, Shell Foundation, and Xerox Corporation.

Rajeev Motwani and Joseph Naor were supported in part by Grant No. 92-00225 from the United States-Israel Binational Science Foundation (BSF), Jerusalem, Israel.

REFERENCES

[Ali95]   F. Alizadeh. Interior point methods in semidefinite programming with applications to combinatorial optimization. *SIAM Journal on Optimization*, 5(1):13–51, 1995.

[Alo94]   N. Alon. Personal Communication, August 1994.

[AK94]   N. Alon and N. Kahale. Approximating the independence number via the Θ-function. Manuscript, November 1994.

[AS92]   N. Alon and J. Spencer. *The Probabilistic Method*. Wiley Interscience, New York, 1992.

[ALMSS92]   S. Arora, C. Lund, R. Motwani, M. Sudan, and M. Szegedy. Proof verification and hardness of approximation problems. In *Proceedings of the 33rd Annual IEEE Symposium on Foundations of Computer Science*, pages 14–23, 1992.

[AS92]   S. Arora and S. Safra. Probabilistic checking of proofs: A new characterization of NP. In *Proceedings of the 33rd Annual IEEE Symposium on Foundations of Computer Science*, pages 2–13, 1992.

[BGJR88]   F. Barahona, M. Grötschel, M. Jünger, and G. Reinelt. An application of combinatorial optimization to statistical physics and circuit layout design. *Operations Research*, 36:493–513, 1988.

[Bar96]   F. Barahona. Network design using cut inequalities. *SIAM Journal on Optimization*, to appear, 1996.

[BGLR93]   M. Bellare, S. Goldwasser, C. Lund, and A. Russell. Efficient multi-prover interactive proofs with applications to approximation problems. In *Proceedings of the 25th Annual ACM Symposium on Theory of Computing*, pages 113-131, 1993.

[BGS95]   M. Bellare, O. Goldreich, and M. Sudan. Free bits and non-approximability. In *Proceedings of the 36th Annual IEEE Symposium on Foundations of Computer Science*, pages 422-431, 1995.

[BS94]   M. Bellare and M. Sudan. Improved non-approximability results. In *Proceedings of the 26th Annual ACM Symposium on Theory of Computing*, pages 184–193, 1994.

[BR91]   B. Berger and J. Rompel. Simulating $(\log^c n)$-wise independence in NC. *Journal of the ACM*, 38:1026–1046, 1991.

[BS92]   P. Berman and G. Schnitger. On the complexity of approximating the independent set problem. *Information and Computation*, 96:77–94, 1992.

[BV94]   D. Bertsimas and R. Vohra. Linear programming relaxations, approximation algorithms and randomization: a unified view of covering problems. Technical Report OR 285-94, MIT, 1994.

[Blu94]   A. Blum. New approximation algorithms for graph coloring. *Journal of the ACM*, 41:470–516, 1994.

[BM77]   J. A. Bondy and U.S. R. Murty. *Graph Theory with Applications*. American Elsevier, 1977.

[BH92]   R.B. Boppana and M.M. Halldórsson. Approximating maximum independent sets by excluding subgraphs. *BIT*, 32:180–196, 1992.

[CY95]   J. Cheriyan and B. Yu. Approximation algorithms for feasible cut and multicut problems. In *Proceedings of the 3rd Annual European Symposium on Algorithms*, pages 394–408, 1995.

[DP93]   C. Delorme and S. Poljak. Laplacian eigenvalues and the maximum cut problem. *Mathematical Programming*, 62:557–574, 1993.

[DR89]   G.S. Ditlow and P. Raghavan. Timing-driven partitioning of PLAs. IBM Technical Disclosure Bulletin, 31, 1989.

[Fei95]   U. Feige. Randomized graph products, chromatic numbers, and the Lovász ϑ-function. In *Proceedings of the 27th Annual ACM Symposium on Theory of Computing*, pages 635–640, 1995.

[FG95]   U. Feige and M.X. Goemans. Approximating the value of two prover proof systems, with applications to MAX 2SAT and MAX DICUT. In *Proceedings of the Third Israel Symposium on the Theory of Computing and Systems*, pages 182–189, 1995.

[FGLSS91] U. Feige, S. Goldwasser, L. Lovász, S. Safra, and M. Szegedy. Approximating clique is almost *NP*-complete. In *Proceedings of the 32nd Annual IEEE Symposium on Foundations of Computer Science*, pages 2–13, 1991.

[FK94]   U. Feige and J. Kilian. Two prover protocols – low error at affordable rates. In *Proceedings of the 26th Annual ACM Symposium on Theory of Computing*, pages 172–183, 1994.

[Fel68]   William Feller. *An Introduction to Probability Theory and Its Applications*. John Wiley & Sons, New York, 1968.

[FJ95]   A. Frieze and M. Jerrum. Improved approximation algorithms for MAX k-CUT and MAX BISECTION. In *Proceedings of the 4th International Conference on Integer Programming and Combinatorial Optimization*, pages 1-9, 1995.

[Fur95]   M. Furer. Improved hardness results for approximating the chromatic number. In *Proceedings of the 36th Annual IEEE Symposium on Foundations of Computer Science*, pages 414–421, 1995.

[GK87]   S. Gao and M. Kaufmann. Channel routing of multiterminal nets. In *Proceedings of the 28th Annual IEEE Symposium on Foundations of Computer Science*, pages 316–325, 1987.

[GJ76]   M.R. Garey and D.S. Johnson. The complexity of near-optimal coloring. *Journal of the ACM*, 23:43–49, 1976.

[GVY93]   N. Garg, V.V. Vazirani, and M. Yannakakis. Approximate max-flow min-(multi) cut theorems and their applications. In *Proceedings of the 25th Annual ACM Symposium on Theory of Computing*, pages 698–707, 1993.

[GW94a]   M.X. Goemans and D.P. Williamson. New 3/4-approximation algorithms for MAX SAT. *SIAM Journal of Discrete Mathematics*, 7:656–666, 1994.

[GW94b]   M.X. Goemans and D.P. Williamson. 0.878-approximation algorithms for MAX-CUT and MAX-2SAT. In *Proceedings of the 26th Annual ACM Symposium on Theory of Computing*, pages 422–431, 1994.

[GV83]   G.H. Golub and C.F. van Loan. *Matrix Computations*. The Johns Hopkins University Press, Baltimore, MD, 1983.

[GLS81]   M. Grötschel, L. Lovász, and A. Schrijver. The ellipsoid method and its consequences in combinatorial optimization. *Combinatorica*, 1:169–197, 1981.

[GLS87]   M. Grötschel, L. Lovász, and A. Schrijver. *Geometric Algorithms and Combinatorial Optimization*. Springer-Verlag, Berlin, 1987.

[Joh74]   D.S. Johnson. Approximation algorithms for combinatorial problems. *Journal of Computer and System Sciences*, 9:256–278, 1974.

[KLS93]   S. Khanna, N. Linial, and S. Safra. On the hardness of approximating the chromatic number. In *Proceedings of the 2nd Israeli Symposium on Theory and Computing Systems*, pages 250–260, 1993.

[KMS94]   D. Karger, R. Motwani, and M. Sudan. Approximate graph coloring by semidefinite programming. In *Proceedings of the 35th Annual IEEE Symposium on Foundations of Computer Science*, pages 2–13, 1994.

[KS92]   P.N. Klein and S. Sairam. A parallel randomized approximation scheme for shortest paths. In *Proceedings of the 24th Annual ACM Symposium on Theory of Computing*, pages 750–758, 1992.

[KST90]   P.N. Klein, C. Stein, and E. Tardos. Leighton-Rao might be practical: faster approximation algorithms for concurrent flow with uniform capacities. In *Proceedings of the 22nd Annual ACM Symposium on Theory of Computing*, pages 310–321, 1990.

[KG95]   J. Kleinberg and M.X. Goemans. The Lovász theta function and a semidefinite programming relaxation of vertex cover. Manuscript, April 1995.

[Knu71]   D. E. Knuth. *The Art of Computer Programming*. Addison-Wesley, Reading, MA, 1971.

[Knu94]   D. E. Knuth. The sandwich theorem. *The Electronic Journal of Combinatorics*, 1:1–48, 1994.

[KP93]   G. Kortsarz and D. Peleg. Generating low-degree 2-spanners. Technical Report CS93-07, The Weizmann Institute of Science, 1993.

[LA87]   P.J.M. van Laarhoven and E.H.L. Aarts. *Simulated Annealing: Theory and Applications*. Mathematics and its Applications. Reidel Publishing Company, 1987.

[LV92]   J.-H. Lin and J.S. Vitter. ϵ-approximations with minimum packing constraint violation. In *Proceedings of the 24th Annual ACM Symposium on Theory of Computing*, pages 771–782, 1992.

[Lov79]   L. Lovász. On the Shannon capacity of a graph. *IEEE Transactions on Information Theory*, IT-25:1–7, 1979.

[Lov94]   L. Lovász. Personal Communication, March 1994.

[LY94]   C. Lund and M. Yannakakis. On the hardness of approximating minimization problems. *Journal of the ACM*, 41:960–981, 1994.

[MR95]   S. Mahajan and H. Ramesh, Derandomizing semidefinite programming based approximation algorithms. In *Proceedings of the 36th Annual IEEE Symposium on Foundations of Computer Science*, pages 162–169, 1995.

[MNN94]   R. Motwani, J. Naor, and M. Naor. The probabilistic method yields deterministic parallel algorithms. *Journal of Computer and System Sciences*, 49:478–516, 1994.

[MR95]   R. Motwani and P. Raghavan. *Randomized Algorithms*. Cambridge University Press, New York, 1995.

[NR95]   M. Naor and R.M. Roth. Optimal file sharing in distributed networks. *SIAM Journal on Computing*, 24:158–183, 1995.

[NT75]   G.L. Nemhauser and L.E. Trotter. Vertex Packing: Structural Properties and Algorithms. *Mathematical Programming*, 8:232–248, 1975.

[NN90]   V. Nesterov and A. Nemirovskii. Self-concordant functions and polynomial time methods in convex programming. Central Economical and Mathematical Institute, U.S.S.R. Academy of Science, Moscow, 1990.

481

[NN94]   V. Nesterov and A. Nemirovskii. *Interior-point polynomial algorithms in convex programming.* SIAM, Philadelphia, 1994.

[NRT87]   A.P-C. Ng, P. Raghavan, and C.D. Thompson. Experimental results for a linear program global router. *Computers and Artificial Intelligence*, 6(3):229–242, 1987.

[PY91]   C.H. Papadimitriou and M. Yannakakis. Optimization, approximation and complexity classes. *Journal of Computer and System Sciences*, 43:425–440, 1991.

[PST91]   S.A. Plotkin, D.B. Shmoys, and E. Tardos. Fast approximation algorithms for fractional packing and covering problems. *Mathematics of Operations Research* 20:257–301, 1995.

[PR94]   W.R. Pulleyblank and P. Raghavan. Personal communication, 1994.

[Rag88]   P. Raghavan. Probabilistic construction of deterministic algorithms: Approximating packing integer programs. *Journal of Computer and System Sciences*, 37:130–143, October 1988.

[RT87]   P. Raghavan and C.D. Thompson. Randomized rounding. *Combinatorica*, 7:365–374, 1987.

[Ren70]   A. Rényi. *Probability Theory.* Elsevier, New York, 1970.

[SG76]   S. Sahni and T. Gonzalez. *P*-complete approximation problems. *Journal of the ACM*, 23:555–565, 1976.

[SSS95]   J.P. Schmidt, A. Siegel, and A. Srinivasan. Chernoff-Hoeffding bounds for applications with limited independence. *SIAM Journal on Discrete Math*, 8:223-250, 1995.

[Sin92]   A. Sinclair. *Algorithms for Random Generation and Counting: A Markov Chain Approach.* Progress in Theoretical Computer Science. Birkhauser, Boston, 1992.

[Spe85]   J. Spencer. Six standard deviations suffice. *Transactions of the American Mathematical Society*, 289(2):679–706, June 1985.

[Spe87]   J. Spencer. *Ten Lectures on the Probabilistic Method.* SIAM, 1987.

[Sri95]   A. Srinivasan. Improved approximation guarantees for packing and covering programs. In *Proceedings of the 27th Annual ACM Symposium on Theory of Computing*, pages 268–276, 1995.

[Sri96]   A. Srinivasan. An extension of the Lovász local lemma, and its applications to integer programming. In *Proceedings of the 7th Annual ACM-SIAM Symposium on Discrete Algorithms*, 1996.

[Sze94a] M. Szegedy. A note on the θ number of Lovász and the generalized Delsarte bound. In *Proceedings of the 35th Annual IEEE Symposium on Foundations of Computer Science*, pages 36–39, 1994.

[Sze94b] M. Szegedy. Personal Communication. March 1994.

[Wig83]   A. Wigderson. Improving the performance guarantee for approximate graph coloring. *Journal of the ACM*, 30:729–735, 1983.

[Yan92]   M. Yannakakis. On the approximation of maximum satisfiability. In *Proceedings of the 3rd ACM-SIAM Symposium on Discrete Algorithms*, pages 1–9, 1992.

THE MARKOV CHAIN MONTE CARLO METHOD: AN APPROACH TO APPROXIMATE COUNTING AND INTEGRATION

Mark Jerrum   **Alistair Sinclair**

In the area of statistical physics, Monte Carlo algorithms based on Markov chain simulation have been in use for many years. The validity of these algorithms depends crucially on the rate of convergence to equilibrium of the Markov chain being simulated. Unfortunately, the classical theory of stochastic processes hardly touches on the sort of non-asymptotic analysis required in this application. As a consequence, it had previously not been possible to make useful, mathematically rigorous statements about the quality of the estimates obtained.

Within the last ten years, analytical tools have been devised with the aim of correcting this deficiency. As well as permitting the analysis of Monte Carlo algorithms for classical problems in statistical physics, the introduction of these tools has spurred the development of new approximation algorithms for a wider class of problems in combinatorial enumeration and optimization. The "Markov chain Monte Carlo" method has been applied to a variety of such problems, and often provides the only known efficient (i.e., polynomial time) solution technique.

INTRODUCTION

12.1

This chapter differs from the others in being concerned more with problems of counting and integration, and correspondingly less with optimization. The problems we address still tend to be complete, but now for the complexity class of counting problems known as #P, rather than for the more familiar class NP of decision problems. It also differs from most of the others in being centred around a general paradigm for designing approximation algorithms, rather than around a specific problem domain. We shall refer to this paradigm as the "Markov chain Monte Carlo method." It has been widely used for many years in several application areas, most notably in computational physics and combinatorial optimization. However, these algorithms have been almost entirely heuristic in nature, in the sense that no rigorous guarantees could be given for the quality of the approximate solutions they produced. Only relatively recently have analytical tools been developed that allow Markov chain Monte Carlo algorithms to be placed on a firm foundation with precise performance guarantees. This has led to an upsurge of interest in this area in computer science, and in the development of the first provably efficient approximation algorithms for several fundamental computational problems. This chapter aims to describe these new tools, and give the reader a flavor of the most significant applications.

The Markov chain Monte Carlo method provides an algorithm for the following general computational task. Let Ω be a very large (but finite) set of combinatorial structures (such as the set of possible configurations of a physical system, or the set of feasible solutions to a combinatorial optimization problem), and let π be a probability distribution on Ω. The task is to sample an element of Ω at random according to the distribution π.

In addition to their inherent interest, combinatorial sampling problems of this kind have many computational applications. The most notable of these are the following:

  I. Approximate counting: i.e., estimate the cardinality of Ω. A natural generalization is *discrete integration*, where the goal is to estimate a weighted sum of the form $\sum_{x \in \Omega} w(x)$, where w is a positive function defined on Ω.

  II. Statistical physics: here Ω is the set of configurations of a statistical mechanical system, and π is a natural probability distribution on Ω (such as the Gibbs distribution), in which the probability of a configuration is related to its energy. The task is to sample configurations according to π, in order to examine properties of a "typical" configuration and to estimate the expectations of certain natural random variables (such as the mean energy of a configuration). Computations of this kind are typically known as "Monte Carlo experiments."

  III. Combinatorial optimization: here Ω is the set of feasible solutions to an optimization problem, and π is a distribution that assigns, in some natural way, higher weight to solutions with a better objective function value. Sampling from π thus favors better solutions. An example of this approach is the popular optimization heuristic known as "simulated annealing."

In all the above applications, more or less routine statistical procedures are used to infer the desired computational information from a sequence of independent random samples from the distribution π. (This point will be illustrated by examples later in the chapter.) In algorithms of this kind, therefore, it is the sampling itself which presents the major challenge.

The Markov chain Monte Carlo method solves the sampling problem as follows. We construct a Markov chain having state space Ω and stationary distribution π. The Markov chain is designed to be *ergodic*, i.e., the probability distribution over Ω converges asymptotically to π, regardless of the initial state. Moreover, its transitions correspond to simple random perturbations of structures in Ω, and hence are simple to simulate. Now we may sample from π as follows: starting from an arbitrary state in Ω, simulate the Markov chain for some number, T, of steps, and output the final state. The ergodicity means that, by taking T large enough, we can ensure that the distribution of the output state is arbitrarily close to the desired distribution π.

In most applications it is not hard to construct a Markov chain having the above properties. What is not at all obvious, however, is how to choose the number of simulation steps T, which is the crucial factor in the running time of any algorithm that uses the chain. Of course, if the algorithm is to be efficient, then T must be very much smaller than the size of Ω; equivalently, we require that the Markov chain be close to its stationary distribution after taking a very short random walk through Ω. Loosely, we shall call a Markov chain having this property "rapidly mixing," and the number of steps required for the distribution to become close to π the "mixing time" of the chain.

In heuristic applications of the Markov chain Monte Carlo method, T is usually chosen by empirical observation of the Markov chain, or by an appeal to combinatorial or physical intuition. This means that no precise claim can be made about the distribution of the samples, so no performance guarantee can be given for the associated approximation algorithms. This observation holds for almost all existing Monte Carlo experiments in physics, and for almost all applications of simulated annealing in combinatorial optimization. It is a considerable challenge for theoretical computer science to analyze the mixing time in such applications, and hence to place these algorithms on a firm foundation.

Unfortunately, the classical theory of stochastic processes hardly touches upon the sort of non-asymptotic analysis required in this situation. In recent years, however, novel analytical tools have been developed that allow the mixing time of Markov chains of this kind to be determined quite precisely. This in turn has led to the first rigorous analysis of the running time of various approximation algorithms based on the Markov chain Monte Carlo method, as well as to the design of entirely new algorithms of this type. This chapter aims to present some of these analytical tools, and to describe their most important algorithmic applications.

The remainder of the chapter is organized as follows. Section 12.2 illustrates how the Markov chain Monte Carlo method can be applied to a combinatorial problem that is very simple to state, namely the problem of counting the number of solutions to an instance of the Knapsack problem. Section 12.3 describes two tools for bounding the mixing time of Markov chains that have proved successful in a number of applications (though not as yet in the case of the Knapsack solution counting problem). An illustration of how these tools might be applied is provided by a toy example, which is a radically simplified version of the Knapsack problem. Section 12.4 introduces a more substantial and better motivated application drawn from the field of statistical physics, namely, estimating the partition function of a monomer-dimer system. This computational problem includes, as a special case, approximately counting matchings of all sizes in a graph. Section 12.5 then catalogues various other problems to which the Markov chain Monte Carlo method has been successfully applied. The concluding Section 12.6 formulates the simulated annealing heuristic as an instance of the Markov chain Monte Carlo method, and indicates how the techniques described in Sections 12.3 and 12.4 can, in certain cases, give rigorous results on the performance of the heuristic.

AN ILLUSTRATIVE EXAMPLE

12.2

To introduce and motivate the Markov chain Monte Carlo method, consider the following problem: given $a = (a_0, \ldots, a_{n-1}) \in \mathbb{N}^n$ and $b \in \mathbb{N}$, estimate the number N of $0,1$-vectors $x \in \{0, 1\}^n$ satisfying the inequality $a \cdot x = \sum_{i=0}^{n-1} a_i x_i \le b$. If the vector a gives the sizes of n items to be packed into a knapsack of capacity b, the quantity to be estimated can be interpreted as the number of combinations of items that can be fitted into the knapsack, which we shall refer to as "Knapsack solutions." Although this problem is perhaps not of pressing practical importance, it does provide a convenient demonstration of the method. No efficient deterministic algorithm is known for accurately counting Knapsack solutions and there is convincing complexity-theoretic evidence that none exists. In this regard at least, the chosen example is more realistic than the familiar classical demonstration of the Monte Carlo method, which involves estimating π by casting a needle onto a ruled surface [Usp37].

The nature of the "convincing evidence" mentioned above is that the problem of counting Knapsack solutions is complete for Valiant's complexity class #P [GJ79, Val79b] with respect to polynomial-time Turing reductions. The class #P is the counting analogue of the more familiar class NP of decision problems. A #P-complete problem is computationally equivalent (via polynomial-time Turing reductions) to computing the number of satisfying assignments of a boolean formula in CNF, or the number of accepting computations of a polynomial-time nondeterministic Turing machine. Obviously, computing the number of accepting computations is at least as hard as deciding whether an accepting computation exists, so #P certainly contains NP. Less obviously, as Toda [Tod89] has demonstrated, #P also essentially contains the entire Meyer-Stockmeyer polynomial-time hierarchy. Thus, in structural terms, and maybe in fact, a #P-complete problem is computationally even harder than an NP-complete one [Jer94].

A classical Monte Carlo approach to solving the Knapsack problem would be based on an estimator of the following type. Select uniformly at random (u.a.r.) a vector $x \in \{0, 1\}^n$ from the corners of the n-dimensional boolean hypercube; if $a \cdot x \le b$ then return 2^n, otherwise return 0. The outcome of this experiment is a random variable whose expectation is precisely N, the value we are required to estimate. In principle, we need only perform sufficiently many trials and take the mean of the results to obtain a reliable approximation to N within any desired accuracy. In practice, the method fails badly, as we can see by taking $a = (1, \ldots, 1)$ and $b = n/3$. Note that, with these values, the expected number of trials before the first non-zero outcome is exponential in n. Thus, a sequence of trials of "reasonable" length will typically yield a mean of 0, even though the actual number of Knapsack solutions is exponentially large. Clearly, the variance of the estimator is far too large for it to be of any practical value.

Before considering other, potentially better approaches, we should pause to consider what distinguishes a good algorithm from a bad one. In the theoretical computer science tradition, we consider an efficient algorithm to be one that terminates in a number of steps that is bounded by a polynomial in the length of the input. More formally, suppose $f : \Sigma^* \to \mathbb{N}$ is a function mapping problem instances (encoded as words over some convenient alphabet Σ) to natural numbers. For example, in the case of the Knapsack problem, f might map (encodings of) the pair $a \in \mathbb{N}^n$ and $b \in \mathbb{N}$ to the number of solutions of $a \cdot x \le b$ in the set $x \in \{0, 1\}^n$. It should be clear that any combinatorial enumeration problem can be cast in this framework. A *randomized approximation scheme* for f is a randomized algorithm that takes as input a word (instance) $x \in \Sigma^n$ and $\varepsilon > 0$, and produces as output a number Y (a random variable) such that[1]

$$\Pr\big((1 - \varepsilon)f(x) \le Y \le (1 + \varepsilon)f(x)\big) \ge \tfrac{3}{4}. \tag{12.1}$$

A randomized approximation scheme is said to be *fully polynomial* [KL83] if it runs in time polynomial in n (the input length) and ε^{-1}. We shall abbreviate the rather unwieldy phrase "Fully Polynomial Randomized Approximation Scheme" to FPRAS.

The above provides a clear-cut definition of an "efficient approximation algorithm" that has at least a certain degree of intuitive appeal. The naive Monte Carlo algorithm described earlier is not efficient in the FPRAS sense, which is reassuring. On the other hand, it is certainly debatable whether an algorithm with running time n^{10} constitutes an efficient solution in anything other than a theoretical sense. In this chapter, we always use the FPRAS as our notion of efficient approximation algorithm; while this has the advantage of providing us with clear goals, it is obvious that in practical applications some more demanding notion of "efficient approximation" would be necessary.

Returning to the Knapsack problem, we might try applying the Markov chain Monte Carlo method as follows. Consider the Markov chain $\mathfrak{M}_{\mathrm{Knap}}$ with state space $\Omega = \{x \in \{0, 1\}^n : a \cdot x \le b\}$, i.e., the set of all Knapsack solutions, and transitions from each state $x = (x_0, \ldots, x_{n-1}) \in \Omega$ defined by the following rule:

I. with probability $\tfrac{1}{2}$ let $y = x$; otherwise,

II. select i u.a.r. from the range $0 \le i \le n - 1$ and let $y' = (x_0, \ldots, x_{i-1}, 1 - x_i, x_{i+1}, \ldots, x_{n-1})$;

III. if $a \cdot y' \le b$, then let $y = y'$, else let $y = x$;

the new state is y. Informally, the process $\mathfrak{M}_{\mathrm{Knap}}$ may be interpreted as a random walk (with stationary moves) on the boolean hypercube, truncated by the hyperplane $a \cdot x = b$.

---

[1]There is no significance in the constant $\tfrac{3}{4}$ appearing in the definition, beyond its lying strictly between $\tfrac{1}{2}$ and 1. Any success probability greater than $\tfrac{1}{2}$ may be boosted to $1 - \delta$ for any desired $\delta > 0$ by performing a small number of trials and taking the median of the results; the number of trials required is $O(\ln \delta^{-1})$ [JVV86].

The Markov chain $\mathfrak{M}_{\text{Knap}}$ is ergodic, since all pairs of states intercommunicate via the state $(0, \ldots, 0)$, and the presence of loops ensures aperiodicity; it is readily checked that the stationary distribution is uniform over Ω. This observation immediately suggests a procedure for selecting Knapsack solutions almost u.a.r.: starting in state $(0, \ldots, 0)$, simulate $\mathfrak{M}_{\text{Knap}}$ for sufficiently many steps that the distribution over states is "close" to uniform, then return as result the current state. Of course, sampling from Ω is not quite the same as estimating the size of Ω (which is our goal), but the second task can be related to the first using a simple trick, which we now describe.[2]

We keep the vector a fixed, but allow the bound b to vary, writing $\Omega(b)$ and $\mathfrak{M}_{\text{Knap}}(b)$ to make explicit the dependence of the Markov chain on b. Assume without loss of generality that $a_0 \leq a_1 \leq \cdots \leq a_{n-1}$, and define $b_0 = 0$ and $b_i = \min\left\{b, \sum_{j=0}^{i-1} a_j\right\}$, for $1 \leq i \leq n$. It may easily be verified that $|\Omega(b_{i-1})| \leq |\Omega(b_i)| \leq (n+1)|\Omega(b_{i-1})|$, for $1 \leq i \leq n$, the key observation being that any element of $\Omega(b_i)$ may be converted into an element of $\Omega(b_{i-1})$ by changing the rightmost 1 to a 0. Now write

$$|\Omega(b)| = |\Omega(b_n)| = \frac{|\Omega(b_n)|}{|\Omega(b_{n-1})|} \times \frac{|\Omega(b_{n-1})|}{|\Omega(b_{n-2})|} \times \cdots \times \frac{|\Omega(b_1)|}{|\Omega(b_0)|} \times |\Omega(b_0)|, \tag{12.2}$$

where, of course, $|\Omega(b_0)| = 1$. The reciprocals $\rho_i = |\Omega(b_{i-1})|/|\Omega(b_i)|$ of each of the ratios appearing in (12.2) may be estimated by sampling almost uniformly from $\Omega(b_i)$ using the Markov chain $\mathfrak{M}_{\text{Knap}}(b_i)$, and computing the fraction of the samples that lie within $\Omega(b_{i-1})$.

Consider the random variable associated with a single trial — i.e., one run of the Markov chain $\mathfrak{M}_{\text{Knap}}(b_i)$ — that is defined to be 1 if the final state is a member of $\Omega(b_{i-1})$, and 0 otherwise. If we were able to simulate $\mathfrak{M}_{\text{Knap}}(b_i)$ "to infinity," the expectation of this random variable would be precisely ρ_i. In reality, we must terminate the simulation at some point, thereby introducing a small though definite bias that ought to be accounted for. To avoid obscuring the main ideas, let us ignore this technical complication for the time being; details of this kind will be attended to when we address a more realistic example in Section 12.4. With the simplifying assumption of zero bias, the expectation of an individual trial is ρ_i, and its variance, since it is a $0,1$-variable, is $\rho_i(1 - \rho_i)$. Suppose we perform $t = 17\varepsilon^{-2}n^2$ trials, and let $\overline{X}_i$ denote the sample mean. In analyzing the efficiency of Monte Carlo estimators, the quantity to focus on is the ratio of the variance of the estimator to the square of its expectation; in this instance we have

$$\frac{\text{Var}\,\overline{X}_i}{\rho_i^2} = \frac{1 - \rho_i}{t\rho_i} \leq \frac{n}{t} = \frac{\varepsilon^2}{17n},$$

where the inequality follows from earlier-noted bound $\rho_i = |\Omega(b_{i-1})|/|\Omega(b_i)| \geq (n+1)^{-1}$.

Suppose the above process is repeated for each of the n ratios in equation (12.2), and denote by Z the random variable $Z = \overline{X}_n \overline{X}_{n-1} \ldots \overline{X}_1$ which is the product of the various sample means. Then, since the random variables $\overline{X}_i$ are independent, the expectation

---

[2]For a more detailed discussion of the problem of inferring information from observations of a Markov chain, see [Ald87, Gill93, Kah94].

of Z is $E Z = \rho_n \rho_{n-1} \ldots \rho_1 = |\Omega(b)|^{-1}$, and

$$\frac{\operatorname{Var} Z}{(E Z)^2} = \prod_{i=1}^{n} \left[1 + \frac{\operatorname{Var} \overline{X}_i}{\rho_i^2} \right] - 1 \leq \left[1 + \frac{\varepsilon^2}{17n} \right]^n - 1 \leq \frac{\varepsilon^2}{16},$$

assuming $\varepsilon \leq 1$. By Chebyshev's inequality, this implies that

$$\Pr\left((1 - \varepsilon/2)|\Omega(b)|^{-1} \leq Z \leq (1 + \varepsilon/2)|\Omega(b)|^{-1} \right) \geq \tfrac{3}{4},$$

so the random variable $Y = Z^{-1}$ satisfies (12.1), i.e., it yields a randomized approximation scheme for the number of Knapsack solutions. The idea of expressing the quantity to be estimated as a product of small factors in the style of (12.2) and then estimating each of the factors by separate Monte Carlo experiments, is one that has repeatedly proved useful in this area, since it provides a general tool for reducing approximate counting to sampling.

Observe that the total number of trials (Markov chain simulations) used is $nt = 17\varepsilon^{-2}n^3$, which is polynomial in n and ε^{-1}. The method described above is therefore an FPRAS for the number of Knapsack solutions, provided the Markov chain $\mathfrak{M}_{\text{Knap}}$ is "rapidly mixing," that is to say, is close to stationarity after a number of steps that is polynomial in n. This is a non-trivial condition, since the size of the state space Ω is exponential in n. Given the relative simplicity of the Markov chain $\mathfrak{M}_{\text{Knap}}$, it is humbling that the question of whether $\mathfrak{M}_{\text{Knap}}$ is rapidly mixing is even now unresolved. The wider question of whether there exists an FPRAS of any kind for the Knapsack problem is also unresolved, though the Markov chain simulation approach sketched above seems to offer the best hope. Using it, Dyer et al. [DFKKPV93] were able to obtain a randomized approximation scheme for the number of Knapsack solutions whose running time is $\varepsilon^{-2} \exp\left(O(\sqrt{n}\, (\log n)^{5/2}) \right)$, and this is asymptotically the fastest known.

OPEN PROBLEM 12.1   Is the Markov chain $\mathfrak{M}_{\text{knap}}$ rapidly mixing (i.e., is its mixing time bounded by a polynomial in the dimension n — see next section) for all choices of the bound b and item sizes a?

TWO TECHNIQUES FOR BOUNDING THE MIXING TIME

12.3

It will be clear from Section 12.2 that successful application of the Markov chain Monte Carlo method rests on obtaining good bounds on the time taken for a Markov chain to become close to stationarity.

There are a number of ways of quantifying "closeness" to stationarity, but they are all essentially equivalent in this application. Let $\mathfrak{M}$ be an ergodic Markov chain on state space Ω with transition probabilities $P : \Omega^2 \to [0, 1]$. Let $x \in \Omega$ be an arbitrary state, and denote by $P^t(x, \cdot)$ the distribution of the state at time t given that x is the initial state. Denote by π the stationary distribution of $\mathfrak{M}$. Then the *variation distance* at time t with respect to the initial state x is defined to be

$$\Delta_x(t) = \max_{S \subseteq \Omega} |P^t(x, S) - \pi(S)| = \frac{1}{2} \sum_{y \in \Omega} |P^t(x, y) - \pi(y)|.$$

Note that the variation distance provides a uniform bound, over all events $S \subseteq \Omega$, of the difference in probabilities of occurrence of event S under the stationary and t-step distributions. The rate of convergence of $\mathfrak{M}$ to stationarity may then be measured by the function

$$\tau_x(\varepsilon) = \min\{t : \Delta_x(t') \le \varepsilon \text{ for all } t' \ge t\},$$

which we shall refer to as the "mixing time" of the Markov chain.

The classical approach to bounding $\tau_x(\varepsilon)$ is via a "coupling" argument. This approach is very successful in the context of highly symmetric Markov chains (e.g., those associated with card shuffling [Ald81, Dia88]), but seems difficult to apply to the kind of "irregular" Markov chains that arise in the analysis of Monte Carlo algorithms. Two exceptions are the analyses of Aldous [Ald90] and Broder [Bro89] for a Markov chain on spanning trees of a graph, and of Matthews [Mat91] for a Markov chain related to linear extensions of a partial order. A glance at the latter paper will give an impression of the technical complexities that can arise.[3]

We should point out that the coupling method has very recently shown signs of staging a comeback. Jerrum [Jer95] has presented a simple application to sampling vertex colorings of a low-degree graph. Propp and Wilson [PW95] have some novel and attractive thoughts on applying coupling when the state space of the Markov chain has a natural lattice structure; their ideas are encouraging, and provide one of the ingredients in Luby, Randall, and Sinclair's [LRS95] analysis of a Markov chain on dimer coverings of certain planar (geometric) lattice graphs. Also, Bubley, Dyer, and Jerrum [BDJ96] have applied coupling to demonstrate rapid mixing of a certain random walk in a convex body, a situation we return to in Section 12.5.2. Finally, coupling has been used in a Markov chain approach to protocol testing by Mihail and Papadimitriou [MP94]. Despite this activity, it is not yet clear how far the coupling method can be pushed in the analysis of complex Markov chains.

In this section we consider two recently proposed alternatives to coupling, which tend to give weaker bounds but which are applicable in a wider range of situations. Historically [Sin93, SJ89], these two methods were not separate, but were developed together in a composite approach to bounding $\tau_x(\varepsilon)$; however, for practical purposes it is better to view them now as distinct approaches. We describe the "canonical path" argument first, and complete the section with a treatment of the "conductance" argument. For further discussion of these approaches, and various refinements of them, see, e.g., [DS91, Sin92, DSC93, Kah95].

We shall assume throughout the rest of the section that $\mathfrak{M}$ is *reversible*, that is to say, satisfies the *detailed balance* condition:

$$Q(x, y) = \pi(x)P(x, y) = \pi(y)P(y, x), \quad \text{for all } x, y \in \Omega;$$

furthermore, we assume the loop probabilities $P(x, x)$ are at least $\frac{1}{2}$ for all $x \in \Omega$. Since

---

[3]For a more direct approach to this problem, using a conductance argument as described below, see [KK90].

the Markov chain $\mathfrak{M}$ is a constructed one, it is not at all difficult to arrange that these two conditions are met.

12.3.1   CANONICAL PATHS

To describe the canonical path argument, we view $\mathfrak{M}$ as an undirected graph with vertex set Ω and edge set $E = \{\{x, y\} \in \Omega^{(2)} : Q(x, y) > 0\}$; this makes sense because of the reversibility condition. For each (ordered) pair $(x, y) \in \Omega^2$, we specify a canonical path γ_{xy} from x to y in the graph (Ω, E); the canonical path γ_{xy} corresponds to a sequence of legal transitions in $\mathfrak{M}$ that leads from initial state x to final state y. Denote by $\Gamma = \{\gamma_{xy} : x, y \in \Omega\}$ the set of all canonical paths. For the method to yield good bounds, it is important to choose a set of paths Γ that avoids the creation of "hot spots:" edges of the graph that carry a particularly heavy burden of canonical paths. The degree to which an even loading has been achieved is measured by the quantity

$$\bar{\rho} = \bar{\rho}(\Gamma) = \max_e \frac{1}{Q(e)} \sum_{\gamma_{xy} \ni e} \pi(x)\pi(y)|\gamma_{xy}|,$$

where the maximum is over oriented edges e of (Ω, E), and $|\gamma_{xy}|$ denotes the length of the path γ_{xy}.

Intuitively, we might expect a Markov chain to be rapidly mixing if it contains no "bottlenecks," i.e., if it admits a choice of paths Γ for which $\bar{\rho}(\Gamma)$ is not too large. This intuition is formalized in the following result from Sinclair [Sin92], which is a slight modification of a theorem of Diaconis and Stroock [DS91].

PROPOSITION 12.1   Let $\mathfrak{M}$ be a finite, reversible, ergodic Markov chain with loop probabilities $P(x, x) \geq \frac{1}{2}$ for all states x. Let Γ be a set of canonical paths with maximum edge loading $\bar{\rho} = \bar{\rho}(\Gamma)$. Then the mixing time of $\mathfrak{M}$ satisfies $\tau_x(\varepsilon) \leq \bar{\rho}(\ln \pi(x)^{-1} + \ln \varepsilon^{-1})$, for any choice of initial state x.[4]

Proof.   Combine Proposition 1 of [Sin92] and Theorem 5 of [Sin92].   ∎

We demonstrate the canonical path method by applying it to a radically simplified version of the Knapsack Markov chain from Section 12.2. Instead of a random walk on the truncated boolean hypercube, we consider a random walk on the the the full hypercube. This can be viewed as the degenerate case of the Knapsack Markov chain which obtains when $\sum_i a_i \leq b$, i.e., the knapsack is large enough to contain all items simultaneously.

Let $x = (x_0, x_1, \ldots, x_{n-1})$ and $y = (y_0, y_1, \ldots, y_{n-1})$ be arbitrary states in $\Omega = \{0, 1\}^n$. The canonical path γ_{xy} from x to y is composed of n edges, 0 to $n-1$, where edge i is simply $\big((y_0, \ldots, y_{i-1}, x_i, x_{i+1}, \ldots x_{n-1}), (y_0, \ldots, y_{i-1}, y_i, x_{i+1}, \ldots x_{n-1})\big)$, i.e., we flip the value of the ith bit from x_i to y_i. Note that some of the edges may be loops (if $x_i = y_i$). To compute $\bar{\rho}$, fix attention on a particular (oriented) edge

$$e = (w, w') = \big((w_0, \ldots, w_i, \ldots w_{n-1}), (w_0, \ldots, w'_i, \ldots w_{n-1})\big),$$

and consider the number of canonical paths γ_{xy} that include e. The number of possible

---

[4]This Proposition also has a suitably stated converse; see Theorem 8 of [Sin92].

choices for x is 2^i, as the final $n - i$ positions are determined by $x_j = w_j$, for $j \geq i$, and by a similar argument the number of possible choices for y is 2^{n-i-1}. Thus, the total number of canonical paths using a particular edge e is 2^{n-1}; furthermore, $Q(e) = \pi(w)P(w, w') \geq 2^{-n}(2n)^{-1}$, and the length of every canonical path is exactly n. Plugging all these bounds into the definition of $\bar{\rho}$ yields $\bar{\rho} \leq n^2$. Thus, by Proposition 12.1, the mixing time for the random walk on the boolean hypercube is $\tau_x(\varepsilon) \leq n^2((\ln 2)n + \ln \varepsilon^{-1})$. We call this Markov chain "rapidly mixing" because its mixing time grows only polynomially with the input size n (even though the size of the state space is exponential in n). The above bound is some way off the exact answer [Dia88], which is $\tau_x(\varepsilon) = O(n(\ln n + \ln \varepsilon^{-1}))$, and the slackness we see here is typical of the method.

On reviewing the canonical path argument, we perceive what appears to be a major weakness. In order to compute the key quantity $\bar{\rho}$, we needed in turn to compute quantities such as $Q(e)$ that depend crucially on the size of the state space Ω. In the hypercube example this does not present a problem, but in more interesting examples we do not know the size of the state space: indeed, our ultimate goal will often be to estimate this very quantity. Fortunately, it is possible to finesse this obstacle by implicit counting using a carefully constructed injective map. The idea will be illustrated by application to the hypercube example.

Let edge $e = (w, w')$ be as before, and denote by $\text{cp}(e) = \{(x, y) : \gamma_{xy} \ni e\}$ the set of all (endpoints of) canonical paths that use edge e. Define the map $\eta_e : \text{cp}(e) \to \Omega$ as follows: if $(x, y) = ((x_0, \ldots, x_{n-1}), (y_0, \ldots, y_{n-1})) \in \text{cp}(e)$ then

$$\eta_e(x, y) = (u_0, \ldots, u_{n-1}) = (x_0, \ldots, x_{i-1}, w_i, y_{i+1}, \ldots, y_{n-1}).$$

The crucial feature of the map η_e is that it is injective. To see this, observe that x and y may be unambiguously recovered from $(u_0, \ldots, u_{n-1}) = \eta_e(x, y)$ through the explicit expressions

$$x = (u_0, \ldots, u_{i-1}, w_i, w_{i+1}, \ldots, w_{n-1})$$

and

$$y = (w_0, \ldots, w_{i-1}, w_i', u_{i+1}, \ldots, u_{n-1}).$$

Using the injective map η_e it is possible to evaluate $\bar{\rho}$ without recourse to explicit counting. Noting[5] that $\pi(x)\pi(y) = \pi(w)\pi(\eta_e(x, y))$, we have

$$\frac{1}{Q(e)} \sum_{\gamma_{xy} \ni e} \pi(x)\pi(y)|\gamma_{xy}| = \frac{1}{\pi(w)P(w, w')} \sum_{\gamma_{xy} \ni e} \pi(w)\pi(\eta_e(x, y))|\gamma_{xy}|$$

$$= \frac{n}{P(w, w')} \sum_{\gamma_{xy} \ni e} \pi(\eta_e(x, y)) \leq \frac{n}{P(w, w')} \leq 2n^2,$$

where the penultimate inequality follows from the facts that η_e is injective, and that π is a probability distribution. Since the above argument is valid uniformly over the choice of e, we deduce $\bar{\rho} \leq 2n^2$. The factor of 2 as compared with the direct argument was lost to slight redundancy in the encoding: the map η_e was not quite a bijection.

---

[5]This is a trivial observation when the stationary distribution is uniform, as it is here, but it is sometimes possible, by judicious choice of η_e, to contrive such an identity even when the stationary distribution is non-uniform. See Section 12.4 for an example.

12.3.2   CONDUCTANCE

As advertised earlier, we now consider an alternative "conductance" approach to bounding $\tau_x(\varepsilon)$, which has proved useful in situations where the Markov chain can be given a geometric interpretation [DFK91]. The *conductance* [SJ89] of Markov chain $\mathfrak{M}$ is defined by

$$\Phi = \Phi(\mathfrak{M}) = \min_{\substack{S \subset \Omega \\ 0 < \pi(S) \le 1/2}} \frac{Q(S, \overline{S})}{\pi(S)}, \tag{12.3}$$

where $Q(S, \overline{S})$ denotes the sum of $Q(x, y)$ over edges $\{x, y\} \in E$ with $x \in S$ and $y \in \overline{S} = \Omega - S$. The conductance may be viewed as a weighted version of edge expansion of the graph (Ω, E) associated with $\mathfrak{M}$. Alternatively, the quotient appearing in (12.3) can be interpreted as the conditional probability that the chain in equilibrium escapes from the subset S of the state space in one step, given that it is initially in S; thus, Φ measures the readiness of the chain to escape from any small enough region of the state space, and hence, to make rapid progress towards equilibrium. This intuitive connection can be given a precise quantitative form as follows. (See [Ald87, Alon86, AM85, Che70, LS88] for related results.)

PROPOSITION 12.2   Let $\mathfrak{M}$ be a finite, reversible, ergodic Markov chain with loop probabilities $P(x, x) \ge \frac{1}{2}$ for all states x. Let Φ be the conductance of $\mathfrak{M}$ as defined in (12.3). Then the mixing time of $\mathfrak{M}$ satisfies $\tau_x(\varepsilon) \le 2\Phi^{-2}(\ln \pi(x)^{-1} + \ln \varepsilon^{-1})$, for any choice of initial state x.

Proof.   Combine Proposition 1 of [Sin92] and Theorem 2 of [Sin92]. ∎

From Proposition 12.2 it will be apparent that good lower bounds on conductance translate to good upper bounds on the mixing time $\tau_x(\varepsilon)$. As we shall see presently, it is possible to bound the conductance of the random walk on the hypercube by considering the geometry of the hypercube and applying an "isoperimetric inequality."

For $x \in \Omega = \{0, 1\}^n$ and $S \subseteq \Omega$, define

$$C(x) = \left\{ \xi = (\xi_0, \ldots, \xi_{n-1}) : |\xi_i - x_i| \le \tfrac{1}{2}, \text{ for all } i \right\},$$

and $C(S) = \bigcup_{x \in S} C(x)$. Observe that the mapping C provides a geometric interpretation of each set S of states as a body in n-dimensional space, and that within this interpretation the entire state space Ω is a hypercube $K = C(\Omega)$ of side 2. Each possible transition from a state in S to a state in $\overline{S}$ contributes one unit of area (i.e., $(n-1)$-dimensional volume) to $\partial C(S) - \partial K$, where ∂ denotes boundary, and each transition occurs with probability $\frac{1}{2n}$; thus,

$$Q(S, \overline{S}) = \frac{1}{2n|\Omega|} \mathrm{vol}_{n-1}(\partial C(S) - \partial K), \tag{12.4}$$

where vol_d denotes d-dimensional volume.

Intuitively, if $\mathrm{vol}_n C(S)$ is large (but less than $\frac{1}{2} \mathrm{vol}_n K$), then $\partial C(S) - \partial K$ must also be large. It is this kind of intuition that is captured and formalized in an isoperimetric inequality. Rather than working with the Euclidean norm and using a classical isoperimetric inequality, it is advantageous in this instance to work with the l_∞-norm $\|\xi\|_\infty = \max\{|\xi_0|, \ldots, |\xi_{n-1}|\}$ and its dual the l_1-norm $\|\xi\|_\infty^* = \|\xi\|_1 = |\xi_0| + \cdots + |\xi_{n-1}|$, and invoke a very refined isoperimetric inequality due to Dyer and Frieze [DF91], which holds for arbitrary norms.

Observe that $\mathrm{vol}_n\, C(S) = |S|$, $\mathrm{vol}_n\, K = 2^n$, and $\mathrm{diam}\, K = 2$, where diam denotes diameter in the l_∞-norm. From Theorem 3 of [DF91], taking F to be identically 1, we have, for $|S| \leq \frac{1}{2}|\Omega|$,

$$\frac{\mathrm{vol}_n\, C(S)}{\mathrm{vol}_{n-1}(\partial C(S) - \partial K)} \leq \tfrac{1}{2}\,\mathrm{diam}\, K;$$

it follows immediately that $\mathrm{vol}_{n-1}(\partial C(S) - \partial K) \geq |S|$. Combining this inequality with equation (12.4) yields

$$Q(S, \overline{S}) \geq \frac{|S|}{2n|\Omega|} = \frac{\pi(S)}{2n}.$$

From the definition of conductance, $\Phi \geq \frac{1}{2n}$, and hence, by Proposition 12.2, $\tau_x(\varepsilon) \leq 8n^2\big((\ln 2)n + \ln \varepsilon^{-1}\big)$. It will be seen that for this example the two bounds obtained using the conductance and canonical paths arguments differ by just a small constant factor.

A MORE COMPLEX EXAMPLE: MONOMER-DIMER SYSTEMS

12.4

In this section we describe a significant computational problem to which the Markov chain Monte Carlo method has been successfully applied to yield an efficient approximation algorithm, or FPRAS. (This is in contrast to the Knapsack problem discussed in Section 12.2, which is still open.) Moreover, the Markov chain Monte Carlo method is to date the *only* approach that yields a provably efficient algorithm for this problem. This application will illustrate the full power of the analysis techniques described in the previous section. Our presentation is an improved version of one we originally gave in [JS89, Sin93].

The problem in question is a classical one from statistical physics, known as the *monomer-dimer problem*. In a monomer-dimer system, the vertices of a finite undirected graph $G = (V, E)$ are covered by a non-overlapping arrangement, or *configuration* of monomers (molecules occupying one site, or vertex of G) and dimers (molecules occupying two vertices that are neighbors in G). Typically, G is a regular lattice in some fixed number of dimensions. Three-dimensional systems occur classically in the theory of mixtures of molecules of different sizes [Gugg52] and in the cell-cluster theory of the liquid state [CdBS55]; in two dimensions, the system is used to model the adsorption of diatomic molecules on a crystal surface [Rob35]. For a more detailed account of the history and significance of monomer-dimer systems, the reader is referred to the seminal paper of Heilmann and Lieb [HL72] and the references given there.

It is convenient to identify monomer-dimer configurations with matchings in the graph G; a *matching* in G is a subset $M \subseteq E$ such that no two edges in M share an endpoint. Thus, a matching of cardinality k, or a k-*matching*, corresponds precisely to a monomer-dimer configuration with k dimers and $2(n - k)$ monomers, where $2n = |V|$ is the number of vertices in G.[6] To each matching M, a *weight* $w(M) = \lambda^{|M|}$ is assigned, where λ is a positive real parameter that reflects the contribution of a dimer to the energy of the system. The *partition function* of the system is defined as

$$Z(\lambda) \equiv Z_G(\lambda) = \sum_M w(M) = \sum_{k=0}^{n} m_k \lambda^k, \qquad (12.5)$$

where $m_k \equiv m_k(G)$ is the number of k-matchings in G (or equivalently, the number of monomer-dimer configurations with k dimers). For a physical interpretation of (12.5), see [HL72].[7]

The partition function is a central quantity in statistical physics, and captures essentially everything one needs to know about the thermodynamics of the system, including quantities such as the free energy and the specific heat, and the location of phase transitions. With this in mind, in the remainder of this section we will develop an algorithm for computing Z_G at an arbitrary point $\lambda \geq 0$. We should also point out that $Z_G(\lambda)$ is of independent combinatorial interest, being nothing other than the generating function for matchings, or *matching polynomial* of G [LP86]. Thus, for example, $Z_G(1)$ enumerates all matchings in G, and the coefficient m_k enumerates matchings of cardinality k. We shall have more to say about these connections in Section 12.5.1.

Our starting point is the observation that no feasible method is known for computing Z *exactly* for general monomer-dimer systems; indeed, for any fixed value of $\lambda > 0$, the problem of computing $Z_G(\lambda)$ exactly for a given graph G is complete for the class #P of enumeration problems, which, as we explained in Section 12.2, may be regarded as convincing evidence that no polynomial time exact algorithm can exist for this problem [Val79b].[8] It is therefore pertinent to ask whether there exists an FPRAS for this problem. In this context, by an FPRAS we mean an algorithm which, given a pair (G, λ), and a parameter $\varepsilon > 0$, outputs a number Y such that

$$\Pr\big((1 - \varepsilon)Z_G(\lambda) \leq Y \leq (1 + \varepsilon)Z_G(\lambda)\big) \geq \tfrac{3}{4},$$

and runs in time polynomial in n and $\lambda' = \max\{1, \lambda\}$.[9]

---

[6]The assumption that the number of vertices in G is even is inessential and is made for notational convenience.

[7]More generally, there may be a weight λ_e associated with each edge $e \in E$, and the weight of M is then $w(M) = \prod_{e \in M} \lambda_e$. The algorithm we present here extends in a straightforward fashion to this more general setting.

[8]An efficient algorithm *does* exist for computing the leading coefficient m_n exactly, provided the graph G is planar. This quantity has an interpretation as the partition function of a system of *hard dimers*, in which no monomers are permitted. This algorithm, due independently to Fisher, Kasteleyn, and Temperley [Fish61, Kast61, TF61] in 1961, is a landmark achievement in the design of combinatorial algorithms. Unfortunately, it does not seem to extend either to non-planar graphs or to other coefficients.

[9]By analogy with the definition given in Section 12.2, this assumes that the edge weight λ is presented in unary. Thus, if the running time of the algorithm is to be polynomial in the size of the system, n, then the edge weight λ must be polynomially bounded in n. This is not a severe restriction in practice when computing the partition function.

For a given graph G, we will construct an FPRAS for Z_G by Monte Carlo simulation of a suitable Markov chain $\mathfrak{M}_{\text{match}}(\lambda)$, parameterized on the edge weight λ. The state space, Ω, is the set of all matchings in G, and the transitions are constructed so that the chain is ergodic with stationary distribution π_λ given by

$$\pi_\lambda(M) = \frac{\lambda^{|M|}}{Z(\lambda)}. \tag{12.6}$$

(Since G is fixed from now on, we drop the subscript from Z.) In other words, the stationary probability of each matching (monomer-dimer configuration) is proportional to its weight in the partition function (12.5). The Markov chain $\mathfrak{M}_{\text{match}}(\lambda)$, if simulated for sufficiently many steps, provides a method of sampling matchings from the distribution π_λ.

Distributions of this form are natural in statistical physics and are usually referred to as *canonical* or *Gibbs* distributions. Note that an alternative interpretation of the partition function is as the normalizing factor in this distribution. Sampling from this distribution at various values of λ has many applications, such as estimating the expectation of certain natural quantities associated with a configuration (e.g., the mean number of monomers, or the mean distance between a pair of monomers in a dense configuration of dimers). As we shall see shortly, it also allows one to approximate the partition function itself.

It is not hard to construct a Markov chain $\mathfrak{M}_{\text{match}}(\lambda)$ with the right asymptotic properties. Consider the chain in which transitions from any matching M are made according to the following rule:

I. with probability $\frac{1}{2}$ let $M' = M$; otherwise,

II. select an edge $e = \{u, v\} \in E$ u.a.r. and set

$$M' = \begin{cases} M - e & \text{if } e \in M; \\ M + e & \text{if both } u \text{ and } v \text{ are unmatched in } M; \\ M + e - e' & \text{if exactly one of } u \text{ and } v \text{ is matched in } M \\ & \quad \text{and } e' \text{ is the matching edge}; \\ M & \text{otherwise}; \end{cases}$$

III. go to M' with probability $\min\{1, \pi_\lambda(M')/\pi_\lambda(M)\}$.

It is helpful to view this chain as follows. There is an underlying graph defined on the set of matchings Ω in which the neighbors of matching M are all matchings M' that differ from M via one of the following local perturbations: an edge is removed from M (a *type 1* transition); an edge is added to M (a *type 2* transition); or a new edge is exchanged with an edge in M (a *type 0* transition). Transitions from M are made by first selecting a neighbor M' u.a.r., and then actually making, or *accepting* the transition with probability $\min\{1, \pi_\lambda(M')/\pi_\lambda(M)\}$. Note that the ratio appearing in this expression is easy to compute: it is just λ^{-1}, λ or 1 respectively, according to the type of the transition.

As the reader may easily verify, this acceptance probability is constructed so that the transition probabilities $P(M, M')$ satisfy the detailed balance condition

$$Q(M, M') = \pi_\lambda(M)P(M, M') = \pi_\lambda(M')P(M', M), \quad \text{for all } M, M' \in \Omega,$$

i.e., $\mathfrak{M}_{\text{match}}(\lambda)$ is reversible with respect to the distribution π_λ. This fact, together with the observation that $\mathfrak{M}_{\text{match}}(\lambda)$ is irreducible (i.e., all states communicate, for example via the empty matching) and aperiodic (by step 1, the self-loop probabilities $P(M, M)$

are all non-zero), ensures that $\mathfrak{M}_{\text{match}}(\lambda)$ is ergodic with stationary distribution π_λ, as required.[10]

Having constructed a family of Markov chains with stationary distribution π_λ, our next task is to explain how samples from this distribution can be used to obtain a reliable statistical estimate of $Z(\lambda)$ at a specified point $\lambda = \widehat{\lambda} \geq 0$. Our strategy is to express $Z(\widehat{\lambda})$ as the product

$$Z(\widehat{\lambda}) = \frac{Z(\lambda_r)}{Z(\lambda_{r-1})} \times \frac{Z(\lambda_{r-1})}{Z(\lambda_{r-2})} \times \cdots \frac{Z(\lambda_2)}{Z(\lambda_1)} \frac{Z(\lambda_1)}{Z(\lambda_0)} \times Z(\lambda_0), \qquad (12.7)$$

where $0 = \lambda_0 < \lambda_1 < \lambda_2 < \cdots < \lambda_{r-1} < \lambda_r = \widehat{\lambda}$ is a suitably chosen sequence of values. Note that $Z(\lambda_0) = Z(0) = 1$. We will then estimate each factor $Z(\lambda_i)/Z(\lambda_{i-1})$ in this product by sampling from the distribution π_{λ_i}. This approach is analogous to that described in Section 12.2 for the Knapsack problem (see Equation (12.2)). For reasons that will become clear shortly, we will use the sequence of values $\lambda_1 = |E|^{-1}$ and $\lambda_i = (1 + \frac{1}{n})^{i-1}\lambda_1$ for $1 \leq i < r$. The length r of the sequence is taken to be minimal such that $(1 + \frac{1}{n})^{r-1}\lambda_1 \geq \widehat{\lambda}$, so we have the bound

$$r \leq \lceil 2n(\ln\widehat{\lambda} + \ln|E|) \rceil + 1. \qquad (12.8)$$

To estimate the ratio $Z(\lambda_i)/Z(\lambda_{i-1})$, we will express it, or rather its reciprocal, as the expectation of a suitable random variable. Specifically, define the random variable $f_i(M) = \left(\frac{\lambda_{i-1}}{\lambda_i}\right)^{|M|}$, where M is a matching chosen from the distribution π_{λ_i}. Then we have

$$\mathrm{E}\,f_i = \sum_M \left(\frac{\lambda_{i-1}}{\lambda_i}\right)^{|M|} \frac{\lambda_i^{|M|}}{Z(\lambda_i)} = \frac{1}{Z(\lambda_i)} \sum_M \lambda_{i-1}^{|M|} = \frac{Z(\lambda_{i-1})}{Z(\lambda_i)}.$$

Thus, the ratio $\rho_i = Z(\lambda_{i-1})/Z(\lambda_i)$ can be estimated by sampling matchings from the distribution π_{λ_i} and computing the sample mean of f_i. Following (12.7), our estimator of $Z(\widehat{\lambda})$ will be the product of the reciprocals of these estimated ratios. Summarizing this discussion, our algorithm can be written down as follows:

ALGORITHM $\mathcal{A}$

Step 1: Compute the sequence $\lambda_1 = |E|^{-1}$ and $\lambda_i = \left(1 + \frac{1}{n}\right)^{i-1}\lambda_1$ for $1 \leq i < r$, where r is the least integer such that $\left(1 + \frac{1}{n}\right)^{r-1}\lambda_1 \geq \widehat{\lambda}$. Set $\lambda_0 = 0$ and $\lambda_r = \widehat{\lambda}$.

Step 2: For each value $\lambda = \lambda_1, \lambda_2, \ldots, \lambda_r$ in turn, compute an estimate X_i of the ratio ρ_i as follows:

  (a) by performing S independent simulations of the Markov chain $\mathfrak{M}_{\text{match}}(\lambda_i)$, each of length T_i, obtain an independent sample of size S from (close to) the distribution π_{λ_i};

---

[10]The device of performing random walk on a connected graph with acceptance probabilities of this form is well known in Monte Carlo physics under the name of the "Metropolis process" [Met53]. Clearly, it can be used to achieve any desired stationary distribution π for which the ratio $\pi(u)/\pi(v)$ for neighbors u, v can be computed easily. It is also the standard mechanism used in combinatorial optimization by simulated annealing: see Section 12.6.

(b) let X_i be the sample mean of the quantity $\left(\frac{\lambda_{i-1}}{\lambda_i}\right)^{|M|}$.

Step 3:   Output the product $Y = \prod_{i=1}^{r} X_i^{-1}$.

To complete the description of the algorithm, we need to specify the sample size S in Step 2, and the number of simulation steps T_i required for each sample. Our goal is to show that, with suitable values for these quantities, Algorithm $\mathcal{A}$ is an FPRAS for $Z(\lambda)$.

The issue of the sample size S is straightforward. Using elementary statistical calculations, we can show the following:

PROPOSITION 12.3   In Algorithm $\mathcal{A}$, suppose the sample size S in Step 2 is $S = \lceil 130e\varepsilon^{-2}r \rceil$, and that the simulation length T_i is large enough that the variation distance of $\mathfrak{M}_{\text{match}}(\lambda_i)$ from its stationary distribution π_{λ_i} is at most $\varepsilon/5er$. Then the output random variable Y satisfies

$$\Pr\left((1-\varepsilon)Z(\widehat{\lambda}) \leq Y \leq (1+\varepsilon)Z(\widehat{\lambda})\right) \geq \tfrac{3}{4}.$$

Since r is a relatively small quantity (essentially linear in n: see (12.8)), this result means that a modest sample size at each stage suffices to ensure a good final estimate Y, provided of course that the samples come from a distribution that is close enough to π_{λ_i}.

It is in determining the number of simulation steps, T_i, required to achieve this that the meat of the analysis lies: of course, this is tantamount to investigating the mixing time of the Markov chain $\mathfrak{M}_{\text{match}}(\lambda_i)$. Our main task in this section will be to show:

PROPOSITION 12.4   The mixing time of the Markov chain $\mathfrak{M}_{\text{match}}(\lambda)$ satisfies

$$\tau_X(\varepsilon) \leq 4|E|n\lambda'\left(n(\ln n + \ln \lambda') + \ln \varepsilon^{-1}\right).$$

The proof of this result will make use of the full power of the machinery introduced in Section 12.3. Note that Proposition 12.4 is a very strong statement: it says that we can sample from (close to) the complex distribution π_λ over the exponentially large space of matchings in G, by performing a Markov chain simulation of length only a low-degree polynomial in the size of G.[11]

According to Proposition 12.3, we require a variation distance of $\varepsilon/5er$, so Proposition 12.4 tells us that it suffices to take

$$T_i = \lceil 4|E|n\lambda_i'\left(n(\ln n + \ln \lambda_i') + \ln(5er/\varepsilon)\right) \rceil. \tag{12.9}$$

This concludes our specification of the Algorithm $\mathcal{A}$.

Before proceeding to prove the above statements, let us convince ourselves that together they imply that Algorithm $\mathcal{A}$ is an FPRAS for $Z(\lambda)$. First of all, Proposition 12.3 ensures that the output of Algorithm $\mathcal{A}$ satisfies the requirements of an FPRAS for Z. It remains only to verify that the running time is bounded by a polynomial in $n, \widehat{\lambda}'$, and ε^{-1}. Evidently, the running time is dominated by the number of Markov chain simulations

---

[11]Incidentally, we should point out that Proposition 12.4 immediately tells us that we can sample monomer-dimer configurations from the canonical distribution π_λ, in time polynomial in n and λ'. This is in itself an interesting result, and allows estimation of the expectation of many quantities associated with monomer-dimer configurations.

steps, which is $\sum_{i=1}^{r} ST_i$; since T_i increases with i, this is at most rST_r. Substituting the upper bound for r from (12.8), and values for S from Proposition 12.3 and T_r from (12.9), we see that the overall running time of Algorithm $\mathcal{A}$ is bounded by[12]

$$O\left(n^4 |E|\widehat{\lambda}'(\ln n\widehat{\lambda}')^3 \varepsilon^{-2}\right),$$

which grows only polynomially with n, $\widehat{\lambda}'$ and ε^{-1}. We have therefore proved

THEOREM 12.1   Algorithm $\mathcal{A}$ is an FPRAS for the partition function of an arbitrary monomer-dimer system.

We return now to prove Proposition 12.3 and Proposition 12.4. The first of these can be dispensed with quickly. It rests on the standard observation that the sample size S required at each value $\lambda = \lambda_i$ to ensure that our final estimate is good with high probability depends on the *variances* of the random variables f_i, or more precisely on the quantities $(\text{Var } f_i)/(\text{E } f_i)^2$. Intuitively, if these quantities are not too large, a small sample will suffice. Since f_i takes values in the range $[0, 1]$, it is clear that $\text{Var } f_i \leq \text{E } f_i = \rho_i$, so that $(\text{Var } f_i)/(\text{E } f_i)^2 \leq \rho_i^{-1}$. Now, from the definition of Z and λ_i we have for $1 \leq i \leq r$,

$$\rho_i^{-1} = \frac{Z(\lambda_i)}{Z(\lambda_{i-1})} = \frac{\sum_k m_k \lambda_i^k}{\sum_k m_k \lambda_{i-1}^k} \leq \left(\frac{\lambda_i}{\lambda_{i-1}}\right)^n \leq \left(1 + \frac{1}{n}\right)^n \leq e. \tag{12.10}$$

Also, it is easy to see (using the fact that matchings are subsets of E) that $Z(|E|^{-1}) \leq e$, so (12.10) holds for $i = 0$ also. Thus, we have $(\text{Var } f_i)/(\text{E } f_i)^2 \leq e$ for all i. This explains our choice of values for the λ_i.

Armed with this bound on the variances of the f_i, one can prove Proposition 12.3 by a routine statistical calculation. The details are unedifying and are deferred to the Appendix.

We turn now to the more challenging question of proving Proposition 12.4. Our strategy will be to carefully choose a collection of canonical paths $\Gamma = \{\gamma_{XY} : X, Y \in \Omega\}$ in the Markov chain $\mathfrak{M}_{\text{match}}(\lambda)$ for which the "bottleneck" measure $\bar{\rho}(\Gamma)$ of Section 12.3 is small. We can then appeal to Proposition 12.1 to bound the mixing time. Specifically, we shall show that our paths satisfy

$$\bar{\rho}(\Gamma) \leq 4|E|n\lambda'. \tag{12.11}$$

Since the number of matchings in G is certainly bounded above by $(2n)!$, the stationary probability $\pi_\lambda(X)$ of any matching X is bounded below by $\pi_\lambda(X) \geq 1/(2n)!\lambda'^n$. Using (12.11) and the fact that $\ln n! \leq n \ln n$, the bound on the mixing time in Proposition 12.4 can now be read off Proposition 12.1.

It remains for us to find a set of canonical paths Γ satisfying (12.11). For a pair of matchings X, Y in G, we define the canonical path γ_{XY} as follows. Consider the symmetric difference $X \oplus Y$. A moment's reflection should convince the reader that this consists of a disjoint collection of paths in G (some of which may be closed cycles),

---

[12]In deriving the O-expression, we have assumed w.l.o.g. that $T_r = O\left(|E|n^2\widehat{\lambda}' \ln n\widehat{\lambda}'\right)$. This follows from (12.9) with the additional assumption that $\ln \varepsilon^{-1} = O(n \ln n)$. This latter assumption is justified since the problem can always be solved exactly by exhaustive enumeration in time $O(n(2n)!)$, which is $O(\varepsilon^{-2})$ if $\ln \varepsilon^{-1}$ exceeds the above bound.

each of which has edges that belong alternately to X and to Y. Now suppose that we have fixed some arbitrary ordering on all simple paths in G, and designated in each of them a so-called "start vertex," which is arbitrary if the path is a closed cycle but must be an endpoint otherwise. This ordering induces a unique ordering $P_1, P_2, \ldots, P_m$ on the paths appearing in $X \oplus Y$. The canonical path from X to Y involves "unwinding" each of the P_i in turn as follows. There are two cases to consider:

(i) P_i *is not a cycle.* Let P_i consist of the sequence $(v_0, v_1, \ldots, v_l)$ of vertices, with v_0 the start vertex. If $(v_0, v_1) \in Y$, perform a sequence of type 0 transitions replacing (v_{2j+1}, v_{2j+2}) by (v_{2j}, v_{2j+1}) for $j = 0, 1, \ldots$, and finish with a single type 2 transition if l is odd. If on the other hand $(v_0, v_1) \in X$, begin with a type 1 transition removing (v_0, v_1) and proceed as before for the reduced path $(v_1, \ldots, v_l)$.

(ii) P_i *is a cycle.* Let P_i consist of the sequence $(v_0, v_1, \ldots, v_{2l+1})$ of vertices, where $l \geq 1$, v_0 is the start vertex, and $(v_{2j}, v_{2j+1}) \in X$ for $0 \leq j \leq l$, the remaining edges belonging to Y. Then the unwinding begins with a type 1 transition to remove (v_0, v_1). We are left with an open path O with endpoints v_0, v_1, one of which must be the start vertex of O. Suppose v_k, $k \in \{0, 1\}$, is *not* the start vertex. Then we unwind O as in (i) above but treating v_k as the start vertex. This trick serves to distinguish paths from cycles, as will prove convenient shortly.

This concludes our definition of the family of canonical paths Γ. Figure 12.1 will help the reader picture a typical transition t on a canonical path from X to Y. The path P_i (which happens to be a cycle) is the one currently being unwound; the paths $P_1, \ldots, P_{i-1}$ to the left have already been processed, while the ones $P_{i+1}, \ldots, P_m$ are yet to be dealt with.

We now proceed to bound the "bottleneck" measure $\bar{\rho}(\Gamma)$ for these paths, using the injective mapping technology introduced in Section 12.3. Let t be an arbitrary edge in the Markov chain, i.e., a transition from M to $M' \neq M$, and let $\mathrm{cp}(t) = \{(X, Y) : \gamma_{XY} \ni t\}$ denote the set of all canonical paths that use t. (We use the notation t in place of e here to avoid confusion with edges of G.) Just as in Section 12.3, we shall obtain a bound on the total weight of all paths that pass through t by defining an injective mapping $\eta_t : \mathrm{cp}(t) \rightarrow \Omega$. By analogy with the hypercube example in Section 12.3, what we would like to do is to set $\eta_t(X, Y) = X \oplus Y \oplus (M \cup M')$; the intuition for this is that $\eta_t(X, Y)$ should agree with X on paths that have already been unwound, and with Y on paths that have not yet been unwound (just as $\eta_e(x, y)$ agreed with x on positions $1, \ldots, i-1$ and with y on positions $i+1, \ldots, n-1$). However, there is a minor complication concerning the path that we are currently processing: in order to ensure that $\eta_t(X, Y)$ is indeed a matching, we may — as we shall see — have to remove from it the edge of X adjacent to the start vertex of the path currently being unwound: we shall call this edge e_{XYt}. This leads us to the following definition of the mapping η_t:

$$\eta_t(X, Y) = \begin{cases} X \oplus Y \oplus (M \cup M') - e_{XYt}, & \text{if } t \text{ is type 0 and the} \\ & \text{current path is a cycle;} \\ X \oplus Y \oplus (M \cup M'), & \text{otherwise.} \end{cases}$$

Figure 12.2 illustrates the encoding $\eta_t(X, Y)$ that would result from the transition t on the canonical path sketched in Figure 12.1.

Let us check that $\eta_t(X, Y)$ is always a matching. To see this, consider the set of edges $A = X \oplus Y \oplus (M \cup M')$, and suppose that some vertex, u say, has degree two in A. (Since $A \subseteq X \cup Y$, no vertex degree can exceed two.) Then, A contains edges $\{u, v_1\}, \{u, v_2\}$ for

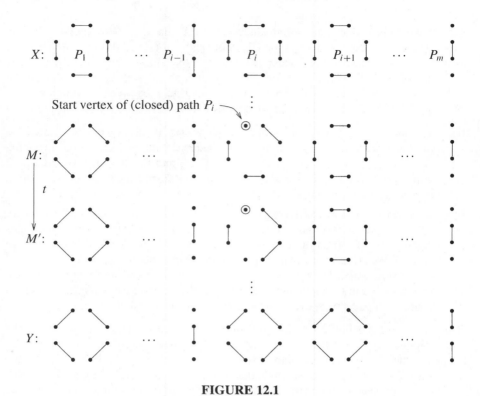

FIGURE 12.1

A transition t in the canonical path from X to Y.

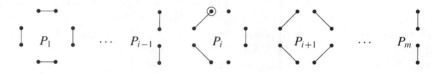

FIGURE 12.2

The corresponding encoding $\eta_t(X, Y)$.

distinct vertices v_1, v_2, and since $A \subseteq X \cup Y$, one of these edges must belong to X and the other to Y. Hence, both edges belong to $X \oplus Y$, which means that neither can belong to $M \cup M'$. Following the form of $M \cup M'$ along the canonical path, however, it is clear that there can be at most one such vertex u; moreover, this happens precisely when the current path is a cycle, u is its start vertex, and t is type 0. Our definition of η_t removes one of the edges adjacent to u in this case, so all vertices in $\eta_t(X, Y)$ have degree at most one, i.e., $\eta_t(X, Y)$ is indeed a matching.

We now have to check that η_t is injective. It is immediate from the definition of η_t

that the symmetric difference $X \oplus Y$ can be recovered from $\eta_t(X, Y)$ using the relation

$$X \oplus Y = \begin{cases} \eta_t(X, Y) \oplus (M \cup M') + e_{XYt}, & \text{if } t \text{ is type 0 and the} \\ & \text{current path is a cycle;} \\ \eta_t(X, Y) \oplus (M \cup M'), & \text{otherwise.} \end{cases}$$

Note that, once we have formed the set $\eta_t(X, Y) \oplus (M \cup M')$, it will be apparent whether the current path is a cycle from the sense of unwinding. (Note that e_{XYt} is the unique edge that forms a cycle when added to the path.) Given $X \oplus Y$, we can at once infer the sequence of paths $P_1, P_2, \ldots, P_m$ that have to be unwound along the canonical path from X to Y, and the transition t tells us which of these, P_i say, is the path currently being unwound. The partition of $X \oplus Y$ into X and Y is now straightforward: X has the same parity as $\eta_t(X, Y)$ on paths $P_1, \ldots, P_{i-1}$, and the same parity as M on paths $P_{i+1}, \ldots, P_m$. Finally, the reconstruction of X and Y is completed by noting that $X \cap Y = M - (X \oplus Y)$, which is immediate from the definition of the paths. Hence, X and Y can be uniquely recovered from $\eta_t(X, Y)$, so η_t is injective.

We are almost done. However, the fact that η_t is injective is not sufficient in this case because, in contrast to the hypercube example, the stationary distribution π_λ is highly non-uniform. What we require in addition is that η_t be "weight-preserving," in the sense that $Q(t)\pi_\lambda(\eta_t(X, Y)) \approx \pi_\lambda(X)\pi_\lambda(Y)$. More precisely, we will show in a moment that

$$\pi_\lambda(X)\pi_\lambda(Y) \le 2|E|\lambda'^2 Q(t)\pi_\lambda(\eta_t(X, Y)). \tag{12.12}$$

First, let us see why we need a bound of this form in order to estimate $\bar{\rho}$. We have

$$\frac{1}{Q(t)} \sum_{\gamma_{XY} \ni t} \pi_\lambda(X)\pi_\lambda(Y)|\gamma_{XY}| \le 2|E|\lambda'^2 \sum_{\gamma_{XY} \ni t} \pi_\lambda(\eta_t(X, Y)) |\gamma_{XY}|$$

$$\le 4|E|n\lambda'^2 \sum_{\gamma_{XY} \ni t} \pi_\lambda(\eta_t(X, Y))$$

$$\le 4|E|n\lambda'^2, \tag{12.13}$$

where the second inequality follows from the fact that the length of any canonical path is bounded by $2n$, and the last inequality from the facts that η_t is injective and π_λ is a probability distribution.

It remains for us to prove inequality (12.12). Before we do so, it is helpful to notice that $Q(t) = (2|E|)^{-1} \min\{\pi_\lambda(M), \pi_\lambda(M')\}$, as may easily be verified from the definition of $\mathfrak{M}_{\text{match}}(\lambda)$. We now distinguish four cases:

(i) *t is a type 1 transition.* Suppose $M' = M - e$. Then $\eta_t(X, Y) = X \oplus Y \oplus M$, so, viewed as multisets, $M \cup \eta_t(X, Y)$ and $X \cup Y$ are identical. Hence, we have

$$\pi_\lambda(X)\pi_\lambda(Y) = \pi_\lambda(M)\pi_\lambda(\eta_t(X, Y))$$

$$= \frac{2|E|Q(t)}{\min\{\pi_\lambda(M), \pi_\lambda(M')\}} \times \pi_\lambda(M)\pi_\lambda(\eta_t(X, Y))$$

$$= 2|E|Q(t) \max\{1, \pi_\lambda(M)/\pi_\lambda(M')\}\pi_\lambda(M)\pi_\lambda(\eta_t(X, Y))$$

$$\le 2|E|\lambda' Q(t)\pi_\lambda(\eta_t(X, Y)),$$

from which (12.12) follows.

(ii)   *t is a type 2 transition.* This is handled by a symmetrical argument to (i) above, with the roles of M and M' interchanged.

(iii)   *t is a type 0 transition and the current path is a cycle.* Suppose $M' = M + e - e'$, and consider the multiset $M \cup \eta_t(X, Y)$. Then, $\eta_t(X, Y) = X \oplus Y \oplus (M + e) - e_{XY_t}$, so the multiset $M \cup \eta_t(X, Y)$ differs from $X \cup Y$ only in that e and e_{XY_t} are missing from it. Thus, we have

$$\pi_\lambda(X)\pi_\lambda(Y) \leq \lambda'^2 \pi_\lambda(M)\pi_\lambda(\eta_t(X, Y))$$

$$= 2|E|\lambda'^2 Q(t)\pi_\lambda(\eta_t(X, Y)),$$

since in this case $\pi_\lambda(M) = \pi_\lambda(M')$, and so $Q(t) = (2|E|)^{-1}\pi_\lambda(M)$. Therefore, (12.12) is again satisfied.

(iv)   *t is a type 0 transition and the current path is not a cycle.* This is identical with (iii) above, except that the edge e_{XY_t} does not appear in the analysis. Accordingly, the bound is

$$\pi_\lambda(X)\pi_\lambda(Y) \leq 2|E|\lambda' Q(t)\pi_\lambda(\eta_t(X, Y)).$$

This concludes our proof of (12.12). We may now deduce from (12.13), that $\bar{\rho}(\Gamma) \leq 4|E|n\lambda'^2$. However, one additional observation will allow us to improve the bound to $\bar{\rho}(\Gamma) \leq 4|E|n\lambda'$, which is what we claimed in (12.11). Looking at the above case analysis we see that, in all cases except case (iii), (12.12), and hence (12.13), actually hold with λ'^2 replaced by λ'. But in case (iii) we can argue that $\eta_t(X, Y)$ must have such a restricted form that $\sum_{\gamma_{XY} \ni t} \pi_\lambda(\eta_t(X, Y))$ is bounded above by λ'^{-1}. Using this fact in the final inequality in (12.13), we get the improved upper bound of $4|E|n\lambda'$ in this case, and hence, in all cases. This will complete our verification of the bound (12.11) on $\bar{\rho}(\Gamma)$.

To justify the above claim, note that $\eta_t(X, Y)$ has at least two unmatched vertices, namely the start vertex of the current cycle and the vertex that is common to both e and e'. Moreover, in $\eta_t(X, Y) \oplus M$ these vertices are linked by an alternating path that starts and ends with an edge of M. So we may associate with each matching $\eta_t(X, Y)$ another matching, say $\eta_t'(X, Y)$, obtained by augmenting $\eta_t(X, Y)$ along this path. But this operation is uniquely reversible, so all matchings $\eta_t'(X, Y)$ created in this way are distinct. Moreover, $\pi_\lambda(\eta_t(X, Y)) = \lambda\pi_\lambda(\eta_t'(X, Y))$. Hence, we have $\sum \pi_\lambda(\eta_t(X, Y)) = \lambda^{-1}\sum \pi_\lambda(\eta_t'(X, Y)) \leq \lambda'^{-1}$, so $\sum \pi_\lambda(\eta_t(X, Y)) \leq \lambda'^{-1}$ as claimed.

MORE APPLICATIONS

12.5

In this section we review some further applications of the techniques described in Section 12.3 to problems in combinatorial enumeration and integration. In each case, as with the monomer-dimer problem of Section 12.4, the Markov chain Monte Carlo method provides the only known basis for an efficient algorithm in the FPRAS sense.

12.5.1 THE PERMANENT

Historically, the first major application of the methods of Section 12.3 was to the approximation of the permanent function. The *permanent* of an $n \times n$ integer matrix $A = (a_{ij} : 0 \le i, j \le n - 1)$ is defined by

$$\text{per } A = \sum_{\pi} \prod_{i=0}^{n-1} a_{i,\pi(i)},$$

where the sum is over all permutations π of $[n] = \{0, \ldots, n - 1\}$. For convenience, we take A to be a $0,1$-matrix, in which case the permanent of A has a simple combinatorial interpretation: namely, per A is equal to the number of perfect matchings (1-factors) in the bipartite graph $G = (V_1, V_2, E)$, where $V_1 = V_2 = [n]$, and $(i, j) \in E$ iff $a_{ij} = 1$. Valiant [Val79a] demonstrated that evaluating the permanent of a $0,1$-matrix is complete for the class #P; thus, just as in the case of the monomer-dimer partition function, we cannot expect to find an algorithm that solves the problem exactly in polynomial time.[13] Interest has therefore centered on finding computationally feasible approximation algorithms.

It turns out that the Markov chain Monte Carlo method can be used to construct such an algorithm (in the FPRAS sense) for almost all instances of this problem. To state the result precisely, we will use the perfect matching formulation. Let $G = (V_1, V_2, E)$ be a bipartite graph with $|V_1| = |V_2| = n$. A special role will be played in the result by the number of *near-perfect* matchings in G, i.e., matchings with exactly two unmatched vertices. Following the notation of the previous section, let us write $m_k = m_k(G)$ for the number of k-matchings in G. Then the number of perfect matchings is m_n, and the number of near-perfect matchings is m_{n-1}. Jerrum and Sinclair [JS89] showed that there exists a randomized approximation scheme for the number of perfect matchings m_n whose running time is polynomial in n, ε^{-1} and the ratio m_{n-1}/m_n.

Note that this algorithm is not in general an FPRAS, since there exist $(n+n)$-vertex graphs G for which the ratio m_{n-1}/m_n is exponential in n. However, it turns out that these examples are wildly atypical in the sense that the probability that a randomly selected G on $n + n$ vertices violates the inequality $m_{n-1}/m_n \le 4n$ tends to 0 as $n \to \infty$.[14] Thus, the above algorithm constitutes an FPRAS for almost all graphs; moreover, the condition that the ratio m_{n-1}/m_n be bounded by a specified polynomial in n can be tested for an arbitrary graph in polynomial time [JS89]. It is also known [Bro86] that *every* sufficiently dense graph (specifically, those in which every vertex has degree at least $\frac{1}{2}n$) satisfies $m_{n-1}/m_n = O(n^2)$. Moreover, it has recently been shown by Kenyon, Randall, and Sinclair [KRS96] that the ratio m_{n-1}/m_n is guaranteed to be small for a wide class of homogeneous graphs G, including the important case of geometric lattice graphs in any number of dimensions. We should also point out that, although the above description has been couched in terms of matchings in bipartite graphs because of the connection with the permanent, everything extends to general $2n$-vertex graphs.

---

[13]In contrast, as is well known, the *determinant* of an $n \times n$ matrix can be evaluated in $O(n^3)$ arithmetic operations using Gaussian elimination.

[14]For more refined results along these lines, see Frieze [Friez89] or Motwani [Mot89].

It was Broder [Bro86, Mih89a] who first proposed a Markov chain Monte Carlo approach to approximating the permanent via Markov chain simulation. His idea was to sample perfect matchings in a bipartite graph G almost u.a.r. by simulating a Markov chain whose states are perfect and near-perfect matchings in G; then, using a reduction similar in spirit to the one described in Section 12.2 for the Knapsack problem, the number of perfect matchings could be counted. Broder's Markov chain was first proved to be rapidly mixing (under the above condition on G) by Jerrum and Sinclair [JS89], using a canonical paths argument as in Section 12.3.

An alternative, more natural approximation algorithm for the permanent follows quite painlessly from our results about the monomer-dimer problem derived in the previous section. Note that m_n is precisely the leading coefficient of the partition function $Z_G(\lambda)$ of the monomer-dimer system associated with G (see (12.5)). In the previous section, we saw how to sample matchings in G from the distribution

$$\pi_\lambda(M) = \frac{\lambda^{|M|}}{Z_G(\lambda)} = \frac{\lambda^{|M|}}{\sum_{k=0}^n m_k \lambda^k} \tag{12.14}$$

for any desired $\lambda > 0$, in time polynomial in n and $\lambda' = \max\{\lambda, 1\}$, by Monte Carlo simulation of the Markov chain $\mathfrak{M}_{\text{match}}(\lambda)$. We also saw how this fact can be used to compute $Z_G(\lambda)$ to good accuracy in time polynomial in n and λ'. Suppose then that we have computed a good estimate $\widehat{Z}_G(\lambda)$ of $Z_G(\lambda)$. Then we can get a good estimator for m_n by sampling matchings from the distribution π_λ and computing the proportion, X, of the sample that are perfect matchings; since $EX = m_n \lambda^n / Z_G(\lambda)$, our estimator is $Y = X \lambda^{-n} \widehat{Z}_G(\lambda)$.

The sample size required to ensure a good estimate depends on the variance of a single sample, or more precisely on the quantity $(EX)^{-1}$. Clearly, by making λ large enough, we can make this quantity, and hence the sample size, small: this corresponds to placing very large weight on the perfect matchings, so that their proportion can be estimated well by random sampling. How large does λ have to be? This analysis is eased by the beautiful fact that the sequence $m_0, m_1, \ldots, m_n$ is *log-concave*, i.e., $m_{k-1} m_{k+1} \le m_k^2$ for $k = 1, 2, \ldots, n-1$. (This is well known [HL72]; a direct combinatorial proof may be found in [JS89].) As a consequence, it follows that $m_{k-1}/m_k \le m_{n-1}/m_n$ for all k, and hence that $m_k/m_n \le (m_{n-1}/m_n)^{n-k}$. This means that, if we take $\lambda \ge m_{n-1}/m_n$, we get

$$EX = \frac{m_n \lambda^n}{Z_G(\lambda)} = \frac{m_n \lambda^n}{\sum_{k=0}^n m_k \lambda^k} \ge \frac{1}{n+1}, \tag{12.15}$$

which implies that the sample size required grows only linearly with n. Thus, it is enough to take λ about as large as the ratio m_{n-1}/m_n. Since the time required to generate a single sample grows linearly with λ (see Proposition 12.4), the running time of the overall algorithm is polynomial in n, ε^{-1} and the ratio m_{n-1}/m_n, as claimed.

OPEN PROBLEM 12.2   Is there an FPRAS for the permanent of a general 0,1 matrix? Note that this problem is not phrased as a question about the mixing time of a specific Markov chain, and certainly the chain $\mathfrak{M}_{\text{match}}(\lambda)$ described here is not directly applicable: as we have seen, it seems to be useful only when the ratio m_{n-1}/m_n for the associated bipartite graph is polynomially bounded. However, the Markov chain Monte Carlo method seems to offer the best hope for a positive resolution of this question. Essentially, the issue is whether the Markov chain $\mathfrak{M}_{\text{match}}(\lambda)$ can be suitably adapted to provide a general solution, or perhaps used as a "black box" following some ingenious preprocessing of the input matrix. (This latter idea has been used in a weaker way by Jerrum and Vazirani [JV92] to obtain a randomized approximation scheme for the general 0,1 permanent whose running time, while still not polynomial, is asymptotically significantly faster than that of more naïve methods.)

We conclude our discussion of the permanent by mentioning some extensions. First of all, it is not hard to see, again using the log-concavity property, that the above technique can be extended to approximate the entire sequence (m_k), or equivalently all the coefficients of the monomer-dimer partition function [JS89]. The running time per coefficient is no worse than for m_n. Secondly, many other approximate enumeration (and sampling) problems can be reduced to enumeration of perfect matchings; examples include counting Hamiltonian cycles in dense or random graphs (Dyer, Frieze, and Jerrum [DFJ94], Frieze and Suen [FS92]), counting graphs with given degree sequence (Jerrum and Sinclair [JS90a], Jerrum, McKay, and Sinclair [JMS92]), and counting Eulerian orientations of an undirected graph (Mihail and Winkler [MW91]).

12.5.2 VOLUME OF CONVEX BODIES

A problem that has attracted much attention in the context of the Markov chain Monte Carlo method is that of estimating the volume of a convex body in high-dimensional space. Computing the volume of a polytope in $n = 3$ dimensions is not a computationally demanding task, but the effort required rises dramatically as the number n of dimensions increases. This empirical observation is supported by a result of Dyer and Frieze [DF88] to the effect that evaluating the volume of a polytope *exactly* is #P-hard.

In contrast, by applying the Markov chain Monte Carlo method, Dyer, Frieze, and Kannan [DFK91] were able to construct an FPRAS for the volume of a convex body in Euclidean space of *arbitrary* dimension. The convex body K in question is presented to the algorithm using a very general mechanism called a *membership oracle*: given a point x, the membership oracle simply reveals whether or not $x \in K$. Other ways of specifying the body K — for example as a list of vertices or $(n - 1)$-dimensional facets — can be recast in the oracle formulation. The algorithm must also be provided with a guarantee in the form of two balls, one contained in K and of non-zero radius, and the other containing K. This seemingly technical condition is essential, for without such a guarantee the task is hopeless.

There are several difficult technical points in the construction and analysis of the volume approximation algorithm of Dyer et al., but, at a high enough level of abstraction, the method is quite simple to describe. The idea is to divide space into n-dimensional (hyper)cubes of side δ, and to perform a random walk on the cubes that lie within the body K. Suppose the random walk is at cube C at time t. A cube C' that is orthogonally adjacent to C is selected uniformly at random; if $C' \in K$ then the walk moves to C', otherwise it stays at C. It is easy to check that the walk (or something close to it) is ergodic, and that the stationary distribution is uniform on cubes in K. The cube size δ is selected so as to provide an adequate approximation to K, while permitting the random walk to "explore" the state space within a reasonable time. Rapid mixing (i.e., in time polynomial in n) is proved via the conductance argument of Section 12.3, by considering the geometry of the state space of the random walk and applying classical isoperimetric inequalities.

Once the sampling problem has been solved, the volume of K can be computed by the technique of Section 12.2. Let $B_0 \subset B_1 \subset \cdots \subset B_m$ be a sequence of concentric balls chosen so that $B_0 \subseteq K \subseteq B_m$ and the volume of B_i exceeds that of B_{i-1} by (say) a factor of 2. Consider the sequence of convex bodies

$$B_0 = K \cap B_0 \subseteq K \cap B_1 \subseteq \cdots \subseteq K \cap B_m = K. \tag{12.16}$$

The volume of the first is known, while the ratios of volumes of successive bodies can be estimated by Monte Carlo sampling using simulation of the random walk described earlier. Random sampling is effective in this context because the volumes of adjacent bodies in sequence (12.16) differ by a factor of at most 2. By multiplying the estimates for the various ratios, the volume of the final body $K \cap B_m = K$ may be computed to any desired degree of approximation.

Although there are many situations in which a source of random bits seems to aid computation, the current example is particularly interesting in that randomness is of *provable* value. It has been shown by Elekes [Elek86] that a deterministic algorithm that is restricted to a subexponential number of oracle calls is unable to obtain a good (say, to within a ratio of 2) approximation to the volume of a convex body.

The close relationship of volume estimation to (approximate) multi-dimensional integration has provided strong practical impetus to research in this area. Since the appearance of the original paper of Dyer et al., much effort has gone into extending the algorithm to a wider class of problems, and into reducing its running time, which, though polynomial in n, is still rather high in practical terms. Applegate and Kannan [AK91] have generalized the algorithm to the integration of log-concave functions over convex regions in arbitrary dimensional space, while Dyer and Frieze [DF91], and Lovász and Simonovits [LS93] have devised many improvements that have successively reduced the time complexity of the algorithm. The success of the latter pursuit may be judged from the dramatic improvement in the dependence of the time-complexity on the dimension n: from $O(n^{27})$ for the original algorithm of Dyer et al., to $\widetilde{O}(n^7)$ as claimed recently by Kannan, Lovász, and Simonovits [KLS94a].[15] Some of the ideas that have led to these improvements are sketched below; for more detail the reader is referred to Kannan's survey article [Kan94], and the references therein.

One source of inefficiency in the early approach was that the random walk in K could, in principle, get stuck for long periods near "sharp corners" of K. Indeed, in the first algorithm, Dyer et al. found it necessary to "round off" the corners of K before simulating the random walk. Applegate and Kannan obtained a substantial improvement in efficiency by providing the random walk with a fuzzy boundary. Rather than estimating the volume of K directly, their version of the algorithm estimates the integral of a function F that takes the value 1 on K, and decays to 0 gracefully outside K. The random walk on cubes is modified so that its stationary distribution is approximately proportional

---

[15]The $\widetilde{O}(\ )$ notation hides not merely constants, but also arbitrary powers of $\log n$. Kannan et al.'s algorithm requires just $\widetilde{O}(n^5)$ oracle calls, but the cost of effecting a single step of their random walk may be as high as $O(n^2)$.

to the function F. As we saw in Section 12.4, in the context of the matching Markov chain $\mathfrak{M}_{\text{match}}(\lambda)$, this end is easily achieved by using a Metropolis-style rule to determine transition probabilities. Provided F decays sufficiently rapidly outside K, the integral of F over the whole of $\mathbb{R}^n$ will be a close approximation to the volume of K.

Another strategy that has been employed in the pursuit of efficiency is to attempt to reduce the length m of sequence (12.16), which amounts to arranging for the extreme balls B_0 and B_m to be as close as possible in volume. In the earlier papers, the body K is subjected to a linear transformation that allows the transformed convex body to be sandwiched between balls whose radii differ by a factor $O(n^{3/2})$. By contenting themselves with a less demanding notion of "approximate sandwiching," Kannan, Lovász, and Simonovits [KLS94b] have recently reduced this factor to $O(\sqrt{n})$, which is best possible. Observe that this improvement in the sandwiching ratio reduces the length of sequence (12.16) roughly by a factor n.

Finally, much thought has gone into potentially more efficient random walks for sampling from within K. This is an attractive line of inquiry, as the original "cubes walk," which only ever makes short steps, intuitively seems rather inefficient. Lovász and Simonovits [LS93] consider instead a "ball walk" with continuous state space, which operates as follows. Suppose $x \in K$ is the position of the walk at time t, and denote by $B(x, \delta)$ the ball with centre x and radius δ. The probability density of the position of the walk at time $t + 1$, conditional on its position at time t being x, is uniform over the region $K \cap B(x, \delta)$, and zero outside. The parameter δ is chosen to exploit the trade-off discussed briefly in the context of the cubes walk. The conductance argument can be extended to the continuous case without essential change. The ball walk saves a factor n in the number of oracle calls; unfortunately, as the moves of the random walk are now more complex than before, there is no saving in net time complexity (i.e., excluding oracle calls).

An interesting problem related to volume estimation is that of approximately counting contingency tables: given $m + n$ positive integers $r_1, \ldots, r_m$ and $c_1, \ldots, c_n$, compute an approximation to the number of $m \times n$ non-negative integer matrices with row-sums $r_1, \ldots, r_m$ and column-sums $c_1, \ldots, c_n$. This problem arises in the interpretation of the results of certain kinds of statistical experiment; see, for example, Diaconis and Efron [DE85].

It is easy to see that the contingency tables with given row- and column-sums are in 1-1 correspondence with integer lattice points contained in an appropriately defined polytope of dimension $nm - n - m$. We might hope that a sufficiently uniform distribution on lattice points could be obtained by sampling from the (continuous) convex polytope and rounding to a nearby lattice point. Dyer, Kannan, and Mount [DKM95] show that this can be done, provided that the row- and column-sums are sufficiently large; specifically, that each sum is at least $(n + m)nm$. The case of small row- and column-sums remains open. There is no hope of an FPRAS for unrestricted 3-dimensional contingency tables (unless $NP = RP$), as Irving and Jerrum [IJ94] have shown that deciding feasibility (i.e, whether there is at least one realization of the contingency table) is NP-complete in 3-dimensions, even when the row- column- and file-sums are all either 0 or 1.

OPEN PROBLEM 12.3 An elegant direct approach to sampling contingency tables has been proposed by Diaconis. Consider the Markov chain $\mathfrak{M}_{\text{CT}}$, whose state space is the set of all matrices with specified row and column sums, and whose transition probabilities are defined as follows. Let the current state (matrix) be $A = (a_{ij})$. Select a pair of rows (i, i') with $i \neq i'$, and a pair of columns (j, j') with $j \neq j'$, both u.a.r. Form a new matrix A' from A by incrementing by one the array elements $a_{ij}, a_{i'j'}$, and decrementing by one the elements $a_{ij'}, a_{i'j}$. Note that A' has the same row- and column-sums as A. If A' is non-negative then we accept it as the next state; otherwise the chain remains at state A. It is easy to verify that $\mathfrak{M}_{CT}$ is ergodic and reversible with uniform stationary distribution. Moreover, it appears to work well in practice as a uniform sampling procedure for contingency tables. However, its mixing time is not known to be bounded by any polynomial in the size of the input. (For obvious reasons, we must assume that the row- and column-sums are expressed in unary notation when defining the input size.)

12.5.3   STATISTICAL PHYSICS

We have already seen, in Section 12.4, a detailed example of the use of the Markov chain Monte Carlo method in statistical physics. It was in fact in this area that the first computational use of the technique was made, and today Markov chain simulations related to physical systems account for vast quantities of CPU time on high performance machines. These methods, while often ingenious, are hardly ever statistically rigorous, so the numerical results obtained from them have to be treated with some degree of caution. One of the most exciting applications of the analytical techniques presented here is the potential they open up for the rigorous quantification of these methods. In this subsection, we sketch the progress that has been made in this direction to date.

The most intensively studied model in statistical physics is the *Ising model*, introduced in the 1920s by Lenz and Ising as a means of understanding the phenomenon of ferromagnetism. An instance of the Ising model is specified by giving a set of *n sites*, a set of *interaction energies* V_{ij} for each unordered pair of sites i, j, a *magnetic field intensity B*, and an *inverse temperature* β. A *configuration* of the system defined by these parameters is one of the 2^n possible assignments σ of ± 1 *spins* to each site. The energy of a configuration σ is given by the *Hamiltonian* $H(\sigma)$, defined by

$$H(\sigma) = -\sum_{\{i,j\}} V_{ij}\sigma_i\sigma_j - B\sum_k \sigma_k.$$

The more interesting part of $H(\sigma)$ is the first sum, which consists of a contribution from each pair of sites. The contribution from the pair i, j is dependent on the interaction energy V_{ij}, and whether the spins at i and j are equal or unequal. The second sum has a contribution from each site i whose sign depends on the sign of the spin at i. In physically realistic applications, the sites are arranged in a regular fashion in 2- or 3-dimensional space, and V_{ij} is non-zero only for "adjacent" sites. From a computational point of view, this special structure seems difficult to exploit. For more detail on this and other models in statistical physics, viewed from a computational perspective, consult the survey by Welsh [Wel90].

A central problem in the theory is evaluating the *partition function* $Z = \sum_\sigma \exp(-\beta H(\sigma))$, where the sum is over all possible configurations σ. This is analogous to the monomer-dimer partition function in Section 12.4, which is also a weighted sum over configurations. The significance of Z is that it is the normalizing factor in the *Gibbs distribution*, which assigns probability $\exp(-\beta H(\sigma))/Z$ to each state (configuration) σ in the steady state. Other problems relate to the evaluation of the expectation of certain random variables of σ, when σ is sampled according to the Gibbs distribution: the *mean magnetic moment* and *mean energy* are two such.

When the interaction energies are unconstrained (this corresponds to a so-called *spin glass*) the partition function is hard even to approximate [JS93], so we restrict attention to the important *ferromagnetic* case, where $V_{ij} \geq 0$ for all pairs $\{i, j\}$ of sites. Even here, *exact* computation of the partition function is #*P*-complete [JS93], so it is again natural to ask whether an FPRAS exists. Jerrum and Sinclair [JS93] answered this question in the affirmative, and in addition presented an FPRAS for the mean magnetic moment and mean energy. Applying the Markov chain Monte Carlo method to the Ising model required an additional twist, as the "natural" random walk on configurations, in which two configurations are adjacent if they differ in just one spin, is *not* rapidly mixing.[16] The twist is to simulate an apparently unrelated Markov chain on a different set of configurations — based on edges rather than vertices — which happens to have essentially the same partition function as the Ising model proper. Using the canonical paths argument, it can be shown that the new, edge-based Markov chain is rapidly mixing. The twist just described is one factor that makes this application one of the most intricate so far devised.

In addition to the Ising model and monomer-dimer systems, other models in statistical physics that have been solved in the FPRAS sense are the *six-point ice model* [MW91] and the *self-avoiding walk model* for linear polymers [BS85, RS94]. The former problem is again connected with matchings in a graph, but rather remotely, and a fair amount of work is required to establish and verify the connection [MW91]. The latter makes use of a Markov chain that is much simpler in structure to those considered here [BS85], and whose analysis requires a far less sophisticated application of the canonical paths approach. The analysis in fact relies on a famous conjecture regarding the behavior of self-avoiding walks: the resulting algorithm is somewhat novel in that it either outputs reliable numerical answers, or produces a counterexample to the conjecture [RS94].

12.5.4 MATROID BASES: AN OPEN PROBLEM

A particularly appealing open problem in this area, and one that would be very rich in terms of consequences, is to determine useful bounds on the mixing time of the *basis-exchange* Markov chain for a general matroid. (A matroid is an algebraic structure that provides an abstract treatment of the concept of linear independence.) The states of this Markov chain are the bases (maximum independent sets) of a given matroid, and a transition is available from base B to base B' if the symmetric difference of B and B' consists of precisely two elements of the ground set. All transition probabilities are equal, so the chain is ergodic and reversible with uniform stationary distribution.

---

[16]A more elaborate random walk on spin configurations proposed by Swendsen and Wang [SW87] *may* be rapidly mixing, but nothing rigorous is known.

A concrete example is provided by the *graphic matroid* associated with an undirected graph G. In this case, the bases are spanning trees of G, and a transition from a given tree T is effected by adding a single edge (selected u.a.r.) to T, thus creating a cycle, and then breaking the cycle by deleting one of its edges (selected u.a.r.). The basis-exchange Markov chain is known to be rapidly mixing for graphic matroids, and, somewhat more generally, for matroids satisfying a certain "balance condition" (see Feder and Mihail [FM92]). A proof of rapid mixing in the general case would imply the existence of an FPRAS for a number of important problems in combinatorial enumeration, all of which are #*P*-complete, including counting connected spanning subgraphs of a graph (network reliability), forests of given size in a graph, and independent subsets of vectors in a set of n-vectors over GF(2).

THE METROPOLIS ALGORITHM AND SIMULATED ANNEALING

12.6

We conclude this survey with a rather different application of the Markov chain Monte Carlo method. Like the applications we have discussed so far, Markov chain simulation will again be used to sample from a large combinatorial set according to some desired probability distribution. However, whereas up to now we have used this random sampling to estimate the expectations of suitably defined random variables over the set, we will now use it to optimize a function. This is the key ingredient of several randomized search heuristics in combinatorial optimization, the most celebrated of which is known as simulated annealing.

As usual, let Ω be a large combinatorial set, which we think of now as the set of feasible solutions to some optimization problem. Let $f : \Omega \to \mathbb{R}^+$ be an objective function defined on Ω; our goal is to find a solution $x \in \Omega$ for which the value $f(x)$ is maximum (or, symmetrically, minimum). As an illustrative example, let us take the maximum cut problem. Here Ω is the set of partitions of the vertices of a given undirected graph $G = (V, E)$ into two sets S and $\overline{S} = V - S$. Our goal is to find a partition that maximizes the number of edges between S and $\overline{S}$.

Here is a very general approach to problems of this kind. First, we define a connected, undirected graph H on vertex set Ω: this graph is often referred to as a *neighborhood structure*. Typically, the neighbors of a solution $x \in \Omega$ are close to x under some measure of distance that is natural to the combinatorial structures in question: for example, in the maximum cut problem, the neighbors of a particular partition $(S, \overline{S})$ might be all partitions of the form $(S - s, \overline{S} + s)$ and $(S + t, \overline{S} - t)$ obtained by moving one element across the partition. Next we construct a Markov chain in the form of a biased random walk on the graph H of a special form. Let $d(x)$ denote the degree of vertex x in H, and let D be an upper bound on the maximum degree. Then transitions from any state $x \in \Omega$ are made as follows:

I. with probability $\frac{1}{2}$ let $y = x$; otherwise,

II. select $y \in \Omega$ according to the distribution

$$\Pr(y) = \begin{cases} \frac{1}{D} & \text{if } y \text{ is a neighbor of } x; \\ 1 - \frac{d(x)}{D} & \text{if } y = x; \\ 0 & \text{otherwise;} \end{cases}$$

III. go to y with probability $\min\{1, \alpha^{f(y)-f(x)}\}$.

Here $\alpha \geq 1$ is a fixed parameter whose role will become clear shortly. We shall refer to this Markov chain as $\mathfrak{MC}(\alpha)$. Note that $\mathfrak{MC}(\alpha)$ always accepts transitions to neighbors with better values of f, but rejects transitions to poorer neighbors with a probability that depends on α.[17]

Let us observe some general properties of this Markov chain. First, since H is connected, the chain is irreducible, and since all self-loop probabilities are non-zero it is aperiodic; hence, it is ergodic. Now define

$$\pi_\alpha(x) = \frac{\alpha^{f(x)}}{Z(\alpha)}, \qquad \text{for } x \in \Omega, \tag{12.17}$$

where $Z(\alpha)$ is a normalizing factor to make π_α a probability distribution. Then it is an easy matter to check that the chain is reversible with respect to π_α, i.e., the transition probabilities $P(x, y)$ satisfy the detailed balance condition

$$\pi_\alpha(x)P(x, y) = \pi_\alpha(y)P(y, x), \qquad \text{for all } x, y \in \Omega.$$

All this implies that the Markov chain converges to the stationary distribution π_α. A Markov chain of this form is known as a *Metropolis process*, in honor of one of its inventors [Met53].

Now let us examine the stationary distribution more closely. From (12.17) it is clear that, for any value of $\alpha \geq 1$, π_α is a monotonically increasing function of $f(x)$. Hence, it favors better solutions. Moreover, the effect of this bias increases with α: as $\alpha \to \infty$, the distribution becomes more sharply peaked around optimal solutions. At the other extreme, when $\alpha = 1$ the distribution is uniform over Ω.

Our optimization algorithm is now immediate: simply simulate the Markov chain $\mathfrak{MC}(\alpha)$ for some number, T, of steps, starting from an arbitrary initial solution, and output the best solution seen during the simulation. We shall refer to this algorithm as the *Metropolis algorithm at* α. How should we choose the parameter α? For sufficiently large T, we can view the algorithm as essentially sampling from the stationary distribution π_α. If we want to be reasonably sure of finding a good solution, we want to make α small so that π_α is well concentrated. On the other hand, intuitively, as α increases the chain becomes less mobile and more likely to get stuck in local optima: indeed, in the limit as $\alpha \to \infty$, $\mathfrak{MC}(\alpha)$ simply becomes a very naïve "randomized greedy" algorithm. This tradeoff suggests that we should use an intermediate value of α.

To precisely quantify the performance of the Metropolis algorithm at a given value of α, we would need to analyze the expected hitting time from the initial solution to the set of optimal (or near-optimal) solutions. However, we can get an upper bound on the time taken to find a good solution by analyzing the mixing time. Certainly, if $\mathfrak{MC}(\alpha)$ is close to stationarity after T steps, then the probability that we find a good solution is at

---

[17]In the case where we wish to minimise f, everything we say carries over with α replaced by α^{-1}.

least the weight of such solutions in the stationary distribution π_α. We shall illustrate this approach by adapting the matching example of Section 12.4, for which we have already developed all the necessary technology.

Consider the classical optimization problem of finding a matching of maximum cardinality in a graph. Thus Ω is the set of all matchings in a graph $G = (V, E)$, and we are trying to maximize the function $f : \Omega \to \mathbb{R}$ given by $f(M) = |M|$. It is well known that this problem can be solved in polynomial time, but the algorithm for non-bipartite graphs is far from trivial [Edm65]. We shall show that the much simpler Metropolis algorithm solves the problem for most graphs, and finds a good approximate solution for all graphs, with high probability in polynomial time. The key to the algorithm's success is a carefully chosen value of the parameter α.

We have in fact already defined a suitable Metropolis process for the maximum matching problem: it is the Markov chain $\mathfrak{M}_{\text{match}}(\lambda)$ from Section 12.4. A glance at the definition of this chain reveals that it is a Metropolis process whose neighborhood structure is defined by edge additions, deletions, and exchanges, and with $D = |E|$ and $\alpha = \lambda$. We saw in Section 12.4 that $\mathfrak{M}_{\text{match}}(\lambda)$ gets very close to its stationary distribution, π_λ, in time polynomial in λ and the number of vertices in G.

Let us first consider the case of $2n$-vertex graphs G for which the ratio m_{n-1}/m_n is polynomially bounded, i.e., $m_{n-1}/m_n \le q(n)$ for some fixed polynomial q.[18] (Of course, for such graphs maximum matchings are perfect matchings.) As we have seen in Section 12.5.1, this actually covers almost all graphs, as well as several interesting special families such as dense graphs. We also saw in Section 12.5.1 that, if we take $\lambda = q(n) \ge m_{n-1}/m_n$, then the weight of perfect matchings in the stationary distribution π_λ is at least $\frac{1}{n+1}$ (see equation (12.15)). Hence, by running the Metropolis algorithm $O(n)$ times (or, alternatively, by increasing λ by a constant factor), we can be almost certain of finding a perfect matching. The running time for each run is polynomial in n and $\lambda = q(n)$, and hence, polynomial in n. The same result holds more generally for graphs with a maximum matching of size k_0, provided that m_{k_0-1}/m_{k_0} is polynomially bounded.

The above analysis breaks down for arbitrary graphs because the value of λ required to find a maximum matching could be very large. However, for arbitrary graphs, we can prove the weaker result that the Metropolis algorithm will find an *approximately* maximum matching in polynomial time. Let G be an arbitrary graph, and suppose we wish to find a matching in G of size at least $k = \lceil (1 - \varepsilon)k_0 \rceil$, where k_0 is the size of a maximum matching in G and $\varepsilon \in (0, 1)$. We claim that, if we run the Metropolis algorithm for a polynomial number of steps with $\lambda = |E|^{(1-\varepsilon)/\varepsilon}$, then with probability at least $\frac{1}{n+1}$ we will find such a matching. (Note, however, that the running time is exponential in the accuracy parameter ε^{-1}.) Once again, the success probability can be boosted by repeated trials, or by increasing λ by a small constant factor.

To justify the above claim, we use the log-concavity property of matchings and the fact that $m_{k_0} \ge 1$ to deduce that

$$m_{k-1} = m_{k_0} \prod_{j=k}^{k_0} \frac{m_{j-1}}{m_j} \ge \left(\frac{m_{k-1}}{m_k} \right)^{k_0-k+1} \tag{12.18}$$

But since j-matchings in G are subsets of E of size j, there is also the crude upper bound

---

[18]Recall that m_k denotes the number of k-matchings in G.

$m_{k-1} \leq |E|^{k-1}$. Hence, from (12.18) we conclude that

$$\frac{m_{k-1}}{m_k} \leq |E|^{(1-\varepsilon)/\varepsilon} = \lambda.$$

Now we use log-concavity again to argue that, for $0 \leq i < k$, we have $m_i/m_k \leq (m_{k-1}/m_k)^{k-i} \leq \lambda^{k-i}$. It follows that the weight of i-matchings in the stationary distribution π_λ is bounded above by the weight of the k-matchings. Hence, the probability of being at a matching of size k or more is at least $\frac{1}{n+1}$, as we claimed.

Rigorous results like this about the performance of the Metropolis algorithm on non-trivial optimization problems are few and far between. The above result on approximating maximum matchings was obtained via a more complex argument by Sasaki and Hajek [SH88], who also show that this result is best possible in the sense that the Metropolis algorithm cannot be expected to find a truly maximum matching in arbitrary graphs in polynomial time, even if the algorithm is allowed to vary the parameter α in an arbitrarily complicated fashion. Negative results of a similar flavor for other problems can be found in [Sas91] and [Jer92]. Jerrum and Sorkin [JS93] prove a positive result for the graph bisection problem analogous to the one above for finding a maximum matching in random graphs: they show that, for almost every input graph in a suitable random graph model, the Metropolis algorithm run at a carefully chosen value of the parameter α will find a minimum bisection of the graph in polynomial time with high probability. Their approach is different from the one presented here, in that they argue directly about the hitting time rather than analyzing the mixing time as we have done. Finally, a recent paper of Kannan, Mount, and Tayur [KMT94] shows how the Metropolis algorithm can be used to efficiently find approximate solutions to a class of convex programming problems.

We close with a brief discussion of the popular optimization heuristic known as simulated annealing, first proposed in [KGV83]. This heuristic is widely used in combinatorial optimization: for a comprehensive survey of experimental results, see for example [JAMS88, JAMS91]. Essentially, the idea is to simulate the Metropolis process while at the same time varying the parameter α according to a heuristic scheme. Thus, a simulated annealing algorithm is specified by a Metropolis process $\mathfrak{MC}(\alpha)$, together with an increasing function $\alpha : \mathbb{N} \to [1, \infty)$. At time t, the process makes a transition according to $\mathfrak{MC}(\alpha(t))$; we can therefore view it as a *time-inhomogeneous* Markov chain on Ω. After some specified number of steps, the algorithm terminates and returns the best solution encountered so far.

The function α is usually referred to as a *cooling schedule*, in accordance with the interpretation of α^{-1} as a "temperature." Increasing α thus corresponds to decreasing temperature, or cooling. The term "simulated annealing" derives from the analogy with the physical annealing process, in which a substance such as glass is heated to a high temperature and then gradually cooled, thereby "freezing" into a state whose energy is locally minimum. If the cooling is done sufficiently slowly, this state will tend to be a *global* energy minimum, corresponding to maximum strength of the solid.

This more complex process is even harder to analyze than the Metropolis algorithm itself. Since the Markov chain is not time-homogeneous, even the question of asymptotic convergence is non-trivial. Holley and Stroock [HS88] proved the existence of a cooling schedule that guarantees convergence to a global optimum: however, the schedule is so slow that the time taken to converge is comparable with the size of Ω, which makes the algorithm uncompetitive with naïve exhaustive search. It remains an outstanding open problem to exhibit a natural example in which simulated annealing with any non-trivial cooling schedule provably outperforms the Metropolis algorithm at a carefully chosen fixed value of α.

Acknowledgments Mark Jerrum was supported in part by a Nuffield Foundation Science Research Fellowship, Grant GR/F 90363 of the UK Science and Engineering Research Council, and EU Esprit Working Group No. 7097, "RAND". Alistair Sinclair was supported in part by NSF Grant CCR-9505448 and a UC Berkeley Faculty Research Grant.

REFERENCES

[Ald81]   D. Aldous. Random walks on finite groups and rapidly mixing Markov chains, *Séminaire de Probabilités XVII*, Springer Lecture Notes in Mathematics 986, 1981/82, 243–297.

[Ald82]   D. Aldous. Some inequalities for reversible Markov chains, *Journal of the London Mathematical Society*, 25(2):564–576, 1982.

[Ald87]   D. Aldous. On the Markov chain simulation method for uniform combinatorial distributions and simulated annealing, *Probability in the Engineering and Informational Sciences*, 1:33–46, 1987.

[Ald90]   D. Aldous. The random walk construction for spanning trees and uniform labeled trees, *SIAM Journal on Discrete Mathematics*, 3:450–465, 1990.

[AD86]   D. Aldous and P. Diaconis. Shuffling cards and stopping times, *American Mathematical Monthly*, 93:333–348, 1986.

[Alon86]   N. Alon. Eigenvalues and expanders, *Combinatorica*, 6:83–96, 1986.

[AM85]   N. Alon and V.D. Milman. λ_1, isoperimetric inequalities for graphs and superconcentrators, *Journal of Combinatorial Theory Series B*, 38:73–88, 1985.

[AK91]   D. Applegate and R. Kannan. Sampling and integration of near log-concave functions, *Proceedings of the 23rd Annual ACM Symposium on Theory of Computing*, 156–163, 1991.

[BS85]   A. Berretti and A.D. Sokal. New Monte Carlo method for the self-avoiding walk, *Journal of Statistical Physics*, 40:483–531, 1985.

[Bro86]   A.Z. Broder. How hard is it to marry at random? (On the approximation of the permanent), *Proceedings of the 18th Annual ACM Symposium on Theory of Computing*, ACM Press, 50–58, 1986. Erratum in *Proceedings of the 20th Annual ACM Symposium on Theory of Computing*, p. 551, 1988.

[Bro89]   A.Z. Broder. Generating random spanning trees, *Proceedings of the 30th Annual IEEE Symposium on Foundations of Computer Science*, 442–447, 1989.

[BDJ96]   R. Bubley, M. Dyer, and M. Jerrum. *A new approach to polynomial-time random walks for volume computation* (preprint), 1996.

[Che70]   J. Cheeger. A lower bound for the smallest eigenvalue for the Laplacian, *Problems in Analysis* (R.C. Gunning, ed.), Princeton University Press, Princeton NJ, 1970, 195–199.

[CdBS55]   E.G.D. Cohen, J. de Boer, and Z.W. Salsburg. A cell-cluster theory for the liquid state II, *Physica*, XXI:137–147, 1955.

[DLMV88]   P. Dagum, M. Luby, M. Mihail, and U. V. Vazirani. Polytopes, permanents and graphs with large factors, *Proceedings of the 29th Annual IEEE Symposium on Foundations of Computer Science*, 412–421, 1988.

[Dia88]   P. Diaconis. *Group representations in probability and statistics*, Lecture Notes Monograph Series Vol. 11, Institute of Mathematical Statistics, Hayward, CA, 1988.

[DE85]   P. Diaconis and B. Efron. Testing for independence in a two-way table, *Annals of Statistics*, 13:845–913, 1985.

[DSC93]   P. Diaconis and L. Saloff-Coste. Comparison techniques for reversible Markov chains, *Annals of Applied Probability*, 3:696–730, 1993.

[DS91]   P. Diaconis and D. Stroock. Geometric bounds for eigenvalues of Markov chains, *Annals of Applied Probability*, 1:36–61, 1991.

[DF88]   M.E. Dyer and A.M. Frieze. On the complexity of computing the volume of a polyhedron, *SIAM Journal on Computing*, 17:967–975, 1988.

[DF91]   M. Dyer and A. Frieze. Computing the volume of convex bodies: a case where randomness provably helps, *Probabilistic Combinatorics and its Applications*, Proceedings of AMS Symposia in Applied Mathematics, 44:123–170, 1991.

[DFJ94]   M. Dyer, A. Frieze, and M. Jerrum. Approximately counting Hamilton cycles in dense graphs, *Proceedings of the 4th Annual ACM-SIAM Symposium on Discrete Algorithms*, 336–343, 1994. Full version to appear in *SIAM Journal on Computing*.

[DFK91]   M. Dyer, A. Frieze, and R. Kannan. A random polynomial time algorithm for approximating the volume of convex bodies, *Journal of the ACM*, 38:1–17, 1991.

[DFKKPV93] M. Dyer, A. Frieze, R. Kannan, A. Kapoor, L. Perkovic, and U. Vazirani. A mildly exponential time algorithm for approximating the number of solutions to a multidimensional knapsack problem, *Combinatorics, Probability and Computing*, 2:271–284, 1993.

[DKM95]   M. Dyer, R. Kannan, and J. Mount. *Sampling contingency tables* (preprint), 1995.

[Edm65]   J. Edmonds. Paths, trees and flowers, *Canadian Journal of Mathematics*, 17:449–467, 1965.

[Elek86]   G. Elekes. A geometric inequality and the complexity of computing volume, *Discrete and Computational Geometry*, 1:289–292, 1986.

[FM92]   T. Feder and M. Mihail. Balanced matroids, *Proceedings of the 24th Annual ACM Symposium on Theory of Computing*, 26–38, 1992.

[Fish61]   M.E. Fisher. Statistical mechanics of dimers on a plane lattice, *Physics Review*, 124:1664–1672, 1961.

[Friez89]   A.M. Frieze. *A note on computing random permanents* (unpublished manuscript), 1989.

[FS92]   A. Frieze and S. Suen. Counting the number of Hamiltonian cycles in random digraphs, *Random Structures and algorithms*, 3:235–241, 1992.

[GJ79]   M.R. Garey and D.S. Johnson. *Computers and Intractability: A Guide to the Theory of NP-Completeness*, Freeman, San Francisco, CA, 1979, p. 176.

[Gill93]   D. Gillman. A Chernoff bound for random walks on expander graphs, *Proceedings of the 34th Annual IEEE Conference on Foundations of Computer Science*, 680–691, 1993.

[Gugg52]   E.A. Guggenheim. *Mixtures*, Clarendon Press, Oxford, 1952.

[HL72]   O.J. Heilmann and E.H. Lieb. Theory of monomer-dimer systems, *Communications in Mathematical Physics*, 25:190–232, 1972.

[HS88]   R. Holley and D.W. Stroock. Simulated annealing via Sobolev inequalities, *Communications in Mathematical Physics*, 115:553–569, 1988.

[IJ94]   R.W. Irving and M.R. Jerrum. 3-D statistical data security problems, *SIAM Journal on Computation*, 23:170-184, 1994.

[Jer87]   M.R. Jerrum. Two-dimensional monomer-dimer systems are computationally intractable, *Journal of Statistical Physics*, 48:121–134, 1987. Erratum in *Journal of Statistical Physics*, 59:1087–1088, 1990.

[Jer92]   M.R. Jerrum. Large cliques elude the Metropolis process, *Random Structures and Algorithms*, 3:347–359, 1992.

[Jer93b]   M. Jerrum. Uniform sampling modulo a group of symmetries using Markov chain simulation, *Expanding Graphs*, DIMACS Series in Discrete Mathematics and Computer Science 10 (J. Friedman, ed.), American Mathematical Society, 1993, 37–47.

[Jer94]   M. Jerrum. The computational complexity of counting, *Proceedings of the International Congress of Mathematicians, Zürich 1994*, Birkhäuser, Basel, 1995, 1407–1416.

[Jer95]   M. Jerrum. A very simple algorithm for estimating the number of k-colourings of a low-degree graph, *Random Structures and Algorithms*, 7:157–165, 1995.

[JMS92]   M. Jerrum, B. McKay, and A. Sinclair. When is a graphical sequence stable? *Random Graphs* 2 (A. Frieze and T. Łuczak, eds), Wiley, 1992, 101–115.

[JS89]   M.R. Jerrum and A.J. Sinclair. Approximating the permanent, *SIAM Journal on Computing*, 18:1149–1178, 1989.

[JS90a]   M.R. Jerrum and A.J. Sinclair. Fast uniform generation of regular graphs, *Theoretical Computer Science*, 73:91–100, 1990.

[JS93]   M. Jerrum and A. Sinclair. Polynomial-time approximation algorithms for the Ising model, *SIAM Journal on Computing*, 22:1087–1116, 1993.

[JS94]   M. Jerrum and G.B. Sorkin. Simulated annealing for graph bisection, *Proceedings of the 34th Annual IEEE Conference on Foundations of Computer Science*, Computer Society Press, 94–103, 1993.

[JVV86]   M.R. Jerrum, L.G. Valiant, and V.V. Vazirani. Random generation of combinatorial structures from a uniform distribution, *Theoretical Computer Science*, 43:169–188, 1986.

[JV92]   M. Jerrum and U. Vazirani. A mildly exponential approximation algorithm for the permanent, *Proceedings of the 33rd Annual IEEE Conference on Foundations of Computer Science*, Computer Society Press, 320–326, 1992.

[JAMS88]   D.S. Johnson, C.R. Aragon, L.A. McGeogh, and C. Schevon. Optimization by simulated annealing: an experimental evaluation; Part I, graph partitioning, *Operations Research*, 37:865–892, 1988.

[JAMS91]   D.S. Johnson, C.R. Aragon, L.A. McGeogh, and C. Schevon. Optimization by simulated annealing: an experimental evaluation; part II, graph coloring and number partitioning, *Operations Research*, 39:378–406, 1991.

[Kah94]   N. Kahale. *Large deviation bounds for Markov chains*, DIMACS Technical Report 94-39, June 1994. To appear in *Combinatorics, Probability and Computing*.

[Kah95]   N. Kahale. *A semidefinite bound for mixing rates of Markov chains*, DIMACS Technical Report 95-41, September 1995.

[Kan94]   R. Kannan. Markov chains and polynomial time algorithms. *Proceedings of the 35th Annual IEEE Symposium on Foundations of Computer Science*, 656–671, 1994.

[KLS94a]   R. Kannan, L. Lovász, and M. Simonovits. *Random walks and a faster algorithm for convex sets* (manuscript).

[KLS94b]   R. Kannan, L. Lovász, and M. Simonovits. Isoperimetric problems for convex sets and a localization lemma, *Discrete and Computational Geometry*, 13:541–559, 1995.

[KMT94]   R. Kannan, J. Mount, and S. Tayur. A randomized algorithm to optimize over certain convex sets, *Mathematics of Operations Research*, 20:529–550, 1995.

[KL83]   R.M. Karp and M. Luby. Monte-Carlo algorithms for enumeration and reliability problems, *Proceedings of the 24th Annual IEEE Symposium on Foundations of Computer Science*, 56–64, 1983.

[KK90]   A. Karzanov and L. Khachiyan. *On the conductance of order Markov chains*, Technical Report DCS 268, Rutgers University, June 1990.

[Kast61]   P.W. Kasteleyn. The statistics of dimers on a lattice I: The number of dimer arrangements on a quadratic lattice, *Physica*, 27:1209–1225, 1961.

[KRS96]   C. Kenyon, D. Randall, and A. Sinclair. Approximating the number of monomer-dimer coverings of a lattice, *Journal of Statistical Physics*, 83:637–659, 1996.

[KGV83]   S. Kirkpatrick, C.D. Gelatt, and M.P. Vecchi. Optimization by simulated annealing, *Science*, 220:671–680, 1983.

[LS88]   G.F. Lawler and A.D. Sokal. Bounds on the L^2 spectrum for Markov chains and Markov processes: a generalization of Cheeger's inequality, *Transactions of the American Mathematical Society*, 309:557–580, 1988.

[LP86]   L. Lovász and M.D. Plummer. *Matching Theory*, North-Holland, Amsterdam, 1986.

[LS93]   L. Lovász and M. Simonovits. Random walks in a convex body and an improved volume algorithm, *Random Structures and Algorithms*, 4:359–412, 1993.

[LRS95]   M. Luby, D. Randall, and A. Sinclair. Markov chain algorithms for planar lattice structures, *Proceedings of the 36th Annual IEEE Symposium on Foundations of Computer Science*, 150–159, 1995.

[Mat91]   P. Matthews. Generating random linear extensions of a partial order, *The Annals of Probability*, 19:1367–1392, 1991.

[Met53]   N. Metropolis, A.W. Rosenbluth, M.N. Rosenbluth, A.H. Teller, and E. Teller. Equation of state calculation by fast computing machines, *Journal of Chemical Physics*, 21:1087–1092, 1953.

[Mih89a]   M. Mihail. On coupling and the approximation of the permanent, *Information Processing Letters*, 30:91–95, 1989.

[Mih89b]   M. Mihail. Conductance and convergence of Markov chains: a combinatorial treatment of expanders, *Proceedings of the 30th Annual IEEE Symposium on Foundations of Computer Science*, 526–531, 1989.

[MP94]   M. Mihail and C.H. Papadimitriou. On the random walk method for protocol testing, *Proceedings of the 6th International Conference on Computer Aided Verification*, Springer Lecture Notes in Computer Science 818, 1994, 132–141.

[MW91]   M. Mihail and P. Winkler. On the number of Eulerian orientations of a graph, *Proceedings of the 3rd Annual ACM-SIAM Symposium on Discrete Algorithms*, 138–145, 1992.

[Mot89]   R. Motwani. Expanding graphs and the average-case analysis of algorithms for matchings and related problems, *Proceedings of the 21st Annual ACM Symposium on Theory of Computing*, ACM Press, 550–561, 1989.

[PW95]   J. Propp and D. Wilson. *Exact sampling with coupled Markov chains and applications to statistical mechanics* (preprint), 1995. To appear in *Random Structures & Algorithms*, 1996.

[RS94]   D. Randall and A.J. Sinclair. Testable algorithms for self-avoiding walks, *Proceedings of the 5th Annual ACM-SIAM Symposium on Discrete Algorithms*, ACM Press, 593–602, 1994.

[Rob35]   J.K. Roberts. Some properties of adsorbed films of oxygen on tungsten, *Proceedings of the Royal Society of London A*, 152:464–480, 1935.

[Sas91]   G.H. Sasaki. The effect of the density of states on the Metropolis algorithm, *Information Processing Letters*, 37:159–163, 1991.

[SH88]   G.H. Sasaki and B. Hajek. The time complexity of maximum matching by simulated annealing, *Journal of the ACM*, 35:387–403, 1988.

[Sin92]   A. Sinclair. Improved bounds for mixing rates of Markov chains and multicommodity flow, *Combinatorics, Probability and Computing*, 1:351–370, 1992.

[Sin93]   A.J. Sinclair. *Randomised algorithms for counting and generating combinatorial structures*, Advances in Theoretical Computer Science, Birkhäuser, Boston, 1993.

[SJ89]   A.J. Sinclair and M.R. Jerrum. Approximate counting, uniform generation and rapidly mixing Markov chains, *Information and Computation*, 82:93–133, 1989.

[SW87]   R.H. Swendsen and J-S. Wang. Nonuniversal critical dynamics in Monte Carlo simulations, *Physical Review Letters*, 58:86–88, 1987.

[TF61]   H.N.V. Temperley and M.E. Fisher. Dimer problem in statistical mechanics—an exact result, *Philosophical Magazine*, 6:1061–1063, 1961.

[Tod89]   S. Toda. On the computational power of PP and $\oplus$P, *Proceedings of the 30th Annual IEEE Symposium on Foundations of Computer Science*, Computer Society Press, 514–519, 1989.

[Usp37]   J.V. Uspensky. *Introduction to mathematical probability*, McGraw Hill, 1937.

[Val79a]   L.G. Valiant. The complexity of computing the permanent, *Theoretical Computer Science*, 8:189–201, 1979.

[Val79b]   L.G. Valiant. The complexity of enumeration and reliability problems, *SIAM Journal on Computing*, 8:410–421, 1979.

[Wel90]   D.J.A. Welsh. The computational complexity of some classical problems from statistical physics, *Disorder in Physical Systems*, Oxford University Press, 1990, 307–321.

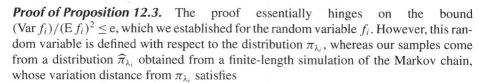

APPENDIX

Proof of Proposition 12.3. The proof essentially hinges on the bound $(\operatorname{Var} f_i)/(\operatorname{E} f_i)^2 \le e$, which we established for the random variable f_i. However, this random variable is defined with respect to the distribution π_{λ_i}, whereas our samples come from a distribution $\widehat{\pi}_{\lambda_i}$ obtained from a finite-length simulation of the Markov chain, whose variation distance from π_{λ_i} satisfies

$$\|\widehat{\pi}_{\lambda_i} - \pi_{\lambda_i}\| \le \frac{\varepsilon}{5er}. \tag{A.1}$$

We shall therefore work with the random variable $\widehat{f}_i$, defined analogously to f_i except that the matching M is selected from the distribution $\widehat{\pi}_{\lambda_i}$ rather than π_{λ_i}. Since $\widehat{f}_i$ takes values in $(0, 1]$, its expectation $\operatorname{E} \widehat{f}_i = \widehat{\rho}_i$ clearly satisfies $|\widehat{\rho}_i - \rho_i| \le \varepsilon/5er$, which by (12.10) implies

$$\left(1 - \frac{\varepsilon}{5r}\right)\rho_i \le \widehat{\rho}_i \le \left(1 + \frac{\varepsilon}{5r}\right)\rho_i. \tag{A.2}$$

Moreover, again using (12.10), the variance of $\widehat{f}_i$ satisfies

$$(\operatorname{Var} \widehat{f}_i)/(\operatorname{E} \widehat{f}_i)^2 \le \widehat{\rho}_i^{\,-1} \le 2\rho_i^{-1} \le 2e, \tag{A.3}$$

where we have also used (A.2) crudely to deduce that $\widehat{\rho}_i \ge \frac{1}{2}\rho_i$.

We can now compute the sample size needed to ensure a good final estimate. Let $X_i^{(1)}, \ldots, X_i^{(S)}$ be a sequence of S independent copies of the random variable $\widehat{f}_i$ obtained by sampling S matchings from the distribution $\widehat{\pi}_{\lambda_i}$, and let $\overline{X}_i = S^{-1}\sum_{j=1}^{S} X_i^{(j)}$ be the sample mean. Clearly, $\operatorname{E} \overline{X}_i = \operatorname{E} \widehat{f}_i = \widehat{\rho}_i$, and $\operatorname{Var} \overline{X}_i = S^{-1} \operatorname{Var} \widehat{f}_i$. Our estimator of $\rho = Z(\widehat{\lambda})^{-1}$ is the random variable $X = \prod_{i=1}^{r} \overline{X}_i$. The expectation of this estimator is $\operatorname{E} X = \prod_{i=1}^{r} \widehat{\rho}_i = \widehat{\rho}$, which by (A.2) satisfies

$$\left(1 - \frac{\varepsilon}{4}\right)\rho \le \widehat{\rho} \le \left(1 + \frac{\varepsilon}{4}\right)\rho. \tag{A.4}$$

Also, by (A.3), the variance satisfies

$$\begin{aligned}
\frac{\operatorname{Var} X}{(\operatorname{E} X)^2} &= \prod_{i=1}^{r}\left(1 + \frac{\operatorname{Var} \overline{X}_i}{(\operatorname{E} \overline{X}_i)^2}\right) - 1 \\
&\le \left(1 + \frac{2e}{S}\right)^r - 1 \\
&\le \exp(2er/S) - 1 \\
&\le \varepsilon^2/64,
\end{aligned}$$

provided we choose the sample size $S = \lceil 130e\varepsilon^{-2}r \rceil$. (Here we are using the fact that $\exp(x/65) \le 1 + x/64$ for $0 \le x \le 1$.) Now Chebyshev's inequality applied to X yields

$$\Pr(|X - \widehat{\rho}| > (\varepsilon/4)\widehat{\rho}) \le \frac{16}{\varepsilon^2}\frac{\operatorname{Var} X}{(\operatorname{E} X)^2} \le \frac{1}{4},$$

so we have, with probability at least $\frac{3}{4}$,

$$\left(1 - \frac{\varepsilon}{4}\right)\widehat{\rho} \le X \le \left(1 + \frac{\varepsilon}{4}\right)\widehat{\rho}. \tag{A.5}$$

Combining (A.4) and (A.5) we see that, with probability at least $\frac{3}{4}$, $Y = X^{-1}$ lies within ratio $1 \pm \varepsilon$ of $\rho^{-1} = Z(\widehat{\lambda})$, which completes the proof. ∎

13

ONLINE COMPUTATION

Sandy Irani   **Anna R. Karlin**

This chapter presents an introduction to the competitive analysis of online algorithms. In an online problem, data is supplied to the algorithm incrementally, one unit at a time. The online algorithm must also produce the output incrementally: after seeing t units of input, it must output the tth unit of output. Since decisions about the output are made with incomplete knowledge about the entire input, an online algorithm often can not produce an optimal solution. Such an algorithm can only hope to approximate the performance of the optimal algorithm that sees all the inputs in advance. An online algorithm is said to be competitive if its performance is close to that of the optimal offline algorithm on each input.

We introduce the basic principles underlying the design and analysis of online algorithms and illustrate these ideas with results for three different problems: paging, metrical task systems, and the k-server problem. We then give detailed descriptions of two recent results. The first is the analysis of the work-function algorithm for the k-server problem ([KP94a]), and the second is the exponential function technique for virtual circuit routing ([AAF$^+$93]). Finally, we discuss new directions in the analysis of online algorithms intended to overcome some of the shortcomings of traditional competitive analysis.

INTRODUCTION

13.1

Suppose you are about to go skiing for the first time in your life. Naturally, you ask yourself whether to rent skis or to buy them. Renting skis costs, say, $30, whereas buying skis costs, say, $300. If you knew how many times you would go skiing in the future (ignoring complicating factors such as inflation, and changing models of skis), then your choice would be clear. If you knew you would go at least 10 times, you would be financially better off buying skis right from the beginning, whereas if you knew you would go less than 10 times, you would be better off renting skis every time.

Alas, the future is unclear, and you must make a decision nonetheless. In this sense, you are faced with an *online problem*, and must deal with events (in this case ski trips) as they arrive without knowledge (or with only limited knowledge) of future events. An *online algorithm* is an algorithm which must solve an online problem.

Online algorithms are approximation algorithms of a certain sort: they attempt to approximate the performance of the optimal offline algorithm *OPT* for the problem. *OPT* is the algorithm that knows the future in its entirety, and deals with events as they arrive at minimum total cost.

For the ski-rental problem, we observe that if an adversary determines exactly at what point you will never go skiing again, it can ensure that you pay at least twice what you could have paid, regardless of your strategy. Indeed, suppose your algorithm is to continue renting until you have skied j times, and then to buy skis. The adversary will then simply wait until you buy skis, and then make sure you never ski again. Since you pay $30j + 300$, and you could have paid $\min(30j, 300)$, you pay at least twice the optimal offline cost.

Furthermore, there is a trivial online algorithm that is guaranteed to achieve this bound: rent until you've skied 10 times, then buy. In so doing, if you ski j times, where $j \leq 10$, you pay $30j$, exactly the optimal offline cost. If $j > 10$, you pay $2 \cdot 300$, twice the optimal offline cost.

The principle underlying this algorithm is often referred to as *the ski principle*. Although it may seem like a good idea to take the action which is cheapest in the short term, online algorithms must hedge their bets. Indeed, it may be that by taking an expensive action at some point, the algorithm pays less in future events. In essence, the ski principle says that once the algorithm has incurred enough total cost by executing a number of cheap actions, the algorithm can afford to take a more expensive action, which can be amortized against the collection of cheap actions.

Online problems are pervasive in computer science, in such diverse areas as scheduling, routing, memory management, dynamic data structures, dynamic graph algorithms, and robot motion planning. This chapter is a survey of techniques used in competitive algorithms which we illustrate using problems from several applications. The chapter is organized as follows. In Section 13.2 we introduce the basic definitions of competitive analysis and several motivating example problems. In Section 13.3 we present the theoretical underpinnings of deterministic competitive algorithms. In Section 13.4 we present the theory underlying randomized competitive algorithms. In Sections 13.5 and 13.6 we give detailed proofs of two recent exciting results in online algorithms.

Section 13.5 presents the proof of the recent tour-de-force of competitive algorithms, the proof that the work-function algorithm is $2k - 1$ competitive for the k-server problem. Section 13.6 presents the exponential function technique for virtual circuit routing, alias online multicommodity flow, and gives an historical overview of the area. In Section 13.7 we discuss some of the shortcomings of competitive analysis and recent work which addresses some of these problems. Finally, in Section 13.8, we give some open problems and directions for future research.

THREE EXAMPLES OF COMPETITIVE ANALYSIS

13.2

We will be using three examples to illustrate the various notions that arise in online algorithms. These are: the paging problem, the k-server problem, and metrical task systems. Each problem is a special case of the next.

13.2.1 PAGING

The paging problem is the most fundamental and practically important online problem in computer science. Consider a two-level store consisting of a fast memory (the *cache*) that can hold k pages, and a slow memory that can store n pages. The n pages in slow memory represent the virtual memory pages. A *paging algorithm* is presented with a sequence of requests to virtual memory pages. If the page requested is in fast memory (a *hit*), no cost is incurred; but if not (a *fault*), the algorithm must bring it into the fast memory at unit cost. The algorithm must decide which of the k pages currently in fast memory to evict in order to make room for the newly requested page.

If we knew the future, the decision would be clear. It has long been known that the optimal offline algorithm, called *MIN*, is the algorithm which always evicts the page whose next request is furthest in the future. Unfortunately, in practice paging decisions are made without knowledge of future requests. A paging algorithm is *online* if it makes the decision of which page to evict without knowing which pages will be requested in the future. We will discuss one commonly used online paging algorithm called *Least-Recently-Used (LRU)*. On a fault, *LRU* evicts the page in memory whose most recent access was earliest.

How do we evaluate the performance of such an online paging algorithm?

A traditional worst-case analysis of paging is completely uninformative, since any paging algorithm can be made to fault on every single request by an adversary which always requests the most recently discarded page. Hence, from the worst-case point of view, all online paging algorithms are equivalent. However, in practice some algorithms perform much better than others and a theoretical analysis should reflect this difference.

Alternatively, one could employ average-case analysis. The problem here is that one must postulate a statistical model for the input. It is difficult to come up with a fixed probability distribution that captures realistic instances, since the patterns of access tend to change dynamically with time and across applications. Nonetheless, several of the early analyses of paging algorithms were done assuming such fixed probability distributions.

Motivated by these observations, Sleator and Tarjan proposed the idea of *competitive analysis*.[1] In competitive analysis, we compare the performance of the online algorithm against the performance of the optimal offline algorithm on every input, and consider the worst-case ratio. Let $\text{cost}_A(\sigma)$ be the cost incurred by an online algorithm A on the input sequence σ. In the case of paging, σ is a sequence of page requests, and $\text{cost}_A(\sigma)$ is the number of page faults incurred by algorithm A on the sequence σ. Let *OPT* be the optimal offline algorithm, and let $\text{cost}_{OPT}(\sigma)$ be the cost incurred by the optimal offline algorithm on input σ.

We say that the online algorithm A is c-competitive if there exists a constant b such that on every request sequence σ,

$$\text{cost}_A(\sigma) \le c \cdot \text{cost}_{OPT}(\sigma) + b.$$

In some sense $\text{cost}_{OPT}(\sigma)$ measures the inherent difficulty of σ, and we only ask an online algorithm to perform well relative to the difficulty of the input. The *competitive ratio* of the algorithm A, denoted c_A, is the infimum over c such that A is c-competitive. An algorithm is said to be *strongly competitive* if it achieves the best possible competitive ratio for a problem. The competitive ratio has become the standard measuring stick for online algorithms in recent years and has been used by the vast majority of recent work in online algorithms.

Notice that we are not placing any computational restrictions on the algorithm – we are simply measuring, from an information theoretic point of view, what kind of solution quality can be obtained given the fact that the decisions have to be made with partial information. How the competitive ratio changes as various computational constraints are imposed is an interesting and largely unexplored issue.

13.2.2   THE K-SERVER PROBLEM

In the k-server problem, introduced by Manasse, McGeoch, and Sleator [MMS90], we must choose how k mobile servers will serve each of a sequence of requests. More specifically, we have k servers each of which occupies a single point in a fixed metric space M. The metric space is known to the online algorithm in advance. Repeatedly, a *request*, a point $x \in M$, appears. Each request must be *served* before the next request appears. To serve the request x, the algorithm must move a server to x unless it already has a server at x. Whenever the algorithm moves a server from point a to point b, it incurs a *cost* of $d_{a,b}$, the distance between a and b in the metric space. The goal is to minimize the total distance moved by all the servers.

The k-server problem encompasses many interesting problems as special cases, for example paging and motion planning for 2-headed disks. To see that the paging problem is a special case of the k-server problem, consider the k-server problem on a *uniform* metric space where the distance between each distinct pair of points is 1. Each point in the space corresponds to a virtual page, and each of the k servers corresponds to one of

---

[1]Competitive analysis was implicit in early work on bin-packing in the sixties.

the k cache locations. The k points occupied by servers correspond to the k pages in the cache. When a request is made for a page which already resides in the cache, the cost to serve it is 0 since it is covered by a server already. When a request is made for a page p not in the cache, some server moves a distance 1 from say q in order to serve the request. This corresponds to the page p replacing q in the cache.

If all the requests are known in advance but the requests must still be served in the order they appear in the sequence (i.e. the problem is offline), there is an algorithm to determine the optimal strategy which takes time $O(kn^2)$ where n is the number of requests in the sequence [CKPV91]. Thus, the difficulty of the problem arises solely from its online nature.

13.2.3   METRICAL TASK SYSTEMS

Metrical task system, introduced by Borodin, Linial, and Saks [BLS87], are a general model for describing a wide class of problems in which a sequence of tasks must be performed. A *task system* is a triple $(S, [[d]], \mathcal{T})$, where S is a finite set of states and $[[d]]$ is a matrix representing distances between each pair of states. (The distance between any two states i and j is denoted $d_{i,j}$.) The distances obey the triangle inequality, and the distance from a state to itself is 0. $\mathcal{T}$ is a set of tasks. A task $T \in \mathcal{T}$ is a non-negative vector indicating the cost of processing that task in each of the states; $T(i)$ is the cost of processing the task T in state i. The input is a sequence of tasks from $\mathcal{T}$: $\sigma = T^1, T^2, \ldots, T^N$, where $T^i \in \mathcal{T}$ for all i. The objective of the algorithm is to determine a state in which to process each task, balancing the cost of moving with the cost of processing the tasks. The algorithm produces a schedule $\pi : \{1, \ldots, N\} \to S$, where $\pi(j)$ is the state in which T^j is processed. If the algorithm is online, then the choice of $\pi(j)$ depends only on $T^1, \ldots, T^j$. The cost of a schedule π on σ is the sum of the cost of moving from state to state (the *moving costs*) and the cost of processing the tasks (the *stationary costs*):

$$\text{cost}(\pi, \sigma) = \sum_{i=1}^{N} d_{\pi(i-1),\pi(i)} + \sum_{i=1}^{N} T^i(\pi(i)).$$

$\pi(0)$ is some fixed initial state. We denote by $A(\sigma)$ the schedule produced by algorithm A on input σ. The *cost* of algorithm A on σ, denoted $\text{cost}_A(\sigma)$, is $\text{cost}(A(\sigma), \sigma)$. The cost of the optimal off-line algorithm for the sequence π is

$$\text{cost}_{OPT}(\sigma) = \min_{\pi} \text{cost}(\pi, \sigma).$$

In most of the interesting examples of task systems, the distances are symmetric (i.e. $d_{i,j} = d_{j,i}$ for all i and j). In this case, the task system is a *metrical task system*. Many online problems in the literature can be described as metrical task systems, including paging and the k-server problem. For example, to express the k-server problem as a metrical task system, we choose the set of states S to be the set of multisets of k points in the metric space in which the servers move. The distance between two states is the minimum total distance k servers would have to move if they were originally occupying one k-set and had to move to the other. This is just the minimum matching between the two k-sets. $\mathcal{T}$ consists of a collection of task vectors, one for each point p in the metric space, where

$$T_p(S) = \begin{cases} 0, & \text{if } p \in S \\ \infty. & \text{if } p \notin S \end{cases}$$

Thus, in order to satisfy the request T_p without incurring a cost of ∞, the algorithm must be in a configuration such that at least one server is occupying the point p.

The k-server problem is not the only problem that can be expressed as a metrical task system. The model is powerful enough to completely formulate a large class of the online problems of interest. Examples include: paging, layered graph traversal, operations on dynamic data structures, and maintaining data in a multiprocessing environment ([BaFiRa92, BlaSle89, KMRS88, MMS90, PY89, DS85, ST85, Westbr92]).

THEORETICAL UNDERPINNINGS: DETERMINISTIC ALGORITHMS

13.3

13.3.1   LOWER BOUNDS

A standard technique in proving lower bounds is to employ an adversary which plays against an arbitrary algorithm and concocts an input which forces it to incur a high cost. In proving a lower bound for the best possible competitive ratio, an algorithm can achieve on a problem; an adversary has two tasks. The adversary generates an input sequence for A and then performs the sequence of operations himself. The adversary's goal is to find a sequence which forces the algorithm to incur a high cost which he can service at a low cost. Such an adversary is commonly referred to as a *cruel adversary*. A cruel adversary is not a rigorous concept, but roughly speaking, such an adversary chooses the next task so that the online algorithm incurs a non-negative cost while the optimal offline algorithm incurs no extra cost whenever possible. In the setting of metrical task systems, if the algorithm is in state j, then the adversary would choose the next task so that $T(j) = c > 0$ and $T(i) = 0$ for all $i \neq j$.

We illustrate the concept of a cruel adversary with a very simple example.

THEOREM 13.1 [ST85]   If A is any deterministic online paging algorithm, then $c_A \geq k$.

Proof.   We assume that A and OPT both start with the same set of pages in the fast memory. The adversary restricts its request sequence to a set of $k + 1$ pages: the k pages initially residing in fast memory and one other page. The adversary always requests the page that is outside of A's fast memory. This process can be continued for an arbitrary number of requests, resulting in an arbitrarily long sequence σ on which A faults on every request.

We must now show that $\text{cost}_{OPT}(\sigma) \le \lceil |\sigma| / k \rceil$. At each fault, the adversary adopts the following strategy: evict the page whose first request occurs farthest in the future. Suppose a page x is evicted by OPT. The next fault occurs the next time x is requested. The adversary is guaranteed that all the other pages in the adversary's fast memory will be requested before x is requested again. There will be at least $k - 1$ pages requested between any two faults, so the adversary faults at most on every k^{th} request. ∎

Note that by requesting only $k + 1$ distinct pages, the adversary ensures that the offline cost is minimal.

It is worth remarking that this proof was made particularly simple by the fact that determining the optimal offline cost was straightforward. For many online problems, this is not the case. Indeed, many of the online problems that have been studied are *NP*-complete. Fortunately, it is sufficient to provide an upper bound for the adversary's cost in proving a lower bound on the competitive ratio.

A useful technique for finding an upper bound on the optimal cost is averaging over a collection of algorithms. That is, we find a collection of algorithms $A_1, \ldots, A_m$, such that when a cruel adversary constructs a sequence σ designed to hurt any online algorithm A, the cumulative cost of the m algorithms on sequence σ is at most c times the cost of A on σ, i.e.

$$\sum_{1 \le i \le m} A_i[\sigma] \le c A[\sigma].$$

Since there is an algorithm in the set $A_1, \ldots A_m$ whose cost is at most the average, such a result implies a lower bound of $\frac{m}{c}$ on the competitive ratio.

This is a remarkably powerful technique as illustrated by the following example which gives a lower bound for an online algorithm for the k-server problem in *any* metric space.

THEOREM 13.2 [MMS90] Let A be any online algorithm for the k-server problem. Then the competitiveness of A is at least k.

Proof. The adversary chooses $k + 1$ points: the k points initially occupied by the servers, which we denote by $\{p_1, \ldots, p_k\}$, and one other point, p_{k+1}. The adversary will only request points from that set. Let A be a deterministic algorithm for the k server problem. On each request, the adversary requests the point where A does not have a server. The adversary continues this process for N requests, where N can be arbitrarily large. Let $\sigma = p_{i_1}, p_{i_2}, \ldots, p_{i_N}$ be the resulting sequence. The cost of A on the sequence is

$$\text{cost}_A(\sigma) = \sum_{j=1}^{N-1} d_{p_{i_j}, p_{i_{j+1}}}.$$

We will upper bound the cost of OPT by showing k algorithms $A_1, \ldots, A_k$ whose total cost on σ is equal to A's cost on σ. On the initial request to p_{k+1}, A_i moves the server from point p_i to point p_{k+1}. From this point on, the set of algorithms maintain the invariant that each algorithm has a server on the point which was last requested. In addition, no two algorithms have the same point vacant.

When p_{i_j} is requested, exactly one algorithm must move a server. That algorithm moves a server from $p_{i_{j-1}}$ to p_{i_j}, and the invariants are maintained. The total cost incurred by all k algorithms is:

$$\sum_{l=1}^{k} \mathrm{cost}_{A_l}(\sigma) = \sum_{j=1}^{k} d_{p_j, p_{k+1}} + \sum_{j=1}^{N-1} d_{p_{i_j}, p_{i_{j+1}}} = \sum_{j=1}^{k} d_{p_j, p_{k+1}} + \mathrm{cost}_A(\sigma).$$

The constant is $\sum_{j=1}^{k} d_{p_j, p_{k+1}}$, which we will denote by c accounts for the first move of each algorithm. We have that $k\mathrm{cost}_{OPT}(\sigma) \leq k\min_l\{\mathrm{cost}_{A_l}(\sigma)\} \leq \sum_{l=1}^{k} \mathrm{cost}_{A_l}(\sigma)$. Thus, $k\mathrm{cost}_{OPT}(\sigma) \leq \mathrm{cost}_A(\sigma) + c$. Since the sequence can be arbitrarily costly, and hence the $\mathrm{cost}_A(\sigma)$ can be made arbitrarily large, the constant c is negligible.   ■

13.3.2   DESIGN PRINCIPLES

The design of online algorithms is still something of an art. There are, however, a few recurring themes which have been useful in a variety of settings. These are

- greedy algorithms,
- balancing costs,
- forcing the offline cost to increase, and
- combining online algorithms.

We consider each of these in turn.

13.3.2.1   Greedy algorithms

In a somewhat vacuous sense, all online algorithms are greedy, since an online algorithm is defined by a function f of the current request, the current state, and the history. Essentially the algorithm evaluates the function for each possible way of serving the current request, and chooses the action which minimizes the value of the function. Nonetheless, there are some natural greedy-type algorithms that work well in certain situations.

The first is the *local greedy* algorithm. This algorithm chooses an action which minimizes the cost to serve the current request. This algorithm performs abysmally in some situations. For example, for the k-server problem, it has no bounded competitive ratio. On the other hand, there are online problems for which it is optimal, including some load balancing problems and constructing online Steiner trees. In addition, there are weighted local greedy algorithms. One such example is the exponential function technique used for virtual circuit routing which is discussed in detail in Section 13.6.

The second is the *retrospective* algorithm. This algorithm keeps track of history and what states *OPT* would be in if the sequence seen so far (including the current request) were the entire sequence. The online algorithm then moves to the closest one of these states. This algorithm is 2-competitive for ski-rental, but has no bounded competitive ratio for the k-server problem. A good illustration of a retrospective algorithm was developed independently in [KP93] and [KMV94] for online minimum weight bipartite matching.

Third is the celebrated *work function* algorithm (WFA)[BLS87, CL92, KP94a]. This is a combination of the first two types of greedy algorithms. It works as follows. Let

$opt_t(s)$ be the optimal cost of serving the first t requests and ending up in state s. If the WFA is in state s_t after serving the tth request, then it serves the $(t+1)st$ request in state s_{t+1} where s_{t+1} is the state minimizing $opt_{t+1}(s_{t+1}) + d_{s_t,s_{t+1}}$. This algorithm is known to have optimal competitiveness or near optimal competitiveness for several online problems including the k-server problem. In Section 13.5, we give the proof that the work function algorithm is $(2k-1)$-competitive for the k-server problem.

There are also situations in which the WFA is not competitive. Burley shows that the WFA is not competitive for the problem of Layered Graph Traversals (see [Bur93]). Interestingly, he shows that for this problem, a slightly altered version of the algorithm is competitive, where the state for the $t+1^{st}$ request is chosen to minimize $\alpha \cdot opt_{t+1}(s_{t+1}) + d_{s_t,s_{t+1}}$, for some $\alpha > 1$. It is a major open problem to characterize online problems for which each of these types of algorithms is competitive.

13.3.2.2   Balancing costs

The principle of balancing costs has already been discussed in the introduction under the name of the "ski principle." Suppose the online algorithm has two choices for how to service a request. If the future is one way, then one of the choices will ultimately be cheaper, whereas if the future is another way, the other choice will ultimately be cheaper. Balancing costs says that an online algorithm should roughly try to incur the same cost on each of the possible futures.

Another example of an algorithm that employs this idea is a k-server algorithm called *BALANCE*, due to Manasse, McGeoch, and Sleator [MMS90], which is optimal for metric spaces consisting of $k+1$ points. *BALANCE* maintains the cumulative distance D_i traveled by the ith server. Let d_i denote the distance from server i to the next request. *BALANCE* sends the server to next request which minimizes $D_i + d_i$.

Clearly, *BALANCE* is attempting to keep the total distance moved by the various servers more or less equal. By doing so, it guards against futures in which different servers are active. Additional intuition for this algorithm comes from considering why the local greedy algorithm fails. By simply moving the server that is closest to the request, the online algorithm may ping-pong a server a between two points alternately requested, simply because moving a far away server b in is locally expensive. The *BALANCE* algorithm does not permit this to happen because as soon as server a ping-pongs for a total cost greater than that of moving b to the request, *BALANCE* moves b.

We prove that *BALANCE* has optimal competitiveness for metric spaces with $k+1$ points.

THEOREM 13.3 [MMS90]   Let c_{BAL} be the competitive ratio of *BALANCE* on a metric space with $k+1$ points. Then, $c_{BAL} \leq k$.

Proof.   At any point in time, there is exactly one point which is not occupied by one of *BALANCE*'s servers. This point is called the *hole*. We can assume that the request sequence always requests *BALANCE*'s hole. A request to another point will cost *BALANCE* nothing and can only serve to increase *OPT*'s cost.

The points in the space are numbered $\{1, \ldots, k+1\}$. Let s_i denote the configuration which has a server on every point except i. Let $opt_t(s_i)$ be the optimal way of serving the first t requests and ending up in configuration s_i. Note that the cost of moving from s_i to s_j is $d_{i,j}$ and, thus, $opt_t(s_i) \le opt_t(s_j) + d_{i,j}$.

Let D_i^t denote the distance traversed after the first t requests by *BALANCE*'s server which occupies point i. If *BALANCE* does not have a server on point i, then D_i^t is undefined. Let h^t denote the location of *BALANCE*'s hole after t requests. The $t + 1^{st}$ request is to point h^t. We make the following claim:

CLAIM 13.1   For $i \ne h^t$, $D_i^t \le opt_t(s_i)$.

We first prove the theorem modulo the claim. The total work done by *BALANCE* through time t is

$$\sum_{i \ne h^t} D_i^t \le \sum_{i \ne h^t} opt_t(s_i) \le k[\min_{1 \le i \le k+1} opt_t(s_i)] + k\max_{i \ne j} d_{i,j} \le k[\text{ cost of } OPT] + b.$$

where b depends only on the distances in the metric space and not on the length of the sequence.

We prove the claim by induction on t. The claim is clearly true for $t = 0$. Now consider a request to h^t at time $t + 1$. Let min be the point which minimizes $\min_{i \ne h^t} \{D_i^t + d_{i,h^t}\}$. *BALANCE* sends the server on min to h^t. Thus, $h^{t+1} \leftarrow min$ and $D_{h^t}^{t+1} \leftarrow D_{min}^t + d_{min,h^t}$. Furthermore, $opt_{t+1}(s_{h^t}) \leftarrow \min_{i \ne h^t} opt_t(s_i) + d_{i,h^t}$. Since by the inductive hypothesis, for $i \ne h^t$, $opt_t(s_i) \ge D_i^t$, we get that $opt_{t+1}(s_{h^t}) \ge D_{h^t}^{t+1}$. The rest of the D's and values of $opt_{t+1}(s_j)$, for $j \ne h^t$ remain unchanged.   ∎

The balancing principle in its simplest form does not always work, however. In particular, if there are more than $k + 1$ points in the metric space, then *BALANCE* is not competitive, even when there are only two servers. Irani and Rubinfeld show in [IR91] that a simple variant of *BALANCE* which minimizes $D_i + 2d_i$ is 10-competitive for two servers. Chrobak and Larmore show in [CL91a] that this variant is no better than 6-competitive. Kleinberg shows in [Kle94] a lower bound of 3.82 for the competitive ratio of any 'balance-like' algorithm for two servers. A balance-like algorithm sends the server which minimizes $D_i + f(d_i)$ for some function f.

13.3.2.3   Forcing cruel adversary cost to increase

An online algorithm can choose an action to take in order to make sure that it will "hasten" the time at which the offline cost will increase.

An example of this paradigm is a general class of paging algorithms called *marking* algorithms. A marking algorithm proceeds in phases. At the beginning of a phase all the nodes are unmarked. Whenever a page is requested, it is marked. On a fault, the marking algorithm evicts an unmarked page (chosen by a rule specified by the algorithm), and brings in the requested page. A phase ends just before the first fault after every page in the fast memory is marked (equivalently, a phase ends just before a request to the $k + 1^{st}$ distinct page requested in the phase). At this point, all the nodes become unmarked and a new phase begins.

Note that the phases are completely determined by the sequence and not by the choice of which unmarked page the algorithm evicts. The intuition behind the marking algorithms is that an adversary can force any deterministic online paging algorithm to fault on every request. Given this fact, the algorithm can only hope to pick pages to evict so that if the adversary always picks a page outside the algorithm's fast memory, his cost will also increase. This idea is made more explicit in the proof below.

THEOREM 13.4 [KMRS88]   Any marking algorithm is k-competitive.

Proof.   The proof is based on the simple observation that the optimal algorithm must incur at least one fault in a phase. To see this, divide the sequence in segments that start on the second request of a phase and end with the first request of the next phase. The claim is that any algorithm must fault at least once in a segment. At the beginning of a segment, the algorithm has the most recent request in its fast memory (this is just the first request of the phase). If it does not fault during the remainder of the phase, then it must have all k pages requested during the phase residing in its fast memory. The first request of the next phase (the last request of the segment) is, by definition, to a page not in this set. Thus, the optimal algorithm must fault.

Meanwhile, the marking algorithm will incur only k faults in a phase. This follows from the fact that there are exactly k distinct pages requested in one phase. Furthermore, once a page has been requested, it becomes marked and will not be evicted for the remainder of the phase. Thus, a marking algorithm will never fault more than once on a given page during a phase.   ■

Another way to view this principle is that, in some sense, a marking algorithm uses the recent past to predict the future. All of the marked pages have been requested more recently than any of the unmarked pages. On the assumption that pages that have been recently requested will be more likely to be requested again (i.e. the sequence exhibits locality of reference), a marking algorithm will not evict any marked page. Thus, an online algorithm can take advantage of any local repetitions in the input sequence. An algorithm which can do this will be favored by a competitive analysis for the following reason. The offline algorithm will have a lower cost on sequences that exhibit locality of reference and will tend to have a higher cost on sequences in which many different pages are requested in turn. Since the online algorithm is evaluated in comparison to the offline algorithm, it must fare well on those sequences for which the offline algorithm has a low cost. These are exactly the sequences that exhibit locality of reference. *Least-Recently-Used* (which is also a marking algorithm) uses the recent history of requests to predict the future even more explicitly.

For another example of this principle, see the Move-to-Front heuristic for maintaining a linked list in [ST85]. A more involved use, in conjunction with the balancing costs principle, is the Traversal algorithm in [BLS87].

13.3.2.4   Online choice of online algorithms

Let $A_1, \ldots, A_m$ be a set of online algorithms for a problem P with input set I. Assume that P can be represented as a metrical task system. Each A_i has a competitive ratio a with respect to the optimum offline algorithm, but only for a *subset* of the possible inputs such that the union of these subsets covers I. Given this setup, one can construct a generic deterministic (resp. randomized) online algorithm for P which is $a(2em + 1)$-competitive (resp. $O(a \log m)$-competitive) over all possible inputs, where e is the base of the natural logarithm. This is sometimes referred to as the *MIN* operator on online algorithms.

Fiat *et al.* observed in [FRR90] that the deterministic version of the *MIN* operator is essentially the solution to the "*m* cow paths problem" analyzed in [BYCR93] and [PY89]. In this problem there are m paths of unknown finite length which all share a common starting point. The goal is to reach the end of one of them, travelling at most some constant times the length of the minimum path. The operator, described here for metrical task systems, works as follows. Let s be the starting configuration for all algorithms and $\sigma = \langle T^1, T^2, \ldots, T^N \rangle$ be the sequence of tasks. Let σ_j denote the first j tasks in the sequence σ.

The cost of A_i on the first j requests when starting in configuration s is denoted by $\text{cost}_{A_i}(s, \sigma_j)$. Let $\text{state}_{A_i}(s, \sigma_j)$ denote the state that A_i is in after serving σ_j. The algorithm $MIN = MIN\{A_0, \ldots, A_{m-1}\}$ is always currently following one of the algorithms. That is to say, after serving σ_j, the algorithm is in state $\text{state}_{A_i}(s, \sigma_j)$ for some i. The initial algorithm is chosen arbitrarily. *MIN* keeps a bound B which is initially set to $m/(m-1)$. Suppose *MIN* is following A_i when the jth request is received. That is, *MIN* is in state $\text{state}_{A_i}(s, \sigma_{j-1})$. All costs are scaled so that $\min_{1 \le i \le m} \text{cost}_{A_i}(s, \sigma_j) = 1$. Before serving T^j, *MIN* checks $\text{cost}_{A_i}(s, \sigma_j)$ against B. If $\text{cost}_{A_i}(s, \sigma_j) > B$, then *MIN* goes to the configuration of $A_{(i+1) (\text{mod } m)}$ just before serving T^j (i.e., $\text{state}_{A_{(i+1)(\text{mod } m)}}(s, \sigma_j)$) and starts following A_{i+1}. Each time a switch is performed, $B \leftarrow Bm/(m-1)$. We state here, without proof, the result implied by [BYCR93].

THEOREM 13.5   Given any m algorithms for a metrical task system, let $MIN = MIN\{A_0, \ldots, A_{m-1}\}$. For any sequence of tasks σ and any initial starting configuration s, $\text{cost}_{MIN}(s, \sigma) \le (2em + 1) \cdot \min_{1 \le i \le m}\{\text{cost}_{A_i}(s, \sigma)\}$.

The randomized *MIN* operator was presented and analyzed in [FFK+91], and later improved in [ABM93]. [ABM93] also gives an improved deterministic *MIN* operator in which an $O(\sum_{i=1}^m a_i)$-competitive algorithm is obtained, where each A_i is a_i-competitive for its portion of the inputs.

13.3.3   BOUNDING COMPETITIVENESS

13.3.3.1   Potential functions

The most common technique for proving upper bounds on the competitive ratio is to construct a *potential function*. Suppose that A is an online algorithm. We use a potential function to analyze A as follows. Fix an input sequence σ of m operations and run A and *OPT* simultaneously on σ. The potential function maps the configurations of A and *OPT* to a real number Φ. Let Φ_i denote the value of the potential function after *OPT* and A have served the first i requests of the sequence. Let t_i denote the cost of A on the ith operation, and o_i the cost of *OPT* on the ith operation. The *amortized* cost of A for the ith operation, denoted a_i, is defined to be $t_i + \Phi_i - \Phi_{i-1}$. An upper bound for the cost of A

on the entire sequence is proven by bounding the amortized cost of A for each operation. Suppose we can find a nonnegative potential function whose initial value is 0 such that for every i, $1 \le i \le m$, $a_i \le c \cdot o_i$. Then,

$$\text{cost}_A(\sigma) = \sum_{i=1}^{m} t_i \le \Phi_m - \Phi_0 + \sum_{i=1}^{m} t_i = \sum_{i=1}^{m} (t_i - \Phi_{i-1} + \Phi_i)$$

$$= \sum_{i=1}^{m} a_i \le c \sum_{i=1}^{m} o_i = c \cdot \text{cost}_{OPT}(\sigma).$$

The use of a potential function to analyze a sequence of operations is called *amortized analysis* [Tar85] because the cost of each operation is amortized (i.e. averaged) across the entire sequence of requests. An individual operation may be costly for A relative to the cost of OPT, however the average cost of an operation over the sequence can be bounded by twice the average optimal cost. Note that the term "average" refers to the average over the sequence and does not imply any statistical assumptions about the input sequence. Potential functions are often used in online algorithms because typically the input to an online problem is a sequence of operations and the goal is to upper bound the cost of an algorithm over the entire sequence.

The key to making such a proof work lies in the choice of an appropriate potential function. Typically, a potential function will measure the "distance" from the online algorithm's configuration to OPT's configuration. We illustrate these ideas using a potential function proof that LRU is a strongly competitive paging algorithm.

We define for each page p, a value $a[p]$. $a[p] = 0$ if and only if p is not in the fast memory. If $a[p] > 0$, then $a[p]$ denotes p's place in the LRU queue. Since initially the cache is empty, we start with $a[p] = 0$ for all p. When LRU copies a new page into the fast memory, it decrements $a[p]$ for every p in the fast memory, ejects the page whose a value is 0. For the new page p', it sets $a[p'] \leftarrow k$. If a page p is requested which is already in LRU's fast memory, then for every p' such that $a[p'] > a[p]$, LRU will decrement $a[p']$. Then it sets $a[p] \leftarrow k$.

Let S be the set of pages that OPT has in its fast memory. The potential function is defined to be

$$\Phi = \sum_{p \in S} (k - a[p]).$$

Consider a single page request. Let Δcost_{LRU} denote the cost of LRU and let Δcost_{OPT} denote the cost of OPT to satisfy the request. The change in potential is denoted $\Delta\Phi$. Since both fast memories start out empty, $\Phi_0 = 0$. Furthermore, $\Phi_i \ge 0$ for all i because $a[P] \le k$ for all P. Thus, it follows from the following lemma that LRU is k-competitive.

LEMMA 13.1 [KMRS88] For any request in any sequence of page requests,

$$\Delta\text{cost}_{LRU} + \Delta\Phi \le k(\Delta\text{cost}_{OPT}).$$

Proof. Consider a request for a page p. We divide the request into two steps: in Step 1, we let OPT satisfy the request and then in Step 2, we let LRU satisfy the request. We prove the lemma for each step separately.

- **Step** 1: Let *OPT* satisfy the request. If *OPT* does not fault, $\Delta\Phi = \Delta\mathrm{cost}_{OPT} = \Delta\mathrm{cost}_{LRU} = 0$. If *OPT* does fault, the right-hand side of the inequality is k. Thus, we have to show that $\Delta\Phi \leq k$. *OPT* loads a new page p and evicts one page p'. In the worst case, p is not in *LRU*'s fast memory and p' is. In this case $\Delta\Phi = (k - a[p]) - (k - a[p']) \leq k$.

- **Step** 2: Now let *LRU* satisfy the request. If *LRU* does not fault, then we have to show that $\Delta\Phi \leq 0$. Let $a[p] = i$. We know that $p \in S$. So Φ decrease by $k - i$ due to the change in $a[p]$. The a value for at most $k - i$ other pages will change and each of these will decrease by at most 1. Thus, $\Delta\Phi \leq 0$.

    If *LRU* does fault, the left hand side of the inequality is 1. Thus, we have to show that $\Delta\Phi \leq -1$. For every page that is both in *LRU* and *OPT*'s fast memory, the potential function increases by 1 (because the a value is decremented by 1). There are at most $k - 1$ of them because *OPT* has the newly requested page and *LRU* does not. The new page p is already in *OPT*'s fast memory, and the a value for this page goes from 0 to k, causing Φ to decrease by k. Thus, $\Delta\Phi \leq (k - 1) - k = -1$.   ∎

13.3.3.2   Existence and construction of potential functions

Although potential functions are often difficult to find, it is not difficult to show that they always exist [2]. Consider an arbitrary metrical task system and the graph G constructed as follows. There is a vertex corresponding to each pair (s_A, s_{opt}) where s_A is a state of the online algorithm A, *including* all its variables, and s_{opt} is a state of *OPT*. There is an edge e from (s_1, s_2) to (s_3, s_4) if there is a task T such that A services T in state s_1 by moving to s_3, and if *OPT can* service T in state s_2 by moving to s_4.

Suppose that "c" is the competitive ratio we are trying to prove. Then, the edge e is labelled with a cost, denoted $cost(e)$, equal to c times the adversary cost for the task minus the online cost, i.e.

$$c(e) = c * (d(s_2, s_4) + T(s_4)) - (d(s_1, s_3) + T(s_3)).$$

Let s_0 be the starting state of the algorithms A and *OPT*, and let G' be the subgraph of G reachable from (s_0, s_0). If the algorithm A is c-competitive, the graph G' cannot have a negative cycle. If it does, then there is a sequence of requests and a behavior of the adversary such that around this cycle, the adversary cost is less than $1/c$ times the online algorithm, which violates c-competitiveness.

It is a standard trick (see [Tar83]) that in a directed graph with no negative cycles, there exists a labeling of the vertices with a potential $\Phi(v)$ such that if the cost of an edge (v, w) is replaced by:

$$newcost(v, w) = cost(v, w) + \Phi(v) - \Phi(w)$$

then all the new costs are non-negative. In fact, it is easy to construct such a potential function. Choose any starting vertex v (from which all vertices can be reached), and choose $\Phi(v) = 0$. Then for each vertex w, the value of $\Phi(w)$ is the length of the shortest path in the graph from v to w, where the length of a path is the sum of the costs of

---

[2]This has been observed independently by several researchers. The presentation here is due to D.D. Sleator.

the edges in the path. This Φ is of course the potential function needed to prove the c-competitiveness of the online algorithm.

The above formulation allows the use of linear programming to directly derive the minimum value of c. Let c and the $\Phi(v)$'s be the variables of a linear program. Then we wish to Minimize c under the constraint that the *newcosts* are all non-negative. This approach may be impractical, however, since the graph G' may be too large. Nonetheless, variants of this idea have been used to prove bounds for small instances of the k-server problem (see [KMMO90, LR94]).

In general, potential functions have been found by trial and error. In most cases, the potential function is a linear combination of certain simple functionals measuring the distance between the online and the offline paper. Bern, Greene, and Ragunathan automate part of the task of designing a potential function for problems in online cache sharing by using linear programming to find the optimal coefficients once their choice of components had been determined (see [BGR93]).

THEORETICAL UNDERPINNINGS: RANDOMIZED ALGORITHMS

13.4

A randomized online algorithm is an online algorithm that makes random choices as it responds to requests. Since the cost incurred by a randomized algorithm on a request sequence depends on the results of the coin tosses the algorithm makes, it is a random variable. Therefore, the performance of such an algorithm is assessed by considering its expected cost on a request sequence.

For randomized online algorithms, there is no unique notion of an adversary. The issue which distinguishes different adversaries is the extent to which they know the outcomes of random choices made by the algorithm and how they themselves service the sequence they generate.

We divide adversaries into two types:

- An *oblivious adversary* must choose the entire request sequence σ, without any knowledge either of the outcome of the coin tosses or of the specific actions taken as a result of the coin tosses. However, the oblivious adversary does know the algorithm itself including the probability distribution of actions taken for a given input.

- An *adaptive adversary* is one that chooses each request in the input string σ based on knowledge of all actions taken so far, and of the outcome of all previous coin tosses.

Under the category of adaptive adversaries, one can distinguish between two types of adversaries, depending on how the adversary itself serves the sequence.

- An *adaptive offline* adversary waits until the entire sequence σ has been generated and services it optimally. In other words, the cost incurred by this adversary is the optimal offline cost on the entire sequence σ.

- An *adaptive online* adversary must itself serve the sequence σ that it generates in an *online* fashion.

Competitiveness is then defined as follows: A randomized online algorithm A is *c-competitive against oblivious (resp. adaptive online, adaptive offline) adversaries* if there exists an α such that for all oblivious (resp. adaptive online, adaptive offline) adversaries, ADV,

$$E[\mathrm{cost}_A(\sigma) - c \cdot \mathrm{cost}_{ADV}(\sigma)] \le \alpha$$

where σ is the sequence generated by the adversary in its interaction with A and $\mathrm{cost}_{ADV}(\sigma)$ is the cost incurred by the adversary. The *competitive ratio of a randomized algorithm against adversaries of type ADV* is

$$c_A^{ADV} \equiv \inf_c\{c \,|\, A \text{ is } c\text{-competitive against all adversaries of type } ADV\}$$

Here the expectation is taken over all choices made by the online algorithm. Since the actions of an oblivious adversary can not depend on any of the random choices of the algorithm, its behavior is deterministic; the sequence σ it generates as well as its cost $\mathrm{cost}_{OBL}(\sigma)$ is not a random variable. A randomized algorithm A is c-competitive against all oblivious adversaries if there is a constant b such that for all input sequences σ,

$$E[\mathrm{cost}_A(\sigma)] \le c \cdot \mathrm{cost}_{OPT}(\sigma) + b.$$

For the other two adversaries, σ depends on the coin tosses of A. This means that the costs $\mathrm{cost}_{ADOFF}(\sigma)$ and $\mathrm{cost}_{ADON}(\sigma)$ are themselves random variables, so the expectation calculated above applies to the adversary cost as well.

The least powerful of the adversaries is the oblivious, because an adaptive adversary has the option of deciding the request sequence in advance and answering it optimally. The most powerful of the adaptive adversaries is the adaptive offline since the adaptive offline adversary can always choose to service the sequence online. Let $\mathcal{C}_{OBL}$ (respectively $\mathcal{C}_{ADON}, \mathcal{C}_{ADOFF}$) be the best competitive ratio achievable against any oblivious (resp. adaptive online, adaptive offline) adversary on a problem. That is, $\mathcal{C}_{OBL} = \inf_A c_A^{OBL}$, $\mathcal{C}_{ADON} = \inf_A c_A^{ADON}$, and $\mathcal{C}_{ADOFF} = \inf_A c_A^{ADOFF}$. Let $\mathcal{C}_{DET}$ be the best competitive ratio achievable by a deterministic algorithm for the task system. We have that:

$$\mathcal{C}_{OBL} \le \mathcal{C}_{ADON} \le \mathcal{C}_{ADOFF} \le \mathcal{C}_{DET}.$$

The distinction between the three adversaries was made by Raghavan and Snir in [RS89] and by Ben-David, Borodin, Karp, Tardos, and Wigderson in [BDBK+90].

13.4.1   EXAMPLE: PAGING

13.4.1.1   Memoryless randomized paging

The lower bound of k for the competitive ratio of any deterministic paging algorithm shown in Section 13.3.1 can easily be extended to apply to randomized algorithms against an adaptive online adversary. Thus, no advantage can be gained in using randomization against an adaptive adversary. It is natural then to ask whether a randomized algorithm fares better against an oblivious adversary. The difference is, in fact, quite dramatic as we shall see later in this section. First, we begin our discussion of randomized paging algorithms with the simplest randomized algorithm: on a fault, evict a random page from the cache. This is a memoryless algorithm: the only information used in making replacement decisions is which pages are currently in the cache.

It turns out that this particular use of randomization does not yield a lower competitive ratio than that achieved by the deterministic algorithms we have discussed, even against an oblivious adversary: this algorithm is k-competitive against any oblivious adversary. The lower bound is a special case of the following theorem proved by Coppersmith, Doyle, Raghavan, and Snir[CDRS93].

THEOREM 13.6 Any memoryless k-server algorithm A on any metric space has competitive ratio at least k against an oblivious adversary.

13.4.1.2   The randomized marking algorithm

Although no memoryless randomized algorithm has competitiveness below k against oblivious adversaries, there do exist nonmemoryless randomized algorithms which beat the deterministic bound. Fiat, Karp, Luby, McGeogh, and Young [FKL+91] were able to show that a randomized version of the marking algorithm has competitive ratio $2\mathcal{H}(k)$ against an oblivious adversary, where $\mathcal{H}(k)$ is the kth harmonic number $\sum_{1 \le i \le k} \frac{1}{k}$. The algorithm, called *RMA* (for Randomized Marking Algorithm), works as follows:

Initially, all pages are unmarked.

- If there is a request for a page not in the cache, bring the page in, replace a random unmarked page, and mark the new page. (If all pages were already marked, unmark all of them first.)

- If the request is for a page that is in the cache, then mark it.

THEOREM 13.7 The randomized marking algorithm *RMA* has competitive ratio $2\mathcal{H}(k)$ against any oblivious adversary, where H_k is the kth harmonic number.

Proof.   Assume *OPT* and *RMA* start with the same cache contents. As before, we divide the sequence σ into phases. The ith phase ends immediately before the $k + 1^{st}$ distinct page is request in the phase. We will analyze the cost of both *OPT* and *RMA* phase by phase. Note that once a page is marked, it is not evicted from the cache for the remainder of the phase. Therefore, if we denote the set of pages requested in phase i by P_i, then at the end of a phase i, the contents of *RMA*'s cache is exactly P_i. Furthermore, *RMA* will not fault twice on the same page within a phase. Thus, we need only account for faults incurred on the first request to any given page in a phase.

Let m_i be the number of *new* requests in phase i, (i.e. the number of pages requested in phase i that were not requested in phase $i - 1$). A request in the first phase is also new if it is not one of the pages initially in the cache. Since any new page is not in *RMA*'s cache at the beginning of a phase, *RMA* must fault once on every new page requested. Now we must analyze the expected number of faults on requests to *old* pages (i.e., pages which are not new). What is the probability that *RMA* faults on the jth old page requested? Let's suppose that just before the jth old page is requested, there have been ℓ new pages requested so far in the phase. It is easy to show by induction that at this time there are exactly ℓ pages in P_{i-1} that are not in the cache. Furthermore, these are distributed uniformly at random among the $k - (j - 1)$ unmarked pages in P_{i-1}. Since the adversary has fixed the request in advance, the probability that it is not in the cache is exactly $\ell/k - (j - 1)$. Since ℓ is always at most m_i, the probability of a fault on the request to the jth old page is at most $\frac{m_i}{k-(j-1)}$.

Therefore, the expected cost of the marking algorithm in the ith phase is

$$E[\text{cost}_{RMA_i}(\sigma)] \leq m_i + \sum_{1 \leq i \leq k - m_i} \frac{m_i}{k - i + 1} \leq m_i \mathcal{H}(k).$$

Summing up over all phases, we get that the expected cost for the algorithm over the entire sequence is $E[\text{cost}_{RMA}(\sigma)] \leq \mathcal{H}(k) \sum_i m_i$.

For the offline algorithm we claim that $\text{cost}_{OPT}(\sigma) \geq \sum_i \frac{m_i}{2}$.

Consider the $(i - 1)^{st}$ and i^{th} phases. The number of distinct pages requested in both phases is $k + m_i$. Since *OPT* has only k pages in the cache at the beginning of the $(i - 1)^{st}$ phase, it must incur at least m_i faults during the two phases. Applying this argument to every pair of adjacent phases, we have that $\text{cost}_{OPT}(\sigma) \geq \sum_i m_{2i}$ and $\text{cost}_{OPT}(\sigma) \geq \sum_i m_{2i+1}$. Therefore, *OPT* has cost at least the average of these, i.e. $\text{cost}_{OPT}(\sigma) \geq \sum_i m_i/2$. Thus, $E[\text{cost}_{RMA}(\sigma)] \leq 2\mathcal{H}(k)\text{cost}_{OPT}(\sigma)$. ∎

A much more complicated algorithm was shown to be $\mathcal{H}(k)$ competitive by Mc-Geoch and Sleator[MS91]

13.4.2   LOWER BOUNDS

A common technique for proving lower bounds on the competitive ratio of a randomized online algorithm against oblivious adversaries is to examine the performance of deterministic algorithms on inputs from a given probability distribution $\mathcal{P}$ over request sequences, σ.

DEFINITION 13.1   Let $\mathcal{P}$ be a probability distribution on request sequences σ. An algorithm A is *c-competitive against $\mathcal{P}$* if there exists a constant, b, such that

$$E_{\mathcal{P}}(\text{cost}_A(\sigma)) \leq c \cdot E_{\mathcal{P}}(\text{cost}_{OPT}(\sigma)) + b$$

DEFINITION 13.2   Let $c_A^{\mathcal{P}}$ denote the infimum over all c such that A is c-competitive against $\mathcal{P}$, and let c_R^{OBL} denote the competitive ratio of a randomized algorithm R against *OBL*.

The basic theorem that allows us to prove lower bounds for randomized online algorithms is the following.

THEOREM 13.8 $\inf_R c_R^{OBL} = \sup_{\mathcal{P}} \inf_A c_A^{\mathcal{P}}$.

In other words, the competitive ratio of the best randomized algorithm against oblivious adversaries is equal to the competitive ratio of the best deterministic algorithm, A, on inputs generated from the "worst" probability distribution. The proof of this theorem follows from the minimax theorem of game theory and was first observed by Yao [Yao80] in the context of ordinary complexity theory, and by Borodin, Linial, and Saks [BLS87] in the context of online algorithms.

13.4.2.1 Example: paging

We now illustrate the use of Theorem 13.8 for proving lower bounds on c_R^{OBL} by showing a lower bound for randomized paging algorithms against an oblivious adversary. The bound comes close to matching the upper bound shown in Section 13.4.1.2. The following theorem is due to Fiat, Karp, Luby, McGeoch, Sleator, and Young [FKL$^+$91].

THEOREM 13.9 [FKL$^+$91] Let R be any randomized paging algorithm. If the number of pages is greater than or equal to $k + 1$, where k is the size of the cache, the competitive ratio of R against any oblivious adversary is greater than or equal to $\mathcal{H}(k)$.

Proof. We will find our lower bound on c_R^{OBL} by exhibiting a probability distribution $\mathcal{P}$ for which $c_A^{\mathcal{P}} \geq \mathcal{H}(k)$ for all deterministic algorithms A. Let S be a set of $k + 1$ pages which include the k pages initially in the cache. Take $\mathcal{P}$ to be the uniform distribution on the $k + 1$ pages in S. That is, a sequence σ of m requests is generated by independently selecting each request at random from S. Clearly, the expected performance of any deterministic algorithm on inputs generated from this distribution is

$$E_{\mathcal{P}}[\text{cost}_A(\sigma)] = \frac{m}{k + 1} \tag{13.1}$$

for $|\sigma| = m$. To see this, note that the probability that a given requested page is not in the cache is $\frac{1}{k+1}$. We now need an upper bound on the expected performance of OPT.

Once again, we divide the sequence of page requests into non-overlapping phases such that each phase contains maximal runs of requests to at most k distinct pages. As we have seen, if there are r distinct phases then the optimal algorithm can service the sequence with at most $r + 1$ faults. At the beginning of a phase OPT replaces the one page currently in the cache that will not be requested in the phase. Therefore, if $N(m)$ is the random variable which is the number of phases in a sequence σ of length m (generated from $\mathcal{P}$), then the expected offline cost satisfies

$$E_{\mathcal{P}}(\text{cost}_{OPT}) \leq E(N(m) + 1). \tag{13.2}$$

Since the durations of successive phases are independent, identically distributed random variables, we have by the elementary renewal theorem [3] that

$$\lim_{m \to \infty} \frac{m}{E(N(m))} = E(X_i),$$

where $E(X_i)$ is the expected length of the ith phase.

---

[3]For a detailed treatment of renewal theory, see for example Feller's book [Fel50] or almost any book on probability theory and stochastic processes.

The expected length of a phase, $E(X_i)$, is easily seen to be $(k+1)\mathcal{H}(k)$ (this is a so-called "coupon collectors problem.")

Therefore, we have that

$$\lim_{m\to\infty} \frac{E_{\mathcal{P}}(\text{cost}_A)}{E_{\mathcal{P}}(\text{cost}_{OPT})} \geq \frac{m/k+1}{m/E(X_i)} \geq \frac{E(X_i)}{k+1} = \frac{(k+1)\cdot\mathcal{H}(k)}{k+1} = \mathcal{H}(k).$$

Applying Theorem 13.8 yields a lower bound of $\mathcal{H}(k)$ on c_R^{OBL}.   ■

13.4.3   THE RELATIONSHIPS BETWEEN THE ADVERSARIES

The power of a randomized online algorithm is measured by the competitive ratio it achieves and the strength of the adversary it plays against. The relationships between the three adversaries we have described was studied by Ben-David, Borodin, Karp, Tardos, and Wigderson [BDBK+90] in a general model called *request-answer games*. Practically every online problem can be formulated as a request-answer game. We do not define this model here; for further details see [BDBK+90]. For the purposes of the subsequent discussion we present the results of [BDBK+90] for online problems which can be posed as metrical task systems (a more restrictive model than request-answer games).

We review the definitions of the three adversaries in a game-theoretic context: the interaction between an adversary and the online algorithm can be viewed as a game. Consider the game tree where the root node has level 0 and represents the starting state of both algorithm and adversary. Nodes at level $2i$ represent possible states of the online algorithm after i requests have been processed. Branches from nodes at an even level to a node at the next level down represent the possible choices of requests the adversary can make. Each such arc is labeled with the name of the request. Branches from nodes at an odd level to a node at the next level down represent the possible ways the online algorithm can serve the request in its current state. Each such arc is labeled with the probability that the online algorithm will take it. Figure 13.1 gives an example of part of such a tree.

The fact that all the adversaries know the online algorithm and the probability distributions it uses means that all adversaries know the entire game tree in advance. Each adversary then consists of a requesting component and a servicing component. The requesting component is a choice of one request r_v from each node v at an even level in the tree. In other words, if the online algorithm reaches v, the next request that adversary gives it is r_v. The requesting component of an adversary can be expressed as a pruned game tree where every node at an even level has exactly one child. The different adversaries are then distinguished as follows:

- For an *oblivious* adversary, for all v at level $2i$ in the tree r_v is the same, so that no matter what the state of the algorithm is, the ith request is the same. In other words, the adversary is oblivious to the random choices (and hence the exact state) of the online algorithm in generating the next request. The oblivious adversary services the resulting sequence optimally.

- *adaptive* adversaries may choose any request from any even-leveled node in the tree. It is adaptive because each request r_v is tailored to the node v itself, i.e. the decision of the next request to give depends on the history and state of the online algorithm.

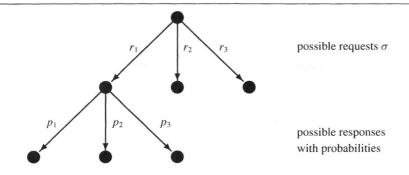

possible requests σ

possible responses
with probabilities

FIGURE 13.1

*Game tree description of interaction between the
randomized online algorithm and adversary.*

- An *adaptive online* adversary is further restricted to make a choice as to how it would serve that request at the time it makes the request, i.e. without knowledge of which path in the game tree will be taken from that node (or equivalently without knowledge of future coin tosses of the online algorithm).

- An *adaptive offline* adversary serves the sequence of requests optimally at the end.

13.4.3.1 Adaptive offline versus adaptive online and oblivious

We saw that the use of randomization against an oblivious adversary gave us an *exponential* improvement in the competitive ratio for paging, relative to deterministic algorithms. In fact, the performance of a randomized online algorithm depends on the adversary against whom it plays. Nevertheless, there are certain relationships between the performance of algorithms against different adversaries. The first result of Ben-David *et al.* shows that the existence of algorithms, one of which does "well" against any oblivious adversary and one of which does "well" against any adaptive online adversary (not necessarily the same algorithm), implies the existence of an algorithm that does "well" against any adaptive offline adversary.

THEOREM 13.10 Let G be an online algorithm that has a competitive ratio of α against adaptive online adversaries and suppose that there exists an online algorithm H which has a competitive ratio of β against oblivious adversaries. Then G is itself $\alpha\beta$-competitive against adaptive offline adversaries.

The intuition for this result is the following slightly fallacious argument. For any adaptive offline adversary A, consider the adaptive online adversary A' whose requesting component is the same as that of A, but which services requests according to the algorithm H. Then we have that G's expected cost on the sequence generated by A' is at most α times that of A', or equivalently α times that of H. But H's expected cost on this sequence is itself β times the optimal offline cost, or equivalently β times that of A. Therefore, G's expected cost is at most $\alpha\beta$ times that of A, for any adaptive offline adversary A.

This theorem is tight in the sense that there exist G and H as in the theorem such that G is no better than $\alpha\beta$ competitive against adaptive offline adversaries: we discussed a randomized paging algorithm that has competitive ratio $\mathcal{H}(k)$ against oblivious adversaries. In addition, the randomized paging algorithm which evicts a random page in the cache on a page fault, has competitive ratio k against adaptive online adversaries. Furthermore, the competitive ratio of the random eviction algorithm is no better than $k\mathcal{H}(k)$. The above theorem implies that the competitive ratio of this latter algorithm against adaptive offline adversaries is at most $k\mathcal{H}(k)$ and this is indeed the case. For paging, however, there exist other algorithms (even deterministic) which are k-competitive against adaptive offline adversaries.

It is possible to show, though, that for any α and β, there is an online problem such that there is an algorithm which is α-competitive against any adaptive online adversary and there is a β-competitive algorithm against any oblivious adversary. There is no algorithm that has a competitive ratio less than $\alpha\beta$ against every adaptive offline adversary. The proof of this is not presented here, but can be found in [BDBK$^+$90]. One interesting aspect of the proof is that the problem for which the property holds is not a metrical task system. It is not known if the analogous result holds for metrical task systems. In fact, it is not even known if there is a metrical task system for which there exists an algorithm whose competitive ratio against adaptive online adversaries is strictly less than the competitive ratio of the best algorithm against adaptive offline adversaries.

13.4.3.2   Adaptive offline versus deterministic

Since the adaptive offline adversary is the most powerful of the three that we have considered for randomized algorithms, an interesting question is whether online algorithms are aided by randomization at all when pitted against such an adversary. Intuitively, one expects the answer to be no, and the next theorem shows that this is indeed the case.

THEOREM 13.11   Let G be an α-competitive online algorithm against *ADOFF*. Then there is a deterministic algorithm that has competitive ratio α.

In general, Theorem 13.11 is not constructive. Deng and Mahajan show in [DM91] that there are games for which there is a simple and computable c-competitive randomized algorithm against adaptive online adversaries for some c but any deterministic algorithm which achieves any bounded competitive ratio is not computable. However, Ben-David *et al.* in [BDBK$^+$90] show that for a wide class of randomized algorithms, the corresponding deterministic algorithm is indeed computable. Theorems 13.11 and 13.10 can be combined to give the following two corollaries:

COROLLARY 13.1   Let G be a randomized algorithm that is α-competitive against any adaptive online adversary. If there is a β-competitive algorithm against an oblivious adversary, then there exists a deterministic $(\alpha \cdot \beta)$-competitive algorithm.

COROLLARY 13.2   Let G be a randomized algorithm that is α-competitive against any adaptive online adversary. Then there exists a deterministic (α^2)-competitive algorithm.

THE K-SERVER PROBLEM REVISITED
13.5

13.5.1   HISTORY

The k-server problem was posed in 1988 by Manasse, McGeoch, and Sleator [MMS90]. They proved a lower bound of k on the competitive ratio, and an upper bound of k for the special cases where $k = 2$ and where $n = k + 1$. They conjectured that there is a k-competitive algorithm for any metric space. Since then, proving k-server conjecture has been a primary focus for researchers in online algorithms. For some time, it was even unknown whether there was an algorithm that achieves a competitiveness which can be bounded by any function of k on all metric spaces. In response to this, researchers focused on algorithms for specific types of metric spaces (e.g. trees, the circle) [CKPV91, CL91b, CDRS93, Kar, AKPW92]. Finally, in 1990 Fiat, Rabani, and Ravid [FRR90] proved that a certain algorithm has competitive ratio which was a function of k only, albeit rather large: $O(k^k)$! This was improved by Grove in 1991 [Gro91] who showed that a simple and natural randomized algorithm has competitive ratio $O(k2^k)$.

In 1994, Koutsoupias and Papadimitriou [KP94a] proved that an algorithm that had long been conjectured [CL92] to be strongly competitive is $(2k - 1)$-competitive. This is undoubtedly the most celebrated result in the area of online algorithms to date. In this section, we present the key features of their proof.

13.5.2   NOTATION AND PROPERTIES OF WORK FUNCTIONS

We use the following notation:

- S is the set of points in the underlying metric space.
- S^k is the set of all size k multisets of points in S.
- $\forall X, Y \in S^k$, $D(X, Y)$ is the minimum cost of moving from X to Y (i.e. the minimum matching between the points in X and the points in Y.)
- σ is the request sequence, and σ_t is the tth request in σ ($\sigma_t \in S$).
- $\text{opt}_t(\sigma, X)$ is the minimum cost of serving the first t requests in σ, ending up in state X, assuming that X_0 is the starting configuration.

$\text{opt}_t(\sigma, X)$ can be computed using dynamic programming as follows:

- Base case: $\text{opt}_0(\sigma, X) = D(X, X_0)$.

- Induction step:
  If $\sigma_t \in X$, $\mathrm{opt}_t(\sigma, X) = \mathrm{opt}_{t-1}(\sigma, X)$.
  If $\sigma_t \notin X$, $\mathrm{opt}_t(\sigma, X) = \min_{Y \mid \sigma_t \in Y} \left[\mathrm{opt}_t(\sigma, Y) + D(X, Y) \right]$.

The two cases in the induction step can be combined to give

$$\mathrm{opt}_t(\sigma, X) = \min_{Y \mid \sigma_t \in Y} \left[\mathrm{opt}_{t-1}(\sigma, Y) + D(Y, X) \right].$$

The functions $\mathrm{opt}_t(\sigma, \cdot)$ are typically called *work functions*, and are usually denoted by w_t. Our change of notation is in order to emphasize the fact that they represent the optimal cost of servicing a sequence of requests.

We will need the following easy-to-prove properties of work functions:

I. $\forall X, Y$, $\mathrm{opt}_t(\sigma, X) \leq \mathrm{opt}_t(\sigma, Y) + D(Y, X)$.

II. $\mathrm{opt}_t(\sigma, X) = \min_{x \in X} \left[\mathrm{opt}_t(\sigma, X - x + \sigma_t) + d(x, \sigma_t) \right]$, since

$$\begin{aligned}
\mathrm{opt}_t(\sigma, X) &= \min_{Y \mid \sigma_t \in Y} \left[\mathrm{opt}_t(\sigma, Y) + D(X, Y) \right] \\
&= \min_{x \in X} \left[\mathrm{opt}_t(\sigma, Y) + d(\sigma_t, x) + D(X - x + \sigma_t, Y) \right] \\
&\geq \min_{x \in X} \left[\mathrm{opt}_t(\sigma, X - x + \sigma_t) + d(\sigma_t, x) \right].
\end{aligned}$$

III. $\mathrm{opt}_t(\sigma, X) \geq \mathrm{opt}_{t-1}(\sigma, X)$.

13.5.3   THE WORK FUNCTION ALGORITHM *WFA*

We review the work function algorithm described earlier. Suppose that after $t - 1$ requests, the algorithm is in state X_{t-1}, and the next request σ_t is r.

The Work Function Algorithm serves the request by moving to the configuration X with $r \in X$ that minimizes $\underbrace{\mathrm{opt}_t(\sigma, X)}_{\text{retrospective}} + \underbrace{D(X, X_{t-1})}_{\text{local greedy}}$.

This algorithm is a combination of two natural algorithms neither of which is competitive by itself. The second term corresponds to the *local greedy* algorithm: the one which serves the request in the cheapest possible way, ignoring history altogether. The first term corresponds to the *retrospective* algorithm, the one which tries to chase the optimal offline algorithm (by moving into a state which minimizes the *OPT* cost so far). The problem with the latter is that it may be very expensive to chase *OPT*; an algorithm which does this may find that this expense was unnecessary only a few requests later. Thus, the second term prevents the algorithm from incurring large local costs in attempting to mimic *OPT*'s behavior.

Using property 3, we can observe that the state X which minimizes the above equation only differs from the algorithm's present configuration X_{t-1} in the location of one server. Thus, *WFA* serves the request by moving a server at x to r where x minimizes

$$\min_{x \in X} \left[\mathrm{opt}_t(\sigma, X_{t-1} + r - x) + d(r, x) \right] = \mathrm{opt}_t(\sigma, X_{t-1})$$

Note that $X_{t-1} + r - x = X_t$, and so we have

$$\min_{x \in X} \left[\text{opt}_t(\sigma, X_t) + d(r, x) \right] = \text{opt}_t(\sigma, X_{t-1}) \qquad (13.3)$$

A more general version of this algorithm was initially proposed by Borodin, Linial, and Saks [BLS87] in 1987 for metrical task systems. It was subsequently studied extensively by Chrobak and Larmore [CL92], for the special case of the k-server problem. Their experiments suggested that it is k-competitive, which they were able to prove for some special cases. They also introduced some ideas for approaching the problem that ultimately turned out to be important. We now present the 1994 result of Koutsoupias and Papadimitriou [DK93] showing that there exists a constant c, such that for any input σ,

$$WFA(\sigma) \le (2k - 1)OPT(\sigma) + c. \qquad (13.4)$$

13.5.4   PROOF OF $(2K - 1)$-COMPETITIVENESS

We will be able to assume that the online and offline algorithms start and end in the same configuration. Indeed, suppose that X_f is the final configuration of OPT, and WFA finishes serving the sequence in a different configuration from X_f. Then we can append the sequence σ with requests to points in X_f until WFA moves to X_f. (Any algorithm that does not eventually move its servers to X_f has no bounded competitive ratio.) The cost of WFA on the appended sequence is greater than or equal to the cost of WFA on the original sequence, and the cost of OPT on the appended sequence is equal to the cost of OPT on the original, therefore it is sufficient to prove equation 13.4 for the appended sequence.

13.5.4.1   Offline pseudo-cost

Define the *offline pseudo-cost* or amortized offline cost, $\widetilde{\text{opt}}_t$ on the tth step to be

$$\widetilde{\text{opt}}_t = \text{opt}_t(\sigma, X_t) - \text{opt}_{t-1}(\sigma, X_{t-1}).$$

This is the amortized offline cost for the tth step, since

$$\sum_t \widetilde{\text{opt}}_t = \text{opt}_f(\sigma, X_f) - \text{opt}_0(\sigma, X_0) = \text{cost}_{OPT}(\sigma).$$

We bound WFA_t, the cost incurred by the work function algorithm on the tth request, plus $\widetilde{\text{opt}}_t$, the amortized offline cost for the tth request.

Suppose that WFA moves from x to r in order to service σ_t. Then,

$$\begin{aligned}
WFA_t + \widetilde{\text{opt}}_t &= d(x, r) + \text{opt}_t(\sigma, X_t) - \text{opt}_{t-1}(\sigma, X_{t-1}) \\
&= \text{opt}_t(\sigma, X_{t-1}) - \text{opt}_{t-1}(\sigma, X_{t-1}) \\
&\le \max_X \left[\text{opt}_t(\sigma, X) - \text{opt}_{t-1}(\sigma, X) \right].
\end{aligned}$$

where the second equation follows from equation (13.3).

Let EC_t, the *extended cost* of the tth request, be defined by

$$EC_t = \max_X \big[\text{opt}_t(\sigma, X) - \text{opt}_{t-1}(\sigma, X)\big].$$

We have that $WFA_t + \widetilde{\text{opt}}_t \le EC_t$.

The proof will proceed by proving an upper bound on the extended cost of the tth request. The advantage of working with extended costs is that it allows us to entirely ignore the real configuration of the online algorithm. We have simply to show that a certain inequality holds for all work functions. Of course, a potential disadvantage of approaching the problem this way is that we may be overestimating the cost incurred by *WFA*.

13.5.4.2 Approach

We seek a potential function $\Phi : X \to \mathcal{R}^+$ satisfying the following two conditions:

$$WFA_t + \widetilde{\text{opt}}_t \le EC_t \le \Phi_t - \Phi_{t-1}, \tag{13.5}$$

and

$$\Phi_f - \Phi_0 \le (k+1)\text{cost}_{OPT}(\sigma) + c. \tag{13.6}$$

The existence of such a potential function implies that

$$
\begin{aligned}
\text{cost}_{WFA}(\sigma) + \text{cost}_{OPT}(\sigma) &= \sum_t (WFA_t + \widetilde{\text{opt}}_t) \\
&\le \sum_t EC_t = \sum_t \max_X \big[\text{opt}_t(\sigma, X) - \text{opt}_{t-1}(\sigma, X)\big] \\
&\le \sum_t (\Phi_t - \Phi_{t-1}) = \Phi_f - \Phi_0 \\
&\le (k+1)\text{cost}_{OPT}(\sigma) + c.
\end{aligned}
$$

which would mean that *WFA* is k-competitive.

13.5.4.3 The case $n = k+1$

For the special case of $n = k+1$, the approach just outlined works easily. Take $\Phi_t = \sum_X \text{opt}_t(\sigma, X)$.
Then $\Delta\Phi = \Phi_t - \Phi_{t-1} \ge \sum_X \big[\text{opt}_t(\sigma, X) - \text{opt}_{t-1}(\sigma, X)\big] \ge EC_t$, and

$$
\begin{aligned}
\Phi_f - \Phi_0 &\le \sum_X \text{opt}_f(\sigma, X) \le \sum_X \big[\text{opt}_f(\sigma, X_f) + D(X, X_f)\big] \\
&\le (k+1)\big[\text{opt}_t(\sigma, X_f)\big] + max_{i,j}\big[(k+1)d(i,j)\big] \\
&= (k+1)\text{cost}_{OPT}(\sigma) + c.
\end{aligned}
$$

Thus, we have the conditions we need to show that *WFA* is k-competitive. Unfortunately, this potential function gives a very poor bound on the competitive ratio when $n > k+1$.

13.5.5   THE DUALITY LEMMA

In order to find a potential function satisfying conditions 13.5 and 13.6, we must get a handle on the properties of the configuration where the extended cost is achieved. Intuitively, we expect the extended cost to be achieved on an X with the following properties:

I. Points in X must be fairly far from r. If they are very close, or even worse $r \in X$, then $\mathrm{opt}_t(\sigma, X)$ will not be significantly larger than $\mathrm{opt}_{t-1}(\sigma, X)$.

II. $\mathrm{opt}_{t-1}(\sigma, X)$ must not be too large. Indeed, let Z be a configuration such that $r \in Z$. We have that $\mathrm{opt}_{t-1}(\sigma, X) \le \mathrm{opt}_{t-1}(\sigma, Z) + D(X, Z)$. We claim that this inequality must be strict. Otherwise, if $\mathrm{opt}_{t-1}(\sigma, X) = \mathrm{opt}_{t-1}(\sigma, Z) + D(X, Z)$, then $\mathrm{opt}_t(\sigma, X) = \min_{Y:r \in Y}(\mathrm{opt}_{t-1}(\sigma, Y) + D(X, Y)) \le \mathrm{opt}_{t-1}(\sigma, Z) + D(X, Z) = \mathrm{opt}_{t-1}(\sigma, X)$. Since work functions cannot decrease, this would imply that $\mathrm{opt}_t(\sigma, X) = \mathrm{opt}_{t-1}(\sigma, X)$, contradicting the assumption that the extended cost is achieved on X.

These two observations motivate the following definition. A configuration X is said to be a *minimizer of r with respect to* $\mathrm{opt}_{t-1}(\sigma, \cdot)$ if X minimizes:

$$\mathrm{opt}_{t-1}(\sigma, X) - \sum_{x \in X} d(r, x).$$

The first term corresponds to the second property, and the second term corresponds to the first property. The crucial lemma conveying this intuition is the Duality Lemma, so named because it relates a maximum (the extended cost) to a minimum (a minimizer).

LEMMA 13.2 The Duality Lemma   Let the configuration X be a minimizer of r with respect to $\mathrm{opt}_{t-1}(\sigma, \cdot)$. Then:

- The extended cost of serving r at the tth step occurs on X.
- If X is a minimizer of r with respect to $\mathrm{opt}_{t-1}(\sigma, \cdot)$, then X is also a minimizer of r with respect to $\mathrm{opt}_t(\sigma, \cdot)$.

We defer a discussion of the proof of the duality lemma to Section 13.5.7.

13.5.6   THE POTENTIAL FUNCTION

We now have the machinery in place to find a potential function whose change at time t is an upper bound on the extended cost of the tth step i.e., we will use the duality lemma to find a Φ such that $\Phi_t - \Phi_{t-1} \ge EC_t$, and such that $\Phi_f - \Phi_0 \le (2k)OPT(\sigma) + c$. We use the duality lemma in order to define a potential function satisfying these conditions.

Define $k + 1$ configurations $U, B_1, B_2, \dots, B_k$ as follows:

$$U = (u_1, u_2, \dots, u_k)$$

and

$$B_i = (b_{i1}, b_{i2}, \dots, b_{ik}), \ i = 1, \dots, k.$$

We define the potential function in terms of a function ψ where

$$\psi(\text{opt}_t, U, B_1, B_2, \ldots, B_k) = k\text{opt}_t(\sigma, U) + \sum_{i=1}^{k}\left[\text{opt}_t(\sigma, B_i) - \sum_{j=1}^{k}d(u_i, b_{ij})\right] \tag{13.7}$$

The potential function ϕ_t is then defined as the minimum value of ψ over all possible configurations U and $B_1, B_2, \ldots, B_k$.

$$\phi_t = \min_{U, B_1, \ldots, B_k} \psi(\text{opt}_t, U, B_1, \ldots, B_k) \tag{13.8}$$

The following lemma shows that we can assume that the U for which ϕ_t is minimized contains the most recent request $\sigma_t = r$, and that one of the configurations B_i for which ϕ_t is minimized is a minimizer of $\sigma_t = r$ with respect to opt_{t-1}.

LEMMA 13.3   Assume ϕ_t occurs at configurations $\tilde{U}, \tilde{B}_1, \ldots, \tilde{B}_k$. Let A be a minimizer of $\sigma_t = r$ with respect to opt_{t-1}. Then $\phi_t \geq \psi_t$ where $\psi_t = \psi(\text{opt}_t, \tilde{U} - u_i + r, \tilde{B}_1, \ldots, \tilde{B}_{i-1}, A, \tilde{B}_{i+1}, \ldots, \tilde{B}_k)$.

Proof.

$$\phi_t = \psi(\text{opt}_t, \tilde{U}, \tilde{B}_1, \ldots, \tilde{B}_k) = k\text{opt}_t(\sigma, \tilde{U}) + \sum_{l=1}^{k}\left[\text{opt}_t(\sigma, \tilde{B}_l) - \sum_{j=1}^{k}d(u_l, \tilde{b}_{lj})\right] \tag{13.9}$$

Since $\text{opt}_t(\sigma, \tilde{U}) = \min_{u \in \tilde{U}}\left[\text{opt}_t(\sigma, \tilde{U} - u + r) + d(u, r)\right]$ by property 2, there is a point, call it u_i, where such a minimum occurs. Substituting $\text{opt}_t(\sigma, \tilde{U}) = \text{opt}_t(\sigma, \tilde{U} - u_i + r) + d(u_i, r)$ into Equation 13.9 and applying the triangle inequalities $d(u_i, r) - d(r, b_{ij}) \geq -d(r, b_{ij})$ for $j = 1, \ldots, k$, yields the fact that

$$\phi_t = \psi(\text{opt}_t, \tilde{U} - u_i + r, \tilde{B}_1, \ldots, \tilde{B}_k)$$
$$\geq \psi(\text{opt}_t, \tilde{U} - u_i + r, \tilde{B}_1, \ldots, \tilde{B}_{i-1}, A, \tilde{B}_{i+1}, \ldots, \tilde{B}_k).$$

The last inequality comes from the fact that A is a minimizer of r with respect to opt_t and so $\text{opt}_t(\sigma, \tilde{B}_i) - \sum_{j=1}^{k}d(r, \tilde{b}_{ij})$ is minimized when $B_i = A$. ∎

LEMMA 13.4   The change in the potential function at time t is an upper bound on the extended cost at time t, i.e. $EC_t \leq \phi_t - \phi_{t-1}$.

Proof.   Suppose that ϕ_t occurs at configurations $\tilde{U}, \ldots, \tilde{B}_k$, Let A be a minimizer of r with respect to opt_{t-1}. Then $\phi_t \geq \psi_t$ by Lemma 13.3. Consequently, $\phi_t - \phi_{t-1} \geq \psi_t - \psi_{t-1}$. Therefore,

$$\phi_t - \phi_{t-1} \geq \psi_t - \psi_{t-1} \geq k\left[\text{opt}_t(\sigma, \tilde{U} - u_i + r) - \text{opt}_{t-1}(\sigma, \tilde{U} - u_i + r)\right]$$
$$+ \sum_{l=1, l \neq i}^{k}\left[\text{opt}_t(\sigma, \tilde{B}_l) - \text{opt}_{t-1}(\sigma, \tilde{B}_l)\right] + \text{opt}_t(\sigma, A) - \text{opt}_{t-1}(\sigma, A)$$
$$\geq \text{opt}_t(\sigma, A) - \text{opt}_{t-1}(\sigma, A) = EC_t.$$

The next to the last step follows from the fact that work functions are nondecreasing with time, while the last step follows from the the first part of the Duality Lemma (Lemma 13.2). ∎

Putting everything together, we have:

THEOREM 13.12   *WFA* is $(2k - 1)$-competitive.

Proof. $WFA(\sigma) + \text{opt}(\sigma) = \sum_t (WFA_t + \widetilde{opt}_t) \leq \sum_t EC_t \leq \sum_t (\phi_t - \phi_{t-1}) = \phi_f - \phi_o.$
The second inequality follows from Lemma 13.4. It can be easily shown that $\phi_o = c$ for some constant c. Note that

$$\phi_f \leq \psi(\text{opt}_f, X_f, \dots, X_f) = 2k\text{opt}_f(\sigma, X_f) - \sum_{i=1}^{k}\sum_{j=1}^{k} d(x_i^f, x_j^f)$$

$$\leq 2k\text{opt}_f(\sigma, X_f) \leq 2k\text{opt}(\sigma).$$

Combining the above we get $\phi_f - \phi_o \leq 2k\text{opt}(\sigma) + c$. Solving for $WFA(\sigma)$ shows that $WFA(\sigma) \leq (2k - 1)\text{opt}(\sigma) + c$. Therefore, *WFA* is $(2k - 1)$-competitive.   ∎

13.5.7   QUASI-CONVEXITY AND THE DUALITY LEMMA

It is not difficult to show by working backwards from the statement of the duality lemma (Section 13.5.5) that the following property of work functions is sufficient to yield a proof. We omit the details.

LEMMA 13.5   For any two configurations A, B, with $a \in A$,

$$\text{opt}_t(\sigma, A) - \text{opt}_t(\sigma, B) \geq \min_{b \in B}\left[\text{opt}_t(\sigma, A - a + b) + \text{opt}_t(\sigma, B - b + a)\right] \tag{13.10}$$

In order to prove Lemma 13.5, a more general fact is proven: that the functions $\text{opt}_t(\sigma, \cdot)$ are *quasi-convex*. The property of quasi-convexity is defined as follows:

DEFINITION 13.3   The functions $\text{opt}_t(\sigma, \cdot)$ are *quasi-convex* if and only if $\forall A, B$ configurations, there exists a bijective map $h : A \to B$ such that for every bipartition of A into X and Y, *i.e.*, $A = X \cup Y$ and $X \cap Y = \phi$, we have

$$\text{opt}_t(\sigma, A) + \text{opt}_t(\sigma, B) \geq \text{opt}_t(\sigma, X \cup h(Y)) + \text{opt}_t(\sigma, h(X) \cup Y)$$

and furthermore the bijection h preserves the intersection of A and B, i.e. $h(r) = r$, $\forall r \in A \cap B$.

This quasi-convexity property implies the desired previous lemma, since we can take the specific bipartition where $X = \{a\}$ and $Y = A - \{a\}$.
We outline the proof of the following lemma.

LEMMA 13.6 $\text{opt}_t(\sigma, \cdot)$ is quasi-convex.

Proof.   The proof by induction on the length of the sequence. The base case is trivial. Suppose that work functions opt_{t-1} are quasiconvex. By definition, we have

$$\text{opt}_t(\sigma, A) = \min_{a \in A}(\text{opt}_{t-1}(\sigma, A - a + r) + d(a, r)) \tag{13.11}$$

$$\text{opt}_t(\sigma, B) = \min_{b \in B}(\text{opt}_{t-1}(\sigma, B - b + r) + d(b, r)) \tag{13.12}$$

Choose the specific a, b that minimize the above expressions, and set $A' \equiv A - a + r$, $B' \equiv B - b + r$.

Suppose that X', Y' and $\{a\}$ are a tripartition of A. Apply the induction hypothesis to A' and B' with the partition $X = X' \cup \{r\}$ and $Y = Y'$. Then there is a bijection $h : A' \to B'$ that maps r to itself, with the property that

$$\text{opt}_{t-1}(\sigma, A') + \text{opt}_{t-1}(\sigma, B') \geq \text{opt}_{t-1}(\sigma, h(X') \cup \{r\} \cup Y) + \text{opt}_{t-1}(\sigma, X' \cup \{r\} \cup h(Y))$$

Extend the bijection $h : a \mapsto b$; then add $d(a, r) + d(b, r)$ to both sides of the above equation to get

$$\text{opt}_t(\sigma, A) + \text{opt}_t(\sigma, B) \geq \text{opt}_t(\sigma, h(X') \cup \{b\} \cup Y) + \text{opt}_t(\sigma, X' \cup \{a\} \cup h(Y)),$$

i.e.,

$$\text{opt}_t(\sigma, A) + \text{opt}_t(\sigma, B) \geq \text{opt}_t(\sigma, h(X) \cup Y) + \text{opt}_t(\sigma, X \cup h(Y)),$$

as desired.   ∎

ONLINE LOAD BALANCING AND VIRTUAL CIRCUIT ROUTING

13.6

Consider the following generic load balancing problem: there is some fixed set of servers and a sequence of tasks which arrive through time. Each task, upon its arrival, is to be assigned to a subset of the servers who will perform the task. When a server is used to perform a task, the load on that server increases while the task is being performed. The amount of this increase may depend both on the task and the server. An offline algorithm knows in advance the sequence of tasks that will arrive into the system. An online algorithm learns about a task only at the moment of its arrival. Depending on the model, servers can represent various devices: processors, communication links, input/output ports, etc. A task can be a job to be executed, a message to be sent, or a commodity to be shipped.

There are two natural optimization problems that arise from this scenario. The first is simply to minimize the maximum load on any server at any point in time. The second is to assume that each server has a fixed capacity. Tasks will either be accepted or rejected by the system and all accepted tasks must be assigned in a manner which respects the capacity constraints of each server. The goal is to complete the set of tasks with the most value (i.e. maximize *throughput*). The value of completing a given task must be specified by the model.

There are static and dynamic versions of load balancing. In the static version of the problem, tasks only arrive. Each task must be assigned (or rejected) upon its arrival and after all the tasks have arrived, the value or cost achieved by the algorithm can be determined. A more difficult but more realistic setting incorporates a notion of time in which tasks are arriving and terminating. As each task arrives, it must be assigned to a set of servers which perform the task. Upon completion of a task, it leaves the system. The static version can be viewed as a special case of the dynamic problem in which there are only tasks of infinite duration. The typical interpretation of the static version is that the load of a job is actually the time it takes to complete it. Thus, the final load on any server is the time it takes for one server to complete all the tasks assigned to it.

There are two natural notions of preemption. In the first, an algorithm may reassign a task on a different set of servers some time after it has already been assigned. Clearly, there must be some cost associated with such a change. Otherwise, the online algorithm can continually reassign jobs to match the optimal assignment on the sequence seen so far. Typically, the goal is to devise the best algorithm given some number of allowed reschedulings. The second notion of preemption is suited only for the problem of maximizing throughput. Here a task may be aborted in the middle of execution, say to make room for a more valuable task. No credit is accrued for uncompleted tasks.

Now what remains to be specified for each model is what a task looks like – that is, which subsets of servers can perform it and at what costs. Below is a description of some of the models that have been studied in the recent literature in online algorithms:

- **Multiprocessors:** There are m servers. Each task is described by a duration d and a vector $(p_1, \ldots, p_m)$ of loads. Each task is assigned to exactly one server. If the task is assigned to server i then the load of server i increases by p_i for the duration d of the task. Four variations of this model have been studied:

  - Uniform: For all i, j, $p_i = p_j$.
  - Related: Each server has a speed s_i and $p_i/p_j = s_j/s_i$ for all i, j.
  - Subset: Each task can be performed by any server from a given subset. That is, $p_i = c$ or $p_i = \infty$ where c depends only on the task.
  - Unrelated: Each p_i can be any non-negative number.

- **Virtual Circuit Routing:** Each server represents an edge in a network. A task specifies two nodes s and t in the network, a duration and bandwidth request p. The algorithm chooses a path from s to t. The load on each of the edges in the path increases by p for the duration of the task. (In this context, the load is often referred to as the *bandwidth*).

In Sections 13.6.1 and 13.6.2 below, we present two algorithms: one for load balancing on unrelated machines and the other for virtual circuit routing. Both results are due to Aspnes, Azar, Fiat, Plotkin, and Waarts ([AAF$^+$93]). The algorithms are non-preemptive and seek to minimize the maximum load. The algorithms are competitive for the static version (i.e. jobs only arrive into the system). The behavior and analysis of the two algorithms are very similar in that they both employ a function which is the sum of a set of numbers that are exponential in the current load on each processor/edge. The algorithm chooses the assignment so as to minimize this function. Interestingly, this function has played a role in other settings outside of online algorithms. A good example of the use of the exponential potential functions for offline optimization problems is the series of papers on multicommodity flow, starting with [SM90]. (See [PST95] and references therein).

Another feature which both algorithms share is that they are based upon an algorithm which knows the optimal cost for the sequence in advance. We will call this optimal cost Λ. The algorithm must simply make sure that its own cost never exceeds $c\Lambda$ in order to get a competitive ratio of c. The algorithm assigns incoming tasks in a manner that guarantees that if its own cost exceeds $c\Lambda$, then the optimal cost must exceed Λ. A simple doubling trick suffices to remove the assumption that the algorithm knows Λ.

13.6.1   LOAD BALANCING ON UNRELATED MACHINES

Let $\sigma = \langle p(1), \ldots, p(k) \rangle$ denote a sequence of jobs which the algorithm receives. Let S_i denote the set of jobs allocated to processor i at the end of the sequence. It will be convenient to keep track of the current load on processor i after the first j jobs have arrived: $l_i(j) = \sum_{1 \le r \le j : r \in S_i} p_i(r)$. The cost to the algorithm is the maximum total load assigned to any processor:

$$\max_{1 \le i \le m} l_i(k).$$

We start with the assumption that the algorithm U knows a Λ such that for the sequence σ of jobs to be assigned, $\text{cost}_{OPT}(\sigma) \le \Lambda$. We will show that U has a maximum load of $O(\Lambda \log n)$ for that sequence. Let $\tilde{x}$ denote the normalization of x by Λ (i.e., $\tilde{x} = x/\Lambda$). Suppose the algorithm is about to assign the next job $p(j)$. U assigns the new job so as to make $\sum_{i=1}^{n} a^{\tilde{l}_i(j)}$ as small as possible for some fixed a. Let β be some number which is $O(\log n)$. The exact constant in the O as well as a will be chosen later. Upon receiving $p(j)$, U assigns $p(j)$ to the processor i that minimizes

$$a^{\tilde{l}_i(j-1) + \tilde{p}_i(j)} - a^{\tilde{l}_i(j-1)}.$$

If $l_i(j-1) + p_i(j) \ge \beta\Lambda$, then U *fails*.

LEMMA 13.7   If $\text{cost}(\sigma) \le \Lambda$, then β and a can be chosen so that U never fails. Thus, the competitive ratio is $O(\log n)$.

Proof.   We define a potential function:

$$\Phi(j) = \sum_{i=1}^{n} a^{\tilde{l}_i(j)} (\gamma - \tilde{l}_i^*(j)).$$

The constant $\gamma > 1$ will also be chosen later.

We will prove that after each job is assigned, the potential function does not increase. But first, let's see how this fact yields the lemma. Since $\Phi(0) = \gamma n$ and $l_i^*(j) \le \Lambda$, we know that at any point j,

$$\gamma n = \Phi(0) \ge \Phi(j) = \sum_{i=1}^{n} a^{\tilde{l}_i(j)} (\gamma - \tilde{l}_i^*(j)) \ge \sum_{i=1}^{n} a^{\tilde{l}_i(j)} (\gamma - 1)$$

Taking the log of both sides, we get that

$$\text{cost}_U \le \max_i l_i(k) \le \Lambda \log_a \left(\frac{\gamma n}{\gamma - 1} \right) = O(\Lambda \log n).$$

Now to prove that $\Phi(j) - \Phi(j-1) \le 0$, suppose that OPT assigns $p(j)$ to i and U assigns $p(j)$ to i'.

$$\begin{aligned}
\Phi(j) - \Phi(j-1) &= (\gamma - \tilde{l}_{i'}^*(j-1))(a^{\tilde{l}_{i'}(j-1)+\tilde{p}_{i'}(j)} - a^{\tilde{l}_{i'}(j-1)}) - a^{\tilde{l}_i(j)}\tilde{p}_i(j) \\
&\le \gamma(a^{\tilde{l}_{i'}(j-1)+\tilde{p}_{i'}(j)} - a^{\tilde{l}_{i'}(j-1)}) - a^{\tilde{l}_i(j-1)}\tilde{p}_i(j) \\
&\le \gamma(a^{\tilde{l}_i(j-1)+\tilde{p}_i(j)} - a^{\tilde{l}_i(j-1)}) - a^{\tilde{l}_i(j-1)}\tilde{p}_i(j) \\
&= a^{\tilde{l}_i(j-1)}(\gamma(a^{\tilde{p}_i(j)} - 1) - \tilde{p}_i(j))
\end{aligned}$$

The first inequality comes from the fact that $\tilde{l}_i(j) \ge \tilde{l}_i(j-1)$. The second inequality comes from the fact that i' minimizes the expression $(a^{\tilde{l}_{i'}(j-1)+\tilde{p}_{i'}(j)} - a^{\tilde{l}_{i'}(j-1)})$.

Since OPT assigns $p(j)$ to i, we know that $0 \le p_i(j) \le \Lambda$ and $0 \le \tilde{p}_i(j) \le 1$. Thus, we want to choose a and γ so that for any $x \in [0, 1]$, $\gamma(a^x - 1) \le x$. This is true for $a = 1 + 1/\gamma$. γ is then chosen to minimize $\beta = \log_a \left(\frac{\gamma n}{\gamma - 1} \right)$. ∎

We can obtain an algorithm U' which does not need to know Λ in advance by sacrificing only an extra factor of 4 in the competitive ratio. The algorithm always has a current guess for the optimal cost which it calls Λ. The algorithm initially assigns $\Lambda = \min_i p_i(1)$. The algorithm makes assignments according to U. Whenever the algorithm fails, Λ is doubled and the algorithm starts again, assigning according to U and ignoring all tasks assigned previous to the last doubling.

13.6.2   ONLINE VIRTUAL CIRCUIT ROUTING

The circuit routing problem is a generalization of the load balancing problem on unrelated machines. Each edge can be thought of as a processor. In this case, the load of a task is the bandwidth required in the connection. A subset of the edges can perform a given task if the edges form a path between the two endpoints specified in the request. Using a path for a connection increases the load on each edge by the bandwidth requirement of the request. The goal is to minimize the maximum load on any edge at any point in time. We will show an algorithm which is $O(\log n)$-competitive. The bound on the competitive ratio is tight to within a constant factor.

We are given a graph $G = (V, E)$ with $|V| = n$ and $|E| = m$. Each edge e has a non-negative capacity u_e. The request sequence σ is a sequence of k requests

$$\langle [s(1), t(1), p(1)], [s(2), t(2), p(2)], \ldots, [s(k), t(k), p(k)] \rangle.$$

$s(i)$ and $t(i)$ denote the endpoints of the ith request and $p(i)$ denotes the bandwidth requirement of the request. The request is satisfied by a path P_i from $s(i)$ to $t(i)$. Let $\mathcal{P} = \{P_1, P_2, \ldots, P_k\}$ denote the set of paths the online algorithm (which we call *Route*) chooses to satisfy the k requests in the sequence. The *relative load* in edge e after j requests have arrived is: $l_e(j) = \sum_{i:e \in P_i, \ i \le j} p(i)/u_e$.

The cost of *Route* on the sequence is then: $\text{cost}_{Route}(\sigma) = \max_{1 \leq i \leq m} l_i(k)$. Similarly, define $\mathcal{P}^* = \{P_1^*, P_2^*, \dots, P_k^*\}$ to be the set of paths the optimal offline algorithm chooses to satisfy the first k requests. $l_e^*(j)$ and $\text{cost}(\sigma)$ are defined analogously for the optimal algorithm.

The algorithm *Route* seeks to minimize $\sum_{e \in E} a^{\bar{l}_e(j)}$. Again, we assume that we are given Λ, such that $\text{cost}(\sigma) \leq \Lambda$. Upon receiving a request (s, t, p), the algorithm *Route* assigns a cost c_e to each edge where $c_e = a^{\bar{l}_e + \bar{p}/u_e} - a^{\bar{l}_e}$.

With these costs assigned to each edge, *Route* picks the path P from s to t of minimum cost. If $\exists e \in P$ such that $l_e + p/u_e > \beta \Lambda$, then *Route* fails. The proof of the following lemma is virtually identical to Lemma 13.7 for scheduling on unrelated machines.

LEMMA 13.8   If $\text{cost}(\sigma) \leq \Lambda$, then β and a can be chosen so that U never fails. Thus, the competitive ratio is $O(\log n)$.

The assumption that *Route* knows Λ can be taken care of in the same manner as U in the previous section.

13.6.3   RECENT RESULTS

13.6.3.1   Minimizing maximum bandwidth

Graham initiated the study of competitive online load balancing in [Gra66] with the proof that the greedy algorithm is 2-competitive for the static problem on uniform machines. Interestingly, although the first algorithm for this problem happened to be online, this version of load balancing is studied in the context of approximation algorithms for *NP*-hard offline scheduling problems. (See Chapter 1 for a survey.) Recently, the problem reemerged in the context of online algorithms when the bound on the competitive ratio was improved to a constant less than 2 in [BFKV92, KPT94]. The improved bound uses a different algorithm, since the greedy algorithm can do no better than 2. Aspnes *et al.* in [AAF+93] give an asymptotically optimal $O(\log n)$-competitive algorithm for unrelated machines, where n is the number of machines in the system (described in Section 13.6.1). This is generalized (as shown in Section 13.6.2) for routing virtual circuits in a network to obtain a competitive ratio which is logarithmic in the number of edges in the network. In [ANR92], Azar, Naor, and Rom show that the greedy algorithm is $O(\log n)$-competitive for the subset model even though it has an $\Omega(n)$ competitive ratio in the unrelated machines case shown by Burley.

For the dynamic version, Azar *et al.* in [AzK93] give a constant competitive algorithm for related machines, even when the durations of the tasks are unknown at the time they must be assigned. This can not be further generalized due to the result of Azar, Broder, and Karlin who show that a lower bound of $\Omega(\sqrt{n})$ for the competitive ratio of any online load balancer for the subset model in [ABK92]. When the durations of the jobs are known, this can be vastly improved to $O(\log nT)$ even on unrelated machines as shown in [AzK93]. (T is the ratio of maximum to minimum job length in the sequence.)

All of the algorithms mentioned up to this point are non-preemptive: once the job has been assigned, it remains assigned to those servers until it terminates. The ability to reassign jobs can be of great advantage to an algorithm, even if it is not permitted to reassign all the jobs. Phillips and Westbrook in [PW93] consider the subset model of [ABK92] where task lengths are unknown and some preemptions may be performed. They showed an $O(\log n/\rho)$-competitive algorithm that uses ρm reassignments on a sequence of m tasks. This compares well with the $\Omega(\sqrt{n})$ lower bound for an online algorithm with no reassignments.

We note here that we use the term "load balancing" to refer to problems where a job must be scheduled upon its arrival into the system. We use the term "scheduling" to refer to problems where the jobs can be held in a buffer until they can be executed. Typically, however, the time to execute a job is not known until it terminates. Online scheduling with the goal of minimizing makespan has been extensively studied (see [DJ81, Jaf80, SWW91, FST94, FKST93]).

13.6.3.2 Maximizing throughput

For the problem of maximizing throughput, models differ as to how a value is assigned to each task. In the most general version, each task arrives with a parameter specifying its value. The algorithm's gain is the sum of the value of all successfully completed jobs. In some applications, however, better bounds can be achieved when the value of a job is a function of its other parameters; for example, duration or load times duration. In the circuit routing problem, the value may also be a function of the distance between the two end nodes in the network. These measures attempt to capture bandwidth utilization.

Baruah *et al.* examine a processor scheduling problem in [BKM$^+$91] where the goal is to maximize throughput. They consider a real-time system with one processor which can perform only one task at a time (i.e., the load of every job is 1 and the capacity of the server is 1). However, in their model a task does not necessarily have to be accepted or rejected upon its arrival into the system. Rather, each task has a deadline, and the algorithm accrues the value of all jobs completed before their deadline. The algorithm may choose to abort a currently running job in favor of a job with more value. In this case, the aborted job, if completed, must be restarted from the beginning. They give a constant competitive algorithm when the value of a job is proportional to its duration.

The remainder of the work on throughput maximization is for routing virtual circuits in networks. This area has become known as *call control*. Call control is similar to the multicommodity flow problem discussed in Chapter 5. The main difference between the two are that multicommodity flow is an offline problem where all the jobs arrive at time 0 and last forever. In addition, in multicommodity flow, the scheduler is allowed to schedule fractions of jobs and receive the corresponding fraction of credit.

For the call control problem, Awerbuch, Azar, and Plotkin in [AAP93] show a deterministic, non-preemptive $O(\log \mu)$-competitive circuit routing algorithm in this model, where μ is the product of the ratio of the maximum to minimum job duration, the ratio of the maximum to minimum job value and the number of nodes in the network. They also show that this is the best that any deterministic, non-preemptive routing algorithm can achieve. Their algorithm has the drawback that every task is constrained to require bandwidth at most $1/\log \mu$ of the capacity of any edge (a necessary assumption for deterministic, non-preemptive algorithms). Canetti and Irani show in [CI] a lower bound of $\Omega(\sqrt{\log \mu/\log\log \mu})$ for this problem which applies even to randomized, preemptive algorithms. Their bound also applies to a variety of fixed capacity load balancing problems in the literature. In [ABFR94], Awerbuch *et al.* remove the constraint on task bandwidth for networks with a tree topology via a randomized, non-preemptive routing algorithm. They obtain an algorithm which is $O(\log L \log T \log n)$-competitive, where n is the number of nodes in the network and L is the ratio of maximum to minimum bandwidth of a request in the sequence. [AGLR94] consider the static version of call control where at most one request can be routed on an edge. They improve upon the bounds in [ABFR94] for trees and also develop algorithms for meshes and hypercubes.

An interesting technique called *classify and randomly select* is employed in [ABFR94]. We describe the technique here with respect to the duration of a request, although it can be used with respect to any parameter of the requests in the sequence. Suppose there is an algorithm $\mathcal{A}$ which is c-competitive when the durations of the requests in the sequence vary only by a factor of 2. We can use $\mathcal{A}$ to obtain an algorithm which is $(c \log T)$-competitive for any request sequence. (Recall that T is the ratio of maximum to minimum job duration). The requests are partitioned into $\log T$ bins according to their duration. The requests in a single bin differ in duration by at most a factor of 2. At the beginning of the sequence, the algorithm selects a bin at random and rejects all requests from other bins. The algorithm then uses $\mathcal{A}$ to decide which requests in the selected bin to execute. The expected total value of all the tasks in the selected bin is at least $(1/\log T)$ times the total value of all the tasks. Since $\mathcal{A}$ is c-competitive for the sequence of tasks in the selected bin, the new algorithm is $c \log T$-competitive on the entire sequence. This technique can be applied to the algorithms of [AGLR94] so that they apply to the dynamic version with only an extra factor of $O(\log T)$ in the competitive ratio.

Preemptive call control algorithms are addressed in [GG92, GGK$^+$93, BNCK$^+$]. Garay and Gopal, who initiate the study of preemptive call control in [GG92], show that if the duration of a call is unknown, then no bounded competitive ratio can be achieved even by preemptive algorithms. Still, constant competitive preemptive algorithms exist for simple networks and measures of call value. Garay *et al.* show in [GGK$^+$93] constant competitive algorithms for several measures of call value on a single link and a line network when at most one call can be accommodated on any link. Bar-Noy *et al.* in [BNCK$^+$] generalize their results by showing a constant competitive algorithm on a single link when the value of a call is the bandwidth times the duration, and every call has a bandwidth requirement which is at most a limited fraction of the capacity of the link.

VARIANTS OF COMPETITIVE ANALYSIS

13.7

Competitive analysis of online algorithms has provided a meaningful way to do a worst-case analysis of online algorithms without assuming a probability distribution over inputs. This means of evaluation has provided new insight to the design of online algorithms as well as to decision making with incomplete information, in general. Moreover, the problems that have been studied in this context have typically been motivated by applications, and many of the algorithms studied have been implemented and widely used (even long before competitive analysis existed). However, there is valid criticism of the model which points to the fact that results are often unrealistically pessimistic. Since many online algorithms fare equally badly in this model, an algorithm which performs well in practice may have the same competitive ratio as one which performs poorly. While it is true that similar problems plague complexity in general, the disparity between theoretical results and practical observations is more disturbing with competitive analysis. Since many of the problems addressed in online algorithms are very applied, there is a higher standard for an algorithm to be considered "practical." The reason for the discrepancy between theory and practice is that somehow pitting an online algorithm that knows nothing about the future against an adversary that is unlimited in its computational resources, as well as its available information, is perhaps an unfair comparison. Various efforts have been made to address these concerns, either by limiting the power of the adversary or providing the online algorithm with more information.

Most of this work has addressed the paging problem where practitioners voice reservations about the competitive analysis, citing its inability to discern between *LRU* and *FIFO* (algorithms whose performances differ markedly in practice), and the fact that the theoretical competitiveness of *LRU* is much larger than observed in practice. In addition, it is not necessarily the case that there is no information about the request sequence available in advance. One would like to use some knowledge of a program's access pattern to improve paging performance on the sequence generated by that program.

A graph theoretic model to describe locality of reference in request sequences was devised in [BIRS91] and later developed in [IKP92]. Instead of requiring that an online algorithm perform well on all input sequences, they define a restricted set of input sequences and analyze the competitive ratio over the restricted set of sequences. The *access graph* for a program $G = (V, E)$ is a graph in which each node corresponds to one of the pages that a program can reference. The sequence of page references must obey locality constraints imposed by the edges of G: following a request to a page (node) u, the next request must be either to u or to a node v such that (u, v) is in E. The graph is known to the online paging algorithm but the particular path taken by the request sequence is revealed online. The intuition is that the access pattern of a program is governed by the data structures and instruction sequences of a program which can be modelled by a graph. Furthermore, this information is available to the paging algorithm before execution. A simple algorithm is devised in [BIRS91] and shown to be close to the best online algorithm for every possible undirected access graph. The algorithm is in fact within a constant factor of the best online algorithm for every access graph as shown in [IKP92].

Karlin, Phillips, and Raghavan take this one step farther in [KPR92] by not only providing the online algorithm with the graph but also probabilities along the edges of the graph: they analyze paging algorithms where the request sequence is generated by a Markov chain. Each node in the Markov chain is a virtual memory page. Since the distribution is completely known to the online algorithm, the goal is simply to minimize the fault rate (expected number of faults per request) instead of the cost in comparison to the offline algorithm. Although the optimal online algorithm (which minimizes the fault rate) is available to the online algorithm in information theoretic terms, it is in general, not efficient to compute. Thus, the goal is to approximate this algorithm. The authors prove that many intuitive algorithms do not have a fault rate that is within a constant of the best online algorithm. They show a somewhat more complicated algorithm which does achieve this goal. Lund, Phillips, and Reingold [CLR94] subsequently presented a simpler algorithm for distributional paging.

Koutsoupias and Papadimitriou also suggest two refinements of competitive analysis in [KP94a]. Although most of their results pertain to paging, their measures could potentially shed light on online computation in many other domains. The first of these is *the diffuse adversary model* where the input is generated by a distribution $\mathcal{D}$. Although the online algorithm does not know the exact distribution, it does know that it is chosen from a class Δ of distributions. The adversary can pick the worst $\mathcal{D} \in \Delta$ for an online algorithm A. Once this choice is made, the cost of A on input σ is compared to the optimal offline cost on σ, where σ is picked according to $\mathcal{D}$. The competitive ratio of A is

$$\max_{\mathcal{D} \in \Delta} \frac{E_{\sigma \in \mathcal{D}}[\text{cost}_A(\sigma)]}{E_{\sigma \in \mathcal{D}}[\text{cost}(\sigma)]}.$$

Naturally, the more restricted Δ is, the more information the online algorithm has. Notice that when Δ is the set of all distributions, this is just the usual competitive ratio.

The second measure called *comparative analysis* compares an algorithm to a less powerful algorithm than the optimal offline algorithm. Consider two classes of algorithms $\mathcal{A}$ and $\mathcal{B}$. Typically, $\mathcal{A} \subseteq \mathcal{B}$. $\mathcal{B}$ may have a more powerful information regime or more computational resources. The comparative ratio of $\mathcal{A}$ and $\mathcal{B}$,

$$c(\mathcal{A}, \mathcal{B}) = \max_{B \in \mathcal{B}} \min_{A \in \mathcal{A}} \max_{\sigma} \frac{\text{cost}_A(\sigma)}{\text{cost}_B(\sigma)}.$$

The comparative ratio is probably best viewed as a two player game. Player $\mathcal{B}$ (typically the adversary) picks an algorithm $B \in \mathcal{B}$. Player $\mathcal{A}$ (typically the online algorithm) picks an algorithm $A \in \mathcal{A}$. Then player B picks the input σ so as to maximize the ratio of A's cost on σ to B's cost on σ. Note that if $\mathcal{B}$ is the set of all algorithms (offline and online), and $\mathcal{A}$ is the set of all online algorithms, then $c(\mathcal{A}, \mathcal{B})$ is simply the best competitive ratio for the given problem.

One feature achieved by comparative analysis is that it allows us to address the anomaly observed in competitive analysis of the k-server problem that an online algorithm does not gain anything with additional lookahead. That is, for any l, a k-server algorithm with lookahead l has the same competitive ratio of an online algorithm with no lookahead. The reason is that an adversary which plays against the algorithm with lookahead l can repeat each request $l + 1$ times, removing any advantage of the lookahead and not increasing the offline cost. However, if an online algorithm competes against a class of algorithms with limited lookahead, it does gain some advantage with additional lookahead. The authors give tight bounds for $c(\mathcal{L}_0, \mathcal{L}_l)$ for task systems and paging, where $\mathcal{L}_i$ is the class of all online algorithms with lookahead i.

Raghavan introduces the notion of a *statistical adversary* in [Rag91] which he uses to address a problem in portfolio management. The idea behind the statistical adversary is that it is free to pick any input as long as it obeys certain statistical properties. The statistical adversary is a compromise between probabilistic analysis and competitive analysis where an unrestricted adversary generates the input. In the portfolio problem, an investor chooses between investing his money in a risk-free asset and a risky asset. The price of the risk-free asset remains fixed while the price of the risky asset changes from day to day. The adversary which determines the sequence of prices for the risky asset is free to choose any sequence as along as it has a fixed mean and fixed variance and only fluctuates within some predetermined bounds. The statistical adversary has also been by Cooperstock, El-Yaniv, and Leighton who study foreign currency exchange in [JC93]. They use competitive analysis with a statistical adversary who is restricted to those sequences for which the offline solution is no more than a fixed value.

CONCLUSIONS AND DIRECTIONS FOR FUTURE RESEARCH

13.8

We have presented the basic principles underlying the design and analysis of competitive online algorithms. It is clear that the performance of online algorithms is of fundamental interest in computer science. Numerous problems in operating systems, architecture, parallel and distributed systems, compilers, graphics, robotics and other areas must be dealt with in an online fashion. Any light shed on the design and analysis of these algorithms by theoreticians is of interest to practitioners.

There have been many online problems studied in this framework. We have presented the best results to date for two problems: the k-server problem and virtual circuit routing. We have omitted presentations of numerous other interesting results, many of which are referenced in the bibliography.

Many interesting problems in this area remain open. First, there are questions that relate to specific online problems. Some of the major outstanding open problems in online algorithms include showing that the work-function algorithm is k-competitive for the k-server problem (obtaining a strongly competitive algorithm for the k-server problem with excursions) and finding a proof of the dynamic optimality conjecture for splay trees. [4] The list goes on and on.

More general results which apply to broad classes of online algorithms, or other general techniques, would represent a more significant advance in the state of the art. For example, a precise characterization of the class of metrical task systems for which the work-function algorithm (or variants of it) is strongly competitive would be extremely interesting.

In terms of randomized algorithms, the field is wide open. As in the case of deterministic algorithms, there are nearly no general results, other than those of Borodin *et al.* Moreover, almost all of the specific results for randomized algorithms against oblivious adversaries apply to metrical task systems with uniform distance matrices. Very little is known about randomized algorithms for problems which can be described as a metrical task system with nonuniform distances.

Finally, variants of competitive analysis have only just begun to be studied. Restrictions on adversary request sequences such as those implied by statistical adversaries,

---

[4]See [MMS90] for a definition of the k-server problem with excursions. See [DS85] for a description of splay trees and the dynamic optimality conjecture.

sequences generated from access graphs and the diffuse adversary model, in addition to other kinds of comparisons between information regimes such as comparative analysis, represent important directions for future research.

Acknowledgments We gratefully acknowledge comments, discussions, papers, and references given to us by Alan Borodin, Marek Chrobak, Ran El-Yaniv, Amos Fiat, Howard Karloff, Elias Koutsoupias, Prabhakar Raghavan and Danny Sleator. The second author would like to thank the students in her 1994 course on online algorithms at the University of Washington, especially Eric Anderson, Ruth Anderson, Donald Chinn, Marc Fiuczynski, Melanie Fulgham, Tracy Kimbrel, Omid Madani, Erik Selberg, Jayram Thathachar, and Elizabeth Walkup.

REFERENCES

[AAF+93]   J. Aspens, Y. Azar, A. Fiat, S. Plotkin, and O. Waarts. Online load balancing with applications to machine scheduling and virtual circuit routing. In *Proc. 25th ACM Symposium on the Theory of Computing*, 623–631, 1993.

[AAP93]   B. Awerbuch, Y. Azar, and S. Plotkin. Throughput-competitive online routing. In *34th IEEE Symposium on Foundations of Computer Science*, 32–40, 1993.

[ABFR94]   B. Awerbuch, Y. Bartal, A. Fiat, and A. Rosén. Competitive non-preemptive call control. In *Proc. of 5th ACM-SIAM Symposium on Discrete Algorithms*, 312–320, 1994.

[ABK92]   Y. Azar, A. Broder, and A. Karlin. Online load balancing. In *Proc. 33rd IEEE Symposium on Foundations of Computer Science*, 218–225, 1992. To appear in *Theoretical Computer Science*.

[ABM93]   Y. Azar, A. Broder, and M. Manasse. Online choice of online algorithms. In *Proc. 4th ACM-SIAM Symposium on Discrete Algorithms*, 432–440, 1993.

[AGLR94]   B. Awerbuch, R. Gawlick, T. Leighton, and Y. Rabani. Online admission control and circuit routing for high performance comp uting and communication. In *Proceedings of the 34th Annual Symposium on the Foundations of Computer Science*, 412–423, 1994.

[AKPW92]   N. Alon, R. Karp, D. Peleg, and D. West. A graph-theoretic game and its application to the k-server problem. In *DIMACS Series in Discrete Mathematics and Theoretical Computer Science*, 7:1–9, 1992.

[ANR92]   Y. Azar, J. Naor, and R. Rom. The competitiveness of online assignments. In *Proc. 3rd ACM-SIAM Symposium on Discrete Algorithms*, 203–210, 1992.

[AzK93]   Y. Azar, B. Kalyanasundaram, S. Plotkin, K. Pruhs, and O. Waarts. Online load balancing of temporary tasks. In *Workshop on Algorithms and Data Structures*, 119–130, 1993.

[BDBK+90]   S. Ben-David, A. Borodin, R. Karp, G. Tardos, and A. Widgerson. On the power of randomization in online algorithms. In *Proc. 22nd Symposium on Theory of Algorithms*, 379–386, 1990.

[BFKV92]   Y. Bartal, A. Fiat, H. Karloff, and R. Vohra. New algorithms for an ancient scheduling problem. In *Proc. 24th ACM Symposium on Theory of Algorithms*, 51–58, 1992. To appear in *Journal of Computer and System Sciences*.

[BaFiRa92] Y. Bartal, A. Fiat, and Y. Rabani. Competitive algorithms for distributed data management. In *Proc. of the 24th Symposium on Theory of Computation*, 39–48, 1992.

[BGR93] M. Bern, D. Greene, and A. Ragunathan. Online algorithms for cache sharing. In *Proceedings of the 25th Annual Symposium on the Theory of Computing*, 422–430, 1993.

[BIRS91] A. Borodin, S. Irani, P. Raghavan, and B. Schieber. Competitive paging with locality of reference. In *Proc. 23rd ACM Symposium on Theory of Computing*, 249–259, 1991. To appear in *Journal of Computer and System Sciences*.

[BKM$^+$91] S. Baruah, G. Koren, B. Mishra, A. Ragunathan, L. Rosier, and D. Shasha. Online scheduling in the presence of overload. In *Proceedings of the 31st Annual Symposium on the Foundations of Computer Science*, 100–110, 1991.

[BLS87] A. Borodin, N. Linial, and M. Saks. An optimal online algorithm for metrical task systems. In *Proc. 19th Annual ACM Symposium on Theory of Computing*, 373–382, 1987.

[BNCK$^+$] A. Bar-Noy, R. Canetti, S. Kutten, Y. Mansour, and B. Schieber. Bandwidth allocation with preemption. Manuscript.

[BlaSle89] D. L. Black and D. D. Sleator. Competitive algorithms for replication and migration problems. CMU Technical ReportCMU-CS-89-201, Department of Computer Science, Carnegie-Mellon University, 1989.

[Bur93] W. Burley. Traversing layered graphs using the work function algorithm. Manuscript, 1993.

[BYCR93] R. Baeza-Yates, J. Culberson, and G. Rawlins. Searching in the plane. *Information and Computation*, 106(2):234–252, 1993. Preliminary version in Proc. 1st Scandinavian Workshop on Algorithm Theory, Lecture Notes in Computer Science 318, Springer-Verlag, Berlin, 1988, 176–189. Also Tech. Report CS-87-68, University of Waterloo, Department of Computer Science, October, 1987.

[CDRS93] D. Coppersmith, Peter Dolye, P. Raghavan, and M. Snir. Random walks on weighted graphs and applications to online algorithms. *Journal of the ACM*, 1993.

[CI] R. Canetti and S. Irani. On the power of preemption in randomized scheduling. Submitted for publication.

[CKPV91] M. Chrobak, H. Karloff, T. H. Payne, and S. Vishwanathan. New results on server problems. *SIAM Journal on Discrete Mathematics*, 4:172–181, 1991. Also in *Proceedings of the 1st Annual ACM-SIAM Symposium on Discrete Algorithms*, San Francisco, 1990, pp. 291-300.

[CL91a] M. Chrobak and L. L. Larmore. On fast algorithms for two servers. *Journal of Algorithms*, 12:607–614, 1991.

[CL91b] M. Chrobak and L. L. Larmore. An optimal online algorithm for k servers on trees. *SIAM Journal on Computing*, 20:144–148, 1991.

[CL92] M. Chrobak and L. L. Larmore. The server problem and online games. In *DIMACS Series in Discrete Mathematics and Theoretical Computer Science*, 7:11–64, 1992.

[CLR94] S. Phillips C. Lund and N. Reingold. IP over connection-oriented networks and distributional paging. In *Proceedings of the 34th Annual Symposium on the Foundations of Computer Science*, 424–434, 1994.

[DJ81] E. Davis and J.M. Jaffe. Algorithms for scheduling tasks on unrelated processors. *Journal of the ACM*, 28:712–736, 1981.

[DK93]   X. Deng and E. Koutsoupias. Competitive implementations of parallel programs. In *Proc. 4th ACM-SIAM Symposium on Discrete Algorithms*, 455–461, 1993.

[DM91]   X. Deng and S. Mahajan. Randomization vs. computability in online problems. In *Proceedings of the 23rd Annual Symposium on the Theory of Computing*, 289–298, 1991.

[DS85]   R.E. Tarjan D.D. Sleator. Self-adjusting binary search trees. *Journal of the ACM*, 32(3):652–686, 1985.

[Fel50]   W. Feller. *An Introduction to Probability Theory and Its Applications*. John Wiley and Sons, 1950.

[FFK+91]   A. Fiat, D. Foster, H. Karloff, Y. Rabani, Y. Ravid, and S. Vishwanathan. Competitive algorithms for layered graph traversal. In *Proc. 32nd IEEE Symposium on Foundations of Computer Science*, 288–297, 1991.

[FKL+91]   A. Fiat, R. Karp, M. Luby, L. A. McGeoch, D. Sleator, and N.E. Young. Competitive paging algorithms. *Journal of Algorithms*, 12:685–699, 1991.

[FKST93]   A. Feldmann, M. Y. Kao, J. Sgall, and S. H. Teng. Optimal online scheduling of parallel jobs with dependencies. In *Proc. 25th ACM Symposium on Theory of Computing*, 642–651, 1993.

[FRR90]   A. Fiat, Y. Rabani, and Y. Ravid. Competitive k-server algorithms. In *Proc. 22nd IEEE Symposium on Foundations of Computer Science*, 454–463, 1990.

[FST94]   A. Feldmann, J. Sgall, and S.H. Teng. Dynamic scheduling on parallel machines. *Theoret. Comput. Sci.*, 1994. To appear in the special issue on dynamic and online algorithms. Also in 32nd IEEE Symposium on Foundations of Computer Science, 1991, 111–120.

[GG92]   J.A. Garay and I.S. Gopal. Call preemption in communication networks. In *Proceedings of INFOCOM 1992*, 1992.

GGK+93]   J. Garay, I.S. Gopal, S. Kutten, Y. Mansour, and M. Yung. Efficient online call control algorithms. In *Proc. 2nd Israel Symposium on Theory of Computing and Systems*, 285 – 293, 1993.

[Gra66]   R. Graham. Bounds for certain multiprocessor anomalies. *Bell Systems Technical Journal*, 45:1563–1581, 1966.

[Gro91]   E. Grove. The harmonic k-server algorithm is competitive. In *Proc. 23rd ACM Symposium on Theory of Computing*, 260–266, 1991.

[IKP92]   S. Irani, A. Karlin, and S. Phillips. Strongly competitive algorithms for paging with locality of reference. In *3rd Annual ACM-SIAM Symposium on Discrete Algorithms*, 228–236, 1992.

[IR91]   S. Irani and R. Rubinfeld. A competitive 2-server algorithm. *Information Processing Letters*, 39:85–91, 1991.

[Jaf80]   J.M. Jaffe. Efficient scheduling of tasks without full use of processor resources. *Theoretical Computer Science*, 12:1–17, 1980.

[JC93]   T. Leighton J. Cooperstock, R. El-Yaniv. The statistical adversary allows online foreign exchange wit. Unpublished manuscript, 1993.

[Kar]   R. Karp. A $2k$-competitive algorithm for the circle. Unpublished manuscript.

[Kle94]   J. Kleinberg. A lower bound for two-server balancing algorithms. *Information Processing Letters*, 1994.

[KMMO90] A. Karlin, M. Manasse, L. McGeoch, and S. Owicki. Randomized competitive algorithms for non-uniform problems. In *1st Annual ACM-SIAM Symposium on Discrete Algorithms*, 301–309, 1990. To appear in *Algorithmica*.

[KMRS88] A. Karlin, M. Manasse, L. Rudolph, and D. Sleator. Competitive snoopy caching. *Algorithmica*, 3:79–119, 1988.

[KMV94] S. Khuller, S. G. Mitchell, and V. V. Vazirani. Online algorithms for weighted bipartite matching and stable marriages. *Theoret. Comput. Sci.*, 127:255–267, 1994.

[KP93] B. Kalyanasundaram and K. Pruhs. Online weighted matching. *Journal of Algorithms*, 478–488, 1993.

[KP94a] E. Koutsoupias and C. Papadimitriou. On the k-server conjecture. In *Proc. 25th Symposium on Theory of Computing*, 507–511, 1994.

[KP94b] E. Koutsoupias and C. Papadimitriou. Beyond competitive analysis. In *Proceedings of the 34th Annual Symposium on the Foundations of Computer Science*, 1994.

[KPR92] A. Karlin, S. Phillips, and P. Raghavan. Markov paging. In *Proc. 33rd IEEE Symposium on Foundations of Computer Science*, 208–217, 1992.

[KPT94] D. R. Karger, S. J. Phillips, and E. Torng. A better algorithm for an ancient scheduling problem. In *Proc. of the 5th ACM-SIAM Symposium on Discrete Algorithms*, 132–140, 1994.

[LR94] C. Lund and N. Reingold. Linear programs for randomized online algorithms. In *Proc. 5th ACM-SIAM Symposium on Discrete Algorithms*, 1994. 382–391.

[MMS90] M. Manasse, L. A. McGeoch, and D. Sleator. Competitive algorithms for server problems. *Journal of Algorithms*, 11:208–230, 1990. Also in *Proc. 20th Annual ACM Symposium on Theory of Computing*, 322-333, 1988.

[MS91] L. McGeoch and D. Sleator. A strongly competitive randomized paging algorithm. *J. Algorithms*, 6:816–825, 1991.

[PW93] S. Phillips and J. Westbrook. Online load balancing and network flow. In *Proc. 25th ACM Symposium on Theory of Computing*, 402–411, 1993.

[PST95] S.A. Plotkin, D.B. Shmoys, E. Tardos. Fast approximation algorithms for fractional packing and covering problems. In *Mathematics of Operations Research*, May 1995, 20(2):257-301.

[PY89] C. H. Papadimitriou and M. Yannakakis. Shortest paths without a map. In *16th International Colloquium on Automata, Languages, and Programming, Lecture Notes in Computer Science* 372:610–620. Springer-Verlag, 1989.

[Rag91] P. Raghavan. A statistical adversary for online algorithms. In *DIMACS Series in Discrete Mathematics and Theoretical Computer Science*, 79–83, 1991.

[RS89] P. Raghavan and M. Snir. Memory versus randomization in online algorithms. In *16th International Colloquium on Automata, Languages, and Programming, Lecture Notes in Computer Science* 372:687–703, Springer-Verlag, 1989.

[SM90] F. Shahrokhi, D.W. Matula. The maximum concurrent flow problem. In *Journal of the Association for Computing Machinery*, April 1990, 37(2):318–34.

[SWW91] D.B. Shmoys, J. Wien, and D.P. Williamson. Scheduling parallel machines online. In *Proceedings of the 31st Annual Symposium on the Foundations of Computer Science*, 131–140, 1991.

[ST85]   D. Sleator and R. E. Tarjan. Amortized efficiency of list update and paging rules. *Communications of the ACM*, 28:202–208, 1985.

[Tar83]   R. E. Tarjan. *Data Structures and Network Algorithms*. SIAM, Philadelphia, 1983.

[Tar85]   R.E. Tarjan. Amortized computational complexity. *SIAM Journal on Discrete Mathematics*, 6(2):306–318, 1985.

[Westbr92] J. Westbrook. Randomized algorithms for multiprocessor page migration. *DIMACS Series in Discrete Mathematics and Theoretical Computer Science*, 7:135–150, 1992.

[Yao80]   A.C. Yao. Probabilistic computations: Towards a unified measure of complexity. In *Proc. 12th ACM Symposium on Theory of Computing*, 222–227, 1980.

GLOSSARY OF PROBLEMS

[MA] Minimum-cost arborescence
Instance: A directed graph $G = (V, A)$, nonnegative costs c_a for $a \in A$, and a root vertex r.
Objective: Find the minimum-cost spanning tree directed out of r.
[4.3]

[AFS] Arc feedback set in directed graphs
Instance: A directed graph $G = (V, A)$ with arc weights w_a for $a \in A$.
Objective: Find a subset of arcs $A' \subseteq A$ so that the subgraph $(V, A \setminus A')$ is acyclic, and such that $\sum_{a \in A'} w_v$ is minimized.
[5.4, 9.2.1, 9.2.3]

[α-BC] α-balanced cut
Instance: An undirected graph $G = (V, E)$ with $|V| = n$, and a non-negative cost $c(e)$ for each $e \in E$.
Objective: Find a partition of the vertex set into S and $V - S$ such that $\alpha n \leq |S| \leq (1 - \alpha)n$ so as to minimize $\sum_{e \in \delta(S)} c(e)$, where $\delta(S) = \{(u, v) = e \in E : u \in S, v \notin S\}$. In other words, delete the minimum-cost subset of edges so that the graph is disconnected into two components each of size at least αn.
[5.1, 5.5, 5.6]

[α-BNS] α-balanced node separator
Instance: An undirected graph $G = (V, E)$ such that $|V| = n$.
Objective: Find a minimum cardinality subset of nodes X such that each connected component of $V - X$ has at most $(1 - \alpha)n$ vertices.
[5.5.2]

[#BASES] Number of bases of a matroid
Instance: A matroid M over a ground set U, specified by an independence oracle, i.e., a black box which, given any subset $S \subseteq U$, determines whether S is independent.
Objective: Count the number of bases of M.
[12.5.4]

[BICC] Minimum biclique cover
Instance: A bipartite graph $G = (V, E)$.
Objective: Find a minimum system of complete bipartite subgraphs which is a cover, i.e., each edge of G is contained in at least one of the complete bipartite subgraphs.
[10.6]

[k-CEN] *k*-center
Instance: A graph $G = (V, E)$ with edge weights $w_{(i,j)}$ for $(i, j) \in E$, and a parameter $k < |V|$.
Objective: Find a set S, $|S| = k$ so that $\max_{v \in V} \min_{s \in S} w_{(v,s)}$ is minimized.
[9.2.3, 9.4.1]

[k-CENW] Weighted *k*-center
Instance: A graph $G = (V, E)$ with edge weights $w_{(i,j)}$ for $(i, j) \in E$, and node weights w_v for $v \in V$. A parameter k.
Objective: Find a set S, $\sum_{v \in S} w_v \leq k$ so that $\max_{v \in V} \min_{s \in S} w_{(v,s)}$ is minimized.
[9.4.2]

[CE] Chordal extension
Instance: An undirected graph $G = (V, E)$.
Objective: Find a minimum cardinality subset of edges F such that $\bar{G} = (V, E \cup F)$ is a chordal graph; that is, in $\bar{G}$ each cycle of length at least 4 has an edge connecting a pair of vertices that are not consecutive in the cycle.
[5.5.2]

[CNF] Fractional chromatic number or fractional coloring
Instance: A graph $G = (V, E)$.
Objective: Find a collection of independent sets $I_1, \ldots I_t$ of G and corresponding nonnegative (possibly fractional) values $\lambda_1, \ldots \lambda_t$, so that the sum of the λ_i's is minimized, and for every node v of G the sum of values assigned to the independent sets containing v is at least 1.
[10.6]

[CLIQ] Maximum clique
Instance: A graph $G = (V, E)$.
Objective: Find a subset S of the vertices such that every pair of vertices in S is an edge in G and such that $|S|$ is maximized.
[10.0, 10.1, 10.2, 10.5, 10.6, 10.8, 10.9]

[CC] Clique cover
Instance: A graph $G = (V, E)$.
Objective: Assign a color (namely, an integer) to each vertex such that any two adjacent vertices have the same color and such that the number of different colorings is minimized.
[10.6]

[CP] Clique partition
Instance: A graph $G = (V, E)$.
Objective: Partition the set V into the smallest number of parts so the subgraph induced on each part is a clique.
[9.4.2.1]

[R-CLIQUE] R-clique
Instance: An integer r and an r-partite graph $G = (V, E)$.
Objective: Find a clique in G of maximum size.
[10.1, 10.5, 10.6]

[k-CLU] k-cluster
Instance: A graph $G = (V, E)$ with edge weights $w_{(i,j)}$ for $(i, j) \in E$, and a parameter $k < |V|$.
Objective: Partition V into k subsets $V_1, \ldots, V_k$ such that $\sum_{i=1}^{k} \sum_{i,j \in V_i} w_{(i,j)}$ is minimized.
[9.2.3]

[k-CMM] k-Cluster minmax or minmax diameter k-clustering
Instance: A graph $G = (V, E)$ with edge weights $w_{(i,j)}$ for $(i, j) \in E$, and a parameter $k < |V|$.
Objective: Partition V into k subsets $V_1, \ldots, V_k$ such that $\max_{i=1,\ldots,k} \min_{i,j \in V_i} w_{(i,j)}$ is minimized.
[9.4.2]

[DIAMkCLU] Minmax diameter k-clustering
Instance: Points $S = \{s_1, s_2, \ldots, s_n\}$ in the plane, and a parameter $k \leq n$.
Objective: Partition S into k subsets $S_1, S_2, \ldots, S_k$ such that $max_{1 \leq i \leq k} diameter(S_i)$ is minimized, where $diameter(S_i) = \max_{s_j, s_l \in S_i} |s_j s_l|$.
[8.5.1]

[EkCEN] Minmax radius k-clustering
Instance: Points $S = \{s_1, s_2, \ldots, s_n\}$ in the plane, and a parameter $k \leq n$.
Objective: Partition S into k subsets $S_1, S_2, \ldots, S_k$ such that $max_{1 \leq i \leq k} radius(S_i)$ is minimized, where $radius(S_i)$ is the radius of the smallest disk covering S_i.
[8.5.1]

[COL] Coloring a graph—the chromatic number
Instance: A graph $G = (V, E)$.
Objective: Assign a color (namely, an integer) to each vertex such that no two adjacent vertices have the same color and such that the number of different colors is minimized.
[9.6, 10.1, 10.5, 10.8]

[COL-EDGE] Edge coloring—the chromatic index
Instance: A graph $G = (V, E)$.
Objective: Assign a color (namely, an integer) to each edge such that no two adjacent edges have the same color and such that the number of different colors is minimized.
[9.5.2, 9.6]

[#CT] Number of contingency tables
Instance: A sequence of $m + n$ positive integers $r_1, \ldots, r_m$ and $c_1, \ldots, c_n$.
Objective: The number of $m \times n$ non-negative integer matrices with row-sums $r_1, \ldots, r_m$ and column-sums $c_1, \ldots, c_n$.
[12.5.2]

[CO] Covering
Instance: Let $\mathcal{Z}_+$ denote the non-negative integers, A be an $m \times n$ matrix over $\mathcal{Z}_+$, b be a vector over $\mathcal{Z}_+^m$, and x and w be vectors over $\mathcal{Z}_+^n$.
Objective: Minimize $w^T \cdot x$ subject to $Ax \geq b$.
[11.2.2]

[CS] Covering with disks
Instance: Points $P = \{p_1, p_2, \ldots, p_n\}$ in the plane. A disk of prescribed radius r.
Objective: Place minimum number of disks so that each point is in at least one of the disks.
[9.3.3]

[CS] Covering with squares
Instance: Points $P = \{p_1, p_2, \ldots, p_n\}$ in the plane. A square of prescribed size and prescribed orientation.
Objective: Place minimum number of squares so that each point is in at least one of the squares.
[9.3.3]

[k-CUT] k-cut
Instance: A graph $G = (V, E)$, edge weights w_e for all $e \in E$, a parameter k.
Objective: Partition V into k nonempty parts $V_1, \ldots, V_k$ so that the sum of edge weights with two endpoints in different parts is minimum.
[9.2.3]

[kDMST] Degree-constrained minimum spanning tree
Instance: Points $S = \{s_1, s_2, \ldots, s_n\}$ in the plane, along with a parameter k.
Objective: Find a tree with vertex set S and maximum degree at most k of minimum total length.
[7, 8.7.6]

[DS] Dominating set
Instance: A graph $G = (V, E)$, vertex weights w_v for all $v \in V$.
Objective: Find a subset of vertices $D \subseteq V$ so that every $v \in V$ has at least one vertex in S adjacent to it and such that $\sum_{v \in S} w_v$ is minimized.
[9.4.1, 10.5]

[λ-ECU] λ edge-connected subgraph (unweighted)
Instance: A graph $G = (V, E)$ and an integer λ. Assume that G is λ edge connected.
Objective: Find a spanning subgraph $H = (V, E_H)$ of G that is λ edge connected, so that the number of edges in H is minimized.
[6.2.2]

[λ-EC] λ **edge connected subgraph**

Instance: A graph $G = (V, E)$ with edge weights $w(i, j)$ for $(i, j) \in E$, and an integer λ.
Objective: Find a spanning subgraph $H = (V, E_H)$ of G that is λ edge connected, so
that H has minimum total weight.
[4.4, 4.7, 6.2.1]

[λ-ECA] λ **edge connectivity augmentation**

Instance: A graph $G = (V, E)$ with edge weights $w(i, j)$ for $(i, j) \in E$, and a subgraph
$G_0 = (V, E_0)$ and an integer λ.
Objective: Find a set of edges $Aug \subseteq E$ to add to G_0, so that the graph $(V, E_0 \cup Aug)$
is λ edge connected and Aug has minimum total weight.
[4.4, 4.7, 6.5.1]

[EC] **Edge covering**

Instance: A graph $G = (V, E)$, and nonnegative costs c_e for $e \in E$.
Objective: Find a minimum-cost set of edges so that each vertex is adjacent to at least
one edge.
[4.5.1]

[EMAXCUT] **Euclidean max cut**

Instance: Points $S = \{s_1, s_2, \ldots, s_n\}$ in the plane.
Objective: Partition S into two subsets S_1 and S_2 such that $\sum_{s_i \in S_1, s_j \in S_2} |s_i - s_j|$ is
maximized.
[8.5.1]

[EMST] **Euclidean minimum spanning tree**

Instance: Points $S = \{s_1, s_2, \ldots, s_n\}$ in the plane.
Objective: Find a tree of minimum total Euclidean length with vertex set S.
[8.1.2, 8.3.1]

[EkMST] **Euclidean k-minimum spanning tree**

Instance: Points $S = \{s_1, s_2, \ldots, s_n\}$ in the plane, and a parameter $k \le n$.
Objective: Find a subset $S' \subset S$ with $|S'| = k$ that minimizes $|MST(S')|$, the total length
of a Euclidean minimum spanning tree on S'.
[8.5.2]

[ETSP] **Euclidean traveling salesman**

Instance: Points $S = \{s_1, s_2, \ldots, s_n\}$ in the plane.
Objective: Find a permutation σ that minimizes the sum of Euclidean distances
$|s_{\sigma(1)}s_{\sigma(2)}| + |s_{\sigma(2)}s_{\sigma(3)}| + \cdots + |s_{\sigma(n-1)}s_{\sigma(n)}| + |s_{\sigma(n)}s_{\sigma(1)}|$.
[8.2]

[EMAXTSP] **Euclidean maximum traveling salesman**

Instance: Points $S = \{s_1, s_2, \ldots, s_n\}$ in the plane.
Objective: Find a permutation σ that maximizes the sum of Euclidean distances
$|s_{\sigma(1)}s_{\sigma(2)}| + |s_{\sigma(2)}s_{\sigma(3)}| + \cdots + |s_{\sigma(n-1)}s_{\sigma(n)}| + |s_{\sigma(n)}s_{\sigma(1)}|$.
[8.1.2, 8.7.8]

[ESMT] Euclidean Steiner tree
Instance: Points $S = \{s_1, s_2, \ldots, s_n\}$ in the plane.
Objective: Find a tree of minimum total Euclidean length that includes S in its vertex set.
[8.3]

[ECOV] Minimum exact cover
Instance: A set I of m elements to be covered and a collection of sets $S_j \subseteq I$, $j \in J = \{1, \ldots, n\}$.
Objective: Find a subcollection of sets C, $C \subset J$, that forms an exact cover, i.e., $\cup_{j \in C} S_j = I$, S_j and $S_{j'}$ are disjoint for distinct $j, j' \in C$ and such that $|C|$ is minimized.
[10.6]

[EP] Exact partitioning
Instance: A graph $G = (V, E)$, nonnegative costs c_e for $e \in E$, and a parameter k.
Objective: Find a minimum-cost set of edges that partitions the vertices into trees/paths/cycles such that each tree/path/cycle has at exactly k vertices.
[4.6.5]

[FSS] Flow shop scheduling
Instance: A set of operations O_{ij} with processing times p_{ij}, $i = 1, \ldots, m$, $j = 1, \ldots, n$.
Objective: Find an assignment of starting times s_{ij} for the operations so that for each j, $s_{ij} + p_{ij} \leq s_{i+1,j}$ (i.e., the operations of job j are scheduled without overlap in the order $O_{1j}, \ldots, O_{mj}$) and so that the processing of operations on a machine do not overlap, so as to minimize the makespan of the schedule (the time at which all processing completes).
[1.5.3]

[k-FS] Maximum k-function-satisfiability
Instance: Truth tables for m boolean functions, each a function of a set of k variables out of $y_1, y_2, \ldots, y_n$.
Objective: An assignment the variables that maximizes the number of functions that evaluate to 1.
[10.7.2]

[GEMB] Graph embedding
Instance: A graph $G = (V, E)$ with $|V| = n$ and points $S = \{s_1, s_2, \ldots, s_n\}$ in the plane.
Objective: Find a permutation σ (that is, a one-to-one mapping from V to S) that minimizes the total edge length $\sum_{(i,j) \in E} |s_{\sigma(i)} s_{\sigma(j)}|$.
[8.7.5]

[HS] Minimum hitting set
Instance: A ground set E, subsets $T_1, \ldots, T_p$ of E, nonnegative costs c_e for $e \in E$.
Objective: Find a minimum-cost set $A \subseteq E$ such that $A \cap T_i \neq \emptyset$ for $i = 1, \ldots, p$.
[4.3,10.6]

[HT] Hypergraph transversal
Instance: A hypergraph $H = (V, E)$.
Objective: Find a minimum cardinality set of nodes S that covers all the edges of H, i.e., every edge contains at least one member of S.
[10.6]

[IS] Independent set
Instance: A graph $G = (V, E)$, vertex weights w_v for all $v \in V$.
Objective: Find a subset of vertices $S \subseteq V$ so that no two vertices in S are adjacent and such that $\sum_{v \in S} w_v$ is minimized.
[3.1, 3.7, 9.3.3]

[IP] Integer programming
Instance: A matrix $A \in \mathcal{Z}^{m \times n}$ and two vectors $c \in \mathcal{Z}^n$ and $b \in \mathcal{Z}^m$.
Objective: Find a vector $x \in \mathcal{Z}^n$ satisfying $A \cdot x \leq b$ that maximizes $c \cdot x$.
[Chapters 1, 3, 4, 5, 9, 11]

[IP2] Integer programming with two variables per inequality
Instance: A matrix $A \in \mathcal{Z}^{m \times n}$ with each row containing at most two nonzero elements, and two vectors $c \in \mathcal{Z}^n$ and $b \in \mathcal{Z}^m$.
Objective: Find a vector $x \in \mathcal{Z}^n$ satisfying $A \cdot x \leq b$ that maximizes $c \cdot x$.
[3.8]

[JSS] Job shop scheduling
Instance: A set of operations $O_1, \ldots, O_K$ with processing time p_k; n jobs and m machines. Each operation has an associated job j and machine i. The set of operations associated with job j must be processed in a particular (job-dependent) order.
Objective: Find a schedule (an assignment of starting times for all operations) so that: for all jobs, the processing of operations associated with the job does not overlap; for all machines, the processing of operations associated with the machine does not overlap; and the ordering of each job's operations is observed. Minimize the makespan (the time at which all processing completes).
[1.5.3,1.6.3]

[KNAP] Knapsack (0/1 Knapsack)
Instance: A set of elements U with weights p_u, a_u for each $u \in U$. A parameter B.
Objective: Find a subset $U' \subseteq U$ such that $\sum_{u \in U'} a_u \leq B$ so as to maximize $\sum_{u \in U'} p_u$.
[9.1, 9.3.1]

[#KNAP] Number of Knapsack solutions
Instance: A vector $a = (a_0, \ldots, a_{n-1}) \in \mathbb{N}^n$ of "item sizes" and a "knapsack capacity" $b \in \mathbb{N}$.
Objective: The number N of 0,1-vectors $x \in \{0, 1\}^n$ satisfying the inequality $a \cdot x = \sum_{i=0}^{n-1} a_i x_i \leq b$.
[12.2]

[LABELCOVER$_{max}$] Labelcover (max. version)
Instance: (i) A regular bipartite graph $G = (V_1, V_2, E)$. (ii) An integer N. This defines the set of *labels*, which are integers in $\{1, 2, \ldots, N\}$. (iii) For each edge $e \in E$ a partial function $\Pi_e : \{1, 2, \ldots, N\} \to \{1, 2, \ldots, N\}$.
Objective: Find a labeling (see Section 10.1.2) that assigns one label per vertex, and maximizes the fraction of covered edges.
[10.1, 10.3, 10.4, 10.6, 10.8]

[LABELCOVER$_{min}$] Labelcover (min. version)
Instance: (i) A regular bipartite graph $G = (V_1, V_2, E)$. (ii) An integer N. This defines the set of *labels*, which are integers in $\{1, 2, \ldots, N\}$. (iii) For each edge $e \in E$ a partial function $\Pi_e : \{1, 2, \ldots, N\} \to \{1, 2, \ldots, N\}$.
Objective: Find a labeling (see Section 10.1.2) that covers all edges, and minimizes the number of labels assign to V_1.
[10.1,10.3,10.4,10.6,10.8]

[LCS] Largest congruent subsets
Instance: Finite point sets $P_1, P_2, \ldots, P_k$ in $\mathbf{R}^d$, with $d \geq 1$ fixed.
Objective: Find a point set $S = \{s_1, s_2, \ldots, s_m\}$ of maximum cardinality such that S is congruent to a subset $P_i' \subseteq P_i$ for each i.
[8.7.3]

[LHE] Learning halfspaces with error
Instance: A set of inequalities over Q: $a_i^T \cdot x < b$ for $i = 1, \ldots, m$.
Objective: Find the smallest set of inequalities whose removal makes the system feasible.
[10.6]

[LAP] Lattice approximation problem
Instance: An $n \times n$ matrix $\mathbf{A}$ all of whose entries are 0 or 1, and a column vector $\mathbf{p}$ with n entries, all of which are in the interval $[0, 1]$.
Objective: Find a column vector $\mathbf{q}$ with n entries, all of which are from the set $\{0, 1\}$, so as to minimize $\| \mathbf{A} \cdot (\mathbf{p} - \mathbf{q}) \|_\infty$.
[11.2]

[mcLA] Minimum cut linear arrangement
Instance: An undirected graph $G = (V, E)$ with $|V| = n$, and a non-negative cost $c(e)$ for each $e \in E$.
Objective: Find a permutation σ from $\{1, 2, \ldots, n\}$ to V so as to minimize $\max_{i=1,\ldots,n} \sum_{e \in S_i} c(e)$, where $S_i = \{e \in E : e = (\sigma(j), \sigma(k)), \text{ where } j \leq i \text{ and } k > i\}$.
[5.1, 5.5.2]

[LP] Linear programming
Instance: A matrix $A \in \mathcal{Z}^{m \times n}$ and two vectors $c \in \mathcal{Z}^n$ and $b \in \mathcal{Z}^m$.
Objective: Find a vector $x \in \mathcal{R}^n$ satisfying $A \cdot x \leq b$ that maximizes $c \cdot x$.
[1, 3, 4, 5, 9, 11]

[LB] Load balancing
Instance: A set of m servers, and a sequence of tasks T_i, where each task has an associated load vector $p_i(1), \ldots p_i(m)$ and a duration d_i.
Objective: Assign each task to a server so as to minimize the maximum load on any server at any point in time, where the load on server j increases by $p_i(j)$ for a duration d_i, if T_i is assigned to server j. In the online version of this problem, the decision of where to assign a task is made without knowledge of future tasks and their characteristics. [13.6, 13.6.1]

[LONGEST PATH] Longest path
Instance: A graph $G = (V, E)$.
Objective: Find a simple path in G such that the length (number of edges) of the path is maximized.
[10.6]

[MM] Maximum matching
Instance: An undirected graph G.
Objective: A set of edges of G of maximum cardinality such that each vertex of G is adjacent to at most one edge in M.
[12.6]

[3DM] Maximum 3-dimensional matching
Instance: Set $T \subset X \times Y \times Z$, where X, Y, and Z are disjoint.
Objective: A matching for T, i.e., a subset $M \subset T$ such that no elements in M agree in any coordinate, and such that the cardinality of the matching, i.e., $|M|$, is maximized.
[10.6]

[MAX CUT] Maximum cut
Instance: A graph $G = (V, E)$.
Objective: Find a subset C of the vertices that maximizes the number of edges that have one vertex in C and one not in C.
[9.2, 10.2, 11.3.1]

[M3CS] Maximum 3-colorable subgraph
Instance: Graph $G = (V, E)$.
Objective: A subset $E' \subset E$ such that the subgraph $G' = (V, E')$ is 3-colorable, i.e., there is a coloring for G' of cardinality at most 3 and such that the cardinality of the subgraph, i.e., $|E'|$, is maximized.
[10.6]

[MAX 2SAT] Maximum 2-satisfiability
Instance: A CNF formula, where each clause contain at most 2 variables.
Objective: Find an assignment that maximizes the number of satisfied clauses.
[Chapter 10]

[MAX-3SAT] Maximum 3-satisfiability
Instance: A CNF formula, where each clause contain at most 3 variables.
Objective: Find an assignment that maximizes the number of satisfied clauses.
[Chapter 10]

[MAX-3SAT(5)] Maximum 3-satisfiability with up to 5 occurrences per variable
Instance: A CNF formula, where each clause contains at most 3 variables and each variable occurs in at most 5 clauses.
Objective: Find an assignment that maximizes the number of satisfied clauses.
[10.1, 10.4]

[MπS] Maximum π subgraph
Instance: Graph $G = (V, E)$. The property π must be hereditary, i.e., every subgraph of G' satisfies π whenever G satisfies π, and non-trivial, i.e., it is satisfied for infinitely many graphs and false for infinitely many graphs.
Objective: A subset $V' \subset V$ such that the subgraph induced by V' has the property π, and such that the cardinality of the induced subgraph, i.e., $|V'|$, is maximized.
[10.6]

[MAX TSP] Maximum traveling salesperson problem
Instance: A graph $G = (V, E)$, edge weights w_e for all $e \in E$.
Objective: Find a subset of edges $T \subseteq E$ forming a tour that visits each node exactly once, so that $\sum_{e \in T} w_e$ is maximized.
[9.2.2]

[MAXNCM] Maximum non-crossing matching
Instance: Points $S = \{s_1, s_2, \ldots, s_n\}$, with n even, in the plane.
Objective: Find a perfect matching on S in which no two edges cross, with maximum total length.
[8.7.8]

[MAXNCST] Maximum non-crossing spanning tree
Instance: Points $S = \{s_1, s_2, \ldots, s_n\}$ in the plane.
Objective: Find a spanning tree on S in which no two edges cross, with maximum total length.
[8.7.8]

[MAXNCHP] Maximum non-crossing Hamiltonian path
Instance: Points $S = \{s_1, s_2, \ldots, s_n\}$ in the plane.
Objective: Find a path that visits each point of S, in which no two edges cross, with maximum total length.
[8.7.8]

[MAXNCC] Maximum non-crossing cycle
Instance: Points $S = \{s_1, s_2, \ldots, s_n\}$ in the plane.
Objective: Find a tour that visits each point of S, in which no two edges cross, with maximum total length.
[8.7.8]

[MAX-SATISFY] Maximum satisfy
Instance: A linear system of m equations in n variables with rational coefficients.
Objective: Find the largest feasible subsystem.
[10.6]

[k-MED] k-median
Instance: A graph $G = (V, E)$ with edge weights $w_{(i,j)}$ for $(i, j) \in E$, and a parameter $k < |V|$.
Objective: Find a set S, $|S| = k$ so that $\sum_{v \in V} \min_{s \in S} w_{(v,s)}$ is minimized.
[9.2.3]

[METRIC TSP] Metric traveling salesman problem
Instance: A graph $G = (V, E)$ that satisfies the triangle inequality, edge weights w_e for all $e \in E$.
Objective: Find a subset of edges $T \subseteq E$ forming a tour that visits each node exactly once, so that $\sum_{e \in T} w_e$ is minimized.
[10.6]

[MDST] Minimum degree spanning tree
Instance: An arbitrary, connected graph $G = (V, E)$.
Objective: Find a spanning tree of G whose maximal degree is the smallest among all spanning trees of G.
[Chapter 7]

[MDStT] Minimum degree Steiner tree
Instance: An arbitrary, connected graph $G = (V, E)$, and $D \subseteq V$.
Objective: Find a Steiner tree of G that spans at least the set D, whose maximal degree is the smallest among all Steiner trees of G.
[7.1, 7.5]

[MDfj] Minimum degree f-join
Instance: An arbitrary, connected graph $G = (V, E)$, and a proper cut function f.
Objective: Find an f-join of G – a forest that crosses all active cuts of f, whose maximal degree is the smallest among all f-joins of G.
[7.1, 7.5]

[MD2CC] Minimum degree two connected subgraph
Instance: An arbitrary, two-connected graph $G = (V, E)$.
Objective: Find a two-connected spanning subgraph of G whose degree is the smallest among all two-connected spanning subgraphs of G.
[7.1, 7.5]

[MDEST] Minimum degree Euclidean spanning tree
Instance: A Euclidean graph $G = (V, E)$ specified by a set of points in $\mathbf{R}^d$, a degree bound δ.
Objective: Find a minimum-weight spanning tree of degree at most δ.
[7.1, 7.6]

[MEG] Minimum equivalent digraph
Instance: A directed graph $G = (V, E)$.
Objective: Find a subgraph $H = (V, E_H)$ with the property that there is a path in H from u to v if and only if there is a path in G from u to v, so that the number of edges in H is minimized.
[6.4]

[MM] Minimum makespan
Instance: A set of jobs $J = \{1, \ldots, n\}$ with associated processing times $p_1, \ldots, p_n$; a positive integer $m < n$.
Objective: Partition J into subsets $J_1, \ldots, J_m$ such that $\max_{1 \le i \le m} \sum_{j \in J_i} p_j$ is minimized.
[1.1, 1.3.2, 9.3.2]

[MMP] Minimum makespan scheduling with precedence constraints
Instance: A set of n jobs with processing times $p_1, \ldots, p_n$, m identical machines, and a partial ordering $\prec$ on the job set.
Objective: Find a schedule (an assignment of jobs to machines and starting times) with minimum makespan (the time at which all processing completes) with the property that if $j \prec k$ then job k does not begin processing until job j has completed processing.
[1.3.1]

[MMU] Minimum makespan scheduling on unrelated machines
Instance: A set of n jobs and a set of m machines and processing times p_{ij} (the processing time of job j on machine i), $i = 1, \ldots, m$, $j = 1, \ldots, n$.
Objective: Partition the jobs into subsets assigned to each machines $N_1, \ldots, N_m$ so that the makespan, $\max_{1 \le i \le m} \sum_{j \in N_i} p_{ij}$, is minimized.
[1.4]

[MWPM] Minimum-weight perfect matching
Instance: A graph $G = (V, E)$, and nonnegative costs c_e for $e \in E$.
Objective: Find a minimum-cost set of edges such that each vertex is adjacent to exactly one edge.
[4.6.3]

[MST] Minimum spanning tree
Instance: A graph $G = (V, E)$, and nonnegative costs c_e for $e \in E$.
Objective: Find a minimum-cost tree spanning all vertices.
[4.3, 4.5]

[MWT] Minimum weight triangulation
Instance: Points $S = \{s_1, s_2, \ldots, s_n\}$ in the plane.
Objective: Find a triangulation of S with minimum total Euclidean length. A triangulation is a planar straight-line graph with vertex set S in which the outer face is equal to the convex hull of S and each other face is a triangle.
[8.4.1]

[MWST] Minimum weight Steiner triangulation
Instance: Points $S = \{s_1, s_2, \ldots, s_n\}$ in the plane.
Objective: Find a triangulation of a superset of S with minimum total Euclidean length.
[8.4.2]

[MULTICOM] Multicommodity-flow
Instance: A tree $T = (V, E)$, a capacity function $c : E \to N$ and k pairs of vertices (s_i, t_i).
Objective: Find a flow $f_i \in N$ for each pair (s_i, t_i) such that for each $e \in E$, $\sum_{i=1}^{k} f_i q_i(e) \leq c(e)$, where $q_i(e) = 1$ iff e belongs to the unique path from s_i to t_i, and such that $\sum_{i=1}^{k} f_i$ is maximized.
[5.2, 10.6]

[MCOV] Multicover
Instance: A set I of m elements to be covered each b_i times. A collection of sets $S_j \in I$, $j \in J = \{1, \ldots, n\}$. Weights w_j for each $j \in J$.
Objective: Find a subcollection of sets C that form a multicover—each $i \in I$ is in at least b_i sets of C and such that $\sum_{j \in C} w_j$ is minimized.
[3.1, 3.6]

[MCUT] Undirected multicut problem
Instance: An undirected graph $G = (V, E)$, $c : E \to \mathbf{R}^+$ a capacity function, and (s_i, t_i), $1 \leq i \leq k$, k source-sink pairs.
Objective: Find a minimum weight set of edges that separates each source from its corresponding sink, i.e, the removal of a multicut disconnects the graph into connected components such that no source-sink pair is contained in the same connected component.
[4.8.1, 5.2, 5.3.2, 5.6, 11.2.2]

[MCUT] Multiway cut
Instance: A graph $G = (V, E)$, a set $S \subset V$ of terminals, and a weight function $w : E \to N$.
Objective: A multiway cut, i.e., a set $E' \subset E$ such that the removal of E' from E disconnects each terminal from all the others and so that $\sum_{e \in E'} w_e$ is minimized.
[10.6]

[NCODE] Nearest codeword
Instance: Linear binary code C of length n and a string x of length n.
Objective: A codeword y of C with the smallest Hamming distance between x and y, i.e., $d(x, y)$.
[10.6]

[NLVP] Nearest lattice vector problem
Instance: A set of independent vectors $\{b_1, b_2, \ldots, b_m\}$ in $\mathcal{Z}^k$, and a point $b_0 \in \mathcal{Q}^k$.
Objective: Find the lattice vector nearest (in the Euclidean norm) to b_0.
[10.4.3]

[NETSCH] Network scheduling
Instance: A set of m machines, a set of n jobs, non-negative machine-dependent job release dates r_{ij} and processing times p_{ij}, $i = 1, \ldots, m$, $j = 1, \ldots, n$.
Objective: Determine a schedule (an assignment of jobs to machines and time slots so that each job begins processing no earlier than its release date) that minimizes the makespan (the time at which all processing completes). *Note*: the problem can be interpreted as a network of processors, such that each job is located at some processor. The jobs can then either be scheduled on the processor where they are located or else routed along a shortest path in the network to another processor and scheduled there. [1.4.3]

[PA] Packing
Instance: Let $\mathcal{Z}_+$ denote the non-negative integers, A be an $m \times n$ matrix over $\mathcal{Z}_+$, b be a vector over $\mathcal{Z}_+^m$, and x and w be vectors over $\mathcal{Z}_+^n$.
Objective: Maximize $w^T \cdot x$ subject to $Ax \leq b$.
[11.2.2]

[FPACK] Fractional packing
Instance: A matrix $A \in \mathbf{R}^{m \times n}$, a vector $b \in \mathbf{R}^m$, and an arbitrary polytope $Q \in \mathbf{R}^n$ with the property that $Az \geq 0$ for each $z \in Q$
Objective: Find $\lambda \in \mathbf{R}^+$ and $z \in Q$ so that $Az \leq \lambda b$ so as to minimize λ.
[5.2.3, 5.3.5, 5.4.1]

[PS] Packing with squares
Instance: A set of grid points in the plane. A $k \times k$-square is one containing k^2 grid points.
Objective: Place largest number of $k \times k$-squares with axis aligned so that no two squares are overlapping.
[9.3.3]

[SQUP] Packing squares with fixed corners
Instance: Points $P = \{p_1, p_2, \ldots, p_n\}$ in the plane.
Objective: Place squares of maximum size at the points so that no two squares overlap. Squares are all equal size and axis aligned, and the square S_i at point p_i must be in one of the four orientations that makes p_i a corner of S_i.
[8.7.2]

[MWCP] Minimum weight convex partition
Instance: Points $S = \{s_1, s_2, \ldots, s_n\}$ in the plane.
Objective: Find a convex partition of S with minimum total Euclidean length. A convex partition is a planar straight-line graph with vertex set S in which the outer face is equal to the convex hull of S and each other face is convex.
[8.4.1]

[lcP] Lower-capacitated partitioning

Instance: A graph $G = (V, E)$, nonnegative costs c_e for $e \in E$, and a parameter k.
Objective: Find a minimum-cost set of edges that partitions the vertices into trees/paths/cycles such that each tree/path/cycle has at least k vertices.
[4.5.2]

[ISING] Partition function of an Ising system

Instance: A set of n *sites*, an *interaction energy* V_{ij} for each unordered pair of sites i, j, a *magnetic field intensity* B, and an *inverse temperature* β.
Objective: A *configuration* of the system is one of the 2^n possible assignments σ of ± 1 *spins* to each site. The energy of a configuration σ is given by the *Hamiltonian* $H(\sigma)$, defined by $H(\sigma) = -\sum_{\{i,j\}} V_{ij} \sigma_i \sigma_j - B \sum_k \sigma_k$. Compute the value of the *partition function* $Z = \sum_\sigma \exp(-\beta H(\sigma))$.
[12.5.3]

[M-D] Partition function of a monomer-dimer system

Instance: A graph G and a number $\lambda > 0$.
Objective: Compute the *partition function* $Z = \sum_{k=0}^{n} m_k \lambda^k$, where m_k is the number of k-matchings in G.
[12.4]

[P] Paging problem

Instance: A cache size k, an initial set of at most k pages in the cache, and a sequence of page requests $p_1, \ldots, p_N$.
Objective: Minimize the total number of faults incurred, where a fault is incurred on page request i if page p_i is not in the cache at the time of that request. In this case, some page that is in the cache must be chosen for replacement by p_i. In the online version of this problem, replacement decisions are made without knowledge of future page requests.
[13.2.1, 13.3.1, 13.3.2.3, 13.3.3.1, 13.4.1, 13.4.2.1, 13.7]

[PERM] Permanent of a matrix

Instance: A matrix $A = (a_{ij} : 0 \le i, j \le n - 1)$.
Objective: Compute the *permanent of A*, namely, per $A = \sum_\pi \prod_{i=0}^{n-1} a_{i,\pi(i)}$, where the sum is over all permutations π of $\{0, 1, \ldots, n - 1\}$.
[12.5.1]

[PFSS] Permutation flow shop scheduling

Instance: A set of operations O_{ij} with processing times $p_{ij}, i = 1, \ldots, m, j = 1, \ldots, n$.
Objective: Find a permutation of $1, \ldots, n$ that minimizes the makespan of the schedule associated with scheduling each machine's operations according to the permutation to obtain a flow shop schedule (see flow shop scheduling).
[1.5.2, 1.6.3]

[PS] Maximum planar subgraph

Instance: A graph $G = (V, E)$.
Objective: A subset $V' \subset V$ such that the induced subgraph is planar and v' is maximized.
[10.6]

[nfPPC] Non-fixed point-to-point connection problem
Instance: A graph $G = (V, E)$, nonnegative costs c_e for $e \in E$, and a set of sources $C \subset V$ and destinations $D \subseteq V$, where $C \cap D = \emptyset$ and $|C| = |D|$.
Objective: Find a minimum-cost set of edges such that each connected component contains the same number of sources and destinations.
[4.6.4]

[PSSEP] Point set separation
Instance: Points $P = \{p_1, p_2, \ldots, p_k\}$ and $Q = \{q_1, q_2, \ldots, q_l\}$ in $\mathbf{R}^3$.
Objective: Find a terrain that separates P and Q and has a minimum number of facets. A terrain T is a polyhedral surface that is intersected exactly once by each line parallel to the z-axis; it separates P and Q if for each $1 \le i \le k$ and $1 \le j \le l$ a path from p_i to q_j must intersect T.
[8.6.3]

[PSINT] Point set interpolation
Instance: Points $P = \{p_1, p_2, \ldots, p_k\}$ in $\mathbf{R}^3$.
Objective: Find a terrain that passes within vertical distance ε of each point of P and has a minimum number of facets. A terrain T is a polyhedral surface that is intersected exactly once by each line parallel to the z-axis.
[8.6.3]

[PBIS] Polygon bisection
Instance: A simple polygon P in the plane.
Objective: Partition P into two equal-area subsets P_1 and P_2 such that the shared boundary $\partial P_1 \cap \partial P_2$ has minimum length.
[8.7.4]

[PGSEP] Polygon separation
Instance: Disjoint, simple polygons $P_1, P_2, \ldots, P_k$ in the plane.
Objective: Find a planar straight-line graph G that separates the polygons (without intersecting them) and has a minimum number of edges. That is, for each $i \ne j$, $1 \le i, j \le k$, any path from a point in P_i to a point in P_j must cross an edge or vertex of G.
[8.6.1]

[PHSEP] Polyhedron separation
Instance: Convex polytopes P and R in $\mathbf{R}^3$, with $P \subseteq R$.
Objective: Find a polytope Q with $P \subseteq Q \subseteq R$ with a minimum number of facets.
[8.6.2]

[PC-ST] Prize collecting Steiner tree problem
Instance: A graph $G = (V, E)$, nonnegative costs c_e for $e \in E$, a root vertex r, and nonnegative penalties π_v for $v \in V$.
Objective: Find a tree containing r that minimizes the sum of the costs of the edges in the tree plus the penalties of the vertices not spanned by the tree.
[4.8.2]

[PC-TSP] Prize collecting traveling salesman problem
Instance: A graph $G = (V, E)$, nonnegative costs c_e for $e \in E$, a root vertex r, and nonnegative penalties π_v for $v \in V$.
Objective: Find a tour containing r that minimizes the sum of the costs of the edges in the tour plus the penalties of the vertices not in the tour.
[4.8.2]

[QP] Quadratic programming
Instance: A matrix $A \in \mathcal{Z}^{m \times 2n}$ and a matrix $C \in \mathcal{Z}^{n \times n}$ and $b \in \mathcal{Z}^m$.
Objective: Find vectors $x, y \in \mathbf{R}^n$ satisfying $A(x, y) \le b$ that maximizes xCy.
[10.6]

[RECC] Rectangle covering
Instance: An orthogonal (that is, only horizontal and vertical sides) polygon in the plane, P.
Objective: Find a minimum number of (possibly overlapping) rectangles with union equal to P.
[8.7.1]

[MSU] Scheduling unrelated machines to minimize weighted sum of completion times
Instance: A set of n jobs and a set of m machines and processing times p_{ij} (the processing time of job j on machine i), $i = 1, \ldots, m$, $j = 1, \ldots, n$; job weights $w_1, \ldots, w_n$
Objective: Schedule the jobs on the m machines so that $\sum_{j=1}^n w_j C_j$ is minimized, where C_j is the completion time of job j.
[1.7.3]

[1RjLmax] Sequencing with release dates and and delivery times
Instance: A set of n jobs with non-negative release dates r_j, processing times p_j, and delivery times q_j, $j = 1, \ldots, n$.
Objective: Schedule the jobs on a single machine so that each job starts at time $s_j \ge r_j$ and no two jobs' processing times overlap (i.e., for all j and k, either $s_j + p_j \le s_k$ or $s_k + p_k \le s_j$), so as to minimize $\max_{1 \le j \le n} s_j + p_j + q_j$. (Note: from the standpoint of optimization, this problem is equivalent to that in which each job has a due date d_j instead of a delivery time q_j and the object is to minimize the maximum lateness $L_j := s_j + p_j - d_j$.)
[1.2]

[MSPrec] Sequencing with precedence constraints to minimize sum of weighted completion times
Instance: A set of n jobs with positive weights w_j and processing times p_j, and a partial order $\prec$ on the job set.
Objective: Find a permutation π of $\{1, \ldots, n\}$ consistent with $\prec$ that minimizes $\sum_{j=1}^n w_{\pi(j)} \left(\sum_{i=1}^j p_{\pi(i)} \right)$.
[1.7.2]

[MSRj] Sequencing with release dates to minimize sum of weighted completion times

Instance: A set of n jobs with positive weights w_j, processing times p_j, and non-negative release dates r_j.

Objective: Find a permutation π of $\{1, \ldots, n\}$ that minimizes

$\sum_{j=1}^n w_{\pi(j)} \left(\max_{1 \le i \le j} r_{\pi(i)} + \sum_{k=i}^j p_{\pi(k)} \right)$.

[1.7.1, 1.7.2]

[SpC] Sparsest cut

Instance: An undirected graph $G = (V, E)$, $c : E \to \mathbf{R}^+$ a cost function, (s_i, t_i), $i = 1, \ldots, k$, k source-sink vertex pairs (terminals), and a demand $d(i)$, $i = 1, \ldots, k$.

Objective: Find a subset $S \subseteq V$ so as to minimize the ratio between the cost of the set of edges connecting S and $V - S$ and the total demand of all commodities i for which $|\{s_i, t_i\} \cap S| = 1$.

[5.1, 5.3, 5.5.1]

[RSMT] Rectilinear Steiner tree

Instance: Points $S = \{s_1, s_2, \ldots, s_n\}$ in the plane.

Objective: Find a tree of minimum total rectilinear length (or equivalently, a minimum-length tree containing only horizontal and vertical edges) that includes S in its vertex set.

[8.3]

[RBSEP] Red-blue separation

Instance: Points $R = \{r_1, r_2, \ldots, r_k\}$ and $B = \{b_1, b_2, \ldots, b_l\}$ in the plane.

Objective: Find a polygon that separates R and B and has a minimum number of sides.

[8.2.3, 8.6.3]

[SAT] Satisfiability

Instance: A CNF formula.

Objective: Find a satisfying assignment.

[10.0, 10.1, 10.3, 10.4, 10.5, 10.7]

[2-SAT] 2-satisfiability

Instance: A 2-satisfiability boolean formula on variables $x_1, \ldots, x_n$ with weights w_j for $j = 1, \ldots, n$.

Objective: Find an assignment satisfying all clauses such that $\sum_{x_j = T} w_j$ is minimized.

[3.1, 3.8]

[k-S] k-Server problem

Instance: An integer k, a metric space M, a set of k points in this space each initially occupied by a server, and a request sequence $p_1, \ldots, p_N$ of points in M.

Objective: Minimize the total distance moved by all servers in order to service this sequence, where the i-th request is served by moving some server from its current location to point p_i. In the online version of this problem, the decision of which server to move in order to service a request is made without knowledge of future requests.

[13.2.2, 13.3.1, 13.3.2.2, 13.5]

[SB] Set balancing

Instance: An $n \times n$ matrix $\mathbf{A}$ all of whose entries are 0 or 1, and a column vector $\mathbf{p}$ with n entries, all of which are 0.5.
Objective: Find a column vector $\mathbf{q}$ with n entries, all of which are from the set $\{0, 1\}$, so as to minimize $\| \mathbf{A} \cdot (\mathbf{p} - \mathbf{q}) \|_\infty$.
[11.2]

[SC] Set cover

Instance: A set I of m elements to be covered and a collection of sets $S_j \in I$, $j \in J = \{1, \ldots, n\}$. Weights w_j for each $j \in J$.
Objective: Find a subcollection of sets C that form a cover, i.e., $\cup_{j \in C} S_j = I$ and such that $\sum_{j \in C} w_j$ is minimized.
[3.1–3.5, 11.2.2]

[SP] Set packing

Instance: Collection C of finite sets.
Objective: A set packing, i.e., a collection of disjoint sets $C' \subset C$. such that $|C'|$ is maximized.
[3.1, 10.6, 11.2.2]

[SLV] Shortest lattice vector

Instance: A set of independent vectors $\{b_1, b_2, \ldots, b_m\}$ in $\mathcal{Z}^k$.
Objective: Find the shortest lattice vector, i.e., $c_1, c_2, \ldots, c_m$ in $\mathcal{Z}$ such that the norm of $\sum_{i=1}^m c_i b_i$ is minimized.
[10.6]

[SP] Shortest *s-t* path

Instance: A graph $G = (V, E)$, nonnegative costs c_e for $e \in E$, and vertices s, t.
Objective: Find the shortest path from s to t.
[4.3, 4.6.2]

[SPS] Shortest paths in space

Instance: Polyhedra in $\mathbf{R}^3$ along with two points s and t that lie outside the union of all interiors of polyhedra.
Objective: Find a shortest path between s and t that lies outside the union of all interiors of polyhedra.
[8.7.7]

[SS] Shortest superstring

Instance: A collection of strings, $s_1, \ldots, s_n$.
Objective: Find a string S of minimum length so that each s_i is a substring of S, for $i = 1, \ldots, n$.
[9.2.2]

[SMT] Steiner tree
Instance: A graph $G = (V, E)$ with edge weights w_e for $e \in E$, and a set of "terminals" $T \subset V$.
Objective: Find a connected subgraph $G' = (V', E')$ with $T \subseteq V'$ that minimizes the total length $\sum_{e \in E'} w_e$.
[4.4, 4.6, 7.2, 7.3, 8.3]

[gSMT] Generalized Steiner tree
Instance: A graph $G = (V, E)$ with edge weights w_e for $e \in E$, and sets of terminals $T_i \subset V, i = 1, \ldots, p$.
Objective: Find a minimum-weight set of edges $E' \subseteq E$ such that for each $i = 1, \ldots, p$, all the vertices in T_i are connected in (V, E').
[4.4, 4.6]

[S-TP] Storage-time product
Instance: A directed acyclic graph $G = (V, E)$, a non-negative weight $w(e)$ for each edge $e \in E$, and a positive processing time $p(v)$ for each $v \in V$.
Objective: Find a topological ordering of the vertices, i.e., if there is a path from u to v in G, then u must come earlier in the ordering, such that if v_i denotes the vertex that is ith in the ordering, then the total cost $\sum_{e=(v_i, v_j) \in E} c(e)(\sum_{k=i}^{j-1} p(v_k))$ is minimized.
[5.5.2]

[SCSS] Strongly connected spanning subgraph
Instance: A strongly connected directed graph $G = (V, E)$ with weights $w(i, j)$ for $(i, j) \in E$.
Objective: Find a strongly connected spanning subgraph $H = (V, E_H)$, so that H has minimum total weight.
[6.4]

[k-SUP] k-supplier
Instance: A graph $G = (V, E)$ with edge weights $w_{(i,j)}$ for $(i, j) \in E$, a partition of V into two sets: a set of *suppliers* S, and a set of *customers* C, and a parameter $k < |V|$.
Objective: Find a subset $\bar{S} \subseteq S, |\bar{S}| = k$ so that $\max_{v \in V} \min_{s \in \bar{S}} w_{(v,s)}$ is minimized.
[9.4.1]

[SNDP] Survivable network design problem
Instance: A graph $G = (V, E)$, nonnegative costs c_e for $e \in E$, and nonnegative r_{ij} for $i, j \in V$.
Objective: Find a minimum-cost set of edges $E' \subseteq E$ such that for each $i, j \in V$, there are at least r_{ij} edge-disjoint paths between i and j in (V, E').
[4.4, 4.7]

[vcSNDP] Vertex-connected survivable network design problem
Instance: A graph $G = (V, E)$, nonnegative costs c_e for $e \in E$, and nonnegative r_{ij} for $i, j \in V$.
Objective: Find a minimum-cost set of edges $E' \subseteq E$ such that for each $i, j \in V$, there are at least r_{ij} vertex-disjoint paths between i and j in (V, E').
[4.8.3]

[TSP] Traveling salesman problem
Instance: A graph $G = (V, E)$, edge weights w_e for all $e \in E$.
Objective: Find a subset of edges $T \subseteq E$ forming a tour that visits each node exactly once, so that $\sum_{e \in T} w_e$ is minimized.
[8.2, 9.4.2]

[TSPN] TSP with neighborhoods
Instance: Simple polygons $P_1, P_2, \ldots, P_k$ in the plane.
Objective: Find a minimum length tour that touches each polygon. In other words, find a point s_i in each P_i and a permutation σ that minimizes $|s_{\sigma(1)}s_{\sigma(2)}| + |s_{\sigma(2)}s_{\sigma(3)}| + \cdots + |s_{\sigma(k-1)}s_{\sigma(k)}| + |s_{\sigma(k)}s_{\sigma(1)}|$.
[8.2.3]

[TJ] T-join
Instance: A graph $G = (V, E)$, nonnegative costs c_e for $e \in E$, and a subset of vertices T.
Objective: Find a minimum-cost set of edges that has odd degree at vertices in T and even degree at vertices not in T.
[4.6.2]

[MUNSAT] Minimum unsatisfying linear subsystem
Instance: System $Ax = b$ of linear equations, where A is an integer $m \times n$-matrix, and b is an integer m-vector.
Objective: Find a rational n-vector $x \in \mathcal{Q}^n$ minimizing the number of equations that are not satisfied by x.
[10.6]

[λ-VCU] λ vertex connected subgraph (unweighted)
Instance: A graph $G = (V, E)$ and an integer λ. Assume that G is λ vertex connected.
Objective: Find a spanning subgraph $H = (V, E_H)$ of G that is λ vertex connected, so that the number of edges in H is minimized.
[4.8.3, 6.3.2]

[λ-VC] λ vertex connected subgraph
Instance: A graph $G = (V, E)$ with edge weights $w(i, j)$ for $(i, j) \in E$, and an integer λ.
Objective: Find a spanning subgraph $H = (V, E_H)$ of G that is λ vertex connected, so that H has minimum total weight.
[6.3.1]

[λ-VCA] λ vertex connectivity augmentation
Instance: A graph $G = (V, E)$ with edge weights $w(i, j)$ for $(i, j) \in E$, and a subgraph $G_0 = (V, E_0)$ and an integer λ.
Objective: Find a set of edges $Aug \subseteq E$ to add to G_0, so that the graph $(V, E_0 \cup Aug)$ is λ vertex connected and Aug has minimum total weight.
[4.8.3, 6.5.2]

[VC] Vertex cover
Instance: A graph $G = (V, E)$, vertex weights w_v for all $v \in V$.
Objective: Find a subset of vertices $C \subseteq V$ that forms a cover so that each edge $e \in E$ has at least one of its endpoints in C and such that $\sum_{v \in C} w_v$ is minimized.
[3, 4.3, 9.2.1, 9.3.3]

[VFS] Vertex feedback set in undirected graphs
Instance: A graph $G = (V, E)$, vertex weights w_v for all $v \in V$.
Objective: Find a subset of vertices $F \subseteq V$ so that the subgraph induced on $V \setminus F$ is acyclic and so that $\sum_{v \in F} w_v$ is minimized.
[9.2.1]

[VRMM] Vehicle routing minmax
Instance: A graph $G = (V, E)$, edge weights w_e for all $e \in E$, a distinguished node, depot-d, and a parameter k.
Objective: Find a partition of the nodes in $V \setminus \{d\}$ to $V_1, \ldots, V_k$ and a subset of edges $T_k \subseteq E$ forming k tours each containing node d and each node of V_i exactly once, so that $\max_{e \in T_k} w_e$ is minimized.
[9.4.2]

[VCR] Virtual circuit routing
Instance: A graph $G = (V, E)$, where each edge $e \in E$ has a nonnegative capacity u_e, and a sequence of requests $(s(i), t(i), p(i), d(i))$, $1 \leq i \leq N$, where $s(i), t(i) \in V$.
Objective: For each i, assign the i-th request to a path P_i in the graph between $s(i)$ and $t(i)$ so as to minimize the maximum relative load on any edge at any point in time, where the relative load on edge e increases by $p(i)/u_e$ for the duration $d(i)$ if e is on the path P_i. An alternative version of this problem is to choose a subset of the requests to accept, and for each of these a path between its endpoints, so that all capacity constraints are met and so that the sum of the loads $p(i)$ of accepted requests is maximized (throughput maximization). In the online version of both of these, the decision for each request is made without knowledge of future requests.
[13.6, 13.6.1]

[VOL] Volume of a convex body
Instance: A convex body K in n-dimensional Euclidean space, specified by a membership oracle, together with a certain guarantee (see Section 12.5.2).
Objective: Compute the volume of K.
[12.5.2]

[WSMM] Wandering salesman minmax
Instance: A graph $G = (V, E)$, edge weights w_e for all $e \in E$. A pair of specified nodes, a starting node s and destination node t.
Objective: Find a subset of edges $P \subseteq E$ forming a path from s to t that visits each node exactly once, so that $\max_{e \in P} w_e$ is minimized.
[9.4.2]

INDEX